Volume III: U.S. Navy, U.S. Marine Corps and U.S. Coast Guard Aircraft Lost During World War II - Listed by Aircraft Type

Douglas E. Campbell, Ph.D.

Volume III: U.S. Navy, U.S. Marine Corps and U.S. Coast Guard Aircraft Lost During World War II - Listed by Aircraft Type

ISBN 978-1-257-90689-5

Direct all inquiries to Dr. Douglas Campbell at dcamp@syneca.com.

Cover design by Michelle Rekstad at Rekstad Graphics, rekstad@aol.com

Dedication

As names such as LTJG George H.W. Bush, ENS George H. Gay, LCDR Edward H. "Butch" O'Hare, MAJ Gregory "Pappy" Boyington and aces such as LT Eugene A. Valencia, LT Alexander Vraciu and others popped up for entry into the master database, it became apparent that the dedication goes out to all those who fought for peace and freedom, many losing their lives in the process.

Acknowledgments

My thanks go out to the staff at the Naval History and Heritage Command (including their National Museum of the U.S. Navy, the Naval Aviation History Office and Naval Aviation News at the Washington Navy Yard, Washington, D.C.; and the Command's National Aviation Museum in Pensacola, FL); the staff at the National Archives & Records Administration (NARA); the staff at the Smithsonian's National Air and Space Museum (a special thanks to former employee CAPT Tim Wooldridge (US Navy, retired)), the staff at the Tailhook Association and the Hook magazine; and my printing consultant and friend Stephen J. Chant in Burlington, VT.

Foreword

The foundation of the aircraft information in this volume comes from what the US Navy calls "Aircraft History Cards" – although called by other names by both the Navy and by other military organizations. The Navy also called them "Aircraft Records" and the US Air Force calls them "Individual Aircraft Record Cards". So what is published here is simply reference material; a dictionary if you will.

For the Navy during World War II, the "Aircraft History Cards" were hand-written compilations of the inventory history of each individual aircraft, showing the location or controlling unit/squadron and status of that aircraft at the end-of-the-month inventory period. In case an individual aircraft was lost in any manner during the month, the Aircraft History Card many times also noted the date lost, the pilot's name and his status. Unfortunately, no inventory information was recorded for most aircraft during late 1943 through mid-1944, apparently due to confusion with record-keeping policies and systems. This gap was closed by searching individual squadron histories. I am sure not all gaps were filled and any substantiated information that can be provided would be helpful for the next edition. Many Aircraft History Cards also display a variety of ways of recording this information by hand, some indecipherable. But as always, even given that this project began with a thick stack of microfiche and even given the hand-written nature of the information, the errors found in this volume are mine.

Those readers who find this type of research on Naval Aircraft Histories interesting should also go to the Internet and look at these sites:

- "US Navy and US Marine Corps Aircraft Serial Numbers and Bureau Numbers--1911 to Present" by Joe Baugher at http://www.joebaugher.com/navy_serials/navyserials.html

- "Bureau (Serial) Numbers of Naval Aircraft" which is Appendix J from *United States Naval Aviation 1910-1995.* http://www.history.navy.mil/branches/org4-24.htm
- Aviation Archaeological Investigation and Research (AAIR) is a primary source on the Web to purchase U.S. military aircraft accident reports, individual aircraft record (history) cards, and aviation archaeology information. Go to http://www.aviationarchaeology.com/

Table of Contents

Introduction.......... 1

Aircraft Lost Listed by Aircraft Manufacturer and Type.......... 11

BEECH GB-1.......... 11

BEECH GB-2.......... 11

BEECH JRB-1.......... 12

BEECH JRB-2.......... 12

BEECH JRB-3.......... 12

BEECH JRB-4.......... 12

BEECH SNB-1.......... 12

BEECH SNB-2C.......... 13

BELLANCA CH-400.......... 13

BOEING PB2B-2.......... 13

BREWSTER F2A-3.......... 14

BREWSTER F3A-1.......... 14

CANADIAN CAR & FOUNDRY CO. (CCF) SBW-1.......... 15

CANADIAN CAR & FOUNDRY CO. (CCF) SBW-3.......... 15

CESSNA JRC-1.......... 17

CONSOLIDATED 21-A.......... 17

CONSOLIDATED PB2Y-2.......... 18

CONSOLIDATED PB2Y-3 19

CONSOLIDATED PB2Y-3R 19

CONSOLIDATED PB4Y-1 19

CONSOLIDATED PB4Y-1P 25

CONSOLIDATED PB4Y-2 26

CONSOLIDATED PBY (VARIANT UNKNOWN) 27

CONSOLIDATED PBY-1 27

CONSOLIDATED PBY-2 28

CONSOLIDATED PBY-3 28

CONSOLIDATED PBY-4 29

CONSOLIDATED PBY-5 29

CONSOLIDATED PBY-5A 34

CONSOLIDATED PBY-6A 37

CONSOLIDATED RY-2 37

CONVAIR OY-1 37

CURTISS R5C-1 39

CURTISS SB2C (VARIANT UNKNOWN) 39

CURTISS SB2C-1 39

CURTISS SB2C-1A 42

CURTISS SB2C-1C 43

CURTISS SB2C-3 48

CURTISS SB2C-3E 59

CURTISS SB2C-4 59

CURTISS SB2C-4E 63

CURTISS SB2C-5 68

CURTISS SBC-4 69

CURTISS SC-1 69

CURTISS SNC-1 71

CURTISS SO3C-1 71

CURTISS SO3C-2 72

CURTISS SO3C-3 72

CURTISS SOC (VARIANT UNKNOWN) 72

CURTISS SOC-1 73

CURTISS SOC-2 75

CURTISS SOC-3 76

CURTISS SOC-3A 77

CURTISS XSBC-4 78

DOUGLAS DC-3A 78

DOUGLAS R3D-2 78

DOUGLAS R4D-1 78

DOUGLAS R4D-5 79

DOUGLAS R4D-6 79

DOUGLAS R5D-2 80

DOUGLAS R5D-3 80

DOUGLAS RD-3 80

DOUGLAS SBD (VARIANT UNKNOWN) 80

DOUGLAS SBD-1 81

DOUGLAS SBD-2 82

DOUGLAS SBD-3 84

DOUGLAS SBD-4 94

DOUGLAS SBD-5 100

DOUGLAS SBD-6 116

DOUGLAS TBD-1 120

FAIRCHILD GK-1 124

FAIRCHILD PILGRIM 100B 125

FAIRCHILD CANADA SBF-1 125

GENERAL MOTORS FM-1 125

GENERAL MOTORS FM-2 127

GENERAL MOTORS FM-2P 155

GENERAL MOTORS TBM (VARIANT UNKNOWN) 155

GENERAL MOTORS TBM-1 155

GENERAL MOTORS TBM-1C 156

GENERAL MOTORS TBM-3 182

GENERAL MOTORS TBM-3C 198

GENERAL MOTORS TBM-3D 198

GENERAL MOTORS TBM-3E 199

GENERAL MOTORS TBM-3P 201

GOODYEAR FG-1 201

GOODYEAR FG-1A 204

GOODYEAR FG-1D 205

GRUMMAN F4F-3 212

GRUMMAN F4F-3A 214

GRUMMAN F4F-4 215

GRUMMAN F4F-4P 230

GRUMMAN F4F-7 230

GRUMMAN F4F-7P 231

GRUMMAN F6F-3 231

GRUMMAN F6F-3N 260

GRUMMAN F6F-3P 261

GRUMMAN F6F-5 262

GRUMMAN F6F-5E 307

GRUMMAN F6F-5N 309

GRUMMAN F6F-5P 318

GRUMMAN J2F-1 319

GRUMMAN J2F-2 320

GRUMMAN J2F-2A 320

GRUMMAN J2F-3 320

GRUMMAN J2F-4 320

GRUMMAN J2F-5 321

GRUMMAN J2F-6 322

GRUMMAN J4F-2 323

GRUMMAN JF-1 323

GRUMMAN JRF-1 323

GRUMMAN JRF-1A 324

GRUMMAN JRF-4 324

GRUMMAN JRF-5 324

GRUMMAN TBF (VARIANT UNKNOWN) 325

GRUMMAN TBF-1 325

GRUMMAN TBF-1C 337

GRUMMAN TBF-1D 343

GRUMMAN TBF-1P 343

HOWARD GH-2 344

HOWARD NH-1 344

LOCKHEED ELECTRA 345

LOCKHEED JO-1 345

LOCKHEED JO-2 345

LOCKHEED PBO-1 346

LOCKHEED PV-1 346

LOCKHEED PV-1(N) 351

LOCKHEED PV-2 352

LOCKHEED PV-3....352

LOCKHEED R3O-2....352

LOCKHEED R5O-4....352

LOCKHEED R5O-5....353

LOCKHEED R5O-6....353

MARTIN JM-1....353

MARTIN JM-2....354

MARTIN PBM-1....355

MARTIN PBM-3C....355

MARTIN PBM-3D....357

MARTIN PBM-3R....360

MARTIN PBM-3S....360

MARTIN PBM-5....361

MARTIN PBM-5E....362

NAVAL AIRCRAFT FACTORY (NAF) N3N-3....363

NAVAL AIRCRAFT FACTORY (NAF) OS2N-1....363

NAVAL AIRCRAFT FACTORY (NAF) SON-1....367

NAVAL AIRCRAFT FACTORY (NAF) SON-1A....368

NORTH AMERICAN PBJ-1C....368

NORTH AMERICAN PBJ-1D....369

NORTH AMERICAN PBJ-1H....370

NORTH AMERICAN PBJ-1J....370

NORTH AMERICAN SNJ-3 371

NORTH AMERICAN SNJ-4 371

NORTH AMERICAN SNJ-5 373

NORTH AMERICAN SNJ-6 373

NORTHROP BT-1 373

PIPER AE-1 373

PIPER NE-1 374

REARWIN SPEEDSTER 374

SIKORSKY JR2S-2 374

SIKORSKY JRS-1 375

STEARMAN N2S-3 375

STINSON MODEL SM 376

TIMM N2T-1 376

VOUGHT F4U (VARIANT UNKNOWN) 376

VOUGHT F4U-1 376

VOUGHT F4U-1D 393

VOUGHT F4U-4 411

VOUGHT O3U-3 415

VOUGHT OS2U-1 415

VOUGHT OS2U-2 416

VOUGHT OS2U-3 416

VOUGHT SB2U-1 422

VOUGHT SB2U-2..423

VOUGHT SB2U-3..423

VULTEE SNV-1 423

WACO YKS-6..424

WACO YKS-7..424

Introduction

This has been a 3-volume set of books many years in the making, and throughout the years the information gathered has grown, conflicted, and somewhat sorted itself out, although one wonders if there will ever be a completely agreed-upon history on such an expansive subject. Rather than bore you with the development of the volumes, I would just like to explain a few administrative details first.

The master aircraft losses database from which the aircraft loss data is reproduced within the following three volumes is a research project undertaken by my company, Syneca Research Group, Inc. (www.syneca.com). As of this printing, there are 15,069 aircraft stored in this database which so far represents the total number of U.S. Navy, Marine Corps and Coast Guard aircraft lost between 7 December 1941 and 15 August 1945, and lost outside the continental United States (CONUS). The database was sorted three ways and each sort is reflected by each volume. The first volume lists all the aircraft lost that were assigned or attached to ships. The ships are listed alphabetically. The second volume lists all the aircraft lost sorted alphabetically by squadron attached. The third and final volume depicts all the aircraft lost sorted alphabetically by manufacturer and type of aircraft. The third volume is the only volume in which the listing of every aircraft, (i.e., all 15,069 aircraft), was printed; the other two volumes are subsets of the database and each of these two volumes represent approximately half of the database listed in Volume III.

The fields in the listings are the same in all three volumes and are described as follows:

- **TYPE:** This is the type or class designation of the aircraft lost. The naval designation system for aircraft used during World War II was the same used by the U.S. Navy, Marine Corps and Coast Guard. Volume III is the alphabetical listing of every aircraft type listed by manufacturer, then by manufacturer's type/variant and within each aircraft type/variant the data is also sorted by date lost.
- **BUNO:** This is the aircraft's Bureau Number, or Serial Number, used by the U.S. Navy, Marine Corps and Coast Guard during World War II and still in use today. This is a unique number assigned to each aircraft and is usually painted on the vertical tail section or on the rear fuselage of every aircraft.
- **SQDRN:** This is the squadron to which the aircraft lost had been attached. In many instances the squadron to which the aircraft was attached was a Naval Air Station (NAS), or a Marine Corps Air Base (MCAB), or flying under Station Operations, or assigned to a Naval Attaché, or just attached to a salvage unit awaiting the scrap heap at or near the end of the war. Some were even lost being transported by ship before being assigned to a squadron and these aircraft are listed as Unassigned. In many instances, though, the exact operational squadron could be determined and are listed in this field. Volume II is a listing of aircraft lost by actual squadron attached. The squadrons are broken down alphabetically within their respective service. Within each squadron the aircraft are also sorted by date lost. Much like the *Dictionary of*

American Naval Fighting Ships (*DANFS* for short), the Naval History and Heritage command, located at the Washington Navy Yard in the District of Columbia, was researching and publishing the Dictionary of American Naval Aviation Squadrons. Volume One, published in 1995, contains the histories of VA, VAH, VAK, VAL, VAP and VFA Squadrons and was authored by Roy Grossnick. Volume Two, published in 2000, contains the histories of VP, VPB, VP(H) and VP(AM) Squadrons and was authored by Michael D. Roberts. Both of these volumes are available on the command website, www.history.navy.mil under Resources & Research - Aviation. These squadron histories are a vast undertaking and resources are tight - Volume Three is currently on hold. However, the Archives Branch can answer small requests and they also welcome visitors and researchers. In this 3-volume set, Volume I (Listed by Ships Attached) includes the histories of the ships; Volume II (Listed by Squadron) does not include the histories of the squadron as this is a life-long undertaking. Volume III (Listed by Aircraft Type) does include a brief mention of the history of the type and variant of the aircraft lost.

- **FROM:** This is a two-fold field in that if the aircraft lost was assigned to a ship, that ship is listed here. If not attached to a ship, than the squadron was located at a land-based airfield, in most cases a field on one of the numerous islands located in the Pacific, and that field or island is also listed here. Volume I is an alphabetical listing of the ships to which the aircraft lost were attached.

Histories of these ships were copied from the DANFS. *DANFS* is the primary reference work for the basic facts about ships used by the United States Navy. *DANFS* was originally released by the Naval Historical Center (NHC, now the Naval History and Heritage Command) in bound hardcover volumes, ordered by ship name, from Volume I (A–B) published in 1959 to Volume VIII (W–Z) published in 1981. Volume I (A–B) subsequently went out of print. In 1991 a revised *Volume I Part A*, covering only ship names beginning with A, was released. Work continues on revisions of the remaining volumes. *DANFS* is a work of the U.S. government and its content is in the public domain.

- **DOWN:** This is a listing of the area in which the aircraft was lost. In almost every case the best that could be identified is the nearest island to where the ship was when the plane attached to the ship was lost (e.g., Midway), the location over land where the plane when lost (e.g., Tokyo), the battle in which the aircraft was participating when lost (e.g., Battle of Midway), or even the body of water the aircraft was lost in (e.g., Battle of the Philippine Sea would be simply Philippine Sea). The exact latitude and longitude of where every aircraft went down is rarely possible, except when the aircraft went down with a sinking ship.
- **AREA:** This is a generalized area of the world where the aircraft was lost. For example, Hawaii is in the Eastern Central Pacific (ECENPAC). EMPIRE is the Empire of Japan and PHIL is the Philippines.

- **DATE:** This is the date in which the aircraft was lost. In some instances, the scrapping of aircraft was only reported monthly, so you may see a number of scrapped aircraft being reported on the last day of a month; however, these aircraft are not linked with an operational squadron but rather with a Carrier Aircraft Service Unit (CASU) or Assembly & Repair (A&R) department.
- **PILOT:** This is the pilot's name and rank or rate who was with the aircraft when the aircraft was lost. Many of the names may be incomplete or misspelled as the reference materials used was very poorly reproduced. In some instances, no pilot is listed but rather a statement such as (DECK LOSS-KAMIKAZE) or (DECK LOSS-TYPHOON); this is self-explanatory. In some others the field is left blank, but a name needs to eventually go into it.
- **FATE:** This is the fate of the pilot reported at the time the plane was lost. It is a single letter represented as follows:

  U - Unknown

  S - Saved

  M - Missing

  D – Deceased

  Although the fate of many of those reported Missing or Unknown were eventually changed to Deceased, what is represented here was the status of the pilot's fate when the original report was made.

A brief understanding to Volume 1 is in order here. Ship types (those ships that lost aircraft) represented in this section are identified as follows:

ACV - Auxiliary Aircraft Carrier

AV - Seaplane Tender
AVD - Seaplane Tender Destroyer
AVP - Small Seaplane tender
BB - Battleship
CA - Heavy Cruiser
CB - Large Cruiser
CL - Light Cruiser
CV - Aircraft Carrier
CVE - Escort Aircraft Carrier
CVL - Small Aircraft Carrier
PG - Gunboat

In some instances, the designation of the ship changed during the course of the war; such as an ACV being redesignated a CVE. In these cases, the ship is listed twice, once under each designation, and the appropriate squadrons are listed under each separate (but identical) ship. In other instances, you will find the same ship's name listed twice but with different number designations, such as USS WASP (CV-7) and USS WASP (CV-18); this means two different ships with the same name rather than one ship with two different designations. This also usually means the first ship was lost in battle during the war and another ship was subsequently renamed to that original ship's name.

A brief understanding to Volume II is also required. This section is simply listed by each squadron in alphabetical order, and within each squadron by date lost. The squadrons are as follows:

Bombing Squadrons (VB)
Bomber-Fighter Squadrons (VBF)
Cargo/Transport Squadrons (VC)
Cargo/Transport-Scout Squadrons (VCS)

Photographic Squadrons (VD)

Night Fighter Squadrons (VF(N))

Fighter Squadrons (VF)

Fighter-Bomber Squadrons (VFB)

Transport-Bomber Squadrons (VGB)

Transport-Fighter Squadrons (VGF)

Transport-Scout Squadrons (VGS)

Hospital Squadrons (VH)

Utility Squadrons (VJ)

Navy Training Squadrons (VN)

Navy Observation Squadrons (VO)

Navy Observation Spotter Squadrons (VOC)

Navy Observation-Fighter Squadrons (VOF)

Navy Patrol Squadrons (VP)

Navy Patrol Bomber Squadrons (VPB)

Navy Transport Squadrons (VR)

Navy Scout Squadrons (VS)

Navy Night Torpedo Squadrons (VT(N))

Navy Torpedo Squadrons (VT)

Marine Bombing Squadrons (VMB)

Marine Bomber-Fighter Squadrons (VMBF)

Marine Photographic Squadrons (VMD)

Marine Night Fighter Squadrons (VMF(N))

Marine Fighter Squadrons (VMF)

Marine Utility Squadrons (VMJ)

Marine Observation Squadrons (VMO)

Marine Transport Squadrons (VMR)

Marine Scout Squadrons (VMS)

Marine Scout-Bomber Squadrons (VMSB)

Marine Torpedo-Bomber Squadrons (VMTB)

Marine Target Drone Squadrons (VMTD)

NOTE: Normally, the U.S. Coast Guard comes under the direct responsibility of the Department of Transportation. During times of war, however, the Coast Guard becomes an entity of the Department of Defense and is relegated to the U.S. Navy.

A brief understanding to Volume III is also required. An aircraft type, or designation, used during World War II is listed as follows:

Letter	Class	Example
A	Ambulance	AE-1 (used only in 1943)
B	Bomber	BT-1 (used up to 1943)
BT	Bomber-Torpedo	BT2D-1
DS	Anti-Submarine Drone	DSN-1
F	Fighter	F6C-1
G	Transport, Single-engine	GB-1 (used in 1941)
H	Helicopter	HO2S-1
H	Hospital	XHL-1 (used only in 1942)
J	Utility	J2F-1
JR	Utility Transport	JRF-5
L	Glider	LNS-1
N	Trainer	N2S-1
O	Observation	O2U-1
OS	Observation-Scout	OS2U-1
P	Patrol	PB-1
PB	Patrol Bomber	PBY-5
R	Transport	RR-5
S	Scout	SU-2
SB	Scout-Bomber	SBD-3
SN	Scout-Trainer	SNJ-2

Letter	Class	Example
SO	Scout-Observation	SOC-1
TB	Torpedo-Bomber	TBD-1
TD	Target Drone	TD2C-1
TS	Torpedo-Scout	XTSF-1 (used only in 1943)

Although this initial effort took many years of research and data entry, it is by no means complete; it has only come time to sort and print out the database and get the information out to those interested. It is now up to the reader to fill in any missing information - especially missing full names of pilots and corrected misspellings of names. For any corrections, additions or deletions to the database sent to me, all I can do is thank you and publish your name in the next edition of this 3-volume set.

Aircraft Lost Listed by Aircraft Manufacturer and Type

BEECH GB-1

At the height of the Great Depression, aircraft executive Walter H. Beech and airplane designer T. A. "Ted" Wells joined forces to collaborate on a project many considered foolhardy - a large, powerful, and fast biplane built specifically for the business executive. The Beechcraft Model 17, popularly known as the "Staggerwing" was first flown on November 4, 1932, setting the standard for private passenger airplanes for many years to come. It was considered, during its time, to be the premier executive aircraft flying, much as the Gulfstream executive jets are considered in contemporary times.

In the mid-1930s, Beech began a major redesign of the aircraft, to create the Model D17 Staggerwing. The D17 featured a lengthened fuselage that improved the aircraft's landing characteristics by increasing the leverage generated by the elevator. They relocated the ailerons to the upper wings, eliminating any interference with the air flow over the flaps. Braking was improved with a foot-operated brake synchronized to the rudder pedals. These modifications enhanced the Staggerwing's performance and by the start of World War II, Beechcraft had sold more than 424 Model 17s.

Early in World War II, the need for a compact executive-type transport or courier aircraft became apparent, and in 1942 the United States Army Air Forces ordered the first of 270 Model 17s for service within the United States. These differed only in minor details from the commercial model. To meet urgent wartime needs, the government also purchased or leased (impressed) additional "Staggerwings" from private owners including 118 more for the Army Air Force plus others for the United States Navy. In Navy service the planes were designated as GB-1 and GB-2. Aircraft lost:

DATE	BUNO	SQDRN	BASE	LOST	AREA	PILOT	FATE
06/01/44	09800	COCO SOLO			NORLANT		
03/23/45	1593	STATION OPR		PORT LYAUTEY	MOROCCO		

BEECH GB-2

See description above. Aircraft lost:

DATE	BUNO	SQDRN	BASE	LOST	AREA	PILOT	FATE
08/02/44	32996	POOL	EBON	ESPIRITU SANTO	SOPAC		
09/04/44	33010	STAG-1	RUSSELLS	BANIKA	SOPAC	LT L.R. POWELL	U
12/31/44	32992	CAC		ESPIRITU SANTO	SOPAC		

BEECH JRB-1

The Beechcraft Model 18, or "Twin Beech" as it is better known, is a 6-to-11 seat, twin-engine, low-wing, conventional-gear aircraft that was manufactured by the Beech Aircraft Corporation of Wichita, Kansas. This model saw military service during and after World War II in a number of versions including the UC-45J Navigator and the SNB-1 Kansan for the Navy. The Navy's Beech JRB-1 was a variant of Beechcraft's Model B-18S with seating for eight passengers, photographic equipment and fitted with fairing over cockpit for improved visibility. There were 11 built. Aircraft lost:

DATE	BUNO	SQDRN	BASE	LOST	AREA	PILOT	FATE
05/14/45	2544	VJ-8		RUSSELLS	SOPAC		
05/14/45	2547	VJ-8		RUSSELLS	SOPAC		
07/13/45	2546	POOL	PEARL	HAWAII	ECENPAC		

BEECH JRB-2

Like as stated above, the Navy's Beech JRB-2 was a variant of Beechcraft's Model B-18S but rather than being configured for aerial photography like the -1, it was configured for light transport for the US Navy. There were 15 built. Aircraft lost:

DATE	BUNO	SQDRN	BASE	LOST	AREA	PILOT	FATE
04/01/44	4722			PEKOA FIELD	SOPAC		

BEECH JRB-3

The Navy's Beech JRB-3 was a variant of Beechcraft's Model B-18S with a modified interior design called the C-45B - with seating for eight passengers and configured for photographic equipment. There were 23 built. Aircraft lost:

DATE	BUNO	SQDRN	BASE	LOST	AREA	PILOT	FATE
10/01/44	76749	COMSERV 7			SW PAC		

BEECH JRB-4

The Navy's Beech JRB-4 was a utility transport version, equivalent to UC-45F. The UC-45F was a standardized seven-seat version based on Model C18S, with a longer nose than preceding models. There were 328 built. Aircraft lost:

DATE	BUNO	SQDRN	BASE	LOST	AREA	PILOT	FATE
11/09/44	90554	VJ-19	PEARL	HAWAII	ECENPAC	ENS FRANKLIN C. FORD	S
11/11/44	76766	3RD MAW	EWA	HAWAII	ECENPAC		
04/30/45	90566	POOL	PEARL	HAWAII	ECENPAC		
07/25/45	44574	NAB	OROTE FIELD	GUAM	WCENPAC		

BEECH SNB-1

The Beechcraft Model 18, or "Twin Beech", as it is better known, is a 6-11 seat, twin-engine, low-wing, conventional-gear aircraft that was manufactured by the Beech Aircraft Corporation of Wichita, Kansas. This model saw military service during and after World War II in a number of versions. Upon the U.S. entry into World War II, work was began in earnest on a variant specifically for training military pilots, bombardiers and navigators. The effort resulted in the Army AT-7 and Navy SNB. Further development led to the AT-11 and SNB-2 navigation trainers and the C-45 military transport. The SNB-1 variant was built specifically for the US Navy, similar to Beech's AT-11. There were 110 built. Aircraft lost:

DATE	BUNO	SQDRN	BASE	LOST	AREA	PILOT	FATE
07/16/45	39981	POOL	PEARL	HAWAII	ECENPAC		

BEECH SNB-2C

The Beech SNB-2C was a variant built specifically for the US Navy, similar to AT-7C (R-985-AN3 engines). Aircraft lost:

DATE	BUNO	SQDRN	BASE	LOST	AREA	PILOT	FATE
03/15/44	51321	CASU-10	ESPIRITU SANTO	PALLIKULO	SOPAC		
10/14/44	51325	AFIU	MOMOTE	MOMOTE	SW PAC	ENS RAY A. DELROSSO	S
03/01/45	51136	NACTU	BARBERS POINT	HAWAII	ECENPAC	LTJG JOHN D. HAIGLER	S
07/24/45	29596	AROU-1		MOMOTE	SW PAC		
08/04/45	23817	POOL	PEARL	HAWAII	ECENPAC		

BELLANCA CH-400

The Bellanca CH-400 Skyrocket was a six-seat utility aircraft built in the United States in the 1930s, a continuation of the design lineage that had started with the Bellanca WB-2. Retaining the same basic airframe of the preceding CH-200 and CH-300, the CH-400 was fitted with a more powerful Pratt & Whitney Wasp radial engine. Three examples were purchased by the US Navy under the designation RE. Two were used for radio research, and one as an air ambulance for the US Marine Corps. This latter aircraft was reconfigured to carry two stretchers.

The "List of Serial Numbers Assigned Navy Aircraft," compiled by the Aviation Statistics office of the Deputy Chief of Naval Operations (Air), states that this particular Bellanca was a "miscellaneous acquisition." Any further information on this from the reader would be helpful. Aircraft lost:

DATE	BUNO	SQDRN	BASE	LOST	AREA	PILOT	FATE
01/12/43	09785				NORPAC		

BOEING PB2B-2

The Consolidated PBY Catalina was an American flying boat of the 1930s and 1940s produced by Consolidated Aircraft. It was one of the most widely used multi-role aircraft of World War II. PBYs served with every branch of the United States Armed Forces and in the air forces and navies of many other nations.

During World War II, PBYs were used in anti-submarine warfare, patrol bombing, convoy escorts, search and rescue missions (especially air-sea rescue), and cargo transport. The PBY was the most successful aircraft of its kind; no other flying boat was produced in greater numbers. The PB2B-2 was the Boeing-Canada built version of the PBY-5 but with the taller fin of the PBN-1. While 67 were built and most supplied to the British RAF/RAAF as the Catalina VI, 8 remained with the United States Navy. Aircraft lost:

DATE	BUNO	SQDRN	BASE	LOST	AREA	PILOT	FATE
02/28/45	44243	VH-2		TENAPAG	WCENPAC		
07/27/45	44244	VH-2		SAIPAN	WCENPAC	LT ROBERT O. NICHOLAS	D

BREWSTER F2A-3

The Navy ordered 108 F2A-3 Buffalo aircraft from Brewster Aeronautical Corporation on January 21, 1941, and took delivery of these between July and December of the same year. Features of this design included increased armor protection for the pilot and for the fuel tank, and improved equipment. The weight of this aircraft adversely affected the aircraft's performance. Navy Squadron VF-2 operated F2A-3s aboard the USS LEXINGTON (CV-2), and VS-201 took a small number aboard the escort carrier USS LONG ISLAND; one Marine fighting squadron, VMF-221, flew the majority of F2A-3s. When VMF-211 was deployed in May 1942 to Palmyra Atoll in the South Pacific they were equipped with the Brewster F2A-3. The fighter achieved little operational success, its only major battle being that at Midway when VMF-221 suffered major losses. Aircraft lost:

DATE	BUNO	SQDRN	BASE	LOST	AREA	PILOT	FATE
12/07/41	01544	VF-2	USS LEXINGTON	PEARL	ECENPAC		
12/07/41	01567	VMF-221	EWA	HAWAII	ECENPAC		
12/10/41	01557	VF-2	USS LEXINGTON	PEARL	ECENPAC		
12/26/41	01529	VF-2	USS LEXINGTON	PEARL	ECENPAC	ACMM H.L. RUTHERFORD	U
12/29/41	01543	MAG-21	EWA	MIDWAY	ECENPAC		
12/29/41	01540	VF-2	USS LEXINGTON	PEARL	ECENPAC	LTJG FRED BORISS	U
02/15/42	01554	MAG-21	EWA	MIDWAY	ECENPAC		
02/19/42	01527	VMF-221		MIDWAY	ECENPAC		
02/24/42	01574	VMF-211	EWA	HAWAII	ECENPAC	2NDLT R.A. CORRY	S
03/05/42	01573	VMF-212	EWA	HAWAII	ECENPAC		
04/06/42	01572	VMF-212	EWA	HAWAII	ECENPAC	1STLT ROGERS	S
04/06/42	01518	VMF-221		MIDWAY	ECENPAC	MAJ PARKS	M
04/06/42	01520	VMF-221		MIDWAY	ECENPAC	CAPT CURTIN	M
04/06/42	01522	VMF-221		MIDWAY	ECENPAC	CAPT HENNESSY	M
04/06/42	01524	VMF-221		MIDWAY	ECENPAC	CAPT MCCARTHY	M
04/06/42	01525	VMF-221		MIDWAY	ECENPAC	CAPT ALRORD	M
04/06/42	01528	VMF-221		MIDWAY	ECENPAC	LT BENSON	M
04/06/42	01537	VMF-221		MIDWAY	ECENPAC	LT BUTLER	M
04/06/42	01541	VMF-221		MIDWAY	ECENPAC	LT LINDSAY	M
04/06/42	01542	VMF-221		MIDWAY	ECENPAC	LT LUCAS	M
04/06/42	01548	VMF-221		MIDWAY	ECENPAC	LT MADOLE	M
04/06/42	01559	VMF-221		MIDWAY	ECENPAC	LT MAHANNAH	M
04/06/42	01563	VMF-221		MIDWAY	ECENPAC	LT SANDOVAL	M
04/06/42	01569	VMF-221		MIDWAY	ECENPAC	LT PINKETON	M

BREWSTER F3A-1

In production longer than any other U.S. fighter of World War II, the gull-winged Vought F4U Corsair had several claims to fame. It was credited with an 11:1 ratio of kills to losses in action against Japanese aircraft and was the last piston-engined fighter in production for any of the U.S. services. Its greatest attribute, though, was the excellence of its overall performance, making it certainly the finest carrier-based fighter of any used by the combatants in World War II, and perhaps the best of any U.S. fighters in the conflict. The demand for these aircraft was so great that Brewster and Goodyear were awarded contracts to build similar aircraft. Of the initial Corsair production of 4,699 aircraft, sources claim that 738 were built by Brewster and given the designate F3A-1. The author, however, found that 745 Bureau Numbers were assigned to these aircraft (BuNos 04515-04774 (270 aircraft); 08550-08797 (248 aircraft); 11067-11293 (227 aircraft)). Aircraft lost:

DATE	BUNO	SQDRN	BASE	LOST	AREA	PILOT	FATE
05/29/44	04685	COMAIR-PAC	PEARL	HAWAII	ECENPAC		
06/12/44	11201	COMAIR-PAC	PEARL	HAWAII	ECENPAC		
07/28/44	04647	COMAIR-PAC	PEARL	HAWAII	ECENPAC		

CANADIAN CAR & FOUNDRY CO. (CCF) SBW-1

The Curtiss SB2C Helldiver was a carrier-based dive bomber aircraft produced for the United States Navy during World War II (see the Curtiss SB2C variants). The program suffered many delays; however, production tempo accelerated with production at Columbus, Ohio and two Canadian factories: one being the Canadian Car and Foundry which built 894 (designated SBW-I, SBW-3, SBW-4, SBW-4E and SBW-5), these models being respectively equivalent to their Curtiss-built counterparts. There were 38 built. Aircraft lost:

DATE	BUNO	SQDRN	BASE	LOST	AREA	PILOT	FATE
06/20/44	21199	VB-2	USS HORNET	W OF SAIPAN	CENPAC	LTJG H. WELLS	M
06/20/44	21211	VB-2	USS HORNET	W OF SAIPAN	CENPAC	ENS C.E. HIIGEL	S
07/13/44	21219		USS CORE	ENIWETOK	CENPAC		
07/27/44	21213	VB-8	USS BUNKER HILL	PALAU	CENPAC		
07/27/44	21215	VB-8	USS BUNKER HILL	PALAU	CENPAC		
08/09/44	21206	CASU-35		ENIWETOK	CENPAC		
09/09/44	21203	VB-8	USS BUNKER HILL	MINDANAO SEA	PHIL	LT ARTHUR D. JONES	M
09/16/44	21210	VB-8	USS BUNKER HILL	PALAU	CENPAC		
09/16/44	21221	VB-8	USS BUNKER HILL	PALAU	CENPAC		
09/17/44	21205	VB-4	HILO	HAWAII	ECENPAC		
09/23/44	21216	VB-8	USS BUNKER HILL	OKINAWA	EMPIRE		
10/05/44	21217	VB-8	USS BUNKER HILL	ULITHI	WCENPAC		
10/05/44	21227	VB-8	USS BUNKER HILL	ULITHI	WCENPAC		

CANADIAN CAR & FOUNDRY CO. (CCF) SBW-3

This was the Canadian built version of the SB2C-3. There were 413 built. Aircraft lost:

DATE	BUNO	SQDRN	BASE	LOST	AREA	PILOT	FATE
10/10/44	21296	VB-14	USS WASP	OKINAWA	EMPIRE		
10/19/44	21283	VB-14	USS WASP	LUZON	PHIL		

DATE	BUNO	SQDRN	BASE	LOST	AREA	PILOT	FATE
10/20/44	21236	VB-100	PEARL	HAWAII	ECENPAC	ENS HOYT BURNS	S
10/24/44	21267	VB-18	USS INTREPID	LOS NEGROS	PHIL		
10/24/44	21271	VB-18	USS INTREPID	LOS NEGROS	PHIL	LT WILSON C. MCNEILL	M
10/25/44	21293	VB-11	USS HORNET		PHIL	LT STRAHAN	S
10/26/44	21329	VB-14	USS WASP	LUZON	PHIL	LTJG JUDSON H. DOANE	S
10/29/44	21318	VB-18	USS INTREPID	LUZON	PHIL		
10/29/44	21268	VB-7	USS HANCOCK	MANILA	PHIL		
10/30/44	21246	COMAIR-PAC	PEARL	HAWAII	ECENPAC		
10/30/44	21261	COMAIR-PAC	PEARL	HAWAII	ECENPAC		
11/05/44	21360	VB-14	USS WASP	LUZON	PHIL	LTJG HEIDEN	M
11/13/44	21282	VB-100	PEARL	HAWAII	ECENPAC	ENS ROBERT A. HOLMES	S
11/13/44	21322	VB-11	USS HORNET		PHIL	ENS CARDONS	S
11/14/44	21290	VB-81	USS WASP	LEYTE GULF	PHIL	ENS EDWIN C. MOORE	S
11/17/44	21304	VB-100	USS SARATOGA	HAWAII	ECENPAC	ENS ELWOOD W. GEORGE	S
11/25/44	21287	VB-18	USS INTREPID		PHIL	LTJG H.E. JOHNSON	S
11/25/44	21292	VB-18	USS INTREPID		PHIL	(DECK LOSS-KAMIKAZE)	
11/25/44	21353	VB-4	USS ESSEX	LEYTE GULF	PHIL	(DECK LOSS-KAMIKAZE)	
11/26/44	21402	VB-7	USS HANCOCK	MANILA	PHIL		
12/07/44	21350	AR & OH		MANUS	SW PAC		
12/16/44	21374	VB-80	USS TICONDER-OGA	LUZON	PHIL	ENS J.E. KLUCZINSKI	D
12/18/44	21355	UNAS-SIGNED	USS CAPE ESPERANC E	PHILIPPINE SEA	PHIL	(DECK LOSS-TYPHOON)	
12/18/44	21356	UNAS-SIGNED	USS ALTAMAHA	PHILIPPINE SEA	PHIL	(DECK LOSS-TYPHOON)	
12/18/44	21357	UNAS-SIGNED	USS ALTAMAHA	PHILIPPINE SEA	PHIL	(DECK LOSS-TYPHOON)	
12/28/44	21306	A.A.	PEARL	HAWAII	ECENPAC		
12/31/44	21370	A.A.	PEARL	HAWAII	ECENPAC		
01/16/45	21406	VB-20	USS LEX-INGTON	HONG KONG	EMPIRE		
01/16/45	21377	VB-7	USS HANCOCK	HONG KONG	EMPIRE	LTJG C.S. SNEAD	M
02/05/45	21301	CASU(F)-43		GUAM	WCENPAC		
02/18/45	21291	VB-87	KAHULUI	HAWAII	ECENPAC	LTJG JACK BESSE	S
03/14/45	21414	VB-17	USS HORNET	ENR HONSHU	EMPIRE		
03/16/45	21286	VB-6	USS HANCOCK	ENR KYUSHU	EMPIRE	LTJG GREHAN	S
03/18/45	21332	VB-6	USS HANCOCK	KYUSHU	EMPIRE	LT R.E. GARDINER	M
03/18/45	21348	VB-6	USS HANCOCK	KYUSHU	EMPIRE	LTJG R.L. SOMERVILLE	S
03/18/45	21390	VB-6	USS HANCOCK	KYUSHU	EMPIRE	LTJG R.D. MOORE	S
03/24/45	21431	CASU(F)-12		GUAM	WCENPAC	1STLT H.W. HACKETT	S
03/28/45	21279	VB-17	USS HORNET	KYUSHU	EMPIRE		
04/02/45	21411	VMSB-245		ULITHI	WCENPAC	1STLT LLOYD C. WALSH	S
04/07/45	21438	VB-17	USS HORNET	OKINAWA	EMPIRE		
04/21/45	21298	VMSB-245		ULITHI	WCENPAC	2NDLT LEO K. BROWN	S
04/29/45	21408	VMSB-151		ENGEBI	WCENPAC		
05/02/45	21395	AROU-1		MOMOTE	SW PAC		
05/05/45	21392	VS-53	HAWAII		ECENPAC	ENS JOHN F. GORTON	S
05/06/45	21524	VS-66		MAJURO	WCENPAC	LTJG GREGORY G. PRIVITELLI	S
05/07/45	21258	NAS	HILO	HAWAII	ECENPAC	LTJG J.E. THORGERSON	D
05/17/45	21263	CASU(F)-12		GUAM	WCENPAC		

DATE	BUNO	SQDRN	BASE	LOST	AREA	PILOT	FATE
05/17/45	21343	CASU(F)-12		GUAM	WCENPAC		
05/17/45	21365	CASU(F)-12		GUAM	WCENPAC		
05/18/45	21533	VS-52	ROI	WOTJE	CENPAC		
05/31/45	21233	COMAIR-PAC	PEARL	HAWAII	ECENPAC		
05/31/45	21238	COMAIR-PAC	PEARL	HAWAII	ECENPAC		
05/31/45	21262	COMAIR-PAC	PEARL	HAWAII	ECENPAC		
05/31/45	21312	COMAIR-PAC	PEARL	HAWAII	ECENPAC		
05/31/45	21407	VB-88		SAIPAN	WCENPAC	LTJG WALTER N. LEONARD	S
06/09/45	21421	VMSB-245		ULITHI	WCENPAC	1STLT RBT L.W. FLAVELLE	S
06/21/45	21351	CASU(F)-14		SAIPAN	WCENPAC		
06/21/45	21461	VS-66		ROI	WCENPAC	LTJG FRANK C. HART, JR.	S
06/29/45	21368	VMSB-245		ULITHI	WCENPAC	1STLT SIMPSON BULL	D
07/17/45	21419	VMSB-245		ULITHI	WCENPAC		

CESSNA JRC-1

The Cessna AT-17 Bobcat was a twin-engined advanced trainer aircraft designed and made in the United States, and used during World War II to bridge the gap between single-engine trainers and twin-engine combat aircraft. The AT-17 was powered by two Jacobs R-755-9 radial piston engines. The AT-17 was a military version of the commercial Cessna T-50 light transport. The Cessna Airplane Company first produced the wood and tubular steel, fabric-covered T-50 in 1939 for the civilian market, as a lightweight and low cost twin for personal use where larger aircraft such as the Beech 18 would be too expensive. A low-wing cantilever monoplane, it featured retractable main landing gear and wing trailing-edge flaps, both electrically actuated. The wing structure was built up of laminated spruce spar beams with spruce and plywood ribs. The fixed tail wheel is non-steerable and full-swiveling. The prototype T-50 made its maiden flight on 26 March 1939. In 1940, the US Army Air Corps ordered them under the designation AT-8 as multi-engine advanced trainers.

Thirty-three AT-8s were built for the U.S. Army Air Corps, and production continued under the designation AT-17 reflecting a change in equipment and engine types. In 1942, the U.S Army Air Force (the successor to the Air Corps from June 1941) adopted the Bobcat as a light personnel transport and those delivered after January 1, 1943 were designated UC-78s. By the end of World War II, Cessna had produced more than 4,600 Bobcats for the U.S. military, 67 of which were transferred to the United States Navy as JRC-1s. Aircraft lost:

DATE	BUNO	SQDRN	BASE	LOST	AREA	PILOT	FATE
06/10/44	64479	NAS		SAN JUAN	NORLANT	AP1/C JAMES D. LANG	S
06/20/45	64452	POOL	KANEOHE	HAWAII	ECENPAC		

CONSOLIDATED 21-A

There are two stories with this one aircraft lost in Alaska. One story is that this was owned by the United States Coast Guard and was called both the Consolidated N4Y-1 and the Model 21-A – a two-seat biplane used for training purposes. The other source states that this was a Grumman JRF-4 "Goose" that had been acquired from a civilian source to help in the war effort. The Grumman Model G-21 story is that in 1936, a group of wealthy residents of Long Island, including E. Roland Harriman, approached Grumman and commissioned an aircraft that they could use to fly to New York City. In response the Grumman Model G-21 was designed as a light amphibian transport. The typical Grumman rugged construction was matched to an all-metal, high-winged monoplane powered by two 450 horsepower (340 kW) Pratt & Whitney R-985 Wasp Jr. SB nine-cylinder, air-cooled radial engines mounted on the leading edge of high-set wings. The deep fuselage served also as a hull and was equipped with hand-cranked retractable landing gear. First flight of the prototype took place on May 29, 1937. The G-21 held six passengers. Of the twelve built, all were converted to G-21A standards. The G-21A had an increased gross weight of 8,000 lb (3,636 kg). There were 30 built. Any further information on this by the reader would be appreciated. Aircraft lost:

DATE	BUNO	SQDRN	BASE	LOST	AREA	PILOT	FATE
00/00/00	99078	STATION OPR	KODIAK	ALASKA	NORPAC		

CONSOLIDATED PB2Y-2

The PB2Y Coronado was a large flying boat patrol bomber designed by Consolidated Aircraft. As of 2011, one Coronado remains at the Pensacola, Florida National Museum of Naval Aviation. After deliveries of the PBY Catalina, also a Consolidated aircraft, began in 1935, the United States Navy began planning for the next generation of patrol bombers.

The next generation prototype design was finalized as the PB2Y-2, with a large cantilever wing, twin tail, and four Pratt & Whitney R-1830 radial engines. The two inner engines were fitted with four-bladed reversible pitch propellers; the outer engines had standard three-bladed feathering props. The prototype Coronado first flew in December 1937.

Like the PBY Catalina before it, the PB2Y's wingtip floats retracted to reduce drag and increase range, with the floats' buoyant hulls acting as the wingtips when retracted. Coronados served in combat in the Pacific, in both bombing and anti-submarine roles, but transport and hospital aircraft were the most common. The PB2Y was used for trans-Atlantic flights, staging through the RAF base at Darrell's Island, Bermuda, and Puerto Rico, though the aircraft were used to deliver vital cargo and equipment in a transportation network that stretched down both sides of the Atlantic, from Newfoundland, to Brazil, and to Nigeria, and other parts of Africa. After the war ended four were scuttled off the coast of Bermuda in 1946.

Coronados served as a major component in the Naval Air Transport Service (NATS) during World War II in the Pacific theater. Most had originally been acquired as combat patrol aircraft, but the limitations noted above quickly relegated them to transport service in the American naval air fleet also. The PB2Y-2 was the evaluation variant with four 1020hp R-1830-78 engines, a modified hull and six 0.5in guns. Only 6 were built. Aircraft lost:

DATE	BUNO	SQDRN	BASE	LOST	AREA	PILOT	FATE
05/06/42	1633	VP-13	PEARL	HAWAII	ECENPAC	LT B.F. MCLEOD	D
02/15/44	1635	HEDRON-2	KANEOHE	OFF SAN DIEGO	CENPAC	LTJG F.E. STRUTHERS	S

CONSOLIDATED PB2Y-3

The Consolidated PB2Y-3 was the production variant of the -2 (see above) with four 1200hp R-1830-88 engines and eight 0.5in guns. There were 210 built. Aircraft lost:

DATE	BUNO	SQDRN	BASE	LOST	AREA	PILOT	FATE
05/23/43	7113	VP-15		BERMUDA	NORLANT	LT HAROLD W. LOUGH	M
10/13/43	7146	VP-1	SALINAS	ECUADOR	CENPAC		
10/18/43	7147	VP-207	PUERTO CASTILLA	HONDURAS	CENLANT	LT ALAN G. OVERTON	M
11/07/43	7108	VP-15		BERMUDA	NORLANT	LTJG EMERICK	S
01/01/44	7106	VP-15		BERMUDA	NORLANT		
02/14/44	7170	VP-207	KANEOHE	EBEYE	WCENPAC	LT W.E. CANNON	S
07/17/44	7143	VP-1		GALAPAGOS	CENPAC	LT W.D. CAUTHAN	M
09/10/44	7186	VH-1		SAIPAN	WCENPAC		
09/14/44	7068	VH-1		EBEYE	WCENPAC	LTJG HARKNESS	S
12/31/44	7131	VPB-1		COCO SOLO	CENLANT		
02/12/45	7075	VR-2		EBEYE	WCENPAC	LT HAROLD A. BOWMAN	D
02/28/45	7076	VPB-13		SAIPAN	WCENPAC		
03/12/45	7063	VPB-13		SAIPAN	WCENPAC		
03/29/45	7056	VPB-13		SAIPAN	WCENPAC		
03/31/45	7152	VPB-13		SAIPAN	WCENPAC		
05/05/45	7145	VPB-13		KEREMA RHETTO	EMPIRE		
05/10/45	7160	VPB-13		KEREMA RHETTO	EMPIRE		
05/23/45	7104	VP-15		BERMUDA	NORLANT	LTJG V.G. MACKENZIE	S
05/23/45	7072	VPB-13	USS KENNETH WHITING	KEREMA RHETTO	EMPIRE		
06/02/45	7132	VPB-13		KEREMA RHETTO	EMPIRE		
06/28/45	7167	VPB-13		KEREMA RHETTO	EMPIRE		
07/17/45	7055	CASU(F)-48		SAIPAN	WCENPAC		
08/05/45	7154	VPB-13		KEREMA RHETTO	EMPIRE		
08/11/45	7053	CASU(F)-48		SAIPAN	WCENPAC		
08/11/45	7074	CASU(F)-48		SAIPAN	WCENPAC		
08/11/45	7103	CASU(F)-48		SAIPAN	WCENPAC		

CONSOLIDATED PB2Y-3R

Thirty-one of the 210 PB2Y-3s were converted by the Rohr Aircraft Corporation as freighters with faired-over turrets, side loading hatch, and seating for 44 passengers. Fred Rohr, who created the fuel tanks for Charles Lindbergh's *Spirit of St. Louis*, founded Rohr Aircraft Corporation on August 6, 1940 with the help of Reuben H. Fleet. The company was acquired by the BFGoodrich Company in 1997. Aircraft lost:

DATE	BUNO	SQDRN	BASE	LOST	AREA	PILOT	FATE
05/07/44	7096	NATS			N AFRICA	CAPT K.A. WHITSIT	S
07/31/44	7233	NATS		FUNAFUTI	CENPAC	JAMES W. GENTRY	D
04/28/45	7198	PAN AM		HAWAII	ECENPAC	WILLIAM D. KNOX	S
05/09/45	7195	VR-10	HONOLULU	HAWAII	ECENPAC		
05/09/45	7226	VR-2		HAWAII	ECENPAC	LT C.E. TAUCH	S

CONSOLIDATED PB4Y-1

The Consolidated PB4Y-1 Liberator was a World War II era long-range patrol bomber of the United States Navy derived from the Consolidated B-24 Liberator. The U.S. Navy designation was applied to 976 “navalized” B-24D, J, L and M models built at Consolidated's San Diego factory, as well as one North American-built B-24G. Later aircraft were equipped with a bow turret. The Navy, Coast Guard and Marine Corps took these 977 PB4Y-1's and most were sent to 24 different VB (Bombing) and VPB (Patrol Bombing) squadrons. Operating in the Atlantic and Pacific, the PB4Y-1's destroyed 13 Axis submarines. Aircraft lost:

DATE	BUNO	SQDRN	BASE	LOST	AREA	PILOT	FATE
02/04/43	31948	VB-101	GUADAL-CANAL	KAHILI	SOPAC		
02/04/43	31970	VB-101	GUADAL-CANAL	KAHILI	SOPAC		
03/05/43	31947	VB-101	GUADAL-CANAL	GUADAL-CANAL	SOPAC		
03/05/43	31950	VB-101	GUADAL-CANAL	GUADAL-CANAL	SOPAC		
04/05/43	31969	FAW-1			SOPAC		
04/07/43	31989	VB-102		HAWAII	ECENPAC	LT GEORGE H.S. BONN	D
04/10/43	32017	VB-103	DUNKES-WELL		NORLANT		
06/24/43	32046	VB-103	DUNKES-WELL		NORLANT	LT H.K. REESE	M
07/06/43	31992	VB-102		GUADAL-CANAL	SOPAC	LT C.R. VAN VOORHIS	M
07/17/43	31952	VB-102		GUADAL-CANAL	SOPAC	LTJG HASKETT	M
07/23/43	32042	VB-105	DUNKES-WELL	BERMUDA	NORLANT	LT EMIL EDWARD COOLMAN	D
07/24/43	32054	VB-107	NATAL	NATAL	SOLANT	LT G.E. WAUGH	M
08/07/43	32037	VB-103	DUNKES-WELL		NORLANT	LTJG WALTER HENRY	U
08/12/43	32064	VB-107	NATAL	NATAL	SOLANT		
08/22/43	63916	VB-105	DUNKES-WELL		NORLANT	LT THOMAS EVERETT	U
09/02/43	32033	VB-103	DUNKES-WELL	BAY OF BISCAY	ENGLAND	LT KEITH W. WICKSTOM	U
09/04/43	32022	VB-103	ST. EVAL	BAY OF BISCAY	ENGLAND	LTJG J.H. ALEXANDER	S
09/10/43	32048	VB-104	GUADAL-CANAL	GUADAL-CANAL	SOPAC		
09/10/43	63925	VB-105	ICELAND		NORLANT	LTJG GEORGE W. BROWN	M
09/18/43	32039	VB-103	ST. EVAL		EUROPE	LTJG KRAUSE	S
09/20/43	32076	VB-104	GUADAL-CANAL	GUADAL-CANAL	SOPAC		
09/21/43	32036	VB-103	DUNKES-WELL		EUROPE	LTJG J.H. ALEXANDER	U
09/26/43	63952	VB-110	DUNKES-WELL		NORLANT		
10/13/43	32034	VB-111		ICELAND	NORLANT	LT DURANT	M
10/15/43	32052	VB-107	NATAL	NATAL	SOLANT	LT LEONARD SHIRLEY	S
10/20/43	32102	VB-106	FUNAFUTI	CANTON	EMPIRE	LT SAMUEL I. PATELLA	M
10/22/43	63917	VB-105		BAY OF BISCAY	EUROPE	LT T.R. EVERT	M
10/23/43	63915	VB-105	DUNKES-WELL	DUNKES-WELL	ENGLAND	LT J.C. HILLMAN	D
11/08/43	63919	VB-110	DUNKES-WELL	BAY OF BISCAY	ENGLAND	LT W.E. GRUMBLES	M
11/12/43	32032	VB-103	DUNKES-WELL	BAY OF BISCAY	ENGLAND	LTJG B. BROWNELL	M
11/15/43	32012	VB-104	CARNEY FIELD	GUADAL-CANAL	SOPAC	LTJG M.M. HONEY	M
11/18/43	32123	VB-108	CANTON	NW OF FUNAFUTI	CENPAC	LT P. HARDY	S
11/28/43	32144	VMD-254	PALMYRA		ECENPAC	LCOL E.P. PENNEBAKER	S
11/30/43	63931	VB-112	PORT LYAUTEY	FARO S PORTUGAL	SW EUROPE	LT R.L. TRUM	M
11/30/43	63950	VB-112	PORT LYAUTEY	MOROCCO	NW AFR	LTJG J.M. HILL	M
12/03/43	32014	VB-103	DUNKES-WELL	OKEHAMPTO N	ENGLAND	LT F.A. LUCAS	D
12/12/43	32099	VB-108	APAMAMA	NUKUFETAU	SOPAC	LCDR J.A.J. MCCORMACK	M
12/13/43	32040	VB-103	DUNKES-WELL		EUROPE	LT C.F. RIEF	S
12/15/43	32093	VB-106	CARNEY FIELD	GUADAL-CANAL	SOPAC	LT A.L. SEAMAN	S

DATE	BUNO	SQDRN	BASE	LOST	AREA	PILOT	FATE
12/18/43	63934	VB-110	DUNKES-WELL	MANCHESTER	EUROPE	LTJG G.H. CHARNS	S
12/25/43	32092	VB-106	GUADAL-CANAL	KOLI POINT	SOPAC	ENS SNEAD	D
12/28/43	32120	VB-108	NUKUFE-TAU	KWAJALEIN	CENPAC	LT V.E. NIEBRAGGE	M
12/28/43	63926	VB-110	DUNKES-WELL	OKEHAMPTON	ENGLAND	LT W.W. PARISH	D
12/28/43	32035	VB-113	ST. MAEGAN		EUROPE	LT R.A. THOMPSON	M
12/29/43	32183	VB-103	DUNKES-WELL	BAY OF BISCAY	ENGLAND	ENS ANDERSON	S
01/01/44	32065	VB-107	NATAL	ASCENSION IS.	SOLANT	CAPT N.S. BLOUNT	M
01/01/44	32136	VB-109	APAMAMA		CENPAC		
01/03/44	32141	VB-109	APAMAMA	TAROA	CENPAC		
01/08/44	32077	VB-104	GUADAL-CANAL	GUADAL-CANAL	SOPAC		
01/13/44	32139	VB-109	APAMAMA	MARSHALLS	CENPAC	LT COLEMAN	M
01/29/44	32074	VB-104	GUADAL-CANAL	RUSSELLS	SOPAC	LT D.L. MCHAGER	S
02/10/44	32085	VB-106	MUNDA	KOLI POINT	SOPAC	LT E.B. MITCHELL	S
02/10/44	31981	VD-1			PAC		
02/13/44	32117	VB-109	APAMAMA	WOTJE	CENPAC	LT J.H. HERRON	M
02/14/44	32191	VB-103	DUNKES-WELL	BAY OF BISCAY	ENGLAND	LTJG K.L. WRIGHT	S
02/26/44	31990	HEDRON-2	KANEOHE	HAWAII	ECENPAC		
02/26/44	32016	HEDRON-2	PALMYRA	HAWAII	ECENPAC		
02/26/44	63929	VB-105	DUNKES-WELL		EUROPE	LT R.L. NORTL	M
03/07/44	32079	VB-104	MUNDA	MUNDA	SOPAC	LTJG W.D. SEARLS	M
03/09/44	32069	VB-104	MUNDA	KAPINGIMARANGI	SOPAC	LTJG A.E. ANDERSON	M
03/12/44	63946	VB-110	DUNKES-WELL	CHERBOURG	EUROPE	LTJG W.H. RYAN	M
03/17/44	32038	VB-105	DUNKES-WELL	FALBENNY WALES	EUROPE	LTJG A.P. ADAMS	S
03/20/44	32209	VB-103	DUNKES-WELL	BAY OF BISCAY	ENGLAND	LTJG J.C. KESSEL	M
03/21/44	32100	VB-108	TARAWA		SOPAC		
03/22/44	32219	VB-106	MUNDA	KOLI POINT	SOPAC	LT R.J. O'DONNELL	M
03/27/44	32210	VB-110	DUNKES-WELL	CHIVENER	EUROPE	LTJG R.B. WEIHANS	S
03/31/44	63940	VB-110	DUNKES-WELL	BAY OF BISCAY	ENGLAND	LTJG O.R. MOORE	M
03/31/44	63948	VB-110	DUNKES-WELL	BAY OF BISCAY	ENGLAND	LT H. BARTON	M
04/06/44	32172	VB-106	NADZAB	NEW GUINEA	SW PAC	LT D.C. DAVIS	S
04/12/44	32235	VB-113		TRINIDAD	CENLANT	LTJG R.B. LANE	D
04/17/44	32187	VB-114	PORT LYAUTEY	MOROCCO	NW AFR	LT F.M. KELLEY	S
04/22/44	32222	VB-115	MUNDA	PULUWAT	SOPAC	LT W.R. DOERR	M
04/28/44	32170	VB-115	MUNDA		SOPAC	ENS E. CARLSON	S
05/01/44	32175	VB-106	NADZAB	NEW GUINEA	SW PAC	LT A.L. SEAMAN	D
05/06/44	32278	VB-101	KANEOHE	HAWAII	ECENPAC	LTJG W.H. GREEN	S
05/15/44	32215	VB-115	GREEN	RABAUL	SOPAC	LT H.M. DAWES	S
05/17/44	32115	VB-115	GREEN	RABAUL	SOPAC		
05/20/44	32159	VB-115	GREEN	DUKE OF YORK	SOPAC	LT S.B. PITT	M
05/27/44	32201	VB-103	DUNKES-WELL		EUROPE		
05/28/44	32171	VB-106	NADZAB	MOMOTE	SW PAC	LT E.J. MORRISON	D
06/05/44	32150	VB-115	WAKDE		SW PAC		
06/05/44	32177	VB-115	WAKDE		SW PAC		
06/05/44	32275	VB-115	WAKDE		SW PAC		
06/26/44	38769	VB-116		ENIWETOK	CENPAC	LT W.H. MILLER	S
07/05/44	32169	VB-114		DUNKES-WELL	ENGLAND		
07/21/44	32121	VB-109	ENIWETOK	ENIWETOK	CENPAC		
07/29/44	32108	VB-109	ENIWETOK	PONAPE	CENPAC	CDR H.H. MILLER	S
08/02/44	32138	VB-108	TARAWA	ENIWETOK	CENPAC		
08/04/44	32263	VB-109	ENIWETOK	SAIPAN	WCENPAC	LT E.H. KASPERSON	M
08/08/44	38739	VB-117	KANEOHE	HAWAII	ECENPAC	ENS A.B. HEARD	S
08/09/44	38766	VB-116		ENIWETOK	CENPAC	LT R.C. ANDERSON	D
08/12/44	32271	HEDRON-7	ENGLAND		EUROPE	LT J.P. KENNEDY, JR.	M

DATE	BUNO	SQDRN	BASE	LOST	AREA	PILOT	FATE
08/19/44	32307	VB-116		ENIWETOK	CENPAC		
08/19/44	32308	VB-116		ENIWETOK	CENPAC		
08/19/44	32327	VB-116		ENIWETOK	CENPAC		
08/23/44	32323	VB-102		CHICHI JIMA	CENPAC	LT T.R. CLARK, JR.	D
08/24/44	38753	VB-110	BRECON-SHIRE		EUROPE	LT J.G. BYRNES	D
08/31/44	63954	FAW-7	ENGLAND		EUROPE		
09/08/44	32322	VB-102		TINIAN	WCENPAC	LT LAWRENCE D. CONDON	S
09/09/44	32319	VB-102		TINIAN	WCENPAC	LTJG FRANCIS J. LENCIONI	S
09/14/44	38799	FAW-7	ENGLAND	ICELAND	NORLANT	LT JAMES O. TRUDEAU	S
09/19/44	32310	VPB-116		TINIAN	WCENPAC	LT L.D. SULLIVAN	S
10/11/44	38776	VPB-116		SAIPAN	WCENPAC	LT W.H. STIMSON	M
10/18/44	38835	VPB-104		HAWAII	ECENPAC	LTJG J.D. SHEA	S
10/19/44	32280	VPB-101	OWI		SW PAC	CDR JUSTIN A. MILLER	S
10/23/44	32277	VPB-101	OWI		SW PAC	LT HAROLD H. LEWIS	M
10/25/44	32266	VPB-101	OWI		SW PAC	ENS ROBERT W. ALLEN	D
10/26/44	32216	VPB-101	OWI		SW PAC	LT ALBERT R. SIEBER	S
10/26/44	32299	VPB-101	OWI		SW PAC	LR RUSSELL E. BOWEN	M
10/26/44	32243	VPB-115		MOROTAI	PHIL	LT E.F.K. JENNINGS	S
11/05/44	32272	VPB-101	MOROTAI		SW PAC		
11/05/44	38848	VPB-101	MOROTAI		SW PAC		
11/06/44	38795	VPB-104	MOROTAI		SW PAC		
11/11/44	38774	VPB-104	MOROTAI		SW PAC	LT MAURICE K. HILL	D
11/12/44	38798	VPB-105		DUNKES-WELL	ENGLAND	ENS JAMES R. ATWILL	S
11/12/44	38760	VPB-117		TINIAN	WCENPAC	LT HERBERT G. BOX	S
11/15/44	38903	VPB-101	OWI		SW PAC		
11/21/44	38841	VPB-101	MOROTAI		SW PAC	LT T.R. WILLIAMS	S
11/23/44	38814	VPB-104	MOROTAI		SW PAC		
11/23/44	32221	VPB-116		TINIAN	WCENPAC		
11/23/44	32306	VPB-116		TINIAN	WCENPAC		
11/25/44	32260	VPB-101	MOROTAI		SW PAC	LTJG WALTON K. ROGERS	S
11/26/44	32281	VPB-103		DUNKES-WELL	ENGLAND		
11/29/44	38829	VPB-101	MOROTAI		SW PAC	LT DAVID M. CARROLL	U
12/05/44	38823	VPB-117		LEYTE GULF	PHIL		
12/06/44	38816	VPB-104		LEYTE GULF	PHIL	LTJG JEFFREY D. HEMPHILL	U
12/09/44	32200	VPB-103		DUNKES-WELL	ENGLAND		
12/10/44	38773	VPB-117		LEYTE GULF	PHIL	LT B.M. BROOKS	M
12/12/44	38927	VPB-104		LEYTE GULF	PHIL		
12/19/44	32328	VPB-106		HAWAII	ECENPAC	LTJG BURTON H. KNUST	S
12/26/44	38860	VPB-116		TINIAN	WCENPAC		
12/27/44	38784	VPB-103		ENGLAND	EUROPE	LT CHARLES M. WEYLAND	S
12/30/44	38849	VPB-104		LEYTE GULF	PHIL		
12/31/44	38768	FAW-2	KANEOHE	HAWAII	ECENPAC		
12/31/44	63951	HEDRON-15		MOROCCO	NW AFR		
12/31/44	63959	HEDRON-15		MOROCCO	NW AFR		
12/31/44	38742	VPB-117		LEYTE GULF	PHIL		
01/02/45	38813	VPB-104		LEYTE GULF	PHIL	LTJG W. W. SUTHERLAND	S
01/03/45	38947	VPB-105		ENGLAND	EUROPE	LT GEORGE E. PANTAND	U
01/07/45	38754	VPB-104		LEYTE GULF	PHIL		
01/10/45	38900	VPB-111		TINIAN	WCENPAC	LT R.L. FLEMING	S
01/11/45	38876	VPB-104		LEYTE GULF	PHIL		
01/12/45	38914	VPB-116		TINIAN	WCENPAC	LT ELLIOT SCHRADER	S
01/14/45	63944	VPB-105		MOROCCO	NW AFR	LT RALPH D. SPAULDING	D
01/15/45	38840	VPB-101		LOS NEGROS	PHIL	LCDR SMITH	U
01/17/45	38972	VPB-104		LEYTE GULF	PHIL		
01/24/45	38807	VPB-104		LEYTE GULF	PHIL		
01/31/45	38780	CASU(F)-44		TINIAN	WCENPAC		
01/31/45	38791	CASU(F)-44		TINIAN	WCENPAC		
02/05/45	65294	VPB-111		MOROTAI	PHIL	LT H.E. SIRES	M
02/06/45	32279	A.A.	KANEOHE	HAWAII	ECENPAC		
02/06/45	32331	A.A.	KANEOHE	HAWAII	ECENPAC		

DATE	BUNO	SQDRN	BASE	LOST	AREA	PILOT	FATE
02/06/45	38856	VPB-104		LEYTE GULF	PHIL	LTJG EARL BITTENBENDER	S
02/11/45	32082	A.A.	KANEOHE	HAWAII	ECENPAC		
02/11/45	32273	A.A.	KANEOHE	HAWAII	ECENPAC		
02/11/45	32302	A.A.	KANEOHE	HAWAII	ECENPAC		
02/11/45	38757	VPB-117		LEYTE GULF	PHIL	LTJG JAN B. CARTER	S
02/11/45	38759	VPB-117		LEYTE GULF	PHIL		
02/12/45	63928	VPB-110		DUNKES-WELL	ENGLAND		
02/12/45	38736	VPB-117		LEYTE GULF	PHIL		
02/14/45	38898	VPB-117		LEYTE GULF	PHIL		
02/17/45	38735	VPB-117		PALAWAN	PHIL	LCDR HAROLD M. MCGAUGHEY	M
02/17/45	38741	VPB-117		PALAWAN	PHIL	LTJG HOMER B. HEARD	S
02/18/45	32276	VPB-104		LEYTE GULF	PHIL	LT WILLIAM E. GOODMAN	M
02/18/45	38924	VPB-104		LEYTE GULF	PHIL	LTJG RICHARD S. JAMESON	S
02/23/45	38891	VPB-117		LEYTE GULF	PHIL		
03/02/45	38933	VPB-104		LUZON	PHIL		
03/03/45	32325	VPB-102		TINIAN	WCENPAC		
03/03/45	32326	VPB-102		TINIAN	WCENPAC		
03/03/45	38800	VPB-116		TINIAN	WCENPAC		
03/05/45	38838	VPB-110		DUNKES-WELL	ENGLAND		
03/09/45	38874	VPB-104		CLARK FIELD	PHIL		
03/10/45	38792	VPB-102		TINIAN	WCENPAC		
03/15/45	63941	FAW-7	ENGLAND	DUNKES-WELL	ENGLAND		
03/16/45	38842	A.A.	KANEOHE	HAWAII	ECENPAC		
03/21/45	63943	VPB-114		AZORES	NORLANT		
03/23/45	38867	VPB-102		TINIAN	WCENPAC	LTJG HOOPER	S
03/25/45	32184	VPB-107		UPOTTERY	NW EUROPE		
03/26/45	32203	VPB-107		UPOTTERY	NW EUROPE		
03/26/45	32207	VPB-107		UPOTTERY	NW EUROPE		
03/26/45	32211	VPB-107		UPOTTERY	NW EUROPE		
03/27/45	38828	VPB-102		TINIAN	WCENPAC	LT WAYEN D. BORMAN	S
03/29/45	38811	VPB-105		DUNKES-WELL	ENGLAND	LT EUGENE J. RICE	S
03/30/45	32212	VPB-103		DUNKES-WELL	ENGLAND		
03/30/45	38925	VPB-117		MINDORO STRAIT	PHIL	LT THOMAS J. HYLAND	S
03/31/45	32188	VPB-103		DUNKES-WELL	ENGLAND		
04/01/45	38794	VPB-104		CLARK FIELD	PHIL		
04/04/45	38873	VPB-116		TINIAN	WCENPAC		
04/06/45	38893	VPB-200		HAWAII	ECENPAC	LTJG TERENCE P. CASIDY	S
04/10/45	38804	CASU(F)-44		TINIAN	WCENPAC		
04/11/45	38844	VPB-116		TINIAN	WCENPAC		
04/13/45	38803	VPB-116		TINIAN	WCENPAC		
04/14/45	38845	VPB-116		TINIAN	WCENPAC		
04/17/45	38819	VPB-102		TINIAN	WCENPAC		
04/18/45	38896	VPB-111		LEYTE GULF	PHIL		
04/20/45	38906	VPB-111		LEYTE GULF	PHIL		
04/23/45	38871	VPB-102		TINIAN	WCENPAC		
04/30/45	38733	VPB-111		LEYTE GULF	PHIL		
04/30/45	38746	VPB-111		LEYTE GULF	PHIL		
04/30/45	38737	VPB-117		MINDORO STRAIT	PHIL		
04/30/45	38743	VPB-117		MINDORO STRAIT	PHIL		
04/30/45	38744	VPB-117		MINDORO STRAIT	PHIL		
04/30/45	38758	VPB-117		MINDORO STRAIT	PHIL		
05/09/45	38857	VPB-102		TINIAN	WCENPAC	LT R.M. BARNES	S
05/09/45	38932	VPB-102		TINIAN	WCENPAC	LT R.L. HOLAHAN	D
05/13/45	38869	VPB-104		LUZON	PHIL	LT THOMAS MCAULIFF	S
05/13/45	38870	VPB-104		LUZON	PHIL	LT STANLEY A. WOOD	S

DATE	BUNO	SQDRN	BASE	LOST	AREA	PILOT	FATE
05/13/45	38979	VPB-104		LUZON	PHIL	LTJG JOHN J. MALLOY	D
05/14/45	38875	VPB-104		LUZON	PHIL	LT IRA B. WEST	S
05/14/45	38863	VPB-117		MINDORO STRAIT	PHIL	LTJG P.J. SULLIVAN	S
05/18/45	38854	VPB-116		IWO JIMA	EMPIRE	LTJG GRALAND	S
05/18/45	90478	VPB-116		IWO JIMA	EMPIRE	LT RICHARD J. GOLDNER	M
05/19/45	32332	POOL	KANEOHE	HAWAII	ECENPAC		
05/19/45	38890	VPB-104		LUZON	PHIL	LT RICHARD S. JAMISON	M
05/21/45	38740	AROU-2		SAMAR	PHIL		
05/21/45	38749	AROU-2		SAMAR	PHIL		
05/21/45	38750	AROU-2		SAMAR	PHIL		
05/25/45	38899	CASU-11		OKINAWA	EMPIRE		
05/26/45	38843	VPB-102		TINIAN	WCENPAC		
06/01/45	32165	COMFAIR		LUZON	PHIL		
06/01/45	32194	FAW-7	ENGLAND	DUNKES-WELL	ENGLAND		
06/04/45	32179	FAW-7	ENGLAND	DUNKES-WELL	ENGLAND		
06/04/45	32192	FAW-7	ENGLAND	DUNKES-WELL	ENGLAND		
06/04/45	32193	FAW-7	ENGLAND	DUNKES-WELL	ENGLAND		
06/04/45	32195	FAW-7	ENGLAND	DUNKES-WELL	ENGLAND		
06/04/45	32198	FAW-7	ENGLAND	DUNKES-WELL	ENGLAND		
06/04/45	32202	FAW-7	ENGLAND	DUNKES-WELL	ENGLAND		
06/04/45	32204	FAW-7	ENGLAND	DUNKES-WELL	ENGLAND		
06/04/45	32206	FAW-7	ENGLAND	DUNKES-WELL	ENGLAND		
06/04/45	32237	FAW-7	ENGLAND	DUNKES-WELL	ENGLAND		
06/04/45	32246	FAW-7	ENGLAND	DUNKES-WELL	ENGLAND		
06/04/45	32249	FAW-7	ENGLAND	DUNKES-WELL	ENGLAND		
06/04/45	32250	FAW-7	ENGLAND	DUNKES-WELL	ENGLAND		
06/04/45	32253	FAW-7	ENGLAND	DUNKES-WELL	ENGLAND		
06/04/45	32254	FAW-7	ENGLAND	DUNKES-WELL	ENGLAND		
06/04/45	32255	FAW-7	ENGLAND	DUNKES-WELL	ENGLAND		
06/04/45	32256	FAW-7	ENGLAND	DUNKES-WELL	ENGLAND		
06/04/45	32257	FAW-7	ENGLAND	DUNKES-WELL	ENGLAND		
06/04/45	32258	FAW-7	ENGLAND	DUNKES-WELL	ENGLAND		
06/04/45	32268	FAW-7	ENGLAND	DUNKES-WELL	ENGLAND		
06/04/45	32282	FAW-7	ENGLAND	DUNKES-WELL	ENGLAND		
06/04/45	32283	FAW-7	ENGLAND	DUNKES-WELL	ENGLAND		
06/04/45	32288	FAW-7	ENGLAND	DUNKES-WELL	ENGLAND		
06/04/45	32289	FAW-7	ENGLAND	DUNKES-WELL	ENGLAND		
06/04/45	32290	FAW-7	ENGLAND	DUNKES-WELL	ENGLAND		
06/04/45	32292	FAW-7	ENGLAND	DUNKES-WELL	ENGLAND		
06/04/45	32293	FAW-7	ENGLAND	DUNKES-WELL	ENGLAND		
06/04/45	32294	FAW-7	ENGLAND	DUNKES-WELL	ENGLAND		
06/04/45	32295	FAW-7	ENGLAND	DUNKES-WELL	ENGLAND		

DATE	BUNO	SQDRN	BASE	LOST	AREA	PILOT	FATE
06/04/45	32296	FAW-7	ENGLAND	DUNKES-WELL	ENGLAND		
06/04/45	32297	FAW-7	ENGLAND	DUNKES-WELL	ENGLAND		
06/04/45	32335	FAW-7	ENGLAND	DUNKES-WELL	ENGLAND		
06/04/45	63945	FAW-7	ENGLAND	DUNKES-WELL	ENGLAND		
06/04/45	63955	FAW-7	ENGLAND	DUNKES-WELL	ENGLAND		
06/05/45	38761	VPB-104		CLARK FIELD	PHIL		
06/05/45	38789	VPB-104		CLARK FIELD	PHIL		
06/07/45	32324	POOL	KANEOHE	HAWAII	ECENPAC		
06/07/45	38801	VPB-104		CLARK FIELD	PHIL		
06/10/45	38905	VPB-102		IWO JIMA	EMPIRE		
06/12/45	38762	POOL	KANEOHE	HAWAII	ECENPAC		
06/13/45	38913	VPB-111		PALAWAN	PHIL	LTJG L.T. BASS	M
06/14/45	38978	VPB-117		MINDORO STRAIT	PHIL	LTJG J.P. DOUGAN	U
06/15/45	38787	POOL	KANEOHE	HAWAII	ECENPAC		
06/17/45	38895	VPB-111		PALAWAN	PHIL	LTJG W.C. BRAND	S
06/20/45	38976	VPB-111		PALAWAN	PHIL	LT DENNIS J. QUINLAN	D
06/22/45	38934	VPB-117		MINDORO STRAIT	PHIL	LTJG STANLEY WARREN SAYRE	D
06/26/45	38859	VPB-104		CLARK FIELD	PHIL		
06/26/45	38889	VPB-104		CLARK FIELD	PHIL		
06/29/45	90482	VPB-116		IWO JIMA	EMPIRE	LCDR J. GERBERDING	M
06/30/45	38861	VPB-117		MINDORO STRAIT	PHIL		
07/01/45	38907	VPB-117		MINDORO STRAIT	PHIL	LTJG ROBERT E. HEPTING	M
07/02/45	38918	VPB-102		TINIAN	WCENPAC		
07/04/45	38882	VPB-117		MINDORO STRAIT	PHIL	LT WILLIAM C. LUCE	S
07/05/45	38945	VPB-111		PALAWAN	PHIL		
07/06/45	38935	VPB-102		TINIAN	WCENPAC	LT O.G. ANDREWS	S
07/06/45	38926	VPB-104		CLARK FIELD	PHIL		
07/09/45	46725	VPB-104		CLARK FIELD	PHIL	LTJG CHARLES L. CROZIER	S
07/10/45	38959	VPB-102		TINIAN	WCENPAC		
07/15/45	38783	CASU(F)-44		TINIAN	WCENPAC		
07/18/45	38948	FAW-7	ENGLAND	DUNKES-WELL	ENGLAND		
07/23/45	32320	POOL	KANEOHE	HAWAII	ECENPAC		
07/28/45	38855	VPB-116		TINIAN	WCENPAC		
07/28/45	38858	VPB-116		TINIAN	WCENPAC		
07/28/45	38868	VPB-116		TINIAN	WCENPAC		
07/28/45	38915	VPB-116		TINIAN	WCENPAC		
07/28/45	38922	VPB-116		TINIAN	WCENPAC		
07/30/45	38965	VPB 102		TINIAN	WCENPAC		
07/31/45	38974	VPB-104		CLARK FIELD	PHIL		
07/31/45	38745	VPB-117		MINDORO STRAIT	PHIL		
07/31/45	38852	VPB-117		MINDORO STRAIT	PHIL		
07/31/45	38946	VPB-117		MINDORO STRAIT	PHIL	LT RAYMOND L. KLASSY	S
08/01/45	46730	VPB-104		CLARK FIELD	PHIL		
08/01/45	46736	VPB-104		CLARK FIELD	PHIL		
08/10/45	90471	VPB-102		IWO JIMA	EMPIRE		
08/11/45	38920	VPB-102		IWO JIMA	EMPIRE		

CONSOLIDATED PB4Y-1P

The Consolidated PB4Y-1P was the photographic reconnaissance variant developed from the PB4Y-1 (see above). Aircraft lost:

DATE	BUNO	SQDRN	BASE	LOST	AREA	PILOT	FATE
02/15/43	31958	VMD-154			SOPAC		
07/07/43	32005	VD-3		HAWAII	ECENPAC	LCDR ALFRED WILSTAM	D

DATE	BUNO	SQDRN	BASE	LOST	AREA	PILOT	FATE
07/24/43	31980	VD-1		GUADAL-CANAL	SOPAC		
09/19/43	31997	VD-1	GUADAL-CANAL	NAURU	CENPAC		
01/04/44	32019	VD-3	APAMAMA	KWAJALEIN	CENPAC	LT L.M. ALLEN	M
02/14/44	31995	VD-1			PAC		
03/05/44	31999	VMD-254	GUADAL-CANAL	GUADAL-CANAL	SOPAC		
04/30/44	32240	VD-1	KOLI	ULITHI	WCENPAC	LT FAIRBANKS	S
05/30/44	32174	VD-1	KOLI	MOMOTE	SW PAC		
12/08/44	38805	VD-5		GUAM	WCENPAC	CDR A.D. FRASER	S
03/06/45	38815	VD-5		GUAM	WCENPAC		
05/22/45	38802	VD-5		GUAM	WCENPAC		

CONSOLIDATED PB4Y-2

The Consolidated PB4Y-2 Privateer was a World War II era long range patrol bomber of the United States Navy also derived, like the PB4Y-1, from the Consolidated B-24 Liberator. The Privateer entered Navy service during late 1944. Squadrons VPB-118 and VPB-119 were the first Fleet squadrons to equip with the Privateer. The first overseas deployment began on 6 January 1945, when VPB-118 left for operations in the Marianas. On 2 March 1945 VPB-119 began "offensive search" missions out of Clark Field, Luzon in the Philippines, flying sectored searches of the seas and coastlines extending from the Gulf of Tonkin in the south, along the Chinese coast, and beyond Okinawa in the North.

The Navy eventually took delivery of 739 Privateers, the majority after the end of the war, although several squadrons saw service in the Pacific theater in the reconnaissance, search and rescue, electronic countermeasures, communication relay and anti-shipping roles (the latter with the "Bat" guided bomb.). Aircraft lost:

DATE	BUNO	SQDRN	BASE	LOST	AREA	PILOT	FATE
10/01/44	59415	VPB-119				LTJG OSCAR L. SMITH, JR.	U
01/12/45	59477	VPB-121	KANEOHE	HAWAII	ECENPAC		
02/16/45	59386	VPB-106			WCENPAC	LTJG BURTON H. KNUST	S
03/02/45	59429	VPB-119		LUZON	PHIL	LT LEONARD J. REICHART	D
03/04/45	59436	A.A.	KANEOHE	HAWAII	ECENPAC		
03/06/45	59402	VPB-118		IWO JIMA	EMPIRE	ENS R.R. WIRTH	S
03/07/45	59474	VPB-121		ENIWETOK	CENPAC	LT W. MCELWER	M
03/08/45	59467	VPB-109			PHIL	LT R.M. ALZEN KEILER	U
03/09/45	59497	VPB-106		TINIAN	WCENPAC	LTJG EDWARD W. ASHLEY	M
03/22/45	59426	VPB-119		CHINA COAST	EMPIRE	LTJG V.J. EVANS	S
03/22/45	59558	VPB-119		CLARK FIELD	PHIL		
03/29/45	59543	VPB-119		CHINA COAST	EMPIRE	LTJG W.G. VOGELSLANG	S
04/01/45	59452	VPB-119		LUZON	PHIL	LCDR R.C. BALES	M
04/08/45	59442	VPB-108		TINIAN	WCENPAC	LT WILLIAM RONALD HAZLETT	S
04/11/45	59414	VPB-119		LUZON	PHIL	LTJG A.L. ALTHANS	M
04/13/45	59401	VPB-118		TINIAN	WCENPAC		
04/22/45	59380	VPB-119		TINIAN	WCENPAC		
04/28/45	59387	POOL	KANEOHE	HAWAII	ECENPAC		
05/01/45	59559	VPB-119		LUZON	PHIL	LT JOHN W. HOLT	M
05/06/45	59378	VPB-118		OKINAWA	EMPIRE	LT MONTGOMERY	S
05/06/45	59449	VPB-118		OKINAWA	EMPIRE	LT J. ALLEN LASATER	M
05/07/45	59388	VPB-118		OKINAWA	EMPIRE	LCDR A.P. FARWELL, JR.	S
05/09/45	59444	VPB-108		TINIAN	WCENPAC	LCDR J. ELLISON MULDROW	M
05/19/45	59422	VPB-119		LUZON	PHIL	LTJG VOGELSLAND	M
05/24/45	59396	VPB-106		PALAWAN	PHIL		
05/25/45	59526	VPB-109		OKINAWA	EMPIRE		
05/25/45	59529	VPB-109		OKINAWA	EMPIRE		

DATE	BUNO	SQDRN	BASE	LOST	AREA	PILOT	FATE
05/25/45	59533	VPB-109		OKINAWA	EMPIRE		
05/25/45	59392	VPB-118		TINIAN	WCENPAC	ENS A.F. GINDEN	S
05/28/45	59470	VPB-121		ENIWETOK	CENPAC		
05/29/45	59479	VPB-200		HAWAII	ECENPAC	LT H.G. MORRIS	M
05/30/45	59530	VPB-109		OKINAWA	EMPIRE	LT L.E. KENNEDY	D
06/01/45	59563	VPB-106		PALAWAN	PHIL	CDR H.F. MEARS	M
06/02/45	59405	VPB-118		OKINAWA	EMPIRE		
06/05/45	59445	VPB-108		TINIAN	WCENPAC	LT M.T. EBRIGHT	S
06/06/45	59513	VPB-124		TINIAN	WCENPAC	WILLIAM CLYDE LAWSON	U
06/09/45	59500	VPB-123		OKINAWA	EMPIRE		
06/11/45	59446	VPB-108		IWO JIMA	EMPIRE	LT WILLIAM RONALD HAZLETT	S
06/14/45	59412	VPB-106		PALAWAN	PHIL	LCDR GREEN CLAY GOODLOE	M
06/17/45	59427	VPB-119		CLARK FIELD	PHIL	LT FRANK D. MURPHY	S
06/17/45	59549	VPB-124		TINIAN	WCENPAC		
06/19/45	59438	VPB-123		OKINAWA	EMPIRE		
06/24/45	59546	VPB-119		CLARK FIELD	PHIL		
06/24/45	59553	VPB-119		CLARK FIELD	PHIL		
06/26/45	59532	VPB-124		OKINAWA	EMPIRE	LTJG J.R. CRIST	U
06/26/45	59557	VPB-124		OKINAWA	EMPIRE	CDR C.E. HOUSTON	M
06/27/45	59535	VPB-124		OKINAWA	EMPIRE	LT J.E. VINCENT	M
06/30/45	59384	CASU-9		PALAWAN	PHIL		
06/30/45	59389	CASU-9		PALAWAN	PHIL		
07/02/45	59534	VPB-124		OKINAWA	EMPIRE	LT G.E. MILLER	S
07/07/45	59538	VPB-124		OKINAWA	EMPIRE	LT R.J. BROWER	M
07/22/45	59458	VPB-118		OKINAWA	EMPIRE	LT L.P. MCCUTCHEON	S
07/23/45	59550	VPB-118		OKINAWA	EMPIRE	LT SHORTLIDGE	S
07/24/45	59519	VPB-124		OKINAWA	EMPIRE	LT J.E. RAMSEY	M
07/24/45	59747	VPB-124		OKINAWA	EMPIRE	LT G.E. MILLER	M
07/27/45	59488	POOL	KANEOHE	HAWAII	ECENPAC		
07/27/45	59448	VPB-118		OKINAWA	EMPIRE	LT DUBA	S
07/29/45	59404	VPB-118		YONTAN	PHIL		
07/30/45	59433	VPB-106		PALAWAN	PHIL	LT JOSEPH WM. SWIENCICKI	M
08/05/45	59521	VPB-109		OKINAWA	EMPIRE	LT JOHN D. KEELING	M
08/06/45	59410	VPB-118		OKINAWA	EMPIRE		
08/08/45	59556	VPB-118		OKINAWA	EMPIRE	LTJG J.R. PARK	M
08/11/45	59495	VPB-121		IWO JIMA	EMPIRE	LT J.B. RAINEY, JR.	M
08/13/45	59441	VPB-108		TINIAN	WCENPAC		

CONSOLIDATED PBY (VARIANT UNKNOWN)

DATE	BUNO	SQDRN	BASE	LOST	AREA	PILOT	FATE
02/25/42		VP-22		N.E.I.	SW PAC	LTJG W.S. ROBINSON	M
06/12/42		VP-43	DUTCH HARBOR	KISKA	NORPAC		
06/12/42		VP-43	DUTCH HARBOR	KISKA	NORPAC	LT HOOD	M
06/12/42		VP-43	DUTCH HARBOR	KISKA	NORPAC		
12/25/42		FAW-10			SW PAC		
12/25/42		FAW-10			SW PAC		
12/25/42		FAW-10			SW PAC		

CONSOLIDATED PBY-1

The Consolidated PBY Catalina was an American flying boat of the 1930s and 1940s produced by Consolidated Aircraft. It was one of the most widely used multi-role aircraft of World War II. PBYs served with every branch of the United States Armed Forces and in the air forces and navies of many other nations.

During World War II, PBYs were used in anti-submarine warfare, patrol bombing, convoy escorts, search and rescue missions (especially air-sea rescue), and cargo transport. The PBY was the most successful aircraft of its kind; no other flying boat was produced in greater numbers.

The initialism of "P.B.Y." was determined in accordance with the U.S. Navy aircraft designation system of 1922; *PB* representing "Patrol Bomber" and *Y* being the code used for the aircraft's manufacturer, Consolidated Aircraft. PBYs were the most extensively used ASW aircraft in both the Atlantic and Pacific Theaters of World War II, and were also used in the Indian Ocean, flying from the Seychelles and from Ceylon. Their duties included escorting convoys to Murmansk. By 1943, U-boats were well-armed with anti-aircraft guns and two Victoria Crosses were won by Catalina pilots pressing home their attacks on U-boats in the face of heavy fire: In their role as patrol aircraft, Catalinas participated in some of the most notable engagements of World War II. The aircraft's parasol wing and large waist blisters allowed for a great deal of visibility and combined with its long range and endurance, made it well suited for the task.

PBYs were also employed by every branch of the US military as rescue aircraft. A PBY piloted by Lt. Cmdr. Adrian Marks (USN) rescued 56 sailors from the USS *Indianapolis* after the ship was sunk during World War II. PBYs continued to function in this capacity for decades after the end of the war. The initial production variant of the PBY-1 came with two 900hp R-1830-64 engines. There were 60 PBY-1's built. Aircraft lost:

DATE	BUNO	SQDRN	BASE	LOST	AREA	PILOT	FATE
01/14/44	0126	VJ-16		SAN JUAN	CENLANT		

CONSOLIDATED PBY-2

The Consolidated PBY-2 was simply the -1 with some equipment changes and improved performance. There were 50 built. Aircraft lost:

DATE	BUNO	SQDRN	BASE	LOST	AREA	PILOT	FATE
08/23/44	0487	NAS	BERMUDA	BERMUDA	NORLANT		

CONSOLIDATED PBY-3

The Consolidated PBY-3 was simply the -1 variant but now powered by two 1,000 hp R-1830-66 engines. There were 66 built. Aircraft lost:

DATE	BUNO	SQDRN	BASE	LOST	AREA	PILOT	FATE
12/07/41	0852	VP-22	KANEOHE	HAWAII	ECENPAC		
12/07/41	0853	VP-22	KANEOHE	HAWAII	ECENPAC		
12/07/41	0873	VP-22	KANEOHE	HAWAII	ECENPAC		
12/07/41	0874	VP-22	KANEOHE	HAWAII	ECENPAC		
12/07/41	0875	VP-22	KANEOHE	HAWAII	ECENPAC		
12/07/41	0882	VP-22	KANEOHE	HAWAII	ECENPAC		
12/07/41	0898	VP-22	KANEOHE	HAWAII	ECENPAC		
12/07/41	0899	VP-22	KANEOHE	HAWAII	ECENPAC		
12/07/41	0900	VP-22	KANEOHE	HAWAII	ECENPAC		
12/12/41	0842	PAT WING-2	KANEOHE	HAWAII	ECENPAC		
02/11/42	0881	PAT WING-2	PEARL	HAWAII	ECENPAC		
09/24/42	0884	VP-32	GUANTAN-AMO BAY	CUBA	CENLANT		
02/28/45	0885	FAW-3	COCO SOLO	COCO SOLO	CENLANT		

CONSOLIDATED PBY-4

The Consolidated PBY-4 was simply the -1 variant but now powered by two 1,050 hp R-1830-72 engines. There were 33 built (including one initial as a XBPY-4 which later became the XBPY-5A). Aircraft lost:

DATE	BUNO	SQDRN	BASE	LOST	AREA	PILOT	FATE
12/07/41	1226	VP-22	PEARL	HAWAII	ECENPAC		
12/08/41	1229	VP-101	USS WM B. PRESTON	CAVITE	PHIL	ENS R.G. TILLS	D
12/08/41	1231	VP-101	DAVAO		SW PAC		
12/08/41	1230	VP-102	USS WM B. PRESTON	CAVITE	PHIL		
12/08/41	1232	VP-102	DAVAO		SW PAC		
12/09/41	1234	VP-101	DAVAO		SW PAC	ENS R. SNYDER	U
12/12/41	1236	VP-101	USS CHILDS	CAVITE	PHIL		
12/12/41	1240	VP-101	USS CHILDS	CAVITE	PHIL		
12/12/41	1243	VP-101	USS CHILDS	CAVITE	PHIL		
12/12/41	1235	VP-102	USS CHILDS	CAVITE	PHIL		
12/12/41	1237	VP-102	USS CHILDS	CAVITE	PHIL		
12/12/41	1239	VP-102	USS CHILDS	CAVITE	PHIL		
12/12/41	1242	VP-102	USS CHILDS	CAVITE	PHIL		
12/25/41	1217	VP-101	USS CHILDS	CAVITE	PHIL		
12/25/41	1218	VP-101	USS CHILDS	CAVITE	PHIL		
12/25/41	1220	VP-102	USS CHILDS	CAVITE	PHIL		
12/27/41	1221	VP-101	USS CHILDS	JOLO	SW PAC		
12/27/41	1222	VP-101	USS CHILDS	JOLO	SW PAC	LT B.R. HASTINGS	M
12/27/41	1223	VP-101	USS CHILDS	JOLO	SW PAC	LTJG J.B. DAWLEY	S
12/27/41	1224	VP-101	USS CHILDS	JOLO	SW PAC	ENS E.L. CHRISTMAN	S
01/04/42	1225	VP-101			PHIL		
01/11/42		FAW-10	N.E.I.	MONADO	SW PAC	LTJG F.M. RALSTON	S
01/15/42		VP-101			SW PAC		
01/15/42		VP-102	N.E.I.		SW PAC		
01/15/42		VP-22	JAVA		SW PAC		
01/16/42	1228	VP-22	JAVA		SW PAC	LTJG C.H. HOLT	S
02/04/42	1227	VP-102	JAVA		SW PAC	ENS C.B. HENDRICKS	M
02/19/42		VP-102	DARWIN		SW PAC		
02/19/42		VP-102	DARWIN		SW PAC		
12/08/42	1216	VP-10			SW PAC		
12/08/42	1219	VP-10			SW PAC		

CONSOLIDATED PBY-5

The Consolidated PBY-5 was simply the -1 variant but now powered by either two 1200hp R-1830-82 or -92 engines and provisioned for extra fuel tanks. There were 683 built (plus one built at New Orleans). One went to the United States Coast Guard. Aircraft lost:

DATE	BUNO	SQDRN	BASE	LOST	AREA	PILOT	FATE
12/07/41	2420	PAT WING-2	KANEOHE	HAWAII	ECENPAC		
12/07/41	2421	PAT WING-2	KANEOHE	HAWAII	ECENPAC		

DATE	BUNO	SQDRN	BASE	LOST	AREA	PILOT	FATE
12/07/41	2423	PAT WING-2	KANEOHE	HAWAII	ECENPAC		
12/07/41	2425	PAT WING-2	KANEOHE	HAWAII	ECENPAC		
12/07/41	2430	PAT WING-2	KANEOHE	HAWAII	ECENPAC		
12/07/41	2431	PAT WING-2	KANEOHE	HAWAII	ECENPAC		
12/07/41	2435	PAT WING-2	KANEOHE	HAWAII	ECENPAC		
12/07/41	2436	PAT WING-2	KANEOHE	HAWAII	ECENPAC		
12/07/41	2437	PAT WING-2	KANEOHE	HAWAII	ECENPAC		
12/07/41	2439	PAT WING-2	KANEOHE	HAWAII	ECENPAC		
12/07/41	2440	PAT WING-2	KANEOHE	HAWAII	ECENPAC		
12/07/41	2441	PAT WING-2	KANEOHE	HAWAII	ECENPAC		
12/07/41	2444	PAT WING-2	KANEOHE	HAWAII	ECENPAC		
12/07/41	2445	PAT WING-2	KANEOHE	HAWAII	ECENPAC		
12/07/41	2448	PAT WING-2	KANEOHE	HAWAII	ECENPAC		
12/07/41	2357	VP-14	KANEOHE	HAWAII	ECENPAC		
12/07/41	2359	VP-14	KANEOHE	HAWAII	ECENPAC		
12/07/41	2361	VP-14	KANEOHE	HAWAII	ECENPAC		
12/07/41	2362	VP-14	KANEOHE	HAWAII	ECENPAC		
12/07/41	2364	VP-14	KANEOHE	HAWAII	ECENPAC		
12/07/41	2365	VP-14	KANEOHE	HAWAII	ECENPAC		
12/07/41	2369	VP-14	KANEOHE	HAWAII	ECENPAC		
12/07/41	2451	VP-14	KANEOHE	HAWAII	ECENPAC		
12/07/41	2291	VP-22	PEARL	HAWAII	ECENPAC		
12/07/41	2293	VP-22	PEARL	HAWAII	ECENPAC		
12/07/41	2301	VP-22	PEARL	HAWAII	ECENPAC		
12/07/41	2302	VP-22	PEARL	HAWAII	ECENPAC		
12/07/41	2303	VP-22	PEARL	HAWAII	ECENPAC		
12/07/41	2308	VP-22	PEARL	HAWAII	ECENPAC		
12/08/41	2325	VP-71	HALIFAX		NORLANT	ENS PAUL H. ALTER	D
12/09/41	2337	VP-73	ICELAND	ICELAND	NORLANT		
12/16/41	2426	PAT WING-2	NIHAU	HAWAII	ECENPAC	ENS REYNOLDS	D
12/27/41	2339	PAT WING-2	KANEOHE	HAWAII	ECENPAC		
01/08/42	2338	VP-73	ICELAND	ICELAND	NORLANT		
01/09/42	2368	VP-52	GALAPA-GOS		EPAC	ENS WILLIAM T. SUTHERLAND	M
01/10/42	2452	PAT WING-2	KANEOHE	HAWAII	ECENPAC		
01/11/42		FAW-3	COCO SOLO		CARIB		
01/11/42		VP-11		HAWAII	ECENPAC	ENS G.S. STEWARD	M
01/12/42	2432	VP-11		HAWAII	ECENPAC	LCDR F.R. JONES	S
01/12/42	2395	VP-31	SAN JUAN		CENLANT	LTJG CLARENCE E. MELVIN	S
01/15/42		VP-73	USS ALBE-MARLE	ICELAND	NORLANT		
01/15/42	2326	VP-73	USS ALBE-MARLE	ICELAND	NORLANT		
01/15/42	2331	VP-73	USS ALBE-MARLE	ICELAND	NORLANT		
01/16/42		VP-82	ARGENTIA		NORLANT		
01/23/42					ECENPAC	LTJG H.W. ARNDT	S
01/29/42		FAW-2	PEARL	HAWAII	ECENPAC	ENS B.W. STALLCUP	M
01/29/42		VP-82	ARGENTIA		NORLANT		
02/04/42	2304	VP-22	N.E.I.		SW PAC	ENS BULL	D
02/04/42	2309	VP-22	N.E.I.		SW PAC		
02/04/42	2321	VP-22	N.E.I.		SW PAC		
02/10/42	2413	VP-24	PEARL	HAWAII	ECENPAC		
02/17/42	2345	VP-72	KANEOHE	HAWAII	ECENPAC	LTJG CARL O. FISCHER	U
02/18/42	2306	VP-22	DARWIN		SW PAC	LT T.H. MOORER	S
02/18/42		VP-73	ICELAND	ICELAND	NORLANT		

DATE	BUNO	SQDRN	BASE	LOST	AREA	PILOT	FATE
02/24/42		VP-22	N.E.I.		SW PAC	LTJG JOHN M. ROBERTSON	M
04/05/42	2422	VP-14	PEARL	HAWAII	ECENPAC	LTJG MEYER	S
04/10/42	2386	VP-23	ALASKA	ALASKA	NORPAC	ENS MURPHY	S
04/18/42	2409	VP-101	AUSTRALIA		SW PAC	LTJG W.E. HARDY	S
04/30/42	2400	VP-31	SAN JUAN		CENLANT		
05/16/42	2322	VP-43	MEXICO		CARIB	LT R.S. ROBERT	U
05/18/42			EWA	HAWAII	ECENPAC	LT HENDERSON	U
05/19/42	2455	VP-101	AUSTRALIA		SW PAC	ENS WILLIAM C. ROPER	S
05/27/42	2418	VP-101	AUSTRALIA		SW PAC		
05/27/42	2453	VP-11	JOHNSTON ISLAND	HAWAII	ECENPAC	LTJG M.V. RICKETTS	S
05/29/42	2294	VP-71	LOYALTY IS.		SOPAC	LTJG J.W. ERHARD	S
05/29/42	2393	VP-71	LOYALTY IS.		SOPAC	LT G.G. MEAD	S
06/01/42	4439	VP-43	HALF MOON BAY		NORPAC	ENS WAYNE W. CAMPBELL	D
06/04/42	4436	VP-42	DUTCH HARBOR	ALASKA	NORPAC		
06/04/42	4443	VP-42	DUTCH HARBOR	ALASKA	NORPAC		
06/04/42	4457	VP-42	DUTCH HARBOR	ALASKA	NORPAC		
06/04/42	4490	VP-42	DUTCH HARBOR	ALASKA	NORPAC		
06/04/42	4511	VP-42	DUTCH HARBOR	ALASKA	NORPAC		
06/04/42		VP-44	MIDWAY		ECENPAC	ENS R.S. WHITMAN	D
06/08/42	2329	VP-81			CENLANT	LTJG M.W. NICHOLSON	S
06/09/42	2358	VP-81			CENLANT	ENS JAMES L. SMITH	S
06/15/42	2454	VP-11	KANEOHE	HAWAII	ECENPAC		
06/15/42	4428	VP-23	ALASKA	ALASKA	NORPAC		
07/09/42	2305	VP-31	TRINIDAD		CENLANT		
07/12/42	2399	VP-31	TRINIDAD		CENLANT	LTJG WALTER V. WINIKA	S
07/13/42		FAW-2	PEARL	HAWAII	ECENPAC		
07/30/42	4463	VP-32	NAZAN BAY		NORPAC	ENS KELLY	S
07/30/42	4499	VP-41	NAZAN BAY		NORPAC	LTJG RAVEN	M
08/08/42	2350	VP-72			SOPAC	LT L.W. THURLOW	S
08/19/42	2389	FAW-2	PEARL	HAWAII	ECENPAC	LT MATHEWS	S
08/19/42	4474	VP-33	COCO SOLO		CENLANT	ENS HARRY H. FORD	D
08/20/42	4468	VP-34	COCO SOLO		CENLANT	LCDR REN. S. CALDERHEAD	D
08/25/42	4469	VP-43	DUTCH HARBOR	ALASKA	NORPAC	LTJG S.O. RAITHELL	M
08/26/42	2360	VP-14	PEARL	HAWAII	ECENPAC		
08/26/42	4427	VP-51			NORPAC		
09/07/42	2376	VP-81			CENLANT	LT ROBERT W. CUMMINGS	D
09/23/42	2388	VP-11			SOPAC		
09/23/42	2410	VP-11			SOPAC		
09/23/42	2419	VP-11			SOPAC		
09/23/42	2450	VP-11			SOPAC		
09/23/42	4429	VP-23			SOPAC		
09/23/42	4430	VP-23			SOPAC		
09/28/42	4477	VP-61	NAZAN BAY		NORPAC	ENS M.E. HUMPHREYS	S
09/29/42	2382	VP-81			CENLANT	LCDR THOMAS B. HALEY	S
10/02/42	4466	VP-43	KOROVIN BAY	ALASKA	NORPAC		
10/05/42	4476	VP-43		ALASKA	NORPAC		
10/15/42	2341	FAW-1			SOPAC		
10/15/42	2344	FAW-1			SOPAC		
10/15/42	2412	FAW-1			SOPAC		
10/15/42	4433	FAW-1			SOPAC		
10/23/42	2297	VP-91	OAHU	HAWAII	ECENPAC		
11/02/42	4486	VP-61	DUTCH HARBOR	ALASKA	NORPAC		
11/04/42	4497	FAW-4	DUTCH HARBOR	ALASKA	NORPAC		
11/04/42	4508	VP-61	KODIAK	ALASKA	NORPAC		
11/06/42	4454	VP-33	COCO SOLO		CENLANT		

DATE	BUNO	SQDRN	BASE	LOST	AREA	PILOT	FATE
11/11/42	2342	FAW-1			SOPAC		
11/11/42	2355	FAW-1			SOPAC		
11/11/42	2416	FAW-1			SOPAC		
11/15/42	4507	FAW-1			SOPAC		
11/15/42	4509	FAW-1			SOPAC		
11/20/42	4425	VP-43	DUTCH HARBOR	ALASKA	NORPAC		
11/20/42	4491	VP-91	YANIKORO		SOPAC	LTJG E.J. MANSUETO	S
11/21/42	4513	FAW-1			SOPAC		
11/26/42	2407	VP-101	PERTH	AUSTRALIA	SW PAC	LT ROY J. KROGH	S
12/16/42	8135	VP-54	SAN DIEGO	ENR HAWAII	ECENPAC	LT ORRIN J. MCCAUSLAND	M
12/28/42	2343	VP-91			SOPAC		
12/30/42	4435	FAW-1			SOPAC		
01/05/43	4482	VP-53			CENLANT	AP1/C W.E. EDWARDS	S
01/11/43	4502	VP-72			SOPAC		
01/12/43	4452	VP-33					
01/12/43	4459	VP-41			NORPAC		
01/17/43	4440	FAW-4	DUTCH HARBOR	ALASKA	NORPAC		
01/24/43	4431	FAW-10			SW PAC		
01/30/43	2367	VP-52			NORLANT		
02/20/43	2408	FAW-1			SOPAC		
02/25/43	2295	FAW-1			SOPAC		
02/28/43	4506	VP-91			SOPAC		
03/10/43	2334	FAW-2	PEARL	HAWAII	ECENPAC	LT SAMUEL I. OGDEN	M
03/16/43	2449	FAW-10			SOPAC		
03/23/43	8444	VP-52			SW PAC		
03/24/43	8136	VP-44	USS CURTISS	FLORIDA IS.	SOPAC	LT JARLATH J. LYONS	S
03/28/43	4461	VP-101		AUSTRALIA	SW PAC		
03/29/43	2354	VP-13	JOHNSTON ISLAND	HAWAII	ECENPAC	LTJG ROBERT T. O'DONNELL	D
04/02/43	2385	VP-81	TRINIDAD	B.W.I.	CENLANT	LT STAN R. QUACKENBUSH	S
04/28/43	8229	VP-101		AUSTRALIA	SW PAC	LT J. HARVEY	M
05/13/43	4445	FAW-2	PEARL	HAWAII	ECENPAC	FLOYD KOONTZ	U
05/15/43	8129	VP-44			SOPAC		
05/30/43	8175	VP-63			NORLANT		
05/31/43	2391	VP-11			SOPAC		
06/28/43	2405	VP-53			NORLANT	LTJG S. A. TWOOD	S
06/30/43	8252	VP-23		ESPIRITU SANTO	SOPAC		
06/30/43	8374	VP-71			WCENPAC		
07/01/43	8228	PATSU-1	GUADAL-CANAL		SOPAC		
07/04/43	8293	VP-11	AUSTRALIA		SW PAC	ENS J.E. HETHERMAN	D
07/12/43	8246	VP-24	TULAGI		SOPAC	LTJG ROBERT C. ALLEN	D
07/24/43	8294	FAW-10			SW PAC		
07/24/43	8409	VP-45			NORPAC	LT WEHMEYER	S
07/30/43	8253	VP-23			SOPAC	LT WILLIAM J. GERITZ	S
08/01/43	8231	VP-63		BAY OF BISCAY	ENGLAND	LT W.P. TANNER, JR.	S
08/02/43	8513	VP-33			ECENPAC		
08/17/43	2446	VP-101		NEW GUINEA	SW PAC	LT T. W. MARSHALL	S
08/23/43	8408	VP-45			NORPAC	JORDAL	S
08/26/43		VP-14	PEARL	HAWAII	ECENPAC		
09/19/43	8327	VP-11			SW PAC		
10/01/43	8451	VP-14			SOPAC		
10/05/43	2424	VP-101			ECENPAC		
10/05/43	8326	VP-101			ECENPAC		
10/05/43	8407	VP-45		ATTU	NORPAC		
10/11/43	8328	VP-11	USS SAN PABLO	JENKINS BAY	SOPAC	LTJG THOMAS L. HINE	S
10/14/43	2415	VP-206	COCO SOLO		ECENPAC		
10/26/43	2447	VP-101		NEW GUINEA	SW PAC	LT E.B. GRAFF	D
11/01/43	8130	VP-34	HERON HAVEN	AUSTRALIA	SW PAC		
11/08/43	8458	VP-23	TULAGI		SOPAC		
11/13/43	8442	VP-52	QUEENS-LAND	TOWNSVILLE	SW PAC	LT LAHODNEY	S
11/19/43	8388	VP-91	TULAGI	MALAITA ISLAND	SOPAC	LT M.M. MOONEY	D

DATE	BUNO	SQDRN	BASE	LOST	AREA	PILOT	FATE
11/22/43	8428	VP-28	NEW GUINEA	NAMOAI BAY	SW PAC	ENS J.F. RYDER	M
12/07/43	8372	VP-14	ESPIRITU SANTO	TIKOPEA	SOPAC	LTJG N. CLARK	D
12/10/43	8541	VP-72	FUNAFUTI		SOPAC		
12/27/43	8329	VP-11		ARAWE	SOPAC	LT G.B. KENNINGTON	S
01/05/44	8377	VP-14	BOUGAIN-VILLE	SHORT-LANDS	SOPAC	LTJG K.L. MARLIN	S
01/09/44	8436	VP-34	SAMARAI	N. IRELAND	SW PAC	LTJG WRIGHT	M
01/09/44	8172	VP-63	PORT LYAUTEY	MOROCCO	NW AFR	LT W.E. SHOLES	D
01/12/44	8540	VP-72	TARAWA	JALUIT	CENPAC	CDR S.J. LAWRENCE	S
01/14/44	8463	VP-14	TULAGI	TOROKINA	SOPAC	LTJG R.K. BROWN	S
01/14/44	8510	VP-72	TARAWA	JALUIT	CENPAC	LT R.L. FINUCANE	S
01/16/44	8443	VP-14	TREASURY	TOROKINA	SOPAC		
01/22/44	8386	VP-91	ESPIRITU SANTO		SOPAC		
02/02/44	8486	VP-91	ESPIRITU SANTO		SOPAC		
02/06/44	8434	VMJ-253	NOUMEA		SOPAC	WHEELER	D
02/06/44	8432	VP-52	PORT MORESBY	DARU ISLAND	SW PAC		
02/14/44	8378	VP-34	QUEENS-LAND		SW PAC		
02/16/44	8132	FAW-2	CANTON		CENPAC	ARM2/C A.A. NEELY	M
02/17/44	2380	VP-72		MAKIN	CENPAC		
02/18/44	8506	VP-72		MAJURO	CENPAC	LT FITCH	S
02/27/44	8354	VP-34	QUEENS-LAND	PALM ISLAND	SW PAC		
03/07/44	8134	VP-101	PERTH	AUSTRALIA	SW PAC	ENS GREAGOR	S
03/11/44	8522	VP-33		HOLLANDIA	SW PAC	LTJG R. MCK. CHILDO	M
03/18/44	2414	VP-71	FUNAFUTI		SOPAC		
04/04/44	8339	VP-11	PERTH	AUSTRALIA	SW PAC	LTJG D.L. HAND	S
04/21/44	4426	VP-101		GREEN	SOPAC		
04/23/44	4504	VP-72		NE OF TRUK	CENPAC		
04/30/44	8297	VP-52	ADMIRAL-TY IS.	ULITHI	WCENPAC		
05/01/44	8431	VP-52		NEW GUINEA	SW PAC	LT VICTOR J. WEAVER	S
05/20/44	8509	VP-34	NEW GUINEA		SW PAC	LT PIERCE	S
05/21/44	8505	COM7THFLT	BRISBANE	AUSTRALIA	SW PAC		
06/03/44	8518	VP-33	HOLLANDIA		SW PAC	LT A.L. WILCOX	S
06/12/44	8469	VP-14	HALAVO	OFF KANEOHE	ECENPAC		
07/16/44	8361	VP-200	HAWAII		ECENPAC	LT C.A. ROARK	S
07/22/44	8174	VP-63	PORT LYAUTEY	MOROCCO	NW AFR	LTJG M.T. VOPATAK	S
07/24/44	8137	VP-34		HALMAHERA	SW PAC	LT R.W. BALL	M
08/10/44	0140	VH-1		KWAJALEIN	CENPAC	LTJG DONALD H. HALL	S
08/10/44	4501	VP-101		GREEN	SOPAC	LT JESSE I. MCMILLAN	D
08/13/44	8331	VP-11	WOENUI	HALMAHERA	SW PAC	LT T.H. RAGSDALE	M
08/14/44	8494	VP-34	DUTCH NEW GUINEA	WOENDI	SW PAC	LTJG FRANK M. POTTS	S
09/04/44	8512	VPB-33		MANADO	SW PAC	LT ALLAN L. WILCOX	M
09/06/44	4492	VPP-29		CAPE ST GEORGE	SOPAC	LT W.C. BARNETT	S
09/09/44	8244	VP-33		DUTCH GUINEA	SW PAC	LTJG JOHN R. RAMSEY	M
10/01/44	8233	VPB-29	MOROTAI		SW PAC	LT JOHN P. SCHENCK	M
10/07/44	8143	VPB-29	OWI		SW PAC		
10/25/44	8363	VPB-34		SAMAR	PHIL	LCDR V.V. UTEOFF	S
10/30/44	8170	VPB-34		SAMAR	PHIL		
10/30/44	8492	VPB-34		SAMAR	PHIL		
10/31/44	8148	COMAIR-PAC	PEARL	HAWAII	ECENPAC		
11/03/44	8375	VPB-33	LEYTE GULF		PHIL		
11/06/44	8484	VPB-34	SAN PEDRO BAY		SW PAC		
11/11/44	8520	VPB-33	LEYTE GULF		PHIL		

DATE	BUNO	SQDRN	BASE	LOST	AREA	PILOT	FATE
11/27/44	8283	VPB-34	LEYTE GULF		PHIL		
12/05/44	8138	VPB-33		WOENDI	SW PAC	LTJG GEORGE H. FAVORITE	U
01/01/45	8429	VPB-33		MANUS	SW PAC		
01/12/45	8368	VPB-33		MANUS	SW PAC		
01/16/45	8249	VPB-33	LEYTE GULF		PHIL		
02/08/45	8167	COMAIR-PAC	PEARL	HAWAII	ECENPAC		
03/16/45	8441	KANEOHE	HAWAII		ECENPAC		
03/18/45	2411	VP-71			PHIL		
03/26/45	8256	FAW-2	KANEOHE	HAWAII	ECENPAC		
04/18/45	8362	POOL	KANEOHE	HAWAII	ECENPAC		
05/09/45	8168	VH-1		SAIPAN	WCENPAC		
07/01/45	8355	VPB-63	BRITISH GAMBIA		NW AFR	LT ELMER D. MOONE	S

CONSOLIDATED PBY-5A

The Consolidated PBY-5A was the amphibious version of the PBY-5 with two 1,200 hp R-1830-92 engines. Of the 803 built, the first 124 had one 0.3in bow gun, the remainder had two bow guns. Some of the 803 built included diversions to the United States Army Air Corps, the Royal Air Force (RAF, as the Catalina IIIA) and one to the United States Coast Guard. Aircraft lost:

DATE	BUNO	SQDRN	BASE	LOST	AREA	PILOT	FATE
03/28/42	2462	VP-73	ICELAND	ICELAND	NORLANT	ENS RALPH B. BOYD	S
03/29/42	7299	VP-41			NORPAC		
04/05/42	2487	VP-91	OAHU	HAWAII	ECENPAC	ENS HOWE	D
04/11/42	2476	VP-91	OAHU	HAWAII	ECENPAC		
04/23/42	7286	VP-42	DUTCH HARBOR	ALASKA	NORPAC	ENS FREDERICK A. SMITH	D
04/27/42	5007				ECENPAC		
05/20/42	7249	VP-92			CENLANT		
05/25/42	5018	VP-24	PEARL	HAWAII	ECENPAC		
06/03/42	7280	VP-42	DUTCH HARBOR	ALASKA	NORPAC	LTJG CAMPBELL	S
06/04/42		VP-24	MIDWAY		ECENPAC	ENS PROPST	S
06/04/42	7282	VP-42	DUTCH HARBOR	ALASKA	NORPAC		
06/04/42	7292	VP-42	DUTCH HARBOR	ALASKA	NORPAC	ENS MITCHELL	D
06/04/42	4979	VP-42	DUTCH HARBOR	ALASKA	NORPAC		
06/04/42	4993	VP-42	DUTCH HARBOR	ALASKA	NORPAC		
06/04/42	5008	VP-42	DUTCH HARBOR	ALASKA	NORPAC		
06/07/42	4404	VP-93	NEWFOUN DLAND		NORLANT	LTJG RIPPEY	M
06/11/42	7294	VP-42	DUTCH HARBOR	KISKA	NORPAC		
06/12/42	7275	VP-42	DUTCH HARBOR	KISKA	NORPAC	ENS EDWIN R. WINTERS	M
06/13/42	7252	VP-83	BRAZIL		SOLANT	LT CHESTER A. SKIDMORE	M
06/14/42	4975	VP-44	PEARL	HAWAII	ECENPAC		
06/15/42	5025	VP-24	PEARL	HAWAII	ECENPAC		
06/15/42	2960	VP-51	PEARL	HAWAII	ECENPAC		
06/16/42	7298	VP-41	DUTCH HARBOR	ALASKA	NORPAC		
06/20/42	7291	VP-42	COLD BAY	ALASKA	NORPAC	LTJG D.A. BROUGH	S
06/20/42	2458	VP-73			NORLANT	LT WILLIAM COLE	S
06/20/42	2954	VP-93			NORLANT		
07/17/42	5026	VP-12	PEARL	HAWAII	ECENPAC		
07/30/42	4414	VP-51	NAZAN BAY		NORPAC	ENS HERRON	S
08/28/42	2456	FAW-7	ENGLAND	ICELAND	NORLANT		
09/07/42	4980	VP-61			NORPAC		

DATE	BUNO	SQDRN	BASE	LOST	AREA	PILOT	FATE
09/21/42	7247	VP-92	STOCKING ISLAND	BERMUDA	NORLANT	ENS R.J. FINNIE	U
09/27/42	2949	FAW-2	PEARL	HAWAII	ECENPAC		
09/30/42	5039	VP-24	HAWAII		ECENPAC		
10/15/42	5020	FAW-2	PEARL	HAWAII	ECENPAC		
11/07/42	2968	MAG-13	WALLIS ISLAND		SOPAC	MSGT A.J. ROSCOE	S
11/07/42	2969	MAG-13	WALLIS ISLAND		SOPAC		
11/10/42	2971	VP-73	WALES		EUROPE		
11/13/42	7274	VP-92		CASABLANCA	NW AFR		
11/26/42	2951	VP-23	PEARL	HAWAII	ECENPAC	LTJG WILLIAM L. JOHNSON	M
12/10/42	7272	FAW-4	DUTCH HARBOR	ALASKA	NORPAC	LTJG CLASPEY	U
12/13/42	2961	FAW-10	PERTH	AUSTRALIA	SW PAC		
12/13/42	5027	VP-24	MOKAPUI	HAWAII	ECENPAC	LTJG RALPH D. POLING	S
12/17/42	2966	FAW-10		AUSTRALIA	SW PAC		
12/20/42	7244	VP-83	BRAZIL		SOLANT	LTJG V.G. HASSELL	S
12/22/42	4408	VP-42			NORPAC		
12/23/42	7285	VP-42			NORPAC		
12/27/42	4402	VP-84	ICELAND	ICELAND	NORLANT	LT HARVEY H. INCE	D
01/05/43	4407	VP-41			NORLANT		
01/16/43	7257	VP-92		MOROCCO	NW AFR		
01/23/43	2957	VP-24	HAWAII		ECENPAC		
01/23/43	7302	VP-84		ICELAND	NORLANT		
01/27/43	7278	VP-93		GREENLAND	NORLANT		
02/12/43	8033	VP-71	CANTON		CENPAC		
02/14/43	2965	PATSU-1	GUADAL-CANAL		SOPAC		
03/03/43	2977	VPB-126		GREENLAND	NORLANT	LTJG VERNON D. STANLEY	D
03/10/43	7297	VP-43		KODIAK	NORPAC	LT R.C. GISH	D
03/24/43	2952	VP-71			SOPAC		
03/25/43	8052	VP-54			SOPAC		
03/31/43	8054	VP-31			NORLANT		
04/11/43	7251	VP-92		MOROCCO	NW AFR	LTJG JOHN H. MULLER	D
04/30/43	2488	FAW-1			SOPAC		
05/15/43	4403	FAW-1			SOPAC		
05/18/43	7289	VP-43		SITKA	NORPAC		
05/18/43	7271	VP-44		SITKA	NORPAC	LT LEEDS	M
05/24/43	4411	VP-43		ALASKA	NORPAC	LT P.C. SPENCER	D
06/03/43	4405	VP-94			SOLANT	LTJG DONALD M. FAULKNER	S
06/05/43	8078	VP-54			SOPAC		
06/12/43	7273	VP-84		ICELAND	NORLANT	LTJG DOUGLAS S. VIEIRA	D
07/16/43	4981	FAW-2	PEARL	HAWAII	ECENPAC	LT BURGES SMITH	S
07/17/43	8051	VP-54	GUADAL-CANAL		SOPAC	LTJG ANDERSON	S
07/23/43	8055	FAW-4	ADAK	ALASKA	NORPAC		
07/23/43	33978	VP-43		ADAK	NORPAC		
07/23/43	4400	VP-61	ADAK	ALASKA	NORPAC		
08/20/43	5040	VJ-2			SOPAC	LCDR R.S. CALDERHEAD	D
09/25/43	34019	VP-43	KISKA	ALASKA	NORPAC	LTJG THROCKMORTON	D
10/01/43	8047	VP-73		MOROCCO	NW AFR	LTJG FUCHS	U
10/02/43	33967	VP-72	KANEOHE	HAWAII	ECENPAC	LT MCDANIEL	S
10/04/43	33999	VP-43		ALASKA	NORPAC	LTJG C. ESSIG	D
10/05/43	33965	MAG-13		TUTUILA	SOPAC	LT PAUL J. SAX	D
10/08/43	8113	FAW-4	ADAK	ALASKA	NORPAC	LT JOLLY	S
11/06/43	34035	VP-53	SAN DIEGO	OFF KANEOHE	ECENPAC	LTJG S.P. EDWARDSON	M
11/06/43	8070	VP-54	GUADAL-CANAL		SOPAC	LT M.T. SCHALL	M
11/13/43	8102	VP-53	FUNAFUTI		SOPAC		
11/18/43	8034	ARU DIAL			SOPAC		
11/18/43	8038	ARU DIAL			SOPAC		
11/23/43	7265	VP-92	PORT LYAUTEY	MOROCCO	NW AFR	LT E.G. LARSEN	D
11/27/43	8118	FAW-4	DUTCH HARBOR	ALASKA	NORPAC	LT W.D. BLISS	S
11/29/43	2472	VP-94		SOUTH AMERICA	SOLANT		
12/19/43	5015	VP-53	FUNAFUTI		SOPAC	LTJG C.E. BREMER	S

DATE	BUNO	SQDRN	BASE	LOST	AREA	PILOT	FATE
12/28/43	33968	HEDRON-2	MAKIN	RAKER	CENPAC	LT K.M. ASHCRAFT	M
01/08/44	33963	FAW-2	PEARL	HAWAII	ECENPAC		
01/17/44	34018	VP-62	AMCHITKA	ALASKA	NORPAC	LTJG A.R. PORTER	M
01/18/44	33969	VP-43	ATTU	ALASKA	NORPAC	LTJG M.J. NOE	D
01/28/44	33982	VP-53	FUNAFUTI		SOPAC		
02/20/44	5043	VJ-2	PEARL	HAWAII	ECENPAC		
03/08/44	48259	VP-12	ONDONGA	CHOISEUL	SOPAC	LTJG C. BURKHARDT	D
03/09/44	8104	HEDRON-9/2		BERMUDA	NORLANT		
03/24/44	48341	VP-53	MAJURO	WOTJE	CENPAC		
03/28/44	8075	VP-102	HAWAII		ECENPAC		
03/31/44	34017	VP-43	ATTU	ALASKA	NORPAC	LT N.P. WYMAN	M
04/06/44	8044	HEDRON-11	HAITI		NORLANT	LT W.T. SISSON	S
04/25/44	46542	VP-34		WOLEAI	CENPAC		
04/27/44	46507	2ND MAW		NEW IRELAND	SOPAC		
05/01/44	48398	VP-61	ATTU	ALASKA	NORPAC	LTJG G.F. HEIDLAGE	M
05/09/44	46500	VP-24	MIDWAY		ECENPAC	LTJG W. HAMPTON	M
05/10/44	46520	VP-45	NATAL	FORTALEZA	SOLANT	LCDR C. ADKINSON	M
05/12/44	48280	VP-44	ESPIRITU SANTO		SOPAC	LTJG C.J. ASTILL	D
05/31/44	34033	VP-61	ATTU	KISKA	NORPAC	SQUIRES	S
06/10/44	48339	VP-53		TAROA	CENPAC		
06/15/44	48427	VP-61	ATTU	ALASKA	NORPAC	LT F.A. WOODY	M
06/27/44	48326	VP-24	MAJURO	WOTJE	CENPAC		
06/30/44	33980	FAW-2	OAHU	HAWAII	ECENPAC		
08/27/44	33961	VP-45		BRAZIL	SOLANT	LTJG JEROME C. EMORY	S
10/08/44	48303	VPB-71			CENPAC	CDR NORMAN C. GILLETTE	S
10/15/44	34013	VP-63	PORT LYAUTEY	MOROCCO	NW AFR	LT ROBERT R. BEDELL	U
10/19/44	48370	VPB-92	SAN JUAN		NORLANT	LT ROBERT B. KERR	S
10/26/44	46471	VPB-23	ENIWETOK		CENPAC		
10/30/44	46473	VPB-23	ENIWETOK		CENPAC	LT ROBIN E. LARSON	S
11/27/44	4973	BLMPHDRN-4	BRAZIL		SOLANT	LTJG R.W. GRACE	M
12/06/44	46512	VPB-71		LEYTE GULF	PHIL		
12/31/44	7254	VC-82			WCENPAC		
12/31/44	48331	VPB-24		TARAWA	CENPAC		
12/31/44	46528	VPB-71		MOROTAI	PHIL		
12/31/44	46549	VPB-71		MOROTAI	PHIL		
01/12/45	48289	VPB-63	PORT LYAUTEY	MOROCCO	NW AFR	LT WILLIAM D. RAY	S
01/30/45	8093	FAW-15	PORT LYAUTEY	MOROCCO	NW AFR	LT LAUREN W. HAWES	D
01/31/45	2479	FAW-16		BELEM	SOLANT		
02/01/45	48268	VPB-100	KANEOHE	HAWAII	ECENPAC	LT ROBERT ERICKSON	D
02/01/45	46464	VPB-23		SAIPAN	WCENPAC	LT OSCAR T. OWRE	S
02/02/45	46529	VPB-71		LUZON	PHIL	LT A.J. LEHMICKE	M
03/05/45	2950	CASU-9		PALAWAN	PHIL		
03/17/45	46525	VPB-45		ASCENSION IS.	SOLANT	LT WALTER SOEHNER	D
03/22/45	48443	VPB-71		SAMAR	PHIL		
03/23/45	2468	FAW-7	ENGLAND	DUNKES-WELL	ENGLAND		
04/09/45	48405	CASU(F)-12		GUAM	WCENPAC		
04/11/45	5042	MAG-13		MAJURO	CENPAC		
05/15/45	48395	ACORN-30 PL		JINAMOC	PHIL		
05/15/45	48409	ACORN-30 PL		JINAMOC	PHIL		
05/18/45	5041	VJ-14	HAWAII		ECENPAC	LT H.I. PEMBERTON	S
05/24/45	48384	VPB-43		ATTU	NORPAC	LTJG DEAN D. MAGOWAN	S
05/31/45	7259	FAW-16		RECIFE	BRAZIL		
06/02/45	46468	VPB-23		IWO JIMA	EMPIRE	LT MILFORD G. MANN	M
07/21/45	46499	CASU(F)-11		YONTAN	PHIL		
07/21/45	48264	CASU(F)-58		SANGLEY POINT	PHIL		
08/01/45	46463	VPB-23		PELELIU	WCENPAC		
08/02/45	46472	VPB-23		PELELIU	WCENPAC		
08/10/45	46517	VPB-71		SAMAR	PHIL		
08/10/45	48399	VPB-71		SAMAR	PHIL		

CONSOLIDATED PBY-6A

The Consolidated PBY-6A was the amphibious version with two 1,200 hp R-1830-92 engines and a taller fin and rudder. There was a radar scanner fitted above the cockpit and two 0.5 in nose guns. Of the 175 built, 21 were transferred to the Soviet Navy. Aircraft lost:

DATE	BUNO	SQDRN	BASE	LOST	AREA	PILOT	FATE
08/10/45	64012	VPB-53			PHIL		

CONSOLIDATED RY-2

The Consolidated C-87 Liberator Express was a transport derivative of the B-24 Liberator heavy bomber built during World War II for the United States Army Air Forces. A total of 287 C-87s were factory-built alongside the B-24 at the Consolidated Aircraft plant in Fort Worth, Texas. Converted former C-87s were the basis for a United States Navy VIP transport designated as the RY. Five former USAAF C-87s were fitted for 20 passengers and designated RY-2; a further 15 were cancelled. All five were lost.

DATE	BUNO	SQDRN	BASE	LOST	AREA	PILOT	FATE
06/08/44	39017	VR-11	HONOLULU	HAWAII	ECENPAC	LCDR J.H. SNEED	S
07/16/45	39013	VB-13	MANUS	MANUS	SW PAC		
07/16/45	39014	VB-13	MANUS	MANUS	SW PAC		
07/16/45	39015	VB-13	MANUS	MANUS	SW PAC		
07/16/45	39016	VB-13	MANUS	MANUS	SW PAC		

CONVAIR OY-1

The Stinson Aircraft Company was founded in Dayton, Ohio, in 1920 by aviator Edward "Eddie" Stinson. One of his more popular aircraft produced was the Model 105 Voyager/L-5 Sentinel, a three-passenger aircraft featuring a strut-braced wing mounted on the top of the fuselage and capable of flying at about 105 miles per hour (169 km/h). The little HW-75 proved an immediate success attracting a flood of orders the manufacturer was hard-pressed to match. The aircraft featured innovations such as slotted wing flaps, and fixed wing slots for better handling at lower speeds. The 105 Voyager was substantially redesigned to become the U.S. Army's L-5 Sentinel, one of the most used and least recognized U.S. aircraft in World War II. Serving as a short field liaison aircraft, the L-5 supported missions such as artillery spotting, medical evacuation, aerial reconnaissance, and passenger transport. Stinson delivered 3,590 between November 1942 and September 1945 under a variety of designations from L-5, L-5B, L-5C, L-5E and L-5G. The U.S. Navy and Marine Corps received 306 Sentinels from the Army, designating their models as the OY-1 and OY-2. Aircraft lost:

DATE	BUNO	SQDRN	BASE	LOST	AREA	PILOT	FATE
03/06/44	60480	VMO-2		HAWAII	ECENPAC		
03/14/44	60465	VMO-1		GUADAL-CANAL	SOPAC	2NDLT R.N. HARRIS	S
03/16/44	60479	VMO-2		HAWAII	ECENPAC		
03/19/44	60493	VMO-3		ESPIRITU SANTO	SOPAC		
04/13/44	60460	VMO-1		GUADAL-CANAL	SOPAC	2NDLT G.R. SKOGNO	S
05/04/44	60472	VMO-2		KAMULEATU	ECENPAC	2NDLT J.O. MILLS	D
05/29/44	75166	VMO-5		HAWAII	ECENPAC		

DATE	BUNO	SQDRN	BASE	LOST	AREA	PILOT	FATE
06/15/44	60495	VMO-3		RUSSELLS	SOPAC		
06/19/44	75159	VMO-4		SAIPAN	WCENPAC		
06/22/44	60500	VMO-4		SAIPAN	WCENPAC		
06/22/44	60502	VMO-4		SAIPAN	WCENPAC		
06/24/44	60498	VMO-4		SAIPAN	WCENPAC		
06/26/44	75160	VMO-5		HAWAII	ECENPAC		
07/30/44	60504	VMO-4	SAIPAN	TINIAN	WCENPAC	LT J.A. CAMERON	D
08/31/44	60464	VMO-1		GUAM	WCENPAC	1STLT W.P. BRODERICK	U
09/22/44	75167	VMO-5		HAWAII	ECENPAC	LT L.H. GREENBURG	S
09/29/44	60501	VMO-4	EWA	HAWAII	ECENPAC		
10/22/44	60467	VMO-1		GUAM	WCENPAC		
10/22/44	60469	VMO-1		GUAM	WCENPAC		
10/25/44	60486	VMO-3		PELELIU	WCENPAC		
10/25/44	60492	VMO-3		PELELIU	WCENPAC		
10/31/44	75169	COMAIR-PAC	PEARL	HAWAII	ECENPAC		
11/03/44	75170	VMO-5	HILO	HAWAII	ECENPAC	LT JAMES J. LOCKWOOD	S
11/29/44	2761	VMO-4	EWA	HAWAII	ECENPAC	LT NED J. FROST	S
12/01/44	60505	VMO-5		HAWAII	ECENPAC		
12/21/44	2762	VMO-4	EWA	HAWAII	ECENPAC		
12/21/44	60497	VMO-4	EWA	HAWAII	ECENPAC		
12/22/44	2777	VMO-5	EWA	HAWAII	ECENPAC	CDR E.S. KEATS	S
12/31/44	60475	VMO-2		SAIPAN	WCENPAC		
02/11/45	2750	VMO-1		GUAM	WCENPAC	LT RALPH G. LESTER	D
02/11/45	2774	VMO-1		GUAM	WCENPAC		
02/21/45	2758	VMO-4			WCENPAC		
02/21/45	2760	VMO-4			WCENPAC		
02/28/45	60503	VMO-4			WCENPAC		
03/13/45	75168	VMO-5		GUAM	WCENPAC		
03/24/45	2776	VMO-5		GUAM	WCENPAC		
03/31/45	60490	VMO-3		OKINAWA	EMPIRE		
03/31/45	2757	VMO-4		GUAM	WCENPAC		
03/31/45	2764	VMO-4		GUAM	WCENPAC		
03/31/45	2765	VMO-4		GUAM	WCENPAC		
03/31/45	60499	VMO-4		GUAM	WCENPAC		
03/31/45	60506	VMO-4		GUAM	WCENPAC		
04/08/45	2788	VMO-6		OKINAWA	EMPIRE		
04/09/45	2786	VMO-6		OKINAWA	EMPIRE		
04/10/45	2787	VMO-6		OKINAWA	EMPIRE		
04/11/45	60463	VMO-1		GUAM	WCENPAC	2NDLT THOMAS R. DRINKWATER	U
04/16/45	2756	VMO-3		OKINAWA	EMPIRE		
04/20/45	2778	VMO-6		OKINAWA	EMPIRE		
04/24/45	60494	VMO-3		OKINAWA	EMPIRE		
04/30/45	2759	CASU(F)-48		SAIPAN	WCENPAC		
04/30/45	3889	VMO-8		GUAM	WCENPAC		
05/21/45	2782	VMO-6		OKINAWA	EMPIRE		
05/21/45	2785	VMO-6		OKINAWA	EMPIRE		
05/31/45	60484	VMO-2		SAIPAN	WCENPAC		
06/02/45	60478	VMO-2		SAIPAN	WCENPAC		
06/02/45	75172	VMO-8		GUAM	WCENPAC		
06/04/45	3865	VMO-7		OKINAWA	EMPIRE		
06/06/45	60489	VMO-3		OKINAWA	EMPIRE		
06/08/45	3891	VMO-2		SAIPAN	WCENPAC	2NDLT GERALD R. TAYLOR	D
06/08/45	2781	VMO-6		OKINAWA	EMPIRE		
06/10/45	3875	VMO-7		JINAMOC	PHIL	2NDLT PAUL G. DUES	S
06/28/45	2783	VMO-6		OKINAWA	EMPIRE	2NDLT KEITH A. KELLIER	S
06/30/45	60461	VMO-1		GUAM	WCENPAC		
06/30/45	60466	VMO-1		GUAM	WCENPAC		
06/30/45	60487	VMO-3		OKINAWA	EMPIRE		
06/30/45	60488	VMO-3		OKINAWA	EMPIRE		
06/30/45	60496	VMO-3		OKINAWA	EMPIRE		
07/03/45	60474	VMO-8		GUAM	WCENPAC		
07/03/45	60482	VMO-8		GUAM	WCENPAC		
07/03/45	75180	VMO-8		GUAM	WCENPAC		
07/11/45	75162	VMO-5		HAWAII	ECENPAC	1STLT RICHARD H. JUVE	S
07/11/45	75165	VMO-5		HAWAII	ECENPAC	1STLT ROBERT GORMAN	S
07/14/45	3896	VMO-4		HAWAII	ECENPAC	2NDLT RICHARD CHYNOWETH	S

DATE	BUNO	SQDRN	BASE	LOST	AREA	PILOT	FATE
07/21/45	3885	VMO-2		SAIPAN	WCENPAC	1STLT FRANK A. MILLIKAN	S
08/05/45	3927	VMO-3			EMPIRE		
08/07/45	75163	VMO-5		KAMUDA	ECENPAC	1STLT FRANK LUEDERS	S

CURTISS R5C-1

The Curtiss-Wright C-46 Commando was a twin-engined transport aircraft originally derived from a commercial high-altitude airliner design. It was instead used as a military transport during World War II by the United States Army Air Forces as well as the U.S. Navy/Marine Corps under the designation R5C. Known to the men who flew them as "The Whale," or the "Curtiss Calamity," the C-46 served a similar role as its counterpart, the Douglas C-47 Skytrain, but was not as extensively produced. The R5C-1 military transport aircraft was used by the US Marine Corps. Similar to the C-46A Commando, there were 160 built. Aircraft lost:

DATE	BUNO	SQDRN	BASE	LOST	AREA	PILOT	FATE
02/05/44	39497	VMJ-252	MIDWAY		ECENPAC	1STLT W.L. TWITS	S
04/03/44	39501	VMJ-252	APAMAMA		CENPAC	CAPT R.S. LAMBERT	S
02/08/45	39525	CASU(F)-20		ROI	WCENPAC		
05/24/45	39607	VMR-253		GUAM	WCENPAC		
05/24/45	39608	VMR-253		OKINAWA	EMPIRE		
05/24/45	39580	VMR-353		SAIPAN	WCENPAC		
06/27/45	39596	VMR-253		ULITHI	WCENPAC	MAJ JACK F. MCCOLLUM	S
07/04/45	39561	VMR-252		GUAM	WCENPAC	1STLT DONALD J. GARIN	S

CURTISS SB2C (VARIANT UNKNOWN)

DATE	BUNO	SQDRN	BASE	LOST	AREA	PILOT	FATE
09/16/44		VB-81	HAWAII		ECENPAC	ENS PHILLIP W. BARTLETT	S

CURTISS SB2C-1

The Curtiss SB2C Helldiver was a carrier-based dive bomber aircraft produced for the United States Navy during World War II, replacing the Douglas SBD Dauntless. Despite its size, the SB2C was much faster than the SBD it replaced. The U.S. Navy would not accept the SB2C until 880 modifications to the design and the changes on the production line had been made, delaying the Curtiss Helldiver's combat debut. The SB2C-1 could deploy slats mechanically linked with undercarriage actuation extended from the outer third of the wing leading edge to aid lateral control at low speeds. The early prognosis of the SB2C was unfavorable as it was strongly disliked by aircrews because it was much bigger and heavier than the SBD it replaced.

In the first Battle of the Philippine Sea, 45 Helldivers were lost because they ran out of fuel on the return to their carriers.

The litany of faults that the Helldiver bore included the fact that it was underpowered, had a shorter range than the SBD, was equipped with an unreliable electrical system and was often poorly manufactured. The Curtis-Electric propeller and the complex hydraulic system had frequent maintenance problems. One of the faults remaining with the aircraft all of its operational life would be poor longitudinal stability from a fuselage that was too short, to fit aircraft carrier elevators. The Helldiver's aileron response was also poor and handling suffered greatly under 90 knots airspeed. Since the speed of approach to land on a carrier was supposed to be 85 knots this proved problematic. The 800 changes demanded by the Navy, and to make the aircraft able to take on a combat role, resulted in a 42% weight increase explaining much of the problem.

An oddity of the SB2Cs with 1942 to 1943-style tricolor camouflage was that the undersides of the outer wing panels carried dark topside camouflage because the undersurfaces were visible from above when the wings were folded.

It was the advent of air to ground rockets which allowed the precision attack of ship and shore based targets without the stress and hence weight/performance issues that dive bombers had to endure that ensured that the SB2C was the last all-purpose dive bomber built. Production version for United States Navy with four 0.50 in (12.7 mm) wing guns and one 0.30 in (7.62 mm) dorsal gun. There were 200 built under the initial contract (BuNos 00001 – 00200). Aircraft lost:

DATE	BUNO	SQDRN	BASE	LOST	AREA	PILOT	FATE
05/26/43	00120	VB-5	USS YORK-TOWN	TRINIDAD	CENLANT		
05/28/43	00154	VB-5	USS YORK-TOWN	TRINIDAD	CENLANT		
07/18/43	00190	VB-17	USS BUNKER HILL		NORLANT		
07/19/43	00171	VB-17	USS BUNKER HILL		NORLANT		
07/19/43	00186	VB-17	USS BUNKER HILL		NORLANT		
09/11/43	00072	VB-17	USS BUNKER HILL		NORLANT		
09/12/43	00090	VB-17	USS BUNKER HILL		NORLANT		
10/13/43	00095	VB-17	USS BUNKER HILL		ECENPAC		
10/25/43	00138	VB-17	USS BUNKER HILL		WCENPAC		
11/11/43	00024	VB-17	USS BUNKER HILL	RABAUL	SOPAC	LTJG W.L. GERNER	S
11/11/43	00067	VB-17	USS BUNKER HILL	RABAUL	SOPAC		
11/11/43	00078	VB-17	USS BUNKER HILL	RABAUL	SOPAC		
11/11/43	00180	VB-17	USS BUNKER HILL	RABAUL	SOPAC	LTJG C.W. THOMSON	M
11/19/43	00076	VB-17	USS BUNKER HILL	TARAWA	CENPAC	ENS F.A. HOUGHTON	S
12/01/43	00028	VB-17	USS BUNKER HILL	MAKIN	CENPAC		
12/01/43	00198	VB-17	USS BUNKER HILL	MAKIN	CENPAC		
12/04/43	00025	VB-8	USS INTREPID	BERMUDA	NORLANT	ENS R.A. HORN	S
12/05/43	00166	VB-8	USS INTREPID	BERMUDA	NORLANT	LT A.F. SEAVER	S

DATE	BUNO	SQDRN	BASE	LOST	AREA	PILOT	FATE
12/09/43	00081	VB-17	USS BUNKER HILL	NAURU	CENPAC	ENS E.D. WILLIAMS	U
12/12/43	00071	VB-8	USS INTREPID	W OF CENT AMER.	CENPAC	ENS W.C. BALLANCE	S
12/13/43	00144	VB-8	USS INTREPID	W OF CENT AMER.	CENPAC	LT M.D. CARMODY	S
12/20/43	00162	VB-8	USS INTREPID	W OF CENT AMER.	CENPAC	LTJG H.S. SHARP	S
01/01/44	00018	VB-17	USS BUNKER HILL	KAVIENG	SOPAC	LT G.H. FREED	M
01/11/44	00196	VB-8	OAHU	MOLOKAI	ECENPAC	ENS R.S. WRIGHT	M
01/24/44	00112	VB-17	USS BUNKER HILL	MARSHALLS	CENPAC		
01/29/44	00087	VB-17	USS BUNKER HILL	KWAJALEIN	CENPAC	ENS C.O. JOHNSON	D
01/31/44	00195	VB-17	USS BUNKER HILL	KWAJALEIN	CENPAC	LT J.D. WALKER	S
02/16/44	00037	VB-17	USS BUNKER HILL	TRUK	CENPAC	LTJG R.L. TEMME	S
02/16/44	00091	VB-17	USS BUNKER HILL	TRUK	CENPAC	ENS G.A. GIBBS	S
02/16/44	00093	VB-17	USS BUNKER HILL	TRUK	CENPAC	LTJG G.L. GLASS	D
02/19/44	00177	VB-2	HILO	HAWAII	ECENPAC	LTJG W.E. FINGER	S
02/28/44	00189	VB-2	BARBERS POINT	HAWAII	ECENPAC		
02/29/44	00151	VB-1	KANEOHE	HAWAII	ECENPAC	ENS F.E. SCHULTZ	D
03/01/44	00107	VB-8	PUUNENE	HAWAII	ECENPAC		
03/02/44	00041	VB-17	USS BUNKER HILL	PEARL	ECENPAC		
03/30/44	00132	VB-18	HILO	HAWAII	ECENPAC	ENS F.P. BORO	S
04/03/44	00036	VB-2	USS HORNET	HAWAII	ECENPAC		
04/05/44	00118	VB-18	HILO	HAWAII	ECENPAC		
04/08/44	00150	VB-100	USS WASP	PEARL	ECENPAC	LT MCD. TYRE	S
04/11/44	00033	VB-1	KANEOHE	HAWAII	ECENPAC		
04/19/44	00109	VB-18	HILO	HAWAII	ECENPAC	ENS C.M. MEYER	S
04/20/44	00164	VB-1	KANEOHE	HAWAII	ECENPAC		
04/20/44	00174	VB-18	HILO	HAWAII	ECENPAC	ENS A.H. ROHLEDER	S
04/22/44	00143	VB-100	BARBERS POINT	HAWAII	ECENPAC	ENS G.D. MCKAY	S
04/24/44	00062	VB-100	BARBERS POINT	HAWAII	ECENPAC		
04/25/44	00104	VB-100	BARBERS POINT	HAWAII	ECENPAC	ENS H.O. MAXWELL	S
04/27/44	00098	VB-100	BARBERS POINT	HAWAII	ECENPAC	ENS F. SIECZKOWSKA	S
05/25/44	00043	VB-100	BARBERS POINT	HAWAII	ECENPAC		
06/05/44	00147	VB-100	BARBERS POINT	HAWAII	ECENPAC	ENS F.M. CRAWFORD	S
06/06/44	00035	VB-100	BARBERS POINT	HAWAII	ECENPAC	ENS L.F. KINCAID	S
06/16/44	00074	VB-100	BARBERS POINT	HAWAII	ECENPAC		
06/17/44	00123	VB-100	BARBERS POINT	HAWAII	ECENPAC		
06/24/44	00084	VB-100	BARBERS POINT	HAWAII	ECENPAC		
06/24/44	00089	VB-100	BARBERS POINT	HAWAII	ECENPAC		
06/24/44	00181	VB-100	BARBERS POINT	HAWAII	ECENPAC		
06/29/44	00142	VB-100	BARBERS POINT	HAWAII	ECENPAC		

DATE	BUNO	SQDRN	BASE	LOST	AREA	PILOT	FATE
07/13/44	00152	A.A.	BARBERS POINT	HAWAII	ECENPAC		
07/13/44	00119	VB-100	BARBERS POINT	HAWAII	ECENPAC		
07/31/44	00097	COMAIR-PAC	PEARL	HAWAII	ECENPAC		
08/05/44	00158	VB-7	USS HANCOCK	PANAMA	CENLANT		
08/10/44	00032	VB-100	BARBERS POINT	HAWAII	ECENPAC	ENS R.M. CLARK	U
08/10/44	00061	VB-100	BARBERS POINT	HAWAII	ECENPAC	ENS W.E. GRESHAM	D
12/12/44	00057	A.A.	BARBERS POINT	HAWAII	ECENPAC		
12/12/44	00060	A.A.	BARBERS POINT	HAWAII	ECENPAC		

CURTISS SB2C-1A

The original designation for this variant was the United States Army Air Corps which they called the Curtiss A-25A. When the Army no longer had a dive-bombing mission, some 410 of these variants were transferred to the United States Marine Corps. Some references claim that this variant never saw combat, being used primarily as trainers, but the Aviation History Cards reflect three assigned to VMSB-332 and lost in Torokina. The Marines did not care much for this variant either and most just sat in Hawaii until stricken from the roles near the end of the war. Aircraft lost:

DATE	BUNO	SQDRN	BASE	LOST	AREA	PILOT	FATE
09/30/44	75448	VMSB-332		TOROKINA	SOPAC		
09/30/44	75486	VMSB-332		TOROKINA	SOPAC		
09/30/44	75549	VMSB-332		TOROKINA	SOPAC		
05/17/45	75233	POOL	HAWAII		ECENPAC		
05/17/45	75349	POOL	HAWAII		ECENPAC		
05/17/45	75360	POOL	HAWAII		ECENPAC		
05/17/45	75380	POOL	HAWAII		ECENPAC		
05/17/45	75389	POOL	HAWAII		ECENPAC		
05/17/45	75394	POOL	HAWAII		ECENPAC		
05/17/45	75402	POOL	HAWAII		ECENPAC		
05/17/45	75405	POOL	HAWAII		ECENPAC		
05/17/45	75420	POOL	HAWAII		ECENPAC		
05/17/45	75450	POOL	HAWAII		ECENPAC		
05/17/45	75452	POOL	HAWAII		ECENPAC		
05/17/45	75460	POOL	HAWAII		ECENPAC		
05/17/45	75464	POOL	HAWAII		ECENPAC		
05/17/45	75465	POOL	HAWAII		ECENPAC		
05/17/45	75469	POOL	HAWAII		ECENPAC		
05/17/45	75472	POOL	HAWAII		ECENPAC		
05/17/45	75480	POOL	HAWAII		ECENPAC		
05/17/45	75484	POOL	HAWAII		ECENPAC		
05/17/45	75488	POOL	HAWAII		ECENPAC		
05/17/45	75489	POOL	HAWAII		ECENPAC		
05/17/45	75490	POOL	HAWAII		ECENPAC		
05/17/45	75517	POOL	HAWAII		ECENPAC		
05/17/45	75542	POOL	HAWAII		ECENPAC		
05/17/45	75548	POOL	HAWAII		ECENPAC		
05/17/45	75555	POOL	HAWAII		ECENPAC		
05/17/45	75556	POOL	HAWAII		ECENPAC		
05/17/45	75557	POOL	HAWAII		ECENPAC		
05/17/45	75558	POOL	HAWAII		ECENPAC		
05/17/45	75559	POOL	HAWAII		ECENPAC		
05/17/45	75560	POOL	HAWAII		ECENPAC		
05/17/45	75572	POOL	HAWAII		ECENPAC		
05/17/45	75581	POOL	HAWAII		ECENPAC		
05/17/45	76781	POOL	HAWAII		ECENPAC		
05/17/45	76784	POOL	HAWAII		ECENPAC		
05/17/45	76792	POOL	HAWAII		ECENPAC		
05/17/45	76804	POOL	HAWAII		ECENPAC		
05/17/45	76818	POOL	HAWAII		ECENPAC		

CURTISS SB2C-1C

The Curtiss SB2C-1C variant was the SB2C-1 with two 20 mm (0.79 in) wing-mounted cannons and hydraulically operated flaps. There were 778 built. Aircraft lost:

DATE	BUNO	SQDRN	BASE	LOST	AREA	PILOT	FATE
01/07/44	00222	VB-15	USS HORNET	BERMUDA	NORLANT		
01/07/44	00273	VB-15	USS HORNET	BERMUDA	NORLANT	ENS A.M. DECESSARO	S
01/14/44	18194		ESPIRITU SANTO		SOPAC		
01/22/44	18235	VB-15	USS HORNET	BERMUDA	NORLANT	ENS E.H. FLETCHER	D
01/23/44	18255	VB-15	USS HORNET	BERMUDA	NORLANT	ENS E.N. PETERSON	D
02/02/44	18279	VB-14	USS WASP	PUERTO RICO	CENLANT	LT F.C. BRANDENBURG	S
02/16/44	00251	VB-14	USS WASP	TRINIDAD	CENLANT	ENS R.B. PETHICK	S
02/19/44	18227	VB-14	USS WASP	TRINIDAD	CENLANT	LTJG J. MAGEE	S
02/21/44	18299	VB-15	USS HORNET	PANAMA	CENPAC	ENS C.N. PLATT	S
02/22/44	01196	VB-15	USS HORNET	PANAMA	CENPAC	ENS W.S. DEMING	S
02/23/44	01190	VB-15	USS HORNET	PANAMA	CENPAC	ENS J.E. PEABODY	D
03/07/44	18322	VB-8	PUUNENE	HAWAII	ECENPAC	ENS B.R. BARCLAY	S
03/13/44	18432		USS ALTAMAHA	PEARL	ECENPAC		
03/21/44	00260	VB-13	USS FRANKLIN	TRINIDAD	CENLANT	LT L.E. TEW	S
03/25/44	18206	VB-13	USS FRANKLIN	TRINIDAD	CENLANT	ENS R. HOWARD	S
03/28/44	18346	VB-8	USS BUNKER HILL	PALAU	CENPAC	ENS G.W. SNEDICKER	S
03/28/44	18347	VB-8	USS BUNKER HILL	PALAU	CENPAC	LTJG C.H. SMITH	S
03/30/44	01024	VB-2	USS HORNET	PALAU	CENPAC	LTJG J.B. HOUSTON	D
03/30/44	18201	VB-13	USS FRANKLIN	TRINIDAD	CENLANT	ENS C.R. PINGREY	S
03/30/44	18454	VB-2	USS HORNET	PALAU	CENPAC	LTJG C.W. HARDIN	D
03/30/44	18456	VB-2	USS HORNET	PALAU	CENPAC	LT D.H. RANSOM	S
03/30/44	18328	VB-8	USS BUNKER HILL	PALAU	CENPAC	ENS C.F. MAYER	S
03/30/44	18409	VB-8	USS BUNKER HILL	PALAU	CENPAC	LTJG C.W. SMITH	S
03/30/44	18471	VB-8	USS BUNKER HILL	PALAU	CENPAC	ENS T.P. NEELY	S
03/31/44	01022	VB-8	USS BUNKER HILL	PALAU	CENPAC	ENS A.R. COFFIN	S
03/31/44	18341	VB-8	USS BUNKER HILL	PALAU	CENPAC		
03/31/44	18427	VB-8	USS BUNKER HILL	PALAU	CENPAC	ENS R.A. BENSHIMAL	S
04/01/44	18488	VB-13	USS FRANKLIN	TRINIDAD	CENLANT	ENS J.D. BOGAN	S
04/01/44	18264	VB-2	USS HORNET	WOLEAI	CENPAC	ENS D.R. SILLS	D
04/05/44	18253	VB-2	USS HORNET	HAWAII	ECENPAC		
04/07/44	00306	VB-14	USS WASP	PEARL	ECENPAC	ENS R.C. WERNTZ	D
04/14/44	01200	POOL	EBON		SOPAC		
04/21/44	00217	VB-2	USS HORNET	WAKDE	SW PAC	LTJG J.W. BAMBER	S

DATE	BUNO	SQDRN	BASE	LOST	AREA	PILOT	FATE
04/21/44	00341	VB-2	USS HORNET	SAMAR	PHIL	LTJG SCLEURER	S
04/21/44	00345	VB-2	USS HORNET	WAKDE	SW PAC	LTJG A.S. BOSWORTH	D
04/21/44	01136	VB-2	USS HORNET	WAKDE	SW PAC	LTJG ISABELLA	S
04/21/44	01175	VB-2	USS HORNET	WAKDE	SW PAC	LTJG A.F. DOHERTY	S
04/21/44	18435	VB-2	USS HORNET	SAMAR	PHIL	LTJG W.E. FINGER	D
04/21/44	18444	VB-2	USS HORNET	SAMAR	PHIL	LTJG H.H. WATSON	D
04/21/44	18512	VB-2	USS HORNET	WAKDE	SW PAC	LTJG K.E. SHERWOOD	M
04/28/44	00228	VB-14	USS WASP	OAHU	ECENPAC	LT F.C. BRANDENBURG	S
04/28/44	00264	VB-8	USS BUNKER HILL	TRUK	CENPAC	LTJG A.A. FOOTE	M
04/29/44	00265	VB-8	USS BUNKER HILL	TRUK	CENPAC	LT P.W. HUNTSMAN	S
04/29/44	00309	VB-8	USS BUNKER HILL	TRUK	CENPAC	LTJG P. SACHON	S
04/29/44	01043	VB-8	USS BUNKER HILL	TRUK	CENPAC	LTJG L.D. SCHEFF	S
04/30/44	00337	VB-14	USS WASP	ENR MARCUS	CENPAC		
04/30/44	18423	VB-2	USS HORNET	TRUK	CENPAC	LTJG J.F. FRITTS	S
05/01/44	18552	VB-1	KANEOHE	HAWAII	ECENPAC		
05/01/44	00303	VB-2	USS HORNET	ENR KWAJALEIN	CENPAC	LTJG J.F. FRITTS	S
05/02/44	01047	VB-20	BARBERS POINT	HAWAII	ECENPAC	ENS R.C. KNOECKEL	S
05/02/44	01063	VB-20	BARBERS POINT	HAWAII	ECENPAC	LTJG R. LEWIS	D
05/10/44	18217	VB-15	USS ESSEX	ENR MARCUS	CENPAC		
05/15/44	00323	VB-3	PUUNENE	HAWAII	ECENPAC		
05/15/44	18343	VB-3	PUUNENE	HAWAII	ECENPAC		
05/16/44	01053	VB-14	USS WASP	MARCUS	CENPAC		
05/19/44	18404	VB-15	USS ESSEX	MARCUS	CENPAC	ENS J.H. DIXON	M
05/19/44	18522	VB-15	USS ESSEX	MARCUS	CENPAC	ENS T.A. WOODS	S
05/23/44	18351	VB-11	HILO	HAWAII	ECENPAC	ENS W.S. CULVER	D
05/23/44	18470	VB-15	USS ESSEX	WAKE	WCENPAC	ENS C.W. CRELLIN	S
06/01/44	18193	VB-11	HILO	HAWAII	ECENPAC	ENS R.M. ELLIS	U
06/01/44	18420	VB-11	HILO	HAWAII	ECENPAC	LT T.J. WARREN	D
06/03/44	18284	VB-14	USS WASP	MAJURO	CENPAC	LT H.J. WALKER	S
06/03/44	00269	VB-2	USS HORNET	MAJURO	CENPAC	LTJG G.H. ROBERTSON	S
06/08/44	18533	VB-1	USS YORK-TOWN	MAJURO	CENPAC		
06/08/44	18336	VB-8	USS BUNKER HILL	ENR OROTE	CENPAC	ENS A. SCOPELITIES	D
06/12/44	01028	VB-15	USS ESSEX	PAGAN	CENPAC	ENS J.G. FOOTE	S
06/12/44	00339	VB-2	USS HORNET	GUAM	WCENPAC	LTD.T. GALVIN	S
06/12/44	00344	VB-2	USS HORNET	GUAM	WCENPAC	LT J.F. FRITTS	M
06/12/44	18207	VB-1	USS YORK-TOWN	GUAM	WCENPAC	LT S.W. ROBERTS	S
06/12/44	18545	VB-1	USS YORK-TOWN	GUAM	WCENPAC	LT R.E. JAMES	S
06/12/44	18458	VB-15	USS ESSEX	PAGAN	CENPAC	ENS C.J. VANDERWALL	D
06/13/44	00290	VB-2	USS HORNET	GUAM	WCENPAC	LTJG A.F. DOHERTY	S
06/13/44	01089	VB-1	USS YORK-TOWN	GUAM	WCENPAC	LTJG BLANCHARD	U
06/13/44	18290	VB-2	USS HORNET	GUAM	WCENPAC	LTJG R.A. YAUSSI	S
06/13/44	18332	VB-2	USS HORNET	GUAM	WCENPAC	LTJG D.H. RANSOM	S
06/13/44	18453	VB-2	USS HORNET	GUAM	WCENPAC	LTJG T.J. TAYLOR	S

DATE	BUNO	SQDRN	BASE	LOST	AREA	PILOT	FATE
06/13/44	18478	VB-15	USS ESSEX	ENR BONINS	CENPAC		
06/14/44	18457	VB-1	USS YORK-TOWN	ENR BONINS	CENPAC		
06/14/44	00304	VB-15	USS ESSEX	ENR BONINS	CENPAC		
06/14/44	00215	VB-8	USS BUNKER HILL	OROTE	CENPAC		
06/15/44	00322	VB-15	USS ESSEX	BONINS	CENPAC		
06/15/44	00342	VB-15	USS ESSEX	BONINS	CENPAC	ENS THEODORE CLEMENT	M
06/15/44	00261	VB-2	USS HORNET	BONINS	CENPAC	LT D.T. GALVIN	M
06/15/44	00277	VB-8	USS BUNKER HILL	OROTE	CENPAC		
06/15/44	01155	VB-1	USS YORK-TOWN	BONINS	CENPAC	ENS J.T. DELMORE	S
06/15/44	18590	VB-15	USS ESSEX	BONINS	CENPAC	ENS C.W. CRELLIN	S
06/16/44	18531	VB-1	USS YORK-TOWN	BONINS	CENPAC	ENS T. ELLIOTT	S
06/17/44	01062	VB-15	USS ESSEX	ENR GUAM	CENPAC		
06/19/44	00302	VB-8	USS BUNKER HILL	MARIANAS	CENPAC	LTJG P.I. TOUW	M
06/19/44	00329	VB-8	USS BUNKER HILL	MARIANAS	CENPAC	LTJG R.S. BENSHIMOL	M
06/19/44	01072	VB-14	USS WASP	W OF SAIPAN	CENPAC		
06/19/44	01077	VB-2	USS HORNET	GUAM	WCENPAC	LTJG K.E. LAWRENCE	M
06/19/44	01088	VB-1	USS YORK-TOWN	GUAM	WCENPAC	ENS J.T. DELMORE	M
06/19/44	18335	VB-8	USS BUNKER HILL	MARIANAS	CENPAC	ENS W.H. RANSOM	D
06/19/44	18520	VB-1	USS YORK-TOWN	GUAM	WCENPAC	LTJG O.W. DIEM	S
06/19/44	18566	VB-1	USS YORK-TOWN	GUAM	WCENPAC	LT S.W. ROBERTS	M
06/20/44	01083	VB-1	USS YORK-TOWN	W OF SAIPAN	CENPAC		
06/20/44	01084	VB-14	USS WASP	W OF SAIPAN	CENPAC	LTJG D.N. SCATUORCHIO	S
06/20/44	01092	VB-1	USS YORK-TOWN	W OF SAIPAN	CENPAC		
06/20/44	01132	VB-1	USS YORK-TOWN	W OF SAIPAN	CENPAC		
06/20/44	01133	VB-2	USS HORNET	W OF SAIPAN	CENPAC	ENS E.D. SONNENBERG	S
06/20/44	01147	VB-2	USS HORNET	W OF SAIPAN	CENPAC	LTJG T.J. TAYLOR	S
06/20/44	01174	VB-14	USS WASP	W OF SAIPAN	CENPAC	ENS A.W. BERG	S
06/20/44	01192	VB-14	USS WASP	W OF SAIPAN	CENPAC	LTJG J.R. AMUSSEN	S
06/20/44	01197	VB-1	USS YORK-TOWN	W OF SAIPAN	CENPAC		
06/20/44	00310	VB-1	USS YORK-TOWN	W OF SAIPAN	CENPAC		
06/20/44	18514	VB-1	USS YORK-TOWN	W OF SAIPAN	CENPAC		
06/20/44	18543	VB-1	USS YORK-TOWN	W OF SAIPAN	CENPAC		
06/20/44	18563	VB-1	USS YORK-TOWN	W OF SAIPAN	CENPAC		
06/20/44	18569	VB-1	USS YORK-TOWN	W OF SAIPAN	CENPAC		
06/20/44	00247	VB-14	USS WASP	W OF SAIPAN	CENPAC	LTJG H.J. HAFF	M
06/20/44	00301	VB-14	USS WASP	W OF SAIPAN	CENPAC	ENS T.F.A. STANLEY	M
06/20/44	18195	VB-14	USS WASP	W OF SAIPAN	CENPAC	ENS H. CONNETT	M
06/20/44	18244	VB-14	USS WASP	W OF SAIPAN	CENPAC	LT J.E. KANE	S
06/20/44	18273	VB-14	USS WASP	W OF SAIPAN	CENPAC	LCDR J.D. BLITCH	S
06/20/44	18285	VB-14	USS WASP	W OF SAIPAN	CENPAC	LTJG A.T. WALRAVEN	M
06/20/44	18287	VB-14	USS WASP	W OF SAIPAN	CENPAC	ENS R.P. PETHICK	M
06/20/44	18561	VB-14	USS WASP	W OF SAIPAN	CENPAC	LTJG M.F. BROWNE	S
06/20/44	00334	VB-2	USS HORNET	W OF SAIPAN	CENPAC	LT H.L. BUELL	S

DATE	BUNO	SQDRN	BASE	LOST	AREA	PILOT	FATE
06/20/44	18269	VB-2	USS HORNET	W OF SAIPAN	CENPAC	LTJG A.F. DOHERTY	S
06/20/44	18304	VB-2	USS HORNET	W OF SAIPAN	CENPAC	LTJG D.S. STEAR	S
06/20/44	18446	VB-2	USS HORNET	W OF SAIPAN	CENPAC	LTJG J. MCGEE	S
06/20/44	18455	VB-2	USS HORNET	W OF SAIPAN	CENPAC	LTJG R.E. SCHEURER	S
06/20/44	18481	VB-2	USS HORNET	W OF SAIPAN	CENPAC	LTJG B. BUSH	S
06/20/44	18498	VB-2	USS HORNET	W OF SAIPAN	CENPAC	LTJG H.A. EWING	S
06/20/44	18529	VB-2	USS HORNET	W OF SAIPAN	CENPAC	LTJG R.A. YAUSSI	S
06/20/44	00291	VB-8	USS BUNKER HILL	W OF SAIPAN	CENPAC	LTJG R.D. HORNE	S
06/20/44	18331	VB-8	USS BUNKER HILL	W OF SAIPAN	CENPAC	LTJG W.F. PILCHER	S
06/20/44	18358	VB-8	USS BUNKER HILL	W OF SAIPAN	CENPAC	LTJG P.W. HUNTSMAN	S
06/20/44	18384	VB-8	USS BUNKER HILL	W OF SAIPAN	CENPAC	LTJG J.O. MCINTIRE	M
06/20/44	18405	VB-8	USS BUNKER HILL	W OF SAIPAN	CENPAC	LT ARTHUR D. JONES	S
06/20/44	18417	VB-8	USS BUNKER HILL	W OF SAIPAN	CENPAC	LTJG C.D. SMITH	M
06/20/44	18460	VB-8	USS BUNKER HILL	W OF SAIPAN	CENPAC	LTJG R.E. STERLING	M
06/20/44	18467	VB-8	USS BUNKER HILL	W OF SAIPAN	CENPAC	LTJG L.D. SCHEFF	S
06/20/44	18540	VB-8	USS BUNKER HILL	W OF SAIPAN	CENPAC	LT A.F. MOOTY	S
06/20/44	18587	VB-8	USS BUNKER HILL	W OF SAIPAN	CENPAC	LTJG H.S. SHARP	S
06/20/44	18588	VB-8	USS BUNKER HILL	W OF SAIPAN	CENPAC	LCDR J.D. ARBES	S
06/21/44	01044	VB-15	USS ESSEX	SAIPAN	WCENPAC	ENS W.F. NOLTE	D
06/24/44	01090	VB-2	USS HORNET	PAGAN	CENPAC	LTJG P. GARBLER	S
06/24/44	18464	VB-15	USS ESSEX	GUAM	WCENPAC	LTJG J.W. BARNITZ	S
06/26/44	18249	VB-11	HILO	HAWAII	ECENPAC		
06/30/44	18411		HAWAII		ECENPAC		
07/02/44	01049	VB-14	USS WASP	ENR IWO JIMA	CENPAC	ENS CLYDE SLAY, JR.	D
07/02/44	18338	VB-18	KANEOHE	HAWAII	ECENPAC	LT F.A. MCALLISTER	M
07/02/44	18591	VB-18	KANEOHE	HAWAII	ECENPAC	ENS A.E. WATKINS	M
07/03/44	01014	VB-11	KANEOHE	HAWAII	ECENPAC	ENS J. ANDERSON	D
07/04/44	01124	VB-2	USS HORNET	BONINS	CENPAC		
07/04/44	01169	VB-1	USS YORK-TOWN	CHICHI JIMA	CENPAC	ENS O.M. HINTZ	M
07/04/44	01191	VB-14	USS WASP	IWO JIMA	EMPIRE		
07/04/44	18547	VB-1	USS YORK-TOWN	CHICHI JIMA	CENPAC	LT W.K. WRIGHT	M
07/04/44	18548	VB-1	USS YORK-TOWN	CHICHI JIMA	CENPAC	ENS J. DRYSDALE	M
07/04/44	00272	VB-14	USS WASP	IWO JIMA	EMPIRE	ENS C.E. BRADY	D
07/04/44	00363	VB-2	USS HORNET	BONINS	CENPAC	ENS G.M. ARMBRUSTER	S
07/04/44	18570	VB-2	USS HORNET	BONINS	CENPAC	ENS W.L. CONNELL	M
07/08/44	00282	VB-14	USS WASP	GUAM	WCENPAC		
07/09/44	18277	VB-2	USS HORNET	MARIANAS	CENPAC	ENS A.F. REYNOLDS	S

DATE	BUNO	SQDRN	BASE	LOST	AREA	PILOT	FATE
07/10/44	00317	VB-2	USS HORNET	ROTA	CENPAC	ENS W.R. DOUGHTY	S
07/12/44	18573	VB-11	KANEOHE	HAWAII	ECENPAC	ENS T.W. OOGLE	D
07/13/44	00315	VB-1	USS YORK-TOWN	GUAM	WCENPAC	LTJG F.L. CUNES	S
07/13/44	18318	VB-8	USS BUNKER HILL	ENR OROTE	CENPAC		
07/15/44	00231	VB-11	KANEOHE	HAWAII	ECENPAC		
07/16/44	00324	VB-1	USS YORK-TOWN	ROTA	CENPAC	LTJG MULLEN	D
07/16/44	00293	VB-14	USS WASP	GUAM	WCENPAC	LTJG GRUBON	S
07/16/44	18256	VB-14	USS WASP	GUAM	WCENPAC		
07/16/44	18270	VB-14	USS WASP	GUAM	WCENPAC	LTJG HEIDEN	S
07/16/44	18578	VB-14	USS WASP	GUAM	WCENPAC	ENS GODMAN	S
07/17/44	18340	VB-1	USS YORK-TOWN	GUAM	WCENPAC	LTJG O.W. DIEM	M
07/18/44	01071	VB-1	USS YORK-TOWN	GUAM	WCENPAC	ENS J.O. MCCALL	M
07/18/44	01039	VB-2	USS HORNET	GUAM	WCENPAC	LT J. KENNETH POWERS	S
07/19/44	01015	VB-2	USS HORNET	MARIANAS	CENPAC	LTJG J.W. BAMBER	S
07/20/44	18500	VB-15	USS ESSEX	GUAM	WCENPAC	LT H.R. SIEHERT	D
07/21/44	00320	VB-14	USS WASP	GUAM	WCENPAC	ENS D.C. HUNICKE	M
07/23/44	00235	VB-15	USS ESSEX	TINIAN	WCENPAC	LTJG C.R. JORDAN	S
07/25/44	01068	VB-15	USS ESSEX	GUAM	WCENPAC	LT H.H. KRAMER	S
07/26/44	00370	VB-8	USS BUNKER HILL	PALAU	CENPAC		
07/26/44	01172	VB-14	USS WASP	PALAU	CENPAC	ENS WRZESINKI	S
07/27/44	00321	VB-1	USS YORK-TOWN	YAP	CENPAC	LTJG J.K. BELING	S
07/27/44	18583	VB-2	USS HORNET	YAP	CENPAC	ENS G.M. ARMBRUSTER	D
07/31/44	01073	VB-100	USS SAVO ISLAND	HAWAII	ECENPAC	ENS W.T. KISSEL	S
08/04/44	18342	VB-8	USS BUNKER HILL	IWO JIMA	EMPIRE		
08/08/44	00278	CASU-4	PUUNENE	HAWAII	ECENPAC	LT J.H. BURNETTE	S
08/09/44	00285	CASU-35		ENIWETOK	CENPAC		
08/09/44	18387	CASU-35		ENIWETOK	CENPAC		
08/09/44	18441	CASU-35		ENIWETOK	CENPAC		
08/09/44	18483	CASU-35		ENIWETOK	CENPAC		
08/09/44	18490	CASU-35		ENIWETOK	CENPAC		
08/09/44	18527	CASU-35		ENIWETOK	CENPAC		
08/09/44	18580	CASU-35		ENIWETOK	CENPAC		
08/09/44	18597	CASU-35		ENIWETOK	CENPAC		
08/11/44	00242	CASU-13		LOS NEGROS	PHIL	PAUL BUGANICH (CAP)	M
08/16/44	18403	VB-100	OAHU	HAWAII	ECENPAC	ENS J.R. SIMPSON	S
08/16/44	18412	VB-100	OAHU	HAWAII	ECENPAC	ENS H.R. BRANTLEY	S
08/21/44	18241	VB-100	OAHU	HAWAII	ECENPAC	LTJG R.R. YOUNT	U
08/31/44	18510		USS COPAHEE	MARIANAS	CENPAC		
08/31/44	00338	VB-3	PUUNENE	HAWAII	ECENPAC	ENS JAMES B. SKINNER	S
09/01/44	18360	A.A.	BARBERS POINT	HAWAII	ECENPAC		
09/01/44	18400	VB-4	HILO	HAWAII	ECENPAC	LT WILLIAM E. DILL	S
09/04/44	00249	NAS	BARBERS POINT	HAWAII	ECENPAC		
09/04/44	00362	VB-3	PUUNENE	HAWAII	ECENPAC	LTJG AUTHUR N. AVERY	S
09/11/44	18525	VB-4	HILO	HAWAII	ECENPAC		
09/16/44	00223	VB-8	USS BUNKER HILL	PALAU	CENPAC		
09/16/44	18399	VB-4	HILO	HAWAII	ECENPAC	ENS KENNETH PETERS	S
09/16/44	01011	VB-8	USS BUNKER HILL	PALAU	CENPAC		
09/16/44	01025	VB-8	USS BUNKER HILL	PALAU	CENPAC		

DATE	BUNO	SQDRN	BASE	LOST	AREA	PILOT	FATE
09/16/44	01182	VB-8	USS BUNKER HILL	PALAU	CENPAC		
09/18/44	01091	VB-8	USS BUNKER HILL	OKINAWA	EMPIRE		
09/21/44	01013	VB-8	USS BUNKER HILL	OKINAWA	EMPIRE	LTJG R.D. HORNE	D
09/23/44	01094	VB-8	USS BUNKER HILL	OKINAWA	EMPIRE		
09/23/44	18192	VB-8	USS BUNKER HILL	OKINAWA	EMPIRE		
09/24/44	01128	VB-8	USS BUNKER HILL	OKINAWA	EMPIRE	LTJG P.L. EVANOFF	S
10/05/44	00258	VB-8	USS BUNKER HILL	ULITHI	WCENPAC		
10/05/44	00330	VB-8	USS BUNKER HILL	ULITHI	WCENPAC		
10/05/44	01009	VB-8	USS BUNKER HILL	ULITHI	WCENPAC		
10/05/44	01035	VB-8	USS BUNKER HILL	ULITHI	WCENPAC		
10/05/44	01045	VB-8	USS BUNKER HILL	ULITHI	WCENPAC		
10/05/44	01153	VB-8	USS BUNKER HILL	ULITHI	WCENPAC		
10/05/44	01164	VB-8	USS BUNKER HILL	ULITHI	WCENPAC		
10/05/44	01180	VB-8	USS BUNKER HILL	ULITHI	WCENPAC		
10/05/44	01202	VB-8	USS BUNKER HILL	ULITHI	WCENPAC		
10/18/44	01198	A.A.	ESPIRITU SANTO	ESPIRITU SANTO	SOPAC		
10/18/44	01066	CASU-13		PONAM	SW PAC		
01/04/45	18392	A.A.	BARBERS POINT	HAWAII	ECENPAC		
01/04/45	18506	A.A.	BARBERS POINT	HAWAII	ECENPAC		
01/13/45	18391	A.A.	PEARL	HAWAII	ECENPAC		
01/27/45	18356	CASU-31	HILO	HAWAII	ECENPAC		
01/30/45	00349	A.A.	PEARL	HAWAII	ECENPAC		
01/30/45	18349	A.A.	PEARL	HAWAII	ECENPAC		
01/30/45	18398	A.A.	PEARL	HAWAII	ECENPAC		
01/30/45	18586	A.A.	PEARL	HAWAII	ECENPAC		
05/31/45	18321	COMAIR-PAC	PEARL	HAWAII	ECENPAC		
05/31/45	18367	COMAIR-PAC	PEARL	HAWAII	ECENPAC		

CURTISS SB2C-3

The problems of the Curtiss SB2C-1 and its variants began to be solved with the introduction of the SB2C-3 beginning in 1944 which used the R-2600-20 Double Cyclone engine with 1,900 HP and the Curtis 4-bladed propeller. This substantially solved the chronic lack of power that had plagued the aircraft. The Helldivers would participate in battles over Marianas, Leyte (partly responsible for sinking the *Mu-*

sashi), Taiwan, Iwo Jima, and Okinawa (in the sinking of the *Yamato*). They were also used in the Navy attacks on the Ryuku Islands and the Japanese home island of Honshu in tactical attacks on airfields, communications, and shipping in 1945. They were also used extensively in patrols during the period between the dropping of the atomic bombs and the official Japanese surrender, and in the immediate pre-occupation period. There were 1,112 built. Aircraft lost:

DATE	BUNO	SQDRN	BASE	LOST	AREA	PILOT	FATE
06/12/44	18728	VB-13	USS FRANKLIN	PUUNENE	ECENPAC	LT R.J. WEBER	S
06/19/44	18928	VB-7	USS HANCOCK	TRINIDAD	CENLANT	ENS THOMAS F. RAY	S
06/29/44	18694	VB-80	USS TICONDER-OGA	TRINIDAD	CENLANT	LT B.P. HELL	S
07/01/44	18985	VB-20	BARBERS POINT	HAWAII	ECENPAC		
07/04/44	18704	VB-13	USS FRANKLIN	BONINS	CENPAC	ENS J.E. MILLER	S
07/04/44	18726	VB-13	USS FRANKLIN	BONINS	CENPAC	LTJG M.J. BOWER	M
07/04/44	18725	VB-14	USS WASP	IWO JIMA	EMPIRE		
07/07/44	18740	COMAIR-PAC	PEARL	HAWAII	ECENPAC		
07/07/44	18875	VB-19	USS LEX-INGTON	GUAM	WCENPAC		
07/07/44	18967	VB-19	USS LEX-INGTON	GUAM	WCENPAC		
07/13/44	18993	VB-18	KANEOHE	HAWAII	ECENPAC	LT C.A. HELLMAN	S
07/18/44	18687	VB-13	USS FRANKLIN	MARIANAS	CENPAC	ENS PERSHING C. PICKERS	S
07/18/44	18858	VB-17	HILO	HAWAII	ECENPAC		
07/19/44	18862	VB-19	USS LEX-INGTON	GUAM	WCENPAC	LT P.R. STRADLEY	S
07/19/44	18994	VB-20	PUUNENE	HAWAII	ECENPAC		
07/20/44	18997	VB-19	USS LEX-INGTON	GUAM	WCENPAC	ENS P.A. GENELINGER	M
07/21/44	18693	VB-13	USS FRANKLIN	MARIANAS	CENPAC		
07/21/44	19004	VB-20	USS ENTER-PRISE	MAINA	CENPAC		
07/26/44	18628	VB-13	USS FRANKLIN	PALAU	CENPAC	LTJG B.C. BARKSDALE	S
07/26/44	19484	VB-14	USS WASP	PALAU	CENPAC	LTJG J.R. AMUSSEN	S
07/26/44	18665	VB-19	USS LEX-INGTON	PALAU	CENPAC		
07/26/44	18816	VB-19	USS LEX INGTON	PALAU	CENPAC		
07/26/44	18841	VB-19	USS LEX-INGTON	PALAU	CENPAC		
07/26/44	18851	VB-19	USS LEX-INGTON	PALAU	CENPAC		
07/27/44	18692	VB-13	USS FRANKLIN	PALAU	CENPAC	LTJG G. MARQUARDT	S
07/27/44	18752	VB-19	USS LEX-INGTON	PALAU	CENPAC	LT E.B. STELLA	S
07/31/44	19568	CASU-30		MAJURO	CENPAC		
07/31/44	19685	VB-100	USS SAVO ISLAND	HAWAII	ECENPAC		
08/04/44	19306	VB-13	USS FRANKLIN	BONINS	CENPAC	ENS D. HEIZER	S
08/04/44	18874	VB-19	USS LEX-INGTON	IWO JIMA	EMPIRE	ENS ROY F. MAJORS	M
08/04/44	18909	VB-19	USS LEX-INGTON	IWO JIMA	EMPIRE	ENS WILLIAM S. EMERSON	S
08/05/44	19187	VB-13	USS FRANKLIN	CHICHI JIMA	CENPAC	LCDR C.B.A. HOLMSTROM	M
08/05/44	18840	VB-19	USS LEX-INGTON	IWO JIMA	EMPIRE	ENS ROBERT G. SMITH	S
08/05/44	18845	VB-19	USS LEX-INGTON	IWO JIMA	EMPIRE	LT D.F. HELM	S

DATE	BUNO	SQDRN	BASE	LOST	AREA	PILOT	FATE
08/05/44	18896	VB-19	USS LEX-INGTON	IWO JIMA	EMPIRE	ENS JOHN A. CAVENAUGH	S
08/05/44	19594	VB-2	USS HORNET	CHICHI JIMA	CENPAC	LTJG ROBERTSON	S
08/05/44	18611	VB-7	USS HANCOCK	PANAMA	CENLANT	ENS LORING MCGEE	D
08/05/44	18612	VB-7	USS HANCOCK	PANAMA	CENLANT	ENS A. ROSEN	S
08/05/44	18662	VB-7	USS HANCOCK	PANAMA	CENPAC	ENS J.H. SHEPLEY	U
08/09/44	18712	VB-100	BARBERS POINT	HAWAII	ECENPAC		
08/11/44	19535		USS NASSAU	ENR ADMIR.	SW PAC	LTJG JUDSON H. DOANE	S
08/29/44	19333	VB-14	USS WASP	PALAU	CENPAC		
08/31/44	18667	VB-100	OAHU	HAWAII	ECENPAC		
08/31/44	19238	VB-20	USS ENTER-PRISE	CHICHI JIMA	CENPAC	ENS LESLIE S. HORNBECK	S
09/01/44	19284	VB-18	USS INTREPID	ENR PALUS	CENPAC	LTJG J.M. SHUMWAY	S
09/01/44	19405	VB-20	USS ENTER-PRISE	BONINS	CENPAC	ENS STUART M. FERGUSON	M
09/02/44	19361	VB-20	USS ENTER-PRISE	BONINS	CENPAC		
09/03/44	18855	VB-19	USS LEX-INGTON	ENR ULITHI	CENPAC	LTJG WILLIAM T. GOOD	S
09/03/44	18812	VB-80	USS TICONDER-OGA	BALBOA	ECENPAC		
09/03/44	18750	VB-81	HAWAII		ECENPAC		
09/04/44	19651	VB-19	USS LEX-INGTON	ENR ULITHI	CENPAC	LTJG ROBERT S. SMITH	S
09/06/44	19229	VB-20	USS ENTER-PRISE	YAP	CENPAC		
09/07/44	19231	VB-18	USS INTREPID	PALUS	SW PAC	LT MORRIS A. ANDERSON	S
09/07/44	18850	VB-19	USS LEX-INGTON	ULITHI	WCENPAC	ENS ROBERT F. GRIFFIN	S
09/08/44	18907	VB-19	USS LEX-INGTON	ULITHI	WCENPAC	LT WILLIAM H. CRAVENS	S
09/08/44	18984	VB-81	HAWAII		ECENPAC	ENS ERWIN H. TUMLER	S
09/09/44	19335	VB-15	USS ESSEX	MINDANAO SEA	PHIL	LTJG FRED MATTHEWS	S
09/10/44	19286	VB-2	USS HORNET	ENR CEBU	CENPAC		
09/10/44	19173	VB-20	USS ENTER-PRISE	PALAU	CENPAC	LCDR G.D. GIBSON	M
09/11/44	19185	CASU-13		PONAM	SW PAC	LTJG ARNOLD E. ELZIG	U
09/11/44	19683	CASU-13		PONAM	SW PAC		
09/12/44	18653	VB-13	USS FRANKLIN	PALAU	CENPAC		
09/12/44	18743	VB-13	USS FRANKLIN	PALAU	CENPAC		
09/12/44	19154	VB-13	USS FRANKLIN	PALAU	CENPAC		
09/12/44	19201	VB-13	USS FRANKLIN	PELELIU	WCENPAC	ENS J.J. KEHOE	S
09/12/44	19083	VB-14	USS WASP	CEBU	PHIL	LTJG WISNYSER	S
09/12/44	19299	VB-14	USS WASP	CEBU	PHIL	LT WALDRON C. WORKMAN	M
09/12/44	19221	VB-7	USS HANCOCK	PEARL	ECENPAC	ENS THOMAS F. RAY	S
09/13/44	19394	VB-15	USS ESSEX	LOS NEGROS	PHIL	LT PHILIP E. GOLDEN	D
09/13/44	19412	VB-18	USS INTREPID	LOS NEGROS	PHIL	ENS DANIEL WEIZER	S
09/14/44	19186	VB-14	USS WASP	LOS NEGROS	PHIL	ENS REARDON	S
09/14/44	19470	VB-14	USS WASP	LOS NEGROS	PHIL	LTJG GEORGE C. DAVIS	S
09/15/44	18999	VB-81	HAWAII		ECENPAC	ENS ROBERT A. PATT	S
09/18/44	18719	CASU(F)-38		KANEOHE	ECENPAC		

DATE	BUNO	SQDRN	BASE	LOST	AREA	PILOT	FATE
09/19/44	19260	VB-18	USS INTREPID	LOS NEGROS	PHIL	LTJG A.L. CHAUVEL	S
09/21/44	19105	VB-14	USS WASP	LOS NEGROS	PHIL	LT S. GRUBIN	M
09/21/44	19316	VB-14	USS WASP	LOS NEGROS	PHIL	LT J.H. HEATH	M
09/22/44	19069	VB-2	USS HORNET		CENPAC		
09/22/44	19263	VB-2	USS HORNET		CENPAC		
09/23/44	19106	VB-81	HAWAII		ECENPAC	ENS ROBERT D. ROMER	S
09/24/44	19194	VB-18	USS INTREPID	LOS NEGROS	PHIL	LTJG EVERETT R. BUNCH	M
09/24/44	19427	VB-18	USS INTREPID	LOS NEGROS	PHIL	LT RALPH H. PEATLE	M
09/24/44	19430	VB-18	USS INTREPID	LOS NEGROS	PHIL	LT WALTER J.D. MADDEN	M
09/25/44	19091	A.A.	BARBERS POINT	HAWAII	ECENPAC		
09/25/44	19078	NAS	BARBERS POINT	HAWAII	ECENPAC		
09/25/44	18925	VB-2	USS HORNET		CENPAC		
10/02/44	19182	CASU-4	PUUNENE	HAWAII	ECENPAC		
10/02/44	18822	VB-80	USS TICONDER-OGA	PEARL	ECENPAC	ENS HOWARD J. STERNS	M
10/02/44	19272	VB-80	USS TICONDER-OGA	PEARL	ECENPAC	LTJG WILLIAM N. WEPPERT	M
10/03/44	18992	VB-81	HAWAII		ECENPAC	ENS C.F. BRIGGS	S
10/04/44	19681	VB-7	USS HANCOCK	ENR MANILA	PHIL	ENS C.N. CAMPBELL	S
10/04/44	18821	VB-80	USS TICONDER-OGA	PEARL	ECENPAC	ENS K.K. NOMEIKO	S
10/08/44	18949	VB-15	USS ESSEX	PESCADORES	CENPAC		
10/09/44	18626	VB-7	USS HANCOCK	ENR MANILA	PHIL		
10/10/44	19506	VB-13	USS FRANKLIN	PALAU	CENPAC	ENS T.G. HOREK	M
10/10/44	19197	VB-14	USS WASP	OKINAWA	EMPIRE	ENS JOSEPH T. GATES	S
10/10/44	19205	VB-18	USS INTREPID	ENR FORMOSA	CENPAC		
10/10/44	19301	VB-18	USS INTREPID	ENR FORMOSA	CENPAC	LTJG DANIEL W. BAKER	S
10/10/44	18892	VB-19	USS LEX-INGTON		CENPAC		
10/10/44	19654	VB-7	USS HANCOCK	ENR MANILA	PHIL	LT J.L. MCCALLEN	M
10/10/44	18903	VB-80	USS TICONDER-OGA	PEARL	ECENPAC	LTJG BILLIE P. HALL	U
10/11/44	19590	VB-80	USS TICONDER-OGA	PEARL	ECENPAC	LTJG JOHN F. BUTLER	S
10/12/44	19624	VB-13	USS FRANKLIN	FORMOSA	EMPIRE	LT R.J. WEBER, JR.	M
10/12/44		VB-14	USS WASP	FORMOSA	EMPIRE	LTJG SEDBIORCHIO	S
10/12/44		VB-18	USS INTREPID	FORMOSA	EMPIRE	LTJG ERNEST A. SMITH	M
10/12/44		VB-18	USS INTREPID	FORMOSA	EMPIRE	LT FRED MORAS	S
10/12/44	18966	VB-18	USS INTREPID	FORMOSA	EMPIRE	LT LEIF W. LARSON	S
10/12/44	19189	VB-18	USS INTREPID	FORMOSA	EMPIRE	LTJG A.K. ROHLEDER	S
10/12/44	19234	VB-18	USS INTREPID	FORMOSA	EMPIRE	LT JOHN A. THREAT	S
10/12/44	19312	VB-18	USS INTREPID	FORMOSA	EMPIRE	LTJG JOHN W. GRUCHWALD	M
10/12/44	19422	VB-18	USS INTREPID	FORMOSA	EMPIRE	CDR MARK ESLICK, JR.	M
10/12/44	19318	VB-20	USS ENTER-PRISE	FORMOSA	EMPIRE	ENS G. MUINCH	S

DATE	BUNO	SQDRN	BASE	LOST	AREA	PILOT	FATE
10/12/44	19436	VB-20	USS ENTER-PRISE	FORMOSA	EMPIRE	LT S.M. THARP	S
10/12/44		VB-7	USS HANCOCK	ENR MANILA	PHIL	LT W. FLUTEY	S
10/12/44	19504	VB-8	USS BUNKER HILL	FORMOSA	EMPIRE	LTJG P. NEWMAN	D
10/12/44	19649	VB-8	USS BUNKER HILL	FORMOSA	EMPIRE	LTJG R.J. MEAD	S
10/12/44	19688	VB-8	USS BUNKER HILL	FORMOSA	EMPIRE	LTJG H.S. SHARP	S
10/13/44	19184	VB-15	USS ESSEX	PESCADORES	CENPAC	LTJG EARL G. MALLETTE	S
10/13/44	19000	VB-18	USS INTREPID	FORMOSA	EMPIRE	LT E.H. EISENGREEN	M
10/13/44	19239	VB-18	USS INTREPID	FORMOSA	EMPIRE	LTJG CARL M. MEYER	S
10/13/44	19490	VB-7	USS HANCOCK	MANILA	PHIL	LTJG E.S. BEVIS	M
10/13/44	19168	VB-8	USS BUNKER HILL	FORMOSA	EMPIRE	LT G.C. MICHEL	S
10/13/44	19572	VB-8	USS BUNKER HILL	FORMOSA	EMPIRE	LTJG P.L. EVANOFF	M
10/14/44	19101	VB-14	USS WASP	LUZON	PHIL	ENS E.J. WALASEK	M
10/14/44	19386	VB-18	USS INTREPID	ENR LOS NEGROS	CENPAC		
10/14/44	19695	VB-7	USS HANCOCK	MANILA	PHIL		
10/14/44	19702	VB-8	USS BUNKER HILL	FORMOSA	EMPIRE	LTJG J.E. MCBRIDE	S
10/15/44	19676	VB-13	USS FRANKLIN	LUZON	PHIL	(DECK LOSS-KAMIKAZE)	
10/15/44	18617	VB-7	USS HANCOCK	MANILA	PHIL		
10/16/44	18868	VB-11	USS HORNET		CENPAC		
10/16/44	19320	VB-11	USS HORNET		CENPAC		
10/16/44	19385	VB-13	USS FRANKLIN	LUZON	PHIL	(DECK LOSS-KAMIKAZE)	
10/16/44	19220	VB-4	USS SARATOGA	HAWAII	ECENPAC	LTJG FRANCIS MOSES	S
10/17/44	19461	VB-14	USS WASP	LUZON	PHIL		
10/17/44	19174	VB-4	USS SARATOGA	HAWAII	ECENPAC	ENS BILLY NYE KINDER	S
10/18/44	19243	VB-20	USS ENTER-PRISE	MANILA	PHIL		
10/18/44	19340	VB-20	USS ENTER-PRISE	MANILA	PHIL		
10/18/44	19379	VB-20	USS ENTER-PRISE	MANILA	PHIL		
10/18/44	19417	VB-20	USS ENTER-PRISE	MANILA	PHIL	ENS LESLIE S. HORNBECK	M
10/18/44	19429	VB-20	USS ENTER-PRISE	MANILA	PHIL		
10/18/44	19094	VB-4	USS SARATOGA	HAWAII	ECENPAC	LTJG HERBERT W. FIFFE	D
10/18/44	19532	VB-7	USS HANCOCK	LUZON	PHIL	LT E.M. MCCARTY	S
10/18/44	19355	VB-8	USS BUNKER HILL	LUZON	PHIL	LTJG D. JOHNSTON	M

DATE	BUNO	SQDRN	BASE	LOST	AREA	PILOT	FATE
10/18/44	19541	VB-8	USS BUNKER HILL	LUZON	PHIL		
10/18/44	18691	VB-80	USS TICONDER-OGA	PEARL	ECENPAC	ENS L.B. CASE, JR.	S
10/18/44	19152	VB-80	USS TICONDER-OGA	PEARL	ECENPAC	LTJG R.E. PEARSON	S
10/19/44	19652	VB-11	USS HORNET	LUZON	PHIL	LTJG W.S. SAILOR	U
10/19/44	19547	VB-13	USS FRANKLIN	MANILA BAY	PHIL		
10/20/44	19052	VB-14	USS WASP	LUZON	PHIL	ENS CRAWFORD	S
10/20/44	19530	VB-82	USS BENNING-TON	NORLANT	ENS P.M. BUDINGER	S	
10/21/44	19540	VB-18	USS INTREPID	LOS NEGROS	PHIL	LT B.W. WILLIAMS	S
10/23/44	19273	VB-82	USS BENNING-TON	NORLANT	ENS J.A. BERKLEY	S	
10/24/44	19452	VB-13	USS FRANKLIN	LUZON	PHIL	LT H.D. BARNETT, JR.	M
10/24/44	19139	VB-15	USS ESSEX	LUZON	PHIL	CDR JAMES H. MINI	S
10/24/44	19625	VB-15	USS ESSEX	LUZON	PHIL	LTJG CONRAD W. CRELLIN	S
10/24/44	19440	VB-18	USS INTREPID	LOS NEGROS	PHIL		
10/24/44	19478	VB-18	USS INTREPID	LOS NEGROS	PHIL		
10/24/44	19660	VB-18	USS INTREPID	LOS NEGROS	PHIL	ENS JOHN J. BOYLE	M
10/24/44	18660	VB-19	USS LEX-INGTON	LEYTE GULF	PHIL	CDR MCGOWAN	D
10/24/44	19543	VB-19	USS LEX-INGTON	LEYTE GULF	PHIL	LT E.E. NEWMAN	S
10/25/44	18671	VB-100	BARBERS POINT	HAWAII	ECENPAC		
10/25/44	18757	VB-11	USS HORNET		PHIL	LTJG TOLER	S
10/25/44	19553	VB-11	USS HORNET		PHIL	ENS ARMSTRONG	S
10/25/44	19631	VB-11	USS HORNET		PHIL	LTJG AUBEL	S
10/25/44	19707	VB-11	USS HORNET		PHIL	LT SCHWAB	S
10/25/44	19521	VB-13	USS FRANKLIN	LUZON	PHIL	LTJG D.A. MCPHIE	M
10/25/44	19677	VB-13	USS FRANKLIN	LUZON	PHIL	LT J.H. FINROW	M
10/25/44	18962	VB-14	USS WASP	LUZON	PHIL	LT HERBERT J. WELKER	M
10/25/44	19198	VB-15	USS ESSEX	LUZON	PHIL	LT ROGER F. NOYES	S
10/25/44	19368	VB-18	USS INTREPID	ENR LUZON	PHIL	LT DONALD L. WILSON	S
10/25/44	19455	VB-19	USS LEX-INGTON	LEYTE GULF	PHIL	LT NEIMEYER	S
10/25/44	19389	VB-20	USS ENTER-PRISE	LUZON	PHIL		
10/25/44	18633	VB-7	USS HANCOCK	MANILA	PHIL	ENS RUCH	S
10/25/44	18646	VB-7	USS HANCOCK	MANILA	PHIL	ENS C.A. ROBERTSON	S
10/25/44	18669	VB-7	USS HANCOCK	MANILA	PHIL	LT B.S. SAMPSELL	M
10/25/44	18679	VB-7	USS HANCOCK	MANILA	PHIL	LTJG KINSELLA	S
10/25/44	18690	VB-7	USS HANCOCK	MANILA	PHIL		
10/25/44	18711	VB-7	USS HANCOCK	MANILA	PHIL	LCDR J.L. ERICKSON	S
10/25/44	19507	VB-7	USS HANCOCK	MANILA	PHIL	LTJG ALDERS	S
10/26/44	19203	VB-14	USS WASP	LUZON	PHIL		

DATE	BUNO	SQDRN	BASE	LOST	AREA	PILOT	FATE
10/26/44		VB-18	USS INTREPID	ENR LUZON	PHIL		
10/26/44	19170	VB-18	USS INTREPID	ENR LUZON	PHIL		
10/26/44	19208	VB-18	USS INTREPID	ENR LUZON	PHIL		
10/26/44	19258	VB-7	USS HANCOCK	MANILA	PHIL	LTJG ENNIS	S
10/26/44	19614	VB-82	USS BENNING-TON		NORLANT	ENS D.R. HOPE	S
10/29/44	19249	VB-18	USS INTREPID	LUZON	PHIL		
10/29/44	19457	VB-18	USS INTREPID	LUZON	PHIL		
10/29/44	18686	VB-7	USS HANCOCK	MANILA	PHIL	LCDR J.L. ERICKSON	U
10/29/44	19038	VB-7	USS HANCOCK	MANILA	PHIL	LT J.H. BELL	M
10/29/44	19248	VB-7	USS HANCOCK	MANILA	PHIL		
10/29/44	19298	VB-7	USS HANCOCK	MANILA	PHIL	LTJG SUNDAY	S
10/29/44	19432	VB-7	USS HANCOCK	MANILA	PHIL		
10/29/44	19598	VB-7	USS HANCOCK	MANILA	PHIL	LTJG ENNIS	S
10/30/44	19411	COMAIR-PAC	PEARL	HAWAII	ECENPAC		
11/02/44	19428	VMSB-343	MIDWAY		ECENPAC	LT RUSSELL B. AITKEN	D
11/05/44	18783	CASU-32	KAHULUI	HAWAII	ECENPAC		
11/05/44	19282	VB-14	USS WASP	LUZON	PHIL	ENS RUSSELL O. BURNHAM	M
11/05/44	19438	VB-14	USS WASP	LUZON	PHIL	LTJG GEORGE C. DAVIS	M
11/05/44	18882	VB-19	USS LEX-INGTON	LEYTE GULF	PHIL	LT D.F. BARKER	M
11/05/44	19462	VB-19	USS LEX-INGTON	LEYTE GULF	PHIL	LTJG J.W. EVATT	M
11/05/44	18609	VB-7	USS HANCOCK	LUZON	PHIL	LTJG ENNIS	S
11/06/44	19384	VB-11	USS HORNET		PHIL	LT WILSON	S
11/06/44	19661	VB-11	USS HORNET		PHIL		
11/06/44	19358	VB-15	USS ESSEX	LUZON	PHIL	LTJG WILLIAM S. RISING	S
11/06/44	19534	VB-18	USS INTREPID	LUZON	PHIL	LTJG MORRIS A. ANDERSON	S
11/09/44	19705	VB-4	USS BUNKER HILL	LUZON	PHIL	ENS H. MAKELA	S
11/11/44		VB-15	USS ESSEX	MANILA	PHIL		
11/11/44	19206	VB-15	USS ESSEX	MANILA	PHIL	ENS JOHN AVERY	U
11/11/44	19230	VB-15	USS ESSEX	MANILA	PHIL	ENS MELVIN GRAY LIVESAY	U
11/11/44	19392	VB-15	USS ESSEX	MANILA	PHIL	LT DAVID R. HALL	S
11/11/44	19398	VB-15	USS ESSEX	MANILA	PHIL	LT ROBERT G. PRICE	S
11/11/44	19464	VB-15	USS ESSEX	MANILA	PHIL	LTJG JOHN STORRS FOOTE	D
11/11/44	19656	VB-4	USS BUNKER HILL	LUZON	PHIL		
11/11/44	19181	VB-9	USS SARATOGA	HAWAII	ECENPAC	LTJG GUILFORD N. ROSS	S
11/12/44		VB-3	USS YORK-TOWN	MANILA	PHIL	LT H.D. COLLYER	S
11/13/44	19586	VB-11	USS HORNET		PHIL		
11/13/44	19397	VB-15	USS ESSEX	MANILA	PHIL	LTJG W.L. MOORE	S
11/13/44	19474	VB-15	USS ESSEX	MANILA	PHIL	LT R.F. NOYES	U
11/13/44		VB-30	USS TICONDER-OGA	MANILA	PHIL	ENS JOHN S. MANCHESTER	S
11/13/44	19160	VB-4	USS BUNKER HILL		PHIL		

DATE	BUNO	SQDRN	BASE	LOST	AREA	PILOT	FATE
11/13/44	19353	VB-4	USS BUNKER HILL		PHIL		
11/13/44	19414	VB-4	USS BUNKER HILL		PHIL		
11/13/44	19419	VB-4	USS BUNKER HILL		PHIL	LTJG A.F. SUMMER	M
11/13/44	19668	VB-4	USS BUNKER HILL		PHIL		
11/13/44	18817	VB-80	USS TICONDER-OGA	MANILA	PHIL		
11/13/44	19036	VB-80	USS TICONDER-OGA	MANILA	PHIL		
11/14/44	19007	VB-100	PEARL	HAWAII	ECENPAC	ENS CHARLES M. MARTIN	S
11/14/44	19153	VB-15	USS ESSEX	MANILA	PHIL	LTJG R.L. TURNER	D
11/14/44	19538	VB-4	USS BUNKER HILL		PHIL	LTJG DONALD DONDERO	S
11/16/44	19145	VB-80	USS TICONDER-OGA	MANILA	PHIL	ENS HOWARD A. MCBRIDE	S
11/17/44	19087	VB-100	USS SARATOGA	HAWAII	ECENPAC	ENS DELPERT A. ANDERSON	S
11/18/44	19079	VB-9	KAHULUI	HAWAII	ECENPAC	ENS ROBERT L. VERRALL	S
11/19/44	19423	VB-7	USS HANCOCK	MANILA	PHIL		
11/19/44	19334	VB-81	USS WASP	LEYTE GULF	PHIL	LCDR WALTER L. DOUGLAS	M
11/23/44	19142	NFTG	USS PRINCE WILLIAM	OFF NORFOLK	CENLANT	ENS M.E. MONTGOMERY	S
11/23/44	19439	VB-4	USS ESSEX	ENR LEYTE GULF	PHIL		
11/24/44	19199	VB-100	PEARL	HAWAII	ECENPAC	ENS CHARLES M. MARTIN	S
11/24/44	18763	VB-80	USS TICONDER-OGA	LUZON	PHIL	LT RUDOLPH H. KOCH	S
11/25/44	18766	VB-18	USS INTREPID		PHIL	(DECK LOSS-KAMIKAZE)	
11/25/44	19166	VB-18	USS INTREPID		PHIL	(DECK LOSS-KAMIKAZE)	
11/25/44	19274	VB 18	USS INTREPID		PHIL	(DECK LOSS-KAMIKAZE)	
11/25/44	19328	VB-18	USS INTREPID		PHIL	(DECK LOSS-KAMIKAZE)	
11/25/44	19647	VB-4	USS ESSEX	LEYTE GULF	PHIL	LTJG RUSSELL L. DEPUTY	D
11/25/44	19674	VB-4	USS ESSEX	LEYTE GULF	PHIL	ENS BILLY NYE KINDER	U
11/25/44	19680	VB-4	USS ESSEX	LEYTE GULF	PHIL	LT WILLIAM E. DILL	S
11/25/44	19549	VB-80	USS TICONDER-OGA	LUZON	PHIL	ENS JOHN E. DOYLE	M
11/30/44	19065	VB-100	PEARL	HAWAII	ECENPAC		
12/05/44	19698	CASU-13		PONAM	SW PAC		
12/10/44	19336	VB-81	USS WASP	ULITHI	WCENPAC		
12/12/44	18976	VB-17	USS SARATOGA	HAWAII	ECENPAC	ENS WILLIAM L. OGLESBY	S
12/15/44	19704	VB-20	USS LEX-INGTON	LUZON	PHIL	LT R.S. WILCOX	D
12/16/44	19374	VB-20	USS LEX-INGTON	LUZON	PHIL	LT H.C. HOGAN	M
12/16/44	19694	VB-7	USS HANCOCK	LUZON	PHIL		
12/18/44	19454	UNASSIGN ED	USS ALTAMAHA	PHILIPPINE SEA	PHIL	(DECK LOSS-TYPHOON)	
12/18/44	19486	UNASSIGN ED	USS ALTAMAHA	PHILIPPINE SEA	PHIL	(DECK LOSS-TYPHOON)	

DATE	BUNO	SQDRN	BASE	LOST	AREA	PILOT	FATE
12/18/44	19488	UNASSIGNED	USS ALTAMAHA	PHILIPPINE SEA	PHIL	(DECK LOSS-TYPHOON)	
12/18/44	19491	UNASSIGNED	USS ALTAMAHA	PHILIPPINE SEA	PHIL	(DECK LOSS-TYPHOON)	
12/18/44	19492	UNASSIGNED	USS CAPE ESPERANCE	PHILIPPINE SEA	PHIL	(DECK LOSS-TYPHOON)	
12/18/44	19499	UNASSIGNED	USS CAPE ESPERANCE	PHILIPPINE SEA	PHIL	(DECK LOSS-TYPHOON)	
12/18/44	19502	UNASSIGNED	USS CAPE ESPERANCE	PHILIPPINE SEA	PHIL	(DECK LOSS-TYPHOON)	
12/18/44	19503	UNASSIGNED	USS CAPE ESPERANCE	PHILIPPINE SEA	PHIL	(DECK LOSS-TYPHOON)	
12/18/44	19510	UNASSIGNED	USS ALTAMAHA	PHILIPPINE SEA	PHIL	(DECK LOSS-TYPHOON)	
12/18/44	19513	UNASSIGNED	USS CAPE ESPERANCE	PHILIPPINE SEA	PHIL	(DECK LOSS-TYPHOON)	
12/18/44	19514	UNASSIGNED	USS CAPE ESPERANCE	PHILIPPINE SEA	PHIL	(DECK LOSS-TYPHOON)	
12/18/44	19516	UNASSIGNED	USS CAPE ESPERANCE	PHILIPPINE SEA	PHIL	(DECK LOSS-TYPHOON)	
12/18/44	19517	UNASSIGNED	USS CAPE ESPERANCE	PHILIPPINE SEA	PHIL	(DECK LOSS-TYPHOON)	
12/18/44	19520	UNASSIGNED	USS ALTAMAHA	PHILIPPINE SEA	PHIL	(DECK LOSS-TYPHOON)	
12/18/44	19529	UNASSIGNED	USS CAPE ESPERANCE	PHILIPPINE SEA	PHIL	(DECK LOSS-TYPHOON)	
12/18/44	19557	UNASSIGNED	USS CAPE ESPERANCE	PHILIPPINE SEA	PHIL	(DECK LOSS-TYPHOON)	
12/18/44	19565	UNASSIGNED	USS CAPE ESPERANCE	PHILIPPINE SEA	PHIL	(DECK LOSS-TYPHOON)	
12/18/44	19626	UNASSIGNED	USS CAPE ESPERANCE	PHILIPPINE SEA	PHIL	(DECK LOSS-TYPHOON)	
12/18/44	19635	UNASSIGNED	USS CAPE ESPERANCE	PHILIPPINE SEA	PHIL	(DECK LOSS-TYPHOON)	
12/18/44	19637	UNASSIGNED	USS CAPE ESPERANCE	PHILIPPINE SEA	PHIL	(DECK LOSS-TYPHOON)	
12/18/44	19665	UNASSIGNED	USS ALTAMAHA	PHILIPPINE SEA	PHIL	(DECK LOSS-TYPHOON)	
12/19/44	19088	NAS	HILO	HAWAII	ECENPAC		
01/03/45	18761	VB-80	USS TICONDEROGA	FORMOSA	EMPIRE		
01/03/45	19525	VB-80	USS TICONDEROGA	FORMOSA	EMPIRE		
01/07/45	19176	VB-11	USS HORNET	FORMOSA	EMPIRE	LT RICHARD GLEW AUBEL	M
01/07/45	19505	VB-80	USS TICONDEROGA	FORMOSA	EMPIRE	LT EDWARD H. BAGLEY	M
01/09/45	19232	VB-80	USS TICONDEROGA	FORMOSA	EMPIRE	LT RALPH PALMER	M
01/12/45	19512	VB-11	USS HORNET	SOUTH CHINA SEA	PHIL		
01/12/45	18877	VB-80	USS TICONDEROGA	FORMOSA	EMPIRE		
01/15/45	19613	VB-11	USS HORNET	FORMOSA	EMPIRE	WILLIAM MALLOY RIVERA	S

DATE	BUNO	SQDRN	BASE	LOST	AREA	PILOT	FATE
01/15/45	19708	VB-11	USS HORNET	FORMOSA	EMPIRE	LTJG LOGAN	S
01/15/45	19483	VB-20	USS LEXINGTON	HAINAN	EMPIRE	LTJG H.H. KOSTER	M
01/16/45	19687	VB-11	USS HORNET	HONG KONG	EMPIRE	LTJG E.W. MCGOWAN	S
01/16/45	18768	VB-20	USS LEXINGTON	HAINAN	EMPIRE	LTJG DAVID F. HUGHES	U
01/16/45	18922	VB-20	USS LEXINGTON	HONG KONG	EMPIRE	LTJG J.E. TSARNAS	M
01/16/45	18756	VB-80	USS TICONDEROGA	HAINAN	EMPIRE	LTJG ROBERT F. DICKENSON	M
01/17/45	19303	VB-20	USS LEXINGTON	HAINAN	EMPIRE		
01/17/45	19699	VB-20	USS LEXINGTON	HAINAN	EMPIRE		
01/18/45	19016	VB-6	HAWAII	HAWAII	ECENPAC	ENS WILLIAM GLADEN	S
01/21/45	19570	VB-20	USS LEXINGTON	FORMOSA	EMPIRE	LTJG R.P. OLSON	M
01/21/45	18632	VB-80	USS TICONDEROGA	FORMOSA	EMPIRE	LTJG GEORGE J. WALSH	S
01/21/45	18742	VB-80	USS TICONDEROGA	FORMOSA	EMPIRE		
01/21/45	18832	VB-80	USS TICONDEROGA	FORMOSA	EMPIRE		
01/21/45	19062	VB-80	USS TICONDEROGA	FORMOSA	EMPIRE		
01/21/45	19636	VB-80	USS TICONDEROGA	FORMOSA	EMPIRE		
01/30/45	18649	A.A.	PEARL	HAWAII	ECENPAC		
01/30/45	18654	A.A.	PEARL	HAWAII	ECENPAC		
01/30/45	18697	A.A.	PEARL	HAWAII	ECENPAC		
01/30/45	18702	A.A.	PEARL	HAWAII	ECENPAC		
01/30/45	18872	A.A.	PEARL	HAWAII	ECENPAC		
01/30/45	18902	A.A.	PEARL	HAWAII	ECENPAC		
01/30/45	18914	A.A.	PEARL	HAWAII	ECENPAC		
01/30/45	18934	A.A.	PEARL	HAWAII	ECENPAC		
01/30/45	18955	A.A.	PEARL	HAWAII	ECENPAC		
01/30/45	19171	A.A.	PEARL	HAWAII	ECENPAC		
01/30/45	19183	A.A.	PEARL	HAWAII	ECENPAC		
01/30/45	19190	A.A.	PEARL	HAWAII	ECENPAC		
01/30/45	19191	A.A.	PEARL	HAWAII	ECENPAC		
01/30/45	19195	A.A.	PEARL	HAWAII	ECENPAC		
01/30/45	19275	A.A.	PEARL	HAWAII	ECENPAC		
01/30/45	19304	A.A.	PEARL	HAWAII	ECENPAC		
01/30/45	19465	A.A.	PEARL	HAWAII	ECENPAC		
01/30/45	19546	A.A.	PEARL	HAWAII	ECENPAC		
01/30/45	19559	A.A.	PEARL	HAWAII	ECENPAC		
01/30/45	19634	A.A.	PEARL	HAWAII	ECENPAC		
01/30/45	18777	NAS	HILO	HAWAII	ECENPAC		
01/30/45	19164	VB-86	HAWAII	HAWAII	ECENPAC	ENS T.E. JENSON	S
02/05/45	18773	VB-17	USS HORNET	ULITHI	WCENPAC		
02/08/45	18769			GUAM	WCENPAC		
02/10/45	18844	CASU(F)-43		GUAM	WCENPAC		
02/10/45	19177	VMSB-332	HAWAII		ECENPAC	1STLT JOHN W. NAHAN	S
02/12/45	19156	VB-80	USS HANCOCK	IWO JIMA	EMPIRE	ENS R.R. READE	S
02/15/45	19415		BARBERS POINT	HAWAII	ECENPAC		
02/15/45	19057	VB-85	USS SHANGRI-LA	HAWAII	ECENPAC	LTJG JOHN E. FREEMONT	S
02/17/45	19193	COMAIRPAC	PEARL	HAWAII	ECENPAC		
02/22/45	19573	COMAIRPAC	PEARL	HAWAII	ECENPAC		
02/22/45	18670	VB-80	USS HANCOCK	IWO JIMA	EMPIRE	ENS EDWIN C. SINCOX	S

DATE	BUNO	SQDRN	BASE	LOST	AREA	PILOT	FATE
03/01/45	19435	VB-9	USS LEX-INGTON	IE SHIMA	EMPIRE	ENS BEATY	S
03/03/45	19047	VB-88	USS SHANGRI-LA	HAWAII	ECENPAC	ENS R.W. RUSSELL	U
03/05/45	19519	CASU(F)-12		GUAM	WCENPAC		
03/18/45	19508	VB-6	USS HANCOCK	KYUSHU	EMPIRE	LTJG HORACE COX	S
03/18/45	19642	VB-6	USS HANCOCK	KYUSHU	EMPIRE	LTJG D.C. HELMER	S
03/18/45	19655	VB-6	USS HANCOCK	KYUSHU	EMPIRE	ENS J.W. DRAGOES	M
03/19/45	19561	VB-17	USS HORNET	HONSHU	EMPIRE	LT DOUGLAS J. YERXA	M
03/19/45	19658	VB-17	USS HORNET	HONSHU	EMPIRE	LTJG WILLIAM A. LAWN	M
03/19/45	19480	VB-6	USS HANCOCK	KYUSHU	EMPIRE	LTJG D.A. BARROWS	M
03/21/45	19070	VB-1	KANEOHE	HAWAII	ECENPAC	LCDR A.B. HAMIN	S
03/22/45	19703	VB-99		GUAM	WCENPAC		
03/31/45	18700	CASU(F)-43		GUAM	WCENPAC		
04/03/45	19409	CASU(F)-12		GUAM	WCENPAC		
04/04/45	19563	VB-17	USS HORNET	OKINAWA	EMPIRE		
04/07/45	19288	VB-17	USS HORNET	OKINAWA	EMPIRE	LCDR R.M. WARE	S
04/10/45	19467	VMSB-343		MIDWAY	ECENPAC	1STLT DANIAL DAVIS	S
04/17/45	19479	CASU(F)-12		GUAM	WCENPAC		
04/19/45	19431	VB-17	USS HORNET	OKINAWA	EMPIRE		
04/19/45	19693	VB-99		SAIPAN	WCENPAC		
04/20/45	19584	CASU(F)-12		GUAM	WCENPAC		
04/20/45	19673	CASU(F)-12		GUAM	WCENPAC		
05/03/45	19381	VMSB-343		MIDWAY	ECENPAC	1STLT WILLIAM R. LANEY	D
05/08/45	19165	CASU(F)-47		SAIPAN	WCENPAC		
05/17/45	19644	CASU(F)-12		GUAM	WCENPAC		
05/18/45	18736	AROU-1		MOMOTE	SW PAC		
05/18/45	19426	CASU(F)-12	GUAM		SW PAC		
05/18/45	18663	AROU-1		MOMOTE	SW PAC		
05/18/45	18733	AROU-1		MOMOTE	SW PAC		
05/24/45	19313	AROU-1		MOMOTE	SW PAC		
05/24/45	19434	AROU-1		MOMOTE	SW PAC		
05/29/45	19172	VB-88		SAIPAN	WCENPAC	ENS MILLARD M. MUSTAINE	S
05/31/45	19098	COMAIR-PAC	PEARL	HAWAII	ECENPAC		
05/31/45	19102	COMAIR-PAC	PEARL	HAWAII	ECENPAC		
05/31/45	19155	COMAIR-PAC	PEARL	HAWAII	ECENPAC		
05/31/45	19235	COMAIR-PAC	PEARL	HAWAII	ECENPAC		
05/31/45	19241	COMAIR-PAC	PEARL	HAWAII	ECENPAC		
05/31/45	19250	COMAIR-PAC	PEARL	HAWAII	ECENPAC		
05/31/45	19296	COMAIR-PAC	PEARL	HAWAII	ECENPAC		
05/31/45	19323	COMAIR-PAC	PEARL	HAWAII	ECENPAC		
05/31/45	19451	COMAIR-PAC	PEARL	HAWAII	ECENPAC		
05/31/45	19466	COMAIR-PAC	PEARL	HAWAII	ECENPAC		
05/31/45	19477	COMAIR-PAC	PEARL	HAWAII	ECENPAC		
05/31/45	19536	COMAIR-PAC	PEARL	HAWAII	ECENPAC		
05/31/45	19539	COMAIR-PAC	PEARL	HAWAII	ECENPAC		
05/31/45	19545	COMAIR-PAC	PEARL	HAWAII	ECENPAC		
05/31/45	19615	COMAIR-PAC	PEARL	HAWAII	ECENPAC		

DATE	BUNO	SQDRN	BASE	LOST	AREA	PILOT	FATE
05/31/45	19450	VB-88		SAIPAN	WCENPAC	LTJG A.E. LEVENSON	S
06/06/45	18919	VB-100	PEARL	HAWAII	ECENPAC	ENS W.T. COOPER	S
06/09/45	19640	VB-99		SAIPAN	WCENPAC		
06/11/45	19204	POOL	KAHULUI	HAWAII	ECENPAC		
06/16/45	18607	CASU(F)-12		GUAM	WCENPAC		
06/16/45	19373	CASU(F)-12		GUAM	WCENPAC		
06/16/45	19494	CASU(F)-12		GUAM	WCENPAC		
06/16/45	19706	CASU(F)-12		GUAM	WCENPAC		
06/30/45	19495	CASU(F)-12		GUAM	WCENPAC		
06/12/44	19376. 46495	VB-13	USS FRANKLIN	PUUNENE	ECENPAC	LT R.J. WEBER	S

CURTISS SB2C-3E

The Curtiss SB2C-3E variant was the SB2C-3 fitted with the APS-4 radar. Aircraft lost:

DATE	BUNO	SQDRN	BASE	LOST	AREA	PILOT	FATE
08/08/44	18615	VB-7	USS HANCOCK	PANAMA	CENLANT	LT ROBERT F. BEGERON	S
09/20/44	18631	VB-7	USS HANCOCK	HAWAII	ECENPAC	LT RALPH E. RICE	S

CURTISS SB2C-4

The Curtiss SB2C-4 variant was the SB2C-1 fitted with wing racks for eight 5 in (127 mm) rockets or 1,000 lb (454 kg) bombs. There were 2,045. Aircraft lost:

DATE	BUNO	SQDRN	BASE	LOST	AREA	PILOT	FATE
06/30/44	19712	VB-80	USS TICONDER-OGA	TRINIDAD	CENLANT		
11/13/44	19831	VB-3	USS YORK-TOWN	MANILA	PHIL	LTJG E.F. ANDERSON	S
11/16/44	20296	VB-87	USS RANDOLPH	TRINIDAD	CENLANT		
11/22/44	19763	VB-9	USS MAKASSAR STR.	HAWAII	ECENPAC	ENS EDWARD L. WATKINS	S
11/24/44	20547	VB-85	USS SHANGRI-LA	TRINIDAD	CENLANT	ENS EVERETT W. STOCKMAN	S
11/27/44	20038	VB-87	USS RANDOLPH	TRINIDAD	CENLANT	ENS RICHARD W. NIELSEN	M
11/29/44	20164	VB-85	USS SHANGRI-LA	TRINIDAD	CENLANT	LT BOROS	D
12/01/44	19746	VB-83	PUUNENE	HAWAII	ECENPAC	LTJG BILLY JESS SHEARON	D
12/04/44	20154	VB-85	USS SHANGRI-LA	TRINIDAD	CENLANT	ENS GEORGE I. MATHER	S
12/05/44	19942	VC-87	USS SALAMAUA	ADMIRALTIES	SW PAC	ENS ELI PINTER	M
12/06/44	19923	VB-100	PEARL	HAWAII	ECENPAC	ENS EDWARD N. JENNINGS	D
12/16/44	19926	VB-83	PUUNENE	HAWAII	ECENPAC	ENS WALTER W. GORMAN	S
12/16/44	19936	VB-83	PUUNENE	HAWAII	ECENPAC	ENS CARMAN J. JACOBSON	M
12/28/44	19782	A.A.	PEARL	HAWAII	ECENPAC		
01/06/45	19818	VB-3	USS YORK-TOWN	MANILA	PHIL	LTJG H.S. LAURINAT	S
01/07/45	19744	VB-3	USS YORK-TOWN	MANILA	PHIL	LTJG KARL R. BEARTSCHY	M
01/07/45	19825	VB-3	USS YORK-TOWN	MANILA	PHIL		
01/12/45	19901	CASU-32	KAHULUI	HAWAII	ECENPAC		

DATE	BUNO	SQDRN	BASE	LOST	AREA	PILOT	FATE
01/13/45	19851	VB-3	USS YORK-TOWN	MANILA	PHIL		
01/15/45	19741	VB-3	USS YORK-TOWN	FORMOSA	EMPIRE	LT ROGERS L. JENKINSON	M
01/16/45	19820	VB-3	USS YORK-TOWN	HONG KONG	EMPIRE	LTJG JOHN H. LAVENDER	M
01/17/45	19731	VB-83	PUUNENE	HAWAII	ECENPAC	ENS C.W. KING	S
01/23/45	20583	VB-82	USS BENNING-TON		WCENPAC		
02/13/45	20601	COMAIR-PAC	PEARL	HAWAII	ECENPAC		
02/17/45	20198	VB-12	USS RANDOLPH	TOKYO	EMPIRE		
02/18/45	20594	VB-82	USS BENNING-TON	IWO JIMA	EMPIRE	LT A.W. LUNDBLADE	M
02/21/45	20214	VB-87	KAHULUI	HAWAII	ECENPAC	ENS JOHN STUART HOGE	S
02/22/45	20581	VB-82	USS BENNING-TON	IWO JIMA	EMPIRE		
02/23/45	20299	VB-12	USS RANDOLPH	TOKYO	EMPIRE		
03/06/45	20227	VB-87	USS SHANGRI-LA	PEARL	ECENPAC	LT GORDON A. DURNA	S
03/07/45	20815	VB-10	USS INTREPID	HAWAII	ECENPAC	LT FARRINGTON	S
03/09/45	20744	COMAIR-PAC	PEARL	HAWAII	ECENPAC		
03/10/45	19720	COMAIR-PAC	PEARL	HAWAII	ECENPAC		
03/11/45	20061	VB-12	USS RANDOLPH	ULITHI	WCENPAC		
03/11/45	20179	VB-12	USS RANDOLPH	ULITHI	WCENPAC		
03/11/45	20181	VB-12	USS RANDOLPH	ULITHI	WCENPAC		
03/11/45	20183	VB-12	USS RANDOLPH	ULITHI	WCENPAC		
03/11/45	20285	VB-12	USS RANDOLPH	ULITHI	WCENPAC		
03/11/45	20330	VB-12	USS RANDOLPH	ULITHI	WCENPAC		
03/14/45	20079	VB-9	USS YORK-TOWN	ENR OKINAWA	EMPIRE		
03/15/45	20773	VB-5	USS FRANKLIN	ENR HONSHU	EMPIRE		
03/15/45	20578	VB-82	USS BENNING-TON	KYUSHU	EMPIRE	ENS E.E. MATT	S
03/18/45	20555	VB-82	USS BENNING-TON	KYUSHU	EMPIRE	LT CARLYLE NEROTON	M
03/18/45	19808	VB-86	USS WASP	KYUSHU	EMPIRE	LCDR WILLIAM W. BUSH	S
03/18/45	19785	VB-9	USS YORK-TOWN	OKINAWA	EMPIRE	ENS W.R. HANAWALT	S
03/19/45	20237	VB-5	USS FRANKLIN	HONSHU	EMPIRE	(DECK LOSS-KAMIKAZE)	
03/19/45	20795	VB-5	USS FRANKLIN	HONSHU	EMPIRE	(DECK LOSS-KAMIKAZE)	
03/19/45	20864	VB-5	USS FRANKLIN	HONSHU	EMPIRE	(DECK LOSS-KAMIKAZE)	
03/19/45	20925	VB-5	USS FRANKLIN	HONSHU	EMPIRE	(DECK LOSS-KAMIKAZE)	
03/19/45	19762	VB-6	USS HANCOCK	KYUSHU	EMPIRE	ENS P.H. WHITEFORD	S
03/19/45	20071	VB-83	USS ESSEX	HONSHU	EMPIRE		
03/21/45	20587	CASU-4	PUUNENE	HAWAII	ECENPAC	LTJG THOMAS CAVIN	S
03/24/45	20127	VB-82	USS BENNING-TON	OKINAWA	EMPIRE		
03/24/45	19775	VB-9	USS YORK-TOWN	OKINAWA	EMPIRE	LTJG BAILANS	M

DATE	BUNO	SQDRN	BASE	LOST	AREA	PILOT	FATE
03/24/45	19811	VB-9	USS YORKTOWN	OKINAWA	EMPIRE		
03/27/45	20081	VMSB-333	EWA	HAWAII	ECENPAC	1STLT SIDNEY L. MEEK	S
03/28/45	21033	VB-84	USS BUNKER HILL	DAITO	EMPIRE	LT W.T. JACKS	S
03/29/45	19981	VB-6	USS HANCOCK	OKINAWA	EMPIRE	LTJG R.L. SOMERVILLE	S
03/30/45	19758	VB-10	USS INTREPID	OKINAWA	EMPIRE		
03/30/45	19778	VB-6	USS HANCOCK	OKINAWA	EMPIRE		
03/30/45	19814	VB-84	USS BUNKER HILL	OKINAWA	EMPIRE	LTJG W.I. ANDERSON	S
03/31/45	19939	VB-100	PEARL	HAWAII	ECENPAC	ENS EUGENE A. WATKINS	S
03/31/45	20930	VB-83	USS ESSEX	OKINAWA	EMPIRE		
04/01/45	20265	VB-6	USS HANCOCK	OKINAWA	EMPIRE	LT J.T. MALONEY	S
04/01/45	20847	VB-83	USS ESSEX	OKINAWA	EMPIRE		
04/02/45	20245	VMSB-231	MAJURO	MAJURO	CENPAC	1STLT GEORGE B. CHIPMAN	S
04/04/45	19830	VB-6	USS HANCOCK	OKINAWA	EMPIRE	ENS E.R. WENDT	S
04/05/45	19828	VB-9	USS YORKTOWN	IWO JIMA	EMPIRE	MAY	S
04/07/45	20714	VB-17	USS HORNET	OKINAWA	EMPIRE		
04/07/45	20060	VB-82	USS BENNINGTON	OKINAWA	EMPIRE	ENS JACK CARL FULLER	M
04/07/45	20738	VB-83	USS ESSEX	ENR TOKUNA	EMPIRE		
04/07/45	20277	VB-9	USS YORKTOWN	KYUSHU	EMPIRE	LT H.W. WORLEY	D
04/16/45	19776	VB-10	USS INTREPID	KOKUBO	EMPIRE		
04/16/45	20119	VB-10	USS INTREPID	KOKUBO	EMPIRE		
04/16/45	20300	VB-10	USS INTREPID	KOKUBO	EMPIRE		
04/16/45	20760	VB-10	USS INTREPID	KOKUBO	EMPIRE		
04/16/45	21058	VB-10	USS INTREPID	KOKUBO	EMPIRE		
04/17/45	20294	VB-83	USS ESSEX	OKINAWA	EMPIRE	LTJG S.C. SWENSON	D
04/20/45	20551	VB-82	USS BENNINGTON	OKINAWA	EMPIRE	LTJG H.A. MCBRIDE	D
04/21/45	20540	VB-12	USS RANDOLPH	OKINAWA	EMPIRE		
04/21/45	20023	VB-83	USS ESSEX	OKINAWA	EMPIRE	LTJG S.W. MITCHELL	S
04/22/45	19774	VB-9	USS YORKTOWN	OKINAWA	EMPIRE		
04/22/45	19949	VS-61	BIAK	PELELIU	WCENPAC	ENS DAVID G. SAWYER	S
04/25/45	19749	VB-100	PEARL	HAWAII	ECENPAC	LTJG ARTHUR F. DOHERTY	S
04/25/45	19761	VB-17	USS HORNET	OKINAWA	EMPIRE		
04/26/45	19769	VB-83	USS ESSEX	OKINAWA	EMPIRE		
04/29/45	20538	VB-85	USS SHANGRI-LA	KIKAI	EMPIRE		
04/29/45	20258	VMSB-231	MAJURO	MAJURO	CENPAC		
05/03/45	19806	VB-9	USS YORKTOWN	OKINAWA	EMPIRE	LTJG BEATY	S
05/06/45	20105	VB-2	USS TICONDEROGA	HILO	ECENPAC	ENS ROBERT M. COOK	U
05/06/45	20250	VB-2	USS TICONDEROGA	HILO	ECENPAC	ENS RICHARD C. DYER	S
05/10/45	19800	VB-9	USS YORKTOWN	EMPIRE			

DATE	BUNO	SQDRN	BASE	LOST	AREA	PILOT	FATE
05/10/45	19804	VB-9	USS YORK-TOWN	EMPIRE			
05/11/45	20025	VB-84	USS BUNKER HILL	OKINAWA	EMPIRE	(DECK LOSS-KAMIKAZE)	
05/11/45	20059	VB-84	USS BUNKER HILL	OKINAWA	EMPIRE	(DECK LOSS-KAMIKAZE)	
05/11/45	20063	VB-84	USS BUNKER HILL	OKINAWA	EMPIRE	(DECK LOSS-KAMIKAZE)	
05/11/45	20124	VB-84	USS BUNKER HILL	OKINAWA	EMPIRE	(DECK LOSS-KAMIKAZE)	
05/11/45	20279	VB-84	USS BUNKER HILL	OKINAWA	EMPIRE	(DECK LOSS-KAMIKAZE)	
05/11/45	20619	VMSB-331		MARSHALLS	WCENPAC	1STLT CHARLES R. JAMESON	M
05/18/45	20975	VB-83	USS ESSEX	KYUSHU	EMPIRE	ENS R.O. COBURN	S
05/18/45	19952	VS-69	BARBERS POINT	HAWAII	ECENPAC	LTJG JAY S. PIREY, JR.	S
05/20/45	20003	VB-2	USS MAN-ILA BAY	HAWAII	ECENPAC	ENS JAMES C. RIDDLE	S
05/21/45	19977	VB-94	KAHULUI	HAWAII	ECENPAC	ENS LAWRENCE B. HAINS	S
05/22/45	20086	VB-2	HILO	HAWAII	ECENPAC		
05/22/45	20099	VB-94	KAHULUI	HAWAII	ECENPAC	ENS MERLE E. PENNINGTON	S
05/29/45	20579	VB-82	USS BENNING-TON	OKINAWA	EMPIRE		
06/05/45	20756	POOL	USS ATTU	OKINAWA	EMPIRE		
06/05/45	19986	VB-82	USS BENNING-TON		EMPIRE	(DECK LOSS-TYPHOON)	
06/05/45	20983	VB-82	USS BENNING-TON		EMPIRE	(DECK LOSS-TYPHOON)	
06/06/45	20111	VMSB-333	EWA	HAWAII	ECENPAC		
06/06/45	20113	VMSB-333	EWA	HAWAII	ECENPAC		
06/07/45	20077	VB-9	USS YORK-TOWN	OKINAWA	EMPIRE	ENS WILLIAM R. WATSON	D
06/07/45	20019	VMSB-244		MINDANAO SEA	PHIL	MCGOWAN	S
06/07/45	20276	VMSB-244		COTOBATO	PHIL		
06/14/45	20004	VMSB-244		MINDANAO SEA	PHIL	1STLT FREDERICK D. MARTIN	M
06/15/45	20248	CASU(F)-12		GUAM	WCENPAC		
06/16/45	20253	CASU(F)-12		GUAM	WCENPAC		
06/20/45	20286	VMSB-231	MAJURO	MAJURO	CENPAC	1STLT WILLIAM J. BALLEN	U
06/25/45	19930	VB-95	KAHULUI	HAWAII	ECENPAC	ENS JOHN J. PICCOLO	S
06/27/45	19756	VB-100	PEARL	HAWAII	ECENPAC	ENS WILLIAM G. PENNETT	S
07/03/45	19740	VB-8	PUUNENE	HAWAII	ECENPAC	ENS ORIE N. SPEGAL	S
07/04/45	20264	CASU(F)-12		GUAM	WCENPAC	LT A.M. DENNY, JR.	S
07/08/45	20024	POOL	PEARL	HAWAII	ECENPAC		
07/10/45	20775	VB-16	USS RANDOLPH	TOKYO	EMPIRE		
07/14/45	19819	POOL	PEARL	HAWAII	ECENPAC		
07/14/45	20955	VB-16	USS RANDOLPH	TSUGARU STR.	EMPIRE	LT R.F. BURCH	S
07/14/45	82996	VB-16	USS RANDOLPH	TSUGARU STR.	EMPIRE	ENS K.E. MOORE	S
07/14/45	21036	VB-6	USS HANCOCK		EMPIRE	ENS ROBERT C. WICKSTRAND	S
07/14/45	21164	VB-85	USS SHANGRI-LA	HOKKAIDO	EMPIRE	LTJG HOWARD E EAGLESTON	M
07/14/45	21021	VB-94	USS LEX-INGTON		EMPIRE	ENS EDWARD W. WILLIAMS	S
07/18/45	21171	VB-94	USS LEX-INGTON		EMPIRE	ENS MERLE E. PENNINGTON	M
07/22/45	19955	POOL	PEARL	HAWAII	ECENPAC	ENS JAMES N. DETTY	D

DATE	BUNO	SQDRN	BASE	LOST	AREA	PILOT	FATE
07/24/45	21126	VB-85	USS SHANGRI-LA	KURE	EMPIRE		
07/24/45	65047	VB-87	USS TICONDER-OGA	KURE	EMPIRE	LTJG W.W. TIMMIS	S
07/25/45	20009	CASU(F)-15		SAIPAN	WCENPAC	ENS P.D. O'KEEFE	U
07/25/45	20033	VB-83	USS ESSEX	KURE	EMPIRE	ENS THOMAS D. SAMARAS	D
07/28/45	83021	VB-16	USS RANDOLPH	SHIKOKU	EMPIRE	LT C.T. WILLIAMS	M
07/28/45	20074	VB-88	USS YORK-TOWN	KURE	EMPIRE	LTJG PERRY L. MITCHELL	M
07/28/45	20323	VS-66		ROI	WCENPAC	ENS EUGENE N. STEGMANN	D
07/30/45	20572	VB-85	USS SHANGRI-LA	KURE	EMPIRE	LCDR A.L. MALTBY	S
08/14/45	20564	CASU(F)-12		GUAM	WCENPAC		

CURTISS SB2C-4E

The Curtiss SB2C-4E variant was the SB2C-4 fitted with the APS-4 radar. Aircraft lost:

DATE	BUNO	SQDRN	BASE	LOST	AREA	PILOT	FATE
12/18/44	20536	VB-18	USS BENNING-TON	CUBA	CENLANT	LTJG D.E. ARNHOLT	S
01/22/45	20577	VB-82	USS BENNING-TON		WCENPAC	LTJG W.E. MURPHY	S
02/16/45	20308	VB-12	USS RANDOLPH	TOKYO	EMPIRE	ENS C.H. BROWN	S
02/16/45	20833	VB-84	USS BUNKER HILL	TOKYO	EMPIRE	LT STRICKLAND	S
02/17/45	20831	VB-12	USS RANDOLPH	TOKYO	EMPIRE	CDR RALPH A. EMBREE	S
02/17/45	20698	VB-84	USS BUNKER HILL	TOKYO	EMPIRE	LTJG STAFFORD	S
02/19/45	20681	VB-5	HAWAII	HAWAII	ECENPAC	ENS GEORGE M. STANLEY	S
02/27/45	20965	VB-10	USS INTREPID	HAWAII	ECENPAC		
02/28/45	20832	VB-5	USS FRANKLIN	HAWAII	ECENPAC	LT D.H. STEGNER	S
03/04/45	20734	VB-10	USS INTREPID	HAWAII	ECENPAC		
03/14/45	20828	VB-10	USS INTREPID	HAWAII	ECENPAC		
03/14/45	20735	VB-83	USS ESSEX	OKINAWA	EMPIRE		
03/15/45	20699	VB-82	USS BENNING-TON	KYUSHU	EMPIRE	ENS R.L. CORY	U
03/18/45	20622	VB-86	USS WASP	KYUSHU	EMPIRE	LCDR PHILLIPS	S
03/19/45		VB-10	USS INTREPID	HONSHU	EMPIRE	ENS ROBERT N. BRINICK	M
03/19/45		VB-10	USS INTREPID	HONSHU	EMPIRE		
03/19/45	20137	VB-5	USS FRANKLIN	HONSHU	EMPIRE	(DECK LOSS-KAMIKAZE)	
03/19/45	20740	VB-5	USS FRANKLIN	HONSHU	EMPIRE	(DECK LOSS-KAMIKAZE)	
03/19/45	20962	VB-5	USS FRANKLIN	HONSHU	EMPIRE	(DECK LOSS-KAMIKAZE)	
03/19/45		VB-82	USS BENNING-TON	HONSHU	EMPIRE	LT DONALD D. WORDEN	M
03/19/45	20702	VB-83	USS ESSEX	HONSHU	EMPIRE		

DATE	BUNO	SQDRN	BASE	LOST	AREA	PILOT	FATE
03/19/45	20711	VB-83	USS ESSEX	HONSHU	EMPIRE	LTJG W.S. LAY	D
03/19/45	20788	VB-83	USS ESSEX	HONSHU	EMPIRE	LTJG D.E. WILLIS	D
03/19/45	20790	VB-84	USS BUNKER HILL	KURE	EMPIRE	LT CARPER	S
03/19/45	20803	VB-84	USS BUNKER HILL	KURE	EMPIRE	LTJG JOHN D. WELSH	M
03/19/45	20772	VB-86	USS WASP	KURE	EMPIRE	ENS H.R. EYER	M
03/21/45	20818	VB-84	USS BUNKER HILL	KURE	EMPIRE		
03/22/45	20724	VS-46	PEARL	HAWAII	ECENPAC	LT HAROLD A. LEWIS	S
03/23/45	20761	VB-84	USS BUNKER HILL	OKINAWA	EMPIRE	LT BARROWS	S
03/24/45	20799	VB-17	USS HORNET	ENR KYUSHU	EMPIRE		
03/24/45	20741	VB-83	USS ESSEX	OKINAWA	EMPIRE		
03/24/45	20829	VB-84	USS BUNKER HILL	OKINAWA	EMPIRE	LTJG C.J.C. DAVIES	S
03/26/45	20956	VB-10	USS INTREPID	HONSHU	EMPIRE	LTJG STANLEY W. POWELL	D
03/26/45	20967	VB-10	USS INTREPID	HONSHU	EMPIRE		
03/27/45	20638	VB-10	USS INTREPID	OKINAWA	EMPIRE	LCDR R.R. PUCHAN	S
03/28/45	20753	VB-10	USS INTREPID	OKINAWA	EMPIRE		
03/29/45	20348	VB-84	USS BUNKER HILL	OKINAWA	EMPIRE	LTJG R.O. TURPIN	M
03/29/45	20704	VB-84	USS BUNKER HILL	OKINAWA	EMPIRE	LTJG H.B. DITTO	M
03/31/45	20730	VB-83	USS ESSEX	OKINAWA	EMPIRE	LTJG CARLSON	S
03/31/45	20801	VB-83	USS ESSEX	OKINAWA	EMPIRE	LT ROBERT B. MOON	D
03/31/45	20789	VB-84	USS BUNKER HILL	OKINAWA	EMPIRE		
04/05/45	20932	VB-10	USS INTREPID	ISHIGAKI	EMPIRE		
04/06/45	20732	VB-83	USS ESSEX	IWO JIMA	EMPIRE	ENS ARTHUR L. THOMAS	M
04/07/45	20767	VB-84	USS BUNKER HILL	KYUSHU	EMPIRE		
04/09/45	20683	VB-12	USS RANDOLPH	OKINAWA	EMPIRE		
04/11/45	20739	VB-83	USS ESSEX	TOKUNO	EMPIRE		
04/16/45	20782	VB-10	USS INTREPID	KOKUBO	EMPIRE		
04/16/45	20861	VB-10	USS INTREPID	KOKUBO	EMPIRE		
04/16/45	20945	VB-10	USS INTREPID	KOKUBO	EMPIRE		
04/16/45	20994	VB-10	USS INTREPID	KOKUBO	EMPIRE		
04/17/45	20763	VB-84	USS BUNKER HILL	OKINAWA	EMPIRE	ENS G.E. PORTER	S
04/18/45	20814	VB-17	USS HORNET	OKINAWA	EMPIRE		
04/18/45	65258	VB-83	USS ESSEX	OKINAWA	EMPIRE		
04/20/45	20693	VB-84	USS BUNKER HILL	OKINAWA	EMPIRE	LTJG H.R. GORDINIER	M
04/21/45	20656	VB-12	USS RANDOLPH	OKINAWA	EMPIRE		
04/28/45	19732	VB-84	USS BUNKER HILL	OKINAWA	EMPIRE		
04/29/45	20729	VB-12	USS RANDOLPH	OKINAWA	EMPIRE		

DATE	BUNO	SQDRN	BASE	LOST	AREA	PILOT	FATE
04/29/45	20755	VB-85	USS SHANGRI-LA	KIKAI	EMPIRE	LTJG R.W. ELMORE	M
04/30/45	20993	VB-84	USS BUNKER HILL	OKINAWA	EMPIRE		
05/01/45	21189	VB-87	KAHULUI	HAWAII	ECENPAC	ENS LEE RAY JENNINGS	S
05/02/45	20210	VB-1	NAVY NO. 27	HAWAII	ECENPAC	LTJG J.M. BARDELMEIER	S
05/02/45	20812	VB-2	USS KASAAN BAY	PEARL	ECENPAC	ENS JOSEPH T. STEINMETZ	S
05/04/45	20727	VB-12	USS RANDOLPH	IE SHIMA	EMPIRE		
05/05/45	20324	VB-12	USS RANDOLPH	IE SHIMA	EMPIRE		
05/05/45	20764	VB-12	USS RANDOLPH	IE SHIMA	EMPIRE		
05/05/45	20278	VB-85	USS SHANGRI-LA	IWO JIMA	EMPIRE	ENS W.J. DOERING	S
05/11/45	20701	VB-82	USS BENNING-TON	OKINAWA	EMPIRE		
05/11/45	20787	VB-82	USS BENNING-TON	OKINAWA	EMPIRE	LCDR HUGH WOOD, JR.	S
05/11/45	20685	VB-84	USS BUNKER HILL	OKINAWA	EMPIRE	(DECK LOSS-KAMIKAZE)	
05/11/45	20688	VB-84	USS BUNKER HILL	OKINAWA	EMPIRE	(DECK LOSS-KAMIKAZE)	
05/11/45	20695	VB-84	USS BUNKER HILL	OKINAWA	EMPIRE	(DECK LOSS-KAMIKAZE)	
05/11/45	20749	VB-84	USS BUNKER HILL	OKINAWA	EMPIRE	(DECK LOSS-KAMIKAZE)	
05/11/45	20752	VB-84	USS BUNKER HILL	OKINAWA	EMPIRE	(DECK LOSS-KAMIKAZE)	
05/11/45	20765	VB-84	USS BUNKER HILL	OKINAWA	EMPIRE	(DECK LOSS-KAMIKAZE)	
05/11/45	20817	VB-84	USS BUNKER HILL	OKINAWA	EMPIRE	(DECK LOSS-KAMIKAZE)	
05/11/45	20952	VB-84	USS BUNKER HILL	OKINAWA	EMPIRE	(DECK LOSS KAMIKAZE)	
05/11/45	65167	VB-84	USS BUNKER HILL	OKINAWA	EMPIRE	(DECK LOSS-KAMIKAZE)	
05/11/45	65225	VB-84	USS BUNKER HILL	OKINAWA	EMPIRE	(DECK LOSS-KAMIKAZE)	
05/18/45	20750	VB-12	USS RANDOLPH	KYUSHU	EMPIRE		
05/18/45	21043	VB-17	USS HORNET	KYUSHU	EMPIRE	LT J.D. WALKER	M
05/18/45	20542	VB-82	USS BENNING-TON	OKINAWA	EMPIRE	LR R.A. KNOPF	S
05/18/45	20839	VB-83	USS ESSEX	KYUSHU	EMPIRE	LCDR D.R. BERRY	S
05/18/45	65158	VMSB-331		MARSHALLS	WCENPAC	1STLT J.A. MALERICH, JR.	S
05/22/45	20700	VB-92	USS TRIPOLI	PEARL	ECENPAC	LTJG ALBERT E. MITCHELL	S
05/24/45	20556	VB-88		SAIPAN	WCENPAC	LT L.J. MILLER	S
05/28/45	20708	VB-82	USS BENNING-TON	OKINAWA	EMPIRE	LTJG KREGER	S

DATE	BUNO	SQDRN	BASE	LOST	AREA	PILOT	FATE
05/28/45	20893	VB-82	USS BENNING-TON	OKINAWA	EMPIRE	LT D.E. ARNHOLT	S
05/29/45	65017	VB-87	USS TICONDER-OGA	ENR KYUSHU	EMPIRE	ENS LEE RAY JENNINGS	S
05/29/45	20721	VB-92	KAHULUI	HAWAII	ECENPAC	LT JOHN H. LOHM	U
06/01/45	64998	POOL	PEARL	HAWAII	ECENPAC		
06/01/45	21064	VMSB-331		MAJURO	CENPAC	2NDLT MERRILL E. STEVENS	S
06/05/45	20690	POOL	USS ATTU	OKINAWA	EMPIRE		
06/05/45	20539	VB-82	USS BENNING-TON		EMPIRE	(DECK LOSS-TYPHOON)	
06/05/45	20558	VB-82	USS BENNING-TON		EMPIRE	(DECK LOSS-TYPHOON)	
06/05/45	20707	VB-82	USS BENNING-TON		EMPIRE	(DECK LOSS-TYPHOON)	
06/05/45	20751	VB-82	USS BENNING-TON		EMPIRE	(DECK LOSS-TYPHOON)	
06/06/45	19979	CASU(F)-15		SAIPAN	WCENPAC		
06/06/45	20798	POOL	USS BOUGAIN-VILLE		EMPIRE	(DECK LOSS-TYPHOON)	
06/06/45	20852	POOL	USS BOUGAIN-VILLE		EMPIRE	(DECK LOSS-TYPHOON)	
06/06/45	20873	POOL	USS BOUGAIN-VILLE		EMPIRE	(DECK LOSS-TYPHOON)	
06/06/45	20885	POOL	USS BOUGAIN-VILLE		EMPIRE	(DECK LOSS-TYPHOON)	
06/06/45	82964	VB-87	USS TICONDER-OGA	OKINAWA	EMPIRE	ENS BREWITTS	S
06/08/45	64997	VB-6	USS HANCOCK	PEARL	ECENPAC		
06/10/45	20867	VB-9	USS YORK-TOWN	MINAMI DAITO	EMPIRE	ENS JAMES A. PROCUNIER	S
06/10/45	82958	VS-69	BARBERS POINT	HAWAII	ECENPAC	LTJG DOUGLAS L. GRANT, JR.	S
06/15/45	65194	VB-94	USS LEX-INGTON	WAKE	WCENPAC		
06/16/45	20811	CASU(F)-12		GUAM	WCENPAC		
06/16/45	20890	CASU(F)-12		GUAM	WCENPAC		
06/16/45	20901	CASU(F)-12		GUAM	WCENPAC		
06/18/45	20720	VB-6	USS HANCOCK	PEARL	ECENPAC		
06/20/45	20842	VB-83	USS ESSEX		EMPIRE		
06/20/45	21115	VB-94	USS LEX-INGTON	WAKE	WCENPAC	ENS JAMES W. SWEENEY	S
06/27/45	20036	VB-88	USS YORK-TOWN	LEYTE GULF	PHIL	LCDR JAMES S. ELKINS, JR.	M
06/29/45	82961	VB-1	USS BENNING-TON	LEYTE GULF	PHIL	ENS ALLEN C. DAVIS	S
06/30/45	20298	CASU-4	PUUNENE	HAWAII	ECENPAC		
07/02/45	20694	VB-16	USS RANDOLPH		EMPIRE		
07/02/45	20794	VB-16	USS RANDOLPH		EMPIRE	ENS K.E. MOORE	S
07/03/45	20757	VB-87	USS TICONDER-OGA	GUAM	WCENPAC	ENS RICHARD P. BREWITT	S
07/07/45	65232	VB-85	USS SHANGRI-LA	ENR HOKKAIDO	EMPIRE	LT THOMAS P. CAVIN	S
07/08/45	21182	VB-6	USS HANCOCK		EMPIRE	ENS ROBERT C. WICKSTRAND	S

DATE	BUNO	SQDRN	BASE	LOST	AREA	PILOT	FATE
07/10/45	65212	VB-1	USS BENNING-TON	KURE	EMPIRE	ENS HAROLD J.E. MEYER	S
07/10/45	21179	VB-94	USS LEX-INGTON		EMPIRE	WILLIAM E. NICHOLSON	S
07/11/45	20905	VB-8	PUUNENE	HAWAII	ECENPAC	LT THOMAS N. KELLY	D
07/11/45	20928	VB-8	PUUNENE	HAWAII	ECENPAC	ENS WALT O GUDJOHNSON	D
07/14/45	20692	VB-16	USS RANDOLPH	TSUGARU STR.	EMPIRE	LTJG LANGLEY	M
07/14/45	20845	VB-16	USS RANDOLPH	TSUGARU STR.	EMPIRE	ENS L.A. WITAKER	M
07/14/45	65015	VB-88	USS YORK-TOWN	HOKKAIDO	EMPIRE	LTJG A.E. LEVENSON	S
07/15/45	20748	VB-83	USS ESSEX	IE SHIMA	EMPIRE		
07/16/45	21040	VMSB-331		MAJURO	CENPAC	2NDLT HARV. SNELLBACKER	D
07/17/45	20317	CASU(F)-12		GUAM	WCENPAC		
07/18/45	20783	CASU(F)-15		SAIPAN	WCENPAC		
07/18/45	20920	VB-1	USS BENNING-TON	KURE	EMPIRE	LTJG J.M. BARDELMEIER	S
07/18/45	21000	VB-1	USS BENNING-TON	KURE	EMPIRE	ENS R.E. CHRIST	M
07/18/45	20718	VB-16	USS RANDOLPH	YOKOSUKA	EMPIRE	ENS DEAN	S
07/18/45	20737	VB-6	USS HANCOCK		EMPIRE	LTJG R.L. SOMERVILLE	S
07/18/45	21186	VB-6	USS HANCOCK		EMPIRE	ENS HOWARD H. HARRISON	S
07/18/45	65157	VB-6	USS HANCOCK		EMPIRE	DECOSTE	S
07/18/45	20684	VB-83	USS ESSEX	IE SHIMA	EMPIRE	ENS ERNEST W. BAKER	M
07/18/45	21062	VB-85	USS SHANGRI-LA	YOKOSUKA	EMPIRE	LCDR A.L. MALTBY	S
07/23/45	20625	VB-14	KAHULUI	HAWAII	ECENPAC		
07/24/45	20636	VB-1	USS BENNING-TON	KURE	EMPIRE	ENS WILLIAM TROYAN	M
07/24/45	20762	VB-1	USS BENNING-TON	KURE	EMPIRE	LT K.C. HALL	S
07/24/45	21034	VB-1	USS BENNING-TON	KURE	EMPIRE	ENS ALLEN C. DAVIS	M
07/24/45	65242	VB-16	USS RANDOLPH	SHIKOKU	EMPIRE		
07/24/45	82955	VB-16	USS RANDOLPH	SHIKOKU	EMPIRE	LTJG D.L. HERRON	S
07/24/45	19767	VB-83	USS ESSEX	KURE	EMPIRE		
07/24/45	20802	VB-85	USS SHANGRI-LA	KURE	EMPIRE	LT ALFRED G. SYMONDS, JR.	M
07/24/45	20853	VB-85	USS SHANGRI-LA	KURE	EMPIRE	LTJG RICHARD WALTER	M
07/24/45	20866	VB-85	USS SHANGRI-LA	KURE	EMPIRE	LTJG REXFORD W. JONES	S
07/24/45	20969	VB-87	USS TICONDER-OGA	KURE	EMPIRE	LTJG W.R. BREHM	S
07/24/45	21002	VB-87	USS TICONDER-OGA	KURE	EMPIRE	LTJG E.L. VAUGHN	M
07/24/45	21059	VB-87	USS TICONDER-OGA	KURE	EMPIRE	LT A.L. MATTESON, JR.	D
07/24/45	65147	VB-87	USS TICONDER-OGA	KURE	EMPIRE	LTJG E.L. WHEELER	S
07/24/45	21075	VB-88	USS YORK-TOWN	KURE	EMPIRE	LT E.C. MILLER	S

DATE	BUNO	SQDRN	BASE	LOST	AREA	PILOT	FATE
07/24/45	21160	VB-88	USS YORK-TOWN	KURE	EMPIRE	LT E.R. TILTON	S
07/24/45	65170	VB-94	USS LEX-INGTON		EMPIRE	ENS LAWRENCE B. HAINS	S
07/25/45	20934	VB-94	USS LEX-INGTON		EMPIRE	ENS GEORGE S. POLLARD	S
07/28/45	20747	VB-1	USS BENNING-TON	KURE	EMPIRE	LTJG J.R. WAGNER, JR.	S
07/28/45	21152	VB-1	USS BENNING-TON	KURE	EMPIRE	LCDR A.B. HAMM	M
07/28/45	82981	VB-16	USS RANDOLPH	SHIKOKU	EMPIRE	LTJG G. TRUSSELL	M
07/28/45	20856	VB-83	USS ESSEX		EMPIRE		
07/28/45	20187	VB-85	USS SHANGRI-LA	KURE	EMPIRE	LT EDWARD F. GIBSON	M
07/28/45	20902	VB-85	USS SHANGRI-LA	KURE	EMPIRE	LTJG MITCHELL	S
07/28/45	21079	VB-87	USS TICONDER-OGA	KURE	EMPIRE	LTJG RAYMOND H. PORTER	M
07/28/45	65162	VB-87	USS TICONDER-OGA	KURE	EMPIRE	LTJG R.F. PUCCI	S
07/28/45	20946	VB-94	USS LEX-INGTON		EMPIRE	LT JOSEPH G. COSTIGAN	M
07/29/45	65100	CASU(F)-12		GUAM	WCENPAC		
07/31/45	20365	MAG-13		MAJURO	CENPAC	CAPT N.L. SHIELDS	S
08/04/45	20731	VB-16	USS RANDOLPH	SHIKOKU	EMPIRE		
08/04/45	65234	VMSB-331		MARSHALLS	CENPAC	1STLT DONALD W. MODESITT	D
08/09/45	65138	VB-16	USS RANDOLPH	SHIKOKU	EMPIRE	LTJG E.U. PORUPSKY	D
08/09/45	65164	VB-16	USS RANDOLPH	SHIKOKU	EMPIRE	ENS MCNAMARA	S
08/09/45	20976	VB-6	USS HANCOCK		EMPIRE	ENS HOWARD H. HARRISON	S
08/09/45	65181	VB-6	USS HANCOCK		EMPIRE	LTJG JOHN E. FREEMAN, JR.	S
08/09/45	65221	VB-83	USS ESSEX		EMPIRE	ENS PAUL BACCI	D
08/09/45	65006	VB-87	USS TICONDER-OGA	TOKYO	EMPIRE		
08/09/45	65141	VB-87	USS TICONDER-OGA	TOKYO	EMPIRE		
08/10/45	83002	VB-16	USS RANDOLPH	SHIKOKU	EMPIRE	ENS K.E. MOORE	S
08/13/45	65222	VB-1	USS BENNING-TON	TOKYO	EMPIRE	ENS BEDMAN	S
08/13/45	20953	VB-87	USS TICONDER-OGA	TOKYO	EMPIRE		
08/13/45	65111	VB-94	USS LEX-INGTON		EMPIRE	LTJG WILLIAM KNOBLES	S
08/14/45	20846	CASU(F)-12		GUAM	WCENPAC		
08/14/45	21105	CASU(F)-12		GUAM	WCENPAC		
08/15/45	65202	VB-6	USS HANCOCK		EMPIRE	ENS EDWARD E. HAWKS	S

CURTISS SB2C-5

The Curtiss SB2C-5 variant was the SB2C-4 with increased fuel capacity, frameless sliding canopy, a tailhook fixed in the extended position, and deletion of the ASB radar. There were 970 built. Aircraft lost:

DATE	BUNO	SQDRN	BASE	LOST	AREA	PILOT	FATE
05/31/45	83208	VB-89	USS ANTIETAM	CANAL ZONE	CENLANT	ENS M.L. NIDTHUN	S
06/08/45	83211	VB-89	USS ANTIETAM	HAWAII	ECENPAC		
06/27/45	83250	VB-86	USS WASP	PEARL	ECENPAC	ENS W.O. SPAUR	D
07/03/45	83143	VB-86	USS WASP		EMPIRE	LTJG ROBERT JOHNSON	D
07/03/45	83380	VB-86	USS WASP		EMPIRE		
07/14/45	83237	VB-86	USS WASP		EMPIRE	LTJG JOHN S. SHIRLEY, JR.	D
07/17/45	83190	VB-89	KAHULUI	HAWAII	ECENPAC		
07/17/45	83213	VB-89	KAHULUI	HAWAII	ECENPAC		
07/18/45	83204	VB-8	PUUNENE	HAWAII	ECENPAC	ENS LARRY M. STRONG	D
07/24/45	83506	VB-150	USS LAKE CHAM-PLAIN	CULEBRA IS.	CENLANT		
07/28/45	83148	VB-86	USS WASP	KURE	EMPIRE	LCDR WILLIAM W. BUSH	S
07/28/45	83221	VB-86	USS WASP	KURE	EMPIRE	LTJG T.E. JENSON	M
07/28/45	83246	VB-86	USS WASP	KURE	EMPIRE	LTJG J.D. BROWN	M
07/28/45	83458	VB-86	USS WASP	KURE	EMPIRE	LTJG E.M. NASON, JR.	S
08/02/45	83187	VB-86	USS WASP	YOKOSUKA	EMPIRE		
08/04/45	83156	CASU(F)-12		GUAM	WCENPAC	LT E.F. HANIQUET	S
08/04/45	83426	VB-10	USS INTREPID	ENR WAKE	WCENPAC		
08/06/45	83399	VB-10	USS INTREPID	WAKE	WCENPAC		
08/06/45	83453	VB-10	USS INTREPID	WAKE	WCENPAC		
08/09/45	83318	VB-14	KAHULUI	HAWAII	ECENPAC	LTJG J.D. BARTLETT	S
08/09/45	83154	VB-86	USS WASP	YOKOSUKA	EMPIRE	LTJG JOHN P. NAUGHTON	S
08/12/45	83173	VB-13	PUUNENE	HAWAII	ECENPAC	ENS J.M. COWART	S

CURTISS SBC-4

The Curtiss SBC Helldiver was a two-place scout bomber built by the Curtiss-Wright Corporation. It was the last military biplane procured by the United States Navy. The Navy took deliveries of the new aircraft in mid-1937 with the first batch of carrier-based aircraft going to USS YORKTOWN, but time and technology caught up to the advanced biplane. It was relegated to menial duties and mostly as an advanced trainer for training units in Florida. However, some saw service with the US Marines in the South Pacific. The -4 was a production variant with a 950 hp R-1820-34. There were 174 built. Aircraft lost:

DATE	BUNO	SQDRN	BASE	LOST	AREA	PILOT	FATE
02/10/42	1829	MAG-13	TUTUILA		SOPAC	2NDLT WILLIAM P. PARRISH	S
06/15/42	1843	VMO-151		SAMOA	SOPAC		
03/13/43	1287	MAG-13		TUTUILA	SOPAC	LT SHEPARD	S

CURTISS SC-1

The Curtiss SC Seahawk was a scout seaplane designed by the Curtiss Aeroplane and Motor Company for the United States Navy. The existing Curtiss SO3C Seamew and the Vought OS2U Kingfisher were 1937 designs that, by 1942 needed to be replaced. The first serial production Seahawks were delivered on 22 October 1944, to the USS GUAM. All 577 aircraft eventually produced for the Navy were delivered on conventional landing gear and flown to the appropriate Naval Air Station, where floats were fitted for service as needed.

Capable of being fitted with either float or wheeled landing gear, the Seahawk was arguably America's best floatplane scout of World War II. However, its protracted development time meant it entered service too late to see significant action in the war. It was not until June 1945, during the pre-invasion bombardment of Borneo, that the Seahawk was involved in military action. By the end of the war, seaplanes were becoming less desirable, with the Seahawk being replaced soon afterward by helicopters. Aircraft lost:

DATE	BUNO	SQDRN	BASE	LOST	AREA	PILOT	FATE
11/13/44	35310	CB-2	USS GUAM	TRINIDAD	CENLANT		
12/05/44	35304	VCS-16	USS ALASKA	W OF PANAMA	SEPAC	ENS E.B. CLARK, JR.	S
01/21/45	35311	VCS-16	USS GUAM	ENR PANAMA	NORLANT	LT LESTER A. REDDING	S
02/10/45	35362	BB-63	USS MISSOURI	ULITHI	WCENPAC	LT EVER. N. FROTHINGHAM	D
02/17/45	35368	CL-49	USS ST. LOUIS	HAWAII	ECENPAC		
02/22/45	35352	CL-67	USS TOPEKA	GULF OF PARIA	NORLANT	ENS J.H. MCCUTCHEON	U
03/01/45	35303	CB-1	USS ALASKA	IWO JIMA	EMPIRE		
03/13/45	35403	CASU(F)-51	USS ST. LOUIS	ULITHI	WCENPAC	ENS RALPH V.E. EICKHOFF	S
03/23/45	35380	CB-2	USS GUAM	ENR OKINAWA	EMPIRE	LTJG SPENCER H. WINSOR	S
03/27/45	35340	COMAIR-PAC	PEARL	HAWAII	ECENPAC		
03/31/45	35392	CL-67	USS TOPEKA	WEST INDIES	CENLANT	ENS FREDERICK B. THOMAS	S
04/16/45	35372	CL-49	USS ST. LOUIS	OKINAWA	EMPIRE	ENS ARTHUR J. GUNDERSON	S
04/19/45	35337	CL-63	USS MOBILE	ENR LEYTE GULF	EMPIRE		
04/21/45	35463	CL-43	USS NASHVILLE	WAKDE	SW PAC		
04/30/45	35370	COMAIR-PAC	PEARL	HAWAII	ECENPAC		
04/30/45	35334	POOL	PEARL	HAWAII	ECENPAC		
04/30/45	35365	POOL	PEARL	HAWAII	ECENPAC		
05/03/45	35397	CA-32	USS NEW ORLEANS		EMPIRE		
05/03/45	35425	CL-43	USS NASHVILLE	ENR ESPIRITU	PHIL	ENS JACK E. HASTINGS	S
05/04/45	35332	CL-104	USS ATLANTA	OFF OKINAWA	EMPIRE	LTJG WILLIAM G. LAKE	S
05/15/45	35484	CA-136	USS CHICAGO	ENR PEARL	CENLANT	LT BENJAMIN SPARKS, JR.	S
05/17/45	35325	CL-91	USS OKLAHOMA CITY	PEARL	ECENPAC	LTJG SKIER NORMAN	S
05/18/45	35359	BB-63	USS MISSOURI	GUAM	WCENPAC		
05/22/45	35369	POOL	PEARL	HAWAII	ECENPAC		
05/23/45	35486	BB-60	USS ALABAMA	OKINAWA	EMPIRE		
05/24/45	35438	CA-136	USS CHICAGO	ENR PEARL	ECENPAC	LTJG VERNON L. POULIOT	S
05/26/45	35411	SOSU-1	PEARL	HAWAII	ECENPAC	LTJG JOHN H. LUDWING	D
05/30/45	35367	CASU(F)-51		ULITHI	WCENPAC		
05/30/45	35335	CL-63	USS MOBILE	LEYTE GULF	PHIL		
05/30/45	35350	COMAIR-PAC	PEARL	HAWAII	ECENPAC		
06/05/45	35436	CA-28	USS LOUIS-VILLE	OKINAWA	EMPIRE	(DECK LOSS-KAMIKAZE)	
06/06/45	35356	CASU(F)-12		GUAM	WCENPAC		
06/08/45	35588	CA-27	USS CHESTER	ENR ULITHI	EMPIRE		
06/08/45	35418	CASU(F)-12		GUAM	WCENPAC		
06/09/45	35336	ACORN-30 PL		JINAMOC	PHIL		
06/09/45	35446	ACORN-30 PL		JINAMOC	PHIL		

DATE	BUNO	SQDRN	BASE	LOST	AREA	PILOT	FATE
06/22/45	35531	ACORN-30 PL		JINAMOC	PHIL	LTJG HAROLD C. MOLHOOK	U
06/28/45	35354	CA-45	USS WICHITA	SAIPAN	WCENPAC	LT R.K. HELLETT, JR.	S
06/28/45	35360	CASU(F)-12		GUAM	WCENPAC		
07/12/45	35341	CASU(F)-48		SAIPAN	WCENPAC		
07/15/45	35309	SOSU-1	PEARL	HAWAII	ECENPAC		
07/29/45	35407	CB-2	USS GUAM	OKINAWA	EMPIRE	ENS J.S. MILLER	S
07/30/45	35600	CA-35	USS INDIANA	MARIANAS	CENPAC		
07/30/45	35630	CA-35	USS INDIANA	MARIANAS	CENPAC		
07/30/45	35635	CA-35	USS INDIANA	MARIANAS	CENPAC		
07/31/45	35419	CA-136	USS CHICAGO		EMPIRE		
07/31/45	35527	CA-45	USS WICHITA	GUAM	WCENPAC		
08/01/45	35666	ACORN-30 PL	USS PENNSYL-VANIA	WAKE	WCENPAC	LTJG G.F. GOSSMAN	U
08/02/45	35518	CL-69	USS BOSTON	HONSHU	EMPIRE		
08/04/45	35555	CL-92	USS LITTLE ROCK	OFF CUBA	CENLANT		
08/09/45	35544	BB-44	USS CALIFORN-IA	TINIAN	WCENPAC		
08/11/45	35413	CB-1	USS ALASKA		EMPIRE	LTJG JOHN H. WAMSLEY	M
08/12/45	35495	CASU(F)-12		GUAM	WCENPAC		
08/13/45	35524	CASU(F)-48		SAIPAN	WCENPAC		
08/13/45	35432	POOL	PEARL	HAWAII	ECENPAC		

CURTISS SNC-1

The Curtiss-Wright CW-22 was a 1940s American general-purpose advanced training monoplane aircraft built by the Curtiss-Wright Corporation. It was operated by the United States Navy as a scout trainer with the designation SNC-1 Falcon. To help to meet the expanding need for training planes the Navy ordered 150 planes in November 1940. Further orders brought the total to 305 aircraft which were designated SNC-1 Falcon. (BuNo's 6290-6439, 05085-05234, 32987-32991). Aircraft lost:

DATE	BUNO	SQDRN	BASE	LOST	AREA	PILOT	FATE
08/31/44	6314	NAS	GUANTAN-AMO BAY	CUBA	CENLANT		

CURTISS SO3C-1

The Curtiss SO3C Seamew was developed by the Curtiss-Wright Corporation as a replacement for the SOC Seagull as the United States Navy's standard floatplane scout. Curtiss named the SO3C the *Seamew* but in 1941 the US Navy began calling it by the name *Seagull*, the same name as the aircraft it replaced (the Curtiss SOC biplane), causing some confusion. From the time it entered service the SO3C suffered two serious flaws: in-flight stability problems and problems with the unique Ranger air-cooled V-shaped inline 520 hp engine. Poor flight performance and a poor maintenance record led to the SO3C being withdrawn from US Navy first line units by 1944. There were 141 of the -1's built. Aircraft lost:

DATE	BUNO	SQDRN	BASE	LOST	AREA	PILOT	FATE

DATE	BUNO	SQDRN	BASE	LOST	AREA	PILOT	FATE
08/27/42	4750	CL-56	USS COLUMBIA	OFF NEW YORK	CENLANT	ENS GEORGE W. KIELY	U
09/05/42	4748	CL-56	USS COLUMBIA		CENLANT	ENS G.F. RUSH	U
11/05/42	4775	COMAIR-PAC	PEARL	HAWAII	ECENPAC	HUGH PRICE	M
01/01/43	4834				SOPAC		
01/06/43	4857	CL-58	USS DENVER		NORLANT	ENS DONALD ALLISON	U
01/09/43	4871	CL-56	USS COLUMBIA	RENNELL IS.	SOPAC		
01/24/43	4804	CL-58	USS DENVER			LT E.M. POST	D
01/24/43	4861	CL-58	USS DENVER			A.B. HASELTINE	S
02/22/43	4825			NOUMEA	SOPAC		
02/25/43	4867	CL-55	USS CLEVE-LAND	ENR VILA	SOPAC		
03/19/43	4786	FAW-2	PEARL	HAWAII	ECENPAC		
04/07/43	4793	COMAIR-PAC	PEARL	HAWAII	ECENPAC		
07/31/43	4763	COMAIR-PAC	PEARL	HAWAII	ECENPAC		
08/31/43	4782	FAW-2	PEARL	HAWAII	ECENPAC	ENS GEORGE W. PORTZ, JR.	M
09/18/43	4865	COMAIR-PAC	PEARL	HAWAII	ECENPAC		
11/03/44	4788	VJ-11	EFATE		SOPAC		
11/26/44	4840	VJ-11	EFATE		SOPAC		
11/28/44	4824	VJ-11	EFATE		SOPAC		

CURTISS SO3C-2

The Curtiss SO3C-2 variant was the same as the -1 with the exception of some minor strengthening and the attachment of arrestor gear for carrier operations. There were 200 built for the Navy. Aircraft lost:

DATE	BUNO	SQDRN	BASE	LOST	AREA	PILOT	FATE
09/02/43	4887	VS-35			NORLANT		
04/01/44	4909	COMAIR-PAC	PEARL	HAWAII	ECENPAC		
11/13/44	04194	VJ-11	EFATE		SOPAC		
11/26/44	4943	VJ-11	EFATE		SOPAC		
11/27/44	04190	VJ-11	EFATE		SOPAC		
11/27/44	04192	VJ-11	EFATE		SOPAC		
11/28/44	4904	VJ-11	EFATE		SOPAC		

CURTISS SO3C-3

The Curtiss SO3C-3 included a more powerful Ranger 600 hp engine. There were 39 built for the Navy. Aircraft lost:

DATE	BUNO	SQDRN	BASE	LOST	AREA	PILOT	FATE
10/01/43	04237	CL-80	USS BILOXI		NORLANT		
12/08/43	04213	SOSU-1	PEARL	HAWAII	ECENPAC	ENS A.G. MENGEL	S
11/06/44	04250	VJ-11	EFATE		SOPAC		
11/23/44	04304	VJ-11	EFATE		SOPAC		

CURTISS SOC (VARIANT UNKNOWN)

DATE	BUNO	SQDRN	BASE	LOST	AREA	PILOT	FATE
04/19/42		VS-3	PEARL	HAWAII	ECENPAC	LT TANMY	S

DATE	BUNO	SQDRN	BASE	LOST	AREA	PILOT	FATE
10/11/42		CL-47	USS BOISE	CAPE ESPERAN.	SOPAC		

CURTISS SOC-1

The Curtiss SOC Seagull was a United States single-engined scout observation biplane aircraft designed for the United States Navy. The aircraft served on battleships and cruisers in a seaplane configuration, being launched by catapult and recovered from a sea landing. The wings folded back against the fuselage for storage aboard ship. When based ashore or on carriers the single float was replaced by fixed wheeled landing gear. The first ship the SOC was assigned to was the USS MARBLEHEAD in November 1935; by the end of the decade, the SOC had replaced its predecessor throughout the fleet. Production came to an end in 1938. By 1941, most battleships had transitioned to the Vought OS2U Kingfisher and cruisers were expected to replace their aging SOCs with the third generation SO3C Seamew. The SO3C, however, suffered from a weak engine and plans to adopt it as a permanent replacement were scrapped. The SOC, despite being a craft from an earlier generation, went on to credibly execute its missions of gunfire observation and limited range scouting missions.

Through the first six months of naval service, the SOC was known as the XO3C-1. The designation was changed to SOC when it was decided to merge its scouting and observation roles. The SOC was not called the *Seagull* until 1941, when the U.S. Navy began the wholesale adoption of popular names for aircraft in addition to their alpha-numeric designations. The name 'Seagull' had earlier been given to two civil Curtiss aircraft, a Curtiss Model 18 and a Model 25, both converted Curtiss MF flying boats.

When operating as a seaplane, returning SOCs would land on the relatively smooth ocean surface created on the sheltered side of the vessel as it made a wide turn, after which the aircraft would be winched back onto the deck. The initial production version, the SOC-1, had a 500 hp R-1340-18 engine enclosed in a cowling and its float or wheel undercarriage was interchangeable. There were 135 of the -1's built. Aircraft lost:

DATE	BUNO	SQDRN	BASE	LOST	AREA	PILOT	FATE
12/08/41	9983	VGS-30	USS OMAHA	PEARL	ECENPAC		
12/08/41		VS-71	USS CLEVE-LAND	CENLANT	(PRE-COMMISSION)		
12/27/41	9977	CA-24	USS PEN-SACOLA	PEARL	ECENPAC		
12/31/41	9976	CAVITE			SW PAC		
01/23/42	9901				SW PAC		
01/28/42	9980	VCS-6	USS MEMPHIS		ECENPAC		
02/01/42	9974	CA-25	USS SALT LAKE CITY	WOTJE	CENPAC		
03/05/42	9929	CA-24	USS PEN-SACOLA	PEARL	ECENPAC		
04/08/42	9925	CA-27	USS CHESTER	ENR GUADAL-CANAL	SOPAC		
06/26/42	9936	VCS-6	USS MEMPHIS	MARTINIQUE	CENLANT		
07/03/42	9964	VCS-4	USS INDIANA	HAWAII	ECENPAC		
07/08/42	9872	VCS-4	USS LOUIS-VILLE	PEARL	ECENPAC		

DATE	BUNO	SQDRN	BASE	LOST	AREA	PILOT	FATE
07/18/42	9943	BB-58	USS INDIANA	HAWAII	ECENPAC		
08/07/42	9945	BB-58	USS INDIANA	KISKA	NORPAC		
08/07/42	9935	VCS-6	USS MEMPHIS	MARTINIQUE	CENLANT		
08/09/42	9955	CA-25	USS SALT LAKE CITY	SAVO IS.	SOPAC		
08/09/42	9874	CA-71	USS QUINCY	SAVO IS.	SOPAC		
08/09/42	9927	CA-71	USS QUINCY	SAVO IS.	SOPAC		
08/09/42	9933	CA-71	USS QUINCY	SAVO IS.	SOPAC		
08/09/42	9946	CL-64	USS VIN-CENNES	SAVO IS.	SOPAC		
10/04/42	9862	CA-31	USS AUGUSTA	ENR EUROPE	NORLANT	ENS JAMES ALOYSIUS	U
10/04/42	9918	CL-49	USS ST. LOUIS	HAWAII	ECENPAC		
10/11/42	9967	CA-25	USS SALT LAKE CITY	CAPE ESPERANCE	SOPAC		
10/11/42	9990	CA-38	USS SAN FRANCIS-CO	CAPE ESPERANCE	SOPAC		
10/14/42	9905	CA-25	USS SALT LAKE CITY	PEARL	ECENPAC		
10/16/42	9876	VGS-6	USS NEW ORLEANS	PEARL	ECENPAC		
11/15/42	9926	VGS-6	USS MINNEAP-OLIS	PEARL	ECENPAC		
11/25/42	9961		USS INDE-PENDENCE	PEARL	ECENPAC		
12/15/42	9954	VCX-64	TANNEM-BOGO IS.		SOPAC	LTJG POLK	S
12/16/42	9881	CA-27	USS CHESTER	ENR SYDNEY AUS	SW PAC		
01/14/43	9911	VCS-64	USS NORTH-AMPTON	THANNEM-BOGA	SOPAC	LT BRACKETT	D
01/14/43	9978	VCS-64	USS NORTH-AMPTON	THANNEM-BOGA	SOPAC	LT HAUGE	M
01/30/43	9962	VCS-64	USS NORTH-AMPTON	THANNEM-BOGA	SOPAC	LT DOBLER	M
02/08/43	9861				SW PAC		
02/08/43	9969	VCS-4	USS LOUIS-VILLE	RENNELL IS.	SOPAC		
03/05/43	9973	CL-43	USS NASHVILLE	NEW GEORGIA	SOPAC		
03/26/43	9947	CA-25	USS SALT LAKE CITY	KOMANDORS KIS	NORPAC		
04/14/43	9883	CL-46	USS PHOENIX		SW PAC		
04/27/43	9877	VCS-6	USS WICHITA	ATTU	NORPAC		
05/29/43	9942	CL-49	USS ST. LOUIS	HAWAII	ECENPAC		
06/27/43	9904	CL-56	USS COLUMBIA	ENR NEW GEORGIA	SOPAC		
07/01/43	9875	CL-58	USS DENVER		SOPAC	LT ENGLISH	S
07/04/43	9950	CL-48	USS HONOLULU	LUNGA POINT	SOPAC	ENS HOFFMAN	S
07/24/43	9937	CL-55	USS CLEVE-LAND	FLORIDA IS.	SOPAC		
09/13/43	9932	CA-38	USS SAN FRANCIS-CO		NORPAC		
10/10/43	9866	CA-35	USS INDIANA	ENR PEARL	WCENPAC		

DATE	BUNO	SQDRN	BASE	LOST	AREA	PILOT	FATE
10/13/43	9988	CA-32	USS NEW ORLEANS	WAKE	WCENPAC		
10/18/43	9941	CA-31	USS AUGUSTA	ENR EUROPE	NORLANT		
12/18/43	9972	SOSU-1	PEARL	HAWAII	ECENPAC		
12/24/43	9938	VCS-12	USS COLUMBIA	RENNELL IS.	SOPAC	LTJG G.W. HANSON	S
01/01/44	9893	VCS-12	USS COLUMBIA	PURVIS BAY	CENPAC	LT D.J. LUNDE	S
01/26/44	9907	VCS-4	USS LOUIS-VILLE	MARSHALLS	CENPAC	ENS D.W. GANDY	S
02/17/44	9896	VCS-4	USS LOUIS-VILLE	MARSHALLS	CENPAC	ENS A.J. TRIMBLE	S
06/15/44	9906	VCS-6	USS NEW ORLEANS	MARIANAS	CENPAC		
07/05/44	9984	VCS-4	USS LOUIS-VILLE	SAIPAN	WCENPAC		
07/20/44	9919	CA-36	USS MINNEAP-OLIS	GUAM	WCENPAC	ENS DALE PARKER	D
07/24/44	9928	VCS-4	USS LOUIS-VILLE	TINIAN	WCENPAC	ENS B.B. CRAVEN	D
07/31/44	9864	COMAIR-PAC	PEARL	HAWAII	ECENPAC		
07/31/44	9870	COMAIR-PAC	PEARL	HAWAII	ECENPAC		
09/12/44	9879	CL-56	USS COLUMBIA	ENR PALUS	ECENPAC	LT GEORGE W. HANSON	S
10/22/44	9900	CL-48	USS HONOLULU	LEYTE GULF	PHIL		
10/25/44	9869	CA-28	USS LOUIS-VILLE	LEYTE GULF	PHIL		
12/18/44	9920	CA-32	USS NEW ORLEANS		CENPAC		
01/25/45	9951	CL-55	USS CLEVE-LAND	ENR CORREGIDOR	WCENPAC		
01/30/45	9989	CA-38	USS SAN FRANCIS-CO	ULITHI	WCENPAC		
02/04/45	9982	SEAPL BASE		NOUMEA	SOPAC		
02/15/45	9953	CA-31	USS AUGUSTA	ENR EAST COAST	CENLANT	ENS ELBERT E. HOWARD	S
03/04/45	9916	SEAPL BASE		MANUS	SW PAC		
03/22/45	9889	CASU(F)-12		GUAM	WCENPAC		
03/31/45	9886	CA-38	USS SAN FRANCIS-CO	NAHA	EMPIRE		
03/31/45	9903	COMAIR-PAC	PEARL	HAWAII	ECENPAC		
05/25/45	9939	ACORN-30 PL		JINAMOC	PHIL		
05/30/45	9958	CASU(F)-51		ULITHI	WCENPAC		
05/31/45	9891	COMAIR-PAC	PEARL	HAWAII	ECENPAC		
06/06/45	9908	CASU(F)-12		GUAM	WCENPAC		
06/22/45	9934	ACORN-30 PL		JINAMOC	PHIL		
06/28/45	9930	ACORN-30 PL		JINAMOC	PHIL		
07/11/45	9894	ACORN-30 PL		TACLOBAN	PHIL		

CURTISS SOC-2

References state that the Curtiss SOC-2 variant was basically, with minor changes, the SOC-1. It flew with an R-1340-22 engine and came from the factory in wheeled configuration only, although based on the squadrons attached many had to have been re-fitted by the Navy with floats. There were 40 built. Aircraft lost:

DATE	BUNO	SQDRN	BASE	LOST	AREA	PILOT	FATE
12/31/41	393		CAVITE		SW PAC		
02/19/42	404	VCS-4	USS LOUIS-VILLE	PEARL	ECENPAC		
02/21/42	421	CA-29	USS CHICAGO	SUVA BAY	SE PAC		
03/11/42	394	CA-38	USS SAN FRANCIS-CO	PEARL	ECENPAC		
03/14/42	417	CL-41	USS PHILADEL-PHIA	OFF ICELAND	NORLANT		
05/10/42	400	CL-43	USS NASHVILLE	HAWAII	ECENPAC		
06/20/42	410		USS INDE-PENDENCE	PEARL	ECENPAC		
07/15/42	406	VCS-4	USS PORTLAND	PEARL	ECENPAC		
08/09/42	389	CL-64	USS VIN-CENNES	SAVO IS.	SOPAC		
12/16/42	399	CA-27	USS CHESTER	ENR SYDNEY AUS	SW PAC		
01/03/43	420	CL-56	USS COLUMBIA	ENR RENNELL IS.	SOPAC		
01/05/43	413	VCS-64	USS NORTH-AMPTON	THANNEM-BOGA	SOPAC	LT REICHEL	M
01/24/43	422	CL-56	USS COLUMBIA	RENNELL IS.	SOPAC		
03/20/43	408	CL-42	USS SAVANNAH	ENR NEW YORK	SOLANT		
02/05/44	405	VCS-4	USS NEW ORLEANS	KWAJALEIN	CENPAC		
02/21/44	424	VCS-4	USS PORTLAND	ENIWETOK	CENPAC		
11/27/44	423	CL-49	USS ST. LOUIS	SURIGAO STRAIT	SW PAC		
03/22/45	388	CASU(F)-12		GUAM	WCENPAC		
04/30/45	390	POOL	PEARL	HAWAII	ECENPAC		
08/01/45	395	ACORN-30 PL		TACLOBAN	PHIL		

CURTISS SOC-3

The Curtiss SOC-3 was similar to SOC-2, but with interchangeable undercarriage. There were 83 built by Curtiss as SOC-3 with another 44 built by the Naval Aircraft Factory as the SON-1. Aircraft lost:

DATE	BUNO	SQDRN	BASE	LOST	AREA	PILOT	FATE
12/31/41	1064		CAVITE		SW PAC		
12/31/41	1103		CAVITE		SW PAC		
02/09/42	1102		HAWAII	HAWAII	ECENPAC	W.H. BURACKER	S
02/28/42	1066	CL-81	USS HOUSTON	OFF JAVA	SW PAC	(SHIP SANK)	
02/28/42	1068	CL-81	USS HOUSTON	OFF JAVA	SW PAC	(SHIP SANK)	
04/16/42		TF-99				ENS FRANCIS M. DILLON	U
04/21/42	1085				ECENPAC		
05/09/42	1106	CA-37	USS TUSCA-LOOSA	OFF NORWAY	NORLANT		
06/14/42		CL-48	USS HONOLULU	HAWAII	ECENPAC	ENS G.S. SMITH	U
06/16/42	1065	VP-101		AUSTRALIA	SW PAC		
06/18/42	1134	CL-48	USS HONOLULU	HAWAII	ECENPAC	ENS B.M. STEPHENSON	M

DATE	BUNO	SQDRN	BASE	LOST	AREA	PILOT	FATE
08/09/42	1075	CA-71	USS QUINCY	SAVO IS.	SOPAC		
08/09/42	1123	CL-64	USS VIN-CENNES	SAVO IS.	SOPAC		
08/09/42	1072	CL-90	USS ASTORIA	SAVO IS.	SOPAC		
08/09/42	1087	CL-90	USS ASTORIA	SAVO IS.	SOPAC		
08/15/42	1096	CL-47	USS BOISE		SOPAC		
08/24/42	1107	CL-9	USS RICHMOND	CHILE	SOPAC		
09/01/42	1139	CL-47	USS BOISE		ECENPAC		
09/04/42	1071	CL-47	USS BOISE		ECENPAC		
09/29/42	1089	CL-46	USS PHOENIX		SW PAC		
11/08/42			USS RANGER	CASABLANCA	NW AFR		
07/04/43	1084	CL-50	USS HELENA	VELLA LAVELLA	SOPAC		
08/11/43	1120	CL-43	USS NASHVILLE	ENR PEARL	ECENPAC		
12/23/43	1080	VCS-15	USS NASHVILLE	MARCUS	CENPAC	ENS W.F. DRIVER	S
05/05/44	1117	VCS-6	USS WICHITA	MAJURO	CENPAC	ENS L.P. MERLINO	S
05/06/44	1070	VCS-9	USS HONOLULU		SOPAC		
05/11/44	1082	VCS-8	USS BROOKLYN	ENR ANZIO	MED		
06/04/44	1074	VCS-6	USS WICHITA	SAIPAN	WCENPAC	CDR P.E. EMICK	S
08/21/44	1083	VCS-8	USS PHILADEL-PHIA	FRANCE	EUROPE	LT FRANCIS A. CAHILL	M
09/12/44	1121	CL-58	USS DENVER		CENPAC		
01/10/45	1100	CA-33	USS PORTLAND	LINGAYEN GULF	PHIL		
04/09/45	1125	CA-37	USS TUSCA-LOOSA	OKINAWA	EMPIRE	LT W.P. LATHROP, JR.	M
04/30/45	1112	POOL	PEARL	HAWAII	ECENPAC		
08/01/45	1079	ACORN-30 PL		TACLOBAN	PHIL		

CURTISS SOC-3A

All SOC-4s were transferred to the U.S. Navy in 1942 which modified them by adding a deck arrester gear and they were subsequently re-designated as the SOC-3A.

DATE	BUNO	SQDRN	BASE	LOST	AREA	PILOT	FATE
07/10/43	1130	CL-41	USS PHILADEL-PHIA	SICILY	MED		
07/10/43	1091	CL-42	USS SAVANNAH	GELA, SICILY	EUROPE	LT CHARLES A. ANDERSON	D
07/10/43	1097	CL-42	USS SAVANNAH	GELA, SICILY	EUROPE	LTJG JOHN G. OSBORN	S
07/10/43	1146	CL-42	USS SAVANNAH	GELA, SICILY	EUROPE		
02/01/44	1067	VCS-6	USS MINNEAP-OLIS	KWAJALEIN	CENPAC		
10/29/44	1136	CL-58	USS DENVER	PORT PURVIS	SW PAC		
11/24/44	1133	CASU(F)-18		EBEYE	WCENPAC		
01/01/45	1137	CA-36	USS MINNEAP-OLIS	ENR LUZON	WCENPAC		
02/07/45	1135	A.A.	PEARL	HAWAII	ECENPAC		

CURTISS XSBC-4

The Curtiss SBC Helldiver was a two-place scout bomber built by the Curtiss-Wright Corporation. It was the last military biplane procured by the United States Navy (see the Curtiss SBC variant write-ups). A single SBC-3 was re-engined with a 950 hp (710 kW) R-1820-22 and redesignated the XSBC-4. It was lost near Kodiak, AK.

DATE	BUNO	SQDRN	BASE	LOST	AREA	PILOT	FATE
07/08/44	0582	NAS	KODIAK	ALASKA	NORPAC		

DOUGLAS DC-3A

This aircraft was acquired by the Navy from Pan Am and assigned a Navy Bureau Number. It is unknown as to how it was lost. Any further information from the reader would be helpful. Aircraft lost:

DATE	BUNO	SQDRN	BASE	LOST	AREA	PILOT	FATE
02/16/44	99099	PAN AM		YAMATAGA	NORPAC		

DOUGLAS R3D-2

The Douglas DC-5, the least known of the famous DC airliner series, was a 16-22 seat, twin-propeller aircraft intended for short airline routes. However, by the time it entered commercial service in 1940, many airlines were canceling orders; consequently, only five civilian DC-5s were ever built. With the Douglas Aircraft Company already converting to war production, the military version of the DC-5 was produced and called the R3D-2. Four of the five DC-5's built were converted for the US Marine Corps as a 22-seat paratrooper version. Aircraft lost:

DATE	BUNO	SQDRN	BASE	LOST	AREA	PILOT	FATE
12/07/41	1904	VMJ-252	PEARL	HAWAII	ECENPAC		

DOUGLAS R4D-1

The Douglas C-47 Skytrain or Dakota is a military transport aircraft that was developed from the Douglas DC-3 airliner. It was used extensively during World War II. The C-47 was vital to the success of many Allied campaigns, in particular those at Guadalcanal and in the jungles of New Guinea and Burma where the C-47 (and its USN/USMC version, the R4D) made it possible for Allied troops to counter the mobility of the light-traveling Japanese army. Aircraft lost:

DATE	BUNO	SQDRN	BASE	LOST	AREA	PILOT	FATE
10/09/42	01981	VMJ-253	NEW CALEDONIA		SOPAC	MAJ KIMBALL	D
11/15/42	01648	VMJ-253			SOPAC		
11/15/42	01978	VMJ-253			SOPAC		
12/29/42	4696	VMJ-253			SOPAC		
01/09/43	4694	VMJ-253			SOPAC		
04/26/43	05055	VMJ-152			SOPAC	CAPT CUNNINGHAM	S
04/27/43	37666	MAG-25	NEW CALEDONIA	GUADALCANAL	SOPAC		
06/28/43	01984	MAG-25		FIJI ISLAND	SOPAC	LT B.C. NYGRAW	S
07/03/43	01990	NAS	DUTCH HARBOR	ALASKA	NORPAC		
08/02/43	4706	MAG-25			SOPAC		

DATE	BUNO	SQDRN	BASE	LOST	AREA	PILOT	FATE
11/19/43	01988	VR-7		RIO DE JANIERO	SOLANT		
05/01/44	3143	VMJ-353			CENPAC	CAPT T.M. PORTER	S

DOUGLAS R4D-5

The Douglas R4D-5 was the Navy's equivalent to the C-47A. The difference from the earlier R4D-1 variant was that the 12-volt electrical system was replaced with a 24-volt system. Aircraft lost:

DATE	BUNO	SQDRN	BASE	LOST	AREA	PILOT	FATE
00/00/00	17184	VMR-253		GUAM	WCENPAC	LT BURL E. RULAND	S
02/18/43	17236	MAG-13		OWI	SW PAC	LT DAVID D. CAMERON	S
06/08/43	12406	MAG-25			SOPAC		
07/07/43		FAW-11			SOLANT		
07/17/43	12411	VMJ-152		NOUMEA	SOPAC	LT CHARLES BRUSH	U
07/22/43	12405	VMJ-253			SOPAC		
08/23/43	39072	COMAIR-PAC	PEARL	HAWAII	ECENPAC		
08/27/43	12433	MAG-25			SOPAC		
12/27/43	12432	VMJ-153	TONIUTA	ESPIRITU SANTO	SOPAC	CAPT R.H. KNOTTS	M
03/06/44	12430	VR-3	ZANDERY		NORLANT		
05/19/44	39073	VMJ-152	TOROKINA	GUADAL-CANAL	SOPAC	R.O. HARELSON	M
07/12/44	17180	VMR-153		GUADAL-CANAL	SOPAC	MAJ E. MEGSON	D
07/22/44	17128	VR-7	RECIFE	MACE ISLAND	SOLANT	ENS R.M. WILHOLME	D
07/23/44	39090	COMAIR-7THFL		PORT MORESBY	SW PAC	LT J.D. GROSS	M
07/28/44	39089	COMAIR-7THFL		BIAK	SW PAC		
08/01/44	12408	VMR-153		NOUMEA	SOPAC		
09/20/44	12431	VMR-153		TOROKINA	SOPAC		
10/01/44	39093	VR-1	NOVA SCOTIA		NORLANT		
10/02/44	39075	COMAIR-PAC	PEARL	HAWAII	ECENPAC		
10/07/44	39086	VMR-153	VELLA LAVELLA		SW PAC		
12/22/44	39069	VMR-253		GUAM	WCENPAC		
01/09/45	12413	VMR-152		BOUGAIN-VILLE	SOPAC		
01/09/45	39059	VMR-153		TORONIA	SW PAC		
01/15/45	17234	VR-13		TACLOBAN	PHIL	CDR B.J. MCKNIGHT	D
02/12/45	17148	VMR-353		KWAJALEIN	CENPAC		
02/15/45	39068	COMAIR-7THFL		MOMOTE	SW PAC		
04/19/45	39067	COM7TH-FLT	PERTH	AUSTRALIA	SW PAC		
04/28/45	17222	ADAK		ALASKA	NORPAC		
05/17/45	17133	VB-13	MOMOTE	MOMOTE	SW PAC	LTJG W.W. STILLWELL	S
05/24/45	17162	2ND MAW		OKINAWA	EMPIRE		
05/28/45	17208	VMR-153		EMIRAU	SW PAC	MURPHY C. NICHOL	S
05/30/45	17240	FAW-15	PORT LYAUTEY	MOROCCO	NW AFR	LCDR BAREFOOT	S
06/30/45	17161	3RD MAW	EWA	HAWAII	ECENPAC		
07/26/45	17185	VMJ-2		IE SHIMA	EMPIRE	1STLT J.B. MCCULLOUGH	S
08/04/45	17232	VR-13	BIAK		SW PAC	LT WILLIAM WESTERVELT	D

DOUGLAS R4D-6

157 C-47Bs were transferred to the US Navy and redesignated the R4D-6. Aircraft lost:

DATE	BUNO	SQDRN	BASE	LOST	AREA	PILOT	FATE
03/05/45	50748	COMAIR-7THFL		MOMOTE	SW PAC		
03/19/45	50770	COMAIR-7THFL		MOMOTE	SW PAC	LT DONALD N. MCINTECK	S
05/30/45	50803	HDRN AF-MF	EWA	HAWAII	ECENPAC		
06/07/45	17277	COM7TH-FLT		SAMAR	PHIL	LTJG JOSEPH M. BARKLEY	U
07/28/45	50750	MAG-32		ZAMBOANGA	PHIL	1STLT CHARLES F. MAYER	S

DOUGLAS R5D-2

The Douglas C-54 Skymaster was a four-engined transport aircraft used by the United States Army Air Forces and US Navy in World War II. First military version of the civilian C-54 came with strengthened airframe, increased fuel capacity, and a provision for passengers or cargo. The US Navy equivalent was called the R5D. Of the 252 C-54As built, 56 were transferred to the United States Navy and redesignated the R5D-1. The Douglas C-54B had increased fuel capacity in the wing. Of the 220 C-54B's built, 30 were transferred to the United States Navy and redesignated the R5D-2. Aircraft lost:

DATE	BUNO	SQDRN	BASE	LOST	AREA	PILOT	FATE
06/07/45	90395	VR-11	HONOLULU	HAWAII	ECENPAC		

DOUGLAS R5D-3

Same as C-54B (R5D-2 above) but with R-2000-11 engines. Of the 380 built, 95 C-54Ds were transferred to the United States Navy and redesignated the R5D-3. Aircraft lost:

DATE	BUNO	SQDRN	BASE	LOST	AREA	PILOT	FATE
03/31/45	56491	VR-11		GUAM	WCENPAC		
04/09/45	50872	VR-11	YONTAN	OKINAWA	EMPIRE	LCDR J.H. HURST	S

DOUGLAS RD-3

The Douglas Dolphin was an amphibious flying boat - a high-wing monoplane, with two radial engines mounted above the wing. Its six to eight passengers looked out picture windows and their baggage was stored in a 30-cubic-foot area. While only 58 were built, they served a wide variety of roles: private "yacht," airliner, military transport, and search and rescue. The Dolphin retracted its landing gear for water landings and evolved into 17 variants to meet military or civilian needs. The U.S. Army, Navy and Coast Guard bought the Dolphin in quantities; the Navy's version was known as the RD-3. Aircraft lost:

DATE	BUNO	SQDRN	BASE	LOST	AREA	PILOT	FATE
12/23/41	9532		PEARL	HAWAII	ECENPAC		
06/23/43	9531	NAS	COCO SOLO	COCO SOLO	CENLANT		

DOUGLAS SBD (VARIANT UNKNOWN)

DATE	BUNO	SQDRN	BASE	LOST	AREA	PILOT	FATE

DATE	BUNO	SQDRN	BASE	LOST	AREA	PILOT	FATE
04/30/42		VS-2	USS LEXINGTON	SW OF WAKE	WCENPAC		
09/18/43		VC-31	USS CABOT		NORLANT		
11/20/43		VB-65	PEARL	HAWAII	ECENPAC		
11/21/43				SEGI CHANNEL	SOPAC	ENS M.E. HOAGY	S
02/02/44		VB-98	ESPIRITU SANTO	AOBA IS.	SOPAC		
02/26/44		VS-52	KANEOHE	HAWAII	ECENPAC		
02/27/44		COMAIRSOPAC	GUADALCANAL	GUADALCANAL	SOPAC		
02/27/44		VB-60			CENPAC		
07/04/44		VB-16	USS LEXINGTON	GUAM	WCENPAC	LTJG C.L. BROWN	S
07/04/44		VB-16	USS LEXINGTON	GUAM	WCENPAC	LT R.N. MCMACKLIN	S
07/05/44					SOPAC	(SALVAGED)	

DOUGLAS SBD-1

The Douglas SBD Dauntless was a naval dive bomber made by Douglas during World War II. The SBD was the United States Navy's main dive bomber from mid-1940 until late 1943, when it was largely replaced by the SB2C Helldiver. The Northrop BT-1 provided the basis for the SBD, which began manufacture in 1940. Ed Heinemann led a team of designers who considered a development with a 1,000 hp (750 kW) Wright Cyclone powerplant. A year earlier, both the U.S. Navy and Marine Corps had placed orders for the new dive bombers, designated the SBD-1 and SBD-2 (the latter had increased fuel capacity and different armament). The SBD-1 went to the Marine Corps in late 1940, and the SBD-2 went to the Navy in early 1941. U.S. Navy and Marine Corps SBDs saw their first action at Pearl Harbor. A total of 18 SBDs from the carrier USS ENTERPRISE arrived over Pearl Harbor during the Japanese attack, and Scouting Squadron Six (VS-6) lost six aircraft, while Bombing Squadron Six (VB-6) lost one. Most Marine SBDs of Marine Scout Bombing Squadron 232 (VMSB-232) were destroyed on the ground at Ewa Mooring Mast Field. On 10 December 1941, USS ENTERPRISE SBDs sank the Japanese submarine *I-70*. In February-March 1942, SBDs from the carriers USS LEXINGTON, USS YORKTOWN and USS ENTERPRISE took part in various strikes on Japanese installations in the Gilbert Islands, Marshall Islands, New Guinea, at Rabaul, on Wake and on Marcus Island.

The type's first major use was in the Battle of the Coral Sea, when SBDs and TBDs sank the Japanese carrier *Shōhō*. SBDs were also used as anti-torpedo combat air patrol (CAP) and scored several times against Japanese aircraft trying to attack USS LEXINGTON and USS YORKTOWN.

Their relatively heavy gun armament - two forward firing .50 in (12.7 mm) M2 Browning machine guns and either one or two rear flexible-mount .30 in (7.62 mm) M1919 Browning machine guns - was effective against the lightly built Japanese fighters, and many pilot-gunner combinations took an aggressive attitude to fighters which attacked them. However, the SBD's most important contribution to the American war effort probably came during the Battle of Midway in early June 1942, when SBD dive bomber attacks sank or fatally damaged all four of the Japanese aircraft carriers, three of them in the space of just six minutes (*Akagi*, *Kaga*, *Sōryū*, and later in the day *Hiryū*) as well as heavily damaging two Japanese cruisers (including *Mikuma*).

At Midway, Marine SBDs were not as effective. One squadron, VMSB-241, operating from Midway Island, was not trained in the "helldiving" technique; instead, the new pilots resorted to the slower but easier glide bombing technique, which led to heavy losses. The carrier-borne squadrons, on the other hand, were much more effective, combined with their F4F Wildcat fighter escorts.

Next, SBDs participated in the Guadalcanal campaign, both from American carriers and Henderson Field on Guadalcanal Island. Dauntlesses contributed to the heavy loss of Japanese shipping during the campaign, including the carrier *Ryūjō* near the Solomon Islands on 24 August, damaging three others during the six-month campaign. SBDs proceeded to sink one cruiser and nine transports during the decisive Naval Battle of Guadalcanal.

During the decisive period of the Pacific Campaign, the SBD's strengths and weaknesses became evident. Interestingly, while the American strength was dive bombing, the Japanese stressed their Nakajima B5N2 "Kate" torpedo bombers, which had caused the bulk of the damage at Pearl Harbor.

In the Atlantic Ocean, the SBD saw action during Operation Torch, the Allied landings in North Africa, in November 1942. The Dauntlesses operated from USS RANGER and two of the five escort carriers that participated in Torch. Eleven months later, SBDs again from USS RANGER attacked German shipping around Bodø, Norway. Although it was becoming obsolete by 1941, the SBD was used until 1944, when the Dauntless undertook its last major action during the Battle of the Philippine Sea. However, some Marine squadrons in the Pacific used Dauntlesses until the end of the war. The SBD-1 variant was the US Marine Corps version without self-sealing fuel tanks. There were 57 SBD-1's built. Aircraft lost:

DATE	BUNO	SQDRN	BASE	LOST	AREA	PILOT	FATE
12/07/41	1626	VMSB-232	EWA	HAWAII	ECENPAC		
12/07/41	1630	VMSB-232	EWA	HAWAII	ECENPAC		
12/07/41	1736	VMSB-232	EWA	HAWAII	ECENPAC		
12/07/41	1737	VMSB-232	EWA	HAWAII	ECENPAC		
12/07/41	1744	VMSB-232	EWA	HAWAII	ECENPAC		
12/07/41	1745	VMSB-232	EWA	HAWAII	ECENPAC		
12/07/41	1746	VMSB-232	EWA	HAWAII	ECENPAC		
12/07/41	1752	VMSB-232	EWA	HAWAII	ECENPAC		
12/07/41	1753	VMSB-232	EWA	HAWAII	ECENPAC		
04/24/42	1741	VMSB-231			ECENPAC		
07/18/42	1629	VMSB-234	PEARL	HAWAII	ECENPAC		
08/08/42	1596	VMSB-234	PEARL	HAWAII	ECENPAC	MARINE GUNNER WIRTA	S
08/14/42	1751	VMSB-232	USS ENTER-PRISE	HAWAII	ECENPAC		
08/21/42	1749	VMSB-234	PEARL	HAWAII	ECENPAC		
09/01/42	1622			MEXICO	CEN AMER	ENS RAY W. GRIMES	D
09/15/42	1754	VMSB-234	PEARL	HAWAII	ECENPAC		
10/20/42	1738	VMSB-234	PEARL	HAWAII	ECENPAC	CAPT WAYNE CARGILL	S
08/31/44	1755	VJ-3					

DOUGLAS SBD-2

The Douglas SBD-2 was the Navy's original production version with increased fuel capacity and different armament but without self-sealing fuel tanks. There were 87 of the SBD's built. Aircraft lost:

DATE	BUNO	SQDRN	BASE	LOST	AREA	PILOT	FATE
12/07/41	2112	VB-2	USS LEX-INGTON	PEARL	ECENPAC		

DATE	BUNO	SQDRN	BASE	LOST	AREA	PILOT	FATE
12/07/41	2181	VB-6	USS ENTER-PRISE	PEARL	ECENPAC		
12/07/41	2110	VMSB-232	EWA	HAWAII	ECENPAC		
12/07/41	2146	VS-2	USS LEX-INGTON	PEARL	ECENPAC		
12/07/41	2158	VS-6	USS ENTER-PRISE	PEARL	ECENPAC		
12/07/41	2159	VS-6	USS ENTER-PRISE	PEARL	ECENPAC	ENS WALTER M. WILLIS	M
12/07/41	2160	VS-6	USS ENTER-PRISE	PEARL	ECENPAC		
02/01/42	2120	VB-6	USS ENTER-PRISE	ROI	WCENPAC	ENS J. DOHERTY	U
02/01/42	2114	VS-6	USS ENTER-PRISE	ROI	WCENPAC		
02/01/42	2155	VS-6	USS ENTER-PRISE	ROI	WCENPAC		
02/01/42	2172	VS-6	USS ENTER-PRISE	ROI	WCENPAC		
02/02/42	2164	VB-6	USS ENTER-PRISE	ROI	WCENPAC	ENS FRED T. WEBER	S
02/24/42	2174	VS-6	USS ENTER-PRISE	WAKE	WCENPAC	ENS PERCY W. FORMAN	M
02/26/42	2140	VB-6	USS ENTER-PRISE	PEARL	ECENPAC	LTJG L.J.M. CHECK	S
03/04/42	2152	VS-6	USS ENTER-PRISE	MARCUS	CENPAC	LTJG HART D. HILTON	M
03/10/42	2130	VS-2	USS LEX-INGTON	SALAMAUA	SW PAC	ENS JOSEPH P. JOHNSON	M
04/01/42	2170	VS-6	KANEOHE	HAWAII	ECENPAC	ENS CARL W. THOMAS	S
04/02/42	2136	VB-6	USS ENTER-PRISE	HAWAII	ECENPAC	ENS S.C. HOGAN	S
04/21/42	2179	VB-8	USS HORNET	PEARL	ECENPAC	LT G.D. RANDALL	D
05/07/42	2132	VB-5	USS YORK-TOWN	MISIMA	SOPAC		
05/08/42	2104	VB 2	USS LEX-INGTON	CORAL SEA	SOPAC	(SHIP SANK)	
05/08/42	2113	VB-2	USS LEX-INGTON	CORAL SEA	SOPAC	(SHIP SANK)	
05/08/42	2115	VB-2	USS LEX-INGTON	CORAL SEA	SOPAC	(SHIP SANK)	
05/08/42	2116	VB-2	USS LEX-INGTON	CORAL SEA	SOPAC	(SHIP SANK)	
05/08/42	2121	VB-2	USS LEX-INGTON	CORAL SEA	SOPAC	(SHIP SANK)	
05/08/42	2127	VB-2	USS LEX-INGTON	CORAL SEA	SOPAC	(SHIP SANK)	
05/08/42	2143	VB-2	USS LEX-INGTON	CORAL SEA	SOPAC	(SHIP SANK)	
05/08/42	2157	VB-2	USS LEX-INGTON	CORAL SEA	SOPAC	(SHIP SANK)	
05/08/42	2163	VB-2	USS LEX-INGTON	CORAL SEA	SOPAC	(SHIP SANK)	
05/08/42	2176	VB-2	USS LEX-INGTON	CORAL SEA	SOPAC	(SHIP SANK)	
05/08/42	2186	VB-2	USS LEX-INGTON	CORAL SEA	SOPAC	(SHIP SANK)	
05/08/42	2188	VB-2	USS LEX-INGTON	CORAL SEA	SOPAC	(SHIP SANK)	
05/29/42		VMSB-241	PEARL	HAWAII	ECENPAC	ENS G.D. MILLIMAN	M

DATE	BUNO	SQDRN	BASE	LOST	AREA	PILOT	FATE
06/04/42	2105	VB-6	USS ENTER-PRISE	MIDWAY	ECENPAC	ENS T.F. SCHNEIDER	M
06/04/42	2123	VB-6	USS ENTER-PRISE	MIDWAY	ECENPAC	ENS E.A. GREENE	M
06/04/42	2125	VB-6	USS ENTER-PRISE	MIDWAY	ECENPAC	ENS W.F. VANDIVIER	M
06/04/42	2145	VB-6	USS ENTER-PRISE	MIDWAY	ECENPAC	ENS B.S. VARIAN	M
06/04/42	2153	VB-6	USS ENTER-PRISE	MIDWAY	ECENPAC	ENS D.W. HALSEY	M
06/04/42	2180	VB-6	USS ENTER-PRISE	MIDWAY	ECENPAC	LTJG J.J. VAN BUREN	M
06/04/42	2103	VMSB-241		MIDWAY	ECENPAC	2NDLT ALBERT TWEEDY	M
06/04/42	2119	VMSB-241		MIDWAY	ECENPAC	2NDLT T.J. GRATZEK	M
06/04/42	2122	VMSB-241		MIDWAY	ECENPAC	2NDLT M.A. WARD	M
06/04/42	2129	VMSB-241		MIDWAY	ECENPAC	MAJ LOFTON R. HENDERSON	M
06/04/42	2139	VMSB-241		MIDWAY	ECENPAC	2NDLT BRUNO HAGEDORN	M
06/04/42	2148	VMSB-241		MIDWAY	ECENPAC	2NDLT H.G. SCHLENDERING	S
06/04/42	2169	VMSB-241		MIDWAY	ECENPAC	CAPT RICHARD BLAIN	S
06/04/42	2184	VMSB-241		MIDWAY	ECENPAC	2NDLT BRUCE HEK	M
06/25/42	2173	VB-8	USS HORNET	MIDWAY	ECENPAC		
07/23/42	2126	VMSB-234	PEARL	HAWAII	ECENPAC		
10/02/42		VS-71		SANTA ISABEL	SOPAC	LTJG PERRITTE	M
10/02/42	2167	VS-71		SAN CRISTOBAL	SOPAC	ENS GARRETT	D
10/12/42	2141	VMSB-233	PEARL	HAWAII	ECENPAC	LT PAUL PETRUCKA	D

DOUGLAS SBD-3

The Douglas SBD-3 variant provided increased protection, self-sealing fuel tanks, and four machine guns. There were 584 built. Aircraft lost:

DATE	BUNO	SQDRN	BASE	LOST	AREA	PILOT	FATE
00/00/00		VS-54	GUADAL-CANAL	GUADAL-CANAL	SOPAC	LTJG A. HAUSER	U
12/07/41	4639	VS-2	USS LEX-INGTON	PEARL	ECENPAC		
12/07/41	4570	VS-6	USS ENTER-PRISE	PEARL	ECENPAC		
12/07/41	4572	VS-6	USS ENTER-PRISE	PEARL	ECENPAC		
12/11/41	4613	VB-3	PEARL	HAWAII	ECENPAC		
12/24/41	4591	VS-3	PEARL	HAWAII	ECENPAC		
01/24/42	4577	VB-3	PEARL	HAWAII	ECENPAC		
01/24/42	4578	VB-3	PEARL	HAWAII	ECENPAC		
02/01/42	4522	VB-6	USS ENTER-PRISE	TAROA	CENPAC		
02/01/42	4562	VS-5	USS YORK-TOWN	JALUIT	CENPAC	LTJG G.L. BELLINGER	M
02/01/42	4567	VS-5	USS YORK-TOWN	JALUIT	CENPAC		
02/01/42	4626	VS-5	USS YORK-TOWN	MAKIN	CENPAC	LTJG M.P. FISHEL	S
02/01/42	4645	VS-6	USS ENTER-PRISE	ROI	WCENPAC		

DATE	BUNO	SQDRN	BASE	LOST	AREA	PILOT	FATE
02/01/42	4676	VS-6	USS ENTER-PRISE	ROI	WCENPAC		
02/09/42	4674	VB-6	USS ENTER-PRISE	PEARL	ECENPAC		
02/19/42	4528	VB-3	USS LEX-INGTON	PEARL	ECENPAC		
02/24/42	4668	VB-5	USS YORK-TOWN	WAKE	WCENPAC	LT ELBERT M. STEVER	S
02/24/42	4524	VS-6	USS ENTER-PRISE	WAKE	WCENPAC	TOAFF	S
03/02/42	4583	VS-6	USS ENTER-PRISE	MARCUS	CENPAC		
03/07/42	4654	VS-6	USS ENTER-PRISE	WAKE	WCENPAC		
03/22/42	4582	VS-3	USS ENTER-PRISE	WAKE	WCENPAC		
04/07/42	4598	VB-6	USS ENTER-PRISE	HAWAII	ECENPAC	ENS A.L. RAUSCH	S
04/09/42	4670	VB-5	USS YORK-TOWN	HAWAII	ECENPAC	ENS HENRY C. TRAVERS	S
04/18/42	4603	VB-6	USS ENTER-PRISE	HAWAII	ECENPAC	ENS LISTON R. COMER	S
04/20/42	4590	VB-6	USS ENTER-PRISE	HAWAII	ECENPAC	LT L.S. SMITH	U
04/25/42	4585	VS-6	KANEOHE	HAWAII	ECENPAC		
04/27/42	4574	VB-5	USS YORK-TOWN	HAWAII	ECENPAC	LTJG ARTHUR L. DOWNING	S
05/07/42	4523	VS-2	USS LEX-INGTON	MISIMA	SOPAC	LT EDWARD ALLEN	M
05/07/42	4531	VS-2	USS LEX-INGTON	MISIMA	SOPAC	LTJG ANTHONY J. QUIGLEY	S
05/08/42	4655	VB-2	USS LEX-INGTON	CORAL SEA	SOPAC	(SHIP SANK)	
05/08/42		VB-5	USS YORK-TOWN	CORAL SEA	SOPAC	LTJG FLOYD E. MOAN	S
05/08/42	4597	VB-5	USS YORK-TOWN	CORAL SEA	SOPAC	LT JOHN J. POWERS	D
05/08/42	4685	VB-5	USS YORK-TOWN	CORAL SEA	SOPAC		
05/08/42	4691	VB-5	USS YORK-TOWN	CORAL SEA	SOPAC		
05/08/42	4534	VS-2	USS LEX-INGTON	CORAL SEA	SOPAC	(SHIP SANK)	
05/08/42	4537	VS-2	USS LEX-INGTON	CORAL SEA	SOPAC	(SHIP SANK)	
05/08/42	4557	VS-2	USS LEX-INGTON	CORAL SEA	SOPAC	LTJG R.O. HALE	M
05/08/42	4623	VS-2	USS LEX-INGTON	CORAL SEA	SOPAC	ENS WINGFIELD	M
05/08/42	4631	VS-2	USS LEX-INGTON	CORAL SEA	SOPAC	ENS H. WOOD	M
05/08/42	4632	VS-2	USS LEX-INGTON	CORAL SEA	SOPAC	CDR AULT	M
05/08/42	4633	VS-2	USS LEX-INGTON	CORAL SEA	SOPAC	LTJG FRANK R. MCDONALD	S
05/08/42	4638	VS-2	USS LEX-INGTON	CORAL SEA	SOPAC	(SHIP SANK)	
05/08/42	4641	VS-2	USS LEX-INGTON	CORAL SEA	SOPAC	(SHIP SANK)	
05/08/42	4533	VS-5	USS YORK-TOWN	CORAL SEA	SOPAC		
05/08/42	4539	VS-5	USS YORK-TOWN	CORAL SEA	SOPAC		
05/08/42	4630	VS-5	USS YORK-TOWN	CORAL SEA	SOPAC		

DATE	BUNO	SQDRN	BASE	LOST	AREA	PILOT	FATE
05/08/42	4651	VS-5	USS YORK-TOWN	CORAL SEA	SOPAC		
05/08/42	4686	VS-5	USS YORK-TOWN	CORAL SEA	SOPAC		
05/09/42	4635	VB-5	USS YORK-TOWN	CORAL SEA	SOPAC		
05/15/42	4536	VB-3	BARBERS POINT	HAWAII	ECENPAC	ENS WALTER E. AUSTIN	S
05/15/42	3205	VS-6	USS ENTER-PRISE	ENR CORAL SEA	ECENPAC	LTJG KLINE	S
05/17/42	4595	VS-6	USS ENTER-PRISE	ENR CORAL SEA	ECENPAC	ENS WILLIAM R. PITTMAN	S
05/18/42	4527	VB-8	USS HORNET	PEARL	ECENPAC		
05/21/42	3194	VB-8	USS HORNET	PEARL	ECENPAC	ENS R.P. GEE	S
05/21/42	4646	VS-6	USS ENTER-PRISE	ENR CORAL SEA	ECENPAC	ENS L.J. MUERY	S
05/29/42		VB-5	HAWAII	HAWAII	ECENPAC		
05/29/42	3187	VS-8	USS HORNET	NW OF WAKE	ECENPAC		
05/31/42		VMSB-241	PEARL	HAWAII	ECENPAC		
06/04/42	4518	VB-3	USS YORK-TOWN	MIDWAY	ECENPAC	LCDR M.F. LESLIE	S
06/04/42	4530	VB-3	USS YORK-TOWN	MIDWAY	ECENPAC	LT P.A. HOLMBERG	S
06/04/42	4538	VB-3	USS YORK-TOWN	MIDWAY	ECENPAC	ENS J.C. BUTLER	M
06/04/42	4551	VB-3	USS YORK-TOWN	MIDWAY	ECENPAC	LT O.B. WISEMAN	M
06/04/42	4663	VB-3	USS ENTER-PRISE	MIDWAY	ECENPAC		
06/04/42	3237	VB-3	USS ENTER-PRISE	MIDWAY	ECENPAC		
06/04/42	3248	VB-3	USS ENTER-PRISE	MIDWAY	ECENPAC		
06/04/42	4532	VB-6	USS ENTER-PRISE	MIDWAY	ECENPAC		
06/04/42	4542	VB-6	USS ENTER-PRISE	MIDWAY	ECENPAC	ENS G.H. GOLDSMITH	M
06/04/42	4581	VB-6	USS ENTER-PRISE	MIDWAY	ECENPAC	LTJG W.E. ROBERTS	M
06/04/42	4620	VB-6	USS ENTER-PRISE	MIDWAY	ECENPAC	ENS T.W. RAMSEY	M
06/04/42	4682	VB-6	USS ENTER-PRISE	MIDWAY	ECENPAC	ENS FRED T. WEBER	M
06/04/42	4576	VB-8	USS HORNET	MIDWAY	ECENPAC	ENS T.J. WOOD	S
06/04/42	4611	VB-8	USS HORNET	MIDWAY	ECENPAC	ENS T.J. AUMAN	S
06/04/42	4636	VB-8	USS HORNET	MIDWAY	ECENPAC	ENS T.T. GUILLORY	S
06/04/42	4559	VS-5	USS YORK-TOWN	MIDWAY	ECENPAC	(SHIP SANK)	
06/04/42	4588	VS-5	USS YORK-TOWN	MIDWAY	ECENPAC	(SHIP SANK)	
06/04/42	4622	VS-5	USS YORK-TOWN	MIDWAY	ECENPAC	(SHIP SANK)	
06/04/42		VS-6	USS ENTER-PRISE	MIDWAY	ECENPAC		
06/04/42	4526	VS-6	USS ENTER-PRISE	MIDWAY	ECENPAC		

DATE	BUNO	SQDRN	BASE	LOST	AREA	PILOT	FATE
06/04/42	4600	VS-6	USS ENTER-PRISE	MIDWAY	ECENPAC	ENS C.D. PFEIFFER	M
06/04/42	4612	VS-6	USS ENTER-PRISE	MIDWAY	ECENPAC	ENS J.C. LOUGH	M
06/04/42	4615	VS-6	USS ENTER-PRISE	MIDWAY	ECENPAC	ENS J.R. MCCARTHY	M
06/04/42	3206	VS-6	USS ENTER-PRISE	MIDWAY	ECENPAC	LT C.R. WARE	M
06/04/42	3207	VS-6	USS ENTER-PRISE	MIDWAY	ECENPAC	ENS J.M. VAMMEN	M
06/04/42	3208	VS-6	USS ENTER-PRISE	MIDWAY	ECENPAC		
06/04/42	3224	VS-6	USS ENTER-PRISE	MIDWAY	ECENPAC	ENS F.H. O'FLAHERTY	M
06/04/42	3225	VS-6	USS ENTER-PRISE	MIDWAY	ECENPAC	ENS F.A. SHELTON	M
06/04/42	3376	VS-6	USS ENTER-PRISE	MIDWAY	ECENPAC	ENS J.W. ROBERTS	M
06/05/42	4604	VB-8	USS HORNET	MIDWAY	ECENPAC		
06/05/42	4634	VS-5	USS YORK-TOWN	MIDWAY	ECENPAC	(SHIP SANK)	
06/06/42	4662	VB-8	USS HORNET	MIDWAY	ECENPAC		
06/06/42	4677	VS-8	USS HORNET	MIDWAY	ECENPAC	ENS DONALD T. GRISWOLD	U
06/07/42	3283	VS-3	(DET 14)	HAWAII	ECENPAC	ENS MANLEY	S
06/08/42	4664	VB-8	USS HORNET	MIDWAY	ECENPAC	ENS ROBERT D. MILLIMAN	U
06/08/42	3193	VB-8	USS HORNET	MIDWAY	ECENPAC	ENS NICKERSON	S
06/14/42	4683	VB-3				ENS O.H. SCHNEIDER	D
06/16/42	4690	VB-3				ENS COONER	D
06/17/42	4649	VP-101		AUSTRALIA	SW PAC	LTJG LEROY C. DEED	D
06/18/42	3299	COMPON					
07/10/42	4624	VS-2			ECENPAC		
07/19/42	4571	VB-8	USS HORNET	ENR HAWAII	ECENPAC	ENS GUS G. BEBAS	M
07/21/42	4616	VB-6	USS ENTER-PRISE	ENR SAN. CRUZ	ECENPAC		
08/04/42	4580	VB-3	USS SARATOGA	ENR GUADAL.	SOPAC	ENS J.A. RUTLEDGE	S
08/05/42	3230	VS-72	USS HORNET		SOPAC	ENS HELMUTH F. HOERNER	S
08/06/42	3317	VS-2	USS SARATOGA	GUADAL-CANAL	SOPAC	ENS W.R. BELL	M
08/07/42	3320	VS-71	USS WASP	TULAGI	SOPAC	LT DUDLEY H. ADAMS	S
08/12/42	4548	VS-8		MIDWAY	ECENPAC		
08/19/42	3191	VB-8	USS HORNET	HAWAII	ECENPAC	LCDR A.B. TUCKER	D
08/23/42	3334	VS-72	USS HORNET		SOPAC		
08/24/42		VB-6	USS ENTER-PRISE	E. SOLOMONS	SOPAC		
08/24/42	3229	VMSB-232		GUADAL-CANAL	SOPAC		
08/24/42	3290	VS-5	USS ENTER-PRISE	E. SOLOMONS	SOPAC	ENS R.D. GIBSON	S
08/24/42	3309	VS-5	USS ENTER-PRISE	E. SOLOMONS	SOPAC	ENS J.R. JORGENSON	S
08/24/42	3374	VS-71	USS WASP	E. SOLOMONS	SOPAC	LTJG HOWARD	S

DATE	BUNO	SQDRN	BASE	LOST	AREA	PILOT	FATE
08/31/42	3336	VS-71	USS WASP	RAMOS ISLAND	SOPAC	MITCHELL	U
09/02/42	4584	VS-3	USS SARATOGA	ESPIRITU SANTO	SOPAC	ENS DAVIDSON	S
09/06/42	3342	VMSB-232		GUADAL-CANAL	SOPAC	LT MCALLISTER	U
09/06/42	3356	VMSB-232		GUADAL-CANAL	SOPAC	MAJ F.L. BROWN	U
09/07/42	4658	VMSB-241			SOPAC	CAPT ACERS	S
09/13/42	4608	VS-3	USS SARATOGA	ESPIRITU SANTO	SOPAC	ENS WAGER	M
09/14/42	4667	VMSB-232		GUADAL-CANAL	SOPAC	LT KAUFMAN	D
09/15/42	3351	VS-71	USS WASP	SAN CRISTOBAL	SOPAC	ENS ROBERT A. ESCHER	S
09/15/42	3330	VS-72	USS WASP	SAN CRISTOBAL	SOPAC	(SHIP SANK)	
09/15/42	3337	VS-72	USS WASP	SAN CRISTOBAL	SOPAC	(SHIP SANK)	
09/15/42	3362	VS-72	USS WASP	SAN CRISTOBAL	SOPAC	(SHIP SANK)	
09/16/42	3243	VS-3	USS SARATOGA	ESPIRITU SANTO	SOPAC	ENS C. NEWTON	U
09/17/42	4669	VMSB-231			SOPAC	LT A. SMITH	M
09/17/42	4629	VS-72	USS HORNET		SOPAC		
09/18/42	3347	VMSB-232		GUADAL-CANAL	SOPAC	LT THOMAS	M
09/20/42	3293	VMSB-231			SOPAC	CAPT IDEN	D
09/20/42	3294	VMSB-231			SOPAC	LT ZUBER	S
09/23/42	3312	VMSB-241			SOPAC		
09/27/42	6641	VS-41	USS RANGER	OFF NORFOLK	CENLANT	ENS GEORGE F. DALTON	U
09/28/42		VMSB-231				LT LESLIE	M
09/28/42	3348	VMSB-232		GUADAL-CANAL	SOPAC		
09/29/42	6560	VGS-29	USS SANTEE	OFF BERMUDA	NORLANT		
09/29/42	6535	VMSB-241	USS COPAHEE	NEW CALEDONIA	SOPAC	2NDLT G.H. ELLIOTT	D
09/30/42	4673	VMSB-232		GUADAL-CANAL	SOPAC		
10/01/42	4544	VB-10	HILO	HAWAII	ECENPAC		
10/02/42	3311	VMSB-141		ROSES	SOPAC	LT AYRES	M
10/03/42	6507	VMSB-141		NOUMEA	SOPAC	LT H.O. HULL	S
10/05/42	3319	VS-71		NEKATA BAY	SOPAC	LCDR ELDRIDGE	S
10/08/42	3255	VMSB-141		GUADAL-CANAL	SOPAC	LT L.R. NORMAN	M
10/09/42	3257	VMSB-141		NOUMEA	SOPAC	S/SGT J.D. COOK	M
10/09/42	3263	VMSB-141		NOUMEA	SOPAC	FROMHOLD	D
10/10/42	6511	VMSB-141		NOUMEA	SOPAC	LT L.C. SMITH	S
10/13/42	6552	VGS-26	USS SAN-GAMON	OFF BERMUDA	NORLANT		
10/14/42	3349	VMSB-232		GUADAL-CANAL	SOPAC		
10/14/42	3352	VMSB-232		GUADAL-CANAL	SOPAC		
10/14/42	3379	VMSB-232		GUADAL-CANAL	SOPAC		
10/14/42	3381	VMSB-232		GUADAL-CANAL	SOPAC		
10/14/42	3384	VMSB-232		GUADAL-CANAL	SOPAC		
10/14/42	3215	VS-71		GUADAL-CANAL	SOPAC		
10/14/42	3339	VS-71		GUADAL-CANAL	SOPAC		
10/14/42	6514	VS-71		GUADAL-CANAL	SOPAC		
10/14/42	6532	VS-71		GUADAL-CANAL	SOPAC		
10/14/42	3222	VS-72		GUADAL-CANAL	SOPAC		
10/14/42	3345	VS-72		GUADAL-CANAL	SOPAC		

DATE	BUNO	SQDRN	BASE	LOST	AREA	PILOT	FATE
10/14/42	3363	VS-72		GUADAL-CANAL	SOPAC		
10/14/42	3366	VS-72		GUADAL-CANAL	SOPAC		
10/15/42	3315	VS-71		GUADAL-CANAL	SOPAC		
10/15/42	3322	VS-71		GUADAL-CANAL	SOPAC		
10/15/42	3324	VS-71		GUADAL-CANAL	SOPAC		
10/16/42	3284						
10/16/42	3254	VMSB-141		GUADAL-CANAL	SOPAC	LT WATERMAN	D
10/16/42	3265	VMSB-141		GUADAL-CANAL	SOPAC	SGT KOMSACK	U
10/16/42	6510	VMSB-141		GUADAL-CANAL	SOPAC	2NDLT TURTORA	D
10/16/42		VMSB-231			SOPAC		
10/16/42		VMSB-231			SOPAC		
10/16/42	3295	VMSB-231			SOPAC		
10/16/42	3332	VMSB-231			SOPAC		
10/16/42	3340	VMSB-231			SOPAC		
10/16/42	3346	VMSB-231			SOPAC		
10/16/42	3355	VMSB-231			SOPAC		
10/16/42	4642	VS-3		GUADAL-CANAL	SOPAC		
10/16/42	3216	VS-3		GUADAL-CANAL	SOPAC		
10/16/42	3218	VS-3		GUADAL-CANAL	SOPAC		
10/16/42	3231	VS-3		GUADAL-CANAL	SOPAC		
10/16/42	3242	VS-3		GUADAL-CANAL	SOPAC		
10/16/42	3247	VS-3		GUADAL-CANAL	SOPAC		
10/16/42	3274	VS-8		GUADAL-CANAL	SOPAC	LTJG CHRISTOPFERSEN	U
10/17/42	3310	VMSB-141		GUADAL-CANAL	SOPAC	2NDLT GILLESPIE	D
10/17/42	3361	VS-71		SAN ISABEL	SOPAC	LT MASTER	S
10/18/42	3217	VS-3		GUADAL-CANAL	SOPAC		
10/18/42	3221	VS-3		GUADAL-CANAL	SOPAC		
10/18/42	3246	VS-3		GUADAL-CANAL	SOPAC		
10/18/42	3302	VS-3		GUADAL-CANAL	SOPAC		
10/21/42	4545	VB-10	USS ENTER-PRISE	ENR GUADAL.	SOPAC	LT R.F. MILLS	M
10/21/42	6555	VGS-29	USS SANTEE	OFF BERMUDA	NORLANT	ENS JOHN H. BALLENTINE	U
10/22/42	6582	VMSB-141		GUADAL-CANAL	SOPAC	SGT ENIFFELL	D
10/23/42	3304	VS-3		GUADAL-CANAL	SOPAC		
10/25/42	4586	VB-6	USS ENTER-PRISE	SANTA CRUZ	SOPAC		
10/25/42	4602	VB-6	USS ENTER-PRISE	SANTA CRUZ	SOPAC		
10/25/42	3209	VB-6	USS ENTER-PRISE	SANTA CRUZ	SOPAC		
10/26/42	3325	VB-8	USS HORNET	SANTA CRUZ	SOPAC	LTJG PHILIP F. GRANT	U
10/26/42	6530	VMSB-141		GUADAL-CANAL	SOPAC	LT BAUMET	D
10/26/42	4656	VS-8	USS HORNET	SANTA CRUZ	SOPAC	LCDR WILLIAM J. WIDHELM	S
10/27/42	4625	VB-8	USS HORNET	SANTA CRUZ	SOPAC	(SHIP SANK)	

DATE	BUNO	SQDRN	BASE	LOST	AREA	PILOT	FATE
10/27/42	3186	VS-8	USS HORNET	SANTA CRUZ	SOPAC	(SHIP SANK)	
10/27/42	3189	VS-8	USS HORNET	SANTA CRUZ	SOPAC	(SHIP SANK)	
10/27/42	3190	VS-8	USS HORNET	SANTA CRUZ	SOPAC	(SHIP SANK)	
10/27/42	3196	VS-8	USS HORNET	SANTA CRUZ	SOPAC	(SHIP SANK)	
10/27/42	3199	VS-8	USS HORNET	SANTA CRUZ	SOPAC	(SHIP SANK)	
10/27/42	3200	VS-8	USS HORNET	SANTA CRUZ	SOPAC	(SHIP SANK)	
10/27/42	3203	VS-8	USS HORNET	SANTA CRUZ	SOPAC	(SHIP SANK)	
10/31/42	3270	VMSB-141		GUADAL-CANAL	SOPAC	LT MEENTS	D
11/02/42	3210	VMSB-132		GUADAL-CANAL	SOPAC	LT NEWMAN	M
11/02/42	6523	VMSB-132		GUADAL-CANAL	SOPAC	LT GENTRY	M
11/02/42	3329	VS-71		GUADAL-CANAL	SOPAC	LCDR ELDRIDGE	D
11/02/42	3335	VS-71		GUADAL-CANAL	SOPAC	LTJG LERMAN	M
11/02/42	3367	VS-71		GUADAL-CANAL	SOPAC		
11/02/42	6590	VS-71		GUADAL-CANAL	SOPAC		
11/07/42	3273	VMSB-141		NOUMEA	SOPAC	LT SULLIVAN	M
11/08/42	6546	VGS-26	USS SAN-GAMON	PORT LYAUTEY	MOROCC O		
11/08/42	6678	VMSB-141		NOUMEA	SOPAC	1STLT ASHCRAFT	D
11/08/42	6619	VS-41	USS RANGER	FEDALA	NW AFR	LCDR CARVER	S
11/08/42	6627	VS-41	USS RANGER	FEDALA	NW AFR	ENS DUFFY	M
11/10/42	6557	VGS-29	USS SANTEE	SAFI	NW AFR	ENS E.M. TOWER, JR.	S
11/10/42	3280	VMSB-141			SOPAC	LT HAHN	S
11/11/42	6592		USS NASSAU	GUADAL-CANAL	SOPAC		
11/13/42	6571	VMSB-141			SOPAC	LT KNAPP	U
11/13/42	6572	VMSB-141			SOPAC	LT SANDRETTO	U
11/14/42	6528			GUADAL-CANAL	SOPAC		
11/14/42	6680			GUADAL-CANAL	SOPAC		
11/14/42	6693			GUADAL-CANAL	SOPAC		
11/14/42	6595	VB-10	USS ENTER-PRISE	GUADAL-CANAL	SOPAC	ENS P.M. HALLORAN	M
11/14/42	6643	VB-10	USS ENTER-PRISE	GUADAL-CANAL	SOPAC	LT V.W. WELCH	M
11/14/42	6644	VB-10	USS ENTER-PRISE	GUADAL-CANAL	SOPAC	LT T.D. WAKEHAM	U
11/14/42	6645	VB-10	USS ENTER-PRISE	GUADAL-CANAL	SOPAC	ENS J.H. CARROUM	S
11/14/42	4610	VS-10	USS ENTER-PRISE	GUADAL-CANAL	SOPAC		
11/14/42	6653	VS-10	USS ENTER-PRISE	GUADAL-CANAL	SOPAC	LTJG W.E. JOHNSON	M
11/15/42	6504	VB-10	USS ENTER-PRISE	GUADAL-CANAL	SOPAC		
11/15/42	6593	VB-10	USS ENTER-PRISE	GUADAL-CANAL	SOPAC		
11/15/42	3338	VMO-251			SOPAC		

DATE	BUNO	SQDRN	BASE	LOST	AREA	PILOT	FATE
11/15/42	3188	VS-10		GUADAL-CANAL	SOPAC		
11/15/42	3220	VS-10		GUADAL-CANAL	SOPAC		
11/15/42	3253	VS-10		GUADAL-CANAL	SOPAC		
11/15/42	6492	VS-10		GUADAL-CANAL	SOPAC		
11/15/42	6494	VS-10		GUADAL-CANAL	SOPAC		
11/19/42	3197	VMSB-241	HAWAII		ECENPAC	2NDLT M.A. VESTAL	S
11/19/42	3318	VMSB-241	HAWAII		ECENPAC	2NDLT R.E. GORTON	S
11/23/42	6620	VS-41	USS RANGER	OFF NORFOLK	CENLANT		
12/01/42	6662	VMSB-132		GUADAL-CANAL	SOPAC	CAPT SPANG	D
12/07/42	6689	VMSB-142		GUADAL-CANAL	SOPAC	MAJ SAILER	D
12/08/42	6646	VB-10	USS ENTER-PRISE	GUADAL-CANAL	SOPAC		
12/08/42	6635	VGS-29	USS SANTEE	HAMPTON VA	SOLANT		
12/08/42	6695	VMO-251		GUADAL-CANAL	SOPAC	LT GEORGE S. KOHLER	D
12/11/42	3344	VMSB-132		GUADAL-CANAL	SOPAC	LT ROHRL	D
12/14/42	4592	VMSB-142		GUADAL-CANAL	SOPAC	LT KELLOGG	S
12/16/42	3258	VMSB-132		GUADAL-CANAL	SOPAC	LT F.L. CHRISTEN	M
12/16/42	6667	VMSB-142		GUADAL-CANAL	SOPAC	CAPT CARNEY, USN	D
12/19/42	3378	VS-8			ECENPAC		
12/21/42	4552	VB-3	USS SARATOGA	NOUMEA	SOPAC		
12/21/42	6661	VMO-251		ESPIRITU SANTO	SOPAC	LT ROY L. BOOTH	S
12/29/42	4640			EFATE	SOPAC		
12/29/42	3292			EFATE	SOPAC		
12/29/42	4520	VB-10	USS ENTER-PRISE	GUADAL-CANAL	SOPAC		
12/29/42	6594	VB-10	USS ENTER-PRISE	GUADAL-CANAL	SOPAC		
12/29/42	6603	VB-3	USS SARATOGA	EFATE	SOPAC		
12/29/42	3192	VB-8		EFATE	SOPAC		
12/29/42	3275	VB 8		EFATE	SOPAC		
12/29/42	3314	VB-8		EFATE	SOPAC		
12/29/42	3380	VMSB-231			SOPAC		
12/29/42	6495	VS-10		GUADAL-CANAL	SOPAC		
12/29/42	6497	VS-10		GUADAL-CANAL	SOPAC		
12/29/42	6500	VS-10		GUADAL-CANAL	SOPAC		
12/29/42	6501	VS-10		GUADAL-CANAL	SOPAC		
12/29/42	6596	VS-10		GUADAL-CANAL	SOPAC		
12/29/42	3327	VS-72		EFATE	SOPAC		
12/29/42	3341	VS-72		EFATE	SOPAC		
12/29/42	3365	VS-72		EFATE	SOPAC		
12/31/42	3286			EFATE	SOPAC		
12/31/42	4565	VB-8		EFATE	SOPAC		
12/31/42	4579	VB-8		EFATE	SOPAC		
12/31/42	6570	VMSB-141			SOPAC		
12/31/42	6573	VMSB-141			SOPAC		
12/31/42	6574	VMSB-141			SOPAC		
12/31/42	3360	VMSB-231		EFATE	SOPAC		
12/31/42	3285	VS-3		GUADAL-CANAL	SOPAC		
12/31/42	4563	VS-72		EFATE	SOPAC		

DATE	BUNO	SQDRN	BASE	LOST	AREA	PILOT	FATE
12/31/42	4547	VS-8			SOPAC		
12/31/42	4568	VS-8			SOPAC		
12/31/42	4593	VS-8			SOPAC		
12/31/42	3223	VS-8			SOPAC		
12/31/42	3277	VS-8			SOPAC		
01/01/43	3261	VMSB-132		GUADAL-CANAL	SOPAC	LT W.E. ECK	U
01/09/43	6568	VGS-28	USS CHE-NANGO	ENR NOUMEA	SOPAC	ENS HOGAN	S
01/10/43	3213	VB-3	USS SARATOGA	NOUMEA	SOPAC	LTJG R.K. CAMPBELL	S
01/15/43	3198	VMSB-142		GUADAL-CANAL	SOPAC	LT WIGGINS	S
01/21/43	6567	VC-29	USS SANTEE	ENR RECIFE	SOLANT		
01/23/43	3251	VMSB-132		GUADAL-CANAL	SOPAC		
01/23/43	3382	VMSB-132		GUADAL-CANAL	SOPAC		
01/23/43	6506	VMSB-132		GUADAL-CANAL	SOPAC		
01/23/43	6647	VMSB-132		GUADAL-CANAL	SOPAC		
01/23/43	6675	VMSB-132		GUADAL-CANAL	SOPAC		
01/23/43	3343	VMSB-233			SOPAC	T/SGT RALPH P. ACKERMAN	D
01/23/43	3308	VMSB-241		MIDWAY	ECENPAC		
01/31/43	4607	MAG-14	GUADAL-CANAL	GUADAL-CANAL	SOPAC		
02/01/43	6650	VMSB-234		GUADAL-CANAL	SOPAC	LT WILLIAMS	M
02/08/43	3250	VMSB-132		GUADAL-CANAL	SOPAC		
02/23/43	3235	VMSB-132		GUADAL-CANAL	SOPAC		
02/23/43	3271	VMSB-132		GUADAL-CANAL	SOPAC		
02/23/43	3288	VMSB-132		GUADAL-CANAL	SOPAC		
02/23/43	3296	VMSB-132		GUADAL-CANAL	SOPAC		
02/23/43	3297	VMSB-132		GUADAL-CANAL	SOPAC		
02/23/43	3306	VMSB-132		GUADAL-CANAL	SOPAC		
02/23/43	6674	VMSB-132		GUADAL-CANAL	SOPAC		
02/23/43	6687	VMSB-132		GUADAL-CANAL	SOPAC		
02/25/43	6610	VB-11	HILO	HAWAII	ECENPAC		
02/25/43	6679	VGS-28	USS CHE-NANGO	SOLOMONS	SOPAC		
02/25/43	4687	VMSB-132		GUADAL-CANAL	SOPAC		
02/25/43	6516	VMSB-132		GUADAL-CANAL	SOPAC		
03/02/43	6550	VC-26			SOPAC		
03/10/43	6692	VB-3	USS SARATOGA	NOUMEA	SOPAC		
03/15/43	4599	VMJ-252	PEARL	HAWAII	ECENPAC	LT E. JIEDE	U
03/19/43	3249	VB-20			SOPAC		
03/21/43	6499	VB-20			SOPAC		
03/25/43	6589	VB-11		GUADAL-CANAL	SOPAC		
04/03/43	3303	VMSB-244		SAND IS.	SOPAC	CAPT EDWARD HARPER	M
04/08/43	6700	VS-28			SOPAC		
04/15/43	3233	VMSB-233			SOPAC	LT WHITE	M
04/22/43	3298	VMSB-244			WCENPAC		
04/23/43	3256	VB-8		EFATE	SOPAC		
04/23/43	6631	VC-26	USS SAN-GAMON	SOLOMONS	SOPAC		
04/26/43	3241	VB-10	USS ENTER-PRISE	SOLOMONS	SOPAC		

DATE	BUNO	SQDRN	BASE	LOST	AREA	PILOT	FATE
05/02/43	6584	VB-10	USS ENTER-PRISE	SOLOMONS	SOPAC		
05/14/43	3238	VMSB-244			WCENPAC	LT GIRARD	S
05/14/43	3301	VMSB-244			WCENPAC		
05/15/43	4596	VMSB-244		MIDWAY	ECENPAC		
06/05/43	6520	VB-21		SHORT-LANDS	SOPAC	LARSON	U
06/22/43	10641	VC-23	USS PRINCE-TON	CARIBBEAN	CENLANT		
06/28/43	6566	VC-26	USS SAN-GAMON	SOLOMONS	SOPAC		
06/30/43	6538	VB-11		GUADAL-CANAL	SOPAC		
06/30/43	6599	VB-11		GUADAL-CANAL	SOPAC		
06/30/43	6512	VB-21			SOPAC		
06/30/43	6540	VB-21			SOPAC		
06/30/43	6579	VB-21			SOPAC		
06/30/43	4550	VMSB-132		GUADAL-CANAL	SOPAC	1STLT G.B. HERLIHY	S
06/30/43	6636	VMSB-132		GUADAL-CANAL	SOPAC	1STLT S.K. OTTERSON	S
07/29/43	3239	VMSB-244		MIDWAY	ECENPAC		
07/29/43	3305	VMSB-244		MIDWAY	ECENPAC	LT WANGER	S
08/01/43	6521	VB-11		GUADAL-CANAL	SOPAC		
08/26/43	6598	VMSB-234		GUADAL-CANAL	SOPAC		
09/15/43	6591	VMSB-236		BAMBAN	SOPAC		
09/18/43	6525	VJ-9			SOPAC		
09/21/43	6605	VMSB-236		BAMBAN	SOPAC	LT CULLER	U
10/23/43		VC-38		SOLOMONS	SOPAC	LTJG J.C. NASON	U
10/23/43		VC-38		SOLOMONS	SOPAC		
11/04/43	6684			SOLOMONS	SOPAC		
01/04/44	6526	VS-70	ADAK	SHEMYAD	NORPAC	LTJG R.E. HYMULLA	M
03/01/44	6518	VS-54	GUADAL-CANAL	GUADAL-CANAL	SOPAC		
04/02/44	6670	VS-54	GUADAL-CANAL	BOUGAIN-VILLE	SOPAC		
05/20/44	3326	POOL	ESPIRITU SANTO		SOPAC		
05/20/44	6602	POOL	ESPIRITU SANTO		SOPAC		
06/15/44	6543	POOL	ESPIRITU SANTO		SOPAC		
07/03/44	3259	ARU SOLS			SOPAC	(SALVAGED)	
07/08/44	4609	POOL	PALLIKULO AIRFIELD		SOPAC		
07/08/44	3266	POOL	PALLIKULO AIRFIELD		SOPAC		
07/15/44	3267	AV-14	USS KEN. WHITING	PEARL	ECENPAC	2NDLT ROBERT E. CURTIS	S
07/31/44	4555	COMAIR-PAC	PEARL	HAWAII	ECENPAC		
08/01/44	6519	VMSB-234			SOPAC		
08/02/44	4573	VJ-10	PALLIKULO AIRFIELD		SOPAC		
08/02/44	3228	VJ-10	PALLIKULO AIRFIELD		SOPAC		
08/02/44	3357	VJ-10	PALLIKULO AIRFIELD		SOPAC		
08/02/44	3377	VJ-10	PALLIKULO AIRFIELD		SOPAC		
08/02/44	6656	VJ-10	PALLIKULO AIRFIELD		SOPAC		
08/31/44	3219						
09/01/44	4569	COMAIR-PAC	PEARL	HAWAII	ECENPAC		
10/20/44	4688	STAG-1	RUSSELLS		SOPAC		
10/20/44	3278	STAG-1	RUSSELLS		SOPAC		
10/20/44	3375	STAG-1	RUSSELLS		SOPAC		
10/20/44	6659	STAG-1	RUSSELLS		SOPAC		
10/20/44	6669	STAG-1	RUSSELLS		SOPAC		

DATE	BUNO	SQDRN	BASE	LOST	AREA	PILOT	FATE
10/20/44	6698	STAG-1	RUSSELLS		SOPAC		
10/26/44		VB-18	USS INTREPID	ENR LUZON	PHIL		
11/14/44	3282	AWT ACTION	GUADAL-CANAL		SOPAC		
11/30/44	6527	AWT ACTION	GUADAL-CANAL		SOPAC		
02/16/45	6537	VJ-3	PUUNENE	HAWAII	ECENPAC		
02/16/45	6588	VJ-3	PUUNENE	HAWAII	ECENPAC		

DOUGLAS SBD-4

The earlier variants of the SBD were only equipped with a 6-volt electrical system. The SBD-4 provided a 12-volt (from 6) electrical system. There were 780 built. Aircraft lost:

DATE	BUNO	SQDRN	BASE	LOST	AREA	PILOT	FATE
09/19/42	10616	VS-5	USS ENTER-PRISE	GUADAL-CANAL	SOPAC	ENS FINK	U
12/17/42	6853	4TH MBDAW	SAMOA		SE PAC	LT FORD	S
12/27/42	6772	4TH MBDAW	SAMOA		SE PAC	LT DEAL	S
12/28/42	6895	4TH MBDAW	SAMOA		SE PAC	LT BASSINGER	S
01/02/43	6892	MAG-13		TUTUILA	SOPAC	2NDLT H.J. TARE EVEWDEN	S
01/02/43	6787	VMSB-233			SOPAC	LT THOMPSON	S
01/08/43	6790	VMSB-233		GUADAL-CANAL	SOPAC	LT AVAET	M
01/10/43	6788	VMSB-234		GUADAL-CANAL	SOPAC	CAPT WHITTEN	S
01/13/43	6786	VMSB-234		GUADAL-CANAL	SOPAC	LT RODGERS	S
01/16/43	6837	MAG-13		TUTUILA	SOPAC	LT JOHN W. HANNA	S
01/20/43	6769	VMSB-142		GUADAL-CANAL	SOPAC	MAJ RICHARD	S
01/21/43	6796	MAG-11	ESPIRITU SANTO		SOPAC	LT WALTER A. ECKMABRES	D
01/22/43	6745	VMSB-142		GUADAL-CANAL	SOPAC	LT BASS	M
01/23/43	6771	MAG-14	GUADAL-CANAL	GUADAL-CANAL	SOPAC	2NDLT WM H HRONEK JR	D
02/01/43	6782	VMSB-234		GUADAL-CANAL	SOPAC	CAPT MOORE	M
02/01/43	6793	VMSB-234		GUADAL-CANAL	SOPAC	LT MOSS	M
02/04/43	6862	VMSB-234		GUADAL-CANAL	SOPAC	LT MURPHY	S
02/04/43	10351	VMSB-234		GUADAL-CANAL	SOPAC	LT RUSSELL	M
02/20/43	6939	VMSB-144		GUADAL-CANAL	SOPAC	2NDLT B.C. YOUNG	D
02/23/43	6743	MAG-14	GUADAL-CANAL	GUADAL-CANAL	SOPAC		
02/25/43	6703	VMSB-144		GUADAL-CANAL	SOPAC		
02/26/43	6874	VS-16			SOLANT		
03/01/43	10319	VMSB-243	JOHNSTON ISLAND	HAWAII	ECENPAC	2NDLT AUG. C BUETENOLD	D
03/05/43	6741	MAG-11	ESPIRITU SANTO		SOPAC		
03/12/43	10390	MAG-11	ESPIRITU SANTO		SOPAC		
03/15/43	6768	MAG-11	ESPIRITU SANTO		SOPAC		
03/29/43	10403	VMSB-243	JOHNSTON ISLAND	HAWAII	ECENPAC	LT GEORGE W. JOHNSON	D
04/03/43	10679	VMSB-233			SOPAC	LT O'SULLIVAN	D
04/05/43	6914	VB-12			WCENPAC		

DATE	BUNO	SQDRN	BASE	LOST	AREA	PILOT	FATE
04/06/43	6704	VMSB-142		GUADAL-CANAL	SOPAC		
04/06/43	6736	VMSB-142		GUADAL-CANAL	SOPAC		
04/06/43	6751	VMSB-144		GUADAL-CANAL	SOPAC	2NDLT JOHN H. FOULD	D
04/06/43	10402	VMSB-233			SOPAC	LT WHITE	S
04/06/43	10660	VMSB-233			SOPAC	2NDLT W.F. HACKNER	S
04/07/43	6926	VMSB-142		GUADAL-CANAL	SOPAC	LT WEBER	D
04/07/43	6754	VMSB-233			SOPAC	LT WEBER	D
04/15/43	6971	VB-10	USS ENTER-PRISE	SOLOMONS	SOPAC		
04/17/43	6857	VB-41	USS RANGER		NORLANT		
04/21/43	10537	VMSB-142		GUADAL-CANAL	SOPAC	LT FINCH	S
04/30/43	6775	VB-13	PUUNENE	HAWAII	ECENPAC		
04/30/43	10333	VB-20			SOPAC		
05/02/43	6839	VMSB-151	USS ENTER-PRISE	SOLOMONS	SOPAC		
05/07/43	6812	VB-42	USS RANGER		NORLANT		
05/08/43	6964	VB-11		GUADAL-CANAL	SOPAC		
05/14/43	6843	VB-12			WCENPAC		
05/15/43	6934	MAG-22	PEARL	HAWAII	ECENPAC	LT JAMES E. DAVIS	M
05/15/43	10462	VB-9	USS ESSEX	HAWAII	ECENPAC		
05/19/43	10618	VMSB-241		FUNAFUTI	CENPAC	CUFFORD R. PERKINS	D
05/25/43	6856	VMSB-144		EFATE	SOPAC	1STLT S.V. TAYLOR	D
05/25/43	10535	VMSB-144		EFATE	SOPAC	1STLT GEORGE W. JUFFMAN	D
05/26/43	10626	VF-28	USS CHE-NANGO	SOLOMONS	SOPAC		
05/26/43	10585	VMSB-151			SOPAC	LT DEXTER	D
05/26/43	10644	VMSB-151			SOPAC	CAPT SUHLETTE	S
05/28/43	10354	VMSB-144		EFATE	SOPAC	1STLT A.L. SCOGGINS	D
06/02/43	6962	VMSB-132		NEW HEBRIDES	SOPAC	M/GUN KENNETH S. GORDAN	M
06/02/43	10338	VMSB-132		NEW HEBRIDES	SOPAC	LT KEN H. DIEFFENBACH	S
06/02/43	10697	VMSB-132		NEW HEBRIDES	SOPAC	MT/S HOWARD H. HICKS	M
06/03/43	10463	VB-16	USS LEX-INGTON	OFF MASS.	NORLANT		
06/26/43	10547	VMSB-234		SOLOMONS	SOPAC		
06/26/43	10567	VMSB-234		SOLOMONS	SOPAC		
06/27/43	10795	VC-22	USS INDE-PENDENCE	OFF PANAMA	CENLANT		
06/30/43	6718	VB-11		GUADAL-CANAL	SOPAC		
06/30/43	6951	VMSB-132		GUADAL-CANAL	SOPAC	1STLT R.D. BACHTEL	S
06/30/43	6966	VMSB-132		GUADAL-CANAL	SOPAC	1STLT MCGUCKIN	S
07/03/43	10662	VC-2			NORLANT		
07/17/43	10586	VMSB-132		KAHILI	SOPAC	LTJG HUGHES	M
07/21/43	10774	VB-41	USS RANGER		NORLANT	LCDR KLINGMAN	S
07/21/43	6969	VMSB-141		ESPIRITU SANTO	SOPAC	CAPT WHITE	D
07/23/43	10348	VMSB-144		GUADAL-CANAL	SOPAC	LT DOUGHERTY	S
07/26/43	10785	VB-42	USS RANGER		NORLANT		
07/27/43	10745	VC-24	USS BELLEAU WOOD	ENR PEARL	ECENPAC		
07/31/43	10337	VMSB-141		RUSSELLS	SOPAC	LT H. KEMP	U
08/01/43	10655	VB-11		GUADAL-CANAL	SOPAC		
08/01/43	10666	VMSB-141		RUSSELLS	SOPAC	LT WOODLEY	S
08/03/43	10518	VB-19	KAHULUI	HAWAII	ECENPAC		

DATE	BUNO	SQDRN	BASE	LOST	AREA	PILOT	FATE
08/05/43	6735	MAG-21	RUSSELLS		SOPAC	LT CLIFFORD	D
08/06/43	6972	VMSB-234		GUADAL-CANAL	SOPAC	LT LEROY SMITH	S
08/07/43	6716	VMSB-141			SOPAC	LT GILFORD TAYLOR	M
08/09/43	6980	VMSB-235			SOPAC	LT CHARLES RUMBOLD	S
08/30/43	10472	VB-9	USS ESSEX	ENR MARCUS IS	ECENPAC		
08/30/43	10635	VMSB-144			ECENPAC		
09/04/43	10322	VMSB-234		GUADAL-CANAL	SOPAC	CAPT BLACKMAN	M
09/05/43	10355	VMSB-144			SOPAC		
09/06/43	10344	VMSB-144			ECENPAC		
09/16/43	10427	VB-9	USS ESSEX	PEARL	ECENPAC		
09/16/43		VMSB-235		GUADAL-CANAL	SOPAC	LT KEEN	S
09/18/43	10681	VMSB-144		EFATE	SOPAC	LT A.M. DANIELS	S
09/20/43	6907	VMSB-151		GUADAL-CANAL	SOPAC		
09/20/43	6910	VMSB-151		GUADAL-CANAL	SOPAC		
09/25/43	10366	VC-22	USS INDE-PENDENCE	PEARL	ECENPAC		
09/29/43	10634	VMSB-236			SOPAC		
09/30/43	10387	VMSB-132	HAWAII		ECENPAC	LT JAMES M. WILSON	U
09/30/43	10317	VMSB-133	JOHNSTON ISLAND	HAWAII	ECENPAC		
09/30/43	10665	VMSB-231			SOPAC		
10/05/43	10359	VS-57	NOUMEA		SOPAC		
10/06/43	6948	VB-9	USS ESSEX	WAKE	WCENPAC		
10/06/43	10435	VB-9	USS ESSEX	WAKE	WCENPAC	LTJG FRITH	U
10/07/43	6988	VMSB-141			SOPAC	LT KRUER	U
10/11/43	6846	VMSB-236		GUADAL-CANAL	SOPAC	MAJ FRED W. LANE, JR.	U
10/11/43	10615	VMSB-236		GUADAL-CANAL	SOPAC	CAPT AMOS BELMAP	U
10/14/43	10437	VMSB-245	OAHU	HAWAII	ECENPAC	LT JOHN H. MATHISON	U
10/15/43	6717	VMSB-132	HAWAII		ECENPAC		
10/20/43	10620	VMSB-241			SOPAC	LT JAMES T. HALL	U
10/22/43	10562	VS-58		NEW HEBRIDES	SOPAC	LT MARVIN GREENBERG	U
10/23/43	6763	VMSB-244		GUADAL-CANAL	SOPAC		
10/23/43	10460	VS-53	PEARL	HAWAII	ECENPAC		
10/26/43	6715	VMSB-236		NEW HEBRIDES	SOPAC		
10/27/43	6725	VS-69	PEARL	HAWAII	ECENPAC		
11/09/43	6936	VMSB-144		MUNDA	SOPAC	LT CARR	S
11/09/43	10737	VMSB-235		EFATE	SOPAC	LT KEEN	M
11/13/43	10432	VC-69	PEARL	HAWAII	ECENPAC		
11/17/43	10502	VMSB-133	JOHNSTON ISLAND	HAWAII	ECENPAC	1STLT S. BARTO	D
11/19/43		VS-58		EFATE	SOPAC	LT M.W. SESSUMO	D
11/27/43	10593	VJ-53	PEARL	HAWAII	ECENPAC		
11/28/43	10326	VS-52			CENPAC		
12/10/43	10451	VB-9	USS ESSEX	PEARL	ECENPAC		
12/10/43	10521	VB-9	USS ESSEX	PEARL	ECENPAC		
12/16/43	10560	VMSB-235		GUADAL-CANAL	SOPAC		
12/20/43	10477	VMSB-236	MUNDA	BONINS	CENPAC	LT LACEY	M
12/23/43	6953	COMAIRSO PAC	GUADAL-CANAL	GUADAL-CANAL	SOPAC		
12/31/43		VMSB-151	WALLIS ISLAND		SOPAC		
12/31/43	10553	VS-57	NOUMEA		SOPAC		
01/05/44	6990		HAWAII		ECENPAC	MAJ L.A. CHRISTOFFERSON	S
01/05/44	10690	VMSB-236	MUNDA	RABAUL	SOPAC	GODBEY	S
01/07/44	6770	VMSB-236	MUNDA	RABAUL	SOPAC	2NDLT J.T. SOWLE	S
01/10/44	6738	VMSB-236	TOROKINA	GIZO	SOPAC	LT COLLINS	S
01/15/44	10375	CASU-1	PEARL	HAWAII	ECENPAC		
01/18/44	10693	VS-58	HAVANNAH	EFATE	SOPAC		
01/18/44	10561	VS-65	FUNAFUTI		SOPAC		
01/25/44	6923	VMSB-133	JOHNSTON ISLAND	HAWAII	ECENPAC	1STLT H.R. ANDERSON	D
01/27/44	6799	VMSB-236	MUNDA	MONOITU	SOPAC	1STLT E.B. COHEN	M

DATE	BUNO	SQDRN	BASE	LOST	AREA	PILOT	FATE
01/27/44	10421	VS-57	NEW CALEDON-IA		SOPAC		
01/28/44	10396	VS-57	NEW CALEDON-IA		SOPAC		
01/28/44	10564	VS-66			CENPAC	LTJG E.L. PENNER	S
01/31/44	10555	VMSB-236	MUNDA	RABAUL	SOPAC	CAPT E.D. HILL	M
02/06/44	10417	VS-57	NOUMEA		SOPAC		
02/16/44	6899	VB-6	USS INTREPID	TRUK	CENPAC	LT P.E. TUPAO	M
02/16/44	6958	VMSB-133	JOHNSTON ISLAND	HAWAII	ECENPAC	1STLT G.W.D. HUTCHINGS	S
02/19/44	10350	VMSB-244	PIVA	BUKA	SOPAC	1STLT H. KEMP	D
02/26/44	6825	HEDRON-2	KANEOHE	HAWAII	ECENPAC		
03/01/44	6902	VS-66	TARAWA		CENPAC		
03/03/44	6731	VS-53	PEARL	HAWAII	ECENPAC		
03/15/44	6783	ACORN-25 PL	NEW GEORGIA		SOPAC		
03/31/44	10739	VS-57	NOUMEA		SOPAC		
04/02/44	10699	HEDRON-21	ESPIRITU SANTO	EFATE	SOPAC	2NDLT A.R. MILLER	M
04/10/44	10609	VC-40	PIVA	BOUGAIN-VILLE	SOPAC		
04/13/44	10391	VB-98	TOROKINA	KAVIENG	SOPAC	ENS D.L. KELLY	M
04/15/44	10385	VS-64	SEGI	CHOISEUL	SOPAC		
04/19/44	10325	POOL	ESPIRITU SANTO		SOPAC	1STLT H.J. LAWRENCE	S
04/20/44		VMSB-241	EFATE		SOPAC	1STLT C.P. BRICE	D
04/20/44		VS-64	SEGI		SOPAC		
04/23/44		VS-43	GUANTAN-AMO BAY	CUBA	CENLANT	ENS H.R. BECKER	D
04/27/44	10656	VS-64	SEGI		SOPAC		
04/28/44		VS-57	NOUMEA		SOPAC		
04/29/44	10438	VMSB-332	MIDWAY		ECENPAC	LT T. KYLKO	S
04/29/44	10648	VS-57	ESPIRITU SANTO		SOPAC	ENS G.R. MILLS	D
05/01/44	6761	VS-55	ESPIRITU SANTO	ESPIRITU SANTO	SOPAC		
05/19/44	6737	VS-54	GUADAL-CANAL	GUADAL-CANAL	SOPAC	LT H.A. LEWIS	S
05/21/44	10540	VS-67	NANDI	EFATE	SOPAC	ENS T.J. STOREY	S
05/23/44	6937	VS-54	GUADAL-CANAL	GUADAL-CANAL	SOPAC	ENS L.B. CLARK	D
05/31/44	6804	FAW-2	PEARL	HAWAII	ECENPAC		
06/03/44	6974	POOL	PALLIKULO AIRFIELD		SOPAC		
06/03/44	10604	POOL	PALLIKULO AIRFIELD		SOPAC		
06/03/44	10629	POOL	PALLIKULO AIRFIELD		SOPAC		
06/06/44	6809	POOL	PALLIKULO AIRFIELD		SOPAC		
06/07/44	6961	POOL	PALLIKULO AIRFIELD		SOPAC		
06/08/44	10411	CASU-10	ESPIRITU SANTO	PALLIKULO	SOPAC		
06/10/44	6978	VS-58	HAVANNAH		SOPAC		
06/14/44	10580	VS-57	ESPIRITU SANTO		SOPAC		
06/27/44	10412	VS-47		PALMYRA	ECENPAC	ENS V.F. DIANA	M
07/07/44	6730	AROU		ESPIRITU SANTO	SOPAC		
07/07/44	6888	AROU		ESPIRITU SANTO	SOPAC		
07/08/44	6991	CASU-40		ESPIRITU SANTO	SOPAC		
07/22/44	6766	ARU SOLS			SOPAC		
07/23/44	10647	CASU-41		GUADAL-CANAL	SOPAC		
07/26/44	10669	FAW-1	ESPIRITU SANTO		SOPAC		
07/27/44	6776	ARU SOLS			SOPAC		
07/27/44	10768	NAS	JOHNSTON ISLAND	HAWAII	ECENPAC		

DATE	BUNO	SQDRN	BASE	LOST	AREA	PILOT	FATE
07/31/44	6721	NAS	MIDWAY		ECENPAC		
07/31/44	6805	NAS	MIDWAY		ECENPAC		
07/31/44	10444	NAS	MIDWAY		ECENPAC		
08/01/44	10532	VS-65	FUNAFUTI	NOUMEA	SOPAC		
08/01/44	10559	VS-65	FUNAFUTI	NOUMEA	SOPAC		
08/01/44	10569	VS-65	FUNAFUTI	NOUMEA	SOPAC		
08/01/44	10589	VS-65	FUNAFUTI	NOUMEA	SOPAC		
08/01/44	10598	VS-65	FUNAFUTI	NOUMEA	SOPAC		
08/01/44	10617	VS-65	FUNAFUTI	NOUMEA	SOPAC		
08/01/44	10630	VS-65	FUNAFUTI	NOUMEA	SOPAC		
08/01/44	10631	VS-65	FUNAFUTI	NOUMEA	SOPAC		
08/01/44	10651	VS-65	FUNAFUTI	NOUMEA	SOPAC		
08/01/44	10758	VS-65	FUNAFUTI	NOUMEA	SOPAC		
08/01/44	10759	VS-65	FUNAFUTI	NOUMEA	SOPAC		
08/08/44	6705	CASU-40		ESPIRITU SANTO	SOPAC		
08/08/44	6710	CASU-40		ESPIRITU SANTO	SOPAC		
08/08/44	6747	CASU-40		ESPIRITU SANTO	SOPAC		
08/08/44	6749	CASU-40		ESPIRITU SANTO	SOPAC		
08/08/44	6871	CASU-40		ESPIRITU SANTO	SOPAC		
08/08/44	6981	CASU-40		ESPIRITU SANTO	SOPAC		
08/08/44	6984	CASU-40		ESPIRITU SANTO	SOPAC		
08/11/44	6758	CASU-39	ESPIRITU SANTO	ESPIRITU SANTO	SOPAC		
08/15/44	10433	COMAIRSO PAC	GUADAL- CANAL	ESPIRITU SANTO	SOPAC		
08/15/44	10507	COMAIRSO PAC	GUADAL- CANAL	ESPIRITU SANTO	SOPAC		
08/15/44	10673	COMAIRSO PAC	GUADAL- CANAL	ESPIRITU SANTO	SOPAC		
08/16/44	6711	NAS	JOHNSTON ISLAND	HAWAII	ECENPAC		
08/16/44	6720	NAS	JOHNSTON ISLAND	HAWAII	ECENPAC		
08/16/44	6755	NAS	JOHNSTON ISLAND	HAWAII	ECENPAC		
08/16/44	6987	NAS	JOHNSTON ISLAND	HAWAII	ECENPAC		
08/16/44	10436	NAS	JOHNSTON ISLAND	HAWAII	ECENPAC		
08/16/44	10474	NAS	JOHNSTON ISLAND	HAWAII	ECENPAC		
08/16/44	10524	NAS	JOHNSTON ISLAND	HAWAII	ECENPAC		
08/16/44	10767	NAS	JOHNSTON ISLAND	HAWAII	ECENPAC		
08/27/44	6740		ESPIRITU SANTO		SOPAC		
08/27/44	6802		ESPIRITU SANTO		SOPAC		
08/27/44	6810		ESPIRITU SANTO		SOPAC		
08/27/44	6814		ESPIRITU SANTO		SOPAC		
08/27/44	6829		ESPIRITU SANTO		SOPAC		
08/27/44	6845		ESPIRITU SANTO		SOPAC		
08/27/44	6880		ESPIRITU SANTO		SOPAC		
08/27/44	6931		ESPIRITU SANTO		SOPAC		
09/01/44	10584	VS-65		FUNAFUTI	CENPAC		
09/01/44	10642	VS-65		FUNAFUTI	CENPAC		
09/01/44	10755	VS-65		FUNAFUTI	CENPAC		
09/01/44	10760	VS-65		FUNAFUTI	CENPAC		
09/08/44	10548	CASU-40		ESPIRITU SANTO	SOPAC	CAPT LAVERE E. WALLACE	S

DATE	BUNO	SQDRN	BASE	LOST	AREA	PILOT	FATE
09/11/44	10698	POOL	GUADAL-CANAL		SOPAC		
09/14/44	10702	POOL	GUADAL-CANAL		SOPAC		
09/18/44	6760	POOL	KANEOHE	HAWAII	ECENPAC		
09/18/44	10453	POOL	KANEOHE	HAWAII	ECENPAC		
09/20/44	6744		ESPIRITU SANTO		SOPAC		
09/20/44	6780		ESPIRITU SANTO		SOPAC		
09/20/44	6828		ESPIRITU SANTO		SOPAC		
09/20/44	10416		ESPIRITU SANTO		SOPAC		
09/20/44	10600		ESPIRITU SANTO		SOPAC		
09/20/44	10687		ESPIRITU SANTO		SOPAC		
09/27/44	6708	POOL	GUADAL-CANAL		SOPAC		
09/27/44	10334	POOL	GUADAL-CANAL		SOPAC		
09/27/44	10506	POOL	GUADAL-CANAL		SOPAC		
09/27/44	10640	POOL	GUADAL-CANAL		SOPAC		
10/15/44	6947	ACORN-7 PL	EMIRAU		SW PAC		
10/18/44	6963		ESPIRITU SANTO		SOPAC		
10/19/44	6820	A & R	MAJURO	MAJURO	CENPAC		
10/19/44	6836	A & R	MAJURO	MAJURO	CENPAC		
10/19/44	6886	A & R	MAJURO	MAJURO	CENPAC		
10/19/44	10612	A & R	MAJURO	MAJURO	CENPAC		
10/20/44	6739	STAG-1	RUSSELLS		SOPAC		
10/20/44	6781	STAG-1	RUSSELLS		SOPAC		
10/20/44	6815	STAG-1	RUSSELLS		SOPAC		
10/20/44	6927	STAG-1	RUSSELLS		SOPAC		
10/20/44	6952	STAG-1	RUSSELLS		SOPAC		
10/20/44	10384	STAG-1	RUSSELLS		SOPAC		
10/20/44	10386	STAG-1	RUSSELLS		SOPAC		
10/20/44	10393	STAG-1	RUSSELLS		SOPAC		
10/20/44	10401	STAG-1	RUSSELLS		SOPAC		
10/20/44	10407	STAG-1	RUSSELLS		SOPAC		
10/20/44	10607	STAG-1	RUSSELLS		SOPAC		
10/20/44	10636	STAG-1	RUSSELLS		SOPAC		
10/20/44	10743	STAG-1	RUSSELLS		SOPAC		
10/23/44	10689	SERVRON-14		GREEN	SOPAC		
10/30/44	6975	A.A.	ESPIRITU SANTO	ESPIRITU SANTO	SOPAC		
10/31/44	10674	A.A.	PEARL	HAWAII	ECENPAC		
10/31/44	10552	ACORN-19 PL	RUSSELLS		SOPAC		
10/31/44	6816	COMAIR-PAC	PEARL	HAWAII	ECENPAC		
10/31/44	10324	COMAIR-PAC	PEARL	HAWAII	ECENPAC		
10/31/44	10339	COMAIR-PAC	PEARL	HAWAII	ECENPAC		
10/31/44	10358	SERVRON-14		GREEN	SOPAC		
11/01/44	6778	COMAIR-PAC	PEARL	HAWAII	ECENPAC		
11/02/44	10478	STATION OPR	MIDWAY		ECENPAC		
11/05/44	6885	AWT ACTION	ESPIRITU SANTO		SOPAC		
11/15/44	6785	ACORN-25 PL	GREEN		SOPAC		
11/24/44	10550	AWT ACTION	GUADAL-CANAL		SOPAC		
11/30/44	10479	AWT ACTION	PEARL	HAWAII	ECENPAC		

DATE	BUNO	SQDRN	BASE	LOST	AREA	PILOT	FATE
12/16/44	6709	NAS	JOHNSTON ISLAND	HAWAII	ECENPAC		
12/16/44	6777	NAS	JOHNSTON ISLAND	HAWAII	ECENPAC		
12/16/44	6941	NAS	JOHNSTON ISLAND	HAWAII	ECENPAC		
12/16/44	6943	NAS	JOHNSTON ISLAND	HAWAII	ECENPAC		
12/16/44	6944	NAS	JOHNSTON ISLAND	HAWAII	ECENPAC		
12/16/44	10399	NAS	JOHNSTON ISLAND	HAWAII	ECENPAC		
12/16/44	10409	NAS	JOHNSTON ISLAND	HAWAII	ECENPAC		
12/16/44	10443	NAS	JOHNSTON ISLAND	HAWAII	ECENPAC		
12/18/44	6938	VS-47		PALMYRA	ECENPAC		
12/18/44	10318	VS-47		PALMYRA	ECENPAC		
12/18/44	10327	VS-47		PALMYRA	ECENPAC		
12/18/44	10328	VS-47		PALMYRA	ECENPAC		
12/18/44	10332	VS-47		PALMYRA	ECENPAC		
12/18/44	10342	VS-47		PALMYRA	ECENPAC		
12/18/44	10360	VS-47		PALMYRA	ECENPAC		
12/21/44	10418	VS-47		PALMYRA	ECENPAC		
03/02/45	6714	COMAIR-PAC	PEARL	HAWAII	ECENPAC		
03/25/45	6912	NAB	MANUS		SW PAC	ENS HAROLD J. BASE	D
04/29/45	6967	CASU-41		GUADAL-CANAL	SOPAC		
06/30/45	10336	COMAIR-PAC	PEARL	HAWAII	ECENPAC		

DOUGLAS SBD-5

The Douglas SBD-5 was the most produced variant of all the SBDs. They were primarily produced at the Douglas plant at Tulsa, Oklahoma. They were equipped with a 1,200 hp engine and increased ammunition. There were 2,965 built. Aircraft lost:

DATE	BUNO	SQDRN	BASE	LOST	AREA	PILOT	FATE
00/00/00	28312	VMSB-244			WCENPAC		
00/00/00	54503	VS-57	NOUMEA	NOUMEA	SOPAC		
12/21/42	28597	CASU-10	USS CHE-NANGO	PANAMA	CENPAC		
12/23/42	28916	CASU-4	USS CHE-NANGO	PANAMA	CENPAC		
06/30/43	28454	VB-5	USS YORK-TOWN	TRINIDAD	CENLANT		
06/30/43	10814	VMSB-132		GUADAL-CANAL	SOPAC	CAPT J.H. STOCK	S
06/30/43	10822	VMSB-132		GUADAL-CANAL	SOPAC	1STLT R.N. MCARDLE	M
06/30/43	10953	VMSB-132		GUADAL-CANAL	SOPAC	LT MCDERMOTT	S
07/01/43	28189	VB-9	USS ESSEX	PEARL	ECENPAC		
07/05/43	10861	VB-3	USS SARATOGA	NOUMEA	SOPAC	ENS T.F. KENNY, JR.	D
07/10/43	28180	VB-6	USS ENTER-PRISE	HAWAII	ECENPAC		
07/17/43	10918	VMSB-236		ESPIRITU SANTO	SOPAC	CAPT LEONARD H. MAILLOUX	D
07/20/43	10867	VC-29	USS SANTEE	AZORES	NORLANT		
07/20/43	28097	VMSB-132		TULAGI	SOPAC	LT MCGUCKIN	S
07/26/43	28270	VMSB-132		GUADAL-CANAL	SOPAC	T/SGT LEWIS	S
07/28/43	10873	VC-29	USS SANTEE	ENR NORFOLK	NORLANT		

DATE	BUNO	SQDRN	BASE	LOST	AREA	PILOT	FATE
07/28/43	10877	VC-29	USS SANTEE	ENR NORFOLK	NORLANT		
07/30/43	28343	VB-5	USS YORKTOWN	PEARL	ECENPAC		
07/31/43	10841	VB-12			WCENPAC		
08/03/43	10827	VB-3	USS SARATOGA	NOUMEA	SOPAC		
08/05/43	28190	VB-6	USS ENTERPRISE	HAWAII	ECENPAC		
08/11/43	28108	VB-1	HILO	HAWAII	ECENPAC		
08/11/43	28467	VB-1	HILO	HAWAII	ECENPAC		
08/11/43	28472	VB-1	HILO	HAWAII	ECENPAC		
08/12/43	28311	VB-6	USS ENTERPRISE	HAWAII	ECENPAC		
08/22/43	10950	VB-5	USS YORKTOWN	ENR MARCUS IS.	WCENPAC	ENS W.A. JOHNSON	D
08/22/43	10952	VB-5	USS YORKTOWN	ENR MARCUS IS.	WCENPAC	ENS MCGINNIS	S
08/30/43	28331	VB-16	USS LEXINGTON	PEARL	ECENPAC		
08/30/43	28386	VB-16	USS LEXINGTON	PEARL	ECENPAC		
08/30/43	28401	VB-16	USS LEXINGTON	PEARL	ECENPAC		
09/12/43	28364	VB-16	USS LEXINGTON	PEARL	ECENPAC	LTJG J.F. STRATTON	S
09/18/43	11026	VB-16	USS LEXINGTON	APAMAMA	WCENPAC	LTJG PAUL H. PRANDINI	M
09/18/43	28088	VB-16	USS LEXINGTON	TARAWA	CENPAC	ENS T.H. BROWN	M
10/01/43	10892	VC-31	USS CABOT		NORLANT	ENS J.H. BUSHNELL	U
10/01/43	28079	VC-40	GUADALCANAL	ESPIRITU SANTO	SOPAC		
10/04/43	11011	VB-4	USS RANGER	VESTFJORD	NORLANT	LTJG TUCKER	U
10/04/43	28636	VB-4	USS RANGER	VESTFJORD	NORLANT	LTJG DAVIS	U
10/04/43	28537	VC-24	USS BELLEAU WOOD	WAKE	WCENPAC	LT K.P. SPEER	U
10/05/43	28128	VB-5	USS YORKTOWN	WAKE	WCENPAC	LTJG JOEL W. ESHOO	U
10/06/43	28185	VB-16	USS LEXINGTON	WAKE	WCENPAC	LTJG W.E. MCCARTHY	U
10/06/43	28085	VB-5	USS YORKTOWN	WAKE	WCENPAC	LTJG R. BYRON	U
10/06/43	28328	VB-5	USS YORKTOWN	WAKE	WCENPAC	LTJG R.M. GREGG	U
10/06/43	28536	VB-9	USS ESSEX	WAKE	WCENPAC	LTJG E.C. KIDD	U
10/10/43	28385	VB-5	USS YORKTOWN	HAWAII	ECENPAC		
10/11/43	28199	VMSB-244		GUADALCANAL	SOPAC	LT MURRAY	U
10/15/43	28303	VMSB-231		MIDWAY	ECENPAC	LT CLYDE VAN DUSEN	U
10/16/43	10839	MAG-23	EWA	HAWAII	ECENPAC		
10/23/43	10914	VC-38		SOLOMONS	SOPAC		
10/27/43	10966	VMSB-236		NEW HEBRIDES	SOPAC	LT C.C. WOLFE	U
10/30/43	29095	VMSB-341		TUTUILA	SOPAC	LT LOUIS F. ZIMMERMAN	D
10/31/43	28135	VB-1	HILO	HAWAII	ECENPAC		
11/01/43	10923	VB-12	USS SARATOGA	BUKA	SOPAC	LTJG R.D. HIGHTOWER	S
11/01/43	28424	VB-16	USS LEXINGTON	PEARL	ECENPAC		
11/01/43	28637	VB-6	USS ENTERPRISE	PUUNENE	ECENPAC		
11/01/43	28649	VB-9	USS ESSEX	ENR RABAUL	SOPAC		
11/05/43	28404	VB-12	USS SARATOGA	RABAUL	SOPAC	LTJG A.L. TEALL	M
11/05/43	10970	VC-38		SEGI FIELD	SOPAC		

DATE	BUNO	SQDRN	BASE	LOST	AREA	PILOT	FATE
11/10/43	35946			ESPIRITU SANTO	SOPAC	1STLT R.G. PHILLIPS	D
11/10/43	28447	VB-9	USS ESSEX	RABAUL	SOPAC	LTJG J.W. WALKER	M
11/10/43	35931	VC-24		MUNDA	SOPAC	LT F.B. MCINTYRE	M
11/12/43	28305	VMSB-231		MIDWAY	ECENPAC	1STLT A.W. COLE	S
11/16/43	35952	VB-10	PUUNENE	HAWAII	ECENPAC	ENS G.F. STOCKHAM	D
11/16/43	36084	VB-10	PUUNENE	HAWAII	ECENPAC	ENS F.P. KENNY	D
11/16/43	35969	VMSB-331		NUKUFETAU	SOPAC		
11/17/43	10958	VB-12	USS SARATOGA	NW OF ESPIRITU	SOPAC	ENS D.N. KINGMAN	D
11/18/43	28608	VB-9	USS ESSEX	BITITU	CENPAC	LTJG B.K. CONRATE	D
11/19/43	28455	VB-1	HILO	HAWAII	ECENPAC	ENS G.A. TALBOT	D
11/19/43	10948	VB-12	USS SARATOGA	NAURU	CENPAC	LTJG J.S. CURTIN	S
11/19/43	28174	VB-16	USS LEX-INGTON	MILLE	CENPAC	ENS C.T. WILLIAMS	S
11/19/43	28469	VB-16	USS LEX-INGTON	MILLE	CENPAC	LTJG KIRKENDAHL	S
11/19/43	28368	VMSB-144		MUNDA	SOPAC		
11/20/43	28233	VB-6	USS ENTER-PRISE	MAKIN	CENPAC	LTJG J.R. HEISINGTON	S
11/22/43	10903	VB-16	USS LEX-INGTON	MILLE	CENPAC	ENS O'CALLAHAN	S
11/22/43	28926	VB-16	USS LEX-INGTON	MILLE	CENPAC	LTJG W.E. HARRISON	S
11/23/43	29049	MAG-31		SAMAAN AREA	SOPAC		
11/23/43		VMSB-243		BARAKOMA	SOPAC	CAPT COLEMAN	S
11/25/43	29062	MAG-31		WALLIS ISLAND	SOPAC		
11/25/43	35965	VMSB-331		NUKUFETAU	SOPAC		
11/25/43	36035	VMSB-331		NUKUFETAU	SOPAC		
12/01/43	11002	VMSB-236		MUNDA	SOPAC	MAJ PARIS	S
12/01/43	35976	VMSB-236		MUNDA	SOPAC	1STLT E.R. WHITELY	M
12/04/43	36088	VB-10	PUUNENE	HAWAII	ECENPAC	LT BLOCH	M
12/04/43	28496	VB-16	USS LEX-INGTON	KWAJALEIN	CENPAC		
12/05/43	28344	VB-16	USS LEX-INGTON	KWAJALEIN	CENPAC		
12/05/43	28388	VB-16	USS LEX-INGTON	KWAJALEIN	CENPAC		
12/05/43	10869	VMSB-236		EFATE	SOPAC		
12/06/43	36045	VB-10	PUUNENE	HAWAII	ECENPAC		
12/06/43	36099	VB-10	PUUNENE	HAWAII	ECENPAC		
12/09/43	28324	VB-16	USS LEX-INGTON	ENR PEARL	ECENPAC	ENS PRICHARD	M
12/11/43	28287	VB-12	USS SARATOGA	PEARL	ECENPAC		
12/11/43	10821	VB-16	USS LEX-INGTON	PEARL	ECENPAC		
12/11/43	28629	VB-9	USS ESSEX	PEARL	ECENPAC		
12/11/43	28661	VMSB-235		MUNDA	SOPAC		
12/13/43	28187	VB-16	USS LEX-INGTON	PEARL	ECENPAC		
12/14/43	28374	VB-1	USS YORK-TOWN	HILO	ECENPAC		
12/15/43	35925	VB-98		MUNDA	SOPAC		
12/16/43		VB-98		MUNDA	SOPAC	LT CULLEN (VMSB-236)	S
12/16/43		VB-98		MUNDA	SOPAC		
12/16/43		VMSB-235		MUNDA	SOPAC	LT QUINLAN	S
12/16/43	28451	VMSB-235		MUNDA	SOPAC		
12/16/43	35968	VMSB-236		MUNDA	SOPAC	LTJG R. OUGHTON	S
12/16/43	10816	VMSB-244	EFATE	EFATE	SOPAC	CAPT G.D. RYAN	M
12/17/43	28473	VB-1	USS YORK-TOWN	HILO	ECENPAC	ENS D.L. WILSON	S
12/18/43	35961	VC-40	GUADAL-CANAL	BOUGAIN-VILLE	SOPAC	2NDLT R.T FROST (VMSB-235)	M
12/20/43	28523	VB-98		MUNDA	SOPAC		
12/24/43	36097	VB-10	PUUNENE	HAWAII	ECENPAC		
12/24/43	36098	VB-10	PUUNENE	HAWAII	ECENPAC		
12/30/43	28091	VMSB-235	GUADAL-CANAL	GUADAL-CANAL	SOPAC		
12/30/43	28663	VS-57	NOUMEA		SOPAC		
12/31/43	36268	VB-10	PUUNENE	HAWAII	ECENPAC		

DATE	BUNO	SQDRN	BASE	LOST	AREA	PILOT	FATE
12/31/43		VMSB-235	MUNDA	RABAUL	SOPAC		
12/31/43	35949	VMSB-235	EMIRAU		SOPAC		
01/01/44	28411	VC-40	MUNDA	RABAUL	SOPAC		
01/02/44	28165	VB-6	USS ENTER-PRISE	PEARL	ECENPAC		
01/02/44	35935	VB-98	TOROKINA	RABAUL	SOPAC	ENS L.A. SHEPARD	S
01/04/44	35994	VB-10	USS ENTER-PRISE	PEARL	ECENPAC		
01/04/44	36271	VB-10	USS ENTER-PRISE	PEARL	ECENPAC		
01/05/44	36568	VB-10	USS ENTER-PRISE	PEARL	ECENPAC		
01/05/44	36220	VMSB-341	TOROKINA	RABAUL	SOPAC		
01/06/44	36007	VB-10	USS ENTER-PRISE	OAHU	ECENPAC	LT W. CLARK	M
01/07/44	36227	VB-98	MUNDA	RABAUL	SOPAC		
01/07/44	28359	VMSB-235	MUNDA	RABAUL	SOPAC		
01/07/44	28295	VMSB-236	MUNDA	RABAUL	SOPAC	CAPT E.D. HILL	S
01/07/44	10842	VMSB-341	PIVA	RABAUL	SOPAC		
01/08/44	35947	VMSB-235	MUNDA	RABAUL	SOPAC		
01/08/44	36100	VMSB-331			CENPAC		
01/09/44	35938	VB-98	MUNDA	RABAUL	SOPAC	LTJG E.L. ALSTOTT	S
01/10/44	35972	COMAIRSO PAC	GUADAL-CANAL	GUADAL-CANAL	SOPAC		
01/10/44	36455	VB-12	USS SARATOGA	PEARL	ECENPAC		
01/10/44	28543	VB-98	ESPIRITU SANTO	AOBA IS.	SOPAC	LT L.E. KENNAN	D
01/10/44	35926	VB-98	ESPIRITU SANTO	AOBA IS.	SOPAC		
01/12/44	29092	VMSB-151	WALLIS ISLAND		SOPAC	1STLT F.P. GRIFFITH	D
01/12/44	28967	VS-69	PEARL	HAWAII	ECENPAC		
01/14/44	35971	VMSB-236	MUNDA	RABAUL	SOPAC	LT B.R. RAMSEY	M
01/14/44	36230	VMSB-341	MUNDA	RABAUL	SOPAC	LT H.R. TUCK	M
01/15/44	28895	VMSB-236	MUNDA	MONOITU	SOPAC		
01/15/44	35966	VMSB-341	MUNDA	MONOITU	SOPAC	LT L.F. CARROLL	M
01/17/44	29142	VB-9	USS ESSEX	MARSHALLS	CENPAC		
01/17/44	35933	VB-98	MUNDA	RABAUL	SOPAC		
01/17/44	28316	VMSB-341	MUNDA	RABAUL	SOPAC	LT R.E. BISHOP	M
01/23/44	28223	VC-35	USS CHE-NANGO	MARSHALLS	CENPAC	ENS W.R. PURYEAR	S
01/24/44	28438	VS-69	PEARL	MOLOKAI	ECENPAC	ENS A.F. LILIENTHAL	S
01/25/44	10855	VC-37	USS SAN-GAMON	KWAJALEIN	CENPAC	(DECK LOSS-AIRCRASH)	
01/25/44	36676	VC-37	USS SAN-GAMON	KWAJALEIN	CENPAC	(DECK LOSS-AIRCRASH)	
01/26/44	36231	VMSB-341	PIVA	RABAUL	SOPAC	1STLT H.H. COONLEY	M
01/29/44	36505	VB-9	USS ESSEX	ROI	WCENPAC		
01/29/44	29148	VMSB-235	EFATE	QUOIN HILL	SOPAC		
01/31/44		COMAIR-SOPAC	GUADAL-CANAL	GUADAL-CANAL	SOPAC		
01/31/44	28256	VB-98	MUNDA	RABAUL	SOPAC		
01/31/44	36931	VC-35	USS CHE-NANGO	ROI	WCENPAC	LTJG HOLLOWAY	S
01/31/44	36814	VC-60	USS SU-WANNEE	ROI	WCENPAC	LT B.W. STRONG	D
01/31/44	36816	VC-60	USS SU-WANNEE	ROI	WCENPAC	ENS W.T. SACKRIDER	D
01/31/44	36708	VMSB-235	EFATE	EFATE	SOPAC		
02/01/44	36190	VMSB-235	PIVA	RABAUL	SOPAC		
02/02/44	28530	VMSB-235	EFATE	QUOIN HILL	SOPAC		
02/04/44	28924	VMSB-341	MUNDA	RABAUL	SOPAC		
02/05/44	36462	VB-12	USS SARATOGA	ENIWETOK	CENPAC		
02/07/44	36026	VB-98	ESPIRITU SANTO	LUGAN FIELD	SOPAC	LTJG J.H. LANKFORD	D
02/10/44	28570	VMSB-241	PIVA	RABAUL	SOPAC	1STLT P.C. WELLS	M
02/10/44	36483	VS-43	GUANTANA MO BAY	CUBA	CENLANT	ENS G.E. COX	S

DATE	BUNO	SQDRN	BASE	LOST	AREA	PILOT	FATE
02/11/44	36672	VB-98	ESPIRITU SANTO	LUGAN FIELD	SOPAC		
02/12/44	35954	VMSB-241	PIVA	RABAUL	SOPAC	1STLT J.M. SANDERS	M
02/14/44	36537	VB-16	USS LEX-INGTON	PEARL	ECENPAC	LT T.E. DUPREE	S
02/14/44	36034	VC-38	TOROKINA	RABAUL	SOPAC		
02/16/44	28133	VB-6	USS INTREPID	TRUK	CENPAC		
02/16/44	28335	VB-6	USS INTREPID	TRUK	CENPAC	LT J.P. PHILLIPS	S
02/16/44	28628	VB-6	USS INTREPID	TRUK	CENPAC		
02/16/44	28644	VB-6	USS INTREPID	TRUK	CENPAC		
02/17/44	36234	VB-10	USS ENTER-PRISE	TRUK	CENPAC	ENS D. DEAN	M
02/17/44	28346	VMSB-234		EFATE	SOPAC		
02/17/44	28566	VMSB-244	PIVA	KORAVIA	SOPAC		
02/17/44	29084	VMSB-244	EFATE	EFATE	SOPAC		
02/17/44	11016	VS-69	PEARL	HAWAII	ECENPAC	LTJG A.F. LILIENTHAL	D
02/19/44	36754	VC-35	USS CHE-NANGO	ENIWETOK	CENPAC		
02/20/44	36225	VB-1	KANEOHE	HAWAII	ECENPAC	ENS E.R. ELLINGBOE	D
02/20/44	36293	VB-1	KANEOHE	HAWAII	ECENPAC	ENS J.E. GRAHAM	D
02/20/44	28460	VB-98	TOROKINA	AUGUSTA BAY	SOPAC		
02/22/44	36777	VC-37	USS SAN-GAMON	ENIWETOK	CENPAC	ENS M.H. BERGMEIER	D
02/22/44	28674	VMSB-244	PIVA	BUKA	SOPAC	CAPT C.E. EATON	S
02/24/44	28151	VMSB-241	PIVA	RABAUL	SOPAC	1STLT C.L. STEWARD	S
02/26/44	28175	VB-6	USS INTREPID	PEARL	ECENPAC		
02/26/44	28372	VMSB-244	TOROKINA	RABAUL	SOPAC	CAPT M.H. PORTERFIELD	S
02/27/44	36898	COMAIR-SOPAC	GUADAL-CANAL	GUADAL-CANAL	SOPAC		
02/27/44	36903	COMAIR-SOPAC	GUADAL-CANAL	GUADAL-CANAL	SOPAC		
02/27/44	36908	COMAIR-SOPAC	GUADAL-CANAL	GUADAL-CANAL	SOPAC		
02/29/44	28301	VMSB-244	TOROKINA	RABAUL	SOPAC		
02/29/44		VS-52	KANEOHE	HAWAII	ECENPAC		
02/29/44		VS-52	KANEOHE	HAWAII	ECENPAC		
02/29/44	36752	VS-52	KANEOHE	HAWAII	ECENPAC		
03/01/44	36345	VMSB-151	WALLIS ISLAND		SOPAC		
03/02/44	29120	VMSB-241	TOROKINA	BOUGAIN-VILLE	SOPAC	CAPT L.A. WALLACE	M
03/03/44	36481	VB-16	USS LEX-INGTON	ERMAJURO	CENPAC	ENS J.W. CHANDLER	S
03/04/44	28688	VB-16	USS LEX-INGTON	ERMAJURO	CENPAC	LTJG A.H. BURROUGH	S
03/05/44	36732	VC-35	USS CHE-NANGO	PEARL	ECENPAC		
03/06/44	36075	VMSB-331	MARSHALL S		CENPAC		
03/09/44	35964	VC-40	PIVA	TOROKINA	SOPAC	1STLT W.G. GILBERT	M
03/13/44	10978	VMSB-341	EFATE	RABAUL	SOPAC	1STLT H.H. FRITZIE	D
03/14/44	36720	VMSB-241	PIVA	TOROKINA	SOPAC	1STLT H. OSTRUM	D
03/15/44	29090	VMSB-235	EFATE	EFATE	SOPAC		
03/17/44	28321	VB-1	KANEOHE	HAWAII	ECENPAC		
03/17/44	36019	VC-40	PIVA	TOROKINA	SOPAC	LTJG D.G. FUTRELL	M
03/17/44	36463	VMSB-231	MAJURO	WOTJE	CENPAC	CAPT H.V. COOK	D
03/17/44	10836	VMSB-244	TOROKINA	MONTUPENA PT.	SOPAC	LTJG BURNS	S
03/17/44	28210	VS-69	BARBERS POINT	HAWAII	ECENPAC	ENS C.G. BAKER	S
03/18/44	36540	VB-16	USS LEX-INGTON	MILLE	CENPAC	LTJG A.H. SPARROW	M
03/23/44	28437	VB-305	PIVA	KAHILI	SOPAC	LTJG FRANK J. SMITH	M
03/23/44	36515	VB-305	PIVA	KAHILI	SOPAC		
03/23/44	28432	VC-40	SEGI	BOUGAIN-VILLE	SOPAC	J.E. CARBEY	S
03/23/44	28425	VMSB-332	EWA	HAWAII	ECENPAC	2NDLT R. SHUMACHER	D

DATE	BUNO	SQDRN	BASE	LOST	AREA	PILOT	FATE
03/24/44	36583	VB-305	PIVA	TOROKINA	SOPAC	LTJG A.L. PATERSON	D
03/24/44	28309	VB-5	USS YORK-TOWN	ENR PALAU	CENPAC		
03/24/44	10935	VMSB-243	TOROKINA	KAVIENG	SOPAC	2NDLT J. TENNYSON	M
03/25/44		VC-40	PIVA	RABAUL	SOPAC	CAPT J WINDSOR (VMSB-235)	S
03/25/44	36436	VMSB-231	MAJURO	WOTJE	CENPAC		
03/30/44	28103	VB-10	USS ENTER-PRISE	PALAU	CENPAC		
03/30/44	36134	VB-10	USS ENTER-PRISE	PALAU	CENPAC		
03/30/44	28275	VB-16	USS LEX-INGTON	PALAU	CENPAC	ENS COOK	S
03/30/44	10954	VB-5	USS YORK-TOWN	PALAU	CENPAC	LTJG F.E. HOLLAND	S
03/30/44	28203	VMSB-243	GREEN		SOPAC	LT E.T. LAROE	S
03/30/44	36445	VMSB-331	MAJURO	WOTJE	CENPAC	2NDLT D.D. MORGAN	S
03/31/44	28707	COMAIR-SOPAC	GUADAL-CANAL	GUADAL-CANAL	SOPAC		
04/01/44	54202	COMAIR-SOPAC	GUADAL-CANAL	GUADAL-CANAL	SOPAC		
04/02/44	54375	HEDRON-21	ESPIRITU SANTO	EFATE	SOPAC	2NDLT C.F. MILLER	M
04/03/44	36226	CASU-38	KANEOHE	HAWAII	ECENPAC		
04/03/44	36907	VB-4	USS RANGER	OFF NEW YORK	NORLANT	LT J.R. FULNECKY	M
04/04/44	28452	COMAIR-SOPAC	GUADAL-CANAL	BOUGAIN-VILLE	SOPAC	LANDON	U
04/09/44	28351	VB-100	BARBERS POINT	HAWAII	ECENPAC	ENS P.F. CUNARD	S
04/11/44	54272	VS-59	BARRANGU ILA		NORLANT	ENS C.B. TETER	D
04/16/44	36485	VS-37		CURACAO	CENLANT	LT B. SIMPSON	S
04/16/44	35945	VS-51	TUTUILA		SOPAC	ENS C.W. EATON	S
04/17/44	28710	VMSB-235	EFATE	EFATE	SOPAC		
04/17/44	36360	VMSB-331	MAJURO		CENPAC	1STLT W.C. MILLER	S
04/18/44	28083	VMSB-243	GREEN	NEW BRITAIN	SOPAC	2NDLT J.E. SHREIBAK	M
04/18/44	54211	VMSB-243	GREEN	NEW BRITAIN	SOPAC	CAPT W.B. REARDON	D
04/19/44	28517	VB-305	GREEN	MAKIN	CENPAC	ENS G.M. MCGEHEE	S
04/19/44	36885	VB-305	GREEN	MAKIN	CENPAC		
04/20/44	36410	VMSB-231	MAJURO	WOTJE	CENPAC	1STLT D.R. HAYES	D
04/20/44		VMSB-241	EFATE		SOPAC	1STLT J. KEESE	D
04/20/44	36539	VS-43	GUANTANA MO BAY	CUBA	CENLANT	LT C.M. EVANS	S
04/23/44	11062	NAS	HILO	HAWAII	ECENPAC	LT E.C. NAMOEKI	S
04/25/44	36086	VMSB-235	TOROKINA	RABAUL	SOPAC	CAPT R. SEELY	S
04/25/44	54165	VMSB-245	OAHU	HAWAII	ECENPAC	1STLT D.M. SMITH	S
04/27/44	36923	COMAIR-SOPAC	GUADAL-CANAL	GUADAL-CANAL	SOPAC		
04/27/44	28681	VB-19	KAHULUI	HAWAII	ECENPAC		
04/28/44	36257	VMSB-133	EWA	HAWAII	ECENPAC		
04/29/44	36295	VB-16	USS LEX-INGTON	TRUK	CENPAC	LTJG F.R. LEVIN	S
04/30/44	28245				CENPAC		
04/30/44	36332				CENPAC		
04/30/44	28111	VB-16	USS LEX-INGTON	TRUK	CENPAC		
04/30/44	36277	VB-16	USS LEX-INGTON	TRUK	CENPAC	LT B. KIRKPATRICK	S
04/30/44	36901	VB-306	SEGI	RABAUL	SOPAC	ENS G.V. HENDSTRAND	M
05/01/44	28333	VB-5	USS YORK-TOWN	TRUK	CENPAC		
05/01/44	36501	VB-5	USS YORK-TOWN	TRUK	CENPAC		
05/01/44	36644	VMSB-235	PIVA	RABAUL	SOPAC	MAJ G.L. TODD	S
05/01/44	35974	VMSB-331	MAJURO	TAROA	CENPAC	1STLT J.H. HOUSTON	D
05/02/44	10913	VMSB-341	GREEN	RABAUL	SOPAC	CAPT W.L. JORDAN	D
05/02/44	54221	VMSB-341	GREEN	RABAUL	SOPAC	1STLT W.W. HARKINS	M
05/04/44	36665	VMSB-133	EWA	HAWAII	ECENPAC	CAPT G.H. SCHLUCKEBIER	S
05/04/44	36678	VMSB-133	EWA	HAWAII	ECENPAC	1STLT R.D. HASSLER	S
05/05/44	28125	VC-40	TOROKINA	TOROKINA	SOPAC		
05/05/44	11055	VMSB-243	HAVANNAH		SOPAC		

DATE	BUNO	SQDRN	BASE	LOST	AREA	PILOT	FATE
05/10/44	29060	COMAIR-PAC	PEARL	HAWAII	ECENPAC		
05/10/44	36674	VMSB-133	EWA	HAWAII	ECENPAC	1STLT E.C. MALAFA	D
05/11/44	36696	VMSB-231	MAJURO	MALOELAP	CENPAC	1STLT G.F. MAY	S
05/11/44	10911	VMSB-332	MIDWAY		ECENPAC	2NDLT J. LORENZ	S
05/14/44	36733	VMSB-236	TOROKINA		SOPAC		
05/17/44	54103	VB-306	PIVA	RABAUL	SOPAC	LT J.M. ANDERSON, JR.	M
05/17/44	28161	VMSB-244	GREEN	RABAUL	SOPAC	CAPT J.A. ANDERSON	M
05/18/44	36228	VMSB-241	EMIRAU	LAKURAFANG E	SOPAC	1STLT C.A. BACON	S
05/21/44	36233	VMSB-241	EMIRAU	RABAUL	SOPAC	2NDLT W. NOSER	S
05/21/44	28957	VS-44	GUANTANA MO BAY	CUBA	CENLANT	ENS G. MCMORROW	S
05/23/44	10865	VMSB-241	EMIRAU		SOPAC		
05/25/44	28693	VMSB-236	TOROKINA		SOPAC		
05/26/44	28269	HEDRON-32	EWA	HAWAII	ECENPAC	COL J.E. YOUNG	S
05/26/44	36449	VMSB-151	ENGEBI		WCENPAC	1STLT L.A. COCKERLAM	S
05/26/44	36789	VS-52	KWAJALEIN		CENPAC	ENS W.A. CULHANE	S
05/28/44	28104	COMAIR-PAC	PEARL	HAWAII	ECENPAC		
05/28/44	54208	VMSB-244	GREEN	RABAUL	SOPAC	2NDLT R.D. ZEHRUNG	S
05/30/44	36630	VMSB-241	EMIRAU	KAVIENG	SOPAC	CAPT M.E. MONLEY	S
05/30/44	36661	VMSB-241	EMIRAU	KAVIENG	SOPAC	1STLT D.N. STEPHENSON	S
05/30/44	54217	VMSB-241	EMIRAU	KAVIENG	SOPAC	2NDLT H.J. SCHROEDER	M
05/31/44	35930	COMAIR-SOPAC	GUADAL-CANAL	GUADAL-CANAL	SOPAC		
06/01/44	10936	COMAIR-PAC	PEARL	HAWAII	ECENPAC		
06/01/44	28061	COMAIR-PAC	PEARL	HAWAII	ECENPAC		
06/01/44	28172	COMAIR-PAC	PEARL	HAWAII	ECENPAC		
06/01/44	36288	VB-100	BARBERS POINT	HAWAII	ECENPAC		
06/01/44	36338	VMSB-151	ENGEBI		WCENPAC		
06/03/44	28535	VMSB-236	PIVA		SOPAC	1STLT B.H. KERR	D
06/09/44	10916	VMSB-142	EWA	HAWAII	ECENPAC	1STLT D.J. HALLAMEYER	S
06/09/44		VMSB-231	MAJURO	MILLE	CENPAC	CAPT J.K. BELL	S
06/09/44	36503	VS-66	MAKIN	MILLE	CENPAC	ENS V.R. MCELMURRY	M
06/10/44	36821	VB-306	ESPIRITU SANTO		SOPAC		
06/11/44	36258	VB-16	USS LEX-INGTON	SAIPAN	WCENPAC	LT B.T. MENNIS	S
06/12/44	36078	VB-10	USS ENTER-PRISE	SAIPAN	WCENPAC	LT J.G. LEONARD	M
06/12/44	35955	VB-16	USS LEX-INGTON	SAIPAN	WCENPAC	LTJG G.F. BRANSON	D
06/13/44	36289	VB-10	USS ENTER-PRISE	SAIPAN	WCENPAC		
06/13/44	28979	VMSB-235	PIVA	CAPE ST. GEO.	SOPAC	1STLT C.W. LUNDELL	S
06/15/44	28371	VB-16	USS LEX-INGTON	SAIPAN	WCENPAC	LT C.T. SCHRADER	S
06/15/44	54384	VB-16	USS LEX-INGTON	SAIPAN	WCENPAC	LTJG D.R. GILLESPIE	S
06/16/44	10934	VB-16	USS LEX-INGTON	SAIPAN	WCENPAC	LT B.T. MENNIS	S
06/16/44	36913	VMSB-235	TOROKINA	SIMPSON HARBR	SOPAC	1STLT M. ALFORD	M
06/17/44	29080	VS-51	TUTUILA	TAFUNA	SOPAC	ENS L. MULHEIAN	S
06/18/44	54088	VMSB-245	MAKIN	EMIRAU	SW PAC	1STLT J.H. MATHIAS	S
06/19/44	36285	VB-16	USS LEX-INGTON	GUAM	WCENPAC	LTJG J.L. MARSH	S
06/19/44	54115	VB-16	USS LEX-INGTON	GUAM	WCENPAC		
06/19/44	36069	VMSB-331	MAJURO	TAROA	CENPAC	1STLT R.A. TERRELL	S
06/19/44	54250	VS-37		CURACAO	CENLANT	ENS J.J. ZUNKEWICZ	S
06/20/44		COMFAIR	GUADAL-CANAL	GUADAL-CANAL	SOPAC		

DATE	BUNO	SQDRN	BASE	LOST	AREA	PILOT	FATE
06/20/44	36129	VB-10	USS ENTER-PRISE	W OF SAIPAN	CENPAC	LT L.L. RANGE	S
06/20/44	28304	VB-16	USS LEX-INGTON	W OF SAIPAN	CENPAC	LT T.E. DUPREE	S
06/20/44	28419	VB-16	USS LEX-INGTON	W OF SAIPAN	CENPAC	LTJG W.E. HARRISON	S
06/20/44	36010	VB-16	USS LEX-INGTON	W OF SAIPAN	CENPAC	LTJG J.A. SHIELDS	D
06/26/44	11054	VB-16	USS LEX-INGTON	ENR GUAM	CENPAC	LT R.A. HARPER	S
06/26/44	36495	VMSB-331	MAJURO	TAROA	CENPAC	2NDLT H.H. SPARKS	S
06/26/44	54096	VMSB-331	MAJURO	MILLE	CENPAC	1STLT R.D. ARMSTRONG	S
06/27/44	36806	COMAIR-PAC	PEARL	HAWAII	ECENPAC		
06/30/44	28068	ARU SOLS			SOPAC		
06/30/44	29091	ARU SOLS			SOPAC		
06/30/44	36928	ARU SOLS			SOPAC		
06/30/44	10828	VS-54	GUADAL-CANAL	GUADAL-CANAL	SOPAC		
06/30/44	54218	VS-54	GUADAL-CANAL	GUADAL-CANAL	SOPAC	LT JACK P. MASON	S
07/01/44	35944	VB-10	USS ENTER-PRISE	GUAM	WCENPAC	LTJG DETEMBLE	S
07/01/44	54527	VMSB-331	MAJURO	TAROA	CENPAC	1STLT T.J. ROSS	S
07/02/44	54510	VS-46	FORD ISLAND	HAWAII	ECENPAC	CAPT E.W. BOSWELL	S
07/03/44	30929	ARU SOLS			SOPAC	(SALVAGED)	
07/03/44	36753	ARU SOLS			SOPAC	(SALVAGED)	
07/03/44		VMSB-235			SOPAC	LT BECKNER	M
07/04/44	36755	VMSB-333	EWA	HAWAII	ECENPAC	2NDLT R.D. MATTHEWS	S
07/10/44	54291	VMSB-235			SOPAC		
07/10/44	36621	VMSB-341			SOPAC		
07/11/44	28257	ARU SOLS			SOPAC	(SALVAGED)	
07/11/44	28675	VS-69	BARBERS POINT	HAWAII	ECENPAC	ENS M.J. THONO	S
07/12/44	10983	VMSB-142	EWA	HAWAII	ECENPAC		
07/12/44	36687	VMSB-245	MAKIN	MILLE	CENPAC	1STLT J.C. JEWELL	S
07/14/44	28390	VS-69	BARBERS POINT	HAWAII	ECENPAC	LT WILLIAM G. GRENSOW	U
07/17/44	36839	VB-305	ESPIRITU SANTO	MAKIN	CENPAC	LT W.N. MCAFEE	D
07/18/44	35979	CAC	MANUS		SW PAC		
07/26/44	29021	VMSB-236	MUNDA		SOPAC		
08/01/44	10808	ARU SOLS			SOPAC		
08/01/44	35963	ARU SOLS		GUADAL-CANAL	SOPAC		
08/01/44	36477	COMAIR7T HFL		BIAK	SW PAC		
08/01/44	54222	VMSB-251		MUNDA	SOPAC	1STLT J.C. EIKNER	S
08/01/44		VMSB-333	MIDWAY		ECENPAC	1STLT R.D. FITZGERALD	D
08/04/44	28956	VMSB-151		ENIWETOK	CENPAC		
08/04/44	36283	VMSB-151		ENIWETOK	CENPAC		
08/09/44	10856	NAS	MIDWAY		ECENPAC		
08/09/44	10899	NAS	MIDWAY		ECENPAC		
08/09/44	10922	NAS	MIDWAY		ECENPAC		
08/09/44	10941	NAS	MIDWAY		ECENPAC		
08/09/44	11048	NAS	MIDWAY		ECENPAC		
08/09/44	28065	NAS	MIDWAY		ECENPAC		
08/09/44	28086	NAS	MIDWAY		ECENPAC		
08/09/44	28154	NAS	MIDWAY		ECENPAC		
08/09/44	28178	NAS	MIDWAY		ECENPAC		
08/09/44	28236	NAS	MIDWAY		ECENPAC		
08/09/44	28274	NAS	MIDWAY		ECENPAC		
08/09/44	28276	NAS	MIDWAY		ECENPAC		
08/09/44	28283	NAS	MIDWAY		ECENPAC		
08/09/44	28294	NAS	MIDWAY		ECENPAC		
08/09/44	28315	NAS	MIDWAY		ECENPAC		
08/09/44	28400	NAS	MIDWAY		ECENPAC		
08/11/44	36508	ARU SOLS			SOPAC		
08/18/44	28378	VMF-311	ROI	ROI	WCENPAC	MAJ H.G. DALTON	S
08/18/44	35932	VMSB-243		KARAUAT	SW PAC	MAJ H.L. CHAITIN	M
08/18/44	36629	VS-66	MAKIN	MAKIN	CENPAC	LTJG J.D. MCLAUGHLIN	M

DATE	BUNO	SQDRN	BASE	LOST	AREA	PILOT	FATE
08/25/44	54226	MAG-14	GREEN	GREEN	SOPAC		
08/25/44	36740	VMSB-236	BOUGAIN-VILLE		SOPAC		
08/28/44		VMSB-235		GREEN	SOPAC	1STLT A.D. GLENN	D
08/29/44	36698	MAG-32	EWA	HAWAII	ECENPAC	2NDLT M.S. MESSER	S
08/31/44	28701	VB-100	OAHU	HAWAII	ECENPAC		
09/08/44	36471	VMSB-231	MAJURO	MAJURO	CENPAC	1STLT A.W. COLE	S
09/12/44	36093	VMSB-151		ENIWETOK	CENPAC	2NDLT R.M. BALCH	S
09/12/44	36664	VS-44	GUANTANA MO BAY	CUBA	CENLANT	LT JAMES D. WALLACE	S
09/13/44	36384	CASU-32	KAHULUI	HAWAII	ECENPAC		
09/14/44	29073	VS-51	TUTUILA	SAMOA	SOPAC	ENS J.D. EZECHEL, JR.	S
09/16/44	54129	VMSB-331		WOTJE	CENPAC	2NDLT R.L. NELSON	S
09/18/44	54120	VMSB-331		MAJURO	CENPAC	LT ROBERT J. MCEVOY	S
09/20/44	28557		ESPIRITU SANTO		SOPAC		
09/20/44	54351	VS-37		CURACAO	CENLANT	ENS HAROLD N. GETZ	M
09/23/44	35940	SERVRON-4		GREEN	SOPAC		
09/23/44	54427	VS-61		MOKERANG	SW PAC	ENS TAYLOR C. SIMPSON	S
09/24/44	28117	COMAIR-PAC	PEARL	HAWAII	ECENPAC		
09/26/44	36825	NAB	ENIWETOK		CENPAC		
09/26/44		VMSB-241		MUNDA	SOPAC		
09/27/44	28070		ESPIRITU SANTO		SOPAC		
09/27/44	10826	POOL	GUADAL-CANAL		SOPAC		
09/27/44	10895	POOL	GUADAL-CANAL		SOPAC		
09/27/44	11047	POOL	GUADAL-CANAL		SOPAC		
09/27/44	29009	POOL	GUADAL-CANAL		SOPAC		
09/27/44	28898	VS-48		ALASKA	NORPAC	ENS DONALD MCDANIEL	M
09/27/44	28910	VS-48		ALASKA	NORPAC	ENS MALCOLM K. CRONIN	M
09/28/44	28363		ESPIRITU SANTO		SOPAC		
09/29/44	54571	VFB-1	PORT LYAUTEY	MOROCCO	NW AFR	LT A. VAN EFFENTERRE	S
09/30/44	29016	VS-57	NOUMEA	NOUMEA	SOPAC		
09/30/44	29113	VS-57	NOUMEA	NOUMEA	SOPAC		
10/04/44	54388	VS-46	PEARL	HAWAII	ECENPAC	ENS JOHN S. MACKLIN	S
10/06/44	54327	VMSB-244	NEW BRITAIN		SW PAC		
10/12/44	54409	VS-61	NAVY NO. 3205		CENPAC	ENS C.F. SOJKA	S
10/19/44	28617	NAS	KANEOHE	HAWAII	ECENPAC		
10/24/44	54277	VS-46	PEARL	HAWAII	ECENPAC	ENS JOSEPH E. PARRIOTT	U
10/26/44	54229	A & R	GUADAL-CANAL	GUADAL-CANAL	SOPAC		
10/26/44	10896	NAS	MIDWAY		ECENPAC		
10/26/44	11065	NAS	MIDWAY		ECENPAC		
10/26/44	28145	NAS	MIDWAY		ECENPAC		
10/31/44	28930	COMAIR-PAC	PEARL	HAWAII	ECENPAC		
11/01/44	10947	COMAIR-PAC	PEARL	HAWAII	ECENPAC		
11/01/44	36362	VS-65		ESPIRITU SANTO	SOPAC	ENS CHARLES D. SHUMAN	S
11/04/44	10964	AWT ACTION	GUADAL-CANAL		SOPAC		
11/04/44	28126	AWT ACTION	GUADAL-CANAL		SOPAC		
11/04/44	28646	AWT ACTION	GUADAL-CANAL		SOPAC		
11/05/44	28290	AWT ACTION	ESPIRITU SANTO		SOPAC		
11/08/44	28527	AWT ACTION	GUADAL-CANAL		SOPAC		

DATE	BUNO	SQDRN	BASE	LOST	AREA	PILOT	FATE
11/08/44	28548	AWT ACTION	GUADAL-CANAL		SOPAC		
11/08/44	28560	AWT ACTION	GUADAL-CANAL		SOPAC		
11/08/44	10956	VS-48	AMCHITKA	ALASKA	NORPAC		
11/19/44	10904	CASU(F)-42		PITYILU	SW PAC		
11/20/44	36768	VMSB-245	GUADAL-CANAL		SOPAC	2NDLT ALLAN M. BARBER	D
11/24/44	36256	AWT ACTION	ESPIRITU SANTO		SOPAC		
11/24/44	36348	AWT ACTION	ESPIRITU SANTO		SOPAC		
11/24/44	54512	VS-46	PEARL	HAWAII	ECENPAC	ENS JAMES F. LLOYD	S
11/26/44	54245	CASU(F)-42		PITYILU	SW PAC		
11/26/44	54422	MAG-32	EMIRAU	LOS NEGROS	PHIL	LT GEORGE H. FLETCHER	S
11/27/44	28522	AWT ACTION	GUADAL-CANAL		SOPAC		
11/29/44	28664	CASU(F)-41		GUADAL-CANAL	SOPAC		
12/02/44	35993	A.A.	GUADAL-CANAL	GUADAL-CANAL	SOPAC		
12/04/44	29066	A.A.	ESPIRITU SANTO	ESPIRITU SANTO	SOPAC		
12/04/44	29089	A.A.	ESPIRITU SANTO	ESPIRITU SANTO	SOPAC		
12/04/44	29094	A.A.	ESPIRITU SANTO	ESPIRITU SANTO	SOPAC		
12/04/44	29106	A.A.	ESPIRITU SANTO	ESPIRITU SANTO	SOPAC		
12/08/44	35924	A.A.	GUADAL-CANAL	GUADAL-CANAL	SOPAC		
12/08/44	36757	A.A.	GUADAL-CANAL	GUADAL-CANAL	SOPAC		
12/09/44	28848	A.A.	GUADAL-CANAL	GUADAL-CANAL	SOPAC		
12/10/44	28459	VMO-155		KWAJALEIN	CENPAC		
12/11/44	28299	A.A.	ESPIRITU SANTO	ESPIRITU SANTO	SOPAC		
12/11/44	28656	A.A.	ESPIRITU SANTO	ESPIRITU SANTO	SOPAC		
12/11/44	28691	A.A.	ESPIRITU SANTO	ESPIRITU SANTO	SOPAC		
12/11/44	28923	A.A.	ESPIRITU SANTO	ESPIRITU SANTO	SOPAC		
12/11/44	28981	A.A.	ESPIRITU SANTO	ESPIRITU SANTO	SOPAC		
12/11/44	29081	A.A.	ESPIRITU SANTO	ESPIRITU SANTO	SOPAC		
12/11/44	29082	A.A.	ESPIRITU SANTO	ESPIRITU SANTO	SOPAC		
12/11/44	36279	A.A.	ESPIRITU SANTO	ESPIRITU SANTO	SOPAC		
12/11/44	36529	A.A.	ESPIRITU SANTO	ESPIRITU SANTO	SOPAC		
12/11/44	36563	A.A.	ESPIRITU SANTO	ESPIRITU SANTO	SOPAC		
12/11/44	36575	A.A.	ESPIRITU SANTO	ESPIRITU SANTO	SOPAC		
12/11/44	36577	A.A.	ESPIRITU SANTO	ESPIRITU SANTO	SOPAC		
12/11/44	36873	A.A.	ESPIRITU SANTO	ESPIRITU SANTO	SOPAC		
12/11/44	36889	A.A.	ESPIRITU SANTO	ESPIRITU SANTO	SOPAC		
12/11/44	36807	COMAIR-PAC	PEARL	HAWAII	ECENPAC		
12/13/44	36514	A.A.	GUADAL-CANAL	GUADAL-CANAL	SOPAC		
12/13/44	36525	A.A.	GUADAL-CANAL	GUADAL-CANAL	SOPAC		
12/13/44	36604	A.A.	GUADAL-CANAL	GUADAL-CANAL	SOPAC		
12/13/44	54128	CASU-30		MAJURO	CENPAC		
12/15/44	54181	VMSB-333	EWA	HAWAII	ECENPAC	2NDLT PETER CLINCH	M

DATE	BUNO	SQDRN	BASE	LOST	AREA	PILOT	FATE
12/16/44	28917	VMF-441	ROI		CENPAC	2NDLT JOHN DALTON	S
12/17/44	36352	VMSB-245		MAJURO	CENPAC	LT ALBERT W. MCGARR	D
12/18/44	10967	NAS	MIDWAY		ECENPAC		
12/18/44	28319	NAS	MIDWAY		ECENPAC		
12/19/44	11058	A.A.	PEARL	HAWAII	ECENPAC		
12/19/44	28528	A.A.	PEARL	HAWAII	ECENPAC		
12/19/44	28616	A.A.	PEARL	HAWAII	ECENPAC		
12/19/44	28677	A.A.	PEARL	HAWAII	ECENPAC		
12/20/44	29157	A.A.	GUADAL-CANAL	GUADAL-CANAL	SOPAC		
12/26/44	54442	CASU-41		GUADAL-CANAL	SOPAC	1STLT JOHN T. CURTIN	S
12/28/44	11059	A.A.	PEARL	HAWAII	ECENPAC		
12/28/44	28345	A.A.	PEARL	HAWAII	ECENPAC		
12/28/44	36115	A.A.	PEARL	HAWAII	ECENPAC		
12/28/44	36378	A.A.	PEARL	HAWAII	ECENPAC		
12/28/44	36561	A.A.	PEARL	HAWAII	ECENPAC		
12/28/44	36597	A.A.	PEARL	HAWAII	ECENPAC		
12/28/44	54209	A.A.	PEARL	HAWAII	ECENPAC		
12/31/44	36419	VMSB-231	MAJURO	MAJURO	CENPAC	2NDLT JACK S. WHITAKER	D
01/01/45	36702	VMSB-244		EMIRAU	SW PAC	MAJ JOHN L. DEXTER	S
01/06/45	28621	A.A.	PEARL	HAWAII	ECENPAC		
01/09/45	36906	POOL	ESPIRITU SANTO	ESPIRITU SANTO	SOPAC		
01/09/45	36926	POOL	ESPIRITU SANTO	ESPIRITU SANTO	SOPAC		
01/13/45	54146	VMF-422	ENGEBI	ENGEBI	WCENPAC		
01/15/45	28925	A.A.	GUADAL-CANAL	GUADAL-CANAL	SOPAC		
01/15/45	28812	VMF-224		ROI	WCENPAC	1STLT GLENN G. RILEY	S
01/17/45	28538	POOL	ESPIRITU SANTO	ESPIRITU SANTO	SOPAC		
01/17/45	29088	POOL	ESPIRITU SANTO	ESPIRITU SANTO	SOPAC		
01/17/45	36267	VMF-111	ROI	ROI	WCENPAC		
01/18/45	54295	POOL	PEARL	HAWAII	ECENPAC		
01/20/45	36102	MAG-23		MIDWAY	ECENPAC		
01/20/45	36548	MAG-23		MIDWAY	ECENPAC		
01/20/45	54054	MAG-23		MIDWAY	ECENPAC		
01/22/45	54343	CAC	MANUS		SW PAC		
01/29/45	54535	SERVRON-22		ENGEBI	WCENPAC		
01/30/45	36612	A.A.	PEARL	HAWAII	ECENPAC		
01/30/45	36657	A.A.	PEARL	HAWAII	ECENPAC		
01/30/45	54108	CASU-30		MAJURO	CENPAC		
01/30/45	54353	VMSB-244		EMIRAU	SW PAC		
02/04/45	36719	CASU(F)-20		ROI	WCENPAC		
02/10/45		A.A.	GUADAL-CANAL	GUADAL-CANAL	SOPAC		
02/20/45	36734	CASU(F)-20		ROI	WCENPAC		
02/23/45	29103	VS-66	TARAWA		WCENPAC	LTJG FRANK C. HART, JR.	S
02/24/45	54541	VMSB-151		ENGEBI	WCENPAC		
02/27/45	36728	CASU(F)-20		ROI	WCENPAC		
02/27/45	36376	VS-52	ROI	ROI	WCENPAC	ENS RICHARD PIERMAN	M
03/05/45	28116	CASU-32	KAHULUI	HAWAII	ECENPAC		
03/05/45	54414	VMSB-244		LUZON	PHIL	2NDLT D. W. MCMULLON	D
03/08/45	54223	COMAIR-PAC	PEARL	HAWAII	ECENPAC		
03/09/45	54210	VMSB-243		LUZON	PHIL	2NDLT THOMAS M. PEPE	M
03/12/45	36822	VMSB-243		LUZON	PHIL		
03/14/45	28579	CASU(F)-13		PITYILU	SW PAC		
03/14/45	36633	CASU(F)-20		ROI	WCENPAC		
03/14/45	54154	CASU(F)-20		ROI	WCENPAC		
03/15/45	54219	VS-65		ESPIRITU SANTO	SOPAC		
03/17/45	36487	CASU(F)-20		ROI	WCENPAC		
03/17/45	36741	CASU(F)-20		ROI	WCENPAC		
03/17/45	54156	CASU(F)-20		ROI	WCENPAC		
03/21/45	54516	COMAIR-PAC	PEARL	HAWAII	ECENPAC		
03/23/45	28407	CASU(F)-20		ROI	WCENPAC		

DATE	BUNO	SQDRN	BASE	LOST	AREA	PILOT	FATE
03/23/45	36669	CASU(F)-20		ROI	WCENPAC		
03/23/45	36706	CASU(F)-20		ROI	WCENPAC		
03/25/45	36453	VS-48	DUTCH HARBOR	KODIAK	NORPAC	ENS WILLIAM E. BELCHER	D
03/28/45	36625	STATION OPR	MIDWAY	HAWAII	ECENPAC		
03/28/45	54311	VMSB-243		LUZON	PHIL	LT JENSEN	S
03/28/45	54359	VMSB-243		LUZON	PHIL	LT ARTHUR N. GUNTHER	S
03/31/45	28611	COMAIR-PAC	PEARL	HAWAII	ECENPAC		
04/04/45	54183	NAB	TARAWA	TARAWA	CENPAC	2NDLT R.C. PATTILLO	S
04/06/45	54508	CASU(F)-20		ROI	WCENPAC		
04/06/45	54051	VMSB-151		ENGEBI	WCENPAC	2NDLT SAMUEL T. DOWLEN	S
04/07/45	28430	CASU-32	KAHULUI	HAWAII	ECENPAC		
04/07/45	54292	VS-46	PEARL	HAWAII	ECENPAC		
04/10/45	28555	POOL	GUADAL-CANAL	GUADAL-CANAL	SOPAC		
04/12/45	28854	CASU(F)-20		ROI	WCENPAC		
04/13/45	36603	CASU(F)-20		ROI	WCENPAC		
04/15/45	28624	CASU-1	USS BLOCK ISLAND	HAWAII	ECENPAC	CAPT ARTHUR T. WOOD	S
04/16/45	36611	VMSB-243		LINGAYEN GULF	PHIL	MCKOY	U
04/16/45	36772	VMSB-343		MIDWAY	ECENPAC	2NDLT WM M. CRUTCHER	S
04/19/45	36763	VMSB-244		LINGAYEN GULF	PHIL		
04/23/45	28936	POOL	BARBERS POINT	HAWAII	ECENPAC		
04/24/45	36773	NAF	FUNAFUTI	FUNAFUTI	CENPAC		
04/24/45	28582	POOL	KANEOHE	HAWAII	ECENPAC		
04/25/45	28690	CASU(F)-20		ROI	WCENPAC		
04/25/45	28978	CASU(F)-20		ROI	WCENPAC		
04/25/45	29022	CASU(F)-20		ROI	WCENPAC		
04/25/45	29069	CASU(F)-20		ROI	WCENPAC		
04/25/45	29087	CASU(F)-20		ROI	WCENPAC		
04/25/45	29099	CASU(F)-20		ROI	WCENPAC		
04/25/45	35934	CASU(F)-20		ROI	WCENPAC		
04/25/45	36065	CASU(F)-20		ROI	WCENPAC		
04/25/45	36108	CASU(F)-20		ROI	WCENPAC		
04/25/45	36143	CASU(F)-20		ROI	WCENPAC		
04/25/45	36254	CASU(F)-20		ROI	WCENPAC		
04/25/45	36264	CASU(F)-20		ROI	WCENPAC		
04/25/45	36353	CASU(F)-20		ROI	WCENPAC		
04/25/45	36372	CASU(F)-20		ROI	WCENPAC		
04/25/45	36381	CASU(F)-20		ROI	WCENPAC		
04/25/45	36421	CASU(F)-20		ROI	WCENPAC		
04/25/45	36468	CASU(F)-20		ROI	WCENPAC		
04/25/45	36489	CASU(F)-20		ROI	WCENPAC		
04/25/45	36500	CASU(F)-20		ROI	WCENPAC		
04/25/45	36545	CASU(F)-20		ROI	WCENPAC		
04/25/45	36595	CASU(F)-20		ROI	WCENPAC		
04/25/45	36616	CASU(F)-20		ROI	WCENPAC		
04/25/45	36617	CASU(F)-20		ROI	WCENPAC		
04/25/45	36619	CASU(F)-20		ROI	WCENPAC		
04/25/45	36667	CASU(F)-20		ROI	WCENPAC		
04/25/45	36668	CASU(F)-20		ROI	WCENPAC		
04/25/45	36679	CASU(F)-20		ROI	WCENPAC		
04/25/45	36681	CASU(F)-20		ROI	WCENPAC		
04/25/45	36695	CASU(F)-20		ROI	WCENPAC		
04/25/45	36699	CASU(F)-20		ROI	WCENPAC		
04/25/45	36717	CASU(F)-20		ROI	WCENPAC		
04/25/45	36721	CASU(F)-20		ROI	WCENPAC		
04/25/45	36738	CASU(F)-20		ROI	WCENPAC		
04/25/45	36791	CASU(F)-20		ROI	WCENPAC		
04/25/45	36810	CASU(F)-20		ROI	WCENPAC		
04/25/45	54052	CASU(F)-20		ROI	WCENPAC		
04/25/45	54061	CASU(F)-20		ROI	WCENPAC		
04/25/45	54069	CASU(F)-20		ROI	WCENPAC		
04/25/45	54070	CASU(F)-20		ROI	WCENPAC		
04/25/45	54075	CASU(F)-20		ROI	WCENPAC		
04/25/45	54104	CASU(F)-20		ROI	WCENPAC		

DATE	BUNO	SQDRN	BASE	LOST	AREA	PILOT	FATE
04/25/45	54141	CASU(F)-20		ROI	WCENPAC		
04/25/45	54144	CASU(F)-20		ROI	WCENPAC		
04/25/45	54153	CASU(F)-20		ROI	WCENPAC		
04/25/45	54178	CASU(F)-20		ROI	WCENPAC		
04/25/45	54200	CASU(F)-20		ROI	WCENPAC		
04/25/45	54214	CASU(F)-20		ROI	WCENPAC		
04/25/45	54318	CASU(F)-20		ROI	WCENPAC		
04/25/45	54517	CASU(F)-20		ROI	WCENPAC		
04/25/45	36609	VMSB-244		LINGAYEN GULF	PHIL		
04/27/45	36601	VMSB-244		LINGAYEN GULF	PHIL		
04/28/45	28932	POOL	KANEOHE	HAWAII	ECENPAC		
04/29/45	28890	VS-53	PEARL	HAWAII	ECENPAC	ENS CARLTON G. HAZARD	S
04/30/45	28844	ACORN-19 PL	RUSSELLS		SOPAC		
04/30/45	28078	POOL	PEARL	HAWAII	ECENPAC		
04/30/45	28325	POOL	PEARL	HAWAII	ECENPAC		
04/30/45	28446	POOL	GUADAL-CANAL	GUADAL-CANAL	SOPAC		
04/30/45	28676	POOL	PEARL	HAWAII	ECENPAC		
04/30/45	28809	POOL	PEARL	HAWAII	ECENPAC		
04/30/45	28816	POOL	PEARL	HAWAII	ECENPAC		
04/30/45	36217	POOL	PEARL	HAWAII	ECENPAC		
04/30/45	36347	POOL	PEARL	HAWAII	ECENPAC		
04/30/45	36662	POOL	GUADAL-CANAL	GUADAL-CANAL	SOPAC		
04/30/45	36736	POOL	GUADAL-CANAL	GUADAL-CANAL	SOPAC		
04/30/45	36833	POOL	PEARL	HAWAII	ECENPAC		
04/30/45	54294	POOL	PEARL	HAWAII	ECENPAC		
04/30/45	54373	POOL	PEARL	HAWAII	ECENPAC		
04/30/45	54504	POOL	PEARL	HAWAII	ECENPAC		
04/30/45	36623	VMSB-244		LINGAYEN GULF	PHIL		
04/30/45	36841	VMSB-244		LINGAYEN GULF	PHIL		
04/30/45	54363	VMSB-244		LINGAYEN GULF	PHIL		
04/30/45	54398	VMSB-244		LINGAYEN GULF	PHIL		
04/30/45	54485	VMSB-244		LINGAYEN GULF	PHIL		
04/30/45	54498	VMSB-244		LINGAYEN GULF	PHIL		
05/01/45	54067	POOL	KANEOHE	HAWAII	ECENPAC		
05/01/45	54440	VMSB-244		COTOBATO	PHIL	LT POORE	U
05/01/45	10851	VS-65		ESPIRITU SANTO	SOPAC		
05/01/45	28516	VS-65		ESPIRITU SANTO	SOPAC		
05/01/45	36516	VS-65		ESPIRITU SANTO	SOPAC		
05/01/45	36651	VS-65		ESPIRITU SANTO	SOPAC		
05/01/45	36766	VS-65		ESPIRITU SANTO	SOPAC		
05/01/45	36924	VS-65		ESPIRITU SANTO	SOPAC		
05/01/45	54198	VS-65		ESPIRITU SANTO	SOPAC		
05/01/45	54212	VS-65		ESPIRITU SANTO	SOPAC		
05/01/45	54215	VS-65		ESPIRITU SANTO	SOPAC		
05/01/45	54232	VS-65		ESPIRITU SANTO	SOPAC		
05/01/45	54273	VS-65		ESPIRITU SANTO	SOPAC		
05/01/45	54308	VS-65		ESPIRITU SANTO	SOPAC		
05/01/45	54309	VS-65		ESPIRITU SANTO	SOPAC		

DATE	BUNO	SQDRN	BASE	LOST	AREA	PILOT	FATE
05/01/45	54324	VS-65		ESPIRITU SANTO	SOPAC		
05/01/45	54392	VS-65		ESPIRITU SANTO	SOPAC		
05/01/45	54461	VS-65		ESPIRITU SANTO	SOPAC		
05/01/45	54514	VS-65		ESPIRITU SANTO	SOPAC		
05/02/45	28456	POOL	KANEOHE	HAWAII	ECENPAC		
05/02/45	36286	POOL	KANEOHE	HAWAII	ECENPAC		
05/03/45	10921	POOL	GUADAL-CANAL	GUADAL-CANAL	SOPAC		
05/03/45	28933	VS-57	NOUMEA	NOUMEA	SOPAC		
05/03/45	36862	VS-57	NOUMEA	NOUMEA	SOPAC		
05/03/45	36884	VS-57	NOUMEA	NOUMEA	SOPAC		
05/03/45	36891	VS-57	NOUMEA	NOUMEA	SOPAC		
05/03/45	36895	VS-57	NOUMEA	NOUMEA	SOPAC		
05/03/45	36915	VS-57	NOUMEA	NOUMEA	SOPAC		
05/03/45	36918	VS-57	NOUMEA	NOUMEA	SOPAC		
05/03/45	54189	VS-57	NOUMEA	NOUMEA	SOPAC		
05/03/45	54201	VS-57	NOUMEA	NOUMEA	SOPAC		
05/03/45	54350	VS-57	NOUMEA	NOUMEA	SOPAC		
05/03/45	54361	VS-57	NOUMEA	NOUMEA	SOPAC		
05/03/45	54424	VS-57	NOUMEA	NOUMEA	SOPAC		
05/03/45	54455	VS-57	NOUMEA	NOUMEA	SOPAC		
05/03/45	54464	VS-57	NOUMEA	NOUMEA	SOPAC		
05/03/45	54502	VS-57	NOUMEA	NOUMEA	SOPAC		
05/04/45	35936	POOL	GUADAL-CANAL	GUADAL-CANAL	SOPAC		
05/04/45	36897	POOL	GUADAL-CANAL	GUADAL-CANAL	SOPAC		
05/06/45	36896	NAF	FUNAFUTI	FUNAFUTI	CENPAC		
05/06/45	36910	NAF	FUNAFUTI	FUNAFUTI	CENPAC		
05/15/45	36606	VFB-53		GREEN	SOPAC		
05/15/45	28162	VS-53	PEARL	HAWAII	ECENPAC		
05/18/45	28355	POOL	KAHULUI	HAWAII	ECENPAC		
05/19/45	36263	POOL	KANEOHE	HAWAII	ECENPAC		
05/21/45	54323	AROU-1		MOMOTE	SW PAC		
05/23/45	54175	VJ-16	GUANTANA MO BAY	CUBA	CENLANT	LT WM ADAMS MORTIMER	S
05/24/45	36793	VMSB-244		COTOBATO	PHIL	LT CRAWFORD	S
05/25/45	54332	VMSB-151		ENGEBI	WCENPAC		
05/26/45	36764	MAG-23	HAWAII		ECENPAC	ENS FRANK E. HAND	S
05/29/45	36383	VS-48	DUTCH HARBOR	ALASKA	NORPAC	ENS FRANCIS N. HELMES	S
05/30/45	36769	MAG-32		ZAMBOAN-GA	PHIL		
05/30/45	54220	MAG-32		ZAMBOAN-GA	PHIL		
05/30/45	54231	MAG-32		ZAMBOAN-GA	PHIL		
05/30/45	54336	MAG-32		ZAMBOAN-GA	PHIL		
05/30/45	54360	MAG-32		ZAMBOAN-GA	PHIL		
05/30/45	54366	MAG-32		ZAMBOAN-GA	PHIL		
05/30/45	54437	MAG-32		ZAMBOAN-GA	PHIL		
05/30/45	54454	MAG-32		ZAMBOAN-GA	PHIL		
05/31/45	36858	COMAIR-PAC	PEARL	HAWAII	ECENPAC		
05/31/45	54289	COMAIR-PAC	PEARL	HAWAII	ECENPAC		
05/31/45	54290	COMAIR-PAC	PEARL	HAWAII	ECENPAC		
05/31/45	54513	COMAIR-PAC	PEARL	HAWAII	ECENPAC		
05/31/45	54344	NAF	TUTUILA	TUTUILA	SOPAC		
05/31/45	54435	NAF	TUTUILA	TUTUILA	SOPAC		
05/31/45	54462	NAF	TUTUILA	TUTUILA	SOPAC		
06/01/45	36628	NAS	MIDWAY	MIDWAY	ECENPAC		
06/01/45	54152	POOL	PEARL	HAWAII	ECENPAC		
06/01/45	54270	POOL	PEARL	HAWAII	ECENPAC		
06/01/45	54287	POOL	PEARL	HAWAII	ECENPAC		
06/02/45	36845	CASU(F)-20		ROI	WCENPAC		
06/02/45	54058	CASU(F)-20		ROI	WCENPAC		
06/02/45	54071	CASU(F)-20		ROI	WCENPAC		
06/02/45	54354	CASU(F)-20		ROI	WCENPAC		
06/02/45	54387	CASU(F)-20		ROI	WCENPAC		
06/02/45	54417	CASU(F)-20		ROI	WCENPAC		
06/02/45	54443	CASU(F)-20		ROI	WCENPAC		

DATE	BUNO	SQDRN	BASE	LOST	AREA	PILOT	FATE
06/02/45	54539	CASU(F)-20		ROI	WCENPAC		
06/06/45	28623	POOL	KANEOHE	HAWAII	ECENPAC		
06/06/45	36301	POOL	BARBERS POINT	HAWAII	ECENPAC		
06/06/45	36547	POOL	BARBERS POINT	HAWAII	ECENPAC		
06/06/45	36684	POOL	BARBERS POINT	HAWAII	ECENPAC		
06/07/45	54145	POOL	KANEOHE	HAWAII	ECENPAC		
06/08/45	36222	VMSB-243		ZAMBOAN-GA	PHIL	LT HECKMAN	S
06/09/45	54062	CASU(F)-20		ROI	WCENPAC		
06/09/45	54358	CASU(F)-20		ROI	WCENPAC		
06/09/45	54523	CASU(F)-20		ROI	WCENPAC		
06/12/45	11056	POOL	PEARL	HAWAII	ECENPAC		
06/16/45	28408	COMAIR-PAC	PEARL	HAWAII	ECENPAC		
06/26/45	54507	POOL	PEARL	HAWAII	ECENPAC		
06/27/45	10831	AROU-1		MOMOTE	SW PAC		
06/27/45	10891	AROU-1		MOMOTE	SW PAC		
06/27/45	10924	AROU-1		MOMOTE	SW PAC		
06/27/45	10931	AROU-1		MOMOTE	SW PAC		
06/27/45	28366	AROU-1		MOMOTE	SW PAC		
06/27/45	28569	AROU-1		MOMOTE	SW PAC		
06/27/45	28575	AROU-1		MOMOTE	SW PAC		
06/27/45	29085	AROU-1		MOMOTE	SW PAC		
06/27/45	35929	AROU-1		MOMOTE	SW PAC		
06/27/45	36055	AROU-1		MOMOTE	SW PAC		
06/27/45	36077	AROU-1		MOMOTE	SW PAC		
06/27/45	36511	AROU-1		MOMOTE	SW PAC		
06/27/45	36562	AROU-1		MOMOTE	SW PAC		
06/27/45	36599	AROU-1		MOMOTE	SW PAC		
06/27/45	36608	AROU-1		MOMOTE	SW PAC		
06/27/45	36671	AROU-1		MOMOTE	SW PAC		
06/27/45	36722	AROU-1		MOMOTE	SW PAC		
06/27/45	36723	AROU-1		MOMOTE	SW PAC		
06/27/45	36767	AROU-1		MOMOTE	SW PAC		
06/27/45	36785	AROU-1		MOMOTE	SW PAC		
06/27/45	36826	AROU-1		MOMOTE	SW PAC		
06/27/45	36888	AROU-1		MOMOTE	SW PAC		
06/27/45	36911	AROU-1		MOMOTE	SW PAC		
06/27/45	36925	AROU-1		MOMOTE	SW PAC		
06/27/45	54113	AROU-1		MOMOTE	SW PAC		
06/27/45	54362	AROU-1		MOMOTE	SW PAC		
06/27/45	54367	AROU-1		MOMOTE	SW PAC		
06/27/45	54380	AROU-1		MOMOTE	SW PAC		
06/27/45	54393	AROU-1		MOMOTE	SW PAC		
06/27/45	54405	AROU-1		MOMOTE	SW PAC		
06/27/45	54416	AROU-1		MOMOTE	SW PAC		
06/27/45	54426	AROU-1		MOMOTE	SW PAC		
06/27/45	54429	AROU-1		MOMOTE	SW PAC		
06/27/45	54431	AROU-1		MOMOTE	SW PAC		
06/27/45	54438	AROU-1		MOMOTE	SW PAC		
06/27/45	54451	AROU-1		MOMOTE	SW PAC		
06/27/45	54452	AROU-1		MOMOTE	SW PAC		
06/27/45	54459	AROU-1		MOMOTE	SW PAC		
06/27/45	54460	AROU-1		MOMOTE	SW PAC		
06/27/45	54468	AROU-1		MOMOTE	SW PAC		
06/27/45	54486	AROU-1		MOMOTE	SW PAC		
06/27/45	54489	AROU-1		MOMOTE	SW PAC		
06/27/45	54491	AROU-1		MOMOTE	SW PAC		
06/27/45	54493	AROU-1		MOMOTE	SW PAC		
06/27/45	54501	AROU-1		MOMOTE	SW PAC		
06/27/45	54505	AROU-1		MOMOTE	SW PAC		
06/27/45	54522	AROU-1		MOMOTE	SW PAC		
06/27/45	28102	POOL	KANEOHE	HAWAII	ECENPAC		
06/28/45	29129	CASU(F)-12		GUAM	WCENPAC		
06/29/45	36232	POOL	KAHULUI	HAWAII	ECENPAC		
06/30/45	28442	MCAS	EWA	HAWAII	ECENPAC		
06/30/45	28389	POOL	BARBERS POINT	HAWAII	ECENPAC		
06/30/45	28094	VB-100	PEARL	HAWAII	ECENPAC		
06/30/45	28353	VB-100	PEARL	HAWAII	ECENPAC		
06/30/45	54239	VS-66	TARAWA	TARAWA	CENPAC		
07/01/45	54500	VJ-8			PHIL	LTJG C. RACZKOWSKI	S
07/03/45	36287	AROU-2		SAMAR	PHIL		

DATE	BUNO	SQDRN	BASE	LOST	AREA	PILOT	FATE
07/03/45	36506	AROU-2		SAMAR	PHIL		
07/03/45	54233	AROU-2		SAMAR	PHIL		
07/03/45	54329	AROU-2		SAMAR	PHIL		
07/03/45	54341	AROU-2		SAMAR	PHIL		
07/03/45	54346	AROU-2		SAMAR	PHIL		
07/03/45	54349	AROU-2		SAMAR	PHIL		
07/03/45	54352	AROU-2		SAMAR	PHIL		
07/03/45	54355	AROU-2		SAMAR	PHIL		
07/03/45	54356	AROU-2		SAMAR	PHIL		
07/03/45	54364	AROU-2		SAMAR	PHIL		
07/03/45	54419	AROU-2		SAMAR	PHIL		
07/03/45	54423	AROU-2		SAMAR	PHIL		
07/03/45	54436	AROU-2		SAMAR	PHIL		
07/03/45	54458	AROU-2		SAMAR	PHIL		
07/03/45	54463	AROU-2		SAMAR	PHIL		
07/03/45	28414	NAS	KAHULUI	HAWAII	ECENPAC		
07/06/45	28642	POOL	PEARL	HAWAII	ECENPAC		
07/07/45	36297	POOL	KAHULUI	HAWAII	ECENPAC		
07/09/45	28326	NAS	HAWAII	HAWAII	ECENPAC		
07/13/45	54511	AROU-1		MOMOTE	SW PAC		
07/13/45	54540	AROU-1		MOMOTE	SW PAC		
07/13/45	54509	AROU-2		SAMAR	PHIL		
07/13/45	29140	CASU(F)-12		GUAM	WCENPAC		
07/13/45	29154	CASU(F)-12		GUAM	WCENPAC		
07/14/45	54325	POOL	KAHULUI	HAWAII	ECENPAC		
07/15/45	10938	NAS	BARBERS POINT	HAWAII	ECENPAC		
07/15/45	54310	VJ-9		SAMAR	PHIL		
07/16/45	10949	NAS	KANEOHE	HAWAII	ECENPAC		
07/16/45	28397	NAS	KANEOHE	HAWAII	ECENPAC		
07/17/45	28289	NAS	KAHULUI	HAWAII	ECENPAC		
07/17/45	54234	NAS	BARBERS POINT	HAWAII	ECENPAC		
07/19/45	36087	POOL	BARBERS POINT	HAWAII	ECENPAC		
07/19/45	36122	POOL	BARBERS POINT	HAWAII	ECENPAC		
07/19/45	36631	POOL	BARBERS POINT	HAWAII	ECENPAC		
07/19/45	54057	POOL	BARBERS POINT	HAWAII	ECENPAC		
07/19/45	54121	POOL	BARBERS POINT	HAWAII	ECENPAC		
07/19/45	54389	POOL	BARBERS POINT	HAWAII	ECENPAC		
07/21/45	28349	NAS	KANEOHE	HAWAII	ECENPAC		
07/21/45	36565	POOL	PEARL	HAWAII	ECENPAC		
07/23/45	10853	POOL	KANEOHE	HAWAII	ECENPAC		
07/25/45	36266	POOL	KANEOHE	HAWAII	ECENPAC		
07/26/45	36542	POOL	MIDWAY	MIDWAY	ECENPAC		
07/26/45	36649	POOL	MIDWAY	MIDWAY	ECENPAC		
07/26/45	36673	POOL	MIDWAY	MIDWAY	ECENPAC		
07/26/45	36675	POOL	MIDWAY	MIDWAY	ECENPAC		
07/26/45	36694	POOL	MIDWAY	MIDWAY	ECENPAC		
07/26/45	36704	POOL	MIDWAY	MIDWAY	ECENPAC		
07/26/45	36707	POOL	MIDWAY	MIDWAY	ECENPAC		
07/26/45	36731	POOL	MIDWAY	MIDWAY	ECENPAC		
07/26/45	36808	POOL	MIDWAY	MIDWAY	ECENPAC		
07/26/45	36835	POOL	MIDWAY	MIDWAY	ECENPAC		
07/30/45	28433	NAS	KANEOHE	HAWAII	ECENPAC		
07/30/45	36729	NAS	KANEOHE	HAWAII	ECENPAC		
07/31/45	10987	POOL	BARBERS POINT	HAWAII	ECENPAC		
07/31/45	28580	POOL	BARBERS POINT	HAWAII	ECENPAC		
07/31/45	28849	POOL	BARBERS POINT	HAWAII	ECENPAC		
07/31/45	28951	POOL	BARBERS POINT	HAWAII	ECENPAC		
07/31/45	28955	POOL	BARBERS POINT	HAWAII	ECENPAC		
07/31/45	28966	POOL	BARBERS POINT	HAWAII	ECENPAC		
07/31/45	28970	POOL	BARBERS POINT	HAWAII	ECENPAC		

DATE	BUNO	SQDRN	BASE	LOST	AREA	PILOT	FATE
07/31/45	29097	POOL	BARBERS POINT	HAWAII	ECENPAC		
07/31/45	36191	POOL	BARBERS POINT	HAWAII	ECENPAC		
07/31/45	36363	POOL	BARBERS POINT	HAWAII	ECENPAC		
07/31/45	36598	POOL	BARBERS POINT	HAWAII	ECENPAC		
07/31/45	36818	POOL	PEARL	HAWAII	ECENPAC		
07/31/45	54262	POOL	BARBERS POINT	HAWAII	ECENPAC		
07/31/45	54321	POOL	BARBERS POINT	HAWAII	ECENPAC		
08/07/45	36132	POOL	SAN JUAN	CUBA	CENLANT		
08/07/45	36154	POOL	SAN JUAN	CUBA	CENLANT		
08/07/45	36905	POOL	SAN JUAN	CUBA	CENLANT		
08/07/45	54518	POOL	SAN JUAN	CUBA	CENLANT		
08/07/45	54524	POOL	SAN JUAN	CUBA	CENLANT		
08/09/45	28110	POOL	PEARL	HAWAII	ECENPAC		
08/13/45	36677	POOL	MIDWAY	MIDWAY	ECENPAC		
08/13/45	36909	POOL	MIDWAY	MIDWAY	ECENPAC		
08/13/45	36932	POOL	MIDWAY	MIDWAY	ECENPAC		
08/13/45	54065	POOL	MIDWAY	MIDWAY	ECENPAC		
08/13/45	54077	POOL	MIDWAY	MIDWAY	ECENPAC		
08/14/45	54433	AROU-2		SAMAR	PHIL		
08/14/45	36765	POOL	CEBU		PHIL		
08/14/45	54421	POOL	CEBU		PHIL		

DOUGLAS SBD-6

The Douglas SBD-6 was the final version produced. This variant provided more improvements, including a 1,350 hp (1,010 kW) engine, but production ended in summer 1944. There were 450 built. Aircraft lost:

DATE	BUNO	SQDRN	BASE	LOST	AREA	PILOT	FATE
08/08/44	54793	VMSB-235		GREEN	SOPAC	CAPT W.F. HALL	U
08/23/44	54751	VMSB-236		GREEN	SOPAC	1STLT J.W. BLOCKER	U
10/05/44	54756	VMSB-142	EMIRAU		SW PAC	LT ROBERT B. MCNEIL	S
10/09/44	54834	VMSB-142	EMIRAU		SW PAC		
10/14/44	54788	VMSB-142	NEW IRELAND		SW PAC	LT J.C. COLEMAN	D
10/19/44	54724	VMSB-245	MAJURO	MAJURO	CENPAC	LT GEORGE M. JACKSON	S
10/23/44	54654	VS-69	BARBERS POINT	HAWAII	ECENPAC	ENS DOUGLAS L. GRANT	S
11/01/44	54785	VMSB-133	TOROKINA		SOPAC	MAJ MAX B. CUNKINHEARD	D
11/09/44	54759	VMSB-341	GREEN		SOPAC	LT PHILIP S. DOTY	S
11/10/44	54819	VMSB-142	EMIRAU		SW PAC		
11/19/44	54792	VMSB-236	TOROKINA		SOPAC	LT JACK LAPATO	U
12/10/44	54607	VMSB-245		MAJURO	CENPAC		
12/10/44	55035	VMSB-245		MAJURO	CENPAC	1STLT HAROLD G. MITCHELL	S
01/07/45	54726	VMSB-245		MARSHALLS	CENPAC	2NDLT GEORGE JACKSON, JR	S
01/26/45	54942	VS-61		ADMIRALTIES	SW PAC	CDR F.F. GOOGOME	M
01/28/45	54784	VMSB-133		LUZON	PHIL	1STLT C.R. LEWIS	M
02/02/45	54889	VMSB-241		LUZON	PHIL	2NDLT WILLIAM A. GANTT	M
02/03/45	54769	VMSB-236		LINGAYEN GULF	PHIL	CAPT G.H. SCHLUCKEBIER	S
02/08/45	54647	VMSB-341		LINGAYEN GULF	PHIL	2NDLT EDWARD E. FRYER	S
02/08/45	54864	VS-47		JOHNSTON IS.	ECENPAC	ENS GAEL A. RHOADES	S
02/10/45	54693	VS-69	BARBERS POINT	HAWAII	ECENPAC	LTJG HARRY A. BINFORD, JR.	S
02/11/45	54706	VMSB-142		LINGAYEN GULF	PHIL	LT W.R. MCKEE	S
02/11/45	54767	VMSB-142		LINGAYEN GULF	PHIL		

DATE	BUNO	SQDRN	BASE	LOST	AREA	PILOT	FATE
02/11/45	54626	VMSB-236		LINGAYEN GULF	PHIL		
02/11/45	54828	VMSB-236		LINGAYEN GULF	PHIL		
02/11/45	54899	VMSB-236		LINGAYEN GULF	PHIL	1STLT JAMES C. EIKNEO	D
02/12/45	54775	VMSB-241		LUZON	PHIL	LT JACOBS	S
02/13/45	54794	VMSB-142		LINGAYEN GULF	PHIL		
02/14/45	54946	SERVRON-32		LINGAYEN GULF	PHIL		
02/19/45	54829	VMSB-133		LUZON	PHIL	2NDLT DONALD M. JOHNSON	M
02/19/45	54809	VMSB-241		LUZON	PHIL	LT J.N. CASHMAN	S
03/01/45	54822	VMSB-236		LINGAYEN GULF	PHIL	LT LACKEY	S
03/02/45	54910	VMSB-241		LUZON	PHIL	1STLT RALPH D. CONSTANT	M
03/02/45	54786	VMSB-341		LINGAYEN GULF	PHIL		
03/06/45	54745	VMSB-341		LUZON	PHIL	CAPT CANAAN	S
03/08/45	54806	VMSB-133		LUZON	PHIL	LT TAYLOR	S
03/08/45	54842	VMSB-142		LUZON	PHIL	MAJ H.R. BARR	S
03/16/45	54772	VMSB-236		LINGAYEN GULF	PHIL	1STLT W.D. SMART	S
03/21/45	54796	VMSB-341		LUZON	PHIL	2NDLT CARLTON M. GREEN	S
03/24/45	54803	VMTB-143		LINGAYEN GULF	PHIL	2NDLT CHARLES T. RUE	U
03/27/45	54771	VMSB-341		MINDANAO SEA	PHIL	LT BURRELL	S
04/10/45	54679	POOL	KANEOHE	HAWAII	ECENPAC		
04/17/45	54871	VJ-16	COCO SOLO	COCO SOLO	CENLANT	LTJG ALLEN B. SNYDER	S
04/19/45	54953	SERVRON-32		ZAMBOANGA	PHIL		
04/23/45	54861	VMSB-241		LINGAYEN GULF	PHIL	1STLT D.E. GERALD	S
04/24/45	54966	POOL	KANEOHE	HAWAII	ECENPAC		
04/24/45	54944	VMSB-241		LINGAYEN GULF	PHIL	1STLT HAROLD J. MOORE	D
04/24/45	54967	VS-69	BARBERS POINT	HAWAII	ECENPAC	ENS ARTHUR C. BOYLESTON	S
04/24/45	55031	VS-69	BARBERS POINT	HAWAII	ECENPAC	LTJG HARRY A. BINFORD, JR.	U
04/26/45	54801	VMSB-133		LINGAYEN GULF	PHIL		
05/01/45	54622	POOL	KANEOHE	HAWAII	ECENPAC		
05/02/45	54739	VMSB-133		COTOBATO	PHIL		
05/02/45	54778	VMSB-133		COTOBATO	PHIL		
05/07/45	54729	VMSB-231	MAJURO	MAJURO	CENPAC	2NDLT HANSEL B. SWINN	S
05/09/45	54886	VMSB-341		ZAMBOANGA	PHIL		
05/16/45	54684	VMSB-241		COTOBATO	PHIL		
05/20/45	55006	AROU-2		SAMAR	PHIL		
05/25/45	54810	VMSB-236		MINDANAO SEA	PHIL	1STLT CHARLES KOLARID, JR	D
05/25/45	54914	VMSB-236		MINDANAO SEA	PHIL	2NDLT CARL C. DRAPER	D
05/27/45	54932	VMSB-236		ZAMBOANGA	PHIL		
05/29/45	54922	VMSB-241		COTOBATO	PHIL		
05/30/45	54712	MAG-32		ZAMBOANGA	PHIL		
05/30/45	54931	MAG-32		ZAMBOANGA	PHIL		
05/30/45	54797	VMSB-133		COTOBATO	PHIL		
05/31/45	54672	COMAIR-PAC	PEARL	HAWAII	ECENPAC		
05/31/45	54687	COMAIR-PAC	PEARL	HAWAII	ECENPAC		
06/03/45	54954	AROU-2		SAMAR	PHIL		
06/07/45	55017	AROU-1		MOMOTE	SW PAC	ENS DOUGLAS N. PLACE	S
06/08/45	54820	VMSB-241		MINDANAO SEA	PHIL	1STLT CLIFFORD A. FROST	S
06/09/45	54753	CASU(F)-20		ROI	WCENPAC		
06/09/45	54663	POOL	PEARL	HAWAII	ECENPAC		

DATE	BUNO	SQDRN	BASE	LOST	AREA	PILOT	FATE
06/09/45	54849	POOL	PEARL	HAWAII	ECENPAC		
06/16/45	54990	VMSB-241		MINDANAO SEA	PHIL	1STLT PHILIP S. DYER	S
06/17/45	55033	NAB		SAMAR	PHIL	ENS C.L. GAMBLE	S
06/17/45	54760	VMSB-142		ZAMBOANGA	PHIL		
06/20/45	54798	VMSB-341		ZAMBOANGA	PHIL	LT SURRATT	S
06/21/45	54716	POOL	BARBERS POINT	HAWAII	ECENPAC		
06/28/45	54660	POOL	PEARL	HAWAII	ECENPAC		
06/28/45	54674	POOL	PEARL	HAWAII	ECENPAC		
06/28/45	54919	POOL	PEARL	HAWAII	ECENPAC		
06/28/45	55015	POOL	PEARL	HAWAII	ECENPAC		
07/02/45	54959	VMSB-243		ZAMBOANGA	PHIL		
07/06/45	54666	POOL	PEARL	HAWAII	ECENPAC		
07/06/45	54682	POOL	PEARL	HAWAII	ECENPAC		
07/06/45	54701	POOL	PEARL	HAWAII	ECENPAC		
07/06/45	55020	POOL	PEARL	HAWAII	ECENPAC		
07/09/45	54992	VMSB-243		ZAMBOANGA	PHIL		
07/10/45	54837	VMSB-142		ZAMBOANGA	PHIL		
07/10/45	54802	VMSB-236		ZAMBOANGA	PHIL		
07/11/45	54911	VMSB-133		MALABANG	PHIL		
07/11/45	54962	VMSB-243		ZAMBOANGA	PHIL		
07/13/45	CASU (F)-12			GUAM	WCENPAC		
07/13/45	CASU (F)-12			GUAM	WCENPAC		
07/13/45	54637	CASU(F)-12		GUAM	WCENPAC		
07/13/45	54696	CASU(F)-12		GUAM	WCENPAC		
07/13/45	54730	CASU(F)-12		GUAM	WCENPAC		
07/13/45	54763	CASU(F)-12		GUAM	WCENPAC		
07/13/45	54964	CASU(F)-12		GUAM	WCENPAC		
07/13/45	54969	CASU(F)-12		GUAM	WCENPAC		
07/13/45	54993	CASU(F)-12		GUAM	WCENPAC		
07/13/45	54994	CASU(F)-12		GUAM	WCENPAC		
07/13/45	54996	CASU(F)-12		GUAM	WCENPAC		
07/13/45		POOL	PEARL	HAWAII	ECENPAC		
07/14/45	54997	CASU(F)-12		GUAM	WCENPAC		
07/14/45	55001	POOL	PEARL	HAWAII	ECENPAC		
07/18/45	54978	CASU(F)-12		GUAM	WCENPAC		
07/18/45	54680	POOL	PEARL	HAWAII	ECENPAC		
07/18/45	55037	POOL	PEARL	HAWAII	ECENPAC		
07/18/45	55041	POOL	PEARL	HAWAII	ECENPAC		
07/19/45	55024	CASU(F)-12		GUAM	WCENPAC		
07/19/45	54658	POOL	BARBERS POINT	HAWAII	ECENPAC		
07/25/45	55048	CASU(F)-12		GUAM	WCENPAC		
07/27/45	54975	CASU(F)-12		GUAM	WCENPAC		
07/27/45	54976	CASU(F)-12		GUAM	WCENPAC		
07/30/45	54634	VMSB-341		ZAMBOANGA	PHIL	LT MCCORMICK	S
07/31/45	54662	POOL	PEARL	HAWAII	ECENPAC		
07/31/45	54698	POOL	PEARL	HAWAII	ECENPAC		
07/31/45	54710	POOL	BARBERS POINT	HAWAII	ECENPAC		
08/03/45	54977	CASU(F)-12		GUAM	WCENPAC		
08/03/45	54613	POOL	CEBU		PHIL		
08/03/45	54623	POOL	CEBU		PHIL		
08/03/45	54650	POOL	CEBU		PHIL		
08/03/45	54665	POOL	CEBU		PHIL		
08/03/45	54711	POOL	CEBU		PHIL		
08/03/45	54717	POOL	CEBU		PHIL		
08/03/45	54735	POOL	CEBU		PHIL		
08/03/45	54749	POOL	CEBU		PHIL		
08/03/45	54758	POOL	CEBU		PHIL		
08/03/45	54781	POOL	CEBU		PHIL		
08/03/45	54783	POOL	CEBU		PHIL		
08/03/45	54799	POOL	CEBU		PHIL		
08/03/45	54804	POOL	CEBU		PHIL		
08/03/45	54807	POOL	CEBU		PHIL		
08/03/45	54821	POOL	CEBU		PHIL		
08/03/45	54823	POOL	CEBU		PHIL		
08/03/45	54832	POOL	CEBU		PHIL		
08/03/45	54858	POOL	CEBU		PHIL		
08/03/45	54869	POOL	CEBU		PHIL		
08/03/45	54880	POOL	CEBU		PHIL		
08/03/45	54882	POOL	CEBU		PHIL		

DATE	BUNO	SQDRN	BASE	LOST	AREA	PILOT	FATE
08/03/45	54893	POOL	CEBU		PHIL		
08/03/45	54896	POOL	CEBU		PHIL		
08/03/45	54898	POOL	CEBU		PHIL		
08/03/45	54905	POOL	CEBU		PHIL		
08/03/45	54907	POOL	CEBU		PHIL		
08/03/45	54927	POOL	CEBU		PHIL		
08/03/45	54943	POOL	CEBU		PHIL		
08/03/45	54955	POOL	CEBU		PHIL		
08/03/45	54958	POOL	CEBU		PHIL		
08/03/45	54983	POOL	CEBU		PHIL		
08/03/45	54987	POOL	CEBU		PHIL		
08/03/45	54991	POOL	CEBU		PHIL		
08/03/45	55003	POOL	CEBU		PHIL		
08/03/45	55004	POOL	CEBU		PHIL		
08/03/45	55005	POOL	CEBU		PHIL		
08/03/45	55007	POOL	CEBU		PHIL		
08/03/45	55009	POOL	CEBU		PHIL		
08/03/45	55018	POOL	CEBU		PHIL		
08/03/45	54973	VMSB-243		ZAMBOANGA	PHIL		
08/03/45	54836	VS-47		JOHNSTON IS.	ECENPAC		
08/03/45	54853	VS-47		JOHNSTON IS.	ECENPAC		
08/03/45	54854	VS-47		JOHNSTON IS.	ECENPAC		
08/03/45	54878	VS-47		JOHNSTON IS.	ECENPAC		
08/03/45	54883	VS-47		JOHNSTON IS.	ECENPAC		
08/03/45	54884	VS-47		JOHNSTON IS.	ECENPAC		
08/03/45	54901	VS-47		JOHNSTON IS.	ECENPAC		
08/04/45	54947	AROU-1		MOMOTE	SW PAC		
08/05/45	54620	POOL	CEBU		PHIL		
08/05/45	54625	POOL	CEBU		PHIL		
08/05/45	54667	POOL	CEBU		PHIL		
08/05/45	54692	POOL	CEBU		PHIL		
08/05/45	54752	POOL	CEBU		PHIL		
08/05/45	54754	POOL	CEBU		PHIL		
08/05/45	54765	POOL	CEBU		PHIL		
08/05/45	54768	POOL	CEBU		PHIL		
08/05/45	54773	POOL	CEBU		PHIL		
08/05/45	54774	POOL	CEBU		PHIL		
08/05/45	54776	POOL	CEBU		PHIL		
08/05/45	54777	POOL	CEBU		PHIL		
08/05/45	54789	POOL	CEBU		PHIL		
08/05/45	54800	POOL	CEBU		PHIL		
08/05/45	54805	POOL	CEBU		PHIL		
08/05/45	54808	POOL	CEBU		PHIL		
08/05/45	54825	POOL	CEBU		PHIL		
08/05/45	54850	POOL	CEBU		PHIL		
08/05/45	54857	POOL	CEBU		PHIL		
08/05/45	54895	POOL	CEBU		PHIL		
08/05/45	54897	POOL	CEBU		PHIL		
08/05/45	54902	POOL	CEBU		PHIL		
08/05/45	54926	POOL	CEBU		PHIL		
08/05/45	54951	POOL	CEBU		PHIL		
08/05/45	54963	POOL	CEBU		PHIL		
08/05/45	54965	POOL	CEBU		PHIL		
08/05/45	54974	POOL	CEBU		PHIL		
08/05/45	54984	POOL	CEBU		PHIL		
08/05/45	55012	POOL	CEBU		PHIL		
08/05/45	55039	POOL	CEBU		PHIL		
08/07/45		POOL	SAN JUAN	CUBA	CENLANT		
08/07/45		POOL	SAN JUAN	CUBA	CENLANT		
08/07/45		POOL	SAN JUAN	CUBA	CENLANT		
08/07/45	54609	POOL	SAN JUAN	CUBA	CENLANT		
08/07/45	54689	POOL	SAN JUAN	CUBA	CENLANT		
08/07/45	54722	POOL	CEBU		PHIL		
08/07/45	54727	POOL	CEBU		PHIL		
08/07/45	54811	POOL	CEBU		PHIL		
08/07/45	54812	POOL	CEBU		PHIL		
08/07/45	54815	POOL	CEBU		PHIL		
08/07/45	54826	POOL	CEBU		PHIL		
08/07/45	54859	POOL	CEBU		PHIL		
08/07/45	54887	POOL	CEBU		PHIL		
08/07/45	54938	POOL	SAN JUAN	CUBA	CENLANT		
08/07/45	54949	POOL	CEBU		PHIL		
08/07/45	54968	POOL	CEBU		PHIL		
08/07/45	54985	POOL	CEBU		PHIL		
08/07/45	54988	POOL	CEBU		PHIL		

DATE	BUNO	SQDRN	BASE	LOST	AREA	PILOT	FATE
08/07/45	55029	POOL	CEBU		PHIL		
08/07/45	55046	POOL	CEBU		PHIL		
08/07/45	55023	VMSB-341		ZAMBOANGA	PHIL		
08/09/45	54941	VMSB-142		ZAMBOANGA	PHIL		
08/09/45	55040	VMSB-142		ZAMBOANGA	PHIL		
08/11/45	54615	POOL	CEBU		PHIL		
08/11/45	54685	POOL	CEBU		PHIL		
08/11/45	54699	POOL	CEBU		PHIL		
08/11/45	54757	POOL	CEBU		PHIL		
08/11/45	54791	POOL	CEBU		PHIL		
08/11/45	54795	POOL	CEBU		PHIL		
08/11/45	54814	POOL	CEBU		PHIL		
08/11/45	54827	POOL	CEBU		PHIL		
08/11/45	54833	POOL	CEBU		PHIL		
08/11/45	54921	POOL	CEBU		PHIL		
08/11/45	54925	POOL	CEBU		PHIL		
08/11/45	54950	POOL	CEBU		PHIL		
08/11/45	54956	POOL	CEBU		PHIL		
08/11/45	54957	POOL	CEBU		PHIL		
08/11/45	55022	POOL	CEBU		PHIL		
08/13/45	54612	POOL	CEBU		PHIL		
08/13/45	54614	POOL	CEBU		PHIL		
08/13/45	54631	POOL	CEBU		PHIL		
08/13/45	54635	POOL	CEBU		PHIL		
08/13/45	54640	POOL	CEBU		PHIL		
08/13/45	54648	POOL	CEBU		PHIL		
08/13/45	54657	POOL	CEBU		PHIL		
08/13/45	54695	POOL	CEBU		PHIL		
08/13/45	54697	POOL	CEBU		PHIL		
08/13/45	54703	POOL	CEBU		PHIL		
08/14/45	54664	POOL	CEBU		PHIL		
08/14/45	54675	POOL	CEBU		PHIL		
08/14/45	54676	POOL	CEBU		PHIL		
08/14/45	54681	POOL	CEBU		PHIL		
08/14/45	54709	POOL	CEBU		PHIL		
08/14/45	54736	POOL	CEBU		PHIL		
08/14/45	54750	POOL	CEBU		PHIL		
08/14/45	54952	POOL	CEBU		PHIL		
08/14/45	54960	POOL	CEBU		PHIL		
08/14/45	54970	POOL	CEBU		PHIL		
08/14/45	54971	POOL	CEBU		PHIL		
08/14/45	54972	POOL	CEBU		PHIL		
08/14/45	54986	POOL	CEBU		PHIL		
08/14/45	54995	POOL	CEBU		PHIL		
08/14/45	54998	POOL	CEBU		PHIL		
08/14/45	55008	POOL	CEBU		PHIL		
08/14/45	55011	POOL	CEBU		PHIL		
08/14/45	55013	POOL	CEBU		PHIL		
08/14/45	54708	VS-47		JOHNSTON IS.	ECENPAC		
08/14/45	54725	VS-47		JOHNSTON IS.	ECENPAC		
08/14/45	54831	VS-47	HAWAII		ECENPAC		
08/14/45	54856	VS-47	HAWAII		ECENPAC		
08/14/45	54874	VS-47	HAWAII		ECENPAC		
08/14/45	54876	VS-47	HAWAII		ECENPAC		
08/14/45	54877	VS-47	HAWAII		ECENPAC		
08/14/45	54879	VS-47	HAWAII		ECENPAC		
08/14/45	54948	VS-47	HAWAII		ECENPAC		

DOUGLAS TBD-1

The Douglas TBD Devastator was a torpedo bomber of the United States Navy, ordered in 1934, first flying in 1935 and entering service in 1937. At that point, it was the most advanced aircraft flying for the USN and possibly for any navy in the world. However, the fast pace of aircraft development caught up with it, and by the time of the Japanese attack on Pearl Harbor the TBD was already outdated. It performed well in some early battles, but in the Battle of Midway the Devastators launched against the Japanese fleet were almost totally wiped out. The type was immediately withdrawn from front line service, replaced by the Grumman TBF Avenger.

In the early days of the Pacific war, the TBD acquitted itself well during February and March 1942, with TBDs from USS ENTERPRISE and USS YORKTOWN attacking targets in the Marshall and Gilbert Islands, Wake Island and Marcus Island, while TDBs from USS YORKTOWN and USS LEXINGTON struck Japanese shipping off New Guinea on 10 March. In the Battle of the Coral Sea Devastators helped sink the *Shōhō* on 7 May, but failed to hit the *Shōkaku* the next day.

Problems were discovered with the Mark 13 torpedo at this point. Many were seen to hit the target yet fail to explode; there was also a tendency to run deeper than the set depth. It took over a year for the problems to be corrected. These problems were not fixed by the time of the Battle of Midway on 4 June 1942.

At Midway, a total of 41 Devastators, a majority of the type still operational, were launched from USS HORNET, USS ENTERPRISE and USS YORKTOWN to attack the Japanese fleet. The sorties were not well coordinated, in part because Rear Admiral Raymond A. Spruance ordered a strike on the enemy carriers immediately after they were discovered, rather than spend the time to assemble a well-ordered attack among the different types of aircraft: fighters, bombers, torpedo planes, reasoning that attacking the Japanese would prevent a counterstrike against the US carriers. The TBDs from USS HORNET and USS ENTERPRISE lost contact with their fighter escort and started their attacks without fighter protection.

The Devastator proved to be a death trap for its crews: slow and scarcely maneuverable, with light defensive weaponry and poor armor relative to the weapons of the time; its speed on a glide-bombing approach was a mere 200 mph (320 km/h), making it easy prey for fighters and defensive guns alike. The aerial torpedo could not even be released at speeds above 115 mph (185 km/h). Torpedo delivery requires a long, straight-line attack run, making the aircraft vulnerable, and the slow speed of the aircraft made them easy targets for the Mitsubishi A6M Zeros. Only four TBDs made it back to USS ENTERPISE, none to USS HORNET and two to USS YORKTOWN, without scoring a torpedo hit.

Nonetheless, their sacrifice was not completely in vain, as several TBDs managed to get within a few ship-lengths range of their targets before dropping their torpedoes, being close enough to be able to strafe the enemy ships and force the Japanese carriers to make sharp evasive maneuvers. Furthermore, the actions of the Devastator aircrews that day drew the Japanese air cover out of position. This window of opportunity was exploited by the late-arriving Douglas SBD Dauntless dive bombers led by Lieutenant Commander C. Wade McClusky and Max Leslie, and three of the four Japanese carriers were fatally damaged shortly afterwards.

The Navy immediately withdrew the TBD from front-line units after Midway; in any case, there were only 39 aircraft left. They remained in service briefly in the Atlantic and in training squadrons until 1944. The original prototype finished its career at NAS Norman, Oklahoma, and the last TBD in the U.S. Navy was used by the Commander of Fleet Air Activities-West Coast. When his TBD was scrapped in November 1944, there were no more. None survived the war and there are none known to exist on dry land today.

In fairness to the Devastator, the newer TBF Avengers were similarly ineffective, losing five out of six aircraft without scoring a hit at Midway. The Avengers' only successes in 1942 would be against the light carrier *Ryūjō* and the battleship *Hiei*. In the initial part of the Pacific War, the poor performances of US torpedo bombers was due to the vulnerability of that type in general against AAA fire and defending fighters, plus the inexperience of American pilots and lack of coordinated fighter cover. It took growing American air superiority, improved attack coordination, and more experienced pilots, before the Avengers were able to successfully accomplish their roles in subsequent battles against Japanese surface forces.

After the debacle at Midway, the surviving TBD Devastators in VT-4 and VT-7 remained in service for a short time before being shipped back to the United States where the aircraft were relegated to training duties for pilots and mechanics or were destroyed following use as instructional airframes for fire-fighting training. By late 1944, no TBD Devastators were left in the US Navy inventory. The production variant was powered by an 850 hp (630 kW) R-1830-64. There were 129 built. Aircraft lost:

DATE	BUNO	SQDRN	BASE	LOST	AREA	PILOT	FATE
01/08/42	371	VT-3	USS SARATOGA	PEARL	ECENPAC		
01/10/42	281	VT-3	USS SARATOGA	PEARL	ECENPAC	ENS EAGLE C. GILLEN	S
01/18/42	335	VT-6	USS ENTER-PRISE	PEARL	ECENPAC		
02/01/42	298	VF-5	USS YORK-TOWN	JALUIT	CENPAC		
02/01/42	352	VT-5	USS YORK-TOWN	JALUIT	CENPAC		
02/01/42	1507	VT-5	USS YORK-TOWN	JALUIT	CENPAC		
02/01/42	1515	VT-5	USS YORK-TOWN	JALUIT	CENPAC		
02/01/42	274	VT-6	USS ENTER-PRISE	MARSHALLS	CENPAC		
05/04/42	317	VF-5	USS YORK-TOWN	TULAGI	SOPAC		
05/04/42	333	VT-5	USS YORK-TOWN	TULAGI	SOPAC		
05/08/42	271	VT-2	USS LEX-INGTON	CORAL SEA	SOPAC	(SHIP SANK)	
05/08/42	273	VT-2	USS LEX-INGTON	CORAL SEA	SOPAC	(SHIP SANK)	
05/08/42	275	VT-2	USS LEX-INGTON	CORAL SEA	SOPAC	(SHIP SANK)	
05/08/42	290	VT-2	USS LEX-INGTON	CORAL SEA	SOPAC	(SHIP SANK)	
05/08/42	291	VT-2	USS LEX-INGTON	CORAL SEA	SOPAC	(SHIP SANK)	
05/08/42	300	VT-2	USS LEX-INGTON	CORAL SEA	SOPAC	(SHIP SANK)	
05/08/42	313	VT-2	USS LEX-INGTON	CORAL SEA	SOPAC	(SHIP SANK)	
05/08/42	320	VT-2	USS LEX-INGTON	CORAL SEA	SOPAC	(SHIP SANK)	
05/08/42	339	VT-2	USS LEX-INGTON	CORAL SEA	SOPAC	(SHIP SANK)	
05/08/42	346	VT-2	USS LEX-INGTON	CORAL SEA	SOPAC	(SHIP SANK)	
05/08/42	1514	VT-2	USS LEX-INGTON	CORAL SEA	SOPAC	(SHIP SANK)	
05/08/42	1516	VT-2	USS LEX-INGTON	CORAL SEA	SOPAC	(SHIP SANK)	
05/30/42	370	VT-6	USS ENTER-PRISE	ENR MIDWAY	ECENPAC		
06/04/42	285	VT-3	USS YORK-TOWN	MIDWAY	ECENPAC	LCDR LANCE E. MASSEY	M
06/04/42	286	VT-3	USS YORK-TOWN	MIDWAY	ECENPAC	(SHIP SANK)	
06/04/42	303	VT-3	USS YORK-TOWN	MIDWAY	ECENPAC	(SHIP SANK)	
06/04/42	310	VT-3	USS YORK-TOWN	MIDWAY	ECENPAC	(SHIP SANK)	

DATE	BUNO	SQDRN	BASE	LOST	AREA	PILOT	FATE
06/04/42	312	VT-3	USS YORK-TOWN	MIDWAY	ECENPAC	(SHIP SANK)	
06/04/42	340	VT-3	USS YORK-TOWN	MIDWAY	ECENPAC	(SHIP SANK)	
06/04/42	341	VT-3	USS YORK-TOWN	MIDWAY	ECENPAC	(SHIP SANK)	
06/04/42	343	VT-3	USS YORK-TOWN	MIDWAY	ECENPAC	(SHIP SANK)	
06/04/42	354	VT-3	USS YORK-TOWN	MIDWAY	ECENPAC	(SHIP SANK)	
06/04/42	361	VT-3	USS YORK-TOWN	MIDWAY	ECENPAC	(SHIP SANK)	
06/04/42	375	VT-3	USS YORK-TOWN	MIDWAY	ECENPAC	(SHIP SANK)	
06/04/42	381	VT-3	USS YORK-TOWN	MIDWAY	ECENPAC	(SHIP SANK)	
06/04/42	1511	VT-3	USS YORK-TOWN	MIDWAY	ECENPAC	(SHIP SANK)	
06/04/42	1513	VT-3	USS YORK-TOWN	MIDWAY	ECENPAC	(SHIP SANK)	
06/04/42	289	VT-6	USS ENTER-PRISE	MIDWAY	ECENPAC	LCDR E.E. LINDSEY	D
06/04/42	294	VT-6	USS ENTER-PRISE	MIDWAY	ECENPAC	ENS R.M. HOLDER	D
06/04/42	327	VT-6	USS ENTER-PRISE	MIDWAY	ECENPAC	MACH A.W. WINCHELL	D
06/04/42	342	VT-6	USS ENTER-PRISE	MIDWAY	ECENPAC	LT P.J. RILEY	D
06/04/42	365	VT-6	USS ENTER-PRISE	MIDWAY	ECENPAC	ENS J.W. BROCK	D
06/04/42	366	VT-6	USS ENTER-PRISE	MIDWAY	ECENPAC	LTJG J.T. EVERSOLE	D
06/04/42	367	VT-6	USS ENTER-PRISE	MIDWAY	ECENPAC	LT A.V. ELY	D
06/04/42	378	VT-6	USS ENTER-PRISE	MIDWAY	ECENPAC	ENS F.C. HODGES	D
06/04/42	1505	VT-6	USS ENTER-PRISE	MIDWAY	ECENPAC	LTJG L. THOMAS	D
06/04/42	284	VT-8	USS HORNET	MIDWAY	ECENPAC	ENS JOHN P. GRAY	D
06/04/42	293	VT 8	USS HORNET	MIDWAY	ECENPAC	ENS W.H.W. CREAMER	D
06/04/42	295	VT-8	USS HORNET	MIDWAY	ECENPAC	ENS WM A. ABERCROMBIE	D
06/04/42	297	VT-8	USS HORNET	MIDWAY	ECENPAC	ENS WILLIAM R. EVANS	D
06/04/42	308	VT-8	USS HORNET	MIDWAY	ECENPAC	LTJG JEFF D. WOODSON	D
06/04/42	311	VT-8	USS HORNET	MIDWAY	ECENPAC	ROBERT B. MILES	D
06/04/42	321	VT-8	USS HORNET	MIDWAY	ECENPAC	ENS HAROLD J. ELLISON	D
06/04/42	324	VT-8	USS HORNET	MIDWAY	ECENPAC	ENS JACK O. WILKIE	D
06/04/42	329	VT-8	USS HORNET	MIDWAY	ECENPAC	ENS CHARLES E. BRANNON	D
06/04/42	364	VT-8	USS HORNET	MIDWAY	ECENPAC	ENS ALBERT K. EARNEST	D
06/04/42	372	VT-8	USS HORNET	MIDWAY	ECENPAC	ENS OSWALD J. GAYNIER	D
06/04/42	1506	VT-8	USS HORNET	MIDWAY	ECENPAC	ENS VICTOR A. LEWIS	D
06/04/42	1509	VT-8	USS HORNET	MIDWAY	ECENPAC	ENS GEORGE H. GAY	S
06/04/42	1518	VT-8	USS HORNET	MIDWAY	ECENPAC	ENS LANGDON K FIEBERLING	D

DATE	BUNO	SQDRN	BASE	LOST	AREA	PILOT	FATE
06/04/42	476	VT-8	USS HORNET	MIDWAY	ECENPAC	LT RAYMOND A. MOORE	D
03/15/43	306	VC-29	USS SANTEE	ENR NORFOLK	CENLANT		

FAIRCHILD GK-1

The Fairchild Model 24, was a four-seat, single-engine monoplane light transport aircraft that was used by the United States Army Air Corps as the UC-61 and by the Royal Air Force. The Model 24 was itself a development of previous Fairchild models and became a successful civil and military utility aircraft.

Fairchild Aircraft was hit hard by the Great Depression in the early 1930s as airline purchases disappeared. Consequently the company's attention turned to developing a reliable and rugged small aircraft for personal and business use. The Fairchild 22 became somewhat of a hit and led directly to the new and much improved Model 24 which gained rapid popularity in the early 1930s, noted for its pleasant handling characteristics and roomy interior. Having adapted many components from the automotive industry (expansion-shoe brakes and roll-down cabin windows), the aircraft was also affordable and easy to maintain. In production continuously from 1932 to 1948 the aircraft remained essentially unchanged aerodynamically and internally, with the simple addition of extra passenger seating and optional equipment. The first models were equipped with only two seats, but in 1933 a third seat was installed and by 1938 a fourth was added. The interior was first created for the Model 24 in 1937 by noted American industrial designer Raymond Loewy. A minor airframe revision was made in 1938 with the redesign of the vertical fin and re-designation from C8 to F24G onwards.

In an innovative concept, the aircraft was available with two powerplants, Warner's reliable Scarab and Fairchild's in-house 200 hp Ranger series in the F24C-8-D, E and F. Initially the 1932 model Fairchild 24C-8-B used a reliable and popular Warner 125 hp radial engine, and the Fairchild 24C-8-C used the Warner 145 hp radial. American Cirrus and Menasco Pirate inline engines were also occasionally used in some earlier Fairchild 24s. Later models such as the popular 24Ws upgraded to the 165 hp Warner Super Scarab.

Designed for operations from relatively unimproved grass airfields, the sturdy undercarriage construction used a vertical oil dampened cylinder above the wheel with a pivoting strut attached to the lower fuselage. The result was a complex but undeniably solid undercarriage that could absorb large amounts of shock and was also adapted for the fitting of twin floats for water-based operations.

The Fairchild 24 built by Kreider-Reisner Aircraft, Hagerstown, Maryland, a division of Fairchild Aviation Corporation, remained in production from 1932 to 1948, essentially the same airframe but with various powerplant and configuration enhancements. In all, Fairchild constructed over 1500 Model 24s, with an additional 280 being constructed by the Texas Engineering & Manufacturing Company (TEMCO) in Dallas when that company purchased the manufacturing rights after World War II.

In civil use, the aircraft was a quick sales success with prominent businessmen and Hollywood actors purchasing the aircraft. In 1936, the US Navy ordered Model 24s designated as GK-1 and JK-1 research and instrument trainers. K. Some aircraft were fitted with two 100 pound bombs for what became successful missions against

German U-boats off the east coast of the United States in the early stages of the World War II. Aircraft lost:

DATE	BUNO	SQDRN	BASE	LOST	AREA	PILOT	FATE
09/04/44	09791	NAS	EWA	HAWAII	ECENPAC		
09/09/44	09795	NAS	BARBERS POINT	HAWAII	ECENPAC		

FAIRCHILD PILGRIM 100B

Sometimes mistakenly referred to as "American Pilgrim 100B" because all Fairchild Pilgrim 100's were supposedly flown by American Airlines. However, this particularly civilian aircraft (Tail Number NC-7249) was leased from Pan Am. It hit a snow-covered ridge near Nome, AK. 6 killed.

DATE	BUNO	SQDRN	BASE	LOST	AREA	PILOT	FATE
04/07/44	99098	PAN AM	NOME	ALASKA	NORPAC	R.L. PULLIS	D

FAIRCHILD CANADA SBF-1

The Curtiss SB2C Helldiver was a carrier-based dive bomber aircraft produced for the United States Navy during World War II (see the Curtiss SB2C variants). The program suffered so many delays that the Grumman TBF Avenger entered service before the Helldiver, even though the Avenger had begun its development two years later. Nevertheless, production tempo accelerated with production at Columbus, Ohio and two Canadian factories, one being the Fairchild Aircraft Ltd. (Canada) which produced a total of 300 (under the designations XSBF-I, SBF-I, SBF-3 and SBF-4E), these models being respectively equivalent to their Curtiss-built counterparts. There were 50 SBF-1's built. Aircraft lost:

DATE	BUNO	SQDRN	BASE	LOST	AREA	PILOT	FATE
07/18/44	31651	VB-8	USS BUNKER HILL	OROTE	CENPAC	LTJG J.H. WEBER	S
08/09/44	31644	CASU-35		ENIWETOK	CENPAC		
08/09/44	31645	CASU-35		ENIWETOK	CENPAC		
09/09/44	31640	VB-8	USS BUNKER HILL	MINDANAO SEA	PHIL		
09/16/44	31653	VB-8	USS BUNKER HILL	PALAU	CENPAC		
10/05/44	31637	VB-8	USS BUNKER HILL	ULITHI	WCENPAC		
10/05/44	31639	VB-8	USS BUNKER HILL	ULITHI	WCENPAC		
10/05/44	31649	VB-8	USS BUNKER HILL	ULITHI	WCENPAC		

GENERAL MOTORS FM-1

The Grumman Aircraft Engineering Co. had provided the U.S. Navy with carrier-based biplane fighters since 1931. When America entered World War II on December 7, 1941, most of the carrier fighter squadrons were equipped with Grumman F4F-3 Wildcats, and the Wildcat bore the brunt of the carrier-based fighting in the Pacific until the introduction of its successor, the Grumman F6F Hellcat in late 1943. In early 1942, a new version, the F4F-4 was introduced with folding wings, which allowed more of the Wildcats to be carried on each carrier. With the fixed wing versions, a fighter squadron numbered only 18 planes, however the folding wings allowed 27 planes to be carried per squadron. As the heavier and faster F6F Hellcat began to replace the Wildcat on the larger fleet carriers in late 1943, the Wildcat continued to fight from the shorter decks of the escort or "jeep" carriers. Production of the F4F-4 was shifted to General Motors Eastern Division, in New Jersey, where they produced the FM-1 and FM-2 versions of the Wildcat. Aircraft lost:

DATE	BUNO	SQDRN	BASE	LOST	AREA	PILOT	FATE
06/15/43	15106	VF-24		HAWAII	ECENPAC		
06/24/43	15003	VMF-111			SOPAC		
07/14/43	15012	MASG-42					
08/22/43	15286	VC-25	USS CROATAN		NORLANT		
08/31/43	15386				SOPAC		
09/01/43	15388	VMF-441		FUNAFUTI	SOPAC		
09/03/43	15244	VC-19			NORLANT		
09/03/43	15363	VMF-441		FUNAFUTI	SOPAC	LT DAVID G. SOUTHER	D
10/09/43	15505	VC-1			NORLANT		
11/05/43	15160	VMF-111		FUNAFUTI	SOPAC		
11/06/43	15395	VMF-441		NANOMEA	SOPAC		
11/09/43	15119	VC-39	USS LISCOME BAY	PEARL	ECENPAC		
11/09/43	15334	VC-33	USS CORAL SEA	PEARL	ECENPAC		
11/12/43	15072	VC-33	USS CORAL SEA	GILBERTS	CENPAC	LTJG F.K. BUNKNER	S
11/15/43	15384	VMF-111		NUKUFETAU	SOPAC	CAPT BICKEL	S
11/15/43	15748	VC-39	USS LISCOME BAY	ENR GILBERTS	CENPAC	ENS FAIRMAN	M
11/19/43	15512	VC-1	USS BLOCK ISLAND	NORLANT	ENS F.H. GLEASON	S	
11/19/43	15627	VC-41	USS CORREGID OR	MAKIN	CENPAC	ENS B.B. JOHNSON	S
11/21/43	15650	VC-41	USS CORREGID OR	MAKIN	CENPAC	LTJG F.R. JONES	D
11/23/43	15222	VC-39	USS LISCOME BAY	GILBERTS	CENPAC	LTJG F.J. BLAIR	D
11/23/43	15228	VC-39	USS LISCOME BAY	GILBERTS	CENPAC		
11/23/43	15653	VC-41	USS CORREGID OR	MAKIN	CENPAC	ENS H.A. CARAVACCI	S
11/24/43	15117	VC-33	USS CORAL SEA	MAKIN	CENPAC		
11/24/43	15248	VC-39	USS LISCOME BAY	GILBERTS	CENPAC		
11/24/43	15253	VC-39	USS LISCOME BAY	GILBERTS	CENPAC		
11/24/43	15315	VC-33	USS CORAL SEA	MAKIN	CENPAC	LTJG E.K. HUSHER	S
11/24/43	15547	VC-39	USS LISCOME BAY	GILBERTS	CENPAC		
11/24/43	15750	VC-39	USS LISCOME BAY	GILBERTS	CENPAC		

DATE	BUNO	SQDRN	BASE	LOST	AREA	PILOT	FATE
11/24/43	15751	VC-39	USS LISCOME BAY	GILBERTS	CENPAC		
11/24/43	15755	VC-39	USS LISCOME BAY	GILBERTS	CENPAC		
11/24/43	15756	VC-39	USS LISCOME BAY	GILBERTS	CENPAC		
11/27/43	15300	VC-19	USS BOGUE		NORLANT	ENS J.D. KAPEIKIN	S
11/30/43	15194	VC-33	USS CORAL SEA	ENR MARSHALLS	CENPAC		
12/04/43	15746	VF-60	USS SUWAN-NEE	ENR ROI	CENPAC		
12/16/43	15498	VC-6	USS CORE	ENR LIVERPOOL	NORLANT	ENS R.E. COLEGROVE	D
12/23/43	15201	VC-55	USS CARD		N AFRICA		
12/23/43	15489	VC-66	USS TRIPOLI	PEARL	ECENPAC	ENS MCNEELAND	S
12/23/43	46783	VC-66	USS TRIPOLI	PEARL	ECENPAC	ENS H.B. DEGENKOLB	D
12/26/43	15510	VC-58	USS BLOCK ISLAND	NORLANT			
01/11/44	15054	VC-58	USS BLOCK ISLAND	N AFRICA	ENS F.P. RIDLEY	D	
01/14/44	15671	VF-35	USS CHENAN-GO	PEARL	ECENPAC		
01/17/44	15375	VC-1	USS CROATAN	BERMUDA	NORLANT	ENS T.F. KENDRICK	S
01/17/44	15662	VC-69	USS WAKE ISLAND	COSTA RICA	NORLANT	ENS W.W. WRIGHT	S
01/20/44	15034	CNAOT JAX	USS TRIPOLI	ENR CANAL Z.	CENPAC		
01/27/44	15061	VC-7	USS MANILA BAY	ENR MARSHALLS	CENPAC		
01/29/44	15617	VC-33	USS CORAL SEA	MARSHALLS	CENPAC	LTJG E.S. TAYLOR	S
02/01/44	46761	VC-66	USS NASSAU	HAWAII	ECENPAC		
02/01/44	46770	VC-63	USS NATOMA BAY	MAJURO	CENPAC	ENS L.R. VENABLE	S
02/07/44	46747	VC-66	USS NASSAU	TAROA	CENPAC	ENS S. TAKIS	S
02/07/44	46812	VC-63	USS NATOMA BAY	MAJURO	CENPAC	LTJG E.J. BECKER	S
04/13/44	15379	VMF-111		ROI	CENPAC		

GENERAL MOTORS FM-2

The General Motors FM-2 was the last and most powerful Wildcat, often being called the "Wilder" Wildcat, as it had a more powerful Wright R-1820 engine of 1,350 hp and weighed about 350 pounds less than the F4F-4. Aircraft lost:

DATE	BUNO	SQDRN	BASE	LOST	AREA	PILOT	FATE
10/26/43	47373	VC-9	USS CARD		NORLANT	ENS D.J. STEWART	M
01/02/44	56847	VC-80	USS MANILA BAY	PEARL	ECENPAC		
01/13/44	16135	VC-7	USS MANILA BAY	PEARL	ECENPAC	ENS W.H. FORESTELLS	S

DATE	BUNO	SQDRN	BASE	LOST	AREA	PILOT	FATE
01/15/44	16129	VC-7	USS MANILA BAY	PEARL	ECENPAC	LT L.H. PECK	U
02/07/44	74239	VC-8	HAWAII	HAWAII	ECENPAC	ENS SAMUEL R. LAKES	
02/20/44	16367	VF-4	USS RANGER	OFF RHODE IS.	NORLANT	LTJG H.F. EDWARDS D	
03/12/44	15978	VC-68	USS WHITE PLAINS	OFF ALAMEDA	CENPAC	ENS E.P. VAN HISE S	
03/13/44	16022	VF-26	USS SANTEE	PEARL	ECENPAC	ENS O.D. HAVERFIELD	S
03/28/44	16033	VF-26	USS SANTEE	ADMIRALTIES	SW PAC	LT R.P. WRIGHT	S
03/28/44	16267	VF-26	USS SANTEE	ADMIRALTIES	SW PAC	ENS R. SCHULTE	D
04/04/44	16081	VC-36	USS CORE	AZORES	NORLANT	LT R.E. TOLLARD	D
04/10/44	16023	VC-63	USS NATOMA BAY	ENR EMIRAU	SOPAC		
04/14/44	16406	VC-63	USS NATOMA BAY	EMIRAU	SW PAC	LTJG E.R. LANGE	M
04/14/44	16423	VC-63	USS NATOMA BAY	EMIRAU	SW PAC	LTJG L.R. VENABLE S	
04/16/44	16634	VC-41	USS CORREGI-DOR	ENR HOLLANDIA	CENPAC		
04/17/44	16216	VF-26	USS SANTEE	FLORIDA IS.	SOPAC	ENS H.V. SCHULTZ	S
04/22/44	16577	VC-33	USS CORAL SEA	AITAPE	SW PAC	LTJG H.A. SPENCER D	
04/23/44	16010	VC-33	USS CORAL SEA	AITAPE	SW PAC		
04/23/44	16095	VC-41	USS CORREGI-DOR	HOLLANDIA	SW PAC		
04/24/44	16334	VC-9	USS SOLO-MONS	BRAZIL	SOLANT	ENS M.C. JONES	S
04/25/44	16102	VC-7	USS MANILA BAY	NEW GUINEA	SW PAC	LTJG D.E. BRUBAKERS	
04/26/44	16565	VC-41	USS CORREGI-DOR	HOLLANDIA	SW PAC		
04/27/44	16588	VC-33	USS CORAL SEA	ENR ADMIRALT.	SW PAC	ENS L.O. MCKEE	S
04/29/44	16254	VC-42	USS CROATAN		NORLANT	ENS J.J. BONDANK	S
04/30/44	16238	CASU-13		PONAM	SW PAC		
04/30/44	16403	COMAIR-PAC	PEARL	HAWAII	ECENPAC		
05/02/44	16082	VC-33	USS CORAL SEA	AITAPE	SW PAC		
05/02/44	16258	VC-65	USS NATOMA BAY	OAHU	ECENPAC	ENS T.J. WILSON	S
05/06/44	16080	VC-14	USS HOGGATT BAY	ENR MAJURO	CENPAC	ENS A. MALINOFF	S
05/12/44	16360	VC-63	USS NATOMA BAY	MAKIN	CENPAC	ENS J.D. WILCOX	S
05/17/44	16173	VC-14	USS HOGGATT BAY	ENR MAJURO	CENPAC	LTJG E.J. MITCHELLS	
05/18/44	16140	VC-3	USS KALININ BAY	MAJURO	CENPAC	LT L.E. JOHNSON	S
05/18/44	16154	COMAIR-PAC	PEARL	HAWAII	ECENPAC		

DATE	BUNO	SQDRN	BASE	LOST	AREA	PILOT	FATE
05/18/44	16317	VC-10	USS GAMBIER BAY	PEARL	ECENPAC	ENS J.F. LISCHER	S
05/18/44	16391	VC-4	USS WHITE PLAINS	BARBERS POINT	ECENPAC		
05/18/44	16575	COMAIR-PAC	PEARL	HAWAII	ECENPAC		
05/30/44	16093	VC-68	USS FANSHAW BAY	MARSHALLS	CENPAC		
05/30/44	16130	VC-8	USS GUADAL-CANAL		NORLANT	LTJG FRANCIS H. BEHLEN III	S
05/30/44	16486	VC-63	USS NATOMA BAY	BARKING SANDS	ECENPAC		
05/31/44		VC-55	USS BLOCK ISLAND	N AFRICA		LTJG J.G. MCDANIELS	U
06/01/44	15963	VC-55	USS BLOCK ISLAND	31-13N/023-03W	NORLANT	(SHIP SANK)	
06/01/44	15970	VC-55	USS BLOCK ISLAND	31-13N/023-03W	NORLANT	(SHIP SANK)	
06/01/44	15975	VC-55	USS BLOCK ISLAND	31-13N/023-03W	NORLANT	(SHIP SANK)	
06/01/44	15984	VC-55	USS BLOCK ISLAND	31-13N/023-03W	NORLANT	(SHIP SANK)	
06/01/44	15985	VC-55	USS BLOCK ISLAND	31-13N/023-03W	NORLANT	(SHIP SANK)	
06/01/44	15991	VC-55	USS BLOCK ISLAND	31-13N/023-03W	NORLANT	(SHIP SANK)	
06/01/44	15995	VC-55	USS BLOCK ISLAND	31-13N/023-03W	NORLANT	(SHIP SANK)	
06/01/44	15997	VC-55	USS BLOCK ISLAND	31-13N/023-03W	NORLANT	(SHIP SANK)	
06/01/44	16000	VC-55	USS BLOCK ISLAND	31-13N/023-03W	NORLANT	(SHIP SANK)	
06/01/44	16277	VC-5	USS KITKUN BAY	ENR SAIPAN	CENPAC		
06/03/44	16273	VC-4	USS WHITE PLAINS	BARBERS POINT	ECENPAC	ENS E.M. BILLINGHURST	S
06/03/44	47019	VC-4	USS WHITE PLAINS	BARBERS POINT	ECENPAC		
06/08/44	46996	VC-68	USS FANSHAW BAY	ENIWETOK	CENPAC		
06/08/44	47016	VC-65	USS MIDWAY	ENIWETOK	CENPAC		
06/09/44	15977	VC-6	USS TRIPOLI	ENR N. SCOTIA	NORLANT	ENS W.B. BOGLE	D
06/11/44	16492	VC-3	USS KALININ BAY	ENIWETOK	CENPAC	LT S.B. FRANCOVICHS	
06/13/44	16761	VC-14	USS HOGGATT BAY	EMIRAU	SW PAC	ENS R.C. BROEDEL	D
06/14/44	16271	VC-10	USS GAMBIER BAY	ENR MARSHALLS	CENPAC	LT JAMES F. OLIVERS	
06/15/44	16150	VC-10	USS GAMBIER BAY	MARSHALLS	CENPAC	LT J.R. STEWART	S
06/15/44	16187	VC-9	USS SOLO-MONS	OFF RECIFE	SOLANT	ENS H.L. HANDSHUH M	

DATE	BUNO	SQDRN	BASE	LOST	AREA	PILOT	FATE
06/15/44	16200	VC-4	USS WHITE PLAINS	SAIPAN	WCENPAC	LTJG BALESS	
06/15/44	16234	VC-9	USS SOLO-MONS	OFF RECIFE	SOLANT	ENS P.H. WALKER	M
06/15/44	16262	VC-10	USS GAMBIER BAY	MARSHALLS	CENPAC	LT HERMAN J. HARDESS	S
06/16/44	16218	VC-4	USS WHITE PLAINS	SAIPAN	WCENPAC	LT E. STRANGLER	S
06/16/44	16260	VC-33	USS CORAL SEA	ENR SAIPAN	CENPAC		
06/16/44	16295	VC-5	USS KITKUN BAY	MARIANAS	CENPAC	LT J.F. RICHARDSONS	
06/16/44	16791	VC-41	USS CORREGI-DOR	TINIAN	WCENPAC	ENS G.L. COLLINS	M
06/16/44	47427	VC-10	USS GAMBIER BAY	MARSHALLS	CENPAC	ENS LEE G. GIGER	S
06/17/44	16060	VC-65	USS MIDWAY	E. OF SAIPAN	CENPAC		
06/17/44	16123	VC-3	USS KALININ BAY	SAIPAN	WCENPAC		
06/17/44	16205	VC-65	USS MIDWAY	E. OF SAIPAN	CENPAC		
06/17/44	16224	VC-3	USS KALININ BAY	SAIPAN	WCENPAC		
06/17/44	16269	VC-4	USS WHITE PLAINS	W OF SAIPAN	CENPAC		
06/17/44	16296	VC-5	USS KITKUN BAY	MARIANAS	CENPAC	ENS J.L. KROUSE	S
06/17/44	16416	VC-4	USS WHITE PLAINS	W OF SAIPAN	CENPAC	LCDR R.C. EVINS	M
06/17/44	16422	VC-65	USS MIDWAY	E. OF SAIPAN	CENPAC		
06/17/44	16710	VC-68	USS FANSHAW BAY	SAIPAN	WCENPAC		
06/17/44	46858	VC-68	USS FANSHAW BAY	SAIPAN	WCENPAC		
06/17/44	46913	VC-5	USS KITKUN BAY	MARIANAS	CENPAC	LT H.L. COLE	M
06/17/44	46965	VC-4	USS WHITE PLAINS	W OF SAIPAN	CENPAC		
06/17/44	46977	VC-4	USS WHITE PLAINS	W OF SAIPAN	CENPAC		
06/17/44	47017	VC-65	USS MIDWAY	E. OF SAIPAN	CENPAC	ENS L.F. WOODHOUSEM	
06/17/44	47026	VC-4	USS WHITE PLAINS	W OF SAIPAN	CENPAC	ENS E.M. BILLINGHURST	S
06/17/44	47027	VC-4	USS WHITE PLAINS	W OF SAIPAN	CENPAC		
06/17/44	47028	VC-4	USS WHITE PLAINS	W OF SAIPAN	CENPAC		
06/17/44	47073	VC-10	USS GAMBIER BAY	TINIAN	WCENPAC	ENS B.F. DILLARD	S
06/17/44	55069	VC-10	USS GAMBIER BAY	TINIAN	WCENPAC	ENS LEE G. GIGER	S
06/18/44	16180	VC-5	USS KITKUN BAY	MARIANAS	CENPAC	LT W.H. JOHNSON	S
06/18/44	16257	VC-33	USS CORAL SEA	SAIPAN	WCENPAC		

DATE	BUNO	SQDRN	BASE	LOST	AREA	PILOT	FATE
06/18/44	16441	VC-41	USS CORREGI-DOR	SAIPAN	WCENPAC	LTJG GUZZINS	S
06/18/44	16541	VC-41	USS CORREGI-DOR	SAIPAN	WCENPAC	ENS B.F. HUDSON	M
06/18/44	16548	VC-33	USS CORAL SEA	SAIPAN	WCENPAC	LT E. BRADSHAW	D
06/18/44	46959	VC-5	USS KITKUN BAY	MARIANAS	CENPAC	ENS J.L. KROUSE	S
06/18/44	47039	VC-10	USS GAMBIER BAY	MARIANAS	CENPAC	ENS JOSEPH D. MCGRAW	S
06/18/44	47289	VC-11	USS NEHENTA BAY	HAWAII	ECENPAC		
06/19/44	16198	VC-10	USS GAMBIER BAY	MARIANAS	CENPAC	LT D.W. GILLIATT	D
06/20/44	16126	VF-26	USS SANTEE	ESPIRITU SANTO	SOPAC	LT R.P. WRIGHT	D
06/20/44	16276	VC-33	USS CORAL SEA	TINIAN	WCENPAC	LT G.A. SUNDGUIST	S
06/20/44	16294	VC-33	USS CORAL SEA	SAIPAN	WCENPAC		
06/22/44	16589	VC-33	USS CORAL SEA	SAIPAN	WCENPAC		
06/24/44	16026	GREEN		RABAUL	SOPAC		
06/24/44	16289	VC-10	USS GAMBIER BAY	ENR TINIAN	CENPAC	ENS JOSEPH D. MCGRAW	S
06/29/44	16767	VC-3	USS KALININ BAY	SAIPAN	WCENPAC	LT R. ANDERSON	S
06/29/44	46920	COMAIR-PAC	PEARL	HAWAII	ECENPAC		
06/30/44	47024	COMAIR-PAC	PEARL	HAWAII	ECENPAC		
07/01/44	16190	COM7THFL T	PERTH	AUSTRALIA	SW PAC		
07/03/44	16658	VC-33	USS CORAL SEA	E. OF SAIPAN	CENPAC		
07/05/44	46953	VC-3	USS KALININ BAY	SAIPAN	WCENPAC		
07/06/44	16244	VC-14	USS HOGGATT BAY	MARSHALLS	CENPAC	ENS J.F. GROSSER	S
07/06/44	16785	VC-3	USS KALININ BAY	E. OF SAIPAN	CENPAC	ENS J.T. CUZZART	S
07/07/44		VC-3	USS KALININ BAY	TINIAN	WCENPAC	ENS P. VAN HISE	S
07/07/44	46988	VC-3	USS KALININ BAY	TINIAN	WCENPAC	LT R.T. BROWN	M
07/08/44	47036	VC-14	USS HOGGATT BAY	MARSHALLS	CENPAC	LTJG E.J. MITCHELL	S
07/10/44	16536	VF-100	BARBERS POINT	HAWAII	ECENPAC		
07/10/44	47003		ESPIRITU PL	PALLIKULO A/F	SOPAC		
07/10/44	47324	VC-3	USS KALININ BAY	TINIAN	WCENPAC	ENS V. YARASHES	M
07/11/44	16125	VF-26	USS SANTEE	ESPIRITU SANTO	SOPAC	ENS C.A. WHEELER	S

DATE	BUNO	SQDRN	BASE	LOST	AREA	PILOT	FATE
07/12/44	16085				CENPAC		
07/15/44	16021	VC-14	USS HOGGATT BAY	MARSHALLS	CENPAC		
07/15/44	16346	VC-5	USS KITKUN BAY	SAIPAN	WCENPAC	LCDR R.L. FOWLER	S
07/15/44	47267	VC-10	USS GAMBIER BAY		WCENPAC	ENS P.P. ZEOLA	S
07/15/44	55351	VC-21	USS MARCUS ISLAND	PEARL	ECENPAC	ENS A.B. FLORY	S
07/16/44	16576	VC-81		ENR PEARL	ECENPAC		
07/17/44	16174	VC-41	USS CORREGID OR	ENR GUAM	CENPAC		
07/17/44	47330	VC-5	USS KITKUN BAY	SAIPAN	WCENPAC	LT P.B. GARRISON	S
07/18/44	16659	VC-76	USS PETROF BAY	ENR PEARL	ECENPAC	LT J.G. BOYD	D
07/18/44	55281	VC-5	USS KITKUN BAY	SAIPAN	WCENPAC	LT R.C. WHITE	S
07/22/44	16164	VC-14	USS HOGGATT BAY	MARSHALLS	CENPAC		
07/24/44	16344	VC-11	USS NEHENTA BAY	MARIANAS	CENPAC		
07/25/44	16400	VC-41	USS CORREGI-DOR	GUAM	WCENPAC	ENS H.L. LOTCH	S
07/26/44	46930	VC-14	USS HOGGATT BAY	MARSHALLS	CENPAC		
07/27/44	16266	VC-19	USS GUADAL-CANAL		NORLANT	LT C.E. FETSCH	S
07/27/44	47035	VC-10	USS GAMBIER BAY		CENPAC		
07/30/44	46839	VC-65	ISLEY FIELD	SAIPAN	WCENPAC		
07/31/44	15990	VC-9	USS SOLO-MONS	OFF RECIFE	SOLANT		
07/31/44	16001	VC-9	USS SOLO-MONS	OFF RECIFE	SOLANT		
07/31/44	47021	VC-65	USS MIDWAY	TINIAN	WCENPAC		
08/01/44	46941	VF-4	NAVY NO. 24	HAWAII	ECENPAC		
08/02/44	47271	VC-82			CENPAC		
08/03/44	16155	VC-66	KAHULUI	HAWAII	ECENPAC	LT CHARLES T. EDWARDS	U
08/03/44	16371	VC-11	USS NEHENTA BAY	MARIANAS	CENPAC		
08/03/44	47308	VC-11	USS NEHENTA BAY	MARIANAS	CENPAC		
08/06/44	55461	VC-27	OAHU	HAWAII	ECENPAC		
08/08/44	55513	VC-21	USS MARCUS ISLAND	PEARL	ECENPAC	LTJG SHERWOOD L. WILSON	M
08/09/44	16158	CASU-35		ENIWETOK	CENPAC		
08/09/44	16159	CASU-35		ENIWETOK	CENPAC		
08/09/44	16473	CASU-35		ENIWETOK	CENPAC		
08/09/44	47075	CASU-35		ENIWETOK	CENPAC		
08/09/44	47245	CASU-35		ENIWETOK	CENPAC		
08/09/44	47305	CASU-35		ENIWETOK	CENPAC		
08/09/44	47316	CASU-35		ENIWETOK	CENPAC		
08/09/44	47418	CASU-35		ENIWETOK	CENPAC		

DATE	BUNO	SQDRN	BASE	LOST	AREA	PILOT	FATE
08/11/44	16106	VC-58	USS WAKE ISLAND	ENR NORFOLK	NORLANT	LTJG CHARLES E. BETTIG	S
08/12/44	55427	VC-21	USS MARCUS ISLAND	ENR TULAGI	CENPAC	LT ROBERT C. CLARK	S
08/12/44	55495	VC-21	USS MARCUS ISLAND	ENR TULAGI	CENPAC	ENS WALTER L. KNEEL	S
08/13/44	16298	VC-5	USS KITKUN BAY	ENIWETOK	CENPAC		
08/15/44	47071	VF-100	BARBERS POINT	HAWAII	ECENPAC		
08/18/44	16263	VF-26	USS SANTEE	ADMIRALTIES	SW PAC	ENS FRANK A. CLOUGH	S
08/19/44	16053	VF-26	USS SANTEE	ADMIRALTIES	SW PAC		
08/19/44	16235	VF-26	USS SANTEE	ADMIRALTIES	SW PAC	ENS R.J. MASTERSON	S
08/22/44	16056	VC-11	USS NEHENTA BAY	S. OF ENIWETOK	CENPAC	ENS HARLAN R. FISKE	D
08/23/44	16479	VC-4	USS WHITE PLAINS	NEW HEBRIDES	SOPAC	ENS LANCE DYER	D
08/25/44	16157	VF-26	USS SANTEE	PONAM	SW PAC		
08/27/44	16008	VC-13	USS CORE	OFF BERMUDA	NORLANT	LT EDWARD V. BROWN	S
08/27/44	16077	VC-13	USS CORE	OFF BERMUDA	NORLANT	LT JULIUS R. BROWNSTEIN	S
08/27/44	16245	VC-13	USS CORE	OFF BERMUDA	NORLANT	LTJG THOMAS N. BLANKS	S
08/27/44	16255	VC-13	USS CORE	OFF BERMUDA	NORLANT	LT DONALD B. GREGG	S
08/27/44	16392	VC-10	USS GAMBIER BAY		CENPAC		
08/27/44	16789	VC-13	USS CORE	OFF BERMUDA	NORLANT	LT ALDEN V. JOHNSON	S
08/28/44	46894	VC-68	USS FANSHAW BAY	MANUS	SW PAC	ENS W.J. JOHNSON	M
08/29/44	55386	VC-75	USS OMMANEY BAY	ENR TULAGI	SOPAC	ENS WILLIAM F. FARRELL, JR.	M
08/29/44	55456	VC-77	USS RUDYERD BAY	ENR MANUS	SW PAC	ENS J.S. BATTLES	S
09/01/44	47211	CASU-35		ENIWETOK	CENPAC		
09/01/44	55444	VC-21	USS MARCUS ISLAND	GUADAL-CANAL	SOPAC	ENS WILLIAM M. MCLENMORE	U
09/01/44	55570	VC-78	USS SAGINAW BAY	ESPIRITU SANTO	SOPAC	LT F.J. NUGENT	S
09/02/44	16083		ESPIRITU PL	PALLIKULO A/F	SOPAC		
09/02/44	47257		ESPIRITU PL	PALLIKULO A/F	SOPAC		
09/05/44	16165	CASU-30		MAJURO	CENPAC		
09/05/44	16411	CASU-42		PITYILU	SW PAC		
09/07/44	55303	VC-27	USS SAVO ISLAND	FLORIDA IS.	SOPAC		
09/08/44	47111	VC-21	USS MARCUS ISLAND	ENR PELELIU	CENPAC	LTJG WILLIAM M. MORAN, JR.	S
09/08/44	47140	VC-81	USS NATOMA BAY	PEARL	ECENPAC		
09/09/44	55620	VC-77	USS RUDYERD BAY	PALAU	CENPAC	ENS JOHN R. WIDMER	S
09/11/44	16009	CASU-13		PONAM	SW PAC		
09/11/44	16197	CASU-13		PONAM	SW PAC		

DATE	BUNO	SQDRN	BASE	LOST	AREA	PILOT	FATE
09/12/44	55401	VC-27	USS SAVO ISLAND	PALAU	CENPAC	LTJG F.M. LEIGHTY	S
09/13/44	55535	VC-20	USS KADASHAN BAY	ENR PALAU	CENPAC	ENS HOWARD H. PEOPLES	S
09/14/44	46938	VC-14	USS HOGGATT BAY	PELELIU	WCENPAC	ENS KEITH L. MARTZ	U
09/14/44	55161	VC-14	USS HOGGATT BAY	PELELIU	WCENPAC		
09/15/44	16286	VF-26	USS SANTEE	MOROTAI	PHIL	ENS WILLIAM H. WILLIS	S
09/15/44	55510	MANUS			SW PAC		
09/16/44	16199	VF-26	USS SANTEE	KASILE BAY	SW PAC	ENS HAROLD A. THOMPSON	S
09/16/44	16349	VC-66	USS FANSHAW BAY	MOROTAI	PHIL	LTJG REYNOLD RODRIGIEZ	D
09/16/44	55396	VC-27	USS SAVO ISLAND	PALAU	CENPAC	ENS R.H. DORMAN	S
09/16/44	55497	VC-75	USS OMMANEY BAY	PALAU	CENPAC		
09/16/44	55501	VC-78	USS SAGINAW BAY	PELELIU	WCENPAC	ENS R.B. LUNSFORD	S
09/18/44	47159	VC-81	USS NATOMA BAY	ENR MANUS	CENPAC		
09/18/44	47310	POOL		GUADAL-CANAL	SOPAC		
09/19/44	16763	VC-82		HAWAII	ECENPAC	ENS MCKINNEY	S
09/20/44	55214	VC-76	USS PETROF BAY	PELELIU	WCENPAC	ENS KENNETH W. LESHER	S
09/20/44	55412	VC-21	USS MARCUS ISLAND	PELELIU	WCENPAC		
09/20/44	55415	VC-5	USS KITKUN BAY	PELELIU	WCENPAC	LT W.H. JOHNSON	S
09/21/44	55265	VC-21	USS MARCUS ISLAND	PELELIU	WCENPAC	ENS JOHN T. JEFFS	D
09/21/44	55615	VC-83	KANEOHE	HAWAII	ECENPAC	ENS PAUL L. PAGE	S
09/23/44		POOL		GUADAL-CANAL	SOPAC		
09/23/44	46929	POOL		GUADAL-CANAL	SOPAC		
09/23/44	55433	VC-21	USS MARCUS ISLAND	PELELIU	WCENPAC		
09/24/44	16003	CASU-42		PITYILU	SW PAC		
09/24/44	47018	VC-80	USS MANILA BAY	HAWAII	ECENPAC	ENS WAYNE P. SQUIRES	S
09/24/44	47098	VC-80	USS MANILA BAY	HAWAII	ECENPAC		
09/25/44	16380	VC-66	USS FANSHAW BAY	ENR MANUS	SW PAC		
09/25/44	46933	VC-66	USS FANSHAW BAY	ENR MANUS	SW PAC		
09/27/44	16427	VC-3	USS KALININ BAY	ENR PALAU	CENPAC	LT SIMPSON	S
09/27/44	16782	VC-65	USS MIDWAY	PALUS	SW PAC		
10/01/44	16686	A & R	MAJURO	MAJURO	CENPAC		
10/01/44	46850	VC-21	USS MARCUS ISLAND	PELELIU	WCENPAC		

DATE	BUNO	SQDRN	BASE	LOST	AREA	PILOT	FATE
10/01/44	47091	VC-80	USS MANILA BAY	HAWAII	ECENPAC	ENS WAYNE P. SQUIRES	D
10/02/44	47100	VC-81	USS NATOMA BAY	MANUS	SW PAC	ENS ROBERT D. MCFARLAND	S
10/02/44	47300	VC-81	USS NATOMA BAY	MANUS	SW PAC	LT W.L. MATHSON, JR.	S
10/04/44	55411	VC-21	USS MARCUS ISLAND	MANUS	SW PAC		
10/04/44	55438	VC-21	USS MARCUS ISLAND	MANUS	SW PAC		
10/04/44	55491	VC-75	USS OMMANEY BAY	ENR SAMAR	CENPAC		
10/06/44	55548	VC-77	USS RUDYERD BAY	PHILIPPINES	PHIL		
10/06/44	55606	VC-77	USS RUDYERD BAY	PHILIPPINES	PHIL		
10/09/44	16383	VC-8	USS CARD		NORLANT	ENS WARREN P. WICKMIRE	S
10/10/44	47248	FAW-16		PITANGA	SOLANT		
10/10/44	55643	VC-69	USS GUADAL-CANAL		NORLANT	LTJG ROBERT K. LEHMAN	U
10/12/44	16156	CASU-42		PITYILU	SW PAC		
10/12/44	16240	CASU-42		PITYILU	SW PAC		
10/12/44	55626	CASU-42		PITYILU	SW PAC		
10/13/44	16019	CASU-42		PITYILU	SW PAC		
10/13/44	16443	CASU-42		PITYILU	SW PAC		
10/13/44	55478	CASU-42		PITYILU	SW PAC		
10/17/44	47168	VC-21	USS MARCUS ISLAND	ENR LEYTE GULF	PHIL		
10/17/44	55290	VC-21	USS MARCUS ISLAND	ENR LEYTE GULF	PHIL	LT ROBERT C. CLARKE	S
10/18/44	47002	VC-81	USS NATOMA BAY	LEYTE GULF	PHIL	LT MAC J. ROEBUCK	S
10/18/44	55425	VC-77	USS RUDYERD BAY	PHILIPPINES	PHIL	ENS GERALD E. BROOMQUIST	S
10/18/44	55533	VC-79	USS SARGENT BAY	ENR MANUS	SW PAC	ENS W.D. BOTSKY	D
10/18/44	73647	VC-84	USS MAKIN ISLAND	ULITHI	WCENPAC		
10/19/44	47223	VC-81	USS NATOMA BAY	LEYTE GULF	PHIL	LT A.C. HUNTER	D
10/19/44	55600	VC-78	USS SAGINAW BAY	LEYTE GULF	PHIL		
10/19/44	55633	VC-69	USS GUADAL-CANAL		NORLANT	LT RICHARD W. WENZELL	S
10/19/44	56789	VC-4	USS WHITE PLAINS	LEYTE GULF	PHIL	LTJG FRANCIS J. MALONEY	S
10/20/44	16274	VC-5	USS KITKUN BAY	LEYTE GULF	PHIL	LTJG D.W. HYDE	S
10/20/44	55519	VC-20	USS KADASHAN BAY	LEYTE GULF	PHIL		
10/20/44	55635	VC-83	USS CORREGID OR	HAWAII	ECENPAC		

DATE	BUNO	SQDRN	BASE	LOST	AREA	PILOT	FATE
10/20/44	56804	VC-79	USS SARGENT BAY	ENR MANUS	SW PAC	ENS JOSEPH J. PEPCZYNSKI	S
10/20/44	73769	VC-84	USS MAKIN ISLAND	ULITHI	WCENPAC		
10/21/44	16508	CASU-42		PITYILU	SW PAC		
10/21/44	16622	VC-75	USS OMMANEY BAY	ENR SAMAR	PHIL		
10/21/44	73616	VC-85	USS LUNGA POINT	ENR LEYTE GULF	CENPAC		
10/22/44	16395	VC-8	USS CARD		NORLANT	ENS ERWIN J. MOTT	S
10/22/44	46979	VC-20	USS KADASHAN BAY	LEYTE GULF	PHIL		
10/22/44	47361	VC-21	USS MARCUS ISLAND	LEYTE GULF	PHIL	ENS CHARLES R. BRADFORD	S
10/22/44	55255	VC-27	USS SAVO ISLAND	LEYTE GULF	PHIL	ENS A.F. UTHOFF	S
10/22/44	55413	VC-80	USS MANILA BAY	LEYTE GULF	PHIL		
10/22/44	55422	VC-20	USS KADASHAN BAY	LEYTE GULF	PHIL		
10/22/44	56860	VC-68	USS FANSHAW BAY	LEYTE GULF	PHIL	LTJG J.R.W. LANDRY	S
10/23/44	16524	VC-21	USS MARCUS ISLAND	LEYTE GULF	PHIL	LT GERALD LEE BRIDGE	S
10/23/44	47006	VF-26	USS SANTEE	MINDANAO SEA	PHIL	ENS WILLIAM L. PHIFER	D
10/23/44	47222	VC-75	USS OMMANEY BAY	SAMAR	PHIL		
10/24/44	46973	VC-27	USS SAVO ISLAND	LEYTE GULF	PHIL	ENS R.A. MAYHEW	D
10/24/44	46994	VC-3	USS KALININ BAY	LEYTE GULF	PHIL	LT W.E. SIMPSON	D
10/24/44	47177	VF-26	USS SANTEE	MINDANAO SEA	PHIL		
10/24/44	47346	VC-3	USS KALININ BAY	LEYTE GULF	PHIL	ENS W.D. MCDANIEL	S
10/24/44	47351	VC-80	USS MANILA BAY	LEYTE GULF	PHIL		
10/25/44	16027	VC-10	USS GAMBIER BAY	LEYTE GULF	PHIL	ENS J.T. TURNER	S
10/25/44	16297	VC-10	USS GAMBIER BAY	LEYTE GULF	PHIL	ENS J.J. TURNER	S
10/25/44	16347	VC-3	USS KALININ BAY	LEYTE GULF	PHIL	LT L.H. PORTERFIELD	S
10/25/44	16386	VC-3	USS KITKUN BAY	LEYTE GULF	PHIL	ENS PAUL HOPFNER	S
10/25/44	16570	VC-65	USS ST. LO	LEYTE GULF	PHIL	(SHIP SANK)	
10/25/44	16681	VC-65	USS ST. LO	LEYTE GULF	PHIL	(SHIP SANK)	
10/25/44	46919	VC-65	USS ST. LO	LEYTE GULF	PHIL	(SHIP SANK)	
10/25/44	46944	VC-65	USS ST. LO	LEYTE GULF	PHIL	LT GORDON A. GABBERT	S
10/25/44	46950	VC-65	USS ST. LO	LEYTE GULF	PHIL	LT JOSEPH T. RILEY	M
10/25/44	46982	VC-65	USS ST. LO	LEYTE GULF	PHIL	(SHIP SANK)	
10/25/44	47121	VC-27	USS SAVO ISLAND	LEYTE GULF	PHIL	ENS STUBBSS	
10/25/44	47135	VC-80	USS MANILA BAY	LEYTE GULF	PHIL		

DATE	BUNO	SQDRN	BASE	LOST	AREA	PILOT	FATE
10/25/44	47187	VC-80	USS MANILA BAY	LEYTE GULF	PHIL	LT W.L. FISHER	S
10/25/44	47247	VC-3	USS KITKUN BAY	LEYTE GULF	PHIL	ENS GEOFREY B. KING	S
10/25/44	47298	VC-80	USS MANILA BAY	LEYTE GULF	PHIL	ENS ROBERT A. COLE	S
10/25/44	47304	VC-3	USS KITKUN BAY	LEYTE GULF	PHIL	ENS MURPHY	S
10/25/44	47393	VC-3	USS KITKUN BAY	LEYTE GULF	PHIL	LTJG ROBERT T. SELL	S
10/25/44	55136	VC-65	USS ST. LO	LEYTE GULF	PHIL	(SHIP SANK)	
10/25/44	55366	VC-68	USS FANSHAW BAY	LEYTE GULF	PHIL		
10/25/44	55378	VC-27	USS SAVO ISLAND	LEYTE GULF	PHIL	ENS F.M. DEIGHTY	S
10/25/44	55379	VC-27	USS SAVO ISLAND	LEYTE GULF	PHIL	ENS STERLING P. ROSS	M
10/25/44	55417	VC-27	USS SAVO ISLAND	LEYTE GULF	PHIL	LT R.J. MULCAMY, JR.	S
10/25/44	55434	VC-21	USS MARCUS ISLAND	LEYTE GULF	PHIL	LT Z.D. HAUCK	S
10/25/44	55441	VC-10	USS GAMBIER BAY	LEYTE GULF	PHIL	LTJG C.F. HUNTING	S
10/25/44	55452	VC-5	USS KITKUN BAY	LEYTE GULF	PHIL		
10/25/44	55469	VC-27	USS SAVO ISLAND	LEYTE GULF	PHIL	ENS ROBERT C. ASHCRAFT	S
10/25/44	55472	VC-20	USS KADASHAN BAY	LEYTE GULF	PHIL	ENS ROY H. DUNCAN	M
10/25/44	55480	VC-65	USS ST. LO	LEYTE GULF	PHIL	(SHIP SANK)	
10/25/44	55489	VC-21	USS MARCUS ISLAND	LEYTE GULF	PHIL	LT W.W. GARNER	M
10/25/44	55496	VC-68	USS FANSHAW BAY	LEYTE GULF	PHIL		
10/25/44	55508	VC-68	USS FANSHAW BAY	LEYTE GULF	PHIL		
10/25/44	55578	VC-68	USS FANSHAW BAY	LEYTE GULF	PHIL		
10/25/44	55603	VC-76	USS PETROF BAY	SAN BERNADINO	PHIL	ENS CURTRIGHT	S
10/25/44	56801	VC-80	USS MANILA BAY	LEYTE GULF	PHIL	LT W.C. DEITCHMAN	S
10/26/44	16116	VC-27	USS SAVO ISLAND	LEYTE GULF	PHIL	ENS BARNETT	S
10/26/44	16431	VC-75	USS OMMANEY BAY	CEMOTEA SEA	PHIL		
10/26/44	47149	VC-81	USS NATOMA BAY	LEYTE GULF	PHIL	ENS W.J. DEVLIN	D
10/26/44	47195	VC-81	USS NATOMA BAY	LEYTE GULF	PHIL	ENS C.D. TATE	S
10/26/44	47209	VC-81	USS NATOMA BAY	LEYTE GULF	PHIL	ENS JOHN O'DONNELL	S
10/26/44	47259	VF-26	USS SANTEE	PHILIPPINE SEA	PHIL	(DECK LOSS-KAMIKAZE)	

DATE	BUNO	SQDRN	BASE	LOST	AREA	PILOT	FATE
10/26/44	55367	VF-26	USS SANTEE	PHILIPPINE SEA	PHIL	(DECK LOSS-KAMIKAZE)	
10/26/44	55419	VC-68	USS FANSHAW BAY	LEYTE GULF	PHIL		
10/26/44	55482	VC-76	USS PETROF BAY	VISAYAN	PHIL	LT FORSYTHE	S
10/26/44	55537	VC-20	USS KADASHAN BAY	LEYTE GULF	PHIL	ENS F.W. PINCERTON	M
10/26/44	55590	VC-75	USS OMMANEY BAY	CEMOTEA SEA	PHIL	LT MARCUSSEN	S
10/26/44	56819	VC-78	USS SAGINAW BAY	LEYTE GULF	PHIL		
10/26/44	56935	VC-80	USS MANILA BAY	LEYTE GULF	PHIL	LT JAMES ALLAN ZELLS	S
10/27/44	47344	VF-26	USS SANTEE	PHILIPPINE SEA	PHIL	LT DAVID C. MCNEILL	S
10/27/44	55217	VC-76	USS PETROF BAY	VISAYAN	PHIL	ENS JOSEPH C. CHEW	S
10/27/44	55488	VF-26	USS SANTEE	PHILIPPINE SEA	PHIL	LT KENNETH F. BOWELL	S
10/27/44	55526	VC-76	USS PETROF BAY	VISAYAN	PHIL		
10/27/44	55607	VC-76	USS PETROF BAY	VISAYAN	PHIL		
10/28/44	46927	VC-11	USS NEHENTA BAY		PHIL	LT JOHN T. TROUTWINE	S
10/28/44	47162	VC-80	USS MANILA BAY	LEYTE GULF	PHIL	ENS CHARLES C. ZUEL	S
10/28/44	55361	VC-20	USS KADASHAN BAY	LEYTE GULF	PHIL		
10/28/44	55443	VC-27	USS SAVO ISLAND	LEYTE GULF	PHIL		
10/28/44	56826	VC-78	USS SAGINAW BAY	LEYTE GULF	PHIL		
10/29/44	16567	VC-82	USS ANZIO		CENPAC		
10/29/44	47175	VC-82	USS ANZIO		CENPAC		
10/29/44	47302	VC-80	USS MANILA BAY	LEYTE GULF	PHIL	ENS WILLIAM R. CRAVENS	M
10/29/44	47321	VC-21	USS MARCUS ISLAND	LEYTE GULF	PHIL	ENS JAMES B. JANES	D
10/29/44	55470	VC-27	USS SAVO ISLAND	LEYTE GULF	PHIL	ENS CHARLES W. SNYDER	D
10/30/44	47107	VC-88	USS MAKASSAR STRAIT	ENR HAWAII	ECENPAC		
10/31/44	16036	A.A.	PEARL	HAWAII	ECENPAC		
10/31/44	16070	A.A.	PEARL	HAWAII	ECENPAC		
10/31/44	16591	COMAIR-PAC	PEARL	HAWAII	ECENPAC		
10/31/44	47431	COMAIR-PAC	PEARL	HAWAII	ECENPAC		
10/31/44	56743	COMAIR-PAC	PEARL	HAWAII	ECENPAC		
10/31/44	56969	VC-88	USS MAKASSAR STRAIT	HAWAII	ECENPAC	LT EVERETT A. KAMP	S
10/31/44	73599	COMAIR-PAC	PEARL	HAWAII	ECENPAC		
10/31/44	73622	COMAIR-PAC	PEARL	HAWAII	ECENPAC		

DATE	BUNO	SQDRN	BASE	LOST	AREA	PILOT	FATE
10/31/44	73714	COMAIR-PAC	PEARL	HAWAII	ECENPAC		
11/02/44	57005	AR & OH		MANUS	SW PAC		
11/07/44	46923	VC-80	USS MANILA BAY	MANUS	SW PAC	ENS R.F. KLEIN	S
11/07/44	47261	VC-80	USS MANILA BAY	MANUS	SW PAC	ENS RICHARD D. ROYAL	S
11/09/44	56810	VC-68	USS FANSHAW BAY	ENR PEARL	WCENPAC	LCDR S.S. ROGERS	S
11/09/44	73746	VC-87	USS SALAMAUA	HAWAII	ECENPAC	ENS ROBERT B. PORTER	S
11/10/44	55135	A & R	PEARL	HAWAII	ECENPAC		
11/11/44	16517	VC-82	USS ANZIO		WCENPAC		
11/11/44	47406	VC-82	USS ANZIO		WCENPAC		
11/13/44	73765	VC-9	USS WAKE ISLAND	ENR PANAMA	CENLANT	LT D.W. LANGSTON	S
11/14/44	16544	CASU(F)-13		PONAM	SW PAC		
11/14/44	16653	VC-14	USS HOGGATT BAY	MARIANAS	CENPAC	LT CLYDE A. ELLIOTT	S
11/14/44	73576	VC-85	USS LUNGA POINT	LEYTE GULF	PHIL	ENS ADRIAN S. BAZZELL	S
11/15/44	16232	CASU(F)-42		PITYILU	SW PAC		
11/15/44	16670	CASU(F)-42		PITYILU	SW PAC		
11/15/44	46838	VC-11	USS NEHENTA BAY		PHIL	ENS DANIEL C. DOWNS	S
11/15/44	47000	CASU(F)-42		PITYILU	SW PAC		
11/15/44	47014	CASU(F)-42		PITYILU	SW PAC		
11/15/44	56707	CASU(F)-42		PITYILU	SW PAC		
11/15/44	73688	VC-86	USS BISMARCK SEA	MANILA	PHIL	ENS FRANCIS W. LAWTON	S
11/15/44	73798	VC-87	USS SALAMAUA	HAWAII	ECENPAC	ENS ROBERT B WILLIAMS, JR.	S
11/16/44	47354	VC-11	USS NEHENTA BAY		WCENPAC	LT W.W. FORSYTHE	S
11/16/44	75063	VC-42	USS SHAMROCK BAY	BALBOA	ECENPAC	LT ARNOLD A. JOHNSTON	S
11/17/44	47340	VC-80	USS MANILA BAY	MANUS	SW PAC	ENS R.F. KLEIN	U
11/17/44	73678	VC-86	USS BISMARCK SEA	MINDANAO SEA	PHIL	ENS WILLIAM H. BEATTY	D
11/17/44	73702	VC-86	USS BISMARCK SEA	MINDANAO SEA	PHIL	ENS HUNTER H. BODLE	S
11/19/44	73594	VC-91	KANEOHE	HAWAII	ECENPAC	ENS EDWARD P. NIXON	S
11/19/44	73595	VC-91	KANEOHE	HAWAII	ECENPAC		
11/20/44	56821	VC-83	USS CORREGI-DOR	HAWAII	ECENPAC		
11/20/44	73672	VC-86	USS BISMARCK SEA	MINDANAO SEA	PHIL		
11/26/44	55410	VC-75	USS OMMANEY BAY	PONAM	SW PAC	ENS DOUGLAS S. ADAMS	S
11/26/44	73728	VC-85	USS LUNGA POINT	ENR MANUS	WCENPAC		
11/28/44	47196	VC-11	USS NEHENTA BAY		WCENPAC		
11/28/44	56701	CASU(F)-42		PITYILU	SW PAC		
11/28/44	73691	CASU(F)-42		PITYILU	SW PAC		
11/30/44	47422	AWT ACTION	PEARL	HAWAII	ECENPAC		

DATE	BUNO	SQDRN	BASE	LOST	AREA	PILOT	FATE
11/30/44	55087	AWT ACTION	PEARL	HAWAII	ECENPAC		
11/30/44	73509	VC-9	USS WAKE ISLAND	HAWAII	ECENPAC		
12/10/44	47312	VF-100	USS MAKASSAR STRAIT	HAWAII	ECENPAC	ENS JAMES E. SAULSBURG	S
12/10/44	73906	A.A.	PEARL	HAWAII	ECENPAC		
12/11/44	16564	CASU(F)-42		PITYILU	SW PAC		
12/11/44	56738	CASU(F)-42		PITYILU	SW PAC		
12/11/44	56813	VC-81	USS NATOMA BAY	ENR LOS NEGR.	PHIL	LT W.L. MATHSON, JR.	S
12/13/44	47193	VC-81	USS NATOMA BAY	LOS NEGROS	PHIL	ENS JOHN F. SARGENT	S
12/13/44	56956	VC-81	USS NATOMA BAY	LOS NEGROS	PHIL		
12/14/44	55544	VC-81	USS NATOMA BAY	LOS NEGROS	PHIL	ENS DARYL V. JOHNSTONE	S
12/14/44	57003	VC-80	USS MANILA BAY	LOS NEGROS	PHIL		
12/16/44	47210	VC-80	USS MANILA BAY	LOS NEGROS	PHIL		
12/16/44	47293	VF-100	USS MAKASSAR STR.	HAWAII	ECENPAC	ENS WILLIAM M. LIMES	S
12/16/44	55440	VC-27	USS SAVO ISLAND	MINDANAO SEA	PHIL	ENS FRED J. MOELTER	M
12/16/44	55534	VC-20	USS KADASHAN BAY		PHIL		
12/16/44	73516	VC-86	USS BISMARCK SEA	ENR LINGAYEN	WCENPAC		
12/16/44	73582	VC-84	USS MAKIN ISLAND	ENR LEYTE GULF	SW PAC		
12/16/44	74009	A.A.	PEARL	HAWAII	ECENPAC		
12/17/44	56863	VC-20	USS KADASHAN BAY		PHIL		
12/17/44	73722	VC-86	USS BISMARCK SEA	ENR LINGAYEN	WCENPAC		
12/17/44	73764	VC-88	USS HOGGATT BAY	MARIANAS	CENPAC	ENS STUART REX DRAPER	S
12/17/44	73778	VC-88	USS HOGGATT BAY	MARIANAS	CENPAC	ENS ROBERT J. HENNEN	S
12/18/44	16504	VC-82	USS ANZIO	LEYTE GULF	PHIL		
12/18/44	47327	VC-11	USS NEHENTA BAY		PHIL	(DECK LOSS-TYPHOON)	
12/18/44	56818	VC-82	USS ANZIO	LEYTE GULF	PHIL		
12/18/44	56967	VC-76	USS PETROF BAY	NEW GUINEA	SW PAC	ENS LEWIS W. THOMPSON	S
12/18/44	57002	VC-76	USS PETROF BAY	NEW GUINEA	SW PAC	ENS THOMAS E. MARSHALL	S
12/18/44	73520	VC-11	USS NEHENTA BAY		PHIL	(DECK LOSS-TYPHOON)	
12/18/44	73717	VC-82	USS ANZIO	LEYTE GULF	PHIL		
12/20/44	56933	VC-92	USS TULAGI	MARIANAS	CENPAC	ENS L.T. BROWN	S
12/20/44	73644	VC-87	USS SALAMAUA	ADMIRALTIES	SW PAC	LTJG JAMES T. ISLEY	U
12/20/44	73771	VC-87	USS SALAMAUA	ADMIRALTIES	SW PAC	ENS J. COOK	U

DATE	BUNO	SQDRN	BASE	LOST	AREA	PILOT	FATE
12/21/44	55349	VC-93		HAWAII	ECENPAC	LT IVAN EDWARD SCHERER	S
12/23/44	16691	VF-100	USS SARATOGA	HAWAII	ECENPAC	ENS GEORGE D. WENTWORTH	S
12/25/44	55485	HEDRON-2	KANEOHE	HAWAII	ECENPAC		
12/26/44	74019	VC-69	USS MISSION BAY	ENR CUBA	NORLANT	ENS HAROLD L. MILLER	S
12/27/44	73610	VC-94	USS SHAMROCK BAY	MANUS	SW PAC	ENS JOHN (NMN) HOCZA	S
12/27/44	73876	VC-94	USS SHAMROCK BAY	MANUS	SW PAC	ENS PHILIP SASEEN	D
12/28/44	56918	CASU-42		PITYILU	SW PAC		
12/28/44	56978	CASU-42		PITYILU	SW PAC		
12/28/44	57023	CASU-42		PITYILU	SW PAC		
12/28/44	73564	CASU-42		PITYILU	SW PAC		
12/28/44	73565	CASU-42		PITYILU	SW PAC		
12/28/44	73628	A.A.	PEARL	HAWAII	ECENPAC		
12/28/44	73920	A.A.	PEARL	HAWAII	ECENPAC		
12/28/44	73995	CASU-42		PITYILU	SW PAC		
01/01/45	47191	A.A.	SAMAR	SAMAR	PHIL		
01/01/45	73809	VC-94	USS SHAMROCK BAY	MANUS	SW PAC		
01/02/45	57022	VC-95	USS BOGUE	BERMUDA	NORLANT	ENS GRONINGER	S
01/02/45	57032	VC-92	USS TULAGI	LINGAYEN GULF	PHIL		
01/03/45	57034	VC-21	USS MARCUS ISLAND	LINGAYEN GULF	PHIL	ENS RICHARD BLEHA	S
01/03/45	73679	VOC-1	USS WAKE ISLAND	SULU SEA	PHIL	LTJG ROBERT B. LYON	S
01/04/45	55224	VC-75	USS OMMANEY BAY	MINDORO STR.	PHIL	(SHIP SANK)	
01/04/45	55448	VC-75	USS OMMANEY BAY	MINDORO STR.	PHIL	(SHIP SANK)	
01/04/45	55479	VC-75	USS OMMANEY BAY	MINDORO STR.	PHIL	(SHIP SANK)	
01/04/45	55498	VC-75	USS OMMANEY BAY	MINDORO STR.	PHIL	(SHIP SANK)	
01/04/45	55506	VC-75	USS OMMANEY BAY	MINDORO STR.	PHIL	(SHIP SANK)	
01/04/45	55520	VC-75	USS OMMANEY BAY	MINDORO STR	PHIL	(SHIP SANK)	
01/04/45	55522	VC-75	USS OMMANEY BAY	MINDORO STR.	PHIL	(SHIP SANK)	
01/04/45	55586	VC-75	USS OMMANEY BAY	MINDORO STR.	PHIL	(SHIP SANK)	
01/04/45	56798	VC-75	USS OMMANEY BAY	MINDORO STR.	PHIL	(SHIP SANK)	
01/04/45	56820	VC-75	USS OMMANEY BAY	MINDORO STR.	PHIL	(SHIP SANK)	
01/04/45	56839	VC-75	USS OMMANEY BAY	MINDORO STR.	PHIL	(SHIP SANK)	
01/04/45	56876	VC-75	USS OMMANEY BAY	MINDORO STR.	PHIL	(SHIP SANK)	
01/04/45	56923	VC-75	USS OMMANEY BAY	MINDORO STR.	PHIL	(SHIP SANK)	
01/04/45	56934	VC-92	USS TULAGI	MINDANAO SEA	PHIL		

DATE	BUNO	SQDRN	BASE	LOST	AREA	PILOT	FATE
01/04/45	56942	VC-75	USS OMMANEY BAY	MINDORO STR.	PHIL	(SHIP SANK)	
01/04/45	56946	VC-75	USS OMMANEY BAY	MINDORO STR.	PHIL	(SHIP SANK)	
01/04/45	56985	VC-75	USS OMMANEY BAY	MINDORO STR.	PHIL	(SHIP SANK)	
01/04/45	56998	VC-75	USS OMMANEY BAY	MINDORO STR.	PHIL	(SHIP SANK)	
01/04/45	57020	VC-75	USS OMMANEY BAY	MINDORO STR.	PHIL	(SHIP SANK)	
01/04/45	57041	VC-75	USS OMMANEY BAY	MINDORO STR.	PHIL	(SHIP SANK)	
01/04/45	73569	VC-91	USS KITKUN BAY	LUZON	PHIL	LCDR BERNARD D. MACK	S
01/04/45	73736	VC-87	USS SALAMAUA	ENR LINGAYEN	PHIL		
01/04/45	73792	VC-88	USS HOGGATT BAY	LUZON	PHIL	ENS ROBERT J. . HENNEN	S
01/04/45	74002	VC-92	USS TULAGI	MINDANAO SEA	PHIL		
01/05/45	56823	VC-80	USS MANILA BAY	MINDORO STR.	PHIL	(DECK LOSS-KAMIKAZE)	
01/05/45	73533	VC-86	USS BISMARCK SEA	LUZON	PHIL		
01/05/45	73551	VC-91	USS KITKUN BAY	LUZON	PHIL	LCDR BERNARD D. MACK	M
01/06/45	16660	VC-21	USS MARCUS ISLAND	LINGAYEN GULF	PHIL	ENS RICHARD BLAND	S
01/06/45	47190	VC-81	USS NATOMA BAY	LUZON	PHIL	LTJG JOHN SARGENT	D
01/06/45	56904	VC-96	HAWAII	HAWAII	ECENPAC	LTJG T.H. GOODSON	S
01/06/45	57070	VC-88	USS HOGGATT BAY	LUZON	PHIL	ENS LESLIE O. PORTHER	S
01/06/45	73593	VC-90	USS STEAMER BAY	LINGAYEN GULF	PHIL		
01/06/45	73612	VC-90	USS STEAMER BAY	LINGAYEN GULF	PHIL		
01/06/45	73733	VC-86	USS BISMARCK SEA	LUZON	PHIL		
01/07/45	56861	VC-80	USS MANILA BAY	ENR LINGAYEN	PHIL		
01/07/45	56915	VC-92	USS TULAGI	SO. CHINA SEA	PHIL		
01/07/45	57068	VC-88	USS HOGGATT BAY	LINGAYEN GULF	PHIL	ENS FREDERICK D. TAYLOR	S
01/07/45	73537	VC-84	USS MAKIN ISLAND	LUZON	PHIL		
01/07/45	73542	VC-92	USS TULAGI	SO. CHINA SEA	PHIL		
01/07/45	73638	VC-86	USS BISMARCK SEA	LUZON	PHIL		
01/07/45	73658	VC-86	USS BISMARCK SEA	LUZON	PHIL		

DATE	BUNO	SQDRN	BASE	LOST	AREA	PILOT	FATE
01/07/45	73811	VC-88	USS HOGGATT BAY	LINGAYEN GULF	PHIL	LTJG WM J. ARMSTRONG	S
01/07/45	73966	VOC-1	USS WAKE ISLAND	MANILA	PHIL	LTJG CLIFFORD E. CASE	S
01/08/45	46962	VC-21	USS MARCUS ISLAND	LINGAYEN GULF	PHIL	ENS QUENTIN B. EVANS	S
01/08/45	47326	VC-80	USS MANILA BAY	SO. CHINA SEA	PHIL	LT JAMES ALLAN ZELLS	S
01/08/45	55503	VC-20	USS KADASHAN BAY		PHIL		
01/08/45	56796	A.A.	SAMAR	SAMAR	PHIL		
01/08/45	57016	VC-21	USS MARCUS ISLAND	LINGAYEN GULF	PHIL	ENS CHARLES B. BRADFORD	U
01/08/45	73522	VC-86	USS BISMARCK SEA	LUZON	PHIL		
01/08/45	73543	VC-84	USS MAKIN ISLAND	LINGAYEN GULF	PHIL		
01/08/45	73617	VC-91	USS KITKUN BAY	LUZON	PHIL	WILLIAM FRANK JORDAN	S
01/08/45	73720	VC-88	USS HOGGATT BAY	LINGAYEN GULF	PHIL	LTJG C.L. NEWBURN	S
01/08/45	73959	VC-90	USS STEAMER BAY	LINGAYEN GULF	PHIL		
01/09/45	56722	VC-80	USS MANILA BAY	SO. CHINA SEA	PHIL		
01/09/45	73528	VC-84	USS MAKIN ISLAND	LINGAYEN GULF	PHIL		
01/09/45	73589	VC-91	USS KITKUN BAY	LUZON	PHIL		
01/09/45	74027	VC-91	USS KITKUN BAY	LUZON	PHIL		
01/09/45	75153	VC-86	USS BISMARCK SEA	LUZON	PHIL		
01/10/45	55476	VC-27	USS SAVO ISLAND	LINGAYEN GULF	PHIL		
01/10/45	55486	VC-21	USS MARCUS ISLAND	LINGAYEN GULF	PHIL		
01/10/45	55582	VC-21	USS MARCUS ISLAND	LINGAYEN GULF	PHIL		
01/10/45	55610	VC-81	USS NATOMA BAY	LUZON	PHIL		
01/10/45	56797	VC-78	USS SAGINAW BAY	LINGAYEN GULF	PHIL		
01/10/45	56868	VC-81	USS NATOMA BAY	LUZON	PHIL		
01/10/45	56912	VC-78	USS SAGINAW BAY	LINGAYEN GULF	PHIL		
01/10/45	56996	VC-21	USS MARCUS ISLAND	LINGAYEN GULF	PHIL		
01/10/45	73531	VC-84	USS MAKIN ISLAND	LINGAYEN GULF	PHIL	LTJG K.B. FINKE	S
01/10/45	73639	VC-84	USS MAKIN ISLAND	LINGAYEN GULF	PHIL		
01/10/45	73738	VC-87	USS SALAMAUA	LINGAYEN GULF	PHIL	(DECK LOSS-KAMIKAZE)	

DATE	BUNO	SQDRN	BASE	LOST	AREA	PILOT	FATE
01/11/45	47419	CASU(F)-42		PITYILU	SW PAC		
01/11/45	73530	VC-84	USS MAKIN ISLAND	LINGAYEN GULF	PHIL	ENS J.G. BABB	S
01/11/45	73577	VC-88	USS HOGGATT BAY	LINGAYEN GULF	PHIL	ENS JAMES H. O'CONNOR	S
01/11/45	73623	VC-91	USS KITKUN BAY	LUZON	PHIL	LTJG JAMES A. JONES	S
01/11/45	73981	VC-90	USS STEAMER BAY	LINGAYEN GULF	PHIL		
01/11/45	74039	VC-84	USS MAKIN ISLAND	LINGAYEN GULF	PHIL	ENS B. HOBSON	S
01/12/45	46888	VC-21	USS MARCUS ISLAND	LINGAYEN GULF	PHIL		
01/12/45	56699	A.A.	PITYILU	PITYILU	SW PAC		
01/12/45	56746	VC-88	USS HOGGATT BAY	LINGAYEN GULF	PHIL		
01/12/45	56971	VC-76	USS PETROF BAY	MANILA	PHIL	CDR JAMES W. MCCOULEY	S
01/12/45	73598	VC-90	USS STEAMER BAY	LINGAYEN GULF	PHIL	LT ROY C. LYNN	S
01/12/45	73667	VC-88	USS HOGGATT BAY	LINGAYEN GULF	PHIL		
01/12/45	73707	VC-84	USS MAKIN ISLAND	LINGAYEN GULF	PHIL	ENS THOMAS A. WALL	D
01/12/45	73871	VC-88	USS HOGGATT BAY	LINGAYEN GULF	PHIL		
01/13/45	47119	VC-81	USS NATOMA BAY	SAN FABIAN	PHIL	ENS ROBERT D. MCFARLAND	S
01/13/45	55332	VC-21	USS MARCUS ISLAND	LINGAYEN GULF	PHIL	ENS CHESTER C. CHAPMAN	D
01/13/45	55561	VC-76	USS PETROF BAY	MANILA	PHIL	LT BENJAMIN J. CURRIE	S
01/13/45	56803	VC-78	USS SAGINAW BAY	LINGAYEN GULF	PHIL		
01/13/45	73536	VC-87	USS SALAMAUA	LINGAYEN GULF	PHIL	(DECK LOSS - KAMIKAZE)	
01/13/45	73721	VC-84	USS MAKIN ISLAND	LINGAYEN GULF	PHIL		
01/13/45	73749	VC-82	USS ANZIO	LUZON	PHIL	LTJG J.F. LEWIS	S
01/13/45	73787	VOC-1	USS WAKE ISLAND	MANILA	PHIL	LTJG FRED WILLIAM FENSEL	M
01/14/45	55595	VC-76	USS PETROF BAY	MANILA	PHIL	LT HOWARD P. BARKS	S
01/14/45	73554	VC-90	USS STEAMER BAY	SO. CHINA SEA	PHIL		
01/14/45	73605	VC-90	USS STEAMER BAY	SO. CHINA SEA	PHIL	ENS CHARLES F. WILSON	S
01/15/45	55374	VC-27	USS SAVO ISLAND	LINGAYEN GULF	PHIL		
01/15/45	55571	VC-27	USS SAVO ISLAND	LINGAYEN GULF	PHIL		
01/15/45	56805	VC-27	USS SAVO ISLAND	LINGAYEN GULF	PHIL		
01/15/45	56882	VC-27	USS SAVO ISLAND	LINGAYEN GULF	PHIL		
01/15/45	73867	VC-88	USS HOGGATT BAY	LINGAYEN GULF	PHIL	LTJG EDWARD A. WHITE	S

DATE	BUNO	SQDRN	BASE	LOST	AREA	PILOT	FATE
01/16/45	56857	VC-92	USS TULAGI	LINGAYEN GULF	PHIL		
01/16/45	56872	VC-92	USS TULAGI	LINGAYEN GULF	PHIL		
01/16/45	56981	VC-27	USS SAVO ISLAND	LINGAYEN GULF	PHIL		
01/16/45	56991	VC-27	USS SAVO ISLAND	LINGAYEN GULF	PHIL		
01/16/45	57012	VC-27	USS SAVO ISLAND	LINGAYEN GULF	PHIL		
01/16/45	73643	VC-88	USS HOGGATT BAY	LINGAYEN GULF	PHIL		
01/16/45	73767	VC-11	USS NEHENTA BAY	ENR HAWAII	PHIL	LTJG GRANT L. DONNELLY	S
01/16/45	73789	VC-79	USS SARGENT BAY	ULITHI	WCENPAC		
01/16/45	74363	VOC-2	USS RANGER	PEARL	ECENPAC	LT BERT FRANCIS WALKER	D
01/17/45	73562	VC-85	USS LUNGA POINT	LINGAYEN GULF	PHIL	LTJG A. WEINTRAUT	S
01/17/45	73627	VC-86	USS BISMARCK SEA	ENR IWO JIMA	PHIL		
01/17/45	73662	VC-86	USS BISMARCK SEA	ENR IWO JIMA	PHIL		
01/17/45	73766	VC-85	USS LUNGA POINT	LINGAYEN GULF	PHIL	ENS H.E. DYEDAHL	S
01/18/45	73734	VC-84	USS MAKIN ISLAND	ENR ULITHI	PHIL		
01/19/45	56834	VC-76	USS PETROF BAY	LUZON	PHIL	LTJG F.F. BURKE	S
01/19/45	73944	VC-94	USS SHAMROCK BAY	LUZON	PHIL		
01/20/45	47301	VC-79	USS SARGENT BAY	ULITHI	WCENPAC		
01/20/45	55350	VC-80	USS MANILA BAY	SO. CHINA SEA	PHIL		
01/21/45	47407	VC-77	USS RUDYERD BAY	LINGAYEN GULF	PHIL	LTJG GERALD BLOOMQUIST	S
01/27/45	74234	A.A.	PEARL	HAWAII	ECENPAC		
01/27/45	74236	A.A.	PEARL	HAWAII	ECENPAC	ENS ELBRIDGE V. GOODRELL	S
01/30/45	47204	A.A.	PITYILU	PITYILU	SW PAC		
01/30/45	47315	A.A.	PITYILU	PITYILU	SW PAC		
01/30/45	56709	A.A.	PITYILU	PITYILU	SW PAC		
01/30/45	57058	CASU(F)-42		PITYILU	SW PAC		
01/31/45	56803	VC-81	USS NATOMA BAY	MINDORO STR.	PHIL		
01/31/45	73915	A.A.	PEARL	HAWAII	ECENPAC		
01/31/45	73997	A.A.	PEARL	HAWAII	ECENPAC		
02/02/45	56880	VC-91	USS SAVO ISLAND	ENR LEYTE GULF	PHIL		
02/03/45	55580	VC-58	USS CORE		NORLANT	(DECK LOSS-ROUGH WEATHER)	
02/06/45	56920	VOC-2		HAWAII	ECENPAC	LT E.H. SPENCER	S
02/06/45	73683	CASU(F)-13		PITYILU	SW PAC		
02/06/45	73709	CASU(F)-13		PITYILU	SW PAC		
02/07/45	73698	CASU(F)-12		GUAM	WCENPAC	ENS GUISEPPO SCHEMBRIO	S
02/08/45	16663	A.A.	GUAM	GUAM	WCENPAC		
02/09/45	57057	CASU-4	PUUNENE	HAWAII	ECENPAC	LTJG J.V. CANTERBURY	S
02/09/45	74087	VC-8	USS TRIPOLI	HAWAII	ECENPAC	ENS REGIS D. BOWERS	S

DATE	BUNO	SQDRN	BASE	LOST	AREA	PILOT	FATE
02/09/45	74283	VC-8	USS TRIPOLI	HAWAII	ECENPAC	ENS DONALD L. FARRIS	S
02/10/45	74279	VC-13	HILO	HAWAII	ECENPAC	ENS H.E. THORPE	S
02/10/45	74428	VC-97	USS MAKASSAR STR.	BONINS	CENPAC	LT PAUL J. GEORGE	S
02/11/45	73624	VC-97	USS MAKASSAR STR.	BONINS	CENPAC	LTJG ROBERT D. THOMPSON	S
02/13/45	57027	VOC-2	USS TRIPOLI	HAWAII	ECENPAC	LTJG JOHN F. CANTERBURY	S
02/15/45	56916	VC-76	USS PETROF BAY	IWO JIMA	EMPIRE		
02/16/45	16162	VC-83	USS SARGENT BAY	IWO JIMA	EMPIRE		
02/16/45	56919	VC-81	USS NATOMA BAY	IWO JIMA	EMPIRE	ENS DANIEL P. VALDEY	M
02/16/45	73574	VC-85	USS LUNGA POINT	IWO JIMA	EMPIRE	ENS FRANK J. STEVENSON	S
02/16/45	73911	VC-83	USS SARGENT BAY	IWO JIMA	EMPIRE		
02/17/45	46918	CASU(F)-43		GUAM	WCENPAC		
02/17/45	73563	VOC-1	USS WAKE ISLAND	IWO JIMA	EMPIRE	LTJG THOMAS LEO MURPHY	M
02/17/45	73945	VC-88	USS SAGINAW BAY	ENR IWO JIMA	EMPIRE		
02/18/45	56895	VOC-2	USS KASAAN BAY	HAWAII	ECENPAC	ENS JAMES A. PANTON	S
02/19/45	55602	VC-77	USS RUDYERD BAY	IWO JIMA	EMPIRE	ENS RICHARD C. SMALLWOOD	S
02/19/45	73518	VC-90	USS STEAMER BAY	NANPO SHOTO	EMPIRE		
02/19/45	73666	VC-88	USS SAGINAW BAY	IWO JIMA	EMPIRE	ENS LESLIE O. PORTHER	S
02/19/45	73784	VC-82	USS ANZIO	CHICHI JIMA	CENPAC	LTJG K.D. PEARSON	S
02/19/45	73965	A.A.	GUAM	GUAM	WCENPAC		
02/20/45	73888	VC-88	USS SAGINAW BAY	IWO JIMA	EMPIRE	ENS GEORGE C. TRIPLETT	S
02/20/45	74242	VC-8	USS TRIPOLI	HAWAII	ECENPAC	ENS JOSEPH GALLAGHER	S
02/21/45	16493	A.A.	PEARL	HAWAII	ECENPAC		
02/21/45	56793	VOC-1	USS WAKE ISLAND	IWO JIMA	EMPIRE		
02/21/45	56943	VC-97	HAWAII	HAWAII	ECENPAC		
02/21/45	73532	VC-86	USS BISMARCK SEA	IWO JIMA	EMPIRE	(SHIP SANK)	
02/21/45	73549	VC-86	USS BISMARCK SEA	IWO JIMA	EMPIRE	(SHIP SANK)	
02/21/45	73567	VC-86	USS BISMARCK SEA	IWO JIMA	EMPIRE	(SHIP SANK)	
02/21/45	73575	VC-86	USS BISMARCK SEA	IWO JIMA	EMPIRE	(SHIP SANK)	
02/21/45	73596	VC-86	USS BISMARCK SEA	IWO JIMA	EMPIRE	(SHIP SANK)	
02/21/45	73608	VC-86	USS BISMARCK SEA	IWO JIMA	EMPIRE	(SHIP SANK)	

DATE	BUNO	SQDRN	BASE	LOST	AREA	PILOT	FATE
02/21/45	73613	VC-86	USS BISMARCK SEA	IWO JIMA	EMPIRE	(SHIP SANK)	
02/21/45	73620	VC-86	USS BISMARCK SEA	IWO JIMA	EMPIRE	(SHIP SANK)	
02/21/45	73629	VC-86	USS BISMARCK SEA	IWO JIMA	EMPIRE	(SHIP SANK)	
02/21/45	73674	VC-86	USS BISMARCK SEA	IWO JIMA	EMPIRE	(SHIP SANK)	
02/21/45	73704	VC-86	USS BISMARCK SEA	IWO JIMA	EMPIRE	(SHIP SANK)	
02/21/45	73729	VC-77	USS RUDYERD BAY	IWO JIMA	EMPIRE	LTJG S.D. MCGURK	D
02/21/45	73752	VC-86	USS BISMARCK SEA	IWO JIMA	EMPIRE	(SHIP SANK)	
02/21/45	73762	VC-86	USS BISMARCK SEA	IWO JIMA	EMPIRE	(SHIP SANK)	
02/21/45	73773	VC-86	USS BISMARCK SEA	IWO JIMA	EMPIRE	(SHIP SANK)	
02/21/45	73807	VC-86	USS BISMARCK SEA	IWO JIMA	EMPIRE	(SHIP SANK)	
02/21/45	73910	VC-86	USS BISMARCK SEA	IWO JIMA	EMPIRE	(SHIP SANK)	
02/21/45	73934	VC-86	USS BISMARCK SEA	IWO JIMA	EMPIRE	(SHIP SANK)	
02/21/45	73952	VC-86	USS BISMARCK SEA	IWO JIMA	EMPIRE	(SHIP SANK)	
02/21/45	73976	VC-86	USS BISMARCK SEA	IWO JIMA	EMPIRE	(SHIP SANK)	
02/21/45	74018	VC-86	USS BISMARCK SEA	IWO JIMA	EMPIRE	(SHIP SANK)	
02/22/45	73808	VC-88	USS SAGINAW BAY	IWO JIMA	EMPIRE	LTJG EDWARD A. WHITE	S
02/22/45	74203	CASU-31	USS SHIPLEY BAY	HAWAII	ECENPAC	ENS WARREN P. WICKMIRE	S
02/23/45	73527	VC-90	USS STEAMER BAY	IWO JIMA	EMPIRE		
02/24/45	56987	POOL	BARBERS POINT	HAWAII	ECENPAC		
02/24/45	73912	VOC-1	USS WAKE ISLAND	IWO JIMA	EMPIRE	LTJG WILLIAM C. MCKEEVER	S
02/24/45	73942	VC-97	USS MAKASSAR STR.	RYUKYU	EMPIRE	LTJG CLIFFORD L. GIEBLER	S
02/26/45	73996	VC-83	USS SARGENT BAY	IWO JIMA	EMPIRE		
02/27/45	56949	VC-76	USS PETROF BAY	IWO JIMA	EMPIRE	LTJG WILLIAM O. GREEN	S
03/01/45	73558	VC-94	USS SHAMROCK BAY	IWO JIMA	EMPIRE		
03/01/45	73868	VC-97	USS MAKASSAR STR.	IWO JIMA	EMPIRE	LTJG JOHN G. ARTHUR	S
03/02/45	47279	VF-99		GUAM	WCENPAC		
03/03/45	56866	VC-81	USS NATOMA BAY	BONINS	CENPAC	LTJG CLAUDE TATE	S

DATE	BUNO	SQDRN	BASE	LOST	AREA	PILOT	FATE
03/03/45	74037	VC-81	USS NATOMA BAY	BONINS	CENPAC	LTJG J.M. HUSTON	D
03/03/45	74214	VOC-2	USS FANSHAW BAY	ENR ULITHI	WCENPAC	ENS RODERICK J. SUTTON	S
03/04/45	56924	VC-76	USS PETROF BAY	GUAM	WCENPAC	LTJG WILLIAM H. RISHART	S
03/05/45	73699	VC-8	USS KASAAN BAY	HAWAII	ECENPAC	LTJG VIRGIL R. BRASLER	S
03/06/45	55524	VC-77	USS RUDYERD BAY	IWO JIMA	EMPIRE	LTJG SCHORNSTEIN	S
03/06/45	73936	VC-88	USS SAGINAW BAY	IWO JIMA	EMPIRE	LTJG JAMES H. O'CONNOR	S
03/07/45	16513	VF-100	USS TRIPOLI	BARBERS POINT	ECENPAC	ENS W.D. HANDLE	S
03/07/45	73635	VC-88	USS SAGINAW BAY	IWO JIMA	EMPIRE	LT GERALD MUEHLER	S
03/07/45	73685	VC-88	USS SAGINAW BAY	IWO JIMA	EMPIRE	LTJG KEMP	S
03/07/45	73883	VC-88	USS SAGINAW BAY	IWO JIMA	EMPIRE	LTJG STEWART R. DRAPER	S
03/07/45	74189	VC-82	USS ANZIO	IWO JIMA	EMPIRE		
03/08/45	55462	VC-77	USS RUDYERD BAY	IWO JIMA	EMPIRE	LT EBER W. BESSETT	S
03/08/45	55532	VC-77	USS RUDYERD BAY	IWO JIMA	EMPIRE	LT KNUDSON	U
03/10/45	73550	VC-84	USS MAKIN ISLAND	IWO JIMA	EMPIRE		
03/10/45	73656	VC-84	USS MAKIN ISLAND	IWO JIMA	EMPIRE		
03/10/45	73742	VC-84	USS MAKIN ISLAND	IWO JIMA	EMPIRE		
03/10/45	73755	COMAIR-PAC	PEARL	HAWAII	ECENPAC		
03/10/45	73758	VC-84	USS MAKIN ISLAND	IWO JIMA	EMPIRE		
03/11/45	74526	CASU(F)-12		GUAM	WCENPAC	ENS ROBERT E. FUTTING	S
03/15/45	46949	NAS	KANEOHE	HAWAII	ECENPAC		
03/15/45	73779	VC-94	USS SHAM-ROCK BAY	OKINAWA	EMPIRE	LTJG JAMES E. STOTZ	S
03/15/45	74031	VC-94	USS SHAM-ROCK BAY	OKINAWA	EMPIRE	ENS JOHN N. PURDY	S
03/16/45	74176	VC-63	HILO	HAWAII	ECENPAC	LTJG T.A. RIDDELL	S
03/19/45	46854	VC-13	USS ANZIO	LEYTE GULF	PHIL		
03/19/45	74199	VC-13	USS ANZIO	LEYTE GULF	PHIL	ENS JOHN J. SHARER	S
03/21/45	73690	VC-84	USS MAKIN ISLAND	ENR OKINAWA	EMPIRE		
03/21/45	73757	VF-100	USS TRIPOLI	HAWAII	ECENPAC	ENS T.A. CLARKSON	S
03/23/45	55587	VC-96	USS RUDYERD BAY	IWO JIMA	EMPIRE		
03/25/45		VC-88	USS SAGINAW BAY	OKINAWA	EMPIRE	LTJG STEWART R. DRAPER	S
03/25/45	47331	VC-87	USS MARCUS ISLAND	OKINAWA	EMPIRE	ENS FREDERICK W. VIRRELL	M
03/25/45	55546	VC-87	USS MARCUS ISLAND	OKINAWA	EMPIRE	R.E. PRAETOR	S
03/25/45	74209	VOC-2	USS FANSHAW BAY	KEREMA RHET.	EMPIRE	ENS MERRILL W. BUCKNER	S

DATE	BUNO	SQDRN	BASE	LOST	AREA	PILOT	FATE
03/25/45	74399	VOC-1	USS WAKE ISLAND	OKINAWA	EMPIRE	LT J.M. ALSTON	M
03/26/45	55528	VC-87	USS MARCUS ISLAND	OKINAWA	EMPIRE	FRANK E. OGDEN	S
03/27/45	73797	VC-84	USS MAKIN ISLAND	OKINAWA	EMPIRE	LTJG WESTON LEON SCOTT	D
03/27/45	74030	VOC-1	USS WAKE ISLAND	OKINAWA	EMPIRE	LTJG L.W. THOMPSON	M
03/27/45	74455	VC-93	USS PETROF BAY	OKINAWA	EMPIRE	LT O.T. DENNETT	S
03/27/45	74492	VC-93	USS PETROF BAY	OKINAWA	EMPIRE	ENS R.A. KINNAID	S
03/28/45	46980	POOL	BARBERS POINT	HAWAII	ECENPAC		
03/28/45	74065	VOC-2	USS FANSHAW BAY	OKINAWA	EMPIRE		
03/29/45	73581	VC-85	USS LUNGA POINT	RYUKYU	EMPIRE	ENS DONALD E. BUTCHER	S
03/29/45	73584	VC-90	USS STEAMER BAY	OKINAWA	EMPIRE		
03/30/45	73695	VC-84	USS MAKIN ISLAND	OKINAWA	EMPIRE	ENS WARDINGS	S
03/30/45	73929	VC-83	USS SARGENT BAY	OKINAWA	EMPIRE		
03/30/45	74286	VC-93	USS PETROF BAY	OKINAWA	EMPIRE	ENS GORDON A. COLLIPRIST	M
03/31/45	47249	VF-99		GUAM	WCENPAC		
03/31/45	57042	VC-93	USS PETROF BAY	OKINAWA	EMPIRE	ENS ROBERT H. ALLISON	S
03/31/45	73696	VC-90	USS STEAMER BAY	OKINAWA	EMPIRE		
03/31/45	74174	VC-92	USS TULAGI	OKINAWA	EMPIRE	ENS H.C. COX	S
04/01/45	73924	VC-88	USS SAGINAW BAY	OKINAWA	EMPIRE	ENS WILLIAM G. MANCE	D
04/02/45	47306	VC-87	USS MARCUS ISLAND	NEAR OKINAWA	EMPIRE	DONALD G. WELLS	S
04/02/45	56962	VC-9	USS NATOMA BAY	OKINAWA	EMPIRE	ENS ALEXANDER X. CIOLEK	S
04/02/45	74159	VC-90	USS STEAMER BAY	OKINAWA	EMPIRE	ENS R.J. UNVERSAW	D
04/03/45	55474	VC-96	USS RUDYERD BAY	OKINAWA	EMPIRE	ENS CECIL A. BROWN, JR.	S
04/03/45	56929	CASU(F)-12		GUAM	WCENPAC		
04/03/45	73583	CASU(F)-12		GUAM	WCENPAC		
04/03/45	73648	VC-85	USS LUNGA POINT	RYUKYU	EMPIRE		
04/03/45	73893	VOC-1	USS MARCUS ISLAND	NEAR OKINAWA	EMPIRE		
04/03/45	73904	CASU(F)-12		GUAM	WCENPAC		
04/03/45	74011	VOC-1	USS MARCUS ISLAND	NEAR OKINAWA	EMPIRE		
04/03/45	74059	VC-88	USS SAGINAW BAY	OKINAWA	EMPIRE	LT EVERETT A. KAMP	S

DATE	BUNO	SQDRN	BASE	LOST	AREA	PILOT	FATE
04/03/45	74090	VC-96	USS RUDYERD BAY	OKINAWA	EMPIRE		
04/05/45	56828	VC-91	USS SAVO ISLAND	OKINAWA	EMPIRE		
04/05/45	73677	VC-85	USS LUNGA POINT	RYUKYU	EMPIRE	ENS DONALD E. BUTCHER	S
04/06/45		VC-85	USS LUNGA POINT	IE SHIMA	EMPIRE	LTJG ADRIAN S. BAZZELL	D
04/06/45	57011	VC-92	USS TULAGI	KEREMA RHET.	EMPIRE	LTJG S.G. CHAPIN	S
04/06/45	73987	VOC-2	USS FANSHAW BAY	OKINAWA	EMPIRE	LTJG A.W. JONES	M
04/07/45	73601	VOC-1	USS MARCUS ISLAND	NEAR OKINAWA	EMPIRE	LTJG DAVID E. ROBINSON	S
04/07/45	73875	VOC-2	USS FANSHAW BAY	OKINAWA	EMPIRE	LT LEWIS W. GASKILL	S
04/09/45	56835	VC-9	USS NATOMA BAY	OKINAWA	EMPIRE		
04/09/45	73849	VC-94	USS SHAM-ROCK BAY	OKINAWA	EMPIRE	LCDR FRANKLIN PATTERSON	D
04/09/45	74501	VC-9	USS NATOMA BAY	OKINAWA	EMPIRE		
04/10/45	73703	VC-88	USS SAGINAW BAY	ENR IE SHIMA	EMPIRE		
04/10/45	74168	VC-84	USS MAKIN ISLAND	OKINAWA	EMPIRE	LT THOMAS S. SEDAKER	S
04/10/45	74208	VC-63	HILO	HAWAII	ECENPAC	ENS NEIL CRAIG	S
04/11/45	74261	VOC-2	USS FANSHAW BAY	OKINAWA	EMPIRE	LT C.B. MCAFEE	S
04/12/45	55260	VC-93	USS PETROF BAY	OKINAWA	EMPIRE	ENS CHARLES J. JANSON	M
04/12/45	55398	VC-93	USS PETROF BAY	OKINAWA	EMPIRE	ENS PAUL R. BAUMGARTNER	S
04/12/45	74072	CASU-1	PEARL	HAWAII	ECENPAC	ENS CLAYTON J. BORNE, JR.	S
04/12/45	74086	VC-63	HILO	HAWAII	ECENPAC	LT R.E. LUND	S
04/13/45	57074	VC-92	USS TULAGI	MIYAKO JIMA	EMPIRE	LTJG NORBERT LINK	U
04/13/45	73813	VC-94	USS SHAM-ROCK BAY	OKINAWA	EMPIRE		
04/13/45	86676	VC-94	USS SHAM-ROCK BAY	OKINAWA	EMPIRE		
04/14/45	74085	VC-97	USS MAKASSAR STR.	OKINAWA	EMPIRE	LTJG ROBERT D. THOMPSON	S
04/14/45	75093	VC-88	USS SAGINAW BAY	IE SHIMA	EMPIRE	LT PHILLIP VAUGHN MOTT	M
04/15/45	55584	CASU(F)-15		SAIPAN	WCENPAC		
04/15/45	73803	VC-93	USS PETROF BAY	IE SHIMA	EMPIRE	LTJG ALFRED GODFERY	S
04/15/45	73949	VOC-1	USS MARCUS ISLAND	IE SHIMA	EMPIRE	ENS MICHAEL ED. KRAINT	M
04/16/45	74188	VC-93	USS PETROF BAY	IE SHIMA	EMPIRE	LCDR CHESTER P. SMITH	S
04/16/45	74224	VC-93	USS PETROF BAY	IE SHIMA	EMPIRE	LTJG IVAN ED. SCHERER	S

DATE	BUNO	SQDRN	BASE	LOST	AREA	PILOT	FATE
04/17/45	74465	VC-96	USS RUDYERD BAY	OKINAWA	EMPIRE		
04/18/45	73611	VOC-1	USS MARCUS ISLAND	IE SHIMA	EMPIRE	LTJG WM HOMER BETHEA	M
04/18/45	74196	VOC-1	USS MARCUS ISLAND	IE SHIMA	EMPIRE	LTJG DENISON	S
04/21/45	73785	VC-97	USS MAKASSAR STR.	OKINAWA	EMPIRE	LTJG JOHN G. ARTHUR	S
04/21/45	74028	VC-97	USS MAKASSAR STR.	OKINAWA	EMPIRE		
04/21/45	74193	VC-92	USS TULAGI	OKINAWA	EMPIRE	ENS J.C. FLYNN	S
04/22/45	74041	VOC-1	USS MARCUS ISLAND	OKINAWA	EMPIRE	LTJG GEORGE W. ZACHMAN	M
04/22/45	74105	VC-83	USS SARGENT BAY	OKINAWA	EMPIRE	LCDR BILLY V. GATES	M
04/23/45	74035	VC-94	USS SHAM-ROCK BAY	KEREMA RHET.	EMPIRE		
04/24/45	56999	VC-91	USS SAVO ISLAND	OKINAWA	EMPIRE		
04/26/45	74049	VOC-1	USS MARCUS ISLAND	OKINAWA	EMPIRE	LTJG WILLIAM C. MCKEEVER	S
04/27/45	73857	VC-97	USS MAKASSAR STR.	OKINAWA	EMPIRE		
04/27/45	73873	VC-97	USS MAKASSAR STR.	OKINAWA	EMPIRE		
04/27/45	74429	VC-84	USS MAKIN ISLAND	OKINAWA	EMPIRE		
04/28/45	56907	VC-91	USS SAVO ISLAND	OKINAWA	EMPIRE	LTJG J.W. WILSON	S
04/28/45	57067	VC-97	USS MAKASSAR STR.	OKINAWA	EMPIRE		
04/28/45	74401	VOC-2	USS FANSHAW BAY	IWO JIMA	EMPIRE	LT WARREN LEVI MCNETT	M
05/01/45	73634	VC-97	USS MAKASSAR STR.	OKINAWA	EMPIRE	LT TOM JEROME CONNELLY	D
05/01/45	74292	VC 70	USS SALAMAUA	HAWAII	ECENPAC	ENS RICHARD C. FINN	D
05/03/45	16612	VF-100	USS TRIPOLI	PEARL	ECENPAC	ENS JOHN (NMN) LOTT	S
05/03/45	74180	VC-96	USS RUDYERD BAY	OKINAWA	EMPIRE	LTJG CHARLES H. HARPER	S
05/04/45	73884	VOC-2	USS FANSHAW BAY	OKINAWA	EMPIRE	ENS JOHN C. HYDE	M
05/04/45	73953	VC-92	USS TULAGI	OKINAWA	EMPIRE	ENS JACK L. BLACKBURN	D
05/05/45	74682	VC-8	USS NEHENTA BAY	HAWAII	ECENPAC	ENS WILLIAM A. SMALL	S
05/06/45	74115	VC-92	USS TULAGI	OKINAWA	EMPIRE	LTJG S.G. CHAPIN	S
05/07/45	57030	CASU(F)-15		SAIPAN	WCENPAC		
05/07/45	73587	VC-97	USS SHIP-LEY BAY	OKINAWA	EMPIRE		
05/07/45	74033	CAG-99	USS NEHENTA BAY	GUAM	WCENPAC	ENS MARLYN V. BELL	D
05/10/45	55070	VF-100	EWA	HAWAII	ECENPAC	ENS JOHN J. WEIGHT	S

DATE	BUNO	SQDRN	BASE	LOST	AREA	PILOT	FATE
05/10/45	74081	VC-95	USS MISSION BAY	OFF NEW YORK	NORLANT	LTJG HAROLD A. KIDWELL	S
05/11/45	56875	VC-9	USS NATOMA BAY	OKINAWA	EMPIRE	LT ROBERT C. PALMQUIST	S
05/11/45	57028	CASU-4	PUUNENE	HAWAII	ECENPAC	ENS JOSEPH A. VIRELLIO	S
05/11/45	57073	VC-97	USS SHIP-LEY BAY	OKINAWA	EMPIRE	LTJG RICHARD J. DUNN	S
05/11/45	74110	VC-97	USS SHIP-LEY BAY	OKINAWA	EMPIRE	ENS WARREN F. SCHAUB	S
05/13/45	73782	VC-97	USS SHIP-LEY BAY	OKINAWA	EMPIRE	LTJG CLIFFORD L. GLEBLER	S
05/14/45	74490	VC-91	USS MAKIN ISLAND	OKINAWA	EMPIRE		
05/15/45	73682	VF-99		SAIPAN	WCENPAC		
05/15/45	74164	VC-92	USS TULAGI	OKINAWA	EMPIRE	ENS J.L. LOGAN	S
05/15/45	74420	VC-83	USS SARGENT BAY	OKINAWA	EMPIRE	LTJG JOHN MORRIS	S
05/15/45	74810	VC-71	PUUNENE	HAWAII	ECENPAC		
05/15/45	74822	VC-71	PUUNENE	HAWAII	ECENPAC	ENS THOMAS J. SHARP, JR.	S
05/16/45	74156	VOC-2	USS FANSHAW BAY	OKINAWA	EMPIRE	LTJG BERNARD MCDERMOTT	S
05/17/45	73891	VC-8	USS NEHENTA BAY	OKINAWA	EMPIRE		
05/17/45	73922	VC-90	USS STEAMER BAY	OKINAWA	EMPIRE	LT H.H. EPES, JR.	S
05/17/45	74198	VC-8	USS NEHENTA BAY	OKINAWA	EMPIRE	LT FRANCIS H. BEHLEN III	S
05/17/45	74250	VC-97	USS SHIP-LEY BAY	ENR GUAM	EMPIRE		
05/18/45	73836	VOC-2	USS FANSHAW BAY	OKINAWA	EMPIRE	LT RICHARD F. FLETCHER	M
05/19/45	74058	VC-99	USS HOGGATT BAY	IE SHIMA	EMPIRE	LTJG ALBERT G. WRIGHT	S
05/19/45	74483	VC-93	USS PETROF BAY	ENR IWO JIMA	EMPIRE	LTJG KEITH C. BROWN	S
05/20/45	74197	VC-13	USS ANZIO	OKINAWA	EMPIRE	LT D.R. HAGOOD	S
05/20/45	74427	VC-88		SAIPAN	WCENPAC	LTJG R.E. TRAUBEHE, JR.	S
05/23/45	73585	VOC-2	USS FANSHAW BAY	OKINAWA	EMPIRE	LT IRVING M. APPLEBAUM	S
05/23/45	73649	VC-96	USS RUDYERD BAY	GUAM	WCENPAC	LCDR W.S. WOOLEN	S
05/23/45	73725	VC-99	USS HOGGATT BAY	OKINAWA	EMPIRE		
05/23/45	73925	VOC-2	USS FANSHAW BAY	OKINAWA	EMPIRE	LT C.B. MCAFEE	S
05/26/45	73834	CASU(F)-12		GUAM	WCENPAC		
05/26/45	73941	CASU(F)-12		GUAM	WCENPAC		
05/26/45	73951	CASU(F)-12		GUAM	WCENPAC		
05/26/45	73971	CASU(F)-12		GUAM	WCENPAC		
05/26/45	74004	CASU(F)-12		GUAM	WCENPAC		
05/26/45	74247	FAW-2	KANEOHE	HAWAII	ECENPAC	ENS JEROME N. GOTTLEIB	M
05/27/45	74422	VOC-1	USS WAKE ISLAND	OKINAWA	EMPIRE		
05/30/45	74177	VC-83	USS SARGENT BAY	OKINAWA	EMPIRE		

DATE	BUNO	SQDRN	BASE	LOST	AREA	PILOT	FATE
05/31/45	56921	VF-100	EWA	HAWAII	ECENPAC		
05/31/45	73653	CASU-11		OKINAWA	EMPIRE		
05/31/45	73745	VF-100	EWA	HAWAII	ECENPAC	ENS E.H. LEEMING	S
06/03/45	74544	VC-70	USS SALAMAUA	OKINAWA	EMPIRE	LTJG SHELLINGTON	S
06/04/45	73521	VOC-1	USS WAKE ISLAND	OKINAWA	EMPIRE	LTJG MCKEEVER	M
06/05/45	74243	VC-70	USS SALAMAUA	OKINAWA	EMPIRE	(DECK LOSS-TYPHOON)	
06/06/45	47167	VF-99		SAIPAN	WCENPAC		
06/06/45	47212	VF-99		SAIPAN	WCENPAC		
06/06/45	56932	VF-100	USS SARATOGA	PEARL	ECENPAC	ENS R.C. HECK	S
06/07/45	47094	VF-99		SAIPAN	WCENPAC		
06/07/45	73630	VC-13	USS ANZIO	OKINAWA	EMPIRE		
06/07/45	73715	VC-9	USS NATOMA BAY	OKINAWA	EMPIRE	(DECK LOSS-KAMIKAZE)	
06/07/45	74089	POOL	PEARL	HAWAII	ECENPAC		
06/07/45	74191	POOL	PEARL	HAWAII	ECENPAC		
06/07/45	75028	VC-83	USS SARGENT BAY	SAKISHIMA	EMPIRE	ENS H.O. CULLEN	S
06/09/45	74686	VC-8	USS NEHENTA BAY	OKINAWA	EMPIRE	ENS LEE R. FARMER, JR.	S
06/10/45	47127	VF-100		HAWAII	ECENPAC	ENS W.K. MARTIN	S
06/13/45	74288	VOC-1	USS WAKE ISLAND	OKINAWA	EMPIRE	LT RENE EMILE POUCEL	U
06/15/45	16171	AROU-1		MOMOTE	SW PAC		
06/15/45	73930	VC-93	USS STEAMER BAY	IWO JIMA	EMPIRE	ENS ROBERT H. ALLISON	S
06/15/45	73967	VC-93	USS STEAMER BAY	IWO JIMA	EMPIRE	LTJG D.H. SHERLOCK	S
06/15/45	74118	VC-93	USS STEAMER BAY	IWO JIMA	EMPIRE	ENS G.J. VIGEANT, JR.	D
06/15/45	75101	VC-97	USS SHIPLEY BAY	MIYAKO SHIMA	EMPIRE	LTJG W.F. WATERS	M
06/16/45	74566	AROU-2		SAMAR	PHIL	ENS CLARANCE J. RIVES	D
06/17/45	74524	VC-8	USS NEHENTA BAY	OKINAWA	EMPIRE	LTJG WILLIAM A. SMALL	S
06/19/45	56959	CASU-4	PUUNENE	HAWAII	ECENPAC	LTJG HERRICK CASH	S
06/19/45	73750	VC-99	USS HOGGATT BAY	OKINAWA	EMPIRE		
06/19/45	73812	VC-96	USS SHAMROCK BAY	OKINAWA	EMPIRE	LTJG THANE G. HEIDERSHAT	S
06/19/45	74012	CASU-4	USS CORREGIDOR	HAWAII	ECENPAC	ENS JAMES PIERCE DANA	S
06/19/45	74484	VC-99	USS HOGGATT BAY	OKINAWA	EMPIRE		
06/21/45	73661	VC-93	USS STEAMER BAY	IWO JIMA	EMPIRE	LT ROBERT IRA MYERS	S
06/21/45	74287	VC-99	USS HOGGATT BAY	IE SHIMA	EMPIRE	LTJG ALBERT ED. D SVARSTA	D
06/21/45	74491	VC-8	USS NEHENTA BAY	MIYARA	EMPIRE	LTJG VIRGIL L. BRASLER	S
06/22/45	74003	VC-99	USS HOGGATT BAY	MIYAKO	EMPIRE	LTJG WARREN H. LOVE	S
06/22/45	74644	VC-8	USS NEHENTA BAY	IE SHIMA	EMPIRE		

DATE	BUNO	SQDRN	BASE	LOST	AREA	PILOT	FATE
06/22/45	75037	VC-93	USS STEAMER BAY	ISHIGAKI	EMPIRE	LCDR CHESTER P. SMITH	S
06/24/45	73847	VF-99		SAIPAN	WCENPAC		
06/24/45	74474	VC-96	USS SHAM-ROCK BAY	ENR SAN PEDRO	EMPIRE		
06/26/45	47228	POOL	PEARL	HAWAII	ECENPAC		
06/28/45	74515	CASU(F)-12		GUAM	WCENPAC		
06/30/45	75023	CASU(F)-12		GUAM	WCENPAC		
07/01/45	56688	VC-83	USS SARGENT BAY	LEYTE GULF	PHIL	ENS W.R. REID	S
07/11/45	55222	VF-100		HAWAII	ECENPAC	ENS G.A. KEWIN	M
07/11/45	74438	ACORN-30 PL		TACLOBAN	PHIL		
07/11/45	74536	VC-70	USS SALAMAUA	OKINAWA	EMPIRE		
07/12/45	73671	VC-13	USS ANZIO		EMPIRE		
07/12/45	74923	VC-63	USS KITKUN BAY	EMPIRE	LT H. TONRY	S	
07/17/45	55567	SOSU-1	PEARL	HAWAII	ECENPAC	LT G. LINCOLN ROCKWELL	S
07/18/45	74814	VC-83	USS SARGENT BAY	LEYTE GULF	PHIL	ENS W.J. COOMBE	D
07/19/45	74114	VC-41	USS MAKIN ISLAND		EMPIRE		
07/19/45	74244	VC-98	USS LUNGA POINT	OKINAWA	EMPIRE	LTJG CHARLES R. NORTH	S
07/20/45	75119	VC-70	USS SALAMAUA	OKINAWA	EMPIRE	LTJG C.E. HASTINGS	D
07/26/45	74690	VC-41	USS MAKIN ISLAND		EMPIRE		
07/29/45	73686	MAG-24	MALABANG	MALABANG	PHIL		
07/29/45	74296	VC-99	USS HOGGATT BAY	LEYTE GULF	PHIL	LTJG WARREN H. LOVE	S
07/29/45	74407	VC-99	USS HOGGATT BAY	LEYTE GULF	PHIL	LT MAURICE D. BURCHFIELD	S
07/31/45	46986	POOL	PEARL	HAWAII	ECENPAC		
07/31/45	56728	POOL	PEARL	HAWAII	ECENPAC		
07/31/45	56928	POOL	PEARL	HAWAII	ECENPAC		
07/31/45	73730	POOL	PEARL	HAWAII	ECENPAC		
08/01/45	73914	ACORN-30 PL		TACLOBAN	PHIL		
08/02/45	56841	VC-33		SAMAR	PHIL	LT M.W. PLUNKETT	S
08/05/45	74038	VC-98	USS LUNGA POINT		WCENPAC		
08/05/45	74508	VC-8	USS NEHENTA BAY	ENR ALEUTIANS	NORPAC		
08/05/45	74626	VC-8	USS NEHENTA BAY	ENR ALEUTIANS	NORPAC		
08/06/45	55248	CASU-31	HILO	HAWAII	ECENPAC	LT F.E. KURZ	S
08/06/45	74982	VC-41	USS MAKIN ISLAND	EMPIRE	LT G.V. KNUDSON	M	
08/08/45	74873	VC-70	USS SALAMAUA	LEYTE GULF	PHIL	LTJG ARTHUR B. BROERMAN	S
08/08/45	86310	VC-65		HAWAII	ECENPAC	ENS H.W. BELL	S
08/11/45	75057	VC-8	USS NEHENTA BAY	ENR ALEUTIANS	NORPAC	LTJG JOSEPH GALLAGHER	S
08/11/45	75059	VC-8	USS NEHENTA BAY	ENR ALEUTIANS	NORPAC		
08/13/45	73810	CASU(F)-12		GUAM	WCENPAC		
08/13/45	73957	VC-8	USS NEHENTA BAY	ENR ALEUTIANS	NORPAC		
08/14/45	74222	POOL	PEARL	HAWAII	ECENPAC		

GENERAL MOTORS FM-2P

The U.S. Navy converted several FM-2's to FM-2P's for photoreconnaissance. Aircraft lost:

DATE	BUNO	SQDRN	BASE	LOST	AREA	PILOT	FATE
06/10/45	74781	VC-63	USS KITKUN BAY	ENR ULITHI	WCENPAC	LTJG R.C. BUNTEN	S
06/17/45	74824	VC-71	USS MANILA BAY	OKINAWA	EMPIRE	LTJG BERYL L. LAHNER	U
06/19/45	74169	VC-71	USS MANILA BAY	OKINAWA	EMPIRE		
06/28/45	74518	CASU(F)-12		GUAM	WCENPAC		
06/28/45	74798	VC-63	USS KITKUN BAY	ENR ULITHI	WCENPAC	ENS WALTER R. WINIECKI	S
07/11/45	74486	CASU(F)-12		GUAM	WCENPAC		

GENERAL MOTORS TBM (VARIANT UNKNOWN)

DATE	BUNO	SQDRN	BASE	LOST	AREA	PILOT	FATE
02/21/45		VT(N)-53	USS SARATOGA	TOKYO	EMPIRE		

GENERAL MOTORS TBM-1

The Grumman TBF Avenger was a torpedo bomber developed initially for the United States Navy and Marine Corps (see write-ups on the TBM and its variants). General Motors was subcontracted by Grumman to help build this aircraft, thus TBM was the designation for the Avengers manufactured by GM. There were 550 built by GM. Aircraft lost:

DATE	BUNO	SQDRN	BASE	LOST	AREA	PILOT	FATE
11/21/43	24959	VC-41	USS CORREGI-DOR	MAKIN	CENPAC	ENS F.C. BERMINGHAM	D
11/24/43	24652	VC-39	USS LISCOME BAY	GILBERTS	CENPAC		
11/24/43	24669	VC-39	USS LISCOME BAY	GILBERTS	CENPAC		
11/24/43	24681	VC-39	USS LISCOME BAY	GILBERTS	CENPAC		
11/24/43	24691	VC-39	USS LISCOME BAY	GILBERTS	CENPAC		
11/24/43	24692	VC-39	USS LISCOME BAY	GILBERTS	CENPAC		
11/24/43	24858	VC-39	USS LISCOME BAY	GILBERTS	CENPAC		
11/24/43	24963	VC-39	USS LISCOME BAY	GILBERTS	CENPAC		
11/24/43	25015	VC-39	USS LISCOME BAY	GILBERTS	CENPAC		

DATE	BUNO	SQDRN	BASE	LOST	AREA	PILOT	FATE
11/24/43	25018	VC-39	USS LISCOME BAY	GILBERTS	CENPAC		
12/16/43	24917	VT-1	USS YORK-TOWN	HILO	ECENPAC	ENS M.H. MCROY	S
01/23/44	24907	VC-35	USS CHE-NANGO	MARSHALLS	CENPAC	LTJG W.H. APPLEBY	S
02/07/44	24674	VC-63	USS NATOMA BAY	MAJURO	CENPAC	ENS R.J. GORANSON	M
03/08/44	25035	COMAIR-PAC	PEARL	HAWAII	ECENPAC		
03/08/44	24602	STAG-1	RUSSELLS	RUSSELLS	SOPAC		
04/07/44	24940	VC-41	USS CORREGI-DOR	EMIRAU	SW PAC	ENS J.T. TRUESDELL	S
05/27/44	24912	VC-41	USS CORREGI-DOR	ENR MARIANAS	SOPAC		
06/24/44	24848	ARU SOLS			SW PAC		
06/24/44	24910	ARU SOLS			SW PAC		
07/01/44	24599	STAG-1	SUNLIGHT FIELD		CENPAC	LT J.L. BARNES	S
09/03/44	24825	VC-85	USS LUNGA POINT		CENPAC	ENS S.R. O'NEIL	S
10/10/44	24911	CAC	MANUS		SW PAC		
10/26/44	24600	STAG-1	RUSSELLS		SOPAC	LT P.I. ELDER	S
04/06/45	484	VJ-7	PEARL	HAWAII	ECENPAC	ENS CLARENCE H. BARNETT	S
06/20/45	AROU-2			SAMAR	PHIL		
06/20/45	24746	POOL	PEARL	HAWAII	ECENPAC		
06/28/45	24604	POOL	BARBERS POINT	HAWAII	ECENPAC		
06/28/45	24613	POOL	BARBERS POINT	HAWAII	ECENPAC		
06/28/45	24619	POOL	BARBERS POINT	HAWAII	ECENPAC		
06/28/45	24640	POOL	BARBERS POINT	HAWAII	ECENPAC		
06/28/45	24664	POOL	BARBERS POINT	HAWAII	ECENPAC		
06/28/45	24927	POOL	BARBERS POINT	HAWAII	ECENPAC		
07/16/45	24598	AROU-2		SAMAR	PHIL		
07/20/45	24920	AROU-1		MOMOTE	SW PAC		

GENERAL MOTORS TBM-1C

The General Motors TBM-1C was the equivalent to the Grumman TBF-1C. There were 2,336 built by GM. Aircraft lost:

DATE	BUNO	SQDRN	BASE	LOST	AREA	PILOT	FATE
00/00/00	73423					LT CLAUDE L. HOLSTIN	U
07/02/43	25407	VT-3	USS SARATOGA	NOUMEA	SOPAC		
11/24/43	25072	VC-39	USS LISCOME BAY	GILBERTS	CENPAC		
11/24/43	25074	VC-39	USS LISCOME BAY	GILBERTS	CENPAC		
11/24/43	25075	VC-39	USS LISCOME BAY	GILBERTS	CENPAC		
12/14/43	25203	VT-31	USS CABOT	PEARL	ECENPAC		
01/18/44	25208	VC-8	USS SOLO-MONS	OFF CALIFORNIA	CENPAC	LT C.B. HANEY	S

DATE	BUNO	SQDRN	BASE	LOST	AREA	PILOT	FATE
01/19/44	25468	VC-69	USS WAKE ISLAND	COSTA RICA	NORLANT	ENS R. SEABURY	D
01/24/44	25379	VC-63	USS NATOMA BAY	MAJURO	CENPAC	ENS R.J. MANN	S
01/24/44	25160	VT-30	USS MONTEREY	ENR MARSHALLS	CENPAC	ENS R.E. MAHONEY	S
01/25/44	25422	VC-37	USS SAN-GAMON	KWAJALEIN	CENPAC	(DECK LOSS-AIRCRASH)	
01/26/44	25427	VC-37	USS SAN-GAMON	KWAJALEIN	CENPAC	(DECK LOSS-AIRCRASH)	
01/28/44	25119	VT-2	HILO	HAWAII	ECENPAC		
01/29/44	25109	VT-12	USS SARATOGA	WOTJE	CENPAC	LTJG D.E. LAIRD	S
01/29/44	25391	VT-12	USS SARATOGA	WOTJE	CENPAC	ENS H.D. HANSON	M
01/29/44	25199	VT-5	USS YORK-TOWN	TAROA	CENPAC	LTJG W. MEAHAN	M
01/30/44	25211	VC-66	USS NASSAU	MAJURO	CENPAC	LTJG W.A. BENNETT	D
01/31/44	25225	VC-38		ESPIRITU SANTO	SOPAC		
01/31/44	25214	VT-31	USS CABOT	MARSHALLS	CENPAC		
02/02/44	25147	VT-12	USS SARATOGA	MARSHALLS	CENPAC		
02/03/44	25384	VC-60	USS SU-WANNEE	ROI	WCENPAC	LTJG P.A. GOLSH	S
02/03/44	25656	VC-8	USS SOLO-MONS	ENR BALBOA	CENPAC	ENS J.D. WALLENG	S
02/06/44	25390	VT-12	USS SARATOGA	MARSHALLS	CENPAC		
02/08/44	25133	VC-51	USS SAN JACINTO	TRINIDAD	CENLANT	LT L.R. HOLE	S
02/10/44	25303	VMTB-143	TOROKINA	RABAUL	SOPAC	LT K.F. GUNDLACH	M
02/13/44	25176	VC-38	TOROKINA	RABAUL	SOPAC		
02/13/44	25296	VC-38	TOROKINA	RABAUL	SOPAC		
02/13/44	25377	VC-38	TOROKINA	RABAUL	SOPAC		
02/13/44	25198	VMTB-143	TOROKINA	RABAUL	SOPAC		
02/13/44	25329	VMTB-233	PIVA	BOUGAIN-VILLE	SOPAC		
02/14/44	25316	VMTB-233	TOROKINA	RABAUL	SOPAC	1STLT A.M. HATHWAY	M
02/14/44	25327	VMTB-233	TOROKINA	RABAUL	SOPAC	1STLT J.L. FOWLER	M
02/16/44	25270	VT-6	USS INTREPID	TRUK	CENPAC	LT J.E. BRIDGES	M
02/17/44	25293	VT-5	USS YORK-TOWN	TRUK	CENPAC	ENS J.J. O'SULLIVAN	S
02/19/44	25182	VT-12	USS SARATOGA	ENIWETOK	CENPAC		
02/20/44	25290	VC-38	TOROKINA	RABAUL	SOPAC	LTJG H.T. LEAKE	D
02/20/44	25469	VT-2	HILO	HAWAII	ECENPAC	ENS J.R. FULWIDER	S
02/20/44	25212	VT-23	USS PRINCE-TON	ENIWETOK	CENPAC	LTJG G.W. SPEAR	S
02/21/44	25385	VC-37	USS SAN-GAMON	ENIWETOK	CENPAC	LTJG J.H. MURRAY	S
02/22/44	25371	VMTB-143	TOROKINA	KERAV.	SOPAC		
02/22/44	25186	VT-9	USS ESSEX	SAIPAN	WCENPAC	LTJG C.R. WILLIAMS	M
02/28/44	25135	VT-51	USS SAN JACINTO	TRINIDAD	CENLANT	ENS J.O. GUY	S
02/29/44	25268	VMTB-233		ESPIRITU SANTO	SOPAC		
03/02/44	25425	VC-15	USS TULAGI	BALBOA	ECENPAC	ENS M.D. GALLOWAY	S
03/09/44	25219	COMAIR-PAC	PEARL	HAWAII	ECENPAC		
03/09/44	25149	VT-10	USS ENTER-PRISE	AT SEA	CENPAC	ENS R.W. KIMBREL	S
03/10/44	25111	VT-12	USS SARATOGA	ESPIRITU SANTO	SOPAC		
03/17/44	25413	COMAIR-PAC	PEARL	HAWAII	ECENPAC		
03/18/44	25420	VMTB-134		TOBERA	SOPAC	1STLT D.W. SMITH	S

DATE	BUNO	SQDRN	BASE	LOST	AREA	PILOT	FATE
03/19/44	17012	VC-58	USS GUADAL-CANAL	MADEIRA	NORLANT	LTJG L.L. MCCORD	S
03/21/44	25701	VC-58	USS GUADAL-CANAL	MADEIRA	NORLANT	LTJG W.F. PATTISON	S
03/26/44	25483	VC-42	USS CROATAN		NORLANT	LTJG J.B. NELSON	M
03/30/44	25217	VT-2	USS HORNET	PALAU	CENPAC	LT H. BEREOLOS	D
03/30/44	25280	VT-2	USS HORNET	PALAU	CENPAC		
03/30/44	25215	VT-31	USS CABOT	PALAU	CENPAC	LTJG J.S. JENKINS	M
03/31/44	25286	VC-40	PIVA	RABAUL	SOPAC	LT R.P. LECKLIDER	S
03/31/44	17079	VC-58	USS GUADAL-CANAL		NORLANT	LTJG W.E. DAVIS	S
03/31/44	25200	VT-2	USS HORNET	PALAU	CENPAC		
03/31/44	25273	VT-2	USS HORNET	PALAU	CENPAC	ENS H.W. BERNARD	S
04/01/44	25373	VMTB-134		ESPIRITU SANTO	SOPAC		
04/01/44	25443	VT-16	USS LEX-INGTON	WOLEAI	CENPAC	ENS W.H. LARSEN	S
04/04/44	25406	VMTB-134		GREEN	SOPAC	1STLT M.M. GLIDDEN	D
04/04/44	25550	VT-35	USS CHE-NANGO	ESPIRITU SANTO	SOPAC		
04/06/44	25382	VC-66	USS ALTAMAHA	MARSHALLS	CENPAC		
04/07/44	25434	VMTB-134		GREEN	SOPAC	1STLT J.E. BALL	M
04/10/44	25177	VMTB-242	PIVA	BOUGAIN-VILLE	SOPAC		
04/11/44	16858	VC-68	USS FANSHAW BAY	MAJURO	CENPAC	ENS HENNESSY	S
04/12/44	25122	VT-305	GREEN	BOUGAIN-VILLE	SOPAC	ENS D.E. WHITE	S
04/13/44	25220	MAG-24	PIVA	PIVA	SOPAC		
04/14/44	17031	VC-10	USS GAMBIER BAY	PEARL	ECENPAC	ENS K.E. CARTER	S
04/14/44	25325	VC-63	USS NATOMA BAY	EMIRAU	SW PAC	LTJG W.R. NUTT	S
04/14/44	25326	VMTB-242		NEW IRELAND	SOPAC	CAPT C.A. MAIN	S
04/14/44	25696	VT-50	USS BATAAN	ENR HOLLANDIA	CENPAC	ENS J.J. FITE	S
04/17/44	25275	VC-66	USS ALTAMAHA	MARSHALLS	CENPAC		
04/17/44	25541	VMTB-242	TOROKINA	RABAUL	SOPAC	1STLT F.E. LEE	S
04/18/44	16811	VC-3	USS KALININ BAY	MAJURO	CENPAC	LT W.D. CROCKETT	S
04/18/44	45456	VC-3	USS KALININ BAY	MAJURO	CENPAC	ENS R.E. EDWARDS	S
04/18/44	25674	VMTB-131		ESPIRITU SANTO	SOPAC	1STLT W.G. GIESKE	D
04/18/44	25240	VMTB-134		NEW BRITAIN	SOPAC	1STLT D.W. SMITH	S
04/21/44	25138	VT-305	GREEN	BOUGAIN-VILLE	SOPAC	ENS W.F. MILBURN	M
04/21/44	16899	VT-5	USS YORK-TOWN	WAKDE	SW PAC	ENS L.E. BENSON	S
04/22/44	25335	VT-37	USS SAN-GAMON	AITAPE	SW PAC	LT P.G. FARLEY	S
04/23/44	25546	VT-10	USS ENTER-PRISE	HOLLANDIA	SW PAC	LTJG C.R. LARGESS	S
04/25/44	25265	VT-31	USS CABOT	ENR TRUK	CENPAC	LT E.A. WOOD	S
04/28/44	45628	VC-3	USS KALININ BAY	MAJURO	CENPAC	ENS T.E. FRANCO	S

DATE	BUNO	SQDRN	BASE	LOST	AREA	PILOT	FATE
04/29/44	25474	VT-24	USS BELLEAU WOOD	TRUK	CENPAC	LTJG E.W. WOOD	D
04/30/44	45561	VT-10	USS ENTER-PRISE	TRUK	CENPAC	LT R.B. NELSON	S
04/30/44	25657	VT-2	USS HORNET	TRUK	CENPAC		
04/30/44	25675	VT-5	USS YORK-TOWN	TRUK	CENPAC	LCDR R. UPSON	M
04/30/44	25442	VT-50	USS BATAAN	TRUK	CENPAC	CDR A.R. MATTER	S
05/01/44	17039	VT-28	BARKING SANDS	KAUAI	ECENPAC	LT A.V. MCHOLLAND	D
05/02/44	17008	VC-55	USS BLOCK ISLAND	CANARIES	NORLANT	LTJG L.W. GLEASON	S
05/04/44	45458	ARU SOLS			SOPAC		
05/13/44	25549	VC-14	USS HOGGATT BAY	ENR MAJURO	CENPAC	ENS W.T. BONE	S
05/13/44	25408	VC-69	USS BOGUE	CAPE VERDE	NORLANT	ENS A.D. BOHLEN	S
05/15/44	25121	VT-51	USS SAN JACINTO	MARCUS	CENPAC	ENS J.J. WYKES	M
05/17/44	25213	VT-10	USS ENTER-PRISE	BARBERS POINT	ECENPAC	LT V.V. EASON	S
05/17/44	45555	VT-10	USS ENTER-PRISE	BARBERS POINT	ECENPAC	ENS R.A. CHANEY	D
05/17/44	25429	VT-12	USS SARATOGA	SOURABAYA	SE ASIA	LT W.E. ROWBOTHAM	M
05/17/44	16952	VT-3	PUUNENE	HAWAII	ECENPAC	ENS J. SWANK	S
05/19/44	25658	VC-65	USS NATOMA BAY	MOLOKAI	ECENPAC	LT STANLEY H. COOK	S
05/26/44	25388	VC-14	USS HOGGATT BAY	EMIRAU	SW PAC	LTJG JAMES W. HARTZELL	S
05/31/44	45652	VC-10	USS GAMBIER BAY	PEARL	ECENPAC	LTJG O.H. WHEELER	S
06/01/44	17002	VC-55	USS BLOCK ISLAND	31-13N/023-03W	NORLANT	(SHIP SANK)	
06/01/44	17004	VC-55	USS BLOCK ISLAND	31-13N/023-03W	NORLANT	(SHIP SANK)	
06/01/44	17006	VC-55	USS BLOCK ISLAND	31-13N/023-03W	NORLANT	(SHIP SANK)	
06/01/44	17009	VC-55	USS BLOCK ISLAND	31-13N/023-03W	NORLANT	(SHIP SANK)	
06/01/44	17010	VC-55	USS BLOCK ISLAND	31-13N/023-03W	NORLANT	(SHIP SANK)	
06/01/44	17011	VC-55	USS BLOCK ISLAND	31-13N/023-03W	NORLANT	(SHIP SANK)	
06/01/44	25709	VC-55	USS BLOCK ISLAND	31-13N/023-03W	NORLANT	(SHIP SANK)	
06/01/44	45491	VC-55	USS BLOCK ISLAND	31-13N/023-03W	NORLANT	(SHIP SANK)	
06/01/44	25637	VT-28	USS MONTEREY	MARSHALLS	CENPAC	ENS R.L. PEUGH	S
06/02/44	25416	VC-10	USS GAMBIER BAY	ENR MARSHALLS	CENPAC	LT ROBERT E. WEATHERHOLT	S
06/02/44	25418	VC-10	USS GAMBIER BAY	ENR MARSHALLS	CENPAC		

DATE	BUNO	SQDRN	BASE	LOST	AREA	PILOT	FATE
06/04/44	45468	VC-5	USS KIT-KUN BAY	MARSHALLS	CENPAC	LTJG M. LAWTY	D
06/05/44	45509	VT-35	USS CHE-NANGO	KWAJALEIN	CENPAC		
06/06/44	25300	ARU SOLS			SOPAC		
06/07/44	16848	VC-3	USS KALININ BAY	MAJURO	CENPAC		
06/08/44	25197	VT-31	USS CABOT	SAIPAN	WCENPAC	ENS C.W. MANTELL	D
06/11/44	17028	VT-20	BARBERS POINT	HAWAII	ECENPAC	ENS J.I. PORTER	M
06/12/44	25370	VC-14	USS HOGGATT BAY	EMIRAU	SW PAC	ENS E.H. WEILAND	S
06/12/44	25424	VT-1	USS YORK-TOWN	GUAM	WCENPAC	LT N.N. MERRELL	M
06/12/44	16918	VT-15	USS ESSEX	SAIPAN	WCENPAC	LTJG J. CHAMBERS	S
06/12/44	25158	VT-2	USS HORNET	GUAM	WCENPAC	LTJG T.M. PORTEOFRELE	S
06/12/44	16933	VT-8	USS BUNKER HILL	MARIANAS	CENPAC	LTJG F.R. SWENSON	M
06/13/44	17019	VT-1	USS YORK-TOWN	GUAM	WCENPAC	ENS WILLIAMS	S
06/13/44	16866	VT-10	USS ENTER-PRISE	MARIANAS	CENPAC	CDR W.I. MARTIN	S
06/13/44	25288	VT-16	USS LEX-INGTON	SAIPAN	WCENPAC	CDR R.H. ISELY	M
06/14/44	25579	VC-8	USS GUADAL-CANAL		NORLANT		
06/14/44	45657	VT-25	USS COWPENS	BONINS	CENPAC	LT W.S. WATSON	S
06/14/44	17042	VT-28	USS MONTEREY	TINIAN	WCENPAC	ENS R.G. GREENE	M
06/14/44	25611	VT-7	USS HANCOCK		NORLANT	LT C.C. TAYLOR	S
06/15/44	45613	VC-9	USS SOLO-MONS	OFF RECIFE	SOLANT	LTJG W.F. CHAMBERLAIN	S
06/15/44	25671	VT-1	USS YORK-TOWN	BONINS	CENPAC	LTJG J.H. KEELER	M
06/15/44	16877	VT-50	USS BATAAN	BONINS	CENPAC	LTJG A. ST. G. HALL	S
06/16/44	45658	VC-10	USS GAMBIER BAY	MARSHALLS	CENPAC	ENS R.C. CROCKER	S
06/16/44	45556	VT-16	USS LEX-INGTON	SAIPAN	WCENPAC	LTJG N.R. LANDON	M
06/16/44	45522	VT-32	USS LANGLEY	PAGAN	CENPAC		
06/17/44	25537	VC-10	USS GAMBIER BAY	TINIAN	WCENPAC	ENS J.B. HOLLOMAN	S
06/17/44	25540	VC-4	USS WHITE PLAINS	SAIPAN	WCENPAC		
06/17/44	16804	VC-5	USS KIT-KUN BAY	MARIANAS	CENPAC		
06/17/44	17051	VC-68	USS FANSHAW BAY	SAIPAN	WCENPAC	LT STIENMETZ	S
06/17/44	45446	VC-68	USS FANSHAW BAY	SAIPAN	WCENPAC	ENS WODEHOUSE	M
06/17/44	25124	VT-51	USS SAN JACINTO	SAIPAN	WCENPAC		
06/18/44	25670	VC-10	USS GAMBIER BAY	MARIANAS	CENPAC	ENS W.C. SHOYER	S
06/18/44	25321	VT-24	USS BELLEAU WOOD	MARIANAS	CENPAC		
06/18/44	45552	VT-25	USS COWPENS	SAIPAN	WCENPAC	ENS E.C. BELL	S

DATE	BUNO	SQDRN	BASE	LOST	AREA	PILOT	FATE
06/19/44	45593	VT-2	USS HORNET	GUAM	WCENPAC	ENS FRANK T. LONG	S
06/19/44	25123	VT-51	USS SAN JACINTO	GUAM	WCENPAC		
06/20/44		VC-12	USS CARD		NORLANT	LTJG GLEN SHEAN	S
06/20/44	16835	VC-33	USS CORAL SEA	SAIPAN	WCENPAC	LTJG C.R. RASMUSSEN	S
06/20/44	17055	VC-5	USS KIT-KUN BAY	MARIANAS	CENPAC	ENS J.C. LUCAS	S
06/20/44	25393	VC-69	USS BOGUE		NORLANT	LT R.D. MORRISON	S
06/20/44	25509	VC-69	USS BOGUE		NORLANT	LT GRANT L. NELSON	S
06/20/44	16905	VT-1	USS YORK-TOWN	W OF SAIPAN	CENPAC	LTJG G.F. LUEDEMAN	S
06/20/44	25277	VT-1	USS YORK-TOWN	W OF SAIPAN	CENPAC	LT E.W. NELSON	S
06/20/44	25322	VT-1	USS YORK-TOWN	W OF SAIPAN	CENPAC	LTJG R.T. MAHONEY	S
06/20/44	25328	VT-1	USS YORK-TOWN	W OF SAIPAN	CENPAC		
06/20/44	45539	VT-1	USS YORK-TOWN	W OF SAIPAN	CENPAC	LTJG R.L. CARLSON	D
06/20/44	16903	VT-10	USS ENTER-PRISE	SAIPAN	WCENPAC	LTJG J.A. DOYLE	S
06/20/44	45646	VT-10	USS ENTER-PRISE	SAIPAN	WCENPAC	LT V.V. EASON	S
06/20/44	45697	VT-14	USS WASP	W OF SAIPAN	CENPAC	LTJG WRIGHT	S
06/20/44	45567	VT-16	USS LEX-INGTON	W OF SAIPAN	CENPAC	LTJG W.E. MCLELLAN	S
06/20/44	45602	VT-16	USS LEX-INGTON	W OF SAIPAN	CENPAC	LT C.L. BROWN	S
06/20/44	25269	VT-2	USS HORNET	SAIPAN	WCENPAC		
06/20/44	45649	VT-2	USS HORNET	SAIPAN	WCENPAC	LTJG K.P. SULLIVAN	S
06/20/44	16868	VT-24	USS BELLEAU WOOD	SAIPAN	WCENPAC	ENS W.D. LUTON	S
06/20/44	25283	VT-24	USS BELLEAU WOOD	SAIPAN	WCENPAC	LTJG G.P. BROWN	M
06/20/44	25711	VT-28	USS MONTEREY	SAIPAN	WCENPAC	ENS R.W. BURNETT	S
06/20/44	25528	VT-31	USS CABOT	MARIANAS	CENPAC	ENS J. JONES	S
06/20/44	17090	VT-51	USS SAN JACINTO	SAIPAN	WCENPAC	LCDR D.I. MELVIN	S
06/20/44	25145	VT-51	USS SAN JACINTO	SAIPAN	WCENPAC		
06/20/44	25324	VT-8	USS BUNKER HILL	SAIPAN	WCENPAC	LTJG L.J. MASON	S
06/20/44	25631	VT-8	USS BUNKER HILL	SAIPAN	WCENPAC	LTJG GAGNON	S
06/20/44	45516	VT-8	USS BUNKER HILL	SAIPAN	WCENPAC	LCDR K.F. MUSICK	S
06/20/44	45562	VT-8	USS BUNKER HILL	SAIPAN	WCENPAC	LTJG H.A. BUXTON	S
06/21/44	25609	VT-7	USS HANCOCK	TRINIDAD	CENLANT	ENS R.A. JOHNSON	S
06/22/44	45558	VT-32	USS LANGLEY	SAIPAN	WCENPAC		
06/23/44	25437	VT-37	USS SAN-GAMON	SAIPAN	WCENPAC		
06/26/44	25495	VC-74	USS KASAAN BAY	OFF RHODE IS.	NORLANT		

DATE	BUNO	SQDRN	BASE	LOST	AREA	PILOT	FATE
06/28/44	25471	VC-10	USS GAMBIER BAY	TINIAN	WCENPAC	ENS H.A. PYNDROWSKI	S
06/28/44	25493	VF(N)-79	PEARL	HAWAII	ECENPAC	LT E.M. TOWER	M
06/29/44	17036	VC-10	USS GAMBIER BAY	TINIAN	WCENPAC		
06/29/44	45504	VC-12	USS CARD		NORLANT	LTJG J. HANSETH	S
06/29/44	16925	VC-68	USS FANSHAW BAY	SAIPAN	WCENPAC	LT P.D. MOONEY	D
06/30/44	16794	VC-65	USS MIDWAY	SAIPAN	WCENPAC	ENS T.F. FRANCO	S
06/30/44	25403	VT-35		HAWAII	ECENPAC		
06/30/44	25516	VT-35		HAWAII	ECENPAC		
07/01/44	25278	COMAIR-PAC	PEARL	HAWAII	ECENPAC		
07/01/44	25473	VT-60	USS SU-WANNEE	MARIANAS	CENPAC	ENS H.G. JEDLONG	S
07/02/44	25110	VC-65	USS MIDWAY	SAIPAN	WCENPAC	LT C.W. SCHUNKE	M
07/03/44	45694	VC-4	USS WHITE PLAINS	SAIPAN	WCENPAC	LT THOMAS LUPO	S
07/04/44	45837	VT-14	USS WASP	IWO JIMA	EMPIRE	ENS DRAKE	S
07/04/44	25174	VT-19	ENIWETOK	PONAPE	CENPAC		
07/04/44	45922	VT-80	USS TICONDER-OGA	TRINIDAD	CENLANT	LT C.C. FRANCONI	S
07/05/44	45670	VT-28	USS MONTEREY	PAGAN	CENPAC	ENS R.R. RICHARDSON	D
07/08/44	25633	STAG-1	RUSSELLS	RUSSELLS	SOPAC	LT D.M. GRAHAM	S
07/08/44	25595	VC-11	USS NEHENTA BAY	MARSHALLS	CENPAC		
07/08/44	45667	VT-18	KANEOHE	HAWAII	ECENPAC	LT L.M. CHRISTENSEN	M
07/08/44	25167	VT-8	USS BUNKER HILL	PALAU	CENPAC		
07/09/44	45549	VT-1	USS YORK-TOWN	GUAM	WCENPAC	LTJG SANBORN	M
07/09/44	25415	VT-50	USS BATAAN	MARIANAS	CENPAC		
07/11/44	17084	VT-80	USS TICONDER-OGA	GULF OF PARIA	NORLANT	LT N. ROGERS	S
07/12/44	45598	VT-22		HAWAII	ECENPAC	ENS STEPHEN K. KORNS	S
07/13/44	46191	VT-2	USS HORNET	ENR GUAM	CENPAC	LT D.A. MCCRARY	S
07/13/44	45728	VT-80	USS TICONDER-OGA	WEST INDIES	CENLANT	LT L.S. BALLIETT	S
07/14/44	45447	VC-14	USS HOGGATT BAY	MARSHALLS	CENPAC	ENS JOHN R. BALYAR	S
07/14/44	25660	VC-41	USS CORREGI-DOR	ENR GUAM	CENPAC	LTJG G.A. LOVE	D
07/15/44	45534	VT-28	USS MONTEREY	ROTA	CENPAC	ENS J.A. MILLER	D
07/15/44	25128	VT-305		NEW HEBRIDES	SOPAC	ENS J. BERGERSON	D
07/16/44	16813	VC-12	USS CARD		NORLANT	LTJG LOVELADY	S
07/17/44	25486	VC-58		AZORES	NORLANT	ENS F.L. MOORE	S
07/17/44	25311	VT-2	USS HORNET	GUAM	WCENPAC	ENS R.L. GJESSING	S
07/18/44	45805	VT-15	USS ESSEX	GUAM	WCENPAC	ENS O. BLEECH	U
07/18/44	46215	VT-2	USS HORNET	GUAM	WCENPAC		
07/19/44	25554	VF(N)-79	OAHU	HAWAII	ECENPAC	LT W.R. TAYLOR	S
07/20/44	45940	VT-1	USS YORK-TOWN	GUAM	WCENPAC	LT L.E. WOOD	M
07/20/44	16946	VT-32	USS LANGLEY	GUAM	WCENPAC	LT FRYATT	S

DATE	BUNO	SQDRN	BASE	LOST	AREA	PILOT	FATE
07/21/44	46210	COMAIR-PAC	PEARL	HAWAII	ECENPAC		
07/21/44	45908	VC-10	USS GAMBIER BAY	SAIPAN	WCENPAC	ENS H.A. PYNDROWSKI	S
07/21/44	16805	VT-19	USS LEX-INGTON	GUAM	WCENPAC	ENS A.W. HOLLOWELL	D
07/21/44	25662	VT-19	USS LEX-INGTON	GUAM	WCENPAC	LT C.E. WENDT	D
07/21/44	45668	VT-19	USS LEX-INGTON	GUAM	WCENPAC	LT R.L. SINCLAIR	D
07/21/44	16953	VT-51	USS SAN JACINTO	GUAM	WCENPAC		
07/22/44	45510	VC-10	USS GAMBIER BAY	SAIPAN	WCENPAC	LT J.P. SANDERSON	D
07/22/44	25588	VF(N)-79	OAHU	HAWAII	ECENPAC	ENS JOHN HAIGLER	S
07/23/44	25363	VT-60	USS SU-WANNEE	GUAM	WCENPAC	LTJG W.C. KELLER	S.
07/24/44	25653	VC-11	USS NEHENTA BAY	MARIANAS	CENPAC		
07/24/44	25553	VC-65		TINIAN	WCENPAC	LT STANLEY H. COOK	M
07/25/44	45819	VC-11	USS NEHENTA BAY	TINIAN	WCENPAC		
07/26/44	25484	VC-42		BERMUDA	NORLANT	LT JOHN SULTON, JR.	S
07/26/44	45718	VC-42		BERMUDA	NORLANT		
07/26/44	25285	VT-19	USS LEX-INGTON	PALAU	CENPAC		
07/26/44	45842	VT-19	USS LEX-INGTON	PALAU	CENPAC	LTJG MYERS	U
07/26/44	45654	VT-31	USS CABOT	YAP	CENPAC	LTJG J.B. RUSSELL	S
07/26/44	45647	VT-8	USS BUNKER HILL	PALAU	CENPAC	LTJG L.J. MASON	D
07/27/44	45810	VT-51	USS SAN JACINTO	PALAU	CENPAC		
07/28/44	46225	VC-21	USS MARCUS ISLAND	PEARL	ECENPAC	ENS JOHN CHRYSTAL	S
07/28/44	16934	VC-66	KAHULUI	HAWAII	ECENPAC		
07/30/44	16951	VC-11	USS NEHENTA BAY	TINIAN	WCENPAC	LT R.F. STONER	D
08/01/44	16895	VC-4	USS WHITE PLAINS	TINIAN	WCENPAC	LT HAROLD H. CARSON	D
08/01/44	25207	VT-31	USS CABOT	MARIANAS	CENPAC	ENS H.A. BO	S
08/02/44	45820	VC-83	KANEOHE	HAWAII	ECENPAC		
08/02/44	45901	VT-18	USS INTREPID	MARSHALLS	CENPAC	LT JOHN L. ROBINSON	M
08/02/44	45928	VT-18	USS INTREPID	MARSHALLS	CENPAC	LTJG W.C. BATES	S
08/03/44	25487	VC-42		BERMUDA	NORLANT	LTJG B.C. SISSLER	S
08/03/44	45945	VT-2	USS HORNET	BONINS	CENPAC		
08/03/44	46009	VT-2	USS HORNET	BONINS	CENPAC	ENS V.G. STAUBER	S
08/04/44	45450	COMAIR-PAC	PEARL	HAWAII	ECENPAC		
08/04/44	25205	VT-2	USS HORNET	MUKO JIMA	CENPAC	LT CLARENCE G. CAMPBELL	D
08/04/44	45783	VT-31	USS CABOT	CHICHI JIMA	CENPAC	LTJG HORNBERGER	M
08/05/44	16935	VT-51	USS SAN JACINTO	BONINS	CENPAC		
08/06/44	46263	VC-6	USS TRIPOLI	BRAZIL	SOLANT	ENS D.E. TUCCI	S
08/07/44	16795	VT-21	USS BELLEAU WOOD	GUAM	WCENPAC		

DATE	BUNO	SQDRN	BASE	LOST	AREA	PILOT	FATE
08/08/44	46203	VC-21	USS MARCUS ISLAND	PEARL	ECENPAC	LTJG ANTHONY M. PEYOU	S
08/08/44	45523	VT-11		MOLOKAI	ECENPAC		
08/09/44	16849	CASU-35		ENIWETOK	CENPAC		
08/09/44	16898	CASU-35		ENIWETOK	CENPAC		
08/09/44	25154	CASU-35		ENIWETOK	CENPAC		
08/09/44	25170	CASU-35		ENIWETOK	CENPAC		
08/09/44	25187	CASU-35		ENIWETOK	CENPAC		
08/09/44	25292	CASU-35		ENIWETOK	CENPAC		
08/09/44	25297	CASU-35		ENIWETOK	CENPAC		
08/09/44	25306	CASU-35		ENIWETOK	CENPAC		
08/09/44	25333	CASU-35		ENIWETOK	CENPAC		
08/09/44	25354	CASU-35		ENIWETOK	CENPAC		
08/09/44	25368	CASU-35		ENIWETOK	CENPAC		
08/09/44	25414	CASU-35		ENIWETOK	CENPAC		
08/09/44	25417	CASU-35		ENIWETOK	CENPAC		
08/09/44	25423	CASU-35		ENIWETOK	CENPAC		
08/09/44	25441	CASU-35		ENIWETOK	CENPAC		
08/09/44	25513	CASU-35		ENIWETOK	CENPAC		
08/09/44	25514	CASU-35		ENIWETOK	CENPAC		
08/09/44	25542	CASU-35		ENIWETOK	CENPAC		
08/09/44	25697	CASU-35		ENIWETOK	CENPAC		
08/09/44	45538	CASU-35		ENIWETOK	CENPAC		
08/09/44	45641	CASU-35		ENIWETOK	CENPAC		
08/09/44	45757	CASU-35		ENIWETOK	CENPAC		
08/09/44	45899	CASU-35		ENIWETOK	CENPAC		
08/09/44	45921	CASU-35		ENIWETOK	CENPAC		
08/09/44	45980	CASU-35		ENIWETOK	CENPAC		
08/09/44	46080	CASU-35		ENIWETOK	CENPAC		
08/09/44	46216	CASU-35		ENIWETOK	CENPAC		
08/09/44	46276	CASU-35		ENIWETOK	CENPAC		
08/09/44	46294	CASU-35		ENIWETOK	CENPAC		
08/09/44	46304	CASU-35		ENIWETOK	CENPAC		
08/09/44	46310	CASU-35		ENIWETOK	CENPAC		
08/10/44	25179	VT-100	NAVY NO. 14	HAWAII	ECENPAC	ENS F.B. MCNULTY, JR.	D
08/11/44	16807	VT-15	USS ESSEX	MARIANAS	CENPAC	ENS E.S. FILEPEZAK	D
08/12/44	46221	VC-76	USS PET-ROF BAY	ENR GUADAL-CANAL	CENPAC	ENS R.P. LODHOLZ	S
08/12/44	16912	VT-37	USS SAN-GAMON	MANUS	SW PAC		
08/12/44	45525	VT-37	USS SAN-GAMON	MANUS	SW PAC		
08/12/44	46322	VT-37	USS SAN-GAMON	MANUS	SW PAC		
08/13/44	46274	VF(N)-102	USS INDE-PENDENCE	PEARL	ECENPAC	ENS JOHN E. DAVIS	S
08/15/44	25171	VC-42	USS BOGUE		NORLANT	LTJG W.A. DIXON	M
08/15/44	45630	VT-22		HAWAII	ECENPAC		
08/16/44	46399	VC-19	USS GUADAL-CANAL	BERMUDA	NORLANT	LTJG T.B. BOOZEL, JR.	S
08/16/44	45878	VC-6	USS TRIPOLI	RECIFE	BRAZIL		
08/17/44	45871	VC-19	USS GUADAL-CANAL	BERMUDA	NORLANT	LTJG H.A. HUGHEY	S
08/17/44	73176	VC-21	USS MARCUS ISLAND	ENR TULAGI	CENPAC	ENS EDGAR L. JONES	S
08/18/44	45462	VT-3	USS RANGER	PEARL	ECENPAC	ENS HAROLD H. STEVENS	S
08/19/44	46016	VC-20	USS KADASHAN BAY	GILBERTS	CENPAC		
08/21/44	25548	VC-15	USS CROATAN		NORLANT	LT W.E. RUTHERFORD	D
08/22/44	46237	VC-76	USS PET-ROF BAY	ENR GUADAL-CANAL	CENPAC	LT A.E. SCHWARZ-WALDER	S
08/24/44	46195	VT-29		HAWAII	ECENPAC		
08/25/44	25411	CASU-2	BARBERS POINT	HAWAII	ECENPAC		

DATE	BUNO	SQDRN	BASE	LOST	AREA	PILOT	FATE
08/26/44	25489	VOF-1	USS TULAGI	MOROCCO	NW AFR		
08/26/44	25380	VT-18	USS INTREPID	ENR PALUS	CENPAC	LT R.E. BRISBIN	S
08/27/44	45876	VC-13	USS CORE	OFF BERMUDA	NORLANT	LTJG P.M. ROCKETT	U
08/27/44	46287	VC-13	USS CORE	OFF BERMUDA	NORLANT	ENS JOHN E. CARPENTER	S
08/27/44	46365	VC-13	USS CORE	OFF BERMUDA	NORLANT	ENS FRED J. HURST	S
08/27/44	46390	VC-13	USS CORE	OFF BERMUDA	NORLANT	LT VINCENT ECCLEFIELD	S
08/27/44	46394	VC-13	USS CORE	OFF BERMUDA	NORLANT	ENS THOMAS SMITH	S
08/27/44	25131	VT-100	NAVY NO. 14	HAWAII	ECENPAC	AVN PHILIP S. MORAN	S
08/31/44	25169	VT-11		MOLOKAI	ECENPAC		
08/31/44	45913	VT-18	USS INTREPID	ENR PALUS	CENPAC		
09/01/44	25589	VC-15	USS CROATAN		NORLANT	ENS WILLIAM O. LEWIS	D
09/01/44	46085	VT-13	USS FRANKLIN	IWO JIMA	EMPIRE		
09/01/44	25626	VT-20	USS ENTER-PRISE	CHICHI JIMA	CENPAC		
09/02/44	16928	VT-51	USS SAN JACINTO	CHICHI JIMA	CENPAC		
09/02/44	46214	VT-51	USS SAN JACINTO	CHICHI JIMA	CENPAC	LTJG G.H.W. BUSH	M
09/03/44	25643	VC-15	USS CROATAN		NORLANT	ENS THEODORE L. PERTUIT	S
09/04/44	25156	CASU-30		MAJURO	CENPAC		
09/04/44	45546	POOL	GUADAL-CANAL		SOPAC		
09/04/44	45903	VC-13	USS CORE	OFF BERMUDA	NORLANT	ENS THOMAS SMITH	S
09/04/44	25210	VT-100	USS MAN-ILA BAY	HAWAII	ECENPAC	ENS M.C. ZWIRBLA	U
09/07/44	73371	VT-80	USS TICONDER-OGA	ENR SAN DIEGO	SE PAC	LT WILLIAM J. GARRETT	S
09/08/44	16836	VT-15	USS ESSEX	PALAU	CENPAC	LTJG W.E. HARPER	S
09/08/44	73249	VT-15	USS ESSEX	PALAU	CENPAC	LT C.D. WEBB	U
09/08/44	16923	VT-18	USS INTREPID	PALUS	SW PAC	LT JOHN J. SAVAGE	M
09/08/44	46236	VT-18	USS INTREPID	PALUS	SW PAC	LT GEORGE B. RILEY	S
09/09/44	16897	VT-27	USS PRINCE-TON	MINDANAO SEA	PHIL		
09/10/44	45904	VC-21	USS MARCUS ISLAND	ENR PELELIU	CENPAC		
09/10/44	17018	VT-20	USS ENTER-PRISE	PALAU	CENPAC	LT J. ROSS MANOWN	M
09/10/44	16927	VT-21	USS BELLEAU WOOD	PALUS	SW PAC	ENS JAMES EVERETT	D
09/10/44	45947	VT-27	USS PRINCE-TON	MINDANAO SEA	PHIL	ENS W.J. BURGESS	D
09/10/44	46344	VT-32	USS LANGLEY	ENR PALUS	CENPAC	LTJG WILLIAM H. STIRLING	S
09/11/44	45461	VT-51	USS SAN JACINTO	PALAU	CENPAC		
09/12/44	46074	VT-13	USS FRANKLIN	PALAU	CENPAC		
09/12/44	73167	VT-13	USS FRANKLIN	PALAU	CENPAC		
09/12/44	16846	VT-15	USS ESSEX	PELELIU	WCENPAC	ENS THOMAS L. MAXWELL	M
09/12/44	16800	VT-19	USS LEX-INGTON	MINDANAO SEA	PHIL	LTJG R.H.H. GOFORTH	D

DATE	BUNO	SQDRN	BASE	LOST	AREA	PILOT	FATE
09/12/44	46193	VT-2	USS HORNET	CEBU	PHIL	ENS RICHARDS	S
09/12/44	73439	VT-2	USS HORNET	CEBU	PHIL	ENS GORDER	S
09/12/44	45788	VT-8	USS BUNKER HILL	CEBU	PHIL		
09/13/44	45632	VC-75	USS OMMANEY BAY	PALAU	CENPAC	LTJG J.R. SPRAGUE	S
09/13/44	73255	VC-82		HAWAII	ECENPAC		
09/13/44	16915	VT-13	USS FRANKLIN	PELELIU	WCENPAC		
09/13/44	45813	VT-14	USS WASP	VISAYAN	PHIL	LT GEORGE C. KELLOGG	S
09/13/44	45867	VT-14	USS WASP	VISAYAN	PHIL		
09/13/44	25715	VT-18	USS INTREPID	LOS NEGROS	PHIL	ENS KANIAL LANER	M
09/13/44	73289	VT-19	USS LEX-INGTON	MANILA	PHIL	LTJG JOHN W. MCDONALD	S
09/13/44	16956	VT-20	USS ENTER-PRISE	PELELIU	WCENPAC	ENS D.E. BAXTER	M
09/13/44	45629	VT-22	USS COWPENS	CEBU	PHIL	LT PAUL P. REEDER	U
09/13/44	25261	VT-8	USS BUNKER HILL	CEBU	PHIL	LTJG E.F. FRANZE	S
09/14/44	45636	VC-14	USS HOGGATT BAY	PELELIU	WCENPAC		
09/15/44	45676	VT-51	USS SAN JACINTO	PALAU	CENPAC	LTJG F.N. WATERS	D
09/15/44	46010	VT-81		HAWAII	ECENPAC		
09/15/44	73235	VT-81		HAWAII	ECENPAC		
09/16/44	25173	PEARL		HAWAII	ECENPAC		
09/16/44	45566	VC-14	USS HOGGATT BAY	MARIANAS	CENPAC	LTJG JAMES W. HARTZELL	S
09/16/44	45678	VC-20	USS KADASHAN BAY	PALAU	CENPAC	ENS LUCIUS M. WILLIS	S
09/16/44	46219	VC-21	USS MARCUS ISLAND	PELELIU	WCENPAC		
09/16/44	46049	VC-3	USS KALININ BAY	PALUS	SW PAC	LTJG JOHN J. PERRELL, JR.	S
09/16/44	46288	VC-42	USS BOGUE		NORLANT	ENS SOLTROEDER	S
09/16/44	45785	VT-8	USS BUNKER HILL	PALAU	CENPAC		
09/17/44	25647	VMTB-131		GUAM	WCENPAC	LT D.R. ANDERSON	U
09/17/44	73247	VT-8	USS BUNKER HILL	PALAU	CENPAC	ENS A.W. REESE	S
09/18/44	45688	POOL	GUADAL-CANAL		SOPAC		
09/18/44	45666	VC-75	USS OMMANEY BAY	PALAU	CENPAC		
09/18/44	45677	VC-75	USS OMMANEY BAY	PALAU	CENPAC		
09/18/44	73132	VC-81	USS NATOMA BAY	ENR MANUS	CENPAC		
09/19/44	45802	VC-75	USS OMMANEY BAY	HAWAII	ECENPAC		
09/20/44	45869	VC-66	USS FANSHAW BAY	MOROTAI	PHIL	LTJG FRANCIS J.M. MCCABE	D

DATE	BUNO	SQDRN	BASE	LOST	AREA	PILOT	FATE
09/20/44	45959	VC-66	USS FANSHAW BAY	MOROTAI	PHIL	ENS ROBERT E. MOLLEY	S
09/21/44		VT-14	USS WASP	LOS NEGROS	PHIL		
09/21/44	45773	VT-18	USS INTREPID	LOS NEGROS	PHIL		
09/21/44	45933	VT-18	USS INTREPID	LOS NEGROS	PHIL		
09/21/44	46060	VT-2			PHIL	ENS W.C. REISERT	M
09/21/44	45507	VT-35	USS CHE-NANGO	HALMAHERA	SW PAC	ENS JAMES B. GLADNEY	D
09/21/44	16864	VT-4	USS HANCOCK	HAWAII	ECENPAC	LCDR H. HUTCHESON	D
09/21/44	25151	VT-4	USS HANCOCK	HAWAII	ECENPAC	ENS M.S. STOCKER	D
09/21/44	25395	VT-4	USS HANCOCK	HAWAII	ECENPAC	LT W.H. CARTY	D
09/21/44	73332	VT-7	USS HANCOCK	HAWAII	ECENPAC	LCDR MAC D. THOMPSON	D
09/21/44	17053	VT-81	USS RANGER	PEARL	ECENPAC	LT H.E. BROWN	S
09/22/44	45640	VT-22	USS COWPENS	LUZON	PHIL	ENS E.L. SNELL	D
09/22/44	45496	VT-86	USS WAKE ISLAND	ENR NORFOLK	NORLANT	LT HARRY L. BADGEROW	S
09/22/44	45713	VT-86	USS WAKE ISLAND	ENR NORFOLK	NORLANT	LTJG LOUIS E. SCOTT	S
09/23/44	45679	VC-75	USS OMMANEY BAY	PALAU	CENPAC		
09/23/44	46423	VC-80	USS MAN-ILA BAY	HAWAII	ECENPAC	ENS JOHN EDWIN KLEDER	S
09/24/44	73126	VC-80	USS MAN-ILA BAY	HAWAII	ECENPAC		
09/25/44	16947	VC-66	USS FANSHAW BAY	ENR MANUS	SW PAC		
09/25/44	46052	VC-77	USS RUDYERD BAY	PALAU	CENPAC	LT C.A. COLLINS	S
09/26/44	25127	CASU-13	NAVY NO. 3205		CENPAC	LT R.E. CLEMENTS	S
09/27/44	46418	CASU-1	PEARL	HAWAII	ECENPAC	LT JOSEPH P. LANDERS	M
09/27/44	45986	VC-6	USS TRIPOLI	CAPE VERDE	NORLANT		
09/27/44	46244	VC-6	USS TRIPOLI	CAPE VERDE	NORLANT	LT WILLIAM J. LAYBEN	S
09/27/44	46318	VC-66	USS FANSHAW BAY	ENR PALAU	CENPAC	LT NELSON R. CHARLES	S
09/27/44	25376	VT-35	USS CHE-NANGO	HALMAHERA	SW PAC	LTJG CHARLES E. CARPENTER	S
09/28/44	45990	VC-6	USS TRIPOLI	CAPE VERDE	NORLANT	LT WILLIAM H. GILLESPIE	M
09/30/44	16961		ESPIRITU SANTO		SOPAC		
09/30/44	46384	A.A.	PEARL	HAWAII	ECENPAC		
10/03/44	73316	VC-82	USS ANZIO		CENPAC		
10/03/44	25582	VT(N)-41	USS INDE-PENDENCE	ULITHI	WCENPAC		
10/03/44	45619	VT(N)-41	USS INDE-PENDENCE	ULITHI	WCENPAC		
10/03/44	46255	VT(N)-41	USS INDE-PENDENCE	ULITHI	WCENPAC		
10/03/44	45690	VT-14	USS WASP	ENR OKINAWA	EMPIRE		
10/03/44	46044	VT-31	USS CABOT	LUZON	PHIL		
10/04/44	16955	CASU-42		PITYILU	SW PAC		
10/04/44	45563	CASU-42		PITYILU	SW PAC		
10/04/44	46281	VC-36	USS MISSION BAY		NORLANT	LT MALCOLM J. MILLER	S
10/05/44	45926	VMTB-134		PELELIU	WCENPAC		

DATE	BUNO	SQDRN	BASE	LOST	AREA	PILOT	FATE
10/05/44	46063	VT-14	USS WASP	ENR OKINAWA	EMPIRE		
10/06/44	46279	VC-36	USS MISSION BAY		NORLANT	LTJG VICTOR B. BAER	S
10/07/44	25129	CASU-13		PONAM	SW PAC		
10/07/44	45639	VT-22	USS COWPENS	OKINAWA	EMPIRE		
10/07/44	45499	VT-44	USS LANGLEY	FORMOSA	EMPIRE	LT GEORGE F. SCULLEY	D
10/08/44	45642	VT-22	USS COWPENS	OKINAWA	EMPIRE	LT B.B. LAUGHREN	S
10/08/44	45684	VT-22	USS COWPENS	OKINAWA	EMPIRE		
10/09/44	73284	VC-82	USS ANZIO		CENPAC		
10/10/44	45763	VT-14	USS WASP	OKINAWA	EMPIRE	LTJG FREEMAN	S
10/10/44	16894	VT-15	USS ESSEX	ENR FORMOSA	CENPAC	LTJG HOWARD JOLLY	S
10/10/44	46084	VT-8	USS BUNKER HILL	YAGYI JIMA	WCENPAC	LTJG D.L. CARTER	S
10/11/44	73357	VC-69	USS GUADAL-CANAL		NORLANT	LTJG HAROLD HOWAT	S
10/11/44	46247	VT(N)-41	USS INDE-PENDENCE	OKINAWA	EMPIRE		
10/11/44	45529	VT-44	USS LANGLEY	FORMOSA	EMPIRE		
10/11/44	45702	VT-44	USS LANGLEY	FORMOSA	EMPIRE		
10/12/44	45841	CASU-42		PITYILU	SW PAC		
10/12/44	25666	VF-20	USS ENTER-PRISE	FORMOSA	EMPIRE	LTJG H.L. MURPHY	M
10/12/44	73233	VT-13	USS FRANKLIN	FORMOSA	EMPIRE	ENS ROBERT F. JONES	M
10/12/44	46439	VT-14	USS WASP	FORMOSA	EMPIRE	LTJG FRANKLIN S MCKEEVER	M
10/12/44	45782	VT-15	USS ESSEX	FORMOSA	EMPIRE	ENS R.H. COPELAND	S
10/12/44	45899	VT-18	USS INTREPID	FORMOSA	EMPIRE		
10/12/44	45905	VT-18	USS INTREPID	FORMOSA	EMPIRE		
10/12/44	46206	VT-18	USS INTREPID	FORMOSA	EMPIRE		
10/12/44	73263	VT-44	USS LANGLEY	FORMOSA	EMPIRE	LT H.W. BORER	M
10/12/44	73329	VT-44	USS LANGLEY	FORMOSA	EMPIRE	LCDR H.F. CRAIG	D
10/12/44	46114	VT-7	USS HANCOCK	ENR MANILA	PHIL	ENS S.M. JOHNSON	M
10/12/44	46293	VT-8	USS BUNKER HILL	FORMOSA	EMPIRE		
10/13/44	45655	CASU-42		PITYILU	SW PAC		
10/13/44	25260	VT-11	USS HORNET	FORMOSA	EMPIRE		
10/13/44	46021	VT-14	USS WASP	ENR LUZON	PHIL		
10/13/44	73458	VT-14	USS WASP	ENR LUZON	PHIL		
10/14/44	45971	VT-100	NAVY NO. 14	HAWAII	ECENPAC	ENS PAUL RITTER	S
10/14/44	45448	VT-11	USS HORNET		CENPAC		
10/15/44	73375	VT(N)-90	BARBERS POINT	HAWAII	ECENPAC	ENS JAMES J. MURPHY	D
10/15/44	17033	VT-100		HAWAII	ECENPAC	ENS JOSEPH J. MURPHY	D
10/15/44	16839	VT-21	USS BELLEAU WOOD	LUZON	PHIL		
10/15/44	17087	VT-7	USS HANCOCK	MANILA	PHIL		
10/16/44	73394	VC-68	USS FANSHAW BAY	ENR LEYTE GULF	PHIL		

DATE	BUNO	SQDRN	BASE	LOST	AREA	PILOT	FATE
10/16/44	73204	VC-75	USS OMMANEY BAY	ENR SAMAR	PHIL		
10/16/44	46370	VC-8	USS CARD		NORLANT	ENS WILLIAM J.D. RUICK	S
10/16/44	46419	VC-83	USS CORREGID OR	HAWAII	ECENPAC		
10/16/44	73319	VC-83	USS CORREGI-DOR	HAWAII	ECENPAC		
10/16/44	73216	VT-51	USS SAN JACINTO	LUZON	PHIL		
10/17/44	73221	VT-13	USS FRANKLIN	LUZON	PHIL	ENS J.G. MANNS	S
10/17/44	46031	VT-20	USS ENTER-PRISE	MANILA	PHIL	LTJG G. WILSON	M
10/18/44	16809	VC-65	USS ST. LO	LEYTE GULF	PHIL		
10/18/44	16837	VC-65	USS ST. LO	LEYTE GULF	PHIL		
10/18/44	16863	VC-65	USS ST. LO	LEYTE GULF	PHIL		
10/18/44	73121	VC-80	USS MAN-ILA BAY	LEYTE GULF	PHIL		
10/18/44	73288	VC-80	USS MAN-ILA BAY	LEYTE GULF	PHIL	ENS CHARLES K. TOWER	S
10/18/44	25302	VMTB-242		TINIAN	WCENPAC	LT LAVERNE A. OSTERNDORF	S
10/18/44	16948	VT(N)-90	BARBERS POINT	HAWAII	ECENPAC	ENS CHARLES W. BARTON JR	M
10/18/44	16908	VT-20	USS ENTER-PRISE	LUZON	PHIL		
10/18/44	16938	VT-20	USS ENTER-PRISE	LUZON	PHIL		
10/18/44	45944	VT-20	USS ENTER-PRISE	LUZON	PHIL		
10/18/44	46024	VT-20	USS ENTER-PRISE	LUZON	PHIL	LT CHARLES W. BRETLAND	D
10/18/44	46078	VT-20	USS ENTER-PRISE	MANILA	PHIL	ENS DONALD M. CONAWAY	D
10/18/44	73425	VT-26	USS SANTEE	PHILIPPINE SEA	PHIL	LCDR THOMAS M. BENNETT	S
10/18/44	46067	VT-44	USS LANGLEY	LEYTE GULF	PHIL	ENS DWIGHT R. HOCH	D
10/19/44	46421	VC-81	USS NATOMA BAY	LEYTE GULF	PHIL	ENS G.W. GALENNIE	S
10/19/44	73256	VT-11	USS HORNET	LUZON	PHIL	LT WILLIAM H. WINNER	M
10/19/44	73230	VT-13	USS FRANKLIN	MANILA BAY	PHIL		
10/19/44	73262	VT-13	USS FRANKLIN	MANILA BAY	PHIL	LT E.W. LARKIN	M
10/19/44	46307	VT-14	USS WASP	LUZON	PHIL	LTJG E.F. HOFFMAN	M
10/19/44	46422	VT-14	USS WASP	LUZON	PHIL	LTJG COFFEY	S
10/20/44	45956	VC-21	USS MARCUS ISLAND	LEYTE GULF	PHIL	ENS WILLIAM A. BALK	S
10/20/44	25539	VT(N)-41	USS INDE-PENDENCE	ENR LEYTE GULF	PHIL	LTJG FOREST M. ARCHER	S
10/21/44	46434	VC-80	USS MAN-ILA BAY	LEYTE GULF	PHIL		
10/21/44	46233	VT-18	USS INTREPID	LOS NEGROS	PHIL	LT ALBERT J. LONG	U
10/22/44	46212	VC-21	USS MARCUS ISLAND	LEYTE GULF	PHIL	LT ANTHONY M. PEYOU	S
10/22/44	45814	VT-14	USS WASP	LOS NEGROS	PHIL	LT GEORGE C. KELLOGG	M
10/22/44	16857	VT-35	USS CHE-NANGO	CEBU	PHIL	ENS EMMETT A. SHAW	S

DATE	BUNO	SQDRN	BASE	LOST	AREA	PILOT	FATE
10/23/44	73296	VC-11	USS NEHENTA BAY		PHIL	ENS EDWARD SAIVICKI	U
10/23/44	45569	VC-27	USS SAVO ISLAND	LEYTE GULF	PHIL	ENS W.R. PEDEN	S
10/24/44	73173	COMAIR-PAC	USS PRINCE-TON	LEYTE GULF	PHIL	(SHIP SANK)	
10/24/44	45964	VC-10	USS GAMBIER BAY	LEYTE GULF	PHIL		
10/24/44	46201	VC-5	USS KIT-KUN BAY	LEYTE GULF	PHIL	(SHIP SANK)	
10/24/44	46202	VC-5	USS KIT-KUN BAY	LEYTE GULF	PHIL	(SHIP SANK)	
10/24/44	46429	VC-68	USS FANSHAW BAY	LEYTE GULF	PHIL	(SHIP SANK)	
10/24/44	73320	VC-68	USS FANSHAW BAY	LEYTE GULF	PHIL	(SHIP SANK)	
10/24/44	46444	VT-13	USS FRANKLIN	LUZON	PHIL	LTJG R.H. CLIVE	M
10/24/44	73252	VT-13	USS FRANKLIN	LUZON	PHIL	LT ROBERT FRELIGH	S
10/24/44	46025	VT-15	USS ESSEX	LUZON	PHIL		
10/24/44	46020	VT-18	USS INTREPID	LOS NEGROS	PHIL	ENS W.M. FLETCHER	M
10/24/44	46175	VT-18	USS INTREPID	LOS NEGROS	PHIL	LT GEORGE B. RILEY	M
10/24/44	73203	VT-18	USS INTREPID	LOS NEGROS	PHIL	LTJG R.J. SKELLY	M
10/24/44	46316	VT-19	USS LEX-INGTON	LEYTE GULF	PHIL	ENS R.K. MCADAMS	M
10/24/44	17023	VT-27	USS PRINCE-TON	LEYTE GULF	PHIL	(SHIP SANK)	
10/24/44	25155	VT-27	USS PRINCE-TON	LEYTE GULF	PHIL	(SHIP SANK)	
10/24/44	45560	VT-27	USS PRINCE-TON	LEYTE GULF	PHIL	(SHIP SANK)	
10/24/44	45759	VT-27	USS PRINCE-TON	LEYTE GULF	PHIL	(SHIP SANK)	
10/24/44	45832	VT-27	USS PRINCE-TON	LEYTE GULF	PHIL	(SHIP SANK)	
10/24/44	46011	VT-27	USS PRINCE-TON	LEYTE GULF	PHIL	(SHIP SANK)	
10/24/44	46068	VT-27	USS PRINCE-TON	LEYTE GULF	PHIL	(SHIP SANK)	
10/24/44	46303	VT-27	USS PRINCE-TON	LEYTE GULF	PHIL	(SHIP SANK)	
10/24/44	46337	VT-27	USS PRINCE-TON	LEYTE GULF	PHIL	(SHIP SANK)	
10/24/44	46173	VT-29	USS CABOT	LEYTE GULF	PHIL	ENS DONALD LAMPSON, JR.	M
10/24/44	73195	VT-29	USS CABOT	LEYTE GULF	PHIL	LT J.W. WILLIAMS	M
10/25/44	46205	VC-10	USS GAMBIER BAY	LEYTE GULF	PHIL	ENS GALLAGHER	M
10/25/44	46348	VC-10	USS GAMBIER BAY	LEYTE GULF	PHIL	(SHIP SANK)	
10/25/44	73220	VC-10	USS GAMBIER BAY	LEYTE GULF	PHIL	(SHIP SANK)	

DATE	BUNO	SQDRN	BASE	LOST	AREA	PILOT	FATE
10/25/44	73228	VC-10	USS GAMBIER BAY	LEYTE GULF	PHIL	(SHIP SANK)	
10/25/44	73271	VC-10	USS GAMBIER BAY	LEYTE GULF	PHIL	(SHIP SANK)	
10/25/44	46331	VC-20	USS KADASHAN BAY	LEYTE GULF	PHIL	LCDR J.R. DALE	M
10/25/44	46240	VC-21	USS MARCUS ISLAND	LEYTE GULF	PHIL	LCDR THOMAS O. MURRAY	S
10/25/44	73175	VC-21	USS MARCUS ISLAND	LEYTE GULF	PHIL	ENS WALTER R. WALKER	S
10/25/44	45554	VC-27	USS SAVO ISLAND	LEYTE GULF	PHIL	ENS HARMS	S
10/25/44	46359	VC-4	USS WHITE PLAINS	LEYTE GULF	PHIL		
10/25/44	46416	VC-4	USS WHITE PLAINS	LEYTE GULF	PHIL		
10/25/44	73352	VC-4	USS WHITE PLAINS	LEYTE GULF	PHIL		
10/25/44	46343	VC-5	USS KIT-KUN BAY	LEYTE GULF	PHIL		
10/25/44	25272	VC-60	USS SU-WANNEE	LEYTE GULF	PHIL	(DECK LOSS-KAMIKAZE)	
10/25/44	25400	VC-60	USS SU-WANNEE	LEYTE GULF	PHIL	(DECK LOSS-KAMIKAZE)	
10/25/44	16963	VC-65	USS ST. LO	LEYTE GULF	PHIL	(SHIP SANK)	
10/25/44	25381	VC-65	USS ST. LO	LEYTE GULF	PHIL	(SHIP SANK)	
10/25/44	25547	VC-65	USS ST. LO	LEYTE GULF	PHIL	LCDR R.M. JONES	M
10/25/44	45553	VC-65	USS ST. LO	LEYTE GULF	PHIL	LTJG R.W. WRINCH	M
10/25/44	45935	VC-65	USS ST. LO	LEYTE GULF	PHIL	(SHIP SANK)	
10/25/44	46192	VC-65	USS ST. LO	LEYTE GULF	PHIL	(SHIP SANK)	
10/25/44	46315	VC-65	USS ST. LO	LEYTE GULF	PHIL	ENS BROOKS	M
10/25/44	73182	VC-65	USS ST. LO	LEYTE GULF	PHIL	(SHIP SANK)	
10/25/44	73449	VC-68	USS FANSHAW BAY	LEYTE GULF	PHIL		
10/25/44	46374	VC-69	USS GUADAL-CANAL		NORLANT	LTJG DAVID G. SPRAGUE	S
10/25/44	45519	VC-75	USS OMMANEY BAY	SAMAR	PHIL	ENS BARTELL	S
10/25/44	45825	VC-76	USS PET-ROF BAY	SAN BERNADINO	PHIL	ENS NIEMANN	S
10/25/44	46200	VC-76	USS PET-ROF BAY	SAN BERNADINO	PHIL	ENS FARMER	S
10/25/44	46333	VC-80	USS MAN-ILA BAY	LEYTE GULF	PHIL	LT D.T. DOOLITTLE	S
10/25/44	73270	VC-80	USS MAN-ILA BAY	LEYTE GULF	PHIL		
10/25/44	46323	VC-81	USS NAT-OMA BAY	LEYTE GULF	PHIL	LTJG L.S. CONNER	M
10/25/44	46356	VC-81	USS NAT-OMA BAY	LEYTE GULF	PHIL	ENS C.H. BOLDT	M
10/25/44	46443	VC-81	USS NAT-OMA BAY	LEYTE GULF	PHIL	LT W.B. MORTON	S
10/25/44	73460	VC-81	USS NAT-OMA BAY	LEYTE GULF	PHIL		
10/25/44	73456	VT-13	USS FRANKLIN	LUZON	PHIL	ENS T.P. BROOKS	U
10/25/44	46415	VT-14	USS WASP	LUZON	PHIL		
10/25/44	16833	VT-15	USS ESSEX	LUZON	PHIL		
10/25/44	25672	VT-18	USS INTREPID	ENR LUZON	PHIL		
10/25/44	45769	VT-19	USS LEX-INGTON	LEYTE GULF	PHIL		
10/25/44	73201	VT-19	USS LEX-INGTON	LEYTE GULF	PHIL		
10/25/44	73407	VT-19	USS LEX-INGTON	LEYTE GULF	PHIL	LTJG J. MIDDLETON	M

DATE	BUNO	SQDRN	BASE	LOST	AREA	PILOT	FATE
10/25/44	46297	VT-20	USS ENTER-PRISE	LUZON	PHIL	LT SAVAGE	S
10/25/44	73163	VT-26	USS SANTEE	PHILIPPINE SEA	PHIL	ENS C.R. MILLS	S
10/25/44	73279	VT-26	USS SANTEE	PHILIPPINE SEA	PHIL	ENS C.L. MCGINNIS	S
10/25/44	73325	VT-26	USS SANTEE	PHILIPPINE SEA	PHIL	LTJG W.H. WILSON	S
10/25/44	16901	VT-44	USS LANGLEY	LEYTE GULF	PHIL	LT W. FREITAG	S
10/25/44	16919	VT-44	USS LANGLEY	LEYTE GULF	PHIL	ENS R.P. SMITH	D
10/25/44	46053	VT-44	USS LANGLEY	LEYTE GULF	PHIL	LT W.F. DOHERTY	M
10/25/44	46320	VT-51	USS SAN JACINTO	SIBUYAN SEA	PHIL	LTJG R.B. PLAISTED	S
10/25/44	45879	VT-7	USS HANCOCK	MANILA	PHIL	LT R.C. SCOBELL	M
10/26/44	73429	VC-68	USS FANSHAW BAY	LEYTE GULF	PHIL	ENS SCHUMANN	M
10/26/44	46252	VC-69	USS GUADAL-CANAL		NORLANT		
10/26/44	73265	VC-76	USS PET-ROF BAY	VISAYAN	PHIL		
10/26/44	73245	VC-81	USS NAT-OMA BAY	LEYTE GULF	PHIL	ENS HARRIMAN HATCH	D
10/26/44	25716	VMTB-131		GUAM	WCENPAC	LT LYMAN BATES	S
10/26/44	73240	VT-14	USS WASP	LUZON	PHIL	LT R.L. COLE, JR.	U
10/26/44	73298	VT-14	USS WASP	LUZON	PHIL		
10/26/44	45932	VT-18	USS INTREPID	ENR LUZON	PHIL	ENS N.J. ROCCAFORTE	S
10/26/44	46019	VT-18	USS INTREPID	ENR LUZON	PHIL	LTJG V.A. DELANEY	S
10/26/44	46204	VT-29	USS CABOT	LEYTE GULF	PHIL	LTJG C.F. NORTON	S
10/26/44	16926	VT-60	USS SU-WANNEE	LEYTE GULF	PHIL	(DECK LOSS-KAMIKAZE)	
10/26/44	17017	VT-60	USS SU-WANNEE	LEYTE GULF	PHIL	(DECK LOSS-KAMIKAZE)	
10/26/44	25397	VT-60	USS SU-WANNEE	LEYTE GULF	PHIL	(DECK LOSS-KAMIKAZE)	
10/26/44	46384	VT-7	USS HANCOCK	MANILA	PHIL	LTJG F.G. KEENE	M
10/26/44	46400	VT-7	USS HANCOCK	MANILA	PHIL	LTJG J.H. BRADY	S
10/27/44	25202	VT-9		HAWAII	ECENPAC	ENS THOMAS H. ROBERTS	D
10/28/44	46373	VC-69	USS GUADAL-CANAL		NORLANT	LT GRANT L. NELSON	D
10/28/44	73135	VC-82	USS ANZIO		CENPAC		
10/28/44	73264	VC-82	USS ANZIO		CENPAC		
10/29/44	73127	VC-82	USS ANZIO		CENPAC		
10/29/44	73278	VC-82	USS ANZIO		CENPAC		
10/29/44	25396	VT(N)-90	BARBERS POINT	HAWAII	ECENPAC	ENS J.J. ZAVESKY	S
10/29/44	73117	VT-13	USS FRANKLIN	LEYTE GULF	PHIL		
10/29/44	25410	VT-18	USS INTREPID	LUZON	PHIL		
10/29/44	45542	VT-18	USS INTREPID	LUZON	PHIL	ENS N.J. ROCCAFORTE	M
10/29/44	45924	VT-18	USS INTREPID	LUZON	PHIL		
10/29/44	46062	VT-18	USS INTREPID	LUZON	PHIL	LTJG J.L. RUEIN	S
10/29/44	46176	VT-18	USS INTREPID	LUZON	PHIL		
10/29/44	46241	VT-18	USS INTREPID	LUZON	PHIL		
10/29/44	46302	VT-18	USS INTREPID	LUZON	PHIL		

DATE	BUNO	SQDRN	BASE	LOST	AREA	PILOT	FATE
10/29/44	46357	VT-18	USS INTREPID	LUZON	PHIL		
10/29/44	45866	VT-28	USS MONTEREY	PHILIPPINE SEA	PHIL		
10/29/44	73169	VT-7	USS HANCOCK	MANILA	PHIL		
10/30/44	46003	VT(N)-90	BARBERS POINT	HAWAII	ECENPAC		
10/30/44	46033	VT-100		HAWAII	ECENPAC	ENS C.C. CAMPBELL	S
10/30/44	17030	VT-13	USS FRANKLIN	LEYTE GULF	PHIL	(DECK LOSS-KAMIKAZE)	
10/30/44	73212	VT-13	USS FRANKLIN	LEYTE GULF	PHIL	(DECK LOSS-KAMIKAZE)	
10/30/44	73461	VT-13	USS FRANKLIN	LEYTE GULF	PHIL	(DECK LOSS-KAMIKAZE)	
10/30/44	16942	VT-20	USS ENTER-PRISE	LUZON	PHIL		
10/30/44	16962	VT-20	USS ENTER-PRISE	LUZON	PHIL		
10/30/44	73274	VT-21	USS BELLEAU WOOD		SW PAC	(DECK FIRE)	
11/01/44	45835	VMTB-232		ULITHI	WCENPAC		
11/04/44	73300	VC-82	USS ANZIO		WCENPAC		
11/05/44	73194	VF-11	USS HORNET		PHIL	LT FRANCIS J. GRASSBAUGH	M
11/05/44	46353	VT-15	USS ESSEX	LUZON	PHIL		
11/05/44	45698	VT-4	USS BUNKER HILL	LUZON	PHIL	ENS J.F. ZOOK	S
11/05/44	46041	VT-7	USS HANCOCK	LUZON	PHIL		
11/05/44	46349	VT-7	USS HANCOCK	LUZON	PHIL		
11/06/44	73328	VF-7	USS HANCOCK	LUZON	PHIL		
11/06/44	45506	VT-19	USS LEX-INGTON	LUZON	PHIL	ENS PATTERSON	S
11/06/44	16890	VT-48		HAWAII	ECENPAC		
11/10/44	45946	VMTB-134		PELELIU	WCENPAC	MAJ HARRY V. SCULLIN	D
11/12/44	25405	VT-100		HAWAII	ECENPAC	LTJG G.E. MCLAUGHLIN	S
11/12/44	16884	VT-48	USS PRINCE WILLIAM	OFF NORFOLK	CENLANT	LTJG GOSMER	S
11/12/44	25276	VT-9		HAWAII	ECENPAC	ENS STEVE F. BEDNER	D
11/13/44	73266	VT-11	USS HORNET		PHIL	LCDR RAD. DENNISTON JR	D
11/13/44	73324	VT-11	U33 HORNET		PHIL	ENS BURTON T. OBERG	D
11/13/44	46242	VT-15	USS ESSEX	MANILA	PHIL	LTJG O.R. BLEECH	S
11/13/44	46042	VT-20	USS ENTER-PRISE	MANILA	PHIL	ENS R.E. MCALPINE	M
11/13/44	46081	VT-22	USS COWPENS	MANILA	PHIL	LT SILAS R. JOHNSON	M
11/13/44	73213	VT-22	USS COWPENS	MANILA	PHIL	ENS REILIS	M
11/13/44	45910	VT-28	USS MONTEREY	MANILA	PHIL	ENS WILLIAM LOUDEN	M
11/14/44	73308	VC-83	USS CORREGID OR	HAWAII	ECENPAC	ENS RICHARD G. PERRY	S
11/14/44	46411	VT-20	USS ENTER-PRISE	LUZON	PHIL		
11/14/44	46172	VT-22	USS COWPENS	MANILA	PHIL	ENS STEPHEN K. KORNS	M
11/14/44	45741	VT-44	USS LANGLEY	MANILA	PHIL	ENS ALLEN BRODY	S
11/14/44	46440	VT-45		GUAM	WCENPAC		
11/14/44	34102	VT-51	USS SAN JACINTO	ULITHI	WCENPAC		
11/15/44	16843	CASU(F)-42		PITYILU	SW PAC		

DATE	BUNO	SQDRN	BASE	LOST	AREA	PILOT	FATE
11/15/44	73403	VC-81	USS NATOMA BAY	PITYILU	SW PAC	ENS JAMES J. MCMAHAN	S
11/16/44	73404	CASU(F)-42		PITYILU	SW PAC		
11/16/44	73310	VC-83	USS CORREGIDOR	HAWAII	ECENPAC	LT WILLIAM C. SAUER	S
11/16/44	17069	VT-23	PUUNENE	HAWAII	ECENPAC	ENS HAROLD J. MOONEY	S
11/16/44	25312	VT-8	USS INTREPID	LUZON	PHIL		
11/19/44	46433	COM7THFLT	PERTH	AUSTRALIA	SW PAC		
11/19/44	46355	VT-29	USS CABOT	ENR MANILA	PHIL	LT JOHN H. BALLANTINE, JR.	U
11/20/44	73208	A.A.	PEARL	HAWAII	ECENPAC		
11/20/44	73186	VC-83	USS CORREGIDOR	HAWAII	ECENPAC		
11/20/44	73326	VC-83	USS CORREGIDOR	HAWAII	ECENPAC		
11/20/44	73301	VMTB-242		HAWAII	ECENPAC	LT RAY B. ENGBRETSON	M
11/21/44	25515	VMTB-232		ULITHI	WCENPAC	LT FRED E. DAVIDSON	U
11/21/44	45454	VMTB-232		ULITHI	WCENPAC	LT JOHN A. LAGRU	D
11/21/44	73344	VMTB-232		ULITHI	WCENPAC	1STLT JAMES W. FOX	S
11/21/44	45955	VT-47	PUUNENE	HAWAII	ECENPAC		
11/21/44	16845	VT-9	USS MAKASSAR STR.	HAWAII	ECENPAC	ENS DONALD J. MCKEEBY	S
11/22/44	45800	VC-11	USS NEHENTA BAY		WCENPAC	ENS JEROME J. TILSON	S
11/23/44	73412	VC-21	USS MARCUS ISLAND	MINDORO STR.	PHIL	LT ANTHONY M. PEYOU	S
11/23/44	45919	VC-75	USS OMMANEY BAY	PONAM	SW PAC	LTJG DONALD E. JONES	S
11/23/44	25366	VT-3	USS YORKTOWN	ULITHI	WCENPAC	LTJG DULL	S
11/23/44	46023	VT-83		HAWAII	ECENPAC	ENS WILLIAM J. PAXTON	S
11/24/44	46013	VT-81	USS WASP	ENR ULITHI	WCENPAC	LTJG BAXTER B. SLAUGHTER	S
11/25/44	16944	CASU-13		PONAM	SW PAC	ENS WALTER C. HARRIS	S
11/25/44	25444	VMTB-242		TINIAN	WCENPAC	LT PAUL J. SANDMEYER	S
11/25/44	46360	VT-18	USS INTREPID		PHIL	(DECK LOSS-KAMIKAZE)	
11/25/44	46194	VT-29	USS CABOT	MANILA	PHIL	(DECK LOSS-KAMIKAZE)	
11/25/44	73487	VT-4	USS ESSEX	LEYTE GULF	PHIL	(DECK LOSS-KAMIKAZE)	
11/25/44	73258	VT-44	USS LANGLEY	LUZON	PHIL	ENS ALLEN BRODY	D
11/25/44	46311	VT-7	USS HANCOCK	LUZON	PHIL		
11/25/44	73336	VT-7	USS HANCOCK	LUZON	PHIL		
11/26/44	16906	VC-11	USS NEHENTA BAY		WCENPAC	LT A.H. PAINE	U
11/30/44	45650	AWT ACTION	PEARL	HAWAII	ECENPAC		
12/02/44	45524	VMTB-134		PELELIU	WCENPAC		
12/02/44	25168	VMTB-242		TINIAN	WCENPAC	1STLT JOHN I. NEVANS	S
12/02/44	16803	VT-100	USS MAKASSAR STR.	HAWAII	ECENPAC	ENS L.E. OLESON	D
12/04/44	45464	CASU(F)-13		PONAM	SW PAC		
12/04/44	73335	CASU(F)-13		PONAM	SW PAC		
12/04/44	45982	VC-13	USS KASAAN BAY	ENR HAWAII	ECENPAC		
12/07/44	45675	AR & OH		MANUS	SW PAC		
12/07/44	46232	AR & OH		MANUS	SW PAC		
12/07/44	73128	AR & OH		MANUS	SW PAC		

DATE	BUNO	SQDRN	BASE	LOST	AREA	PILOT	FATE
12/07/44	45660	VMTB-232		ULITHI	WCENPAC	1STLT THOMAS M. SCHRIVER	D
12/10/44	46291	VT-11	USS HORNET	ULITHI	WCENPAC		
12/11/44	45445	1ST MAW		TOROKINA	SOPAC	1STLT CLARENCE A. HESS	S
12/11/44	46015	VC-77	USS RUDYERD BAY	PHILIPPINES	PHIL	LT JOHN J. SCANNELL	S
12/12/44	25392	CASU(F)-13		PITYILU	SW PAC	LT ROBERT L. STIX	S
12/13/44	73397	VT-45	USS SAN JACINTO	MANILA	PHIL		
12/14/44	34105	VC-75	USS OMMANEY BAY	SULU SEA	PHIL		
12/14/44	45618	VT(N)-41	USS INDE-PENDENCE	LUZON	PHIL	ENS JOHN E. LEWIS	S
12/14/44	25157	VT-100		HAWAII	ECENPAC		
12/14/44	46424	VT-29	USS CABOT	LUZON	PHIL	LTJG C.F. NORTON	S
12/15/44	34103	VT-11	USS HORNET	LUZON	PHIL	LTJG JOSEPH W. HYLAND	S
12/15/44	46211	VT-29	USS CABOT	LUZON	PHIL	LT W.H. ANDERSON, JR.	S
12/15/44	46039	VT-7	USS HANCOCK	LUZON	PHIL		
12/16/44	45970	VT-6	PEARL	HAWAII	ECENPAC	ENS A.F. WALTER KRESSE	S
12/17/44	25642	1ST MAW		TOROKINA	SOPAC		
12/17/44	46334	VC-82	USS ANZIO	LEYTE GULF	PHIL		
12/18/44	45550	VC-11	USS NEHENTA BAY		PHIL	(DECK LOSS-TYPHOON)	
12/18/44	73187	VC-11	USS NEHENTA BAY		PHIL	(DECK LOSS-TYPHOON)	
12/18/44	73432	VC-11	USS NEHENTA BAY		PHIL	(DECK LOSS-TYPHOON)	
12/18/44	73168	VC-82	USS ANZIO	LEYTE GULF	PHIL		
12/18/44	73188	VC-82	USS ANZIO	LEYTE GULF	PHIL		
12/18/44	73309	VC-82	USS ANZIO	LEYTE GULF	PHIL		
12/18/44	73414	VC-82	USS ANZIO	LEYTE GULF	PHIL		
12/18/44	45689	VT-22	USS COWPENS	LUZON	PHIL	(DECK LOSS-TYPHOON)	
12/18/44	46178	VT-22	USS COWPENS	LUZON	PHIL	(DECK LOSS-TYPHOON)	
12/18/44	46431	VT-22	USS COWPENS	LUZON	PHIL	(DECK LOSS-TYPHOON)	
12/18/44	45692	VT-28	USS MONTEREY	PHILIPPINE SEA	PHIL	(DECK LOSS-TYPHOON)	
12/18/44	45961	VT-28	USS MONTEREY	PHILIPPINE SEA	PHIL	(DECK LOSS-TYPHOON)	
12/18/44	46235	VT-28	USS MONTEREY	PHILIPPINE SEA	PHIL	(DECK LOSS-TYPHOON)	
12/18/44	73482	VT-28	USS MONTEREY	PHILIPPINE SEA	PHIL	(DECK LOSS-TYPHOON)	
12/18/44	16842	VT-45	USS SAN JACINTO	PHILIPPINE SEA	PHIL	(DECK LOSS-TYPHOON)	
12/18/44	16922	VT-45	USS SAN JACINTO	PHILIPPINE SEA	PHIL	(DECK LOSS-TYPHOON)	
12/18/44	46027	VT-45	USS SAN JACINTO	PHILIPPINE SEA	PHIL	(DECK LOSS-TYPHOON)	
12/18/44	46169	VT-45	USS SAN JACINTO	PHILIPPINE SEA	PHIL	(DECK LOSS-TYPHOON)	
12/18/44	46239	VT-45	USS SAN JACINTO	PHILIPPINE SEA	PHIL	(DECK LOSS-TYPHOON)	
12/18/44	73317	VT-45	USS SAN JACINTO	PHILIPPINE SEA	PHIL	(DECK LOSS-TYPHOON)	
12/19/44	46196	VC-76	USS PET-ROF BAY	NEW GUINEA	SW PAC	ENS RICHARD J. MAROVICH	S
12/19/44	45948	VT-6	PEARL	HAWAII	ECENPAC	ENS BENJAMIN J. STANDEN	S

DATE	BUNO	SQDRN	BASE	LOST	AREA	PILOT	FATE
12/21/44	46347	VC-11	USS NEHENTA BAY		WCENPAC	LT E.R. SCHMARTH	S
12/21/44	73222	VC-20	USS KADASHAN BAY		PHIL	LTJG CHARLES WM ROTH	S
12/21/44	73282	VC-82	USS ANZIO	LEYTE GULF	PHIL		
12/21/44	46335	VJ-7	PEARL	HAWAII	ECENPAC	LTJG ROBERT L. HARTLEY	S
12/22/44	16796	VMTB-131		GUAM	WCENPAC		
12/22/44	16796	VMTB-131		GUAM	WCENPAC		
12/22/44	16812	VMTB-131		GUAM	WCENPAC		
12/22/44	25580	VMTB-131		GUAM	WCENPAC		
12/22/44	25630	VMTB-131		GUAM	WCENPAC		
12/22/44	25665	VMTB-131		GUAM	WCENPAC		
12/22/44	25669	VMTB-131		GUAM	WCENPAC		
12/22/44	25719	VMTB-131		GUAM	WCENPAC		
12/22/44	45460	VMTB-131		GUAM	WCENPAC		
12/22/44	45551	VMTB-131		GUAM	WCENPAC		
12/22/44	73171	VT-4	USS ESSEX	LINGAYEN GULF	PHIL		
12/23/44	46032	VC-77	USS RUDYERD BAY	PHILIPPINES	PHIL	ENS THOMAS W. JOHN	D
12/23/44	46034	VC-93		HAWAII	ECENPAC	LTJG BENJAMIN BEAN	S
12/24/44	25331	CASU(F)-42		PITYILU	SW PAC		
12/27/44	73275	VT-100	BARBERS POINT	HAWAII	ECENPAC		
12/28/44	46476	A.A.	PEARL	HAWAII	ECENPAC		
12/28/44	73478	CASU(F)-13		PITYILU	SW PAC		
12/28/44	73483	CASU(F)-42		PITYILU	SW PAC		
12/30/44	46017	A.A.	PEARL	HAWAII	ECENPAC		
12/30/44	73333	VT-7	USS HANCOCK	ULITHI	WCENPAC		
12/30/44	73341	VT-7	USS HANCOCK	ULITHI	WCENPAC		
12/30/44	73400	VT-7	USS HANCOCK	ULITHI	WCENPAC		
12/31/44	17045	COMAIR-PAC	PEARL	HAWAII	ECENPAC		
12/31/44	25378	VMTB-232		ULITHI	WCENPAC	MAJ ALLEN T. BARNUM	S
12/31/44	46336	VT-7	USS HANCOCK	ENR FORMOSA	WCENPAC		
01/01/45	45532	VC-21	USS MARCUS ISLAND	LINGAYEN GULF	PHIL	ENS ARTHUR ALBERT	S
01/02/45	46340	SERVRON-11		PELELIU	WCENPAC		
01/03/45	73443	A.A.	SAMAR	SAMAR	PHIL		
01/03/45	46058	VT-11	USS HORNET	FORMOSA	EMPIRE	LT T.B. ADAMS	S
01/03/45	46410	VT-20	USS LEX-INGTON	FORMOSA	EMPIRE	LTJG D.F. SEIZ	S
01/03/45	46308	VT-29	USS CABOT	FORMOSA	EMPIRE	ENS J.A. VASHRO	S
01/03/45	46326	VT-45	USS SAN JACINTO	FORMOSA	EMPIRE	ENS C.W. DYSEPT	S
01/03/45	73281	VT-45	USS SAN JACINTO	FORMOSA	EMPIRE	ENS CHARLES H. FRISBIE	M
01/04/45	45521	VC-75	USS OMMANEY BAY	MINDORO STRAIT	PHIL	(SHIP SANK)	
01/04/45	46018	VC-75	USS OMMANEY BAY	MINDORO STRAIT	PHIL	(SHIP SANK)	
01/04/45	46037	VC-75	USS OMMANEY BAY	MINDORO STRAIT	PHIL	(SHIP SANK)	
01/04/45	46207	VC-75	USS OMMANEY BAY	MINDORO STRAIT	PHIL	(SHIP SANK)	
01/04/45	73272	VC-75	USS OMMANEY BAY	MINDORO STRAIT	PHIL	(SHIP SANK)	

DATE	BUNO	SQDRN	BASE	LOST	AREA	PILOT	FATE
01/04/45	73395	VC-75	USS OMMANEY BAY	MINDORO STRAIT	PHIL	(SHIP SANK)	
01/04/45	73405	VC-75	USS OMMANEY BAY	MINDORO STRAIT	PHIL	(SHIP SANK)	
01/04/45	73447	VC-75	USS OMMANEY BAY	MINDORO STRAIT	PHIL	(SHIP SANK)	
01/04/45	73459	VC-75	USS OMMANEY BAY	MINDORO STRAIT	PHIL	(SHIP SANK)	
01/04/45	16806	VT-100		HAWAII	ECENPAC		
01/04/45	46083	VT-20	USS LEXINGTON	FORMOSA	EMPIRE	LTJG W.T. ROSS	U
01/05/45	46358	VC-80	USS MANILA BAY	MINDORO STRAIT	PHIL	(DECK LOSS-KAMIKAZE)	
01/05/45	46417	VC-80	USS MANILA BAY	MINDORO STRAIT	PHIL	(DECK LOSS-KAMIKAZE)	
01/05/45	73125	VC-80	USS MANILA BAY	MINDORO STRAIT	PHIL	(DECK LOSS-KAMIKAZE)	
01/05/45	73304	VC-80	USS MANILA BAY	MINDORO STRAIT	PHIL	(DECK LOSS-KAMIKAZE)	
01/05/45	73347	VC-80	USS MANILA BAY	MINDORO STRAIT	PHIL	(DECK LOSS-KAMIKAZE)	
01/05/45	73406	VC-80	USS MANILA BAY	MINDORO STRAIT	PHIL	(DECK LOSS-KAMIKAZE)	
01/05/45	73426	VC-80	USS MANILA BAY	MINDORO STRAIT	PHIL	(DECK LOSS-KAMIKAZE)	
01/05/45	73476	VC-80	USS MANILA BAY	MINDORO STRAIT	PHIL	(DECK LOSS-KAMIKAZE)	
01/06/45	45907	VC-69	USS MISSION BAY	OFF CUBA	CENLANT	LTJG JOHN B. SCHMIDT	U
01/06/45	73134	VC-81	USS NATOMA BAY	LUZON	PHIL	LTJG VOLTZ	S
01/06/45	17065	VT-20	USS LEXINGTON	LUZON	PHIL		
01/06/45	73160	VT-3	USS YORKTOWN	MANILA	PHIL		
01/06/45	45812	VT-6	PEARL	HAWAII	ECENPAC	ENS RONALD W. MCLELLAN	S
01/07/45	73441	VC-27	USS SAVO ISLAND	LUZON	PHIL		
01/07/45	73350	VC-80	USS MANILA BAY	ENR LINGAYEN	PHIL	LT ALBERT N. MILLER, JR.	S
01/07/45	73178	VT-3	USS YORKTOWN	MANILA	PHIL	LT F.A. FOSS, JR.	M
01/07/45	73283	VT-3	USS YORKTOWN	MANILA	PHIL	LTJG A. FRANCIS LANDRY	M
01/08/45	16909	VC-20	USS KADASHAN BAY		PHIL		
01/08/45	73463	VC-27	USS SAVO ISLAND	LUZON	PHIL	LCDR P.W. JACKSON	S
01/09/45	46346	VT-11	USS HORNET	FORMOSA	EMPIRE	LTJG GORDON W. BELL	M
01/09/45	73218	VT-3	USS YORKTOWN	FORMOSA	EMPIRE	LT F.F. FRAZIER	M
01/09/45	45818	VT-44	USS LANGLEY	FORMOSA	EMPIRE	ENS WILLIAM JOSEPH ALLEN	M
01/10/45	17060	VC-21	USS MARCUS ISLAND	LINGAYEN GULF	PHIL	ENS PHILIP T. BANKSTON	U
01/10/45	73420	VT-81	USS WASP	LUZON	PHIL		
01/12/45	46298	NACTU	USS SARATOGA	HAWAII	ECENPAC	ENS R.F. POLLARD	S
01/12/45	73162	VC-27	USS SAVO ISLAND	LINGAYEN GULF	PHIL		
01/12/45	73322	VT-11	USS HORNET	FR. I.C.	PHIL	LTJG WILLIAM MAIER	M
01/12/45	45900	VT-20	USS LEXINGTON	FR. I.C.	PHIL	LTJG R.H. BRADLEY	M
01/12/45	45653	VT-29	USS CABOT		EMPIRE	ENS JOHN P. WALKER	D

DATE	BUNO	SQDRN	BASE	LOST	AREA	PILOT	FATE
01/12/45	73314	VT-3	USS YORK-TOWN	MANILA	PHIL	LT H.C. SKINNER	M
01/13/45	46257	VT(N)-41	USS INDE-PENDENCE	FR. I.C.	PHIL	LT WILLIAM RICHARD TAYLOR	S
01/14/45	46300	VC-80	USS MAN-ILA BAY	SOUTH CHINA SEA	PHIL	ENS JOHN EDWIN KLEDER	S
01/14/45	45749	VT-22	USS COWPENS	LINGAYEN GULF	PHIL		
01/15/45	45596	VC-27	USS SAVO ISLAND	LINGAYEN GULF	PHIL		
01/15/45	46218	VC-27	USS SAVO ISLAND	LINGAYEN GULF	PHIL		
01/15/45	46030	VT-44	USS LANGLEY	FORMOSA	EMPIRE		
01/15/45	73477	VT-44	USS LANGLEY	FORMOSA	EMPIRE	LT ROSSON, JR.	S
01/16/45	73130	VC-80	USS MAN-ILA BAY	SO. CHINA SEA	PHIL		
01/16/45	73493	VT-11	USS HORNET	HONG KONG	EMPIRE	LTJG EDWIN MCGOWAN	M
01/16/45	46413	VT-20	USS LEX-INGTON	HONG KONG	EMPIRE	LTJG D.F. SEIZ	M
01/16/45	73226	VT-20	USS LEX-INGTON	HONG KONG	EMPIRE	LT M.L. LEEDON	D
01/16/45	45663	VT-22	USS COWPENS	CHINA COAST	EMPIRE	ENS G.W. CLARK	M
01/16/45	46329	VT-22	USS COWPENS	HONG KONG	EMPIRE	LT B.B. LAUGHREN	M
01/16/45	46458	VT-7	USS HANCOCK	HONG KONG	EMPIRE	LTJG R.C. SCOBELL	S
01/16/45	73334	VT-7	USS HANCOCK	HONG KONG	EMPIRE	ENS WILLIAM BARROW	U
01/16/45	73343	VT-7	USS HANCOCK	HONG KONG	EMPIRE	LTJG R.L. HUNT	D
01/16/45	73438	VT-80	USS TICONDER-OGA	HAINAN	EMPIRE		
01/17/45	17014	VC-80	USS MAN-ILA BAY	SO. CHINA SEA	PHIL	LTJG RICHARD P. DEITCHMAN	S
01/17/45	46065	VC-82	USS ANZIO	LUZON	PHIL	LTJG H.D.C. SALTSMAN	S
01/17/45	73211	VC-82	USS ANZIO	LUZON	PHIL		
01/20/45	46057	VC-77	USS RUDYERD BAY	LINGAYEN GULF	PHIL	LTJG JOHN J. SCANNELL	S
01/20/45	45595	VT-6	PEARL	HAWAII	ECENPAC	LT FORREST F. CRANE	S
01/23/45	25479	A.A.	PEARL	HAWAII	ECENPAC		
01/23/45	25206	VT-86		HAWAII	ECENPAC	ENS ROLAND B. FOERSTER	S
01/24/45	73236	VC-82	USS ANZIO	LUZON	PHIL	ENS W.E. PULASKI	U
01/26/45	46278	VC-36	USS CROATAN	BERMUDA	NORLANT		
01/26/45	45817	VMTB-232		ULITHI	WCENPAC	1STLT LEETE JACKSON, JR.	S
01/27/45	25661	CASU-1	PEARL	HAWAII	ECENPAC	LT SAMUEL LEVY JONES	S
01/27/45	73205	VC-21	USS MARCUS ISLAND	LUZON	PHIL	LTJG ORVILLE C. HOOVER	S
01/27/45	73131	VT-11	USS HORNET		WCENPAC		
01/30/45	46312	CASU(F)-51		ULITHI	WCENPAC	LT G.C. TAYLOR	S
01/31/45	46339	CASU(F)-51		ULITHI	WCENPAC		
01/31/45	73391	VC-27	USS SAVO ISLAND	ULITHI	WCENPAC	(DECK LOSS-SCRAPPED)	
02/01/45	46265	VC-58	USS CORE		NORLANT	LT A.R. THOMPSON	S
02/01/45	73379	VC-69	USS MISSION BAY	CUBA	CENLANT	LTJG O.E. FRYE	S
02/05/45	73398	VT-81	USS WASP	IWO JIMA	EMPIRE		
02/08/45	73229	AA & RH		HAWAII	ECENPAC		
02/11/45	73356	VC-58	USS CORE		CENLANT	LT EUGENE F. WALLACE	S
02/11/45	73302	VT(N)-90	USS ENTER-PRISE	ENR TOKYO	WCENPAC		
02/12/45	73358	VC-58	USS CORE		CENLANT		

DATE	BUNO	SQDRN	BASE	LOST	AREA	PILOT	FATE
02/13/45	46831	AA & RH		HAWAII	ECENPAC		
02/13/45	25645	VMTB-131		GUAM	WCENPAC	1STLT ELDON J. SHARP	S
02/14/45	25593	NACTU	BARBERS POINT	HAWAII	ECENPAC	ENS JACK P. EBERLEY	S
02/15/45	25146	VT-99	USS SITKOH BAY	GUAM	WCENPAC	ENS R.W. BRIGHAM	S
02/17/45	73401	VC-76	USS PETROF BAY	IWO JIMA	EMPIRE	ENS HILLARY FAULCANER	S
02/17/45	73490	VC-81	USS NATOMA BAY	IWO JIMA	EMPIRE	ENS C. MCMAHONS	S
02/17/45	73664	VT-12	USS RANDOLPH	IWO JIMA	EMPIRE		
02/17/45	73412	VT-45	USS SAN JACINTO	TOKYO	EMPIRE	LT ALVIN F. RIECK	S
02/18/45	73191	VT-3	USS YORKTOWN	CHICHI JIMA	EMPIRE		
02/18/45	73219	VT-3	USS YORKTOWN	CHICHI JIMA	EMPIRE		
02/18/45	73321	VT-81	USS WASP	BONIN	EMPIRE		
02/19/45	16959	A.A.	GUAM	GUAM	WCENPAC		
02/19/45	73342	A.A.	GUAM	GUAM	WCENPAC		
02/19/45	73442	CASU(F)-12		GUAM	WCENPAC		
02/19/45	46403	VC-58	USS CORE		CENLANT	LTJG C.E. TINGLEY	S
02/19/45	47744	VMTB-232		ULITHI	WCENPAC	2NDLT RAYMOND C. DAELDUS	S
02/19/45	73353	VT(N)-53	USS SARATOGA	TOKYO	EMPIRE		
02/19/45	45950	VT-80		IWO JIMA	EMPIRE	ENS C.V. HIGMAN	S
02/20/45	16965	AA & RH		HAWAII	ECENPAC		
02/20/45	45452	CASU(F)-13		PITYILU	SW PAC		
02/20/45	46075	VC-77	USS RUDYERD BAY	IWO JIMA	EMPIRE	LT T.A. TURNER	S
02/20/45	16796	VC-83	USS SARGENT BAY	IWO JIMA	EMPIRE		
02/21/45	73465	VC-81	USS NATOMA BAY		EMPIRE	ENS GORDON W. KESTERKE	S
02/21/45	16882	VC-98	USS FANSHAW BAY	ENR PEARL	WCENPAC	ENS L.L. ZIEGLER	S
02/21/45	16936	VT-100		HAWAII	ECENPAC		
02/22/45	46216	AA & RH		HAWAII	ECENPAC		
02/22/45	46428	VC-77	USS RUDYERD BAY	IWO JIMA	EMPIRE	LTJG WILLIAM P. CONLEY	M
02/23/45	73180	VC-77	USS RUDYERD BAY	IWO JIMA	EMPIRE	LTJG JOHN J. SCANNELLI	S
02/25/45	45677	VC-82	USS BENNINGTON	IWO JIMA	EMPIRE		
02/27/45	46233	AA & RH		HAWAII	ECENPAC		
02/27/45	46072	VT-99		MARSHALLS	WCENPAC	ENS ROBERT B. LAWSON	U
02/28/45	46335	CASU(F)-31		ULITHI	WCENPAC		
02/28/45	25289	CASU(F)-43		GUAM	WCENPAC		
03/02/45	46189	VC-77	USS RUDYERD BAY	IWO JIMA	EMPIRE		
03/03/45	46045	VC-83	USS SARGENT BAY	CHICHI JIMA	EMPIRE	ENS J.D. PROVOST DURHAM	S
03/08/45	73330	VC-77	USS RUDYERD BAY	IWO JIMA	EMPIRE	ENS TRAVIS L. SCOTT	S
03/08/45	73339	VJ-2		ADMIRALTIES	SW PAC	LTJG ROBERT O. EDDY	S
03/14/45	45870	NACTU	BARBERS POINT	HAWAII	ECENPAC	ENS ARTHUR B. STRATTEN	S
03/19/45	73435	VT-86	USS WASP	KURE	EMPIRE		
03/19/45	73480	VT-86	USS WASP	KURE	EMPIRE		
03/21/45	16924	VT-99		GUAM	WCENPAC	ENS ROBERT G. STOWELL	S

DATE	BUNO	SQDRN	BASE	LOST	AREA	PILOT	FATE
03/21/45	45470	VT-99		GUAM	WCENPAC	ENS JAMES R. YEARSLEY	M
03/27/45	73306	VC-13	USS ANZIO	OKINAWA	EMPIRE	LTJG PAUL J. BARNARD	U
03/27/45	73444	VT-1		HAWAII	ECENPAC	LT JAMES P. LONG	S
03/28/45	46056	VC-13	USS ANZIO	OKINAWA	EMPIRE		
03/28/45	73280	VT-49		HAWAII	ECENPAC	ENS ROBERT W. HUNTER	D
03/29/45	73446	VC-13	USS ANZIO	OKINAWA	EMPIRE	LTJG A.L. SCHROEDER	M
03/31/45	73291	CASU-4	PUUNENE	HAWAII	ECENPAC	ENS J.A. VIRGILIO	S
03/31/45	45941	COMAIR-PAC	PEARL	HAWAII	ECENPAC		
03/31/45	73163	VC-13	USS ANZIO	OKINAWA	EMPIRE		
04/01/45	46213	VC-13	USS ANZIO	OKINAWA	EMPIRE	ENS JOHN E. CARPENTER	S
04/03/45	46180	CASU(F)-13		PITYILU	SW PAC		
04/14/45	45967	VJ-7	PEARL	HAWAII	ECENPAC	ENS EARL AMUNDSON	S
04/15/45	73297	CASU(F)-15		SAIPAN	WCENPAC		
04/24/45	45911	CVG-100		HAWAII	ECENPAC		
04/24/45	45536	VJ-2		PITYILU	SW PAC	ENS RUSSELL F.A. CRIGGS	D
04/25/45	25705	AS & MU		GUAM	WCENPAC	LTJG G.C. CRUMBLER	S
04/27/45	73277	VC-13	USS ANZIO	OKINAWA	EMPIRE		
04/29/45	73269	VMTB-134		PELELIU	WCENPAC	LT STEWART	S
04/30/45	46051	POOL	PEARL	HAWAII	ECENPAC		
05/01/45	16904	VJ-17		GUAM	WCENPAC	CAPT W.R. SHOALTS	S
05/08/45	73223	VJ-2		SAMAR	PHIL	ENS MERVIN E. DRAIN	S
05/09/45	45927	VMTB-134		PELELIU	WCENPAC		
05/10/45	25399	CASU(F)-47		SAIPAN	WCENPAC		
05/19/45	45963	SERVRON-11		PELELIU	WCENPAC		
05/19/45	46230	SERVRON-11		PELELIU	WCENPAC		
05/21/45	25298	VJ-17		GUAM	WCENPAC		
05/23/45	73496	VMTB-134		PELELIU	WCENPAC		
05/29/45	73488	CASU(F)-15		SAIPAN	WCENPAC		
06/03/45	25190	AROU-2		SAMAR	PHIL		
06/05/45	45966	VMTB-134		PELELIU	WCENPAC		
06/06/45	25148	POOL	BARBERS POINT	HAWAII	ECENPAC		
06/06/45	25191	POOL	BARBERS POINT	HAWAII	ECENPAC		
06/06/45	25224	POOL	BARBERS POINT	HAWAII	ECENPAC		
06/12/45	16920	POOL	PEARL	HAWAII	ECENPAC		
06/12/45	25136	POOL	PEARL	HAWAII	ECENPAC		
06/12/45	25221	POOL	PEARL	HAWAII	ECENPAC		
06/12/45	25281	POOL	PEARL	HAWAII	ECENPAC		
06/12/45	25374	POOL	PEARL	HAWAII	ECENPAC		
06/12/45	45568	POOL	PEARL	HAWAII	ECENPAC		
06/12/45	45610	POOL	PEARL	HAWAII	ECENPAC		
06/12/45	46008	POOL	PEARL	HAWAII	ECENPAC		
06/12/45	46314	POOL	PEARL	HAWAII	ECENPAC		
06/12/45	73161	POOL	PEARL	HAWAII	ECENPAC		
06/12/45	73165	POOL	PEARL	HAWAII	ECENPAC		
06/12/45	73190	POOL	PEARL	HAWAII	ECENPAC		
06/12/45	73243	POOL	PEARL	HAWAII	ECENPAC		
06/12/45	17048	VJ-17		GUAM	WCENPAC		
06/12/45	25538	VT-88	USS YORK-TOWN	SAIPAN	WCENPAC	ENS H.W. BRADLUND	S
06/14/45	25150	POOL	PEARL	HAWAII	ECENPAC		
06/14/45	25332	POOL	PEARL	HAWAII	ECENPAC		
06/14/45	25706	POOL	PEARL	HAWAII	ECENPAC		
06/14/45	45687	POOL	PEARL	HAWAII	ECENPAC		
06/15/45	25301	CASU(F)-47		SAIPAN	WCENPAC		
06/15/45	25419	CASU(F)-47		SAIPAN	WCENPAC		
06/15/45	46184	CASU(F)-47		SAIPAN	WCENPAC		
06/16/45	16916	CASU(F)-15		SAIPAN	WCENPAC		
06/20/45		AROU-2		SAMAR	PHIL		
06/20/45	46299	AROU-2		SAMAR	PHIL		
06/20/45	73299	AROU-2		SAMAR	PHIL		
06/20/45	73402	AROU-2		SAMAR	PHIL		
06/20/45	16859	POOL	PEARL	HAWAII	ECENPAC		
06/20/45	17029	POOL	PEARL	HAWAII	ECENPAC		
06/20/45	46035	POOL	PEARL	HAWAII	ECENPAC		
06/20/45	46290	POOL	PEARL	HAWAII	ECENPAC		

DATE	BUNO	SQDRN	BASE	LOST	AREA	PILOT	FATE
06/20/45	46305	POOL	PEARL	HAWAII	ECENPAC		
06/20/45	73174	POOL	PEARL	HAWAII	ECENPAC		
06/20/45	73198	POOL	PEARL	HAWAII	ECENPAC		
06/20/45	73210	POOL	PEARL	HAWAII	ECENPAC		
06/20/45	73224	POOL	PEARL	HAWAII	ECENPAC		
06/20/45	73227	POOL	PEARL	HAWAII	ECENPAC		
06/20/45	73246	POOL	PEARL	HAWAII	ECENPAC		
06/20/45	73251	POOL	PEARL	HAWAII	ECENPAC		
06/20/45	73261	POOL	PEARL	HAWAII	ECENPAC		
06/20/45	73416	POOL	PEARL	HAWAII	ECENPAC		
06/20/45	73428	POOL	PEARL	HAWAII	ECENPAC		
06/20/45	73453	POOL	PEARL	HAWAII	ECENPAC		
06/20/45	73462	POOL	PEARL	HAWAII	ECENPAC		
06/20/45	73475	POOL	PEARL	HAWAII	ECENPAC		
06/20/45	73492	POOL	PEARL	HAWAII	ECENPAC		
06/23/45	25372	CASU(F)-15		SAIPAN	WCENPAC		
06/23/45	45508	CASU(F)-15		SAIPAN	WCENPAC		
06/23/45	45512	CASU(F)-15		SAIPAN	WCENPAC		
06/23/45	45599	CASU(F)-15		SAIPAN	WCENPAC		
06/23/45	45799	CASU(F)-15		SAIPAN	WCENPAC		
06/23/45	45829	CASU(F)-15		SAIPAN	WCENPAC		
06/23/45	45836	CASU(F)-15		SAIPAN	WCENPAC		
06/23/45	46022	CASU(F)-15		SAIPAN	WCENPAC		
06/23/45	46043	CASU(F)-15		SAIPAN	WCENPAC		
06/23/45	46227	CASU(F)-15		SAIPAN	WCENPAC		
06/23/45	46306	CASU(F)-15		SAIPAN	WCENPAC		
06/23/45	46352	CASU(F)-15		SAIPAN	WCENPAC		
06/23/45	46420	CASU(F)-15		SAIPAN	WCENPAC		
06/23/45	46426	CASU(F)-15		SAIPAN	WCENPAC		
06/23/45	73179	CASU(F)-15		SAIPAN	WCENPAC		
06/23/45	73232	CASU(F)-15		SAIPAN	WCENPAC		
06/23/45	73242	CASU(F)-15		SAIPAN	WCENPAC		
06/23/45	73260	CASU(F)-15		SAIPAN	WCENPAC		
06/23/45	73323	CASU(F)-15		SAIPAN	WCENPAC		
06/23/45	73353	CASU(F)-15		SAIPAN	WCENPAC		
06/23/45	73437	CASU(F)-15		SAIPAN	WCENPAC		
06/25/45	45651	VJ-7	PEARL	HAWAII	ECENPAC	ENS NELSON S. NATHANSON	S
06/27/45	45661	VJ-9		PITYILU	SW PAC		
06/29/45	25646	CASU(F)-47		SAIPAN	WCENPAC		
06/29/45	45517	CASU(F)-47		SAIPAN	WCENPAC		
06/29/45	45691	CASU(F)-47		SAIPAN	WCENPAC		
06/29/45	73129	CASU(F)-47		SAIPAN	WCENPAC		
06/29/45	73244	CASU(F)-47		SAIPAN	WCENPAC		
06/30/45	16917	CASU(F)-14		SAIPAN	WCENPAC		
06/30/45	25330	CASU(F)-14		SAIPAN	WCENPAC		
06/30/45	45976	CASU(F)-14		SAIPAN	WCENPAC		
06/30/45	46243	CASU(F)-14		SAIPAN	WCENPAC		
06/30/45	16881	CASU(F)-20		ROI	WCENPAC		
06/30/45	17054	POOL	PEARL	HAWAII	ECENPAC		
06/30/45	25431	POOL	PEARL	HAWAII	ECENPAC		
06/30/45	45463	POOL	PEARL	HAWAII	ECENPAC		
06/30/45	45938	POOL	PEARL	HAWAII	ECENPAC		
06/30/45	46264	POOL	PEARL	HAWAII	ECENPAC		
06/30/45	46409	POOL	PEARL	HAWAII	ECENPAC		
06/30/45	16793	VT-99		SAIPAN	WCENPAC		
06/30/45	25577	VT-99		SAIPAN	WCENPAC		
06/30/45	45696	VT-99		SAIPAN	WCENPAC		
06/30/45	45954	VT-99		SAIPAN	WCENPAC		
06/30/45	46428	VT-99		SAIPAN	WCENPAC		
06/30/45	73185	VT-99		SAIPAN	WCENPAC		
06/30/45	73215	VT-99		SAIPAN	WCENPAC		
06/30/45	73238	VT-99		SAIPAN	WCENPAC		
06/30/45	73239	VT-99		SAIPAN	WCENPAC		
06/30/45	73340	VT-99		SAIPAN	WCENPAC		
06/30/45	73399	VT-99		SAIPAN	WCENPAC		
06/30/45	73495	VT-99		SAIPAN	WCENPAC		
07/05/45	45896	POOL	PEARL	HAWAII	ECENPAC		
07/05/45	46270	POOL	PEARL	HAWAII	ECENPAC		
07/05/45	73273	POOL	PEARL	HAWAII	ECENPAC		
07/05/45	73327	POOL	PEARL	HAWAII	ECENPAC		
07/05/45	73409	POOL	PEARL	HAWAII	ECENPAC		
07/05/45	73427	POOL	PEARL	HAWAII	ECENPAC		
07/05/45	73430	POOL	PEARL	HAWAII	ECENPAC		
07/05/45	25634	VJ-17		GUAM	WCENPAC		

DATE	BUNO	SQDRN	BASE	LOST	AREA	PILOT	FATE
07/08/45	46283	POOL	PEARL	HAWAII	ECENPAC		
07/08/45	73388	POOL	PEARL	HAWAII	ECENPAC		
07/13/45	45537	AROU-2		SAMAR	PHIL		
07/13/45	73498	VMTB-134		PELELIU	WCENPAC		
07/16/45	46055	AROU-2		SAMAR	PHIL		
07/16/45	73445	AROU-2		SAMAR	PHIL		
07/16/45	25428	VT-100	USS SARATOGA	HAWAII	ECENPAC	ENS JOHN K. TOMPSON	S
07/20/45	16964	AROU-1		MOMOTE	SW PAC		
07/20/45	25409	AROU-1		MOMOTE	SW PAC		
07/20/45	45644	AROU-1		MOMOTE	SW PAC		
07/20/45	46174	AROU-1		MOMOTE	SW PAC		
07/20/45	73345	AROU-1		MOMOTE	SW PAC		
07/24/45	46046	CASU(F)-47		SAIPAN	WCENPAC		
07/24/45	46229	CASU(F)-47		SAIPAN	WCENPAC		
07/25/45	45979	AROU-2		SAMAR	PHIL		
07/25/45	73337	AROU-2		SAMAR	PHIL		
07/25/45	73457	AROU-2		SAMAR	PHIL		
07/26/45	16814	CASU(F)-12		GUAM	WCENPAC		
07/26/45	16852	CASU(F)-12		GUAM	WCENPAC		
07/26/45	16911	CASU(F)-12		GUAM	WCENPAC		
07/26/45	16921	CASU(F)-12		GUAM	WCENPAC		
07/26/45	16937	CASU(F)-12		GUAM	WCENPAC		
07/26/45	25184	CASU(F)-12		GUAM	WCENPAC		
07/26/45	25467	CASU(F)-12		GUAM	WCENPAC		
07/26/45	25545	CASU(F)-12		GUAM	WCENPAC		
07/26/45	25629	CASU(F)-12		GUAM	WCENPAC		
07/26/45	25654	CASU(F)-12		GUAM	WCENPAC		
07/26/45	45474	CASU(F)-12		GUAM	WCENPAC		
07/26/45	45527	CASU(F)-12		GUAM	WCENPAC		
07/26/45	45816	CASU(F)-12		GUAM	WCENPAC		
07/26/45	45965	CASU(F)-12		GUAM	WCENPAC		
07/26/45	45973	CASU(F)-12		GUAM	WCENPAC		
07/28/45	16860	POOL	PEARL	HAWAII	ECENPAC		
07/31/45	46047	COMPHIB			PHIL		
08/01/45	25667	1ST MAW		TIENTSIN	EMPIRE		
08/03/45	73159	AROU-2		SAMAR	PHIL		
08/03/45	73192	AROU-2		SAMAR	PHIL		
08/09/45	16893	POOL	PEARL	HAWAII	ECENPAC		
08/09/45	16907	POOL	PEARL	HAWAII	ECENPAC		
08/09/45	17034	POOL	PEARL	HAWAII	ECENPAC		
08/09/45	17037	POOL	PEARL	HAWAII	ECENPAC		
08/09/45	45543	POOL	PEARL	HAWAII	ECENPAC		
08/09/45	45594	POOL	PEARL	HAWAII	ECENPAC		
08/09/45	45937	POOL	PEARL	HAWAII	ECENPAC		
08/09/45	45968	POOL	PEARL	HAWAII	ECENPAC		
08/09/45	46006	POOL	PEARL	HAWAII	ECENPAC		
08/09/45	46228	POOL	PEARL	HAWAII	ECENPAC		
08/09/45	73184	POOL	PEARL	HAWAII	ECENPAC		
08/09/45	73349	SERVRON-24		LINGAYEN GULF	PHIL		
08/13/45	73119	AROU-1		MOMOTE	SW PAC		
08/13/45	73454	AROU-1		MOMOTE	SW PAC		
08/13/45	73494	AROU-1		MOMOTE	SW PAC		

GENERAL MOTORS TBM-3

The General Motors TBM-3 was its TBM-1C with double cooling intakes, an engine upgrade, and some minor changes. There were 4,011 built by GM. Aircraft lost:

DATE	BUNO	SQDRN	BASE	LOST	AREA	PILOT	FATE
00/00/00	68483	VPB-200		HAWAII	ECENPAC	LCDR PAUL F. NAGLE	U
09/21/44	22949	VC-8	USS CARD		NORLANT	LTJG DONALD G. BECK	S
10/07/44	22894	VC-8	USS CARD		NORLANT	LTJG R.K. BURKE	S
10/13/44	22952	VC-69	USS GUADAL-CANAL		NORLANT	LTJG ROBERT M. BASSETT	S
10/13/44	23162	VC-86	USS BISMARCK SEA	ENR LEYTE GULF	CENPAC	ENS HARDY H. SANDVIG	S

DATE	BUNO	SQDRN	BASE	LOST	AREA	PILOT	FATE
10/13/44	23233	VC-86	USS BISMARCK SEA	ENR LEYTE GULF	CENPAC	ENS WILLIAM T. BRANNEN	S
10/17/44	22893	VT-82	USS BENNING-TON		NORLANT	ENS J.G. BAGOT	S
11/04/44	22968	VC-55	USS CROATAN		CENLANT	ENS JOHN D. ANDERSON	D
11/05/44	68554	VT-15	USS ESSEX	LUZON	PHIL	LT R.D. COSGROVE	S
11/05/44	23010	VT-80	USS TICONDER-OGA	CAVITE	PHIL	ENS LAWRENCE C. JEALSEN	M
11/11/44	22915	VT-80	USS TICONDER-OGA	CAVITE	PHIL	ENS C.W. HIGMAN	S
11/11/44	23039	VT-80	USS TICONDER-OGA	CAVITE	PHIL	LTJG ROBERT H. O'REILLY	M
11/14/44	23024	VC-84	USS MAKIN ISLAND	ENR LEYTE GULF	SW PAC		
11/14/44	23152	VC-86	USS BISMARCK SEA	MANILA	PHIL	ENS R. W. EASTERBROCK	D
11/15/44	23256	VC-85	USS LUNGA POINT	LEYTE GULF	PHIL	ENS CLIFFORD E. SEEMAN	S
11/20/44	22970	VT(N)-90	BARBERS POINT	HAWAII	ECENPAC	ENS JAMES L. CRANE	U
11/21/44	23646	VC-42	USS SHAM-ROCK BAY	BALBOA	ECENPAC	LT LAURENCE B. CHUTE	S
11/21/44	23106	VT-9	USS MAKASSAR STR.	HAWAII	ECENPAC	LT WILLIAM H. PEARCE	S
11/25/44	23650	VC-42	USS SHAM-ROCK BAY	BALBOA	ECENPAC	LTJG PATRICK J. CARTER	S
11/25/44	23139	VC-85	USS LUNGA POINT	ENR MANUS	WCENPAC	ENS WILBUR F. BERAVER	D
11/25/44	23230	VC-85	USS LUNGA POINT	ENR MANUS	WCENPAC	LT FRED C. HARRIMAN	S
11/25/44	23174	VC-87	USS SALAMAUA	ENR ADMIRALTIES	SW PAC		
11/27/44	23223	CASU(F)-42		PITYILU	SW PAC		
11/27/44	68468	VC-20	USS KADASHAN BAY	MANUS	SW PAC	ENS HANS L. JENSEN	D
11/27/44	22924	VC-90	USS STEAMER BAY	PEARL	ECENPAC	ENS GEORGE F. ARCHER	S
11/30/44	23155	AWT ACTION	PEARL	HAWAII	ECENPAC		
12/02/44	23221	VT-45	USS SAN JACINTO	ENR MANILA	PHIL		
12/03/44	23347	VC-88	USS HOGGATT BAY	MARIANAS	CENPAC	LT C. L. HERBSTER	S
12/06/44	22880	VC-91	USS KIT-KUN BAY	ENR MANUS	WCENPAC	ENS CLAGGETT H. HAWKINS	D
12/13/44	68606	VC-13	USS KASAAN BAY	ENR HAWAII	ECENPAC		
12/16/44	23371	VC-84	USS MAKIN ISLAND	ENR LEYTE GULF	SW PAC		
12/18/44	22932	UNASSIGN ED	USS CAPE ESPERANC E	PHILIPPINE SEA	PHIL	(DECK LOSS-TYPHOON)	
12/18/44	22940	UNASSIGN ED	USS CAPE ESPER-ANCE	PHILIPPINE SEA	PHIL	(DECK LOSS-TYPHOON)	
12/18/44	23020	UNASSIGN ED	USS CAPE ESPER-ANCE	PHILIPPINE SEA	PHIL	(DECK LOSS-TYPHOON)	

DATE	BUNO	SQDRN	BASE	LOST	AREA	PILOT	FATE
12/18/44	23053	UNASSIGNED	USS CAPE ESPERANCE	PHILIPPINE SEA	PHIL	(DECK LOSS-TYPHOON)	
12/18/44	23098	UNASSIGNED	USS ALTAMAHA	PHILIPPINE SEA	PHIL	(DECK LOSS-TYPHOON)	
12/18/44	23100	UNASSIGNED	USS CAPE ESPER-ANCE	PHILIPPINE SEA	PHIL	(DECK LOSS-TYPHOON)	
12/18/44	23112	UNASSIGNED	USS ALTAMAHA	PHILIPPINE SEA	PHIL	(DECK LOSS-TYPHOON)	
12/18/44	23121	UNASSIGNED	USS CAPE ESPER-ANCE	PHILIPPINE SEA	PHIL	(DECK LOSS-TYPHOON)	
12/18/44	23132	UNASSIGNED	USS CAPE ESPERANCE	PHILIPPINE SEA	PHIL	(DECK LOSS-TYPHOON)	
12/18/44	23168	UNASSIGNED	USS CAPE ESPER-ANCE	PHILIPPINE SEA	PHIL	(DECK LOSS-TYPHOON)	
12/18/44	23172	UNASSIGNED	USS CAPE ESPERANCE	PHILIPPINE SEA	PHIL	(DECK LOSS-TYPHOON)	
12/18/44	23184	UNASSIGNED	USS CAPE ESPERANCE	PHILIPPINE SEA	PHIL	(DECK LOSS-TYPHOON)	
12/18/44	23231	UNASSIGNED	USS CAPE ESPER-ANCE	PHILIPPINE SEA	PHIL	(DECK LOSS-TYPHOON)	
12/18/44	23237	UNASSIGNED	USS ALTAMAHA	PHILIPPINE SEA	PHIL	(DECK LOSS-TYPHOON)	
12/18/44	23266	UNASSIGNED	USS ALTAMAHA	PHILIPPINE SEA	PHIL	(DECK LOSS-TYPHOON)	
12/18/44	23275	UNASSIGNED	USS ALTAMAHA	PHILIPPINE SEA	PHIL	(DECK LOSS-TYPHOON)	
12/18/44	23283	UNASSIGNED	USS ALTAMAHA	PHILIPPINE SEA	PHIL	(DECK LOSS-TYPHOON)	
12/18/44	23284	UNASSIGNED	USS ALTAMAHA	PHILIPPINE SEA	PHIL	(DECK LOSS-TYPHOON)	
12/18/44	23293	UNASSIGNED	USS ALTAMAHA	PHILIPPINE SEA	PHIL	(DECK LOSS-TYPHOON)	
12/18/44	23321	UNASSIGNED	USS ALTAMAHA	PHILIPPINE SEA	PHIL	(DECK LOSS-TYPHOON)	
12/18/44	23250	VT-28	USS MONTEREY	PHILIPPINE SEA	PHIL	(DECK LOSS-TYPHOON)	
12/18/44	23457	VT-28	USS MONTEREY	PHILIPPINE SEA	PHIL	(DECK LOSS-TYPHOON)	
12/18/44	23433	VT-45	USS SAN JACINTO	PHILIPPINE SEA	PHIL	(DECK LOSS-TYPHOON)	
12/21/44	23648	VC-3	HAWAII		ECENPAC	LTJG MALCOLM W. WILLIAMS	S
12/22/44	23477	VMTB-131		GUAM	WCENPAC		
12/26/44	23185	COMAIR-PAC	PEARL	HAWAII	ECENPAC		
12/28/44	23148	CASU(F)-42		PITYILU	SW PAC		
12/28/44	23161	CASU(F)-42		PITYILU	SW PAC		
12/28/44	23238	CASU(F)-42		PITYILU	SW PAC		
12/28/44	68215	VC-94	USS SHAM-ROCK BAY	MANUS	SW PAC	ENS ROBERT F. MASON	S
12/28/44	23018	VT-47	PUUNENE	HAWAII	ECENPAC		
12/30/44	23429	VT-7	USS HANCOCK	ULITHI	WCENPAC		
01/04/45	23449	VC-75	USS OMMANEY BAY	MINDORO STRAIT	PHIL	(SHIP SANK)	
01/06/45	23232	VC-84	USS MAKIN ISLAND	LINGAYEN GULF	PHIL		
01/06/45	23235	VC-92	USS TULAGI	MINDORO STRAIT	PHIL		
01/06/45	23370	VC-92	USS TULAGI	MINDORO STRAIT	PHIL		
01/07/45	23414	VC-84	USS MAKIN ISLAND	LUZON	PHIL	ENS WILLIAM T. WORDEN	S
01/07/45	23469	VC-90	USS STEAMER BAY	LINGAYEN GULF	PHIL	ENS WM. F. FROTHINGHAM	D

DATE	BUNO	SQDRN	BASE	LOST	AREA	PILOT	FATE
01/07/45	23269	VC-92	USS TULAGI	SO. CHINA SEA	PHIL	LT DONALD D. DILLY	M
01/09/45	53213	VC-94	USS SHAMROCK BAY	LUZON	PHIL		
01/10/45	23192	VC-92	USS TULAGI	LINGAYEN GULF	PHIL		
01/10/45	68211	VC-94	USS SHAMROCK BAY	LUZON	PHIL	ENS LAWRENCE D. ABBUTT	D
01/11/45	22933	VC-85	USS LUNGA POINT	LINGAYEN GULF	PHIL	ENS ARTHUR W. GILKEY	M
01/11/45	23188	VC-87	USS SALAMAUA	LINGAYEN GULF	PHIL	LTJG FRED J. STOCK, JR.	S
01/12/45	68224	VC-80	USS MANILA BAY	SOUTH CHINA SEA	PHIL		
01/12/45	68078	VT-45	USS SAN JACINTO	FORMOSA	EMPIRE	ENS PETER LANBROS	S
01/12/45	23229	VT-7	USS HANCOCK	FR. I.C.	PHIL		
01/14/45	23236	VC-87	USS SALAMAUA	LINGAYEN GULF	PHIL	(DECK LOSS-KAMIKAZE)	
01/14/45	23187	VC-88	USS HOGGATT BAY	LINGAYEN GULF	PHIL	ENS FRANKLIN E. FAIRHURST	S
01/14/45	68223	VC-94	USS SHAMROCK BAY	LUZON	PHIL	LTJG E.R. DATHE	S
01/15/45	23300	VC-88	USS HOGGATT BAY	LINGAYEN GULF	PHIL	ENS C.E. MINICK	M
01/15/45	23365	VC-88	USS HOGGATT BAY	LINGAYEN GULF	PHIL	LCDR E.N. WEBB	D
01/15/45	23122	VC-92	USS TULAGI	LINGAYEN GULF	PHIL	LTJG HARPER	S
01/15/45	23099	VT-45	USS SAN JACINTO	FORMOSA	EMPIRE	LT FLOYD J. BARTOGLIA	S
01/15/45	23254	VT-7	USS HANCOCK	ENR H. KONG	EMPIRE		
01/16/45	23163	VC-85	USS LUNGA POINT	LINGAYEN GULF	PHIL	LTJG W.J. MURRAY	S
01/16/45	23399	VMF-313		PONAM	SW PAC	ENS JAMES M. FALKER	S
01/16/45	23445	VMF-313		PONAM	SW PAC	ENS ROBERT E. FITZGERALD	S
01/16/45	22926	VT-80	USS TICONDEROGA	HAINAN	EMPIRE	ENS EDWIN D. RUEGG	M
01/16/45	23253	VT-80	USS TICONDEROGA	HAINAN	EMPIRE		
01/17/45	23164	VC-85	USS LUNGA POINT	LINGAYEN GULF	PHIL	LTJG ROBERT C. REILLY	S
01/17/45	23314	VT-45	USS SAN JACINTO	FORMOSA	EMPIRE		
01/21/45	23539	VT-7	USS HANCOCK	FORMOSA	EMPIRE	LTJG C.R. DEAN	D
01/21/45	22930	VT-80	USS TICONDEROGA	FORMOSA	EMPIRE		
01/21/45	22942	VT-80	USS TICONDEROGA	FORMOSA	EMPIRE		
01/21/45	23031	VT-80	USS TICONDEROGA	FORMOSA	EMPIRE		
01/21/45	23036	VT-80	USS TICONDEROGA	FORMOSA	EMPIRE		
01/21/45	23276	VT-80	USS TICONDEROGA	FORMOSA	EMPIRE	LT JOHN CARMODY	S
01/21/45	23549	VT-80	USS TICONDEROGA	FORMOSA	EMPIRE		

DATE	BUNO	SQDRN	BASE	LOST	AREA	PILOT	FATE
01/22/45	22916	VT-80	USS TICONDER-OGA	FORMOSA	EMPIRE		
01/27/45	68358	VC-8	HAWAII		ECENPAC	ENS HOWARD NAGEL	S
01/30/45	22937	VT(N)-53	USS SARATOGA	IWO JIMA	EMPIRE	ENS WALTER J. BENNETT	D
01/31/45	22919	CASU(F)-51		ULITHI	WCENPAC		
02/03/45	22957	VC-58	USS CORE		NORLANT	LTJG HARRY D. OROUTT	S
02/04/45	23118	POOL		SAMAR	PHIL		
02/06/45	23137	CASU(F)-13		PITYILU	SW PAC		
02/06/45	23154	CASU(F)-13		PITYILU	SW PAC		
02/07/45	68425	VT-24	USS SANTEE	HAWAII	ECENPAC	LTJG TRAVIS N. POWELL	S
02/07/45	68724	VT-24	USS SANTEE	HAWAII	ECENPAC	ENS ALFRED C. HOLMES	S
02/12/45	23075	VC-58	USS CORE		CENLANT	LT DOUGLAS W. BROOKS	S
02/12/45	23511	VC-99	USS TRIPOLI	HAWAII	ECENPAC	ENS A.F. WILHELM	S
02/12/45	68245	VT-82	USS BENNING-TON		WCENPAC	ENS PAUL COCHRAN	S
02/13/45	68482	VT-40	USS SU-WANNEE		SOPAC	LTJG O.F. SLINGERLAND	S
02/15/45	22995	VC-58	USS CORE		CENLANT	LT HOLMITH	S
02/15/45	68371	VT-40	USS SU-WANNEE		SOPAC		
02/16/45	68171	VOC-1	USS WAKE ISLAND	IWO JIMA	EMPIRE	ENS L.A. WOOD	S
02/16/45	23225	VT-17	USS HORNET	TOKYO	EMPIRE		
02/16/45	22959	VT-82	USS BENNING-TON	HACAYO JIMA	EMPIRE	ENS H.S. FLICKENGER	M
02/16/45	68239	VT-82	USS BENNING-TON	HACAYO JIMA	EMPIRE	LCDR D. SARMO	S
02/16/45	67316	VT-84	USS BUNKER HILL	TOKYO	EMPIRE	ENS RICHARD SOUTHERN	M
02/16/45	68451	VT-84	USS BUNKER HILL	TOKYO	EMPIRE	ENS ARTHUR PORTER	M
02/17/45	68303	VT(N)-90	USS ENTER-PRISE	TOKYO	EMPIRE	ENS JOHN W. STUCKEY	S
02/17/45	23476	VT-23	USS LANGLEY	IWO JIMA	EMPIRE	ENS EUGENE C. CONAGISKIE	M
02/18/45	23023	VT(N)-53	USS SARATOGA	TOKYO	EMPIRE		
02/18/45	23517	VT-12	USS RANDOLPH	IWO JIMA	EMPIRE	ENS R.F. ROHLING	S
02/18/45	23637	VT-12	USS RANDOLPH	IWO JIMA	EMPIRE	ENS F.E. HALL	M
02/18/45	22889	VT-82	USS BENNING-TON	IWO JIMA	EMPIRE	ENS R. COSBIE	D
02/18/45	22904	VT-82	USS BENNING-TON	IWO JIMA	EMPIRE	ENS R.T. KING	M
02/18/45	22977	VT-82	USS BENNING-TON	IWO JIMA	EMPIRE		
02/19/45	22928	VC-88	USS SAGINAW BAY	IWO JIMA	EMPIRE		
02/19/45	23014	VC-90	USS STEAMER BAY	NANPO SHOTO	EMPIRE		
02/19/45	68438	VT-33		HAWAII	ECENPAC		
02/19/45	68492	VT-84	USS BUNKER HILL	IWO JIMA	EMPIRE	LT TURNBULL	S
02/20/45	68816	AA & RH		HAWAII	ECENPAC		

DATE	BUNO	SQDRN	BASE	LOST	AREA	PILOT	FATE
02/20/45	23159	VC-88	USS SAGINAW BAY	IWO JIMA	EMPIRE	LT C.L. HERBSTER	S
02/20/45	23281	VT-17	USS WASP	IWO JIMA	EMPIRE		
02/20/45	23303	VT-45	USS SAN JACINTO		EMPIRE		
02/21/45	23005	VC-86	USS BISMARCK SEA	IWO JIMA	EMPIRE	(SHIP SANK)	
02/21/45	23124	VC-86	USS BISMARCK SEA	IWO JIMA	EMPIRE	(SHIP SANK)	
02/21/45	23125	VC-86	USS BISMARCK SEA	IWO JIMA	EMPIRE	(SHIP SANK)	
02/21/45	23140	VC-86	USS BISMARCK SEA	IWO JIMA	EMPIRE	(SHIP SANK)	
02/21/45	23149	VC-86	USS BISMARCK SEA	IWO JIMA	EMPIRE	(SHIP SANK)	
02/21/45	23158	VC-86	USS BISMARCK SEA	IWO JIMA	EMPIRE	(SHIP SANK)	
02/21/45	23183	VC-86	USS BISMARCK SEA	IWO JIMA	EMPIRE	(SHIP SANK)	
02/21/45	23222	VC-86	USS BISMARCK SEA	IWO JIMA	EMPIRE	(SHIP SANK)	
02/21/45	23462	VC-86	USS BISMARCK SEA	IWO JIMA	EMPIRE	(SHIP SANK)	
02/21/45	23588	VC-86	USS BISMARCK SEA	IWO JIMA	EMPIRE	(SHIP SANK)	
02/21/45	68380	VC-86	USS BISMARCK SEA	IWO JIMA	EMPIRE	(SHIP SANK)	
02/21/45	23386	VMTB-242		TINIAN	WCENPAC	2NDLT WILLIAM J. HINES	S
02/21/45	22946	VT(N)-53	USS SARATOGA	TOKYO	EMPIRE		
02/21/45	23017	VT(N)-53	USS SARATOGA	TOKYO	EMPIRE		
02/21/45	23375	VT(N)-53	USS SARATOGA	TOKYO	EMPIRE		
02/21/45	23384	VT(N)-53	USS SARATOGA	TOKYO	EMPIRE		
02/21/45	23554	VT(N)-53	USS SARATOGA	TOKYO	EMPIRE		
02/21/45	23568	VT(N)-53	USS SARATOGA	TOKYO	EMPIRE		
02/21/45	23583	VT(N)-53	USS SARATOGA	TOKYO	EMPIRE		
02/21/45	68283	VT(N)-53	USS SARATOGA	TOKYO	EMPIRE		
02/21/45	23504	VT-12	USS RANDOLPH	TOKYO	EMPIRE		
02/21/45	23636	VT-12	USS RANDOLPH	TOKYO	EMPIRE		
02/21/45	23642	VT-12	USS RANDOLPH	TOKYO	EMPIRE		
02/21/45	68138	VT-12	USS RANDOLPH	TOKYO	EMPIRE		
02/21/45	23295	VT-46	USS COWPENS	IWO JIMA	EMPIRE		
02/21/45	23157	VT-82	USS BENNING-TON	IWO JIMA	EMPIRE		
02/21/45	68475	VT-9	USS LEX-INGTON	IWO JIMA	EMPIRE	LTJG WALTER A. JACOBS	D
02/22/45	23382	VT(N)-90	USS ENTER-PRISE		EMPIRE		

DATE	BUNO	SQDRN	BASE	LOST	AREA	PILOT	FATE
02/22/45	23473	VT(N)-90	USS ENTER-PRISE		EMPIRE	LT E.B. COLLINS, JR.	M
02/22/45	68173	VT-82	USS BENNING-TON	IWO JIMA	EMPIRE		
02/23/45	23649	VC-99	USS FANSHAW BAY	HAWAII	ECENPAC	LTJG WARD J. TAYLOR	S
02/23/45	23436	VT-23	USS LANGLEY	IWO JIMA	EMPIRE	ENS R.W. WETZEL	D
02/24/45	22964	VC-90	USS STEAMER BAY	IWO JIMA	EMPIRE	LTJG JACK F. BLOOMER	M
02/25/45	23076	VC-58	USS CORE		NORLANT	LT SAMUEL D. PARSONS	S
02/25/45	22874	VT-45	USS SAN JACINTO		EMPIRE		
02/25/45	68094	VT-80	USS HANCOCK	IWO JIMA	EMPIRE		
02/26/45	23160		USS WAKE ISLAND		EMPIRE		
02/26/45	68221	VT(N)-90	USS ENTER-PRISE	IWO JIMA	EMPIRE	LT MOORE	S
02/26/45	68287	VT-40	USS SU-WANNEE		WCENPAC		
02/26/45	69461	VT-40	USS SU-WANNEE		WCENPAC		
02/27/45	68755	VT-25	USS CHE-NANGO		SOPAC	ENS ERNEST R. THOMSON	S
02/28/45	23282	VC-85	USS LUNGA POINT	IWO JIMA	EMPIRE	ENS RICHARD S. SHIPPE	S
03/01/45	23046	VC-85	USS LUNGA POINT	IWO JIMA	EMPIRE	LTJG ALBERT M. SARLECH	D
03/01/45	68420	VT-30	USS BELLEAU WOOD	IE SHIMA	EMPIRE	LT JACOB M. REISERT	D
03/01/45	68515	VT-30	USS BELLEAU WOOD	IE SHIMA	EMPIRE	ENS C.D. BAYLES	S
03/01/45	23210	VT-4	USS ESSEX	OKINAWA	EMPIRE	LTJG NORMAN K. VOGT	S
03/01/45	23310	VT-45	USS SAN JACINTO	OKINAWA	EMPIRE	ENS JOHN L. MASON	S
03/05/45	23166	VC-84	USS MAKIN ISLAND	IWO JIMA	EMPIRE	LT GLASGOW	S
03/05/45	23442	VC-84	USS MAKIN ISLAND	IWO JIMA	EMPIRE	ENS HORACE D. HARPER	S
03/06/45	23551	VC-87	USS MARCUS ISLAND	OKINAWA	EMPIRE	LTJG FREDERICK J.T. STOCK	S
03/06/45	68124	VC-88	USS SAGINAW BAY	IWO JIMA	EMPIRE	ENS PROVOST	U
03/07/45	23494	VC-99		KAHULUI	ECENPAC		
03/10/45	23428	VT-12	USS RANDOLPH	ULITHI	WCENPAC	ENS HOWARD M. ALLEN	S
03/11/45	23633	VC-6	USS GUADAL-CANAL	CUBA	CENLANT	ENS HELGE J. AXELSON	S
03/11/45	68310	VT-12	USS RANDOLPH	ULITHI	WCENPAC		
03/11/45	68464	VT-12	USS RANDOLPH	ULITHI	WCENPAC		
03/14/45	68432	VT-84	USS BUNKER HILL	ULITHI	WCENPAC	LTJG FREDERICK R. MORGAN	D
03/14/45	68450	VT-84	USS BUNKER HILL	ULITHI	WCENPAC		
03/15/45	23573	VT(N)-90	USS ENTER-PRISE	HAWAII	ECENPAC		

DATE	BUNO	SQDRN	BASE	LOST	AREA	PILOT	FATE
03/15/45	23315	VT-17	USS HORNET	ENR HONSHU	EMPIRE		
03/15/45	68103	VT-83	USS ESSEX	OKINAWA	EMPIRE		
03/16/45	68526	VMTB-232		YAP	WCENPAC	2NDLT JOSEPH CROWLEY	M
03/18/45	68487	VT-30	USS BELLEAU WOOD	IE SHIMA	EMPIRE	LT FREDERICK C. TETHILL	M
03/18/45	68782	VT-45	USS SAN JACINTO	KYUSHU	EMPIRE	LT WOODROW J. VAN HOREN	S
03/18/45	68493	VT-47	USS BATAAN	KYUSHU	EMPIRE	ENS DAVID C. LOOMIS	M
03/18/45	68499	VT-47	USS BATAAN	KYUSHU	EMPIRE	ENS JAMES A. MARVIN	M
03/18/45	22895	VT-82	USS BENNING-TON	KYUSHU	EMPIRE	ENS SCHOUBOE	S
03/18/45		VT-83	USS ESSEX	KYUSHU	EMPIRE	ENS JOHN L. KIERMAN	D
03/19/45	68113	VC-97	USS MAKASSAR STR.		EMPIRE		
03/19/45	23430	VMTB-242		TINIAN	WCENPAC		
03/19/45	68988	VT-10	USS INTREPID	HONSHU	EMPIRE		
03/19/45	68064	VT-17	USS HORNET	HONSHU	EMPIRE	LTJG T. WESTMORELAND	M
03/19/45	23483	VT-40	USS SU-WANNEE	ULITHI	WCENPAC	ENS RAYMOND T. BURNS	S
03/19/45	68265	VT-5	USS FRANKLIN	HONSHU	EMPIRE	(DECK LOSS-KAMIKAZE)	
03/19/45	68315	VT-5	USS FRANKLIN	HONSHU	EMPIRE	(DECK LOSS-KAMIKAZE)	
03/19/45	68378	VT-5	USS FRANKLIN	HONSHU	EMPIRE	(DECK LOSS-KAMIKAZE)	
03/19/45	68401	VT-5	USS FRANKLIN	HONSHU	EMPIRE	(DECK LOSS-KAMIKAZE)	
03/19/45	68421	VT-5	USS FRANKLIN	HONSHU	EMPIRE	(DECK LOSS-KAMIKAZE)	
03/19/45	68458	VT-5	USS FRANKLIN	HONSHU	EMPIRE	(DECK LOSS-KAMIKAZE)	
03/19/45	68588	VT-5	USS FRANKLIN	HONSHU	EMPIRE	(DECK LOSS-KAMIKAZE)	
03/19/45	68650	VT-5	USS FRANKLIN	HONSHU	EMPIRE	(DECK LOSS-KAMIKAZE)	
03/19/45	68661	VT-5	USS FRANKLIN	HONSHU	EMPIRE	(DECK LOSS-KAMIKAZE)	
03/19/45	68671	VT-5	USS FRANKLIN	HONSHU	EMPIRE	(DECK LOSS-KAMIKAZE)	
03/19/45	68678	VT-5	USS FRANKLIN	HONSHU	EMPIRE	(DECK LOSS-KAMIKAZE)	
03/19/45	68689	VT-5	USS FRANKLIN	HONSHU	EMPIRE	(DECK LOSS-KAMIKAZE)	
03/19/45	68692	VT-5	USS FRANKLIN	HONSHU	EMPIRE	(DECK LOSS-KAMIKAZE)	
03/19/45	68709	VT-5	USS FRANKLIN	HONSHU	EMPIRE	(DECK LOSS-KAMIKAZE)	
03/19/45	68710	VT-5	USS FRANKLIN	HONSHU	EMPIRE	(DECK LOSS-KAMIKAZE)	
03/19/45	68641	VT-83	USS ESSEX	HONSHU	EMPIRE		
03/20/45	23156	VC-97	USS MAKASSAR STR.		EMPIRE		
03/20/45	23555	VT-40	USS SU-WANNEE	ULITHI	WCENPAC	ENS RICHARD A. ADRIAN	S
03/21/45	68180	VC-97	USS MAKASSAR STR.		EMPIRE		
03/21/45	68534	VT-45	USS SAN JACINTO	KYUSHU	EMPIRE		
03/22/45	68583	VT-6	USS HANCOCK	IE SHIMA	EMPIRE		
03/23/45	69051	VC-96	USS RUDYERD BAY	IWO JIMA	EMPIRE		

DATE	BUNO	SQDRN	BASE	LOST	AREA	PILOT	FATE
03/23/45	68900	VT-10	USS INTREPID	OKINAWA	EMPIRE	LT W.J. MILLER	D
03/23/45	68938	VT-10	USS INTREPID	OKINAWA	EMPIRE		
03/23/45	68628	VT-29	USS CABOT	OKINAWA	EMPIRE	ENS A.H. GIDNEY	S
03/23/45	23594	VT-46	USS INDE-PENDENCE	OKINAWA	EMPIRE	ENS ARTHUR ROSENBURGH	S
03/24/45	68593	VC-63	USS MAKASSAR STR.	PEARL	ECENPAC	ENS R.G. DUBUQUE	S
03/24/45	23067	VC-90	USS STEAMER BAY		PHIL		
03/24/45	68510	VC-93	USS PET-ROF BAY	OKINAWA	EMPIRE	ENS JAMES M. WELLS	S
03/24/45	23395	VT-17	USS HORNET	ENR KYUSHU	EMPIRE	LTJG W.D. NIELSON	S
03/24/45	68312	VT-17	USS HORNET	ENR KYUSHU	EMPIRE	ENS W.E. HOOTON	M
03/24/45	68564	VT-30	USS BELLEAU WOOD	IE SHIMA	EMPIRE	LTJG FRANCID HEDGES	D
03/24/45	22924	VT-47	USS BATAAN	OKINAWA	EMPIRE		
03/25/45	68837	VC-83	USS SARGENT BAY	OKINAWA	EMPIRE	LTJG M. BOTEAN	S
03/25/45	68551	VT-17	USS HORNET	OKINAWA	EMPIRE	LT LIVENGOOD	S
03/26/45	68372	VT-47	USS BATAAN	OKINAWA	EMPIRE	ENS KENNETH A. LORING	S
03/26/45	23358	VT-9	USS YORK-TOWN	SHIMA	EMPIRE	LCDR COOKE	M
03/27/45	23095	VC-88	USS SAGINAW BAY	OKINAWA	EMPIRE		
03/27/45	23115	VC-9	USS NAT-OMA BAY	RHET.	EMPIRE	LTJG PETER H. HAZARD	M
03/27/45	68904	VT-10	USS INTREPID	OKINAWA	EMPIRE		
03/27/45	68272	VT-25	USS CHE-NANGO		WCENPAC	ENS FREDERICK S. ROYCE	S
03/27/45	68411	VT-30	USS BELLEAU WOOD	NANSEI SHOTO	EMPIRE		
03/27/45	68090	VT-33	USS SAN-GAMON	KEREMA RHET.	EMPIRE		
03/28/45	23306	VT-23	USS LANGLEY	OKINAWA	EMPIRE		
03/28/45	23576	VT-45	USS SAN JACINTO	OKINAWA	EMPIRE		
03/28/45	67417	VT-45	USS SAN JACINTO	OKINAWA	EMPIRE		
03/28/45	68481	VT-45	USS SAN JACINTO	OKINAWA	EMPIRE		
03/28/45	68813	VT-45	USS SAN JACINTO	OKINAWA	EMPIRE		
03/28/45	23147	VT-49		HAWAII	ECENPAC	ENS THOMAS S. HESTER	S
03/29/45	68562	VC-84	USS MAKIN ISLAND	OKINAWA	EMPIRE		
03/29/45	23265	VT-29	USS CABOT	KYUSHU	EMPIRE	LTJG R.N. MAHONEY	M
03/29/45	68281	VT-84	USS BUNKER HILL	OKINAWA	EMPIRE		
03/29/45	68440	VT-84	USS BUNKER HILL	OKINAWA	EMPIRE	ENS W.A. ELINGS	M
03/29/45	68455	VT-84	USS BUNKER HILL	OKINAWA	EMPIRE	LTJG MELVIN H. GEORGIUS	M
03/30/45	68812	VT-10	USS INTREPID	OKINAWA	EMPIRE		

DATE	BUNO	SQDRN	BASE	LOST	AREA	PILOT	FATE
03/31/45	23640	CASU(F)-31		ULITHI	WCENPAC		
03/31/45	68808	VT-25	USS CHENANGO		WCENPAC		
03/31/45	68521	VT-47	USS BATAAN	OKINAWA	EMPIRE		
04/01/45	23110	VT-29	USS CABOT	OKINAWA	EMPIRE	LTJG C.F. NORTON	S
04/01/45	23397	VT-83	USS ESSEX	OKINAWA	EMPIRE	LCDR STEWART	S
04/01/45	68433	VT-84	USS BUNKER HILL	AMAMI	EMPIRE		
04/02/45	68308	VT-33	USS SANGAMON	OKINAWA	EMPIRE		
04/02/45	68406	VT-33	USS SANGAMON	OKINAWA	EMPIRE		
04/02/45	68426	VT-33	USS SANGAMON	OKINAWA	EMPIRE		
04/02/45	68504	VT-40	USS SUWANNEE	OKINAWA	EMPIRE	LT EVERETTE G. TRULY	S
04/02/45	68452	VT-45	USS SAN JACINTO	OKINAWA	EMPIRE	ENS CARLTON L. SHARP, JR.	M
04/03/45	68188	VC-96	USS RUDYERD BAY	OKINAWA	EMPIRE		
04/03/45	68479	VMTB-233	USS BLOCK ISLAND	HAWAII	ECENPAC	CAPT RICHARD W. JOHNSON	S
04/03/45	68893	VMTB-233	USS BLOCK ISLAND	HAWAII	ECENPAC	2NDLT JACK MARCONI	S
04/03/45	68570	VT-25	USS CHENANGO	OKINAWA	EMPIRE		
04/03/45	68393	VT-45	USS SAN JACINTO	MAYAKO	EMPIRE	LTJG CARL WILBUR DYZORT	M
04/03/45	23218	VT-83	USS ESSEX	OKINAWA	EMPIRE		
04/04/45	23160	VC-92	USS TULAGI	OKINAWA	EMPIRE	ENS PAUL J. GARRISON	S
04/04/45	68791	VT-24	USS SANTEE	OKINAWA	EMPIRE	ENS C.G. BORGLUM	S
04/05/45	68772	VT-24	USS SANTEE	OKINAWA	EMPIRE	ENS ROBERT A. OVELLETTE	S
04/05/45	68560	VT-9	USS YORKTOWN	IWO JIMA	EMPIRE	LTJG E.D. KEMP	S
04/06/45	23392	VT-46	USS INDEPENDENCE	GUNTO	EMPIRE	ENS JOHN A. TASHIRHART	S
04/07/45	23448	VT-17	USS HORNET	OKINAWA	EMPIRE	ENS LEE O'BRIEN	M
04/07/45	68477	VT-17	USS HORNET	OKINAWA	EMPIRE		
04/07/45	68457	VT-30	USS BELLEAU WOOD	KYUSHU	EMPIRE	LTJG W.E. DELANEY	S
04/07/45	68292	VT-47	USS BATAAN	OKINAWA	EMPIRE	LT COLLINS	S
04/07/45	68198	VT-82	USS BENNINGTON	KYUSHU	EMPIRE	LT N.A. WIESE	S
04/07/45	68148	VT-84	USS BUNKER HILL	KYUSHU	EMPIRE	ENS GUTTENBERGER	S
04/07/45	68446	VT-84	USS BUNKER HILL	KYUSHU	EMPIRE	LTJG RICHARD J. WALSH, JR.	M
04/07/45	68648	VT-84	USS BUNKER HILL	KYUSHU	EMPIRE		
04/08/45	22936	VC-85	USS LUNGA POINT	IE SHIMA	EMPIRE	LTJG ROBERT N. CRON	S
04/08/45	23536	VT-25	USS CHENANGO	IE SHIMA	EMPIRE	ENS WALTER J. NASLANKA	S
04/09/45	68580	VC-42	USS CORREGIDOR	WOTJE	CENPAC	LTJG KENNETH R. HARLOW	S

DATE	BUNO	SQDRN	BASE	LOST	AREA	PILOT	FATE
04/10/45	22967	VC-95	USS MISSION BAY		NORLANT	ENS VESTAL L. COOK	S
04/11/45	23533	VT(N)-90	USS ENTER-PRISE	OKINAWA	EMPIRE	CUMMINGS	S
04/12/45	23299	VMTB-242		TINIAN	WCENPAC		
04/12/45	23369	VT(N)-90	USS ENTER-PRISE	OKINAWA	EMPIRE	(DECK LOSS-KAMIKAZE)	
04/13/45	23586	VT(N)-91		HAWAII	ECENPAC	ENS RICHARD S. ALLEN	S
04/14/45	69420	VC-55	USS CROATAN	ARGENTIA	NORLANT	ENS GENE W. RICHARDS	S
04/14/45	23471	VC-92	USS TULAGI	OKINAWA	EMPIRE	HAROLD MORRISSEY	U
04/14/45	68274	VC-96	USS RUDYERD BAY	MIYAKO	EMPIRE	LTJG PHILIP E. BROU	S
04/15/45	23136	CASU(F)-15		SAIPAN	WCENPAC		
04/15/45	68767	VC-97	USS MAKASSAR STR.	OKINAWA	EMPIRE	LT V.L. TEBO, JR.	M
04/15/45	23311	VOC-1	USS MARCUS ISLAND	IE SHIMA	EMPIRE	ENS FRITZ H.E. LARSON	S
04/15/45	23400	VT-83	USS ESSEX	OKINAWA	EMPIRE		
04/16/45	23599	VC-93	USS PET-ROF BAY	IE SHIMA	EMPIRE	LTJG MALCOLM W. WILLIAMS	S
04/16/45	23545	VT-10	USS INTREPID	KOKUBO	EMPIRE		
04/16/45	23560	VT-10	USS INTREPID	KOKUBO	EMPIRE		
04/16/45	68839	VT-10	USS INTREPID	KOKUBO	EMPIRE		
04/16/45	68878	VT-10	USS INTREPID	KOKUBO	EMPIRE		
04/16/45	68886	VT-10	USS INTREPID	KOKUBO	EMPIRE		
04/16/45	68903	VT-10	USS INTREPID	KOKUBO	EMPIRE		
04/16/45	68912	VT-10	USS INTREPID	KOKUBO	EMPIRE		
04/16/45	68929	VT-10	USS INTREPID	KOKUBO	EMPIRE		
04/16/45	68957	VT-10	USS INTREPID	KOKUBO	EMPIRE		
04/16/45	68983	VT-10	USS INTREPID	KOKUBO	EMPIRE		
04/18/45	22888	VC-55	USS CROATAN	ARGENTIA	NORLANT	LT CALVIN E. MANSELL	S
04/19/45	68777	VT-25	USS CHE-NANGO	IE SHIMA	EMPIRE		
04/21/45	68819	VC-83	USS SARGENT BAY	OKINAWA	EMPIRE		
04/23/45	69074	VT-1	KAHULUI	HAWAII	ECENPAC		
04/23/45	23627	VT-23	USS LANGLEY	OKINAWA	EMPIRE		
04/23/45	68688	VT-24	USS SANTEE	IWO JIMA	EMPIRE	ENS JOSEPH F. FLORENCE	M
04/23/45	68197	VT-33	USS SAN-GAMON	MIYAKO	EMPIRE		
04/24/45	69426	VC-19	USS BOGUE		CENLANT	LTJG P.R. WHEELER	S
04/24/45	69432	VC-95	USS MISSION BAY		NORLANT	ENS ANTHONY F. ZERA	D
04/24/45	69440	VC-95	USS MISSION BAY		NORLANT	ENS NEIL H. RICHARDSON	S
04/24/45	69441	VC-95	USS MISSION BAY		NORLANT	ENS HENRY J. TARSKI	S
04/25/45	23513			ARGENTIA	NORLANT		

DATE	BUNO	SQDRN	BASE	LOST	AREA	PILOT	FATE
04/25/45	68561	VT-40	USS SUWANNEE	MIYAKO	EMPIRE	LT FRANK COLLURA	M
04/26/45	68584	VMTB-232		OKINAWA	EMPIRE	1STLT JAMES W. FOX	D
04/26/45	23431	VT-83	USS ESSEX	OKINAWA	EMPIRE		
04/27/45	69008	NACTU	BARBERS POINT	HAWAII	ECENPAC	ENS HAROLD N. STOCKWELL	S
04/27/45	68729	VT-25	USS CHENANGO	IE SHIMA	EMPIRE		
04/27/45	69044	VT-40	USS SUWANNEE	ISHIGAKI	EMPIRE	LT CARROLL R. CAMPBELL	D
04/28/45	68412	VC-84	USS MAKIN ISLAND	IWO JIMA	EMPIRE	LTJG DONALD E. GLASGOW	D
04/28/45	68666	VMTB-232		OKINAWA	EMPIRE	2NDLT J.M. GODBOLD	S
04/29/45	68472	VMTB-232		OKINAWA	EMPIRE	2NDLT LYMAN WILLIS BERG	M
04/29/45	69155	VT-33	USS SANGAMON	IWO JIMA	EMPIRE	LT FRED F. WARREN	S
04/29/45	68509	VT-46	USS INDEPENDENCE	OSHIMA	EMPIRE	LCDR BARRON	S
04/29/45	23201	VT-85	USS SHANGRI-LA	KIKAI	EMPIRE	ENS C. C. BROWNMILLER	M
04/30/45	68736	POOL	PEARL	HAWAII	ECENPAC		
04/30/45	68697	VT-25	USS CHENANGO	IWO JIMA	EMPIRE	ENS V.T. HOLINARO	S
04/30/45	68789	VT-25	USS CHENANGO	IWO JIMA	EMPIRE	ENS J.W. MOODY	S
05/01/45	23114	VT-23	USS LANGLEY	OKINAWA	EMPIRE		
05/02/45	69281	VT-34	USS MONTEREY	ENR KYUSHU	WCENPAC	LTJG FRANK BIRGFELD	D
05/03/45	69235	VT-46	USS INDEPENDENCE	OKINAWA	EMPIRE	LTJG BURTON B. LETULLE	S
05/04/45	23091	VC-12	USS CORE	ENR NEW YORK	NORLANT		
05/04/45		VT-12	USS RANDOLPH	OKINAWA	EMPIRE		
05/04/45	69069	VT-33	USS SANGAMON	KEREMA RHET.	EMPIRE		
05/04/45	69086	VT-33	USS SANGAMON	KEREMA RHET.	EMPIRE		
05/04/45	69100	VT-33	USS SANGAMON	KEREMA RHET.	EMPIRE		
05/04/45	69167	VT-33	USS SANGAMON	KEREMA RHET.	EMPIRE		
05/04/45	69179	VT-33	USS SANGAMON	KEREMA RHET.	EMPIRE		
05/04/45	69232	VT-33	USS SANGAMON	KEREMA RHET.	EMPIRE		
05/04/45	69254	VT-33	USS SANGAMON	KEREMA RHET.	EMPIRE		
05/05/45	23060	CASU(F)-12		GUAM	WCENPAC		
05/05/45	68824	VT-12	USS RANDOLPH	OKINAWA	EMPIRE	LT CURTIS HAMILTON	S
05/05/45	68377	VT-23	USS LANGLEY	OKINAWA	EMPIRE		
05/07/45	68841	VT-25	USS CHENANGO	IWO JIMA	EMPIRE		
05/08/45	23362	CASU(F)-12		GUAM	WCENPAC		
05/09/45	69111	VT-34	USS MONTEREY	NANSEI SHOTO	EMPIRE	ENS MERLE E. SANDERS	D
05/09/45	68463	VT-47	USS BATAAN	TUKUNO	EMPIRE		
05/10/45	68522	VMTB-232		OKINAWA	EMPIRE		
05/10/45	68706	VMTB-233	USS BLOCK ISLAND	MIYAKO	EMPIRE	2NDLT DOUGLAS H. HERRIN	M
05/10/45	68780	VMTB-233	USS BLOCK ISLAND	MIYAKO	EMPIRE	CAPT FRANK TAKAOS	S
05/11/45	68711	VC-93	USS PETROF BAY	OKINAWA	EMPIRE	LTJG LOUIS S. DEVRIES	S
05/11/45	68218	VC-94	USS SHAMROCK BAY	OKINAWA	EMPIRE		

DATE	BUNO	SQDRN	BASE	LOST	AREA	PILOT	FATE
05/11/45	68155	VC-97	USS SHIP-LEY BAY	OKINAWA	EMPIRE	LTJG A.R. GOODALL	S
05/11/45	68434	VT-40	USS SU-WANNEE	IE SHIMA	EMPIRE		
05/11/45	68461	VT-46	USS INDE-PENDENCE	OKINAWA	EMPIRE	LTJG JAMES M. FELKER	S
05/11/45	68549	VT-47	USS BATAAN	OKINAWA	EMPIRE		
05/11/45	23247	VT-84	USS BUNKER HILL	OKINAWA	EMPIRE	(DECK LOSS-KAMIKAZE)	
05/11/45	23288	VT-84	USS BUNKER HILL	OKINAWA	EMPIRE	(DECK LOSS-KAMIKAZE)	
05/11/45	68128	VT-84	USS BUNKER HILL	OKINAWA	EMPIRE	(DECK LOSS-KAMIKAZE)	
05/11/45	68195	VT-84	USS BUNKER HILL	OKINAWA	EMPIRE	(DECK LOSS-KAMIKAZE)	
05/11/45	68370	VT-84	USS BUNKER HILL	OKINAWA	EMPIRE	(DECK LOSS-KAMIKAZE)	
05/11/45	68405	VT-84	USS BUNKER HILL	OKINAWA	EMPIRE	(DECK LOSS-KAMIKAZE)	
05/11/45	68442	VT-84	USS BUNKER HILL	OKINAWA	EMPIRE	(DECK LOSS-KAMIKAZE)	
05/11/45	68459	VT-84	USS BUNKER HILL	OKINAWA	EMPIRE	(DECK LOSS-KAMIKAZE)	
05/11/45	68465	VT-84	USS BUNKER HILL	OKINAWA	EMPIRE	(DECK LOSS-KAMIKAZE)	
05/11/45	68502	VT-84	USS BUNKER HILL	OKINAWA	EMPIRE	(DECK LOSS-KAMIKAZE)	
05/11/45	68847	VT-84	USS BUNKER HILL	OKINAWA	EMPIRE	(DECK LOSS-KAMIKAZE)	
05/11/45	69032	VT-84	USS BUNKER HILL	OKINAWA	EMPIRE	(DECK LOSS-KAMIKAZE)	
05/11/45	69038	VT-84	USS BUNKER HILL	OKINAWA	EMPIRE	(DECK LOSS-KAMIKAZE)	
05/11/45	69045	VT-84	USS BUNKER HILL	OKINAWA	EMPIRE	(DECK LOSS-KAMIKAZE)	
05/11/45	69055	VT-84	USS BUNKER HILL	OKINAWA	EMPIRE	(DECK LOSS-KAMIKAZE)	
05/13/45	68496	VMTB-232		IE SHIMA	EMPIRE	CAPT SNOW	S
05/13/45	68626	VMTB-232		IE SHIMA	EMPIRE	CAPT NAUSS	S
05/13/45	23507	VT-12	USS RANDOLPH	KYUSHU	EMPIRE		
05/13/45	23542	VT-17	USS HORNET	KANOYA	EMPIRE	LT THOMAS C. DURKIN	S
05/13/45		VT-34	USS MONTEREY	KYUSHU	EMPIRE	ENS ALBERT BOWERS	D
05/14/45	69290	VC-71	PUUNENE	HAWAII	ECENPAC		
05/14/45	68513	VMTB-232		OKINAWA	EMPIRE	2NDLT OWEN R. BAIRD	S
05/14/45	68279	VT(N)-90	USS ENTER-PRISE	KYUSHU	EMPIRE		
05/14/45	68311	VT(N)-90	USS ENTER-PRISE	KYUSHU	EMPIRE		
05/14/45	22870	VT-25	USS CHE-NANGO	IWO JIMA	EMPIRE	ENS RICE	S
05/14/45	68714	VT-47	USS BATAAN	KYUSHU	EMPIRE	ENS THOMAS E. HENLEY	M
05/15/45	69195	POOL	USS ATTU	OKINAWA	EMPIRE		
05/15/45	68660	VMTB-232		OKINAWA	EMPIRE		

DATE	BUNO	SQDRN	BASE	LOST	AREA	PILOT	FATE
05/15/45		VT-17	USS HORNET	KYUSHU	EMPIRE		
05/16/45	68324	VMTB-232		IE SHIMA	EMPIRE	1STLT RICHARD MCMAHON	S
05/16/45	69030	VT-25	USS CHE-NANGO	IWO JIMA	EMPIRE		
05/17/45	69307	VC-71	PUUNENE	HAWAII	ECENPAC	LTJG JACK V. BAKER	S
05/17/45	68806	VC-97	USS SHIP-LEY BAY	ENR GUAM	EMPIRE	LT JAMES LOEB	S
05/17/45	69497	VT-87	USS TICONDER-OGA	TAROA	CENPAC	LT E.J. NUFER	S
05/18/45	23601	VOC-2	USS FANSHAW BAY	OKINAWA	EMPIRE	LTJG J.R. MALLARD	M
05/18/45	69185	VT-83	USS ESSEX	IE SHIMA	EMPIRE	LTJG J.A. BOATRIGHT	D
05/18/45	69274	VT-83	USS ESSEX	IE SHIMA	EMPIRE	ENS NICHOLSON	S
05/19/45	69189	VC-99	USS HOGGATT BAY	IE SHIMA	EMPIRE	ENS PAUL A. SIEBOLD	S
05/20/45	22907	AROU-2		SAMAR	PHIL		
05/20/45	68969	VT-50		HAWAII	ECENPAC	ENS A.B. MCGRAW	S
05/23/45	68832	VT-12	USS RANDOLPH	IE SHIMA	EMPIRE	LT J.H. NEWBY	S
05/23/45	68887	VT-12	USS RANDOLPH	IE SHIMA	EMPIRE	LT CURTIS HAMILTON	S
05/23/45	68385	VT-24	USS SANTEE	IWO JIMA	EMPIRE	ENS JAMES A. DAY	S
05/24/45	68368	VT-40	USS SU-WANNEE	OKINAWA	EMPIRE	LT OBED F. SLINGERLAND	D
05/25/45	68273	NACTU	BARBERS POINT	HAWAII	ECENPAC	ENS CARL G. LIBERG	S
05/25/45	68788	NACTU	BARBERS POINT	HAWAII	ECENPAC	ENS ELWOOD E. WHITE	S
05/27/45	68388	VT-24	USS SANTEE	IWO JIMA	EMPIRE		
05/28/45	23526	CASU(F)-52		IWO JIMA	EMPIRE		
05/28/45	68146	VC-99	USS MAKASSAR STR.	SAIPAN	WCENPAC	ENS ELDON L. WERNER	S
05/28/45	68259	VT-2	BARBERS POINT	HAWAII	ECENPAC	ENS JOHN V. STAPLES	S
05/29/45	68497	VMTB-232		OKINAWA	EMPIRE		
05/29/45	68830	VMTB-233	USS BLOCK ISLAND	IE SHIMA	EMPIRE	2NDLT JACK MARCONI	M
05/31/45	23634	CASU-11		OKINAWA	EMPIRE		
05/31/45	68575	VT-40	USS SU-WANNEE	MIYAKO	EMPIRE	ENS CALO	S
05/31/45	68951	VT-40	USS SU WANNEE	MIYAKO	EMPIRE	ENS GLEN O. THOMAS	S
06/03/45	69023	VMTB-143	USS GILBERT IS.	IE SHIMA	EMPIRE	1STLT R.B. CROMWELL	S
06/03/45	68478	VT-82	USS BENNING-TON	OKINAWA	EMPIRE	LCDR E.E. DEGARMO	S
06/04/45	69049	VT-8	PUUNENE	HAWAII	ECENPAC		
06/05/45	23425	POOL	USS ATTU	OKINAWA	EMPIRE		
06/05/45	23530	POOL	USS ATTU	OKINAWA	EMPIRE		
06/05/45	23614	VC-70	USS SALAMAUA	OKINAWA	EMPIRE	(DECK LOSS-TYPHOON)	
06/05/45	68175	VC-70	USS SALAMAUA	OKINAWA	EMPIRE	(DECK LOSS-TYPHOON)	
06/05/45	68230	VC-70	USS SALAMAUA	OKINAWA	EMPIRE	(DECK LOSS-TYPHOON)	
06/05/45	68323	VC-70	USS SALAMAUA	OKINAWA	EMPIRE	(DECK LOSS-TYPHOON)	
06/05/45	68437	VC-70	USS SALAMAUA	OKINAWA	EMPIRE	(DECK LOSS-TYPHOON)	
06/05/45	68723	VC-70	USS SALAMAUA	OKINAWA	EMPIRE	(DECK LOSS-TYPHOON)	
06/05/45	23410	VC-91	USS MAKIN ISLAND	GUAM	WCENPAC		

DATE	BUNO	SQDRN	BASE	LOST	AREA	PILOT	FATE
06/05/45	68519	VC-91	USS MAKIN ISLAND	GUAM	WCENPAC		
06/05/45	68397	VT-30	USS BELLEAU WOOD		EMPIRE		
06/05/45	68441	VT-30	USS BELLEAU WOOD		EMPIRE		
06/05/45	68568	VT-30	USS BELLEAU WOOD		EMPIRE		
06/05/45	68704	VT-30	USS BELLEAU WOOD		EMPIRE		
06/05/45	68848	VT-30	USS BELLEAU WOOD		EMPIRE		
06/05/45	68945	VT-49	USS SAN JACINTO	OKINAWA	EMPIRE	(DECK LOSS-TYPHOON)	
06/06/45	23190	POOL	USS BOUGAIN-VILLE		EMPIRE	(DECK LOSS-TYPHOON)	
06/06/45	68105	POOL	USS BOUGAIN-VILLE		EMPIRE	(DECK LOSS-TYPHOON)	
06/06/45	69040	VC-8	USS NEHENTA BAY	OKINAWA	EMPIRE		
06/06/45	68505	VMTB-131		IE SHIMA	EMPIRE	1STLT CARL E. KANT	M
06/07/45	68818	VT-12	USS RANDOLPH		PHIL		
06/07/45	68821	VT-12	USS RANDOLPH		PHIL		
06/07/45	69061	VT-12	USS RANDOLPH		PHIL		
06/08/45	68359	VC-41	USS TRIPOLI	PEARL	ECENPAC	ENS WILLIAM E. CHICKERING	S
06/08/45	23374	VC-96	USS SHAM-ROCK BAY	OKINAWA	EMPIRE	LTJG PHILIP E. BROU	S
06/12/45	69026	VMTB-143	USS GILBERT ISL.	IE SHIMA	EMPIRE	1STLT KELVERN O. MISAMORE	D
06/13/45	68267	VC-97	USS SHIP-LEY BAY	ENR SHIMA	EMPIRE		
06/14/45	68212	VC-96	USS SHAM-ROCK BAY	OKINAWA	EMPIRE	ENS SHELTON B. CARNWRIGHT	S
06/14/45	68790	VOC-2	USS FANSHAW BAY	MIYAKO	EMPIRE		
06/15/45	23354	CASU-11		OKINAWA	EMPIRE		
06/16/45	68428	CASU(F)-12		GUAM	WCENPAC		
06/16/45	68799	CASU(F)-12		GUAM	WCENPAC		
06/16/45	68863	CASU(F)-12		GUAM	WCENPAC		
06/20/45		VT-83	USS ESSEX		EMPIRE		
06/21/45	68107	CASU(F)-14		SAIPAN	WCENPAC		
06/21/45	68389	VMTB-131		IE SHIMA	EMPIRE		
06/21/45	68906	VMTB-131		IE SHIMA	EMPIRE	1STLT JOHN W. RUSSELL	S
06/22/45	23485	VC-96	USS SHAM-ROCK BAY	MIYAKO	EMPIRE	ENS R.E. WEEKS	M
06/23/45	68467	VMTB-232		OKINAWA	EMPIRE		
06/25/45	68921	VMTB-131		OKINAWA	EMPIRE	1STLT ROBERT A. COOK	S
06/27/45	22910	VT-40	USS SU-WANNEE	LEYTE GULF	PHIL	LTJG R.N. PENDERGRASS	S
07/02/45	68667	VMTB-131		IE SHIMA	EMPIRE	1STLT ROBERT G. STATLER	S
07/05/45	68566	VMTB-232		KADENA	EMPIRE		
07/07/45	23367	VT-24	USS SANTEE	OKINAWA	EMPIRE	(DECK LOSS-AIRCRASH)	
07/07/45	23474	VT-24	USS SANTEE	OKINAWA	EMPIRE	(DECK LOSS-AIRCRASH)	
07/07/45	68923	VT-24	USS SANTEE	OKINAWA	EMPIRE	(DECK LOSS-AIRCRASH)	
07/07/45	69033	VT-24	USS SANTEE	OKINAWA	EMPIRE	(DECK LOSS-AIRCRASH)	

DATE	BUNO	SQDRN	BASE	LOST	AREA	PILOT	FATE
07/08/45	23453	VT-31	USS HOLLANDIA		EMPIRE	LTJG I.V. KINDER	S
07/08/45	23119	VT-83	USS ESSEX		EMPIRE		
07/10/45	68129	VT-1	USS BENNING-TON	KURE	EMPIRE		
07/10/45	69415	VT-16	USS RANDOLPH	TOKYO	EMPIRE	LT N.N. HOLMES	M
07/10/45	69064	VT-34	USS MONTEREY	HONSHU	EMPIRE	ENS JACK T. WASSOR	M
07/11/45	68642	ACORN-30 PL		TACLOBAN	PHIL		
07/14/45	68851	VT-16	USS RANDOLPH	TSUGARU STRAIT	EMPIRE	ENS B.H. NOAH	S
07/14/45	69006	VT-16	USS RANDOLPH	TSUGARU STRAIT	EMPIRE		
07/14/45	68908	VT-47	USS BATAAN	OKINAWA	EMPIRE		
07/14/45	69477	VT-47	USS BATAAN	OKINAWA	EMPIRE	LT DOUGLAS	S
07/14/45	23407	VT-85	USS SHANGRI-LA	HOKKAIDO	EMPIRE	LT RICHARD W. POLAND	S
07/14/45	68854	VT-88	USS YORK-TOWN	HOKKAIDO	EMPIRE		
07/15/45	23567	VT-31	USS BELLEAU WOOD		EMPIRE		
07/18/45	68707	VT-27	USS INDE-PENDENCE	YOKOSUKA	EMPIRE	LTJG HARRY PATTERSON	M
07/20/45	68169	VC-93	USS STEAMER BAY	ENR GUAM	WCENPAC	ENS PAUL R. BAUMGARTNER	S
07/22/45	68178	NACTU	BARBERS POINT	HAWAII	ECENPAC	ENS FRANCIN J. MACMURTRIN	M
07/22/45		VT(N)-91	USS BON HOMME RICHARD		EMPIRE		
07/22/45	23128	VT-31	USS BELLEAU WOOD	HONSHU	EMPIRE	ENS VICTOR J. NORTON	M
07/24/45	68623	VT-49	USS SAN JACINTO	HONSHU	EMPIRE	ENS CLAUDE C. CAFFEY	S
07/24/45	68608	VT-95	HILO	HAWAII	ECENPAC	LTJG FLOYD N. GOSS	D
07/25/45	69270	VT(N)-91	USS BON HOMME RICHARD		EMPIRE	ENS JOSEPH T. WILLIAMS	M
07/26/45	68263	AROU-2		SAMAR	PHIL		
07/28/45	69211	VT-34	USS MONTEREY	KURE	EMPIRE	LTJG L.B. LAMPMAN	S
07/28/45	68856	VT-85	USS SHANGRI-LA	KURE	EMPIRE	LT G.M. BROWN	M
07/29/45	68398	CASU(F)-12		GUAM	WCENPAC		
07/29/45	68443	CASU(F)-12		GUAM	WCENPAC		
07/30/45	23035	VJ-9			SW PAC	CAPT P.V. MINGO	S
07/31/45	22860	POOL	BARBERS POINT	HAWAII	ECENPAC		
08/01/45	69654	CASU-31	HILO	HAWAII	ECENPAC	ENS EARL L. GRANT	S
08/03/45	68233	VT-14		HAWAII	ECENPAC	ENS K.B. MATTHEWS	S
08/06/45	69012	VT-16	USS RANDOLPH	SHIKOKU	EMPIRE	ENS ROBERT E. RIEGER	D
08/09/45	68761	VT-83	USS ESSEX		EMPIRE	LT BOMBYK	S
08/11/45	23393	CASU-11		OKINAWA	EMPIRE		
08/11/45	23268	POOL	PEARL	HAWAII	ECENPAC		
08/11/45	68150	VT-27	USS INDE-PENDENCE		EMPIRE		
08/13/45	22899	CASU(F)-12		GUAM	WCENPAC		
08/13/45	23011	CASU(F)-12		GUAM	WCENPAC		
08/13/45	68898	VT-85	USS SHANGRI-LA	HONSHU	EMPIRE	LT RICHARD W. POLAND	S
08/14/45	69014	SERVRON-14		OKINAWA	EMPIRE		

GENERAL MOTORS TBM-3C

Although several Aircraft History Cards list these missing aircraft as General Motors TBM-3C's, their Bureau Numbers depict them as straight TBM-3 aircraft. Research shows that no TBM-3C variants were manufactured by GM, so either these were re-designated by the Navy while operational or the Cards are in error. Aircraft lost:

DATE	BUNO	SQDRN	BASE	LOST	AREA	PILOT	FATE
12/27/44	23579	COMAIR-PAC	PEARL	HAWAII	ECENPAC		
01/08/45	23613	A.A.	SAMAR	SAMAR	PHIL		
01/12/45	23603	VT-4	USS ESSEX	FR. I.C.	PHIL	LTJG DONALD A. HENRY	S
01/16/45	23422	VT-4	USS ESSEX	HAINAN	EMPIRE	ENS WALKER	S
01/16/45	23574	VT-4	USS ESSEX	HAINAN	EMPIRE	LTJG BINDER	S
01/16/45	68086	VT-4	USS ESSEX	HAINAN	EMPIRE	LTJG THOMAS	S
01/22/45	23404	VT-4	USS ESSEX	FORMOSA	EMPIRE	ENS BISSEL	D

GENERAL MOTORS TBM-3D

The General Motors TBM-3D variant was a TBM-3 converted by adding a centimetric radar in a radome to the starboard wing leading edge. Aircraft lost:

DATE	BUNO	SQDRN	BASE	LOST	AREA	PILOT	FATE
11/30/44	23001	AWT ACTION	PEARL	HAWAII	ECENPAC		
12/25/44	23352	VT(N)-90	BARBERS POINT	HAWAII	ECENPAC	LTJG R.R. JONES	S
12/29/44	68249	VT(N)-90	USS ENTER-PRISE	HAWAII	ECENPAC	LTJG R. LEE	D
12/31/44	23078	VC-12		BERMUDA	NORLANT	ENS M.L. MATSLER	S
01/02/45		VT(N)-53	USS SARATOGA	HAWAII	ECENPAC	ENS K.W. SCOTT	U
01/13/45	23356	VT(N)-90	USS ENTER-PRISE	FR. I.C.	PHIL	ENS JOHN B. HADDENS	S
01/15/45	23558	VT(N)-90	USS ENTER-PRISE	FR. I.C.	PHIL	LTJG S.W. MCCHARRY	S
01/22/45	22981	VT(N)-90	USS ENTER-PRISE	FORMOSA	EMPIRE	LT RUSSELL F. KIPPEN	M
01/22/45	23387	VT(N)-90	USS ENTER-PRISE	FORMOSA	EMPIRE	ENS JOHN P. WOOD	M
01/22/45	68306	VT(N)-90	USS ENTER-PRISE	FORMOSA	EMPIRE	ENS CHESTER C. KOOP	M
01/25/45	23389	VT(N)-90	USS ENTER-PRISE	LUZON	PHIL	ENS KNOX O. SCOTT	S
01/30/45	23030	VT(N)-90	USS ENTER-PRISE	LUZON	PHIL		
01/31/45	23003	A.A.	PEARL	HAWAII	ECENPAC		
01/31/45	23061	A.A.	PEARL	HAWAII	ECENPAC		
05/14/45	23006	VT(N)-90	USS ENTER-PRISE	KYUSHU	EMPIRE		
05/14/45	23069	VT(N)-90	USS ENTER-PRISE	KYUSHU	EMPIRE		
05/14/45	23291	VT(N)-90	USS ENTER-PRISE	KYUSHU	EMPIRE		
05/14/45	23304	VT(N)-90	USS ENTER-PRISE	KYUSHU	EMPIRE		

DATE	BUNO	SQDRN	BASE	LOST	AREA	PILOT	FATE
05/14/45	23348	VT(N)-90	USS ENTER-PRISE	KYUSHU	EMPIRE		
05/14/45	68156	VT(N)-90	USS ENTER-PRISE	KYUSHU	EMPIRE		
05/14/45	68260	VT(N)-90	USS ENTER-PRISE	KYUSHU	EMPIRE		
05/14/45	68271	VT(N)-90	USS ENTER-PRISE	KYUSHU	EMPIRE		
05/14/45	68272	VT(N)-90	USS ENTER-PRISE	KYUSHU	EMPIRE		

GENERAL MOTORS TBM-3E

The General Motors TBM-3E variant was a TBM-3 with a stronger airframe and search radar and with its ventral gun deleted. There were 646 built by GM. Aircraft lost:

DATE	BUNO	SQDRN	BASE	LOST	AREA	PILOT	FATE
05/10/45	85772	CASU(F)-12		GUAM	WCENPAC		
05/26/45	85699	VT-93		GUANTAN. BAY	CENLANT	LTJG R. BARTELL	S
06/01/45	68845	VF-82	USS BENNING-TON	OKINAWA	EMPIRE	LT W.G. REED	S
06/05/45	69331	POOL	USS ATTU	OKINAWA	EMPIRE		
06/05/45	85841	VC-70	USS SALAMAUA	OKINAWA	EMPIRE	(DECK LOSS-TYPHOON)	
06/05/45	69240	VT-49	USS SAN JACINTO	OKINAWA	EMPIRE	(DECK LOSS-TYPHOON)	
06/06/45	69213	POOL	USS BOUGAIN-VILLE		EMPIRE	(DECK LOSS-TYPHOON)	
06/06/45	69257	POOL	USS BOUGAIN-VILLE		EMPIRE	(DECK LOSS-TYPHOON)	
06/06/45	69260	POOL	USS BOUGAIN-VILLE		EMPIRE	(DECK LOSS-TYPHOON)	
06/06/45	69322	POOL	USS BOUGAIN-VILLE		EMPIRE	(DECK LOSS-TYPHOON)	
06/06/45	69350	POOL	USS BOUGAIN-VILLE		EMPIRE	(DECK LOSS-TYPHOON)	
06/06/45	69383	POOL	USS BOUGAIN-VILLE		EMPIRE	(DECK LOSS-TYPHOON)	
06/07/45	69455	VT-12	USS RANDOLPH		PHIL		
06/07/45	85492	VT-17	USS HORNET	OKINAWA	EMPIRE		
06/08/45	69388	VT-6	USS HANCOCK	PEARL	ECENPAC	LT H.J.W. EPPLER	S
06/08/45	85982	VT-6	USS HANCOCK	PEARL	ECENPAC	LTJG JUNGHANS	S
06/09/45	85735	VC-63	USS KIT-KUN BAY	HAWAII	ECENPAC	ENS M.I. POLKOWSKI	S
06/15/45	69414	VC-71	USS MAN-ILA BAY	OKINAWA	EMPIRE	ENS C.D. KLEIN	S
06/16/45	69386	CASU(F)-12		GUAM	WCENPAC		
06/16/45	69393	CASU(F)-12		GUAM	WCENPAC		
06/17/45	86198	AROU-2		SAMAR	PHIL		
06/18/45	85955	VT-86	USS WASP		PHIL	LT JAMES ELIYAH BURK	D
06/18/45	85976	VT-86	USS WASP		PHIL	ENS FREDERICK CAFNER	M

DATE	BUNO	SQDRN	BASE	LOST	AREA	PILOT	FATE
06/30/45	69200	NACTU	BARBERS POINT	HAWAII	ECENPAC		
07/03/45	69516	VT(N)-91	USS BON HOMME RICHARD		EMPIRE	ENS A.R. KLEINHAUF	S
07/07/45	23248	CASU(F)-42		PITYILU	SW PAC	LTJG KEITH NIMS	S
07/07/45	68766	VC-13	USS ANZIO		EMPIRE		
07/07/45	69161	VT(N)-91	USS BON HOMME RICHARD		EMPIRE	LTJG T.H. WITT	S
07/10/45	69137	VT-34	USS MONTEREY	HONSHU	EMPIRE		
07/10/45	69372	VT-34	USS MONTEREY	HONSHU	EMPIRE		
07/10/45	86208	VT-34	USS MONTEREY	HONSHU	EMPIRE		
07/11/45	69493	VC-70	USS SALAMAUA	OKINAWA	EMPIRE	ENS CHARLES F. FONTY	U
07/11/45	69277	VMTB-232		OKINAWA	EMPIRE	2NDLT OWEN R. BAIRD	M
07/14/45	69068	VT-34	USS MONTEREY	HONSHU	EMPIRE		
07/15/45	86132	VT-1	USS BENNING-TON	HOKKAIDO	EMPIRE	JOSEPH DORTSCH	M
07/15/45	86224	VT-34	USS MONTEREY	HONSHU	EMPIRE		
07/18/45	53206	VT-1	USS BENNING-TON	KURE	EMPIRE	LT W.R. EDDINS	S
07/18/45	86110	VT-1	USS BENNING-TON	KURE	EMPIRE	LTJG R.L. PUGET	S
07/19/45	86202	CASU-31	HILO	HAWAII	ECENPAC		
07/24/45	69324	CASU(F)-47		SAIPAN	WCENPAC		
07/24/45	69338	CASU(F)-47		SAIPAN	WCENPAC		
07/24/45	69397	VT-1	USS BENNING-TON	KURE	EMPIRE	LTJG GEORGE A. GUSTIN	D
07/24/45	69176	VT-34	USS MONTEREY	HONSHU	EMPIRE	ENS STEENBERG	D
07/24/45	69211	VT-34	USS MONTEREY	HONSHU	EMPIRE		
07/24/45	69444	VT-6	USS HANCOCK		EMPIRE	LT HYND	S
07/24/45	85853	VT-6	USS HANCOCK		EMPIRE	LTJG CALLON	M
07/24/45	86116	VT-6	USS HANCOCK		EMPIRE	LTJG C.A. TEIGE	M
07/24/45	85526	VT-87	USS TICONDER-OGA	KURE	EMPIRE		
07/26/45	85788	VC-65		HAWAII	ECENPAC	ENS E.J. PAULAVEDUS	D
07/28/45	69401	VMTB-134		PELELIU	WCENPAC		
07/28/45	86157	VT-50	USS COWPENS	KURE	EMPIRE	WILLIAM MAGUIRE	M
07/28/45	86160	VT-50	USS COWPENS	KURE	EMPIRE		
07/28/45	69453	VT-6	USS HANCOCK		EMPIRE	LT J. WILLIAM TEMPLE	S
07/28/45	85953	VT-86	USS WASP	KURE	EMPIRE	ENS C.R. JOHNSON	M
07/28/45	69208	VT-87	USS TICONDER-OGA	KURE	EMPIRE	ENS PAUL STEPHENS	M
07/28/45	86126	VT-94	USS LEX-INGTON		EMPIRE		
07/28/45	86163	VT-94	USS LEX-INGTON		EMPIRE	ENS E.M. SIMMS	M
07/30/45	86164	VT(N)-91	USS BON HOMME RICHARD		EMPIRE	ENS J.T. THORNTON	S
07/30/45	69110	VT-27	USS INDE-PENDENCE	HONSHU	EMPIRE	ENS BRUCE W. ANDERSON	S
07/30/45	69326	VT-27	USS INDE-PENDENCE	HONSHU	EMPIRE	ENS D.R. BENARDINELLI	M

DATE	BUNO	SQDRN	BASE	LOST	AREA	PILOT	FATE
07/30/45	85462	VT-6	USS HANCOCK		EMPIRE	ENS NORMAN B. BITZEGAIO	D
08/04/45	68919	VC-7			WCENPAC	ENS CHARLES SMITH	D
08/04/45	85543	VT(N)-91	USS BON HOMME RICHARD		EMPIRE		
08/05/45	69264	VT-31	USS BELLEAU WOOD		EMPIRE		
08/06/45	85752	CASU(F)-47		SAIPAN	WCENPAC		
08/07/45	85965	POOL	PEARL	HAWAII	ECENPAC		
08/08/45	85798	VC-70	USS SALAMAUA	LEYTE GULF	PHIL	ENS RAYMOND D. SMITH	S
08/09/45	86223	VT-32	USS CABOT		WCENPAC		
08/09/45	69297	VT-83	USS ESSEX		EMPIRE	LTJG LECLAIR	S
08/10/45	69352	VT-6	USS HANCOCK		EMPIRE		
08/10/45	86220	VT-83	USS ESSEX		EMPIRE		
08/10/45	86213	VT-94	USS LEX-INGTON		EMPIRE		
08/11/45	53447	VT-36	USS SIBONEY	HAWAII	ECENPAC		
08/11/45	53464	VT-36	USS SIBONEY	HAWAII	ECENPAC		
08/11/45	85565	VT-6	USS HANCOCK		EMPIRE		
08/13/45	85820	CASU(F)-12		GUAM	WCENPAC		
08/13/45	69231	VC-41	USS MAKIN ISLAND		EMPIRE		
08/13/45	69272	VT-1	USS BENNING-TON	TOKYO	EMPIRE	LTJG LEE M. PASLEY	M
08/13/45	69066	VT-87	USS TICONDER-OGA	TOKYO	EMPIRE		

GENERAL MOTORS TBM-3P

The General Motors TBM-3P variant was the TBM-3 converted for photo-reconnaissance. Aircraft lost:

DATE	BUNO	SQDRN	BASE	LOST	AREA	PILOT	FATE
07/31/45	68080	VC-99	USS HOGGATT DAY	LEYTE GULF	PHIL	ENS PAUL A. SIEBOLD	S

GOODYEAR FG-1

The Chance Vought F4U Corsair was a carrier-capable fighter aircraft that saw service in World War II (see "Vought F4U-1" write-up). Demand for the aircraft soon overwhelmed Vought's manufacturing capability, resulting in production by Goodyear and Brewster: Goodyear-built Corsairs were designated FG. Aircraft lost:

DATE	BUNO	SQDRN	BASE	LOST	AREA	PILOT	FATE
12/31/43	13220	COMAIR-SOPAC	GUADAL-CANAL	GUADAL-CANAL	SOPAC		
01/12/44	13112	VMF-441	TUTUILA	S. OF SAMOA	SOPAC	2NDLT E.H. SEARIGHT	M
01/22/44	13217	COMAIR-PAC	PEARL	HAWAII	ECENPAC		
01/22/44	13270	VMF-321	TOROKINA	RABAUL	SOPAC	1STLT L.T. WARDLE	M
01/22/44	14212	VMF-321	TOROKINA	RABAUL	SOPAC	1STLT E.V. SMITH	S
01/30/44	13265	COMAIR-SOPAC	GUADAL-CANAL	GUADAL-CANAL	SOPAC		
01/30/44	13215	VMF-211	PIVA	RABAUL	SOPAC	MAJ R.L. HOPKINS	D
02/16/44	13272	COMAIR-SOPAC	GUADAL-CANAL	GUADAL-CANAL	SOPAC		

DATE	BUNO	SQDRN	BASE	LOST	AREA	PILOT	FATE
02/16/44	13288	COMAIR-SOPAC	GUADAL-CANAL	GUADAL-CANAL	SOPAC		
02/29/44	13271	VMF-211			SOPAC		
03/12/44	13297	VMF-211			SOPAC		
03/23/44	13248	VMF-216	PIVA	KAHILI	SOPAC	1STLT B.J. BASCH	M
04/08/44	13259	VMF-321	BARAKOMA	KAVIENG	SOPAC	2NDLT J.D. STITH	S
04/23/44	13261	COMAIR-SOPAC	GUADAL-CANAL	GUADAL-CANAL	SOPAC		
04/29/44	13307	VMF-215	PIVA	NEW BRITAIN	SOPAC	1STLT E.B. COCHRAN	M
05/11/44	13473	COMAIR-PAC	PEARL	HAWAII	ECENPAC		
05/17/44	13208	COMAIR-SOPAC	GUADAL-CANAL	GUADAL-CANAL	SOPAC		
05/24/44	13219	VMF-212			SW PAC		
06/07/44	13282	VMF-223	GREEN	RABAUL	SOPAC	2NDLT J.C. PERKINS	M
06/15/44	13289	COMFAIR	GUADAL-CANAL	TULAGI	SOPAC		
07/08/44	14088	VMF-222		ESPIRITU SANTO	SOPAC		
07/16/44	13274	VMF-212		GREEN	SOPAC		
07/21/44	14180	MAG-11		ESPIRITU SANTO	SOPAC		
08/09/44	14242	VMF-312		ESPIRITU SANTO	SOPAC	1STLT H.L. BURGE	M
08/12/44	13994	VMF-115		EMIRAU	SW PAC	LT JOHN C. WILLIS	S
08/14/44	14204	VMF-222		GREEN	SOPAC		
08/31/44	13933	MADC-2					
09/24/44	14011	VMF-218		RABAUL	SW PAC	LT W.H. HODSON	S
10/02/44	14266	VMF-122		PELELIU	WCENPAC	LT JAMES F. SMITH	U
10/13/44	14182	VMF-114		PALAU	WCENPAC	LT VIRGETS	S
10/15/44	14148	VMF-122		PELELIU	WCENPAC	LT CHARLES S. SPIVEY	D
10/24/44	14189	VMF-122		PELELIU	WCENPAC	LT GIRVIS HALTON, JR.	D
10/25/44	14187	MAG-11		PELELIU	WCENPAC		
10/25/44	14194	MAG-11		PELELIU	WCENPAC		
10/25/44	14220	MAG-11		PELELIU	WCENPAC		
10/28/44	14046	VMF-213	EWA	HAWAII	ECENPAC		
11/01/44	14113	VMF-223		TOROKINA	SOPAC	LT GERALD MILLER	S
11/02/44	14197	VMF-122		PELELIU	WCENPAC		
11/06/44	14513	VMF-114		PALAU	WCENPAC	LT BILLY H. CANTRELL	S
11/18/44	13995	VMF-115		EMIRAU	SW PAC		
11/18/44	14237	VMF-121		PELELIU	WCENPAC	LT CARMENA	S
11/19/44	14520	VMF-313		EMIRAU	SW PAC		
11/21/44	14323	VMF-121	PELELIU	YAP	CENPAC	MAJ WILLIAM CLAY, JR.	D
11/21/44	14053	VMF-122		PELELIU	WCENPAC	CAPT MCCULLOH	S
11/28/44	14125	SERVRON-11		PELELIU	WCENPAC		
11/28/44	14047	VMF-114		PELELIU	WCENPAC	1STLT WM L. SONNENBERG	S
12/01/44	14430	VMF-218		LEYTE GULF	PHIL		
12/02/44	14221	VMF-121		PALAU	WCENPAC	LT FISHER	S
12/03/44	14508	VMF-212		CAPE GAZELLE	SW PAC	1STLT HAROLD E. BOYSEN	D
12/05/44	14417	VMF-222		NEW BRITAIN	SW PAC	1STLT MOSZEK ZANGER	M
12/06/44	14538	VMF-115		LEYTE GULF	PHIL		
12/10/44	14403	VMF-115		LEYTE GULF	PHIL	LT N.W. GOURLEY KREIGER	S
12/11/44	14083	VMBF-333	HAWAII	HAWAII	ECENPAC	1STLT JAMES D. ZIMMER	S
12/11/44	14487	VMF-115		LEYTE GULF	PHIL	2NDLT M. GUDOR	S
12/11/44	14253	VMF-218		LEYTE GULF	PHIL	2NDLT R.E. EACOBACCI	M
12/12/44	14380	VMF-313		LEYTE GULF	PHIL		
12/13/44	14436	VMF-313		LEYTE GULF	PHIL	MAJ T. OLSEN	U
12/13/44	14531	VMF-313		LEYTE GULF	PHIL	LT WILLIAM E. BRADY	D
12/15/44	14355	VMF-115		LEYTE GULF	PHIL		
12/18/44	14542	VMF-115		LEYTE GULF	PHIL	LT AUGUST DANNEHL	S
12/18/44	14119	VMF-218		LEYTE GULF	PHIL	LT ROBINSON	S
12/19/44	14498	VMF-218		LEYTE GULF	PHIL	2NDLT RICHARD L. STULTS	M
12/22/44	14150	VMF-218		LEYTE GULF	PHIL		
12/25/44	14003	VMF-218		LEYTE GULF	PHIL		
12/26/44	14055		BARBERS POINT	HAWAII	ECENPAC		
12/26/44	14072	VMF-114		BABELTHAUP	WCENPAC	1STLT WM L. SONNENBERG	S

DATE	BUNO	SQDRN	BASE	LOST	AREA	PILOT	FATE
12/26/44	14378	VMF-218		LEYTE GULF	PHIL	FORYSIAK	S
12/31/44	14488	VMF-223		TOROKINA	SOPAC		
01/01/45	14462	VMF-313		LEYTE GULF	PHIL	LT MASTERS	S
01/03/45	14415	VMF-115		LEYTE GULF	PHIL	MCCALL	U
01/04/45	14233	VMF-121		PALAU	WCENPAC		
01/04/45	14441	VMF-218		LEYTE GULF	PHIL		
01/06/45	14344	VMF-212		GREEN	SOPAC		
01/07/45	14431	VMF-218		LEYTE GULF	PHIL		
01/11/45	14332	VBF-6	HAWAII	HAWAII	ECENPAC	LTJG ROBERT E. HARROLD	M
01/12/45	14476	MAG-12		LEYTE GULF	PHIL		
01/13/45	14527	VMF-115		LEYTE GULF	PHIL	ERWIN	U
01/13/45	14545	VMF-223		SAMAR	PHIL	2NDLT GUY W. OLIVER	S
01/15/45	14230	VBF-86	HAWAII	HAWAII	ECENPAC		
01/15/45	14479	VMF-223		GREEN	SOPAC	2NDLT CLIFFORD E. WOZNIAK	S
01/16/45	14397	VMF-222		GREEN	SOPAC	MAJ GERALD GEIGER	S
01/18/45	14414	VBF-6	HAWAII	HAWAII	ECENPAC	ENS FREDERICK D. HOOKS	S
01/18/45	14533	VBF-6	HAWAII	HAWAII	ECENPAC	LTJG DAVIS F. MOYER	S
01/18/45	14427	VMF-115		LEYTE GULF	PHIL	R. OLSON	S
01/20/45	14019	VMF-218		LEYTE GULF	PHIL		
01/20/45	14061	VMF-218		LEYTE GULF	PHIL		
01/20/45	14295	VMF-324		MIDWAY	ECENPAC	2NDLT WALTER R. MORTON	D
01/21/45	14106	VMF-223		SAMAR	PHIL	2NDLT KENNETH G. POMASL	M
01/24/45	14515	VMF-218		LEYTE GULF	PHIL		
01/24/45	14095	VMF-222		GREEN	SOPAC	2NDLT KARL OERTH	D
01/27/45	14370	VMF-212		SAMAR	PHIL	CAPT MARTIN L. WING	M
02/01/45	14185	VMF-114		PELELIU	WCENPAC	LT J.R. ANDERSON	S
02/01/45	14505	VMF-223		LUZON	PHIL	2NDLT EUGENE F. PRORILX	S
02/06/45	14449	VMF-222		SAMAR	PHIL		
02/09/45	14394	VMF-222		SAMAR	PHIL		
02/13/45	14561	NAS	HILO	HAWAII	ECENPAC		
02/13/45	14572	NAS	HILO	HAWAII	ECENPAC		
02/14/45	14094	VMF-222		SAMAR	PHIL	1STLT LOREN G. WILDER	D
02/14/45	14502	VMF-223		SAMAR	PHIL	LT SYKES	U
02/20/45	14131	VMF-222		SAMAR	PHIL		
02/21/45	14486	VMF-115		LEYTE GULF	PHIL		
02/21/45	14025	VMF-212		SAMAR	PHIL		
02/21/45	14435	VMF-223		SAMAR	PHIL	2NDLT R.L. ZORN	S
02/21/45	14570	VMF-223		SAMAR	PHIL	2NDLT MILTON H. THOMPSON	M
02/22/45	14541	VMF-212		SAMAR	PHIL	CAPT W.W. HAZLETTE	S
02/22/45	14584	VMF-212		SAMAR	PHIL	2NDLT WILLIAM B. GAY	D
02/23/45	14573	VMF-313		LEYTE GULF	PHIL		
02/24/45	14482	VMF-115		LEYTE GULF	PHIL	2NDLT DIXON	S
02/24/45	14322	VMF-218		LEYTE GULF	PHIL		
02/24/45	14495	VMF-223		SAMAR	PHIL	2NDLT MARTIN T. TIERMAN	S
02/28/45	14005	VMB-423		GREEN	SOPAC		
02/28/45	14218	VMB-423		GREEN	SOPAC		
03/01/45	14077	VMF-222		SAMAR	PHIL		
03/04/45	14183	VMF-114		PELELIU	WCENPAC	MAJ ROBERT F. STOUT	M
03/04/45	14257	VMF-121		PELELIU	WCENPAC	1STLT W.F. BROWN	S
03/04/45	14017	VMF-222		MINDANAO	PHIL	2NDLT JACK G. OBRINGER	S
03/05/45	14078	VMF-313		LOS NEGROS	PHIL	LT H.E. CAIN	S
03/06/45	14480	VMF-115		LEYTE GULF	PHIL	LT FOSTER	S
03/11/45	14211	VMF-313		CEBU	PHIL	2NDLT ROBERT FISHER, JR.	D
03/24/45	14193	VMF-223	SAMAR	SAMAR	PHIL	LT PRATT	M
04/02/45	14008	VMF-115		ZAMBOANGA	PHIL	LT GEORGE A. COSHAL	M
04/02/45	14051	VMF-115		ZAMBOANGA	PHIL	LT RAY H. MCDONALD	S
04/02/45	14504	VMF-212		SAMAR	PHIL	2NDLT JOHN D. WOODLOCK	S
04/05/45	14439	VMF-222	SAMAR	SAMAR	PHIL	LT BOLLER	S
04/06/45	14347	VMF-222	SAMAR	SAMAR	PHIL	2NDLT ROBERT F. MAJORS	D
04/07/45	14143	SERVRON-11		PELELIU	WCENPAC		
04/07/45	14438	VMF-313		ZAMBOANGA	PHIL	2NDLT L.B. HAMITY	S

DATE	BUNO	SQDRN	BASE	LOST	AREA	PILOT	FATE
04/12/45	14021	VMF-313		ZAMBOANGA	PHIL	LT J.W. WALLACE	S
04/14/45	14348	VBF-88	HILO	HAWAII	ECENPAC	ENS E.J. HOE	S
04/17/45	14483	CASU-32	KAHULUI	HAWAII	ECENPAC		
04/18/45	14374	VBF-38		HAWAII	ECENPAC	ENS ELMER B. KRAUSE	M
04/18/45	14165	VMF-212	SAMAR	SAMAR	PHIL	2NDLT GEORGE E. DUNCAN	S
04/22/45	14352	VMF-212		LEYTE GULF	PHIL	MSGT DAVID D. WILCOX	S
04/23/45	14503	VMF-212		LEYTE GULF	PHIL	2NDLT E.H. EWALD	S
04/24/45	14549	VMF-212	SAMAR	SAMAR	PHIL	1STLT DONALD T. DOYLE	S
05/05/45	14509	VMF-115	ZAMBOAN-GA	ZAMBOANGA	PHIL	MAJ MORRISON	S
05/06/45	14413	VMF-212	SAMAR	SAMAR	PHIL	2NDLT THOMAS H MCKAY, JR	S
05/07/45	14235	VBF-100		HAWAII	ECENPAC		
05/10/45	14060	VBF-215	EWA	HAWAII	ECENPAC		
05/11/45	14229	VMF-114		PELELIU	WCENPAC		
05/20/45	14308	VMF-212	SAMAR	SAMAR	PHIL		
05/21/45	14267	SAMAR			PHIL		
05/21/45	14160	AROU-1		MOMOTE	SW PAC		
05/21/45	14123	AROU-2		SAMAR	PHIL		
05/23/45	14385	VBF-2	HILO	HAWAII	ECENPAC	LTJG DONALD C. BRANDT	S
05/26/45	14493	VMF-218	ZAMBOAN-GA	ZAMBOANGA	PHIL	2NDLT PAUL R. BLOMQUIST	D
05/31/45	14379	VBF-100		HAWAII	ECENPAC	LTJG WARREN P. KELLEY	S
06/01/45	14100	VBF-100		HAWAII	ECENPAC	ENS WILLIAM J. VON OHLEN	S
06/03/45	14566	VBF-100		HAWAII	ECENPAC	ENS L.B. CONNELL	S
06/05/45	14455	VBF-100	BARBERS POINT	HAWAII	ECENPAC		
06/06/45	14318	POOL	BARBERS POINT	HAWAII	ECENPAC		
06/07/45	14401	VMF-215	OAHU	HAWAII	ECENPAC	2NDLT JOSEPH C. PACE	S
06/13/45	14327	VBF-100		HAWAII	ECENPAC	ENS J.R. DILLINGHAM	S
06/14/45	14528	VMF-115	ZAMBOAN-GA	ZAMBOANGA	PHIL		
06/22/45	14523	VMF-218	ZAMBOAN-GA	ZAMBOANGA	PHIL		
06/26/45	14080	POOL	BARBERS POINT	HAWAII	ECENPAC		
07/08/45	14102	VBF-100	HILO	HAWAII	ECENPAC	LT KENNETH C. ABLES, JR.	M
07/09/45	14283	VBF-14	PEARL	HAWAII	ECENPAC		
07/14/45	14262	AROU-2		SAMAR	PHIL		
07/17/45	14408	VMF-115	ZAMBOAN-GA	ZAMBOANGA	PHIL		
07/18/45	14576	VMF-218	ZAMBOAN-GA	ZAMBOANGA	PHIL		
07/22/45	14388	VMF-218			PHIL	LT BURNS	D
08/05/45	14469	SERVRON-12			PHIL		
08/06/45	14588	VMF-115	ZAMBOAN-GA	ZAMBOANGA	PHIL		
08/14/45	14587	VMF-115	ZAMBOAN-GA	ZAMBOANGA	PHIL		
12/31/43	14572. 49527	COMAIR-SOPAC	GUADAL-CANAL	GUADAL-CANAL	SOPAC		

GOODYEAR FG-1A

Most of the Goodyear FG-1A Corsairs were built for the US Marines to be used as a land based fighter/bomber. These Corsairs had non-folding wings, plus all of the Navy carrier equipment was removed, including the tail hook. Aircraft lost:

DATE	BUNO	SQDRN	BASE	LOST	AREA	PILOT	FATE
01/26/44	13213	VMF-211	PIVA	RABAUL	SOPAC	1STLT H.E. SEGAL	S
02/18/44	13268	MAG-11	ESPIRITU SANTO	MALAKULA IS.	SOPAC	1STLT P.E. WATSON	S
02/24/44	13212	VMF-222	TOROKINA	RABAUL	SOPAC	1STLT J.M. LEACH	M

DATE	BUNO	SQDRN	BASE	LOST	AREA	PILOT	FATE
03/07/44	13262	VMF-222	TOROKINA	RABAUL	SOPAC	LT BEACON	S
03/09/44	13269	VMF-217	VELLA LAVELLA	BARAKOMA	SOPAC	1STLT P.R. HAMMOND	S
10/10/44	14067	VMF-124		HAWAII	ECENPAC	LT J.L. VANDERGRIFT	S
10/10/44	13316	VMO-251	PIVA	RABAUL	SOPAC	LT JAMES B. STURGIS	S
10/19/44	14039	VMF-222		GREEN	SOPAC	LT A.B. VAUGHN	M
10/31/44	14279	VMF-121		YAP	CENPAC	LT G.O. BEALL	M
11/07/44	14015	VMF-222	GREEN	RABAUL	SOPAC		
11/10/44	14145	VMF-121		PELELIU	WCENPAC		
11/10/44	14196	VMF-121		PELELIU	WCENPAC		
11/10/44	14240	VMF-121		PELELIU	WCENPAC		
11/11/44	14236	VMF-222	GREEN	RABAUL	SOPAC	LT GERALD MILLER	M
11/12/44	14140	VMF-121	ULITHI	ULITHI	WCENPAC	LT ROBERT L. GILLIS	M
11/12/44	14026	VMF-222	GREEN	RABAUL	SOPAC	LT ARCHIE C. PERU	M
11/16/44	14029	VMF-222		GREEN	SOPAC	LT HARWOOD K. RYAN	S
12/06/44	14063	VMSB-333		MIDWAY	ECENPAC	1STLT DORAN O. KEMPER	D
01/02/45	14357	VBF-6	HILO	HAWAII	ECENPAC	ENS JOSEPH W. STEWART	S
01/07/45	14311	VBF-83		HAWAII	ECENPAC	LTJG E.O. SCHLOSS	S
01/07/45	14445	VMF-313		LOS NEGROS	PHIL	1STLT K.S. SHERWOOD	M
01/09/45	14081	VMF-313		LUZON	PHIL	CAPT J.R. BLACKSHIRE	D
01/10/45	14209	VBF-6	HAWAII	HAWAII	ECENPAC	ENS WILLIAM N. MILLESON	S
01/11/45	14284	VMF-121		PELELIU	WCENPAC	1STLT VIRGINIUS B. PERRY	D
01/11/45	14579	VMF-313		LUZON	PHIL	2NDLT KIME	S
01/15/45	14478	VMF-212		GREEN	SOPAC		
01/22/45	14056	VMF-114		PELELIU	WCENPAC	1STLT RICHARD S. RASH	S
01/23/45	14152	VMF-223		LUZON	PHIL	2NDLT GLEN J. AMO	M
02/01/45	14286	VBF-86	HAWAII	HAWAII	ECENPAC	ENS ROBERT C. CREGER	D
02/06/45	14382	VMF-324		MIDWAY	ECENPAC	2NDLT AUBREY LIVERMORE	S
02/15/45	14274	VMF-121		PELELIU	WCENPAC		
02/16/45	14042	VBF-100		HAWAII	ECENPAC	ENS LYNN S. MEGILL	S
02/28/45	14453	VMF-223		SAMAR	PHIL	LT UKENA	S
03/03/45	14241	VMF-114		PELELIU	WCENPAC	LT K.A. WALLACE	D
03/08/45	14018	VMF-114		PELELIU	WCENPAC	LT R.S. PASH	S
03/09/45	14557	VMF-212		SAMAR	PHIL		
03/12/45	14490	VMF-313		LEYTE GULF	PHIL	LT HOWE	S
03/15/45	14298	VMF-324		MIDWAY	ECENPAC	2NDLT CHARLES A. CHASE	S
03/21/45	14369	VMF-223		SAMAR	PHIL	1STLT RALPH R. STAYEN	S
03/22/45	14450	VMF-115		ZAMBOAN-GA	PHIL	2NDLT MARION B. COOPER	D
03/22/45	14458	VMF-222		SAMAR	PHIL	2NDLT LANGER	S
03/25/45	14313	VBF-1	KAHULUI	HAWAII	ECENPAC	ENS FRANK A. KOPF	S
03/31/45	14107	VMF-114		PELELIU	WCENPAC	LT CARTRIGHT	S
03/31/45	14271	VMF-121		BABELTHAUP	WCENPAC	1STLT KELLER	S
04/21/45	14121	VBF-1	KAHULUI	HAWAII	ECENPAC	LT M. FALMLEN	S
04/22/45	14342	VBF-1	KAHULUI	HAWAII	ECENPAC	ENS ROBERT PETERSON	D

GOODYEAR FG-1D

The Chance Vought F4U Corsair was a carrier-capable fighter aircraft that saw service in World War II (see the Vought F4U-1 write-up). Demand for the aircraft soon overwhelmed Vought's manufacturing capability, resulting in production by Goodyear and Brewster: Goodyear-built Corsairs were designated FG. Aircraft lost:

DATE	BUNO	SQDRN	BASE	LOST	AREA	PILOT	FATE
01/08/45	76503	VMF-314		HAWAII	ECENPAC	2NDLT CHARLES M. BUDD	S
01/19/45	76495	VBF-83	USS BOUGAIN-VILLE	HAWAII	ECENPAC	ENS JACK L. KOEHLER	D
01/20/45	14410	VMF-222		SAMAR	PHIL		

DATE	BUNO	SQDRN	BASE	LOST	AREA	PILOT	FATE
02/17/45	76446	VMF-123	USS BENNING-TON	TOKYO	EMPIRE		
02/20/45	76542	A.A.	PEARL	HAWAII	ECENPAC		
03/04/45	76557	COMAIR-PAC	PEARL	HAWAII	ECENPAC		
03/12/45	76462	VMF-115		ZAMBOANGA	PHIL	1STLT JON S. SCHNORF	M
03/15/45	76518	VBF-6	USS HANCOCK	ENR KYUSHU	EMPIRE		
03/16/45	76566	VBF-6	USS HANCOCK	ENR KYUSHU	EMPIRE		
03/18/45	76513	VBF-6	USS HANCOCK	KYUSHU	EMPIRE	LTJG T.C. MOURGAS	S
03/19/45	76487	VBF-6	USS HANCOCK	KYUSHU	EMPIRE	LTJG T.C. MOURGAS	S
03/19/45	76533	VBF-6	USS HANCOCK	KYUSHU	EMPIRE	ENS E.R. CALCOTE	M
03/19/45	76473	VF-5	USS FRANKLIN	HONSHU	EMPIRE	(DECK LOSS-KAMIKAZE)	
03/19/45	76521	VMF-5	USS FRANKLIN	HONSHU	EMPIRE	(DECK LOSS-KAMIKAZE)	
03/19/45	76550	VMF-5	USS FRANKLIN	HONSHU	EMPIRE	(DECK LOSS-KAMIKAZE)	
03/19/45	76627	VMF-5	USS FRANKLIN	HONSHU	EMPIRE	(DECK LOSS-KAMIKAZE)	
03/21/45	76579	VF-10	USS INTREPID	HONSHU	EMPIRE		
03/22/45	76480	VBF-6	USS HANCOCK	IE SHIMA	EMPIRE		
03/26/45	76454	VBF-6	USS HANCOCK	OKINAWA	EMPIRE		
03/26/45	76536	VBF-6	USS HANCOCK	OKINAWA	EMPIRE	LT F.W. BOWEN	S
03/26/45	76633	VMF-422		MARSHALLS	CENPAC	1STLT C. KELLENBERGER JR	S
03/30/45	76590	VBF-6	USS HANCOCK	OKINAWA	EMPIRE		
03/31/45	76647	VBF-6	USS HANCOCK	OKINAWA	EMPIRE		
03/31/45	76501	VF-6	USS HANCOCK	OKINAWA	EMPIRE	LTJG R.B. GRAHAM	D
04/01/45	76676	VBF-6	USS HANCOCK	OKINAWA	EMPIRE		
04/01/45	76543	VBF-83	USS ESSEX	OKINAWA	EMPIRE		
04/03/45	76467	VMF-422	ENGEBI	ENGEBI	WCENPAC		
04/06/45	76576	VBF-6	USS HANCOCK	OKINAWA	EMPIRE	ENS J.R. VILSACK	M
04/07/45	76470	VBF-6	USS HANCOCK	OKINAWA	EMPIRE		
04/07/45	76493	VBF-6	USS HANCOCK	OKINAWA	EMPIRE		
04/07/45	76511	VBF-6	USS HANCOCK	OKINAWA	EMPIRE		
04/07/45	76479	VBF-83	USS ESSEX	OKINAWA	EMPIRE	LTJG CRITTES	S
04/07/45	76505	VF-84	USS BUNKER HILL	KYUSHU	EMPIRE	LTJG ANDREW S. BEARWA	M
04/09/45	76478	VBF-83	USS ESSEX	ENR IWO JIMA	EMPIRE		
04/09/45	76502	VMF-112	USS BENNING-TON	OKINAWA	EMPIRE	2NDLT V. BYERLEIN, JR.	S
04/10/45	76489	VBF-83	USS ESSEX	IWO JIMA	EMPIRE	ENS DENNIS GRAY, JR.	M
04/12/45	76574	VMF-112	USS BENNING-TON	IE SHIMA	EMPIRE		
04/12/45	76483	VMF-218	ZAMBOAN-GA	ZAMBOANGA	PHIL	1STLT JOHN W. BERRY	M
04/13/45	76504	VBF-83	USS ESSEX	ENR OKINAWA	EMPIRE		
04/13/45	76675	VMF-112	USS BENNING-TON	IE SHIMA	EMPIRE	2NDLT K.E. HUNTINGTON	S
04/14/45	76703	VBF-83	USS ESSEX	ENR OKINAWA	EMPIRE		

DATE	BUNO	SQDRN	BASE	LOST	AREA	PILOT	FATE
04/16/45	76570	VBF-10	USS INTREPID	KOKUBO	EMPIRE		
04/16/45	76614	VBF-10	USS INTREPID	KOKUBO	EMPIRE		
04/16/45	76654	VBF-10	USS INTREPID	KOKUBO	EMPIRE		
04/16/45	87883	VBF-10	USS INTREPID	KOKUBO	EMPIRE	ENS E.M. BAILEY, JR.	M
04/16/45	76460	VBF-83	USS ESSEX	KYUSHU	EMPIRE	ENS J.M. BOULDIN	M
04/16/45	76624	VBF-83	USS ESSEX	KYUSHU	EMPIRE	ENS TINGNOR	S
04/16/45	76680	VBF-83	USS ESSEX	KYUSHU	EMPIRE	ENS WEAR	S
04/16/45	76471	VMF-122		PELELIU	WCENPAC	MAJ QUINTUS B. NELSON	D
04/18/45	76472	VBF-83	USS ESSEX	OKINAWA	EMPIRE		
04/19/45	76484	VBF-85	USS SHANGRI-LA	ENR OKINAWA	EMPIRE		
04/20/45	76617	CASU(F)-12		GUAM	WCENPAC		
04/23/45	76693	VMF-323		OKINAWA	EMPIRE		
04/30/45	76461	CASU(F)-51		ULITHI	WCENPAC		
05/01/45	87822	VBF-83	USS ESSEX	OKINAWA	EMPIRE		
05/03/45	76613	AROU-1		MOMOTE	SW PAC		
05/04/45	87877	CASU(F)-12	USS WINDHAM BAY	GUAM	WCENPAC	2NDLT C.S. HOWLAND	S
05/04/45	76731	POOL	USS WINDHAM BAY	GUAM	WCENPAC		
05/04/45	87825	VBF-83	USS ESSEX	OKINAWA	EMPIRE	LTJG G.A. GIBBS	M
05/04/45	76683	VBF-85	USS SHANGRI-LA	IE SHIMA	EMPIRE	LT WILLIAM H. MAY	S
05/05/45	76630	VBF-85	USS SHANGRI-LA	IE SHIMA	EMPIRE	LTJG LEONARD D. WELSH	S
05/06/45	76719	CASU(F)-12	USS WINDHAM BAY	GUAM	WCENPAC	ENS PAUL A. VERES	S
05/07/45	76606	VBF-83	USS ESSEX	OKINAWA	EMPIRE		
05/10/45	87876	VF-85	USS SHANGRI-LA	IWO JIMA	EMPIRE	LT DAVID C. KINCANNON	M
05/11/45	76468	VF-84	USS BUNKER HILL	OKINAWA	EMPIRE	(DECK LOSS-KAMIKAZE)	
05/11/45	76485	VF-84	USS BUNKER HILL	OKINAWA	EMPIRE	(DECK LOSS-KAMIKAZE)	
05/11/45	76567	VF-84	USS BUNKER HILL	OKINAWA	EMPIRE	(DECK LOSS-KAMIKAZE)	
05/11/45	76587	VF-84	USS BUNKER HILL	OKINAWA	EMPIRE	(DECK LOSS-KAMIKAZE)	
05/11/45	76602	VF-84	USS BUNKER HILL	OKINAWA	EMPIRE	(DECK LOSS-KAMIKAZE)	
05/11/45	76609	VF-84	USS BUNKER HILL	OKINAWA	EMPIRE	(DECK LOSS-KAMIKAZE)	
05/11/45	76612	VF-84	USS BUNKER HILL	OKINAWA	EMPIRE	(DECK LOSS-KAMIKAZE)	
05/11/45	76455	VMF-221	USS BUNKER HILL	OKINAWA	EMPIRE	(DECK LOSS-KAMIKAZE)	
05/11/45	76457	VMF-221	USS BUNKER HILL	OKINAWA	EMPIRE	(DECK LOSS-KAMIKAZE)	
05/11/45	76488	VMF-451	USS BUNKER HILL	OKINAWA	EMPIRE	(DECK LOSS-KAMIKAZE)	
05/11/45	76611	VMF-451	USS BUNKER HILL	OKINAWA	EMPIRE	(DECK LOSS-KAMIKAZE)	

DATE	BUNO	SQDRN	BASE	LOST	AREA	PILOT	FATE
05/14/45	76506	VMF-123	USS BENNING-TON	KYUSHU	EMPIRE	1STLT HERBERT PFREMMER	S
05/14/45	76571	VMF-312		OKINAWA	EMPIRE	MAJ RICHARD M. DAY	M
05/14/45	87851	VMF-312		OKINAWA	EMPIRE	2NDLT HARRIS C. COHEN	S
05/18/45	76640	VMF-224		OKINAWA	EMPIRE	2NDLT L.J. MICHAELS	S
05/20/45	87856	VBF-83	USS ESSEX	OKINAWA	EMPIRE	ENS R.M. JONES	S
05/22/45	87932	VBF-2	HILO	HAWAII	ECENPAC	ENS ELLSWORTH O. MERCER	S
05/23/45	76569	VMF-113		OKINAWA	EMPIRE	2NDLT EARL E. SANDT	S
05/24/45	76711	VMF-123	USS BENNING-TON	KYUSHU	EMPIRE	1STLT ROBERT J. MCINNIS	S
05/25/45	76663	VMF-312		OKINAWA	EMPIRE	2NDLT MALCOM M. BERNEY	M
05/27/45	87826	VBF-93	USS BOXER	CUBA	CENLANT	ENS O.F. JACKSON	D
05/27/45	87828	VMF-511	USS BLOCK ISLAND	IE SHIMA	EMPIRE	MAJ CLAUDE MAZE	D
05/29/45	87914	VMF-351	USS C. GLOUCES-TER	HAWAII	ECENPAC	CAPT H.F. FITZPATRICK	S
05/30/45	76577	VMF-322		OKINAWA	EMPIRE	2NDLT RAYMOND D. BAKER	M
06/01/45	87850	POOL	USS WINDHAM BAY	OKINAWA	EMPIRE	1STLT BYRON J. COSTELLO	S
06/01/45	87848	VBF-93	LEEWARD FIELD	CUBA	CENLANT	ENS W.R. BROCK	S
06/01/45	76652	VMF-312		OKINAWA	EMPIRE		
06/02/45	88170	VBF-351	USS C. GLOUCES-TER	HAWAII	ECENPAC		
06/02/45	76477	VBF-85	USS SHANGRI-LA	KYUSHU	EMPIRE	LTJG TOENGES	S
06/02/45	76528	VBF-85	USS SHANGRI-LA	KYUSHU	EMPIRE	LTJG C.M. KIRKHAN	M
06/02/45	76540	VBF-85	USS SHANGRI-LA	KYUSHU	EMPIRE	LT H.R. KENNEDY	M
06/03/45	88042	VF-85	USS SHANGRI-LA	KYUSHU	EMPIRE	LT JOHN H. SHROFF	M
06/03/45	76728	VMF-323		OKINAWA	EMPIRE		
06/03/45	76697	VMF-351	USS C. GLOUCES-TER	HAWAII	ECENPAC		
06/03/45	87920	VMF-351	USS C. GLOUCES-TER	HAWAII	ECENPAC	CAPT FRED. S. ROWE, JR.	M
06/05/45	87808	POOL	USS ATTU	OKINAWA	EMPIRE		
06/05/45	87817	POOL	USS ATTU	OKINAWA	EMPIRE		
06/06/45	76562	VMF-422		IE SHIMA	EMPIRE	1STLT RAYMOND A. WRISLEY	S
06/07/45	87842	VBF-93	USS BOXER	CUBA	CENLANT	CDR GEORGE B. NICOL	M
06/07/45	88252	VBF-93	LEEWARD FIELD	CUBA	CENLANT	ENS F.L. LAVESEN	S
06/08/45	87843	VBF-85	USS SHANGRI-LA	KYUSHU	EMPIRE	LTJG N.L. EDWIN	S
06/08/45	87913	VMF-512	USS GILBERT ISLANDS	IE SHIMA	EMPIRE	2NDLT LOGAN M. WHITE	D
06/09/45	76690	VMF-223		OKINAWA	EMPIRE	2NDLT E.C. STANTON	S
06/10/45	76655	VMF-322		OKINAWA	EMPIRE	1STLT E.J. SMYTH	S
06/12/45	87895	VBF-85	USS SHANGRI-LA	ENR LEYTE GULF	EMPIRE	2NDLT V.V. KOENIG	S
06/14/45	76623	VBF-93	USS BOXER		CENLANT	ENS J.R. DRUMHELLER	S

DATE	BUNO	SQDRN	BASE	LOST	AREA	PILOT	FATE
06/14/45	88070	VMF-113		IE SHIMA	EMPIRE	LT A.A. ANTON	S
06/14/45	76452	VMF-115	ZAMBOANGA	ZAMBOANGA	PHIL		
06/15/45	87859	VMF-312		OKINAWA	EMPIRE		
06/15/45	87916	VMF-322		OKINAWA	EMPIRE		
06/16/45	76573	CASU(F)-12		GUAM	WCENPAC		
06/16/45	88002	CASU(F)-12		GUAM	WCENPAC		
06/16/45	88393	VBF-93	USS BOXER		CENLANT	ENS C. EASTON	S
06/16/45	87908	VMF-113		IE SHIMA	EMPIRE	2NDLT WILLIAM C. MADDOX	M
06/17/45	87866	VMF-323		IE SHIMA	EMPIRE	2NDLT W.O. BAKER	M
06/18/45	76481	VMF-422		IE SHIMA	EMPIRE		
06/20/45	88046	VMF-322		OKINAWA	EMPIRE	2NDLT MICHAEL GAYDOS	M
06/22/45	76559	VMF-113		IE SHIMA	EMPIRE	2NDLT R.D. ALLCROFT	M
06/22/45	87905	VMF-113		IE SHIMA	EMPIRE	2NDLT F.B. SMITH	M
06/22/45	87844	VMF-224		OKINAWA	EMPIRE	2NDLT GEORGE R. TREGAY	M
06/22/45	87927	VMF-224		OKINAWA	EMPIRE		
06/22/45	88262	VMF-312		OKINAWA	EMPIRE	MAJ WALTON L. TURNER	D
06/23/45	76474	VMF-323		OKINAWA	EMPIRE	1STLT GUST. BROBERG JR	S
06/24/45	88199	CASU(F)-12		GUAM	WCENPAC	LT J.E. COKER	S
06/25/45	87925	CASU-31	HILO	HAWAII	ECENPAC	ENS JOHN H. BLACK	S
06/29/45	88374	VBF-1	USS BENNINGTON	LEYTE GULF	PHIL	ENS PETER PARTHEMOS	D
06/29/45	76498	VMF-113		IE SHIMA	EMPIRE		
06/29/45	76552	VMF-422		IE SHIMA	EMPIRE	1STLT RICHARD F. HALE	D
06/30/45	76565	POOL	PEARL	HAWAII	ECENPAC		
07/01/45	88254	VMF-224		CHIMU	EMPIRE	LT W.A. ROGERS	D
07/01/45	76660	VMF-312		AWASE	EMPIRE	2NDLT SAMUEL S. SMITH	M
07/01/45	87860	VMF-312		AWASE	EMPIRE	1STLT HOWARD F. HEYLIGER	S
07/01/45	76730	VMF-322		KADENA	EMPIRE	2NDLT PETER N. HOMRICH	M
07/02/45	76650	VBF-83		USS ESSEX	EMPIRE		
07/02/45	88099	VMF-113		IE SHIMA	EMPIRE	MAJ O.H. RAMLO	S
07/02/45	88242	VMF-224		OKINAWA	EMPIRE	CAPT J.P. LYNCH	S
07/03/45	88307	VBF-1	USS BENNINGTON	ENR KURE	EMPIRE	LTJG F.B. PHILLIPS	S
07/04/45	88399	VMF-113		IE SHIMA	EMPIRE	2NDLT MARTIN W. HARKE	S
07/04/45	88441	VMF-113		IE SHIMA	EMPIRE	1STLT RUSSELL HUNCHAR	S
07/04/45	87875	VMF-323		KADENA	EMPIRE	1STLT GUST. BROBERG JR	S
07/04/45	88081	VMF-422		IE SHIMA	EMPIRE		
07/07/45	87810	VBF-85	USS SHANGRI-LA	ENR HOKKAIDO	EMPIRE	LTJG CHARLES W. FOX	S
07/07/45	88220	VBF-88	USS YORKTOWN	ENR JAPAN	EMPIRE	LT C.K. HUGHES	S
07/07/45	88115	VMF-224		OKINAWA	EMPIRE	2NDLT NATHAN H. LAWLESS	M
07/10/45	76720	VBF-1	USS BENNINGTON	KURE	EMPIRE	LTJG THOMAS MCBRIDE	S
07/10/45	87802	VBF-1	USS BENNINGTON	KURE	EMPIRE	LTJG WALTER HENSHAW	S
07/10/45	88323	VBF-1	USS BENNINGTON	KURE	EMPIRE	LTJG F.B. PHILLIPS	S
07/10/45	92109	VBF-88	USS YORKTOWN	ENR JAPAN	EMPIRE	ENS C.E. EMHOFF	M
07/10/45	76727	VMF-323		OKINAWA	EMPIRE		
07/10/45	87821	VMF-323		OKINAWA	EMPIRE	CAPT MCCLEARY	S
07/10/45	88177	VMF-323		OKINAWA	EMPIRE	1STLT WALT K PARMENTER	M
07/11/45	87910	VMF-312		AWASE	EMPIRE		

DATE	BUNO	SQDRN	BASE	LOST	AREA	PILOT	FATE
07/12/45	76537	CASU(F)-12		GUAM	WCENPAC		
07/12/45	88361	VMF-312		IE SHIMA	EMPIRE	CAPT PAUL H. BROWN, JR.	D
07/14/45	87834	VF-85	USS SHANGRI-LA	HOKKAIDO	EMPIRE	ENS L.E. DEVEREAUX	S
07/14/45	87854	VF-85	USS SHANGRI-LA	HOKKAIDO	EMPIRE	LTJG LESTER	S
07/15/45	88295	VBF-1	USS BENNING-TON	HOKKAIDO	EMPIRE	LT R.F. MORGAN	S
07/15/45	76526	VBF-85	USS SHANGRI-LA	HOKKAIDO	EMPIRE	LTJG J.L. PEELEY	S
07/15/45	76692	VBF-85	USS SHANGRI-LA	HOKKAIDO	EMPIRE	LTJG JOHN SANFORD WEEKS	M
07/15/45	87801	VBF-85	USS SHANGRI-LA	HOKKAIDO	EMPIRE	ENS WALLACE C. MOESSMER	S
07/15/45	88052	VBF-88	USS YORK-TOWN	HOKKAIDO	EMPIRE	ENS M.D. SPRINGER	M
07/15/45	88125	VBF-88	USS YORK-TOWN	HOKKAIDO	EMPIRE	ENS R.G. SHEPHERD	M
07/15/45	88299	VBF-88	USS YORK-TOWN	HOKKAIDO	EMPIRE		
07/16/45	76568	VBF-85	USS SHANGRI-LA	HOKKAIDO	EMPIRE	LT JACK A. GUSTAVUS	S
07/17/45	88240	VMF-113		CHIMU	EMPIRE	1STLT W.M. WASKOM	S
07/18/45	76494	VBF-1	USS BENNING-TON	KURE	EMPIRE	LT R.M. LANG	S
07/18/45	88312	VBF-1	USS BENNING-TON	KURE	EMPIRE	ENS WILLIAM H. CARNEY	M
07/18/45	88321	VBF-1	USS BENNING-TON	KURE	EMPIRE	LT RICHARD B. EASON	M
07/18/45	88110	VBF-83	USS ESSEX	IE SHIMA	EMPIRE	LT DAVID A. HORTON	D
07/18/45	88102	VBF-88	USS YORK-TOWN	TOKYO	EMPIRE	LT L.G. CHRISTISON	M
07/18/45	88129	VBF-88	USS YORK-TOWN	TOKYO	EMPIRE	LTJG T.H. GLEASON	D
07/19/45	88087	VBF-513	BARBERS POINT	HAWAII	ECENPAC	1STLT WILLIAM R. WINN	S
07/19/45	76608	VMF-323		KADENA	EMPIRE		
07/20/45	87937	POOL		ADMIRALTY IS.	EMPIRE	ENS DEAN H. ALLISON	S
07/20/45	92038	VBF-85	USS SHANGRI-LA	ENR KURE	EMPIRE		
07/24/45	76670	CASU-31	HILO	HAWAII	ECENPAC		
07/24/45	88062	VBF-1	USS BENNING-TON	KURE	EMPIRE	LT R.C. TABLER	M
07/24/45	88224	VBF-1	USS BENNING-TON	KURE	EMPIRE	ENS R.J. SPECKMAN	M
07/24/45	88245	VBF-1	USS BENNING-TON	KURE	EMPIRE	LT J.W. ROWLEY	S
07/24/45	76516	VBF-85	USS SHANGRI-LA	KURE	EMPIRE		
07/24/45	88440	VBF-85	USS SHANGRI-LA	KURE	EMPIRE	LTJG R.L. REED	S
07/24/45	88080	VBF-88	USS YORK-TOWN	KURE	EMPIRE	LT A.C. SHEFLOE	D
07/24/45	88250	VBF-88	USS YORK-TOWN	KURE	EMPIRE	ENS HECK	S
07/24/45	88367	VBF-88	USS YORK-TOWN	KURE	EMPIRE	ENS FRANK G. RITZ	M

DATE	BUNO	SQDRN	BASE	LOST	AREA	PILOT	FATE
07/24/45	87869	VMF-211			PHIL	2NDLT ANTHONY CRAMER	D
07/24/45	76685	VMF-218			PHIL	1STLT MAURICE E. BROWN	S
07/24/45	76575	VMF-323		AWASE	EMPIRE	2NDLT R.L. HAMMERLY	S
07/25/45	88308	VBF-1	USS BENNING-TON	NAGOYA	EMPIRE	ENS FRANK A. KOPF	S
07/25/45	92116	VBF-1	USS BENNING-TON	NAGOYA	EMPIRE	LTJG FRANK G. KINGSTON	S
07/25/45	88370	VBF-83	USS ESSEX	KURE	EMPIRE		
07/25/45	87794	VMF-512	USS GILBERT ISLANDS	LEYTE GULF	PHIL		
07/27/45	76737	VMF-113		IE SHIMA	EMPIRE	2NDLT HARLEY L. HABERLIE	S
07/28/45	88434	VBF-1	USS BENNING-TON	NAGOYA	EMPIRE	ENS O.P. FISHER	D
07/28/45	92102	VBF-1	USS BENNING-TON	NAGOYA	EMPIRE	ENS J.A. LUNDGREN	S
07/28/45	87868	VBF-85	USS SHANGRI-LA	KURE	EMPIRE	LTJG J.L. PEELEY	S
07/28/45	92033	VBF-85	USS SHANGRI-LA	KURE	EMPIRE	LTJG J.G. HJELSTROM	M
07/28/45	88214	VBF-88	USS YORK-TOWN	KURE	EMPIRE		
07/29/45	76523	VMF-122		PELELIU	WCENPAC		
07/30/45	87884	VBF-85	USS SHANGRI-LA	KURE	EMPIRE	LT R.T. SCHAEFFER	D
07/30/45	92037	VBF-88	USS YORK-TOWN	TOKYO	EMPIRE	LTJG PENN	S
07/30/45	92049	VMF-122		PELELIU	WCENPAC		
07/31/45	76687	MAG-33	KADENA	AWASE	EMPIRE		
08/02/45	76531	VBF-100		HAWAII	ECENPAC		
08/03/45	88063	VMF-351	USS C. GLOUCEST ER	HAWAII	ECENPAC	1STLT J.G. DUER	S
08/06/45	87899	VMF-322		OKINAWA	EMPIRE		
08/08/45	92048	VMF-422		CHIMU	EMPIRE	2NDLT WILLIAM D. WATSON	S
08/09/45	92087	VBF-1	USS BENNING-TON		EMPIRE	ENS VINCENT L. LANDAU	D
08/09/45	76716	VBF-83	USS ESSEX		EMPIRE	LTJG COUMBE	S
08/09/45	88329	VBF-83	USS ESSEX		EMPIRE	LT W.H. HARRIS, JR.	D
08/09/45	88243	VBF-88	USS YORK-TOWN	HONSHU	EMPIRE		
08/09/45	92023	VF-85	USS SHANGRI-LA	ENR HONSHU	EMPIRE		
08/10/45	76732	VBF-83	USS ESSEX		EMPIRE	LTJG CLINTON E. MOORE?	M
08/10/45	88106	VBF-88	USS YORK-TOWN	TOKYO	EMPIRE		
08/10/45	88194	VBF-88	USS YORK-TOWN	TOKYO	EMPIRE		
08/10/45	88219	VBF-88	USS YORK-TOWN	TOKYO	EMPIRE		
08/11/45	88109	VMF-441		CHIMU	EMPIRE	LT JOSEPH L. NEWMAN	S
08/12/45	92117	VMF-512	USS GILBERT ISLANDS		EMPIRE		
08/13/45	76639	CASU(F)-12		GUAM	WCENPAC		
08/13/45	76682	CASU(F)-12		GUAM	WCENPAC		
08/13/45	88317	CASU(F)-12		GUAM	WCENPAC		
08/13/45	76558	MAG-33	KADENA	OKINAWA	EMPIRE		
08/13/45	76667	VBF-1	USS BENNING-TON	TOKYO	EMPIRE	LT SEARCY	S

DATE	BUNO	SQDRN	BASE	LOST	AREA	PILOT	FATE
08/13/45	88227	VBF-1	USS BENNING-TON	TOKYO	EMPIRE	LTJG CHARLES B. MOXLEY	D
08/13/45	88387	VBF-1	USS BENNING-TON	TOKYO	EMPIRE	ENS J.A. LUNDGREN	S
08/13/45	76653	VBF-83	USS ESSEX	TOKYO	EMPIRE		
08/13/45	92242	VBF-83	USS ESSEX	TOKYO	EMPIRE		
08/13/45	88444	VBF-85	USS SHANGRI-LA	HONSHU	EMPIRE	ENS J.H. CHAPMAN, JR.	M
08/15/45	88360	VBF-1	USS BENNING-TON		EMPIRE	LT R.P. ROSS	S
08/15/45	87898	VBF-85	USS SHANGRI-LA	HONSHU	EMPIRE		
08/15/45	88054	VBF-85	USS SHANGRI-LA	HONSHU	EMPIRE	LTJG J.C. DUNN	M
08/15/45	87935	VMF-224		CHIMU	EMPIRE		

GRUMMAN F4F-3

The first flight of the Grumman XF4F-3 was made on February 12, 1939. Although engine cooling proved to be a major problem, the potential of the Grumman fighter had been established with a trial speed was recorded at 333.5 mph at 21,300 ft altitude. In August 1939 the Navy ordered 54 F4F-3s and the first production F4F-3 rolled off the production line in February 1940. A few were subsequently equipped in the field with cameras as F4F-3P reconnaissance aircraft and one was fitted with twin floats as the F4F-3S. By December 1940, 22 F4F-3s had been accepted by the Navy and initial deliveries were being made to VF-4 (USS RANGER) and VF-7 (USS WASP) at the Naval Air Station in Norfolk, VA. During 1941, VF-42 and VF-71 were equipped with F4F-3s as well as Marine Squadrons VMF-121, -211, and -221. In addition to further contracts for the F4F-3, Grumman received a Navy order for 95 F4F-3As, these being powered by R-1830-90 engines with single-stage superchargers (See F4F-3A below). The F4F-3A was mostly used by Navy squadron VF-6 and Marine squadron VMF-111. By the end of 1941 the Navy and Marines together had 183 F4F-3s and 65 F4F-3As. Most of these were still in the United States or aboard the USS RANGER and USS WASP, but Marine squadron VMF-211 was in Ewa, Hawaii, when the Japanese attack was launched and eight of their aircraft were lost on the ground. A detachment of the same squadron lost seven more of their F4F-3s. In the ensuing battle for Wake, five remaining F4F-3s scored a number of victories against Japanese bombers and fighters before they were outnumbered and lost. Production of the F4F-3 totaled 285 (plus the 95 F4F-3As), all by Grumman. Aircraft lost:

DATE	BUNO	SQDRN	BASE	LOST	AREA	PILOT	FATE
12/07/41	3977	VMF-211	EWA	HAWAII	ECENPAC		
12/07/41	3992	VMF-211	EWA	HAWAII	ECENPAC		
12/07/41	4018	VMF-211	EWA	HAWAII	ECENPAC		
12/07/41	4023	VMF-211	EWA	HAWAII	ECENPAC		
12/07/41	4025	VMF-211	EWA	HAWAII	ECENPAC		
12/07/41	4029	VMF-211	EWA	HAWAII	ECENPAC		
12/07/41	4034	VMF-211	EWA	HAWAII	ECENPAC		
12/07/41	4040	VMF-211	EWA	HAWAII	ECENPAC		
12/08/41	4024	VMF-211		WAKE	ECENPAC		
12/08/41	4027	VMF-211		WAKE	ECENPAC		
12/08/41	4028	VMF-211		WAKE	ECENPAC		
12/08/41	4030	VMF-211		WAKE	ECENPAC		
12/08/41	4032	VMF-211		WAKE	ECENPAC		
12/08/41	4039	VMF-211		WAKE	ECENPAC		
12/08/41	4041	VMF-211		WAKE	ECENPAC		

DATE	BUNO	SQDRN	BASE	LOST	AREA	PILOT	FATE
12/11/41	4020	VMF-211		WAKE	ECENPAC	CAPT ELROD	S
12/13/41	4051	VF-5	USS WASP	ENR NORFOLK	NORLANT		
12/14/41	3988	VMF-211		WAKE	ECENPAC		
12/14/41	4019	VMF-211		WAKE	ECENPAC		
12/22/41	3985	VF-3	USS SARATOGA	HAWAII	ECENPAC	LTJG V.M. GADROW	U
12/23/41	3980	VMF-211		WAKE	ECENPAC		
12/23/41	4022	VMF-211		WAKE	ECENPAC		
12/24/41	1853	VF-41	USS RANGER	BERMUDA	NORLANT		
01/08/42	2529	VF-42	USS YORK-TOWN	HAWAII	ECENPAC	ENS WILLIAM W. WOOLLEN	S
01/12/42	1886	VF-42	USS YORK-TOWN	HAWAII	ECENPAC	CDR C.S. SMILEY	S
01/14/42	1860	VF-42	USS YORK-TOWN	HAWAII	ECENPAC	ENS RICHARD L. WRIGHT	S
01/15/42	4015	VF-3	EWA	HAWAII	ECENPAC	ENS LEON W. HAYNES	S
02/20/42	3995	VF-3	USS LEX-INGTON	RABAUL	SOPAC	ENS JOHN W. WILSON	M
02/20/42	4026	VF-3	USS LEX-INGTON	RABAUL	SOPAC	LTJG HOWARD L. JOHNSON	S
02/24/42	4017	VF-6	USS ENTER-PRISE	WAKE	WCENPAC	ENS JOSEPH R. DALY	S
03/14/42	4009	VF-3	USS LEX-INGTON	ENR PEARL	SW PAC	ENS WALTER A. HAAS	S
03/15/42	3867	VF-72	USS WASP	ENR NORFOLK	CENLANT		
04/27/42	1896	VMF-111			SOPAC		
04/28/42	1877	VF-42	USS YORK-TOWN	HAWAII	ECENPAC		
05/02/42	4012	VF-42	USS YORK-TOWN	TULAGI	SOPAC	ENS JOHN P. ADAMS	S
05/02/42	3994	VF-6	USS ENTER-PRISE	ENR CORAL SEA	ECENPAC		
05/02/42	4002	VF-6	USS ENTER-PRISE	ENR CORAL SEA	ECENPAC		
05/04/42	2527	VF-42	USS YORK-TOWN	TULAGI	SOPAC	LTJG ELBERT S. MCCUSKEY	S
05/04/42	2528	VF-42	USS YORK-TOWN	TULAGI	SOPAC	ENS JOHN P. ADAMS	S
05/07/42	4011	VF-2	USS LEX-INGTON	NISIMA	SOPAC	LTJG PAUL G. BAKER	M
05/07/42	2531	VF-42	USS YORK-TOWN	NISIMA	SOPAC	KNOX	M
05/07/42	3972	VF-42	USS YORK-TOWN	NISIMA	SOPAC	ENS WILLIAM W. WOOLEN	M
05/08/42	3970	VF-2	USS LEX-INGTON	CORAL SEA	SOPAC	LTJG RICHARD G. CROMMELIN	S
05/08/42	3978	VF-2	USS LEX-INGTON	CORAL SEA	SOPAC	(SHIP SANK)	
05/08/42	3979	VF-2	USS LEX-INGTON	CORAL SEA	SOPAC	(SHIP SANK)	
05/08/42	3981	VF-2	USS LEX-INGTON	CORAL SEA	SOPAC	(SHIP SANK)	
05/08/42	3982	VF-2	USS LEX-INGTON	CORAL SEA	SOPAC	(SHIP SANK)	
05/08/42	3986	VF-2	USS LEX-INGTON	CORAL SEA	SOPAC	(SHIP SANK)	
05/08/42	3987	VF-2	USS LEX-INGTON	CORAL SEA	SOPAC	(SHIP SANK)	
05/08/42	3993	VF-2	USS LEX-INGTON	CORAL SEA	SOPAC	(SHIP SANK)	
05/08/42	4003	VF-2	USS LEX-INGTON	CORAL SEA	SOPAC	(SHIP SANK)	
05/08/42	4005	VF-2	USS LEX-INGTON	CORAL SEA	SOPAC	(SHIP SANK)	
05/08/42	4016	VF-2	USS LEX-INGTON	CORAL SEA	SOPAC	(SHIP SANK)	
05/08/42	4021	VF-2	USS LEX-INGTON	CORAL SEA	SOPAC	(SHIP SANK)	
05/08/42	4035	VF-2	USS LEX-INGTON	CORAL SEA	SOPAC	(SHIP SANK)	

DATE	BUNO	SQDRN	BASE	LOST	AREA	PILOT	FATE
05/08/42	3999	VF-42	USS YORK-TOWN	CORAL SEA	SOPAC		
06/04/42	1873	4TH MBDAW		SAMOA	SE PAC		
06/04/42	3989	VMF-221		MIDWAY	ECENPAC	LT SWANNBERGER	M
06/04/42	4006	VMF-221		MIDWAY	ECENPAC		
06/09/42	1859	VMF-111			SOPAC		
06/12/42	2512	4TH MBDAW		SAMOA	SE PAC		
06/26/42	4056	VF-6	USS ENTER-PRISE	HAWAII	ECENPAC		
07/09/42	4004	VBF-224			ECENPAC	LT C.S. HUGHES	S
07/21/42	1851	VMF-111		SAMOA	SE PAC	CAPT D.H. YOST	U
07/26/42	1890	VMO-251			SOPAC	LT GEORGE S. KOHLER	S
08/03/42	1863	VMF-111		SAMOA	SE PAC		
08/03/42	1884	VMF-111		SAMOA	SE PAC		
08/03/42	1891	VMF-111		SAMOA	SE PAC		
08/18/42	4037	VGS-12			NORPAC		
08/25/42	1875	VMF-111			SOPAC		
09/10/42	2516	VMO-251			SOPAC		
09/27/42	2515	VMF-111			SOPAC		
10/05/42	1881	VMF-111			SOPAC		
10/05/42	1893	VMF-111			SOPAC		
10/08/42	1889	MAG-13		TUTUILA	SOPAC	S/SGT KOPAS	S
10/13/42	3996	VMF-221		GUADAL-CANAL	SOPAC	LT JOSEPH L. NARR	S
10/19/42	3973	VMF-441			SOPAC	2NDLT HENRY DEAL	S
11/17/42	1850	VMO-251			SOPAC	2NDLT K.L. REUSSER	D
12/01/42	4010	VMF-213	PEARL	HAWAII	ECENPAC	LT ROSS	D
12/21/42	3998	VMO-251	GUADAL-CANAL	ESPIRITU SANTO	SOPAC	2NDLT ROY L. BOOTH	M
01/11/43	3991	MAG-13		TUTUILA	SOPAC	1STLT KENNY FORD	S
01/15/43	1852	VMO-251			SOPAC		
01/23/43	1866	VMF-111			SOPAC		
01/27/43	1849	VMF-112			SOPAC	LT HORACE G. CLEVELAND	D
02/08/43	1864	VMF-215			SOPAC		
05/02/43	4043	VMF-123			SOPAC		
05/11/43	3997	VC-21	USS NASSAU	ATTU	NORPAC		
06/09/43	1876	MAG-11	ESPIRITU SANTO	NEW HEBRID.	SOPAC		
07/15/43	1872	MAG-11	ESPIRITU SANTO		SOPAC		
07/29/43	1845	VMF-123		EFATE	SOPAC		

GRUMMAN F4F-3A

A shortage of two-stage superchargers lead to the development of the F4F-3A, which was basically the F4F-3 but with a 1,200hp (890 kW) Pratt & Whitney R-1830-90 radial engine with a more primitive single-stage two-speed supercharger. The F4F-3A, which was capable of 312 mph (502 km/h) at 16,000 ft (4,900 m), was used side by side with the F4F-3, but its poorer performance made it unpopular with US Navy fighter pilots. Aircraft lost:

DATE	BUNO	SQDRN	BASE	LOST	AREA	PILOT	FATE
12/07/41	3906	VF-6	USS ENTER-PRISE	PEARL	ECENPAC		
12/07/41	3909	VF-6	USS ENTER-PRISE	PEARL	ECENPAC		
12/07/41	3935	VF-6	USS ENTER-PRISE	PEARL	ECENPAC		
12/07/41	3938	VF-6	USS ENTER-PRISE	PEARL	ECENPAC		

DATE	BUNO	SQDRN	BASE	LOST	AREA	PILOT	FATE
12/31/41	3907	VF-6	USS ENTER-PRISE	PEARL	ECENPAC	ENS JOHN C. KELLY	S
02/01/42	3937	VF-6	USS ENTER-PRISE	ROI	WCENPAC	ENS DAVID W. CRISWELL	S
03/28/42	3932	VF-6	USS ENTER-PRISE	HAWAII	ECENPAC	ENS ERIC ALLEN	S
04/21/42	3894	VF-6	USS ENTER-PRISE	HAWAII	ECENPAC	ENS HOWARD S. PACKARD	S
05/08/42	3964	VF-2	USS LEX-INGTON	CORAL SEA	SOPAC	(SHIP SANK)	
05/11/42	3911	VMF-212		NEW CALEDONIA	SOPAC		
05/20/42	3915	VMF-212		NEW CALEDONIA	SOPAC		
05/31/42	3916	VMF-212		NEW CALEDONIA	SOPAC	2NDLT ARTHUR R. FINSCARE	D
08/06/42	3908	MAG-21	EWA	HAWAII	ECENPAC		
08/06/42	3918	VMF-212		NEW CALEDONIA	SOPAC		

GRUMMAN F4F-4

The Grumman F4F Wildcat was an American carrier-based fighter aircraft that began service with both the United States Navy and the British Royal Navy (as the Martlet) in 1940. The Wildcat was the only effective fighter available to the United States Navy and Marine Corps in the Pacific Theater during the early part of World War II in 1941 and 1942, replacing the Brewster Buffalo. With a top speed of 318 mph (512 km/h), the Wildcat was outperformed by the faster and more nimble 331 mph (533 km/h) Mitsubishi Zero, but its ruggedness, coupled with tactics such as the *"Thach Weave"*, resulted in an air combat kill-to-loss ratio of 5.9:1 in 1942 and 6.9:1 for the entire war. Aircraft lost:

DATE	BUNO	SQDRN	BASE	LOST	AREA	PILOT	FATE
02/21/42	01997	VF-6	USS ENTER-PRISE	WAKE	WCENPAC	ENS NORMAN D. HODSON	U
04/10/42	4065	VF-72	USS WASP	ENR GREENOCK	EUROPE		
04/30/42	5101	VF-71	USS WASP	OFF MALTA	CENLANT	ENS P.T. JORGENSEN	U
05/01/42	5131	VF-8	USS HORNET	PEARL	ECENPAC	ENS S.W. GROVES	S
05/02/42	5095	VF-8	USS HORNET	PEARL	ECENPAC	ENS C.M. KELLY	S
05/05/42	5176	VF-6	USS ENTER-PRISE	ENR CORAL SEA	ECENPAC	AP1/C HOMER E. CARTER	U
05/07/42	11799	VF-42	USS YORK-TOWN	NISIMI	SOPAC	BAKER	M
05/08/42	01998	VF-42	USS YORK-TOWN	CORAL SEA	SOPAC		
05/10/42	5051	VF-6	USS ENTER-PRISE	ENR CORAL SEA	ECENPAC	LTJG JOHN G. PRESLER	S
05/15/42	5146	VF-3	BARBERS POINT	HAWAII	ECENPAC		
05/15/42	5173	VF-6	USS ENTER-PRISE	ENR CORAL SEA	ECENPAC	ENS W.M. HOLT	S
05/25/42	5060	VF-6	USS ENTER-PRISE	ENR HAWAII	ECENPAC	LTJG GEYLE L. HERMANN	D
05/31/42	5132	VF-8	USS HORNET	NW OF WAKE	ECENPAC		

DATE	BUNO	SQDRN	BASE	LOST	AREA	PILOT	FATE
06/01/42	11731	VF-3	USS YORK-TOWN	ENR MIDWAY	ECENPAC	LCDR DONALD A. LOVELACE	S
06/01/42	5048	VF-6	USS ENTER-PRISE	ENR MIDWAY	ECENPAC		
06/01/42	5079	VF-6	USS ENTER-PRISE	ENR MIDWAY	ECENPAC		
06/03/42	5182	VF-2	USS SARATOGA	HAWAII	ECENPAC	AP2/C F.W. TUMOSA	S
06/04/42	5080	VF-3	USS YORK-TOWN	MIDWAY	ECENPAC	(SHIP SANK)	
06/04/42	5093	VF-3	USS YORK-TOWN	MIDWAY	ECENPAC	(SHIP SANK)	
06/04/42	5143	VF-3	USS YORK-TOWN	MIDWAY	ECENPAC	(SHIP SANK)	
06/04/42	5145	VF-3	USS YORK-TOWN	MIDWAY	ECENPAC	(SHIP SANK)	
06/04/42	5239	VF-3	USS YORK-TOWN	MIDWAY	ECENPAC	ENS MILTON TOOTLE, JR.	U
06/04/42	5150	VF-42	USS YORK-TOWN	MIDWAY	ECENPAC	ENS G.F. HOPPER	M
06/04/42	5151	VF-42	USS YORK-TOWN	MIDWAY	ECENPAC	ENS H.B. GIBBS	M
06/04/42	5152	VF-42	USS YORK-TOWN	MIDWAY	ECENPAC	(SHIP SANK)	
06/04/42	5165	VF-42	USS YORK-TOWN	MIDWAY	ECENPAC	ENS E.R. BASSETI	M
06/04/42	5170	VF-42	USS YORK-TOWN	MIDWAY	ECENPAC	ENS B.T. MACOMBER	M
06/04/42	5062	VF-6	USS ENTER-PRISE	MIDWAY	ECENPAC	MACH R.H. WARDEN	S
06/04/42	5086	VF-8	USS HORNET	MIDWAY	ECENPAC	LTJG R. GRAY	S
06/04/42	5089	VF-8	USS HORNET	MIDWAY	ECENPAC		
06/04/42	5109	VF-8	USS HORNET	MIDWAY	ECENPAC	ENS C.M. KELLY	S
06/04/42	5113	VF-8	USS HORNET	MIDWAY	ECENPAC		
06/04/42	5115	VF-8	USS HORNET	MIDWAY	ECENPAC		
06/04/42	5116	VF-8	USS HORNET	MIDWAY	ECENPAC		
06/04/42	5117	VF-8	USS HORNET	MIDWAY	ECENPAC	ENS G.R. HILL	S
06/04/42	5118	VF-8	USS HORNET	MIDWAY	ECENPAC	ENS S.W. GROVES	S
06/04/42	5119	VF-8	USS HORNET	MIDWAY	ECENPAC	LCDR S.G. MITCHELL	S
06/04/42	5123	VF-8	USS HORNET	MIDWAY	ECENPAC	LT S.E. RUSHLOW	S
06/04/42	5237	VF-8	USS HORNET	MIDWAY	ECENPAC		
06/05/42	4071	VF-71	USS WASP	OFF MALTA	CENLANT	ENS BEACH PIERCE	S
06/12/42	02005	VF-72	USS SARATOGA	HAWAII	ECENPAC	LTJG R.W. RYND	S
06/16/42	4059	VF-71	USS WASP	ENR SAN DIEGO	CENPAC	ENS RICHARD P. BRISTLE	S
06/18/42	5184	VF-3	USS YORK-TOWN	MIDWAY	ECENPAC	LTJG RALPH M. RICH	M
06/18/42	5178	VF-6	USS ENTER-PRISE	OAHU	ECENPAC	LTJG RALPH MCMASLEY	D
06/23/42	5217	VGB-12	KODIAK	ALASKA	NORPAC	LCDR W. ELLISON PERNREWILL	D
07/01/42	5232	VF-6	USS ENTER-PRISE	HAWAII	ECENPAC	ENS SYL. HOPFERSPERGER	D
07/09/42	5174	VF-6	USS ENTER-PRISE	HAWAII	ECENPAC		

DATE	BUNO	SQDRN	BASE	LOST	AREA	PILOT	FATE
07/15/42	5149	VF-6	USS ENTER-PRISE	HAWAII	ECENPAC	H.M. O'LEARY	S
07/15/42	02103	VMF-223		HAWAII	ECENPAC		
08/04/42	5224	VF-6	USS ENTER-PRISE	SANTA CRUZ	SOPAC	MACH CLAYTON ALLERE, JR.	D
08/06/42	5083	VMF-211		PALMYRA	ECENPAC		
08/06/42	02042	VMF-211		PALMYRA	ECENPAC		
08/07/42	5128	VF-5	USS SARATOGA	GUADAL-CANAL	SOPAC		
08/07/42	5133	VF-5	USS SARATOGA	GUADAL-CANAL	SOPAC	LT J.J. SOUTHERLAND	S
08/07/42	5137	VF-5	USS SARATOGA	GUADAL-CANAL	SOPAC		
08/07/42	5154	VF-5	USS SARATOGA	GUADAL-CANAL	SOPAC	LTJG BOLT	S
08/07/42	5190	VF-5	USS SARATOGA	GUADAL-CANAL	SOPAC	ENS R.L. PRICE	M
08/07/42	5192	VF-5	USS SARATOGA	GUADAL-CANAL	SOPAC	ENS J. DALY	S
08/07/42	5068	VF-6	USS ENTER-PRISE	TULAGI	SOPAC	AP1/C STEPHENSON	M
08/07/42	5071	VF-6	USS ENTER-PRISE	TULAGI	SOPAC	MACH P.L. NAGLE	M
08/07/42	5082	VF-6	USS ENTER-PRISE	TULAGI	SOPAC	LTJG G.E. FIREBAUGH	S
08/07/42	5228	VF-6	USS ENTER-PRISE	TULAGI	SOPAC	MACH J.A. ACHTEN	S
08/07/42	5235	VF-6	USS ENTER-PRISE	TULAGI	SOPAC	MACH R.H. WARDEN	S
08/07/42	5236	VF-6	USS ENTER-PRISE	TULAGI	SOPAC	ENS E.W. COOK	M
08/07/42	4076	VF-71	USS WASP	TULAGI	SOPAC		
08/07/42	5103	VF-71	USS WASP	TULAGI	SOPAC	ENS THADDEUS J. CAPONSKI	S
08/07/42	02111	VF-71	USS WASP	TULAGI	SOPAC		
08/08/42	5202	VF-5	USS SARATOGA	GUADAL-CANAL	SOPAC	ENS F. BLAIR	S
08/14/42`	5244	VF-3	MAUI	HAWAII	ECENPAC	ENS JOHN J. MCCURDY	D
08/14/42	5166	VF-6	USS ENTER-PRISE	HAWAII	ECENPAC	LT ALBERT O. VORSE	S
08/14/42	03404	VMF-224		GUADAL-CANAL	SOPAC	LT KENNEDY	S
08/21/42	5031	VF-71	USS WASP	SOLOMONS	SOPAC		
08/21/42	02077	VMF-223		GUADAL-CANAL	SOPAC	2NDLT CHARLES KENDRICK	S
08/21/42	02101	VMF-223		GUADAL-CANAL	SOPAC	T/SGT JOHN LINDLEY	S
08/23/42	02044	VF-5	USS SARATOGA	E. SOLOMONS	SOPAC	LT R.E. HARMER	S
08/24/42	02066	VF-5	USS SARATOGA	E. SOLOMONS	SOPAC	LT LOESCH	S
08/24/42	02072	VF-5	USS SARATOGA	E. SOLOMONS	SOPAC	LT M. BUFILHO	M
08/24/42	02078	VF-5	USS SARATOGA	E. SOLOMONS	SOPAC	LTJG J.C. SMITH	M
08/24/42	02080	VF-5	USS SARATOGA	E. SOLOMONS	SOPAC	ENS H.A. BASS	M
08/24/42	5049	VF-5	USS SARATOGA	E. SOLOMONS	SOPAC	MM1/C DOYLE C. HERNES	M
08/24/42	02062	VF-5	USS SARATOGA	E. SOLOMONS	SOPAC	ENS RICHARD M. LINQUE	S
08/24/42	02083	VF-5	USS SARATOGA	E. SOLOMONS	SOPAC	MM1/C BEVERLY W. REID	M
08/24/42	5158	VMF-223		GUADAL-CANAL	SOPAC		

DATE	BUNO	SQDRN	BASE	LOST	AREA	PILOT	FATE
08/24/42	02061	VMF-223		GUADAL-CANAL	SOPAC		
08/24/42	02084	VMF-223		GUADAL-CANAL	SOPAC	2NDLT LAWRENCE C. TAYLOR	M
08/24/42	02095	VMF-223		GUADAL-CANAL	SOPAC	LT BAILEY	M
08/26/42	5225		DUTCH HARBOR	ALASKA	NORPAC		
08/26/42	03405	VMF-223		GUADAL-CANAL	SOPAC	2NDLT ROY A. CORRY	M
08/29/42	02075	VMF-223		GUADAL-CANAL	SOPAC	2NDLT EUGENE TROWBRIDGE	S
08/29/42	02086	VMF-223		GUADAL-CANAL	SOPAC		
08/29/42	02087	VMF-223		GUADAL-CANAL	SOPAC		
08/30/42	02133	VF-71	USS WASP	RAMOS ISLAND	SOPAC		
08/30/42	02104	VMF-224		GUADAL-CANAL	SOPAC	LT THOMPSON	M
08/30/42	02122	VMF-224		GUADAL-CANAL	SOPAC	LT BRYANE	M
08/30/42	03438	VMF-224		GUADAL-CANAL	SOPAC	LT AMARINE	S
09/05/42	03399	VF-9	USS RANGER	BERMUDA	NORLANT		
09/05/42	02076	VMF-223		GUADAL-CANAL	SOPAC		
09/05/42	5074	VMF-224		GUADAL-CANAL	SOPAC	LT JEFFRIES	D
09/05/42	5096	VMF-224		GUADAL-CANAL	SOPAC	S/SGT GARRABRANT	M
09/08/42	01993	VGS-9			CENLANT	ENS W.F. CHAMBERLAIN	S
09/08/42	02079	VMF-223		GUADAL-CANAL	SOPAC	LT LEES	S
09/08/42	02082	VMF-223	USS BOGUE	GUADAL-CANAL	SOPAC	LT HUGHES	S
09/08/42				GUADAL-CANAL	SOPAC		
09/08/42				GUADAL-CANAL	SOPAC		
09/08/42	2091	VMF-223		GUADAL-CANAL	SOPAC	LT JEANS	S
09/08/42	5142	VMF-224		GUADAL-CANAL	SOPAC	LT D'ARCY	S
09/08/42	2106	VMF-224		GUADAL-CANAL	SOPAC	LT JOHNSON	S
09/09/42	2099	VMF-223		GUADAL-CANAL	SOPAC	LT CANFIELD	S
09/09/42	2100	VMF-223		GUADAL-CANAL	SOPAC	LT MARION R. CARL	S
09/09/42	2107	VMF-224		GUADAL-CANAL	SOPAC	LT J.M. JONES	M
09/10/42	3491	VMF-223		GUADAL-CANAL	SOPAC	LT POND	M
09/11/42	2109	VMF-224		GUADAL-CANAL	SOPAC	MAJ R.E. GALER	S
09/12/42	3506	VF-10	HAWAII	HAWAII	ECENPAC	ENS E.S. COLSSON	S
09/12/42	5075	VF-5		GUADAL-CANAL	SOPAC	ENS CHARLES RICHERBERGER	D
09/13/42	5084	VF-5		GUADAL-CANAL	SOPAC	ENS INNIS	S
09/13/42	5198	VF-5		GUADAL-CANAL	SOPAC	ENS WILEMAN	D
09/13/42	5100	VMF-223		GUADAL-CANAL	SOPAC	LT PHILLIPS	S
09/13/42	3499	VMF-223		GUADAL-CANAL	SOPAC	LT CHAMBERLAIN	S
09/13/42	3501	VMF-223		GUADAL-CANAL	SOPAC	CONGER	S
09/13/42	4071	VMF-223		GUADAL-CANAL	SOPAC	MCLENNAN	M
09/13/42	4105	VMF-223		GUADAL-CANAL	SOPAC	B.D. HARING	D

DATE	BUNO	SQDRN	BASE	LOST	AREA	PILOT	FATE
09/14/42	5066	VF-3	USS YORK-TOWN	PEARL	ECENPAC	ENS ROBERT C. EVANS	S
09/14/42	2093	VMF-223		GUADAL-CANAL	SOPAC	LT TROWBRIDGE	S
09/15/42	5043	VF-10	HAWAII	HAWAII	ECENPAC	ENS J.L. MCMAHON	S
09/15/42	5205	VF-5		GUADAL-CANAL	SOPAC		
09/15/42	5240	VF-5		GUADAL-CANAL	SOPAC		
09/17/42	5230	VF-10	HAWAII	HAWAII	ECENPAC	ENS GERALD V. DAVIS	D
09/17/42	5191	VF-5		GUADAL-CANAL	SOPAC		
09/23/42	3418	VF-10			SOPAC		
09/28/42	5034	VF-41	USS RANGER	OFF NORFOLK	CENLANT	ENS B.N. MAGHEN	U
09/28/42	2136	VF-41	USS RANGER	OFF NORFOLK	CENLANT	LT T.A. GREEL	S
09/29/42	5185	VF-5		GUADAL-CANAL	SOPAC	ENS SHOEMAKER	U
09/29/42	11729	VGS-12	USS COPAHEE	NEW CALEDON.	SOPAC	2NDLT SIMPSON	S
10/02/42	5168	VF-10	PEARL	HAWAII	ECENPAC	ENS R.L. VON LEHE	D
10/02/42	5195	VF-5		GUADAL-CANAL	SOPAC	ENS GEORGE MORGAN	M
10/02/42	4063	VF-71		GUADAL-CANAL	SOPAC		
10/02/42	4067	VF-71		GUADAL-CANAL	SOPAC		
10/02/42	4073	VF-71		GUADAL-CANAL	SOPAC		
10/02/42	4074	VF-71		GUADAL-CANAL	SOPAC		
10/02/42	3486	VGF-29	USS SANTEE	OFF BERMUDA	NORLANT	ENS J.M. GALLAND	S
10/02/42	2098	VMF-223		GUADAL-CANAL	SOPAC	LT LEES	M
10/02/42	3502	VMF-223		GUADAL-CANAL	SOPAC	SMITH	U
10/02/42	2110	VMF-224		GUADAL-CANAL	SOPAC	LT KENDRICK	D
10/02/42	2112	VMF-224		GUADAL-CANAL	SOPAC	LT GEORGE A. TREPTOW	M
10/02/42	2118	VMF-224		GUADAL-CANAL	SOPAC	MAJ R.E. GALER	S
10/03/42	5141	VF-5		GUADAL-CANAL	SOPAC		
10/03/42	2063	VMF-223		GUADAL-CANAL	SOPAC	LT FRAZIER	S
10/05/42	11747	VF-41	USS RANGER	BERMUDA	NORLANT		
10/05/42	11704	VF-9	USS RANGER	BERMUDA	NORLANT		
10/08/42	5050	VF-5		GUADAL-CANAL	SOPAC		
10/08/42	5073	VF-5		GUADAL-CANAL	SOPAC	LTJG C.W. TUCKER	M
10/08/42	5234	VF-5		GUADAL-CANAL	SOPAC	LTJG ROACH	S
10/09/42	5032	VMF-121		GUADAL-CANAL	SOPAC	LT NARR	S
10/10/42	11702	VF-9	USS RANGER	BERMUDA	NORLANT		
10/11/42	5125	VF-5		GUADAL-CANAL	SOPAC	LTJG MCDONALD	S
10/11/42	5047	VMF-121		GUADAL-CANAL	SOPAC	LT ARTHUR N. NEFF	S
10/13/42	5127	VF-5		GUADAL-CANAL	SOPAC		
10/13/42	5196	VF-5		GUADAL-CANAL	SOPAC		
10/13/42	5201	VF-5		GUADAL-CANAL	SOPAC		
10/13/42	5207	VF-5		GUADAL-CANAL	SOPAC		

DATE	BUNO	SQDRN	BASE	LOST	AREA	PILOT	FATE
10/14/42	5241	VF-5		GUADAL-CANAL	SOPAC		
10/14/42	5242	VF-5		GUADAL-CANAL	SOPAC		
10/14/42	2014	VF-5		GUADAL-CANAL	SOPAC	LCDR ROBERT L. STRICKLAND	D
10/14/42	5033	VF-71		GUADAL-CANAL	SOPAC		
10/14/42	5041	VF-71		GUADAL-CANAL	SOPAC		
10/14/42	5056	VF-71		GUADAL-CANAL	SOPAC		
10/14/42	5058	VMF-121		GUADAL-CANAL	SOPAC	LT KOLLAR C. BRANDON	M
10/14/42	5081	VMF-121		GUADAL-CANAL	SOPAC	LT PAUL S. RUTLEDGE	M
10/14/42	5088	VMF-121		GUADAL-CANAL	SOPAC	T/SGT THOMPSON	M
10/14/42	2126	VMF-223		GUADAL-CANAL	SOPAC		
10/14/42	2127	VMF-223		GUADAL-CANAL	SOPAC		
10/14/42	2130	VMF-223		GUADAL-CANAL	SOPAC		
10/14/42	3415	VMF-223		GUADAL-CANAL	SOPAC		
10/14/42	3424	VMF-223		GUADAL-CANAL	SOPAC		
10/14/42	3500	VMF-223		GUADAL-CANAL	SOPAC		
10/15/42	11743	VF-41	USS RANGER	BERMUDA	NORLANT		
10/15/42	2081	VF-5		GUADAL-CANAL	SOPAC	LTJG ROUSE	S
10/15/42	5070	VF-71		GUADAL-CANAL	SOPAC		
10/15/42	5098	VF-71		GUADAL-CANAL	SOPAC		
10/15/42	5099	VF-71		GUADAL-CANAL	SOPAC		
10/15/42	2123	VMF-224		GUADAL-CANAL	SOPAC	OLLSON	U
10/16/42	5111	VMF-121		GUADAL-CANAL	SOPAC	LT JOHN H. CLARK	S
10/17/42	5122	VMF-121		GUADAL-CANAL	SOPAC	LT WILEY H. CRAFT	M
10/18/42	5108	VF-71		GUADAL-CANAL	SOPAC		
10/18/42	5114	VF-71		GUADAL-CANAL	SOPAC		
10/18/42	2025	VMF-121		GUADAL-CANAL	SOPAC	LT ROBERT F. FLAHERTY	M
10/18/42	3532	VMF-121		GUADAL-CANAL	SOPAC	LT LOWELL D. GROW	S
10/18/42	11656	VMF-121		GUADAL-CANAL	SOPAC	LT EDWARD P. ANDREWS	D
10/19/42	3524	VMF-121		GUADAL-CANAL	SOPAC	LT FLOYD A. LYNCH	M
10/19/42	3528	VMF-121		GUADAL-CANAL	SOPAC	S/SGT JAMES A. PELITON	S
10/19/42	11655	VMF-121		GUADAL-CANAL	SOPAC	LT FRY	M
10/20/42	5135	VF-71		GUADAL-CANAL	SOPAC		
10/20/42	5136	VF-71		GUADAL-CANAL	SOPAC		
10/20/42	11658	VMF-121		GUADAL-CANAL	SOPAC	LT JOHN KING	S
10/20/42	11659	VMF-121		GUADAL-CANAL	SOPAC	LT EUGENE A. NEWER	M
10/20/42	4087	VMF-213	PEARL	HAWAII	ECENPAC	LT HOWER	S
10/21/42	2017	VF-5		GUADAL-CANAL	SOPAC	LTJG HILDEN M. ROUSE	M
10/21/42	5156	VF-71		GUADAL-CANAL	SOPAC		

DATE	BUNO	SQDRN	BASE	LOST	AREA	PILOT	FATE
10/21/42	5045	VMF-212		GUADAL-CANAL	SOPAC	M/GUN HENRY B. HAMILTON	M
10/21/42	2085	VMO-251		GUADAL-CANAL	SOPAC	T/SGT ERNEST L. ANDERSON	M
10/22/42	4090	VF-41	USS RANGER	BERMUDA	NORLANT		
10/22/42	3398	VF-9	USS RANGER	BERMUDA	NORLANT		
10/25/42	5138	VF-10	USS ENTER-PRISE	SANTA CRUZ	SOPAC	LTJG BLAIR	S
10/25/42	5204	VF-10	USS ENTER-PRISE	SANTA CRUZ	SOPAC	LT FRANK D. MILLER	S
10/25/42	5102	VF-71		GUADAL-CANAL	SOPAC		
10/25/42	5183	VF-71		GUADAL-CANAL	SOPAC		
10/25/42	2055	VMF-121		GUADAL-CANAL	SOPAC	LT OSCAR M. BATE, JR.	S
10/25/42	5180	VMF-212		GUADAL-CANAL	SOPAC	LT JACK E. CONGERS	S
10/26/42	5078	VF-10	USS ENTER-PRISE	SANTA CRUZ	SOPAC	ENS RALEIGH E. RHODES	M
10/26/42	5107	VF-10	USS ENTER-PRISE	SANTA CRUZ	SOPAC	ENS ALBERT E. MEAD	M
10/26/42	5148	VF-10	USS ENTER-PRISE	SANTA CRUZ	SOPAC	ENS LONG	U
10/26/42	5153	VF-10	USS ENTER-PRISE	SANTA CRUZ	SOPAC	ENS L.J. FULTON	M
10/26/42	5177	VF-10	USS ENTER-PRISE	SANTA CRUZ	SOPAC	LCDR E.R. KANE	S
10/26/42	5194	VF-10	USS ENTER-PRISE	SANTA CRUZ	SOPAC	ENS DAVIS	U
10/26/42	5245	VF-10	USS ENTER-PRISE	SANTA CRUZ	SOPAC	ENS BARNES	U
10/26/42	5254	VF-10	USS ENTER-PRISE	SANTA CRUZ	SOPAC	ENS J.E. CALDWELL	M
10/26/42	2040	VF-10	USS ENTER-PRISE	SANTA CRUZ	SOPAC	LTJG JOHN A. LEYOLA	M
10/26/42	2102	VF-10	USS ENTER-PRISE	SANTA CRUZ	SOPAC	LT J.C. ECKHARDT	S
10/26/42	3432	VF-10	USS ENTER-PRISE	SANTA CRUZ	SOPAC	LTJG J.D. BILLO	S
10/26/42	5130	VF-72	USS HORNET	SANTA CRUZ	SOPAC	LTJG W.W. ROBERTS	U
10/26/42	5181	VF-72	USS HORNET	SANTA CRUZ	SOPAC	LT THOMAS C. JOHNSON	M
10/26/42	5188	VF-72	USS HORNET	SANTA CRUZ	SOPAC	LT JOHN G. BOWER	M
10/26/42	5197	VF-72	USS HORNET	SANTA CRUZ	SOPAC	LTJG J.R. FRANKLIN	U
10/26/42	5208	VF-72	USS HORNET	SANTA CRUZ	SOPAC	LTJG D.P. LANDRY	U
10/26/42	5209	VF-72	USS HORNET	SANTA CRUZ	SOPAC	LT L.K. BLISS	U
10/26/42	5210	VF-72	USS HORNET	SANTA CRUZ	SOPAC	LTJG R.S. MERRITT	U
10/26/42	5215	VF-72	USS HORNET	SANTA CRUZ	SOPAC	LTJG FORMORER	U
10/27/42	5226	VF-72	USS HORNET	SANTA CRUZ	SOPAC	(SHIP SANK)	
10/27/42	5227	VF-72	USS HORNET	SANTA CRUZ	SOPAC	(SHIP SANK)	

DATE	BUNO	SQDRN	BASE	LOST	AREA	PILOT	FATE
10/27/42	5246	VF-72	USS HORNET	SANTA CRUZ	SOPAC	(SHIP SANK)	
10/27/42	5248	VF-72	USS HORNET	SANTA CRUZ	SOPAC	(SHIP SANK)	
10/27/42	2004	VF-72	USS HORNET	SANTA CRUZ	SOPAC	(SHIP SANK)	
10/27/42	2006	VF-72	USS HORNET	SANTA CRUZ	SOPAC	(SHIP SANK)	
10/27/42	2058	VF-72	USS HORNET	SANTA CRUZ	SOPAC	(SHIP SANK)	
10/27/42	2065	VF-72	USS HORNET	SANTA CRUZ	SOPAC	(SHIP SANK)	
10/27/42	2067	VF-72	USS HORNET	SANTA CRUZ	SOPAC	(SHIP SANK)	
10/29/42	5212	VF-10	HAWAII	HAWAII	ECENPAC		
11/01/42	3448	VMO-251			SOPAC	LT YUNCK	S
11/02/42	2148	VF-71		GUADAL-CANAL	SOPAC	LT THRASH	U
11/03/42	5206	VF-9	USS RANGER	FEDALA	NW AFR		
11/05/42	5171	VF-10		NEW CALEDONIA	SOPAC	ENS M.W. AXELROD	S
11/07/42	5061	VMF-112		GUADAL-CANAL	SOPAC	LT MAAS	S
11/07/42	3453	VMF-121		GUADAL-CANAL	SOPAC	CAPT FOSS	S
11/07/42	3467	VMF-121		GUADAL-CANAL	SOPAC	LT DOYLE	U
11/07/42	3480	VMF-121		GUADAL-CANAL	SOPAC	LT STUB	U
11/07/42	3482	VMF-121		GUADAL-CANAL	SOPAC	LT MANN	S
11/07/42	3483	VMF-121		GUADAL-CANAL	SOPAC	LT SIMPSON	U
11/07/42	3533	VMF-121		GUADAL-CANAL	SOPAC	LT RUDDELL	M
11/07/42	3542	VMF-121		GUADAL-CANAL	SOPAC	LT NARR	M
11/08/42	4084	VF-41	USS RANGER	FEDALA	NW AFR	LT ANDREWS	S
11/08/42	4094	VF-41	USS RANGER	FEDALA	NW AFR		
11/08/42	3461	VF-41	USS RANGER	FEDALA	NW AFR	LT GRALL	S
11/08/42	11703	VF-41	USS RANGER	FEDALA	NW AFR		
11/08/42	11708	VF-41	USS RANGER	FEDALA	NW AFR	ENS HARRIS	S
11/08/42	4089	VF-9	USS RANGER	FEDALA	NW AFR		
11/08/42	2023	VF-9	USS RANGER	FEDALA	NW AFR	ENS THOMAS MACK WILHOITE	M
11/08/42	11908	VGF-26	USS SAN-GAMON	PORT LYAUTEY	MOROC-CO		
11/08/42	4081	VGF-27	USS SUWAN-NEE	CASABLANCA	NW AFR		
11/08/42	2113	VGF-27	USS SUWAN-NEE	CASABLANCA	NW AFR	LCDR T.K. WRIGHT	S
11/08/42	3436	VGF-29	USS SANTEE	SAFI	NW AFR	ENS R.W. PETERSON	S
11/08/42	3462	VGF-29	USS SANTEE	SAFI	NW AFR	ENS UNCAS L. FRETWELL	S
11/08/42	3511	VGF-29	USS SANTEE	SAFI	NW AFR	LCDR J.T. BLACKBURN	S
11/08/42	3512	VGF-29	USS SANTEE	SAFI	NW AFR	ENS J.M. GALLAND	S
11/08/42	11745	VGF-29	USS SANTEE	SAFI	NW AFR	ENS W.P. NAYLOR	S
11/08/42	11763	VGF-29	USS SANTEE	SAFI	NW AFR	ENS E. VAN VRANKEN	S
11/08/42	11767	VGF-29	USS SANTEE	SAFI	NW AFR	LTJG GEORGE N. TRUMPETER	M

DATE	BUNO	SQDRN	BASE	LOST	AREA	PILOT	FATE
11/09/42	11762	VF-41	USS RANGER	FEDALA	NW AFR		
11/09/42	11765	VF-41	USS RANGER	FEDALA	NW AFR	LT AMESBURY	M
11/09/42	11707	VF-9	USS RANGER	FEDALA	NW AFR	ENS GEARHARDT	S
11/09/42	11742	VF-9	USS RANGER	FEDALA	NW AFR	LT MICKA	M
11/09/42	5035	VGF-27	USS SUWAN-NEE	CASABLANCA	NW AFR	LTJG W. SWEETMAN	S
11/10/42	3514	VGF-29	USS SANTEE	SAFI	NW AFR		
11/11/42	5199	VF-71		GUADAL-CANAL	SOPAC		
11/11/42	5259	VF-71		GUADAL-CANAL	SOPAC		
11/11/42	2125	VF-71		GUADAL-CANAL	SOPAC		
11/11/42	2132	VF-71		GUADAL-CANAL	SOPAC		
11/11/42	2145	VF-71		GUADAL-CANAL	SOPAC		
11/11/42	3407	VMF-112		GUADAL-CANAL	SOPAC	S/SGT COCHRAN	M
11/11/42	3427	VMF-112		GUADAL-CANAL	SOPAC	LT PEDERSON	M
11/11/42	5121	VMF-121		GUADAL-CANAL	SOPAC	M/SGT PALKO	M
11/11/42	5167	VMF-121		GUADAL-CANAL	SOPAC		
11/11/42	2064	VMF-121		GUADAL-CANAL	SOPAC		
11/11/42	2121	VMF-121		GUADAL-CANAL	SOPAC		
11/11/42	5200	VMF-212		GUADAL-CANAL	SOPAC		
11/11/42	3503	VMF-224	PEARL	HAWAII	ECENPAC		
11/11/42	3504	VMF-224	PEARL	HAWAII	ECENPAC		
11/11/42	3508	VMF-224	PEARL	HAWAII	ECENPAC		
11/12/42	11906	VGF-26	USS SAN-GAMON	ENR NORFOLK	CENLANT		
11/12/42	3444	VMF-112		GUADAL-CANAL	SOPAC	LT WAMEL	S
11/12/42	3447	VMF-112		GUADAL-CANAL	SOPAC	S/SGT HURST	S
11/12/42	5172	VMF-121		GUADAL-CANAL	SOPAC	LT BATE	S
11/13/42	3452	VMF-112		GUADAL-CANAL	SOPAC	LT BOLLMANN	S
11/14/42	3445	VF-10		GUADAL-CANAL	SOPAC		
11/14/42	3456	VF-10		GUADAL-CANAL	SOPAC		
11/14/42	3518	VF-10		GUADAL-CANAL	SOPAC		
11/14/42	4062	VF-71		GUADAL-CANAL	SOPAC		
11/14/42	4070	VF-71		GUADAL-CANAL	SOPAC		
11/14/42	5120	VF-71		GUADAL-CANAL	SOPAC		
11/14/42	2144	VF-71		GUADAL-CANAL	SOPAC		
11/14/42	2147	VF-71		GUADAL-CANAL	SOPAC		
11/14/42	2150	VF-71		GUADAL-CANAL	SOPAC		
11/14/42	3478	VMF-112		GUADAL-CANAL	SOPAC	S/SGT HURST	S
11/14/42	3454	VMF-212		GUADAL-CANAL	SOPAC	LCOL BAUER	M
11/15/42	11727	VF-6	USS SARATOGA	ENR NOUMEA	SOPAC	LTJG ROBERT M. BISQUE	S

DATE	BUNO	SQDRN	BASE	LOST	AREA	PILOT	FATE
11/15/42	4068	VF-71		GUADAL-CANAL	SOPAC		
11/15/42	3484	VMF-223		GUADAL-CANAL	SOPAC		
11/16/42	2128	VMF-122			SOPAC	LT REUSSERS	S
11/17/42	3434	VMO-251			SOPAC	2NDLT G.B. LOYLE	D
11/19/42	11723	VF-6	USS SARATOGA	ENR NOUMEA	SOPAC	ENS ROBERT B. GROVE	S
11/19/42	5112	VF-72	USS NASSAU	HAWAII	ECENPAC		
11/20/42	1996	VF-11	MAUI	HAWAII	ECENPAC	ENS EARL G. CRAIG	M
11/21/42	3477	VMF-112			SOPAC	LT CLARK	S
11/21/42	3531	VMF-112			SOPAC	T/SGT H. CONTI	D
11/23/42	11787	VGS-11	USS ALTAMAHA	ESPIRITU SANTO	SOPAC	LTJG MURRAY S. BRANNEN	S
12/02/42	12082	VMF-122			SOPAC	LT D. MEYERS	M
12/04/42	3517	VF-10	USS ENTER-PRISE	NOUMEA	SOPAC	ENS GASKILL	S
12/06/42	2050	VMF-211		PALMYRA	ECENPAC	LT T.O. DANIELS	S
12/12/42	3437	VGF-26	USS SAN-GAMON	OFF NORFOLK	CENLANT		
12/13/42	11673	VGS-11	USS ALTAMAHA		SOPAC	ENS BERT CHASE	S
12/16/42	3492	VMF-121		GUADAL-CANAL	SOPAC		
12/16/42	3497	VMO-251	ESPIRITU SANTO	ESPIRITU SANTO	SOPAC		
12/21/42	11734	VF-6	USS SARATOGA	NOUMEA	SOPAC		
12/23/42	3408	VGF-16		HAWAII	ECENPAC		
12/23/42	3541	VMF-121		GUADAL-CANAL	SOPAC	MARINE GUNNER WISER	M
12/23/42	3534	VMO-251			SOPAC	CAPT ANDRE	S
12/24/42	11998	VGF-28		BALBOA	CENLANT	ENS ERNEST D. BROOKS	S
12/28/42	11909	VF-26	USS SANTEE	ENR TRINIDAD	CENLANT	ENS J. GALLAND	S
12/29/42	3540	1ST MAW		GUADAL-CANAL	SOPAC		
12/29/42	2140	VGS-12	USS COPAHEE		SOPAC	ENS M.E. WOODCOCK	S
12/29/42	5065	VMF-121		GUADAL-CANAL	SOPAC		
12/29/42	3466	VMF-121		GUADAL-CANAL	SOPAC		
01/02/43	5124	VMF-121		GUADAL-CANAL	SOPAC	LT CRUM	M
01/02/43	5169	VMF-121		GUADAL-CANAL	SOPAC	LT PETERSON	M
01/05/43	3450	VMF-121		GUADAL-CANAL	SOPAC	LT CARTER	M
01/05/43	3476	VMF-121		GUADAL-CANAL	SOPAC	MARINE GUNNER MORAVES	S
01/09/43	4096	VF-11	HAWAII	HAWAII	ECENPAC		
01/09/43	3455	VMO-251	ESPIRITU SANTO	ESPIRITU SANTO	SOPAC		
01/10/43	11895	VMF-213	PEARL	HAWAII	ECENPAC	LT HODDE	S
01/11/43	11939	VGS-29	USS SANTEE	ENR RECIFE	CENLANT		
01/11/43	3494	VMF-121		GUADAL-CANAL	SOPAC	LT CANNON	M
01/12/43	11669	VF-6	USS SARATOGA	NOUMEA	SOPAC	LT HAROLD E. RUTHERFORD	D
01/12/43	11699	VF-72	USS NASSAU		SOPAC	LTJG H.J. LOWNDS III	D
01/15/43	3509	VMF-121		GUADAL-CANAL	SOPAC	LT NARONTATE	U
01/16/43		MAG-13		TUTUILA	SOPAC	LT ROBERT J. PATTERSON	S
01/21/43	11894	VMF-213	PEARL	HAWAII	ECENPAC	LT C.B. PERKINS	S
01/22/43	11761	VGF-27	USS SUWAN-NEE	PEARL	ECENPAC		
01/23/43	11783	VGS-11	USS ALTAMAHA		SOPAC	ENS ARTHUR BURTON WOLUS	U

DATE	BUNO	SQDRN	BASE	LOST	AREA	PILOT	FATE
01/23/43	11857	VMF-221	EWA	HAWAII	ECENPAC		
01/27/43	5087	VMF-112			SOPAC	E.V. WAGNER	D
01/27/43	2131	VMF-112			SOPAC	LT LYNCH	S
01/29/43	3414	VGF-27	USS SUWAN-NEE	NEW HEBRIDES	SOPAC	LTJG J.P. MCGOVERN	S
01/30/43	11758	VF-10	USS ENTER-PRISE	RENNELL IS.	SOPAC	LT T.E. EDWARDS	D
01/30/43	11714	VMF-213	PEARL	HAWAII	ECENPAC	LT RAWSON	M
01/31/43	3446	VMF-112			SOPAC	LT DEBLANE	S
01/31/43	3523	VMF-112			SOPAC	S/SGT FILTON	S
02/01/43	11687	MAG-11		ESPIRITU SANTO	SOPAC		
02/01/43	11882	VGS-12	USS COPAHEE		SOPAC	L.A. BLISS	S
02/01/43	11657	VMF-112			SOPAC	LT MORAN	S
02/01/43	11843	VMF-221	EWA	HAWAII	ECENPAC	LT HALLMEYER	S
02/04/43	11717	VF-6	USS SARATOGA	NOUMEA	SOPAC		
02/04/43	11869	VF-72	USS NASSAU		SOPAC		
02/04/43	11936	VMF-221	EWA	HAWAII	ECENPAC	CAPT S.G. BEMIS	D
02/07/43	3416	MAG-12		NOUMEA	SOPAC	CAPT WYATT B. CARNEAL	S
02/08/43	11690	VF-72	USS NASSAU		SOPAC		
02/08/43	11782	VF-72	USS NASSAU		SOPAC		
02/10/43	12028	VMF-123		GUADAL-CANAL	SOPAC		
02/11/43	11736	VF-6	USS SARATOGA	NOUMEA	SOPAC	ENS HUGH D. MCINTOSH	M
02/22/43	11934	VGS-11	USS ALTAMAHA		SOPAC		
02/23/43	11983	COMFAIR	GUADAL-CANAL	GUADAL-CANAL	SOPAC		
02/23/43	5106	MAG-14	GUADAL-CANAL	GUADAL-CANAL	SOPAC		
02/23/43	3520	VMF-112			SOPAC		
02/25/43	11694	COMAIR-PAC	GUADAL-CANAL	GUADAL-CANAL	SOPAC		
02/25/43	11774	COMAIR-PAC	GUADAL-CANAL	GUADAL-CANAL	SOPAC		
02/25/43	11795	COMAIR-PAC	GUADAL-CANAL	GUADAL-CANAL	SOPAC		
02/25/43	2049	MAG-14	GUADAL-CANAL	GUADAL-CANAL	SOPAC		
02/25/43	3471	MAG-14	GUADAL-CANAL	GUADAL-CANAL	SOPAC		
02/25/43	11660	MAG-14	GUADAL-CANAL	GUADAL-CANAL	SOPAC		
02/25/43	11715	VMF-112		ESPIRITU SANTO	SOPAC		
02/25/43	11722	VMF-112		ESPIRITU SANTO	SOPAC		
02/25/43	11793	VMF-112		ESPIRITU SANTO	SOPAC		
02/25/43	11898	VMF-214	EWA	HAWAII	ECENPAC		
02/27/43	3409	VF-72			SOPAC		
02/27/43	2057	VMF-211		PALMYRA	ECENPAC		
02/28/43	2141	VGF-27	USS SUWAN-NEE	TONTOUTA	SOPAC	ENS G.R. COOK	S
02/28/43	5203	VMF-112			SOPAC		
02/28/43	1991	VMF-112			SOPAC		
02/28/43	3465	VMF-112			SOPAC		
02/28/43	3470	VMF-112			SOPAC		
02/28/43	3526	VMF-112			SOPAC		
03/04/43	12021	VMF-441		SAMOA	SE PAC	LT R.L. TAGART	M
03/07/43	11752	VMO-251		NOUMEA	SOPAC		
03/07/43	11848	VMO-251		NOUMEA	SOPAC		
03/07/43	11891	VMO-251		NOUMEA	SOPAC		
03/07/43	12036	VMO-251		NOUMEA	SOPAC		
03/07/43	12117	VMO-251		NOUMEA	SOPAC		

DATE	BUNO	SQDRN	BASE	LOST	AREA	PILOT	FATE
03/07/43	12132	VMO-251		NOUMEA	SOPAC		
03/07/43	12141	VMO-251		NOUMEA	SOPAC		
03/08/43	12044	VC-1	USS CARD		CENLANT	ENS WILLIAM B. BUCKELEW	S
03/08/43	11940	VF-11		GUADAL-CANAL	SOPAC		
03/11/43	3530	VMF-112			SOPAC		
03/13/43	12040	VF-41	USS RANGER		NORLANT	ENS ARTHUR J. BALDWIN	S
03/14/43	12035	COMFAIR	GUADAL-CANAL	GUADAL-CANAL	SOPAC		
03/14/43	12068	COMFAIR	GUADAL-CANAL	GUADAL-CANAL	SOPAC		
03/14/43	4098	VMF-213			SOPAC		
03/18/43	11786	VMF-123			SOPAC		
03/19/43	2073	VF-28	USS CHENANGO	SOLOMONS	SOPAC	ENS W. CHARLES BAILEY	D
03/19/43	11907	VF-28	USS CHENANGO	SOLOMONS	SOPAC		
03/23/43	2151	COMFAIR	GUADAL-CANAL	GUADAL-CANAL	SOPAC		
03/23/43	11785	MAG-14	GUADAL-CANAL	GUADAL-CANAL	SOPAC		
03/23/43	11784	VMF-123			SOPAC		
03/24/43	2047	VMF-211		PALMYRA	ECENPAC	CAPT HERBERT T. MERRILL	D
03/25/43	11981	VF-11		GUADAL-CANAL	SOPAC	ENS ROBERT K. HAUSGARTNER	D
03/27/43	12063	MAG-11		ESPIRITU SANTO	SOPAC		
03/27/43	11677	VMF-123			SOPAC		
03/28/43	12172	MAG-14	GUADAL-CANAL	GUADAL-CANAL	SOPAC		
03/31/43	11879	VC-16			SOPAC		
03/31/43	11698	VF-6	USS SARATOGA	NOUMEA	SOPAC		
04/01/43	3410	VF-26	USS SAN-GAMON	SOLOMONS	SOPAC		
04/01/43	3535	VF-26	USS SAN-GAMON	SOLOMONS	SOPAC		
04/01/43	12046	VF-28	USS CHENANGO	SOLOMONS	SOPAC		
04/03/43	11946	VC-12	USS COPAHEE		SOPAC		
04/03/43	3485	VF-28	USS CHENANGO	ENR RUSSELLS	SOPAC		
04/04/43	11930	VC-12	USS COPAHEE		SOPAC	LT T. SAUNDERS	S
04/06/43	4085	VF-28	USS CHENANGO	RUSSELLS	SOPAC		
04/07/43	11867	MAG-12		GUADAL-CANAL	SOPAC		
04/07/43	2060	VMF-211	PEARL	HAWAII	ECENPAC	LT JOHN BLAKE CORRELL	D
04/07/43	11721	VMF-214		CAPE ESPERAN.	PHIL	LT SCARBOROUGH	U
04/07/43	11905	VMF-214		CAPE ESPERAN.	PHIL	CAPT BURNETT	U
04/07/43	2143	VMF-221		RUSSELLS	SOPAC	1STLT W.H. HALLMEYER	S
04/07/43	3529	VMF-221		RUSSELLS	SOPAC	1STLT G.W. ROBERTS	S
04/07/43	11716	VMF-221		RUSSELLS	SOPAC	LT WINFIELD	S
04/07/43	11890	VMF-221		RUSSELLS	SOPAC	2NDLT P.P. PITTMAN	S
04/07/43	12013	VMF-221		RUSSELLS	SOPAC	1STLT E.A. WALSH	S
04/07/43	12049	VMF-221		RUSSELLS	SOPAC	CAPT PAYNE	S
04/07/43	12084	VMF-221		RUSSELLS	SOPAC	1STLT J.E. SWETT	S
04/08/43	5094	VMF-221		RUSSELLS	SOPAC	LT SNIDER	S
04/09/43	12056	VMF-221		RUSSELLS	SOPAC	LT CONNOLLY	S
04/10/43	3412	VF-26	USS SAN-GAMON	SOLOMONS	SOPAC		
04/12/43	11675	VF-6	USS SARATOGA	NOUMEA	SOPAC		
04/14/43	11789	VMF-111			SOPAC		
04/15/43	11911	VMF-214		GUADAL-CANAL	SOPAC	LT LAMPHIER	S
04/18/43	11697	VF-10			WCENPAC		

DATE	BUNO	SQDRN	BASE	LOST	AREA	PILOT	FATE
04/18/43	3413	VF-28	USS CHENANGO	SOLOMONS	SOPAC		
04/20/43	12050	VMF-123			SOPAC		
04/26/43	3474	VF-11		GUADAL-CANAL	SOPAC		
04/26/43	11854	VF-23			NORLANT		
04/26/43	11686	VMO-251		NOUMEA	SOPAC		
04/30/43	11689	VC-11			SOPAC		
04/30/43	11780	VC-11			SOPAC		
04/30/43	4060	VF-22			NORLANT		
04/30/43	11741	VF-41			NORLANT		
04/30/43	11665	VF-72			SOPAC		
04/30/43	11676	VF-72			SOPAC		
04/30/43	11791	VF-72			SOPAC		
04/30/43	4069	VMO-251		NOUMEA	SOPAC		
04/30/43	5059	VMO-251		NOUMEA	SOPAC		
04/30/43	5252	VMO-251		NOUMEA	SOPAC		
05/02/43	11932	MAG-13		TUTUILA	SOPAC		
05/02/43	11757	VF-11		GUADAL-CANAL	SOPAC		
05/04/43	11853	VF-41			NORLANT		
05/05/43	2097	VMF-211	PEARL	HAWAII	ECENPAC	LT WILLIAM L. BEERMAN	S
05/06/43	11992	VF-11		GUADAL-CANAL	SOPAC		
05/07/43	2138	ADVB-204		NOUMEA	SOPAC		
05/07/43	11776	VF-6	USS SARATOGA	NOUMEA	SOPAC		
05/08/43	11875	VMF-123			SOPAC		
05/09/43	12193	VF-16			NORLANT		
05/10/43	12216	VC-18			SOPAC		
05/11/43	3519	VC-21	USS NASSAU	ATTU	NORPAC	ENS A. KOSTRZEWSKY	S
05/11/43	11822	VC-21	USS NASSAU	ATTU	NORPAC	ENS PAUL BEAUMONT	S
05/11/43	3488	VF-26	USS SAN-GAMON	SOLOMONS	SOPAC		
05/14/43	3490	VC-21	USS NASSAU	ATTU	NORPAC	LCDR GREENMAYER	M
05/14/43	11836	VC-21	USS NASSAU	ATTU	NORPAC	ENS KELLY	S
05/14/43	12019	VC-21	USS NASSAU	ATTU	NORPAC	LT DOUGLAS HENDERSON	M
05/14/43	12074	VC-21	USS NASSAU	ATTU	NORPAC	ENS E.D. JACKSON	M
05/16/43	2043	VC-21	USS NASSAU	ATTU	NORPAC	LTJG F.R. REGISTER	M
05/16/43	11834	VC-21	USS NASSAU	ATTU	NORPAC	SGT BREEDEN	D
05/19/43	12154	VF-16			NORLANT		
05/19/43	12020	VF-20	USS CHENANGO	SOLOMONS	SOPAC		
05/20/43	12151	VF-16			NORLANT		
05/20/43	11881	VMO-251		NOUMEA	SOPAC		
05/21/43	11797	VC-11			SOPAC		
05/21/43	2010	VF-26	USS SAN-GAMON	SOLOMONS	SOPAC		
05/27/43	12108	VC-9	USS BOGUE		NORLANT		
05/28/43	3421	VF-10			SOPAC		
05/28/43	12152	VF-16	USS LEX-INGTON	CARIBBEAN	CENLANT		
05/31/43	11777	VMO-251		NOUMEA	SOPAC		
06/02/43	12086	COMFAIR	GUADAL-CANAL	GUADAL-CANAL	SOPAC		
06/02/43	11728	MAG-12		GUADAL-CANAL	SOPAC		
06/03/43	5140	VF-37			SOPAC		
06/04/43	12030	VMF-441		FUNAFUTI	SOPAC	LT WESTERLIND	M
06/06/43	2008	VF-23			NORLANT		
06/07/43	11751	VF-11		GUADAL-CANAL	SOPAC	HUBERTSON	U
06/07/43	11871	VF-11		GUADAL-CANAL	SOPAC	HUBLER	U
06/07/43	11923	VF-11		GUADAL-CANAL	SOPAC		

DATE	BUNO	SQDRN	BASE	LOST	AREA	PILOT	FATE
06/09/43	11877	VF-27			SOPAC		
06/09/43	12038	VMF-221		GUADAL-CANAL	SOPAC		
06/12/43	12119	VF-11		GUADAL-CANAL	SOPAC	ENS VERNON GRAHAM	S
06/16/43	4095	VF-11		GUADAL-CANAL	SOPAC	RICKER	U
06/16/43	3442	VF-11		GUADAL-CANAL	SOPAC	BOSWELL	U
06/16/43	11899	VF-11		GUADAL-CANAL	SOPAC	HULL	U
06/16/43	11937	VF-11		GUADAL-CANAL	SOPAC	PRESALER	U
06/18/43	11710	VF-6	USS SARATOGA	NOUMEA	SOPAC	ENS R.J. MOORE	U
06/22/43	3536	VC-26	USS SAN-GAMON	SOLOMONS	SOPAC		
06/22/43	3443	VC-28	USS CHENANGO	SOLOMONS	SOPAC		
06/22/43	11994	VC-29	USS SANTEE	ENR CASABLAN.	NORLANT		
06/22/43	3464	VF-41			NORLANT		
06/23/43	12020	VMF-441		FUNAFUTI	SOPAC		
06/25/43	5147			GUADAL-CANAL	SOPAC		
06/30/43	11671	VF-11		GUADAL-CANAL	SOPAC		
06/30/43	11888	VF-11		GUADAL-CANAL	SOPAC		
06/30/43	11862	VF-21			SOPAC		
06/30/43	11885	VF-21			SOPAC		
06/30/43	11901	VF-21			SOPAC		
06/30/43	11947	VF-21			SOPAC		
06/30/43	12053	VF-21			SOPAC		
06/30/43	3441	VF-26	USS SAN-GAMON	SOLOMONS	SOPAC	THRASH	M
06/30/43	11666	VMF-123			SOPAC		
06/30/43	12123	VMF-123			SOPAC		
07/01/43	2038	VF-28		RUSSELLS	SOPAC	LT J.A. MAHONEY	D
07/01/43	11779	VF-28		RUSSELLS	SOPAC	ENS WALKER	M
07/01/43	11839	VF-28		RUSSELLS	SOPAC	LT WOODS	M
07/04/43	11868	VF-21		RENDOVA	SOPAC	LTJG HEARD	M
07/09/43	11944	VF-11		GUADAL-CANAL	SOPAC	LTJG CYRUS G. GARY	M
07/09/43	3495	VF-26	USS SAN-GAMON	SOLOMONS	SOPAC		
07/12/43	2012	VF-11		GUADAL-CANAL	SOPAC		
07/13/43	12112	VC-13	USS CORE	27-15N/034-18W	NORLANT		
07/13/43	12118	VF-28		RUSSELLS	SOPAC	ERNEST INGOLD	S
07/14/43	11830	VF-21		RENDOVA	SOPAC		
07/14/43	11833	VF-27		RUSSELLS	SOPAC	LT STEEP	M
07/14/43	12098	VF-27		GUADAL-CANAL	SOPAC		
07/15/43	12059	VF-21		GUADAL-CANAL	SOPAC	ENS BEDINGER	M
07/18/43	5155	VF-28		RUSSELLS	SOPAC	LT DALTON	M
07/18/43	3472	VF-28		RUSSELLS	SOPAC	LT WARING	M
07/18/43	11672	VF-28		RUSSELLS	SOPAC	ENS LANDIS	M
07/18/43	11724	VF-28		RUSSELLS	SOPAC	ENS LEWIS	M
07/18/43	11978	VF-28		RUSSELLS	SOPAC	LT POPE	M
07/18/43	12094	VF-28		RUSSELLS	SOPAC	LT PIERSON	M
07/21/43	12177	VF-28		RUSSELLS	SOPAC		
07/22/43	11678	VF-21		GUADAL-CANAL	SOPAC	HEMSLEY	M
07/22/43	11679	VF-21		GUADAL-CANAL	SOPAC	TORKELSON	M
07/22/43	11975	VF-21		GUADAL-CANAL	SOPAC	VOWCRANTZ	M
07/22/43	12176	VF-21		GUADAL-CANAL	SOPAC	LT SCOL	U
07/25/43	11876	VF-21		GUADAL-CANAL	SOPAC	ROACH	M

DATE	BUNO	SQDRN	BASE	LOST	AREA	PILOT	FATE
07/25/43	11973	VF-21		GUADAL-CANAL	SOPAC	JOHNSON	M
07/25/43	12122	VF-21		GUADAL-CANAL	SOPAC		
07/28/43	3489	VF-29			NORLANT		
07/29/43	3538	VF-29			NORLANT		
07/29/43	12087	VMF-216			WCENPAC		
07/31/43	3430	VF-11		GUADAL-CANAL	SOPAC		
07/31/43	11892	VF-11		GUADAL-CANAL	SOPAC		
07/31/43	11896	VF-11		GUADAL-CANAL	SOPAC		
08/04/43	12090	VF-27	USS SUWAN-NEE	SOLOMONS	SOPAC	LT IRWIN BINK	M
08/04/43	12139	VF-27	USS SUWAN-NEE	SOLOMONS	SOPAC	ENS WILLIAM T. CLIFTON	M
08/06/43	12101	VF-16	USS LEX-INGTON	PEARL	ECENPAC		
08/08/43	11845	VC-1	USS CARD		NORLANT	ENS SPRAGUE	M
08/16/43	12159	VC-13	USS CORE		NORLANT		
08/22/43	12209	VF-4	USS RANGER		NORLANT		
08/26/43	11953	VF-4	USS RANGER		NORLANT		
08/28/43	12204	VC-1	USS CARD		NORLANT	LTJG E.E. JACKSON	S
08/28/43	12136	VMF-111			SOPAC		
08/30/43	11688	VF-21			SOPAC		
08/30/43	11860	VF-21			SOPAC		
08/30/43	11897	VF-21			SOPAC		
08/30/43	11696	VF-27	USS SUWAN-NEE	SOLOMONS	SOPAC		
08/30/43	12165	VF-27	USS SUWAN-NEE	SOLOMONS	SOPAC		
08/30/43	12166	VF-27	USS SUWAN-NEE	SOLOMONS	SOPAC		
08/30/43	11949	VF-28			SOPAC		
08/31/43	11991	VF-29	USS SANTEE	OFF BERMUDA	NORLANT		
08/31/43	11927	VF-4	USS RANGER		NORLANT		
08/31/43	12153	VF-4	USS RANGER		NORLANT		
09/01/43	12014	VMF-441		FUNAFUTI	SOPAC		
09/05/43	11682	CASU-14			SOPAC		
09/08/43	11943	VMF-441		FUNAFUTI	SOPAC	LT FOSTER LEMLY	M
09/10/43	11884	VMF-111			SOPAC		
09/11/43	12107	VC-29	USS SANTEE	ENR CASABLAN.	NORLANT		
09/12/43	12158	VC-9	USS CARD		NORLANT		
09/13/43	12041	VF-29	USS SANTEE	ENR CASABLAN.	NORLANT		
09/28/43	3510	VC-29	USS SANTEE	ENR NORFOLK	NORLANT		
10/04/43	2054	ADVB-204		NOUMEA	SOPAC		
10/04/43	11852	VF-4	USS RANGER	VESTFJORD	NORLANT	LTJG C.R. HOPSON	S
10/09/43	11955	VF-4	USS RANGER	SCAPA FLOW	NORLANT		
10/09/43	12106	VF-4	USS RANGER	SCAPA FLOW	NORLANT		
10/10/43	11933	VMF-111			SOPAC		
10/21/43	2129	VF-29	USS SANTEE	OFF NORFOLK	CENLANT		
11/04/43	12181	VF-29	USS SANTEE	ENR CASABLAN.	NORLANT	LTJG JOHN F. THOMPSON	S
11/05/43	2115	VMF-441		NANOMEA	SOPAC		
11/08/43	11849	VC-13	USS CORE		NORLANT		

DATE	BUNO	SQDRN	BASE	LOST	AREA	PILOT	FATE
11/15/43	5175	VC-41	USS CORREGI-DOR	ENR MAKIN	CENPAC		
11/20/43	12115	VC-13	USS CORE		NORLANT		
11/24/43	2030	VC-39	USS LISCOME BAY	GILBERTS	CENPAC		
11/24/43	11720	VC-39	USS LISCOME BAY	GILBERTS	CENPAC		
11/24/43	12055	VC-39	USS LISCOME BAY	GILBERTS	CENPAC		
11/24/43	12065	VC-39	USS LISCOME BAY	GILBERTS	CENPAC		
11/25/43	3468	CASU-1	HILO	HAWAII	ECENPAC	ENS J.P. LANDES	S
11/25/43	11883	VMF-111	FUNAFUTI	NUKUFETAU	SOPAC		
11/26/43	3433	VF-4	USS RANGER	ICELAND	NORLANT		
12/12/43	12034	HEDRON-M/13		FUTUILA	SOPAC	1STLT H.M. SMOLL	D
01/08/44	11668	CASU-1	FORD ISLAND	HAWAII	ECENPAC	CDR W.B. TOWNSEND	M
01/25/44	11691	VC-33	USS CORAL SEA	MARSHALLS	CENPAC	ENS W.H. GREGORY	S
03/04/44	12062	VC-33	USS CORAL SEA	PEARL	ECENPAC		
04/13/44	11841	COMAIR-PAC	PEARL	HAWAII	ECENPAC		
04/30/44	5054	COMAIR-PAC	PEARL	HAWAII	ECENPAC		
06/03/44	5229	VMF(N)-531		BARAKOMA	SOPAC		
07/11/44	5261	ARU SOLS			SOPAC		
11/30/44	5092	COMAIR-PAC	PEARL	HAWAII	ECENPAC		

GRUMMAN F4F-4P

Simply, the photo-reconnaissance version of the F4F-4. Aircraft lost:

DATE	BUNO	SQDRN	BASE	LOST	AREA	PILOT	FATE
11/13/43	5160	VF-4	USS RANGER	ICELAND	NORLANT		

GRUMMAN F4F-7

The F4F-7 was a long-range photo-reconnaissance variant of the F4F-3 Wildcat, with armor and armament removed. It had the same engine as the -3 but had non-folding "wet" wings that carried an additional 555 gallons of fuel for a total of 685 gallons, increasing its range to 3,700 mi (5,955 km). The extra fuel allowed for nearly 11 hours of endurance. A total of 21 were built. The film processing and photo interpretation was performed by the Navy photo lab aboard the USS CURTISS at anchor at Guadalcanal. Aircraft lost:

DATE	BUNO	SQDRN	BASE	LOST	AREA	PILOT	FATE
04/23/42	5265	4TH MBDAW		SAMOA	SE PAC		
08/24/42	5272	VF-6	USS ENTER-PRISE	E. SOLOMONS	SOPAC	LT ALBERT O. VORSE	S
01/31/43	5270	VMD-154			SOPAC		
06/30/43	5277	CASU-4	PUUNENE	HAWAII	ECENPAC		
12/22/43	5271	MAG-14	ONDONGA	BARAKOMA	SOPAC		
01/07/44	5268	CASU-8		HENDERSON	SOPAC		

GRUMMAN F4F-7P

In 1944 the Navy redesignated the F4F-7 by adding a P (for Photographic) after the designator, but nothing else changed about the aircraft. Aircraft lost:

DATE	BUNO	SQDRN	BASE	LOST	AREA	PILOT	FATE
12/11/44	5277	VMD-254	HAWAII		ECENPAC	GULLIFORD OLIVER	U

GRUMMAN F6F-3

Grumman was working on a successor to the F4F Wildcat well before the Japanese attacked Pearl Harbor. While the F4F was a capable fighter, early air battles revealed the Japanese A6M Zero was more maneuverable and possessed a better rate of climb than the F4F. The F4F did have some advantages over the Zero. Wildcats were able to absorb a tremendous amount of damage compared to the Zero, and had better armament. The F4F was also much faster in a dive than the Zero, an advantage frequently used by Wildcat pilots to elude attacking Zeros. The F6F Hellcat was designed to enhance the favorable aspects of the F4F while having a much higher top speed and greater range, allowing it to outperform the Zero.

The contract for the prototype XF6F-1 was signed on 30 June 1941. The F6F was first designed to use the Wright R-2600 Cyclone engine of 1,700 hp, but based on combat experience of F4F Wildcat and A6M Zero encounters, Grumman decided to further increase the new fighter's performance. Grumman redesigned and strengthened the F6F airframe to incorporate the 2,000hp Pratt & Whitney R-2800 Double Wasp, estimating a 25% increase in performance would result. Instead of the Wildcat's narrow-track, hand-cranked undercarriage retracting into the fuselage, the Hellcat had wide-set, hydraulically-actuated undercarriage struts which twisted through 90° while retracting backward into the wings. The wing was low-mounted instead of mid-mounted and was arranged to allow each panel outboard of the undercarriage bay to fold backwards, parallel with the fuselage, with the leading edges pointing down.

The first Double Wasp-equipped aircraft, the XF6F-3 (02982) made its first flight on 30 July 1942. The first production F6F-3 flew on 3 October 1942 with the type reaching operational readiness with VF-9 on USS ESSEX in February 1943. Two night fighter sub-variants of the F6F-3 were also developed.

Standard armament on the F6F-3 consisted of six .50 in (12.7 mm) M2/AN Browning air-cooled machine guns with 400 rpg; later aircraft gained three hard-points to carry a total bomb-load in excess of 2,000 lb (900 kg). The center hard point also had the ability to carry a single 150 gal (568 l) disposable drop tank. Six 5 in (127 mm) HVARs (High Velocity Aircraft Rocket) could be carried; three under each wing. A bullet-resistant windshield and a total of 212 lb (96 kg) of cockpit armor was fitted, along with armor around the oil tank and oil cooler. Self-sealing fuel tanks further reduced susceptibility to fire and often allowed damaged aircraft to return home.

The US Navy preferred the more docile flight qualities of the F6F compared with the Vought F4U Corsair, especially during carrier take-offs and landings, and the F6F remained the standard USN carrier-borne fighter until the F4U series was finally cleared for carrier operations in late-1944. In addition to its good flight qualities the Hellcat was easy to maintain and had an airframe tough enough to withstand the rigors of routine carrier operations. Like the Wildcat, the Hellcat was designed for ease of manufacture and ability to withstand significant damage. The U.S. Navy's all-time leading ace, Captain David McCampbell USN (Ret) scored all his 34 victories in the Hellcat.

The Hellcat first saw action against the Japanese on 1 September 1943 when fighters off the USS INDEPENDENCE shot down a Kawanishi H8K "Emily" flying boat. Soon after, on 23 and 24 November, Hellcats engaged Japanese aircraft over Tarawa, shooting down a claimed 30 Mitsubishi Zeros for the loss of one F6F. Over Rabaul, New Britain, on 11 November 1943, Hellcats and Corsairs were engaged in day-long fights with many Japanese aircraft including A6M Zeros, claiming nearly 50 aircraft.

Hellcats were involved in practically all engagements with Japanese air power from that point onward. It was the major U.S. Navy fighter type involved in the Battle of the Philippine Sea, where so many Japanese aircraft were shot down that Navy aircrews nicknamed the battle "The Great Marianas Turkey Shoot." The F6F accounted for 75% of all aerial victories recorded by the U.S. Navy in the Pacific.

Navy and Marine F6F pilots flew 66,530 combat sorties and claimed 5,163 kills (56% of all U.S. Naval/Marine air victories of the war) at a recorded cost of 270 Hellcats (an overall kill-to-loss ratio of 19:1). The aircraft performed well against the best Japanese opponents with a claimed 13:1 kill ratio against Mitsubishi A6M, 9.5:1 against Nakajima Ki-84, and 3.7:1 against the Mitsubishi J2M during the last year of the war. The F6F became the prime ace-maker aircraft in the American inventory, with 305 Hellcat aces. The U.S. successes were not only attributed to superior aircraft, but also because they faced increasingly inexperienced Japanese aviators from 1942 onwards, as well as having the advantage of increasing numerical superiority. The last Hellcat rolled out in November 1945, the total production figure being 12,275, of which 11,000 had been built in just two years. This high production rate was credited to the sound original design, which required little modification once production was underway. In the ground attack role, Hellcats dropped 6,503 tons of bombs. Aircraft lost:

DATE	BUNO	SQDRN	BASE	LOST	AREA	PILOT	FATE
05/01/43	4910	VB-9	USS ESSEX		WCENPAC		
06/13/43	4940	VF-30			NORLANT		
06/25/43	4895	VF-3			WCENPAC		
06/27/43	4779	VB-9	USS ESSEX		SOPAC		
06/29/43	8891	VC-16			SOPAC		
06/30/43	8995	VC-22	USS INDE-PENDENCE	PEARL	ECENPAC		
06/30/43	4784	VF-9		HAWAII	ECENPAC		
06/30/43	4935	VF-9		HAWAII	ECENPAC		
07/06/43	4825	VF-3	USS SARATOGA	NOUMEA	SOPAC		
07/12/43	8856	VF-3	USS SARATOGA	NOUMEA	SOPAC		
07/19/43	4903	VF-6			SOPAC		
07/23/43	4936	VF-5	USS YORK-TOWN	PEARL	ECENPAC		
07/31/43	8881	COMAIR-PAC	PEARL	HAWAII	ECENPAC		
08/01/43	4820	VF-5	USS YORK-TOWN	PEARL	ECENPAC		
08/01/43	4863	VF-5	USS YORK-TOWN	PEARL	ECENPAC		
08/02/43	4846	VF-5	USS YORK-TOWN	PEARL	ECENPAC		
08/06/43	4829	VF-3	USS SARATOGA	NOUMEA	SOPAC		
08/06/43	4840	VF-3	USS SARATOGA	NOUMEA	SOPAC		

DATE	BUNO	SQDRN	BASE	LOST	AREA	PILOT	FATE
08/14/43	25799	CASU-10	ESPIRITU SANTO	PALLIKULO	SOPAC		
08/25/43	8946	VF-24		HAWAII	ECENPAC		
08/25/43	8854	VT-12	USS SARATOGA	NOUMEA	SOPAC		
08/26/43	25762	VF-23		HAWAII	ECENPAC		
08/28/43	8970	VF-12	USS SARATOGA	NOUMEA	SOPAC		
08/28/43	9017	VF-12	USS SARATOGA	NOUMEA	SOPAC		
08/30/43	4921	VF-1	KANEOHE	HAWAII	ECENPAC		
08/31/43	8993	VF-12	USS SARATOGA	NOUMEA	SOPAC		
08/31/43	9006	VF-33		MUNDA	SOPAC		
08/31/43	9015	VF-33		MUNDA	SOPAC		
08/31/43	9018	VF-33		MUNDA	SOPAC		
08/31/43	25852	VF-38			SOPAC		
08/31/43	4861	VF-5	USS YORK-TOWN	MARCUS	CENPAC	ENS MORGAN	M
08/31/43	4894	VF-5	USS YORK-TOWN	MARCUS	CENPAC	ENS F.A. TOWNS	D
08/31/43	25937	VF-9	USS ESSEX	MARCUS	CENPAC	LTJG M.A. HADDEN, JR.	S
09/01/43	25831	VF-24	USS BELLEAU WOOD	HAWAII	ECENPAC	LCDR CURTIS	D
09/11/43	25808	VF-23	USS PRINCE-TON	HAWAII	ECENPAC	ENS W.A. DAVIS	S
09/11/43	25902	VF-33	MUNDA	KAHILI	SOPAC	LTJG POTTER	U
09/14/43	8979	VF-33	MUNDA	BALLALE	SOPAC	LTJG BERTUZZI	S
09/14/43	9024	VF-33	MUNDA	BALLALE	SOPAC	LT BROWN	U
09/14/43	25771	VF-5	USS YORK-TOWN	MIDWAY	ECENPAC		
09/15/43	4912	VF-25	USS COWPENS	HAWAII	ECENPAC	LT W. PETERSON	S
09/15/43	25883	VF-33	MUNDA	BALLALE	SOPAC	STLAKER	U
09/15/43	26009	VF-38	MUNDA	BALLALE	SOPAC	LTJG KOSTRAZONSKY	S
09/15/43	4879	VF-6	PEARL	HAWAII	ECENPAC		
09/15/43	25938	VF-6	PEARL	HAWAII	ECENPAC		
09/16/43	VF-38		GUADAL-CANAL	BALLALE	SOPAC	LTJG MOORE	S
09/16/43	25796	VF-38	GUADAL-CANAL	BALLALE	SOPAC	LTJG CORNELL	S
09/16/43	25839	VF-38	GUADAL-CANAL	BALLALE	SOPAC	LCDR ANDERSON	U
09/16/43	25940	VF-38	GUADAL-CANAL	BALLALE	SOPAC	LTJG WAYNE PRESLEY	M
09/16/43	8811	VF-9	USS ESSEX	PEARL	ECENPAC		
09/18/43	8915	VF-16	USS LEX-INGTON	TARAWA	CENPAC	LTJG JOHN ROBINSON	M
09/18/43		VF-23	USS PRINCE-TON	TARAWA	CENPAC		
09/18/43		VF-23	USS PRINCE-TON	TARAWA	CENPAC		
09/18/43	25926	VF-23	USS PRINCE-TON	TARAWA	CENPAC		
09/19/43	26067	VF-31	USS CABOT		NORLANT		
09/22/43	25928	VF-40			SOPAC	LT R.F. GRANT	S
09/25/43	25828	VF-24	USS BELLEAU WOOD	ENR WAKE IS.	CENPAC		
09/26/43	8950	VF-16	USS LEX-INGTON	PEARL	ECENPAC		
09/28/43	25925	VF-6	PEARL	HAWAII	ECENPAC		
10/01/43	9022	VF-12	USS SARATOGA	NOUMEA	SOPAC		
10/01/43	25913	VF-40			SOPAC		
10/03/43	8864	VF-31	USS CABOT		NORLANT	LTJG J.L. WIRTH	S
10/05/43	8828	VF-16	USS LEX-INGTON	WAKE	WCENPAC	LTJG R.G. JOHNSON	M

DATE	BUNO	SQDRN	BASE	LOST	AREA	PILOT	FATE
10/05/43	25917	VF-24	USS BELLEAU WOOD	WAKE	WCENPAC	ENS E.J. PHILLIPS	M
10/05/43	8853	VF-25	USS COWPENS	WAKE	WCENPAC	ENS A.G. MCILWAINE	M
10/05/43	25809	VF-25	USS COWPENS	WAKE	WCENPAC	ENS W.O. STANTON	M
10/05/43	25916	VF-25	USS COWPENS	WAKE	WCENPAC	ENS J.R. OGG	S
10/05/43	4847	VF-5	USS YORK-TOWN	WAKE	WCENPAC	LTJG SATTERFIELD	S
10/06/43	8914	VF-16	USS LEX-INGTON	WAKE	WCENPAC	LTJG W.M. REITER	M
10/06/43	25924	VF-24	USS BELLEAU WOOD	WAKE	WCENPAC		
10/06/43	1781	VF-25	USS COWPENS	WAKE	WCENPAC	LCDR MARK A. GRANT	S
10/06/43	1845	VF-25	USS COWPENS	WAKE	WCENPAC	LT HAROLD J. KICKER	M
10/06/43	4896	VF-25	USS COWPENS	WAKE	WCENPAC	ENS ORSON H. THOMAS	M
10/06/43	8904	VF-25	USS COWPENS	WAKE	WCENPAC	ENS E.R. ARMS	D
10/06/43	8977	VF-25	USS COWPENS	WAKE	WCENPAC	ENS C.N. SEAVER	S
10/06/43	4860	VF-5	USS YORK-TOWN	WAKE	WCENPAC	LTJG T.D. CROW	M
10/06/43	4871	VF-5	USS YORK-TOWN	WAKE	WCENPAC	ENS M.H. TYLER	D
10/06/43	26032	VF-5	USS YORK-TOWN	WAKE	WCENPAC	ENS J.R. BOIUS	D
10/06/43	8849	VF-6	USS INDE-PENDENCE	WAKE	WCENPAC	LTJG E.S. MENDENHALL	S
10/06/43	25936	VF-9	USS ESSEX	WAKE	WCENPAC	LTJG R.M. MCCANN	M
10/08/43	26000	VF-33	USS BRETON		SOPAC		
10/12/43	8876	VF-12	USS SARATOGA	NOUMEA	SOPAC		
10/12/43	8982	VF-12	USS SARATOGA	NOUMEA	SOPAC		
10/15/43	4887	CASU-32	KAHULUI	HAWAII	ECENPAC		
10/15/43	8943	VF-16	USS LEX-INGTON	WAKE	WCENPAC	LT E.A. KRAFT	S
10/16/43	8953	VF-16	USS LEX-INGTON	ENR PEARL	ECENPAC	LTJG D.D. WHITMORE	S
10/19/43	4898	VF-6	PEARL	HAWAII	ECENPAC		
10/20/43	9020	VF-33		KAHILI	SOPAC	LTJG T.C. CORWIN, JR.	M
10/20/43	26005	VF-33		KAHILI	SOPAC	ENS STACEY	S
10/21/43	9021	VF-33		BOUGAIN-VILLE	SOPAC	ENS HARRY A. CANTRELL	M
10/22/43	25997	VF-40		SEGI	SOPAC	ENS R.B. CARMICHAEL	S
10/23/43	25955	VF-1	KANEOHE	HAWAII	ECENPAC		
10/24/43	25899	VF-8	USS INTREPID	BERMUDA	NORLANT		
10/26/43	8800	VF-1	KANEOHE	HAWAII	ECENPAC		
10/31/43	66176	VF-30	PEARL	HAWAII	ECENPAC		
11/01/43	8884	VF-12	USS SARATOGA	BUKA	SOPAC	ENS W.T. WELLES	M
11/01/43	26014	VF-12	USS SARATOGA	BUKA	SOPAC	FERRIS	S
11/01/43	25814	VF-23	USS PRINCE-TON	BOUGAIN-VILLE	SOPAC		
11/01/43	25930	VF-23	USS PRINCE-TON	BOUGAIN-VILLE	SOPAC	LTJG D.N. OLIN	S
11/01/43	65914	VF-30	USS MONTEREY	PEARL	ECENPAC	LT A.E. DIETRICH	S
11/02/43	66021	VF-23	USS PRINCE-TON	RABAUL	SOPAC	ENS L.C. KEENER	M
11/02/43	25884	VF-38	SEGI	NEW GEORGIA	SOPAC	LTJG P. BEAUMONT	S

DATE	BUNO	SQDRN	BASE	LOST	AREA	PILOT	FATE
11/03/43	9000	VF-38	SEGI	BOUGAIN-VILLE	SOPAC		
11/04/43	26004	VF-33	USS BRETON	BOUGAIN-VILLE	SOPAC		
11/04/43	66158	VF-6	PEARL	HAWAII	ECENPAC		
11/05/43	26117	VF-12	USS SARATOGA	RABAUL	SOPAC	LTJG T.G. ATWILL	M
11/05/43	25840	VF-23	USS PRINCE-TON	RABAUL	SOPAC	LT R.E. O'CONNELL	M
11/05/43	25946	VF-23	USS PRINCE-TON	RABAUL	SOPAC	LTJG J.D. MADISON	M
11/05/43	66011	VF-23	USS PRINCE-TON	RABAUL	SOPAC	LT J.A. SMITH	M
11/05/43	26122	VF-37	USS SAN-GAMON	ESPIRITU SANTO	SOPAC		
11/08/43	66098	VF-24	USS BELLEAU WOOD	KAHULUI	ECENPAC		
11/08/43	25857	VF-33	SEGI	AUGUSTA BAY	SOPAC	LTJG KINSELLA	S
11/08/43	25991	VF-33	SEGI	AUGUSTA BAY	SOPAC	ENS M.E. PATTERSON	M
11/08/43	9025	VF-9	USS ESSEX	RABAUL	SOPAC		
11/09/43	66185	VF-2	USS ENTER-PRISE	BARBERS POINT	ECENPAC		
11/09/43	4913	VF-9	USS ESSEX	RABAUL	SOPAC		
11/10/43	25974	VF-2	USS ENTER-PRISE	BARBERS POINT	ECENPAC		
11/10/43	25985	VF-2	USS ENTER-PRISE	BARBERS POINT	ECENPAC		
11/10/43	4911	VF-25	USS COWPENS	KAHULUI	ECENPAC		
11/11/43	26174	VF-12	USS SARATOGA	BOUGAIN-VILLE	SOPAC	LTJG W.W. CULVER	S
11/11/43	26177	VF-18	USS BUNKER HILL	RABAUL	SOPAC	ENS C.J. HUSTED	M
11/11/43	65974	VF-18	USS BUNKER HILL	RABAUL	SOPAC	LTJG W. PARKER	S
11/11/43	66125	VF-18	USS BUNKER HILL	RABAUL	SOPAC	LT MANESS	S
11/11/43	66200	VF-18	USS BUNKER HILL	RABAUL	SOPAC	LT J.A. PIERCE	U
11/11/43	25977	VF-2	USS ENTER-PRISE	BARBERS POINT	ECENPAC		
11/11/43	8834	VF-22	USS INDE-PENDENCE	RABAUL	SOPAC	LT E.W. MARSH	M
11/11/43	26158	VF-33	SEGI	NEW GEORGIA	SOPAC	ENS STOLFA	S
11/11/43	40054	VF-33	SEGI	NEW GEORGIA	SOPAC	LT J.C. KELLEY	M
11/11/43	8930	VF-6	USS INDE-PENDENCE	RABAUL	SOPAC	LTJG R.A. HOBBS	S
11/11/43	66080	VF-6	USS INDE-PENDENCE	RABAUL	SOPAC	ENS B.E. GATES	M
11/11/43	65988	VF-9	USS ESSEX	RABAUL	SOPAC	ENS R.E. KAPP	M
11/15/43	8991	VF-23	USS PRINCE-TON	NAURU	CENPAC		
11/15/43	4883	VF-9	USS ESSEX	GILBERTS	CENPAC	ENS R.J. MILLER	S
11/19/43	26078	VF-10	PEARL	HAWAII	ECENPAC	ENS NEWCOMB	M
11/19/43	40139	VF-10	PEARL	HAWAII	ECENPAC		
11/19/43	25752	VF-2	USS ENTER-PRISE	MAKIN	CENPAC	ENS R.W. HARWOOD	M

DATE	BUNO	SQDRN	BASE	LOST	AREA	PILOT	FATE
11/19/43	26161	VF-2	USS ENTER-PRISE	MAKIN	CENPAC		
11/19/43	4806	VF-24	USS BELLEAU WOOD	MAKIN	CENPAC	LTJG J.P. HERR	S
11/19/43	66202	VF-30	USS MONTEREY	MAKIN	CENPAC	ENS C. CARMEN	S
11/19/43	66195	VF-5	USS YORK-TOWN	MILLE	CENPAC	LT J.B. FURSTENBERG	D
11/19/43	8846	VF-9	USS ESSEX	BITITU	CENPAC		
11/19/43	25927	VF-9	USS ESSEX	BITITU	CENPAC		
11/20/43	66201	VF-16	USS LEX-INGTON	MILLE	CENPAC	ENS R.E. O'CALLAHAN	M
11/20/43	8990	VF-22	USS INDE-PENDENCE	TARAWA	CENPAC		
11/20/43	66077	VF-24	USS BELLEAU WOOD	MAKIN	CENPAC	LT C.J. OVERLAND	S
11/20/43	66078	VF-24	USS BELLEAU WOOD	MAKIN	CENPAC		
11/21/43	8929	VF-16	USS LEX-INGTON	MILLE	CENPAC	ENS L.J. HATCH	S
11/21/43	8940	VF-16	USS LEX-INGTON	MILLE	CENPAC	ENS U.N. JOHNSON	M
11/21/43	4873	VF-25	USS COWPENS	MAKIN	CENPAC	ENS W.D. UPTEGRAFF	S
11/21/43	66242	VF-36	USS COPAHEE	ENR PEARL	ECENPAC	LT R.E. BROWNELL	U
11/22/43	8939	VF-16	USS LEX-INGTON	MILLE	CENPAC	LTJG F.G. SCHWARZ	S
11/22/43	25772	VF-16	USS LEX-INGTON	MILLE	CENPAC	CDR E.M. SNOWDEN	S
11/22/43	26164	VF-18	USS BUNKER HILL	TARAWA	CENPAC	ENS E.J. COURRAGE	S
11/22/43	4933	VF-25	USS COWPENS	MAKIN	CENPAC		
11/22/43	40055	VF-25	USS COWPENS	MAKIN	CENPAC		
11/22/43	66100	VF-25	USS COWPENS	MAKIN	CENPAC		
11/23/43	25777	VF-16	USS LEX-INGTON	MILLE	CENPAC	LTJG XAVIER H.E. BLOME	S
11/23/43	4864	VF-5	USS YORK-TOWN	MILLE	CENPAC		
11/23/43	4870	VF-5	USS YORK-TOWN	MILLE	CENPAC	LT L.A. GRANGER	S
11/23/43	4937	VF-5	USS YORK-TOWN	MILLE	CENPAC		
11/24/43	66198	VF-16	USS LEX-INGTON	MILLE	CENPAC	LTJG E.L. HEACOCK	M
11/24/43	4834	VF-24	USS BELLEAU WOOD	MAKIN	CENPAC	LTJG J.G. SNOWDEN	S
11/24/43	66101	VF-25	USS COWPENS	MAKIN	CENPAC	LTJG A.W.MAGEE	S
11/24/43	25780	VF-30	USS MONTEREY	MAKIN	CENPAC	LTJG W.B. REDING	S
11/24/43	25909	VF-6	USS INDE-PENDENCE	TARAWA	CENPAC	LT G.C. BULLARD	S
11/25/43	40037	VF-10	MAUI	HAWAII	ECENPAC		
11/25/43	40038	VF-10	MAUI	HAWAII	ECENPAC		
11/25/43	26103	VF-18	USS BUNKER HILL	BITITU	CENPAC		
11/26/43	26121	VF-18	USS BUNKER HILL	ENR MARAKEI IS.	CENPAC	LTJG H.W. WILDER	U
11/26/43	66168	VF-2	USS ENTER-PRISE	TARAWA	CENPAC	LCDR EDWARD H. O'HARE	M

DATE	BUNO	SQDRN	BASE	LOST	AREA	PILOT	FATE
11/26/43	25822	VF-23	USS PRINCE-TON	PEARL	ECENPAC		
11/28/43	66007	VF-6	USS INDE-PENDENCE	TARAWA	CENPAC	ENS W.D. UPTEGRAFF	S
11/29/43	26093	VF-18	USS BUNKER HILL	MARAKEI ISLAND	CENPAC		
11/29/43	26099	VF-18	USS BUNKER HILL	MARAKEI ISLAND	CENPAC		
11/30/43	25950	VF-22	KANEOHE	HAWAII	ECENPAC		
11/30/43	40530	VF-36	PEARL	HAWAII	ECENPAC	ENS F.M. BURLEY	S
11/30/43	4877	VF-9	USS ESSEX	PEARL	ECENPAC		
12/01/43	26179	VF-37	USS SAN-GAMON	APAMAMA	WCENPAC		
12/03/43	66177	VF-1	TARAWA	TARAWA	CENPAC		
12/04/43	40096	VF-10	KAHULUI	MAUI	ECENPAC	ENS G.A. CALHOON	D
12/04/43	66153	VF-10	KAHULUI	MAUI	ECENPAC	ENS J.C. ENDRES	S
12/04/43	8921	VF-16	USS LEX-INGTON	KWAJALEIN	CENPAC		
12/04/43	8936	VF-16	USS LEX-INGTON	ROI	WCENPAC		
12/04/43	8942	VF-16	USS LEX-INGTON	KWAJALEIN	CENPAC		
12/04/43	66023	VF-16	USS LEX-INGTON	MARSHALLS	CENPAC	ENS FIZALKOWSKI	S
12/04/43	25750	VF-2	USS ENTER-PRISE	KWAJALEIN	CENPAC	ENS E.D. REDMOND	S
12/04/43	25804	VF-25	USS COWPENS	MARSHALLS	CENPAC		
12/04/43	4939	VF-5	USS YORK-TOWN	KWAJALEIN	CENPAC	LT H.T. GILL	M
12/04/43	25907	VF-5	USS YORK-TOWN	KWAJALEIN	CENPAC	LCDR E.M. OWEN	S
12/04/43	25953	VF-5	USS YORK-TOWN	KWAJALEIN	CENPAC	LT K.B. SATTERFIELD	D
12/04/43	25933	VF-6	KANEOHE	HAWAII	ECENPAC		
12/05/43	66197	VF-16	USS LEX-INGTON	KWAJALEIN	CENPAC		
12/05/43	40042	VF-23	USS PRINCE-TON	PEARL	ECENPAC	ENS J.R. HILL, JR.	S
12/05/43	25893	VF-8	USS INTREPID	BERMUDA	NORLANT	ENS W.A. PRESTIN	D
12/08/43	26088	VF-18	USS BUNKER HILL	NAURU	CENPAC	ENS A.F. SMITH	M
12/10/43	40002	VF-33	ONDONGA	BARAKOMA	SOPAC		
12/11/43	26030	COMAIR-PAC	PEARL	HAWAII	ECENPAC		
12/11/43	66064	VF-16	USS LEX-INGTON	PEARL	ECENPAC		
12/11/43	26089	VF-18	USS BUNKER HILL	PEARL	ECENPAC		
12/11/43	4904	VF-23	USS PRINCE-TON	PEARL	ECENPAC		
12/11/43	66013	VF-23	USS PRINCE-TON	PEARL	ECENPAC		
12/11/43	8984	VF-26	USS PRINCE-TON	PEARL	ECENPAC		
12/11/43	26190	VF-37	USS SAN-GAMON	PEARL	ECENPAC		
12/11/43	40355	VF-39	BARBERS POINT	HAWAII	ECENPAC	ENS E.G. MCHATTON	S
12/11/43	4792	VF-9	USS ESSEX	PEARL	ECENPAC		
12/11/43	4794	VF-9	USS ESSEX	PEARL	ECENPAC		
12/11/43	4817	VF-9	USS ESSEX	PEARL	ECENPAC		
12/13/43	4839	VF-6	PEARL	HAWAII	ECENPAC		

DATE	BUNO	SQDRN	BASE	LOST	AREA	PILOT	FATE
12/14/43	40311	VF-32	USS LANGLEY	ENR HAWAII	CENPAC	ENS H.M. GARVEN	S
12/15/43	4800	VF-9	USS ESSEX	PEARL	ECENPAC	LT J.W. ONSTOTT	S
12/18/43	40099	VF-25	USS COWPENS	PEARL	ECENPAC		
12/20/43	40053	VF-23	USS PRINCE-TON	PUUNENE	ECENPAC	ENS T. WICKLIN	S
12/20/43	4813	VF-25	USS COWPENS	PEARL	ECENPAC	ENS H.A. MORLOCK	S
12/22/43	4848	CASU-32	KAHULUI	HAWAII	ECENPAC		
12/22/43	66174	VF-24	USS BELLEAU WOOD	PEARL	ECENPAC		
12/22/43	40132	VF-40	BARAKOMA	KOLOMBANG ARA	SOPAC	ENS W.L. SIMMONS	M
12/23/43	66061	VF-24	USS BELLEAU WOOD	PEARL	ECENPAC	ENS D.E. FLEISHER	S
12/24/43	66099	VF-25	USS COWPENS	PEARL	ECENPAC		
12/24/43	9028	VF-33	ONDONGA	RABAUL	SOPAC	LTJG D.A. SCOTT	S
12/24/43	25801	VF-33	ONDONGA	RABAUL	SOPAC	ENS J.A. WARREN	M
12/25/43	66124	VF-30	USS MONTEREY	ENR KAVIENG	SOPAC		
12/25/43	26178	VF-33	ONDONGA	RABAUL	SOPAC	LCDR H. RUSSELL	S
12/27/43	25918	VF-5	USS YORK-TOWN	PEARL	ECENPAC		
12/28/43	8847	VF-25	USS COWPENS	HAWAII	ECENPAC		
12/28/43	40406	VF-39	BARBERS POINT	HAWAII	ECENPAC	LTJG G.C. CARRINGTON	S
01/01/44	65908	VF-10	PUUNENE	HAWAII	ECENPAC		
01/01/44	66015	VF-18	USS BUNKER HILL	KAVIENG	SOPAC	ENS J.W. HAYES	D
01/01/44	26159	VF-25	USS COWPENS	KANEOHE	ECENPAC		
01/01/44	8806	VF-30	USS MONTEREY	KAVIENG	SOPAC		
01/01/44	66157	VF-30	USS MONTEREY	KAVIENG	SOPAC		
01/01/44	9005	VF-40	VELLA LAVELLA	RABAUL	SOPAC	LTJG F.G. DUMPHY	M
01/01/44	40502	VF-6	USS ENTER-PRISE	BARBERS POINT	ECENPAC		
01/02/44	25835	VF-24	USS BELLEAU WOOD	PUUNENE	ECENPAC		
01/02/44	40141	VF-9	USS ESSEX	PEARL	ECENPAC	LTJG K.C. MCGOWAN	S
01/03/44	40810	VF-12	USS SARATOGA	HAWAII	ECENPAC		
01/04/44	26100	VF-18	USS BUNKER HILL	KAVIENG	SOPAC	ENS R.W. BOEDLE	M
01/04/44	66108	VF-25	USS COWPENS	KANEOHE	ECENPAC		
01/06/44	25834	VF-32	USS LANGLEY	PEARL	ECENPAC		
01/06/44	40440	VF-39	BARBERS POINT	HAWAII	ECENPAC		
01/07/44	66079	VF-2	USS INTREPID	PEARL	ECENPAC		
01/07/44	9027	VF-33	ONDONGA	CAPE ST. GEO.	SOPAC	LTJG G.W. KITCHEN	M
01/07/44	25920	VF-33	ONDONGA	CAPE ST. GEO.	SOPAC	ENS M. WOLD	M
01/07/44	26042	VF-40	VELLA LAVELLA	CAPE ST. GEO.	SOPAC	LTJG C.P. LEARNED	M
01/07/44	41336	VF-5	USS YORK-TOWN	PEARL	ECENPAC	LTJG WORLING	M
01/09/44	25853	VF-33	ONDONGA	TOBERA	SOPAC	ENS F.E. SCHNEIDER	M
01/10/44	66111	VF-25	USS COWPENS	KANEOHE	ECENPAC		

DATE	BUNO	SQDRN	BASE	LOST	AREA	PILOT	FATE
01/12/44	25722	VF-50	USS BATAAN	ENR TRINIDAD	NORLANT	ENS R.S. FRASER	S
01/13/44	4827	VF-2	USS INTREPID	PEARL	ECENPAC		
01/14/44	40070	VF-36	HILO	HAWAII	ECENPAC		
01/14/44	8855	VF-40	VELLA LAVELLA	RABAUL	SOPAC	LTJG A.J. BARANOUSKI	S
01/14/44	25880	VF-40	VELLA LAVELLA	RABAUL	SOPAC	LTJG T.J. BURTON	S
01/17/44	4837	VF-24	USS BELLEAU WOOD	ENR KWAJALEIN	CENPAC	ENS C.E. BLACKMAN	S
01/17/44	26031	VF-40	BARAKOMA	RABAUL	SOPAC	ENS K.P. BABKIRK	M
01/19/44	66047	VF-50	USS BATAAN	TRINIDAD	CENLANT	ENS D.R. REHM	S
01/22/44	66135	VF-15	USS HORNET	BERMUDA	NORLANT	LTJG A.A. JONES	S
01/22/44	8992	VF-23	USS PRINCE-TON	ENR KWAJAL.		CENPAC	
01/22/44	42277	VF-40	BARAKOMA	RABAUL	SOPAC	ENS W.L. SIMMONS	M
01/23/44	66130	VF-15	USS HORNET	BERMUDA	NORLANT	ENS W.J. CLARK	S
01/24/44	40063	VF-50	USS BATAAN	TRINIDAD	CENLANT	LT W.A. STONER	S
01/25/44	40840	VF-35	USS CHE-NANGO	PEARL	ECENPAC	ENS H.C. SHORT	S
01/25/44	40843	VF-37	USS SAN-GAMON	KWAJALEIN	CENPAC	(DECK LOSS-AIRCRASH)	
01/25/44	40845	VF-37	USS SAN-GAMON	KWAJALEIN	CENPAC	LT R.E. DONNELLY	D
01/25/44	40878	VF-37	USS SAN-GAMON	KWAJALEIN	CENPAC	(DECK LOSS-AIRCRASH)	
01/25/44	40912	VF-37	USS SAN-GAMON	KWAJALEIN	CENPAC	(DECK LOSS-AIRCRASH)	
01/26/44	40295	VF-51	USS SAN JACINTO		CENLANT	LT H.T. FICHMAN	
01/27/44	40387	VF-51	USS SAN JACINTO		CENLANT	LTJG R.G. HENDERSON	S
01/29/44	26079	VF-10	USS ENTER-PRISE	MALOELAP	CENPAC	LTJG E.W. TALIN	S
01/29/44	26186	VF-10	USS ENTER-PRISE	MALOELAP	CENPAC	ENS F.H. JONES	M
01/29/44	40102	VF-10	USS ENTER-PRISE	MALOELAP	CENPAC	ENS B.D. STEWARD	M
01/29/44	40130	VF-10	USS ENTER-PRISE	MALOELAP	CENPAC	LTJG R.G. TABER	S
01/29/44	40337	VF-15	USS HORNET	BERMUDA	NORLANT		
01/29/44	26002	VF-18	USS BUNKER HILL	KWAJALEIN	CENPAC	LT M.P. MOWRY	M
01/29/44	25968	VF-24	USS BELLEAU WOOD	KWAJALEIN	CENPAC	ENS J.R. POWNING	M
01/29/44	26087	VF-24	USS BELLEAU WOOD	KWAJALEIN	CENPAC	ENS R.L. PARKER	M
01/29/44	40301	VF-31	USS CABOT	ROI	WCENPAC	ENS F. HANCOCK, JR.	S
01/29/44	25906	VF-38	BARAKOMA	RABAUL	SOPAC		
01/29/44	4878	VF-6	USS INTREPID	ROI	WCENPAC	LT R.W. NEEL	M
01/29/44	4880	VF-6	USS INTREPID	ROI	WCENPAC	LTJG R.A. HOBBS	S
01/29/44	26106	VF-9	USS ESSEX	ROI	WCENPAC	LTJG S.D. WRIGHT	M
01/30/44	40703	VF-32	USS LANGLEY	KWAJALEIN	CENPAC	LTJG H.V. LADLEY	S
01/31/44	25849	VF-18	USS BUNKER HILL	KWAJALEIN	CENPAC		

DATE	BUNO	SQDRN	BASE	LOST	AREA	PILOT	FATE
01/31/44	40166	VF-23	USS PRINCE-TON	WOTJE	CENPAC	LTJG W.G. BUCKELEW	M
01/31/44	40036	VF-24	USS BELLEAU WOOD	KWAJALEIN	CENPAC	ENS L.E. GRAHAM	S
01/31/44	40978	VF-35	USS CHE-NANGO	ROI	WCENPAC	ENS J.M. RING	S
02/01/44	40121	VF-24	USS BELLEAU WOOD	KWAJALEIN	CENPAC	ENS J.R. CLEM	D
02/01/44	26073	VF-30	USS MONTEREY	MARSHALLS	CENPAC		
02/01/44	66212	VF-30	USS MONTEREY	MARSHALLS	CENPAC	ENS E.T. JOYCE	S
02/01/44	40030	VF-9	USS ESSEX	ROI	WCENPAC	LTJG J.O. BENTON	M
02/03/44	40017	VF-10	USS ENTER-PRISE	KWAJALEIN	CENPAC	LTJG A.L. MASTIN	S
02/03/44	25803	VF-18	USS BUNKER HILL	NAMU ISLAND	CENPAC		
02/03/44	40024	VF-6	USS INTREPID	ENR TRUK	CENPAC	ENS T.A. HALL	D
02/04/44	4930	VF-16	KAHULUI	HAWAII	ECENPAC		
02/04/44	40356	VF-8	PUUNENE	HAWAII	ECENPAC	ENS M.H. HIGH	S
02/05/44	40808	VF-12	USS SARATOGA	ENIWETOK	CENPAC		
02/05/44	40836	VF-12	USS SARATOGA	ENIWETOK	CENPAC		
02/07/44	40319	VF-31	USS CABOT	MAJURO	CENPAC		
02/07/44	40911	VF-37	USS SAN-GAMON	KWAJALEIN	CENPAC		
02/08/44	25900	VF-24	USS BELLEAU WOOD	MAJURO	CENPAC		
02/08/44	66004	VF-24	USS BELLEAU WOOD	MAJURO	CENPAC	LT C.N. QUINLAN	S
02/08/44	40625	VF-8	PUUNENE	HAWAII	ECENPAC		
02/10/44	66049	VF-32	USS LANGLEY	ENIWETOK	CENPAC		
02/11/44	4938	VF-23	USS PRINCE-TON	ENIWETOK	CENPAC	ENS J.B. BOYD	D
02/11/44	65942	VF-32	USS LANGLEY	ENIWETOK	CENPAC		
02/12/44	26017	VF-38	PIVA	RABAUL	SOPAC	LTJG C.W. HAGANS	S
02/12/44	40516	VF-8	PUUNENE	HAWAII	ECENPAC	LT H.Q. GUFATFSON	S
02/12/44	25810	VF-9	USS ESSEX	ENR TRUK	CENPAC	LT L. DECEW	S
02/14/44	4875	VF-24	USS BELLEAU WOOD	ENR TRUK	CENPAC	ENS HARRIGAN	S
02/14/44	40385	VF-51	USS SAN JACINTO	TRINIDAD	CENLANT	ENS T.H. LINDSEY	S
02/16/44	40077	VF-10	USS ENTER-PRISE	TRUK	CENPAC	ENS L.L. COX	M
02/16/44	40667	VF-10	USS ENTER-PRISE	TRUK	CENPAC		
02/16/44	40149	VF-16	KAHULUI	HAWAII	ECENPAC	LT A.L. FRENDBURG	S
02/16/44	40076	VF-25	USS COWPENS	TRUK	CENPAC	LTJG R.J. RAFFMAN	S
02/16/44	8996	VF-5	USS YORK-TOWN	TRUK	CENPAC	LT R.T. STOVER	M
02/16/44	8859	VF-6	USS INTREPID	TRUK	CENPAC		
02/16/44	25921	VF-6	USS INTREPID	TRUK	CENPAC	LCDR J.L. PHILLIPS	M
02/16/44	65894	VF-6	USS INTREPID	TRUK	CENPAC	ENS J.R. OGG	M
02/16/44	66016	VF-6	USS INTREPID	TRUK	CENPAC	LT G.C. BULLARD	M

DATE	BUNO	SQDRN	BASE	LOST	AREA	PILOT	FATE
02/16/44	8838	VF-9	USS ESSEX	TRUK	CENPAC	LT A.B. SMITH	S
02/16/44	40020	VF-9	USS ESSEX	TRUK	CENPAC		
02/16/44	40684	VF-9	USS ESSEX	TRUK	CENPAC	LTJG H.A. SCHIEBLER	M
02/17/44	65891	COMAIR-PAC	GUADAL-CANAL	GUADAL-CANAL	SOPAC		
02/17/44	40108	VF-9	USS ESSEX	TRUK	CENPAC	LTJG G.M. BLAIR	S
02/18/44	40850	VF-35	USS CHE-NANGO	ENIWETOK	CENPAC	S.L. TENBURG	S
02/18/44	25944	VF-9	USS ESSEX	TRUK	CENPAC	ENS R.K. GREEN	U
02/19/44	66160	VF-35	USS CHE-NANGO	ENIWETOK	CENPAC		
02/20/44	40420	VF-33	PALLIKULO AIRFIELD		SOPAC		
02/21/44	65892	VF-18	USS BUNKER HILL	TINIAN	WCENPAC	ENS J.H. CRAWFORD	S
02/21/44	66062	VF-25	USS COWPENS	SAIPAN	WCENPAC	LTJG B.F. FARBER	D
02/21/44	40454	VF-30	USS MONTERR EY	SAIPAN	WCENPAC		
02/22/44	66156	VF-18	USS BUNKER HILL	TINIAN	WCENPAC	LTJG J.H. FORMAN	M
02/22/44	4908	VF-5	USS YORK-TOWN	SAIPAN	WCENPAC	LTJG A.F. DAVIS	M
02/22/44	40671	VF-5	USS YORK-TOWN	SAIPAN	WCENPAC	LT W.L. MCVAY	M
02/22/44	66056	VF-9	USS ESSEX	SAIPAN	WCENPAC	ENS L.A. MATTHEWS	D
02/23/44	40419	VF-18	USS BUNKER HILL	TINIAN	WCENPAC	LT W.W. KELLY	S
02/23/44	40125	VF-9	USS ESSEX	SAIPAN	WCENPAC	LTJG S.W. MCGURK	D
02/24/44	66104	VF-51	USS SAN JACINTO	GULF OF PARIA	NORLANT	LT W.L. POLAND	S
02/25/44	40610	VF-12	USS SARATOGA	ENIWETOK	CENPAC	LTJG J.E. DARDEN	S
02/27/44	40351	CASU-4	PUUNENE	HAWAII	ECENPAC		
02/27/44	25735	VF-2	KANEOHE	PEARL	ECENPAC	ENS J.M. EDWARDS	M
02/27/44	41055	VF-2	KANEOHE	PEARL	ECENPAC	LCDR W.A. DEAN	S
02/29/44	65997	VF-38	PIVA	NEW IRELAND	SOPAC	LTJG L.H. ENGLADE	M
03/03/44	40362	VF-19	PEARL	MAUI	ECENPAC	ENS S.E. SIMONCIK	S
03/05/44	40515	VF-39	MAJURO	EMIDJ	CENPAC	LT N.J. PINEUR	S
03/05/44	40519	VF-39	MAJURO	EMIDJ	CENPAC	ENS C.C. WRIGHT	S
03/06/44	9001	VF-1	KANEOHE	HAWAII	ECENPAC	ENS G.G. ROSS	M
03/07/44	40449	VF-39	MAJURO	MILLE	CENPAC	LT J.W. BUDD	D
03/08/44	26108	VF-24	USS BELLEAU WOOD	MAJURO	CENPAC		
03/10/44	66123	VF-37	USS SAN-GAMON	ENR PEARL	CENPAC		
03/11/44	40510	VF-19	PEARL	PUUNENE	ECENPAC	LT H.J. ROSSI	S
03/11/44	40895	VF-19	PEARL	PUUNENE	ECENPAC	ENS S.E. SIMONCIK	D
03/12/44	41610	VF-15	USS HORNET	PEARL	ECENPAC		
03/13/44	40008	VF-35	USS CHE-NANGO	PEARL	ECENPAC	ENS L.W. BUNDY	M
03/16/44	40864	VF-32	USS LANGLEY	ENR PALAU	CENPAC		
03/16/44	41840	VF-50	USS BATAAN	ENR PEARL	ECENPAC		
03/17/44	9011	VF-34	ESPIRITU SANTO	PALLIKULO	SOPAC	ENS R.G. HILL	S
03/18/44	8919	VF-16	USS LEX-INGTON	MILLE	CENPAC	LT H.R. FIZALKOUSKI	S
03/18/44	41081	VF-16	USS LEX-INGTON	MILLE	CENPAC	LT J.W. BARTOL	S
03/18/44	25751	VF-2	USS HORNET	ENR MAJURO	CENPAC	ENS H.L. CARLSON	D
03/18/44	40621	VF-2	USS HORNET	ENR MAJURO	CENPAC	ENS G.D. WILLIAMS	D
03/18/44	40556	VF-34	TOROKINA	GREEN	SOPAC		
03/19/44	66051	VF-15	MAUI	HAWAII	ECENPAC		
03/19/44	40539	VF-16	USS LEX-INGTON	MAJURO	CENPAC	ENS E.J. RUCINSKI	S

DATE	BUNO	SQDRN	BASE	LOST	AREA	PILOT	FATE
03/19/44	41175	VF-25	USS COWPENS	PALAU	CENPAC		
03/19/44	40701	VF-34	TOROKINA	GREEN	SOPAC		
03/20/44	40103	VF-24	USS BELLEAU WOOD	EMIRAU	SW PAC		
03/20/44	41026	VF-35	USS CHE-NANGO	ENR ADMIRALTIES	SW PAC	ENS R.T. NEWMAN	D
03/21/44	40728	VF-13	USS FRANKLIN	ENR TRINIDAD	NORLANT	ENS J.H. WILSON	S
03/21/44	40136	VF-23	USS PRINCE-TON	ENIWETOK	CENPAC		
03/22/44	40527	VF-24	USS BELLEAU WOOD	PALAU	CENPAC		
03/23/44	40127	VF-16	USS LEX-INGTON	ENR PALAU	CENPAC	LTJG A. VRACIN	S
03/24/44	41609	VF-14	USS WASP	ENR CZ TO CA	CENPAC	ENS E.J. STRESTER	S
03/25/44	4926	VF-100	BARBERS POINT	HAWAII	ECENPAC	ENS W.H. BURNS	S
03/25/44	8821	VF-100	BARBERS POINT	HAWAII	ECENPAC		
03/26/44	41257	VF-2	USS HORNET	ENR PALAU	CENPAC		
03/27/44	40255	VF-39	MAJURO	WOTJE	CENPAC		
03/28/44	41670	VF-50	USS BATAAN	PEARL	ECENPAC	LT C.E. FANNING	S
03/28/44	42002	VF-50	USS BATAAN	PEARL	ECENPAC	LT B.R. CHESTNEY	M
03/29/44	25733	VF-2	USS HORNET	PALAU	CENPAC		
03/29/44	41236	VF-25	USS COWPENS	PALAU	CENPAC		
03/29/44	40437	VF-34	TOROKINA	SW WATEN IS.	SOPAC	ENS K.T. DRISCOLL	M
03/30/44	41195	VF-16	USS LEX-INGTON	PALAU	CENPAC	ENS E.J. RUCINSKI	S
03/30/44	25952	VF-23	USS PRINCE-TON	PALAU	CENPAC	LTJG J.M. WEBB	S
03/30/44	40023	VF-24	USS BELLEAU WOOD	PALAU	CENPAC	ENS D.E. FLEISHER	M
03/30/44	40997	VF-30	USS MONTEREY	PALAU	CENPAC	ENS W.B. GUNNELS	S
03/30/44	25942	VF-40	SEGI	GREEN	SOPAC	ENS R.H. HOWARD	D
03/30/44	66068	VF-5	USS YORK-TOWN	PALAU	CENPAC	ENS R. BLACK	S
03/30/44	66189	VF-5	USS YORK-TOWN	PALAU	CENPAC	ENS J.J. BROSNAHAN	S
03/30/44	40377	VF-8	USS BUNKER HILL	PALAU	CENPAC	ENS R.J. HANZEL	M
03/30/44	41188	VF-8	USS BUNKER HILL	PALAU	CENPAC	LT W.L. GIBBS	S
03/31/44	40653	VF-23	USS PRINCE-TON	PALAU	CENPAC	LTJG J.W. SYME	M
03/31/44	40804	VF-32	USS LANGLEY	PALAU	CENPAC	LT EDMONDSON	S
03/31/44	40925	VF-32	USS LANGLEY	PALAU	CENPAC		
03/31/44	40682	VF-34	TOROKINA	RABAUL	SOPAC	ENS C.R. MILLER	M
03/31/44	8926	VF-35	USS CHE-NANGO	ADMIRALTIES	SW PAC		
03/31/44	66190	VF-5	USS YORK-TOWN	PALAU	CENPAC	LT W.S. DUNN	S
03/31/44	41768	VF-50	USS BATAAN	PEARL	ECENPAC	ENS E.R. TARLETON	S
04/01/44	41295	VF-15	PUUNENE	HAWAII	ECENPAC	ENS G.F. BUTLER	D
04/01/44	25827	VF-16	USS LEX-INGTON	WOLEAI	CENPAC	LTJG ABERCROMBIE	S

DATE	BUNO	SQDRN	BASE	LOST	AREA	PILOT	FATE
04/01/44	40078	VF-16	USS LEXINGTON	WOLEAI	CENPAC	ENS J.H. HUNNICUTT	S
04/01/44	40691	VF-16	USS LEXINGTON	WOLEAI	CENPAC	ENS A.W. SPINDLER	D
04/01/44	25824	VF-8	USS BUNKER HILL	WOLEAI	CENPAC	ENS M.W. DELEADERNIER	M
04/01/44	40695	VF-8	USS BUNKER HILL	WOLEAI	CENPAC	ENS J.R. GALVIN	S
04/02/44	66192	VF-30	USS MONTEREY	WOLEAI	CENPAC	LT R.Z. HUGHES	S
04/02/44	66219	VF-30	USS MONTEREY	WOLEAI	CENPAC		
04/03/44	41447	CASU-1	PEARL	HAWAII	ECENPAC		
04/03/44	41410	VF-1	KANEOHE	HAWAII	ECENPAC	LT W.R. CRUTCHER	D
04/03/44	66182	VF-1	KANEOHE	HAWAII	ECENPAC	ENS J.O. HAMILTON	D
04/03/44	66094	VF-23	USS PRINCETON	PALAU	CENPAC		
04/04/44	40888	VF-34		GREEN	SOPAC	LT J.A. ROSE	D
04/05/44	65906	VF-18	HILO	HAWAII	ECENPAC	ENS V. JACKSON	D
04/06/44	26006	COMAIRSOPAC	GUADALCANAL	GUADALCANAL	SOPAC	ENS T.C. FEARING	M
04/06/44	40719	VF-13	USS FRANKLIN	TRINIDAD	CENLANT	ENS C.M. PRICE	S
04/06/44	40434	VF-24	USS BELLEAU WOOD	MAJURO	CENPAC		
04/07/44	41911	VF-14	USS WASP	PEARL	ECENPAC	ENS E.L. TOTEMEIER	M
04/07/44	40657	VF-18	HILO	HAWAII	ECENPAC	ENS L.S. WOODWARD	S
04/08/44	41894	VF-51	USS SAN JACINTO	ENR PEARL	ECENPAC		
04/10/44	41039	VF-39	MAJURO	TAROA	CENPAC	LTJG E.G. MCHATTON	S
04/11/44	26109	VF-37		ESPIRITU SANTO	SOPAC	ENS L.C. RODEBACK	D
04/13/44	4929	VF-1	KANEOHE	HAWAII	ECENPAC		
04/13/44	40520	VF-16	USS LEXINGTON	MAJURO	CENPAC		
04/14/44	42159	VF-21	HAWAII	HAWAII	ECENPAC		
04/14/44	41243	VF-28	BARKING SANDS	HAWAII	ECENPAC	LT E.S. MATHIS	M
04/14/44	41254	VF-28	BARKING SANDS	HAWAII	ECENPAC	LT J.J. KEOUGH	S
04/15/44	40128	VF-5	USS YORKTOWN	ENR HOLLANDIA	CENPAC	LTJG J.E. SCHILLER	S
04/16/44	40832	CASU-13		ESPIRITU SANTO	SOPAC		
04/16/44	40217	VF-10	USS ENTERPRISE	ENR HOLLANDIA	CENPAC		
04/16/44	25984	VF-2	USS HORNET	ADMIRALTIES	SW PAC	ENS EDWARD J. O'NEAL	S
04/16/44	25858	VF-32	USS LANGLEY	ENR HOLLANDIA	CENPAC		
04/16/44	40240	VF-32	USS LANGLEY	ENR HOLLANDIA	CENPAC		
04/17/44	40061	VF-24	USS BELLEAU WOOD	MAJURO	CENPAC		
04/19/44	40122	VF-11	HILO	HAWAII	ECENPAC	ENS T.B. REED	M
04/19/44	41186	VF-11	HILO	HAWAII	ECENPAC	LTJG T.H. HOLBERTON	S
04/19/44	40052	VF-12	USS SARATOGA	SABANG	SE ASIA		
04/19/44	40917	VF-12	USS SARATOGA	SABANG	SE ASIA	LTJG D.C. KLAHN	S
04/19/44	25761	VF-5	USS YORKTOWN	ENR HOLLANDIA	CENPAC	ENS L.M. COBB	S
04/21/44	26081	VF-10	USS ENTERPRISE	HOLLANDIA	SW PAC	LTJG W.M. HAMPTON	S
04/21/44	40815	VF-16	USS LEXINGTON	HOLLANDIA	SW PAC		
04/22/44	41454	VF-19	KAHULUI	MAUI	ECENPAC	J.R. MILLER	M

DATE	BUNO	SQDRN	BASE	LOST	AREA	PILOT	FATE
04/22/44	43102	VF-2	USS HORNET	WAKDE	SW PAC		
04/22/44	40211	VF-39		MAJURO	CENPAC	LT G.D. ANDERSON	S
04/22/44	40296	VF-8	USS BUNKER HILL	HOLLANDIA	SW PAC	LT E.J. DOONER	S
04/23/44	40370	VF-30	USS MONTEREY	HOLLANDIA	SW PAC	LT G. FORMANEK	D
04/23/44	40254	VF-31	USS CABOT	WAKDE	SW PAC	LTJG J.L. WIRTH	S
04/24/44	40238	VF-31	USS CABOT	HOLLANDIA	SW PAC	LTJG M.L. LOOMIS	S
04/24/44	40321	VF-32	USS LANGLEY	HOLLANDIA	SW PAC		
04/24/44	40513	VF-39		MAJURO	CENPAC		
04/25/44	8824	COMFAIRT U		ARU SOLS	SOPAC		
04/25/44	26011	VF(N)-76	USS HORNET	ENR TRUK	CENPAC		
04/25/44	41020	VF-34	GREEN	ATLIKLIKUN BAY	SOPAC	ENS R.A. RICHARDSON	D
04/25/44	41675	VF-51	USS SAN JACINTO	PEARL	ECENPAC		
04/26/44	41337	VF-1	KANEOHE	HAWAII	ECENPAC	ENS E.W. HANSEN	S
04/27/44	66159	VF-35	USS CHE-NANGO	HOLLANDIA	SW PAC	LT E.W. SIMPSON	S
04/28/44	4955	VF-100	BARBERS POINT	HAWAII	ECENPAC	ENS G.A. HEINMILLER	S
04/28/44	4919	VF-23	USS PRINCE-TON	HOLLANDIA	SW PAC		
04/28/44	40334	VF-24	USS BELLEAU WOOD	ENR TRUK	CENPAC		
04/29/44	40381	VF-10	USS ENTER-PRISE	TRUK	CENPAC	LTJG R.F. KANZE	S
04/29/44	25829	VF-16	USS LEX-INGTON	TRUK	CENPAC	ENS R.D. MCAFEE	M
04/29/44	40994	VF-16	USS LEX-INGTON	TRUK	CENPAC	LTJG A. VRACIN	S
04/29/44	41094	VF-16	USS LEX-INGTON	TRUK	CENPAC	ENS T. CARLISLE	M
04/29/44	65985	VF-16	USS LEX-INGTON	TRUK	CENPAC	LTJG D.J. KENNEY	M
04/29/44	25759	VF-24	USS BELLEAU WOOD	TRUK	CENPAC	ENS R.H. ODEM	D
04/29/44	40565	VF-25	USS COWPENS	TRUK	CENPAC	ENS D.V. ROUCH	M
04/29/44	65972	VF-25	USS COWPENS	TRUK	CENPAC	ENS P.A. PARKER	S
04/29/44	66105	VF-25	USS COWPENS	TRUK	CENPAC	ENS A.H. SANCHEZ	M
04/29/44	40278	VF-30	USS MONTEREY	TRUK	CENPAC	ENS J.J. ODOM	S
04/29/44	8986	VF-31	USS CABOT	TRUK	CENPAC	LTJG D.B. GALT	S
04/29/44	40891	VF-32	USS LANGLEY	TRUK	CENPAC		
04/29/44	9012	VF-34	GREEN	NEW BRITAIN	SOPAC	LT J.P. KNIGHT	S
04/29/44	40806	VF-5	USS YORK-TOWN	TRUK	CENPAC	LT H.R. HILL	S
04/30/44	26001				CENPAC		
04/30/44	40004				CENPAC		
04/30/44	8967	COMAIRSO PAC	GUADAL-CANAL	GUADAL-CANAL	SOPAC		
04/30/44	42421	VF-20	BARBERS POINT	HAWAII	ECENPAC	ENS G.A. WILBUR	D
04/30/44	42676	VF-20	BARBERS POINT	HAWAII	ECENPAC	ENS H.E. SPEARS	D
04/30/44	40326	VF-22	USS LANGLEY	TRUK	CENPAC	LTJG R.T. BARBOR	S
04/30/44	40090	VF-30	USS MONTEREY	TRUK	CENPAC	LT W.B. REDING	S

DATE	BUNO	SQDRN	BASE	LOST	AREA	PILOT	FATE
04/30/44	40232	VF-30	USS MONTEREY	TRUK	CENPAC	LTJG C.L. LOFTIN	S
04/30/44	40398	VF-34		GREEN	SOPAC	ENS PITTS	S
04/30/44	8944	VF-5	USS YORK-TOWN	TRUK	CENPAC	LTJG J.C. COLE	S
04/30/44	25885	VF-8	USS BUNKER HILL	TRUK	CENPAC		
05/01/44	9009	POOL		ESPIRITU SANTO	SOPAC		
05/01/44	66204	VF-10	USS ENTER-PRISE	ENR HAWAII	ECENPAC		
05/01/44	66207	VF-25	USS COWPENS	PONAPE	CENPAC	LTJG F.R. SLIEGLITZ	S
05/01/44	40532	VF-30	USS MONTEREY	TRUK	CENPAC	LT H.A. CAREY	S
05/01/44	40368	VF-39		MAJURO	CENPAC		
05/01/44	41300	VF-50	USS BATAAN	KWAJALEIN	CENPAC	ENS F.V. SMITH	S
05/02/44	40391	VF-24	USS BELLEAU WOOD	PONAPE	CENPAC		
05/03/44	8934	VF-16	USS LEX-INGTON	ENR SAIPAN	CENPAC		
05/03/44	40829	VF-2	USS HORNET	KWAJALEIN	CENPAC	ENS R.B. BLAYDES	S
05/03/44	40157	VF-24	USS BELLEAU WOOD	PONAPE	CENPAC		
05/03/44	41983	VF-27	KAHULUI	HAWAII	ECENPAC	LT H.E. BREDLERTON	S
05/03/44	26085	VF-60	USS SU-WANNEE	ENR MANUS	CENPAC		
05/05/44	41621	VF-14	USS WASP	ENR MARCUS	CENPAC	ENS L. LAMPEN	M
05/05/44	42542	VF-39		MAJURO	CENPAC	LT N.J. PINEUR	D
05/08/44	25993	VF-38	GUADAL-CANAL	GUADAL-CANAL	SOPAC		
05/08/44	26195	VF-40	GREEN	GREEN	SOPAC		
05/10/44	42042	VF-27	KAHULUI	HAWAII	ECENPAC	LT R.P. BUTLER	D
05/13/44	65931	VF-2	USS HORNET	KWAJALEIN	CENPAC	ENS P.A. DOHERTY	S
05/13/44	42124	VF-27	PUUNENE	HAWAII	ECENPAC	ENS S.F. SAWYER	D
05/15/44	42123	VF-27	USS PRINCE-TON	PEARL	ECENPAC	ENS G.J. MCCORMICK	S
05/15/44	42137	VF-9	ATTU	ALASKA	NORPAC		
05/17/44	40348	VF-10	USS ENTER-PRISE	BARBERS POINT	ECENPAC		
05/17/44	26028	VF-100	BARBERS POINT	HAWAII	ECENPAC		
05/18/44	40521	VF-32	USS LANGLEY	MAJURO	CENPAC		
05/19/44	40796	COMAIR-PAC	PEARL	HAWAII	ECENPAC		
05/19/44	41502	VF-15	USS ESSEX	MARCUS	CENPAC	ENS W.T. BURNAM	M
05/20/44	41681	VF-15	USS ESSEX	MARCUS	CENPAC	LTJG L.T. KENNEY	S
05/20/44	41692	VF-15	USS ESSEX	MARCUS	CENPAC		
05/21/44	41504	POOL	DIAL	LUNGA POINT	SOPAC		
05/23/44	43111	VF-15	USS ESSEX	WAKE	WCENPAC		
05/23/44	42603	VF-21	PUUNENE	HAWAII	ECENPAC	ENS R.E. WHITE	S
05/23/44	42632	VF-21	PUUNENE	HAWAII	ECENPAC	LT R.N. MORRISON	D
05/23/44	42677	VF-21	PUUNENE	HAWAII	ECENPAC	LT L.S. RICE	U
05/24/44	41561	VF-14	USS WASP	HAWAII	ECENPAC		
05/24/44	40647	VF-34	RUSSELLS	ARU SOLS	SW PAC		
05/24/44	40963	VF-35	USS CHE-NANGO	ARU SOLS	SW PAC		
05/24/44	40669	VF-40		ARU SOLS	SW PAC		
05/26/44	40615	VF-11	HILO	HAWAII	ECENPAC	ENS W. DEROLF	S
05/26/44	42538	VF-25	USS COWPENS	MAJURO	CENPAC		
05/27/44	25922	POOL		ESPIRITU SANTO	SOPAC		
05/28/44	42281	VF-20	BARBERS POINT	HAWAII	ECENPAC		

DATE	BUNO	SQDRN	BASE	LOST	AREA	PILOT	FATE
05/30/44	41575	VF-14	USS WASP	MAJURO	CENPAC		
05/30/44	41673	VF-14	USS WASP	MAJURO	CENPAC		
05/30/44	8905	VF-18	HILO	HAWAII	ECENPAC		
05/30/44	41045	VF-34		RUSSELLS	SOPAC		
06/01/44	41870	CASU-30		MAJURO	CENPAC		
06/01/44	42307	VF-24	USS BELLEAU WOOD	MAJURO	CENPAC	LT R.S. FELT	D
06/01/44	42329	VF-24	USS BELLEAU WOOD	MAJURO	CENPAC		
06/02/44	41972	VF-14	USS WASP	MAJURO	CENPAC	ENS A.C. NISI	S
06/02/44	41587	VF-3	PUUNENE	HAWAII	ECENPAC	LT H.C. IRVINE	M
06/05/44	41332	SS-11		ESPIRITU SANTO	SOPAC		
06/05/44		VF-35	USS CHE-NANGO	ENR KWAJALEIN	CENPAC		
06/06/44	40802	VF-39	MAJURO	JALUIT	CENPAC	LT A.F. MINIER	D
06/06/44	41922	VF-7	USS HANCOCK		NORLANT		
06/07/44	25994	ARU SOLS			SOPAC		
06/11/44	41285	VF-10	USS ENTER-PRISE	SAIPAN	WCENPAC	LTJG M.P. LONG	S
06/11/44	42322	VF-10	USS ENTER-PRISE	SAIPAN	WCENPAC	LTJG RICHARD W. MASON	S
06/11/44	41651	VF-15	USS ESSEX	SAIPAN	WCENPAC	LTJG L.T. KENNEY	D
06/11/44	40676	VF-16	USS LEX-INGTON	SAIPAN	WCENPAC	LTJG W.E. BURCKHOLTER	D
06/11/44	25768	VF-2	USS HORNET	SAIPAN	WCENPAC	LT H.B. DUFF	M
06/11/44	66069	VF-25	USS COWPENS	SAIPAN	WCENPAC	ENS P.A. PARKER	M
06/11/44	26029	VF-31	USS CABOT	SAIPAN	WCENPAC	ENS R.G. WHITWORTH	S
06/11/44	41646	VF-32	USS LANGLEY	SAIPAN	WCENPAC	LT M.N. WICKENDALL	M
06/11/44	41746	VF-32	USS LANGLEY	SAIPAN	WCENPAC	LTJG D.E. REEVES	M
06/11/44	41154	VF-8	USS BUNKER HILL	SAIPAN	WCENPAC	LT BOYLES	S
06/11/44	41240	VF-8	USS BUNKER HILL	SAIPAN	WCENPAC	LT D.E. CARNEY	M
06/11/44	42522	VF-8	USS BUNKER HILL	SAIPAN	WCENPAC	CAPT W.M. COLLINS	S
06/12/44	41430	VF-1	USS YORK-TOWN	GUAM	WCENPAC	LTJG A.H. PAYTON	D
06/12/44	41452	VF-1	USS YORK-TOWN	GUAM	WCENPAC	LT G.W. STAEHELI	S
06/12/44	42411	VF-14	USS WASP	TINIAN	WCENPAC	ENS VICTOR LOWERY	M
06/12/44	41643	VF-15	USS ESSEX	SAIPAN	WCENPAC	LT M.C. ROACH	D
06/12/44	41105	VF-16	USS LEX-INGTON	SAIPAN	WCENPAC	LTJG J.R. LINDBECK	M
06/12/44	66113	VF-16	USS LEX-INGTON	SAIPAN	WCENPAC	LTJG C.L. HULL	S
06/12/44	40493	VF-2	USS HORNET	GUAM	WCENPAC	LT J.M. SEARCY	S
06/12/44	40788	VF-2	USS HORNET	GUAM	WCENPAC	LT D. LLOYD	D
06/12/44	40803	VF-2	USS HORNET	GUAM	WCENPAC		
06/12/44	40964	VF-24	USS BELLEAU WOOD	GUAM	WCENPAC	LTJG J.G. SNOWDEN	M
06/12/44	40967	VF-24	USS BELLEAU WOOD	GUAM	WCENPAC		
06/12/44	66110	VF-24	USS BELLEAU WOOD	GUAM	WCENPAC		

DATE	BUNO	SQDRN	BASE	LOST	AREA	PILOT	FATE
06/12/44	40443	VF-25	USS COWPENS	PAGAN	CENPAC	LT N.E. PETERSON	S
06/12/44	40979	VF-25	USS COWPENS	PAGAN	CENPAC	LCDR R.H. PRICE	S
06/12/44	66002	VF-25	USS COWPENS	PAGAN	CENPAC	ENS ROBERT T. WRIGHT	S
06/12/44	42187	VF-50	USS BATAAN	ROTA	CENPAC	LT W.E. LEAKE	S
06/12/44	42863	VF-51	USS SAN JACINTO	SAIPAN	WCENPAC	ENS R.D. MCILWAIN	D
06/13/44	4920	VF-1	USS YORK-TOWN	GUAM	WCENPAC	CDR STREAN	S
06/13/44	42534	VF-10	USS ENTER-PRISE	SAIPAN	WCENPAC	ENS M.D. POWELL	M
06/13/44	41926	VF-14	USS WASP	SAIPAN	WCENPAC	ENS MULARSKI	S
06/13/44	41772	VF-15	USS ESSEX	ENR BONINS	CENPAC	LT J.E. BARRY	S
06/13/44	40079	VF-2	USS HORNET	GUAM	WCENPAC	ENS D.C. BRANDT	S
06/13/44	42347	VF-2	USS HORNET	GUAM	WCENPAC		
06/13/44	66188	VF-2	USS HORNET	GUAM	WCENPAC		
06/13/44	42378	VF-28	USS MONTEREY	TINIAN	WCENPAC	LCDR R.W. MEHLE	S
06/13/44	41633	VF-50	USS BATAAN	GUAM	WCENPAC	LT W.Y. IRVIN	S
06/13/44	41756	VF-50	USS BATAAN	GUAM	WCENPAC	LT W.E. LEAKE	S
06/13/44	65916	VF-8	USS BUNKER HILL	OROTE	CENPAC	LT R.D. HANENKRATT	S
06/14/44	42234	VF-14	USS WASP	ROTA	CENPAC	LTJG J.J. SIMMS	M
06/14/44	66136	VF-8	USS BUNKER HILL	OROTE	CENPAC	LT J.J. MCGUIRE	S
06/15/44	41413	VF-1	USS YORK-TOWN	BONINS	CENPAC	ENS H.H. CRABBE	S
06/15/44	41427	VF-1	USS YORK-TOWN	BONINS	CENPAC	ENS J. HOGUE	M
06/15/44	41441	VF-1	USS YORK-TOWN	BONINS	CENPAC	ENS A.P. MORNER	S
06/15/44	41455	VF-1	USS YORK-TOWN	BONINS	CENPAC	LT P.M. HENDERSON	M
06/15/44	40308	VF-10	USS ENTER-PRISE	SAIPAN	WCENPAC	LTJG K.W. KIRCHNEY	M
06/15/44	41639	VF-15	USS ESSEX	IWO JIMA	EMPIRE	LTJG A.A. JONES	D
06/15/44	40223	VF-2	USS HORNET	BONINS	CENPAC		
06/15/44	42594	VF-2	USS HORNET	BONINS	CENPAC	LTJG NOBLE	S
06/15/44	41525	VF-20	BARBERS POINT	HAWAII	ECENPAC	ENS H.N. WARNKE	D
06/15/44	42546	VF-24	USS BELLEAU WOOD	BONINS	CENPAC		
06/15/44	41742	VF-32	USS LANGLEY	BONINS	CENPAC		
06/15/44	42861	VF-32	USS LANGLEY	BONINS	CENPAC		
06/15/44	40974	VF-35	USS CHE-NANGO	MARIANAS	CENPAC	ENS J. LIPTON	S
06/15/44	25818	VF-8	USS BUNKER HILL	OROTE	CENPAC	LT LONGINO	S
06/16/44	41367	VF-1	USS YORK-TOWN	BONINS	CENPAC	ENS J. SPIVEY	M
06/16/44	41108	VF-10	USS ENTER-PRISE	GUAM	WCENPAC	CDR W.R. KANE	S
06/16/44	41667	VF-15	USS ESSEX	IWO JIMA	EMPIRE	LT J.R. IVEY	M
06/16/44	41860	VF-15	USS ESSEX	IWO JIMA	EMPIRE		

DATE	BUNO	SQDRN	BASE	LOST	AREA	PILOT	FATE
06/16/44	41096	VF-24	USS BELLEAU WOOD	BONINS	CENPAC		
06/16/44	41484	VF-27	USS PRINCE-TON	GUAM	WCENPAC	ENS F. KLEFFNER	U
06/16/44	42066	VF-27	USS PRINCE-TON	GUAM	WCENPAC		
06/16/44	42030	VF-50	USS BATAAN	BONINS	CENPAC	ENS F.F. FRANCIS	S
06/16/44	41705	VF-51	USS SAN JACINTO	GUAM	WCENPAC		
06/16/44	41754	VF-51	USS SAN JACINTO	GUAM	WCENPAC	LT B.F. GRIFFIN	S
06/16/44	41799	VF-51	USS SAN JACINTO	GUAM	WCENPAC	ENS W.R. MOONEY	S
06/17/44	4922	VF-100	BARBERS POINT	HAWAII	ECENPAC	ENS C.M. MUELLER	S
06/17/44	41206	VF-16	USS LEX-INGTON	GUAM	WCENPAC	LT M. BRIGHT	M
06/18/44	42021	VF-28	USS MONTEREY	TINIAN	WCENPAC	ENS PERSON	S
06/19/44	43082	VF(N)-76	USS HORNET	GUAM	WCENPAC	ENS W.E. LEVERING	S
06/19/44	41371	VF-1	USS YORK-TOWN	GUAM	WCENPAC	ENS C.R. GARMAN	M
06/19/44	41438	VF-1	USS YORK-TOWN	GUAM	WCENPAC	LT W.C. MOSELEY	S
06/19/44	42675	VF-10	USS ENTER-PRISE	GUAM	WCENPAC	LT H.C. CLEM	M
06/19/44	42200	VF-14	USS WASP	W OF SAIPAN	CENPAC	ENS TAYLOR	S
06/19/44	42449	VF-14	USS WASP	W OF SAIPAN	CENPAC	ENS P.A. NEILL	M
06/19/44	41548	VF-15	USS ESSEX	GUAM	WCENPAC		
06/19/44	41668	VF-15	USS ESSEX	GUAM	WCENPAC	ENS T. TARR	M
06/19/44	42015	VF-15	USS ESSEX	GUAM	WCENPAC	CDR C.W. BREWER	M
06/19/44	42034	VF-15	USS ESSEX	GUAM	WCENPAC	ENS G.H. RADER	M
06/19/44	40535	VF-16	USS LEX-INGTON	GUAM	WCENPAC	LT W.C. BIRKHOLM	S
06/19/44	25879	VF-2	USS HORNET	GUAM	WCENPAC		
06/19/44	41986	VF-2	USS HORNET	GUAM	WCENPAC		
06/19/44	26023	VF-25	USS COWPENS	GUAM	WCENPAC	LTJG F.R. SLIEGLITZ	M
06/19/44	40022	VF-25	USS COWPENS	GUAM	WCENPAC	ENS G.A. MASSANBURG	M
06/19/44	42056	VF-27	USS PRINCE-TON	W OF GUAM	CENPAC	LCDR E.W. WOOD, JR.	M
06/19/44	42121	VF-27	USS PRINCE-TON	W OF GUAM	CENPAC	LTJG V.B. CARTER	M
06/19/44	41798	VF-51	USS SAN JACINTO	GUAM	WCENPAC	ENS T.E. HALLOWELL	M
06/19/44	25760	VF-8	USS BUNKER HILL	MARIANAS	CENPAC	LCDR R.W. HOEL	S
06/19/44	40344	VF-8	USS BUNKER HILL	MARIANAS	CENPAC	ENS E.J. DONNER	M
06/19/44	40373	VF-8	USS BUNKER HILL	MARIANAS	CENPAC		
06/24/44	41362	VF-2	USS HORNET	BONINS	CENPAC	LTJG C. ELLIOTT	M
06/24/44	42083	VF-27	USS PRINCE-TON	MARIANAS	CENPAC	ENS A.H. MUNSON	S
06/24/44	41595	VF-32	USS LANGLEY	SAIPAN	WCENPAC		
06/24/44	25789	VF-37	USS SAN-GAMON	SAIPAN	WCENPAC	ENS JESSE E. MCNINCH	S

DATE	BUNO	SQDRN	BASE	LOST	AREA	PILOT	FATE
06/25/44	41329	VF-1	USS YORKTOWN	PAGAN	CENPAC	ENS J.C. SCHUG	D
06/25/44	40005	VF-25	USS COWPENS	GUAM	WCENPAC	ENS W.C. HARTUNG	S
06/25/44	26123	VF-37	USS SANGAMON	SAIPAN	WCENPAC	ENS L.J. EIGNER	S
06/25/44	40176	VF-37	USS SANGAMON	SAIPAN	WCENPAC	ENS DEAN R. LEAF	S
06/25/44	40943	VF-60	USS SUWANNEE	TINIAN	WCENPAC	LTJG J.C. SIMPSON	D
06/26/44	41436	VF(N)-79	PEARL	HAWAII	ECENPAC	ENS T.H. LEA	S
06/26/44	42307	VF-28	USS MONTEREY	ENIWETOK	CENPAC		
06/28/44	42381	VF-21	USS OMMANEY BAY	PEARL	ECENPAC	ENS H.J. LATE	S
06/28/44	40347	VF-32	USS LANGLEY	PAGAN	CENPAC	LTJG K.D. LARSON	S
06/29/44	25843	ARU SOLS			SOPAC		
06/30/44	40010	COMAIRPAC	PEARL	HAWAII	ECENPAC		
06/30/44	8879	VF-100	BARBERS POINT	HAWAII	ECENPAC	ENS T.L. HENRY	S
07/01/44	42488	VF-15	USS ESSEX	ROTA	CENPAC		
07/01/44	40505	VF-31	USS CABOT	BONINS	CENPAC		
07/01/44	40545	VF-31	USS CABOT	BONINS	CENPAC	LT STEVE G. KOVA	S
07/02/44	41648	VF-15	USS ESSEX	ROTA	CENPAC		
07/03/44	41069	VF(N)-76		IWO JIMA	EMPIRE	ENS T.E. CUNNINGHAM	S
07/03/44	41405	VF-1	USS YORKTOWN	IWO JIMA	EMPIRE	LT N.D. DUBERSTEIN	S
07/03/44	41893	VF-1	USS YORKTOWN	IWO JIMA	EMPIRE	LT A.J. WARD	M
07/03/44	41813	VF-2	USS HORNET	IWO JIMA	EMPIRE		
07/04/44	41448	VF-1	USS YORKTOWN	BONINS	CENPAC	LT W.C. MOSELEY	M
07/04/44	43046	VF-1	USS YORKTOWN	BONINS	CENPAC	LT H.R. CHILTON	S
07/04/44	41879	VF-14	USS WASP	IWO JIMA	EMPIRE	ENS J.H. DOUGHERTON	M
07/04/44	43041	VF-14	USS WASP	IWO JIMA	EMPIRE	ENS A.C. NISI	M
07/04/44	40523	VF-2	USS HORNET	BONINS	CENPAC		
07/04/44	40524	VF-2	USS HORNET	BONINS	CENPAC	LT W.K. BLAIR	S
07/04/44	40259	VF-31	USS CABOT	IWO JIMA	EMPIRE	ENS F. HANCOCK, JR.	M
07/04/44	40307	VF-31	USS CABOT	IWO JIMA	EMPIRE	LTJG H.G. ELEZIAN, JR.	M
07/04/44	40317	VF-31	USS CABOT	IWO JIMA	EMPIRE	LTJG M.L. LOOMIS	M
07/04/44	42626	VF-31	USS CABOT	IWO JIMA	EMPIRE	LTJG WILSON	S
07/04/44	40863	VF-50	USS BATAAN	CHICHI JIMA	CENPAC		
07/04/44	42185	VF-50	USS BATAAN	BONINS	CENPAC	LTJG P.C. THOMAS	S
07/05/44	42193	VF-1	USS YORKTOWN	GUAM	WCENPAC	LT J. LEBOUTILLIER	M
07/05/44	40194	VF-11	OAHU	HAWAII	ECENPAC	ENS RICHARD J. STERLING	S
07/05/44	42107	VF-27	USS PRINCETON	GUAM	WCENPAC	ENS EDWARD W. LYNN	D
07/05/44	42112	VF-27	USS PRINCETON	GUAM	WCENPAC	LT RODGERS	S
07/05/44	42064	VF-28	USS MONTEREY	PAGAN	CENPAC	ENS G.J. BARNES	S
07/05/44		VF-8	USS BUNKER HILL	PALAU	CENPAC		

DATE	BUNO	SQDRN	BASE	LOST	AREA	PILOT	FATE
07/05/44	40554	VF-8	USS BUNKER HILL	PALAU	CENPAC		
07/06/44	43124	VF-50	USS BATAAN	GUAM	WCENPAC	LTJG E.R. TARLETON	S
07/06/44	41932	VF-7	USS HANCOCK		NORLANT	LT W.P. MATHEWS	S
07/08/44	41967	VF-14	USS WASP	GUAM	WCENPAC	LCDR E.W. BIRES	M
07/09/44	42023	VF-21	MAUI	HAWAII	ECENPAC	ENS K.B. ROGERS	D
07/10/44	41626	VF-25	USS COWPENS	MARIANAS	CENPAC		
07/10/44	42101	VF-25	USS COWPENS	MARIANAS	CENPAC		
07/11/44	41818	VF-1	USS YORK-TOWN	GUAM	WCENPAC	ENS L.L. CYPHERS	D
07/12/44	41989	VF-14	USS WASP	GUAM	WCENPAC	ENS F.T. VITENSKY	M
07/12/44	42622	VF-18	USS INTREPID	MARSHALLS	CENPAC		
07/13/44	41431	VF-36	USS COPAHEE	MARIANAS	CENPAC		
07/13/44	42437	VF-60	USS SU-WANNEE	GUAM	WCENPAC	LTJG QUINN LAFARGUE	S
07/14/44	26146	ARU SOLS			SOPAC		
07/14/44	25792	VF-100	BARBERS POINT	HAWAII	ECENPAC	ENS ERICK NYGAARD	S
07/15/44	42313	VF-44	PEARL	HAWAII	ECENPAC	ENS ROWEN F. HALL, JR.	S
07/16/44	41288	VF-100	BARBERS POINT	HAWAII	ECENPAC	ENS W.H. WINGFIELD	M
07/16/44	40547	VF-31	USS CABOT	MARIANAS	CENPAC		
07/17/44	42906	VF-31	USS CABOT	MARIANAS	CENPAC		
07/18/44	42095	VF-19	GUAM	GUAM	WCENPAC	ENS WILLIAM E. STRUNK	D
07/18/44	40450	VF-35	USS CHE-NANGO	GUAM	WCENPAC		
07/18/44	26180	VF-60	USS SU-WANNEE	GUAM	WCENPAC	ENS B.L. MCMANEMIN	S
07/19/44	41811	VF-1	USS YORK-TOWN	GUAM	WCENPAC	ENS R.A. FARNSWORTH	S
07/19/44	42069	VF-11	OAHU	HAWAII	ECENPAC	ENS T.S. WILLIAMS	S
07/19/44	41375	VF-27	USS PRINCE-TON	GUAM	WCENPAC		
07/20/44	41499	VF-1	USS YORK-TOWN	GUAM	WCENPAC	LT R.H. SHIREMAN, JR.	S
07/20/44	42513	VF-13	USS FRANKLIN	GUAM	WCENPAC	ENS H.J. SMITH	S
07/20/44	42296	VF-19	GUAM	GUAM	WCENPAC	ENS D.G. DELUCE, JR.	D
07/20/44	42164	VF-27	USS PRINCE-TON	GUAM	WCENPAC		
07/20/44	40288	VF-31	USS CABOT	MARIANAS	CENPAC		
07/20/44	40931	VF-60	USS SU-WANNEE	GUAM	WCENPAC	LTJG J.D. SHEA	S
07/21/44	40889	VF-35	USS CHE-NANGO	GUAM	WCENPAC	LTJG LEONARD W. SEENSON	S
07/22/44	43031	VF-31	USS CABOT	ENR YAP	CENPAC		
07/22/44	42213	VF-44	PEARL	HAWAII	ECENPAC		
07/23/44	41771	VF-15	USS ESSEX	TINIAN	WCENPAC	ENS A.C. SLACK	S
07/23/44	41777	VF-32	USS LANGLEY	TINIAN	WCENPAC	LTJG J.D. KEYSER	D
07/23/44	42561	VF-32	USS LANGLEY	TINIAN	WCENPAC	LTJG J.D. SULTZER	D
07/23/44	40980	VF-35	USS CHE-NANGO	GUAM	WCENPAC	ENS DOUGLAS K. SINGLETON	S
07/24/44	41510	VF-15	USS ESSEX	TINIAN	WCENPAC	ENS D.E. JOHNSON	U
07/25/44	41139	CAG-4			CENPAC	LTJG J.W.E. WOOD	S
07/25/44	41821	VF-14	USS WASP	PALAU	CENPAC		
07/25/44	41881	VF-14	USS WASP	PALAU	CENPAC	LT W.A. PANNELL	D
07/25/44	41506	VF-4	NAVY NO. 24	HAWAII	ECENPAC	CDR GEORGE O. KLINSMANN	S

DATE	BUNO	SQDRN	BASE	LOST	AREA	PILOT	FATE
07/25/44	41620	VF-51	USS SAN JACINTO	PALAU	CENPAC		
07/26/44	41601	VF-14	USS WASP	PALAU	CENPAC		
07/26/44	41674	VF-14	USS WASP	PALAU	CENPAC		
07/26/44	42375	VF-19	USS LEX-INGTON	PALAU	CENPAC	LT C.E. BARTLETT	S
07/26/44	42098	VF-29	PUUNENE	HAWAII	ECENPAC	ENS ROBERT B. WILLIAMS	S
07/26/44	42821	VF-29	PUUNENE	HAWAII	ECENPAC	ENS T.W. TREMBATH	M
07/26/44	40089	VF-31	USS CABOT	ENIWETOK	CENPAC		
07/26/44	40874	VF-8	USS BUNKER HILL	PALAU	CENPAC		
07/27/44	41695	VF-14	USS WASP	PALAU	CENPAC	ENS C.E. SMITH	S
07/27/44	40673	VF-8	USS BUNKER HILL	PALAU	CENPAC	LCDR R.W. HOEL	S
07/28/44	42057	VF-14	USS WASP	PALAU	CENPAC	ENS J.B. STOKES	S
07/28/44	42090	VF-27	USS PRINCE-TON	ENR ENIWETOK	CENPAC		
07/28/44	40280	VF-31	USS CABOT	YAP	CENPAC	ENS EDWIN FREE	S
07/28/44	40207	VF-35	USS CHE-NANGO	GUAM	WCENPAC	ENS DOUGLAS K. SINGLETON	D
07/29/44	40007	VF-37	USS SAN-GAMON	GUAM	WCENPAC		
07/30/44	25882			BOUGAIN-VILLE	SOPAC		
07/30/44	41613	NAS	BARBERS POINT	HAWAII	ECENPAC		
07/30/44	40582	VF-11	OAHU	HAWAII	ECENPAC	ENS CLARENCE E. SMITH	S
08/01/44	4865	CASU-40		ESPIRITU SANTO	SOPAC		
08/01/44	41268	VF-100	BARBERS POINT	HAWAII	ECENPAC	LT E.J. BECKER	S
08/03/44	41889	VF-2	USS HORNET	BONINS	CENPAC		
08/04/44	41907	VF-14	USS WASP	ENIWETOK	CENPAC		
08/04/44	42031	VF-19	USS LEX-INGTON	IWO JIMA	EMPIRE	LT H.R. BURNETT	M
08/04/44	42356	VF-19	USS LEX-INGTON	IWO JIMA	EMPIRE	ENS B.M. WAKEFIELD	M
08/04/44	40137	VF-2	USS HORNET	BONINS	CENPAC		
08/04/44	40645	VF-31	USS CABOT	ENIWETOK	CENPAC		
08/04/44	41291	VF-8	USS BUNKER HILL	IWO JIMA	EMPIRE	LT JOHN B. CZERNY	M
08/05/44	41598	VF-19	USS LEX-INGTON	IWO JIMA	EMPIRE	LT E.L. LINDSEY	S
08/05/44	41960	VF-19	USS LEX-INGTON	IWO JIMA	EMPIRE	ENS JOSEPH KELLY	S
08/09/44	41600	CASU(F)-31		PITYILU	SW PAC		
08/09/44	25862	CASU-35		ENIWETOK	CENPAC		
08/09/44	25934	CASU-35		ENIWETOK	CENPAC		
08/09/44	40631	CASU-35		ENIWETOK	CENPAC		
08/09/44	40713	CASU-35		ENIWETOK	CENPAC		
08/09/44	40971	CASU-35		ENIWETOK	CENPAC		
08/09/44	41472	CASU-35		ENIWETOK	CENPAC		
08/09/44	41530	CASU-35		ENIWETOK	CENPAC		
08/09/44	41691	CASU-35		ENIWETOK	CENPAC		
08/09/44	41903	CASU-35		ENIWETOK	CENPAC		
08/09/44	42181	CASU-35		ENIWETOK	CENPAC		
08/10/44	40452	CASU-30		MAJURO	CENPAC		
08/10/44	42348	CASU-30		MAJURO	CENPAC		
08/10/44	42433	VF-44	USS RANGER	PEARL	ECENPAC	ENS D.T. WILLIAMS	S
08/11/44	42242	VF(N)-75	USS HANCOCK	PANAMA	CENPAC		
08/11/44	42080	VF-29	PUUNENE	HAWAII	ECENPAC	ENS BOBBY D. COMBS	S

DATE	BUNO	SQDRN	BASE	LOST	AREA	PILOT	FATE
08/17/44	8829	NAS	BARBERS POINT	HAWAII	ECENPAC		
08/20/44	42499	VF-37	USS SAN-GAMON	MANUS	SW PAC		
08/24/44	40248	CAG-11	USS RANGER	PEARL	ECENPAC	CDR G.T. MCCUTCHAN	D
08/24/44	42781	VF(N)-107			NORLANT	LT JOHN D. MACKLIN	S
08/24/44	41794	VF-51	USS SAN JACINTO	ENR CHICHI J.	CENPAC		
08/30/44	41897	COMAIR-PAC	PEARL	HAWAII	ECENPAC		
08/30/44	42363	COMAIR-PAC	PEARL	HAWAII	ECENPAC		
08/30/44	41822	VF-14	USS WASP	ENIWETOK	CENPAC	ENS C.M. MUELLER	D
08/30/44	42555	VF-14	USS WASP	PALAU	CENPAC	CDR G.D. CADY	D
08/30/44	42039	VF-32	USS LANGLEY	ENR PELELIU	CENPAC		
08/31/44	41112	VF(N)-78	USS ENTER-PRISE	CHICHI JIMA	CENPAC		
08/31/44	40933	VF-10	HAWAII	HAWAII	ECENPAC		
08/31/44	8947	VF-100	BARBERS POINT	HAWAII	ECENPAC		
08/31/44	40212	VF-100	BARBERS POINT	HAWAII	ECENPAC		
08/31/44	40609	VF-11			CENPAC		
08/31/44	66236	VF-11			CENPAC		
08/31/44	66116	VF-16			CENPAC		
08/31/44	42045	VF-27	USS PRINCE-TON	ENR PALUS	CENPAC		
09/01/44	40988	NAS	PEARL	HAWAII	ECENPAC		
09/02/44	42073	CASU-30		MAJURO	CENPAC		
09/02/44	41359	VF-51	USS SAN JACINTO	CHICHI JIMA	CENPAC	(DECK CRASH)	
09/02/44	42535	VF-51	USS SAN JACINTO	CHICHI JIMA	CENPAC	(LANDING ACCIDENT)	
09/03/44	42207	CASU-30		MAJURO	CENPAC		
09/04/44	42844	A & R	PEARL	HAWAII	ECENPAC		
09/05/44	41273	VF-4	NAVY NO. 24	HAWAII	ECENPAC	LTJG WM B. MILLWARD, JR	S
09/08/44	42114	VF-15	USS ESSEX	PALAU	CENPAC	ENS L.S. HAMBLIN	D
09/08/44	42616	VF-15	USS ESSEX	PALAU	CENPAC	LT H. KRAMER	D
09/09/44	42324	NACTU	USS RANGER	PEARL	ECENPAC	ENS EDWIN R. JONES	S
09/09/44	42516	VF-15	USS ESSEX	MINDANAO SEA	PHIL	LT J.H. BARKY, JR.	D
09/09/44	41806	VF-51	USS SAN JACINTO	ENR PALAU	CENPAC		
09/10/44	41797	CASU-30		MAJURO	CENPAC		
09/10/44	42550	VF-13	USS FRANKLIN	PELELIU	WCENPAC	ENS W.E. DROUIN	M
09/10/44	41299	VF-15	USS ESSEX	MINDANAO SEA	PHIL	ENS H.L. FOSHEE	S
09/10/44	41647	VF-15	USS ESSEX	MINDANAO SEA	PHIL	LT R.W. DAVIS, JR.	D
09/10/44	41790	VF-15	USS ESSEX	MINDANAO SEA	PHIL	ENS H.C. GREEN	D
09/12/44	41509	VF-15	USS ESSEX	PELELIU	WCENPAC	ENS C.W. PLANT	M
09/12/44	42128	VF-15	USS ESSEX	PELELIU	WCENPAC	ENS H.C. GAVER	S
09/12/44	42176	VF-18	USS INTREPID	VISAYAN	PHIL		
09/12/44	40533	VF-19	USS LEX-INGTON	VISAYAN	PHIL	CDR KARL E. JUNG	S
09/12/44	42890	VF-2	USS HORNET	CEBU	PHIL	ENS T.C. TILLER	S
09/12/44	42539	VF-51	USS SAN JACINTO	PALAU	CENPAC	ENS G.F. DAILY	D
09/13/44	42563	VB-14	USS WASP	LOS NEGROS	PHIL	LT MELVIN A. MOR	M
09/13/44	41876	VF-100	BARBERS POINT	HAWAII	ECENPAC	ENS MARVIN R. CATCHING	M
09/13/44	42146	VF-15	USS ESSEX	LOS NEGROS	PHIL	ENS J.W. BRET	M
09/13/44	42602	VF-31	USS CABOT	PALUS	SW PAC	ENS GEORGE G. BARDIN, JR.	S

DATE	BUNO	SQDRN	BASE	LOST	AREA	PILOT	FATE
09/13/44	41985	VF-8	USS BUNKER HILL	LUZON	PHIL	LCDR R.W. HOEL	S
09/13/44	42663	VF-8	USS BUNKER HILL	VEGASPI	PHIL	LTJG J.D. VANDERHOOF	S
09/14/44	42067	VF-32	USS LANGLEY	PALUS	SW PAC	LTJG CLAIRE BIENVENU	S
09/14/44	42379	VF-4	NAVY NO. 24	HAWAII	ECENPAC	LTJG R.A. HANCHE	M
09/14/44	42131	VF-81		HAWAII	ECENPAC	LT HALLEY D. SELLERS	S
09/14/44	42376	VF-81	USS RANGER	PEARL	ECENPAC	LT L. ORR	D
09/14/44	42824	VF-81	USS RANGER	PEARL	ECENPAC	CDR F.K. UPHAM	S
09/15/44	42871	VF-14	USS WASP	LOS NEGROS	PHIL		
09/16/44	42358	VF-19	USS LEX-INGTON	MANILA	PHIL		
09/16/44	40834	VF-37	USS SAN-GAMON	HALMAHERA	SW PAC	ENS M.G. KNACKSTEDT	S
09/16/44	42036	VF-60	USS SU-WANNEE	MOROTAI	PHIL	ENS P.W. LINDSKOG	S
09/16/44	42351	VF-60	USS SU-WANNEE	MOROTAI	PHIL	ENS W.P. BANNISTER	D
09/17/44	42811	VF-8	USS BUNKER HILL	PALAU	CENPAC		
09/20/44	25845			ESPIRITU SANTO	SOPAC		
09/20/44	25856			ESPIRITU SANTO	SOPAC		
09/20/44	40913			ESPIRITU SANTO	SOPAC		
09/20/44	42184	VF-45		HAWAII	ECENPAC	ENS DALE L. MAYNARD	S
09/21/44	42364	CASU-35		ENIWETOK	CENPAC		
09/21/44	42317	VF-14	USS WASP	LOS NEGROS	PHIL	LT A.L. LORRAINE	M
09/21/44	41996	VF-27	USS PRINCE-TON	LUZON	PHIL	LT WILLIAM E. LAMB	M
09/21/44	41348	VF-32	USS LANGLEY	ENR FORMOSA	CENPAC	LTJG K.D. LARSON	S
09/21/44	41709	VF-32	USS LANGLEY	ENR FORMOSA	CENPAC	LTJG W.E. MILLER	M
09/21/44	42841	VF-32	USS LANGLEY	ENR FORMOSA	CENPAC	ENS V.H. HALVA	D
09/21/44	41850	VF-81		HAWAII	ECENPAC		
09/22/44	42904	VF-32	USS LANGLEY	ENR FORMOSA	CENPAC	LT H.H. HILLIS	S
09/24/44	41579	VF-15	USS ESSEX	PELELIU	WCENPAC	ENS H.C. GAVER	D
09/24/44	42331	VF-19	USS LEX-INGTON	CEBU	PHIL	ENS A.W. HOWE	M
09/24/44	41971	VF-2	USS HORNET		CENPAC	ENS FRANK O'BRIEN	D
09/24/44	43127	VF-8	USS BUNKER HILL	OKINAWA	EMPIRE	LTJG J.D. VANDERHOOF	S
09/25/44	25836	NACTU	NAVY NO. 14	HAWAII	ECENPAC	LTJG BERT H. BROSNAN	S
09/27/44	42514	VF-100	USS RANGER	PEARL	ECENPAC	LT PAUL A. QUARNBERG	S
09/30/44	42645	VF-51	USS SAN JACINTO	OKINAWA	EMPIRE		
09/30/44	42557	VF-8	USS BUNKER HILL	OKINAWA	EMPIRE		
10/01/44	25932	A & R	MAJURO	MAJURO	CENPAC		
10/01/44	43105	A & R	MAJURO	MAJURO	CENPAC		
10/03/44	41304	VF-31	USS CABOT	LUZON	PHIL		
10/03/44	41912	VF-31	USS CABOT	LUZON	PHIL		
10/04/44	42004	CASU-42		PITYILU	SW PAC		
10/04/44	42825	VF-14	USS WASP	ENR OKINAWA	EMPIRE		

DATE	BUNO	SQDRN	BASE	LOST	AREA	PILOT	FATE
10/04/44	43026	VF-14	USS WASP	ENR OKINAWA	EMPIRE		
10/04/44	42443	VF-45		HAWAII	ECENPAC	ENS CHARLES A. SHAW	D
10/05/44	42679	VF-81		HAWAII	ECENPAC	ENS R.J. HALAMEA	S
10/07/44	40973	VF-4	NAVY NO. 24	HAWAII	ECENPAC	LTJG J.W. BENNETT	S
10/08/44	8814	VF-18	USS INTREPID	ENR FORMOSA	CENPAC		
10/08/44	41800	VF-44	USS LANGLEY	FORMOSA	EMPIRE		
10/08/44	42391	VF-51	USS SAN JACINTO	ENR LUZON	CENPAC		
10/09/44	42158	VF-11	USS HORNET		CENPAC		
10/09/44	42451	VF-19	USS LEX-INGTON		CENPAC		
10/09/44	41804	VF-51	USS SAN JACINTO	ENR LUZON	CENPAC		
10/10/44	43100	VF-14	USS WASP	OKINAWA	EMPIRE	LTJG AMUSSEN	S
10/10/44	42202	VF-19	USS LEX-INGTON		CENPAC		
10/10/44	41433	VF-4	NAVY NO. 24	HAWAII	ECENPAC	ENS GWYNN ENGEL	D
10/10/44	41564	VF-44	USS LANGLEY	FORMOSA	EMPIRE	ENS ROBERT W. UPTON	S
10/10/44	41608	VF-44	USS LANGLEY	FORMOSA	EMPIRE		
10/10/44	42040	VF-44	USS LANGLEY	FORMOSA	EMPIRE		
10/11/44	41558	VF-15	USS ESSEX	ENR FORMOSA	CENPAC		
10/12/44	40371	CASU-42		PITYILU	SW PAC		
10/12/44	41844	VF-14	USS WASP	FORMOSA	EMPIRE		
10/12/44	41994	VF-14	USS WASP	FORMOSA	EMPIRE	ENS D.N. FISHER	S
10/12/44	41664	VF-15	USS ESSEX	FORMOSA	EMPIRE	ENS C.A. DORN	M
10/12/44	41382	VF-27	USS PRINCE-TON	FORMOSA	EMPIRE		
10/12/44	42965	VF-8	USS BUNKER HILL	FORMOSA	EMPIRE		
10/13/44	42043	A & R	MAJURO	MAJURO	CENPAC		
10/13/44	42894	VF-11	USS HORNET	FORMOSA	EMPIRE		
10/13/44	41715	VF-15	USS ESSEX	PESCADORES	CENPAC	ENS K.A. FUNN	S
10/14/44	42638	CASU-4	PUUNENE	HAWAII	ECENPAC		
10/14/44	43137	VF-11	USS HORNET		CENPAC	ENS J.C. BLAIR	D
10/14/44	42327	VF-19	USS LEX-INGTON		CENPAC	LTJG C.M. BARTLETT	M
10/14/44	41970	VF-29	USS CABOT	LUZON	PHIL	LTJG B.J. HARRISON	M
10/14/44	41632	VF-51	USS SAN JACINTO	LUZON	PHIL		
10/14/44	66052	VF-81		HAWAII	ECENPAC	LTJG H.B. HALES, JR.	D
10/15/44	41957	VF-14	USS WASP	LUZON	PHIL		
10/15/44	41414	VF-51	USS SAN JACINTO	LUZON	PHIL		
10/15/44	42162	VF-8	USS BUNKER HILL	LUZON	PHIL		
10/15/44	42353	VF-8	USS BUNKER HILL	LUZON	PHIL		
10/17/44	42698	VF-15	USS ESSEX	FORMOSA	EMPIRE		
10/18/44	41987	VF-14	USS WASP	LUZON	PHIL		
10/18/44	41368	VF-20	USS ENTER-PRISE	LUZON	PHIL	ENS HENRY W. BALSIGER	S
10/18/44	42278	VF-20	USS ENTER-PRISE	LUZON	PHIL	ENS W.M. FOYT	U
10/18/44	42711	VF-20	USS ENTER-PRISE	LUZON	PHIL	ENS WALTER A. WOOD	M

DATE	BUNO	SQDRN	BASE	LOST	AREA	PILOT	FATE
10/18/44	43018	VF-35	USS CHENANGO	ENR CEBU	SW PAC	ENS RADLEY E. CLEMENS	S
10/18/44	41908	VF-51	USS SAN JACINTO	LUZON	PHIL		
10/19/44	42551	VF-35	USS CHENANGO	CEBU	PHIL	ENS JESSE O. KENNEDY	D
10/19/44	42037	VF-37	USS SANGAMON	ENR LEYTE GULF	SW PAC	LT FRANK REISER	S
10/19/44	41884	VF-45	USS SARATOGA	HAWAII	ECENPAC	ENS W.J. WESTMORELAND	S
10/19/44	42328	VF-45	USS SARATOGA	HAWAII	ECENPAC		
10/19/44	42670	VF-45	USS SARATOGA	HAWAII	ECENPAC	ENS R.C. WOLVERTON	S
10/20/44	42008	VF-35	USS CHENANGO	CEBU	PHIL		
10/21/44	41724	CASU-42		PITYILU	SW PAC		
10/21/44	42651	CASU-42		PITYILU	SW PAC		
10/21/44	42054	VF-19	USS LEXINGTON	ENR LEYTE GULF	SW PAC	LT B.W. WILLIAMS	S
10/21/44	41629	VF-29	USS CABOT	ENR LEYTE GULF	PHIL	ENS EASTLING	S
10/22/44	43007	VF-14	USS WASP	LOS NEGROS	PHIL		
10/22/44	43048	VF-35	USS CHENANGO	CEBU	PHIL	ENS HENRY P. OUTEN	S
10/22/44	41725	VF-44	USS LANGLEY	LEYTE GULF	PHIL	ENS W.R. BAILEY	S
10/23/44	42368	NAS	BARBERS POINT	HAWAII	ECENPAC		
10/23/44	42496	VF-11	USS HORNET		PHIL		
10/23/44	41483	VF-14	USS WASP	LOS NEGROS	PHIL		
10/23/44	42047	VF-60	USS SUWANNEE	LOS NEGROS	PHIL	LTJG EARL LEMWIG	M
10/24/44	41435	VF-27	USS PRINCETON	LEYTE GULF	PHIL	ENS O.L. SCOTT	M
10/24/44	41512	VF-27	USS PRINCETON	LEYTE GULF	PHIL	(SHIP SANK)	
10/24/44	41593	VF-27	USS PRINCETON	LEYTE GULF	PHIL	(SHIP SANK)	
10/24/44	42003	VF-27	USS PRINCETON	LEYTE GULF	PHIL	(SHIP SANK)	
10/24/44	42519	VF-27	USS PRINCETON	LEYTE GULF	PHIL	(SHIP SANK)	
10/24/44	42521	VF-27	USS PRINCETON	LEYTE GULF	PHIL	(SHIP SANK)	
10/24/44	42548	VF-27	USS PRINCETON	LEYTE GULF	PHIL	(SHIP SANK)	
10/24/44	42621	VF-27	USS PRINCETON	LEYTE GULF	PHIL	(SHIP SANK)	
10/24/44	42814	VF-27	USS PRINCETON	LEYTE GULF	PHIL	(SHIP SANK)	
10/24/44	42830	VF-27	USS PRINCETON	LEYTE GULF	PHIL	(SHIP SANK)	
10/24/44	42902	VF-27	USS PRINCETON	LEYTE GULF	PHIL	(SHIP SANK)	
10/24/44	42908	VF-27	USS PRINCETON	LEYTE GULF	PHIL	(SHIP SANK)	
10/24/44	43037	VF-27	USS PRINCETON	LEYTE GULF	PHIL	(SHIP SANK)	

DATE	BUNO	SQDRN	BASE	LOST	AREA	PILOT	FATE
10/24/44	43103	VF-27	USS PRINCE-TON	LEYTE GULF	PHIL	(SHIP SANK)	
10/24/44	70126	VF-27	USS PRINCE-TON	LEYTE GULF	PHIL	(SHIP SANK)	
10/24/44	42179	VF-44	USS LANGLEY	SAN BERNADINO	PHIL	LTJG JOHN R. MONTAPORT	S
10/24/44	42371	VF-44	USS LANGLEY	SAN BERNADINO	PHIL	ENS W. DAVIS	M
10/25/44	42145	VF-15	USS ESSEX	LUZON	PHIL	LT J.R. STRANE	S
10/25/44	42642	VF-44	USS LANGLEY	LEYTE GULF	PHIL	ENS J.M. RING	D
10/25/44	42454	VF-45		HAWAII	ECENPAC	ENS CLARENCE B. SHAY	S
10/25/44	41990	VF-51	USS SAN JACINTO	SIBUYAN SEA	PHIL		
10/25/44	40180	VF-60	USS SU-WANNEE	LEYTE GULF	PHIL	ENS J.P. RICHARDSON	M
10/25/44	41043	VF-60	USS SU-WANNEE	LEYTE GULF	PHIL	(DECK LOSS-KAMIKAZE)	
10/25/44	41211	VF-60	USS SU-WANNEE	LEYTE GULF	PHIL	(DECK LOSS-KAMIKAZE)	
10/25/44	41745	VF-60	USS SU-WANNEE	LEYTE GULF	PHIL	(DECK LOSS-KAMIKAZE)	
10/25/44	43075	VF-8	USS BUNKER HILL	LUZON	PHIL		
10/26/44	41690	VF-14	USS WASP	LUZON	PHIL		
10/26/44	42884	VF-14	USS WASP	LUZON	PHIL		
10/26/44	42405	VF-35	USS CHE-NANGO	MOROTAI	PHIL	LT SAMUEL W. FORRER	S
10/26/44	42087	VF-37	USS SAN-GAMON	SAMAR	PHIL	LTJG JAMES RITCHIE	M
10/26/44	42157	VF-37	USS SAN-GAMON	SAMAR	PHIL		
10/26/44	41216	VF-60	USS SU-WANNEE	LEYTE GULF	PHIL	(DECK LOSS-KAMIKAZE)	
10/26/44	41283	VF-60	USS SU-WANNEE	LEYTE GULF	PHIL	(DECK LOSS-KAMIKAZE)	
10/26/44	41782	VF-60	USS SU-WANNEE	LEYTE GULF	PHIL	(DECK LOSS-KAMIKAZE)	
10/26/44	42048	VF-60	USS SU-WANNEE	LEYTE GULF	PHIL	(DECK LOSS-KAMIKAZE)	
10/26/44	42406	VF-60	USS SU-WANNEE	LEYTE GULF	PHIL	(DECK LOSS-KAMIKAZE)	
10/27/44	42401	VF-45		HAWAII	ECENPAC	LT CHARLES R. KNOCKEY	S
10/27/44	41000	VF-99		ENIWETOK	CENPAC		
10/28/44	41758	VF-13	USS FRANKLIN	LEYTE GULF	PHIL	LT ROBERT F. BROOKS	M
10/28/44	42837	VF-13	USS FRANKLIN	LEYTE GULF	PHIL	ENS CHARLES N. GIBBS	M
10/28/44	43034	VF-13	USS FRANKLIN	LEYTE GULF	PHIL		
10/28/44	40957	VF-29	USS CABOT	LUZON	PHIL	LTJG JOHN F. THOMPSON	S
10/28/44	42408	VF-51	USS SAN JACINTO	CAPE ENGANO	SW PAC		
10/29/44	42892	VF-13	USS FRANKLIN	LEYTE GULF	PHIL		
10/29/44	41901	VF-15	USS ESSEX	LUZON	PHIL		
10/29/44	42316	VF-29	USS CABOT	LUZON	PHIL	LTJG JOHN F. THOMPSON	S
10/29/44	42394	VF-29	USS CABOT	LUZON	PHIL	ENS EMERAL B. COOK	S
10/29/44	41469	VF-7	USS HANCOCK	MANILA	PHIL	ENS R.G. HANECOK	S
10/29/44	42284	VF-7	USS HANCOCK	MANILA	PHIL		
10/30/44	41539	VF-13	USS FRANKLIN	LEYTE GULF	PHIL	(DECK LOSS-KAMIKAZE)	
10/30/44	42573	VF-13	USS FRANKLIN	LEYTE GULF	PHIL	(DECK LOSS-KAMIKAZE)	

DATE	BUNO	SQDRN	BASE	LOST	AREA	PILOT	FATE
10/30/44	42009	VF-18	USS INTREPID	LUZON	PHIL		
10/30/44	41744	VF-20	USS ENTER-PRISE	LUZON	PHIL		
10/30/44	41535	VF-21	USS BELLEAU WOOD		SW PAC	(DECK FIRE)	
10/30/44	42147	VF-21	USS BELLEAU WOOD		SW PAC	(DECK FIRE)	
10/30/44	41425	VF-51	USS SAN JACINTO	LEYTE GULF	PHIL		
10/30/44	41998	VF-51	USS SAN JACINTO	LEYTE GULF	PHIL		
10/30/44	42058	VF-51	USS SAN JACINTO	LEYTE GULF	PHIL		
10/30/44	42212	VF-51	USS SAN JACINTO	LEYTE GULF	PHIL		
10/30/44	42817	VF-51	USS SAN JACINTO	LEYTE GULF	PHIL		
10/30/44	42833	VF-51	USS SAN JACINTO	LEYTE GULF	PHIL		
10/31/44	26015	COMAIR-PAC	PEARL	HAWAII	ECENPAC		
10/31/44	40066	COMAIR-PAC	PEARL	HAWAII	ECENPAC		
10/31/44	42822	COMAIR-PAC	PEARL	HAWAII	ECENPAC		
10/31/44	41547	POOL			PHIL		
10/31/44	42011	VF-20	USS ENTER-PRISE	LUZON	PHIL		
11/03/44	41344	CASU-38	KANEOHE	HAWAII	ECENPAC	ENS JAMES A. JONES	S
11/05/44	41522	VF-44	USS LANGLEY	MANILA	PHIL	ENS J.J. SMITH	S
11/05/44	42722	VF-45	USS BATAAN	ENR HAWAII	WCENPAC		
11/06/44	42013	VF-19	USS LEX-INGTON	LUZON	PHIL	LTJG W.E. COPELAND	M
11/09/44	41544	VF-100	USS MAKASSAR STR.	HAWAII	ECENPAC	ENS ROBERT L. RAGLUND	D
11/11/44	42154	VF-81	USS WASP	LEYTE GULF	PHIL		
11/13/44	41393	AWT ACTION	BARBERS POINT	HAWAII	ECENPAC		
11/13/44	41582	VF-4	USS BUNKER HILL		PHIL	LTJG C.L. MARTIN, II	S
11/13/44	43097	VF-47	PUUNENE	HAWAII	ECENPAC	ENS JAMES J. CARPENTER	S
11/14/44	41833	VF-81	USS WASP	LEYTE GULF	PHIL	LT DANIEL C. MARSHAL	M
11/16/44	42416	VF-9	KAHULUI	HAWAII	ECENPAC	ENS AUBREY W. ACKLEY	S
11/17/44	42018	VF-45	USS BATAAN	HAWAII	ECENPAC		
11/18/44	41296	CASU(F)-42		PITYILU	SW PAC		
11/19/44	41103	CASU(F)-42		PITYILU	SW PAC		
11/19/44	42359	CASU(F)-42		PITYILU	SW PAC		
11/19/44	42639	VF-11	USS HORNET		PHIL	LT WEST	S
11/19/44	40466	VF-23	USS MAKASSAR STRAIT	HAWAII	ECENPAC		
11/19/44	42177	VMF(N)-541		PELELIU	WCENPAC	LT P.L. MARTELLI	S
11/21/44	41749	2ND MAW		ESPIRITU SANTU	SOPAC	LT DAVID F. EVANS	S
11/22/44	41360	NACTU	BARBERS POINT	HAWAII	ECENPAC		
11/22/44	41843	VF-23	PUUNENE	HAWAII	ECENPAC	ENS WALTER R. ZERNBACK	S
11/22/44	42995	VF-23	PUUNENE	HAWAII	ECENPAC	ENS DONALD L. WATROUS	D
11/25/44	40937	AWT ACTION	BARBERS POINT	HAWAII	ECENPAC		

DATE	BUNO	SQDRN	BASE	LOST	AREA	PILOT	FATE
11/25/44	42106	VF-29	USS CABOT	MANILA	PHIL	ENS WILLIAM H. TURNER	D
11/26/44	41519	VF-80	USS TICONDER OGA	LUZON	PHIL		
11/27/44	40160	A & R	PEARL	HAWAII	ECENPAC		
11/30/44	41267		PEARL	HAWAII	ECENPAC		
11/30/44	41286		PEARL	HAWAII	ECENPAC		
11/30/44	41808		PEARL	HAWAII	ECENPAC		
11/30/44	41866		PEARL	HAWAII	ECENPAC		
11/30/44	42326		PEARL	HAWAII	ECENPAC		
11/30/44	42562		PEARL	HAWAII	ECENPAC		
11/30/44	43098		PEARL	HAWAII	ECENPAC		
11/30/44	42537	CASU-35		ENIWETOK	CENPAC	ENS O.E. SABATKE	S
11/30/44	40195	VF-11	PEARL	HAWAII	ECENPAC		
11/30/44	42767	VF-45	USS BATAAN (CVL-29)	HAWAII	ECENPAC	ENS GEORGE J. HAENN	S
12/07/44	41565	AR & OH		MANUS	SW PAC		
12/08/44	41653	VF-11	PEARL	HAWAII	ECENPAC		
12/10/44	42396		BARBERS POINT	HAWAII	ECENPAC		
12/12/44	66031		BARBERS POINT	HAWAII	ECENPAC		
12/14/44	41407	VF-45	USS SAN JACINTO	MANILA	PHIL		
12/14/44	42099	VF-45	USS SAN JACINTO	MANILA	PHIL		
12/15/44	40644	VF-28	USS MONTEREY	PHILIPPINE SEA	PHIL	(DECK LOSS-TYPHOON)	
12/15/44	42628	VF-28	USS MONTEREY	PHILIPPINE SEA	PHIL	(DECK LOSS-TYPHOON)	
12/15/44	42403	VF-44	USS LANGLEY	LINGAYEN GULF	PHIL	LTJG JOHN R. MONTAPORT	S
12/16/44	41374	VF-9	KAHULUI	HAWAII	ECENPAC		
12/18/44	42598	VF-28	USS MONTEREY	PHILIPPINE SEA	PHIL	(DECK LOSS-TYPHOON)	
12/20/44	42318	VF-100	USS SARATOGA	HAWAII	ECENPAC	ENS LEONARD C. WITT	S
12/20/44	42299	VF-47	PUUNENE	HAWAII	ECENPAC	ENS D.H. RUSSON	D
12/21/44	41573		PEARL	HAWAII	ECENPAC		
12/21/44	42673		PEARL	HAWAII	ECENPAC		
12/21/44	41249	NAS	KAHULUI	HAWAII	ECENPAC		
12/21/44	41465	VF-83		HAWAII	ECENPAC		
12/28/44	40683	VF-99		ENIWETOK	CENPAC	LT FRANK A. MARCHER, JR.	D
12/31/44	40386		BARBERS POINT	HAWAII	ECENPAC		
12/31/44	42667		PEARL	HAWAII	ECENPAC		
12/31/44	41270	VF-47	USS MAKASSAR STR.	HAWAII	ECENPAC	LT G.B. MCCURRY	S
01/03/45	42152	VF-29	USS CABOT	FORMOSA	EMPIRE	LT MARTIN	S
01/03/45	41730	VF-81	USS WASP	FORMOSA	EMPIRE	LT MINOS D. MILLER, JR.	M
01/04/45	41501	VF-47	PUUNENE	HAWAII	ECENPAC	LT RAYMOND L. PODSEDNIK	S
01/07/45	42373	VF-22	USS COWPENS	E. OF LUZON	PHIL	LTJG FRANCIS I. KELLY	S
01/07/45	42707	VF-45	USS SAN JACINTO	LUZON	PHIL	ENS DANIEL R. PAUL	S
01/08/45	42294	VF-11	USS HORNET	FORMOSA	EMPIRE	ENS P.E. KING	S
01/08/45	41931	VF-44	USS LANGLEY	FORMOSA	EMPIRE		
01/09/45	41783	VF-11	USS HORNET	FORMOSA	EMPIRE		
01/09/45	42930	VF-9		PONAM	SW PAC	ENS SAMUEL A. MCDOWELL	S
01/10/45	42097	CASU-43		GUAM	WCENPAC		
01/11/45	42354	VF-33	PEARL	HAWAII	ECENPAC	LTJG JIM STACY	S
01/15/45	42113	VF-3	USS YORK-TOWN	CANTON	EMPIRE	ENS J.G. SCORDO	M

DATE	BUNO	SQDRN	BASE	LOST	AREA	PILOT	FATE
01/16/45	42827	VBF-7	USS HANCOCK	HONG KONG	EMPIRE	LT DANIEL S. KALUS	M
01/16/45	41466	VF-86		HAWAII	ECENPAC		
01/17/45	41365		BARBERS POINT	HAWAII	ECENPAC		
01/17/45	42635	VF-81	USS WASP	HONG KONG	EMPIRE		
01/18/45	42000	VF-100	BARBERS POINT	HAWAII	ECENPAC	ENS TERRY MILLS	S
01/18/45	40833	VF-47	PUUNENE	HAWAII	ECENPAC	ENS GEORGE D. GRAY	S
01/20/45	41731	VF-100	BARBERS POINT	HAWAII	ECENPAC	LTJG JAMES SEAHILL	S
01/20/45	42625	VF-33	PEARL	HAWAII	ECENPAC	LTJG JACK O. WATSON	S
01/21/45	41517	VF-11	USS HORNET		EMPIRE	LCDR FRITZ WOLF	S
01/22/45	41761	VF-29	USS CABOT	MIYAKO	EMPIRE	ENS BOBBY D. COMBS	S
01/23/45	41280	VF-86		HAWAII	ECENPAC	ENS R.P. MCCOY	S
01/26/45	42541	CASU(F)-43		GUAM	WCENPAC		
01/31/45	41628	CASU(F)-51		ULITHI	WCENPAC		
01/31/45	41642	CASU(F)-51		ULITHI	WCENPAC		
01/31/45	42374	COMAIR-PAC	PEARL	HAWAII	ECENPAC		
01/31/45	42402	COMAIR-PAC	PEARL	HAWAII	ECENPAC		
02/02/45	40794		BARBERS POINT	HAWAII	ECENPAC		
02/14/45	42382	VF-100	BARBERS POINT	HAWAII	ECENPAC	ENS H.O. JORDAN	S
02/16/45	71463	VF-4	USS ESSEX	TOKYO	EMPIRE	LTJG WILLIAM C. RHODES	M
02/20/45	41451	COMAIR-PAC	PEARL	HAWAII	ECENPAC		
02/22/45	41439	VF-100	BARBERS POINT	HAWAII	ECENPAC	ENS JOHN P. LAIRD	S
02/23/45	40382	CASU(F)-43		GUAM	WCENPAC		
02/27/45	41878		BARBERS POINT	HAWAII	ECENPAC		
02/28/45	41536	COMAIR-PAC	PEARL	HAWAII	ECENPAC		
03/04/45	42369	CASU(F)-12		GUAM	WCENPAC		
03/05/45	42156	CASU(F)-12		GUAM	WCENPAC		
03/05/45	42644	CASU(F)-12		GUAM	WCENPAC		
03/05/45	42730	CASU(F)-12		GUAM	WCENPAC		
03/06/45	8997	COMAIR-PAC	PEARL	HAWAII	ECENPAC		
03/06/45	41172	COMAIR-PAC	PEARL	HAWAII	ECENPAC		
03/08/45	40793	VF-99		GUAM	WCENPAC	ENS GEORGE STAMBAUGH	D
03/09/45	42141	COMAIR-PAC	PEARL	HAWAII	ECENPAC		
03/10/45	41328	COMAIR-PAC	PEARL	HAWAII	ECENPAC		
03/10/45	41969	COMAIR-PAC	PEARL	HAWAII	ECENPAC		
03/10/45	42431	COMAIR-PAC	PEARL	HAWAII	ECENPAC		
03/14/45	42386	COMAIR-PAC	PEARL	HAWAII	ECENPAC		
03/14/45	40446	POOL	BARBERS POINT	HAWAII	ECENPAC		
03/14/45	40613	POOL	BARBERS POINT	HAWAII	ECENPAC		
03/19/45	40220	NACTU	BARBERS POINT	HAWAII	ECENPAC	LTJG WALKER JOHNSON, JR.	M
03/19/45	42230	NACTU	BARBERS POINT	HAWAII	ECENPAC	LT GREGORY C. SCHROPER	M
03/21/45	40462	VF-99		GUAM	WCENPAC		
03/21/45	40809	VF-99		GUAM	WCENPAC		
03/24/45	8928	VBF-16	USS BON HOMME RICHARD	COSTA RICA	NORLANT	LTJG D.E. SATTERFIELD	S
03/27/45	42547	VF-99		GUAM	WCENPAC	ENS WALLACE M. DOSS	U
04/03/45	42259	VF-100	USS TRIPOLI	HAWAII	ECENPAC		

DATE	BUNO	SQDRN	BASE	LOST	AREA	PILOT	FATE
04/17/45	40822	NACTU	BARBERS POINT	HAWAII	ECENPAC	ENS JAY S. SMITH	M
04/26/45	41152	VF-1	USS KASAAN BAY	HAWAII	ECENPAC	LT THOMAS E. BLOUNT	S
04/29/45	40681	NAB		ENIWETOK	CENPAC		
04/30/45	40700	POOL	PEARL	HAWAII	ECENPAC		
04/30/45	40932	VF-100	USS TRIPOLI	HAWAII	ECENPAC	ENS M.C. MYERS	D
04/30/45	41006	VF-99		SAIPAN	WCENPAC		
05/05/45	40996	VF-99		SAIPAN	WCENPAC		
05/10/45	42565	CASU(F)-12		GUAM	WCENPAC		
05/20/45	40536	VF-99		SAIPAN	WCENPAC		
05/21/45	41220	CASU-38	KANEOHE	HAWAII	ECENPAC	LTJG W.E. MACDONALD	S
06/01/45	42428	POOL	PEARL	HAWAII	ECENPAC		
06/02/45	41591	VF-99		SAIPAN	WCENPAC		
06/07/45	40797	VF-99		SAIPAN	WCENPAC		
06/12/45	42737	CASU(F)-47		SAIPAN	WCENPAC		
07/11/45	42111			ENIWETOK	CENPAC	LCDR J.J. LYONS	D

GRUMMAN F6F-3N

DATE	BUNO	SQDRN	BASE	LOST	AREA	PILOT	FATE
02/22/44	8945	VF(N)-76	USS BUNKER HILL	SAIPAN	WCENPAC	ENS R.W. BICE	M
03/20/44	40982	VF(N)-77	BARBERS POINT	HAWAII	ECENPAC	ENS S.T. SMITH	M
03/31/44	26034	VF-16	USS LEX-INGTON	PALAU	CENPAC	ENS J. GILMAN	S
03/31/44	26050	VF-16	USS LEX-INGTON	PALAU	CENPAC		
05/22/44	26104	VF(N)-76	USS BUNKER HILL	MAJURO	CENPAC	LT J.K. JOLLEFF	M
05/23/44	40464	VF(N)-77	USS ESSEX	WAKE	WCENPAC	ENS B.A. DAVIS	D
06/10/44	40592	VF(N)-77	USS ESSEX	ENR MARIANAS	CENPAC	ENS D.B. KELLY	D
06/19/44	65976	VF(N)-76	USS BUNKER HILL	MARIANAS	CENPAC	LTJG N.L. DAVIDSON	M
06/19/44	40339	VF(N)-77B	USS YORK-TOWN	GUAM	WCENPAC	ENS W.F. WOLF	S
06/30/44	40870	VMF(N)-533	ENIWETOK	PONAPE	CENPAC		
07/13/44	42480	VF-74	USS KASAAN BAY	ALGIERS	NW AFR		
07/15/44	40480	VF-1	USS YORK-TOWN	MARIANAS	CENPAC	ENS J.H. RHODE	M
07/16/44	40400	VF(N)-77	USS ESSEX	ENR GUAM	CENPAC		
07/17/44	43022	VF(N)-79	PEARL	HAWAII	ECENPAC	ENS JOSEPH SAMUEL ALLEN	S
07/19/44	40174	VF(N)-533			CENPAC		
07/25/44	40922	VF(N)-79	USS INDEPEN-DENCE	PEARL	ECENPAC	ENS JOSEPH SAMUEL ALLEN	S
07/26/44	66081	VMF(N)-533		ROI	WCENPAC	2NDLT A.F. DILLAMANO	S
08/02/44	40844	VF(N)-79	USS INDEPEN-DENCE	PEARL	ECENPAC	ENS R.W. KLOCK	S
08/04/44	43106	VF(N)-78		HAWAII	ECENPAC	CDR J.S. GRAY, JR.	S
08/07/44	41157	VMF(N)-534	OROTE FIELD	GUAM	WCENPAC	CAPT PAUL H. TODD	M
08/11/44	42360	CASU-27			NORLANT		
08/11/44	40082	VMF(N)-534		GUAM	WCENPAC	1STLT HURLEY E. CROFT	S
08/19/44	41408	VF(N)-78	USS ENTER-PRISE	HAWAII	ECENPAC	ENS E.J. BOUDINOT	S

DATE	BUNO	SQDRN	BASE	LOST	AREA	PILOT	FATE
08/21/44	42560	VF-74	USS KASAAN BAY	CORSICA	EUROPE	ENS M. FOSTER DEMASTERS	M
08/24/44	40656	VF(N)-77	USS ESSEX	ENR PALAU	CENPAC		
09/05/44	40496	VF(N)-77	USS ESSEX	PALAU	CENPAC		
09/08/44	41968	VF(N)-78	USS ENTER-PRISE	ENR PALAU	CENPAC	ENS BASIL A. BERERIDGE	U
09/15/44	40294	VF-13	USS FRANKLIN	PELELIU	WCENPAC		
09/15/44	40384	VF-13	USS FRANKLIN	PELELIU	WCENPAC		
09/21/44	26131	VF(N)-76	USS LEX-INGTON	MANILA	PHIL	LT W.H. ABERCROMBIE	D
10/09/44	41060	VF(N)-42	HAWAII	HAWAII	ECENPAC	ENS HAROLD G. COLE	S
10/12/44	41209	VF(N)-41	USS INDEPEN-DENCE	OKINAWA	EMPIRE	ENS JOSEPH F. MOORE	M
10/14/44	42133	VMF(N)-541		PALAU	CENPAC	2NDLT M.R. DESCHIPPER	S
10/19/44	41869	VMF(N)-541			CENPAC	2NDLT W.J. COOK	S
10/29/44	41261	VF-18	USS INTREPID	LUZON	PHIL	ENS J.P. HEDRICK	M
10/31/44	42600	COMAIR-PAC	PEARL	HAWAII	ECENPAC		
11/02/44	66000	VMF(N)-534		GUAM	WCENPAC		
11/11/44	40969	VF(N)-42	USS BATAAN	HAWAII	ECENPAC	ENS LEWIS P. DOMINGOS	S
11/17/44	41183	NACTU	BARBERS POINT	HAWAII	ECENPAC		
11/18/44	41394	VF-18	USS INTREPID	LUZON	PHIL		
11/25/44	41222	VF-18	USS INTREPID		PHIL	(DECK LOSS-KAMIKAZE)	
11/26/44	41450	NACTU	BARBERS POINT	HAWAII	ECENPAC		
11/26/44	42450	NACTU	BARBERS POINT	HAWAII	ECENPAC		
11/26/44	43008	NACTU	BARBERS POINT	HAWAII	ECENPAC		
12/02/44	43036	NACTU	BARBERS POINT	HAWAII	ECENPAC	ENS RICHARD R. MELMICK	S
12/12/44	42210	VMF(N)-541			PHIL		
12/18/44	41422		USS KWAJALEIN	PHILIPPINE SEA	PHIL		
01/07/45	42204	VMF(N)-541		TACLOBAN	PHIL		
01/20/45	66059	VMF(N)-534		GUAM	WCENPAC		
01/27/45	66179	VMF(N)-534		GUAM	WCENPAC	ENS ADOLF ELSEVIER	D
01/30/45	40768	VMF(N)-534		GUAM	WCENPAC		
03/03/45	40058	VBF(N)-534		GUAM	WCENPAC		
03/29/45	41198	COMAIR-PAC	PEARL	HAWAII	ECENPAC		
04/04/45	40720	NACTU	BARBERS POINT	HAWAII	ECENPAC	ENS DAVID T. LEMBKE	S
06/02/45	41148	VF-99		SAIPAN	WCENPAC		

GRUMMAN F6F-3P

A small number of standard F6F-5s were also fitted with camera equipment for reconnaissance duties as the F6F-5P. Aircraft lost:

DATE	BUNO	SQDRN	BASE	LOST	AREA	PILOT	FATE
09/17/43	04862	VD-2		CARIBBEAN	CENLANT		
05/05/44	40417	VF-24	USS BELLEAU WOOD	TRUK	CENPAC		
09/07/44	42876	VF-2	USS HORNET	PALAU	CENPAC	LTJG C.L. CARLSON	D
10/12/44	42929	VF-44	USS LANGLEY	FORMOSA	EMPIRE	ENS PAUL E. BARLEY	D

DATE	BUNO	SQDRN	BASE	LOST	AREA	PILOT	FATE
10/28/44	41982	VF-13	USS FRANKLIN	LEYTE GULF	PHIL		
11/14/44	43112	VF-44	USS LANGLEY	PALAU	CENPAC	ENS ROBERT HAYS HEDLEY	S
04/16/45	66119	POOL	BARBERS POINT	HAWAII	ECENPAC		
06/23/45	42153	VF-100		HAWAII	ECENPAC		

GRUMMAN F6F-5

The most common variant of the F6F was the F6F-5. Featured improvements included a more powerful R-2800-10W engine housed in a slightly more streamlined engine cowling, spring-loaded control tabs on the ailerons, deletion of the rear-view windows behind the main canopy, an improved, clear view windscreen, with a flat armored-glass front panel replacing the curved Plexiglas panel and internal armor glass screen, and numerous other less conspicuous changes. Aircraft lost:

DATE	BUNO	SQDRN	BASE	LOST	AREA	PILOT	FATE
05/30/44	58029	VF-13	USS FRANKLIN	HAWAII	ECENPAC		
06/24/44	58271	VF-74	USS KASAAN BAY	OFF RHODE IS.	NORLANT		
07/01/44	58113	VF-13	USS FRANKLIN	MARSHALLS	CENPAC		
07/01/44	58613	VF-80	USS TICONDER-OGA	TRINIDAD	CENLANT	ENS J.W. FRAIJOGL	S
07/03/44	58063	VF-2	USS HORNET	IWO JIMA	EMPIRE	LT R.R. BUTLER	M
07/03/44	58359	VF-2	USS HORNET	IWO JIMA	EMPIRE		
07/03/44	58401	VF-2	USS HORNET	IWO JIMA	EMPIRE	ENS EDWARD J. O'NEAL	M
07/04/44	58321	VF-13	USS FRANKLIN	BONINS	CENPAC	LTJG D.E. JAINES	S
07/04/44	58357	VF-13	USS FRANKLIN	BONINS	CENPAC	LTJG J.B. JOHNSON	S
07/04/44	58348	VF-2	USS HORNET	BONINS	CENPAC		
07/05/44	58603	VF-80	USS TICONDER-OGA	TRINIDAD	CENLANT	LT W.L. MINNICK	D
07/06/44	58377	VF-13	USS FRANKLIN	GUAM	WCENPAC	LT W.T. GOVE	M
07/14/44	58616	VOF-1	USS TULAGI	ALGIERS	NW AFR	ENS E.L. FRIEDT	D
07/19/44	58419	VF-2	USS HORNET	GUAM	WCENPAC		
07/22/44	58351	VF-13	USS FRANKLIN	MARIANAS	CENPAC		
07/22/44	58383	VF-13	USS FRANKLIN	MARIANAS	CENPAC		
07/22/44	58926	VF-46			NORLANT		
07/22/44	58602	VF-51	USS SAN JACINTO	PALAU	CENPAC		
07/24/44	58291	VF-74	USS KASAAN BAY	MED	N AFRICA	ENS MAX B. HALES	S
07/26/44	79483	VF-32	USS CABOT	YAP	CENPAC		
07/26/44	58366	VOF-1	USS TULAGI	CASABLANCA	NW AFR	LT C.E. CASE	S
07/27/44	58361	VF-13	USS FRANKLIN	PALAU	CENPAC	ENS R.H. MARTIN	D
08/01/44	58424	VF-22	USS COWPENS	HAWAII	ECENPAC	LT JOHN C. MAXEY, JR.	D

DATE	BUNO	SQDRN	BASE	LOST	AREA	PILOT	FATE
08/01/44	58282	VOF-1	USS TULAGI	FRANCE	EUROPE		
08/05/44	58315	VF-13	USS FRANKLIN	CHICHI JIMA	CENPAC	LT A.C. HUDSON	M
08/05/44	58371	VF-13	USS FRANKLIN	CHICHI JIMA	CENPAC	ENS R.W. L'ESTRANGE	M
08/06/44	58245	VF-13	USS FRANKLIN	CHICHI JIMA	CENPAC		
08/11/44	58648	VF-21	USS BELLEAU WOOD	GUAM	WCENPAC	ENS R.D. YANCEY	S
08/11/44	70230	VF-7	USS HANCOCK	PANAMA	CENPAC	ENS JOHN G. MCILWEE	S
08/11/44	70308	VF-7	USS HANCOCK	PANAMA	CENPAC	LT WILLIAM H. KENAH, JR.	S
08/13/44	58087	VF-14	USS WASP	ENR PALAU	CENPAC		
08/15/44	58458	VF-22		MARSHALLS	CENPAC		
08/15/44	58731	VF-22		MARSHALLS	CENPAC		
08/15/44	58314	VOF-1	USS TULAGI	MOROCCO	NW AFR	LCDR WILLIAM F. BRINGLE	S
08/15/44	58688	VOF-1	USS TULAGI	MOROCCO	NW AFR	ENS W.C. MCKEEVER	S
08/17/44	58474	VF-3	USS RANGER	PEARL	ECENPAC	LTJG H.A. HUGHEY	S
08/17/44	58484	VF-3	USS RANGER	PEARL	ECENPAC	LT SAMUEL SOLBERGER	S
08/17/44	58536	VF-3	USS RANGER	PEARL	ECENPAC	LT RICHARD ENGLISH	S
08/17/44	58556	VF-3	USS RANGER	PEARL	ECENPAC		
08/17/44	58592	VF-3	USS RANGER	PEARL	ECENPAC	LT CARLOS R. MCKEE	D
08/17/44	58241	VF-74	USS KASAAN BAY	FRANCE	EUROPE	LT R.J. JOHNSON	M
08/17/44	58867	VF-74	USS KASAAN BAY	FRANCE	EUROPE	LTJG J.D. FRANK	M
08/20/44	58109	VF-74	USS KASAAN BAY	FRANCE	EUROPE	LCDR HARRY R. BASE	D
08/20/44	58307	VF-74	USS KASAAN BAY	FRANCE	EUROPE	ENS C.W.S. HULLAND	M
08/20/44	58333	VF-74	USS KASAAN BAY	FRANCE	EUROPE	LTJG W. ARBUCKLE	M
08/20/44	58279	VOF-1	USS TULAGI	FRANCE	EUROPE	LT DAVID S. CROCKETT	U
08/20/44	58300	VOF-1	USS TULAGI	FRANCE	EUROPE	LT JAMES M. ALSTON	M
08/21/44	58024	VF-20		MARSHALLS	CENPAC		
08/21/44	58263	VOF-1	USS TULAGI	FRANCE	EUROPE	LTJG COYNE	M
08/25/44	58173	VOF-1	USS TULAGI	MOROCCO	NW AFR	LCDR WILLIAM F. BRINGLE	U
08/26/44	58646	VOF-1	USS TULAGI	FRANCE	EUROPE	LT BROWN	S
08/30/44	58139	VF-15	USS ESSEX	ENR PALAU	CENPAC		
08/31/44	58529	VF-3			CENPAC		
09/01/44	58354	VF-80	USS TICONDER-OGA	GREAT EXHUMA	CENLANT	ENS R.K.H. WEEKS	S
09/02/44	58295	VF-20	USS ENTER-PRISE	BONINS	CENPAC	ENS J.W. BECKMAN	S
09/03/44	58360	VF-22	USS COWPENS	ENR PALUS	CENPAC		
09/04/44	58714	VF-22	USS COWPENS	ENR PALUS	CENPAC	LT L.L. JOHNSON	S
09/06/44	58471	VF-20	USS ENTER-PRISE	YAP	CENPAC	LTJG H.D. BROWN	M

DATE	BUNO	SQDRN	BASE	LOST	AREA	PILOT	FATE
09/06/44	58675	VF-20	USS ENTER-PRISE	YAP	CENPAC	ENS JOSEPH E. COX	M
09/06/44	58713	VF-20	USS ENTER-PRISE	YAP	CENPAC	ENS H.A. HOLDING	M
09/08/44	58945	CASU-35		ENIWETOK	CENPAC		
09/08/44	58193	VB-2	USS HORNET	PALAU	CENPAC	LT FELDERMAN	S
09/08/44	58140	VF-13	USS FRANKLIN	YAP	CENPAC	ENS R.E. SLINGERLAND	S
09/09/44	58543	VF-21	USS BELLEAU WOOD	MINDANAO SEA	PHIL	LT MARVIN H. MEAD	D
09/10/44	58980	VF-13	USS FRANKLIN	PELELIU	WCENPAC	ENS J.P.R. PARENT	M
09/10/44	58457	VF-19	USS LEX-INGTON	MINDANAO SEA	PHIL	ENS A.E. RUFFCORN	D
09/11/44	58477	VF-18	USS INTREPID	VISAYAN	PHIL	LTJG G.J. ECHEL	S
09/11/44	70370	VF-7	USS HANCOCK	ENR HAWAII	ECENPAC	LTJG WALTER J. SHEEN	S
09/12/44	70115	VF-15	USS ESSEX	PELELIU	WCENPAC	LTJG W.V. HENNING	M
09/12/44	58205	VF-18	USS INTREPID	VISAYAN	PHIL	LT JAMES B. NEIGHBOURS	D
09/13/44	70554	VB-14	USS WASP	LOS NEGROS	PHIL	LT JOHN MAGEE	S
09/13/44	58121	VB-2	USS HORNET	LOS NEGROS	PHIL	LT FELDERMAN	S
09/13/44	70049	VF-8	USS BUNKER HILL	CEBU	PHIL	ENS S.F. CZEKALA	S
09/14/44	58372	VF-2	USS HORNET	LEYTE GULF	PHIL		
09/14/44	58559	VF-31	USS CABOT	PALUS	SW PAC		
09/14/44	58921	VF-31	USS CABOT	PALUS	SW PAC	LTJG D.B. DRISCOLL	S
09/16/44	58043	VF-37	USS SAN-GAMON	HALMAHERA	SW PAC	ENS JESSE E. MCNINCH	D
09/17/44	58719	VF-21	USS BELLEAU WOOD	MOROTAI	PHIL		
09/18/44	58037	VB-2		USS HORNET	CENPAC		
09/20/44	70080	VF-28	USS MONTEREY	RYUKYU	EMPIRE	ENS MELVIN C. SMITH	D
09/21/44	58216	VF-18	USS INTREPID	LOS NEGROS	PHIL	LTJG C.P. AMERMAN	S
09/21/44	70129	VF-2		USS HORNET	CENPAC		
09/21/44	58442	VF-22	USS COWPENS	LUZON	PHIL	LT C.M. CRAIG	S
09/21/44	58479	VF-22	USS COWPENS	LUZON	PHIL	LT M.E. FRELLSON	S
09/22/44	58382	VF-14	USS WASP	LOS NEGROS	PHIL		
09/22/44	58407	VF-18	USS INTREPID	LOS NEGROS	PHIL	ENS W.L. PASSI	M
09/22/44	58472	VF-31	USS CABOT	ENR OKINAWA	CENPAC	ENS M.J. NAYLON, JR.	M
09/24/44	58513	VF-18	USS INTREPID	LOS NEGROS	PHIL	LT WILLIAM H. SARTWELLS	M
09/24/44	58546	VF-27	USS PRINCE-TON	LUZON	PHIL	ENS O.L. SCOTT	S
09/24/44	70111	VF-28	USS MONTEREY	PANAY	SW PAC	ENS WM G. SHACKELFORD	M
09/26/44	58652	CASU-35		ENIWETOK	CENPAC		
09/27/44	58912	VF-13	USS FRANKLIN	PALAU	CENPAC		
09/30/44	58805	VF-21	USS BELLEAU WOOD	PALUS	SW PAC		
10/01/44	58067	A & R	MAJURO	MAJURO	CENPAC		
10/03/44	58817	VF(N)-41	USS INDEPEN-DENCE	ULITHI	WCENPAC		

DATE	BUNO	SQDRN	BASE	LOST	AREA	PILOT	FATE
10/03/44	58021	VF-31	USS CABOT	LUZON	PHIL		
10/03/44	58070	VF-31	USS CABOT	LUZON	PHIL		
10/03/44	58460	VF-31	USS CABOT	LUZON	PHIL		
10/03/44	58587	VF-31	USS CABOT	LUZON	PHIL		
10/05/44	58417	VF-11	USS HORNET		CENPAC	ENS S.J. RICHARDSON	S
10/05/44	70073	VF-28	USS MONTEREY	ENR PHILIPPINES	CENPAC		
10/07/44	58429	VF-22	USS COWPENS	OKINAWA	EMPIRE		
10/07/44	58949	VF-22	USS COWPENS	OKINAWA	EMPIRE		
10/07/44	70176	VF-22	USS COWPENS	OKINAWA	EMPIRE		
10/08/44	58054	VF-22	USS COWPENS	OKINAWA	EMPIRE	ENS A.L. WATTS	S
10/09/44	58956	VF-18	USS INTREPID	ENR FORMOSA	CENPAC		
10/10/44	70130	VF-11	USS HORNET	MIYAKO	EMPIRE	ENS K.C. CHASE	D
10/10/44	58993	VF-13	USS FRANKLIN	PALAU	CENPAC	LTJG W.M. FERNANDO	S
10/10/44	70413	VF-13	USS FRANKLIN	PALAU	CENPAC	ENS J.L.C. HEINRICH	S
10/10/44	58253	VF-18	USS INTREPID	ENR FORMOSA	CENPAC	LTJG JOHN F. MAYER	S
10/10/44	70315	VF-7	USS HANCOCK	ENR MANILA	PHIL		
10/10/44	70328	VF-7	USS HANCOCK	ENR MANILA	PHIL		
10/11/44	58482	VF-22	USS COWPENS	LUZON	PHIL	ENS J.W. BOWEN	M
10/11/44	70415	VF-90	USS STEAMER BAY	ENR PALAU	SW PAC	ENS W.B. RIFFAG	S
10/12/44	70609	VB-14	USS WASP	LUZON	PHIL		
10/12/44	58234	VF-11	USS HORNET		CENPAC	ENS G.E. LINDESMITH	D
10/12/44	70155	VF-11	USS HORNET		CENPAC		
10/12/44	58040	VF-14	USS WASP	LUZON	PHIL		
10/12/44	70093	VF-14	USS WASP	FORMOSA	EMPIRE		
10/12/44	58836	VF-15	USS ESSEX	FORMOSA	EMPIRE	LTJG J.D. VAN ALTENA	S
10/12/44	70152	VF-15	USS ESSEX	FORMOSA	EMPIRE	ENS G.A. BORLEY	S
10/12/44	58106	VF-18	USS INTREPID	FORMOSA	EMPIRE	LTJG W.C. ZIENER	M
10/12/44	58236	VF-18	USS INTREPID	FORMOSA	EMPIRE	LTJG E.J. DIBAPTISTA	S
10/12/44	58240	VF-18	USS INTREPID	FORMOSA	EMPIRE	ENS HARRY F. WEBSTER	M
10/12/44	58518	VF-18	USS INTREPID	FORMOSA	EMPIRE	ENS R.C. DUPONT	M
10/12/44	58661	VF-18	USS INTREPID	FORMOSA	EMPIRE	LTJG I.W. KEELS	M
10/12/44	58036	VF-19	USS LEX-INGTON		CENPAC	LT D.K. TRIPP	M
10/12/44	58095	VF-19	USS LEX-INGTON		CENPAC	LT PASKOSKI	S
10/12/44	58565	VF-19	USS LEX-INGTON		CENPAC	LCDR F.F. COOK, JR.	M
10/12/44	58706	VF-20	USS ENTER-PRISE	FORMOSA	EMPIRE	ENS FRED. D. TRUMBULL	M
10/12/44	58397	VF-21	USS BELLEAU WOOD	LUZON	PHIL		
10/12/44	58411	VF-22	USS COWPENS	FORMOSA	EMPIRE		
10/12/44	58085	VF-8	USS BUNKER HILL	FORMOSA	EMPIRE	LTJG J.J. MCGUIRE	S

DATE	BUNO	SQDRN	BASE	LOST	AREA	PILOT	FATE
10/12/44	58806	VF-8	USS BUNKER HILL	FORMOSA	EMPIRE	LTJG R.J. ROSEN	S
10/12/44	58835	VF-8	USS BUNKER HILL	FORMOSA	EMPIRE	LTJG N.W. IMEL	M
10/13/44	58192	VF-11	USS HORNET	FORMOSA	EMPIRE	CDR F.R. SCHRADER	D
10/13/44	70400	VF-11	USS HORNET	FORMOSA	EMPIRE	ENS L.E. LEE	D
10/13/44	58804	VF-13	USS FRANKLIN	FORMOSA	EMPIRE		
10/13/44	70331	VF-13	USS FRANKLIN	FORMOSA	EMPIRE	LTJG R.H. BRIDGE	M
10/13/44	70377	VF-13	USS FRANKLIN	FORMOSA	EMPIRE		
10/13/44	58217	VF-15	USS ESSEX	PESCADORES	CENPAC		
10/13/44	58723	VF-21	USS BELLEAU WOOD	LUZON	PHIL		
10/13/44	58086	VF-51	USS SAN JACINTO	LUZON	PHIL	ENS E. VANFLEET	U
10/13/44	58235	VF-51	USS SAN JACINTO	LUZON	PHIL		
10/14/44	58828	VF-11	USS HORNET		CENPAC	ENS HENRY PTACEK	M
10/14/44	58950	VF-11	USS HORNET		CENPAC	ENS T. LEPIANKA	S
10/14/44	70454	VF-11	USS HORNET		CENPAC	LTJG S.E. GOLDBERG	D
10/14/44	70544	VF-11	USS HORNET		CENPAC	LT N.W. DAYHOFF	D
10/14/44	58353	VF-13	USS FRANKLIN	LUZON	PHIL		
10/14/44	58396	VF-13	USS FRANKLIN	LUZON	PHIL		
10/14/44	58415	VF-19	USS LEX-INGTON		CENPAC	LTJG R.W. BLAKESLEE	M
10/14/44	58336	VF-20	USS ENTER-PRISE	ENR MANILA	PHIL		
10/14/44	58967	VF-28	USS MONTEREY	PHILIPPINE SEA	PHIL		
10/14/44	58840	VF-44	USS LANGLEY	ENR LEYTE GULF	CENPAC	LTJG JOHN R. MONTAPORT	S
10/14/44	70220	VF-7	USS HANCOCK	MANILA	PHIL	ENS T.F. MIZELL	M
10/14/44	70233	VF-7	USS HANCOCK	MANILA	PHIL	LTJG K.V. KILLIAN	M
10/15/44	58042	VF-11	USS HORNET		CENPAC	ENS R.C. DANCE	D
10/15/44	58044	VF-11	USS HORNET		CENPAC		
10/15/44	58048	VF-13	USS FRANKLIN	LUZON	PHIL	(DECK LOSS-KAMIKAZE)	
10/15/44	58256	VF-13	USS FRANKLIN	LUZON	PHIL	(DECK LOSS-KAMIKAZE)	
10/15/44	58358	VF-13	USS FRANKLIN	LUZON	PHIL	(DECK LOSS-KAMIKAZE)	
10/15/44	58430	VF-13	USS FRANKLIN	LUZON	PHIL	(DECK LOSS-KAMIKAZE)	
10/15/44	58544	VF-13	USS FRANKLIN	LUZON	PHIL	(DECK LOSS-KAMIKAZE)	
10/15/44	70330	VF-14	USS WASP	LUZON	PHIL	ENS JAMES C. JUDGE	M
10/15/44	58020	VF-20	USS ENTER-PRISE	ENR MANILA	PHIL	ENS N.W. SNOW	M
10/15/44	58346	VF-21	USS BELLEAU WOOD	LUZON	PHIL		
10/15/44	58924	VF-28	USS MONTEREY	PHILIPPINE SEA	PHIL		
10/15/44	70237	VF-7	USS HANCOCK	MANILA	PHIL		

DATE	BUNO	SQDRN	BASE	LOST	AREA	PILOT	FATE
10/16/44	70659	VF-11	USS HORNET	ENR LUZON	CENPAC	ENS W.A. BORING	S
10/16/44	58571	VF-29	USS CABOT	LUZON	PHIL		
10/16/44	70128	VF-8	USS BUNKER HILL	LUZON	PHIL	LTJG D.R. REHM	M
10/17/44	58375	VF-13	USS FRANKLIN	LUZON	PHIL	LTJG J. KOPMAN	M
10/17/44	58493	VF-18	USS INTREPID	ENR L. NEGROS	CENPAC	ENS W.H. MURRAY	S
10/17/44	58994	VF-19	USS LEX-INGTON		CENPAC		
10/17/44	70135	VF-28	USS MONTEREY	PHILIPPINE SEA	PHIL		
10/17/44	70222	VF-82	USS BENNING-TON		NORLANT	LTJG BUD B. GEAR	S
10/18/44	58116	VF-11	USS HORNET	MANILA	PHIL	ENS G.C. ANDERSON	D
10/18/44	58839	VF-11	USS HORNET	MANILA	PHIL	ENS W. DEROLF	M
10/18/44	58399	VF-13	USS FRANKLIN	LUZON	PHIL		
10/18/44	58209	VF-14	USS WASP	LUZON	PHIL	LTJG W.E. SCHMIDT	M
10/18/44	70559	VF-14	USS WASP	LUZON	PHIL		
10/18/44	58007	VF-20	USS ENTER-PRISE	LUZON	PHIL	ENS BLYTHE	S
10/18/44	58122	VF-20	USS ENTER-PRISE	LUZON	PHIL	LT JOHN P. LAXTON	M
10/18/44	70229	VF-7	USS HANCOCK	LUZON	PHIL		
10/18/44	70586	VF-7	USS HANCOCK	LUZON	PHIL	LT R.G. RANDALL	S
10/19/44	58363	VF-13	USS FRANKLIN	MANILA BAY	PHIL	LT ERIC MAGNUSSON	M
10/19/44	58019	VF-20	USS ENTER-PRISE	LUZON	PHIL		
10/19/44	70197	VF-82	USS BENNING-TON		NORLANT	ENS L.J. CONNERS	D
10/20/44	58695	VF-21	USS BELLEAU WOOD	LEYTE GULF	PHIL		
10/20/44	58487	VF-22	USS COWPENS	ENR ULITHI	SW PAC	LT G.H. ROBERTS	S
10/20/44	70173	VF-28	USS MONTEREY	PHILIPPINE SEA	PHIL		
10/21/44	70676	VF-19	USS LEX-INGTON	ENR LEYTE GULF	SW PAC	LTJG W.J. MASONER	S
10/21/44	58612	VF-21	USS BELLEAU WOOD	LEYTE GULF	PHIL		
10/21/44	58697	VF-21	USS BELLEAU WOOD	LEYTE GULF	PHIL		
10/21/44	70325	VF-7	USS HANCOCK	ENR MANILA	PHIL		
10/22/44	58470	VF-20	USS ENTER-PRISE	LUZON	PHIL		
10/22/44	70412	VF-27	USS PRINCE-TON	LEYTE GULF	PHIL		
10/22/44	58074	VF-37	USS SAN-GAMON	LEYTE GULF	PHIL	ENS MERVILLA KNACKSTADT	S
10/22/44	70455	VF-37	USS SAN-GAMON	LEYTE GULF	PHIL	LTJG WARREN A. SOMMERS	S
10/24/44	58008	VF-19	USS LEX-INGTON	LEYTE GULF	PHIL	ENS W.H. MARTIN	S
10/24/44	70186	VF-19	USS LEX-INGTON	LEYTE GULF	PHIL	ENS F.P. HUBBUCK	M

DATE	BUNO	SQDRN	BASE	LOST	AREA	PILOT	FATE
10/24/44	58028	VF-20	USS ENTER-PRISE	LUZON	PHIL	CDR FREDERICK E. BAKUTIS	M
10/24/44	58064	VF-27	USS PRINCE-TON	LEYTE GULF	PHIL	(SHIP SANK)	
10/24/44	58080	VF-27	USS PRINCE-TON	LEYTE GULF	PHIL	(SHIP SANK)	
10/24/44	58129	VF-27	USS PRINCE-TON	LEYTE GULF	PHIL	(SHIP SANK)	
10/24/44	58808	VF-27	USS PRINCE-TON	LEYTE GULF	PHIL	(SHIP SANK)	
10/24/44	70831	VF-37	USS SAN-GAMON	SAMAR	PHIL	LTJG KARL W. KONYON	S
10/24/44	70175	VF-44	USS LANGLEY	SAN BERNADINO	PHIL		
10/24/44	58143	VF-80	USS TICONDER-OGA	MARSHALLS	CENPAC	ENS D.F. GREENHAGEN	D
10/25/44	58370	VB-14	USS WASP	LUZON	PHIL	ENS ARTHUR MCLANE, JR.	M
10/25/44	58391	VF-11	USS HORNET		PHIL		
10/25/44	58005	VF-20	USS ENTER-PRISE	LUZON	PHIL	ENS ROBERT K. NELSON	S
10/25/44	58030	VF-20	USS ENTER-PRISE	LUZON	PHIL	ENS G.W. DENBY	S
10/25/44	58983	VF-20	USS ENTER-PRISE	LUZON	PHIL	LCDR J.T. LAWLER	S
10/25/44	58454	VF-21	USS BELLEAU WOOD	CAPE ENGANO	SW PAC		
10/25/44	58018	VF-29	USS CABOT	LEYTE GULF	PHIL	ENS EMERAL B. COOK	S
10/25/44	58012	VF-37	USS SAN-GAMON	SAMAR	PHIL		
10/25/44	58175	VF-37	USS SAN-GAMON	SAMAR	PHIL	LT H.C. TABER	S
10/25/44	58202	VF-37	USS SAN-GAMON	SAMAR	PHIL		
10/25/44	58476	VF-37	USS SAN-GAMON	SAMAR	PHIL		
10/25/44	58650	VF-37	USS SAN-GAMON	SAMAR	PHIL	LTJG BENEDICT	S
10/25/44	58651	VF-37	USS SAN-GAMON	SAMAR	PHIL	LTJG J.L. SLOAN	S
10/25/44	70857	VF-37	USS SAN-GAMON	SAMAR	PHIL	ENS DEAN R. LEAF	S
10/25/44	58955	VF-51	USS SAN JACINTO	SIBUYAN SEA	PHIL	ENS H.E. MATTHEWS	M
10/25/44	70617	VF-7	USS HANCOCK	MANILA	PHIL		
10/26/44	58114	VF-14	USS WASP	LUZON	PHIL	LTJG EUGENE J. STREETER	M
10/26/44	70086	VF-18	USS INTREPID	ENR LUZON	PHIL	ENS HOWARD S. MERCHAM	M
10/26/44	58635	VF-28	USS MONTEREY	PHILIPPINE SEA	PHIL		
10/26/44	70139	VF-3	USS YORK-TOWN	ENR ENIWETOK	CENPAC		
10/26/44	58680	VF-7	USS HANCOCK	MANILA	PHIL	LT WILLIAM H. KENAH, JR.	D
10/26/44	70461	VF-7	USS HANCOCK	MANILA	PHIL	ENS D.A. SCHUMACKER	M
10/27/44	70434	VF-11	USS HORNET		CENPAC	ENS C.R. BRATRIES	D
10/27/44	70533	VF-11	USS HORNET		CENPAC		

DATE	BUNO	SQDRN	BASE	LOST	AREA	PILOT	FATE
10/27/44	58287	VF-13	USS FRANKLIN	LEYTE GULF	PHIL		
10/27/44	71368	VF-85	USS SHIP-LEY BAY	HAWAII	ECENPAC		
10/28/44	58248	VF-13	USS FRANKLIN	LEYTE GULF	PHIL	ENS BENJAMIN J. MILES	M
10/28/44	58665	VF-13	USS FRANKLIN	LEYTE GULF	PHIL		
10/28/44	58475	VF-18	USS INTREPID	LUZON	PHIL	LT GEORGE D. GRIFFITH	M
10/28/44	58011	VF-20	USS ENTER-PRISE	LUZON	PHIL	ENS D.G. REEDER	S
10/28/44	58449	VF-20	USS ENTER-PRISE	LUZON	PHIL	ENS JOHN L. CRITTENDEN	S
10/28/44	71077	VF-3	USS YORK-TOWN	ENR ENIWETOK	CENPAC	LTJG ROBERT E. OVERMIER	D
10/28/44	58243	VF-80	USS TICONDER-OGA	ULITHI	WCENPAC	ENS GEORGE B. JACKSON	D
10/28/44	70312	VF-82	USS BENNING-TON		NORLANT	LT JACK R. SESSIONS	S
10/29/44	58298	VF-13	USS FRANKLIN	LEYTE GULF	PHIL		
10/29/44	58254	VF-18	USS INTREPID	LUZON	PHIL	LT W.R. THOMPSON	M
10/29/44	58409	VF-18	USS INTREPID	LUZON	PHIL	ENS A.P. MOLLENHAUER	M
10/29/44	70605	VF-18	USS INTREPID	LUZON	PHIL	ENS D.A. HAUGHTON	M
10/29/44	70667	VF-18	USS INTREPID	LUZON	PHIL	LT K.G. CRUSOE	M
10/29/44	58463	VF-20	USS ENTER-PRISE	LUZON	PHIL		
10/29/44	58069	VF-29	USS CABOT	LUZON	PHIL	ENS S.W. TROUP	S
10/29/44	58252	VF-29	USS CABOT	LUZON	PHIL	ENS STANLEY DEATH	M
10/29/44	58560	VF-29	USS CABOT	LUZON	PHIL	LT HARRY E. LESLIE	M
10/29/44	70071	VF-7	USS HANCOCK	MANILA	PHIL		
10/29/44	70192	VF-7	USS HANCOCK	MANILA	PHIL	ENS H.J. STOCKERT	M
10/29/44	70193	VF-7	USS HANCOCK	MANILA	PHIL	LTJG R.M. HARRIS	M
10/29/44	70196	VF-7	USS HANCOCK	MANILA	PHIL	ENS L.J. ARCHER	S
10/29/44	70288	VF-7	USS HANCOCK	MANILA	PHIL		
10/30/44	58056	VF-13	USS FRANKLIN	LEYTE GULF	PHIL	(DECK LOSS-KAMIKAZE)	
10/30/44	58195	VF-13	USS FRANKLIN	LEYTE GULF	PHIL	(DECK LOSS-KAMIKAZE)	
10/30/44	58304	VF-13	USS FRANKLIN	LEYTE GULF	PHIL	(DECK LOSS-KAMIKAZE)	
10/30/44	58385	VF-13	USS FRANKLIN	LEYTE GULF	PHIL	(DECK LOSS-KAMIKAZE)	
10/30/44	58554	VF-13	USS FRANKLIN	LEYTE GULF	PHIL	(DECK LOSS-KAMIKAZE)	
10/30/44	70969	VF-13	USS FRANKLIN	LEYTE GULF	PHIL	(DECK LOSS-KAMIKAZE)	
10/30/44	58208	VF-18	USS INTREPID	LUZON	PHIL		
10/30/44	58390	VF-21	USS BELLEAU WOOD		SW PAC	(DECK FIRE)	
10/30/44	58414	VF-21	USS BELLEAU WOOD		SW PAC	(DECK FIRE)	

DATE	BUNO	SQDRN	BASE	LOST	AREA	PILOT	FATE
10/30/44	58504	VF-21	USS BELLEAU WOOD		SW PAC	(DECK FIRE)	
10/30/44	58521	VF-21	USS BELLEAU WOOD		SW PAC	(DECK FIRE)	
10/30/44	58678	VF-21	USS BELLEAU WOOD		SW PAC	(DECK FIRE)	
10/30/44	58685	VF-21	USS BELLEAU WOOD		SW PAC	(DECK FIRE)	
10/30/44	58700	VF-21	USS BELLEAU WOOD		SW PAC	(DECK FIRE)	
10/30/44	58704	VF-21	USS BELLEAU WOOD		SW PAC	(DECK FIRE)	
10/30/44	58707	VF-21	USS BELLEAU WOOD		SW PAC	(DECK FIRE)	
10/30/44	58718	VF-21	USS BELLEAU WOOD		SW PAC	(DECK FIRE)	
10/30/44	58913	VF-21	USS BELLEAU WOOD		SW PAC	(DECK FIRE)	
10/30/44	58528	VF-51	USS SAN JACINTO	LEYTE GULF	PHIL		
10/30/44	58982	VF-51	USS SAN JACINTO	LEYTE GULF	PHIL		
10/30/44	70337	VF-51	USS SAN JACINTO	LEYTE GULF	PHIL		
10/30/44	70303	VF-7	USS HANCOCK	MANILA	PHIL		
10/31/44	58078	COMAIR-PAC	PEARL	HAWAII	ECENPAC		
10/31/44	58557	NAS		HAWAII	ECENPAC		
11/02/44	70057	VF-14	USS BARNES		WCENPAC	LTJG STOKES	S
11/02/44	70182	VF-80	USS TICONDER-OGA	ENR CAVITE	WCENPAC		
11/03/44	58644	VF-11	USS HORNET		WCENPAC		
11/03/44	70894	VF-44	USS LANGLEY	MANILA	PHIL	LT CHARLES V. AUGUST	S
11/05/44	58199	VF-11	USS HORNET		PHIL	ENS W.M. MANN	M
11/05/44	58981	VF-11	USS HORNET		PHIL		
11/05/44	70580	VF-14	USS WASP	LUZON	PHIL	LT W.M. KNIGHT	M
11/05/44	58201	VF-18	USS INTREPID	LUZON	PHIL	LT C.W. DEMASS	M
11/05/44	58496	VF-19	USS LEX-INGTON	LEYTE GULF	PHIL	ENS S.F. MURRAY	S
11/05/44	70686	VF-19	USS LEX-INGTON	LEYTE GULF	PHIL	LT R.S. BOLES	D
11/05/44	70931	VF-19	USS LEX-INGTON	LEYTE GULF	PHIL	(DECK LOSS-KAMIKAZE)	
11/05/44	58512	VF-22	USS COWPENS	LUZON	PHIL	ENS J.E. BACON	M
11/05/44	70625	VF-22	USS COWPENS	LUZON	PHIL	ENS L.R. GUNTHER, JR.	D
11/05/44	58868	VF-28	USS MONTEREY	LUZON	PHIL	ENS R.L. CLARY	M
11/05/44	58330	VF-80	USS TICONDER-OGA	CAVITE	PHIL	ENS R.K.H. WEEKS	M
11/05/44	58873	VF-80	USS TICONDER-OGA	CAVITE	PHIL	ENS WILLIAM N. NETTLES	M
11/05/44	70380	VF-80	USS TICONDER-OGA	CAVITE	PHIL	LT GEORGE F. ECKERT	M

DATE	BUNO	SQDRN	BASE	LOST	AREA	PILOT	FATE
11/05/44	70399	VF-80	USS TICONDER-OGA	CAVITE	PHIL	LT F.G. TYLER	M
11/06/44	58403	VF-15	USS ESSEX	LUZON	PHIL		
11/06/44	58568	VF-15	USS ESSEX	LUZON	PHIL	LTJG W.S. DEMING	S
11/06/44	58845	VF-15	USS ESSEX	LUZON	PHIL	ENS W.B. RIFFLE	S
11/06/44	58894	VF-15	USS ESSEX	LUZON	PHIL	LTJG T.E. THOMPSON	M
11/06/44	58047	VF-7	USS HANCOCK	LUZON	PHIL	LT G.M. SULLIVAN	S
11/06/44	58881	VF-7	USS HANCOCK	LUZON	PHIL	LT H.A. SOLI	S
11/06/44	70353	VF-7	USS HANCOCK	LUZON	PHIL	LTJG N.C DRAPER	S
11/06/44	70369	VF-7	USS HANCOCK	LUZON	PHIL	ENS W.J. GROOMES	S
11/06/44	70376	VF-7	USS HANCOCK	LUZON	PHIL	LTJG J.A. BOYLE	M
11/09/44	58520	VF-3	USS YORK-TOWN	LEYTE GULF	PHIL		
11/09/44	58535	VF-3	USS YORK-TOWN	LEYTE GULF	PHIL		
11/09/44	70618	VF-3	USS YORK-TOWN	LEYTE GULF	PHIL		
11/09/44	71066	VF-3	USS YORK-TOWN	LEYTE GULF	PHIL	ENS J.G. SCORDO	S
11/09/44	58610	VF-80	USS TICONDER-OGA	ENR MANILA	PHIL	LT WILLIAM B. MILLIVARD	S
11/09/44	71336	VF-87	USS RANDOLPH	TRINIDAD	CENLANT		
11/11/44	58656	VF-15	USS ESSEX	MANILA	PHIL	ENS R.W. ERICKSON	S
11/11/44	71029	VF-3	USS YORK-TOWN	MANILA	PHIL	ENS R.S. COLEMAN	S
11/11/44	71096	VF-44	USS LANGLEY	VISAYAN	PHIL		
11/12/44	70901	VF-3	USS YORK-TOWN	MANILA	PHIL	LTJG J.S. TYLER	S
11/12/44	70921	VF-44	USS LANGLEY	ENR MANILA	PHIL		
11/12/44	70585	VF-81	USS WASP	LEYTE GULF	PHIL		
11/12/44	70821	VF-81	USS WASP	LEYTE GULF	PHIL		
11/13/44	70363	VF-15	USS ESSEX	MANILA	PHIL		
11/13/44	58574	VF-20	USS ENTER-PRISE	LUZON	PHIL	LT JOHN D. PETERSEN	M
11/13/44	70100	VF-20	USS ENTER-PRISE	MANILA	PHIL	ENS W.N. ERIKSON	M
11/13/44	70389	VF-20	USS ENTER-PRISE	MANILA	PHIL		
11/13/44	58698	VF-3	USS YORK-TOWN	MANILA	PHIL	LT LEONARD R. ROW	U
11/13/44	58958	VF-4	USS BUNKER HILL		PHIL	ENS S.R. LANNER	M
11/13/44	58548	VF-44	USS LANGLEY	MANILA	PHIL	ENS A.B. NAUMAN	M
11/13/44	58627	VF-80	USS TICONDER-OGA	MANILA	PHIL		
11/13/44	58667	VF-80	USS TICONDER-OGA	MANILA	PHIL	LT W.C. EDWARDS	S
11/14/44	58123	NFTG					
11/14/44	58369	VF-11	USS HORNET	MANILA	PHIL		
11/14/44	58049	VF-20	USS ENTER-PRISE	MANILA	PHIL	ENS ARTHUR M. TUBB	M
11/14/44	58380	VF-20	USS ENTER-PRISE	MANILA	PHIL		

DATE	BUNO	SQDRN	BASE	LOST	AREA	PILOT	FATE
11/14/44	58917	VF-20	USS ENTER-PRISE	MANILA	PHIL	LT T.J. WOODRUFF	M
11/14/44	70886	VF-3	USS YORK-TOWN	MINDORO STR.	PHIL	ENS R.C. VANNESS	M
11/14/44	70941	VF-3	USS YORK-TOWN	MINDORO STR.	PHIL	ENS G.C. MARTIN	U
11/14/44	58596	VF-4	USS BUNKER HILL		PHIL	ENS KENNETH W. WATKINS	M
11/14/44	70387	VF-4	USS BUNKER HILL		PHIL	ENS WILLIAM N. OSTLUND	M
11/14/44	70677	VF-80	USS TICONDER-OGA	MANILA	PHIL		
11/14/44	70171	VF-81	USS WASP	LEYTE GULF	PHIL	LT JOHN B. STAHL	M
11/15/44	58288	VF-18	USS INTREPID	LUZON	PHIL		
11/16/44	58576	VF-28	USS MONTEREY	PHILIPPINE SEA	PHIL		
11/18/44	58483	VF-22	USS COWPENS	LUZON	PHIL		
11/18/44	70811	VF-4	USS BUNKER HILL		WCENPAC		
11/19/44	58453	CASU(F)-42		PITYILU	SW PAC		
11/19/44	58537	VF-18	USS INTREPID	LUZON	PHIL	LTJG J.M. NEWSOME	M
11/19/44	70683	VF-18	USS INTREPID	LUZON	PHIL	LT F.W. TRACEY	S
11/19/44	58013	VF-20	USS ENTER-PRISE	LUZON	PHIL		
11/19/44	58050	VF-20	USS ENTER-PRISE	LUZON	PHIL	ENS ROBERT K. NELSON	M
11/19/44	58885	VF-20	USS ENTER-PRISE	LUZON	PHIL	ENS T.F. MCCUE	M
11/19/44	70626	VF-22	USS COWPENS	LUZON	PHIL	LTJG J.A. BRYCE	S
11/19/44	58849	VF-3	USS YORK-TOWN	LEYTE GULF	PHIL	LT T.W. LINDSEY	M
11/19/44	70587	VF-3	USS YORK-TOWN	LEYTE GULF	PHIL	LT T.A. BACCHUS	M
11/19/44	70842	VF-3	USS YORK-TOWN	LEYTE GULF	PHIL	ENS N.A. LOTZ	M
11/19/44	58871	VF-7	USS HANCOCK	MANILA	PHIL	LT W.G. REEVES	M
11/19/44	70208	VF-7	USS HANCOCK	MANILA	PHIL		
11/19/44	70219	VF-7	USS HANCOCK	MANILA	PHIL		
11/19/44	70379	VF-7	USS HANCOCK	MANILA	PHIL		
11/19/44	70394	VF-7	USS HANCOCK	MANILA	PHIL	LTJG LOWELL V. MASTERS	D
11/19/44		VF-81	USS WASP	LEYTE GULF	PHIL		
11/19/44	70983	VF-81	USS WASP	LEYTE GULF	PHIL	ENS EDWARD J. HADDOCK	M
11/20/44	58694	VF-100	USS MAKASSAR STRAIT	HAWAII	ECENPAC	ENS JOHN H. SCHULTZ	S
11/22/44	58636	VF-20	USS ENTER-PRISE	YAP	CENPAC	LT ZACKARY F. LILLARD	M
11/22/44	70039	VF-22	USS COWPENS	LUZON	PHIL		
11/23/44	70868	VF-4	USS ESSEX	ENR LEYTE GULF	PHIL	LT NORMAN F. RANDOLPH	D
11/24/44	58821	VF-44	USS LANGLEY	ENR LUZON	PHIL	LT JOHN B. TYLER	S
11/24/44	71004	VF-81	USS WASP	ENR ULITHI	WCENPAC	LT CLIFFORD B. WATT	D

DATE	BUNO	SQDRN	BASE	LOST	AREA	PILOT	FATE
11/25/44		VF-18	USS INTREPID		PHIL	(DECK LOSS-KAMIKAZE)	
11/25/44		VF-18	USS INTREPID		PHIL	(DECK LOSS-KAMIKAZE)	
11/25/44	58053	VF-18	USS INTREPID		PHIL	(DECK LOSS-KAMIKAZE)	
11/25/44	58088	VF-18	USS INTREPID		PHIL	(DECK LOSS-KAMIKAZE)	
11/25/44	58091	VF-18	USS INTREPID		PHIL	(DECK LOSS-KAMIKAZE)	
11/25/44	58386	VF-18	USS INTREPID		PHIL	(DECK LOSS-KAMIKAZE)	
11/25/44	58485	VF-18	USS INTREPID		PHIL	(DECK LOSS-KAMIKAZE)	
11/25/44	58486	VF-18	USS INTREPID		PHIL	(DECK LOSS-KAMIKAZE)	
11/25/44	58501	VF-18	USS INTREPID		PHIL	(DECK LOSS-KAMIKAZE)	
11/25/44	58530	VF-18	USS INTREPID		PHIL	(DECK LOSS-KAMIKAZE)	
11/25/44	58683	VF-18	USS INTREPID		PHIL	(DECK LOSS-KAMIKAZE)	
11/25/44	58883	VF-18	USS INTREPID		PHIL	(DECK LOSS-KAMIKAZE)	
11/25/44	70090	VF-18	USS INTREPID		PHIL	(DECK LOSS-KAMIKAZE)	
11/25/44	70146	VF-18	USS INTREPID		PHIL	(DECK LOSS-KAMIKAZE)	
11/25/44	70396	VF-18	USS INTREPID		PHIL	(DECK LOSS-KAMIKAZE)	
11/25/44	70435	VF-18	USS INTREPID		PHIL	(DECK LOSS-KAMIKAZE)	
11/25/44	70558	VF-18	USS INTREPID		PHIL	(DECK LOSS-KAMIKAZE)	
11/25/44	71462	VF-44	USS LANGLEY	LUZON	PHIL	ENS MOSKO	M
11/25/44	58965	VF-7	USS HANCOCK	LUZON	PHIL		
11/25/44	58332	VF-80	USS TICONDER-OGA	LUZON	PHIL		
11/25/44	58673	VF-80	USS TICONDER-OGA	LUZON	PHIL		
11/25/44	71306	VF-87	USS RANDOLPH	TRINIDAD	CENLANT	ENS THOMAS G. SCHAFFER	S
11/25/44	71348	VF-87	USS RANDOLPH	TRINIDAD	CENLANT	ENS EUGENE E. MANDEBERG	S
11/25/44	71415	VF 87	USS RANDOLPH	TRINIDAD	CENLANT		
11/26/44	58911	VF-7	USS HANCOCK	MANILA	PHIL		
11/26/44	70563	VF-7	USS HANCOCK	MANILA	PHIL		
11/28/44	58355	CASU(F)-42		PITYILU	SW PAC		
11/28/44	58859	CASU(F)-42		PITYILU	SW PAC		
11/28/44		VF(N)-43	USS KASAAN BAY	ENR PANAMA	CENLANT	LT C. DENBY-WELKES	U
11/28/44	70091	VF-18	USS INTREPID		WCENPAC	(DECK LOSS-SCRAPPED)	
11/30/44	58532	PEARL		HAWAII	ECENPAC		
11/30/44	58624	PEARL		HAWAII	ECENPAC		
11/30/44	58816	PEARL		HAWAII	ECENPAC		
11/30/44	70439	VF-17	HILO	HAWAII	ECENPAC	ENS KENNETH E. FIEDLER	D
11/30/44	70457	VF-17	HILO	HAWAII	ECENPAC	LTJG EDWARD G. VERNELLE	S
11/30/44	71591	VF-9	KAHULUI	HAWAII	ECENPAC		
12/01/44	71917	VF-33	PEARL	HAWAII	ECENPAC	ENS JOSEPH J. FREINEIT	D
12/03/44	71000	VF-87	USS RANDOLPH	TRINIDAD	CENLANT	ENS THOMAS W. FORTUNE	M
12/04/44	71838	VF-8	HILO	HAWAII	ECENPAC	ENS GLEN M. LARKINS	D
12/05/44	70770	VF-20			WCENPAC		

DATE	BUNO	SQDRN	BASE	LOST	AREA	PILOT	FATE
12/06/44	71369	VF-87	USS RANDOLPH	TRINIDAD	CENLANT	ENS GRANVILLE O'BYROM	S
12/08/44	58824	VF-11	PEARL	HAWAII	ECENPAC		
12/10/44	70865	VF-11	USS HORNET	ULITHI	WCENPAC		
12/10/44	70392	VF-17	USS SARATOGA	HAWAII	ECENPAC	ENS LONNIE C. PACE	S
12/10/44	58620	VF-80	USS TICONDER-OGA	LUZON	PHIL		
12/10/44	70518	VF-81	USS WASP	ULITHI	WCENPAC		
12/12/44	58388		BARBERS POINT	HAWAII	ECENPAC		
12/12/44	70682	VF-20	USS LEX-INGTON	LUZON	PHIL		
12/12/44	70458	VF-3	USS YORK-TOWN	ENR LUZON	PHIL	LTJG LEO J. RILEY	S
12/12/44	58895	VF-4	USS ESSEX	LUZON	PHIL		
12/12/44	70631	VF-4	USS ESSEX	LUZON	PHIL		
12/12/44	58663	VF-80	USS TICONDER-OGA	LUZON	PHIL		
12/12/44	58891	VF-80	USS TICONDER-OGA	LUZON	PHIL		
12/12/44	58550	VF-81	USS WASP	LEYTE GULF	PHIL		
12/13/44	58410	VF-22	USS COWPENS	LUZON	PHIL		
12/13/44	58903	VF-22	USS COWPENS	LUZON	PHIL		
12/13/44	58643	VF-44	USS LANGLEY	LINGAYEN GULF	PHIL	LTJG E. NOWAK	D
12/13/44	70638	VF-44	USS LANGLEY	LINGAYEN GULF	PHIL		
12/13/44	71150	VF-44	USS LANGLEY	LINGAYEN GULF	PHIL		
12/13/44	58060	VF-45	USS SAN JACINTO	MANILA	PHIL		
12/13/44	58900	VF-45	USS SAN JACINTO	MANILA	PHIL		
12/13/44	70148	VF-7	USS HANCOCK	ENR LUZON	PHIL		
12/14/44	58660	VF-11	USS HORNET	MANILA	PHIL	LT WALTER O. ZOECKLEIN	S
12/14/44	70534	VF-11	USS HORNET	MANILA	PHIL	ENS C.L. PARSLEY	S
12/14/44	70556	VF-11	USS HORNET	MANILA	PHIL		
12/14/44	71034	VF-11	USS HORNET	MANILA	PHIL		
12/14/44	71103	VF-11	USS HORNET	MANILA	PHIL		
12/14/44	58510	VF-20	USS LEX-INGTON	LUZON	PHIL	ENS JAMES W. ROBINSON	M
12/14/44	58540	VF-20	USS LEX-INGTON	LUZON	PHIL	LTJG JAMES W. BECKMAN	M
12/14/44	58831	VF-20	USS LEX-INGTON	LUZON	PHIL	LT ALEXANDER VRACIU	M
12/14/44	70109	VF-20	USS LEX-INGTON	LUZON	PHIL	ENS ALBERT L. EHRREICH	S
12/14/44	70890	VF-20	USS LEX-INGTON	LUZON	PHIL	ENS GEORGE W. MCKIMSEY	M
12/14/44	71481	VF-20	USS LEX-INGTON	LUZON	PHIL	ENS JAMES G. DARRACOTT	M
12/14/44	71494	VF-20	USS LEX-INGTON	LUZON	PHIL	ENS R.M. KIMBALL	S
12/14/44	71800	VF-20	USS LEX-INGTON	LUZON	PHIL	LTJG DOUGLAS BAKER	M
12/14/44	72311	VF-22	USS COWPENS	LUZON	PHIL	ENS GEORGE B. WHITEHOUSE	D
12/14/44	58362	VF-29	USS CABOT	LUZON	PHIL	LT JOHN F. THOMPSON	D
12/14/44	58898	VF-29	USS CABOT	LUZON	PHIL	ENS GEORGE E. RECORDS	M

DATE	BUNO	SQDRN	BASE	LOST	AREA	PILOT	FATE
12/14/44	71007	VF-29	USS CABOT	LUZON	PHIL	LTJG WALTER D. BISHOP	M
12/14/44	70112	VF-3	USS YORK-TOWN	LUZON	PHIL	ENS HORNER	S
12/14/44	70942	VF-3	USS YORK-TOWN	LUZON	PHIL	ENS BILLY F. COMMONS	M
12/14/44	71403	VF-3	USS YORK-TOWN	LUZON	PHIL	ENS R.L. JACKSON	S
12/14/44		VF-4	USS ESSEX	LUZON	PHIL		
12/14/44	71390	VF-4	USS ESSEX	LUZON	PHIL	ENS REX TYRON SNIDER	S
12/14/44	71833	VF-4	USS ESSEX	LUZON	PHIL	ENS JAMES R. PARK	S
12/14/44	70995	VF-45	USS SAN JACINTO	MANILA	PHIL	LT JOHN LENDO	M
12/14/44	71427	VF-45	USS SAN JACINTO	MANILA	PHIL	LT THOMAS P. MCCANN	M
12/14/44	58865	VF-7	USS HANCOCK	LUZON	PHIL	ENS W.W. PECK	D
12/14/44	58905	VF-7	USS HANCOCK	LUZON	PHIL		
12/14/44	70887	VF-7	USS HANCOCK	LUZON	PHIL		
12/14/44	70059	VF-81	USS WASP	LEYTE GULF	PHIL		
12/14/44	70862	VF-81	USS WASP	LEYTE GULF	PHIL	LT SANFORD B. PERKINS	M
12/15/44	70557	VF-11	USS HORNET	LUZON	PHIL	ENS W.E. LIZOTTE	S
12/15/44	71032	VF-3	USS YORK-TOWN	LUZON	PHIL	ENS CURTIN	S
12/15/44	71056	VF-3	USS YORK-TOWN	LUZON	PHIL	LTJG ROBERT L. GLAISYER	D
12/15/44	71837	VF-3	USS YORK-TOWN	LUZON	PHIL	ENS URBANO	S
12/15/44	58693	VF-7	USS HANCOCK	LUZON	PHIL		
12/15/44	58864	VF-7	USS HANCOCK	LUZON	PHIL	LTJG V. HICKEY	M
12/15/44	70289	VF-7	USS HANCOCK	LUZON	PHIL	ENS I. TIJA	D
12/15/44	70571	VF-7	USS HANCOCK	LUZON	PHIL		
12/16/44	70986	VF-20	USS LEX-INGTON	LUZON	PHIL		
12/16/44	70356	VF-3	USS YORK-TOWN	LUZON	PHIL	CDR MACBERRIAN WILLIAMS	S
12/16/44	71061	VF-3	USS YORK-TOWN	LUZON	PHIL	LT MARSHALL S. HOPP	S
12/16/44	58083	VF-4	USS ESSEX	LUZON	PHIL	LTJG WATSON	S
12/16/44	58827	VF-4	USS ESSEX	LUZON	PHIL	ENS GLEN R. SWAIM	S
12/10/44	71453	VF-45	USS SAN JACINTO	ENR GUAM	PHIL		
12/16/44	70296	VF-7	USS HANCOCK	LUZON	PHIL	LCDR CALDWELL	S
12/16/44	70322	VF-7	USS HANCOCK	LUZON	PHIL	LTJG B.W. ADAMS	S
12/16/44	71797	VF-80	USS TICONDER-OGA	LUZON	PHIL	ENS FRANKORIE	S
12/16/44	71718	VF-87	USS RANDOLPH	CARIBBEAN	CENLANT	ENS RALPH A. SMITH	M
12/17/44	58311		BARBERS POINT	HAWAII	ECENPAC		
12/17/44	71925	VF-3	USS YORK-TOWN	LUZON	PHIL	ENS A.W. WOLTERS, JR.	D
12/17/44	71919	VF-6	PEARL	HAWAII	ECENPAC	LTJG FRANK E. TURPIE	S
12/18/44	58270		USS KWAJALEIN	PHILIPPINE SEA	PHIL		
12/18/44	71054		USS KWAJALEIN	PHILIPPINE SEA	PHIL		
12/18/44	58590	UNASSIGN ED	USS CAPE ESPERAN.	PHILIPPINE SEA	PHIL	(DECK LOSS-TYPHOON)	
12/18/44	58674	UNASSIGN ED	USS CAPE ESPERAN.	PHILIPPINE SEA	PHIL	(DECK LOSS-TYPHOON)	
12/18/44	70795	UNASSIGN ED	USS CAPE ESPERAN.	PHILIPPINE SEA	PHIL	(DECK LOSS-TYPHOON)	

DATE	BUNO	SQDRN	BASE	LOST	AREA	PILOT	FATE
12/18/44	70919	UNASSIGNED	USS CAPE ESPERAN.	PHILIPPINE SEA	PHIL	(DECK LOSS-TYPHOON)	
12/18/44	71158	UNASSIGNED	USS ALTAMAHA	PHILIPPINE SEA	PHIL	(DECK LOSS-TYPHOON)	
12/18/44	71356	UNASSIGNED	USS CAPE ESPERAN.	PHILIPPINE SEA	PHIL	(DECK LOSS-TYPHOON)	
12/18/44	71388	UNASSIGNED	USS ALTAMAHA	PHILIPPINE SEA	PHIL	(DECK LOSS-TYPHOON)	
12/18/44	71406	UNASSIGNED	USS ALTAMAHA	PHILIPPINE SEA	PHIL	(DECK LOSS-TYPHOON)	
12/18/44	71457	UNASSIGNED	USS CAPE ESPERAN.	PHILIPPINE SEA	PHIL	(DECK LOSS-TYPHOON)	
12/18/44	71480	UNASSIGNED	USS ALTAMAHA	PHILIPPINE SEA	PHIL	(DECK LOSS-TYPHOON)	
12/18/44	71490	UNASSIGNED	USS ALTAMAHA	PHILIPPINE SEA	PHIL	(DECK LOSS-TYPHOON)	
12/18/44	71496	UNASSIGNED	USS ALTAMAHA	PHILIPPINE SEA	PHIL	(DECK LOSS-TYPHOON)	
12/18/44	71501	UNASSIGNED	USS CAPE ESPERAN.	PHILIPPINE SEA	PHIL	(DECK LOSS-TYPHOON)	
12/18/44	71525	UNASSIGNED	USS ALTAMAHA	PHILIPPINE SEA	PHIL	(DECK LOSS-TYPHOON)	
12/18/44	71533	UNASSIGNED	USS ALTAMAHA	PHILIPPINE SEA	PHIL	(DECK LOSS-TYPHOON)	
12/18/44	71569	UNASSIGNED	USS CAPE ESPERAN.	PHILIPPINE SEA	PHIL	(DECK LOSS-TYPHOON)	
12/18/44	71584	UNASSIGNED	USS CAPE ESPERAN.	PHILIPPINE SEA	PHIL	(DECK LOSS-TYPHOON)	
12/18/44	71727	UNASSIGNED	USS ALTAMAHA	PHILIPPINE SEA	PHIL	(DECK LOSS-TYPHOON)	
12/18/44	71793	UNASSIGNED	USS CAPE ESPERAN.	PHILIPPINE SEA	PHIL	(DECK LOSS-TYPHOON)	
12/18/44	71795	UNASSIGNED	USS CAPE ESPERAN.	PHILIPPINE SEA	PHIL	(DECK LOSS-TYPHOON)	
12/18/44	71823	UNASSIGNED	USS ALTAMAHA	PHILIPPINE SEA	PHIL	(DECK LOSS-TYPHOON)	
12/18/44	71824	UNASSIGNED	USS CAPE ESPERAN.	PHILIPPINE SEA	PHIL	(DECK LOSS-TYPHOON)	
12/18/44	71826	UNASSIGNED	USS ALTAMAHA	PHILIPPINE SEA	PHIL	(DECK LOSS-TYPHOON)	
12/18/44	71830	UNASSIGNED	USS ALTAMAHA	PHILIPPINE SEA	PHIL	(DECK LOSS-TYPHOON)	
12/18/44	71831	UNASSIGNED	USS CAPE ESPERAN.	PHILIPPINE SEA	PHIL	(DECK LOSS-TYPHOON)	
12/18/44	71839	UNASSIGNED	USS CAPE ESPERAN.	PHILIPPINE SEA	PHIL	(DECK LOSS-TYPHOON)	
12/18/44	71840	UNASSIGNED	USS ALTAMAHA	PHILIPPINE SEA	PHIL	(DECK LOSS-TYPHOON)	
12/18/44	71852	UNASSIGNED	USS ALTAMAHA	PHILIPPINE SEA	PHIL	(DECK LOSS-TYPHOON)	
12/18/44	71865	UNASSIGNED	USS ALTAMAHA	PHILIPPINE SEA	PHIL	(DECK LOSS-TYPHOON)	
12/18/44	71869	UNASSIGNED	USS ALTAMAHA	PHILIPPINE SEA	PHIL	(DECK LOSS-TYPHOON)	
12/18/44	71874	UNASSIGNED	USS ALTAMAHA	PHILIPPINE SEA	PHIL	(DECK LOSS-TYPHOON)	
12/18/44	71875	UNASSIGNED	USS ALTAMAHA	PHILIPPINE SEA	PHIL	(DECK LOSS-TYPHOON)	
12/18/44	71883	UNASSIGNED	USS ALTAMAHA	PHILIPPINE SEA	PHIL	(DECK LOSS-TYPHOON)	
12/18/44	71886	UNASSIGNED	USS ALTAMAHA	PHILIPPINE SEA	PHIL	(DECK LOSS-TYPHOON)	
12/18/44	71898	UNASSIGNED	USS ALTAMAHA	PHILIPPINE SEA	PHIL	(DECK LOSS-TYPHOON)	
12/18/44	71930	UNASSIGNED	USS ALTAMAHA	PHILIPPINE SEA	PHIL	(DECK LOSS-TYPHOON)	
12/18/44	71933	UNASSIGNED	USS ALTAMAHA	PHILIPPINE SEA	PHIL	(DECK LOSS-TYPHOON)	
12/18/44	71942	UNASSIGNED	USS ALTAMAHA	PHILIPPINE SEA	PHIL	(DECK LOSS-TYPHOON)	
12/18/44	71975	UNASSIGNED	USS ALTAMAHA	PHILIPPINE SEA	PHIL	(DECK LOSS-TYPHOON)	
12/18/44	58262	VF-22	USS COWPENS	LUZON	PHIL	(DECK LOSS-TYPHOON)	

DATE	BUNO	SQDRN	BASE	LOST	AREA	PILOT	FATE
12/18/44	58887	VF-22	USS COWPENS	LUZON	PHIL	(DECK LOSS-TYPHOON)	
12/18/44	70087	VF-22	USS COWPENS	LUZON	PHIL	(DECK LOSS-TYPHOON)	
12/18/44	70131	VF-22	USS COWPENS	LUZON	PHIL	(DECK LOSS-TYPHOON)	
12/18/44	70961	VF-22	USS COWPENS	LUZON	PHIL	(DECK LOSS-TYPHOON)	
12/18/44	58633	VF-28	USS MONTEREY	PHILIPPINE SEA	PHIL	(DECK LOSS-TYPHOON)	
12/18/44	58934	VF-28	USS MONTEREY	PHILIPPINE SEA	PHIL	(DECK LOSS-TYPHOON)	
12/18/44	58966	VF-28	USS MONTEREY	PHILIPPINE SEA	PHIL	(DECK LOSS-TYPHOON)	
12/18/44	70070	VF-28	USS MONTEREY	PHILIPPINE SEA	PHIL	(DECK LOSS-TYPHOON)	
12/18/44	70075	VF-28	USS MONTEREY	PHILIPPINE SEA	PHIL	(DECK LOSS-TYPHOON)	
12/18/44	70102	VF-28	USS MONTEREY	PHILIPPINE SEA	PHIL	(DECK LOSS-TYPHOON)	
12/18/44	70149	VF-28	USS MONTEREY	PHILIPPINE SEA	PHIL	(DECK LOSS-TYPHOON)	
12/18/44	70290	VF-28	USS MONTEREY	PHILIPPINE SEA	PHIL	(DECK LOSS-TYPHOON)	
12/18/44	70372	VF-28	USS MONTEREY	PHILIPPINE SEA	PHIL	(DECK LOSS-TYPHOON)	
12/18/44	70613	VF-28	USS MONTEREY	PHILIPPINE SEA	PHIL	(DECK LOSS-TYPHOON)	
12/18/44	70657	VF-28	USS MONTEREY	PHILIPPINE SEA	PHIL	(DECK LOSS-TYPHOON)	
12/18/44	70817	VF-28	USS MONTEREY	PHILIPPINE SEA	PHIL	(DECK LOSS-TYPHOON)	
12/18/44	71059	VF-28	USS MONTEREY	PHILIPPINE SEA	PHIL	(DECK LOSS-TYPHOON)	
12/18/44	58517	VF-45	USS SAN JACINTO	PHILIPPINE SEA	PHIL	(DECK LOSS-TYPHOON)	
12/19/44	58655	VF-4	USS ESSEX	LUZON	PHIL	(DECK LOSS-TYPHOON)	
12/19/44	70150	VF-81	USS WASP	LEYTE GULF	PHIL		
12/19/44	71365	VF-87	USS RANDOLPH	PANAMA	CENLANT	ENS JEAN T. PROVOST	S
12/20/44	71947	VF-44	USS LANGLEY	ENR FORMOSA	PHIL	ENS DONALD W. HEDGES	S
12/21/44	70572		PEARL	HAWAII	ECENPAC		
12/21/44	71366		PEARL	HAWAII	ECENPAC		
12/21/44	58204	VF-20	USS LEX-INGTON	LUZON	PHIL		
12/21/44	71384	VF-20	USS LEX-INGTON	LUZON	PHIL		
12/21/44	70623	VF-29	USS CABOT	FORMOSA	EMPIRE	ENS ROBERT B. WILLIAMS	S
12/22/44	58986	VF-11	USS HORNET		WCENPAC		
12/23/44	71058	VF-7	USS HANCOCK	ENR ULITHI	WCENPAC		
12/25/44	58478	VF-29	USS CABOT	NANSEI SHOTO	EMPIRE		
12/25/44	71349	VF-87	USS RANDOLPH	HAWAII	ECENPAC	ENS JAMES D. SMITH	S
12/29/44	71044	VF-7	USS HANCOCK	ULITHI	WCENPAC		
12/30/44	58108	COMAIR-PAC	PEARL	HAWAII	ECENPAC		
12/30/44	72378	VF-22	USS COWPENS	LINGAYEN GULF	PHIL		
12/30/44	58838	VF-7	USS HANCOCK	ULITHI	WCENPAC		
12/30/44	70433	VF-7	USS HANCOCK	ULITHI	WCENPAC		
12/31/44	58653		PEARL	HAWAII	ECENPAC		
12/31/44	58668		PEARL	HAWAII	ECENPAC		
12/31/44	70578		PEARL	HAWAII	ECENPAC		
01/01/45	58480	COMAIR-PAC	PEARL	HAWAII	ECENPAC		
01/01/45	70462	VF-20	USS LEX-INGTON	LUZON	PHIL		

DATE	BUNO	SQDRN	BASE	LOST	AREA	PILOT	FATE
01/01/45	72093	VF-23		PONAM	SW PAC	ENS THOMAS F. TORPEY, JR.	D
01/01/45	70103	VF-7	USS HANCOCK	FORMOSA	EMPIRE		
01/03/45	72072	VF-22	USS COWPENS	FORMOSA	EMPIRE		
01/03/45	70040	VF-3	USS YORK-TOWN	FORMOSA	EMPIRE	LT EDWARD GAGE	M
01/03/45	71908	VF-3	USS YORK-TOWN	FORMOSA	EMPIRE	LT W.T. MCNEIL	M
01/03/45	70938	VF-4	USS ESSEX	OKINAWA	EMPIRE	LT HUBERT T. HOUSTON	M
01/03/45	71929	VF-4	USS ESSEX	OKINAWA	EMPIRE		
01/03/45	58935	VF-7	USS HANCOCK	FORMOSA	EMPIRE	LTJG H.R. AUSTIN	M
01/03/45	58969	VF-7	USS HANCOCK	FORMOSA	EMPIRE		
01/03/45	70357	VF-7	USS HANCOCK	FORMOSA	EMPIRE	ENS E.A. TURNER	M
01/03/45	70443	VF-7	USS HANCOCK	FORMOSA	EMPIRE	ENS C.D. SIGENTHALER	D
01/03/45	70560	VF-7	USS HANCOCK	FORMOSA	EMPIRE		
01/03/45	71065	VF-80	USS TICONDER-OGA	FORMOSA	EMPIRE	ENS P.J. MANELLA	M
01/03/45	70532	VF-81	USS WASP	FORMOSA	EMPIRE	LT CHARLES P. REEKS, JR.	M
01/03/45	70595	VF-81	USS WASP	FORMOSA	EMPIRE	LTJG MARION E. WINTER	M
01/04/45	70514	VF-11	USS HORNET	FORMOSA	EMPIRE		
01/04/45	71095	VF-3	USS YORK-TOWN	FORMOSA	EMPIRE	LTJG LEO J. RILEY	S
01/04/45	71014	VF-4	USS ESSEX	OKINAWA	EMPIRE		
01/04/45	58684	VF-44	USS LANGLEY	FORMOSA	EMPIRE	LT L.E. GUY	M
01/04/45	71441	VF-44	USS LANGLEY	FORMOSA	EMPIRE	LT CHARLES V. AUGUST	M
01/04/45	71381	VF-7	USS HANCOCK	FORMOSA	EMPIRE	LTJG F.D. HEACOX	S
01/04/45	72339	VF-7	USS HANCOCK	FORMOSA	EMPIRE	LCDR L.J. CHECK	M
01/06/45	71258	VF(N)-41	USS INDEPEN-DENCE	LUZON	PHIL	ENS EMMETT R. EDWARDS	M
01/06/45	71060	VF-20	USS LEX-INGTON	LUZON	PHIL	ENS W.W. ALLEN	S
01/06/45	72568	VF-22	USS COWPENS	E. OF LUZON	PHIL	ENS GORDON CUMMIN	D
01/06/45	71430	VF-4	USS ESSEX	LUZON	PHIL	LCDR KEENEG KAMMOND	D
01/06/45	72044	VF-45	USS SAN JACINTO	LUZON	PHIL		
01/06/45	72198	VF-45	USS SAN JACINTO	LUZON	PHIL		
01/06/45	59025	VF-81	USS WASP	LUZON	PHIL	ENS ALLEN J. STORER	M
01/06/45	70606	VF-81	USS WASP	LUZON	PHIL	LT DONALD M. BUENSIDE	M
01/06/45	70773	VF-81	USS WASP	LUZON	PHIL		
01/06/45	71364	VF-81	USS WASP	LUZON	PHIL		
01/06/45	71805	VF-81	USS WASP	LUZON	PHIL	LTJG WILLIAM L. TRAYLOR	M
01/06/45	71990	VF-81	USS WASP	LUZON	PHIL	LT I.P. COLLIER	S
01/07/45	58594	VF-11	USS HORNET	FORMOSA	EMPIRE	ENS HAYTER	S
01/07/45	71904	VF-11	USS HORNET	FORMOSA	EMPIRE	ENS J.H. BETHEL, JR.	M
01/07/45	71949	VF-11	USS HORNET	FORMOSA	EMPIRE	LTJG J.P. SIMS	M
01/07/45	70527	VF-20	USS LEX-INGTON	LUZON	PHIL	LTJG DANIEL J. RYAN	M
01/07/45	71464	VF-20	USS LEX-INGTON	LUZON	PHIL		

DATE	BUNO	SQDRN	BASE	LOST	AREA	PILOT	FATE
01/07/45	71563	VF-20	USS LEXINGTON	LUZON	PHIL		
01/07/45	71897	VF-20	USS LEXINGTON	LUZON	PHIL		
01/07/45	70880	VF-22	USS COWPENS	E. OF LUZON	PHIL		
01/07/45	72391	VF-22	USS COWPENS	E. OF LUZON	PHIL	ENS CHARLES H. NORTON	D
01/07/45	70117	VF-3	USS YORKTOWN	MANILA	PHIL	ENS ARTHUR G. BRASS	M
01/07/45	70123	VF-4	USS ESSEX	LUZON	PHIL		
01/07/45	58583	VF-7	USS HANCOCK	LUZON	PHIL		
01/07/45	70300	VF-7	USS HANCOCK	LUZON	PHIL	LTJG A.C. WOCHOMURKA	M
01/07/45	71977	VF-7	USS HANCOCK	LUZON	PHIL		
01/07/45	58323	VF-80	USS TICONDEROGA	FORMOSA	EMPIRE	LTJG R.C. WAGG	M
01/07/45	71465	VF-80	USS TICONDEROGA	FORMOSA	EMPIRE	ENS J.G. COZZA	M
01/08/45	72030	VF-45	USS SAN JACINTO	FORMOSA	EMPIRE		
01/09/45	72445	VF-22	USS COWPENS	LINGAYEN GULF	PHIL	LT O.A. HIGGINS	M
01/09/45	71835	VF-7	USS HANCOCK	FORMOSA	EMPIRE		
01/09/45	58187	VF-80	USS TICONDEROGA	FORMOSA	EMPIRE		
01/09/45	58316	VF-80	USS TICONDEROGA	FORMOSA	EMPIRE		
01/09/45	58338	VF-80	USS TICONDEROGA	FORMOSA	EMPIRE		
01/09/45	70627	VF-80	USS TICONDEROGA	FORMOSA	EMPIRE		
01/10/45	58071	CASU-43		GUAM	WCENPAC		
01/10/45	70168	CASU-43		GUAM	WCENPAC		
01/10/45	70342	CASU-43		GUAM	WCENPAC		
01/10/45	72057	VF-22	USS COWPENS	LINGAYEN GULF	PHIL		
01/10/45	58079	VF-80	USS TICONDEROGA	FORMOSA	EMPIRE	ENS G.M. MCGEHEE	D
01/10/45	58350	VF-80	USS TICONDEROGA	FORMOSA	EMPIRE		
01/11/45	72380	VF-45	USS SAN JACINTO	FORMOSA	EMPIRE		
01/11/45	58555	VF-86		HAWAII	ECENPAC	ENS R.W. CURNAYN	S
01/12/45	70680	VF-11	USS HORNET	FR. I.C.	PHIL	LTJG HOR. D. MORANVILLE	D
01/12/45	71043	VF-11	USS HORNET	FR. I.C.	PHIL		
01/12/45	58062	VF-20	USS LEXINGTON	FR. I.C.	PHIL	ENS M.D. ALLEN	M
01/12/45	58938	VF-20	USS LEXINGTON	FR. I.C.	PHIL	ENS G.E. GORDON	D
01/12/45	71948	VF-20	USS LEXINGTON	FR. I.C.	PHIL	LTJG GALLAGHER	S
01/12/45	71502	VF-22	USS COWPENS	FR. I.C.	PHIL		
01/12/45	71324	VF-4	USS ESSEX	FR. I.C.	PHIL	LT J.G. MCREYNOLDS	S
01/12/45	70045	VF-44	USS LANGLEY	FR. I.C.	PHIL	ENS G.H. BOWSER	D
01/12/45	58843	VF-7	USS HANCOCK	FR. I.C.	PHIL	LTJG W.B. BAHR	M
01/12/45	70105	VF-7	USS HANCOCK	FR. I.C.	PHIL	LT G.M. SULLIVAN	M

DATE	BUNO	SQDRN	BASE	LOST	AREA	PILOT	FATE
01/12/45	70349	VF-7	USS HANCOCK	FR. I.C.	PHIL	LTJG E.A. STRATTON	M
01/13/45	70079	VF-81	USS WASP	FORMOSA	EMPIRE		
01/13/45	70564	VF-81	USS WASP	FORMOSA	EMPIRE		
01/14/45	58847			GUAM	WCENPAC		
01/14/45	70419			GUAM	WCENPAC		
01/14/45	70577			GUAM	WCENPAC		
01/14/45	71132			GUAM	WCENPAC		
01/15/45	58495	VBF-9		ADMIRALTIES	SW PAC	ENS CHARLES G. SPEIGHT	S
01/15/45	72325	VF-4	USS ESSEX	FORMOSA	EMPIRE	CDR GEORGE O. KLINSMANN	D
01/15/45	58273	VF-80	USS TICONDER-OGA	FORMOSA	EMPIRE		
01/15/45	71813	VF-80	USS TICONDER-OGA	FORMOSA	EMPIRE	LCDR A.D. VORSE	S
01/15/45	58041	VF-81	USS WASP	FORMOSA	EMPIRE	LTJG JOHN C. MCNIECE	S
01/15/45	71393	VF-81	USS WASP	FORMOSA	EMPIRE	LT HALLEY D. SELLERS	M
01/15/45	72385	VF-81	USS WASP	FORMOSA	EMPIRE		
01/16/45	58925	VBF-7	USS HANCOCK	HONG KONG	EMPIRE	LTJG R.A. KINSELLA	M
01/16/45	71843	VBF-7	USS HANCOCK	HONG KONG	EMPIRE	LTJG H.D. MAXWELL	M
01/16/45	71782	VF(N)-41	USS INDEPEN-DENCE	FORMOSA	EMPIRE		
01/16/45	70561	VF-11	USS HORNET	HONG KONG	EMPIRE	ENS R.E. WILSON	M
01/16/45	71082	VF-11	USS HORNET	HONG KONG	EMPIRE	ENS M.J. CREHAN	M
01/16/45	70524	VF-20	USS LEX-INGTON	HAINAN	EMPIRE	ENS R.W. BERTSCHI	S
01/16/45	58844	VF-4	USS ESSEX	HAINAN	EMPIRE		
01/16/45	58394	VF-45	USS SAN JACINTO	FORMOSA	EMPIRE		
01/16/45	71504	VF-45	USS SAN JACINTO	FORMOSA	EMPIRE		
01/16/45	71520	VF-45	USS SAN JACINTO	FORMOSA	EMPIRE		
01/16/45	71994	VF-45	USS SAN JACINTO	FORMOSA	EMPIRE		
01/16/45	72211	VF-45	USS SAN JACINTO	FORMOSA	EMPIRE		
01/16/45	72214	VF-45	USS SAN JACINTO	FORMOSA	EMPIRE		
01/16/45	72232	VF-45	USS SAN JACINTO	FORMOSA	EMPIRE		
01/16/45	72366	VF-45	USS SAN JACINTO	FORMOSA	EMPIRE		
01/16/45	72395	VF-45	USS SAN JACINTO	FORMOSA	EMPIRE		
01/16/45	72403	VF-45	USS SAN JACINTO	FORMOSA	EMPIRE		
01/16/45	71513	VF-81	USS WASP	HONG KONG	EMPIRE	LTJG ALBERT BASMAJRAN	M
01/16/45	71858	VF-81	USS WASP	HONG KONG	EMPIRE	LTJG SHORRILL	S
01/16/45	70355	VF-82	USS BENNING-TON	PEARL	ECENPAC	ENS F.M. HOWELL	S
01/17/45	71020	VF-20	USS LEX-INGTON	HONG KONG	EMPIRE		
01/17/45	71478	VF-20	USS LEX-INGTON	HONG KONG	EMPIRE		
01/17/45	70459	VF-4	USS ESSEX	HAINAN	EMPIRE		
01/17/45	72207	VF-45	USS SAN JACINTO	FORMOSA	EMPIRE		
01/17/45	71450	VF-80	USS TICONDER-OGA	HAINAN	EMPIRE		
01/18/45	72105	VF-20	USS LEX-INGTON	ENR FORMOSA	CENPAC		
01/18/45	58984	VF-3	USS YORK-TOWN	HONG KONG	EMPIRE	LT W.B. MCELROY	S

DATE	BUNO	SQDRN	BASE	LOST	AREA	PILOT	FATE
01/18/45	58995	VF-81	USS WASP	ENR FORMOSA	EMPIRE		
01/20/45	58591	VF-100	BARBERS POINT	HAWAII	ECENPAC	ENS ELEAZER C. OVERTON	S
01/20/45	58593	VF-3	USS YORK-TOWN	ENR FORMOSA	EMPIRE	ENS HOWARD PARKER, JR.	D
01/21/45	70388	VF-20	USS LEX-INGTON	FORMOSA	EMPIRE	LTJG M.D. COOLEY	S
01/21/45	71091	VF-20	USS LEX-INGTON	FORMOSA	EMPIRE		
01/21/45	58666	VF-22	USS COWPENS	FORMOSA	EMPIRE	ENS C.M. PETRIE	S
01/21/45	72320	VF-22	USS COWPENS	FORMOSA	EMPIRE		
01/21/45	58947	VF-3	USS YORK-TOWN	FORMOSA	EMPIRE		
01/21/45	71068	VF-3	USS YORK-TOWN	FORMOSA	EMPIRE	LT SAMUEL SOLBERGER	S
01/21/45	71842	VF-3	USS YORK-TOWN	FORMOSA	EMPIRE	ENS NICHOLS	M
01/21/45	71471	VF-4	USS ESSEX	FORMOSA	EMPIRE	LTJG ROBERT W. GINTHER	D
01/21/45	71593	VF-4	USS ESSEX	FORMOSA	EMPIRE	LT W.P. BLACKWELL	S
01/21/45	58962	VF-7	USS HANCOCK	FORMOSA	EMPIRE		
01/21/45	70395	VF-7	USS HANCOCK	FORMOSA	EMPIRE		
01/21/45	70441	VF-7	USS HANCOCK	FORMOSA	EMPIRE		
01/21/45	71913	VF-7	USS HANCOCK	FORMOSA	EMPIRE		
01/21/45	72083	VF-7	USS HANCOCK	FORMOSA	EMPIRE		
01/21/45	58340	VF-80	USS TICONDER-OGA	FORMOSA	EMPIRE		
01/21/45	58356	VF-80	USS TICONDER-OGA	FORMOSA	EMPIRE		
01/21/45	58564	VF-80	USS TICONDER-OGA	FORMOSA	EMPIRE		
01/21/45	58589	VF-80	USS TICONDER-OGA	FORMOSA	EMPIRE		
01/21/45	58614	VF-80	USS TICONDER-OGA	FORMOSA	EMPIRE		
01/21/45	58890	VF-80	USS TICONDER-OGA	FORMOSA	EMPIRE		
01/21/45	70089	VF-80	USS TICONDER-OGA	FORMOSA	EMPIRE		
01/21/45	70158	VF-80	USS TICONDER-OGA	FORMOSA	EMPIRE		
01/21/45	70167	VF-80	USS TICONDER-OGA	FORMOSA	EMPIRE		
01/21/45	70183	VF-80	USS TICONDER-OGA	FORMOSA	EMPIRE		
01/21/45	70336	VF-80	USS TICONDER-OGA	FORMOSA	EMPIRE		
01/21/45	70359	VF-80	USS TICONDER-OGA	FORMOSA	EMPIRE		
01/21/45	70361	VF-80	USS TICONDER-OGA	FORMOSA	EMPIRE		
01/21/45	70408	VF-80	USS TICONDER-OGA	FORMOSA	EMPIRE		

DATE	BUNO	SQDRN	BASE	LOST	AREA	PILOT	FATE
01/21/45	70460	VF-80	USS TICONDER-OGA	FORMOSA	EMPIRE		
01/21/45	70526	VF-80	USS TICONDER-OGA	FORMOSA	EMPIRE		
01/21/45	70545	VF-80	USS TICONDER-OGA	FORMOSA	EMPIRE		
01/21/45	70598	VF-80	USS TICONDER-OGA	FORMOSA	EMPIRE		
01/21/45	70640	VF-80	USS TICONDER-OGA	FORMOSA	EMPIRE		
01/21/45	70876	VF-80	USS TICONDER-OGA	FORMOSA	EMPIRE		
01/21/45	70899	VF-80	USS TICONDER-OGA	FORMOSA	EMPIRE		
01/21/45	70965	VF-80	USS TICONDER-OGA	FORMOSA	EMPIRE		
01/21/45	71378	VF-80	USS TICONDER-OGA	FORMOSA	EMPIRE		
01/21/45	71412	VF-80	USS TICONDER-OGA	FORMOSA	EMPIRE		
01/21/45	71433	VF-80	USS TICONDER-OGA	FORMOSA	EMPIRE		
01/21/45	71486	VF-80	USS TICONDER-OGA	FORMOSA	EMPIRE		
01/21/45	71509	VF-80	USS TICONDER-OGA	FORMOSA	EMPIRE		
01/21/45	71857	VF-80	USS TICONDER-OGA	FORMOSA	EMPIRE		
01/21/45	71901	VF-80	USS TICONDER-OGA	FORMOSA	EMPIRE		
01/21/45	72609	VF-80	USS TICONDER-OGA	FORMOSA	EMPIRE		
01/21/45	70406	VF-81	USS WASP	FORMOSA	EMPIRE		
01/21/45	70878	VF-83		HAWAII	ECENPAC	ENS W.J. KINGSTON, JR.	S
01/21/45	70583	VF-86	USS BATAAN	HAWAII	ECENPAC	ENS A.K. HARRIS	S
01/22/45			PEARL	HAWAII	ECENPAC		
01/22/45	58522	VF-3	USS YORK-TOWN	OKINAWA	EMPIRE		
01/22/45	70347	VF-3	USS YORK-TOWN	OKINAWA	EMPIRE	LCDR W.L. LAMBERSON	M
01/22/45	71046	VF-3	USS YORK-TOWN	OKINAWA	EMPIRE	ENS AYDELOTT	S
01/22/45	71383	VF-4	USS ESSEX	FORMOSA	EMPIRE	LTJG CLAYTON RHODES	S
01/22/45	71885	VF-44	USS LANGLEY	OKINAWA	EMPIRE	LT EDWIN H. SEILER	D
01/22/45	70098	VF-81	USS WASP	NAHA	EMPIRE		
01/22/45	70916	VF-81	USS WASP	NAHA	EMPIRE	ENS NORMAN P. STARK, JR.	S
01/22/45	71439	VF-81	USS WASP	NAHA	EMPIRE		
01/22/45	71582	VF-81	USS WASP	NAHA	EMPIRE		
01/22/45	71731	VF-81	USS WASP	NAHA	EMPIRE	LTJG JAMES H. BABCOCK	M
01/22/45	72482	VF-81	USS WASP	NAHA	EMPIRE		
01/25/45	58558	VF-29	USS CABOT		EMPIRE		
01/26/45	72626	VF-16		TRINIDAD	CENLANT	LT BYRON T. MENNIS	S
01/30/45	72690	CASU(F)-43		GUAM	WCENPAC		

DATE	BUNO	SQDRN	BASE	LOST	AREA	PILOT	FATE
01/31/45	58621	CASU(F)-51		ULITHI	WCENPAC		
01/31/45	58914	CASU(F)-51		ULITHI	WCENPAC		
01/31/45	71791	CASU(F)-51		ULITHI	WCENPAC		
01/31/45	72300	CASU(F)-51		ULITHI	WCENPAC		
01/31/45	41047	COMAIR-PAC	PEARL	HAWAII	ECENPAC		
01/31/45	58492	COMAIR-PAC	PEARL	HAWAII	ECENPAC		
01/31/45	71134	COMAIR-PAC	PEARL	HAWAII	ECENPAC		
01/31/45	71556	COMAIR-PAC	PEARL	HAWAII	ECENPAC		
01/31/45	71836	COMAIR-PAC	PEARL	HAWAII	ECENPAC		
01/31/45	71863	COMAIR-PAC	PEARL	HAWAII	ECENPAC		
01/31/45	71873	COMAIR-PAC	PEARL	HAWAII	ECENPAC		
01/31/45	58523	VF-100	BARBERS POINT	HAWAII	ECENPAC	ENS CLARENCE A. BARNETT	S
01/31/45	72318	VF-12	USS RANDOLPH	ENR ULITHI	WCENPAC	ENS STANLEY H. DAVIDSON	S
02/01/45	71385	VF-86		HAWAII	ECENPAC	ENS R.E. BOUCHET	S
02/02/45	71332	POOL		ADMIRALTIES	SW PAC		
02/02/45	71284	VF-100	BARBERS POINT	HAWAII	ECENPAC	LTJG JOHN RICH. SIMPSON	S
02/03/45	70327	COMAIR-PAC	PEARL	HAWAII	ECENPAC		
02/03/45	71953	COMAIR-PAC	PEARL	HAWAII	ECENPAC		
02/03/45	58198	VF-80	USS HANCOCK		WCENPAC		
02/04/45	58825	VF(N)-41	USS INDEPEN-DENCE	FORMOSA	EMPIRE	LT ERWIN W. BECKEE	S
02/04/45	70326	VF(N)-41	USS INDEPEN-DENCE	FORMOSA	EMPIRE	LTJG JAMES A. BARNETT	S
02/04/45	58511	VF-17	USS HORNET	ULITHI	WCENPAC		
02/04/45	71728	VF-80	USS HANCOCK		WCENPAC		
02/04/45	71940	VF-82	USS BENNING-TON	ENR ULITHI	WCENPAC	LT B.F. LINEHOUSE, JR.	S
02/05/45	72348	VF-12	USS RANDOLPH	ENR ULITHI	WCENPAC	LCDR F.H. MICHAELS	S
02/05/45	58423	VF-17	USS HORNET	ULITHI	WCENPAC		
02/05/45	58681	VF-17	USS HORNET	ULITHI	WCENPAC		
02/05/45	77452	VF-24	USS SANTEE	HAWAII	ECENPAC	ENS WILLIAM H. PRITCHARD	S
02/06/45	72815	VF-30	USS BELLEAU WOOD	ULITHI	WCENPAC		
02/06/45	71988	VF-81	USS WASP	IWO JIMA	EMPIRE		
02/07/45	77457	VF-24	USS SANTEE	HAWAII	ECENPAC	ENS WILLIAM A. SINNOTT	S
02/08/45	58257	COMAIR-PAC	PEARL	HAWAII	ECENPAC		
02/08/45	70195	VF-100	BARBERS POINT	HAWAII	ECENPAC	ENS TOM WINN, JR.	D
02/08/45	72600	VF-46	USS COWPENS	ENR ULITHI	WCENPAC		
02/09/45	58402	VF-6	PEARL	HAWAII	ECENPAC	LTJG JAMES W. DRIVER	S
02/10/45	58944	CASU(F)-43		GUAM	WCENPAC		
02/10/45	70154	CASU(F)-43		GUAM	WCENPAC		
02/10/45	58191	COMAIR-PAC	PEARL	HAWAII	ECENPAC		
02/10/45	72314	VBF-12	USS RANDOLPH	ULITHI	WCENPAC		
02/10/45	77437	VF-25	USS CHENAN-GO	HAWAII	ECENPAC	LTJG ROBERT E. OLSON	S

DATE	BUNO	SQDRN	BASE	LOST	AREA	PILOT	FATE
02/10/45	71626	VF-45	USS SAN JACINTO	ENR TOKYO	EMPIRE		
02/10/45	72915	VF-53	USS SARATOGA	ENR TINIAN	WCENPAC		
02/10/45	71808	VF-83		HAWAII	ECENPAC	ENS H.D. HABENIGHT	D
02/11/45	70302	VBF-9	USS LEX-INGTON	ENR TOKYO	EMPIRE		
02/11/45	70844	VF-28	USS LANGLEY	IWO JIMA	EMPIRE	LTJG CALEGERO S. PUPILLO	D
02/11/45	71011	VF-29	USS CABOT	TOKYO	EMPIRE		
02/11/45	72492	VF-29	USS CABOT	TOKYO	EMPIRE	LTJG JAMES B. VAN FLEET	S
02/11/45	72638	VF-30	USS BELLEAU WOOD	HONSHU	EMPIRE		
02/11/45	72749	VF-30	USS BELLEAU WOOD	HONSHU	EMPIRE		
02/11/45	72958	VF-30	USS BELLEAU WOOD	HONSHU	EMPIRE	ENS KEITH W. CURRY	S
02/11/45	71162	VF-46	USS COWPENS	ENR ULITHI	WCENPAC		
02/11/45	71924	VF-46	USS COWPENS	ENR ULITHI	WCENPAC		
02/11/45	72014	VF-82	USS BENNING-TON	ENR ULITHI	WCENPAC		
02/12/45	58551	VBF-3	USS YORK-TOWN	ENR TOKYO	EMPIRE	LT MARSHALL S. CREEL	D
02/12/45	58833	VBF-3	USS YORK-TOWN	ENR TOKYO	EMPIRE	LTJG NORMAN J. SCHMITZ	D
02/12/45	72042	VF(N)-53	USS SARATOGA	TINIAN	WCENPAC		
02/12/45	71118	VF(N)-90	USS ENTER-PRISE	ENR TOKYO	WCENPAC		
02/12/45	71720	VF-45	USS SAN JACINTO	ENR TOKYO	EMPIRE		
02/12/45	72216	VF-81	USS WASP	ENR TOKYO	EMPIRE		
02/13/45	58427		USS NEHENTA BAY	HAWAII	ECENPAC		
02/13/45	71905	COMAIR-PAC	PEARL	HAWAII	ECENPAC		
02/13/45	72553	VF-24	USS SANTEE	HAWAII	ECENPAC	ENS ALVIN GORDON COOPER	S
02/13/45	71864	VF-83		HAWAII	ECENPAC	ENS P.D. DAVIDSON	S
02/14/45	72923	VF-45	USS SAN JACINTO	ENR TOKYO	EMPIRE		
02/14/45	58595	VF-46	USS COWPENS	ENR ULITHI	EMPIRE		
02/14/45	72040	VF-46	USS COWPENS	ENR ULITHI	EMPIRE		
02/14/45	70820	VF-80	USS HANCOCK	IWO JIMA	EMPIRE	LTJG K.A. BAKER	M
02/16/45	71794	VBF-12	USS RANDOLPH	TOKYO	EMPIRE	LT SAPE LEGATOS	M
02/16/45	72363	VBF-12	USS RANDOLPH	TOKYO	EMPIRE	LT BLEEKER P. SEAMAN, JR.	M
02/16/45	58841	VBF-17	USS HORNET	TOKYO	EMPIRE	LTJG MONTE D. HAROUFF	S
02/16/45	70980	VBF-17	USS HORNET	TOKYO	EMPIRE	ENS GEORGE SALVAGGIO	S
02/16/45	58942	VBF-9	USS LEX-INGTON	TOKYO	EMPIRE	ENS FLOYD E. TURNER	M
02/16/45	72279	VF(N)-53	USS SARATOGA	TOKYO	EMPIRE		
02/16/45	72417	VF-12	USS RANDOLPH	TOKYO	EMPIRE	ENS W.H. ROSSER	S
02/16/45	70592	VF-17	USS HORNET	TOKYO	EMPIRE	LTJG J.P. FARRELL	S
02/16/45	71438	VF-17	USS HORNET	TOKYO	EMPIRE	ENS R.F. CUNNINGHAM	S

DATE	BUNO	SQDRN	BASE	LOST	AREA	PILOT	FATE
02/16/45	70917	VF-3	USS YORK-TOWN	TOKYO	EMPIRE	ENS J.T. GRAHAM	S
02/16/45	71031	VF-45	USS SAN JACINTO	TOKYO	EMPIRE	ENS J.E. HOOD	D
02/16/45	71549	VF-46	USS COWPENS	TOKYO	EMPIRE	ENS O.H. CLARK	M
02/16/45	70962	VF-80	USS HANCOCK	IWO JIMA	EMPIRE	LTJG J.N. MOLITER	M
02/16/45	72354	VF-80	USS HANCOCK	IWO JIMA	EMPIRE	ENS R.E. MAYNARD	M
02/16/45	72710	VF-80	USS HANCOCK	IWO JIMA	EMPIRE	ENS W.O. THOMAS	M
02/16/45	72234	VF-81	USS WASP	TOKYO	EMPIRE	LT J.F. BAUMAN	M
02/16/45	72412	VF-81	USS WASP	TOKYO	EMPIRE	ENS J.T. STANLEY	M
02/16/45	72421	VF-81	USS WASP	TOKYO	EMPIRE	LT J.W.B. GAGE	M
02/16/45	71351	VF-82	USS BENNING-TON	HONSHU	EMPIRE	LT J.F. CARROLL	M
02/16/45	71890	VF-82	USS BENNING-TON	HONSHU	EMPIRE	LT B.A. INGRAHAM	M
02/16/45	71960	VF-82	USS BENNING-TON	HONSHU	EMPIRE	ENS P.K. SPRADLING	M
02/16/45	71978	VF-82	USS BENNING-TON	HONSHU	EMPIRE	ENS J.A. MCCANN	M
02/16/45	71998	VF-82	USS BENNING-TON	HONSHU	EMPIRE	LT D.O. PUCKETT, JR.	M
02/16/45	72008	VF-82	USS BENNING-TON	HONSHU	EMPIRE	LT B.B. GEAR	S
02/16/45	70841	VF-9	USS LEX-INGTON	TOKYO	EMPIRE	LTJG ROBERT L. PARKER	M
02/16/45	71397	VF-9	USS LEX-INGTON	TOKYO	EMPIRE	LT WILLIAM M. KILKENO	D
02/16/45	71445	VF-9	USS LEX-INGTON	TOKYO	EMPIRE	CDR PHILIP H. TORREY, JR.	M
02/17/45	71866	COMAIR-PAC	PEARL	HAWAII	ECENPAC		
02/17/45	72293	VBF-12	USS RANDOLPH	TOKYO	EMPIRE	ENS T. MCADAMS	M
02/17/45	72635	VBF-12	USS RANDOLPH	TOKYO	EMPIRE	ENS W.N. MCCONNELL	M
02/17/45	72499	VBF-17	USS HORNET	TOKYO	EMPIRE		
02/17/45	71297	VF-100	BARBERS POINT	HAWAII	ECENPAC		
02/17/45	72296	VF-12	USS RANDOLPH	TOKYO	EMPIRE	LT L.A. MENARD	M
02/17/45	72411	VF-12	USS RANDOLPH	TOKYO	EMPIRE	LT J.E. TOLLIVER	M
02/17/45	70839	VF-17	USS HORNET	TOKYO	EMPIRE	LTJG E.G. FETZER	M
02/17/45	70875	VF-17	USS HORNET	TOKYO	EMPIRE		
02/17/45	58909	VF-23	USS LANGLEY	IWO JIMA	EMPIRE	ENS KARL T. SMITH	S
02/17/45	71522	VF-23	USS LANGLEY	IWO JIMA	EMPIRE	LCDR DONALD W. WHITE	M
02/17/45	70515	VF-29	USS CABOT	TOKYO	EMPIRE	ENS ROBERT L. BUCHANAN	S
02/17/45	71610	VF-3	USS YORK-TOWN	BONINS	CENPAC	ENS F.C. ONION, JR.	S
02/17/45	71387	VF-4	USS ESSEX	TOKYO	EMPIRE	ENS C.E. GUSTAFSON	S
02/17/45	71446	VF-46	USS COWPENS	TOKYO	EMPIRE	LTJG D.K. BRIGHT	M
02/17/45	58197	VF-81	USS WASP	TOKYO	EMPIRE	ENS CHARLES H. BUTLER	M
02/17/45	71479	VF-81	USS WASP	TOKYO	EMPIRE		
02/17/45	71514	VF-81	USS WASP	TOKYO	EMPIRE	ENS F.H. METZGER	M
02/17/45	58856	VF-9	USS LEX-INGTON	TOKYO	EMPIRE		
02/19/45	58373			GUAM	WCENPAC		

DATE	BUNO	SQDRN	BASE	LOST	AREA	PILOT	FATE
02/19/45	58570			GUAM	WCENPAC		
02/19/45	71730			GUAM	WCENPAC		
02/19/45	58959	VBF-3	USS YORK-TOWN	ENR IWO JIMA	EMPIRE		
02/19/45	71023	VBF-9	USS LEX-INGTON	CHICHI JIMA	CENPAC	ENS WALTER J. SCHISSEUR	M
02/19/45	70779	VF-9	USS LEX-INGTON	CHICHI JIMA	CENPAC		
02/20/45	70988	COMAIR-PAC	PEARL	HAWAII	ECENPAC		
02/20/45	71131	COMAIR-PAC	PEARL	HAWAII	ECENPAC		
02/20/45	71280	COMAIR-PAC	PEARL	HAWAII	ECENPAC		
02/20/45	71987	COMAIR-PAC	PEARL	HAWAII	ECENPAC		
02/20/45	72285	VBF-12	USS RANDOLPH	TOKYO	EMPIRE		
02/21/45	71414	VBF-9	USS LEX-INGTON	IWO JIMA	EMPIRE		
02/21/45	72015	VF-45	USS SAN JACINTO	EMPIRE	ENS M.A. MOSELY	S	
02/21/45	71420	VF-53	USS SARATOGA	TOKYO	EMPIRE		
02/21/45	72699	VF-53	USS SARATOGA	TOKYO	EMPIRE		
02/21/45	72700	VF-53	USS SARATOGA	TOKYO	EMPIRE	ENS C. SZYMBORSKI	S
02/21/45	72724	VF-53	USS SARATOGA	TOKYO	EMPIRE		
02/21/45	72728	VF-53	USS SARATOGA	TOKYO	EMPIRE		
02/21/45	72733	VF-53	USS SARATOGA	TOKYO	EMPIRE	ENS J.P. NELSON	M
02/21/45	72757	VF-53	USS SARATOGA	TOKYO	EMPIRE		
02/21/45	72771	VF-53	USS SARATOGA	TOKYO	EMPIRE		
02/21/45	72773	VF-53	USS SARATOGA	TOKYO	EMPIRE		
02/21/45	72779	VF-53	USS SARATOGA	TOKYO	EMPIRE		
02/21/45	72789	VF-53	USS SARATOGA	TOKYO	EMPIRE		
02/21/45	72871	VF-53	USS SARATOGA	TOKYO	EMPIRE		
02/21/45	72914	VF-53	USS SARATOGA	TOKYO	EMPIRE		
02/21/45	72919	VF-53	USS SARATOGA	TOKYO	EMPIRE		
02/21/45	72936	VF-53	USS SARATOGA	TOKYO	EMPIRE		
02/21/45	72939	VF-53	USS SARATOGA	TOKYO	EMPIRE	ENS L.C. RADFORD	S
02/21/45	72964	VF-53	USS SARATOGA	TOKYO	EMPIRE	LT R.W. LUKE	S
02/21/45	72967	VF-53	USS SARATOGA	TOKYO	EMPIRE		
02/21/45	71632	VF-80	USS HANCOCK	IWO JIMA	EMPIRE		
02/21/45	72413	VF-82	USS BENNING-TON	IWO JIMA	EMPIRE		
02/21/45	72864	VF-9	USS LEX-INGTON	IWO JIMA	EMPIRE		
02/22/45	72110	VBF-12	USS RANDOLPH	TOKYO	EMPIRE		
02/22/45	72276	VBF-12	USS RANDOLPH	TOKYO	EMPIRE		
02/22/45	72843	VBF-12	USS RANDOLPH	TOKYO	EMPIRE		
02/22/45	72401	VF-12	USS RANDOLPH	TOKYO	EMPIRE		
02/22/45	72341	VF-23	USS LANGLEY	IWO JIMA	EMPIRE		

DATE	BUNO	SQDRN	BASE	LOST	AREA	PILOT	FATE
02/22/45	72670	VF-46	USS COWPENS	TOKYO	EMPIRE		
02/23/45	72371		PEARL	HAWAII	ECENPAC		
02/23/45	72890	VF-30	USS BELLEAU WOOD	BONINS	CENPAC	LCDR ROBERT H. LINDNER	M
02/23/45	72303	VF-81	USS WASP	BONINS	CENPAC	LT NORTON W. HURD	S
02/24/45	77393		PEARL	HAWAII	ECENPAC		
02/24/45	72286	VBF-12	USS RANDOLPH	ENR HONSHU	EMPIRE	ENS WILLIAM E.F. INZER	S
02/24/45	70346	VD-5		GUAM	WCENPAC	LCDR LOUIS R. GEHLBACH	D
02/24/45	70442	VF-9	USS LEX-INGTON	NANSEI SHOTO	EMPIRE		
02/25/45	72329	VBF-12	USS RANDOLPH	HONSHU	EMPIRE	LT N.W. SANDLEA	M
02/25/45	72530	VBF-12	USS RANDOLPH	HONSHU	EMPIRE	ENS E. JINDRA	S
02/25/45	70984	VBF-17	USS HORNET		EMPIRE	LTJG S.O. BACH	S
02/25/45	70622	VBF-3	USS YORK-TOWN	TOKYO	EMPIRE	ENS HOAL	S
02/25/45	71476	VBF-9	USS LEX-INGTON	NANSEI SHOTO	EMPIRE		
02/25/45	71561	VF-23	USS LANGLEY	IWO JIMA	EMPIRE		
02/25/45	71750	VF-23	USS LANGLEY	IWO JIMA	EMPIRE		
02/25/45	72451	VF-23	USS LANGLEY	IWO JIMA	EMPIRE		
02/25/45	72576	VF-23	USS LANGLEY	IWO JIMA	EMPIRE		
02/25/45	77387	VF-25	USS CHENAN-GO	ENR SEATTLE	CENPAC	LTJG WARREN GARDEN	S
02/25/45	72408	VF-29	USS CABOT	HONSHU	EMPIRE	ENS JOSEPH F. CRAWFORD	M
02/25/45	58542	VF-3	USS YORK-TOWN	TOKYO	EMPIRE	ENS P.E. KING	S
02/25/45	71541	VF-3	USS YORK-TOWN	TOKYO	EMPIRE		
02/25/45	71816	VF-80	USS HANCOCK	IWO JIMA	EMPIRE		
02/25/45	70547	VF-81	USS WASP	TOKYO	EMPIRE	LTJG JOHN C. MCNIECE	M
02/26/45	72302	VBF-12	USS RANDOLPH	HONSHU	EMPIRE		
02/27/45	72870	VBF-17	USS HORNET		EMPIRE		
02/27/45	71828	VBF-9	USS LEX-INGTON	NANSEI SHOTO	EMPIRE		
02/28/45	58142	COMAIR-PAC	PEARL	HAWAII	ECENPAC		
02/28/45	71815	COMAIR-PAC	PEARL	HAWAII	ECENPAC		
02/28/45	72379	VF-46	USS COWPENS	OKINAWA	EMPIRE		
03/01/45	70863	CASU-32	KAHULUI	HAWAII	ECENPAC	LTJG J.P. LAVIN	S
03/01/45	70869	CASU-32	KAHULUI	HAWAII	ECENPAC	ENS J.D. O'CONNELL	D
03/01/45	70164	VF-17	USS HORNET	OKINAWA	EMPIRE		
03/01/45	71595	VF-30	USS BELLEAU WOOD	IE SHIMA	EMPIRE	ENS R.O. BURNS	M
03/01/45	72585	VF-30	USS BELLEAU WOOD	IE SHIMA	EMPIRE		
03/01/45	72891	VF-30	USS BELLEAU WOOD	IE SHIMA	EMPIRE	ENS W.N. THOMAS	M
03/01/45	72929	VF-30	USS BELLEAU WOOD	IE SHIMA	EMPIRE	ENS G.C. TRACY, JR.	M
03/01/45	71585	VF-4	USS ESSEX	OKINAWA	EMPIRE	LTJG DOUGLAS R. CAHOON	M
03/01/45	71788	VF-4	USS ESSEX	OKINAWA	EMPIRE	LTJG PURYEAR	S

DATE	BUNO	SQDRN	BASE	LOST	AREA	PILOT	FATE
03/01/45	71976	VF-46	USS COWPENS	IE SHIMA	EMPIRE		
03/01/45	72242	VF-46	USS COWPENS	IE SHIMA	EMPIRE		
03/01/45	72349	VF-46	USS COWPENS	IE SHIMA	EMPIRE		
03/01/45	72449	VF-46	USS COWPENS	IE SHIMA	EMPIRE		
03/01/45	72249	VF-80	USS HANCOCK	IE SHIMA	EMPIRE		
03/01/45	71252	VF-82	USS BENNING-TON	MYAKE SHIMA	EMPIRE	ENS F.P. HAHN	S
03/01/45	71526	VF-82	USS BENNING-TON	MYAKE SHIMA	EMPIRE	LT B.F. LINEHOUSE, JR.	M
03/03/45	71130	VF(N)-90	USS ENTER-PRISE	IWO JIMA	EMPIRE	ENS W.I. GILLE	S
03/03/45	58690	VF-100	BARBERS POINT	HAWAII	ECENPAC	ENS ROBERT R. WEEMS, JR	D
03/04/45	58138	COMAIR-PAC	PEARL	HAWAII	ECENPAC		
03/04/45	72256	COMAIR-PAC	PEARL	HAWAII	ECENPAC		
03/04/45	71889	VF-85	USS SHANGRI-LA	HAWAII	ECENPAC	ENS CLARENCE A. HANSEN	S
03/05/45	72725	CASU(F)-12		GUAM	WCENPAC		
03/05/45	71819	VF-88		HAWAII	ECENPAC	ENS TOM B. LOSKI	S
03/06/45	72816	VF-40	USS SUWAN-NEE	TULAGI	SOPAC	LTJG ED. L. BRIDGES, JR.	D
03/08/45	72824	VF-25	USS CHENAN-GO	TULAGI	SOPAC	LTJG DONALD E. HICKS	D
03/09/45	72375	VF-12	USS RANDOLPH	ENR ULITHI	WCENPAC		
03/10/45	71534	CASU(F)-13		PITYILU	SW PAC	ENS JAMES B. MCLENDON	M
03/10/45	77416	VF-24	USS SANTEE	HAWAII	ECENPAC	LTJG HENRY L. SWOPE	S
03/10/45	72382	VF-25	USS CHENAN-GO	GUADAL-CANAL	SOPAC	LT LEONARD R. KOSLOWSKI	S
03/11/45	72334	VF-12	USS RANDOLPH	ULITHI	WCENPAC		
03/11/45	72340	VF-12	USS RANDOLPH	ULITHI	WCENPAC		
03/12/45	77584	CASU-38	USS SHIP-LEY BAY	HAWAII	ECENPAC	LCDR H.J. TRUM	S
03/13/45	72854	VF-24	USS SANTEE	HAWAII	ECENPAC	LTJG CHARLES E. BLACKMAN	S
03/14/45	71362	COMAIR-PAC	PEARL	HAWAII	ECENPAC		
03/14/45	70054	VF-23	USS LANGLEY	IWO JIMA	EMPIRE	ENS R.A. SMITH	S
03/14/45	71426	VF-23	USS LANGLEY	IWO JIMA	EMPIRE		
03/14/45	72430	VF-23	USS LANGLEY	IWO JIMA	EMPIRE		
03/14/45	77627	VF-25	USS CHENAN-GO	SOLOMONS	SOPAC	ENS LOWELL D. PATERSON	S
03/14/45	72681	VF-6	USS HANCOCK	ENR KYUSHU	EMPIRE		
03/14/45	71581	VF-86	USS WASP	ULITHI	WCENPAC		
03/15/45	72834	VF-23	USS LANGLEY	IWO JIMA	EMPIRE		
03/15/45	71881	VF-83	USS ESSEX	OKINAWA	EMPIRE		
03/15/45	71902	VF-83	USS ESSEX	OKINAWA	EMPIRE		
03/15/45	72572	VF-83	USS ESSEX	OKINAWA	EMPIRE		
03/15/45	71530	VF-86	USS WASP	ULITHI	WCENPAC		
03/15/45	71451	VF-9	USS YORK-TOWN	ENR OKINAWA	EMPIRE	ENS R.A. DOOLING	S

DATE	BUNO	SQDRN	BASE	LOST	AREA	PILOT	FATE
03/16/45	70391	NACTU	USS HOLLANDIA	HAWAII	ECENPAC	LT JOHN W. CARTER	D
03/16/45	72818	VF-30	USS BELLEAU WOOD	KYUSHU	EMPIRE		
03/17/45	70537	VBF-87	KAHULUI	HAWAII	ECENPAC	ENS HARRY COON, JR.	S
03/17/45	71970	VF-29	USS CABOT	OKINAWA	EMPIRE	LT JOHN W. ADAMS, JR.	S
03/17/45	72259	VF-6	USS HANCOCK	KYUSHU	EMPIRE		
03/18/45	72238	VBF-17	USS HORNET	KURE	EMPIRE	LT K.B. MESSENGER	S
03/18/45	71062	VF-17	USS HORNET	KURE	EMPIRE	ENS JOHN P. WRAY	M
03/18/45	70348	VF-29	USS CABOT	OKINAWA	EMPIRE	LTJG F.A. WEIR	D
03/18/45	72769	VF-30	USS BELLEAU WOOD	IE SHIMA	EMPIRE	ENS MCIVER	M
03/18/45	72830	VF-30	USS BELLEAU WOOD	IE SHIMA	EMPIRE	ENS FOSTER	M
03/18/45	72835	VF-30	USS BELLEAU WOOD	IE SHIMA	EMPIRE	ENS W.J. CUMMINGS	M
03/18/45	72845	VF-30	USS BELLEAU WOOD	IE SHIMA	EMPIRE	LTJG BALDWIN	S
03/18/45	72867	VF-30	USS BELLEAU WOOD	IE SHIMA	EMPIRE	ENS R.W. MOSHER	M
03/18/45	70588	VF-45	USS SAN JACINTO	ENR KYUSHU	EMPIRE	CDR GORDON E. SCHECTER	M
03/18/45	70365	VF-6	USS HANCOCK	KYUSHU	EMPIRE	LCDR W.E. BECK	M
03/18/45	71448	VF-82	USS BENNING-TON	KYUSHU	EMPIRE	LTJG T.B. CHANDLER	M
03/18/45	72464	VF-82	USS BENNING-TON	KYUSHU	EMPIRE	LT JACK R. SESSIONS	M
03/18/45	71989	VF-83	USS ESSEX	KYUSHU	EMPIRE		
03/18/45	72657	VF-86	USS WASP	KANOYA	EMPIRE		
03/18/45	72013	VF-9	USS YORK-TOWN	KYUSHU	EMPIRE	ENS D.R. IVES	D
03/18/45	72458	VF-9	USS YORK-TOWN	OKINAWA	EMPIRE	LT E.A. VALENCIA	S
03/19/45	58857	VBF-17	USS HORNET	KURE	EMPIRE	LT R.W. MOORE	S
03/19/45	70675	VBF-17	USS HORNET	KURE	EMPIRE	LTJG R.W. KARR	M
03/19/45	70859	VBF-17	USS HORNET	KURE	EMPIRE	LT S.T. KIPP	M
03/19/45	70991	VBF-17	USS HORNET	KURE	EMPIRE	ENS E.W. MATTHEWS	M
03/19/45	71781	VBF-17	USS HORNET	KURE	EMPIRE	LT PRINZ	S
03/19/45	72372	VBF-17	USS HORNET	KURE	EMPIRE	LT C.F. WEISS	M
03/19/45	72488	VBF-17	USS HORNET	HONSHU	EMPIRE		
03/19/45	72569	VBF-17	USS HORNET	KURE	EMPIRE	ENS H.L. HANNAH	M
03/19/45	72910	VBF-17	USS HORNET	KURE	EMPIRE		
03/19/45	71892	VF(N)-46	USS INDEPEN-DENCE	ENR OKINAWA	EMPIRE	LT WILLIAM SCHROEDER	S
03/19/45	71138	VF-17	USS HORNET	KURE	EMPIRE		
03/19/45	71754	VF-17	USS HORNET	KURE	EMPIRE	LTJG F.E. MCCORMICK	M
03/19/45	72504	VF-33	USS SAN-GAMON	ULITHI	WCENPAC		

DATE	BUNO	SQDRN	BASE	LOST	AREA	PILOT	FATE
03/19/45	72466	VF-5	USS FRANKLIN	HONSHU	EMPIRE	(DECK LOSS-KAMIKAZE)	
03/19/45	72628	VF-5	USS FRANKLIN	HONSHU	EMPIRE	(DECK LOSS-KAMIKAZE)	
03/19/45	72004	VF-82	USS BENNING-TON	KYUSHU	EMPIRE	LTJG R.L. PFEIFER	M
03/19/45	72209	VF-82	USS BENNING-TON	HONSHU	EMPIRE	LTJG E.A. MCALLISTER	M
03/19/45	71752	VF-83	USS ESSEX	KURE	EMPIRE		
03/19/45	72235	VF-83	USS ESSEX	KURE	EMPIRE		
03/19/45	72873	VF-83	USS ESSEX	KURE	EMPIRE	ENS W.J. MORTON	S
03/19/45	70630	VF-9	USS YORK-TOWN	KYUSHU	EMPIRE	LTJG R.R. PRIOR	D
03/20/45	72892	VF-30	USS BELLEAU WOOD	IE SHIMA	EMPIRE		
03/20/45	72601	VF-47	USS BATAAN	OKINAWA	EMPIRE	CDR WALKER ETHRIDGE	M
03/20/45	72963	VF-47	USS BATAAN	OKINAWA	EMPIRE	LTJG HOWARD F. ELZINER	S
03/21/45	58575	COMAIR-PAC	PEARL	HAWAII	ECENPAC		
03/21/45	70104	COMAIR-PAC	PEARL	HAWAII	ECENPAC		
03/21/45	71554	COMAIR-PAC	PEARL	HAWAII	ECENPAC		
03/21/45	71386	VBF-17	USS HORNET	ENR KYUSHU	EMPIRE	LTJG W.E. KLEIN	M
03/21/45	72309	VF-12	USS RANDOLPH	ULITHI	WCENPAC	ENS D.O. MARTIN	D
03/21/45	72817	VF-40	USS SUWAN-NEE	ULITHI	WCENPAC	LTJG DALE F. MABRY	S
03/21/45	72539	VF-45	USS SAN JACINTO	KYUSHU	EMPIRE		
03/21/45	71408	VF-99		GUAM	WCENPAC		
03/22/45	71279	VF-1	KANEOHE	HAWAII	ECENPAC	ENS HEATH C. SWISHER	S
03/22/45	71422	VF-17	USS HORNET	ENR KYUSHU	EMPIRE		
03/22/45	77363	VF-24	USS SANTEE	ENR LEYTE GULF	WCENPAC	LTJG LEDIO MAVELANI	S
03/22/45	70999	VF-29	USS CABOT	KYUSHU	EMPIRE		
03/22/45	71019	VF-29	USS CABOT	KYUSHU	EMPIRE	ENS CARL T. CAMPBELL	S
03/22/45	71099	VF-29	USS CABOT	OKINAWA	EMPIRE		
03/22/45	71560	VF-29	USS CABOT	KYUSHU	EMPIRE		
03/22/45	72435	VF-29	USS CABOT	OKINAWA	EMPIRE		
03/22/45	72531	VF-29	USS CABOT	OKINAWA	EMPIRE		
03/23/45	71967	VF-23	USS LANGLEY	OKINAWA	EMPIRE	ENS WILLIAM R. RANKIN	M
03/23/45	72778	VF-23	USS LANGLEY	OKINAWA	EMPIRE	LTJG H. E. HENDRICKSON	M
03/23/45	72562	VF-46	USS INDEPEND ENCE	OKINAWA	EMPIRE	ENS EVERETT ROBINETT	S
03/24/45	77449	NACTU	BARBERS POINT	HAWAII	ECENPAC	ENS PHILLIP T. MCDONALD	S
03/24/45	72067	VBF-16	USS BON HOMME RICHARD	COSTA RICA	NORLANT	LTJG J.L. ARQUETTE	S
03/24/45	71923	VF-46	USS INDEPEN-DENCE	OKINAWA	EMPIRE	LTJG FREDERICK E. LIEBER	D
03/24/45	72287	VF-46	USS INDEPEN-DENCE	OKINAWA	EMPIRE	LTJG WM JOSEPH SCHLEIS	S

DATE	BUNO	SQDRN	BASE	LOST	AREA	PILOT	FATE
03/24/45	72489	VF-46	USS INDEPENDENCE	OKINAWA	EMPIRE	CDR CARL W. ROONEY	S
03/24/45	77579	VF-46	USS INDEPENDENCE	OKINAWA	EMPIRE	LTJG CHARLES K. PURCELL	S
03/24/45	72948	VF-9	USS YORKTOWN	RYUKYU	EMPIRE	LTJG KENT	S
03/25/45	72196	VBF-12	USS RANDOLPH	ULITHI	WCENPAC		
03/25/45	72310	VBF-12	USS RANDOLPH	ULITHI	WCENPAC		
03/25/45	72316	VBF-12	USS RANDOLPH	ULITHI	WCENPAC		
03/25/45	72683	VBF-12	USS RANDOLPH	ULITHI	WCENPAC		
03/25/45	72855	VF-30	USS BELLEAU WOOD	IE SHIMA	EMPIRE	ENS ROBERT G. BERENSON	D
03/25/45	71026	VF-82	USS BENNINGTON	OKINAWA	EMPIRE	ENS J.B. HOAG	S
03/25/45	71922	VF-82	USS BENNINGTON	OKINAWA	EMPIRE	LT R.B. DALTON	S
03/25/45	72370	VF-86	USS WASP	CAROLINES	WCENPAC		
03/25/45	72913	VF-89	USS ANTIETAM		CENLANT	LTJG MASON L. DEWEES	S
03/25/45	72781	VF-99	ULITHI		WCENPAC		
03/26/45	72085	VBF-16	USS BON HOMME RICHARD	HAWAII	ECENPAC	G.F. SOUZA	S
03/26/45	70051	VBF-9	USS YORKTOWN	NAHA	EMPIRE	ENS J.M. SEE	M
03/26/45	71424	VBF-9	USS YORKTOWN	NAHA	EMPIRE	LT F.M. FOX	S
03/26/45	72541	VF-23	USS LANGLEY	OKINAWA	EMPIRE	ENS K.T. SMITH	S
03/26/45	72599	VF-30	USS BELLEAU WOOD	IE SHIMA	EMPIRE		
03/26/45	72468	VF-6	USS HANCOCK	OKINAWA	EMPIRE		
03/26/45	72594	VF-6	USS HANCOCK	OKINAWA	EMPIRE	ENS W.L. MIDYETT	D
03/26/45	72632	VF-6	USS HANCOCK	OKINAWA	EMPIRE	LTJG W.H. KELLER	S
03/26/45	72389	VF-9	USS YORKTOWN	NAHA	EMPIRE	LTJG THOMAS CONNOR	M
03/27/45	71510	VBF-17	USS HORNET	AMAMI	EMPIRE	ENS G.W. MCADOO	U
03/27/45	72564	VBF-9	USS YORKTOWN	NAHA	EMPIRE	ENS T.M. SMYER	S
03/27/45	71600	VF-45	USS SAN JACINTO	IE SHIMA	EMPIRE	LTJG BILLY J.J. PETTIGREW	D
03/27/45	72956	VF-46	USS INDEPENDENCE	ENR KYUSHU	EMPIRE	LTJG AL. WM. C. THOMAS	S
03/27/45	71943	VF-82	USS BENNINGTON	OKINAWA	EMPIRE	LT E.S. HEIM	M
03/28/45	70451	VF-17	USS HORNET	KYUSHU	EMPIRE	LTJG WYMAN C. EDMUND	M
03/28/45	71768	VF-17	USS HORNET	KYUSHU	EMPIRE	ENS S. HARRINGTON	M
03/28/45	72275	VF-30	USS BELLEAU WOOD	DAITO JIMA	EMPIRE	ENS REBER	S
03/28/45	72792	VF-40	USS SUWANNEE	ENR OKINAWA	SOPAC		
03/28/45	72524	VF-45	USS SAN JACINTO	KYUSHU	EMPIRE	LTJG SHAY	S
03/28/45	72575	VF-45	USS SAN JACINTO	KYUSHU	EMPIRE	LTJG SWINBURNE	S

DATE	BUNO	SQDRN	BASE	LOST	AREA	PILOT	FATE
03/28/45	72289	VF-82	USS BENNING-TON	OKINAWA	EMPIRE	ENS P.M. BUDINGER	S
03/28/45	72689	VF-82	USS BENNING-TON	OKINAWA	EMPIRE	ENS F.W. STALLINGS	S
03/28/45	72776	VF-86	USS WASP	CAROLINES	WCENPAC		
03/29/45	70056	COMAIR-PAC	PEARL	HAWAII	ECENPAC		
03/29/45	70937	COMAIR-PAC	PEARL	HAWAII	ECENPAC		
03/29/45	71047	COMAIR-PAC	PEARL	HAWAII	ECENPAC		
03/29/45	72266	COMAIR-PAC	PEARL	HAWAII	ECENPAC		
03/29/45	72010	VF-10	USS INTREPID	KYUSHU	EMPIRE		
03/29/45	70536	VF-23	USS LANGLEY	OKINAWA	EMPIRE	LTJG C. E. WEICKHARDT, JR.	M
03/29/45	71745	VF-23	USS LANGLEY	OKINAWA	EMPIRE	ENS DONALD W. HENKEL	M
03/29/45	71749	VF-23	USS LANGLEY	OKINAWA	EMPIRE	ENS A.B. DENDINGER	D
03/29/45	71771	VF-23	USS LANGLEY	OKINAWA	EMPIRE	ENS BAILEY	S
03/29/45	77461	VF-24	USS SANTEE	OKINAWA	EMPIRE	LT ROBERT BRIGHAM ELLERY	S
03/29/45	77475	VF-24	USS SANTEE	OKINAWA	EMPIRE	LTJG IRVING MAYER	S
03/29/45	71609	VF-29	USS CABOT	KYUSHU	EMPIRE	ENS KELLEHER	S
03/29/45	71154	VF-33	USS SAN-GAMON	KEREMA RETTO	EMPIRE		
03/29/45	72455	VF-46	USS INDEPEN-DENCE	KYUSHU	EMPIRE	LTJG RALPH J. REEDER	M
03/29/45	72409	VF-6	USS HANCOCK	OKINAWA	EMPIRE	LTJG L.L. DAVIS	M
03/29/45	72479	VF-6	USS HANCOCK	OKINAWA	EMPIRE	ENS R.H. BAKER	S
03/29/45	72304	VF-83	USS ESSEX	OKINAWA	EMPIRE		
03/29/45	72582	VF-84	USS BUNKER HILL	OKINAWA	EMPIRE		
03/29/45	71346	VF-87		HAWAII	ECENPAC		
03/30/45	70794	VF-17	USS HORNET	PALAU	CENPAC		
03/30/45	77380	VF-24	USS SANTEE	OKINAWA	EMPIRE	ENS HARRY L. HOTCHKIN	D
03/30/45	77413	VF-24	USS SANTEE	OKINAWA	EMPIRE	LTJG CHARLES E. BLACKMAN	S
03/30/45	71846	VF-29	USS CABOT	OKINAWA	EMPIRE		
03/30/45	71592	VF-6	USS HANCOCK	OKINAWA	EMPIRE		
03/30/45	71543	VF-83	USS ESSEX	OKINAWA	EMPIRE		
03/30/45	70951	VF-9	USS YORK-TOWN	IE SHIMA	EMPIRE	ENS R.E. JEHLI	S
03/31/45	72356	CASU(F)-51		ULITHI	WCENPAC		
03/31/45	72213	VBF-17	USS HORNET	IE SHIMA	EMPIRE	LT R.C. COATES	M
03/31/45	70393	VF-45	USS SAN JACINTO	ENR OKINAWA	EMPIRE		
03/31/45	72987	VF-47	USS BATAAN	OKINAWA	EMPIRE		
03/31/45	71557	VF-83	USS ESSEX	OKINAWA	EMPIRE		
04/01/45	71531	CASU(F)-43		GUAM	WCENPAC		
04/01/45	71767	VF-10	USS INTREPID	OKINAWA	EMPIRE		
04/01/45	72648	VF-12	USS RANDOLPH	ULITHI	WCENPAC		
04/01/45	72921	VF-24	USS SANTEE	OKINAWA	EMPIRE	LTJG GRANT LELAND KELLY	D

DATE	BUNO	SQDRN	BASE	LOST	AREA	PILOT	FATE
04/01/45	71769	VF-40	USS SUWANNEE	OKINAWA	EMPIRE	ENS GEORGE W. WARNER	S
04/01/45	70043	VF-46	USS INDEPENDENCE	ULITHI	WCENPAC		
04/01/45	70553	VF-83	USS ESSEX	OKINAWA	EMPIRE		
04/01/45	72532	VF-83	USS ESSEX	OKINAWA	EMPIRE		
04/02/45	70867	POOL	KANEOHE	HAWAII	ECENPAC		
04/02/45	72851	POOL	USS WINDHAM BAY	OKINAWA	EMPIRE	LTJG J.H. BATEMAN	S
04/02/45	72901	VBF-17	USS HORNET	OKINAWA	EMPIRE	LTJG J.H. CALES	D
04/02/45	70834	VBF-9	USS YORKTOWN	OKINAWA	EMPIRE		
04/02/45	71085	VBF-9	USS YORKTOWN	OKINAWA	EMPIRE		
04/02/45	71010	VF-17	USS HORNET	OKINAWA	EMPIRE		
04/02/45	71932	VF-17	USS HORNET	OKINAWA	EMPIRE	ENS S.F. MCCOLE	M
04/02/45	71903	VF-23	USS LANGLEY	IE SHIMA	EMPIRE		
04/02/45	71022	VF-24	USS SANTEE	OKINAWA	EMPIRE		
04/02/45	72977	VF-24	USS SANTEE	OKINAWA	EMPIRE	LTJG GLEN WM. FREEMAN	S
04/02/45	77390	VF-25	USS CHENANGO	OKINAWA	EMPIRE	ENS ROBERT T. WRIGHT	S
04/02/45	77961	VF-25	USS CHENANGO	OKINAWA	EMPIRE		
04/02/45	72243	VF-30	USS BELLEAU WOOD		EMPIRE		
04/02/45	72596	VF-45	USS SAN JACINTO	OKINAWA	EMPIRE		
04/02/45	71982	VF-82	USS BENNINGTON	OKINAWA	EMPIRE	LTJG C.A. MCCREA	S
04/02/45	72088	VF-82	USS BENNINGTON	OKINAWA	EMPIRE	ENS E.H. SCHMUTZLER	S
04/03/45	58130	CASU(F)-12		GUAM	WCENPAC		
04/03/45	72552	CASU(F)-12		GUAM	WCENPAC		
04/03/45	71907	VBF-17	USS HORNET	OKINAWA	EMPIRE	LT H.E. MITCHELL	D
04/03/45	77511	VBF-17	USS HORNET	OKINAWA	EMPIRE		
04/03/45	70604	VF-17	USS HORNET	OKINAWA	EMPIRE		
04/03/45	72051	VF-17	USS HORNET	OKINAWA	EMPIRE		
04/03/45	71394	VF-25	USS CHENANGO	OKINAWA	EMPIRE		
04/03/45	71980	VF-25	USS CHENANGO	OKINAWA	EMPIRE		
04/03/45	77397	VF-25	USS CHENANGO	OKINAWA	EMPIRE		
04/03/45	71853	VF-29	USS CABOT	IE SHIMA	EMPIRE	LT BARNES	S
04/03/45	71972	VF-29	USS CABOT	IE SHIMA	EMPIRE	LTJG MELVIN COZZONS	S
04/03/45	72471	VF-29	USS CABOT	IE SHIMA	EMPIRE	LT FRATWELL	U
04/03/45	71546	VF-45	USS SAN JACINTO	MAYAKO	EMPIRE	ENS H.W. SWINBURN	S
04/03/45	72324	VF-45	USS SAN JACINTO	MAYAKO	EMPIRE		

DATE	BUNO	SQDRN	BASE	LOST	AREA	PILOT	FATE
04/03/45	71723	VF-47	USS BATAAN	OKINAWA	EMPIRE	ENS OLIVER L. SWISHER	S
04/03/45	72976	VF-47	USS BATAAN	OKINAWA	EMPIRE	LTJG R. L. WESTBROOK III	M
04/03/45	71884	VF-83	USS ESSEX	OKINAWA	EMPIRE		
04/04/45	72248	VBF-9	USS YORK-TOWN	OKINAWA	EMPIRE	ENS HENRY G. HICKS	D
04/04/45	72434	VBF-9	USS YORK-TOWN	OKINAWA	EMPIRE		
04/04/45	72957	VF-40	USS SUWAN-NEE	OKINAWA	EMPIRE	LCDR RICHARD D. SAMPSON	M
04/04/45	58860	VF-6	USS HANCOCK	OKINAWA	EMPIRE		
04/05/45	77945	VBF-17	USS HORNET	OKINAWA	EMPIRE	LTJG D.H. CRIST	S
04/05/45	72330	VF-12	USS RANDOLPH	ULITHI	WCENPAC		
04/05/45	77890	VF-45	USS SAN JACINTO	DAITO JIMA	EMPIRE	LT C.W. WILSON	M
04/05/45	71921	VF-46	USS INDEPEN-DENCE	ENR OKINAWA	EMPIRE	LT ANGUS T. MORRISON	S
04/05/45	71613	VF-9	USS YORK-TOWN	IWO JIMA	EMPIRE	LTJG EATON J. BADEN	M
04/05/45	71957	VF-9	USS YORK-TOWN	IWO JIMA	EMPIRE	ENS H.H. HUDSPETH	S
04/06/45	70151	VF-17	USS HORNET	OKINAWA	EMPIRE	ENS C. IDU	S
04/06/45	72863	VF-25	USS CHENANG O	ENR ISHIGAKI	EMPIRE		
04/06/45	72399	VF-29	USS CABOT		EMPIRE	LTJG JOSEPH L. CHANDLIER	S
04/06/45	72617	VF-47	USS BATAAN	OKINAWA	EMPIRE		
04/06/45	72262	VF-82	USS BENNING-TON	OKINAWA	EMPIRE	ENS H.W. BENSON	S
04/06/45	72298	VF-82	USS BENNING-TON	OKINAWA	EMPIRE	ENS G.M. HUFFMAN	S
04/06/45	71784	VF-83	USS ESSEX	IWO JIMA	EMPIRE	ENS BERUBE	M
04/07/45	72631	VBF-12	USS RANDOLPH	ENR KIKAI	EMPIRE		
04/07/45	72107	VF-45	USS SAN JACINTO	OKINAWA	EMPIRE		
04/07/45	77865	VF-47	USS BATAAN	OKINAWA	EMPIRE	LT SUGGS	S
04/07/45	72407	VF-6	USS HANCOCK	OKINAWA	EMPIRE		
04/07/45	72415	VF-6	USS HANCOCK	OKINAWA	EMPIRE	ENS R.L. CURRETT	M
04/07/45	72459	VF-6	USS HANCOCK	OKINAWA	EMPIRE		
04/07/45	72500	VF-6	USS HANCOCK	OKINAWA	EMPIRE		
04/07/45	72507	VF-6	USS HANCOCK	OKINAWA	EMPIRE		
04/07/45	72578	VF-6	USS HANCOCK	OKINAWA	EMPIRE		
04/07/45	72653	VF-6	USS HANCOCK	OKINAWA	EMPIRE		
04/07/45	72768	VF-6	USS HANCOCK	OKINAWA	EMPIRE		
04/07/45	72770	VF-6	USS HANCOCK	OKINAWA	EMPIRE		
04/07/45	72847	VF-6	USS HANCOCK	OKINAWA	EMPIRE		
04/07/45	72934	VF-6	USS HANCOCK	OKINAWA	EMPIRE		
04/07/45	72980	VF-6	USS HANCOCK	OKINAWA	EMPIRE		
04/07/45	77385	VF-6	USS HANCOCK	OKINAWA	EMPIRE		

DATE	BUNO	SQDRN	BASE	LOST	AREA	PILOT	FATE
04/07/45	77391	VF-6	USS HANCOCK	OKINAWA	EMPIRE		
04/07/45	77528	VF-6	USS HANCOCK	OKINAWA	EMPIRE		
04/08/45	72295	VF-12	USS RANDOLPH	KIKAI	EMPIRE	ENS JAY M. FINLEY	S
04/08/45	72566	VF-25	USS CHENAN-GO	ISHIGAKI	EMPIRE	LCDR RICHARD W. ROBINSON	D
04/09/45	71330	CASU-32	KAHULUI	HAWAII	ECENPAC	LTJG ARTHUR B. KOONTZ, JR.	D
04/09/45	71416	VBF-9	USS YORK-TOWN	OKINAWA	EMPIRE	LT M.C. JACOBS	M
04/09/45	71071	VF-17	USS HORNET	OKINAWA	EMPIRE		
04/09/45	71113	VF-25	USS CHENAN-GO	IE SHIMA	EMPIRE		
04/09/45	77374	VF-25	USS CHENAN-GO	IE SHIMA	EMPIRE		
04/09/45	77407	VF-25	USS CHENANG O	IE SHIMA	EMPIRE	ENS JOHN WILLIAM ENDERS	S
04/09/45	77428	VF-25	USS CHENAN-GO	IE SHIMA	EMPIRE		
04/09/45	77685	VF-25	USS CHENAN-GO	IE SHIMA	EMPIRE	ENS C. HENTON ROGERS, JR.	D
04/09/45	77689	VF-25	USS CHENAN-GO	IE SHIMA	EMPIRE		
04/10/45	72633	VBF-12	USS RANDOLPH	OKINAWA	EMPIRE		
04/10/45	70958	VC-91	USS SAVO ISLAND	OKINAWA	EMPIRE		
04/10/45	71331	VF-100	USS TRIPOLI	HAWAII	ECENPAC		
04/10/45	71350	VF-24	USS SANTEE	IWO JIMA	EMPIRE	LCDR R.J. OSTROM	M
04/11/45	70064	VBF-9	USS YORK-TOWN	OKINAWA	EMPIRE	ENS F. BRIGHT	S
04/11/45	77954	VF-31	HILO	HAWAII	ECENPAC		
04/11/45	77971	VF-31	HILO	HAWAII	ECENPAC		
04/11/45	72761	VF-40	USS SUWAN-NEE	OKINAWA	EMPIRE		
04/11/45	72619	VF-83	USS ESSEX	TOKUNO	EMPIRE		
04/12/45	58374	POOL	BARBERS POINT	HAWAII	ECENPAC		
04/12/45	77548	VBF-17	USS HORNET	OKINAWA	EMPIRE	ENS RAYMOND GROSSO	M
04/12/45	72454	VF-30	USS BELLEAU WOOD	IWO JIMA	EMPIRE		
04/12/45	72837	VF-30	USS BELLEAU WOOD	IWO JIMA	EMPIRE		
04/12/45	72315	VF-82	USS BENNING-TON	IE SHIMA	EMPIRE	ENS TERRY MILLS	S
04/12/45	71434	VF-9	USS YORK-TOWN	OKINAWA	EMPIRE	LT J.E. KUSSMAN	S
04/13/45	78141	CASU(F)-12		GUAM	WCENPAC		
04/13/45	71934	VF-45	USS SAN JACINTO	KYUSHU	EMPIRE		
04/13/45	77521	VF-82	USS BENNING-TON	IE SHIMA	EMPIRE	ENS CHARLES CARTY	S
04/14/45	72469	VBF-12	USS RANDOLPH	DAITO SHIMA	EMPIRE		
04/14/45	72590	VBF-12	USS RANDOLPH	DAITO SHIMA	EMPIRE		

DATE	BUNO	SQDRN	BASE	LOST	AREA	PILOT	FATE
04/14/45	77917	VBF-12	USS RANDOLPH	DAITO SHIMA	EMPIRE		
04/14/45	77625	VF(N)-90	USS ENTER-PRISE	OKINAWA	EMPIRE	(DECK LOSS-KAMIKAZE)	
04/14/45	72322	VF-12	USS RANDOLPH	DAITO SHIMA	EMPIRE		
04/14/45	72394	VF-12	USS RANDOLPH	DAITO SHIMA	EMPIRE	ENS W.K. SANKEY	S
04/14/45	72416	VF-12	USS RANDOLPH	DAITO SHIMA	EMPIRE		
04/14/45	77669	VF-34	KANEOHE	HAWAII	ECENPAC		
04/15/45	70882	CASU(F)-15		SAIPAN	WCENPAC		
04/15/45	72613	CASU(F)-15		SAIPAN	WCENPAC		
04/15/45	58072	VF-17	USS HORNET	OKINAWA	EMPIRE	ENS W.S. SHASTEEN	D
04/15/45	72474	VF-24	USS SANTEE	IWO JIMA	EMPIRE	LTJG LEDIO MAVELANI	S
04/15/45	72027	VF-30	USS BELLEAU WOOD	KYUSHU	EMPIRE		
04/15/45	72785	VF-40	USS SUWAN-NEE	OKINAWA	EMPIRE		
04/15/45	71248	VF-82	USS BENNING-TON	OKINAWA	EMPIRE	LT J.M. FORBES	S
04/15/45	71586	VF-83	USS ESSEX	OKINAWA	EMPIRE		
04/16/45	70046	VBF-9	USS YORK-TOWN	OKINAWA	EMPIRE	LTJG A.R. ENGLISH	S
04/16/45	71598	VF-10	USS INTREPID	KOKUBO	EMPIRE		
04/16/45	70597	VF-17	USS HORNET	OKINAWA	EMPIRE	LTJG C.V. STONE	S
04/16/45	78022	VF-23	USS LANGLEY	OKINAWA	EMPIRE	LCDR MERLIN PADDOCK	M
04/16/45	77487	VF-45	USS SAN JACINTO	KYUSHU	EMPIRE	LT R.L. TAYLOR	M
04/16/45	72984	VF-47	USS BATAAN	KIKAI	EMPIRE	ENS RICHARD STEPHANSKY	S
04/16/45	77383	VF-47	USS BATAAN	KIKAI	EMPIRE	ENS VICTOR B. RINK	S
04/16/45	77863	VF-83	USS ESSEX	KYUSHU	EMPIRE	ENS WARD	S
04/17/45	72106	VF-12	USS RANDOLPH	IE SHIMA	EMPIRE		
04/17/45	72844	VF-12	USS RANDOLPH	IE SHIMA	EMPIRE		
04/17/45	77529	VF-12	USS RANDOLPH	IE SHIMA	EMPIRE		
04/17/45	71997	VF-40	USS SUWAN-NEE	OKINAWA	EMPIRE	LTJG JOHN M. MOLSBERGEN	S
04/17/45	71456	VF-82	USS BENNING-TON	OKINAWA	EMPIRE		
04/17/45	72003	VF-82	USS BENNING-TON	OKINAWA	EMPIRE		
04/17/45	72277	VF-82	USS BENNING-TON	OKINAWA	EMPIRE		
04/18/45	77784	VF-45	USS SAN JACINTO	KYUSHU	EMPIRE	LT J. CAIN	S
04/19/45	72490	VF-23	USS LANGLEY	OKINAWA	EMPIRE		
04/20/45	72056	VBF-16	USS BON HOMME RICHARD	HAWAII	ECENPAC	LTJG EDWIN R. ROSS	S
04/21/45	77515	VF-25	USS CHENAN-GO	IE SHIMA	EMPIRE	ENS DONALD ELMER CORZINE	S
04/21/45	71985	VF-30	USS BELLEAU WOOD	IWO JIMA	EMPIRE	LTJG LEWIS JOHN BEHREND	D

DATE	BUNO	SQDRN	BASE	LOST	AREA	PILOT	FATE
04/22/45	71786	VBF-12	USS RANDOLPH	OKINAWA	EMPIRE		
04/22/45	72290	VBF-12	USS RANDOLPH	OKINAWA	EMPIRE		
04/22/45	72696	VBF-12	USS RANDOLPH	KIKAI	EMPIRE		
04/22/45	71759	VF-82	USS BENNING-TON	OKINAWA	EMPIRE	ENS W.L. STALLINGS	S
04/23/45	72306	VF-23	USS LANGLEY	OKINAWA	EMPIRE		
04/23/45	72584	VF-23	USS LANGLEY	OKINAWA	EMPIRE		
04/23/45	72342	VF-40	USS SUWAN-NEE	MIYARA	EMPIRE	LT ROBERT S. ROTH	S
04/23/45	72272	VF-82	USS BENNING-TON	OKINAWA	EMPIRE	LTJG S.P. STURGIS	S
04/24/45	72317	VF-12	USS RANDOLPH	OKINAWA	EMPIRE		
04/24/45	72754	VF-16	USS BON HOMME RICHARD	HAWAII	ECENPAC	ENS WM M. VANLANDINGHAM S	
04/24/45	72786	VF-16	USS BON HOMME RICHARD	HAWAII	ECENPAC	ENS SIMON J. DRAGO	D
04/25/45	72616	VF-12	USS RANDOLPH	IE SHIMA	EMPIRE	ENS T.J. NORTHCUTT	S
04/25/45	77942	VF-24	USS SANTEE	IWO JIMA	EMPIRE	LTJG GLEN WM. FREEMAN	M
04/26/45	70666	CASU(F)-15		SAIPAN	WCENPAC		
04/26/45	70814	CASU(F)-15		SAIPAN	WCENPAC		
04/26/45	72210	CASU(F)-15		SAIPAN	WCENPAC		
04/26/45	72064	VBF-16	USS KASAAN BAY	HAWAII	ECENPAC	ENS WALDO B. LUMBERT	S
04/27/45	72846	VBF-17	USS HORNET	ENR KYUSHU	EMPIRE		
04/27/45	72672	VBF-9	USS YORK-TOWN	OKINAWA	EMPIRE	LCDR H.B. HOUCK	S
04/27/45	72400	VF-12	USS RANDOLPH	IE SHIMA	EMPIRE		
04/28/45	58119	CASU-1	PEARL	HAWAII	ECENPAC	CAPT RAYMOND CONN	U
04/29/45	71470	VF-33	USS SAN-GAMON	IWO JIMA	EMPIRE	LT WALKER H. BASKETT	M
04/29/45	71437	VF-46	USS INDEPEN-DENCE	OKINAWA	EMPIRE	LTJG SAMUEL A. SPARKS	S
04/29/45	77996	VF-9	USS YORK-TOWN	OKINAWA	EMPIRE	ENS C.S. ARTHUR	S
04/30/45	70437	POOL	PEARL	HAWAII	ECENPAC		
04/30/45	70977	POOL	PEARL	HAWAII	ECENPAC		
04/30/45	71041	POOL	PEARL	HAWAII	ECENPAC		
04/30/45	71314	POOL	PEARL	HAWAII	ECENPAC		
04/30/45	71798	POOL	PEARL	HAWAII	ECENPAC		
04/30/45	72326	POOL	PEARL	HAWAII	ECENPAC		
04/30/45	72523	POOL	PEARL	HAWAII	ECENPAC		
04/30/45	72563	POOL	PEARL	HAWAII	ECENPAC		
04/30/45	72955	POOL	PEARL	HAWAII	ECENPAC		
04/30/45	72452	VBF-12	USS RANDOLPH	IE SHIMA	EMPIRE		
04/30/45	72410	VF-23	USS LANGLEY	OKINAWA	EMPIRE		
04/30/45	71506	VF-83	USS ESSEX	OKINAWA	EMPIRE	ENS R.C. TARLTON	D
04/30/45	71999	VF-9	USS YORK-TOWN	KIKAI	EMPIRE	LTJG R.J. WARNER	S
04/30/45	71421	VF-99		SAIPAN	WCENPAC		
05/02/45	71899	VF-2	HILO	HAWAII	ECENPAC	ENS J.H. DUNCAN	S
05/02/45	77731	VF-34	USS MONTEREY	ENR KYUSHU	WCENPAC		
05/02/45	72624	VF-40	USS SUWAN-NEE	OKINAWA	EMPIRE		

DATE	BUNO	SQDRN	BASE	LOST	AREA	PILOT	FATE
05/02/45	72231	VF-9	USS YORK-TOWN	OKINAWA	EMPIRE		
05/03/45	72345	VBF-12	USS RANDOLPH	IE SHIMA	EMPIRE	ENS L.L. COLIN	S
05/03/45	72470	VF-46	USS INDEPEN-DENCE	OKINAWA	EMPIRE	CDR CARL W. ROONEY	S
05/04/45	71315	POOL	KAHULUI	HAWAII	ECENPAC		
05/04/45	71380	VBF-12	USS RANDOLPH	IE SHIMA	EMPIRE		
05/04/45	77937	VBF-9	USS YORK-TOWN	OKINAWA	EMPIRE		
05/04/45	72498	VF-12	USS RANDOLPH	IE SHIMA	EMPIRE		
05/04/45	72669	VF-12	USS RANDOLPH	IE SHIMA	EMPIRE	ENS JAMES J. FOWLER	S
05/04/45	78298	VF-12	USS RANDOLPH	IE SHIMA	EMPIRE	ENS LEE O. GLIDDEN	S
05/05/45	71360	CASU-4	PUUNENE	HAWAII	ECENPAC	LT CHARLES O. DODSON	S
05/05/45	72250	VBF-12	USS RANDOLPH	IE SHIMA	EMPIRE		
05/06/45	72236	VBF-9	USS YORK-TOWN	OKINAWA	EMPIRE		
05/06/45	70929	VF-2	USS TICONDER-OGA	HAWAII	ECENPAC	ENS L.A. VABULIAS	S
05/06/45	77860	VF-9	USS YORK-TOWN	OKINAWA	EMPIRE		
05/08/45	72024	VF-49	USS SAN JACINTO	ULITHI	WCENPAC	ENS WILLIAM C. HENWOOD	S
05/08/45	72526	VF-49	USS SAN JACINTO	ULITHI	WCENPAC	ENS G.C. POMBEO	S
05/09/45	72886	VF-47	USS BATAAN	OKINAWA	EMPIRE		
05/09/45	72927	VF-47	USS BATAAN	TUKUNO	EMPIRE	ENS JACK D. EZELL	M
05/10/45	58525	VF-100	EWA	HAWAII	ECENPAC	ENS CARL B. BAXTER	S
05/10/45	72288	VF-46	USS INDEPEN-DENCE	IE SHIMA	EMPIRE	ENS ROBERT D. FLOODQUIST	S
05/10/45	72522	VF-49	USS SAN JACINTO	ULITHI	WCENPAC	ENS E.A. CASE	S
05/10/45	77838	VF-49	USS SAN JACINTO	ULITHI	WCENPAC	ENS CHRISTOFSEN	S
05/10/45	72678	VMF-511	USS BLOCK ISLAND	JIMA	EMPIRE	2NDLT BYRON LEE COOK	S
05/11/45	71926	VBF-12	USS RANDOLPH	IE SHIMA	EMPIRE		
05/11/45	77744	VBF-12	USS RANDOLPH	IE SHIMA	EMPIRE		
05/11/45	72726	VF-24	USS SANTEE	IWO JIMA	EMPIRE	ENS ALVIN GORDON COOPER	S
05/11/45	77939	VF-34	USS MONTEREY	KYUSHU	EMPIRE		
05/11/45	71398	VF-40	USS SUWAN-NEE	IE SHIMA	EMPIRE		
05/11/45	72711	VF-40	USS SUWAN-NEE	IE SHIMA	EMPIRE	LTJG DENNINGS	S
05/11/45	72714	VF-40	USS SUWAN-NEE	IE SHIMA	EMPIRE	LTJG GEORGE W. WARNER	S
05/11/45	71493	VF-47	USS BATAAN	OKINAWA	EMPIRE		
05/11/45	77456	VF-83	USS ESSEX	OKINAWA	EMPIRE		
05/11/45	72517	VF-84	USS BUNKER HILL	OKINAWA	EMPIRE	(DECK LOSS-KAMIKAZE)	
05/11/45	72661	VF-84	USS BUNKER HILL	OKINAWA	EMPIRE	(DECK LOSS-KAMIKAZE)	

DATE	BUNO	SQDRN	BASE	LOST	AREA	PILOT	FATE
05/11/45	77464	VF-84	USS BUNKER HILL	OKINAWA	EMPIRE	(DECK LOSS-KAMIKAZE)	
05/12/45	72945	VBF-12	USS RANDOLPH	IE SHIMA	EMPIRE	CDR RALPH A. EMBREE	M
05/12/45	77829	VBF-12	USS RANDOLPH	IE SHIMA	EMPIRE		
05/12/45	78274	VF-87	USS TICONDER-OGA	TAROA	CENPAC	ENS BENJAMIN D. CAIN	S
05/12/45	71634	VF-99		SAIPAN	WCENPAC	ENS MARLYN V. BELL	S
05/13/45	71820	CASU-4	PUUNENE	HAWAII	ECENPAC	LT LOUIS M. KELLY	S
05/13/45	77787	VF-17	USS HORNET	KYUSHU	EMPIRE	ENS JOHN J. GAFFNEY	D
05/13/45	72525	VF-30	USS BELLEAU WOOD	KYUSHU	EMPIRE	LT RUSSELL E. STEPHENS	M
05/13/45	71780	VF-82	USS BENNING-TON	KYUSHU	EMPIRE	ENS J.B. HOAG	S
05/13/45	72448	VF-82	USS BENNING-TON	KYUSHU	EMPIRE	LT PHIL PERABO, JR.	M
05/13/45	72460	VF-83	USS ESSEX	OKINAWA	EMPIRE		
05/14/45	70108	CASU(F)-15		SAIPAN	WCENPAC		
05/14/45	71538	VBF-17	USS HORNET	KYUSHU	EMPIRE	LCDR H.W. NICHOLSON	D
05/14/45	72605	VF-12	USS RANDOLPH	KYUSHU	EMPIRE	ENS J. MORRIS	S
05/14/45	77880	VF-12	USS RANDOLPH	KYUSHU	EMPIRE	ENS R.L. WELTY	M
05/14/45	72567	VF-47	USS BATAAN	KYUSHU	EMPIRE		
05/15/45	71320	NACTU	BARBERS POINT	HAWAII	ECENPAC	ENS HENRY J. O'MEARA	S
05/15/45	72297	VF-102	USS ATTU	OKINAWA	EMPIRE	ENS ROBERT J. RHINEFIELD	S
05/15/45	72671	VF-82	USS BENNING-TON	SHIKOKU	EMPIRE	ENS R.A. MACDONALD	S
05/16/45	77943	VF-82	USS BENNING-TON	MINDANAO SEA	PHIL	LCDR E.W. HESSEL	S
05/17/45	71111	VF-99		SAIPAN	WCENPAC	LTJG LAWRENCE E. OLIVER	S
05/18/45	77198	VF-12	USS RANDOLPH	IE SHIMA	EMPIRE	ENS C.L. WHITE	M
05/18/45	71589	VF-47	USS BATAAN	OKINAWA	EMPIRE		
05/18/45	77936	VF-47	USS BATAAN	OKINAWA	EMPIRE		
05/18/45	78074	VF-47	USS BATAAN	OKINAWA	EMPIRE		
05/18/45	78087	VF-47	USS BATAAN	OKINAWA	EMPIRE		
05/18/45	78041	VF-49	USS SAN JACINTO	IE SHIMA	EMPIRE	ENS FOLZ	S
05/19/45	78490	VF-34	USS MONTEREY	KYUSHU	EMPIRE		
05/19/45	78077	VF-49	USS SAN JACINTO	IE SHIMA	EMPIRE		
05/19/45	78877	VF-49	USS SAN JACINTO	IE SHIMA	EMPIRE	ENS D. BOX BYRON	S
05/20/45	71341	NACTU	USS KASAAN BAY	PEARL	ECENPAC	ENS LOUIS N. CISLO	S
05/20/45	77782	VF-34	USS MONTEREY	KYUSHU	EMPIRE		
05/21/45	78030	CASU(F)-35		ENIWETOK	CENPAC		
05/21/45	72486	CASU-11		OKINAWA	EMPIRE	MAJ WALTER L. EVANS	M
05/21/45	58601	NACTU	BARBERS POINT	HAWAII	ECENPAC	ENS EUGENE BRENDAN LONG	S
05/21/45	78095	VF-49	USS SAN JACINTO	TOKUNO	EMPIRE	ENS C.P. THORNE	S

DATE	BUNO	SQDRN	BASE	LOST	AREA	PILOT	FATE
05/21/45	78161	VF-49	USS SAN JACINTO	TOKUNO	EMPIRE	ENS WILLIAM C. HENWOOD	S
05/21/45	71841	VF-99	USS MAKASSAR STRAIT	SAIPAN	WCENPAC		
05/22/45	71763	CASU-4	PUUNENE	HAWAII	ECENPAC	LT JOHN H. DICK	S
05/22/45	77770	NACTU	BARBERS POINT	HAWAII	ECENPAC	ENS BRYEE BROWN, JR.	S
05/22/45	77502	VF-30	USS BELLEAU WOOD	KONIYA	EMPIRE	LT STURDEVANT	S
05/22/45	78153	VF-82	USS BENNING-TON	IE SHIMA	EMPIRE	ENS J.C. DRESSEL	M
05/22/45	78286	VF-82	USS BENNING-TON	OKINAWA	EMPIRE	ENS P.M. BUDINGER	S
05/22/45	70140	VF-99		SAIPAN	WCENPAC	ENS R.J. HALLIDAY	S
05/23/45	72727	VF-83	USS ESSEX	OKINAWA	EMPIRE		
05/24/45	77589	VF-17	USS HORNET	KYUSHU	EMPIRE	LT EDWARD G. VERNELIE	D
05/24/45	77708	VF-17	USS HORNET	KYUSHU	EMPIRE	LT H.D. COWGERS	S
05/24/45	70120	VMF(N)-534		GUAM	WCENPAC	2NDLT EARL D. VAN KEUREN	S
05/25/45	77679	VBF-9	USS YORK-TOWN	ENR OKINAWA	EMPIRE		
05/25/45	77958	VF-25	USS CHENAN-GO	OKINAWA	EMPIRE	ENS M.T. TEPPEN	M
05/25/45	72193	VF-82	USS BENNING-TON	OKINAWA	EMPIRE	LT W.L. STALLINGS	S
05/26/45	77743	VF-40	USS SUWAN-NEE	ENR MIYAKO	EMPIRE		
05/27/45	58190	VF-88	USS MAKASSAR STR.	SAIPAN	WCENPAC	ENS ROBERT C. BAKER	S
05/28/45	58326	NAS	HILO	HAWAII	ECENPAC	ENS CHANNING S. ROUILLARD	D
05/28/45	78305	VF-40	USS SUWAN-NEE	MIYAKO	EMPIRE	LTJG MAXWELL F. DENMAN	M
05/29/45	72822	VF-17	USS HORNET	OKINAWA	EMPIRE		
05/29/45	71862	VF-2	HILO	HAWAII	ECENPAC		
05/29/45	72795	VF-24	USS SANTEE	IWO JIMA	EMPIRE	LT JOHN F. GRAY	M
05/29/45	78481	VMF(N)-541		PELELIU	WCENPAC	2NDLT H.T. HAYES	M
05/30/45	70297	CASU(F)-15		SAIPAN	WCENPAC	ENS E.C. MURRAY	S
05/30/45	71737	CASU(F)-51		ULITHI	WCENPAC		
05/30/45	78160	CASU(F)-51		ULITHI	WCENPAC		
05/31/45	71342	COMAIR-PAC	PEARL	HAWAII	ECENPAC		
05/31/45	71935	COMAIR-PAC	PEARL	HAWAII	ECENPAC		
05/31/45	72462	COMAIR-PAC	PEARL	HAWAII	ECENPAC		
05/31/45	79243	COMAIR-PAC	PEARL	HAWAII	ECENPAC		
05/31/45	70889	VF-8	HILO	HAWAII	ECENPAC	LT WILLIAM R. FRANK	S
06/01/45	78814	CASU-4	PUUNENE	HAWAII	ECENPAC	ENS CHESTER T. LAWRENCE	S
06/01/45	71370	POOL	PEARL	HAWAII	ECENPAC		
06/01/45	71776	VF-25	USS CHENAN-GO	IWO JIMA	EMPIRE	LT B. PHILLIPS	S
06/02/45	78633	VBF-87	USS TICONDER-OGA	KYUSHU	EMPIRE	LT MERLE M. HERSHEY	S
06/02/45	78145	VBF-9	USS YORK-TOWN	KYUSHU	EMPIRE	ENS ROY G. KUELLER	S
06/02/45	78213	VF-17	USS HORNET	OKINAWA	EMPIRE		

DATE	BUNO	SQDRN	BASE	LOST	AREA	PILOT	FATE
06/02/45	77875	VF-46	USS INDEPENDENCE	KYUSHU	EMPIRE	LTJG M.E. STEWART	S
06/03/45	77545	VF-17	USS HORNET	OKINAWA	EMPIRE		
06/03/45	71969	VF-46	USS INDEPENDENCE	KYUSHU	EMPIRE	LTJG B.R. APGAR	M
06/03/45	77642	VF-46	USS INDEPENDENCE	KYUSHU	EMPIRE	ENS R.T. DYER	M
06/03/45	77849	VF-46	USS INDEPENDENCE	KYUSHU	EMPIRE	ENS ZIGMUND PLECHA	S
06/03/45	77600	VF-9	USS YORKTOWN	OKINAWA	EMPIRE	LTJG HARTWIG	S
06/04/45	70926	CASU-51	HILO	HAWAII	ECENPAC		
06/04/45	78996	VF-87	USS TICONDEROGA	ENR OKINAWA	EMPIRE		
06/05/45	72893	POOL	USS ATTU	OKINAWA	EMPIRE		
06/05/45	77646	POOL	USS BOUGAINVILLE		EMPIRE	(DECK LOSS-TYPHOON)	
06/05/45	78157	POOL	USS BOUGAINVILLE		EMPIRE	(DECK LOSS-TYPHOON)	
06/05/45	78329	POOL	USS BOUGAINVILLE		EMPIRE	(DECK LOSS-TYPHOON)	
06/05/45	78531	POOL	USS ATTU	OKINAWA	EMPIRE		
06/05/45	78545	POOL	USS ATTU	OKINAWA	EMPIRE		
06/05/45	78555	POOL	USS ATTU	OKINAWA	EMPIRE		
06/05/45	78556	POOL	USS ATTU	OKINAWA	EMPIRE		
06/05/45	78567	POOL	USS ATTU	OKINAWA	EMPIRE		
06/05/45	78611	POOL	USS ATTU	OKINAWA	EMPIRE		
06/05/45	72709	VF-17	USS HORNET	OKINAWA	EMPIRE		
06/05/45	72485	VF-30	USS BELLEAU WOOD		EMPIRE		
06/05/45	72862	VF-30	USS BELLEAU WOOD		EMPIRE		
06/05/45	77544	VF-30	USS BELLEAU WOOD		EMPIRE		
06/05/45	77570	VF-30	USS BELLEAU WOOD		EMPIRE		
06/05/45	77845	VF-30	USS BELLEAU WOOD		EMPIRE		
06/05/45	78050	VF-30	USS BELLEAU WOOD		EMPIRE		
06/05/45	78135	VF-30	USS BELLEAU WOOD		EMPIRE		
06/06/45	77598	POOL	PEARL	HAWAII	ECENPAC		
06/06/45	78000	POOL	USS BOUGAINVILLE		EMPIRE	(DECK LOSS-TYPHOON)	
06/06/45	78571	POOL	USS BOUGAINVILLE		EMPIRE	(DECK LOSS-TYPHOON)	
06/06/45	78622	POOL	USS BOUGAINVILLE		EMPIRE	(DECK LOSS-TYPHOON)	
06/06/45	71321	VF-94		HAWAII	ECENPAC	LT JAMES E. GALLAWAY	S
06/07/45	77832	VBF-12	USS RANDOLPH		PHIL		
06/07/45	78061	VBF-12	USS RANDOLPH		PHIL		

DATE	BUNO	SQDRN	BASE	LOST	AREA	PILOT	FATE
06/07/45	78169	VBF-12	USS RANDOLPH		PHIL		
06/07/45	77834	VF-12	USS RANDOLPH		PHIL		
06/07/45	77929	VF-12	USS RANDOLPH		PHIL		
06/07/45	78216	VF-12	USS RANDOLPH		PHIL		
06/07/45	78349	VF-12	USS RANDOLPH		PHIL		
06/07/45	72715	VF-30	USS BELLEAU WOOD		EMPIRE		
06/08/45	72082	VBF-8	PUUNENE	HAWAII	ECENPAC		
06/08/45	78224	VF-82	USS BENNING-TON	KYUSHU	EMPIRE		
06/08/45	78282	VF-87	USS TICONDER-OGA	KYUSHU	EMPIRE	LT MURRAY H. TYLER	S
06/09/45	78422	VF-8	PUUNENE	HAWAII	ECENPAC	ENS VICTOR GHIDINELLI	S
06/09/45	58296	VF-92	OAHU	HAWAII	ECENPAC	ENS WARREN RUSSELL	S
06/10/45	72737	POOL	USS ATTU	PEARL	ECENPAC	ENS R.C. HACKER	S
06/10/45	78104	VF-30	USS BELLEAU WOOD	IWO JIMA	EMPIRE		
06/12/45	71748	CASU(F)-47		SAIPAN	WCENPAC		
06/12/45	78251	CASU-11		OKINAWA	EMPIRE		
06/12/45	77759	VF-49	USS SAN JACINTO	LEYTE GULF	PHIL		
06/16/45	77564	CASU(F)-12		GUAM	WCENPAC		
06/16/45	77862	CASU(F)-12		GUAM	WCENPAC		
06/16/45	58810	NACTU	BARBERS POINT	HAWAII	ECENPAC		
06/16/45	77944	VF-24	USS SANTEE	KYUSHU	EMPIRE		
06/19/45	78693	VF-85	USS SHANGRI-LA	LEYTE GULF	PHIL		
06/20/45	58866	POOL	PEARL	HAWAII	ECENPAC		
06/20/45	71714	POOL	PEARL	HAWAII	ECENPAC		
06/20/45	78129	POOL	PEARL	HAWAII	ECENPAC		
06/20/45	58534	VF-21		HAWAII	ECENPAC	LTJG ELTON BOECK	S
06/20/45	79072	VF-50	USS COWPENS	WAKE	WCENPAC		
06/20/45	72911	VF-53	USS ESSEX		EMPIRE		
06/20/45	78752	VF-94	USS LEX-INGTON	WAKE	WCENPAC	LTJG NEWHY HALE POPE	D
06/21/45	70097	CASU(F)-14		SAIPAN	WCENPAC		
06/21/45	71518	CASU(F)-14		SAIPAN	WCENPAC		
06/21/45	77547	VF-16	USS RANDOLPH	PHIL			
06/21/45	72047	VF-8	PUUNENE	HAWAII	ECENPAC	LT D.E. SNIDER	S
06/22/45	78612	VF-6	USS HANCOCK	PEARL	ECENPAC		
06/22/45	58032	VF-92	KAHULUI	HAWAII	ECENPAC		
06/26/45	77723	VF-31	USS BELLEAU WOOD	LEYTE GULF	PHIL		
06/26/45	77893	VF-49	USS SAN JACINTO	LEYTE GULF	PHIL	LTJG FOLZ	S
06/26/45	79656	VF-6	USS HANCOCK	PEARL	ECENPAC		
06/26/45	79946	VF-89	KAHULUI	HAWAII	ECENPAC	ENS LEONARD L. ALICK	S
06/29/45	79366	NACTU	BARBERS POINT	HAWAII	ECENPAC	LT PAUL E. PUGH	S
06/29/45	72750	VF-1	USS BENNING-TON	LEYTE GULF	PHIL		
06/30/45	78262	CASU-31	HILO	HAWAII	ECENPAC		
06/30/45	78339	VF-94	USS LEX-INGTON	HAWAII	ECENPAC	ENS NORMAN RICH. LOESING	S
07/03/45	79490	VF-94	USS LEX-INGTON		EMPIRE	ENS TOM LA VON NEILSON	S

DATE	BUNO	SQDRN	BASE	LOST	AREA	PILOT	FATE
07/05/45	77897	VF-16	USS RANDOLPH		EMPIRE		
07/05/45	77763	VF-34	USS MONTEREY	HONSHU	EMPIRE		
07/05/45	79268	VF-94	USS LEXINGTON		EMPIRE	ENS EDWARD A. MAGGIOLI	S
07/06/45	78304	VBF-16	USS RANDOLPH		EMPIRE		
07/06/45	77844	VF-34	USS MONTEREY	HONSHU	EMPIRE	ENS R.E. SCHWEDEMANN	S
07/07/45	72663	VF-24	USS SANTEE	OKINAWA	EMPIRE	ENS WILLIAM A. SINNOTT	S
07/07/45	77831	VF-24	USS SANTEE	OKINAWA	EMPIRE	LT ROBERT BRIGHAM ELLERY	D
07/07/45	72838	VF-40	USS SUWANNEE	LEYTE GULF	PHIL	LTJG ROBERT E. CURRY	S
07/08/45	77556	CASU-4	PUUNENE	HAWAII	ECENPAC	ENS RANDALL D. GOEHRING	S
07/08/45	58872	NACTU	USS SARATOGA	HAWAII	ECENPAC	ENS STEWART B. PATTISON	M
07/08/45	71887	NACTU	USS SARATOGA	HAWAII	ECENPAC	ENS GENAVERY R. TALLINI	S
07/08/45	71854	POOL	PEARL	HAWAII	ECENPAC		
07/08/45	71931	POOL	USS HOLLANDIA		EMPIRE		
07/08/45	77938	VF-1	USS BENNINGTON	ENR KURE	EMPIRE		
07/08/45	78054	VF-31	USS BELLEAU WOOD		EMPIRE		
07/08/45	78430	VF-47	USS BATAAN	TOKYO	EMPIRE		
07/08/45	78117	VF-94	USS LEXINGTON		EMPIRE		
07/09/45	78142	ACORN-30 PL		TACLOBAN	PHIL		
07/10/45	77835	ACORN-30 PL		TACLOBAN	PHIL		
07/10/45	78025	ACORN-30 PL		TACLOBAN	PHIL		
07/10/45	78636	ACORN-30 PL		TACLOBAN	PHIL		
07/10/45	72612	CASU(F)-39		SAMAR	PHIL		
07/10/45	79600	VF-16	USS RANDOLPH	TOKYO	EMPIRE	ENS WILLIAM LANGE	M
07/10/45	77541	VF-31	USS BELLEAU WOOD		EMPIRE	ENS E.H. CAYWOOD	M
07/10/45	78292	VF-34	USS MONTEREY	HONSHU	EMPIRE		
07/10/45	77645	VF-47	USS BATAAN	TOKYO	EMPIRE	LT R.I. TALBOT	S
07/10/45	78690	VF-6	USS HANCOCK		EMPIRE	LTJG JAMES S. LONG	S
07/10/45	78155	VF-88	USS YORKTOWN	ENR JAPAN	EMPIRE		
07/10/45	72858	VF-94	USS LEXINGTON		EMPIRE	LTJG P. J. VANDERLINDEN	S
07/11/45	77878	VF-34	USS MONTEREY	HONSHU	EMPIRE		
07/11/45	78949	VF-94	USS LEXINGTON		EMPIRE	LT THOMAS JOSEPH HANLEN	S
07/11/45	71870	VF-99		SAIPAN	WCENPAC		
07/12/45	78806	VF-99		GUAM	WCENPAC	ENS C.F. ARCHER	S
07/13/45	77446	CASU(F)-12		GUAM	WCENPAC		
07/13/45	58115	VF-99		SAIPAN	WCENPAC		
07/14/45	78255	VF-16	USS RANDOLPH	TSUGARU STRAIT	EMPIRE	ENS G.G. HAYNES	M
07/14/45	77587	VF-27	USS INDEPENDENCE		EMPIRE	ENS JULIUS PARKER	S
07/14/45	77947	VF-34	USS MONTEREY	HONSHU	EMPIRE		

DATE	BUNO	SQDRN	BASE	LOST	AREA	PILOT	FATE
07/14/45	78012	VF-47	USS BATAAN	OKINAWA	EMPIRE	LT JOHN WRIGHT	U
07/14/45	77918	VF-88	USS YORK-TOWN	HOKKAIDO	EMPIRE	LCDR RICH. G. CROMMELIN	U
07/14/45	78089	VF-88	USS YORK-TOWN	HOKKAIDO	EMPIRE		
07/15/45	71850	NACTU	BARBERS POINT	HAWAII	ECENPAC	ENS CHARLES L. KLEDER	S
07/15/45	78051	VBF-16	USS RANDOLPH		EMPIRE	LTJG G.W. MCKENZIE	S
07/15/45	78542	VBF-16	USS RANDOLPH		EMPIRE		
07/15/45	77991	VF-34	USS MONTEREY	HONSHU	EMPIRE		
07/15/45	78736	VF-6	USS HANCOCK		EMPIRE	ENS HERD	S
07/15/45	78368	VF-83	USS ESSEX	IE SHIMA	EMPIRE	ENS W.J. KINGSTON, JR.	S
07/15/45	78090	VF-88	USS YORK-TOWN	HOKKAIDO	EMPIRE	LTJG HERMAN B. CHASE	U
07/15/45	72881	VF-94	USS LEX-INGTON		EMPIRE		
07/16/45	71148	POOL	PEARL	HAWAII	ECENPAC		
07/16/45	72001	VBF-16	USS RANDOLPH		EMPIRE		
07/16/45	79499	VF-8	PUUNENE	HAWAII	ECENPAC	LT ANDREW J. KELLY	S
07/16/45	79224	VF-86	USS WASP		EMPIRE	LTJG D.E. MYERS	S
07/17/45	72364	CASU(F)-12		GUAM	WCENPAC		
07/17/45	77710	CASU(F)-12		GUAM	WCENPAC		
07/17/45	77631	VF-50	USS COWPENS	KURE	EMPIRE	LTJG ALBERT E. BRADLEY	S
07/17/45	78667	VF-6	USS HANCOCK		EMPIRE	ENS M.E. KINDER	S
07/18/45	79544	VF-34	USS MONTEREY	HONSHU	EMPIRE	ENS CESAR E. NORTHINGTON	U
07/18/45	78665	VF-6	USS HANCOCK		EMPIRE		
07/18/45	78676	VF-6	USS HANCOCK		EMPIRE	LTJG RICHARD J. OLSEN	U
07/18/45	78886	VF-8	PUUNENE	HAWAII	ECENPAC		
07/18/45	78088	VF-88	USS YORK-TOWN	TOKYO	EMPIRE		
07/20/45	71475	CASU-31	HILO	HAWAII	ECENPAC		
07/23/45	78379	VF-150	USS LAKE CHAM-PLAIN	CULEBRA IS.	CENLANT	ENS R.R. CAMPBELL	S
07/23/45	78014	VF-40	USS SUWAN-NEE	LEYTE GULF	PHIL		
07/23/45	78138	VF-47	USS BATAAN	OKINAWA	EMPIRE		
07/23/45	72902	VF-99		SAIPAN	WCENPAC		
07/24/45	77617	VBF-16	USS RANDOLPH	SHIKOKU	EMPIRE		
07/24/45	78634	VBF-87	USS TICONDER-OGA	KURE	EMPIRE		
07/24/45	78995	VBF-87	USS TICONDER-OGA	KURE	EMPIRE	CDR PORTER W. MAXWELL	M
07/24/45	72365	VF-16	USS RANDOLPH	SHIKOKU	EMPIRE	ENS G.E. HUMPHREY	S
07/24/45	79400	VF-16	USS RANDOLPH	SHIKOKU	EMPIRE	LCDR CHARLES SAWERS	M
07/24/45	79468	VF-16	USS RANDOLPH	SHIKOKU	EMPIRE		
07/24/45	78575	VF-27	USS INDEPEND ENCE		EMPIRE	LT BURDICK V. SCOY BURTCH	S
07/24/45	78237	VF-88	USS YORK-TOWN	KURE	EMPIRE	LTJG KENNETH L. MEYER	U
07/25/45	72623	VBF-16	USS RANDOLPH	SHIKOKU	EMPIRE	LT G.W. PACE	S
07/25/45	77593	VF-1	USS BENNING-TON	KURE	EMPIRE	ENS CHARLES J. STATLER	S

DATE	BUNO	SQDRN	BASE	LOST	AREA	PILOT	FATE
07/25/45	78222	VF-1	USS BENNING-TON	KURE	EMPIRE		
07/25/45	77934	VF-16	USS RANDOLPH	SHIKOKU	EMPIRE	ENS J.J. HANTSCHEL	M
07/25/45	78133	VF-16	USS RANDOLPH	SHIKOKU	EMPIRE	ENS C.B. YODER	S
07/25/45	78154	VF-16	USS RANDOLPH	SHIKOKU	EMPIRE	LT K.W.D. LEE	S
07/25/45	77489	VF-31	USS BELLEAU WOOD		EMPIRE	ENS HERBERT L. LAW	M
07/25/45	78228	VF-31	USS BELLEAU WOOD		EMPIRE	ENS EDWIN R. WHITE	D
07/25/45	78534	VF-31	USS BELLEAU WOOD		EMPIRE	LTJG CHARLES WM ROBISON	S
07/25/45	78110	VF-49	USS SAN JACINTO		EMPIRE	ENS W.A. BANCY	U
07/25/45	78583	VF-49	USS SAN JACINTO		EMPIRE	ENS DOGGETT	S
07/25/45	79583	VF-83	USS ESSEX	KURE	EMPIRE		
07/25/45	79336	VF-86	USS WASP		EMPIRE		
07/25/45	78035	VF-88	USS YORK-TOWN	KURE	EMPIRE		
07/27/45	77628	VF-28	PUUNENE	HAWAII	ECENPAC		
07/28/45	78719	VBF-87	USS TICONDER-OGA	KURE	EMPIRE	ENS WILLIAM N. STANLEY	D
07/28/45	79358	VBF-87	USS TICONDER-OGA	KURE	EMPIRE	ENS THOMAS G. SCHAEFER	M
07/28/45	78715	VF-1	USS BENNING-TON	KURE	EMPIRE	ENS R.J. BONSINGER	S
07/28/45	78359	VF-27	USS INDEPEND ENCE		EMPIRE		
07/28/45	78059	VF-49	USS SAN JACINTO		EMPIRE	LTJG G.M. WILLIAMS	S
07/28/45	78549	VF-50	USS COWPENS	KURE	EMPIRE	ENS R.B. BUFFINGTON	S
07/28/45	79334	VF-86	USS WASP	KURE	EMPIRE		
07/28/45	79339	VF-86	USS WASP	KURE	EMPIRE	LTJG T.H. MORTON	M
07/28/45	78524	VF-87	USS TICONDER-OGA	KURE	EMPIRE	ENS C.H. WALKER	M
07/29/45	77639	CASU(F)-12		GUAM	WCENPAC		
07/29/45	77532	CASU-38	KANEOHE	HAWAII	ECENPAC		
07/30/45	77621	CASU(F)-12		GUAM	WCENPAC		
07/30/45	78085	CASU(F)-12		GUAM	WCENPAC		
07/30/45	78309	CASU(F)-12		GUAM	WCENPAC		
07/30/45	78351	CASU(F)-12		GUAM	WCENPAC		
07/30/45	77921	VBF-16	USS RANDOLPH	SHIKOKU	EMPIRE		
07/30/45	78248	VBF-16	USS RANDOLPH	SHIKOKU	EMPIRE		
07/30/45	78044	VF-1	USS BENNING-TON	NAGOYA	EMPIRE	LTJG E.J. MURPHY	S
07/30/45	77972	VF-16	USS RANDOLPH	SHIKOKU	EMPIRE		
07/30/45	79563	VF-31	USS BELLEAU WOOD		EMPIRE		
07/30/45	79659	VF-34	USS MONTEREY	KURE	EMPIRE		
07/30/45	78036	VF-49	USS SAN JACINTO		EMPIRE		
07/30/45	78345	VF-6	USS HANCOCK		EMPIRE		
07/30/45	78370	VF-6	USS HANCOCK		EMPIRE		
07/30/45	79301	VF-86	USS WASP	YOKOSUKA	EMPIRE		

DATE	BUNO	SQDRN	BASE	LOST	AREA	PILOT	FATE
07/30/45	79337	VF-86	USS WASP	YOKOSUKA	EMPIRE	ENS L.H. AHERN	M
07/30/45	78979	VF-87	USS TICONDER-OGA	TOKYO	EMPIRE	LTJG GEORGE J. MATLOCK	S
07/30/45	72043	VF-88	USS YORK-TOWN	TOKYO	EMPIRE		
07/30/45	78720	VF-94	USS LEX-INGTON		EMPIRE	LT HAROLD H. BROCK	S
07/30/45	78983	VF-94	USS LEX-INGTON		EMPIRE		
07/30/45	78020	VF-95		HAWAII	ECENPAC	LTJG D.W. FISHER	S
07/30/45	70574	VF-99		SAIPAN	WCENPAC		
07/31/45	58850	CASU(F)-14		SAIPAN	WCENPAC		
07/31/45	58939	CASU(F)-47		SAIPAN	WCENPAC		
07/31/45	70352	CASU(F)-47		SAIPAN	WCENPAC		
07/31/45	79895	NAB		KWAJALEIN	CENPAC	ENS JOHN DAVIS	S
07/31/45	58368	POOL	BARBERS POINT	HAWAII	ECENPAC		
07/31/45	71719	POOL	KAHULUI	HAWAII	ECENPAC	LTJG WILSON F. DENNIS	D
07/31/45	78115	VF-16	USS RANDOLPH	SHIKOKU	EMPIRE		
07/31/45	78662	VF-6	USS HANCOCK		EMPIRE		
07/31/45	78235	VF-95		HAWAII	ECENPAC	ENS D.O. CHASE	S
08/02/45	78037	VF-83	USS ESSEX		EMPIRE		
08/03/45	71796	CASU-31	HILO	HAWAII	ECENPAC		
08/03/45	80030	VF-93	USS BOXER	GUAM	WCENPAC		
08/04/45	77578	CASU(F)-12		GUAM	WCENPAC		
08/05/45	78867	VF-27	USS INDEPEND ENCE		EMPIRE		
08/05/45	79459	VF-50	USS COWPENS	KURE	EMPIRE		
08/06/45	58717	VF(N)-52	OAHU	HAWAII	ECENPAC		
08/06/45	78338	VF-6	USS HANCOCK		EMPIRE		
08/07/45	79835	VF-83	USS ESSEX		EMPIRE		
08/09/45	78156	VBF-16	USS RANDOLPH	SHIKOKU	EMPIRE	ENS W.R. ROGERS	M
08/09/45	72265	VF-1	USS BENNING-TON		EMPIRE	ENS CHARLES J. STATLER	D
08/09/45	78596	VF-1	USS BENNING-TON		EMPIRE	LCDR M.C. HOPPMAN	S
08/09/45	78820	VF-31	USS BELLEAU WOOD		EMPIRE		
08/09/45	79632	VF-83	USS ESSEX		EMPIRE	LTJG BATTEN	S
08/10/45	78518	VBF-16	USS RANDOLPH	SHIKOKU	EMPIRE		
08/10/45	79559	VBF-16	USS RANDOLPH	SHIKOKU	EMPIRE	ENS M.W. VOSS	S
08/10/45	77965	VBF-87	USS TICONDER-OGA	TOKYO	EMPIRE		
08/10/45	78990	VBF-87	USS TICONDER-OGA	TOKYO	EMPIRE	LT GRANVILLE W. GOWAN	M
08/10/45	78202	VF-27	USS INDEPEND ENCE		EMPIRE	ENS GEORGE E. VAN HAGEN	S
08/10/45	78548	VF-31	USS BELLEAU WOOD		EMPIRE		
08/10/45	79306	VF-86	USS WASP	YOKOSUKA	EMPIRE	LT WILLIAM S. ANDERSON	M
08/10/45	78998	VF-87	USS TICONDER-OGA	TOKYO	EMPIRE	LT WILLIAM L. PETERSON	M
08/10/45	78200	VF-88	USS YORK-TOWN	TOKYO	EMPIRE	LTJG WILLIAM TUCHIMA	M

DATE	BUNO	SQDRN	BASE	LOST	AREA	PILOT	FATE
08/11/45	77713	VF-31	USS BELLEAU WOOD		EMPIRE		
08/12/45	77853	VF-83	USS ESSEX		EMPIRE		
08/13/45	77830	VF-16	USS RANDOLPH	SHIKOKU	EMPIRE	LT JAMES H. MCPHERSON	M
08/13/45	79817	VF-27	USS INDEPEND ENCE		EMPIRE	ENS WILLIAM A. CONDON	S
08/13/45	79649	VF-31	USS BELLEAU WOOD		EMPIRE	LT SHIMEK	S
08/13/45	78006	VF-49	USS SAN JACINTO	TOKYO	EMPIRE	LTJG WILLIAM C. HENWOOD	S
08/13/45	79496	VF-88	USS YORK-TOWN	TOKYO	EMPIRE	LT WILSON L. DOZIER	M
08/14/45	58006	VF-100		HAWAII	ECENPAC	ENS ARTHUR J. TEAGUE	S
08/14/45	78748	VF-31	USS BELLEAU WOOD		EMPIRE		
08/14/45	77949	VF-83	USS ESSEX		EMPIRE		
08/15/45	58400	CASU(F)-47		SAIPAN	WCENPAC		
08/15/45	79111	VF-26	USS SANTEE	ENR SAN PEDRO	PHIL		
08/15/45	79657	VF-27	USS INDEPEN-DENCE		EMPIRE	ENS EUGENE E. FELLOWS	U
08/15/45	79503	VF-34	USS MONTEREY	HONSHU	EMPIRE		
08/15/45	77599	VF-7				LTJG C. N. WIPPENSTALL	U
08/15/45	77748	VF-83	USS ESSEX		EMPIRE		
08/15/45	77458	VF-88	USS YORK-TOWN	TOKYO	EMPIRE	ENS E.E. MANDEBERG	M
08/15/45	78065	VF-88	USS YORK-TOWN	TOKYO	EMPIRE	LTJG J.G. SAHLOFF	M
08/15/45	78244	VF-88	USS YORK-TOWN	TOKYO	EMPIRE	ENS W.C. HOBBS, JR.	U
08/15/45	79592	VF-88	USS YORK-TOWN	TOKYO	EMPIRE	LT HOWARD M. HARRISON	M
08/15/45	78791	VF-94	USS LEX-INGTON		EMPIRE	LT ARTHUR N. MELHUSE	S

GRUMMAN F6F-5E

The F6F-5E was a night fighter with APS-4 radar. This was a rather clumsy stopgap that was superseded by the F6F–3N and –5N with the more suitable APS-6 radar. Aircraft lost:

DATE	BUNO	SQDRN	BASE	LOST	AREA	PILOT	FATE
12/24/44	71052	VF(N)-90	BARBERS POINT	HAWAII	ECENPAC	LTJG R.F. WRIGHT	S
01/06/45	71110	VF(N)-90	USS ENTER-PRISE	CLARK FIELD	PHIL	LCDR R.J. MCCULLOUGH	S
01/07/45	71080	VF(N)-90	USS ENTER-PRISE	CLARK FIELD	PHIL	ENS C.W. GIBSON	M
01/12/45	71153	VF(N)-90	USS ENTER-PRISE	FR. I.C.	PHIL		
01/19/45	71241	VF-33	PEARL	HAWAII	ECENPAC	ENS R.F. ECKSTEIN	S
02/05/45	71326	VF-33	USS SAN-GAMON	HAWAII	ECENPAC	LTJG JACK C. WATSON	S
02/10/45	71136	VF(N)-90	USS ENTER-PRISE	ENR TOKYO	WCENPAC	ENS W.L. SADLER	D
02/24/45	71147	VF(N)-90	USS ENTER-PRISE	IWO JIMA	EMPIRE	ENS WOODS	S

DATE	BUNO	SQDRN	BASE	LOST	AREA	PILOT	FATE
03/14/45	71125	COMAIR-PAC	PEARL	HAWAII	ECENPAC		
03/14/45	71160	COMAIR-PAC	PEARL	HAWAII	ECENPAC		
03/14/45	71260	COMAIR-PAC	PEARL	HAWAII	ECENPAC		
03/15/45	71112	VF(N)-90	USS ENTER-PRISE	HAWAII	ECENPAC	LT R.D. OTIS	S
03/20/45	71120	VF(N)-90	USS ENTER-PRISE	KYUSHU	EMPIRE		
03/20/45	71141	VF(N)-90	USS ENTER-PRISE	KYUSHU	EMPIRE		
03/20/45	72060	VF(N)-90	USS ENTER-PRISE	KYUSHU	EMPIRE		
03/28/45	71395	VF-17	USS HORNET	KYUSHU	EMPIRE	CDR CHARLES L. CROMMELIN	D
04/18/45	71372	VF-33	USS SAN-GAMON	JIMA	EMPIRE	LTJG JACK H. BATEMAN	M
04/23/45	71156	VF-33	USS SAN-GAMON	MIYARA	EMPIRE		
04/23/45	77351	VF-33	USS SAN-GAMON	MIYARA	EMPIRE		
04/23/45	77415	VF-33	USS SAN-GAMON	IWO JIMA	EMPIRE	LT CLAUDE M. REYNOLDS	S
04/27/45	72461	NACTU	BARBERS POINT	HAWAII	ECENPAC	ENS WILLIAM ODEN LARGON	S
04/30/45	71145	POOL	PEARL	HAWAII	ECENPAC		
05/04/45	71261	VF-33	USS SAN-GAMON	KEREMA RHET.	EMPIRE		
05/04/45	71305	VF-33	USS SAN-GAMON	KEREMA RHET.	EMPIRE		
05/04/45	71355	VF-33	USS SAN-GAMON	KEREMA RHET.	EMPIRE		
05/04/45	71410	VF-33	USS SAN-GAMON	KEREMA RHET.	EMPIRE		
05/04/45	71992	VF-33	USS SAN-GAMON	KEREMA RHET.	EMPIRE		
05/04/45	72080	VF-33	USS SAN-GAMON	KEREMA RHET.	EMPIRE		
05/04/45	72086	VF-33	USS SAN-GAMON	KEREMA RHET.	EMPIRE		
05/04/45	72090	VF-33	USS SAN-GAMON	KEREMA RHET.	EMPIRE		
05/04/45	72431	VF-33	USS SAN-GAMON	KEREMA RHET.	EMPIRE		
05/04/45	72465	VF-33	USS SAN-GAMON	KEREMA RHET.	EMPIRE		
05/04/45	72521	VF-33	USS SAN-GAMON	KEREMA RHET.	EMPIRE		
05/04/45	77358	VF-33	USS SAN-GAMON	KEREMA RHET.	EMPIRE		
05/04/45	77485	VF-33	USS SAN-GAMON	KEREMA RHET.	EMPIRE		
05/04/45	77497	VF-33	USS SAN-GAMON	KEREMA RHET.	EMPIRE		
05/08/45	77438	CASU-51		ULITHI	WCENPAC	LTJG G.F. KEELER	S
05/11/45	77359	NACTU	BARBERS POINT	HAWAII	ECENPAC	ENS KENNETH J. LANGLOIS	S
05/14/45	71117	VF(N)-90	USS ENTER-PRISE	KYUSHU	EMPIRE		
05/14/45	71255	VF(N)-90	USS ENTER-PRISE	KYUSHU	EMPIRE		
05/22/45	71122	NACTU	BARBERS POINT	HAWAII	ECENPAC	LT DOUGLAS RAY BRANTLEY	S
06/02/45	78283	NACTU	USS ROI	PEARL	ECENPAC	ENS JAMES R. KENNEDY	S
07/04/45	78296	NACTU	BARBERS POINT	HAWAII	ECENPAC	ENS WILLIAM R. BARNETT	S

DATE	BUNO	SQDRN	BASE	LOST	AREA	PILOT	FATE
07/05/45	71259	NACTU	BARBERS POINT	HAWAII	ECENPAC	ENS ROBERT E. PICTSOH	U
07/18/45	77450	VF-6	USS HANCOCK		EMPIRE		

GRUMMAN F6F-5N

Fitting AN/APS-6 radar to F6F-5s resulted in the night fighter **F6F-5N**, recognizable with a radar fairing mounted on the outer-starboard wing. Fitting AN/APS-6 radar to F6F-5s resulted in the night fighter **F6F-5N**, recognizable with a radar fairing mounted on the outer-starboard wing. While all F6F-5s were capable of carrying an armament mix of one 20 mm (.79 in) M2 cannon in each of the inboard gun bays (220 rpg), along with two pairs of .50 in (12.7 mm) machine guns (each with 400 rpg), this configuration was only used on many later F6F-5N night fighters. Aircraft lost:

DATE	BUNO	SQDRN	BASE	LOST	AREA	PILOT	FATE
08/23/44	58459	VF-22	USS INDEPEN-DENCE	E. OF ENIWETOK	CENPAC	ENS WILLIAM A. SHIPMAN	D
08/23/44	58975	VF-22	USS INDEPEN-DENCE	E. OF ENIWETOK	CENPAC		
08/31/44	58976	VF(N)-90	OAHU	HAWAII	ECENPAC	ENS RICHARD B. JONES	D
09/12/44	58010	VF-13	USS FRANKLIN	PALAU	CENPAC		
09/12/44	70041	VF-7	USS HANCOCK	PEARL	ECENPAC		
09/21/44	58502	VF(N)-41	USS INDEPEN-DENCE	LUZON	PHIL	ENS HAROLD E. JOHNSON	S
09/21/44	70147	VF(N)-41	USS INDEPEN-DENCE	LUZON	PHIL	LT WILLIAM E. HENRY	S
09/26/44	58334	VF(N)-76	USS LEX-INGTON		CENPAC	LTJG JOHN S. GILMAN	S
10/03/44	58431	VF(N)-41	USS INDEPEN-DENCE	ULITHI	WCENPAC		
10/03/44	58726	VF(N)-41	USS INDEPEN-DENCE	ULITHI	WCENPAC		
10/03/44	58853	VF(N)-41	USS INDEPEN-DENCE	ULITHI	WCENPAC		
10/05/44	58325	VF-13	USS FRANKLIN	PALAU	CENPAC		
10/07/44	58531	VMF(N)-533		ROI	WCENPAC	MAJ HOMER C. HUTCHISON	S
10/11/44	58796	VF(N)-41	USS INDEPEN-DENCE	OKINAWA	EMPIRE		
10/11/44	58970	VF(N)-41	USS INDEPEN-DENCE	OKINAWA	EMPIRE		
10/11/44	58344	VF-14	USS WASP	ENR FORMOSA	CENPAC		
10/12/44	58728	VF(N)-41	USS INDEPEN-DENCE	OKINAWA	EMPIRE	ENS GEORGE W. OBENOW	M
10/12/44	78052	VF(N)-41	USS INDEPEN-DENCE	OKINAWA	EMPIRE	ENS EMMETT R. EDWARDS	S
10/13/44	58305	CASU-42		PITYILU	SW PAC		
10/14/44	58392	VF(N)-41	USS INDEPEN-DENCE	OKINAWA	EMPIRE		
10/14/44	58167	VF-11	USS HORNET		CENPAC	LT E.E. HELGERSON	D

DATE	BUNO	SQDRN	BASE	LOST	AREA	PILOT	FATE
10/14/44	70053	VF-7	USS HANCOCK	MANILA	PHIL		
10/24/44	58724	VF(N)-41	USS INDEPEN-DENCE	LEYTE GULF	PHIL		
10/29/44	58722	VF(N)-41	USS INDEPEN-DENCE	LEYTE GULF	PHIL	CDR TURNER CALDWELL JR	S
10/29/44	58649	VF-13	USS FRANKLIN	LEYTE GULF	PHIL	LT WARREN F. WOLF	M
10/29/44	70294	VF-7	USS HANCOCK	MANILA	PHIL	ENS C.F. SULLIVAN	S
10/31/44	70142	COMAIR-PAC	PEARL	HAWAII	ECENPAC		
10/31/44	70063	NAS		HAWAII	ECENPAC		
11/10/44	70191	VF(N)-90	BARBERS POINT	HAWAII	ECENPAC	ENS J.F. LUNGERHAUSSEN	D
11/19/44	58725	VF(N)-41	USS INDEPEN-DENCE	LUZON	PHIL	ENS JAMES A. BARNETT	S
11/19/44	58352	VF-11	USS HORNET		PHIL	ENS WITZIG	S
11/21/44	70591	VF(N)-42	USS BATAAN	HAWAII	ECENPAC	ENS HAROLD G. COLE	S
11/25/44	58364	VF(N)-41	USS INDEPEN-DENCE	LUZON	PHIL		
11/30/44	70360	PEARL		HAWAII	ECENPAC		
12/03/44	70542		BARBERS POINT	HAWAII	ECENPAC		
12/11/44	71894	VF(N)-42	USS BATAAN	HAWAII	ECENPAC	ENS L.T. SKREBA	S
12/12/44	70414	VF-17	USS SARATOGA	HAWAII	ECENPAC	ENS HAROLD L. PAUL	S
12/12/44	58312	VF-20	USS LEX-INGTON	LUZON	PHIL		
12/13/44	70216	VF-80	USS TICONDER-OGA	LUZON	PHIL	LT C.T. LADWIG	S
12/14/44	71253	VF(N)-41	USS INDEPEN-DENCE	LUZON	PHIL	LT F.E. HANKINS	M
12/14/44	71278	VF(N)-41	USS INDEPEN-DENCE	LUZON	PHIL	ENS JOSEPH SAMUEL ALLEN	M
12/14/44	71309	VF(N)-41	USS INDEPEN-DENCE	LUZON	PHIL	ENS HAROLD E. JOHNSON	M
12/14/44	71316	VF(N)-41	USS INDEPEN-DENCE	LUZON	PHIL		
12/14/44	70662	VF-81	USS WASP	LEYTE GULF	PHIL		
12/15/44	58073	VF(N)-41	USS INDEPEN-DENCE	LUZON	PHIL	LT HOUDEN	S
12/15/44	71142	VF(N)-41	USS INDEPEN-DENCE	LUZON	PHIL	ENS WALLACE E. MILLER	S
12/15/44	71275	VF(N)-41	USS INDEPEN-DENCE	LUZON	PHIL	ENS JACK S. BERKHEIMER	M
12/15/44	70404	VF-4	USS ESSEX	LUZON	PHIL		
12/15/44	58026	VF-7	USS HANCOCK	LUZON	PHIL	LCDR JOHN ERICKSON	U
12/16/44	71155	VF(N)-41	USS INDEPEN-DENCE	LUZON	PHIL	ENS DONALD R. POWERS	D
12/21/44	58730	VF-11	USS HORNET		WCENPAC		
12/31/44	70521	PEARL		HAWAII	ECENPAC		
01/02/45	72201	VF(N)-53		HAWAII	ECENPAC	ENS L.D. HARROLD	S
01/03/45	70565	VF-3	USS YORK-TOWN	FORMOSA	EMPIRE	ENS CLIFFORD S. TOMLINSON	S

DATE	BUNO	SQDRN	BASE	LOST	AREA	PILOT	FATE
01/06/45	71758	VF(N)-41	USS INDEPEN-DENCE	LUZON	PHIL	LT RUSSELL D. OTIS	S
01/06/45	72215	VF(N)-53	USS SARATOGA	HAWAII	ECENPAC	ENS F. COLBERT	S
01/06/45	72261	VF-33	PEARL	HAWAII	ECENPAC	ENS MATTHEW CUMMINGS	S
01/07/45	58004	MAG-11		TACLOBAN	PHIL		
01/07/45	58696	MAG-11		TACLOBAN	PHIL		
01/07/45	71761	VF(N)-90	USS ENTER-PRISE	CLARK FIELD	PHIL	ENS J.G. SOWELL	M
01/07/45	58553	VF-20	USS LEX-INGTON	LUZON	PHIL		
01/12/45	70427	NACTU	BARBERS POINT	HAWAII	ECENPAC	ENS E.G. MCGARRY	D
01/13/45	71735	VF(N)-41	USS INDEPEN-DENCE	FR. I.C.	PHIL	ENS WALLACE E. MILLER	S
01/16/45	71821	VF(N)-41	USS INDEPEN-DENCE	FORMOSA	EMPIRE		
01/16/45	71983	VF(N)-41	USS INDEPEN-DENCE	FORMOSA	EMPIRE	ENS GLEN R. EARL	U
01/16/45	71809	VF(N)-90	USS ENTER-PRISE	HONG KONG	EMPIRE	ENS R.C. WALLENBURGER	S
01/16/45	72089	VF(N)-90	USS ENTER-PRISE	HONG KONG	EMPIRE	ENS E.G. NASH	D
01/16/45	72224	VF(N)-90	USS ENTER-PRISE	HONG KONG	EMPIRE	LTJG R.F. WRIGHT	M
01/16/45	58308	VF-7	USS HANCOCK	HONG KONG	EMPIRE		
01/17/45	72269	VF-33	PEARL	HAWAII	ECENPAC	ENS PAUL R. WATTERS	S
01/17/45	72270	VF-33	PEARL	HAWAII	ECENPAC		
01/20/45	58494	VF-7	USS HANCOCK	FORMOSA	EMPIRE	ENS C.P. SITES	M
01/21/45	71746	VF-80	USS TICONDER-OGA	FORMOSA	EMPIRE		
01/22/45	70426	VF-81	USS WASP	NAHA	EMPIRE		
02/06/45	71287	VF(N)-90	USS ENTER-PRISE	ULITHI	WCENPAC		
02/06/45	71868	VF(N)-90	USS ENTER-PRISE	ULITHI	WCENPAC		
02/11/45	71951	VF(N)-53	USS SARATOGA	ENR TINIAN	WCENPAC		
02/11/45	71789	VF(N)-90	USS ENTER-PRISE	ENR TOKYO	WCENPAC		
02/11/45	72011	VF(N)-90	USS ENTER-PRISE	ENR TOKYO	WCENPAC		
02/13/45	71045	VF(N)-90	USS ENTER-PRISE	ENR TOKYO	WCENPAC	ENS M.A. YORSTON	S
02/13/45	72874	VF-12	USS RANDOLPH	ENR TOKYO	EMPIRE		
02/14/45	70935	VF(N)-53	USS SARATOGA	ENR TOKYO	EMPIRE		
02/16/45	72739	VF(N)-53	USS SARATOGA	TOKYO	EMPIRE	LT STEWART E. DOTY	M
02/16/45	70669	VF(N)-90	USS ENTER-PRISE	TOKYO	EMPIRE	ENS FREDERICK A. HUNZIKER	S
02/16/45	71293	VF(N)-90	USS ENTER-PRISE	TOKYO	EMPIRE	ENS J.R. KENYON, JR.	S

DATE	BUNO	SQDRN	BASE	LOST	AREA	PILOT	FATE
02/16/45	71760	VF(N)-90	USS ENTER-PRISE	TOKYO	EMPIRE		
02/16/45	71822	VF(N)-90	USS ENTER-PRISE	TOKYO	EMPIRE	ENS FRANCIS R. LUSCOMBE	U
02/17/45	71238	VF(N)-90	USS ENTER-PRISE	TOKYO	EMPIRE	ENS M.A. YORSTON	S
02/18/45	72337	VF(N)-53	USS SARATOGA	TOKYO	EMPIRE		
02/19/45	71721	VF(N)-90	USS ENTER-PRISE	IWO JIMA	EMPIRE		
02/21/45	70156	VF(N)-53	USS SARATOGA	TOKYO	EMPIRE		
02/21/45	70319	VF(N)-53	USS SARATOGA	TOKYO	EMPIRE		
02/21/45	71021	VF(N)-53	USS SARATOGA	TOKYO	EMPIRE		
02/21/45	72012	VF(N)-53	USS SARATOGA	TOKYO	EMPIRE		
02/21/45	72033	VF(N)-53	USS SARATOGA	TOKYO	EMPIRE		
02/21/45	72054	VF(N)-53	USS SARATOGA	TOKYO	EMPIRE	ENS WALL	S
02/21/45	72066	VF(N)-53	USS SARATOGA	TOKYO	EMPIRE		
02/21/45	72078	VF(N)-53	USS SARATOGA	TOKYO	EMPIRE		
02/21/45	72101	VF(N)-53	USS SARATOGA	TOKYO	EMPIRE		
02/21/45	72111	VF(N)-53	USS SARATOGA	TOKYO	EMPIRE		
02/21/45	72112	VF(N)-53	USS SARATOGA	TOKYO	EMPIRE		
02/21/45	72253	VF(N)-53	USS SARATOGA	TOKYO	EMPIRE		
02/21/45	72278	VF(N)-53	USS SARATOGA	TOKYO	EMPIRE		
02/21/45	72312	VF(N)-53	USS SARATOGA	TOKYO	EMPIRE		
02/21/45	72556	VF(N)-53	USS SARATOGA	TOKYO	EMPIRE		
02/21/45	72581	VF(N)-53	USS SARATOGA	TOKYO	EMPIRE		
02/21/45	72593	VF(N)-53	USS SARATOGA	TOKYO	EMPIRE		
02/21/45	72666	VF(N)-53	USS SARATOGA	TOKYO	EMPIRE		
02/21/45	70405	VF-3	USS YORK-TOWN	IWO JIMA	EMPIRE		
02/25/45	72384	VF-82	USS BENNING-TON	IWO JIMA	EMPIRE		
02/28/45	72065	VF(N)-90	USS ENTER-PRISE	IWO JIMA	EMPIRE	ENS R.D. HILTON	S
03/01/45	72655	POOL	KANEOHE	HAWAII	ECENPAC		
03/02/45	72373	COMAIR-PAC	PEARL	HAWAII	ECENPAC		
03/02/45	72203	VF-84	USS BUNKER HILL	OKINAWA	EMPIRE		
03/03/45	72204	VF-84	USS BUNKER HILL	OKINAWA	EMPIRE		
03/04/45	72812	VF(N)-90	USS ENTER-PRISE	IWO JIMA	EMPIRE		
03/07/45	72020	VF(N)-90	USS ENTER-PRISE	IWO JIMA	EMPIRE		

DATE	BUNO	SQDRN	BASE	LOST	AREA	PILOT	FATE
03/07/45	72813	VF(N)-90	USS ENTER-PRISE	IWO JIMA	EMPIRE		
03/08/45	71133	VF(N)-90	USS ENTER-PRISE	HAWAII	ECENPAC	ENS MICHAEL E. PETERS	D
03/09/45	72252	COMAIR-PAC	PEARL	HAWAII	ECENPAC		
03/14/45	77373	VF-17	USS HORNET	ENR HONSHU	EMPIRE		
03/14/45	72447	VF-84	USS BUNKER HILL	ULITHI	WCENPAC		
03/14/45	71624	VF-86	USS WASP	ULITHI	WCENPAC		
03/14/45	71877	VF-86	USS WASP	ULITHI	WCENPAC		
03/15/45	72790	VF(N)-90	USS ENTER-PRISE	HAWAII	ECENPAC	LTJG K.D. CLOSE	S
03/16/45	72477	VF-84	USS BUNKER HILL	KURE	EMPIRE		
03/18/45	70855	VF(N)-90	USS ENTER-PRISE	KYUSHU	EMPIRE	LTJG J.W. COLE	S
03/18/45	72397	VF(N)-90	USS ENTER-PRISE	KYUSHU	EMPIRE	LT R.D. OTIS	S
03/18/45	70520	VF-83	USS ESSEX	KYUSHU	EMPIRE		
03/18/45	72032	VF-86	USS WASP	KANOYA	EMPIRE		
03/19/45	77615	NACTU	BARBERS POINT	HAWAII	ECENPAC	ENS W.J. ROBERTS	S
03/19/45	77361	VF-5	USS FRANKLIN	HONSHU	EMPIRE	(DECK LOSS-KAMIKAZE)	
03/19/45	77408	VF-5	USS FRANKLIN	HONSHU	EMPIRE	(DECK LOSS-KAMIKAZE)	
03/19/45	77527	VF-5	USS FRANKLIN	HONSHU	EMPIRE	(DECK LOSS-KAMIKAZE)	
03/19/45	72740	VF-82	USS BENNING-TON	KYUSHU	EMPIRE	LT R.I. BRUCE	S
03/20/45	71802	VF(N)-90	USS ENTER-PRISE	KYUSHU	EMPIRE		
03/20/45	72328	VF(N)-90	USS ENTER-PRISE	KYUSHU	EMPIRE		
03/20/45	72336	VF(N)-90	USS ENTER-PRISE	KYUSHU	EMPIRE		
03/22/45	58267	CASU(F)-12		GUAM	WCENPAC		
03/22/45	77538	CASU(F)-12		GUAM	WCENPAC		
03/22/45	70094	NACTU	BARBERS POINT	HAWAII	ECENPAC	ENS PAUL F. IRVINE	S
03/24/45	72374	VF-33	USS SAN-GAMON	KER. RHETTO	EMPIRE	LT EDWARD L. MILLER	M
03/26/45	77396	VF-6	USS HANCOCK	OKINAWA	EMPIRE	LT R.M. BUCK	D
03/28/45	72791	VF-33	USS SAN-GAMON	KER. RHETTO	EMPIRE	ENS ROBERT N. GORDON	S
03/29/45	72900	COMAIR-PAC	PEARL	HAWAII	ECENPAC		
04/01/45	77491	VMF-511	USS BLOCK ISLAND	HAWAII	ECENPAC	LT ROBERT E. WAGNER	S
04/02/45	70143	POOL	USS WINDHAM BAY	OKINAWA	EMPIRE	ENS L.E. COLVIN	S
04/02/45	71777	VF-17	USS HORNET	OKINAWA	EMPIRE		
04/02/45	72361	VF-33	USS SAN-GAMON	OKINAWA	EMPIRE		
04/02/45	72362	VF-33	USS SAN-GAMON	OKINAWA	EMPIRE		
04/02/45	70125	VF-83	USS ESSEX	OKINAWA	EMPIRE		
04/02/45	58632	VMF(N)-541		ULITHI	WCENPAC		

DATE	BUNO	SQDRN	BASE	LOST	AREA	PILOT	FATE
04/04/45	72899	VF-83	USS ESSEX	OKINAWA	EMPIRE		
04/05/45	72313	VF-10	USS INTREPID	OKINAWA	EMPIRE		
04/07/45	71906	VF-6	USS HANCOCK	OKINAWA	EMPIRE		
04/11/45	77977	VF(N)-90	USS ENTER-PRISE	OKINAWA	EMPIRE	ENS FREDERICK A. HUNZIKER	M
04/12/45	72876	NACTU	BARBERS POINT	HAWAII	ECENPAC	LTJG L.P. DOMINGOS	S
04/12/45	72805	VF(N)-90	USS ENTER-PRISE	OKINAWA	EMPIRE	(DECK LOSS-KAMIKAZE)	
04/12/45	72888	VF(N)-90	USS ENTER-PRISE	OKINAWA	EMPIRE	(DECK LOSS-KAMIKAZE)	
04/12/45	77432	VF(N)-90	USS ENTER-PRISE	OKINAWA	EMPIRE	(DECK LOSS-KAMIKAZE)	
04/12/45	77877	VF(N)-90	USS ENTER-PRISE	OKINAWA	EMPIRE	(DECK LOSS-KAMIKAZE)	
04/13/45	77481	VBF-17	USS HORNET	OKINAWA	EMPIRE		
04/13/45	77372	VF-10	USS INTREPID	OKINAWA	EMPIRE	LT MARK L. ORR	U
04/13/45	71736	VF-82	USS BENNING-TON	IE SHIMA	EMPIRE	ENS RICHARD CHUTE	S
04/13/45	70541	VF-9	USS YORK-TOWN	OKINAWA	EMPIRE		
04/13/45	72528	VMF(N)-542		OKINAWA	EMPIRE		
04/14/45	72574	VMF(N)-543		OKINAWA	EMPIRE	2NDLT BRUCE T. BONMER	D
04/15/45	72729	VMF(N)-543		OKINAWA	EMPIRE	2NDLT CHARLES F. TEMOLE	S
04/16/45	70189	VF-10	USS INTREPID	KOKUBO	EMPIRE		
04/16/45	72544	VF-10	USS INTREPID	KOKUBO	EMPIRE		
04/16/45	72719	VF-10	USS INTREPID	KOKUBO	EMPIRE		
04/16/45	72763	VF-10	USS INTREPID	KOKUBO	EMPIRE		
04/16/45	77580	VF-10	USS INTREPID	KOKUBO	EMPIRE		
04/16/45	78018	VF-10	USS INTREPID	KOKUBO	EMPIRE		
04/16/45	77360	VF-83	USS ESSEX	KYUSHU	EMPIRE	ENS L.E. COLVIN	S
04/16/45	72592	VMF(N)-542		OKINAWA	EMPIRE	LT HILL	D
04/17/45	70781	VF-17	USS HORNET	OKINAWA	EMPIRE		
04/17/45	72629	VMF(N)-543		OKINAWA	EMPIRE	2NDLT EDWIN T. IVERSON	D
04/17/45	72775	VMF(N)-543		OKINAWA	EMPIRE	2NDLT CHARLES ENGMAN JR	S
04/18/45	77670	VF-82	USS BENNING-TON	OKINAWA	EMPIRE	ENS P.H. DORSE	S
04/18/45	77647	VMF(N)-543		GUAM	WCENPAC		
04/21/45	72907	NACTU	BARBERS POINT	HILO	ECENPAC	ENS ARTHUR W. PHINNEY	S
04/22/45	72694	VF-24	USS SANTEE	IWO JIMA	EMPIRE	LTJG IRVING MAYER	S
04/22/45	72006	VF-33	USS SAN-GAMON	JIMA	EMPIRE	LTJG RICHARD F. ECKSTEIN	M
04/23/45	77409	VF-33	USS SAN-GAMON	MIYARA	EMPIRE		
04/23/45	77480	VF-33	USS SAN-GAMON	MIYARA	EMPIRE		
04/25/45	71250	NACTU	BARBERS POINT	HAWAII	ECENPAC	ENS RICHARD N. CROXTON	S
04/27/45	77602	VF-82	USS BENNING-TON	OKINAWA	EMPIRE	LTJG R.T. HAYES	D

DATE	BUNO	SQDRN	BASE	LOST	AREA	PILOT	FATE
04/29/45	72480	VF-12	USS RANDOLPH	IE SHIMA	EMPIRE	LT D.M. HYPES	S
04/30/45	72019	POOL	PEARL	HAWAII	ECENPAC		
04/30/45	72898	POOL	PEARL	HAWAII	ECENPAC		
04/30/45	77395	POOL	PEARL	HAWAII	ECENPAC		
04/30/45	77504	POOL	PEARL	HAWAII	ECENPAC		
05/03/45	72494	NACTU	BARBERS POINT	HAWAII	ECENPAC	LTJG HAROLD GENE COLE	S
05/03/45	72675	VF-12	USS RANDOLPH	IE SHIMA	EMPIRE	ENS OLIVER LAMAR WOOD	M
05/03/45	77558	VF-12	USS RANDOLPH	IE SHIMA	EMPIRE	LT JAMES JULIAN WOOD	M
05/03/45	72908	VF-85	USS SHANGRI-LA	OKINAWA	EMPIRE		
05/04/45	72438	VF-33	USS SAN-GAMON	KEREMA RHET.	EMPIRE		
05/04/45	72446	VF-33	USS SAN-GAMON	KEREMA RHET.	EMPIRE		
05/04/45	72695	VF-33	USS SAN-GAMON	KEREMA RHET.	EMPIRE		
05/04/45	72718	VF-33	USS SAN-GAMON	KEREMA RHET.	EMPIRE		
05/04/45	72730	VF-33	USS SAN-GAMON	KEREMA RHET.	EMPIRE		
05/04/45	72885	VF-33	USS SAN-GAMON	KEREMA RHET.	EMPIRE		
05/04/45	77559	VF-33	USS SAN-GAMON	KEREMA RHET.	EMPIRE		
05/06/45	70340	VF(N)-91		HAWAII	ECENPAC	LT HARRY V. WELDON	S
05/09/45	78623	VF(N)-90	USS ENTER-PRISE	KIKAI	EMPIRE	LTJG J.T. TUCKER	D
05/11/45	78684	VF(N)-91		HAWAII	ECENPAC	LT WARREN F. SMITH	S
05/11/45	71996	VF-84	USS BUNKER HILL	OKINAWA	EMPIRE	(DECK LOSS-KAMIKAZE)	
05/11/45	72195	VF-84	USS BUNKER HILL	OKINAWA	EMPIRE	(DECK LOSS-KAMIKAZE)	
05/11/45	72228	VF-84	USS BUNKER HILL	OKINAWA	EMPIRE	(DECK LOSS-KAMIKAZE)	
05/11/45	72529	VF-84	USS BUNKER HILL	OKINAWA	EMPIRE	(DECK LOSS-KAMIKAZE)	
05/11/45	72707	VF-84	USS BUNKER HILL	OKINAWA	EMPIRE	(DECK LOSS-KAMIKAZE)	
05/11/45	77451	VF-84	USS BUNKER HILL	OKINAWA	EMPIRE	(DECK LOSS-KAMIKAZE)	
05/12/45	77895	VMF-511	USS BLOCK ISLAND		EMPIRE	2NDLT REX H. PLOEN	S
05/14/45	70214	VF(N)-90	USS ENTER-PRISE	KYUSHU	EMPIRE		
05/14/45	71576	VF(N)-90	USS ENTER-PRISE	KYUSHU	EMPIRE		
05/14/45	72426	VF(N)-90	USS ENTER-PRISE	KYUSHU	EMPIRE		
05/14/45	72774	VF(N)-90	USS ENTER-PRISE	KYUSHU	EMPIRE		
05/14/45	77624	VF(N)-90	USS ENTER-PRISE	KYUSHU	EMPIRE		
05/14/45	77636	VF(N)-90	USS ENTER-PRISE	KYUSHU	EMPIRE		

DATE	BUNO	SQDRN	BASE	LOST	AREA	PILOT	FATE
05/14/45	77876	VF(N)-90	USS ENTER-PRISE	KYUSHU	EMPIRE		
05/14/45	77969	VF(N)-90	USS ENTER-PRISE	KYUSHU	EMPIRE		
05/14/45	77992	VF(N)-90	USS ENTER-PRISE	KYUSHU	EMPIRE		
05/14/45	78294	VF(N)-90	USS ENTER-PRISE	KYUSHU	EMPIRE		
05/14/45	78482	VF(N)-90	USS ENTER-PRISE	KYUSHU	EMPIRE		
05/14/45	78483	VF(N)-90	USS ENTER-PRISE	KYUSHU	EMPIRE		
05/14/45	72573	VMF(N)-543		IE SHIMA	EMPIRE	CAPT AUGUST L. AENDT	M
05/15/45	78495	VF(N)-90	USS BOUGAIN-VILLE		WCENPAC	ENS OLIVER N. CALLAWAY	S
05/15/45	77968	VF(N)-91	USS BON HOMME RICHARD	HAWAII	ECENPAC	ENS R.M. STEWARD	S
05/15/45	58679	VMF(N)-541		PELELIU	WCENPAC		
05/16/45	71629	NACTU	BARBERS POINT	HAWAII	ECENPAC	LT CLAUDE A. YORK	S
05/16/45	78100	VF(N)-91	USS BON HOMME RICHARD	PEARL	ECENPAC	LCDR ALPHONSE MINVIELLE	S
05/16/45	71778	VMF(N)-542		OKINAWA	EMPIRE	2NDLT W.W. CAMPBELL	M
05/17/45	78303	VMF(N)-533		OKINAWA	EMPIRE		
05/18/45	72667	VMF(N)-543		OKINAWA	EMPIRE		
05/19/45	71801	VF-17	USS HORNET	KYUSHU	EMPIRE		
05/19/45	72752	VMF(N)-543		OKINAWA	EMPIRE	LT CHARLES A. ENGMAN, JR.	S
05/21/45	72505	VF-12	USS RANDOLPH	IE SHIMA	EMPIRE	LTJG LEWIS	U
05/21/45	77530	VF-12	USS RANDOLPH	IE SHIMA	EMPIRE	ENS DAVID G. HOWARD, JR.	U
05/21/45	78529	VF-12	USS RANDOLPH	IE SHIMA	EMPIRE		
05/24/45	72545	VMF-511	USS BLOCK ISLAND		EMPIRE		
05/24/45	72877	VMF-511	USS BLOCK ISLAND		EMPIRE		
05/24/45	77842	VMF-511	USS BLOCK ISLAND		EMPIRE		
05/26/45	58812	VMF(N)-543		GUAM	WCENPAC		
05/27/45	78079	VF-87	USS TICONDER-OGA	MARSHALLS	CENPAC	ENS EMMET M. COOKE	S
05/28/45	79281	VF(N)-91	USS BON HOMME RICHARD	HAWAII	ECENPAC		
05/28/45	79365	VF(N)-91	USS BON HOMME RICHARD	HAWAII	ECENPAC	LCDR KARL H. STEFAN	S
05/30/45	77419	CASU(F)-51		ULITHI	WCENPAC		
06/01/45	77514	VF-82	USS BENNING-TON	OKINAWA	EMPIRE		
06/04/45	72804	VF(N)-52	OAHU	HAWAII	ECENPAC	ENS RICHARD GORDON DAY	D
06/05/45	78723	VMF(N)-543		OKINAWA	EMPIRE	1STLT AMOR L. TOWNS	M
06/07/45	77581	VF-82	USS BENNING-TON	KYUSHU	EMPIRE		

DATE	BUNO	SQDRN	BASE	LOST	AREA	PILOT	FATE
06/08/45	78513	VMF-511	USS BLOCK ISLAND		EMPIRE	LTJG THOMAS H. HARY	S
06/09/45	72493	VMF(N)-543		OKINAWA	EMPIRE	2NDLT DONALD M. STEELE	M
06/10/45	70339	NACTU	BARBERS POINT	HAWAII	ECENPAC	LT ALAN EVERETT RICH	S
06/10/45	79259	VF(N)-91	USS BON HOMME RICHARD	IWO JIMA	EMPIRE	LT HARRY V. WELDON	S
06/10/45	72291	VMF(N)-542		OKINAWA	EMPIRE	1STLT FRED HILLIARD, JR.	M
06/11/45	72387	VMF(N)-543		OKINAWA	EMPIRE	2NDLT REDFORD COVINGTON	M
06/16/45	77537	VMF-511	USS BLOCK ISLAND	AMAMI	EMPIRE		
06/20/45	70589	POOL	PEARL	HAWAII	ECENPAC		
06/21/45	72782	VMF(N)-543		OKINAWA	EMPIRE	2NDLT E.N. POLAND	S
06/22/45	78670	VF-16	USS RANDOLPH		PHIL		
06/24/45	79172	VF(N)-52	OAHU	HAWAII	ECENPAC	LT GEORGE W. SNIDER	S
06/24/45	78841	VF-87	USS TICONDER-OGA	LEYTE GULF	PHIL	LT CHARLES W. MILLER	S
06/24/45	58111	VMF(N)-541		PELELIU	WCENPAC		
06/26/45	78514	VMF(N)-543		OKINAWA	EMPIRE	2NDLT SPENC. EGGLEFIELD	S
06/28/45	77550	ACORN-30 PL		JINAMOC	PHIL		
07/01/45	77671	VMF(N)-543		KADENA	EMPIRE		
07/03/45	79151	VF(N)-91	USS BON HOMME RICHARD		EMPIRE		
07/03/45	79322	VF(N)-91	USS BON HOMME RICHARD		EMPIRE	LT C.Z. STEWARD	S
07/03/45	78537	VF-16	USS RANDOLPH		EMPIRE	ENS H.D. BLACKBURN	M
07/04/45	77526	VF-85	USS SHANGRI-LA	ENR HOKKAIDO	EMPIRE	ENS WILLARD K. DANDO	M
07/10/45	72457	VF(N)-91	USS BON HOMME RICHARD		EMPIRE	ENS WILLIAM L. WOODS	U
07/13/45	72836	POOL	PEARL	HAWAII	ECENPAC		
07/17/45	78757	VF(N)-91	USS BON HOMME RICHARD		EMPIRE	ENS H.A. SOHRWELD	D
07/17/45	79384	VF(N)-91	USS BON HOMME RICHARD		EMPIRE	LT C.P. CANHAM	M
07/25/45	78316	VF(N)-91	USS BON HOMME RICHARD		EMPIRE	LT WARREN F. SMITH	S
07/25/45	78809	VF(N)-91	USS BON HOMME RICHARD		EMPIRE	ENS J.G. SELWAY	U
07/25/45	77660	VF-1	USS BENNING-TON	KURE	EMPIRE	LTJG J. DANIELS	U
07/25/45	78767	VF-33	USS CHENANG O		EMPIRE		
07/26/45	70273	VF-6	USS HANCOCK		EMPIRE		
07/27/45	71124	VMF(N)-543		PELELIU	WCENPAC	1STLT F.J. SHERWIN	S
07/28/45	78564	VF-16	USS RANDOLPH	SHIKOKU	EMPIRE	LT D.K. OLSEN	S
07/28/45	79572	VF-89	USS ANTIETAM	HAWAII	ECENPAC	ENS DOUGLAS BEATTIE	S
07/29/45	72437	NACTU	BARBERS POINT	HAWAII	ECENPAC	LTJG WILLIAM J. ROBERTS	S
08/02/45	72850	VF-83	USS ESSEX		EMPIRE	ENS JAMES M. BARNES	U
08/04/45	77894	CASU(F)-12		GUAM	WCENPAC		

DATE	BUNO	SQDRN	BASE	LOST	AREA	PILOT	FATE
08/04/45	79912	CASU(F)-12		GUAM	WCENPAC		
08/04/45	80207	CASU(F)-12		GUAM	WCENPAC		
08/06/45	78766	VF-83	USS ESSEX		EMPIRE	ENS WILLIAM K. SOMERS	U
08/14/45	77904	VF-1	USS BENNING-TON		EMPIRE		

GRUMMAN F6F-5P

A small number of standard F6F-5s were also fitted with camera equipment for reconnaissance duties as the F6F-5P. Aircraft lost:

DATE	BUNO	SQDRN	BASE	LOST	AREA	PILOT	FATE
09/13/44	58146	VF-22	USS COWPENS	CEBU	PHIL	LT ROBERT K. ASHFORD	M
10/12/44	58159	VF-22	USS COWPENS	FORMOSA	EMPIRE	LTJG D.C. STANLEY	M
10/15/44	58046	VF-20	USS ENTER-PRISE	ENR MANILA	PHIL	ENS BRUCE HANNA	S
11/28/44	70985	VF-85	USS SHANGRI-LA	TRINIDAD	CENLANT		
12/10/44	58233	VF-7	USS HANCOCK	ENR LUZON	PHIL		
12/12/44	70311	VF-4	USS ESSEX	LUZON	PHIL		
12/30/44	70401	AR & OH		MANUS	SW PAC		
12/31/44	58514	CASU(F)-51		ULITHI	WCENPAC		
01/10/45	58689	CASU-43		GUAM	WCENPAC		
01/12/45	70907	VF-44	USS LANGLEY	FR. I.C.	PHIL	ENS BERNARD R. SMITH	S
01/21/45	70307	VF-9		ADMIRALTIES	SW PAC		
03/19/45	58507	CASU-2	BARBERS POINT	HAWAII	ECENPAC	ENS ARTHUR E. OLEENHOFF	S
03/26/45	72226	VF-10	USS INTREPID	HONSHU	EMPIRE		
03/26/45	72668	VF-30	USS BELLEAU WOOD	IE SHIMA	EMPIRE	LT RAY FRANCES GILLESPIE	S
03/27/45	70825	VF-82	USS BENNING-TON	OKINAWA	EMPIRE	LTJG B.P. SMITH	S
03/31/45	70967	VF-47	USS BATAAN	OKINAWA	EMPIRE		
04/01/45	70291	VF-83	USS ESSEX	OKINAWA	EMPIRE	LTJG LANEY	D
04/16/45	72264	VF-10	USS INTREPID	KOKUBO	EMPIRE		
04/18/45	72680	VF-24	USS SANTEE	IWO JIMA	EMPIRE	ENS ROBERT A. BALLARD	S
05/05/45	70323	CASU(F)-12		GUAM	WCENPAC		
05/05/45	77758	VF-12	USS RANDOLPH	IE SHIMA	EMPIRE		
05/11/45	72478	VF-84	USS BUNKER HILL	OKINAWA	EMPIRE	(DECK LOSS-KAMIKAZE)	
05/21/45	72961	VMF-511	USS BLOCK ISLAND		EMPIRE		
06/02/45	72853	VF-87	USS TICONDER-OGA	KYUSHU	EMPIRE	LT FRANK V. SCOTT, JR.	S
06/16/45	77610	CASU(F)-12		GUAM	WCENPAC		
06/16/45	70797	NACTU	BARBERS POINT	HAWAII	ECENPAC		
07/01/45	77424	VMF-512	USS GILBERT ISLANDS	BALIKPAPAN	BORNEO	1STLT JAMES B. CRAWFORD	D
07/05/45	71055	VMD-354		IWO JIMA	EMPIRE	2NDLT DONALD V. BEAN	S

DATE	BUNO	SQDRN	BASE	LOST	AREA	PILOT	FATE
07/24/45	77562	VF-27	USS INDEPENDENCE		EMPIRE	LT ROBERT O. ZIMMERMAN	U
07/24/45	71773	VF-31	USS BELLEAU WOOD		EMPIRE	ENS WILLIAM B. HALL	D
07/30/45	72422	VF-16	USS RANDOLPH	SHIKOKU	EMPIRE		
07/30/45	77626	VF-94	USS LEXINGTON		EMPIRE	LT LAWSON BAYLIES	M
07/30/45	78226	VMD-354		GUAM	WCENPAC	2NDLT HARRY R. BAUTHEROT	S
07/31/45	72703	VMD-354		GUAM	WCENPAC	1STLT L.D. SLATTERY	U
08/09/45	77512	VF-94	USS LEXINGTON		EMPIRE	LT ROBERT C. MCABEE	S
08/11/45	71542	VF-47	USS BATAAN	OKINAWA	EMPIRE		

GRUMMAN J2F-1

The Grumman J2F Duck (company designation G-15) was an American single-engine amphibious biplane. It was used by each major branch of the U.S. armed forces from the mid-1930s until just after World War II, primarily for utility and air-sea rescue duties.

The J2F-1 Duck first flew on 2 April 1936 powered by a 750 hp (559 kW) Wright R-1820 Cyclone, and was delivered to the U.S. Navy on the same day. The J2F-2 had a Wright Cyclone engine which was boosted to 790 hp (589 kW). Twenty J2F-3 variants were built in 1939 for use by the Navy as executive transports with plush interiors. Due to pressure of work following the United States entry into the war in 1941, production of the J2F Duck was transferred to the Columbia Aircraft Corp of New York. They produced 330 aircraft for the Navy and U.S. Coast Guard.

The J2F was an equal-span single-bay biplane with a large monocoque central float which also housed the retractable main landing gear. The aircraft had strut-mounted stabilizer floats beneath each lower wing. A crew of two or three were carried in tandem cockpits, forward for the pilot and rear for an observer with room for a radio operator if required. It had a cabin in the fuselage for two passengers or a stretcher.

The Duck's main pontoon was blended into the fuselage, making it almost a flying boat despite its similarity to a conventional landplane which has been float-equipped. This configuration was shared with the earlier Loening OL, Grumman having acquired the rights to Loening's hull, float and undercarriage designs. Like the F4F Wildcat, its narrow-tracked landing gear was hand-cranked.

The J2F was used by the U.S. Navy, Marines, Army Air Forces, and Coast Guard; apart from general utility and light transport duties its missions included mapping, scouting/observation, anti-submarine patrol, air-sea rescue work, photographic surveys and reconnaissance, and target tug. Aircraft lost:

DATE	BUNO	SQDRN	BASE	LOST	AREA	PILOT	FATE
07/23/43	0189	NAS	DUTCH HARBOR	ALASKA	NORPAC		
05/16/44	0187	NAS	SAN JUAN	SAN JUAN	SOLANT		
07/08/44	0167	NAS	KODIAK	ALASKA	NORPAC		
07/08/44	0168	NAS	KODIAK	ALASKA	NORPAC		
08/23/44	0183	NAS	KAHULUI	HAWAII	ECENPAC		

GRUMMAN J2F-2

The Grumman J2F-2 was a version of the J2F-1 used mostly by the United States Marine Corps. It was equipped with nose and dorsal guns as well as under-wing bomb racks. There were 21 built. Aircraft lost:

DATE	BUNO	SQDRN	BASE	LOST	AREA	PILOT	FATE
01/21/42	1207	FAW-10	JAVA		SW PAC	LTJG SZABO	S
06/29/42	1209		MIDWAY		ECENPAC		
04/08/43	0781			KANEOHE	ECENPAC		
05/10/43	0788	COMAIR-PAC	PEARL	HAWAII	ECENPAC		
06/14/44	0793	ARU SOLS			SOPAC		
07/24/44	1197	ASWTU FW-2			CENPAC		
08/17/44	0791	NAS	BARBERS POINT	HAWAII	ECENPAC		
08/21/44	0787	NAS	HILO	HAWAII	ECENPAC		
08/28/44	0790		NOUMEA		SOPAC		
08/31/44	0782	NAS	GUANTAN-AMO BAY	CUBA	CENLANT		
08/31/44	1195	VJ-3					
09/20/44	0794	NAS	PEARL	HAWAII	ECENPAC		

GRUMMAN J2F-2A

The Grumman J2F-2A was the J2F-2 with minor changes for use in the United States Virgin Islands. There were 9 built. Aircraft lost:

DATE	BUNO	SQDRN	BASE	LOST	AREA	PILOT	FATE
09/19/42	1204		VIRGIN ISLANDS		CENLANT		

GRUMMAN J2F-3

The Grumman J2F-3 was the J2F-2 but powered by an 850 hp R-1820-26 engine. There were 20 built. Aircraft lost:

DATE	BUNO	SQDRN	BASE	LOST	AREA	PILOT	FATE
10/01/42	1587				ECENPAC		
08/01/44	1576	ARU SOLS		ESPIRITO SANTO	SOPAC		
03/31/45	1582	NAS	ADAK	ALASKA	NORPAC		
04/10/45	1580	POOL	GUADAL-CANAL	GUADAL-CANAL	SOPAC		

GRUMMAN J2F-4

The Grumman J2F-4 was the J2F-2 but powered by an 850 hp R-1820-30 engine and fitted with target towing equipment. There were 32 built. Aircraft lost:

DATE	BUNO	SQDRN	BASE	LOST	AREA	PILOT	FATE
00/00/00	1642				SW PAC		
00/00/00	1658	POOL		GUADAL-CANAL	SOPAC		
12/07/41	1644	VMJ-252	PEARL	HAWAII	ECENPAC		
12/07/41	1656	VMJ-252	PEARL	HAWAII	ECENPAC		
08/16/42	1653	NAS	DUTCH HARBOR	ALASKA	NORPAC		
12/20/42	1640				NORLANT		
07/31/43	1646	NAB		ICELAND	NORLANT		
10/23/44	1655	NAS		TRINIDAD	SOLANT		

DATE	BUNO	SQDRN	BASE	LOST	AREA	PILOT	FATE
11/02/44	1659	VMSB-343		MIDWAY	ECENPAC	LT RENE RINSFIELD	D
02/09/45	1660	ACORN-4 PL			SOPAC		
02/21/45	1641	CASU-4	PUUNENE	HAWAII	ECENPAC		
03/31/45	1650	NAS	ADAK	ALASKA	NORPAC		
04/30/45	1647	POOL	PEARL	HAWAII	ECENPAC		

GRUMMAN J2F-5

The Grumman J2F-5 was the J2F-2 but powered by a 1,050 hp R-1820-54 engine. There were 144 built. Aircraft lost:

DATE	BUNO	SQDRN	BASE	LOST	AREA	PILOT	FATE
02/06/42	690	VJ-12	PEARL	HAWAII	ECENPAC	CLARENCE H. GREENWOOD	U
02/17/42	674		MAUI	HAWAII	ECENPAC		
04/07/42	704		USS WASP	SCAPA FLOW	NORLANT		
04/10/42	730	VJ-2	PEARL	HAWAII	ECENPAC	JAMES W. HARDY	S
04/12/42	673	VJ-1	PEARL	HAWAII	ECENPAC	ENS JAMES E. MONAHAN	S
04/20/42	741	VMS-3		ST. THOMAS V.I.	CENLANT		
06/11/42		4TH MBDAW		SAMOA	SE PAC		
07/01/42	749	VMS-3		ST. THOMAS V.I.	CENLANT	LT KENNETH SMITH	U
07/29/42	676	VJ-2	PEARL	HAWAII	ECENPAC	ENS CLAIR C. DENNIS	S
08/26/42	781	COMAIR-PAC		PEARL	HAWAII	ECENPAC	
09/21/42	689	VJ-4	GUANTAN-AMO BAY	CUBA	CENLANT		
09/22/42	671	VS-1	(DET 14)		SOPAC		
10/02/42	746	VMS-3		ST. THOMAS V.I.	CENLANT	2NDLT H.J. VALENTINE	D
11/15/42	665	VMF-223	GUADAL-CANAL		SOPAC		
11/15/42	723	VMJ-253			SOPAC		
12/16/42	765	COCO SOLO			CENLANT		
12/16/42	795				ECENPAC		
12/19/42	694						
12/25/42	715	VMJ-253			SOPAC		
12/30/42	768	FAW-10			SOPAC		
01/31/43	787	4TH MBDAW		SAMOA	SE PAC	CAPT BABB	S
01/31/43	700	VF-207		SAN JULIEN	CENLANT		
02/16/43	743			SAN JUAN	CENLANT		
02/17/43	799	VJ-2			WCENPAC		
03/25/43	726		USS SARATOGA	NOUMEA	SOPAC		
04/01/43	683	VB-10	USS ENTER-PRISE	SOLOMONS	SOPAC		
04/30/43	734	MAG-14	AUCKLAND	NEW ZEALAND	SOPAC		
06/02/43	706	VB-41	USS RANGER		NORLANT		
06/04/43	664	VJ-9			SOPAC		
06/10/43	760	VJ-10			WCENPAC		
07/24/43	733	VMJ-252	PEARL	HAWAII	ECENPAC	LT BRINDA	S
08/03/43	717	VJ-2			SOPAC		
08/04/43	727	MAG-11		ESPIRITU SANTO	SOPAC		
09/18/43	754	VJ-9		HAVANNAH	SOPAC		
12/11/43	796	CCOP			NORLANT		
12/16/43	675	VS-64		SEGI	SOPAC	LTJG J. METZNER	S
12/23/43	708	ARU SOLS		ADVG 60	SOPAC		
01/15/44	779	ACORN-7 PL		EMIRAU	SW PAC		
02/09/44	714	FAW-1		NEW GEORGIA	SOPAC		

DATE	BUNO	SQDRN	BASE	LOST	AREA	PILOT	FATE
04/30/44	698	VJ-12	PEARL	HAWAII	ECENPAC	ENS J.E. PERDUE	S
05/23/44	685	VS-64			SOPAC		
06/02/44	766				SW PAC		
08/01/44	687	VS-65	FUNAFUTI	NOUMEA	SOPAC		
08/01/44	713	VS-65	FUNAFUTI	NOUMEA	SOPAC		
08/01/44	753	VS-65	FUNAFUTI	NOUMEA	SOPAC		
08/02/44	802	VJ-10		PALLIKULO A/F	SOPAC		
08/02/44	662	VJ-7	PEARL	HAWAII	ECENPAC		
08/11/44	777	ARU SOLS			SOPAC		
08/31/44	736	NAS	JOHNSTON ISLAND	HAWAII	ECENPAC		
09/01/44	731	VS-65		FUNAFUTI	CENPAC		
09/15/44	774	POOL		GUADAL-CANAL	SOPAC		
10/07/44	771	A & R	GUADAL-CANAL	GUADAL-CANAL	SOPAC		
10/12/44	682	VJ-12		GUADAL-CANAL	SOPAC	ENS MOPPENSTALL	S
10/31/44	784	VS-51		TUTUILA	SOPAC		
11/06/44	724	VJ-2		AUSTRALIA	SW PAC	LTJG JAMES B. STACY	S
12/02/44	705	A.A.	GUADAL-CANAL	GUADAL-CANAL	SOPAC		
01/27/45	776	CASU-31	HILO	HAWAII	ECENPAC		
02/06/45	788	1ST MAW		TOROKINA	SOPAC		
02/27/45	697	A.A.	GUADAL-CANAL	GUADAL-CANAL	SOPAC		
04/01/45	762	NAS	MIDWAY	MIDWAY	ECENPAC		
04/03/45	791	POOL	GUADAL-CANAL	GUADAL-CANAL	SOPAC		
05/02/45	667	POOL	KANEOHE	HAWAII	ECENPAC		
05/31/45	750	NAF	TUTUILA	TUTUILA	SOPAC		
06/10/45	740	COMFAIRW G16		RECIFE	BRAZIL		
06/11/45	735	VJ-7	PEARL	HAWAII	ECENPAC	ENS C.P. RANDLE	S
06/13/45	721	NAS		PALMYRA	ECENPAC		
06/19/45	782	NAS	SAN JUAN	SAN JUAN	CENLANT		

GRUMMAN J2F-6

The Grumman J2F-6 was the J2F-5 version built by Columbia Aircraft. It was powered by a 1,050 hp R-1820-64 engine in a long-chord cowling, fitted with underwing bomb racks and provisioned with target towing gear. There were 330 built. Aircraft lost:

DATE	BUNO	SQDRN	BASE	LOST	AREA	PILOT	FATE
00/00/00	36996	AV-15	USS HAMLIN	EMPIRE			
03/08/44	36943	VS-52		ROI	CENPAC		
06/15/44	36954	COMAIR-PAC		PEARL	HAWAII	ECENPAC	
07/05/44	36944	VS-66	MAKIN	MAKIN	CENPAC	ENS W.D. JURASCHEK	S
07/12/44	36950	MAG-11		ESPIRITU SANTO	SOPAC		
10/10/44	36969	VJ-12		ESPIRITU SANTO	SOPAC	LAWRENCE A. DRUMMINE	S
11/01/44	36986	AV-14	USS KEN. WHITING	SAIPAN	WCENPAC	ALTON J. HASSELL	S
11/03/44	36962	VS-57	NOUMEA	NOUMEA	SOPAC		
12/12/44	36946	CASU-30		MAJURO	CENPAC		
12/14/44	37034	NAS	NAVY NO. 28	HAWAII	ECENPAC	LCDR D.E. RICHARDSON	D
03/09/45	37003	VS-61		OWI	SW PAC		
03/16/45	36956	A.A.	GUADAL-CANAL	GUADAL-CANAL	SOPAC		
04/14/45	32651	VJ-17		ENIWETOK	CENPAC		
04/25/45	37005	MCAB	ULITHI	ULITHI	WCENPAC		
04/25/45	32745	NAB	ATTU	ALASKA	NORPAC	ENS BENJAMIN R. STRONG	S
05/03/45	36938	VS-57	NOUMEA	NOUMEA	SOPAC		

DATE	BUNO	SQDRN	BASE	LOST	AREA	PILOT	FATE
05/28/45	36948	SEAPL BASE		RIAK	SW PAC		
05/30/45	32643	CASU(F)-49		PELELIU	WCENPAC	MAJ J.H. REINBURG	S
05/31/45	37033	COMAIR-PAC	PEARL	HAWAII	ECENPAC		
05/31/45	36955	VJ-17		GUAM	WCENPAC		
06/12/45	36949	CASU(F)-12		GUAM	WCENPAC		
07/03/45	32652	AV-17	USS CUMBER. SOUND	ENR ENIWETOK	WCENPAC	CAPT LOUIS PETERSON	S
08/08/45	32648	ACORN-19 PL		MINDORO	PHIL	LT E.S. MILLER	S

GRUMMAN J4F-2

The Grumman G-44 Widgeon is a small, five-person, twin-engine amphibious aircraft. It was designated J4F by the United States Navy and Coast Guard. The Widgeon was originally designed for the civil market. It is smaller but otherwise similar to Grumman's earlier G-21 Goose, and was produced from 1941 to 1955. The aircraft was used during World War II as a small patrol and utility machine by the United States Navy and US Coast Guard. The first prototype flew in 1940, and the first production aircraft went to the United States Navy as an anti-submarine aircraft. In total, 276 were built by Grumman, including 176 for the military. During World War II, they served with the US Navy, Coast Guard, Civil Air Patrol and Army Air Force. Aircraft lost:

DATE	BUNO	SQDRN	BASE	LOST	AREA	PILOT	FATE
10/25/42	34585			TRUJILLO CITY	CENLANT		
03/27/44	32978	NAS		ARGENTIA	NORLANT		
04/23/44	32950	NAS	DUTCH HARBOR	UMKAK	NORPAC	LT L. MCELROY	D
07/20/45	32938	POOL	PEARL	HAWAII	ECENPAC		
07/20/45	32946	POOL	PEARL	HAWAII	ECENPAC		
08/04/45	32944	POOL	PEARL	HAWAII	ECENPAC		

GRUMMAN JF-1

The JF-1 began the long line of amphibious "Duck" aircraft for Grumman. The initial operational production variant had a 700 hp Pratt & Whitney R-1830-62 Twin Wasp engine. There were 27 built (BuNos 9434-9455, 9523-9527). Aircraft lost:

DATE	BUNO	SQDRN	BASE	LOST	AREA	PILOT	FATE
08/31/44	9446	NAS	COCO SOLO	COCO SOLO	CENLANT		

GRUMMAN JRF-1

In 1936, a group of wealthy residents of Long Island approached Grumman and commissioned an aircraft that they could use to fly to New York City. In response the Grumman Model G-21 was designed as a light amphibian transport. The typical Grumman rugged construction was matched to an all-metal, high-winged monoplane powered by two 450 horsepower (340 kW) Pratt & Whitney R-985 Wasp Jr. nine-cylinder, air-cooled radial engines mounted on the leading edge of high-set wings. The deep fuselage served also as a hull and was equipped with hand-cranked retractable landing gear. First flight of the prototype took place on May 29, 1937.

The fuselage also proved versatile as it provided generous interior space that allowed fitting for either a transport or luxury airliner role. Having an amphibious configuration also allowed the G-21 to go just about anywhere, and plans were made to market it as an amphibian airliner. Some had a hatch in the nose, which could remain open in flight.

Grumman promoted also the G-21 as a military transport. The most numerous of the military versions were the United States Navy variants, designated the JRF. The JRF-1 was the production version of XJ3F-1. The XJ3F-1 was a prototype (one built in 1938) eight seat utility amphibian built specifically for the US Navy. Five JRF-1's were built for the US Navy. The amphibian was soon adopted by the Coast Guard and, during World War II, it served in transport, reconnaissance, rescue (including air-sea rescues) and training roles. Aircraft lost:

DATE	BUNO	SQDRN	BASE	LOST	AREA	PILOT	FATE
06/01/44	0163		COCO SOLO		NORLANT		
07/31/44	09782	NAS		PALMYRA	ECENPAC		
08/31/44	1676	NVL ATTACHE		HAVANA	CENLANT		
10/21/44	1675	NAS		TRINIDAD	SOLANT		

GRUMMAN JRF-1A

Similar to the Grumman JRF-1 above but with target towing gear and camera hatch added. Five built for US Navy although list below shows a duplicate BuNo. BuNo's 1671, 1672, 1673, 1678, 1679 were converted to JRF-1A. Help is needed by the reader to redesignate one of the 1673 BuNo's. Aircraft lost:

DATE	BUNO	SQDRN	BASE	LOST	AREA	PILOT	FATE
03/14/42	1673	MCAS	ST. THOMAS V.I.		CENLANT	MAJ ROGER T. CARLESA	S
10/27/43	1679	NAS	PALMYRA		ECENPAC		
08/31/44	1673	NAS	GUANTAN-AMO BAY	CUBA	CENLANT		
08/31/44	1678	NAS	COCO SOLO	COCO SOLO	CENLANT		
08/31/44	1671	VJ-3					
12/04/44	1672	A.A.	ESPIRITU SANTO	ESPIRITU SANTO	SOPAC		

GRUMMAN JRF-4

Similar to the Grumman JRF-1A, the JRF-4 could carry two depth bombs under its wing. Ten were built for the US Navy. Aircraft lost:

DATE	BUNO	SQDRN	BASE	LOST	AREA	PILOT	FATE
07/21/44	3847	HEDRON-15		GIBRALTAR	SW EUR	LT W.E. DAVENPORT	U
05/31/45	3846	NAF	TUTUILA	TUTUILA	SOPAC		

GRUMMAN JRF-5

This was a major production version, incorporating bomb racks from the JRF-4, target towing and camera gear from the JRF-1A and de-icing gear from the JRF-3. There were 184 built. Aircraft lost:

DATE	BUNO	SQDRN	BASE	LOST	AREA	PILOT	FATE

DATE	BUNO	SQDRN	BASE	LOST	AREA	PILOT	FATE
08/10/42	6451	TF-24		NEWFOUND-LAND	NORLANT		
07/21/43	6447	NAS	SITKA	SITKA	NORPAC		
08/12/43	6443	NAS	SANTA LUCIA	CUBA	CENLANT		
08/27/43	34060	COMAIR-SOPAC	GUADAL-CANAL	GUADAL-CANAL	SOPAC		
01/26/44	6446		KANEOHE	HAWAII	ECENPAC		
03/04/44	37780	USCG	SANTA LUCIA	CUBA	CENLANT	LCDR R.L. MELLEN	S
06/02/44	34072	FAW-3	COCO SOLO	COSTA RICA	NORLANT	LT R.K. TOWNSEND	D
07/01/44	34074	FAW-8		SOUTH AMERICA	SOLANT		
10/11/44	37815	ARTU		MANUS	SW PAC		
11/02/44	37785	NAS	PORT LYAUTEY	MOROCCO	NW AFR	LT GEORGE W. SPURLIN	S
11/14/44	34081	NAS	SAN JUAN	SAN JUAN	CENLANT	AP1/C JAMES D. LANG	S
05/02/45	84794	ARTU		MANUS	SW PAC		
08/01/45	84811	ACORN-47 PL			PHIL		

GRUMMAN TBF (VARIANT UNKNOWN)

DATE	BUNO	SQDRN	BASE	LOST	AREA	PILOT	FATE
02/12/44				ENIWETOK	CENPAC		

GRUMMAN TBF-1

The Grumman TBF Avenger (designated TBM for aircraft manufactured by General Motors) was a torpedo bomber developed initially for the United States Navy and Marine Corps, and eventually used by several air or naval arms around the world. It entered U.S. service in 1942, and first saw action during the Battle of Midway. Despite losing five of the six Avengers on its debut, it survived in service to become one of the outstanding torpedo bombers of World War II.

On the afternoon of 7 December 1941, Grumman held a ceremony to open a new manufacturing plant and display the new TBF to the public. Coincidentally, on that day, the Imperial Japanese Navy attacked Pearl Harbor, as Grumman soon found out. After the ceremony was over, the plant was quickly sealed off to guard against possible sabotage. By early June 1942, a shipment of more than 100 aircraft was sent to the Navy, ironically arriving only a few hours after the three carriers quickly departed from Pearl Harbor, so most of them were too late to participate in the pivotal Battle of Midway.

However, six TBF-1s were present on Midway Island, as part of VT-8 (Torpedo Squadron 8), while the rest of the squadron flew Devastators from the Hornet. Unfortunately, both types of torpedo bombers suffered heavy casualties. Out of the six Avengers, five were shot down and the other returning heavily damaged with one of its gunners killed, and the other gunner and the pilot injured. Nonetheless, the US torpedo bombers were credited with drawing away the Japanese combat air patrols so the American dive bombers could successfully hit the Japanese carriers.

On 24 August 1942, the next major naval battle occurred at the Eastern Solomons. Based on the carriers USS SARATOGA and USS ENTERPRISE, the 24 TBFs present were able to sink the Japanese light carrier *Ryūjō* and claim one dive bomber, at the cost of seven aircraft.

The first major "prize" for the TBFs (which had been assigned the name "Avenger" in October 1941, before the Japanese attack on Pearl Harbor) was at the Naval Battle of Guadalcanal in November 1942, when Marine Corps and Navy Avengers helped sink the battleship *Hiei*.

After hundreds of the original TBF-1 models were built, the TBF-1C began production. The allotment of space for specialized internal and wing-mounted fuel tanks doubled the Avenger's range. By 1943, Grumman began to slowly phase out production of the Avenger to produce F6F Hellcat fighters, and the Eastern Aircraft Division of General Motors took-over, with these aircraft being designated TBM. The Eastern Aircraft plant was located in North Tarrytown (re-named Sleepy Hollow in 1996), NY. Starting in mid-1944, the TBM-3 began production (with a more powerful powerplant and wing hardpoints for drop tanks and rockets). The dash-3 was the most numerous of the Avengers (with about 4,600 produced). However, most of the Avengers in service were dash-1s until near the end of the war (in 1945).

Besides the traditional surface role (torpedoing surface ships), Avengers claimed about 30 submarine kills, including the cargo submarine *I-52*. They were one of the most effective sub-killers in the Pacific theatre, as well as in the Atlantic, when escort carriers were finally available to escort Allied convoys. There, the Avengers contributed in warding off German U-Boats while providing air cover for the convoys.

After the "Marianas Turkey Shoot", in which more than 250 Japanese aircraft were downed, Admiral Marc Mitscher ordered a 220-aircraft mission to find the Japanese task force. At the extreme end of their range (300 nmi (560 km) out), the group of Hellcats, TBF/TBMs, and dive bombers took many casualties. However, Avengers from USS BELLEAU WOOD torpedoed the light carrier *Hiyō* as their only major prize. Mitscher's gamble did not pay off as well as he had hoped.

In June 1943, future-President George H.W. Bush became the youngest naval aviator at the time. While flying a TBM with VT-51 (from the USS SAN JACINTO), his TBM was shot down on 2 September 1944 over the Pacific island of Chichi Jima. Both of his crewmates died. However, he released his payload and hit the target before being forced to bail out; he received the Distinguished Flying Cross.

Another famous Avenger aviator was Paul Newman, who flew as a rear gunner. He had hoped to be accepted for pilot training, but did not qualify because of being color blind. Newman was on board the escort carrier USS HOLLANDIA roughly 500 mi (800 km) from Japan when the Enola Gay dropped the first atomic bomb on Hiroshima. The Avenger was the type of torpedo bomber used during the sinking of the two Japanese "super battleships": the *Musashi* and the *Yamato*. The postwar disappearance of a flight of American Avengers, known as Flight 19, was later added to the Bermuda Triangle legend. There were 1,526 -1's built. Aircraft lost:

DATE	BUNO	SQDRN	BASE	LOST	AREA	PILOT	FATE
06/04/42	383	VT-8	USS HORNET	MIDWAY	ECENPAC		
06/04/42	384	VT-8	USS HORNET	MIDWAY	ECENPAC		
06/04/42	391	VT-8	USS HORNET	MIDWAY	ECENPAC		
06/04/42	398	VT-8	USS HORNET	MIDWAY	ECENPAC		
06/04/42	399	VT-8	USS HORNET	MIDWAY	ECENPAC		
06/26/42	410	VT-6	PEARL	HAWAII	ECENPAC		
07/07/42	450	VT-6	PEARL	HAWAII	ECENPAC		
07/15/42	425	VT-3	PEARL	HAWAII	ECENPAC		

DATE	BUNO	SQDRN	BASE	LOST	AREA	PILOT	FATE
07/27/42	412	VT-6	PEARL	HAWAII	ECENPAC		
07/30/42	380	VT-8	USS SARATOGA	SUVA BAY	SE PAC	ENS ROBERT S. EVARTS	S
08/03/42	421	FAW-2	PEARL	HAWAII	ECENPAC		
08/04/42	455	VT-6	KANEOHE	HAWAII	ECENPAC		
08/10/42	402	VT-6	KANEOHE	HAWAII	ECENPAC		
08/18/42	539	VGS-12			NORPAC		
08/18/42	436	VT-6	PEARL	HAWAII	ECENPAC		
08/18/42	472	VT-6	PEARL	HAWAII	ECENPAC		
08/18/42	499	VT-6	PEARL	HAWAII	ECENPAC		
08/18/42	502	VT-6	PEARL	HAWAII	ECENPAC		
08/18/42	505	VT-6	PEARL	HAWAII	ECENPAC		
08/18/42	513	VT-6	PEARL	HAWAII	ECENPAC		
08/21/42	447	VT-6	PEARL	HAWAII	ECENPAC		
08/21/42	471	VT-6	PEARL	HAWAII	ECENPAC		
08/21/42	503	VT-6	PEARL	HAWAII	ECENPAC		
08/22/42	385	VT-8	USS SARATOGA	ENR SOLOMONS	SOPAC	ENS GOOD	D
08/24/42	418	VT-3	USS ENTER-PRISE	E. SOLOMONS	SOPAC	MACH H.L. CORL	M
08/24/42	419	VT-3	USS ENTER-PRISE	E. SOLOMONS	SOPAC	ENS E.B. HOLLEY	S
08/24/42	426	VT-3	USS ENTER-PRISE	E. SOLOMONS	SOPAC	LT J.H. MYERS	U
08/24/42	433	VT-3	USS ENTER-PRISE	E. SOLOMONS	SOPAC	ENS H.L. BENGANER	U
08/24/42	446	VT-3	USS ENTER-PRISE	E. SOLOMONS	SOPAC	ENS BYE	U
08/24/42	395	VT-8	USS SARATOGA	E. SOLOMONS	SOPAC	ENS J. TAURNAN	S
08/24/42	396	VT-8	USS SARATOGA	E. SOLOMONS	SOPAC	ENS E.L. FAYLE	S
08/26/42	422	VT-8	USS SARATOGA	ENR GUADAL.	SOPAC	ENS JAMES H. COOK	S
08/27/42	356	VT-6	USS ENTER-PRISE	GUADAL-CANAL	SOPAC		
08/27/42	466	VT-6	USS ENTER-PRISE	GUADAL-CANAL	SOPAC		
08/30/42	457	VT-6	USS ENTER-PRISE	GUADAL-CANAL	SOPAC		
08/30/42	397	VT-8	USS SARATOGA	GUADAL-CANAL	SOPAC		
10/01/42	388	VT-8		GUADAL-CANAL	SOPAC		
10/01/42	388	VT-8		GUADAL-CANAL	SOPAC		
10/01/42	417	VT-8		GUADAL-CANAL	SOPAC		
10/01/42	417	VT-8		GUADAL-CANAL	SOPAC		
10/01/42	424	VT-8		GUADAL-CANAL	SOPAC		
10/01/42	424	VT-8		GUADAL-CANAL	SOPAC		
10/05/42	382	VT-8		GUADAL-CANAL	SOPAC	ENS DOGGETT	D
10/06/42	401	VT-8		GUADAL-CANAL	SOPAC	ENS J. TAURNAN	S
10/12/42	509	VT-3	PEARL	HAWAII	ECENPAC		
10/12/42	509	VT-3	PEARL	HAWAII	ECENPAC		
10/12/42	514	VT-3	PEARL	HAWAII	ECENPAC	LT ANDREW J. GARDNER	U
10/12/42	590	VT-3	PEARL	HAWAII	ECENPAC		
10/12/42	590	VT-3	PEARL	HAWAII	ECENPAC		
10/14/42	427	VT-7		GUADAL-CANAL	SOPAC		

DATE	BUNO	SQDRN	BASE	LOST	AREA	PILOT	FATE
10/14/42	427	VT-7		GUADAL-CANAL	SOPAC		
10/14/42	429	VT-7		GUADAL-CANAL	SOPAC		
10/14/42	429	VT-7		GUADAL-CANAL	SOPAC		
10/14/42	430	VT-7		GUADAL-CANAL	SOPAC		
10/14/42	430	VT-7		GUADAL-CANAL	SOPAC		
10/14/42	432	VT-7		GUADAL-CANAL	SOPAC		
10/14/42	432	VT-7		GUADAL-CANAL	SOPAC		
10/14/42	434	VT-7		GUADAL-CANAL	SOPAC		
10/14/42	434	VT-7		GUADAL-CANAL	SOPAC		
10/14/42	437	VT-7		GUADAL-CANAL	SOPAC		
10/14/42	437	VT-7		GUADAL-CANAL	SOPAC		
10/14/42	452	VT-7		GUADAL-CANAL	SOPAC		
10/14/42	452	VT-7		GUADAL-CANAL	SOPAC		
10/14/42	459	VT-7		GUADAL-CANAL	SOPAC		
10/14/42	459	VT-7		GUADAL-CANAL	SOPAC		
10/14/42	461	VT-7		GUADAL-CANAL	SOPAC		
10/14/42	461	VT-7		GUADAL-CANAL	SOPAC		
10/15/42	654	VGS-29	USS SANTEE	OFF BERMUDA	NORLANT		
10/15/42	654	VGS-29	USS SANTEE	OFF BERMUDA	NORLANT		
10/23/42	406	VT-8		GUADAL-CANAL	SOPAC	LT HANSON	U
10/26/42	381	VT-10	USS ENTER-PRISE	SANTA CRUZ	SOPAC	ENS J.M. REED	M
10/26/42	1749	VT-10	USS ENTER-PRISE	SANTA CRUZ	SOPAC	LCDR JAMES D. COLLETT	M
10/26/42	1758	VT-10	USS ENTER-PRISE	SANTA CRUZ	SOPAC	LTJG R.G. WYLLIE	S
10/26/42	5885	VT-10	USS ENTER-PRISE	SANTA CRUZ	SOPAC	LT J.W. MCCONNAUGHHAY	S
10/26/42	5903	VT-10	USS ENTER-PRISE	SANTA CRUZ	SOPAC	LT MARVIN D. NORTON	S
10/26/42	6044	VT-10	USS ENTER-PRISE	SANTA CRUZ	SOPAC	LTJG RICHARD K. BATTEN	S
10/26/42	435	VT-6	USS HORNET	SANTA CRUZ	SOPAC	LTJG ELAM	S
10/26/42	445	VT-6	USS HORNET	SANTA CRUZ	SOPAC	LTJG RAPP	S
10/26/42	449	VT-6	USS HORNET	SANTA CRUZ	SOPAC	ENS HOOVER	S
10/26/42	453	VT-6	USS HORNET	SANTA CRUZ	SOPAC	LTJG HUMPHREY L. TALLMAN	S
10/26/42	454	VT-6	USS HORNET	SANTA CRUZ	SOPAC	ENS CRESTO	S
10/26/42	464	VT-6	USS HORNET	SANTA CRUZ	SOPAC	LTJG PARKER	S
10/26/42	468	VT-6	USS HORNET	SANTA CRUZ	SOPAC	LTJG CLARK	S
10/27/42	465	VT-6	USS HORNET	SANTA CRUZ	SOPAC	(SHIP SANK)	

DATE	BUNO	SQDRN	BASE	LOST	AREA	PILOT	FATE
10/27/42	465	VT-6	USS HORNET	SANTA CRUZ	SOPAC	(SHIP SANK)	
10/27/42	467	VT-6	USS HORNET	SANTA CRUZ	SOPAC	(SHIP SANK)	
10/27/42	467	VT-6	USS HORNET	SANTA CRUZ	SOPAC	(SHIP SANK)	
11/08/42	572	VGS-27	USS SU-WANNEE	CASABLANCA	NW AFR	LT G.H. WIGFALL	S
11/08/42	611	VGS-29	USS SANTEE	SAFI	NW AFR	ENS E.M. LOCK	S
11/08/42	624	VGS-29	USS SANTEE	SAFI	NW AFR	ENS C.L. WARNSTAFF	S
11/08/42	545	VGS-9	USS RANGER	FEDALA	NW AFR		
11/08/42	545	VGS-9	USS RANGER	FEDALA	NW AFR		
11/09/42	460	VGS-26	USS SAN-GAMON	PORT LYAUTEY	MOROCC O	LTJG LEOPOLD WEIDLEN	S
11/10/42	608	VGS-27	USS SU-WANNEE	CASABLANCA	NW AFR	ENS R.E. O'NEIL	D
11/10/42	568	VGS-29	USS SANTEE	SAFI	NW AFR	ENS WILLIAM E. WHITE	S
11/10/42	1765	VGS-29	USS SANTEE	SAFI	NW AFR	LTJG DONALD C. RODEEN	S
11/12/42	585	VGS-29	USS SANTEE	SAFI	NW AFR		
11/13/42	557	VMSB-131		GUADAL-CANAL	SOPAC	LT BANGERT	U
11/15/42	1744	VT-10	GUADAL-CANAL	ESPIRITU SANTO	SOPAC	ENS DELNORTE BONDURANT	S
11/16/42	594	VT-3	USS SARATOGA	ENR NOUMEA	SOPAC	ENS E.E. RODENBURG	S
11/17/42	580	VGS-26	USS SAN-GAMON	ENR NORFOLK	CENLANT		
11/19/42	512	VT-5	USS SARATOGA	ENR NOUMEA	SOPAC	ENS E.B. HOLLEY	S
11/30/42	1760	VT-3	USS SARATOGA	ENR NOUMEA	SOPAC		
12/03/42	558	VMSB-131		GUADAL-CANAL	SOPAC	LT PELTO	M
12/08/42	389	VT-8		GUADAL-CANAL	SOPAC		
12/08/42	390	VT-8		GUADAL-CANAL	SOPAC		
12/11/42	582	VGS-28	USS CHE-NANGO	ENR PANAMA	CENLANT		
12/12/42	1770	VGS-28	USS CHE-NANGO	ENR PANAMA	CENLANT		
12/21/42	5938	VGS-11	USS ALTAMAHA	NEW CALEDONIA	SOPAC		
12/29/42	440	VMSB-131		GUADAL-CANAL	SOPAC		
12/29/42	537	VMSB-131		GUADAL-CANAL	SOPAC		
12/29/42	549	VMSB-131		GUADAL-CANAL	SOPAC		
12/29/42	559	VMSB-131		GUADAL-CANAL	SOPAC		
12/31/42	562	VGS-26	USS SAN-GAMON	ENR PANAMA	CENLANT		
01/01/43	598	VMSB-131		GUADAL-CANAL	SOPAC		
01/08/43	5952	VGS-29	USS SANTEE	ENR RECIFE	CENLANT		
01/24/43	5877	VGS-27	USS SU-WANNEE	NEW CALEDONIA	SOPAC	LT HUDDLESTON	S
01/30/43	6004	MAG-12		NOUMEA	SOPAC	2NDLT MARKHAM JOHNSTON	S
01/31/43	554	VT-3	USS SARATOGA	NOUMEA	SOPAC	ENS W.I. WEISS	D
02/01/43	415	VMSB-131		GUADAL-CANAL	SOPAC	CAPT BEAN	M
02/01/43	560	VMSB-131		GUADAL-CANAL	SOPAC	M/SGT JULIEN	M

DATE	BUNO	SQDRN	BASE	LOST	AREA	PILOT	FATE
02/01/43	1742	VMSB-131		GUADAL-CANAL	SOPAC	LT DALTON	M
02/01/43	5901	VMSB-131		GUADAL-CANAL	SOPAC	CAPT MOLVIK	M
02/06/43	6037	VGS-29	USS SANTEE	RECIFE	BRAZIL	ENS F.K. BARRETT	M
02/08/43	431	VGS-11	USS ALTAMAHA		SOPAC		
02/08/43	5963	VGS-11	USS ALTAMAHA		SOPAC		
02/10/43	5956	VC-27	USS SU-WANNEE	SOLOMONS	SOPAC	ENS ROBERT H. STONUM	S
02/15/43	6035	VGS-29	USS SANTEE	RECIFE	BRAZIL		
02/22/43	493	VT-11		FIJI IS.	SOPAC		
02/24/43	1752	VT-10	USS ENTER-PRISE	SOLOMONS	SOPAC	LTJG G.L. WELLS	S
02/27/43	530	VGS-27	USS SU-WANNEE	NOUMEA	SOPAC	ENS BENTON JOHN SKUDA	S
02/27/43	6048	VGS-9	USS BOGUE		CENLANT		
02/28/43	5958	VGS-27	USS SU-WANNEE	NOUMEA	SOPAC	ENS BENTON JOHN SKUDA	S
03/03/43	6109	VMSB-143		GUADAL-CANAL	SOPAC	LT A.R. BERRY	M
03/04/43	555	VT-11		FIJI IS.	SOPAC		
03/10/43	6018	VC-28	USS CHE-NANGO	SOLOMONS	SOPAC		
03/12/43	528	VC-28	USS CHE-NANGO	SOLOMONS	SOPAC	LT W. UNDER (OR WUNDER)	M
03/14/43	5899	VMSB-143		GUADAL-CANAL	SOPAC	LT RAYMOND K. EASTCOTT	M
03/14/43	5964	VMSB-143		GUADAL-CANAL	SOPAC	LT PETER M. PAGE	D
03/14/43	5966	VMSB-143		GUADAL-CANAL	SOPAC	CAPT WILFRED L. PARK	M
03/14/43	6019	VMSB-143		GUADAL-CANAL	SOPAC	LT JOHN H. MARTINDALE	M
03/14/43	6022	VMSB-143		GUADAL-CANAL	SOPAC	LT GLEN I. ANDERSON	M
03/14/43	6092	VMSB-143		GUADAL-CANAL	SOPAC	LT JOSEPH H. KURZ	M
03/16/43	6068	VC-29	USS SANTEE	ENR NORFOLK	CENLANT	ENS CLAUDE N. BARTON	S
03/21/43	6091	VMSB-143		KAHILI	SOPAC	2NDLT MATHESON	M
03/23/43	553	MAG-14	GUADAL-CANAL	GUADAL-CANAL	SOPAC		
03/30/43	1766	VT-9	USS ESSEX	GULF OF PARIA	NORLANT		
04/01/43	5897	VMSB-143		RUSSELLS	SOPAC	LT LEHOW	M
04/01/43	5905	VMSB-143		RUSSELLS	SOPAC	LT PALMER	S
04/01/43	5944	VMSB-143		RUSSELLS	SOPAC	LT FRAZIER	S
04/01/43	6084	VMSB-143		RUSSELLS	SOPAC	WINSTEAD	M
04/03/43	1761	FAW-2	PEARL	HAWAII	ECENPAC		
04/07/43	527	VC-26	USS SAN-GAMON	RUSSELLS	SOPAC	LTJG WEBER	M
04/07/43	569	VC-28	USS CHE-NANGO	RUSSELLS	SOPAC	LT HARDMAN	M
04/07/43		VMSB-131		GUADAL-CANAL	SOPAC	LT HAYTER	M
04/07/43	5970	VMSB-131		GUADAL-CANAL	SOPAC	LT HATFIELD	M
04/07/43	5985	VMSB-131		GUADAL-CANAL	SOPAC	LT NUSUM	M
04/07/43	6226	VMSB-131		GUADAL-CANAL	SOPAC	LT REESE	S
04/07/43	6438	VMSB-131		GUADAL-CANAL	SOPAC	LT MANTHEY	M
04/08/43	1740	VMSB-131		GUADAL-CANAL	SOPAC	LT CLARK	S
04/09/43	438	VMSB-131		GUADAL-CANAL	SOPAC	CAPT BANGERT	U
04/10/43	5972	VMSB-143			SOPAC		
04/14/43	5994	VJ-1	PEARL	HAWAII	ECENPAC		

DATE	BUNO	SQDRN	BASE	LOST	AREA	PILOT	FATE
04/19/43	606	VT-27	GUADAL-CANAL	GUADAL-CANAL	SOPAC	LTJG R.W. BURNS	M
04/19/43	462	VT-3	USS SARATOGA	NOUMEA	SOPAC		
04/30/43	536	VC-9	USS BOGUE		SOLANT		
04/30/43	5898	VMSB-143			SOPAC		
04/30/43	5909	VMSB-143			SOPAC		
04/30/43	5910	VMSB-143			SOPAC		
04/30/43	6254	VT-4	USS RANGER		CENLANT		
04/30/43	409	VT-6	USS SARATOGA	NOUMEA	SOPAC		
04/30/43	469	VT-6	USS SARATOGA	NOUMEA	SOPAC		
05/06/43	6227	VMSB-143	GUADAL-CANAL	MUNDA	SOPAC	LT W.C. SPRADLING	M
05/15/43	610	VT-9	USS ESSEX	HAWAII	ECENPAC		
05/17/43	6239	VMSB-143	GUADAL-CANAL	BOUGAIN-VILLE	SOPAC	SLEYSTER	M
05/18/43	6243	VMSB-143	GUADAL-CANAL	BOUGAIN-VILLE	SOPAC	LT KEIN	M
05/19/43	5969	VT-11	GUADAL-CANAL		SOPAC	SWEETAER	M
05/19/43	6357	VT-11	GUADAL-CANAL		SOPAC	AYERS	M
05/20/43	6121	VC-27	USS SU-WANNEE	SOLOMONS	SOPAC	ENS AUSTIN WEST KELLY	D
05/20/43	5943	VT-11	GUADAL-CANAL		SOPAC		
05/20/43	5962	VT-3	USS SARATOGA	NOUMEA	SOPAC		
05/21/43	6367	VT-5	USS YORK-TOWN	ENR TRINIDAD	CENLANT		
05/22/43	5991	VC-28	USS CHE-NANGO	SOLOMONS	SOPAC	LTJG J.C. MILLON	S
05/24/43	6468	VF-16	USS LEX-INGTON	CARIBBEAN	CENLANT	LTJG RICHARD O. SCHEELE	S
05/28/43	5968	VC-1	USS CARD	ENR CASABLANCA	CENLANT	ROBERT KALMAN HAAS, JR.	M
05/28/43	538	VT-11	GUADAL-CANAL		SOPAC	BURKE	U
05/28/43	5949	VT-11	GUADAL-CANAL		SOPAC	HUGHES	U
05/28/43	47474	VT-16	USS LEX-INGTON	CARIBBEAN	CENLANT	FRANK ELLSWORTH	S
05/30/43	1737	VMSB-143	GUADAL-CANAL		SOPAC	LT BOWIE	M
05/31/43	6165	VB-9	USS ESSEX		WCENPAC	LT THOMAS H. STETSON	S
06/05/43	47473	VT-16	USS LEX-INGTON	OFF MASS.	NORLANT	ENS EUGENE F. TERNASKY	S
06/08/43	6036	VC-27			SOPAC		
06/09/43	6352	VMTB-233		NEW HEBRIDES	SOPAC	MAJ HOWARD F. BOWKER	M
06/09/43	6067	VT-27	GUADAL-CANAL	KAHILI	SOPAC	ENS C.R. ROWLEY, JR.	S
06/10/43	47539	VT-21		KAHILI	SOPAC		
06/15/43	6116	VC-28	USS CHE-NANGO	SOLOMONS	SOPAC		
06/16/43	47448	VT-21		KAHILI	SOPAC	PECK	U
06/21/43	535	VMSB-233			SOPAC	LT HOLLIS	S
06/23/43	6303	VT-4	USS RANGER		NORLANT		
06/26/43	6485	VT-7			WCENPAC	ENS ROBERT ELIOT BUSBY	S
06/26/43	6027	VT-9	USS ESSEX		SOPAC	LT DELMAR WALKER, JR.	S
06/28/43	1736	VT-3	USS SARATOGA	NOUMEA	SOPAC	2NDLT O. PETRIE	S
06/30/43	6361	VC-26	USS SAN-GAMON	SOLOMONS	SOPAC	LTJG LEADBETTER	S
06/30/43	6015	VC-9	USS BOGUE		NORLANT		

DATE	BUNO	SQDRN	BASE	LOST	AREA	PILOT	FATE
07/01/43	6356	VF-3	USS SARATOGA	NOUMEA	SOPAC		
07/02/43	47490	VC-1	USS CARD	ENR NORFOLK	CENLANT	LTJG H.A. CACH	S
07/02/43	47465	VT-7			WCENPAC		
07/05/43	5912	VC-28	USS CHE-NANGO	SOLOMONS	SOPAC		
07/07/43	24016	VC-19			NORLANT		
07/07/43	403	VMTB-233		ESPIRITU SANTO	SOPAC	LT MCGOWAN	D
07/07/43	6166	VT-17			NORLANT		
07/07/43	6063	VT-21	GUADAL-CANAL	KAHILI	SOPAC	LTJG MCKINNEY	M
07/09/43	653	VT-9	USS ESSEX		WCENPAC	FREDERICK L. MARVIL	S
07/14/43	6089	VC-19	USS CROATAN	ENR NORFOLK	NORLANT		
07/14/43	6240	VT-21	GUADAL-CANAL		SOPAC	LT JACOBSON	S
07/16/43	6312	VT-21	GUADAL-CANAL		SOPAC	ENS LAWTY	S
07/17/43	6338	VC-36			NORLANT		
07/17/43	5902	VC-9	USS BOGUE		NORLANT		
07/17/43	6434	VT-21	GUADAL-CANAL		SOPAC	LT JACOBSON	D
07/18/43	5923	VC-26	USS SAN-GAMON	SOLOMONS	SOPAC	MITCHELL	M
07/18/43	47440	VT-6			SOPAC	ENS RICHARD J. WALSH, JR.	S
07/18/43	47450	VT-6			SOPAC		
07/20/43	6271	VT-21		VELLA LAVELLA	SOPAC	ENS WILLIAM R. WINN	M
07/20/43	6314	VT-21		VELLA LAVELLA	SOPAC	LTJG GERALD E. ROBBINS	M
07/20/43	47446	VT-5	USS YORK-TOWN	ENR PEARL	ECENPAC	LT J.W. CONDIT	S
07/21/43	47594	VC-13	USS CORE		NORLANT	ENS DOYLE WILSON HALL	S
07/21/43		VMTB-233		ESPIRITU SANTO	SOPAC	LT HOLLIS	S
07/24/43	6238	VMTB-143	GUADAL-CANAL		SOPAC	MAJ MOLLENKAMP	S
07/24/43	6126	VT-27	GUADAL-CANAL	GUADAL-CANAL	SOPAC	LTJG STONUM	S
07/26/43	47508	VMTB-143	GUADAL-CANAL		SOPAC	LT LABAT	S
07/28/43	574	VC-28	USS CHE-NANGO	ENR WASHINGTON	SOPAC		
07/29/43	6245	VMTB-143	GUADAL-CANAL		SOPAC		
07/31/43	24022	VC-29	USS SANTEE	ENR NORFOLK VA	NORLANT		
08/04/43	6369	VC-24	USS BELLEAU WOOD	HAWAII	ECENPAC		
08/08/43	1750	VC-1	USS CARD		NORLANT	LT SALLENGER	S
08/09/43	47476	VT-16	USS LEX-INGTON	PEARL	ECENPAC		
08/11/43	6081	VT-12	USS SARATOGA	NOUMEA	SOPAC		
08/11/43	6095	VT-12	USS SARATOGA	NOUMEA	SOPAC		
08/11/43	6457	VT-12	USS SARATOGA	NOUMEA	SOPAC		
08/20/43	623	VC-28	USS CHE-NANGO		SOPAC	TAKEN OFF SHIP AT REFIT	
08/20/43	6141	VT-16	USS LEX-INGTON	PEARL	ECENPAC		
08/20/43	6325	VT-16	USS LEX-INGTON	PEARL	ECENPAC		
08/20/43	47489	VT-16	USS LEX-INGTON	PEARL	ECENPAC		
08/24/43	24174	VT-1	HILO	HAWAII	ECENPAC		

DATE	BUNO	SQDRN	BASE	LOST	AREA	PILOT	FATE
08/28/43	5919	VC-23	USS PRINCE-TON	HAWAII	ECENPAC		
08/31/43	6371	VT-5	USS YORK-TOWN	MARCUS	CENPAC	LT J.W. CONDIT	M
09/02/43	6258	VT-24	USS BELLEAU WOOD	HAWAII	ECENPAC	ENS WARREN OMARK	S
09/02/43	47602	VT-6		HAWAII	ECENPAC		
09/03/43	6477	VMTB-233	GUADAL-CANAL	VILA	SOPAC	LITTLE	S
09/04/43	24048	VMTB-233	GUADAL-CANAL	VILA	SOPAC	MAJ O'NEIL	D
09/09/43	6429	VMTB-233	GUADAL-CANAL	VILA	SOPAC		
09/11/43	6350	VMTB-233	GUADAL-CANAL	BAMBAN	SOPAC	LCDR H.H. LARSON	S
09/11/43	6140	VT-16	USS LEX-INGTON	PEARL	ECENPAC		
09/11/43	23888	VT-16	USS LEX-INGTON	PEARL	ECENPAC		
09/16/43	23909	VC-40	GUADAL-CANAL	BALLALE	SOPAC	LTJG ROWLAND D. HAHN	U
09/16/43	6452	VMTB-233	GUADAL-CANAL	BALLALE	SOPAC	LT E.A. CROKER	U
09/18/43	5916	VC-23	USS PRINCE-TON	TARAWA	CENPAC	LTJG C.M. BRANSFIELD	M
09/18/43	6193	VC-23	USS PRINCE-TON	MAKIN	CENPAC		
09/18/43	23865	VC-31	USS CABOT		NORLANT		
09/20/43	6115	VMTB-233	GUADAL-CANAL	GUADAL-CANAL	SOPAC		
09/22/43	47441	VC-23	USS PRINCE-TON	ENR PEARL	WCENPAC	LTJG J.R. MARSH	S
09/24/43	6482	VT-6			WCENPAC		
09/27/43	47578	VC-23	USS PRINCE-TON	ENR PEARL	WCENPAC		
09/27/43	47553	VF-33	USS BRETON		SOPAC		
09/29/43	529	VC-26	USS SAN-GAMON	ESPIRITU SANTO	SOPAC		
09/30/43	47494	VMTB-143	GUADAL-CANAL		SOPAC		
09/30/43	6214	VT-9	USS ESSEX	HAWAII	ECENPAC		
10/02/43	23958	ACV-23	USS BRETON		SOPAC		
10/04/43	6302	VT-4	USS RANGER	VESTFJORD	NORLANT	LTJG J.H. PALMER	M
10/05/43	23964	VT-5	USS YORK-TOWN	WAKE	WCENPAC	LT WILLIAM J. RUEFLE	S
10/05/43	47535	VT-9	USS ESSEX	WAKE	WCENPAC	LTJG G.C. HENRY	S
10/07/43	23867	VC-31	USS CABOT		NORLANT		
10/10/43	6481	VMTB-233		BOUGAIN-VILLE	SOPAC	LT ROMANUS MCCOLE	S
10/10/43	24019	VT-8	USS INTREPID	CARIBBEAN	CENLANT		
10/11/43	492	MAG-21	EFATE	GUADAL-CANAL	SOPAC	LT R.S. MCCALL	S
10/11/43	23880	VT-4	USS RANGER	OFF ICELAND	NORLANT	LT H.W. MCMILLIAM	S
10/19/43	6114	VC-38		SOLOMONS	SOPAC		
10/19/43	6142	VT-16	USS LEX-INGTON	PEARL	ECENPAC		
10/22/43	47533	VC-35			ECENPAC		
10/22/43	47592	VMTB-232		BOUGAIN-VILLE	SOPAC	LT LOACH	S
10/24/43	23963	VC-22	USS INDE-PENDENCE	PEARL	ECENPAC	LTJG W.M. COMAGYA	S
10/26/43	6416	VMTB-232		KAHILI	SOPAC	LT PHILLIP FIELD	M

DATE	BUNO	SQDRN	BASE	LOST	AREA	PILOT	FATE
10/27/43	23881	VC-22	USS INDE-PENDENCE	PEARL	ECENPAC	ENS J.S. BEHRENS	M
10/28/43	6118	VC-38		BOUGAIN-VILLE	SOPAC	LTJG H.W. WILSON	D
10/28/43	6475	VMTB-233		BOUGAIN-VILLE	SOPAC	LTJG DOUGLAS B. LAPIERRE	S
10/29/43	6436	VC-60	USS SU-WANNEE	PEARL	ECENPAC		
10/31/43	24062	VC-60	USS SU-WANNEE	PEARL	ECENPAC		
10/31/43	612	VT-9	USS ESSEX	WAKE	WCENPAC	LT A.C. WHIPPLE	S
11/01/43	23956	VC-22	USS INDE-PENDENCE	OAHU	ECENPAC		
11/01/43	5892	VT-9	USS ESSEX	ENR RABAUL	SOPAC	LTJG R.B. BENTMEYER	S
11/02/43	24071	VC-23	USS PRINCE-TON	RABAUL	SOPAC	LTJG C.C. DYER	M
11/02/43	24176	VC-23	USS PRINCE-TON	RABAUL	SOPAC	LTJG G.W. SPEAR	S
11/02/43	6117	VT-12	USS SARATOGA	RABAUL	SOPAC	LTJG S.A. NYARADY	S
11/03/43	6403	VC-35	USS CHE-NANGO	PEARL	ECENPAC		
11/03/43	24033	VC-35	USS CHE-NANGO	PEARL	ECENPAC		
11/04/43	24122	VC-32	USS LANGLEY	TRINIDAD	CENLANT	ENS K.J. VALGARES	D
11/04/43	6237	VC-33	USS CORAL SEA	ENR PEARL	ECENPAC	ENS G.P. POWERS	S
11/04/43	6316	VMTB-143		BARAKOMA	SOPAC		
11/04/43	24195	VMTB-143		MUNDA KAHILI	SOPAC	1STLT J.W. TUNNELL	M
11/05/43	5920	VC-23	USS PRINCE-TON	RABAUL	SOPAC		
11/05/43	24177	VC-23	USS PRINCE-TON	RABAUL	SOPAC	LTJG W.W. FRATUS	M
11/05/43	6418	VC-37	USS SAN-GAMON	ESPIRITU SANTO	SOPAC		
11/08/43	6359	VMTB-232		MUNDA	SOPAC		
11/11/43	23953	VC-22	USS INDE-PENDENCE	RABAUL	SOPAC		
11/11/43	47579	VC-30	USS MONTEREY	ENR MAKIN	CENPAC	ENS R.J. KEENAN	S
11/11/43	6406	VMTB-233		MUNDA	SOPAC	1STLT P.A. WARD	S
11/11/43	23973	VT-12	USS SARATOGA	BOUGAIN-VILLE	SOPAC	LTJG S.A. NYARADY	M
11/11/43	6353	VT-17	USS BUNKER HILL	RABAUL	SOPAC	LTJG N.C. CARBY	S
11/11/43	47458	VT-9	USS ESSEX	RABAUL	SOPAC	LTJG C. DENBY WILKOS	S
11/11/43	47555	VT-9	USS ESSEX	RABAUL	SOPAC	LTJG J.P. SCHERER	S
11/13/43	23887	VF-16	USS LEX-INGTON	PEARL	ECENPAC	LT C.L. WILSON	S
11/14/43	47608	VC-60	USS SU-WANNEE	PEARL	ECENPAC	ENS G.R. BANKS	S
11/15/43	6267	VT-5	USS YORK-TOWN	PUUNENE	ECENPAC		
11/15/43	47599	VT-9	USS ESSEX	GILBERTS	CENPAC	LT F.H. FOX	D
11/16/43	47551	VMTB-143		MUNDA	SOPAC	1STLT E.R. MCLAUGHLIN	S
11/16/43	6190	VMTB-233		MUNDA	SOPAC	1STLT J. DELANCY	S
11/17/43	6093	VMTB-233		MUNDA TOROKINA	SOPAC	LT L.P. HARRIS	D
11/19/43	6355	VMTB-134		ESPIRITU SANTO	SOPAC	2NDLT C.A. HESS	S
11/19/43	6138	VT-16	USS LEX-INGTON	MILLE	CENPAC	LTJG N.E. WHITE	M
11/19/43	23918	VT-23	USS PRINCE-TON	NAURU	CENPAC	ENS R.S. BATES	S

DATE	BUNO	SQDRN	BASE	LOST	AREA	PILOT	FATE
11/19/43	23877	VT-6	USS ENTER-PRISE	MAKIN	CENPAC	LT J.E. MCINERNY	M
11/20/43	24238	VC-33	USS CORAL SEA	MAKIN	CENPAC	ENS R.F. SCHOLZ	S
11/20/43	24063	VT-16	USS LEX-INGTON	MILLE	CENPAC	LT R.O. CURRY	S
11/22/43	24216	VT-16	USS LEX-INGTON	MILLE	CENPAC	ENS N.R. LANDON	S
11/25/43	6186	VC-60	USS SU-WANNEE	ENR ROI	CENPAC		
11/25/43	47460	VT-6	USS ENTER-PRISE	MAKIN	CENPAC	ENS WALDEN	S
11/26/43	6261	VC-22	USS BELLEAU WOOD	TARAWA	CENPAC	LTJG R.S. CHASE	S
11/30/43	23875	VT-6	USS ENTER-PRISE	PUUNENE	ECENPAC		
11/30/43	24190	VT-6	USS ENTER-PRISE	PUUNENE	ECENPAC		
12/03/43	6024	VMTB-233		MUNDA	SOPAC	1STLT C.O. PYLANT	D
12/05/43	386	VJ-1	PEARL	HAWAII	ECENPAC		
12/05/43	24214	VT-5	USS YORK-TOWN	KWAJALEIN	CENPAC	LT R.F. KELRAIN	D
12/08/43	47589	VC-30	USS MONTEREY	NAURU	CENPAC	ENS T.L. HALL	S
12/09/43	6259	VT-24	USS BELLEAU WOOD	ENR PEARL	CENPAC		
12/11/43	6041	VT-12		PEARL	ECENPAC		
12/23/43	23871	VMTB-232	MUNDA	BOUGAIN-VILLE	SOPAC	1STLT T.L. SPARKS	M
12/27/43	47593	VC-58	USS BLOCK ISLAND		NORLANT	LTJG J.J. MCCONVILLE	S
12/28/43	23873	VMTB-134		ESPIRITU SANTO	SOPAC	1STLT H.A. ELLIOTT	S
12/28/43	47510	VMTB-134		ESPIRITU SANTO	SOPAC	1STLT R.L. MCGANN	S
01/01/44	47531	VT-30	USS MONTEREY	KAVIENG	SOPAC		
01/01/44	47570	VT-30	USS MONTEREY	KAVIENG	SOPAC	ENS G.B. YOUNG	S
01/11/44	23980	VT-23	USS PRINCE-TON	PEARL	ECENPAC	ENS E.P. EUBANK	M
01/14/44	24102	VC-58	USS BLOCK ISLAND		NORLANT	LTJG A.R. THOMPSON	S
01/23/44	6061	VMTB-143	MUNDA	RABAUL	SOPAC	1STLT A.H. JOHNSON	S
01/29/44	47586	VT-30	USS MONTEREY	MARSHALLS	CENPAC	ENS Q.B. HURLBURT	M
01/29/44	6175	VT-5	USS YORK-TOWN	TAROA	CENPAC	ENS T.E. MCGRATH	D
01/29/44	6213	VT-5	USS YORK-TOWN	TAROA	CENPAC	LT D.R. SIMENSEN	M
01/29/44	6265	VT-5	USS YORK-TOWN	TAROA	CENPAC	ENS J.J. O'SULLIVAN	S
01/29/44	47617	VT-6	USS INTREPID	ROI	WCENPAC	LTJG T.M. VAUGHN	D
01/30/44	24207	VT-24	USS BELLEAU WOOD	KWAJALEIN	CENPAC	LTJG G.J. AGAR	D
01/31/44	24504	VC-13	USS GUADAL-CANAL		N AFRICA		
02/01/44	6346	VT-9	USS ESSEX	ROI	WCENPAC		
02/05/44	23969	VMTB-233		RABAUL	SOPAC	1STLT F.W. PAINTER	M
02/05/44	617	VT-31	USS CABOT	MARSHALLS	CENPAC		

DATE	BUNO	SQDRN	BASE	LOST	AREA	PILOT	FATE
02/07/44	6419	VC-33	USS CORAL SEA	KWAJALEIN	CENPAC		
02/14/44	6311	VMTB-233	TOROKINA	RABAUL	SOPAC	1STLT J.F. BARTHORF	M
02/14/44	47506	VMTB-233	TOROKINA	RABAUL	SOPAC	1STLT H.L. CORNELIUS	M
02/16/44	6223	VMTB-233	TOROKINA	RABAUL	SOPAC	LT CORMAN	S
02/16/44	23891	VT-9	USS ESSEX	TRUK	CENPAC	LTJG D.C. KANE	M
02/22/44	47544	VMTB-143	TOROKINA	KERAV.	SOPAC	1STLT W.K. HARRIS	M
02/26/44	6072	VC-60	USS SU-WANNEE	ENIWETOK	CENPAC	ENS F.P. MACKAY	S
02/29/44	24168	VMTB-134		TOROKINA	SOPAC		
03/06/44	595	VJ-2	PEARL	HAWAII	ECENPAC	ENS W.H. JONES	S
03/08/44	24194	VC-40	PIVA	TOROKINA	SOPAC		
03/09/44	647	VT-10	USS ENTER-PRISE	AT SEA	CENPAC	LTJG C.E. HENDERSON	S
03/13/44	1732	VMTB-242		ESPIRITU SANTO	SOPAC		
03/17/44	451	COM7THFLT	PERTH	AUSTRALIA	SW PAC		
04/03/44	24101	VC-66	USS ALTAMAHA	MARSHALLS	CENPAC		
04/10/44	6189	MAG-24	PIVA	BOUGAIN-VILLE	SOPAC		
04/12/44	546	VJ-12	PEARL	HAWAII	ECENPAC	API/C J.E. BOWERS	S
04/12/44	24220	VMTB-134		GREEN	SOPAC		
04/24/44	561	VT-32	USS LANGLEY	NW NEW GUINEA	SW PAC		
04/26/44	47515	FAW-2	KANEOHE	HAWAII	ECENPAC	ENS R.R. JOHNSON	S
04/29/44	24368	VT-24	USS BELLEAU WOOD	TRUK	CENPAC	LT R.M. SWENSSON	M
05/21/44	23987	VT-305		RABAUL	SOPAC	ENS D.D. ATKISS	M
05/30/44	6086	VMTB-232		ESPIRITU SANTO	SOPAC	1STLT A.J. AUNE	S
06/01/44	23952	VC-55	USS BLOCK ISLAND	31-13N/023-03W	NORLANT	(SHIP SANK)	
06/01/44	24202	VC-55	USS BLOCK ISLAND	31-13N/023-03W	NORLANT	(SHIP SANK)	
06/01/44	47614	VC-55	USS BLOCK ISLAND	31-13N/023-03W	NORLANT	(SHIP SANK)	
06/05/44	24279	VT-35	USS CHE-NANGO	KWAJALEIN	CENPAC		
06/18/44	6025	VJ-10		BANIKA	SOPAC		
07/10/44	5936	VMTB-443		ESPIRITU SANTO	SOPAC	1STLT P.H. KEZERIAN	U
07/14/44	5881	VT-100	NAVY NO. 14	HAWAII	ECENPAC	ENS R.E. FALKNER	S
07/18/44	24508	VC-19	USS GUADAL-CANAL		NORLANT	LTJG H.A. HUGHEY	S
07/19/44	47502	VMTB-134		ESPIRITU SANTO	SOPAC		
08/04/44	6171	COMAIR-PAC	PEARL	HAWAII	ECENPAC		
08/07/44	5911	VJ-2		TREASURY	SOPAC	ENS D.C. YEDICA	S
08/11/44	5939	ARU SOLS			SOPAC		
08/11/44	5973	ARU SOLS			SOPAC		
08/28/44	6420	VJ-12		ESPIRITU SANTO	SOPAC		
08/31/44	6222			ESPIRITU SANTO	SOPAC		
09/15/44	474	VJ-12		ESPIRITU SANTO	SOPAC		
09/15/44	588	VJ-12		ESPIRITU SANTO	SOPAC		
09/15/44	6155	VJ-12		ESPIRITU SANTO	SOPAC		
09/25/44	5979			ESPIRITU SANTO	SOPAC		
09/28/44	23982			ESPIRITU SANTO	SOPAC		

DATE	BUNO	SQDRN	BASE	LOST	AREA	PILOT	FATE
09/29/44	23975	STAG-1	RUSSELLS	RUSSELLS	SOPAC	LT C.E. TOBIN	S
10/01/44	6437	ARU SOLS		GUADAL-CANAL	SOPAC		
10/30/44	6473	SERVRON-24		TOROKINA	SOPAC		
11/30/44	5907	VMTB-134		PELELIU	WCENPAC		
12/18/44	24088	NACTU	BARBERS POINT	HAWAII	ECENPAC	LTJG JOSEPH W. JEWELL, JR	S
01/04/45	23907	VJ-12		STERLING	SOPAC		
01/05/45	47471	VS-65		EBON	SW PAC	ENS CLAUDE SUTHERLAND	S
01/15/45	47549	A.A.	GUADAL-CANAL	GUADAL-CANAL	SOPAC		
01/26/45	24143	VJ-7	PEARL	HAWAII	ECENPAC	LTJG MANLOND SMITH	S
02/07/45	405	A.A.	GUADAL-CANAL	GUADAL-CANAL	SOPAC		
02/26/45	6039	A.A.	GUADAL-CANAL	GUADAL-CANAL	SOPAC	ENS S.S. SHAW	U
03/06/45	1759	COMAIR-PAC	PEARL	HAWAII	ECENPAC		
03/06/45	6474	MAW-1		TOROKINA	SOPAC		
03/21/45	408	COMAIR-PAC	PEARL	HAWAII	ECENPAC		
03/31/45	6229	SERVRON-24		LINGAYEN GULF	PHIL		
05/21/45	6058	AROU-1		MOMOTE	SW PAC		
05/21/45	6456	AROU-1		MOMOTE	SW PAC		
06/20/45	23882	POOL	PEARL	HAWAII	ECENPAC		
06/26/45	5990	POOL	PEARL	HAWAII	ECENPAC		
06/28/45	23938	POOL	BARBERS POINT	HAWAII	ECENPAC		
07/16/45	47556	AROU-2		SAMAR	PHIL		
07/20/45	6122	AROU-1		MOMOTE	SW PAC		
07/20/45	6256	AROU-1		MOMOTE	SW PAC		
07/20/45	6336	AROU-1		MOMOTE	SW PAC		
07/20/45	6358	AROU-1		MOMOTE	SW PAC		
07/20/45	6373	AROU-1		MOMOTE	SW PAC		
07/20/45	6432	AROU-1		MOMOTE	SW PAC		
07/20/45	23937	AROU-1		MOMOTE	SW PAC		
07/20/45	23972	AROU-1		MOMOTE	SW PAC		
07/20/45	24038	AROU-1		MOMOTE	SW PAC		
07/20/45	47504	AROU-1		MOMOTE	SW PAC		
07/26/45	23889	CASU(F)-12		GUAM	WCENPAC		
07/26/45	23966	CASU(F)-12		GUAM	WCENPAC		
08/09/45	6370	POOL	PEARL	HAWAII	ECENPAC		

GRUMMAN TBF-1C

The Grumman TBF-1C variant was the TBF-1 with provision for two 0.5 in (12.7 mm) wing guns and with its fuel capacity increased to 726 gal (2,748 l). There were 765 built. Aircraft lost:

DATE	BUNO	SQDRN	BASE	LOST	AREA	PILOT	FATE
08/09/43	24389	VC-1	USS CARD		NORLANT	LTJG THOMAS	S
08/25/43	24274	VT-1	HILO	HAWAII	ECENPAC		
09/04/43	24257	VC-29	USS SANTEE	ENR CASABLANCA	NORLANT		
09/19/43	24356	VT-1	HILO	HAWAII	ECENPAC		
09/27/43	24283	VC-40	GUADAL-CANAL	ESPIRITU SANTO	SOPAC		
10/12/43	24247	VC-29	USS SANTEE	ENR NORFOLK VA	NORLANT		
10/13/43	24421	VC-9	USS CARD		NORLANT		
10/15/43	24342	VMTB-232		NEW HEBRIDES	SOPAC	LT CLAIR V. BERDELL	S
11/01/43	24422	VT-12	USS SARATOGA	BUKA	SOPAC	LT T.B. BASH	S
11/03/43	47815	VC-33	USS CORAL SEA	ENR PEARL	ECENPAC	ENS C.W. MARION	S
11/04/43	24354	VT-1	HILO	HAWAII	ECENPAC		

DATE	BUNO	SQDRN	BASE	LOST	AREA	PILOT	FATE
11/05/43	24401	VT-12	USS SARATOGA	RABAUL	SOPAC	LCDR R.F. FARRINGTON	S
11/11/43	24414	VT-17	USS BUNKER HILL	RABAUL	SOPAC	LT W.F. KRANTZ	M
11/11/43	24512	VT-17	USS BUNKER HILL	RABAUL	SOPAC	LT R.H. HIGLEY	M
11/15/43	24402	VT-17	USS BUNKER HILL	ENR TARAWA	SOPAC	LTJG A.P. O'SULLIVAN	S
11/22/43	24250	VC-29	USS SANTEE	BAY OF BISCAY	NORLANT	LT J. OSTER	S
11/23/43	24360	VMTB-134		ESPIRITU SANTO	SOPAC		
11/25/43	24410	VC-22	USS INDE-PENDENCE	TARAWA	CENPAC		
11/30/43	47755	VT-10	USS ENTER-PRISE	PUUNENE	ECENPAC	ENS J.D. EILAND	M
12/05/43	24488	VT-25	USS COWPENS	MARSHALLS	CENPAC	LT W.S. WATSON	S
12/08/43	47933	VT-32	USS LANGLEY	OFF PANAMA	CENLANT	ENS J.H. MILLIKEN	D
12/10/43	47702	VC-37	USS SAN-GAMON	GILBERTS	CENPAC		
12/11/43	24412			NOUMEA	SOPAC		
12/23/43	47818	VT-10	USS ENTER-PRISE	PUUNENE	ECENPAC	LTJG F. DOELKER	S
12/25/43	24338	VT-17	USS BUNKER HILL	KAVIENG	SOPAC	LTJG H.C. CARBY	S
12/26/43	47658	VC-55	USS CARD		N AFRICA	LTJG R.N. HARLEY	S
01/10/44	24500	VC-13	USS GUADAL-CANAL		N AFRICA		
01/10/44	24502	VC-13	USS GUADAL-CANAL		N AFRICA	LTJG J.F. SCHOLY	D
01/10/44	24432	VT-25	USS COWPENS	PEARL	ECENPAC		
01/14/44	24487	VMTB-232	MUNDA	RABAUL	SOPAC		
01/14/44	24492	VMTB-232	MUNDA	RABAUL	SOPAC	1STLT L.V. SWENSON	M
01/16/44	24426	VC-13	USS GUADAL-CANAL		N AFRICA		
01/16/44	24431	VC-13	USS GUADAL-CANAL		N AFRICA		
01/16/44	24503	VC-13	USS GUADAL-CANAL		N AFRICA		
01/16/44	24267	VT-1	USS YORK-TOWN	HILO	ECENPAC		
01/16/44	47926	VT-32	USS LANGLEY	KANEOHE	ECENPAC	ENS J.W. DEMPSEY	M
01/16/44	47928	VT-32	USS LANGLEY	KANEOHE	ECENPAC		
01/17/44	24489	VMTB-143	MUNDA	RABAUL	SOPAC		
01/17/44	24363	VMTB-232	MUNDA	RABAUL	SOPAC	1STLT H.H. MILLER	M
01/18/44	47761	VT-10	USS ENTER-PRISE	PEARL	ECENPAC	LT V.V. EASON	S
01/19/44	47810	VT-10	USS ENTER-PRISE	PEARL	ECENPAC	LTJG R.G. JONES	S
01/20/44	47972	VC-13	USS GUADAL-CANAL		N AFRICA	LTJG B.M. BEATTIE	M
01/20/44	24343	VT-23	USS PRINCE-TON	MARSHALLS	CENPAC	LTJG J.M. CALDWELL	S
01/23/44	24396	VC-35	USS CHE-NANGO	MARSHALLS	CENPAC		

DATE	BUNO	SQDRN	BASE	LOST	AREA	PILOT	FATE
01/23/44	24480	VMTB-232	MUNDA		RABAUL	SOPAC	
01/23/44	47909	VT-2	HILO	HAWAII	ECENPAC	ENS D.M. MILLIGAN	D
01/25/44	47854	VT-8	PUUNENE	HAWAII	ECENPAC	ENS F.M. SEWALL	S
01/27/44	47739	VC-33	USS CORAL SEA	MARSHALLS	CENPAC		
01/27/44	48089	VC-55	USS CARD		NORLANT	LTJG J.H.J. PEAROE	S
01/29/44	47748	VMTB-143	MUNDA	TOBERA	SOPAC	1STLT D.R. MEUPOLDER	D
01/29/44	24507	VT-17	USS BUNKER HILL	KWAJALEIN	CENPAC	LTJG A.P. O'SULLIVAN	M
01/29/44	47915	VT-17	USS BUNKER HILL	KWAJALEIN	CENPAC	LTJG G.M. BROWN	S
01/30/44	47911	VC-7	USS MAN-ILA BAY	MARSHALLS	CENPAC	LT F.W. ROBINSON	S
01/30/44	24406	VMTB-233		RABAUL	SOPAC	CAPT P.E. LAMALE	M
01/31/44	47868	VC-60	USS SU-WANNEE	ROI	WCENPAC	ENS W.M. KELLER	S
02/03/44	47661	VC-55	USS CARD		NORLANT	LTJG CALVIN E. MANSELL	S
02/03/44	47738	VT-10	USS ENTER-PRISE	KWAJALEIN	CENPAC	LT R.F. KIPPEN	S
02/03/44	24347	VT-17	USS BUNKER HILL	ENIWETOK	CENPAC	LTJG W.D. STACK	M
02/03/44	24458	VT-17	USS BUNKER HILL	ENIWETOK	CENPAC	LTJG J.K. PEARSON	M
02/03/44	24484	VT-17	USS BUNKER HILL	ENIWETOK	CENPAC	LCDR F.M. WHITAKER	M
02/07/44	48122	VC-33	USS CORAL SEA	KWAJALEIN	CENPAC		
02/10/44	24244	VMTB-233		BOUGAIN-VILLE	SOPAC		
02/11/44	47879	VT-32	USS LANGLEY	ENGEBI	WCENPAC	ENS J.H. SAUNDERS	S
02/14/44	24264	VMTB-233	TOROKINA	RABAUL	SOPAC	1STLT J.W. BOYDEN	M
02/14/44	24340	VMTB-233	TOROKINA	RABAUL	SOPAC	1STLT R.W. SHERMAN	M
02/14/44	24475	VT-10	USS ENTER-PRISE	TRUK	CENPAC		
02/16/44	24330	VT-6	USS INTREPID	TRUK	CENPAC		
02/16/44	24362	VT-9	USS ESSEX	TRUK	CENPAC	LTJG C.C. HOOVER	D
02/17/44	47746	VT-10	USS ENTER-PRISE	TRUK	CENPAC		
02/17/44	47973	VT-15	USS HORNET	ENR CANAL ZONE	CENPAC		
02/17/44	47812	VT-17	USS BUNKER HILL	TRUK	CENPAC	LTJG W.B. BIRKES	M
02/17/44	47762	VT-30	USS MONTEREY	TRUK	CENPAC	LT E.C. KNOSPE	D
02/18/44	47697	VT-14	USS WASP	GULF OF PARIA	NORLANT	LT W.T. WILLIAMS	S
02/19/44	47677	VC-1	USS CROATAN		AFRICA	LT F.W. MURRAY	M
02/20/44	24495	VMTB-143	TOROKINA	RABAUL	SOPAC	LTJG H.T. LEAKE	M
03/04/44	24357	VMTB-134		ESPIRITU SANTO	SOPAC		
03/08/44	24479	VT-15	USS HORNET	BARBERS POINT	ECENPAC	ENS R. CHAFFE	S
03/09/44	24253	VC-95	USS BOGUE	ENGLAND	EUROPE	ENS A.H. HEINES	S
03/13/44	48080	VT-26	USS SANTEE	PEARL	ECENPAC	ENS E.D. PETERSON	S
03/17/44	47876	VT-15	USS HORNET	PUUNENE	ECENPAC	ENS B.J. IRWIN	D

DATE	BUNO	SQDRN	BASE	LOST	AREA	PILOT	FATE
03/18/44	48101	VC-63	USS NATOMA BAY	KAVIENG	SOPAC	LT G.M. DOUGLASS	S
03/19/44	47679	VC-6	USS BLOCK ISLAND	CAPE VERDE	NORLANT	LTJG W.T. DOUTY	D
03/20/44	47698	VC-33	USS CORAL SEA	GUADAL-CANAL	SOPAC	LT J.A. ZEHNUNG	D
03/20/44	47917	VF-24	USS BELLEAU WOOD	EMIRAU	SW PAC		
03/25/44	24295	VC-9	USS SOLO-MONS	RECIFE	BRAZIL	LTJG W.F. CHAMBERLAIN	S
03/25/44	24397	VMTB-134	GREEN	RABAUL	SOPAC	1STLT L.H. HERNDON	M
03/25/44	47676	VT-13	USS FRANKLIN	TRINIDAD	CENLANT	ENS W.F. DRIESSEN	S
03/25/44	48050	VT-13	USS FRANKLIN	TRINIDAD	CENLANT	ENS H.R. HUDSON	S
03/26/44	48052	VT-13	USS FRANKLIN	TRINIDAD	CENLANT	ENS J.W. LAWTON	S
03/30/44	47920	VT-16	USS LEX-INGTON	PALAU	CENPAC	LTJG W.E. MCLELLAN	S
03/30/44	47904	VT-2	USS HORNET	PALAU	CENPAC	ENS R.H. WILSON	S
03/30/44	24420	VT-5	USS YORK-TOWN	PALAU	CENPAC	ENS M.G. MOORE	S
03/30/44	47860	VT-8	USS BUNKER HILL	PALAU	CENPAC	LTJG M. LECOMPTE	S
03/31/44	48084	VT-16	USS LEX-INGTON	PALAU	CENPAC	LT R.O. CURRY	M
04/01/44	24387	VC-13	USS TRIPOLI	CAPE VERDE	NORLANT	LTJG J.P. BURKE	S
04/02/44	24490	VC-40	TOROKINA	ST. GEORGE	SOPAC	LTJG R.J. COLLINS	S
04/09/44	47816	VC-36	USS CORE	AZORES	NORLANT	LTJG N.L. BULL	S
04/12/44	24249	VC-13	USS TRIPOLI		N AFRICA	LTJG J.P. BURKE	S
04/12/44	48059	VT-26	USS SANTEE	FLORIDA IS.	SOPAC	ENS C.T. MCGINNIS	S
04/14/44	48109	VC-58	USS GUADAL-CANAL	CAPE VERDE	NORLANT	LTJG R.J. WADE	S
04/20/44	48090	VC-9	USS SOLO-MONS	BRAZIL	SOLANT	ENS M.S. BAKER	S
04/21/44	47728	VT-10	USS ENTER-PRISE	HOLLANDIA	SW PAC	ENS W.J. MILLER	S
04/21/44	47833	VT-8	USS BUNKER HILL	WAKDE	SW PAC	LTJG F.R. SWENSON	S
04/21/44	47980	VT-8	USS BUNKER HILL	WAKDE	SW PAC	LCDR K.F. MUSICK	S
04/22/44	47811	VC-7	USS MAN-ILA BAY	TUMLEO	SW PAC	LT T.G. BONDURANT	S
04/22/44	24333	VT-5	USS YORK-TOWN	WAKDE	SW PAC	ENS O.W. RAMEY	D
04/22/44	47867	VT-8	USS BUNKER HILL	WAKDE	SW PAC	LTJG F.C. HALEY	S
04/23/44	47745	VT-10	USS ENTER-PRISE	HOLLANDIA	SW PAC	LTJG S.W. MCCRARY	S
04/23/44	24361	VT-5	USS YORK-TOWN	HOLLANDIA	SW PAC	LTJG L.J. MILLIGAN	S
04/27/44	47866	VT-8	USS BUNKER HILL	TRUK	CENPAC	LTJG H.A. BUXTON	S
04/29/44	48117	VT-16	USS LEX-INGTON	TRUK	CENPAC	LTJG C.L. WILSON	S
04/29/44	48105	VT-2	USS HORNET	TRUK	CENPAC	LTJG SCAMMELL	S
04/30/44	24275	VMTB-134		GREEN	SOPAC		

DATE	BUNO	SQDRN	BASE	LOST	AREA	PILOT	FATE
04/30/44	47758	VT-10	USS ENTER-PRISE	TRUK	CENPAC	ENS C.L. FARRELL	S
04/30/44	24346	VT-2	USS HORNET	TRUK	CENPAC		
04/30/44	47908	VT-2	USS HORNET	TRUK	CENPAC		
04/30/44	48113	VT-2	USS HORNET	TRUK	CENPAC		
05/11/44	24334	VC-40	TOROKINA	TOROKINA	SOPAC		
05/15/44	47887	COMAIR-PAC	PEARL	HAWAII	ECENPAC		
05/15/44	48058	VC-36	USS CORE	AZORES	NORLANT	LT G. KRAMER	S
05/18/44	24474	VMTB-232		EMIRAU	SW PAC		
05/20/44	48010	VC-36	USS CORE	CANARIES	NORLANT	LT W.A. DAVENPORT	D
05/22/44	48123	VMTB-232		NEW IRELAND	SOPAC	CAPT C.V. BERDEL	S
06/09/44	24281	VT-12	USS SARATOGA	OFF BREMERTON	CENPAC		
06/11/44	24485	VMTB-232		EMIRAU	SW PAC	CAPT RADCLIFFE	S
06/12/44	47805	VT-14	USS WASP	TINIAN	WCENPAC	ENS J.L. MORRISON	S
06/12/44	24476	VT-2	USS HORNET	GUAM	WCENPAC		
06/12/44	24463	VT-25	USS COWPENS	SAIPAN	WCENPAC		
06/12/44	48094	VT-25	USS COWPENS	PAGAN	CENPAC	LTJG W.J. DAY	S
06/12/44	47864	VT-8	USS BUNKER HILL	MARIANAS	CENPAC	LT G.A. WILDHACK	M
06/13/44	24423	VT-16	USS LEX-INGTON	SAIPAN	WCENPAC	LTJG F.M. DELGADO	M
06/14/44	24287	VC-95	USS CROATAN		NORLANT	LT E.M. KOOS	S
06/14/44	47674	VC-95	USS CROATAN		NORLANT		
06/14/44	47696	VT-14	USS WASP	ROTA	CENPAC	LT WEEKS	S
06/15/44	48121	VC-65	USS MIDWAY	SAIPAN	WCENPAC		
06/15/44	47936	VC-9	USS SOLO-MONS	OFF RECIFE	SOLANT	ENS EDWARDS	M
06/15/44	24390	VMTB-232		EMIRAU	SW PAC	CAPT C.V. BERDEL	M
06/15/44	47769	VT-15	USS ESSEX	BONINS	CENPAC	ENS A.D. MCRAE	D
06/15/44	48106	VT-15	USS ESSEX	BONINS	CENPAC	ENS T.W. STERLING	M
06/15/44	47817	VT-2	USS HORNET	BONINS	CENPAC		
06/15/44	47925	VT-32	USS LANGLEY	BONINS	CENPAC		
06/19/44	47882	VT-14	USS WASP	W OF SAIPAN	CENPAC		
06/20/44	24486	VC-33	USS CORAL SEA	TINIAN	WCENPAC	LTJG I.F. PFAHNL	S
06/20/44	47749	VC-33	USS CORAL SEA	TINIAN	WCENPAC	LT R.S. EVARTS	M
06/20/44	47756	VT-1	USS YORK-TOWN	W OF SAIPAN	CENPAC	LTJG F. MAYOCK	S
06/20/44	24468	VT-10	USS ENTER-PRISE	SAIPAN	WCENPAC	LTJG R.W. CUMMINGS	S
06/20/44	47826	VT-10	USS ENTER-PRISE	SAIPAN	WCENPAC	LT C.B. COLLINS	S
06/20/44	47828	VT-14	USS WASP	SAIPAN	WCENPAC	LT W.T. WILLIAMS	S
06/20/44	47979	VT-14	USS WASP	SAIPAN	WCENPAC	ENS C.K. HOFFMAN	S
06/20/44	47829	VT-16	USS LEX-INGTON	W OF SAIPAN	CENPAC	LT H.C. THOMAS	S
06/20/44	24246	VT-24	USS BELLEAU WOOD	SAIPAN	WCENPAC	LTJG B.C. TATE	S
06/20/44	47694	VT-31	USS CABOT	MARIANAS	CENPAC	LTJG D.H. SMITH	S
06/20/44	23968	VT-60	USS SU-WANNEE	PHILIPPINE SEA	PHIL	LTJG HIGGINBOTHAM	D

DATE	BUNO	SQDRN	BASE	LOST	AREA	PILOT	FATE
06/20/44	24478	VT-8	USS BUNKER HILL	SAIPAN	WCENPAC	LTJG W.H. FOLKEDAHL	M
06/20/44	47907	VT-8	USS BUNKER HILL	SAIPAN	WCENPAC		
06/22/44	24286	VC-95	USS CROATAN		NORLANT	LCDR J. ADAMS	S
06/25/44	47806	VT-15	USS ESSEX	GUAM	WCENPAC		
06/25/44	47975	VT-16	USS LEX-INGTON	ENR GUAM	CENPAC	LT C.S. BROOKES	S
07/05/44	47874	VT-8	USS BUNKER HILL	PALAU	CENPAC		
07/09/44	24276	VC-4	USS WHITE PLAINS	SAIPAN	WCENPAC		
07/10/44	48095	VT-28	USS MONTEREY	MARIANAS	CENPAC		
07/11/44	24483	VC-11	USS NEHENTA BAY	MARSHALLS	CENPAC		
07/12/44	47766						
07/12/44	48054	VT-13	USS FRANKLIN	MARIANAS	CENPAC	ENS D.F.Q. TORALOMON	S
07/22/44	47681	VC-19	USS GUADAL-CANAL		NORLANT	ENS WARNER G. BAILEY	S
07/27/44	47905	VT-15	USS ESSEX	GUAM	WCENPAC		
07/27/44	48082	VT-15	USS ESSEX	ROTA	CENPAC	ENS L.R. TIMBERLAKE	S
07/27/44	24344	VT-35		GUAM	WCENPAC	LT C.F. MORGAN	S
07/28/44	47669	VC-19	USS GUADAL-CANAL		NORLANT		
07/31/44	47938	VF(N)-79	USS INDE-PENDENCE	PEARL	ECENPAC	LT W.R. TAYLOR	S
08/05/44	47663	VT-13	USS FRANKLIN	CHICHI JIMA	CENPAC	LTJG HARTZELL F. MCCUE	M
08/09/44	24407	CASU-35		ENIWETOK	CENPAC		
08/09/44	24481	CASU-35		ENIWETOK	CENPAC		
08/09/44	47763	CASU-35		ENIWETOK	CENPAC		
08/09/44	47822	CASU-35		ENIWETOK	CENPAC		
08/09/44	47852	CASU-35		ENIWETOK	CENPAC		
08/09/44	47912	CASU-35		ENIWETOK	CENPAC		
08/09/44	48103	CASU-35		ENIWETOK	CENPAC		
08/10/44	24394	VT-4	HILO	HAWAII	ECENPAC	ENS LYNN C. GRAY	S
08/27/44	47665	VC-19	USS GUADAL-CANAL		NORLANT	ENS WARNER G. BAILEY	S
09/22/44	47969	CASU-2	BARBERS POINT	HAWAII	ECENPAC		
09/23/44	24355	VMTB-242		TINIAN	WCENPAC	LT M.M. GUFFY, JR.	S
09/25/44	48018	VT-44	HAWAII		ECENPAC	ENS WARD H. BURROWS	M
09/27/44	47886	A & R	PEARL	HAWAII	ECENPAC		
09/27/44	48019	VT-26	USS SANTEE	MOROTAI	PHIL	ENS GEORGE J. BALDINI	M
10/09/44	24494	VC-88	HAWAII	HAWAII	ECENPAC		
10/10/44	47700	VT-14	USS WASP	OKINAWA	EMPIRE		
10/11/44	48087	VT-14	USS WASP	ENR FORMOSA	CENPAC		
10/12/44	48093	CASU-42		PITYILU	SW PAC		
10/13/44	47695	VT-14	USS WASP	ENR LUZON	PHIL	LT W.A. DAVIDSON, JR.	M
10/15/44	47764	VT-15	USS ESSEX	FORMOSA	EMPIRE		
10/18/44	47935	VT-15	USS ESSEX	ENR LEYTE GULF	PHIL		
10/24/44	47862	VT-15	USS ESSEX	LUZON	PHIL		
10/24/44	47977	VT-15	USS ESSEX	LUZON	PHIL	LTJG F.E. SOUTHARD	M
10/25/44	48091	VT-26	USS SANTEE	PHILIPPINE SEA	PHIL	ENS E.D. PETERSON	S
11/12/44	24352	VT-9	HAWAII		ECENPAC	ENS DONALD J. MCKEEBY	S
12/29/44	47668	A.A.	PEARL	HAWAII	ECENPAC		
01/08/45	23935	VT-80	USS TICONDER-OGA	FORMOSA	EMPIRE		

DATE	BUNO	SQDRN	BASE	LOST	AREA	PILOT	FATE
01/09/45	24348	VT-86	HAWAII		ECENPAC	LT B.M. EASLEY	S
01/21/45	48100	VC-97	HAWAII	HAWAII	ECENPAC	LTJG J.R. SPENCER	S
01/31/45	23925	CASU-1	PEARL	HAWAII	ECENPAC	LT JOHN J. CINAK	D
02/19/45	73254	VC-77	USS RUDYERD BAY	IWO JIMA	EMPIRE	LCDR FRANK J. PETERSON	S
02/20/45	47743	AA & RH	HAWAII		ECENPAC		
04/04/45	24405	VT-100	HAWAII		ECENPAC	ENS A.W. HITE, JR.	S
04/13/45	47753	VT-100	HAWAII		ECENPAC	ENS JOSEPH H. MYERS	S
04/23/45	48012	VT(N)-53	HILO	HAWAII	ECENPAC	ENS D.L. PIPER	S
04/24/45	48108	VC-79	HAWAII		ECENPAC	ENS JOHN N. FRAZIER	U
05/07/45	47804	COMAIR-PAC	PEARL	HAWAII	ECENPAC	ENS NED E. OWENS	S
05/21/45	47827	AROU-1		MOMOTE	SW PAC		
05/21/45	48097	VT-100	HAWAII		ECENPAC	ENS LEE MEROLLI	S
05/22/45	47699	VJ-18		ULITHI	WCENPAC	ENS EDWARD EDMISTEN	S
06/06/45	47655	POOL	BARBERS POINT	HAWAII	ECENPAC		
06/29/45	47870	CASU(F)-47		SAIPAN	WCENPAC		
06/29/45	48098	CASU(F)-47		SAIPAN	WCENPAC		
06/30/45	48048	POOL	PEARL	HAWAII	ECENPAC		
06/30/45	48014	VT-99		SAIPAN	WCENPAC		
07/15/45	48028	VJ-17		GUAM	WCENPAC	ENS C.S. MEHELICH	M
07/16/45	24269	AROU-2		SAMAR	PHIL		
07/26/45	47830	CASU(F)-12		GUAM	WCENPAC		
07/26/45	47919	CASU(F)-12		GUAM	WCENPAC		
08/07/45	48120	POOL	PEARL	HAWAII	ECENPAC		

GRUMMAN TBF-1D

The Grumman TBF-1D variant was the TBF-1 with a centimetric radar in radome installed on the starboard wing leading edge. Aircraft lost:

DATE	BUNO	SQDRN	BASE	LOST	AREA	PILOT	FATE
04/06/44		VT-13	USS FRANKLIN	TRINIDAD	CENLANT	ENS H.R. HUDSON	S
04/22/44	24261	VC-9	USS SOLO-MONS	BRAZIL	SOLANT	LT C.G. HEWITT	M
07/16/44	24511	VC-19	USS GUADAL-CANAL		NORLANT	LT J.E. OGLE	D
07/22/44	24509	VC-19	USS GUADAL-CANAL		NORLANT	LT G. GOODWIN	S
07/26/44	24255	VC-19	USS GUADAL-CANAL	PUERTO RICO	CENLANT	LT J.S. IRELAND	M
07/26/44	24248	VC-42		BERMUDA	NORLANT		
08/16/44	24506	VC-19	USS GUADAL-CANAL	BERMUDA	NORLANT	LTJG R.B. MCASHAN	S
09/15/44	24277	VC-42	USS BOGUE		NORLANT	LT F.B. UNDERONAN	S

GRUMMAN TBF-1P

The Grumman TBF-1P variant was the TBF-1 converted for photo-reconnaissance. Aircraft lost:

DATE	BUNO	SQDRN	BASE	LOST	AREA	PILOT	FATE
07/18/43	05992	VT-11			SOPAC		
11/01/43	06127	VT-12	USS SARATOGA	BUKA	SOPAC	LTJG J.T. EATON	U
11/05/43	24219	VC-23	USS PRINCE-TON	RABAUL	SOPAC	LTJG G.F. SCOTT	M

DATE	BUNO	SQDRN	BASE	LOST	AREA	PILOT	FATE
02/16/44	06372	VT-5	USS YORK-TOWN	TRUK	CENPAC	ENS BENSON	S

HOWARD GH-2

The Howard Aircraft Corporation DGA-15 was a single-engine civil aircraft produced in the USA from 1939 to 1944. The Howard Aircraft Company (later Howard Aircraft Corporation) was formed in 1936 to build commercial derivatives of the Howard DGA-6, a successful four seat racing aircraft which had won both the Bendix and the Thompson Trophies in 1935, the only aircraft ever to win both races. These successes did indeed bring the DGA series much attention, and Howard produced a series of closely-related differing mainly in the engine type, consisting of the DGA-7, 8, 9, 11 and 12. Offering high performance and comprehensively equipped, these emerged as coveted aircraft owned by corporations, wealthy individuals, and movie stars.

In 1939, the Howard Aircraft Corporation produced a new development of the basic design, the Howard DGA-15. Like its predecessors, the DGA-15 was a single engined high-winged monoplane with a wooden wing and a steel tube truss fuselage, but it was distinguished by a deeper and wider fuselage, allowing five people to be seated in comfort. It was available in several versions, differing in the engine fitted. The DGA-15P was powered by a Pratt & Whitney Wasp Junior radial engine, while the DGA-15J used a Jacobs L6MB and the DGA-15W a Wright R-760-E2 Whirlwind. In an era when airlines were flying DC-3s, the Howards cruising at 160 to 170 mph could match their speed, range and comfort with the rear seat leg room exceeding airline standards with limousine-like capaciousness, and high wing loading allowing the Howards to ride through most turbulence comfortably.

Prior to Pearl Harbor, about 80 DGA-8 through DGA-15 aircraft had been built at the Howard Aircraft Corporation factory on the south side of Chicago Municipal Airport. With America's entry into World War II, most of the civilian Howards were commandeered by the military. The Army used them as officer transports and as ambulance planes, with the designation UC-70. The Navy, in particular, much liked the plane and contracted Howard Aircraft Corporation to build hundreds of the DGA-15Ps to its own specifications. They were used variously as an officer's utility transport (GH-1, GH-3), aerial ambulance (GH-2), and for instrument training (NH-1). A second factory was opened at Dupage County airport, west of Chicago, and about 520 DGA-15's were eventually completed. Aircraft lost:

DATE	BUNO	SQDRN	BASE	LOST	AREA	PILOT	FATE
04/10/44	32336	VR-10	HONOLULU	HAWAII	ECENPAC	LT C.H. DOLSON	S
06/29/44	32789	STATION OPR	HONOLULU	HAWAII	ECENPAC		
10/16/44	32338	3RD MAW	NAVY NO. 61		SOPAC		
12/21/44	32337	VMO-5		HAWAII	ECENPAC		
02/12/45	32374	CASU-2	BARBERS POINT	HAWAII	ECENPAC	LT ROBERT R. HANSON	S
06/26/45	32806	POOL	BARBERS POINT	HAWAII	ECENPAC		

HOWARD NH-1

The Howard Aircraft Corporation DGA-15 was a single-engine civil aircraft produced in the USA from 1939 to 1944. Prior to Pearl Harbor, about 80 DGA-8 through DGA-

15 aircraft had been built at the Howard Aircraft Corporation factory on the south side of Chicago Municipal Airport. With America's entry into World War II, most of the civilian Howards were commandeered by the military. The Army used them as officer transports and as ambulance planes, with the designation UC-70. The Navy, in particular, liked the plane and contracted Howard Aircraft Corporation to build hundreds of the DGA-15Ps to its own specifications. They were used variously as an officer's utility transport (GH-1, GH-3), aerial ambulance (GH-2), and for instrument training (NH-1). A second factory was opened at Dupage County airport, west of Chicago, and about 520 DGA-15's were eventually completed. There were 205 of the NH-1's built. Aircraft lost:

DATE	BUNO	SQDRN	BASE	LOST	AREA	PILOT	FATE
10/31/44	29472	COMAIR-PAC	PEARL	HAWAII	ECENPAC		
02/12/45	29530	VS-46	PEARL	PEARL	HAWAII	J.B. PINKSTON (CAP)	S
03/16/45	29543	NAS	NAVY NO. 24	PEARL	HAWAII	LTJG CARL E. MARSDEN	S
05/14/45	29541	POOL	KANEOHE	PEARL	HAWAII		
07/19/45	29545	POOL	BARBERS POINT	PEARL	HAWAII		

LOCKHEED ELECTRA

This aircraft was acquired by the Navy from Pan Am and assigned a Navy Bureau Number. It is unknown as to how it was lost. Three Electras were acquired in this manner (BuNos 99090-99092). Any further information from the reader would be helpful. Aircraft lost:

DATE	BUNO	SQDRN	BASE	LOST	AREA	PILOT	FATE
03/08/44	99091	PAN AM	FAIRBANKS	ALASKA	NORPAC	CAPT J. OLSONS	U

LOCKHEED JO-1

The Lockheed Model 12 Electra Junior, more commonly known as the Lockheed 12 or L-12, is an eight-seat, six-passenger all-metal twin-engine transport aircraft of the late 1930s designed for use by small airlines, companies, and wealthy private individuals. A scaled-down version of the Lockheed Model 10 Electra, the Lockheed 12 was not popular as an airliner but was widely used as a corporate and government transport. The Lockheed 12 proved much more popular as a transport for company executives or government officials. Oil and steel companies were among the major users. A number were purchased as military staff transports by the United States Army Air Corps, which designated the type as the C-40, and by the United States Navy, which used the designation JO. The JO-1 was a U.S. Navy five-passenger transport based on the Model 12-A Electra Junior. Only one was built and its loss is listed below.

DATE	BUNO	SQDRN	BASE	LOST	AREA	PILOT	FATE
09/04/44	1053	NVL ATTACHE		RIO DE JANERIO	SOLANT		

LOCKHEED JO-2

The Lockheed JO-2 was a U.S. Navy and Marine Corps six-passenger transport also based on the Model 12-A Electra Junior. Five were built. Aircraft lost:

DATE	BUNO	SQDRN	BASE	LOST	AREA	PILOT	FATE
12/07/41	1051	VMJ-252	PEARL	HAWAII	ECENPAC		

LOCKHEED PBO-1

The Lockheed Hudson was an American-built light bomber and coastal reconnaissance aircraft built initially for the Royal Air Force shortly before the outbreak of World War II and primarily operated by the RAF thereafter. The US Navy operated 20 A-28s, redesignated the PBO-1. These were former RAF Hudson IIIAs that were 'repossessed' for use by VP-82 Squadron of the United States Navy. Aircraft lost:

DATE	BUNO	SQDRN	BASE	LOST	AREA	PILOT	FATE
01/19/42	03845	VP-82	ARGENTIA		NORLANT		
01/21/42	03844	VP-82	ARGENTIA		NORLANT	ENS WILLIAM TEPUNI	S
08/01/42			GUANTAN-AMO BAY	CUBA	CENLANT		
09/15/42			TRINIDAD		CENLANT		

LOCKHEED PV-1

The Lockheed PV-1 Ventura was a bomber and patrol aircraft of World War II, used by United States forces in several guises. It was developed from the Lockheed Model 18 Lodestar transport, as a replacement for the Lockheed Hudson bombers then in service with the Royal Air Force. The PV-1 Ventura, built by the Vega Aircraft Company division of Lockheed (hence the 'V' Navy manufacturer's letter that later replaced the 'O' for Lockheed), was a version of the Ventura built for the U.S. Navy. The main differences between the PV-1 and the B-34 were the inclusion of special equipment in the PV-1, adapting it to its patrol-bombing role. The maximum fuel capacity of the PV-1 was increased from 1,345 gal (5,081 l) to 1,607 gal (6,082 l), to increase its range; the forward defensive armament was also reduced for this reason. The most important addition was of an ASD-1 search radar.

Early production PV-1s still carried a bombardier's station behind the nose radome, with four side windows and a flat bomb-aiming panel underneath the nose. Late production PV-1s dispensed with this bombardier position and replaced it with a pack with three 0.50 in (12.7 mm) machine guns underneath the nose. These aircraft could also carry eight 5 in (127 mm) HVAR rockets on launchers underneath the wings.

The PV-1 began to be delivered in 1942 December, and entered service in 1943 February. The first squadron in combat was VP-135, deployed in the Aleutian Islands in 1943 April. They were operated by three other squadrons in this theatre. From the Aleutians, they flew strikes against bases in Paramushiro and Shimushu, Japanese islands in the Kurile chain. Often, PV-1s would lead B-24 bomber formations, since they were equipped with radar. In late 1943, some PV-1s were deployed to the Solomon Islands as night-fighters.

During the early months of 1942, the primary responsibility for anti-submarine warfare in the United States was shouldered by the Army Air Force. This irked the Navy, as it considered this region of battle its burden. To carry out such a task, the Navy was pursuing a long-range, land-based patrol and reconnaissance aircraft with a substantial bombload. This goal was always resisted by the Army Air Force, which carefully protected its monopoly on land-based bombing. This forced the navy to use long-range floatplanes for these roles. The Navy was unable to upgrade to more capable aircraft until the Army Air Force needed the Navy plant in Renton, Washington to manufacture its B-29 Superfortress. In exchange for use of the Renton plant, the Army Air Force would discontinue its objections to naval land-based bombers, and provide planes to the Navy. One of the clauses of this agreement stated that production of the B-34 and B-37 by Lockheed would cease, and instead these resources would be directed at building a 'navalized" version, the PV-1 Ventura. Aircraft lost:

DATE	BUNO	SQDRN	BASE	LOST	AREA	PILOT	FATE
04/02/43	29735	VB-136	ATTU	ALASKA	NORPAC		
04/03/43	29902	FAW-9			NORLANT		
04/27/43	29828		NEW BRUNS-WICK		NORLANT		
05/01/43	29911	FAW-7	ENGLAND	ICELAND	NORLANT		
05/04/43	29768	VB-135	ADAK	ALASKA	NORPAC		
05/10/43	29794	FAW-4	DUTCH HARBOR	ALASKA	NORPAC	LT PERMENTER	M
05/10/43	29847	FAW-4	DUTCH HARBOR	ALASKA	NORPAC		
05/15/43	29900	VB-128			NORLANT		
05/23/43	29746	VB-135	ADAK	ALASKA	NORPAC		
05/23/43	29787	VB-135	ADAK	ALASKA	NORPAC	ENS P.P. PATTERSON	D
06/21/43	33329	VB-131			NORLANT		
06/28/43	29737	VB-135	ADAK	ALASKA	NORPAC		
06/30/43	29899	VB-126			NORLANT		
06/30/43	33187	VB-129	IPATANGA	CARIBBEAN	CENLANT		
07/01/43	33277	VB-150	USS LAKE CHAM-PLAIN	ALASKA	NORPAC		
07/09/43	33147	VB-126			NORLANT		
07/09/43	33419	VB-134			NORLANT		
07/10/43	33097	VB-131		GUANTANA-MO BAY	CENLANT		
08/01/43	29920	VB-127	PORT LYAUTEY	MOROCCO	NW AFR		
08/05/43	33284	VB-133			NORLANT		
08/06/43	33347	COMAIR-PAC	PEARL	HAWAII	ECENPAC		
08/06/43	33220	VB-138			WCENPAC	LT ROBERT E. SLATER	D
08/07/43	29916	VB-128			NORLANT		
08/24/43	29919	VB-128			NORLANT		
08/27/43	29918	VB-129	IPATANGA	SOUTH AMERICA	SOLANT		
09/02/43	34737	VB-130			NORLANT		
09/05/43	33100	VB-128			NORLANT		
09/07/43	29810	VB-137	FUNAFUTI		SOPAC	LT LLOYD E. PARKER	M
09/09/43	29825	VB-137	FUNAFUTI		SOPAC	LTJG LELAND L. DUNN	D
09/10/43	33411	VB-141	CURACAO		CENLANT		
09/12/43	29839	VB-137	FUNAFUTI		SOPAC		
09/12/43	33091	VB-137	FUNAFUTI		SOPAC		
09/13/43	33171	VB-130			NORLANT		
09/15/43	33414	VB-140	RUSSELLS	BALLALE	SOPAC	LT TREWHITT	S
09/16/43	29755	VMF(N)-531	RUSSELLS	SAVO IS.	SOPAC	LT MASON	M
09/25/43	33133	VB-136	ATTU	ALASKA	NORPAC		
09/29/43	33096	VB-127	PORT LYAUTEY	MOROCCO	NW AFR		
10/09/43	33092	VB-127	PORT LYAUTEY	MOROCCO	NW AFR	LT L.M. WEBB	S
10/11/43	33307	VB-140	GUADAL-CANAL	GUADAL-CANAL	SOPAC	LTJG ANTHONY S. BREWER	M
10/11/43	33410	VB-141	CURACAO		CENLANT		
10/16/43	29903	VB-125	CUBA	CARIBBEAN	CENLANT		
10/19/43	33200	VB-140	GUADAL-CANAL	GUADAL-CANAL	SOPAC	LTJG P.C. KERN	S
10/22/43	33134	VB-131	BRITISH GUYANA	CONAKY FIELD	SOLANT	LT PEEVEY	S
10/25/43	29736	VB-125	CUBA	CARIBBEAN	CENLANT		
10/26/43	29835	VB-125	CUBA	CARIBBEAN	CENLANT		
10/28/43	33209	VB-138	RUSSELLS		SOPAC	LTJG G.E. MITCHELL	S
10/31/43	29820	VMF(N)-531	USS SAVO ISLAND	BARAKOMA	SOPAC		

DATE	BUNO	SQDRN	BASE	LOST	AREA	PILOT	FATE
11/09/43	33412	VB-131	SURINAM	SARAMACCA R.	NORLANT	LTJG J.W. POWERS	S
11/09/43	33140	VB-136	ALEUTIANS	SHEMYAD	NORPAC	LT DINSMORE	S
11/10/43	33358	VB-131	PARAHAR-IBO	ZANDERY FIELD	NORLANT	LTJG R.G. WINTHERS	D
11/13/43	34802	VB-138	RUSSELLS		SOPAC	LT W.E. LOHSE	S
11/13/43	34828	VB-141	CURACAO		CENLANT	LT L.M. EVANS	M
11/13/43	34653	VB-145	NATAL		SOLANT	LT E.M. JONES	S
11/14/43	34837	VB-142	MIDWAY		ECENPAC	LT E.L. HAWKINS	S
11/19/43	29853	VB-129	IPATANGA	SOUTH AMERICA	SOLANT		
11/19/43	29910	VB-129	IPATANGA	SOUTH AMERICA	SOLANT		
12/02/43	33189	VB-131	PARAHAR-IBO	ZANDERY FIELD	NORLANT	LT SWONETZ	S
12/03/43	33212	VB-137	TARAWA	TARAWA	CENPAC		
12/03/43	33217	VB-140	GUADAL-CANAL	MUNDA	SOPAC	LT A.J. JONGEWAARD	S
12/09/43	34774	VB-136	ATTU	ALASKA	NORPAC	ENS E. WATSON	S
12/11/43	33428	VB-142	KANEOHE	HAWAII	ECENPAC	LT R.S. BRANE	D
12/13/43	29879	VB-145	NATAL		SOLANT	LTJG H.H. WOODWARD	S
12/16/43	34636	VB-139	AMCHITKA	ALASKA	NORPAC	LT A.G. NEAL	S
12/18/43	34843	VB-138	RUSSELLS		SOPAC	LT C. DILLON	S
12/21/43	34590	VB-141	CURACAO		CENLANT	LTJG W.W. LOMAS	D
12/22/43	34989	VB-132	FRENCH GUYANA	CONAKY FIELD	SOLANT	LT R.G. SHULTS	S
12/23/43	29821	VB-137	TARAWA	NAURU	CENPAC	LT T.J. CUNNINGHAM	M
12/24/43	29824	VB-137	TARAWA	TARAWA	CENPAC		
12/28/43	29815	VB-137	TARAWA	TARAWA	CENPAC		
12/30/43	34745	VB-137	TARAWA	TARAWA	CENPAC		
12/30/43	33346	VB-139	ATTU	ALASKA	NORPAC	LTJG V.C. AUSTIN	S
01/01/44	34801	VB-138	RUSSELLS	RENARD	SOPAC		
01/01/44	33417	VB-141	CURACAO		CENLANT	ENS J. MANKIN	S
01/03/44	49598	VPB-137		MOROTAI	PHIL		
01/05/44	48738	VB-131	SURINAM	ZANDERY FIELD	NORLANT	LTJG B.C. KERN	D
01/10/44	34790	VB-132	PORT LYAUTEY	MOROCCO	NW AFR	LT E.P. WOOD	D
01/11/44	29843	VB-137	TARAWA	TARAWA	CENPAC		
01/20/44	33353	VB-142	TARAWA	EMIDJ	CENPAC	LTJG M.E. VILLA	M
01/29/44	34891	VB-138	RUSSELLS		SOPAC		
02/03/44	33254	VMF-215	PIVA	BUKA	SOPAC		
02/13/44	33285	VB-140	GUADAL-CANAL	GUADAL-CANAL	SOPAC		
02/14/44	33361	VB-144	TARAWA		CENPAC	LT J.W. BAKER	M
02/17/44	33351	VB-131	SURINAM	ZANDERY FIELD	NORLANT	LT M.E. NAFE	D
02/22/44	33340	VB-138	STIRLING	CAPE ST. GEORGE	SOPAC	LTJG A.J. DITTER	D
02/23/44	33384	VB-131	SURINAM	ZANDERY FIELD	NORLANT	ENS C.M. THOMAS	S
03/25/44	33343	VB-139	ATTU	KURILES	NORPAC	LT J.H. MOORE	S
03/25/44	34641	VB-139	ATTU	KURILES	NORPAC	LT W.S. WHITMAN	M
04/04/44	29921	VB-127	PORT LYAUTEY	MOROCCO	NW AFR	LTJG D.L. SCHLATER	D
04/14/44	48697	VB-148	MUNDA	KAHILI	SOPAC	LTJG W.T. HENDERSON	S
04/21/44	34941	VB-143	IPATANGA	BAHIA, BRAZIL	SOLANT	LT J.B. PETERSON	S
04/27/44	48937	VB-135	ADAK	ALASKA	NORPAC	LT J.J. MCNULTY	M
04/29/44	48907	FAW-5	NATAL		SOLANT	LT KINAZOZUK	M
05/01/44	29749	FAW-4	ADAK	ALASKA	NORPAC		
05/03/44	34824	VB-148	MUNDA		SOPAC	LT W.E. DAVIS	M
05/06/44	48733	VB-135	ATTU	KURILES	NORPAC	LTJG A.A. WHEAT	M
05/13/44	48934	VB-135	ATTU	PARAMUSH-IRO	NORPAC	LT H.V. LOGAN	M
05/16/44	34736	VB-147	SURINAM	ZANDERY FIELD	NORLANT	LT S.C. WAHLBERG	M
05/18/44	34640	VB-139	ATTU	ALASKA	NORPAC	LT R.J. LOWE	S
05/23/44	48889	VB-135	ATTU	ALASKA	NORPAC	LT C. CLARK	D
05/26/44	33301	VB-142	MAJURO		CENPAC		
06/01/44	34833	VB-148		EMIRAU	SW PAC		
06/08/44	33357	FAW-6	SITKA	ALASKA	NORPAC		
06/09/44	34742	VB-151	KANEOHE	HAWAII	ECENPAC		
06/10/44	48923	VB-135	ATTU	AGATTU	NORPAC	LTJG J.W. CLARK	S
06/10/44	49417	VB-151	KANEOHE	HAWAII	ECENPAC	LT A. STAAB	M

DATE	BUNO	SQDRN	BASE	LOST	AREA	PILOT	FATE
06/12/44	34883	VB-146	KANEOHE	HAWAII	ECENPAC		
06/14/44	48910	VB-135	ATTU	KURILES	NORPAC	LT R.P. BONE	M
06/14/44	48930	VB-135	ATTU	KURILES	NORPAC	LT H.P. SCHUETTE	U
06/15/44	48809	VB-146	KANEOHE	HAWAII	ECENPAC		
06/17/44	34839	VB-144	ROI	JALUIT	CENPAC		
06/18/44	49469	VB-125	CUBA	SAN JULIAN	CENLANT	LT P.J. BUFOUR	M
06/19/44	48938	VB-135	ATTU	KURILES	NORPAC	LT MAHRT	U
06/20/44	34682	VB-147	TRINIDAD		NORLANT	ENS A.T. BILLIARD	S
06/25/44	49468	VB-147	SAN JUAN		NORLANT	LT G.S. MOORE	S
07/01/44	34789	VB-132	PORT LYAUTEY	MOROCCO	NW AFR	ENS L.H. HATCHETT	S
07/10/44	34884	VB-146		ADMIRALTIES	SW PAC	LT F.S. MASON	S
07/22/44	48928	VB-135	ATTU	KURILES	NORPAC	LTJG J.W. CLARK	M
07/24/44	48909	VB-135	ATTU	KURILES	NORPAC	LT VIVIAN	M
08/02/44	33247	COMAIR-PAC	PEARL	HAWAII	ECENPAC		
08/03/44	34924	VB-125	CUBA	SAN JULIAN	CENLANT	LT ROY I. BEATHARD	S
08/12/44	49525	VB-136	ATTU	ARAIDO IS.	NORPAC	LT LINDELL	U
08/20/44	49507	VB-136	ATTU	KURILES	NORPAC	LTJG J.R. COWLES	M
08/28/44	49508	VB-136	ATTU	KURILES	NORPAC	LTJG J.A. DINGLE	U
08/28/44	34654	VB-145	NATAL		SOLANT	LT C.W. BLEICHER	S
09/08/44	33196	VPB-125		SAN JULIAN	NORLANT		
09/11/44	33278	VB-135	ATTU	KURILES	NORPAC	LTJG MCDONALD	M
09/12/44	33078	VPB-127	PORT LYAUTEY	MOROCCO	NW AFR		
09/17/44	49472	VPB-136		KURILES	NORPAC	LCDR C. WAYNE	U
09/19/44	34690	VPB-127		CORSICA	EUROPE	LTJG A.J. MAYELL	S
09/19/44	34697	VPB-200	HAWAII		ECENPAC	B.T. SCHAFERSMAN	S
09/24/44	34879	VPB-146		ADMIRALTIES	SW PAC	LTJG P.E. CARON	S
09/30/44	33348	COMAIR-PAC	GUADAL-CANAL	GUADAL-CANAL	SOPAC		
10/09/44	33349	VPB-148	EMIRAU		SW PAC	LT GEORGE S. VON WELLER	S
10/16/44	33429	FAW-5	ITALY		EUROPE	LT THOMAS J. GALVIN	D
10/17/44	34913	VPB-132	AGADIR	MOROCCO	NW AFR	LT ALONZO F. WELLMAN	S
10/20/44	34799	VPB-146	PITYILU		SW PAC	LTJG WILLIAM B. TAYLOR	M
10/20/44	34885	VPB-146	PITYILU		SW PAC	LTJG GORDON L. PEEL	D
10/23/44	48894	VPB-150		TINIAN	WCENPAC		
10/28/44	48810	VPB-146	PITYILU		SW PAC	LT WILLIAM J. DECKER	M
11/03/44	34848	VPB-146	PITYILU		SW PAC	LT J.E. CLARK	S
11/04/44	49641	VPB-131	ATTU	ALASKA	NORPAC	LT ROBERY A. ELLINGHOE	M
11/07/44	48897	VPB-146	PITYILU		SW PAC		
11/09/44	34782	VPB-132	AGADIR	MOROCCO	NW AFR		
11/09/44	34783	VPB-132	AGADIR	MOROCCO	NW AFR		
11/09/44	34785	VPB-132	AGADIR	MOROCCO	NW AFR		
11/09/44	34787	VPB-132	AGADIR	MOROCCO	NW AFR		
11/09/44	34788	VPB-132	AGADIR	MOROCCO	NW AFR		
11/09/44	34792	VPB-132	AGADIR	MOROCCO	NW AFR		
11/09/44	34794	VPB-132	AGADIR	MOROCCO	NW AFR		
11/09/44	34795	VPB-132	AGADIR	MOROCCO	NW AFR		
11/09/44	34796	VPB-132	AGADIR	MOROCCO	NW AFR		
11/09/44	34797	VPB-132	AGADIR	MOROCCO	NW AFR		
11/09/44	34940	VPB-132	AGADIR	MOROCCO	NW AFR		
11/09/44	48866	VPB-132	AGADIR	MOROCCO	NW AFR		
11/09/44	48869	VPB-132	AGADIR	MOROCCO	NW AFR		
11/09/44	49636	VPB-132	AGADIR	MOROCCO	NW AFR		
11/13/44	49421	VPB-151		TINIAN	WCENPAC		
11/20/44	49588	VPB-146	PITYILU		SW PAC	LT R.H. HART	S
11/22/44	48743	VPB-130	MANUS		SW PAC		
11/22/44	34798	VPB-146	PITYILU		SW PAC	LTJG H.W. WRIGHT	S
11/26/44	34882	VPB-146	PITYILU		SW PAC	LT C.E. JACKSON	S
11/27/44	33216	VPB-130		MOROTAI	PHIL		
11/27/44	33223	VPB-130	MANUS		SW PAC		
11/27/44	49639	VPB-134		BRAZIL	SOLANT	ENS CHARLES M. ROCKWELL	S
11/29/44	34775	VPB-146	PITYILU		SW PAC		
11/29/44	34874	VPB-146	PITYILU		SW PAC		
11/29/44	49652	VPB-146	PITYILU		SW PAC		
11/30/44	49590	VPB-137	MOKER-ANG		SW PAC		
12/18/44	34993	VPB-134		BRAZIL	SOLANT	LTJG CHARLES C. WOLFE	D

DATE	BUNO	SQDRN	BASE	LOST	AREA	PILOT	FATE
12/19/44	34840	CASU(F)-44		TINIAN	WCENPAC		
12/19/44	49595	VPB-137		MOROTAI	PHIL	LTJG HANCOCK	U
12/20/44	48921	VPB-151		TINIAN	WCENPAC	LT K.C. SANDY, JR.	M
12/22/44	34725	NAB	GUAM	GUAM	WCENPAC		
12/26/44	48877	VPB-150		TINIAN	WCENPAC		
12/31/44	49601	FAW-2	KANEOHE	HAWAII	ECENPAC		
01/03/45	49414	VPB-137		MOROTAI	PHIL		
01/03/45	49416	VPB-137		MOROTAI	PHIL		
01/03/45	49575	VPB-137		MOROTAI	PHIL		
01/03/45	49576	VPB-137		MOROTAI	PHIL		
01/03/45	49578	VPB-137		MOROTAI	PHIL		
01/03/45	49587	VPB-137		MOROTAI	PHIL		
01/03/45	49589	VPB-137		MOROTAI	PHIL		
01/03/45	49591	VPB-137		MOROTAI	PHIL		
01/03/45	49592	VPB-137		MOROTAI	PHIL		
01/03/45	49640	VPB-137		MOROTAI	PHIL		
01/11/45	49559	VPB-149		MIDWAY	ECENPAC	LT ERNEST L. REHBERG	S
01/13/45	49593	VPB-133		ROI	WCENPAC		
01/18/45	49624	VPB-137		ORMOC BAY	PHIL	LTJG PARKER	S
01/19/45	34684	VPB-126	GUANTAN-AMO BAY	NATAL	SOLANT	LT RUSSELL H. SMITH	S
02/09/45	49563	VPB-130		MOROTAI	PHIL	LT JOHN W. SELF	S
02/12/45	49464	VPB-130		MOROTAI	PHIL	LT R.V. UMPHREY	M
02/20/45	49654	VPB-131	ATTU	ALASKA	NORPAC		
02/23/45	49530	VPB-130		MOROTAI	PHIL	LT G.B. NORRIS	S
02/24/45	49562	VPB-137		LEYTE GULF	PHIL		
03/05/45	48929	VPB-151		TINIAN	WCENPAC		
03/12/45	49614	VPB-149		LEYTE GULF	PHIL	LT J.J. BOYD	M
03/12/45	49631	VPB-149		LEYTE GULF	PHIL	LT E.H. BRIGHAM	S
03/18/45	48891	FAW-4	ATTU	ALASKA	NORPAC		
03/21/45	34888	VPB-128		CEBU	PHIL	LCDR WILLIAM TEPUNI	D
03/22/45	49627	VPB-149		LEYTE GULF	PHIL	LCDR C.M. WOOD	M
03/27/45	49596	VPB-133		TINIAN	WCENPAC	LTJG L.A. WILSON	S
03/28/45	33422	VPB-128		PALAWAN	PHIL		
03/28/45	49461	VPB-133		TINIAN	WCENPAC		
04/01/45	48694	CASU(F)-44		TINIAN	WCENPAC		
04/04/45	48892	VPB-137		LEYTE GULF	PHIL		
04/05/45	49597	VPB-137		LUZON	PHIL	LTJG D.E. ISS	M
04/07/45	49648	VPB-131	ATTU	ALASKA	NORPAC	LTJG JAMES F. PATTON	D
04/16/45	29770	VPB-128		PALAWAN	PHIL	LT PAUL T. CYRRET	M
04/22/45	34698	NAS	SAN JUAN	SAN JUAN	CENLANT	LT BURRILL	S
04/22/45	34914	NAS	SAN JUAN	SAN JUAN	CENLANT	LT CAMPBELL	S
04/22/45	34693	VPB-139	ATTU	ALASKA	NORPAC		
04/25/45	48652	VPB-127	PORT LYAUTEY	MOROCCO	NW AFR		
04/26/45	34876	ACORN-8 PL			SW PAC		
04/26/45	33077	VPB-149		SAMAR	PHIL	LT A.J. ST. LOUIS	S
04/30/45	29769	VPB-128		SAMAR	PHIL		
05/04/45	48742	VPB-147		CURACAO	CENLANT	LT H.P. PRATHER	S
05/15/45	34926	VPB-127	PORT LYAUTEY	MOROCCO	NW AFR		
05/15/45	48863	VPB-127	PORT LYAUTEY	MOROCCO	NW AFR		
05/20/45	48886	VPB-133		TINIAN	WCENPAC		
05/21/45	48915	VPB-133		TINIAN	WCENPAC	LT A.L. WOOTEN	S
05/26/45	49615	VPB-147		CURACAO	CENLANT	LT K.W. ROBINSON	S
05/27/45	34730	VPB-133		TINIAN	WCENPAC	LT SCHENK T. CREW	M
05/28/45	49569	VPB-133		TINIAN	WCENPAC	LTJG CHARLES R. PHILLIPS	M
05/28/45	49599	VPB-133		TINIAN	WCENPAC	LCDR V.J. COLEY	S
05/29/45	33219	VPB-133		TINIAN	WCENPAC		
05/31/45	33379	VPB-127	PORT LYAUTEY	MOROCCO	NW AFR	ENS T.E. MCGOWAN	S
05/31/45	33138	VPB-128		PALAWAN	PHIL		
06/06/45	33069	VPB-149		SAMAR	PHIL		
06/14/45	48808	CASU(F)-44		TINIAN	WCENPAC		
06/14/45	48920	CASU(F)-44		TINIAN	WCENPAC		
06/18/45	33225	VPB-133		TINIAN	WCENPAC		
06/21/45	34877	COMAIR-PAC	PEARL	HAWAII	ECENPAC		
07/04/45	29845	POOL	KANEOHE	HAWAII	ECENPAC		
07/04/45	34934	POOL	KANEOHE	HAWAII	ECENPAC		
07/04/45	34983	POOL	KANEOHE	HAWAII	ECENPAC		
07/13/45	33074	AROU-2		SAMAR	PHIL		

DATE	BUNO	SQDRN	BASE	LOST	AREA	PILOT	FATE
07/13/45	34803	AROU-2		SAMAR	PHIL		
07/13/45	49498	AROU-2		SAMAR	PHIL		
07/17/45	29740	AROU-1		MOMOTE	SW PAC		
07/17/45	29804	AROU-1		MOMOTE	SW PAC		
07/17/45	29805	AROU-1		MOMOTE	SW PAC		
07/17/45	29823	AROU-1		MOMOTE	SW PAC		
07/17/45	33211	AROU-1		MOMOTE	SW PAC		
07/17/45	33224	AROU-1		MOMOTE	SW PAC		
07/17/45	33342	AROU-1		MOMOTE	SW PAC		
07/17/45	33360	AROU-1		MOMOTE	SW PAC		
07/17/45	34800	AROU-1		MOMOTE	SW PAC		
07/17/45	48812	AROU-1		MOMOTE	SW PAC		
07/17/45	48896	AROU-1		MOMOTE	SW PAC		
07/17/45	49502	AROU-1		MOMOTE	SW PAC		
07/17/45	49503	AROU-1		MOMOTE	SW PAC		
07/18/45	33067	POOL	KANEOHE	HAWAII	ECENPAC		
07/18/45	33128	POOL	KANEOHE	HAWAII	ECENPAC		
07/18/45	33144	POOL	KANEOHE	HAWAII	ECENPAC		
07/18/45	33350	POOL	KANEOHE	HAWAII	ECENPAC		
07/18/45	48807	POOL	KANEOHE	HAWAII	ECENPAC		
07/18/45	48887	POOL	KANEOHE	HAWAII	ECENPAC		
07/18/45	48917	POOL	KANEOHE	HAWAII	ECENPAC		
07/18/45	48922	POOL	KANEOHE	HAWAII	ECENPAC		
07/18/45	48925	POOL	KANEOHE	HAWAII	ECENPAC		
07/18/45	48935	POOL	KANEOHE	HAWAII	ECENPAC		
07/18/45	49458	POOL	KANEOHE	HAWAII	ECENPAC		
07/23/45	34756	FAW-2	NAVY NO. 28	HAWAII	ECENPAC	LTJG F.B. QUEALEY	S
07/26/45	33071	CASU(F)-44		TINIAN	WCENPAC		
07/26/45	49412	CASU(F)-44		TINIAN	WCENPAC		
07/26/45	49413	CASU(F)-44		TINIAN	WCENPAC		
07/26/45	49623	CASU(F)-44		TINIAN	WCENPAC		
07/26/45	49625	CASU(F)-44		TINIAN	WCENPAC		
07/26/45	49647	CASU(F)-44		TINIAN	WCENPAC		
07/26/45	49650	CASU(F)-44		TINIAN	WCENPAC		
07/26/45	49659	CASU(F)-44		TINIAN	WCENPAC		
07/27/45	48893	VPB-133		TINIAN	WCENPAC		
07/31/45	29840	CASU(F)-44		TINIAN	WCENPAC		
07/31/45	33381	VPB-200	HAWAII		ECENPAC	LTJG E.P. BYARS	D
08/01/45	48695	CASU(F)-35		ENIWETOK	CENPAC		
08/01/45	49419	CASU(F)-44		TINIAN	WCENPAC		
08/07/45	29724	POOL	SAN JUAN	CUBA	CENLANT		
08/07/45	33075	POOL	SAN JUAN	CUBA	CENLANT		
08/15/45	33084	AROU-2		SAMAR	PHIL		
08/15/45	48868	AROU-2		SAMAR	PHIL		
08/15/45	49463	AROU-2		SAMAR	PHIL		
08/15/45	49568	AROU-2		SAMAR	PHIL		
08/15/45	49586	AROU-2		SAMAR	PHIL		
08/15/45	49620	AROU-2		SAMAR	PHIL		
08/15/45	49621	AROU-2		SAMAR	PHIL		
08/15/45	49630	AROU-2		SAMAR	PHIL		
08/15/45	49634	AROU-2		SAMAR	PHIL		
08/15/45	49635	AROU-2		SAMAR	PHIL		
08/15/45	49637	AROU-2		SAMAR	PHIL		
08/15/45	49656	AROU-2		SAMAR	PHIL		

LOCKHEED PV-1(N)

The Lockheed PV-1(N) was simply the PV-1, which was already equipped with radar for night fighting, redesignated with the (N) when assigned to Marine Night Fighting Squadron 531. Aircraft lost:

DATE	BUNO	SQDRN	BASE	LOST	AREA	PILOT	FATE
12/03/43	29857	VMF(N)-531	BARAKOMA	BOUGAIN-VILLE	SOPAC	CAPT D.R. JENKINS	U
02/09/44	33253	VMF(N)-531		BARAKOMA	SOPAC	LT C.W. WATSON	D
02/19/44	33089	VMF(N)-531		GREEN	SOPAC	LT T.H. BANKS	M
03/13/44	33255	VMF(N)-531		RUSSELLS	SOPAC	MAJ R.H. GEORGE	S
03/14/44	34841	VMF(N)-531		HENDERSON	SOPAC	LT BRINGAZE	S
03/21/44	29870	VMF(N)-531	TREASURY	RABAUL	SOPAC	LT W.L. BIRDSALL	D
03/21/44	33079	VMF(N)-531	TREASURY	RABAUL	SOPAC	LT M.M. PIERCE	D

DATE	BUNO	SQDRN	BASE	LOST	AREA	PILOT	FATE
04/07/44	29854	VMF(N)-531	GREEN		SOPAC	CAPT J.H. WEHMER	S

LOCKHEED PV-2

The Lockheed PV-2 "Harpoon" was an updated model with larger fin and wing area. There were 470 built. Aircraft lost:

DATE	BUNO	SQDRN	BASE	LOST	AREA	PILOT	FATE
03/26/45	37065	VPB-139	ATTU	ALASKA	NORPAC	LT LOREN J. DULIN	S
04/02/45	37096	VPB-142	KANEOHE	HAWAII	ECENPAC		
05/08/45	37101	VPB-153		KANEOHE	ECENPAC	LT WM SHERWIN HARSHAW	M
08/05/45	37306	VPB-144		ENIWETOK	CENPAC		

LOCKHEED PV-3

Twenty-seven former RAF Ventura IIs were requisitioned by the US Navy and redesignated the PV-3. Aircraft lost:

DATE	BUNO	SQDRN	BASE	LOST	AREA	PILOT	FATE
12/14/42	33938	VP-82			NORLANT		
01/07/43	33926	VP-82			NORLANT		
02/26/43	33927	VP-82			NORLANT		
03/06/43	33950	VB-126			NORLANT		
03/17/43	33931	VP-82			NORLANT		

LOCKHEED R3O-2

The Lockheed Model 12 Electra Junior, more commonly known as the Lockheed 12 or L-12, is an eight-seat, six-passenger all-metal twin-engine transport aircraft of the late 1930s designed for use by small airlines, companies, and wealthy private individuals. A scaled-down version of the Lockheed Model 10 Electra, the Lockheed 12 was not popular as an airliner but was widely used as a corporate and government transport. A number were purchased as military staff transports by the United States Army Air Corps, which designated the type as the C-40, and by the United States Navy, which used the designation JO, or in one peculiar case, this R3O-2. This particular Model 12-A has a civilian tail number of NC33615 and was impressed into service to the Navy. Rather than being "lost" in terms of being destroyed or scrapped, the R3O-2 was actually put back into the civil registry as NC33615 on September 1, 1944.

DATE	BUNO	SQDRN	BASE	LOST	AREA	PILOT	FATE
09/01/44	02947	NVL ATTACHE		LONDON	ENGLAND		

LOCKHEED R5O-4

The Lockheed Model 18 Lodestar was a 7-seater passenger transport aircraft of the World War II era. The military variant called the R5O-4 was powered by 1,200 hp (895 kW) Wright R-1820-40 engines. Of the 12 aircraft built, they were all impressed form civilian service for the needs of the war effort. Aircraft lost:

DATE	BUNO	SQDRN	BASE	LOST	AREA	PILOT	FATE
02/15/45	12448	NAS	KANEOHE	HAWAII	ECENPAC		

LOCKHEED R5O-5

Lockheed built the C60 "Lodestar II" and the Navy's version of the C-60, called the R5O-5, was powered by 1,200 hp (895 kW) Wright R-1820-40 engines. It was similar to the R5O-4 but had 14-seats. There were 38 aircraft built. Aircraft lost:

DATE	BUNO	SQDRN	BASE	LOST	AREA	PILOT	FATE
11/27/43	12490				SOPAC	ENS L.M. CROCKETT	S

LOCKHEED R5O-6

This was the Navy's version of the C-60A used by the US Marine Corps and redesignated the R5O-6. It was equipped with 18 paratroop seats. There were 35 built. Aircraft lost:

DATE	BUNO	SQDRN	BASE	LOST	AREA	PILOT	FATE
11/11/43	39630	FAW-16	CARABIL-LAS	BRAZIL	SOLANT		
05/17/45	39629	COMAIR-7THFL		MANILA	PHIL	LT DONALD T. RANKIN	S

MARTIN JM-1

The Martin B-26 Marauder was a World War II twin-engine medium bomber built by the Glenn L. Martin Company. First used in the Pacific Theater in early 1942, it was also used in the Mediterranean Theater and in Western Europe. After entering service with the U.S. Army, the aircraft got a reputation as the "Widowmaker" due to the early models' high rate of accidents during takeoff and landings.

The B-26 was a shoulder-winged monoplane of all metal construction, fitted with a tricycle undercarriage. It had a streamlined, circular section fuselage, housing the crew, consisting of a bombardier in the nose, which was armed with a .30 in (7.62 mm) machine gun, a pilot and co-pilot sitting side by side, with positions for radio operator and navigator behind the pilots. A gunner manned a dorsal turret armed with two .50 in (12.7 mm) machine guns (the first powered dorsal turret to be fitted to a US bomber), while an additional .30 in (7.62 mm) machine gun was fitted in the tail.

Two bomb bays were fitted mid-fuselage, capable of carrying 5,800 lb (2,600 kg) of bombs, although in practice such a bomb-load reduced range too much, and the aft bomb bay was usually fitted with additional fuel tanks instead of bombs. It was powered by two Pratt & Whitney R-2800 Double Wasp radial engines in nacelles slung under the wing, driving four-bladed propellers.

The B-26 Marauder was used mostly in Europe but also saw action in the Mediterranean and the Pacific. In early combat the aircraft took heavy losses but was still one of the most successful medium-range bombers used by the U.S. Army Air Forces. The B-26 was initially deployed on combat missions in the South West Pacific in the spring of 1942, but most of the B-26s subsequently assigned to operational theaters were sent to England and the Mediterranean area.

By the end of World War II, it had flown more than 110,000 sorties and had dropped 150,000 tons of bombs, and had been used in combat by British, Free French and

South African forces in addition to U.S. units. In 1945, when B-26 production was halted, 5,266 had been built.

The B-26 began to equip the 22d Bombardment Group at Langley Field, Virginia in February 1941, with a further two Bombardment groups equipping with the B-26 by December. Immediately following the Japanese Attack on Pearl Harbor, the 22d was deployed to the South West Pacific, being sent by ship to Hawaii and then flown to Australia. The 22d flew its first combat mission, an attack on Rabaul which required an intermediate stop at Port Moresby, New Guinea, on 5 April 1942.

Four Marauders from the 38th Bombardment Group deployed to Midway Island in the build-up to the Battle of Midway, and carried out torpedo attacks against the Japanese Fleet on 4 June 1942. Two B-26s were shot down with the remaining two badly damaged, while their torpedoes failed to hit any Japanese ships, although they did shoot down one A6M Zero fighter, and killed two seamen aboard the aircraft carrier *Akagi* with machine gun fire.

The B-26 flew its last combat missions against the German garrison at the Île d'Oléron on 1 May 1945, with the last units disbanding in early 1946.

The first produced model of the B-26 was ordered based upon design alone (no XB-26). The armament on this model consisted of two .30 caliber and two .50 caliber machine guns. The B-26A incorporated changes made on the production line to the B-26, including upgrading the two .30 caliber machine guns in the nose and tail to .50 caliber. The B-26B was an improved version of the –A. Also called AT-23A or TB-26B, 208 B-26Bs were converted into target tugs and gunnery trainers and were designated JM-1 by the Navy. Aircraft lost:

DATE	BUNO	SQDRN	BASE	LOST	AREA	PILOT	FATE
00/00/00	66731	STATION OPR	EWA	HAWAII	ECENPAC		
04/26/44	66671	VJ-12	PEARL	HAWAII	ECENPAC	CAPT J.G. DROLEO	D
05/15/44	66667	COMAIR-PAC		PEARL	HAWAII	ECENPAC	
08/15/44	66673	VJ-12	RUSSELLS	BANIKA	SOPAC	LT THOMAS R. BARALDI	D
08/31/44	66662	VJ-12		ESPIRITU SANTO	SOPAC		
10/27/44	66661	VJ-14		HAWAII	ECENPAC	LTJG CHARLES C. GATLING	S
10/31/44	66607	VJ-2		PITYILU	SW PAC		
11/02/44	66371	MCAS	EWA	HAWAII	ECENPAC	LT PHILIP H. DORGAN	D
11/15/44	66773	FAW-4	ATTU	ALASKA	NORPAC		
12/17/44	66666	VJ-12		ESPIRITU SANTO	SOPAC	LTJG R.A. MILLER	S
12/28/44	66617	VJ-2		ADMIRALTIES	SW PAC	LT ROBERT LEE AUER	D
01/07/45	66724	VJ-16		TRINIDAD	CENLANT	LT RAYMOND P. MARA	D
01/07/45	66741	VMTD-2		GUAM	WCENPAC		
02/05/45	66634	VJ-2		ADMIRALTIES	SW PAC	LT A.W. PORTER	S
02/18/45	75206	VJ-14		HAWAII	ECENPAC	LT NORMAN G. MORSE	S
03/20/45	75186	NAS	ADAK	ALASKA	NORPAC	LTJG WILLIS M. PARKER	D
04/06/45	66787	VJ-17		ENIWETOK	CENPAC		
05/05/45	66611	VJ-17		GUAM	WCENPAC	LT S.W. MARSHALL	S
05/05/45	66612	VJ-2		PITYILU	SW PAC	LT PAUL PAVLOW, JR.	S
06/30/45	66608	VJ-9		PITYILU	SW PAC	LT ROY L. MINNICK	S
07/20/45	66747	VMJ-2		GUAM	WCENPAC		
08/01/45	66658	VJ-7	PEARL	HAWAII	ECENPAC	CAPT REGINALD T. MARRION	S

MARTIN JM-2

The Martin B-26G was a conversion of the B-26F to be used for crew training. Most, possibly all, were delivered to the United States Navy as the JM-2. The one lost below was being flown by a US Marine Corps photo-reconnaissance squadron. Aircraft lost:

DATE	BUNO	SQDRN	BASE	LOST	AREA	PILOT	FATE
07/20/45	90518	VMJ-2		GUAM	WCENPAC		

MARTIN PBM-1

The Martin PBM Mariner was a patrol bomber flying boat of World War II era. It was designed to complement the PBY Catalina in service. A total of 1,366 were built, with the first example flying on 18 February 1939 and the type entering service in September 1940. The first PBM-1s entered service with Patrol Squadron Fifty-Five (VP-55) of the United States Navy on 1 September 1940. Prior to the outbreak of World War II, PBMs were used (together with PBYs) to carry out Neutrality Patrols in the Atlantic, including operations from Iceland. Following the Japanese Attack on Pearl Harbor, PBMs were used on anti-submarine patrols, sinking their first German U-Boat, *U-158* on 30 June 1942. In total, PBMs were responsible, wholly or in part, for sinking 10 U-Boats during World War II. PBMs were also heavily used in the Pacific, operating from bases at Saipan, Okinawa, Iwo Jima and the South-West Pacific.

The United States Coast Guard acquired 27 Martin PBM-3 aircraft during the first half of 1943. In late 1944, the service acquired 41 PBM-5 models and more were delivered in the latter half of 1945. Aircraft lost:

DATE	BUNO	SQDRN	BASE	LOST	AREA	PILOT	FATE
01/08/42	1248	VP-74	BERMUDA	BERMUDA	NORLANT		
01/15/42	1255	VP-73	USS ALBE-MARLE	ICELAND	NORLANT		
01/15/42	1256	VP-73	USS ALBE-MARLE	ICELAND	NORLANT		
06/03/42	1250	VP-74	BERMUDA	BERMUDA	NORLANT	ENS CUSHMAN	M
06/23/44	1254	FAW-11	SAN JUAN	SAN JUAN	CENLANT		
11/01/44	1260	FAW-3	COCO SOLO	COCO SOLO	CENLANT		
04/24/45	1265	FAW-11	SAN JUAN	SAN JUAN	CENLANT		
06/19/45	1262	POOL	SAN JUAN	SAN JUAN	CENLANT		
07/04/45	1249	FAW-3	COCO SOLO	COCO SOLO	CENLANT		

MARTIN PBM-3C

The Martin PBM-3C was an improved patrol version of the -3 with twin .50 in machine guns in nose and dorsal turrets, and single guns in tail turret and waist positions. There was also an AN/APS-15 radar in the radome behind cockpit. There were 274 built. Aircraft lost:

DATE	BUNO	SQDRN	BASE	LOST	AREA	PILOT	FATE
03/18/43	6730	FAW-12	GRAND CAYMAN	WEST INDIES	CENLANT		
03/31/43	6533	VP-207	FAW-11		CENLANT		
05/14/43	6520	VP-207			NORLANT		
06/10/43	6534	VP-205			SOLANT		
07/03/43	6571	VP-74			SOLANT		
08/03/43	6722	VP-205			NORLANT		
08/06/43	6713	VP-205			NORLANT		
08/18/43	6716	VP-210		CARIBBEAN	CENLANT		
09/20/43	6682	VP-202			NORLANT		
09/24/43	1668	VP-212			NORLANT		
10/25/43	6621	VP-212			NORLANT		
12/05/43	6583	FAW-6	GEORGE-TOWN	BRITISH GUINEA	NORLANT		

DATE	BUNO	SQDRN	BASE	LOST	AREA	PILOT	FATE
01/12/44	6644	VP-211		ARATU	SOLANT	ENS DONAHUE	D
03/05/44	6737	VP-204	GUANTAN-AMO BAY	CUBA	CENLANT	LTJG P.W. TOBIN	S
04/17/44	6715	VP-207	COCO SOLO		NORLANT	LT W. VAN ALST	S
06/27/44	6632	VP-203	TRITANGA		SOLANT	LT R.L. JONES	S
07/15/44	6734	VP-209		CARIBBEAN	CENLANT	LTJG R.C. CARLSON	S
07/16/44	6600	VP-209		CARIBBEAN	CENLANT	LT R.D. SPANNUTT	M
07/19/44	6630	VP-208		BAHAMAS	CENLANT		
07/20/44	6569	VP-205		CUBA	CENLANT	LTJG W.H.F. HESSE	S
07/21/44	6679	VP-203		RIO DE JANEIRO	SOLANT	LT L. DEBONIS	M
08/20/44	6717	VP-207		BERMUDA	NORLANT	LTJG STANLEY C. SMITH	M
08/31/44	6726	VP-211		ARATU	SOLANT		
09/17/44	6638	VPB-209		COCO SOLO	CENLANT	LTJG JOHN P. NUGENT	S
09/21/44	1656	FAW-11	SAN JUAN	BRAZIL	SOLANT	LT J.W. SEABORG	S
10/31/44	1658	FAW-11	SAN JUAN	SAN JUAN	CENLANT		
11/21/44	1669	VPB-211	BRAZIL		SOLANT	LT ROBERT H. LIND	M
01/17/45	6689	VH-3		SAIPAN	WCENPAC	LT W.D. EDDY	S
01/20/45	6687	VH-3		SAIPAN	WCENPAC	LT JAMES E. GRINSTEAD	S
02/28/45	6523	CASU(F)-48		SAIPAN	WCENPAC		
03/10/45	6703	VPB-74		GALAPAGOS	CENPAC	LTJG WILLIAM B. ANSBRO	S
04/08/45	6738	POOL	KANOEHE	HAWAII	ECENPAC		
04/10/45	6634	VPB-203		BELEM	SOLANT	LTJG F. BENTLEY JR.	S
04/24/45	6653	VPB-25			PHIL	LT EDWARD DOUDICAN	S
04/28/45	6588	VPB-207		BERMUDA	NORLANT		
05/08/45	6739	CASU(F)-48		SAIPAN	WCENPAC		
05/18/45	6640	POOL	SAN JUAN	SAN JUAN	CENLANT		
05/18/45	6647	POOL	SAN JUAN	SAN JUAN	CENLANT		
06/08/45	6605	NAS	BERMUDA	BERMUDA	NORLANT		
06/09/45	6629	NAS	BERMUDA	BERMUDA	NORLANT		
06/09/45	6749	NAS	BERMUDA	BERMUDA	NORLANT		
06/10/45	6639	NAS	BERMUDA	BERMUDA	NORLANT		
06/11/45	6732	NAS	BERMUDA	BERMUDA	NORLANT		
06/12/45	6674	NAS	BERMUDA	BERMUDA	NORLANT		
06/13/45	6539	NAS	BERMUDA	BERMUDA	NORLANT		
06/13/45	6624	NAS	BERMUDA	BERMUDA	NORLANT		
06/15/45	6642	POOL	SAN JUAN	SAN JUAN	CENLANT		
06/16/45	6599	COCO SOLO		COCO SOLO	CENLANT		
06/16/45	6625	COCO SOLO		COCO SOLO	CENLANT		
06/16/45	1664	COCO SOLO		COCO SOLO	CENLANT		
06/16/45	6614	POOL	SAN JUAN	SAN JUAN	CENLANT		
06/17/45	1652	POOL	SAN JUAN	SAN JUAN	CENLANT		
06/18/45	6509	POOL	SAN JUAN	SAN JUAN	CENLANT		
06/18/45	6637	POOL	SAN JUAN	SAN JUAN	CENLANT		
06/19/45	6633	POOL	SAN JUAN	SAN JUAN	CENLANT		
06/20/45	6529	COCO SOLO		COCO SOLO	CENLANT		
06/20/45	6578	COCO SOLO		COCO SOLO	CENLANT		
06/20/45	6580	COCO SOLO		COCO SOLO	CENLANT		
06/20/45	6608	COCO SOLO		COCO SOLO	CENLANT		
06/20/45	6610	COCO SOLO		COCO SOLO	CENLANT		
06/20/45	6652	COCO SOLO		COCO SOLO	CENLANT		
06/20/45	6676	COCO SOLO		COCO SOLO	CENLANT		
06/20/45	6698	COCO SOLO		COCO SOLO	CENLANT		
06/20/45	6709	COCO SOLO		COCO SOLO	CENLANT		
06/20/45	6711	COCO SOLO		COCO SOLO	CENLANT		
06/20/45	6718	COCO SOLO		COCO SOLO	CENLANT		

DATE	BUNO	SQDRN	BASE	LOST	AREA	PILOT	FATE
06/20/45	6720	COCO SOLO		COCO SOLO	CENLANT		
06/20/45	6748	COCO SOLO		COCO SOLO	CENLANT		
06/20/45	1666	COCO SOLO		COCO SOLO	CENLANT		
06/20/45	6650	POOL	SAN JUAN	SAN JUAN	CENLANT		
06/20/45	6683	POOL	SAN JUAN	SAN JUAN	CENLANT		
06/20/45	6714	POOL	SAN JUAN	SAN JUAN	CENLANT		
06/21/45	6631	POOL	SAN JUAN	SAN JUAN	CENLANT		
06/21/45	6635	POOL	SAN JUAN	SAN JUAN	CENLANT		
06/21/45	1661	POOL	SAN JUAN	SAN JUAN	CENLANT		
06/22/45	6668	POOL	SAN JUAN	SAN JUAN	CENLANT		
06/22/45	6735	POOL	SAN JUAN	SAN JUAN	CENLANT		
06/23/45	6618	POOL	SAN JUAN	SAN JUAN	CENLANT		
06/23/45	6680	POOL	SAN JUAN	SAN JUAN	CENLANT		
06/30/45	6670	POOL	SAN JUAN	SAN JUAN	CENLANT		
06/30/45	6700	POOL	SAN JUAN	SAN JUAN	CENLANT		
06/30/45	6750	POOL	SAN JUAN	SAN JUAN	CENLANT		
07/12/45	6697	POOL	SAN JUAN	SAN JUAN	CENLANT		
07/12/45	6702	POOL	SAN JUAN	SAN JUAN	CENLANT		
07/28/45	6570	CASU(F)-48		SAIPAN	WCENPAC		
07/31/45	6667	COCO SOLO		COCO SOLO	CENLANT		

MARTIN PBM-3D

The Martin PBM-3D was a variant of the original patrol bomber but with increased power (two 1,900 hp (1,417 kW) R-2600-22s) and increased armament (twin 0.50 machine guns in nose, dorsal and tail turrets, plus two waist guns). There were 259 built. Aircraft lost:

DATE	BUNO	SQDRN	BASE	LOST	AREA	PILOT	FATE
01/24/44	48177	VP-202	HAWAII	NW OF TARAWA	CENPAC	LTJG H.J. KACZMAREK	S
02/06/44	48175	VP-202		MAJURO	CENPAC		
02/16/44	48182	VP-202		KWAJALEIN	CENPAC		
02/25/44	48184	VP-202		KWAJALEIN	CENPAC		
03/16/44	48172	VP-202	KWAJALEIN		CENPAC		
04/11/44	48202	VP-16	ALAMEDA	ENR KANEOHE	ECENPAC	LT W.R. BRIGGS	S
06/10/44	48199	VP-16	KANEOHE	HAWAII	ECENPAC	LT J. KENNEDY	S
06/19/44	45242	CASU(F)-34		PARRY IS.	WCENPAC		
06/19/44	48173	VP-16		SAIPAN	WCENPAC	ENS H.C. CULBRETH	S
06/22/44	45216	VP-16	SAIPAN	W OF SAIPAN	CENPAC	LCDR FLACKSTARTE	D
06/24/44	45231	VH-1	SAIPAN	ROTA	CENPAC	LTJG SMITH	S
06/25/44	48185	VP-216		SAIPAN	WCENPAC	LT V.S. HAGEN	S
06/27/44	48208	VP-16	SAIPAN	SAIPAN	WCENPAC	LT DANIEL T. FELIX	S
07/31/44	48205	VP-216	USS CHANDE-LEUR	SAIPAN	WCENPAC	LT R.P. GAVIN	S
08/01/44	48215	VP-202		SAIPAN	WCENPAC	ENS L. HUBERT	S
08/21/44	45262	VP-18	SAIPAN	SAIPAN	WCENPAC	ENS LOWELL H. CONROW	S
08/21/44	45210	VPB-210		SAIPAN	WCENPAC		
09/01/44	45240	VPB-21		ENIWETOK	CENPAC	LT JAMES R. YOUNG	S
09/05/44	45236	VPB-200		FUNAFUTI	CENPAC	LT ROBERT GREENIER	S
09/13/44	45332	VPB-20		HAWAII	ECENPAC	LTJG GEORGE T. HOPKINS	S
09/26/44	45282	VPB-16	USS POCO-MOKE	PALAU	CENPAC	LT R.R. STEINOFF	S
09/28/44	48165	VP-16		SAIPAN	WCENPAC	LT DANIEL W. THOMAS	D
10/02/44	45344	VPB-21		PARRY ISLAND	CENPAC	LTJG PHILLIP Q. ONHOCK	S
10/06/44	45217	VPB-18		SAIPAN	WCENPAC	LTJG TONY J. LAURI	S
10/06/44	48189	VPB-216		KOSSOL PASSAGE	CENPAC	LT ARTHUR W. DOHERTY	D
10/18/44	45279	VPB-216	USS CHANDE-LEUR	SAIPAN	WCENPAC	ENS JAMES L. EYMAN	S

DATE	BUNO	SQDRN	BASE	LOST	AREA	PILOT	FATE
10/22/44	45287	VPB-19		HAWAII	ECENPAC	LT GRADY L. MULLINS	M
10/27/44	45304	VPB-21	USS CHANDE-LEUR		CENPAC	LT J.F. MORAIRTY	S
11/07/44	45361	VPB-16		SAIPAN	WCENPAC		
11/07/44	45307	VPB-21	PALAU		WCENPAC		
11/07/44	45362	VPB-21	PALAU		WCENPAC		
11/24/44	45232	VH-1		SAIPAN	WCENPAC	LT WALTER V. HIGGINS	S
11/26/44	45239	VPB-25	MANUS		SW PAC		
11/28/44	48174	FAW-2	KANEOHE	HAWAII	ECENPAC		
11/30/44	45398	VPB-22	USS KENNETH WHITING	ENR KOSSOL	WCENPAC	LTJG EDWARD B. KNIGHT	S
12/02/44	45288	VPB-20		LEYTE GULF	PHIL		
12/05/44	45386	VPB-19		PARRY IS.	WCENPAC	LT CLAYTON M. REES	U
12/07/44	45220	VPB-20		LEYTE GULF	PHIL		
12/12/44	48194	VPB-20		LEYTE GULF	PHIL		
12/12/44	45300	VPB-22	USS KENNETH WHITING	PALAU	CENPAC	LT EMMETT E. FITTS	S
12/12/44	45382	VPB-28		HAWAII	ECENPAC	LT C.T.M. GOERTZ	M
12/12/44	48194	VPB-20		LEYTE GULF	PHIL		
12/14/44	45308	VPB-22	USS KENNETH WHITING	PALAU	CENPAC	ENS J.W. SCOTT	S
12/24/44	45280	VPB-20		LOS NEGROS	PHIL	LT DOUGLAS B. BADT	S
12/25/44	45297	VPB-22	USS KENNETH WHITING	PALAU	CENPAC	ENS A.G. DENUNCIO	S
12/26/44	45212	VPB-20		MINDORO STRAIT	PHIL	LT JAMES V. FALLON	D
12/26/44	45376	VPB-20		LEYTE GULF	PHIL	LTJG WARREN M. COX	U
12/28/44	45322	VPB-22		ULITHI	WCENPAC	LT EMMETT E. FITTS	S
01/01/45	45301	VPB-25		LEYTE GULF	PHIL		
01/01/45	45305	VPB-25		LEYTE GULF	PHIL		
01/14/45	45266	VPB-25		LEYTE GULF	PHIL	LTJG DONALD A. RIEDL	S
01/16/45	45277	VPB-25	CHINA SEA	LEYTE GULF	PHIL	LT JAMES LEE STEVENSON	S
01/26/45	45309	VPB-25		LEYTE GULF	PHIL	LT JAMES LEE STEVENSON	U
02/05/45	45335	VPB-25		LEYTE GULF	PHIL	LT WELSEY A. STEENSON	S
02/19/45	45399	VPB-25		LEYTE GULF	PHIL	ENS D.W. WRIGHT	S
02/24/45	45246	A.A.	KANEOHE	HAWAII	ECENPAC		
02/24/45	45294	A.A.	KANEOHE	HAWAII	ECENPAC		
02/24/45	45299	VPB-22		ENIWETOK	CENPAC		
02/24/45	48169	A.A.	KANEOHE	HAWAII	ECENPAC		
02/24/45	48192	A.A.	KANEOHE	HAWAII	ECENPAC		
02/28/45	48218	CASU(F)-48		SAIPAN	WCENPAC		
03/01/45	45249	VPB-19		IWO JIMA	EMPIRE		
03/03/45	45244	VPB-17		LEYTE GULF	PHIL		
03/07/45	45281	VPB-17		LEYTE GULF	PHIL		
03/08/45	45388	VPB-28		LINGAYEN GULF	PHIL	LTJG P.J. RICHERT	S
03/12/45	45313	VPB-25		LEYTE GULF	PHIL		
03/13/45	45264	VPB-18		SAIPAN	WCENPAC	ENS MYRON M. JENSEN	S
03/13/45	45378	VPB-28		LINGAYEN GULF	PHIL	LTJG P.J. RICHERT	S
03/14/45	48168	VPB-25		LEYTE GULF	PHIL	LT F.J. BURCK	S
03/16/45	48207	A.A.	KANEOHE	HAWAII	ECENPAC		
03/19/45	45347	A.A.	KANEOHE	HAWAII	ECENPAC		
03/19/45	45352	VPB-17		LINGAYEN GULF	PHIL	LT C.W. JOHNSON	S
03/19/45	48204	A.A.	KANEOHE	HAWAII	ECENPAC		
03/26/45	45387	VPB-28		MINDORO STRAIT	PHIL		
04/14/45	45256	POOL	KANEOHE	HAWAII	ECENPAC		
04/14/45	45334	VPB-17		JINAMOC	PHIL		
04/14/45	48166	POOL	KANEOHE	HAWAII	ECENPAC		
04/14/45	48188	POOL	KANEOHE	HAWAII	ECENPAC		
04/19/45	45207	CASU(F)-34		PARRY IS.	WCENPAC		
04/19/45	45234	CASU(F)-34		PARRY IS.	WCENPAC		
04/27/45	45243	POOL	KANEOHE	HAWAII	ECENPAC		
04/27/45	48197	POOL	KANEOHE	HAWAII	ECENPAC		
05/02/45	45224	POOL	SAN JUAN	SAN JUAN	CENLANT		

DATE	BUNO	SQDRN	BASE	LOST	AREA	PILOT	FATE
05/02/45	48180	POOL	KANEOHE	HAWAII	ECENPAC		
05/07/45	45215	CASU(F)-48		SAIPAN	WCENPAC		
05/07/45	45293	CASU(F)-48		SAIPAN	WCENPAC		
05/07/45	45350	CASU(F)-48		SAIPAN	WCENPAC		
05/07/45	45365	CASU(F)-48		SAIPAN	WCENPAC		
05/07/45	45366	VPB-22		OKINAWA	EMPIRE		
05/15/45	45369	ACORN-30 PL		JINAMOC	PHIL		
05/29/45	45318	POOL	KANEOHE	HAWAII	ECENPAC		
06/02/45	45271	ACORN-30 PL		JINAMOC	PHIL		
06/07/45	45241	BASE B-1 PL		MANUS	SW PAC		
06/10/45	48212	VPB-25		JINAMOC	PHIL		
06/14/45	45319	VPB-25		JINAMOC	PHIL		
06/14/45	45337	VPB-25		JINAMOC	PHIL		
06/17/45	45316	VPB-25		JINAMOC	PHIL		
06/18/45	45211	VPB-22		ULITHI	WCENPAC		
06/18/45	45214	VPB-25		JINAMOC	PHIL		
06/18/45	45225	CASU(F)-34		PARRY IS.	WCENPAC		
06/18/45	45250	VPB-25		JINAMOC	PHIL		
06/18/45	45295	VPB-25		JINAMOC	PHIL		
06/18/45	45317	VPB-25		JINAMOC	PHIL		
06/18/45	45331	VPB-25		JINAMOC	PHIL		
06/18/45	45336	VPB-25		JINAMOC	PHIL		
06/18/45	45339	VPB-25		JINAMOC	PHIL		
06/18/45	45348	VPB-25		JINAMOC	PHIL		
06/18/45	45351	VPB-25		JINAMOC	PHIL		
06/18/45	45353	VPB-25		JINAMOC	PHIL		
06/18/45	45368	VPB-25		JINAMOC	PHIL		
06/19/45	45230	CASU(F)-34		PARRY IS.	WCENPAC		
06/19/45	45330	VPB-25		JINAMOC	PHIL		
06/19/45	45381	VPB-25		JINAMOC	PHIL		
06/21/45	45372	BASE B-1 PL		MANUS	SW PAC		
06/22/45	45341	VPB-22		ULITHI	WCENPAC		
06/23/45	45248	VPB-25		JINAMOC	PHIL		
06/23/45	45269	VPB-25		JINAMOC	PHIL		
06/25/45	45205	COCO SOLO		COCO SOLO	CENLANT		
06/26/45	45395	VPB-25		JINAMOC	PHIL		
06/27/45	45296	VPB-22		ULITHI	WCENPAC		
06/27/45	45321	VPB-22		ULITHI	WCENPAC		
06/30/45	45328	VPB-25		JINAMOC	PHIL		
06/30/45	45329	CASU(F)-12		GUAM	WCENPAC		
07/01/45	45391	VPB-28		LINGAYEN GULF	PHIL		
07/02/45	45379	VPB-28			PHIL		
07/04/45	45290	CASU(F)-34		PARRY IS.	WCENPAC		
07/04/45	45201	CASU(F)-34		PARRY IS.	WCENPAC		
07/11/45	45268	VPB-25		LINGAYEN GULF	PHIL		
07/11/45	45310	VPB-25		LINGAYEN GULF	PHIL		
07/15/45	45380	VPB-28			PHIL		
07/15/45	45384	VPB-28			PHIL		
07/15/45	45393	VPB-28			PHIL		
07/21/45	45289	SEAPL BASE		MANUS	SW PAC		
07/21/45	45370	SEAPL BASE		MANUS	SW PAC		
07/21/45	45392	VPB-28			PHIL		
07/21/45	48217	SEAPL BASE		MANUS	SW PAC		
07/21/45	48222	SEAPL BASE		MANUS	SW PAC		
07/28/45	45275	CASU(F)-48		SAIPAN	WCENPAC		
07/28/45	45314	CASU(F)-48		SAIPAN	WCENPAC		
07/28/45	48164	CASU(F)-48		SAIPAN	WCENPAC		
07/30/45	45340	CASU(F)-34		PARRY IS.	WCENPAC		
07/30/45	45357	CASU(F)-34		PARRY IS.	WCENPAC		
07/30/45	45402	CASU(F)-34		PARRY IS.	WCENPAC		
08/05/45	45394	VPB-28		JINAMOC	PHIL		
08/06/45	45254	CASU(F)-34		PARRY IS.	WCENPAC		
08/06/45	45265	CASU(F)-34		PARRY IS.	WCENPAC		

DATE	BUNO	SQDRN	BASE	LOST	AREA	PILOT	FATE
08/06/45	45267	CASU(F)-34		PARRY IS.	WCENPAC		
08/06/45	45312	CASU(F)-34		PARRY IS.	WCENPAC		
08/06/45	45342	CASU(F)-34		PARRY IS.	WCENPAC		
08/06/45	45358	CASU(F)-34		PARRY IS.	WCENPAC		
08/06/45	45360	CASU(F)-34		PARRY IS.	WCENPAC		
08/08/45	45374	CASU(F)-60		JINAMOC	PHIL		
08/08/45	45385	CASU(F)-60		JINAMOC	PHIL		
08/08/45	45389	CASU(F)-60		JINAMOC	PHIL		
08/08/45	45390	CASU(F)-60		JINAMOC	PHIL		
08/08/45	45400	CASU(F)-60		JINAMOC	PHIL		

MARTIN PBM-3R

The Martin PBM-3R was the unarmed transport version of the PBM-3. There were 18 built as new plus 31 that were converted from PBM-3's. Aircraft lost:

DATE	BUNO	SQDRN	BASE	LOST	AREA	PILOT	FATE
11/24/44	6491	FAW-2	KANEOHE	HAWAII	ECENPAC		
11/24/44	6493	FAW-2	KANEOHE	HAWAII	ECENPAC		
02/12/45	6498	VR-10	HONOLULU	HAWAII	ECENPAC	LTJG W.C. BALLINGER	S
03/17/45	6485	VH-4		LINGAYEN GULF	PHIL		
04/08/45	6457	POOL	KANEOHE	HAWAII	ECENPAC		
04/08/45	6458	POOL	KANEOHE	HAWAII	ECENPAC		
04/08/45	6459	POOL	KANEOHE	HAWAII	ECENPAC		
04/08/45	6468	POOL	KANEOHE	HAWAII	ECENPAC		
04/08/45	6481	POOL	KANEOHE	HAWAII	ECENPAC		
04/08/45	6488	POOL	KANEOHE	HAWAII	ECENPAC		
04/14/45	6467	POOL	KANEOHE	HAWAII	ECENPAC		
04/29/45	6487	VH-5		KANEOHE	ECENPAC		
06/23/45	6489	VH-1		SAIPAN	WCENPAC		
07/28/45	6477	CASU(F)-48		SAIPAN	WCENPAC		
07/28/45	6478	CASU(F)-48		SAIPAN	WCENPAC		
07/28/45	6496	CASU(F)-48		SAIPAN	WCENPAC		

MARTIN PBM-3S

The Martin PBM-3S was built as a dedicated anti-submarine aircraft with reduced armament (2× fixed 0.50 in machine guns in nose, single machine gun in port waist position and single gun in tail turret) but with increased range. There were 94 built as new plus 62 that were converted from PBM-3's. Aircraft lost:

DATE	BUNO	SQDRN	BASE	LOST	AREA	PILOT	FATE
01/23/44	6476	VR-10	FUNAFUTI		SOPAC	LTJG C.H. TALBERT	S
03/14/44	1679	VP-209	COCO SOLO	SALINAS ECUADOR	SE PAC	LT W.J. MCGUIRE	S
05/26/44	1711	VP-210	GUANTAN-AMO BAY	CUBA	CENLANT	LT J.F. SLAVIC	S
07/01/44	1697	VP-210		CARIBBEAN	CENLANT	LT FRANCIS GERTI	D
07/15/44	1726	VP-204		TRINIDAD	CENLANT	LTJG BRUNA	D
08/09/44	48155	VR-2		ESPIRITU SANTO	SOPAC		
12/26/44	48150	VPB-214		CUBA	CENLANT	LTJG THOMAS E. WOOD	S
01/19/45	48128	VPB-213		TRINIDAD	CENLANT	LT GLENN L. CARLSON	S
04/13/45	48161	VH-3		SAIPAN	WCENPAC		
05/08/45	48143	CASU(F)-48		SAIPAN	WCENPAC		
05/18/45	48140	POOL	SAN JUAN	SAN JUAN	CENLANT		
05/31/45	48144	COCO SOLO		COCO SOLO	CENLANT		
06/10/45	1683	NAS	BERMUDA	BERMUDA	NORLANT		
06/16/45	1688	POOL	SAN JUAN	SAN JUAN	CENLANT		
06/16/45	1689	POOL	SAN JUAN	SAN JUAN	CENLANT		
06/16/45	48129	COCO SOLO		COCO SOLO	CENLANT		
06/16/45	48130	COCO SOLO		COCO SOLO	CENLANT		

DATE	BUNO	SQDRN	BASE	LOST	AREA	PILOT	FATE
06/16/45	48138	COCO SOLO		COCO SOLO	CENLANT		
06/16/45	48139	COCO SOLO		COCO SOLO	CENLANT		
06/16/45	48142	COCO SOLO		COCO SOLO	CENLANT		
06/20/45	1678	COCO SOLO		COCO SOLO	CENLANT		
06/20/45	1682	COCO SOLO		COCO SOLO	CENLANT		
06/20/45	48133	COCO SOLO		COCO SOLO	CENLANT		
06/20/45	48137	COCO SOLO		COCO SOLO	CENLANT		
06/20/45	48148	COCO SOLO		COCO SOLO	CENLANT		
06/20/45	48149	COCO SOLO		COCO SOLO	CENLANT		
06/20/45	48151	COCO SOLO		COCO SOLO	CENLANT		
06/23/45	1696	POOL	SAN JUAN	SAN JUAN	CENLANT		
06/23/45	48136	POOL	SAN JUAN	SAN JUAN	CENLANT		
06/29/45	1725	COCO SOLO		COCO SOLO	CENLANT		
06/29/45	48131	POOL	SAN JUAN	SAN JUAN	CENLANT		
06/30/45	1675	POOL	SAN JUAN	SAN JUAN	CENLANT		
06/30/45	1677	POOL	SAN JUAN	SAN JUAN	CENLANT		
06/30/45	1685	POOL	SAN JUAN	SAN JUAN	CENLANT		
06/30/45	48125	POOL	SAN JUAN	SAN JUAN	CENLANT		
07/11/45	1693	POOL	MANUS		SW PAC		
07/12/45	1687	POOL	SAN JUAN	SAN JUAN	CENLANT		
07/13/45	48160	VH-1		SAIPAN	WCENPAC		
07/28/45	48153	CASU(F)-48		SAIPAN	WCENPAC		
07/28/45	48154	CASU(F)-48		SAIPAN	WCENPAC		
07/28/45	48156	CASU(F)-48		SAIPAN	WCENPAC		
08/14/45	48157	POOL		EBEYE	WCENPAC		

MARTIN PBM-5

The -5 version was built by Martin with 2,100 hp (1,566 kW) Pratt & Whitney R-2800 engines. There were 628 built. Aircraft lost:

DATE	BUNO	SQDRN	BASE	LOST	AREA	PILOT	FATE
11/22/44	45422	VPB-208		ENR KANEOHE	ECENPAC		
11/30/44	45415	VPB-200	KANEOHE	HAWAII	ECENPAC		
12/25/44	59017	VPB-27		HAWAII	ECENPAC	LT HARRY BEATY	D
01/23/45	59015	VPB-27		HAWAII	ECENPAC	LTJG THOMAS J.F. CONNOLLY	S
02/19/45	59168	VPB-205		JOHNSTON IS	ECENPAC	LTJG G.O. NUNGESSOR	S
02/22/45	45430	VPB-26		PARRY IS	WCENPAC		
03/17/45	45417	VPB-208		SAIPAN	WCENPAC	LTJG F.J. FRANK	S
03/22/45	59077	VPB-100	KANEOHE	HAWAII	ECENPAC	LTJG WALTER L. HANSON	M
03/25/45	59035	VPB-100	KANEOHE	HAWAII	ECENPAC		
03/29/45	59117	VPB-20		LEYTE GULF	PHIL	LTJG W.O. GLAZE	M
04/02/45	45419	VPB-21		SAIPAN	WCENPAC		
04/12/45	59161	VPB-18		IE SHIMA	EMPIRE	LT DINO MARATI	S
04/13/45	45432	VPB-26		SAIPAN	WCENPAC	ENS JACK E. LANDRETH	S
04/27/45	45413	VPB-208	USS HAMLIN	KEREMA RHET.	EMPIRE	ENS RICHARD C. GARBE	S
04/27/45	59018	VPB-27		KEREMA RHET.	EMPIRE	LTJG OTHO L. EDWARDS	S
05/05/45	59028	VPB-208		KEREMA RHET.	EMPIRE	LCDR A.J. SINTIC	S
05/07/45	59029	VPB-27		KEREMA RHET.	EMPIRE		
05/11/45	59204	VPB-100	KANEOHE	HAWAII	ECENPAC	LTJG ROLAND M. COCKER	S

DATE	BUNO	SQDRN	BASE	LOST	AREA	PILOT	FATE
05/11/45	59031	VPB-21	USS CHANDELEUR	KEREMA RHET.	EMPIRE	LT R.L. SIMMS	S
05/15/45	59042	VPB-18	USS ST. GEORGE	KEREMA RHET.	EMPIRE	LT M.E. HART	S
05/15/45	59122	VPB-18	USS ST. GEORGE	KEREMA RHET.	EMPIRE	LTJG I.E. MARR	M
05/20/45	59099	VPB-18		KEREMA RHET.	EMPIRE	LT F.C. SCHWEIZER	S
05/25/45	59126	VPB-17		TAWI TAWI	PHIL	LTJG FORMAN	S
05/30/45	59107	VPB-18		KEREMA RHET.	EMPIRE	LTJG C.S. BEMIS	S
05/31/45	59038	VPB-18		KEREMA RHET.	EMPIRE	LT J.C. HOUGHTON	S
06/04/45	59062	VPB-20		TAWI TAWI	PHIL	LT GROZER	U
06/05/45	59115	VPB-17		JINAMOC	PHIL	LT HARMEYER	S
06/05/45	45416	VPB-21	USS CHANDELEUR	KEREMA RHET.	EMPIRE		
06/16/45	45439	VPB-26		KEREMA RHET.	EMPIRE	LTJG HERBERT S. FOWLER	S
06/16/45	59097	VPB-26		KEREMA RHET.	EMPIRE	LTJG BOLESIAUS GIESLINSKI	S
06/18/45	59066	VPB-21		KEREMA RHET.	EMPIRE		
06/20/45	45423	VPB-208		KEREMA RHET.	EMPIRE	LT A.A. KEITH	S
06/22/45	59026	VPB-27		KEREMA RHET.	EMPIRE	LTJG J.B. WATSABAUGH	S
06/28/45		VPB-18					
06/30/45	59200	VPB-17		LINGAYEN GULF	PHIL		
06/30/45	59047	VPB-74		GALAPAGOS	CENPAC	LT C.F. FISHER	S
07/05/45	59000	VPB-21		KEREMA RHET.	EMPIRE		
07/06/45	59153	VPB-20		TAWI TAWI	PHIL		
07/15/45	45410	VPB-208		KEREMA RHET.	EMPIRE		
07/15/45	45442	VPB-208		KEREMA RHET.	EMPIRE		
07/24/45	59030	VH-3		KEREMA RHET.	EMPIRE		
07/25/45	59201	VH-4		KEREMA RHET.	EMPIRE		
07/28/45	59071	VPB-208		KEREMA RHET.	EMPIRE	LT CHARLES A. TURNER	D
07/28/45	59128	VPB-21		KEREMA RHET.	EMPIRE		
08/06/45	59019	VPB-27		KEREMA RHET.	EMPIRE		
08/07/45	45412	CASU(F)-48		SAIPAN	WCENPAC		
08/07/45	59023	VPB-27		KEREMA RHET.	EMPIRE	LTJG OTHO L. EDWARDS	M
08/07/45	59154	VPB-27		KEREMA RHET.	EMPIRE	LTJG B.A. GALLAGHER	M
08/08/45	59175	VH-6		CHIMU	EMPIRE		
08/15/45	59176	VH-6		OKINAWA	EMPIRE	LTJG THOMAS B. LADD	S

MARTIN PBM-5E

The Martin PBM-5E was a variant of the PBM-5 with improved radar. Aircraft lost:

DATE	BUNO	SQDRN	BASE	LOST	AREA	PILOT	FATE
05/12/45	59242	VH-3		KEREMA RHET.	EMPIRE		
06/24/45	59280	VH-4		SAIPAN	WCENPAC		
06/29/45	59267	VH-4		SAIPAN	WCENPAC		
07/01/45	59301	VPB-25		LINGAYEN GULF	PHIL		
07/22/45	59286	VH-4		KEREMA RHET.	EMPIRE		
08/02/45	59336	VPB-205		JOHNSTON IS.	ECENPAC	WILLIAM SAMPLE	U

DATE	BUNO	SQDRN	BASE	LOST	AREA	PILOT	FATE
08/11/45	84658	VPB-100	KANEOHE	HAWAII	ECENPAC	LTJG J.W. FLYBAA	S
08/11/45	59346	VPB-19		PARRY IS.	WCENPAC		

NAVAL AIRCRAFT FACTORY (NAF) N3N-3

The N3N was a United States two-place primary training biplane aircraft built by the Naval Aircraft Factory (NAF) in Philadelphia, Pennsylvania during the 1930s. Built to replace the Consolidated NY-2 and NY-3, the N3N was successfully tested as both a conventional airplane and a seaplane. The seaplane used a single float under the fuselage and floats under the outer tips of the lower wing. The conventional airplane used a fixed landing gear. The prototype XN3N-1 was powered by a radial Wright designed Wright J-5 engine. An order for 179 production aircraft was received. Near the end of the first production run the engine was replaced with the 235 hp Wright R-760-2 Whirlwind radial piston engine.

The NAF delivered 997 N3N aircraft beginning in 1935. They included 180 N3N-1s and 816 N3N-3s. Four N3N-3s were delivered to the United States Coast Guard in 1941. Production ended in January 1942 but the type remained in use through the rest of World War II. The N3N was the last biplane in US military service. The N3N was also unique in that it was an aircraft designed and manufactured by an aviation firm wholly owned and operated by the U.S. government (the Navy, in this case) as opposed to private industry. For this, the Navy bought the rights and the tooling for the Wright R-760 series engine and produced their own engines. These Navy-built engines were installed on Navy built airframes. There were 816 built. Aircraft lost:

DATE	BUNO	SQDRN	BASE	LOST	AREA	PILOT	FATE
05/26/45	1987	NAF	DUNKES-WELL	ENGLAND	EUROPE		

NAVAL AIRCRAFT FACTORY (NAF) OS2N-1

The Vought OS2U Kingfisher was an American catapult-launched observation floatplane. It was a compact mid-wing monoplane, with a large central float and small stabilizing floats. Performance was modest, because of its light engine. The OS2U could also operate on fixed, wheeled, tail-dragger landing gear.

The OS2U was the main shipboard observation aircraft used by the United States Navy during World War II, and 1,519 of the aircraft were built. It served on battleships and cruisers of the US Navy, with the United States Marine Corps in Marine Scouting Squadron THREE (VMS-3), and with the United States Coast Guard at coastal air stations. The Naval Aircraft Factory OS2N was the designation of the OS2U-3 aircraft built by the Naval Aircraft Factory in Philadelphia, Pennsylvania. The OS2U first flew on 1 March 1938. The OS2U-3 was powered by a 450 hp (336 kW) Pratt & Whitney R-985-AN-2 or -AN-8 engine.

The first 54 *Kingfisher*s were delivered to the U.S. Navy beginning in August 1940 and six had been assigned to the Pearl Harbor based Battle Force before the end of the same year. The *Kingfisher* was widely used as a shipboard, catapult-launched scout plane on US Navy battleships, heavy cruisers and light cruisers during World War II, as well as playing a major role in support of shore bombardments and air-sea rescue. There were 300 built. Aircraft lost:

DATE	BUNO	SQDRN	BASE	LOST	AREA	PILOT	FATE
06/16/42	1270	VS-1	COCO SOLO (DET 15)		CARIB		
07/08/42	1296	VS-1	(DET 10)		CENLANT		
07/10/42	1295			WEST INDIES	CENLANT	ENS RAYMOND J. COOL	D
07/28/42	1287	VMS-3		ST. THOMAS V.I.	CENLANT	2NDLT D.M. KERWIN	D
08/11/42	1242	VO-3	USS IDAHO	PEARL	ECENPAC		
08/14/42	1227	VO-2	USS PENNSYL-VANIA	OFF CALIFORNIA	CENPAC	ENS EDWARD P. JOYCE	S
09/04/42	1342	VO-3	USS IDAHO	SITKA	NORPAC		
09/17/42	1324	VMS-3		ST. THOMAS V.I.	CENLANT		
09/22/42	1373		GUANTAN-AMO BAY	CUBA	CENLANT		
10/08/42	1326	VMS-3		ST. THOMAS V.I.	CENLANT		
10/11/42	1238	BB-40	USS NEW MEXICO	PEARL	ECENPAC		
10/17/42	1266	FAW-3	COCO SOLO		EPAC		
10/17/42	1293	VS-4	TRINIDAD (DET 10)		CENLANT		
10/21/42	1265	FAW-3	COCO SOLO		EPAC		
10/22/42	1335	VS-1	SITKA (DET 13)	ALASKA	NORPAC		
11/05/42	1408	VS-2	COCO SOLO		CENLANT		
11/10/42	1397	VS-2	JAMAICA		CENLANT		
11/15/42	1320	VO-6	USS SOUTH DAKOTA	GUADAL-CANAL	SOPAC		
11/21/42	1330	FAW-1			SOPAC		
11/25/42	1308		SITKA	ALASKA	NORPAC		
11/25/42	1321	BB-40	USS NEW MEXICO	PEARL	ECENPAC		
11/27/42	1443	VS-2	COCO SOLO (DET 15)		CENLANT		
12/31/42	1355	VS-1	(DET 14)		SOPAC		
01/07/43	1386	CL-13	USS MEMPHIS	ENR GAMBIA	SOLANT		
01/23/43	1427	CL-10	USS CONCORD		ECENPAC		
01/30/43	1387	CL-13	USS MEMPHIS	BAHIA, BRAZIL	SOLANT		
01/30/43	1474	COMFAIR	GUADAL-CANAL	GUADAL-CANAL	SOPAC		
02/23/43	1458	VS-4			NORLANT		
02/26/43	1497	VS-4			NORLANT		
03/29/43	1513	CL-4	USS OMAHA		SOLANT		
04/03/43	1239	A.A.	KODIAK	ALASKA	NORPAC		
04/13/43	1348	VS-63			NORLANT		
04/15/43	1492	VS-64		LUNGA POINT	SOPAC	ENS MCGEORGE	S
04/18/43	1317	A.A.	KODIAK	ALASKA	NORPAC		
04/20/43	1493	VS-54			WCENPAC		
04/30/43	1235	VS-64			SOPAC		
04/30/43	1339	VS-64			SOPAC		
05/03/43	1507	BB-35	USS TEXAS	OKINAWA	EMPIRE		
05/03/43	1459	VS-44			SOLANT		
05/05/43	1312	CL-7	USS RANGER		SOLANT		
05/13/43	1433	CL-6	USS CINCIN-NATI		SOLANT		
05/16/43	1419	VS-58			SOPAC	LT W.W. PHELPS	S
05/20/43	1351	VS-65			SOPAC		
05/23/43	1417	BB-59	USS MASSA-CHUSETTS	SOLOMONS	SOPAC		
05/31/43	1512	VJ-3	USS OMAHA		SOLANT		

DATE	BUNO	SQDRN	BASE	LOST	AREA	PILOT	FATE
05/31/43	1423	VS-66			SOPAC		
06/02/43	1356	VS-51			SOPAC		
06/07/43	1508	VC-29	USS SANTEE	OFF NORFOLK	CENLANT		
06/07/43	1470	VS-65			SOPAC		
07/01/43	1260	COMAIR-PAC	PEARL	HAWAII	ECENPAC		
07/11/43	1277	CL-12	USS MARBLE-HEAD	ENR MED	SOLANT		
08/01/43	1472	VS-64			SOPAC		
08/03/43	1345	VS-53	ROI		WCENPAC		
08/14/43	1328	CL-7	USS RALEIGH	GERTRUDE COVE	NORPAC		
08/23/43	1290	VS-63			NORLANT		
08/24/43	1367	BB-60	USS ALABAMA	HAWAII	ECENPAC		
09/10/43	1451	VB-44			NORLANT		
09/12/43	1385	VMS-3		ST. THOMAS V.I.	CENLANT		
09/15/43	FAW-4	KISKA		ALASKA	NORPAC		
09/19/43	1286	VMS-3		ST. THOMAS V.I.	CENLANT		
09/26/43	FAW-4		DUTCH HARBOR	ALASKA	NORPAC		
09/28/43	FAW-4		DUTCH HARBOR	ALASKA	NORPAC		
09/29/43	1449	VS-60	JAMAICA		CENLANT		
10/01/43	1426	FAW-4	ATTU	ALASKA	NORPAC		
10/02/43	1450	VS-60	JAMAICA	CUBA	CENLANT		
10/26/43	1503	BB-43	USS TENNES-SEE		WCENPAC		
10/30/43	1248	BB-55	USS NORTH CAROLINA		WCENPAC		
11/07/43	1456	VS-44	CURACAO		CENLANT	ENS H.P. DECKER	S
11/09/43	1496	BB-45	USS COLO-RADO	TARAWA	CENPAC		
11/22/43	1314	VS-56	AGATTU	ALASKA	NORPAC	ENS L.W. HARRIGER	S
12/03/43		VS-63	SAN JUAN		NORLANT	ENS W.E. BELRINGER	S
12/25/43	1313	VO-5	USS NEVADA	GREENLAND	NORLANT		
01/31/44	1421	VO-3	USS NEW MEXICO	KWAJALEIN	CENPAC		
02/02/44	1245	VO-3	USS IDAHO	KWAJALEIN	CENPAC		
02/08/44	1369	VO-9	USS ALABAMA	MAJURO	CENPAC		
02/16/44	1425	VS-59	COCO SOLO		NORLANT		
02/17/44	1228	VS-49	DUTCH HARBOR	ADAK	NORPAC	LTJG J.F. JERNIGAN	S
02/17/44	1303	VS-56	ADAK	ADAK	NORPAC		
03/28/44	1301	VS-45	GUANTAN-AMO BAY	CUBA	CENLANT	LTJG D.A. RAYMOND	S
04/21/44	1500	VCS-13	USS BILOXI	WAKDE	SW PAC	LTJG H.F. JOLLY	S
04/29/44	1264	VO-6	USS NORTH CAROLINA	TRUK	CENPAC		
05/15/44	1311	COMAIR-PAC	PEARL	HAWAII	ECENPAC		
06/10/44	1329	VCS-14	USS HOUSTON	W OF PAGAN	CENPAC	ENS D.R. KUNTZ	S
07/14/44	1331	VS-56	ADAK	KASATOCHI	NORPAC	ENS K.I. KOST	D
07/24/44	1448	CL-13	USS MEMPHIS		NORLANT	LTJG T.A. BASTON	S
07/30/44	1304	VO-2	USS TENNES-SEE	TINIAN	WCENPAC	ENS JACQUES GENICE	U
08/15/44	1438	CL-8	USS DETROIT	COCO SOLO	CENLANT		
08/21/44	1255	CL-86	USS VICKS-BURG	CARLISLE BAY	NORLANT	ENS M. NORMAN HANNAN	S

DATE	BUNO	SQDRN	BASE	LOST	AREA	PILOT	FATE
09/14/44	1412	BB-43	USS TENNES-SEE	ANGUAR	CENPAC		
09/14/44	1409	CA-69	USS BOSTON	PALUS	SW PAC	LTJG CHARLES E. GREITZMACHER S	
09/19/44	1479	CL-60	USS SANTA FE		PHIL		
09/20/44	1488	CA-24	USS PEN-SACOLA	WAKE	WCENPAC	LTJG J.A. WILLIAMS	S
10/27/44	1352	BB-43	USS TENNES-SEE	LEYTE GULF	PHIL		
10/30/44	1420	BB-61	USS IOWA	LEYTE GULF	PHIL	ENS A.J. HIGGINS	D
11/18/44	1237	VS-56	ADAK	ALASKA	NORPAC	ENS JOS. B. KLOCKENKEMPER	S
12/01/44	1424	CL-65	USS PASADENA	LUZON	PHIL	LT ROBERT W. BROWNFIELD	S
12/18/44	1278	CL-89	USS MIAMI	LUZON	PHIL	(DECK LOSS-TYPHOON)	
12/19/44	1446	BB-64	USS WISCON-SIN	MINDORO STRAIT	PHIL		
12/23/44	1476	BB-61	USS IOWA	LUZON	PHIL		
12/23/44	1346	CL-13	USS MEMPHIS		CENLANT	LT KENNETH J. MATHIS	S
12/31/44	1251	A.A.	PEARL	HAWAII	ECENPAC		
12/31/44	1274	A.A.	PEARL	HAWAII	ECENPAC		
12/31/44	1482	A.A.	PEARL	HAWAII	ECENPAC		
12/31/44	1486	A.A.	PEARL	HAWAII	ECENPAC		
01/21/45	1343	CL-90	USS ASTORIA	FORMOSA	EMPIRE		
02/18/45	1338	BB-56	USS WASHING-TON	OKINAWA	EMPIRE		
02/19/45	1315	VO-2	USS TENNES-SEE	BONINS	CENPAC	LTJG THOMAS F. MCCORMICK	U
02/21/45	1510	CL-103	USS WILKES BARRE	IWO JIMA	EMPIRE	LTJG V.W. COLLINS	S
02/24/45	1447	CL-4	USS OMAHA		CENLANT	LT THOMAS A. WOOD	S
02/28/45	1337	CASU(F)-51		ULITHI	WCENPAC		
02/28/45	1340	FAW-3	COCO SOLO	COCO SOLO	CENLANT		
03/14/45	1441	CL-6	USS CINCIN-NATI		SOLANT	LTJG P.A. SCHAACK	S
03/28/45	1490	CL-80	USS BILOXI	OKINAWA	EMPIRE		
03/29/45	1428	COMAIR-PAC	PEARL	HAWAII	ECENPAC		
03/31/45	1418	COMAIR-PAC	PEARL	HAWAII	ECENPAC		
03/31/45	1487	COMAIR-PAC	PEARL	HAWAII	ECENPAC		
04/01/45	1354	BB-40	USS NEW MEXICO	OKINAWA	EMPIRE	LTJG HAROLD K. ANDERSON	U
04/03/45	1511	CL-64	USS VIN-CENNES	OKINAWA	EMPIRE		
04/06/45	1416	BB-55	USS NORTH CAROLINA		EMPIRE	ENS ALMAN P. OLIVER	S
04/07/45	1444	CA-71	USS QUINCY	PEARL	ECENPAC	LTJG WILLIAM J. FRANCIS	S
04/24/45	1465	BB-43	USS TENNES-SEE	OKINAWA	EMPIRE		
04/30/45	1468	BB-45	USS COLO-RADO	OKINAWA	EMPIRE		
04/30/45	1494	POOL	PEARL	HAWAII	ECENPAC		
05/01/45	1393	NAS	ATTU	ALASKA	NORPAC		
05/05/45	1475	CASU(F)-12		GUAM	WCENPAC		
05/30/45	1498	CASU(F)-51		ULITHI	WCENPAC		
05/31/45	1481	BB-59	USS MASSA-CHUSETTS		EMPIRE		

DATE	BUNO	SQDRN	BASE	LOST	AREA	PILOT	FATE
05/31/45	1316	COMAIR-PAC	PEARL	HAWAII	ECENPAC		
06/02/45	1504	SOSU-1	PEARL	HAWAII	ECENPAC	ENS RAYMOND J. WHISPELL	S
06/05/45	1249	CA-68	USS BALTI-MORE	OKINAWA	EMPIRE		
06/05/45	1396	CA-71	USS QUINCY	OKINAWA	EMPIRE		
06/05/45	1288	CA-72	USS PITTS-BURGH		EMPIRE		
06/22/45	1395	ACORN-30 PL		JINAMOC	PHIL		
07/03/45	1399	CL-12	USS MARBLE-HEAD		CENLANT		
07/11/45	1495	ACORN-30 PL		TACLOBAN	PHIL		
08/07/45	1217	POOL	SAN JUAN	SAN JUAN	CENLANT		
08/07/45	1291	POOL	SAN JUAN	SAN JUAN	CENLANT		
08/07/45	1297	POOL	SAN JUAN	SAN JUAN	CENLANT		
08/07/45	1462	POOL	SAN JUAN	SAN JUAN	CENLANT		
08/15/45	1243	ACORN-30 PL		TACLOBAN	PHIL		

NAVAL AIRCRAFT FACTORY (NAF) SON-1

The Curtiss SOC Seagull was a United States single-engined scout observation biplane aircraft, designed for the United States Navy (see the SOC variants above). Curtiss delivered 258 SOC aircraft, in versions SOC-1 through SOC-4, beginning in 1935. The SOC-3 design was the basis of the Naval Aircraft Factory SON-1 variant, of which the NAF delivered 64 aircraft from 1940. Aircraft lost:

DATE	BUNO	SQDRN	BASE	LOST	AREA	PILOT	FATE
12/12/41	1154	CL-6	USS CINCIN-NATI	SANTA LUCIA	CENLANT	ENS O.O. ZINK	M
12/17/41	1178	CL-50	USS HELENA	PEARL	ECENPAC		
02/28/42	1190	CL-81	USS HOUSTON	OFF JAVA	SW PAC	(SHIP SANK)	
04/04/42	1174	CL-48	USS HONOLULU	HAWAII	ECENPAC		
04/13/42	1175	VCS-8	BERMUDA		BERMUDA	NORLANT	
08/09/42	1151	CA-71	USS QUINCY	SAVO IS.	SOPAC		
08/09/42	1155	CL-90	USS ASTORIA	SAVO IS.	SOPAC		
08/09/42	1156	CL-90	USS ASTORIA	SAVO IS.	SOPAC		
08/15/42	1152	CL-47	USS BOISE		SOPAC		
10/11/42	1182	CL-50	USS HELENA	CAPE ESPERANCE	SOPAC		
06/16/43	1184	CL-55	USS CLEVE-LAND	ENR SHORT-LANDS	SOPAC		
07/04/43	1148	CL-50	USS HELENA	VELLA LAVELLA	SOPAC		
11/27/43	1168	CA-37	USS TUSCA-LOOSA	OFF ICELAND	NORLANT		
11/08/44	1172	CL-40	USS BROOKLYN	SICILY	MED	LTJG M.G. PICKARD	S
11/27/44	1149	CL-49	USS ST. LOUIS	SURIGAO STRAIT	SW PAC		
01/06/45	1157	CL-56	USS COLUMBIA	LINGAYEN GULF	PHIL	(DECK LOSS-KAMIKAZE)	
04/07/45	1189	CA-35	USS INDIANA		EMPIRE		

NAVAL AIRCRAFT FACTORY (NAF) SON-1A

Some of the 64 Curtiss SOC-3's that were converted to SON-1's by the Naval Aircraft Factory for carrier operations were re-designated as SON-1A but this appears rather arbitrary at best. Aircraft lost:

DATE	BUNO	SQDRN	BASE	LOST	AREA	PILOT	FATE
03/31/45	1147	CA-35	USS INDIANA		EMPIRE		

NORTH AMERICAN PBJ-1C

The North American B-25 Mitchell was an American twin-engined medium bomber manufactured by North American Aviation. It was used by many Allied air forces, in every theater of World War II, as well as many other air forces after the war ended, and saw service across four decades.

The B-25 was named in honor of General Billy Mitchell, a pioneer of U.S. military aviation. The B-25 is the only American military aircraft named after a specific person. By the end of its production, nearly 10,000 B-25s in numerous models had been built. These included a few limited variations, such as the United States Navy's and Marine Corps' PBJ-1 patrol bomber

The PBJ-1C was manufactured as the B-25C, exclusively at the North American Aviation aircraft plant in Inglewood, California. Characteristic features of the -1C included a tricycle landing gear, a gull-wing, and a double fin and rudder empennage. In addition to .50 caliber machine guns, the PBJ-1C was also equipped to carry various types of bombs, depth charges, or an aerial torpedo.

The PBJ-1 had its origin in a deal cut in mid-1942 between the Navy and the USAAF. As part of the deal, fifty B-25Cs and 152 B-25Ds were transferred to the Navy from the USAAF. The planes carried Navy serial numbers beginning with 34998. The first PBJ-1s arrived in February 1943. They were used by Marine Corps pilots, beginning with VMB-413. Many of them were equipped with search radar with a retractable radome fitted in place of the ventral turret.

The PBJs were operated almost exclusively by the Marine Corps as land-based bombers. To operate them, the US Marine Corps established a number of bomber squadrons, beginning with VMB-413, in March 1943 at Cherry Point, North Carolina. Eight VMB squadrons were flying PBJs by the end of 1943, forming the initial Marine Medium Bombardment Group. Four more squadrons were in the process of formation in late 1945, but had not yet deployed by the time the war ended.

Operational use of the Marine Corps PBJ-1s began in March 1944. The Marine PBJs operated from the Philippines, Saipan, Iwo Jima and Okinawa during the last few months of the Pacific war. Their primary mission was the long range interdiction of enemy shipping that was trying to run the blockade which was strangling Japan. The weapon of choice during these missions was usually the five-inch HVAR rocket, eight of which could be carried on underwing racks. Many of the PBJ-1C and D versions carried a rather ugly, bulbous antenna for an APS-3 search radar sticking out of the upper part of the transparent nose. On the PBJ-1H and J, the APS-3 search radar antenna was usually housed inside a ventral or wingtip radome. Some PBJ-1Js had their top turrets removed to save weight, especially toward the end of the war when Japanese fighters had become relatively scarce.

The Navy received a total of 50 PBJ-1Cs between 20 February 1943 and 19 April 1943. All of these aircraft were from the 20 and 25 series production blocks. These aircraft were primarily used stateside by the Marine Corps' Operational Training Squadrons, although two aircraft of this type were deployed to the Southwest Pacific and saw action with VMB-443. Aircraft lost:

DATE	BUNO	SQDRN	BASE	LOST	AREA	PILOT	FATE
07/03/45	35034	VMB-443		EMIRAU	SW PAC	1STLT GEORGE J. KOZLOWSKI	S
07/20/45	35033	SERVRON-61		EMIRAU	SW PAC		

NORTH AMERICAN PBJ-1D

As a note of reference, the B-25D and its naval variant, the PBJ-1D, was an identical aircraft - the only difference being that it was produced solely at the North American aircraft factory in Kansas City, Kansas. This being the case, it is impossible to distinguish a PBJ-1C from a PBJ-1D without establishing the aircraft's Bureau of Aeronautics Number (BuNo), or by examining the manufacturer's data plate for the corresponding AAF Serial Number. The difference between the B-25D and the PBJ-1D was that the -1D has a single .50 in (12.7 mm) machine gun in the tail turret and beam gun positions similar to the B-25H. Many PBJ-1D's were often fitted with airborne search radar and used in the anti-submarine role. Aircraft lost:

DATE	BUNO	SQDRN	BASE	LOST	AREA	PILOT	FATE
01/11/44	35110	VMB-413	PEARL	HAWAII	ECENPAC		
01/21/44	35131	VMB-413	CANTON	TUTUILA	SOPAC		
03/03/44	35145	VMB-423	EWA	OAHU	ECENPAC	1STLT H.E. SEEMAN	D
03/16/44	35139	VMB-413	TREASURY	STERLING	SOPAC		
03/22/44	35117	VMB-413	TREASURY	RABAUL	SOPAC	1STLT W.D. GRAUL	M
03/22/44	35124	VMB-413	TREASURY	RABAUL	SOPAC	MAJ J.K. SMITH	M
04/01/44	35134	VMB-413	TREASURY		SOPAC	1STLT R.A. DREASHER	M
04/20/44	35127	VMB-413	STIRLING	KAVIENG	SOPAC	MAJ D.E. KEELER	D
04/20/44	35083	VMB-423		ESPIRITU SANTO	SOPAC	1STLT A.R. CARLSON	D
04/22/44	35087	VMB-423		ESPIRITU SANTO	SOPAC	1STLT L.A. LALLATHIN	M
04/26/44	35133	VMTB-133	GREEN		SOPAC		
05/05/44	35143	VMB-413	STIRLING	RABAUL	SOPAC	1STLT G.M. SMITH	M
05/18/44	35144	VMB-423	STIRLING		SOPAC	1STLT R.J. WEAVER	S
05/23/44	35125	VMB-423	STIRLING	TREASURY	SOPAC	1STLT R. JONES	S
06/22/44	35109	VMB-423	GREEN	RABAUL	SOPAC	1STLT V.R. KISTNER	M
06/28/44	35141	VMB-423	GREEN	RABAUL	SOPAC	CAPT R.A. EDMONDS	D
06/29/44	35128	VMB-413		CHOISEUL BAY	SOPAC	MILLINGTON	S
08/10/44	35102	VMB-433		EMIRAU	SW PAC	LT T.G. JOHNSON	S
09/02/44	35106	VMB-433		KAVIENG	SOPAC	1STLT CHARLES L. INGLES	M
09/11/44	35100	VMB-433		NEW BRITAIN	SOPAC	1STLT E.E. TERRY, JR.	D
09/11/44	35073	VMB-443		NEW HANOVER	SW PAC	1STLT JOHN M. O'HARA	D
09/16/44	35086	VMB-443		KAVIENG	SOPAC	1STLT B.G. KINNICK	M
09/18/44	35085	VMB-443		EMIRAU	SW PAC	1STLT JOHN L. BRADEN, JR.	M
09/29/44	35181	VMB-413		MUNDA	SOPAC	CAPT HOMER L. DANIEL	S
10/03/44	35132	VMB-423	GREEN		SOPAC		
10/03/44	35140	VMB-423	GREEN		SOPAC		
10/30/44	35080	VMB-443		EMIRAU	SW PAC	LT MULLER	S
10/31/44	35152	VMB-611		EMIRAU	SW PAC		
10/31/44	35197	VMB-611		EMIRAU	SW PAC		
11/11/44	35130	VMB-423	GREEN		SOPAC	LT JASPER H. BATES	U
11/15/44	35165	VMB-611		EMIRAU	SW PAC	LT DAVID A. HIEHMAN	S
11/15/44	35201	VMB-612		SAIPAN	WCENPAC	LT J.W. BOSTICK	M

DATE	BUNO	SQDRN	BASE	LOST	AREA	PILOT	FATE
11/26/44	35149	VMB-612		SAIPAN	WCENPAC	LT GEORGE J. FALCOUT	M
11/26/44	35156	VMB-612		SAIPAN	WCENPAC	LT EDWARD MADVOY	M
01/17/45	35175	VMB-611		EMIRAU	SW PAC	1STLT CHARLES H. LAWRENCE	D
01/26/45	35129	VMB-433		EMIRAU	SW PAC	1STLT WILLIAM B. DUNN	S
02/11/45	35168	VMB-612		SAIPAN	WCENPAC	1STLT C.L. JAMES	U
02/28/45	35151	VMB-413		RASI	SW PAC	MAJ JAMES W. CUNNINGHAM	D
02/28/45	35105	VMB-433		EMIRAU	SW PAC	1STLT DONALD R. HAPHEY	D
03/05/45	35190	VMB-413	EMIRAU	TOBERA	SOPAC	LT WILLIAM J. MUEHLEISEN	S
03/05/45	35123	VMB-433		EMIRAU	SW PAC	LT WILLIAM R. PARKS	S
03/27/45	35118	VMB-433		EMIRAU	SW PAC	1STLT NORMAN V. HENRY, JR.	S
04/08/45	35193	VMB-611		EMIRAU	SW PAC		
04/12/45	35157	VMB-611		ZAMBOAN-GA	PHIL	1STLT CHARLES M. GOOD	S
04/16/45	35161	VMB-612		IWO JIMA	EMPIRE		
04/20/45	35148	VMB-612		IWO JIMA	EMPIRE		
04/20/45	35189	VMB-612		IWO JIMA	EMPIRE		
04/30/45	35065	SERVRON-61		EMIRAU	SW PAC		
04/30/45	35069	SERVRON-61		EMIRAU	SW PAC		
04/30/45	35082	SERVRON-61		EMIRAU	SW PAC		
04/30/45	35108	SERVRON-61		EMIRAU	SW PAC		
05/02/45	35200	VMB-611		ZAMBOAN-GA	PHIL	1STLT ROBERT B. MASON	D
05/02/45	35196	VMB-612		SAIPAN	WCENPAC	1STLT J.F. JARELL, JR.	D
05/03/45	35176	VMB-612		SAIPAN	WCENPAC	MAJ LAWRENCE F. FOX	S
05/25/45	35121	SERVRON-61		EMIRAU	SW PAC		
05/30/45	35164	VMB-611		ZAMBOAN-GA	PHIL	LTCOL GEORGE A. SARLES	M
06/15/45	35147	VMB-443		PELELIU	WCENPAC	1STLT EDWARD E. GARTON	S
06/19/45	35172	VMB-611		ZAMBOAN-GA	PHIL	MAJ DAVIS	S
06/19/45	35194	VMB-611		ZAMBOAN-GA	PHIL	LT GRIFFITH	M
07/10/45	35183	VMB-611		ZAMBOAN-GA	PHIL		
07/18/45	35075	SERVRON-61		EMIRAU	SW PAC		
07/23/45	35079	SERVRON-61		EMIRAU	SW PAC		
08/04/45	35114	VMB-443		EMIRAU	SW PAC	1STLT C.W. SIEBEN	M
08/11/45	35185	VMB-611		ZAMBOAN-GA	PHIL		
08/13/45	35126	VMB-413		EMIRAU	SW PAC		
08/15/45	35101	SERVRON-61		EMIRAU	SW PAC		

NORTH AMERICAN PBJ-1H

The PBJ-1H was the US Navy/US Marine Corps designation for the B-25H. It featured two additional fixed .50 in (12.7 mm) machine guns in the nose and four in fuselage-mounted pods; the heavy M4 cannon was replaced by a lighter 75 mm (2.95 in) T13E1. Aircraft lost:

DATE	BUNO	SQDRN	BASE	LOST	AREA	PILOT	FATE
02/06/45	35275	VMB-613		PONAPE	CENPAC	1STLT WILLIAM J. LOVE	D

NORTH AMERICAN PBJ-1J

The PBJ-1J was the US Navy/US Marine Corps designation for the B-25J-NC (Blocks -1 through -35) with improvements in radio and other equipment. The -1J was often fitted with "package guns" and wingtip search radar for the anti-shipping/anti-submarine role. One PBJ-1H was modified with carrier take-off and landing equipment and successfully tested on the USS Shangri-La, but the Navy did not continue development.

DATE	BUNO	SQDRN	BASE	LOST	AREA	PILOT	FATE
04/20/45	35239	VMB-612		IWO JIMA	EMPIRE	1STLT SAMUEL C. BALTHROP	D
05/30/45	35243	VMB-611		ZAMBOANGA	PHIL	1STLT DOIT L. FISH	M
07/27/45	35242	VMB-612		OKINAWA	EMPIRE	1STLT BYRON C. PETERSON	M
08/01/45	64983	VMB-612		CHIMU	EMPIRE		

NORTH AMERICAN SNJ-3

The North American Aviation T-6 Texan was a single-engine advanced trainer aircraft used to train pilots of the United States Navy, during World War II and into the 1950s. Designed by North American Aviation, the T-6 is known by a variety of designations depending on the model and operating air force. The US Navy designated it as the "SNJ". The Texan originated from the North American NA-16 prototype (first flown on April 1, 1935) which, modified as the NA-26, was submitted as an entry for a USAAC "Basic Combat" aircraft competition in March, 1937. The first model went into production shortly after March 1937 and the US Navy received 16 modified aircraft, designated the SNJ-1, and a further 61 as the SNJ-2 with a different engine. Next came the AT-6A which was powered by the Pratt & Whitney R-1340-49 Wasp radial engine. The US Navy received 270 of these SNJ-3's. Aircraft lost:

DATE	BUNO	SQDRN	BASE	LOST	AREA	PILOT	FATE
00/00/00	7009	COMAIR-PAC	PEARL	HAWAII	ECENPAC		
12/07/41	6794	VMJ-252	PEARL	HAWAII	ECENPAC		
08/14/42	1883				ECENPAC	2NDLT FRED R.P. GROSS	D
10/23/42	1855	VMF-212	GUADAL-CANAL		SOPAC		
04/27/43	1856	VMF-123			SOPAC		
04/30/43	1853	VMO-251			SOPAC		
01/20/44	6852	VMJ-252	EWA	HAWAII	ECENPAC		
02/10/44	1858	CASU-4	PUUNENE	HAWAII	ECENPAC		
09/22/44	6943	MAG-31		ROI	WCENPAC		
03/10/45	1059	A.A.	KANEOHE	HAWAII	ECENPAC		
05/19/45	1860	NAS	PEARL	HAWAII	ECENPAC	LT JOHN F. HART	M
05/19/45	1854	POOL	KANEOHE	HAWAII	ECENPAC		
05/26/45	6908	CASU(F)-12		GUAM	WCENPAC		
08/14/45	1901	POOL	PEARL	HAWAII	ECENPAC		
08/14/45	1902	POOL	PEARL	HAWAII	ECENPAC		

NORTH AMERICAN SNJ-4

Minor design changes in the AT-6A resulted in the North American 88 (NA-88) design. The equivalent of the NA-88 for the Navy was the SNJ-4, of which 2,400 were built for the Navy. Aircraft lost:

DATE	BUNO	SQDRN	BASE	LOST	AREA	PILOT	FATE
09/19/42	10123	MAG-24	EWA	HAWAII	ECENPAC	2NDLT CHARLES H. HYDE, JR	M
02/24/43	26818	VF-207	SAN JULIEN		CENLANT		
02/25/43	26458	VMF-211	PALMYRA		ECENPAC	LT FOULKES	S
02/26/43	5667	1ST MAW		GUADAL-CANAL	SOPAC		
03/19/43	5665	VMSB-131			SOPAC	CAPT STILES	D

DATE	BUNO	SQDRN	BASE	LOST	AREA	PILOT	FATE
04/27/43	26953	NAS	SITKA	SITKA	NORPAC		
05/05/43	27368	VF-31			NORLANT		
05/18/43	5668	1ST MAW		RUSSELLS	SOPAC		
07/31/43	27583	MAG-13		SAMOA	SOPAC		
10/25/43	27607	FAW-11			NORLANT		
12/27/43	27266	AFIU	ESPIRITU SANTO		SOPAC		
01/05/44	27554	MAG-31		ROI	WCENPAC		
01/16/44	26522	VJ-10	PEARL	HAWAII	ECENPAC		
02/12/44	27553	HEDRON-31	ROI		CENPAC		
03/17/44	27364	CASU-10	ESPIRITU SANTO	PALLIKULO	SOPAC		
04/19/44	27562	AFIU-5			SOPAC	2NDLT H.H. LATHROP	S
06/08/44	26815	VS-141	SAN JUAN		NORLANT	LT W.J. GALLAGHER	S
08/02/44	27664	NAS	DUTCH HARBOR	ALASKA	NORPAC		
08/08/44	27152	CASU-40		ESPIRITU SANTO	SOPAC		
08/08/44	27158	CASU-40		ESPIRITU SANTO	SOPAC		
08/08/44	27358	CASU-40		ESPIRITU SANTO	SOPAC		
08/08/44	27359	CASU-40		ESPIRITU SANTO	SOPAC		
08/08/44	27360	CASU-40		ESPIRITU SANTO	SOPAC		
08/08/44	27361	CASU-40		ESPIRITU SANTO	SOPAC		
08/08/44	27362	CASU-40		ESPIRITU SANTO	SOPAC		
08/08/44	27365	CASU-40		ESPIRITU SANTO	SOPAC		
08/08/44	27466	CASU-40		ESPIRITU SANTO	SOPAC		
09/04/44	10127	NAS	MIDWAY		ECENPAC		
09/07/44	10125	VMF-314	MIDWAY		ECENPAC	2NDLT JOHN R. REICHART	S
09/12/44	26561	MAG-32	EWA	HAWAII	ECENPAC		
12/09/44	26463	A.A.	BARBERS POINT	HAWAII	ECENPAC		
01/18/45	27555	SERVRON-31		ROI	WCENPAC		
02/20/45	10137	A.A.	KANEOHE	HAWAII	ECENPAC		
03/10/45	26457	A.A.	EWA	HAWAII	ECENPAC		
03/15/45	27155	COMAIR-PAC	PEARL	HAWAII	ECENPAC		
03/16/45	26466	A.A.	KANEOHE	HAWAII	ECENPAC		
04/01/45	9875	CASU-4	USS TRIPOLI	HAWAII	ECENPAC	LCDR D.A. RATLEY	S
04/03/45	27556	CASU(F)-13		PITYILU	SW PAC		
04/09/45	10122	2ND MAW	HAWAII		ECENPAC	1STLT WILLIAM C. TERRY	S
04/21/45	9965	NAS	NAVY NO. 29	HAWAII	ECENPAC	LT ALBERT C. LUBBERTS	S
04/27/45	9865	POOL	KANEOHE	HAWAII	ECENPAC		
04/27/45	27558	POOL	KANEOHE	HAWAII	ECENPAC		
04/27/45	27563	POOL	KANEOHE	HAWAII	ECENPAC		
05/31/45	9872	COMAIR-PAC	PEARL	HAWAII	ECENPAC		
05/31/45	26791	FAW-3	COCO SOLO	COCO SOLO	CENLANT	AP1/C THOMAS T. BARTOW	S
06/23/45	26910	POOL	PEARL	HAWAII	ECENPAC		
07/18/45	26520	POOL	PEARL	HAWAII	ECENPAC		
07/19/45	26519	POOL	BARBERS POINT	HAWAII	ECENPAC		
07/28/45	26465	POOL	PEARL	HAWAII	ECENPAC		
07/28/45	26521	POOL	PEARL	HAWAII	ECENPAC		
08/14/45	5666	POOL	PEARL	HAWAII	ECENPAC		

NORTH AMERICAN SNJ-5

Modifications to the electrical system produced the North American AT-6D variant, of which 1,357 were built for the Navy as the SNJ-5. Aircraft lost:

DATE	BUNO	SQDRN	BASE	LOST	AREA	PILOT	FATE
03/29/44	51737	CASU-1	PEARL	HAWAII	ECENPAC	LT P.M. EATON	D
10/13/44	51736	CASU-1	PEARL	HAWAII	ECENPAC	LTJG HENRY N. SCHROEDER	S
10/30/44	51733	NAS	KAHILI	HAWAII	ECENPAC	LT WARING ROBERS	D
04/19/45	51984	POOL	KANEOHE	HAWAII	ECENPAC		
07/10/45	91041	NAB	TACLOBAN		PHIL		
08/06/45	51724	CASU-31	HILO	HAWAII	ECENPAC		

NORTH AMERICAN SNJ-6

The North American NA-121 design included a completely clear rearmost section on the canopy, gaving rise to the SNJ-6 for the US Navy. There were 931 built for the Navy. Aircraft lost:

DATE	BUNO	SQDRN	BASE	LOST	AREA	PILOT	FATE
07/26/45		HEDRON-3	EWA	HAWAII	ECENPAC	CAPT SAMUEL D. AARONSON	S

NORTHROP BT-1

John K. Northrop, famed designer of the Lockheed Vega, formed his own company, Northrop Corporation, at Inglewood, CA, and continued producing military and civil aircraft with all-metal designs and advanced structural features. One development was the BT-1 - an aircraft fitted with semi-retractable undercarriage and split trailing-edge flaps. After minor refinements of the XBT-1, 54 production BT-1s were ordered and deliveries began to the VB-5 squadron in April 1938. The BT-1 was the earliest configuration of what would become the famous SBD Dauntless dive-bombers. Aircraft lost:

DATE	BUNO	SQDRN	BASE	LOST	AREA	PILOT	FATE
10/31/44	0624	COMAIR-PAC	PEARL	HAWAII	ECENPAC		

PIPER AE-1

In 1942, the Navy acquired 100 HE-1's (BuNos 30197-30296). These were ambulance versions of the Piper J-5C, with Lycoming O-235-2 engines, designed to carry one stretcher and a pilot. These aircraft were redesignated AE-1 when the H designation was assigned to helicopters in 1943. Aircraft lost:

DATE	BUNO	SQDRN	BASE	LOST	AREA	PILOT	FATE
03/24/44	30274	COMAIR-PAC	PEARL	HAWAII	ECENPAC		
04/08/44	30264	CASU-31	HILO	HAWAII	ECENPAC	LTJG E.J. BECKER	S
11/27/44	30293	AWT ACTION		GUADAL-CANAL	SOPAC		
01/31/45	30221	A.A.	PEARL	HAWAII	ECENPAC		
03/15/45	30238	COMAIR-PAC	PEARL	HAWAII	ECENPAC		
05/26/45	30263	CASU(F)-12		GUAM	WCENPAC		
05/31/45	30289	MCAB	ULITHI	ULITHI	WCENPAC		
08/04/45	30241	POOL	PEARL	HAWAII	ECENPAC		

PIPER NE-1

The Piper J-3 Cub is a small, simple, light aircraft that was built between 1937 and 1947 by Piper Aircraft. With tandem (fore and aft) seating, it was intended for flight training but became one of the most popular and best-known light aircraft of all time. During World War II, the Piper Cub quickly became a familiar sight. First Lady Eleanor Roosevelt took a flight in a J-3 Cub, posing for a series of publicity photos to help promote the CPTP. Newsreels and newspapers of the era often featured images of wartime leaders, such as Generals Dwight Eisenhower, George Patton and George Marshall, flying around European battlefields in Piper Cubs. Civilian-owned Cubs joined the war effort as part of the newly formed Civil Air Patrol (CAP), patrolling the Eastern Seaboard and Gulf Coast in a constant search for German U-boats and survivors of U-boat attacks.

Piper developed a military variant; the variant for the US Navy was designated as the NE. The variety of models, as well as similar, tandem-cockpit accommodation aircraft from Aeronca and Taylorcraft, were collectively nicknamed "Grasshoppers" and used extensively in World War II for reconnaissance, transporting supplies an d medical evacuation. The Navy's NE-1 had dual controls and 230 were built. Aircraft lost:

DATE	BUNO	SQDRN	BASE	LOST	AREA	PILOT	FATE
00/00/00	26351	CAG-5	USS YORK-TOWN		CENPAC		
04/30/43	26212	COMFAIR	GUADAL-CANAL	GUADAL-CANAL	SOPAC		
08/23/43	26235	NAS	ST. THOMAS V.I.		CENLANT		
04/11/44	26389	HQ MCAS	EWA	HAWAII	ECENPAC	2NDLT J.B. DEHAVEN	S
08/31/44	26392		USS INDEPEN-DENCE	ENIWETOK	CENPAC		
08/31/44	26388	NAS	HILO	HAWAII	ECENPAC		
10/31/44	26248	CASU-39	ESPIRITU SANTO	ESPIRITU SANTO	SOPAC		
05/28/45	26422	NAS	GUANTAN-AMO BAY	CUBA	CENLANT	LT H.R. BERNING	S
05/31/45	26350	NAB	TARAWA		WCENPAC		
06/30/45	26357	CASU(F)-12	GUAM		WCENPAC		

REARWIN SPEEDSTER

These two aircraft were acquired by the Navy from Pan Am and assigned Navy Bureau Numbers. It is unknown as to how they were both lost at the same place on the same day. Also, Pan Am purchased a number of Rearwin Cloudsters (approximately 124 were built); only two Speedsters were built and Pan Am was not the owner. Any further information from the reader would be helpful. Aircraft lost:

DATE	BUNO	SQDRN	BASE	LOST	AREA	PILOT	FATE
08/31/44	99096	PAN AM	ALASKA	ALASKA	NORPAC		
08/31/44	99097	PAN AM	ALASKA	ALASKA	NORPAC		

SIKORSKY JR2S-2

The Sikorsky VS-44 was a large four-engined flying boat built in the USA in the early 1940s. The VS-44 was designed primarily for the trans-Atlantic passenger market, with a capacity of 40+ passengers. Only three aircraft were produced: *Excalibur*,

Excambian, and *Exeter*. The outbreak of World War II put civilian transatlantic air services on hold. Now under a Navy contract, with the Navy designation JR2S-1, American Export Airline's three VS-44's continued flying between New York and Foynes, Ireland, carrying passengers, freight and materiel. The first VS-44, *Excalibur*, was BuNo 12390 and crashed on takeoff in 1942 at Botwood, Newfoundland, killing 11 of the 37 aboard. The Aircraft History Card states March 1 1943 which is incorrect. Aircraft lost:

DATE	BUNO	SQDRN	BASE	LOST	AREA	PILOT	FATE
03/01/43	12390		NEW YORK	NEWFOUND-LAND	NORLANT		

SIKORSKY JRS-1

The Sikorsky S-43 was a twin engine amphibious aircraft manufactured in United States during the 1930s by the American firm Sikorsky Aircraft.

The S-43 first flew in 1935, and was a smaller version of the Sikorsky S-42 "Clipper". It accommodated between 18 and 25 passengers, with a separate two-crew forward cockpit. The S-43 was known as the "Baby Clipper" in airline service. In total, approximately 53 S-43s were built, including examples of the twin-tailed S-43B.

The S-43 was used primarily by Pan American World Airways for flights to Cuba and within Latin America. Two were also flown by Reeve Aleutian Airways in Alaska and three were used by Inter-Island Airways of Hawaii, the predecessor to modern-day Hawaiian Airlines, to ferry Pan-Am Clipper passengers and local residents from Honolulu to the other islands.

Five aircraft were acquired by the U.S. Army Air Corps in 1937 under the designation OA-8 and were used for transport of freight and passengers. 17 aircraft were procured by the U.S. Navy between 1937 and 1939 as the JRS-1, two of which served the U.S. Marine Corps. Aircraft lost:

DATE	BUNO	SQDRN	BASE	LOST	AREA	PILOT	FATE
12/07/41	1061	VMJ-252	PEARL	HAWAII	ECENPAC		
04/25/42	1191	VJ-1	PEARL	HAWAII	ECENPAC	LTJG LEONARD WARE	M
04/20/43	1194	VJ-1	PEARL	HAWAII	ECENPAC		
07/22/43	0504	VJ-1			WCENPAC		
07/22/43	0506	VJ-1			WCENPAC		
07/22/43	1056	VJ-1			WCENPAC		
07/22/43	1057	VJ-1			WCENPAC		
07/22/43	1059	VJ-1			WCENPAC		

STEARMAN N2S-3

The Stearman (Boeing) Model 75 is a biplane used as a military trainer aircraft, of which at least 9,783 were built in the United States during the 1930s and 1940s. Stearman Aircraft became a subsidiary of Boeing in 1934. Widely known as the Stearman, Boeing Stearman or Kaydet, it served as a basic trainer for the USN (as the NS & N2S). The N2S is known colloquially as the "Yellow Peril" from its overall-yellow paint scheme. The N2S-3 had the R-670-4 engine. 1,875 were delivered to the US Navy. Aircraft lost:

DATE	BUNO	SQDRN	BASE	LOST	AREA	PILOT	FATE
03/25/44	07008	MAG-11	ESPIRITU SANTO		SOPAC		

STINSON MODEL SM

The Stinson Aircraft Company was an aircraft manufacturing company in the United States between the 1920s and the 1950s. It seems that the Stinson Model SM was one of the many pre-World War II U.S. general aviation aircraft pressed into military service for liaison and observation work during World War II, but it was the only Stinson Model SM so acquired. It was listed as a "miscellaneous acquisition."

DATE	BUNO	SQDRN	BASE	LOST	AREA	PILOT	FATE
10/31/44	09786	NAS	SITKA	ALASKA	NORPAC		

TIMM N2T-1

The Timm N2T Tutor was an American training monoplane built by the Timm Aircraft Corporation, founded by Otto Timm for the United States Navy as the N2T-1. The Timm S-160 (or Timm PT-160K) was a conventional tandem open-cockpit monoplane trainer first flown on the 22 May, 1940. It was powered by a Kinner R-5 radial engine and was a low-wing cantilever monoplane with a tailwheel landing gear. It had an unusual feature in that the airframe structure was made from resin impregnated and molded plywood. The PT-175-K variant was fitted with a Kinner R-53 engine. This was followed by the PT-220-C with a 220hp (164kW) Continental W-670-6 engine and larger tail. The PT-220C was evaluated by the United States Navy, which ordered 262 aircraft as the N2T-1 for operation in the basic training role. Aircraft lost:

DATE	BUNO	SQDRN	BASE	LOST	AREA	PILOT	FATE
05/15/44	32559	COMAIR-PAC	PEARL	HAWAII	ECENPAC		

VOUGHT F4U (VARIANT UNKNOWN)

DATE	BUNO	SQDRN	BASE	LOST	AREA	PILOT	FATE
00/00/00		VF-1	USS BENNING-TON		EMPIRE		

VOUGHT F4U-1

The performance of the Corsair was impressive. The F4U-1 was considerably faster than the F6F Hellcat and only 13 mph (21 km/h) slower than the P-47 Thunderbolt - all three were powered by the R-2800. But while the P-47 achieved its highest speed at 30,020 feet (9,150 m) with the help of an intercooled turbosupercharger, the F4U-1 reached its maximum speed at 19,900 ft (6,100 m), and used a mechanically supercharged engine.

Carrier qualification trials on the escort carrier USS SANGAMON, on 25 September 1942, caused the U.S. Navy to release the type to the United States Marine Corps. Early Navy pilots spoke disparagingly of the F4U as the "hog", "hose nose" or "bent wing widow-maker". After all, the U.S. Navy still had the Grumman F6F Hellcat, which did not have the performance of the F4U but was a far better deck landing aircraft. The Marines needed a better fighter than the F4F Wildcat. For them it was not as important that the F4U could be recovered aboard a carrier, as they usually flew from land bases. Growing pains aside, Marine Corps squadrons readily took to the radical new fighter.

Despite the decision to issue the F4U to Marine Corps units, two Navy units, VF-12 (October 1942) and later VF-17 (April 1943) were equipped with the F4U. By April 1943, VF-12 had successfully completed deck landing qualification. However, VF-12 soon abandoned its aircraft to the Marines. VF-17 kept its Corsairs, but was removed from its carrier, USS BUNKER HILL, due to perceived difficulties in supplying parts at sea. In November 1943, while operating as a shore-based unit in the Solomon Islands, VF-17 reinstalled the tail hooks so its F4Us could land and refuel while providing top cover over the task force participating in the carrier raid on Rabaul. The squadron's pilots landed, refueled, and took off from their former home, USS BUNKER HILL and the USS ESSEX on 11 November 1943.

The U.S. Navy did not get into combat with the type until September 1943. The U.S. Navy finally accepted the F4U for shipboard operations in April 1944, after the longer oleo strut was fitted, which finally eliminated the tendency to bounce. The first Corsair unit to be based effectively on a carrier was the pioneer USMC squadron, VMF-124, which joined *Essex*. They were accompanied by VMF-213. The increasing need for fighter protection against *kamikaze* attacks resulted in more Corsair units being moved to carriers.

From February 1943 onward, the F4U operated from Guadalcanal and ultimately other bases in the Solomon Islands. A dozen USMC F4U-1s of VMF-124, commanded by Major William E. Gise, arrived at Henderson Field (code name "Cactus") on 12 February. The first recorded combat engagement was on 14 February 1943, when Corsairs of VMF-124 under Major Gise assisted P-40s and P-38s in escorting a formation of B-24 Liberators on a raid against a Japanese aerodrome at Kahili. Japanese fighters contested the raid and the Americans got the worst of it, with four P-38s, two P-40s, two Corsairs and two Liberators lost. No more than four Japanese Zeros were destroyed. A Corsair was responsible for one of the kills, although this was due to a midair collision. The fiasco was referred to as the "Saint Valentine's Day Massacre". Although the Corsair's combat debut was not impressive, the Marines quickly learned how to make better use of the aircraft and started demonstrating its superiority over Japanese fighters. By May the Corsair units were getting the upper hand, and VMF-124 had produced the first Corsair ace, Second Lieutenant Kenneth A. Walsh, who would rack up a total of 21 kills during the war.

VMF-113 was activated on 1 January 1943 at Marine Corps Air Station El Toro as part of Marine Base Defense Air Group 41. They were shortly given their full complement of 24 F4U Corsairs. On 26 March 1944, while escorting 4 B-25 bombers on a raid over Ponape, they recorded their first enemy kills when they downed eight Japanese aircraft. In April of that year, VMF-113 was tasked with providing air support for the landings at Ujelang. Since the assault was unopposed the squadron quickly returned to striking Japanese targets in the Marshall Islands for the remainder of 1944.

Corsairs were flown by the famous "Black Sheep" Squadron (VMF-214, led by Marine Major Gregory "Pappy" Boyington) in an area of the Solomon Islands called "The Slot". Boyington was credited with 22 kills in F4Us (of 28 total, including six in an AVG P-40, though his score with the AVG has been disputed). Other noted Corsair pilots of the period included VMF-124's Kenneth Walsh, James E. Swett, and Archie Donohue, VMF-215's Robert M. Hanson and Don Aldrich, and VF-17's Tommy

Blackburn, Roger Hedrick, and Ira Kepford. Nightfighter versions equipped Navy and Marine units afloat and ashore.

At war's end, Corsairs were ashore on Okinawa, combating the *kamikaze*, and also were flying from fleet and escort carriers. VMF-312, VMF-323, VMF-224, and a handful of others met with success in the Battle of Okinawa.

Corsairs also served well as fighter bombers in the Central Pacific and the Philippines. By spring 1944, Marine pilots were beginning to exploit the type's considerable capabilities in the close-support role during amphibious landings. Charles Lindbergh flew Corsairs with the Marines as a civilian technical advisor for United Aircraft Corporation in order to determine how best to increase the Corsair's payload and range in the attack role and to help evaluate future viability of single- versus twin-engine fighter design for Vought. Lindbergh managed to get the F4U into the air with 4,000 pounds (1,800 kg) of bombs, with a 2,000 pounds (910 kg) bomb on the centerline and a 1,000 pounds (450 kg) bomb under each wing. In the course of such experiments, he performed strikes on Japanese positions during the battle for the Marshall Islands.

By the beginning of 1945, the Corsair was a full-blown "mudfighter", performing strikes with high-explosive bombs, napalm tanks, and HVARs. She proved surprisingly versatile, able to operate everything from Bat glide bombs (without sacrificing a load of 2.75 in/70 mm rockets) to 11.75 in (300 mm) Tiny Tim rockets. The aircraft was a prominent participant in the fighting for the Palaus, Iwo Jima and Okinawa.

Statistics compiled at the end of the war indicate that the F4U and FG flew 64,051 operational sorties for the U.S. Marines and U.S. Navy through the conflict (44% of total fighter sorties), with only 9,581 sorties (15%) flown from carrier decks. F4U and FG pilots claimed 2,140 air combat victories against 189 losses to enemy aircraft, for an overall kill ratio of over 11:1. The aircraft performed well against the best Japanese opponents with a 12:1 kill ratio against Mitsubishi A6M and 6:1 against the Nakajima Ki-84, Kawanishi N1K-J and Mitsubishi J2M combined during the last year of the war. The Corsair bore the brunt of fighter-bomber missions, delivering 15,621 tons of bombs during the war (70% of total bombs dropped by fighters during the war). (write-up from Wikipedia). Aircraft lost:

DATE	BUNO	SQDRN	BASE	LOST	AREA	PILOT	FATE
01/23/43	2175	VMF-124		ESPIRITU SANTO	SOPAC		
02/01/43	2172	VMF-124		NOUMEA	SOPAC	LT KENNETH A. WALSH	S
02/14/43	2187	VMF-124			SOPAC	LT GEORGE L. LYON	M
02/14/43	2249	VMF-124			SOPAC	LT HAROLD B. STEWART	M
02/27/43	2171	VMF-124			SOPAC	LT WALTER A. FRANKLIN	D
02/27/43	2191	VMF-124			SOPAC	LT GEORGE L. GATELY	D
03/19/43	2293	MAG-21		RUSSELLS	SOPAC		
03/23/43	2181	VMF-124			SOPAC		
03/26/43	2477	VMF-121		GUADAL-CANAL	SOPAC	LT RODES	S
03/30/43	2236		USS COPAHEE		SOPAC	2NDLT D.H. TATE	S
03/31/43	2179	VMF-124			SOPAC		
03/31/43	2180	VMF-124			SOPAC		
03/31/43	2186	VMF-124			SOPAC		
04/01/43	2206	VMF-124		RUSSELLS	SOPAC	LT JOHNSTON	S
04/01/43	2229	VMF-213		NEW HEBRIDES	SOPAC	LT TATE	S
04/08/43	2311	VMF-222		GUADAL-CANAL	SOPAC	LT TRUEHEART	D
04/12/43	2403	VF-12			WCENPAC		

DATE	BUNO	SQDRN	BASE	LOST	AREA	PILOT	FATE
04/13/43	2286	VMF-213		GUADAL-CANAL	SOPAC	S/SGT W.T. COFFEEN	S
04/13/43	2316	VMF-213		GUADAL-CANAL	WCENPAC	MAJ W. BRITT	D
04/13/43	2377	VMF-213		GUADAL-CANAL	WCENPAC		
04/13/43	2387	VMF-213		GUADAL-CANAL	SOPAC		
04/13/43	2319	VMF-221		RUSSELLS	SOPAC	MAJ BULT	D
04/18/43	2396	VMF-213		RUSSELLS	SOPAC	LT HINES	M
04/24/43	2292	VF-12	PEARL	HAWAII	ECENPAC		
04/24/43	2287	VMF-222	PEARL	HAWAII	ECENPAC	LT WALTER L. JORDAN	S
04/24/43	2308	VMF-222		GUADAL-CANAL	SOPAC	LT JORDAN	S
04/25/43	2399	VMF-213		RUSSELLS	SOPAC	LT ECKART	M
04/25/43	2413	VMF-213		RUSSELLS	SOPAC	LT VEDDER	S
04/30/43	2323	VMF-112		GUADAL-CANAL	SOPAC	1STLT WAYNE W. LAIRD	U
05/01/43	2261	VMF-121		GUADAL-CANAL	SOPAC	LT LAIRD	M
05/02/43	2217	VF-12	PEARL	HAWAII	ECENPAC		
05/02/43	2373	VMF-121		GUADAL-CANAL	SOPAC	LT TRINCHARD	S
05/04/43	2190	VF-12	PEARL	HAWAII	ECENPAC		
05/04/43	2208	VF-12	PEARL	HAWAII	ECENPAC		
05/04/43	2214	VF-12	PEARL	HAWAII	ECENPAC		
05/04/43	2414	VF-12	PEARL	HAWAII	ECENPAC		
05/08/43	2198	VF-12	PEARL	HAWAII	ECENPAC		
05/10/43	2420	VMF-222			WCENPAC		
05/12/43	2205	VF-12	PEARL	HAWAII	ECENPAC		
05/13/43	2170	VMF-112		GUADAL-CANAL	SOPAC	LT SEIFERT	M
05/13/43	2188	VMF-112		GUADAL-CANAL	SOPAC	LT WILCOX	S
05/13/43	2178	VMF-124		GUADAL-CANAL	SOPAC	MAJ WILLIAM GISE	M
05/13/43	2314	VMF-124		GUADAL-CANAL	SOPAC	CANNON	M
05/13/43	2370	VMF-124		GUADAL-CANAL	SOPAC	DALE	U
05/14/43	2276	MAG-22	PEARL	HAWAII	ECENPAC		
05/25/43	2457	VMF-112		RUSSELLS	SOPAC	LT W.S. LOGAN	S
06/01/43	2274	VMF-215		MIDWAY	ECENPAC	LT NEWHALL	S
06/05/43	2499	VMF-112		RUSSELLS	SOPAC		
06/07/43	2331	VMF-112		RUSSELLS	SOPAC	1STLT PERCY	S
06/07/43	2349	VMF-112		RUSSELLS	SOPAC	LT W.S. LOGAN	S
06/07/43	2393	VMF-112		RUSSELLS	SOPAC	MAJ R.B. FRASER	S
06/07/43	2374	VMF-121		GUADAL-CANAL	SOPAC	MAJ VROOME	S
06/07/43	2379	VMF-121		GUADAL-CANAL	SOPAC	LT SNEE	S
06/07/43	2220	VMF-124		RUSSELLS	SOPAC		
06/08/43	2584	FAW-3		COCO SOLO	ECENPAC		
06/08/43	2395	VF-12			WCENPAC		
06/08/43	2416	VMF-124		RUSSELLS	SOPAC		
06/08/43	2464	VMF-124		RUSSELLS	SOPAC		
06/09/43	2491	MAG-11	ESPIRITU SANTO	NEW HEBRIDES	SOPAC	MAJ JAMES R. ANDERSON	S
06/10/43	2382	VMF-121		GUADAL-CANAL	SOPAC	LT BARBER	M
06/11/43	2480	VMF-122		NEW HEBRIDES	SOPAC	LT HARRY E. ATWATER	S
06/12/43	2318	VMF-112			SOPAC		
06/12/43	2343	VMF-121		GUADAL-CANAL	SOPAC		
06/12/43	2456	VMF-121		GUADAL-CANAL	SOPAC	CAPT SCHMITT	M
06/15/43	2509	MAG-22		MIDWAY	ECENPAC		
06/16/43	2519	VMF-112			SOPAC		
06/16/43	2332	VMF-122		GUADAL-CANAL	SOPAC	T/SGT E.F. STATHION	U
06/16/43	2210	VMF-213			SOPAC	LT WILLIAM S. JOHNSON	S
06/18/43	2430	VMF-122		GUADAL-CANAL	SOPAC	LT ERNEST A. POWELL	S

DATE	BUNO	SQDRN	BASE	LOST	AREA	PILOT	FATE
06/19/43	2251	VMF-222		MIDWAY	ECENPAC	T/SGT LAWRENCE ROUD	M
06/20/43	2489	VMF-121		GUADAL-CANAL	SOPAC	LT WILLIAM B. HARLAN	S
06/22/43	2326	MAG-22		MIDWAY	ECENPAC	LT OTHER F. SMITH	S
06/22/43	2611	VMF-211	PEARL	HAWAII	ECENPAC	CAPT JAMES G. OBENSHAIN	D
06/24/43	2684	VMF-211	PEARL	HAWAII	ECENPAC		
06/27/43	2248	VMF-112			SOPAC		
06/28/43	2488	VMF-121		GUADAL-CANAL	SOPAC	1STLT SNEE	D
06/28/43	17468	VMF-121		GUADAL-CANAL	SOPAC	CAPT POINDEXTER	S
06/29/43	2279	VMF-212		MIDWAY	ECENPAC		
06/29/43	2345	VMF-213		GUADAL-CANAL	SOPAC		
06/29/43	2369	VMF-213		GUADAL-CANAL	SOPAC	LT TATE	D
06/29/43	2401	VMF-213		GUADAL-CANAL	SOPAC		
06/29/43	2502	VMF-213		GUADAL-CANAL	SOPAC		
06/30/43	2235	VMF-121	GUADAL-CANAL	RENDOVA	SOPAC	LT DAILEY	S
06/30/43	2453	VMF-121	GUADAL-CANAL	RENDOVA	SOPAC	LT FOXWORTH	M
06/30/43	2580	VMF-121	GUADAL-CANAL	RENDOVA	SOPAC	CAPT BARON	S
06/30/43	2628	VMF-121	GUADAL-CANAL	RENDOVA	SOPAC	CAPT GORDON	M
06/30/43	2267	VMF-122	GUADAL-CANAL	RENDOVA	SOPAC		
06/30/43	2483	VMF-122	GUADAL-CANAL	RENDOVA	SOPAC	MAJ REINBERG	S
06/30/43	2524	VMF-122	GUADAL-CANAL	RENDOVA	SOPAC	LT BOURGEOIS	S
06/30/43	17482	VMF-122	GUADAL-CANAL	RENDOVA	SOPAC	CAPT GARDNER	M
06/30/43	17898	VMF-122	GUADAL-CANAL	RENDOVA	SOPAC	LT BRENNAN	M
06/30/43	2518	VMF-213	GUADAL-CANAL	RENDOVA	SOPAC	MAJ WEISSENBERGER	S
06/30/43	2598	VMF-213	GUADAL-CANAL	RENDOVA	SOPAC	LT M. PECK	D
07/01/43	2495	VMF-121		SOLOMONS	SOPAC	LT RHODES	S
07/01/43	17751	VMF-122		NEW HEBRIDES	SOPAC	LT BOURGEOIS	S
07/01/43	2668	VMF-213		GUADAL-CANAL	SOPAC	CAPT CLOAKE	S
07/02/43	2381	VMF-121		SOLOMONS	SOPAC	CAPT FORD	S
07/02/43	2383	VMF-121		SOLOMONS	SOPAC	LT BARKER	M
07/02/43	2394	VMF-121		SOLOMONS	SOPAC	CAPT TRENCHARD	S
07/02/43	2384	VMF-213		GUADAL-CANAL	SOPAC	LT MILTON V. VEDDER	S
07/03/43	17485	VMF-121		RENDOVA	SOPAC	LT DAILEY	S
07/03/43	2282	VMF-122		NEW HEBRIDES	SOPAC	CAPT RASMUSSEN	D
07/03/43	2237	VMF-213		GUADAL-CANAL	SOPAC	LT SPOEDE	M
07/03/43	2423	VMF-213		GUADAL-CANAL	SOPAC	LT T.R. BROWN	S
07/05/43	2529	VMF-221		GUADAL-CANAL	SOPAC		
07/05/43	2376	VMF-223		MIDWAY	ECENPAC		
07/07/43	17501	VMF-122		RENDOVA	SOPAC	1STLT EWING	S
07/11/43	17517	VMF-213		GUADAL-CANAL	SOPAC	LT THOMAS	S
07/11/43	17521	VMF-213		GUADAL-CANAL	SOPAC	LT A.R. BORG	S
07/11/43	17675	VMF-213		GUADAL-CANAL	SOPAC	LT TREFFOR	U
07/11/43	2490	VMF-221		MUNDA	SOPAC	CAPT SWEET	S
07/11/43	2510	VMF-221		MUNDA	SOPAC	LT SAGE	M
07/11/43	2514	VMF-221		GUADAL-CANAL	SOPAC	LT SEGAL	S

DATE	BUNO	SQDRN	BASE	LOST	AREA	PILOT	FATE
07/14/43	17491	VMF-221		GUADAL-CANAL	SOPAC	LT HACKING	S
07/15/43	2599	VMF-213		GUADAL-CANAL	SOPAC	LT VOTAW	M
07/15/43	2683	VMF-214		ESPIRITU SANTO	SOPAC	LT TOMLINSON	S
07/15/43	17477	VMF-214		ESPIRITU SANTO	SOPAC	LT HOLLMEYER	S
07/17/43	2472	VF-17			NORLANT		
07/17/43	2421	VMF-213		GUADAL-CANAL	SOPAC	1STLT F.R. GARISON	M
07/17/43	2482	VMF-222		MIDWAY	ECENPAC		
07/18/43		VMF-121		GUADAL-CANAL	SOPAC	LT RHODES	M
07/18/43		VMF-122		GUADAL-CANAL	SOPAC	2NDLT RAY	U
07/18/43		VMF-122		GUADAL-CANAL	SOPAC	LT ERNEST A. POWELL	M
07/18/43		VMF-213		GUADAL-CANAL	SOPAC	LT C.C. WINNIA	M
07/18/43		VMF-213		GUADAL-CANAL	SOPAC	LT S.O. HALL	S
07/18/43	2264	VMF-222		MIDWAY	ECENPAC		
07/18/43	2506	VMF-222		MIDWAY	ECENPAC		
07/25/43	2213	VMF-212			WCENPAC		
07/25/43	2275	VMF-212			WCENPAC	LT RAY W. BARTLETT	D
07/25/43	2328	VMF-215		GUADAL-CANAL	SOPAC	MAJ TOMES	S
07/26/43	2537	VMF-215		GUADAL-CANAL	SOPAC	LT MOORE	D
07/26/43	2545	VMF-215		GUADAL-CANAL	SOPAC	CAPT PICKEREL	D
07/26/43	2242	VMF-222		MIDWAY	ECENPAC	LT OTHER F. SMITH	D
07/26/43	2678	VMF-222		MIDWAY	ECENPAC	LT RAY W. BARTLETT	D
07/29/43	2335	VF-17	USS BUNKER HILL	CARIB			
07/29/43	2339	VF-17	USS BUNKER HILL	CARIB			
07/30/43	2375	VMF-215		GUADAL-CANAL	SOPAC	CAPT J.A. NICHOLS	M
07/31/43	2337	VF-17	USS BUNKER HILL	CENLANT			
07/31/43	2289	VMF-212		MIDWAY	ECENPAC		
08/01/43	2508	VMF-123			SOPAC		
08/01/43	2475	VMF-215		GUADAL-CANAL	SOPAC	LT STIDGER	S
08/04/43	2575	VMF-213		NEW HEBRIDES	SOPAC	LT JACK P. DUNN	S
08/06/43	2266	VMF-123			SOPAC		
08/06/43	2492	VMF-214	SHORT-LANDS	BOUGAIN-VILLE	SOPAC	LT W.H. BLAKESLEE	S
08/07/43	2474	VMF-214		RUSSELLS	SOPAC	MAJ W.A. PACE	D
08/08/43	18072	VMF-214		RUSSELLS	SOPAC	LT LAMPHIER	U
08/09/43	17499	FAW-3		COCO SOLO	NORLANT		
08/09/43	49770	VMF-221		GUADAL-CANAL	SOPAC	LT DUNCAN	S
08/11/43	3825	VMF-223		MIDWAY	ECENPAC		
08/12/43	49744	VMF-112		NEW HEBRIDES	SOPAC	LT HARRY E. ATWATER	S
08/12/43	49745	VMF-121			SOPAC		
08/12/43	2615	VMF-215		GUADAL-CANAL	SOPAC	DENING	S
08/13/43	2409	VMF-124		GUADAL-CANAL	SOPAC	LANGER	U
08/13/43	2679	VMF-124		GUADAL-CANAL	SOPAC	LT WALSH	S
08/14/43	2670	VMF-224	PEARL	HAWAII	ECENPAC		
08/15/43	2485	VMF-123		VELLA LAVELLA	SOPAC	LT BLAINE	S
08/15/43	2244	VMF-124		MUNDA	SOPAC	LT HARTER	S
08/15/43	2494	VMF-124		MUNDA	SOPAC	LT HARTSOCK	S

DATE	BUNO	SQDRN	BASE	LOST	AREA	PILOT	FATE
08/16/43	2215	VMF-224	PEARL	HAWAII	ECENPAC	LT HERBERT W. STRASS, JR.	D
08/18/43	49768	VMF-121		MUNDA	SOPAC		
08/18/43	2467	VMF-123		MUNDA	SOPAC	LT FOORD	M
08/18/43	2484	VMF-123		MUNDA	SOPAC	LT JESSUP	S
08/18/43	49788	VMF-214		GUADAL-CANAL	SOPAC	LT BLAINE	S
08/19/43	2533	VMF-215		GUADAL-CANAL	SOPAC	G. SANDERS	S
08/21/43	2288	VMF-123		VELLA LAVELLA	SOPAC	LT NETTLES	M
08/21/43	2310	VMF-123		VELLA LAVELLA	SOPAC	LT STRICKLAND	M
08/21/43	2327	VMF-212	PEARL	HAWAII	ECENPAC		
08/21/43	2567	VMF-223		MIDWAY	ECENPAC	MAJ A.J. ARMSTRONG	S
08/23/43	2473	VMF-222		ESPIRITU SANTO	SOPAC	LT STEPHEN J. YEAGER	S
08/23/43	2719	VMF-222		ESPIRITU SANTO	SOPAC	LT STEPHEN J. YEAGER	S
08/24/43	2281	VMF-124		MUNDA	SOPAC	LT HARTER	D
08/24/43	2166	VMF-212	PEARL	HAWAII	ECENPAC		
08/24/43	2277	VMF-223		MIDWAY	ECENPAC	LT W.J. POOLE	S
08/25/43	3838	VMF-222		ESPIRITU SANTO	SOPAC	LT RICHARD L. HOBBS	S
08/28/43	2634	2ND MAW		MUNDA	SOPAC		
08/28/43	2577	VMF-214		GUADAL-CANAL	SOPAC	LT C.C. LAMPHIER	U
08/30/43	2351	VMF-123		GUADAL-CANAL	SOPAC	LT W.T. MAYBERRY	S
08/30/43	2290	VMF-124		MUNDA	SOPAC	LT KUHN	S
08/30/43	2486	VMF-124		BARAKOMA	SOPAC	LT WALSH	S
08/30/43	2516	VMF-124		BARAKOMA	SOPAC	LT FOWLER	M
09/01/43	2404	VMF-215	GUADAL-CANAL	BALLALE	SOPAC	MAJ JONES	D
09/02/43	2602	VMF-123	MUNDA	KAHILI	SOPAC	LT TOMES	M
09/03/43	2359	VF-17	USS BUNKER HILL		NORLANT		
09/03/43	2192	VMF-213		NEW HEBRIDES	SOPAC	LT W.T. ANDERSON	D
09/09/43	17647	VMF-123	MUNDA	KAHILI	SOPAC		
09/09/43	2552	VMF-213	GUADAL-CANAL	VILA	SOPAC	LT G.C. BENNETT	M
09/09/43	2321	VMF-222	MUNDA	KAHILI	SOPAC	LT J. CRAIG	S
09/09/43	17594	VMF-222	MUNDA	KAHILI	SOPAC	LT W.O. REID	S
09/09/43	56210	VMF-222	MUNDA	KAHILI	SOPAC	LT J. WILLIAMS III	S
09/09/43	56403	VMF-222	MUNDA	KAHILI	SOPAC	LT J.P. MORRIS	S
09/10/43	2211	VMF-222	MUNDA	KAHILI	SOPAC	1STLT JOHN C. THORNTON	S
09/11/43	2536	VMF-123	MUNDA	KAHILI	SOPAC	LT JESSUP	S
09/11/43	2550	VMF-213	RUSSELLS	KAHILI	SOPAC	BENET	U
09/12/43	2338	VMF-213	SHORT-LANDS	BOUGAIN-VILLE	SOPAC	CAPT T.R. BROWN	M
09/13/43	2348	VMF-222		VELLA LAVELLA	SOPAC	1STLT P.J. MORRIS	S
09/13/43	3829	VMF-222		VELLA LAVELLA	SOPAC	MAJ CAINAGEY	S
09/13/43	17435	VMF-222	MUNDA	BALLALE	SOPAC	CAPT W.D. MOORE	M
09/14/43	17545	VMF-224			SOPAC		
09/15/43	17489	VMF-213	GUADAL-CANAL	BALLALE	SOPAC	LT A.R. BORG	S
09/16/43	17527	VMF-214	RUSSELLS	BALLALE	SOPAC	R.T. EWING	M
09/18/43	17831	VMF-213	RUSSELLS	VELLA LAVELLA	SOPAC	1STLT V.L. GLASCOCK	M
09/18/43	17843	VMF-213	RUSSELLS	VELLA LAVELLA	SOPAC	MAJ W.H. CLARKE	M
09/18/43	17886	VMF-213	RUSSELLS	VELLA LAVELLA	SOPAC	LT W.E. STEWART	S
09/19/43	2271	VMF-223		MIDWAY	ECENPAC	LT TIMOTHY CASADY	D
09/20/43	17900	VMF-213	RUSSELLS	VELLA LAVELLA	SOPAC	CAPT J.M. CUPP	S
09/21/43	17901	VMF-214		MUNDA	SOPAC		
09/21/43	17916	VMF-214		MUNDA	SOPAC	LT W.D. HOIER	S
09/23/43	17917	VMF-213	RUSSELLS	BOUGAIN-VILLE	SOPAC	1STLT THOMAS	S

DATE	BUNO	SQDRN	BASE	LOST	AREA	PILOT	FATE
09/23/43	17920	VMF-213	RUSSELLS	BOUGAIN-VILLE	SOPAC	1STLT R.T. ROBERTS	M
09/23/43	55828	VMF-214	RUSSELLS	KAHILI	SOPAC	1STLT R.A. ALEXANDER	S
09/24/43	17670	VF-17	USS BUNKER HILL		CENPAC		
09/25/43	2230	VMF-223		MIDWAY	ECENPAC		
09/25/43	2269	VMF-223		MIDWAY	ECENPAC	LT JAMES LAWRENCE	S
09/26/43	55876	VMF-214	RUSSELLS	KANGU HILL	SOPAC	LT R.N. RINABARGER	S
09/26/43	55943	VMF-214	RUSSELLS	KANGU HILL	SOPAC	LT WILSON	S
09/27/43	56016	VMF-214	TREASURY	KAHILI	SOPAC	LT W.R. HARRIS	M
09/27/43	17936	VMF-215			SOPAC	LT ESCHER	S
09/30/43	55819	VMF-213		MUNDA	SOPAC	LT HENRY HUIDEKOPER	S
10/01/43	2449	VMF-214		NEW HEBRIDES	SOPAC	LT PRESTON P. WOLFE	D
10/02/43	2329	VMF-214		NEW HEBRIDES	SOPAC	MAJ JAMES K. DILL	S
10/03/43	2655	VMF-221		VELLA LAVELLA	SOPAC	CAPT JOHN S. PAYNE	S
10/03/43	17473	VMF-221		VELLA LAVELLA	SOPAC	1STLT J.S. KOETSCH	S
10/11/43	17493	VMF-311	USS NASSAU	SAMOA	SOPAC	LT WM STANLEY ROBSON, JR.	D
10/12/43	17522	VMF-224	USS NASSAU	SAMOA	SOPAC	LT ROBERT W. GRIFFITH	S
10/13/43	17679	VMF-214		MUNDA	SOPAC	LT V.G. RAY	M
10/16/43	2265	2ND MAW		MUNDA	SOPAC		
10/16/43	17844	VMF-214		BOUGAIN-VILLE	SOPAC	1STLT W.T. EMRICH	S
10/17/43	55889	VMF-214		MUNDA	SOPAC	HARPER	U
10/18/43	17424	VMF-214		NEW HEBRIDES	SOPAC	LT OLIVER K. MCMAHAN	M
10/18/43	17557	VMF-221		KAHILI	SOPAC	1STLT MILTON E. SCHNEIDER	M
10/20/43	2315	VMF-214		NEW HEBRIDES	SOPAC	LT HERBERT HOLDEN, JR.	S
10/20/43	50011	VMF-215			SOPAC	LT PETIT	M
10/21/43	55786	VMF-422		MIDWAY	ECENPAC		
10/22/43	2608	VMF-214		NEW HEBRIDES	SOPAC	LT WAYLAND E. BENNETT	D
10/22/43	56082	VMF-215			SOPAC	LT DUVAL	S
10/22/43	17542	VMF-222		MUNDA	SOPAC		
10/26/43	17889	VMF-113	OAHU	HAWAII	ECENPAC	LT ROBERT S. HUTCHINSON	S
10/28/43	17513	VMF-215		VELLA LAVELLA	SOPAC	LT KNIGHT	S
10/30/43	2309	VMF-212		VELLA LAVELLA	SOPAC	CAPT POSKE	S
10/30/43	17462	VMF-212		VELLA LAVELLA	SOPAC	LT JACOBSON	M
11/01/43	17661	VF-17	ONDONGA	POPORANG IS.	SOPAC	LTJG J.H. KEITH	M
11/01/43	2680	VMF-114	EWA	HAWAII	ECENPAC	2NDLT J.W. WALLACE	S
11/01/43	17492	VMF-212		BARAKOMA	SOPAC	1STLT G.W. GRILL	D
11/01/43	2224	VMF-215	RUSSELLS	BARAKOMA	SOPAC	1STLT E.H. MCCALEB	S
11/01/43	17472	VMF-215	VELLA LAVELLA	AUGUSTA BAY	SOPAC	LT R.M. HANSON	S
11/01/43	17523	VMF-215	RUSSELLS	BARAKOMA	SOPAC	2NDLT R.L. KEISTER	M
11/03/43	56398	VF-38		SEGI WALANDE	SOPAC	LTJG L.H. ENGLADE	S
11/03/43	17559	VMF-211	MUNDA	AUGUSTA BAY	SOPAC	MAJ G. MOFFAT	M
11/03/43	17643	VMF-211	MUNDA	AUGUSTA BAY	SOPAC	1STLT R.L. HATFIELD	M
11/03/43	17550	VMF-215		BARAKOMA	SOPAC	CAPT J.R. JORDAN	D
11/05/43	2543	VMF-222		VELLA LAVELLA	SOPAC		
11/07/43	17730	VMF-211		RUSSELLS	SOPAC		
11/08/43	2656	VMF-224	BARAKOMA	AUGUSTA BAY	SOPAC	1STLT E.R. BROWN	S
11/08/43	17546	VMF-224		FUNAFUTI	SOPAC	1STLT W. GAY	D
11/09/43	2642	VMF-321		TUTUILA	SOPAC		
11/11/43	17655	VF-17	ONDONGA	TREASURY	SOPAC	ENS R.H. HILL	S
11/11/43	17671	VF-17	ONDONGA	VELLA LAVELLA	SOPAC	ENS B.W. BAKER	S

DATE	BUNO	SQDRN	BASE	LOST	AREA	PILOT	FATE
11/11/43	17743	VF-17	ONDONGO	VELLA LAVELLA	SOPAC		
11/11/43	2546	VMF-212	BARAKOMA	BUKA	SOPAC	1STLT T.J. HORNER	S
11/14/43	2253	VMF-212	BARAKOMA	VELLA LAVELLA	SOPAC	1STLT W.D. LEE	S
11/15/43	17925	VMF-211		RUSSELLS	SOPAC		
11/15/43	17579	VMF-215	VELLA LAVELLA	BOUGAIN-VILLE	SOPAC	LT L.B. HAZELWOOD	D
11/15/43	2273	VMF-422		MIDWAY	ECENPAC		
11/16/43	17826	VMF-211		RUSSELLS	SOPAC	1STLT E.H. MCCALEB	S
11/17/43	17454	VF-17	ONDONGA	AUGUSTA BAY	SOPAC	LTJG ANDERSON	S
11/17/43	17669	VF-17	ONDONGA	AUGUSTA BAY	SOPAC	ENS B.W. BAKER	M
11/17/43	17617	VMF-215	BARAKOMA	TOROKINA	SOPAC	2NDLT A.J. SNYDER	S
11/20/43	17872	VMF-211		RUSSELLS	SOPAC		
11/20/43	17574	VMF-224		FUNAFUTI	SOPAC		
11/20/43	2233	VMF-422		MIDWAY	ECENPAC	1STLT S.W. DRAKO	D
11/20/43	2650	VMF-422		MIDWAY	ECENPAC	2NDLT E.G. FARRELL	D
11/21/43	17693	VF-17	ONDONGA	AUGUSTA BAY	SOPAC		
11/21/43	17804	VF-17	ONDONGA	AUGUSTA BAY	SOPAC	LT C.A. PILLSBURY	M
11/22/43	17478	VMF-222		VELLA LAVELLA	SOPAC	CAPT J. FITTING	S
11/27/43	17463	VMF-222	BARAKOMA	RABAUL	SOPAC	CAPT J. FITTING	S
11/28/43	17651	VF-17	ONDONGA	MALUPENA PT.	SOPAC	LTJG D.H. GUTENKUNST	S
11/28/43	3803	VMF-214		VELLA LAVELLA	SOPAC	1STLT J.S. BROWN	U
11/28/43	3830	VMF-216	ONDONGA	TOROKINA	SOPAC	CAPT L.M. FAULKNER	S
11/28/43	17450	VMF-223		VELLA LAVELLA	SOPAC		
11/29/43	2212	VMF-114	EWA	HAWAII	ECENPAC	LT R.C. LEHNERT	S
11/29/43	2216	VMF-321		EFATE	SOPAC	1STLT SHODEN	S
11/29/43	2262	VMF-321		EFATE	SOPAC	1STLT NORMAN	S
12/01/43	17632	VMF-223	BARAKOMA	BOUGAIN-VILLE	SOPAC		
12/01/43	17921	VMF-223	BARAKOMA	EMP. AUGUSTA	SOPAC	1STLT R.P. KESSLER	S
12/01/43	17876	VMF-225	EWA	BARBERS POINT	ECENPAC	2NDLT R.C. VIRGIN	D
12/01/43	17486	VMF-311		WALLIS ISLAND	SOPAC	LT AYLWARD	S
12/06/43	2571	VMF-321	EFATE	QUOIN HILL	SOPAC	LT DIXON	S
12/07/43	17750	VMF-216	RUSSELLS	TOROKINA	SOPAC		
12/07/43	17420	VMF-321	EFATE	QUOIN HILL	SOPAC	CAPT MANGEL	U
12/11/43	17400	VMF-212	PEARL	HAWAII	ECENPAC		
12/12/43	17840	VMF-222	VELLA LAVELLA	BOUGAIN-VILLE	SOPAC		
12/13/43	17726	VMF-114	BARBERS POINT	HAWAII	ECENPAC	2NDLT L.J. GAGE	D
12/13/43	2576	VMF-222	VELLA LAVELLA	BOUGAIN-VILLE	SOPAC		
12/13/43	17452	VMF-223	VELLA LAVELLA	BALLALE	SOPAC	1STLT G.A. DAVIS	S
12/14/43	2380	VMF-222	BARAKOMA	BOUGAIN-VILLE	SOPAC	2NDLT N. SMITH	D
12/14/43	2687	VMF-222	BARAKOMA	BOUGAIN-VILLE	SOPAC	1STLT J.W. WITT	S
12/15/43	17884	VMF-222	BARAKOMA	BOUGAIN-VILLE	SOPAC		
12/16/43	2352	VMF-321	EFATE	QUOIN HILL	SOPAC		
12/17/43	17777	VMF-214	VELLA LAVELLA	RABAUL	SOPAC	LT D.J. MOORE	S
12/17/43	2193	VMF-321	EFATE	QUOIN HILL	SOPAC		
12/19/43	17806	VMF-216	TOROKINA	RABAUL	SOPAC	CAPT L.M. FAULKNER	M
12/19/43	17906	VMF-216	TOROKINA	RABAUL	SOPAC	LT KEMPER	M
12/22/43	17736	VMF-216	TOROKINA	RABAUL	SOPAC		
12/23/43	17395	VMF-214	ONDONGA	RABAUL	SOPAC	MAJ P. CARMAGEY	M
12/23/43	17443	VMF-214	ONDONGA	RABAUL	SOPAC	LT B. FOULKES	M
12/23/43	17451	VMF-214	ONDONGA	RABAUL	SOPAC	LT J.E. BRUBAKER	M
12/26/43	17821	VMF-225	EWA	BARBERS POINT	ECENPAC	1STLT J.M. NEARHOOD	S
12/27/43	17734	VMF-216	TOROKINA	RABAUL	SOPAC	2NDLT F.G. PUTNAM	M

DATE	BUNO	SQDRN	BASE	LOST	AREA	PILOT	FATE
12/27/43	17808	VMF-216	TOROKINA	RABAUL	SOPAC	LT DAVEY	D
12/27/43	17845	VMF-216	TOROKINA	RABAUL	SOPAC	1STLT J. KAMPS	D
12/27/43	17942	VMF-223	VELLA LAVELLA	RABAUL	SOPAC	LT B.L. STROHL	S
12/28/43	17908	VMF-214	VELLA LAVELLA	RABAUL	SOPAC	CAPT J.C. DUSTIN	M
12/28/43	49681	VMF-214	VELLA LAVELLA	RABAUL	SOPAC	1STLT D.J. MOORE	M
12/28/43	56420	VMF-214	VELLA LAVELLA	RABAUL	SOPAC	2NDLT H.R. BARTL	M
12/29/43	18011	VF-17		ESPIRITU SANTO	SOPAC	LTJG C.L. SMITH	S
12/29/43	17737	VMF-216	TOROKINA	EMP. AUGUSTA	SOPAC	1STLT M. ALLEN	D
12/29/43	17910	VMF-222	BARAKOMA	RABAUL	SOPAC		
12/30/43	2693	VMF-321		ESPIRITU SANTO	SOPAC		
01/01/44	2189	VMF-321	VELLA LAVELLA	RABAUL	SOPAC	1STLT R.W. BAKER	S
01/02/44	17787	VMF-311		WALLIS ISLAND	SOPAC		
01/02/44	3828	VMF-321	TOROKINA	RABAUL	SOPAC	CAPT N.S. BLOUNT	M
01/03/44	2662	VF(N)-101	PEARL	HAWAII	ECENPAC		
01/03/44	18059	VMF-113		KWAJALEIN	CENPAC		
01/03/44	2723	VMF-214	VELLA LAVELLA	RABAUL	SOPAC	CAPT G.M. ASHMAN	M
01/03/44	17915	VMF-214	VELLA LAVELLA	RABAUL	SOPAC	MAJ G. BOYINGTON	M
01/04/44	17812	VMF-225	EWA	BARBERS POINT	ECENPAC	MAJ D.W. BURKE	D
01/04/44	17938	VMF-321	TOROKINA	RABAUL	SOPAC	CAPT H.F. CARTER	M
01/06/44	18001	VMF-111		TUTUILA	SOPAC	1STLT HOWARD T. BURNS	S
01/07/44	2544	VMF-212		ARU SOLS	SOPAC		
01/08/44	17825	VMF-211	TOROKINA	BUKA	SOPAC	MAJ W.T. CAMPBELL	M
01/11/44	17430	VMF-212	BARAKOMA	RENDOVA	SOPAC	LT C.L. LARSON	M
01/11/44	2578	VMF-321	TOROKINA	RABAUL	SOPAC	MAJ H.J. JACOBS	D
01/12/44	2605	VF(N)-101		MARSHALLS	CENPAC		
01/12/44	3819	VMF-111	TUTUILA	NW OF SAMOA	SOPAC	LT UNDERWOOD	S
01/12/44	18065	VMF-111	TUTUILA	NW OF SAMOA	SOPAC	CAPT D.F. O'SULLIVAN	D
01/13/44	18045	VMF-211	TOROKINA	SHORT-LANDS	SOPAC	CAPT A.R. VETTER	D
01/14/44	18114	VMF-111		TUTUILA	SOPAC		
01/14/44	17807	VMF-211	TOROKINA	RABAUL	SOPAC	1STLT N.R. LANDON	M
01/14/44	17907	VMF-211	TOROKINA	RABAUL	SOPAC	1STLT M.R. TUTTON	S
01/14/44	17922	VMF-211	TOROKINA	RABAUL	SOPAC		
01/14/44	17722	VMF-215	VELLA LAVELLA	RABAUL	SOPAC	2NDLT J.J. KNIGHT	M
01/14/44	17896	VMF-215	VELLA LAVELLA	RABAUL	SOPAC	2NDLT G. KROSS	S
01/14/44	17897	VMF-215	VELLA LAVELLA	RABAUL	SOPAC	1STLT E.N. MOORE	M
01/14/44	17899	VMF-215	VELLA LAVELLA	RABAUL	SOPAC	CAPT G.S. STIDGER	D
01/15/44	17416	VMF-321	TOROKINA	MIKMIK IS.	SOPAC	CAPT M.C. MCGOWN	S
01/17/44	17841	VMF-212	VELLA LAVELLA	RABAUL	SOPAC	1STLT C.M. DWYER	D
01/18/44	17792	VMF-211	TOROKINA	RABAUL	SOPAC	1STLT W.R. CULLER	S
01/18/44	17449	VMF-216	EFATE	QUOIN HILL	SOPAC		
01/18/44	55834	VMF-218		NEW HEBRIDES	SOPAC		
01/19/44	55925	VMF-218		ESPIRITU SANTO	SOPAC	2NDLT R.A. ENDERS	S
01/20/44	2688	VF(N)-101	USS INTREPID	MARSHALLS	CENPAC	LTJG R.N. GREEN	S
01/20/44	2402	VMF-211	TOROKINA	RABAUL	SOPAC		
01/20/44	17448	VMF-321	TOROKINA	RABAUL	SOPAC	CAPT M.C. MCGOWN	M
01/20/44	17914	VMF-321	TOROKINA	RABAUL	SOPAC	1STLT R.H. BRINDOS	M
01/20/44	55835	VMF-321	TOROKINA	RABAUL	SOPAC	1STLT R.W. MARSHALL	M
01/21/44	17650	VF-17		ESPIRITU SANTO	SOPAC	LTJG T.F. KROPF	S
01/22/44	17903	VMF-211	TOROKINA	RABAUL	SOPAC		
01/22/44	2196	VMF-225	EWA	HAWAII	ECENPAC	1STLT J.L. SLEARER	S

DATE	BUNO	SQDRN	BASE	LOST	AREA	PILOT	FATE
01/22/44	17511	VMF-441		NW OF SAMAO	SOPAC		
01/23/44	49891	VMF-212	VELLA LAVELLA	RABAUL	SOPAC	MAJ D.W. BOYLE	M
01/23/44	50166	VMF-321	PIVA	RABAUL	SOPAC	1STLT R.S. MARSH	S
01/24/44	2285	VMF-215	VELLA LAVELLA	RABAUL	SOPAC	MAJ R.G. OWENS	S
01/24/44	17571	VMF-321	PIVA	RABAUL	SOPAC	1STLT R.W. GRIFFITH	S
01/25/44	55869	VF-88	TARAWA	FUNAFUTI	CENPAC		
01/25/44	2283	VMF-216	EFATE	QUOIN HILL	SOPAC	1STLT T.H. FITZGIBBONS	D
01/25/44	17446	VMF-216	EFATE	QUOIN HILL	SOPAC		
01/25/44	55994	VMF-321	PIVA	RABAUL	SOPAC	1STLT W.H. BILLINGS	S
01/25/44	17833	VMF-422	TARAWA	FUNAFUTI	CENPAC	LT R.P. MORAN	D
01/25/44	17945	VMF-422	TARAWA	FUNAFUTI	CENPAC	MAJ J.S. MACLAUGHLIN	M
01/25/44	17990	VMF-422	TARAWA	FUNAFUTI	CENPAC	LT W.A. AYCRIGG	M
01/25/44	18015	VMF-422	TARAWA	FUNAFUTI	CENPAC	LT C.F. LAUESEN	M
01/25/44	18024	VMF-422	TARAWA	FUNAFUTI	CENPAC	CAPT J.F. ROGERS	M
01/25/44	18025	VMF-422	TARAWA	FUNAFUTI	CENPAC	LT E.C. THOMPSON	M
01/25/44	18054	VMF-422	TARAWA	FUNAFUTI	CENPAC	LT T.D. THURNAW	S
01/25/44	18075	VMF-422	TARAWA	FUNAFUTI	CENPAC	LT W.A. WILSON	S
01/25/44	18079	VMF-422	TARAWA	FUNAFUTI	CENPAC	CAPT C.R. JEANS	S
01/25/44	18116	VMF-422	TARAWA	FUNAFUTI	CENPAC	LT R.C. LEHNERT	S
01/25/44	55807	VMF-422	TARAWA	FUNAFUTI	CENPAC		
01/25/44	55817	VMF-422	TARAWA	FUNAFUTI	CENPAC		
01/25/44	55818	VMF-422	TARAWA	FUNAFUTI	CENPAC		
01/25/44	55825	VMF-422	TARAWA	FUNAFUTI	CENPAC		
01/25/44	55872	VMF-422	TARAWA	FUNAFUTI	CENPAC		
01/25/44	55883	VMF-422	TARAWA	FUNAFUTI	CENPAC		
01/25/44	55886	VMF-422	TARAWA	FUNAFUTI	CENPAC		
01/25/44	55892	VMF-422	TARAWA	FUNAFUTI	CENPAC		
01/25/44	55906	VMF-422	TARAWA	FUNAFUTI	CENPAC		
01/25/44	55913	VMF-422	TARAWA	FUNAFUTI	CENPAC		
01/26/44	17659	VF-17	PIVA	RABAUL	SOPAC	LTJG H.R. HOGAN	M
01/26/44	18061	VF-17	PIVA	RABAUL	SOPAC	ENS R.H. HILL	S
01/26/44	55822	VF-17	PIVA	RABAUL	SOPAC	LTJG J.W. FARLEY	M
01/26/44	2185	VMF-217		ESPIRITU SANTO	SOPAC	1STLT W.R. NOWADNICK	S
01/27/44	17676	VF-17	PIVA	RABAUL	SOPAC	LT T.R. BELL	M
01/27/44	17685	VF-17	PIVA	RABAUL	SOPAC	LTJG H.M. BURRISS	S
01/27/44	18064	VF-17	PIVA	RABAUL	SOPAC	ENS L.A. FITZGERALD	S
01/27/44	2470	VMF-321	PIVA	RABAUL	SOPAC	1STLT C.L. ASKEW	M
01/27/44	49974	VMF-321	PIVA	RABAUL	SOPAC	LT TAYLOR	S
01/28/44	17883	VMF-215	PIVA	RABAUL	SOPAC	CAPT D.N. ALDRICH	S
01/29/44	2432	VF(N)-75	TOROKINA	RABAUL	SOPAC		
01/29/44	17646	VMF-212	PIVA	RABAUL	SOPAC	1STLT J.B. DEVAUGHN	M
01/30/44	17666	VF-17	PIVA	RABAUL	SOPAC	LTJG T.F. KROPF	M
01/30/44	17668	VF-17	PIVA	RABAUL	SOPAC	LT S.R. BOACHAM	S
01/30/44	17684	VF-17	PIVA	BOUGAIN-VILLE	SOPAC	LTJG J.C. KOPFORD	S
01/30/44	17686	VF-17	PIVA	BOUGAIN-VILLE	SOPAC	ENS W.P. POPP	S
01/30/44	18070	VF-17	PIVA	BOUGAIN-VILLE	SOPAC	LT D.H. OUTENKUNST	D
01/30/44	55927	VMF-215	PIVA	RABAUL	SOPAC	1STLT J.J. FITZGERALD	M
01/30/44	55827	VMF-217	PIVA	RABAUL	SOPAC	LT RANAGAN	M
01/31/44	18005	VF-17	PIVA	RABAUL	SOPAC	LTJG H.M. BURRISS	M
01/31/44	2595	VMF-212	TOROKINA	RABAUL	SOPAC		
01/31/44	17875	VMF-212	PIVA	RABAUL	SOPAC	1STLT E.H. HUGHES	M
02/03/44	56039	VMF-215	PIVA	RABAUL	SOPAC	1STLT R.M. HANSON	M
02/03/44	18012	VMF-218	PIVA	RABAUL	SOPAC	1STLT J. HENABERY	M
02/03/44	55938	VMF-218	PIVA	RABAUL	SOPAC	1STLT E.C. MILLER	M
02/03/44	2540	VMF-321	EFATE	QUOIN HILL	SOPAC	2NDLT C.B. SELVEY	M
02/03/44	3840	VMF-321	EFATE	QUOIN HILL	SOPAC	2NDLT D.B. POLLOM	M
02/04/44	17949	VF-17	PIVA	RABAUL	SOPAC	ENS P.E. DIVENNEY	M
02/04/44	18057	VF-17	PIVA	RABAUL	SOPAC	LTJG D.T. MALONE	M
02/05/44	55916	VMF-218	PIVA	RABAUL	SOPAC	2NDLT R.S. THOMPSON	M
02/05/44	55982	VMF-218	PIVA	RABAUL	SOPAC		
02/09/44	17729	VMF-211			SOPAC		
02/09/44	2324	VMF-217	PIVA	RABAUL	SOPAC	2NDLT J. KING	M
02/09/44	2517	VMF-222	PIVA	RABAUL	SOPAC		
02/10/44	2566	VMF-218	PIVA	RABAUL	SOPAC	2NDLT J.G. MORRIS	S
02/10/44	2173	VMF-222	PIVA	RABAUL	SOPAC	1STLT J. CRAIG	D
02/11/44	55908	VMF-212	PIVA	RABAUL	SOPAC	1STLT A.S. HARRISON	M
02/12/44	17798	VMF-222	PIVA	RABAUL	SOPAC	1STLT C.P. LASSITER	M

DATE	BUNO	SQDRN	BASE	LOST	AREA	PILOT	FATE
02/13/44	2617	VMF(N)-532	TARAWA	MAKIN	CENPAC	LT R. PFIZENMAIER	S
02/13/44	18022	VMF-212	PIVA	RABAUL	SOPAC	1STLT N.L. NICCO	M
02/13/44	17590	VMF-223	PIVA	BOUGAIN-VILLE	SOPAC		
02/15/44	2350	VMF-217	PIVA	RABAUL	SOPAC	CAPT J.D. HENCH	S
02/16/44	17991	VMF-216	PIVA	RABAUL	SOPAC	CAPT A.H. PHARR	M
02/17/44	17680	VF-17	PIVA	KORAVIA	SOPAC	ENS C.H. DUNN	M
02/17/44	17692	VF-17	PIVA	KORAVIA	SOPAC	LTJG J. MILLER	M
02/19/44	17460	VMF-222	TOROKINA	RABAUL	SOPAC	1STLT R.A. SCHAEFFER	S
02/21/44	17879	VMF-216	PIVA	CAPE ST. GEO.	SOPAC	1STLT W.J. O'BRIEN	S
02/21/44	56132	VMF-218	TOROKINA	W OF TAIOF IS.	SOPAC	MAJ H.A. POHL	S
02/21/44	56155	VMF-223	PIVA	RABAUL	SOPAC	LT LIPOVSKY	S
02/22/44	49955	MAG-12		EFATE	SOPAC	2NDLT J.A. WOODBURN	M
02/22/44	2512	VMF-216	PIVA	BUKA	SOPAC		
02/23/44	2378	MAG-12	EFATE	ERROMANGA IS.	SOPAC	1STLT H.E. HARRIS	S
02/23/44	17433	MAG-21	EFATE	ERROMANGA IS.	SOPAC	2NDLT H.H. HARDIN	D
02/23/44	2632	VMF(N)-532		ROI	CENPAC	LT DOLHONDE	S
02/25/44	56084	VMF-223	PIVA	BUKA	SOPAC	MAJ H.E. STEWART	D
02/27/44	17904	VMF-114	KANEOHE	HAWAII	ECENPAC	1STLT R.G. SMITH	D
02/28/44	17725	VMF-225	EWA	WAIMEA	ECENPAC	1STLT J.H. BOYLAND	S
02/28/44	3826	VMF-422			CENPAC	1STLT T.D. THURNAW	D
02/29/44	17924	VMF-211			SOPAC		
02/29/44	18008	VMF-211			SOPAC		
02/29/44	56141	VMF-211			SOPAC		
02/29/44	55826	VMF-216	PIVA	BOUGAIN-VILLE	SOPAC		
03/02/44	55918	VMF-113	MAKIN	MAJURO	CENPAC	2NDLT C.B. PRATHER	D
03/06/44	2630	VF(N)-101	USS ENTER-PRISE	BARBERS POINT	ECENPAC	ENS C.B. TAYLOR	D
03/06/44	55823	VMF-113		ENGEBI	WCENPAC	1STLT L.R. JOHNSTON	S
03/07/44	56047	VMO-155		MIDWAY	ECENPAC		
03/08/44	17891	ARU SOLS	PIVA	TOROKINA	SOPAC		
03/08/44	56030	CASU(F)-12		GUAM	WCENPAC		
03/08/44	55897	VMF-223	PIVA	TOROKINA	SOPAC		
03/09/44	2479	VMF-212		EFATE	SOPAC	2NDLT R.L. ROUSH	D
03/09/44	2618	VMF-212		EFATE	SOPAC	2NDLT C.E. LONGSHORE	D
03/09/44	17558	VMF-311		KWAJALEIN	CENPAC		
03/09/44	17947	VMF-311		KWAJALEIN	CENPAC		
03/12/44	2574	VMF-217	TOROKINA	RABAUL	SOPAC	CAPT J.D. HENCH	M
03/14/44	18042	VMF-211			SOPAC		
03/14/44	2521	VMF-217	GREEN	CAPE ST. GEO.	SOPAC	1STLT L.E. RUSSELL	M
03/16/44	56000	VMF-216		BARAKOMA	SOPAC	LT R.H. PUTNAM	S
03/17/44	17874	VMF-217		CAPE ST GEO.	SOPAC	1STLT J.G. MARAIST	S
03/18/44	56212	VMF-222		DUKE OF YORK	SOPAC	LT R.Q. BEKINS	S
03/19/44	18046	VMF-223		GREEN	SOPAC	2NDLT E. SHOENING	D
03/20/44	17421	VMF-115		ESPIRITU SANTO	SOPAC	1STLT J.W. ALDRICH	D
03/22/44	56013	VMF-217	ESPIRITU SANTO	AOBA IS.	SOPAC	1STLT W.H. KOAR	S
03/25/44	17656	VMF-225		ESPIRITU SANTO	SOPAC		
03/26/44	17995	VMF-441	ROI	WOTJE	CENPAC	CAPT L.E. MIDKIFF	S
03/28/44	56022	VMF-211	GREEN	DUKE OF YORK	SOPAC	LT THOMAS	S
03/28/44	56139	VMF-211	GREEN	DUKE OF YORK	SOPAC	2NDLT T.C. CZARNOCKI	M
03/28/44	56401	VMF-211	GREEN	DUKE OF YORK	SOPAC	1STLT J.J. RELY	U
03/31/44	17836	VMO-155		MIDWAY	ECENPAC	1STLT H.E. HARVEY	S
04/01/44	18062	VMF-225		ESPIRITU SANTO	SOPAC	1STLT R.F. HARVEY	S
04/02/44	17873	VMF-114	GREEN	ST. GEORGE	SOPAC	CAPT J.K. CONGER	S
04/04/44	17926	VMF-311	ROI	WOTJE	CENPAC	1STLT R.A. HENENDORF	S
04/05/44	2195	VMF-321		BARAKOMA	SOPAC		
04/05/44	56209	VMF-322	FORD ISLAND	HAWAII	ECENPAC	LT D.B. HOUGE	S

DATE	BUNO	SQDRN	BASE	LOST	AREA	PILOT	FATE
04/05/44	56404	VMF-322	FORD ISLAND	HAWAII	ECENPAC	1STLT J.E. INGRUM	D
04/06/44	56148	VMO-155		MIDWAY	ECENPAC	1STLT S.L. LUTTON	S
04/07/44	56263	VMF-217		ESPIRITU SANTO	SOPAC	1STLT H.M. SHAFER	D
04/07/44	56334	VMF-217		ESPIRITU SANTO	SOPAC	2NDLT L.W. DECAMP	S
04/07/44	18056	VMF-422	ENIWETOK	PONAPE	CENPAC	1STLT W.T. REARDON	M
04/07/44	18113	VMF-422	ENIWETOK	PONAPE	CENPAC	1STLT D.K. SKILLIKORN	M
04/09/44	56194	VMF-114	GREEN	KAVIENG	SOPAC	1STLT L.V. STRANDTMAN	S
04/09/44	55986	VMO-155		MIDWAY	ECENPAC	1STLT J. JOHNSON	D
04/09/44	56258	VMO-155		MIDWAY	ECENPAC	MAJ J.E. REYNOLDS	S
04/11/44	56133	VMF-114	GREEN	RABAUL	SOPAC	CAPT C.M. FREEMAN	S
04/11/44	2222	VMF-321		BARAKOMA	SOPAC		
04/11/44	17919	VMF-321		BARAKOMA	SOPAC		
04/12/44	56364	VMF-222		TOROKINA	SOPAC		
04/13/44	55836	VMF-113	ENGEBI	PONAPE	CENPAC	MAJ W.M. WATKINS	S
04/13/44	55928	VMF-211	GREEN	MALAGUNA	SOPAC	STIGALL	S
04/14/44	56384	SERVRON-11		NEW HEBRIDES	SOPAC	2NDLT J.A. FOLEY	S
04/14/44	2624	VMF(N)-532	ENIWETOK	PONAPE	CENPAC	1STLT J.E. BONNER	S
04/14/44	2733	VMF(N)-532	ENIWETOK	PONAPE	CENPAC	1STLT D.W. SPATZ	M
04/14/44	18060	VMF-215	PIVA	PIVA	SOPAC	T/SGT H. MICLALSKI	S
04/14/44	17817	VMF-441	ROI	WOTJE	CENPAC	1STLT J.A. MITCHELL	S
04/17/44	18066	VMF-212		GREEN	SOPAC		
04/18/44	56090	VMF-215	PIVA	HAHELA	SOPAC	1STLT J.K. BURKE	D
04/18/44	56227	VMF-215	PIVA	HAHELA	SOPAC		
04/23/44	18077	VMF-114	GREEN	NEW IRELAND	SOPAC	1STLT W.P. TALEP	M
04/23/44	56093	VMF-215	PIVA	NAMATANAI	SOPAC	1STLT E.B. COCHRAN	S
04/23/44	17497	VMF-311		KWAJALEIN	CENPAC	1STLT F.C. HAWKES	D
04/25/44	55934	VMF-211		NEW IRELAND	SW PAC	MURTO	S
04/26/44	56040	VMF-215	PIVA		SOPAC	2NDLT M.G. HARRELL	D
04/28/44	49666	VMF-312	EWA	HAWAII	ECENPAC	2NDLT H.L. MARSH	S
04/30/44	17398	VF(N)-75		TOROKINA	SOPAC		
04/30/44	56036	VMF-114	GREEN	RABAUL	SOPAC	1STLT J.L. PARMALEE	M
04/30/44	56274	VMF-114	GREEN	RABAUL	SOPAC	1STLT W.H. HOBBS	M
04/30/44	2392	VMF-215	PIVA	RABAUL	SOPAC		
04/30/44	56012	VMF-223		EFATE	SOPAC		
04/30/44	56162	VMF-223		EFATE	SOPAC		
05/01/44	49800	VMF-114	GREEN	RABAUL	SOPAC	1STLT G.J. SMITH	D
05/01/44	56215	VMF-223			SOPAC		
05/03/44	56142	VMF-223			SOPAC		
05/04/44	49699	HEDRON-32	EWA	HAWAII	ECENPAC	1STLT R.N. CONWELL	D
05/04/44	2295	VMF-114	GREEN	KAVIENG	SOPAC	1STLT RICHARD S. RASH	S
05/04/44	56074	VMF-215	PIVA	RABAUL	SOPAC	1STLT R.C. GRAY	S
05/04/44	56269	VMF-223			SOPAC		
05/04/44	18069	VMF-225		ESPIRITU SANTO	SOPAC		
05/05/44	56377	VMF-313		MIDWAY	ECENPAC	2NDLT C. SANDONE	S
05/05/44	2270	VMF-321		EFATE	SOPAC	2NDLT VITTITOE	S
05/05/44	49935	VMF-422		ROI	CENPAC	2NDLT T.W. SCHROEDER	S
05/06/44	49712	MAG-14	GREEN	GREEN	SOPAC		
05/10/44	17932	VMF-225		ESPIRITU SANTO	SOPAC		
05/12/44	55799	VMF-223	GREEN	CAPE LAMBERT	SOPAC	1STLT R.P. MUMME	M
05/13/44	50055	SERVRON-11		ESPIRITU SANTO	SOPAC	1STLT A.M. PAPPAS	M
05/14/44	56400	VMF-218		GREEN	SOPAC		
05/17/44	2710	VF(N)-101	USS ENTER-PRISE	BARBERS POINT	ECENPAC		
05/17/44	56076	VMF-211	ESPIRITU SANTO	AOBA IS.	SOPAC	2NDLT J.E. DATE	S
05/19/44	17782	VMF-312	EWA	HAWAII	ECENPAC	2NDLT R.H. SCHANNAMANN	S
05/19/44	17816	VMF-312	EWA	HAWAII	ECENPAC	2NDLT G.A. HARTIG	M
05/20/44	49828	VMF-218	GREEN	DUKE OF YORK	SOPAC	2NDLT L.J. PILLIOD	D
05/20/44	56104	VMF-222	TOROKINA	KAVIENG	SOPAC		

DATE	BUNO	SQDRN	BASE	LOST	AREA	PILOT	FATE
05/20/44	49822	VMF-225	ESPIRITU SANTO	SAKAW IS.	SOPAC	1STLT B.H. WALLACE	S
05/20/44	49894	VMF-225	ESPIRITU SANTO	SAKAW IS.	SOPAC	2NDLT B.B. DODGE	D
05/22/44	2709	VF(N)-101		ROI	CENPAC		
05/22/44	56395	VMF-115	EMIRAU	NEW IRELAND	SOPAC	LT P.M. HALL, JR.	M
05/22/44	56138	VMF-222	TOROKINA	NEW IRELAND	SOPAC		
05/22/44	17566	VMF-441	ROI	WOTJE	CENPAC	1STLT H. PICKERING	S
05/23/44	56273	VMF-222		EMIRAU	SW PAC		
05/23/44	56240	VMF-223	GREEN	RABAUL	SOPAC	1STLT J.W. LIZER	D
05/24/44	56326	VMF-115		EMIRAU	SW PAC	LT K.L. MYERS	D
05/25/44	17783	VMF-441	ROI	WOTJE	CENPAC	1STLT R.K. MCALLISTER	D
05/26/44	56302	VMF-224	ROI	WOTJE	CENPAC	1STLT V.A. DEMPSEY	S
05/26/44	49988	VMF-311	ROI	WOTJE	CENPAC	1STLT G.W. KIEMER	D
05/27/44	56160	VMO-155		MIDWAY	ECENPAC	CAPT M.E. DANITSCHER	S
05/28/44	18115	VMF-111	MAKIN	MAJURO	CENPAC	2NDLT J.E. THELAN	D
05/28/44	55803	VMF-111	MAKIN	MAJURO	CENPAC	CAPT A.M. BLACKMAN	D
05/29/44	56023	VMF-223	GUADAL-CANAL	GUADAL-CANAL	SOPAC	1STLT C.F. INMAN	M
05/31/44	49829	VMF-114	ESPIRITU SANTO	CUMBERLAND PT	SOPAC	2NDLT F.H. OLMSTEAD	M
06/01/44	17418	VMF(N)-532		ENGEBI	WCENPAC		
06/01/44	49939	VMF-321		EFATE	SOPAC	LT J.P. ADAMS	S
06/05/44	56130	VMF-114		ESPIRITU SANTO	SOPAC		
06/05/44	2228	VMF-124		ESPIRITU SANTO	SOPAC	1STLT L.V. STRANDTMAN	S
06/06/44	56298	VMO-251	ESPIRITU SANTO	GUADAL-CANAL	SOPAC	2NDLT M.D. HATHAWAY	D
06/07/44	49950	VMF-111	MAKIN	MILLE	CENPAC	2NDLT T.W. KESSLER	S
06/07/44	17402	VMF-114	ESPIRITU SANTO	TURTLE BAY	SOPAC	1STLT S.R. WESSMAN	D
06/08/44	49675	VMF-312	BARBERS POINT	HAWAII	ECENPAC	CAPT F.A. BEAVERS	D
06/08/44	55910	VMF-312	BARBERS POINT	HAWAII	ECENPAC	2NDLT R.J. DEVINE	D
06/08/44	17549	VMF-441	ROI	MALOELAP	CENPAC	2NDLT J.M. GLOVER	M
06/08/44	17790	VMF-441	ROI	MALOELAP	CENPAC	2NDLT T. WYATT	S
06/11/44	55830	VMF-113		ENGEBI	WCENPAC	1STLT J.E. ZOELLNER	S
06/11/44	56159	VMF-212	GREEN	RABAUL	SOPAC	2NDLT W.E. GRAY	D
06/15/44	56380	VMF-224	ROI	WOTJE	CENPAC	CAPT TUCKER	S
06/16/44	56332	VMF-223	GREEN	RABAUL	SOPAC	2NDLT L.W. PINGREE	D
06/16/44	56004	VMF-224		KWAJALEIN	CENPAC	LT ATTEBERY	S
06/16/44	49700	VMF-313		MIDWAY	ECENPAC	2NDLT W.E. GARRETT	S
06/17/44	55971	VMF-215		EMIRAU	SW PAC		
06/19/44	56137	VMF-223	GREEN	RABAUL	SOPAC	1STLT J.N. GLENN	D
06/20/44	18120	VMF-111	MAKIN	MILLE	CENPAC	1STLT W.F. PIMLOTT	M
06/24/44	50163	VMF-113	ROI	WOTJE	CENPAC		
06/24/44	49880	VMF-441	ROI	WOTJE	CENPAC	1STLT J.M. NOLAN	D
06/26/44	55936	VMF-211	EMIRAU	KAVIENG	SOPAC	2NDLT C.H. SLATON	S
06/27/44	55866	VMF-113	ROI	WOTJE	CENPAC	CAPT G.H. FRANCK	S
06/27/44	55998	VMF-113	ROI	WOTJE	CENPAC	LT R.H. ZEHNER	D
06/27/44	49692	VMF-215		EMIRAU	SW PAC	MAJ JOHNS	S
06/29/44	56390	VMF-211	EMIRAU	RABAUL	SOPAC	LT FERREE	S
06/29/44	56083	VMF-311	ROI	WOTJE	CENPAC		
06/29/44	49734	VMF-441	ROI	WOTJE	CENPAC		
06/30/44	56190	VMF-222	BOUGAIN-VILLE	BUKA	SOPAC	1STLT D.J. SCHOETZ	S
07/01/44	56018	VMF-314			CENPAC	2NDLT D.W. BAIRD	D
07/02/44	56112	VMO-251	PIVA		SW PAC	LT L.L. NEAL	S
07/03/44	56010	VMF-314		HAWAII	ECENPAC	2NDLT R.H. BURRUS	S
07/05/44	50169	VF-302		ESPIRITU SANTO	SOPAC		
07/06/44	49704	VMF-212	GREEN	RABAUL	SOPAC		
07/07/44	18055	VMF-111	MILLE	MILLE	CENPAC	1STLT HOWARD T. BURNS	D
07/07/44	50056	VMF-422	ENGEBI	WOTJE	CENPAC	1STLT D.H. STOUT	M
07/08/44	49660	VMF-211	EMIRAU	NEW BRITAIN	SOPAC	LT D.S. BISHOP	M
07/09/44	56236	VMF-215		EMIRAU	SW PAC	2NDLT TAYLOR	S
07/10/44	49819	VMO-155		TARAWA	CENPAC	1STLT MILES F. GOODMAN	D
07/11/44	17786	VMF-441	ROI	WOTJE	CENPAC		
07/12/44	56239	VMF-311	ROI	WOTJE	CENPAC	CAPT M.J. CURRAN	S
07/13/44	49693	VMF-212	GREEN	RABAUL	SOPAC		
07/17/44	56001	VMF-113	ROI	WOTJE	CENPAC		

DATE	BUNO	SQDRN	BASE	LOST	AREA	PILOT	FATE
07/17/44	56094	VMF-222		ESPIRITU SANTO	SOPAC		
07/18/44	2641	VMF(N)-532			CENPAC		
07/18/44	49924	VMF-113	ROI	TAROA	CENPAC	2NDLT G.H. WERTS	M
07/18/44	49997	VMF-113	ROI	TAROA	CENPAC	MAJ R.B. ERSKINE	M
07/18/44	55973	VMF-113	ROI	TAROA	CENPAC	1STLT L.W. JOHNSTON	M
07/22/44	50014	VMO-251		NEW IRELAND	SW PAC	1STLT R.F. SPRENGER	M
07/22/44	56163	VMO-251		NEW IRELAND	SW PAC	2NDLT R.C. HOLIDAY	S
07/23/44	50191	VMF-218		GREEN	SOPAC		
07/25/44	56201	VMF-211	EMIRAU	RABAUL	SOPAC	LT FERGUSON	S
07/26/44	17913	VMF-441		KWAJALEIN	CENPAC	1STLT J.W. ROBINSON	D
07/30/44	49836	VMF-311	ROI	WOTJE	CENPAC	CAPT M.J. CURRAN	D
08/01/44	49689	VMF-314		MIDWAY	ECENPAC	LT FURMAN H. KELLER	S
08/03/44	56151	VMO-251	COMAIRNO SOLS	CAPE ST. GEO.	SOPAC	1STLT ORVILLE F. LORCH	M
08/04/44	17781	VMF-422		ENIWETOK	CENPAC	2NDLT R.V. SCHROEDER	D
08/06/44	50047	VMF-323	EWA	HAWAII	ECENPAC	2NDLT G.B. SMITH	D
08/06/44	49902	VMF-441		KWAJALEIN	CENPAC	2NDLT ELMO D. CONE	D
08/07/44	56157	VMF-223		BOUGAIN-VILLE	SOPAC		
08/09/44	49766	VMO-251		BUKA	SW PAC	1STLT F.C. JENNINGS	S
08/11/44	18080	VMF-422		ENIWETOK	CENPAC	LT E.E. WOLVERTON	D
08/11/44	56417	VMO-251		CAPE LAMBERT	SW PAC	LT D.J. SCHOLTZ	S
08/15/44	2199	VMF-223	KIELA	PIVA	SOPAC		
08/18/44	50288	VMF-115	EMIRAU	VUNAKANAU	SW PAC		
08/18/44	49817	VMF-218		GREEN	SOPAC		
08/18/44	56355	VMF-224		ENIWETOK	CENPAC		
08/18/44	56410	VMO-251	PIVA	RABAUL	SOPAC	LT JOHN MCMASTERS	S
08/19/44	55977	VMF-211		EMIRAU	SW PAC	LT S.A. GRUNLAND	M
08/19/44	55814	VMF-422		ENIWETOK	CENPAC	1STLT D.A. DAHLQUIST	D
08/20/44	56113	VMF-224		MARSHALLS	CENPAC		
08/23/44	56025	VMF-441	MAJURO	MILLE	CENPAC	2NDLT KARL B. CHAMBERS	S
08/24/44	56407	VMF-215		EMIRAU	SW PAC	LT H.C. MCGREW	S
08/29/44	50184	VMF-111	MILLE	MILLE	CENPAC	1STLT J.F. MOORE, JR.	S
08/31/44	2434	VF(N)-75			SOPAC		
08/31/44	2436	VF(N)-75			SOPAC		
08/31/44	2441	VF(N)-75			SOPAC		
08/31/44	2681	VF(N)-75			SOPAC		
08/31/44	56261	VMO-251		NEW BRITAIN	SW PAC	1STLT J.A. FOLEY	D
09/01/44	56394	VMF-222		GREEN	SOPAC	1STLT ROBERT L. GILLESPIE	U
09/02/44	49858	VMF(N)-532		SAIPAN	CENPAC	CAPT R. PFIZENMAIER	S
09/03/44	56260	VMF-215		KAVIENG	SW PAC	LT A. PATET, JR.	M
09/03/44	56373	VMF-215		KAVIENG	SW PAC	LT A. POHLMAN	S
09/03/44	56099	VMO-251		RATAVAL	SW PAC	LT FLICKINGER	S
09/04/44	49776	VMF-441		ROI	CENPAC	1STLT FRANK L. MOISTER	S
09/05/44	56323	VMF-215		EMIRAU	SW PAC	LT GAY	U
09/06/44	56096	VMF-212		GREEN	SOPAC	2NDLT LUTHER L. PARKER	S
09/06/44	55837	VMF-223		BOUGAIN-VILLE	SOPAC	2NDLT HADLEY W. BAKER	M
09/07/44	55787	VMF-212		GUADAL-CANAL	SOPAC	LT M.H. THOMPSON	S
09/08/44	49980	VMF-111	MAKIN	MAKIN	CENPAC		
09/11/44	2692	VMF(N)-532		SAIPAN	CENPAC		
09/12/44	56372	VMF-115		NEW BRITAIN	SW PAC	LT R.J. LARSEN	S
09/12/44	56344	VMF-212		BOUGAIN-VILLE	SOPAC	LT M.H. THOMPSON	S
09/12/44	50157	VMO-251		CAPE GAZELLE	SW PAC	1STLT MAC K. ROBINSON	M
09/14/44	18036	VMF-212		TOROKINA	SOPAC	LT D.J. ARONA	S
09/15/44	49929	VMF-212		BOUGAIN-VILLE	SOPAC	2NDLT JAMES LAGGREN	D
09/16/44	50198	VMF-218		GREEN	SOPAC	LT W.D. MAYO	S
09/17/44	56045	VMF-218		GREEN	SOPAC	LT ROSENBLOOM	D
09/21/44	50202	CASU-30		MAJURO	CENPAC		
09/21/44	56229	MAG-21	OROTE FIELD	GUAM	WCENPAC		
09/24/44	17749	VMF-218		RABAUL	SW PAC	LT HERMAN	M
09/25/44	56327	VMF-313		EMIRAU	SW PAC	CAPT MARTIN D. LANE	S
09/29/44	49820	VMF-115		NEW IRELAND	SW PAC	1STLT P.K. MCKINNEY	S

DATE	BUNO	SQDRN	BASE	LOST	AREA	PILOT	FATE
09/29/44	50174	VMF-223		BOUGAIN-VILLE	SOPAC	MAJ MARION MARCH	S
09/30/44	49844	VMF-218		GREEN	SOPAC	LT G.H. JOHNSON	S
10/05/44	50057	VMF-115		EMIRAU	SW PAC	LT AUGUST DANNEHL	S
10/07/44	49884	VMF-115		NEW IRELAND	SW PAC		
10/07/44	49685	VMF-124		HAWAII	ECENPAC	LT ROLAND HIGGINS	S
10/08/44	50171	VMF-111	MAKIN	MAKIN	CENPAC		
10/08/44	56095	VMF-224		JALUIT	CENPAC	MAJ B.S. CLUZON	M
10/08/44	49780	VMF-225		GUAM	WCENPAC	LT J.M. NOARHOOD	D
10/08/44	56305	VMO-251		NEW BRITAIN	SW PAC	LT DAIGLE	S
10/09/44	49809	VMF-441		ROI	CENPAC	LT JAMES M. VREELAND	U
10/10/44	49677	VMF-124		HAWAII	ECENPAC	LT RICHARD F. STROM	U
10/12/44	49933	VMF-217		GUAM	WCENPAC	LT PHILLIP R. HAMMOND	S
10/19/44	56031	VMF-224		ROI	CENPAC	LT R.E. LORGERSON	S
10/21/44	49743	VMF-441		ROI	CENPAC	LT ROBERTSON ROSS	S
10/23/44	55923	CASU-39	ESPIRITU SANTO	ESPIRITU SANTO	SOPAC	ENS ARNOLD MILLER	S
10/23/44	56126	VMF-314		MIDWAY	ECENPAC	CAPT R.S. GREENWOOD, JR.	S
10/24/44	50207	VMF-111	MAKIN	JALUIT	CENPAC	2NDLT D.L. KNUTSON	S
10/26/44	50052	VMF-222	GREEN	RABAUL	SOPAC	2NDLT L.C. WILDER	U
10/31/44	49982	VMF-311		EMIDJ	SW PAC	LT FRANK T. SWEENEY	M
11/05/44	49778	VMF-224	ROI	JALUIT	CENPAC	LT FRANCIS M. FOX	S
11/08/44	49671	VMF-111		KWAJALEIN	CENPAC		
11/08/44	49721	VMF-213	EWA	HAWAII	ECENPAC	LT GEORGE S. KELLER	D
11/08/44	49833	VMF-321		GUAM	WCENPAC		
11/09/44	49762	VMF-115		EMIRAU	SW PAC		
11/09/44	49854	VMF-311		ROI	CENPAC	CAPT J.W. BLAKENEY	S
11/10/44	56353	VMF-212		TOROKINA	SOPAC		
11/13/44	56374	VMF-224		ROI	CENPAC		
11/13/44	49899	VMF-225		GUAM	WCENPAC	LT J.C. BUTLER	D
11/15/44	56375	NACTU	BARBERS POINT	HAWAII	ECENPAC	ENS ROBERT A. DAVIS	S
11/19/44	50194	VMF-212		BUKA	SW PAC	LT KELLEHER	S
11/21/44	56278	CASU(F)-39		NEW HEBRIDES	SOPAC	2NDLT WILEY F. GOFF	S
11/22/44	50176	VMF-114		YAP	ECENPAC	LT ROBERT W. SPAIN	D
11/25/44	50192	VMF-225		GUAM	WCENPAC	LT WILLIAM J. GILL	M
12/01/44	50050	VMF-218		HOLLANDIA	SW PAC		
12/04/44	49733	VMF-216		GUAM	WCENPAC		
12/04/44	49919	VMF-225		GUAM	WCENPAC		
12/06/44	50025	VMF-115		LEYTE GULF	PHIL		
12/09/44	49906	VMF-217		GUAM	WCENPAC		
12/11/44	50212	VMF-115		LEYTE GULF	PHIL	2NDLT WILLIAM J. RAINALTER	S
12/11/44	50187	VMF-218		LEYTE GULF	PHIL	2NDLT W.D. BEAN	S
12/20/44	50150	VMF-225		GUAM	WCENPAC		
12/22/44	50027	SERVRON-22		ENGEBI	WCENPAC		
12/22/44	50214	VMF-218		LEYTE GULF	PHIL		
01/01/45	50001	MAG-12		ZAMBOAN-GA	PHIL		
01/03/45	49741	VMF-111	ROI	ROI	WCENPAC		
01/03/45	49888	VMF-111		KWAJALEIN	CENPAC		
01/03/45	49881	VMF-115		LEYTE GULF	PHIL	1STLT J. HARRISON	S
01/03/45	49802	VMF-223		TOROKINA	SOPAC		
01/06/45	50190	VMF-115		LEYTE GULF	PHIL	BLANCHARD	S
01/06/45	49893	VMF-212		GREEN	SOPAC		
01/11/45	56019	VMF-212		GREEN	SOPAC		
01/13/45	50180	VMF-223		SAMAR	PHIL	2NDLT THOMAS G. LOVETT	S
01/18/45	49825	SERVRON-1		PELELIU	WCENPAC		
01/20/45	50151	VMF-218		LEYTE GULF	PHIL		
01/21/45	50153	VMF-222		SAMAR	PHIL	2NDLT KEN A. VERMILLION	S
01/27/45	49765	VMF-212		SAMAR	PHIL	LT LEO MARTIN	M
01/29/45	49857	VBF-86	USS BATAAN	HAWAII	ECENPAC	LTJG EDWARD J. RUANE	S
01/30/45	49910	A.A.	PEARL	HAWAII	ECENPAC		
01/30/45	49995	A.A.	PEARL	HAWAII	ECENPAC		
01/30/45	56381	A.A.	PEARL	HAWAII	ECENPAC		
01/30/45	56399	A.A.	PEARL	HAWAII	ECENPAC		
01/30/45	49742	CASU-4	PUUNENE	HAWAII	ECENPAC	ENS GEORGE J. HONNIGAN	S

DATE	BUNO	SQDRN	BASE	LOST	AREA	PILOT	FATE
01/31/45	55874	POOL	BARBERS POINT	HAWAII	ECENPAC		
02/01/45	49812	A.A.	PEARL	HAWAII	ECENPAC		
02/01/45	56196	VBF-86	HAWAII	HAWAII	ECENPAC	ENS WALTER STEPAHIN	D
02/10/45	49951	A.A.	PEARL	HAWAII	ECENPAC		
02/10/45	50189	VMF-218		LEYTE GULF	PHIL		
02/12/45	56333	VBF-100	OAHU	HAWAII	ECENPAC	ENS DONALD LANNING	S
02/17/45	49785	VMF-212		SAMAR	PHIL	2NDLT EVERETT A. JONES	S
02/19/45	50228	VMF-212		SAMAR	PHIL	LT D.F. DOYLE	D
02/20/45	50197	VMF-222		SAMAR	PHIL		
02/20/45	50201	VMF-222		SAMAR	PHIL		
02/20/45	50183	VMF-223		SAMAR	PHIL		
02/21/45	49983	VMF-212		SAMAR	PHIL		
02/21/45	56238	VMF-212		SAMAR	PHIL		
02/23/45	50037	CASU-43		GUAM	WCENPAC	R.L. BURNETT	D
02/23/45	49684	VMF-213	EWA	HAWAII	ECENPAC	2NDLT R.L. HAXTHAUSEN	D
02/23/45	49870	VMF-222		SAMAR	PHIL		
02/25/45	49883	VMF-115		LEYTE GULF	PHIL		
02/28/45	49973	VMB-423		GREEN	SOPAC		
03/04/45	49998	VBF-88	USS SHANGRI-LA	HAWAII	ECENPAC		
03/06/45	49801	VMF-225	GUAM		WCENPAC	2NDLT WALTER PANCHISON	S
03/10/45	49920	VMF-114		PELELIU	WCENPAC	1STLT WILLIAM P. ELZEY, JR.	S
03/13/45	49942	VMF-121		PELELIU	WCENPAC	2NDLT THOMAS R. O'BOYLE	D
03/15/45	56100	MAG-13		MAJURO	CENPAC	1STLT E.M. HERRIN	S
03/18/45	49898	VBF-100		HAWAII	ECENPAC		
03/21/45	49986	COMAIR-PAC	PEARL	HAWAII	ECENPAC		
03/24/45	49813	VMF-225		GUAM	WCENPAC		
03/29/45	49663	VBF-88	USS SHIP-LEY BAY	HAWAII	ECENPAC	ENS J.W. HINKLE	U
03/31/45	49736	VMF-114		PELELIU	WCENPAC		
04/04/45	50006	VMF-114		PELELIU	WCENPAC	LT MANTEL	S
04/07/45	49889	POOL	KANEOHE	HAWAII	ECENPAC		
04/07/45	50179	VBF-100		HAWAII	ECENPAC	LTJG FRANK MYERS, JR.	S
04/16/45	50307	VMF-441		OKINAWA	EMPIRE	2NDLT LARRY G. FRIESS	D
04/17/45	49668	VMF-215	EWA	HAWAII	ECENPAC	2NDLT WILLIAM H. HOLDEN	S
04/20/45	49702	VBF-100		HAWAII	ECENPAC		
04/22/45	56277	VMF-215	EWA	HAWAII	ECENPAC	ENS FRANK J. O'MALLEY	S
04/27/45	49904	VBF-100		HAWAII	ECENPAC	ENS CARROLL A. BERG	S
04/30/45	55987	POOL	PEARL	HAWAII	ECENPAC		
05/07/45	49934	CASU(F)-12	USS WINDHAM BAY	GUAM	WCENPAC		
05/21/45	50015	AROU-1		MOMOTE	SW PAC		
05/21/45	50016	AROU-1		MOMOTE	SW PAC		
05/21/45	50035	AROU-1		MOMOTE	SW PAC		
05/21/45	50068	AROU-1		MOMOTE	SW PAC		
05/21/45	50208	AROU-1		MOMOTE	SW PAC		
05/27/45	50059	VBF-99	USS MAKASSAR ST.	SAIPAN	WCENPAC		
05/31/45	50036	COMAIR-PAC	PEARL	HAWAII	ECENPAC		
05/31/45	50026	MAG-21	OROTE FIELD	GUAM	WCENPAC	2NDLT BRUCE R. BADENOCH	S
06/01/45	49949	VBF-2	USS TRIPOLI	PEARL	ECENPAC	LCDR ALBERT W. NEWHALL	S
06/02/45	49834	VBF-2	USS TRIPOLI	HILO	ECENPAC	ENS JOHN R. GRIEBEL	S
06/06/45	49698	CASU(F)-15		SAIPAN	WCENPAC		
06/09/45	49687	VBF-92	USS HANCOCK	PEARL	ECENPAC	ENS ROBERT PROPAK	S
06/12/45	49953	CASU(F)-47		SAIPAN	WCENPAC		

DATE	BUNO	SQDRN	BASE	LOST	AREA	PILOT	FATE
06/14/45	50278	VMF-115	ZAMBOAN-GA	ZAMBOANGA	PHIL		
06/16/45	56267	CASU(F)-20		ROI	WCENPAC		
06/28/45	49938	VBF-100	HILO	HAWAII	ECENPAC	ENS CHARLES S. NICKERSON	S
07/11/45	56189	VBF-14	PEARL	HAWAII	ECENPAC	LT W.J. BROWN	S
07/13/45	49948	POOL	PEARL	HAWAII	ECENPAC		
07/19/45	49711	POOL	BARBERS POINT	HAWAII	ECENPAC		
07/30/45	56143	VBF-100		HAWAII	ECENPAC	ENS MARTIN T. GILL	D

VOUGHT F4U-1D

Of the numerous changes implemented to the F4U-1 (in what would be designated the F4U-1D) the most evident was a substantial increase in firepower. The aircraft's ordinance load-out was upgraded by deleting the centerline rack and the addition of pylons to the anhedral portion of the wings for loads of up to one 1000lb bomb each or a 150-gallon drop tank, and the inclusion of tabs on the wings for eight 5" HVAR rockets (four on each side). The outer pair of machine guns was also increased to 400 rounds per gun, compared to 375 in the -1 and -1A, for a total of 2400 rounds for the Brownings. Toward the end of the war the centerline bomb rack was re-added and strengthened, allowing the aircraft to carry up to a 2000lb bomb in this position or another drop tank. The F4U-1D could also carry two of the massive 11.75" "Tiny Tim" rockets on the main pylons. Depending on configuration, the Corsair could carry up to 4000lbs of bombs in addition to rockets, however, such a configuration was too heavy for carrier operations, and was generally only used when the aircraft was operating from land bases.

This overwhelming firepower made the F4U-1D the Navy and Marine Corps' primary ground attack aircraft from the end of 1944 through the end of the war. Her armament was almost on par with that of the Navy's SB2C Helldiver and TBM Avenger, with the performance to handle enemy fighters. As with earlier models, the -1D's landing gear possessed a dive brake setting, which could be used to control the fighter's airspeed during attack dives. The Corsair's durability also greatly contributed to her success in the attack role.

The F4U-1D made further improvements in addition to the increased ground-attack capability. Early -1Ds retained the partially-framed canopy of the -1A, however this was quickly replaced with a bubble canopy that eliminated these frames entirely. Most -1Ds retained the metal "hood" above the pilot's head but this was also eventually omitted in later -1Ds. Additional controls on top of the dash were added for the handling of the aircraft's ordinance. Some of the fabric covering on the underside of the wings was replaced by metal plate. The wing-mounted fuel tanks were eliminated entirely. Slightly heavier than the -1A, the main pylons on the anhedral of the wing inboard of the landing gear struts were permanently fixed, even when the aircraft was flying clean. As a result the -1D's top speed was reduced, but still exceeded 400mph at altitude.

Marine Corps squadrons in the Pacific began receiving the F4U-1D in late 1944, operating from land bases throughout the South and Central Pacific. Additionally, for the first time Corsairs began to be deployed aboard carriers with US Navy squadrons in numbers, supplementing the Hellcats, Helldivers and Avengers already in service aboard the flattops. The -1D provided a superb ground attack platform with its heavy ordinance loadout, and still retained its capability to take on enemy aircraft.

Marine squadrons to use the -1D included VMF-312; the famed Checkerboarders with their distinctive checkered cowls and tails, VMF-251; formerly an observation squadron flying F4F-3P and F4U-1As, VMF-323 Deathrattlers and VMF-224.

One squadron of note to fly the F4U-1D was VMF-512, a unit undergoing special training with the massive "Tiny Tim" 11.75" rocket (essentially a 500lb naval shell with a rocket engine strapped to it). Their target was the German V-1 launch sites in Europe, intending to use the range of the Tiny Tims to stay clear of German anti-aircraft fire, and take advantage of its high destructive power to obliterate the sites. However, General George C. Marshall, upon hearing the plan, would not listen any further once he learned the attack would be carried out by Marines, and is famously attributed with refusing to "allow Jarheads to fly in my war."

In addition to its ubiquitous use among the Marines, for the first time the Corsair began to deploy in large numbers among Navy squadrons. The most notable, perhaps, was VF-84 under Roger Hendrick. The squadron flew off USS BUNKER HILL Including Hendrick, much of the core of the squadron was made up of veterans of VF-17, however despite being spiritual successors to the Jolly Rogers, they were denied use of the name by the Navy. F4U-1Ds were also assigned to VBF-85 assigned to USS SHANGRI-LA and VF-10 off USS ENTERPRISE.

The F4U-1D became the main Corsair variant fielded by the USN and USMC until the end of the war. The F4U-1D saw combat at most major engagements in the final year of combat, including Iwo Jima and Okinawa, and was used to strike ground targets and enemy shipping throughout the Pacific on the final drive towards Japan. Additionally, F4U-1Ds of VMF-224 flew in the last major dogfights of the war for the Marines, when eight Corsairs encountered estimates of up to 80 N1K2-J Shiden-kai of the elite 343rd Kokutai over Kyushu (information from Wikipedia). Aircraft lost:

DATE	BUNO	SQDRN	BASE	LOST	AREA	PILOT	FATE
12/25/43	57464	VMF-223	VELLA LAVELLA	RABAUL	SOPAC	1STLT B.E. SAHL	M
09/18/44	57365	VMF-323		EMIRAU	SW PAC	1STLT GERALD E. BAKER	D
10/11/44	50392	VMO-155	MAJURO	MAJURO	CENPAC	MAJ F.S. HOFFECKER	S
10/25/44	57386	VMBF-331	MIDWAY	MIDWAY	ECENPAC	MAJ JOSEPH A. GRAY	S
10/29/44	50644	VMO-251		RABAUL	SW PAC	LT ARCHIBALD A. HARRIS	S
11/04/44	50511	VMO-155		KWAJALEIN	CENPAC		
11/05/44	57167	MAG-31		ROI	WCENPAC	CAPT FRANK MICK	S
11/05/44	50498	VMF-441	ROI	WOTJE	CENPAC	LT RICHARD STEVENSON	S
11/08/44	50427	VMF-213	EWA	HAWAII	ECENPAC	LT JOHN R. JOHNSON	D
11/11/44	57637	VF-85	USS LUNGA POINT	LEYTE GULF	PHIL		
11/14/44	57778	VMF-213	EWA	HAWAII	ECENPAC		
11/18/44	50508	VMF-113		ENGEBI	WCENPAC		
11/22/44	57439	VMBF-333	HAWAII	HAWAII	ECENPAC	LT RAY H. JOLLY	D
11/24/44	57575	VMF-213	EWA	HAWAII	ECENPAC	LT VICTOR K. RUSLING	S
11/27/44	50642	MAG-31		ROI	WCENPAC	LT PHILLIP E. CONROY, JR.	S
11/29/44	50514	VMBF-231	MAJURO	MAJURO	CENPAC	JOHN D. HARVLEY, JR.	M
12/01/44	57540	VMF-122		PALAU	WCENPAC	1STLT RICHARD C. ALLISON	D
12/04/44	57174	VMF-224		ROI	CENPAC	2NDLT RUSSELL TORGERSON	S
12/04/44	57333	VMF-323		ESPIRITU SANTO	SOPAC	2NDLT KEITH W. FOUNTAIN	S
12/04/44	50394	VMF-422		ENIWETOK	CENPAC	2NDLT ARTHUR WAGNER	S
12/05/44	57490	VMF-211		LEYTE GULF	PHIL	LT JEROME G. BOHLAND	D

DATE	BUNO	SQDRN	BASE	LOST	AREA	PILOT	FATE
12/07/44	57484	VMF-211		LEYTE GULF	PHIL	LT CATLIN	S
12/07/44	57510	VMF-211		LEYTE GULF	PHIL	LT ALLEN	S
12/07/44	57527	VMF-211		LEYTE GULF	PHIL		
12/07/44	57532	VMF-211		LEYTE GULF	PHIL	LT LOUIS W. REISNERS	M
12/07/44	57609	VMF-211		LEYTE GULF	PHIL	MAJ WITOMSKI	S
12/11/44	57502	VMF-211		LEYTE GULF	PHIL	1STLT HARRY O'HARA	M
12/11/44	57525	VMF-211		LEYTE GULF	PHIL	2NDLT STANLEY PICAK	M
12/12/44	57519	VMF-211		LEYTE GULF	PHIL	LT DUNK	S
12/12/44	57196	VMF-321		GUAM	WCENPAC	MAJ LEWIS S. BUTLER, JR.	D
12/13/44	57754	ABU-1	MOMOTE	MOMOTE	SW PAC	FLTSGT KENNETH MCGOWAN	D
12/16/44	50637	VMSB-231	MAJURO	MAJURO	CENPAC	1STLT HAROLD E. STANARD	S
12/18/44	57626	VF-85	USS SHANGRI-LA	CULEBRA IS.	CENLANT	ENS G.K. CHAPPELL	S
12/19/44	57692	VMF-122		PALAU	WCENPAC		
12/19/44	50396	VMF-441		ROI	CENPAC		
12/19/44	50495	VMF-441		ROI	CENPAC		
12/19/44	50497	VMF-441		ROI	CENPAC	2NDLT JOHN DALTON	S
12/23/44	57560	VMF-213	USS SARATOGA	HAWAII	ECENPAC	2NDLT ALYMER R. BARNUM	S
12/23/44	57699	VMF-213	USS SARATOGA	HAWAII	ECENPAC	1STLT WILLIAM J. WEBSTER	S
12/27/44	57433	VMF-115		LEYTE GULF	PHIL		
12/31/44	57328	VMF-124	USS ESSEX	ENR FORMOSA	CENPAC		
12/31/44	57377	VMF-124	USS ESSEX	ENR FORMOSA	CENPAC		
12/31/44	57623	VMF-124	USS ESSEX	ENR FORMOSA	CENPAC		
12/31/44	82329	VMF-216	EWA	HAWAII	ECENPAC		
01/01/45	82588	VBF-85	USS SHANGRI-LA	GULF OF PICIA	CENLANT	ENS ROBERT F. SHERMAN	S
01/03/45	57207	VMF-124	USS ESSEX	FORMOSA	EMPIRE	1STLT R.W. MULLINS	M
01/04/45	57455	MAG-31		KWAJALEIN	CENPAC	1STLT E.G. TREMBLEY	S
01/04/45	57419	VMF-115		LEYTE GULF	PHIL	1STLT J. HARRISON	U
01/04/45	57690	VMF-124	USS ESSEX	OKINAWA	EMPIRE		
01/04/45	57706	VMF-124	USS ESSEX	OKINAWA	EMPIRE		
01/06/45	57544	VMF-313		LUZON	PHIL	1STLT E.G. ROBINSON	M
01/06/45	57587	VMF-313		LUZON	PHIL	LT J.M. WOLF	M
01/07/45	57351	VMF-213	USS ESSEX	LUZON	PHIL	2NDLT MIKE KOCHUT	M
01/07/45	57392	VMF-213	USS ESSEX	LUZON	PHIL	2NDLT WILLIAM H. CLOWARD	S
01/07/45	57440	VMF-213	USS ESSEX	LUZON	PHIL	1STLT ROBERT M. DORSETT	M
01/07/45	57465	VMF-213	USS ESSEX	LUZON	PHIL	2NDLT ROBERT D. GREEN	S
01/07/45	57480	VMF-213	USS ESSEX	LUZON	PHIL	1STLT DANIAL L. MORTAG	M
01/07/45	57772	VMF-313		LOS NEGROS	PHIL	1STLT C.E. BROOKS	M
01/07/45	57359	VMSB-331	MAJURO	MAJURO	CENPAC	2NDLT CHESTER M. JEROT	S
01/09/45	82462	VMF-123			WCENPAC		
01/09/45	57390	VMF-124	USS ESSEX	SOUTH CHINA SEA	PHIL		
01/11/45	50409	SERVRON-22		ENGEBI	WCENPAC		
01/11/45	57729	VMF-124	USS ESSEX	SOUTH CHINA SEA	PHIL		
01/12/45	57381	VMF-213	USS ESSEX	FR. I.C.	PHIL	2NDLT JOSEPH A. LYNCH	S
01/12/45	50371	VMO-155		KWAJALEIN	CENPAC	1STLT JAMES B. BLACK, JR.	M
01/13/45	57285	VMF-122		PALAU	WCENPAC	1STLT JAMES A. SMITH	S
01/14/45	57851	A.A.	GUAM	GUAM	WCENPAC		
01/14/45	57437	POOL	PEARL	HAWAII	ECENPAC		
01/14/45	57315	VMF-122		PELELIU	WCENPAC	CAPT WARREN E. FISCHER	S
01/15/45	57283	VMF-124	USS ESSEX	FORMOSA	EMPIRE		
01/15/45	57571	VMF-312		ESPIRITU SANTO	SOPAC	2NDLT JOHN C. WEBB	S

DATE	BUNO	SQDRN	BASE	LOST	AREA	PILOT	FATE
01/16/45	50622	VMF-113		ENGEBI	WCENPAC	2NDLT ROBERT E. PAULIN	S
01/16/45	57662	VMF-124	USS ESSEX	HAINAN	EMPIRE	1STLT GEORGE R. STRIMBECK	M
01/16/45	57685	VMF-211		LEYTE GULF	PHIL	FERREE	S
01/16/45	57552	VMF-312		ESPIRITU SANTO	SOPAC	1STLT THOMAS H. MULLIGAN	D
01/17/45	57579	MAG-12		ZAMBOAN-GA	PHIL		
01/17/45	57520	VMF-211		LEYTE GULF	PHIL	LT SANKEY	M
01/17/45	57297	VMO-251		LUZON	PHIL		
01/18/45	57606	VBF-85	USS SHANGRI-LA	ENR PANAMA	NORLANT	ENS MILO G. PARKER, JR.	D
01/18/45	57632	VBF-85	USS SHANGRI-LA	ENR PANAMA	NORLANT	LT WILLIAM V. KASTLER	U
01/20/45	57501	VMF-211		LEYTE GULF	PHIL	LT EVANS	S
01/20/45	57169	VMO-251		SAMAR	PHIL	1STLT NICK A. SIGAN	D
01/20/45	57531	VMO-251		SAMAR	PHIL	LT JAMES B. STURGIS	D
01/21/45	57407	VMF-213	USS ESSEX	FORMOSA	EMPIRE	2NDLT J.T. MOLAN	S
01/21/45	57399	VMF-251		SAMAR	PHIL	2NDLT ROBERT LINDSAY	S
01/22/45	57760	VMF-211		LEYTE GULF	PHIL	CAPT LOUIS W. RANCOURT	D
01/23/45	82340	VMF-217		GUAM	WCENPAC		
01/24/45	50377	VMF-113		ENGEBI	WCENPAC	2NDLT JOHN L. SCOTT	S
01/25/45	57885	VF-85	USS SHANGRI-LA	PANAMA	CENPAC	ENS JAMES A. MACKINNON	S
01/25/45	57348	VMF-422		ENIWETOK	CENPAC		
01/26/45	57581	VF-85	USS SHANGRI-LA	ENR HAWAII	ECENPAC	ENS JAMES L. HARHEN	S
01/26/45	82302	VMF-216	EWA	HAWAII	ECENPAC		
01/28/45	57453	VMO-251		LUZON	PHIL	CAPT HAROLD C. WALLACE	M
01/28/45	57494	VMO-251		LUZON	PHIL	1STLT MICHAEL H. MOYNIHAN	M
01/30/45	57408	A.A.	PEARL	HAWAII	ECENPAC		
01/30/45	57905	VF-84	USS BUNKER HILL	WCENPAC			
02/02/45	57391	VMF-251		LINGAYEN	PHIL		
02/03/45	57804	VMF-122		PELELIU	WCENPAC	1STLT STANLEY POSLUSSNY	S
02/04/45	82291	VMF-216	USS WASP	IWO JIMA	EMPIRE		
02/07/45	57505	VMF-211		LEYTE GULF	PHIL		
02/11/45	57773	VF-84	USS BUNKER HILL	WCENPAC			
02/11/45	57589	VMF-122		YAP	WCENPAC	MAJ PIERCE	S
02/11/45	57874	VMF-124	EWA	HAWAII	ECENPAC		
02/11/45	57497	VMF-211		LEYTE GULF	PHIL		
02/11/45	57295	VMF-441		KWAJALEIN	CENPAC		
02/12/45	57793	VF-84	USS BUNKER HILL	WCENPAC			
02/12/45	57954	VF-84	USS BUNKER HILL	WCENPAC			
02/12/45	50386	VMF-155		MARSHALLS	CENPAC	LT HARRY J. WERNER	S
02/12/45	82313	VMF-217	USS WASP	IWO JIMA	EMPIRE		
02/13/45	82227	NAS	HILO	HAWAII	ECENPAC		
02/13/45	82413	VMF-112	USS BENNING-TON	ULITHI	WCENPAC		
02/13/45	82343	VMF-216	USS WASP	ENR TOKYO	EMPIRE		
02/13/45	82352	VMF-217	USS WASP	ENR TOKYO	EMPIRE		
02/13/45	57826	VMF-221	USS BUNKER HILL	WCENPAC			
02/14/45	82642	VBF-10		HAWAII	ECENPAC		
02/14/45	82522	VMF-123	USS BENNING-TON	ENR HONSHU	EMPIRE	2NDLT WENDALL BROWNING	S

DATE	BUNO	SQDRN	BASE	LOST	AREA	PILOT	FATE
02/14/45	82190	VMF-216	USS BUNKER HILL	WCENPAC			
02/16/45	82533	VF-5	PEARL	HAWAII	ECENPAC		
02/16/45	82430	VMF-112	USS BENNING-TON	TOKYO	EMPIRE	2NDLT J.M. HAMILTON	S
02/16/45	82297	VMF-123	USS BENNING-TON	TOKYO	EMPIRE	2NDLT HARRY BEARLUND	S
02/16/45	82344	VMF-123	USS BENNING-TON	TOKYO	EMPIRE	2NDLT ROBERT M. CIES	M
02/16/45	82346	VMF-123	USS BENNING-TON	TOKYO	EMPIRE	2NDLT W.R. HATHCOX	M
02/16/45	57509	VMF-211		LEYTE GULF	PHIL	LT ELIAS	S
02/16/45	82293	VMF-216	USS WASP	HONSHU	EMPIRE	2NDLT DANIAL V. HAYES	M
02/16/45	57858	VMF-217	USS WASP	HONSHU	EMPIRE	MAJ J.R. AMENDE, JR.	M
02/16/45	82466	VMF-217	USS WASP	HONSHU	EMPIRE	1STLT ROLAND VAUGHN, JR.	M
02/16/45	82470	VMF-217	USS WASP	HONSHU	EMPIRE	1STLT SPENCER D. WEILLS	M
02/16/45	57816	VMF-221	USS BUNKER HILL	TOKYO	EMPIRE	LT WILLIAM H. PEMBLE	M
02/16/45	82181	VMF-311		ROI	CENPAC	2NDLT JOHN H. NEWTON	M
02/16/45	82202	VMF-451	USS BUNKER HILL	TOKYO	EMPIRE		
02/16/45	82631	VMF-451	USS BUNKER HILL	TOKYO	EMPIRE	1STLT FORREST BROWN, JR.	M
02/17/45	82505	VMF-123	USS BENNING-TON	TOKYO	EMPIRE	2NDLT E.H. REHRICHT	M
02/17/45	57834	VMF-451	USS BUNKER HILL	TOKYO	EMPIRE		
02/17/45	57936	VMF-451	USS BUNKER HILL	TOKYO	EMPIRE		
02/17/45	82222	VMF-451	USS BUNKER HILL	TOKYO	EMPIRE		
02/18/45	57324	VMF-211		LEYTE GULF	PHIL		
02/18/45	82192	VMF-451	USS BUNKER HILL	ENR OKINAWA	EMPIRE		
02/19/45	57730	MAG-33		ESPIRITU SANTO	SOPAC		
02/19/45	57774	VMF-211		LEYTE GULF	PHIL		
02/19/45	57769	VMF-218		LEYTE GULF	PHIL	2NDLT I.F. CARTNEY	M
02/20/45	57762	VMF-218		LEYTE GULF	PHIL		
02/22/45	82422	VMF-112	USS BENNING-TON	IWO JIMA	EMPIRE	2NDLT WILLIAM C. WEBB	S
02/22/45	82405	VMF-123	USS BENNING-TON	IWO JIMA	EMPIRE	CAPT DONALD C. OWEN	S
02/23/45	82356	VMF-123	USS BENNING-TON	IWO JIMA	EMPIRE	2NDLT WARREN E. VAUGHN	M
02/24/45	82424	VMF-123	USS BENNING-TON	IWO JIMA	EMPIRE		
02/24/45	82471	VMF-216	USS WASP	ENR TOKYO	EMPIRE		
02/24/45	57941	VMF-221	USS BUNKER HILL	ENR OKINAWA	EMPIRE		
02/25/45	57950	VF-84	USS BUNKER HILL	ENR OKINAWA	EMPIRE	ENS CURTIS LEE JEFFERSON	M

DATE	BUNO	SQDRN	BASE	LOST	AREA	PILOT	FATE
02/25/45	82300	VMF-123	USS BENNING-TON	IWO JIMA	EMPIRE	MAJ EVERETT V. ALWARD	M
02/25/45	82410	VMF-123	USS BENNING-TON	IWO JIMA	EMPIRE	2NDLT VINCENT A. JACOBS	M
02/25/45	57251	VMF-124	USS ESSEX	ENR OKINAWA	EMPIRE	2NDLT D. CARLSON	M
02/25/45	57318	VMF-124	USS ESSEX	HAWAII	ECENPAC		
02/25/45	57335	VMF-124	USS ESSEX	HAWAII	ECENPAC		
02/25/45	57400	VMF-124	USS ESSEX	HAWAII	ECENPAC		
02/25/45	57595	VMF-124	USS ESSEX	HAWAII	ECENPAC		
02/26/45	57620	VBF-85	USS SHANGRI-LA	HAWAII	ECENPAC	ENS PETER J. HOPKINS	S
02/27/45	57878	VBF-85	USS SHANGRI-LA	HAWAII	ECENPAC	ENS WALTER BARTSCHAT, JR.	D
02/27/45	57724	VMF-221	USS BUNKER HILL	MINDANOA	PHIL	MAJ PHILLIP B. MAY	M
02/28/45	57848	VMF-123	USS BENNING-TON	OKINAWA	EMPIRE		
02/28/45	82485	VMF-422		CAROLINE IS.	WCENPAC	LT SOLADAY	S
03/01/45	82487	A.A.	BARBERS POINT	HAWAII	ECENPAC		
03/01/45	82820	VF-10	USS INTREPID	HAWAII	ECENPAC	ENS C.R. GALLAGHER	S
03/01/45	57594	VMF-124	USS ESSEX	OKINAWA	EMPIRE	1STLT C.J. CHOP	S
03/01/45	82476	VMF-217	USS WASP	OKINAWA	EMPIRE	1STLT ROBERT E. WASHBON	S
03/01/45	82196	VMF-221	USS BUNKER HILL	OKINAWA	EMPIRE		
03/01/45	82590	VMF-451	USS BUNKER HILL	OKINAWA	EMPIRE	LT SIMKUNA	S
03/03/45	57796	VMF-218		LUZON	PHIL	CAPT BILLY M. KEAHEY	S
03/04/45	57300	VMF-422	ENGEBI	ENGEBI	WCENPAC	2NDLT ROBERT J. MORS	M
03/05/45	57522	VMF-211		ZAMBOAN-GA	PHIL	2NDLT ANTHONY CRAMER	S
03/05/45	57722	VMF-251		SAMAR	PHIL	CAPT JOSEPH P. HART	S
03/08/45	57373	SERVRON-13		MAJURO	CENPAC	1STLT WILBERT H. GIESEKE	D
03/09/45	82682	COMAIR-PAC	PEARL	HAWAII	ECENPAC		
03/09/45	82764	COMAIR-PAC	PEARL	HAWAII	ECENPAC		
03/09/45	82773	COMAIR-PAC	PEARL	HAWAII	ECENPAC		
03/09/45	57576	VMF-218		LUZON	PHIL		
03/10/45	57807	VMF-122		PELELIU	WCENPAC	2NDLT JAMES R. MISLEY	M
03/11/45	82660	VF-10	USS INTREPID	HAWAII	ECENPAC		
03/14/45	82295	CASU(F)-13		PITYILU	SW PAC		
03/14/45	82331	CASU(F)-13		PITYILU	SW PAC		
03/14/45	57838	COMAIR-PAC	PEARL	HAWAII	ECENPAC		
03/14/45	82327	VBF-86	HAWAII	HAWAII	ECENPAC		
03/14/45	57802	VMF-218		LEYTE GULF	PHIL	2NDLT EMMET C. BOYLE	D
03/15/45	57423	VBF-83	USS ESSEX	OKINAWA	EMPIRE		
03/15/45	57427	VBF-83	USS ESSEX	OKINAWA	EMPIRE		
03/15/45	57684	VBF-83	USS ESSEX	OKINAWA	EMPIRE		
03/15/45	82229	VBF-83	USS ESSEX	OKINAWA	EMPIRE		
03/15/45	57876	VF-84	USS BUNKER HILL	ENR KURE	WCENPAC		
03/15/45	82345	VMF-112	USS BENNING-TON	ENR KYUSHU	EMPIRE	2NDLT G.J. MURRAY	S

DATE	BUNO	SQDRN	BASE	LOST	AREA	PILOT	FATE
03/15/45	57918	VMF-451	USS BUNKER HILL	ENR KURE	EMPIRE		
03/16/45	82198	VMF-221	USS BUNKER HILL	KURE	EMPIRE		
03/17/45	57907	VF-84	USS BUNKER HILL	KURE	EMPIRE		
03/17/45	57378	VMF-111	ENIWETOK	ENIWETOK	CENPAC	2NDLT FRED J. SCHWETJE	S
03/17/45	57458	VMF-122		PELELIU	WCENPAC	1STLT DAVID J. THOMPSON	M
03/18/45	82654	VBF-10	USS INTREPID	KYUSHU	EMPIRE		
03/18/45	57471	VBF-83	USS ESSEX	KYUSHU	EMPIRE	LT JAMES J. STEVENS	M
03/18/45	57603	VBF-83	USS ESSEX	KYUSHU	EMPIRE		
03/18/45	57625	VBF-83	USS ESSEX	KYUSHU	EMPIRE	LTJG W.F. GALNOR	M
03/18/45	57715	VBF-83	USS ESSEX	KYUSHU	EMPIRE		
03/18/45	57719	VBF-83	USS ESSEX	KYUSHU	EMPIRE	LTJG W.O. SIGMAN	M
03/18/45	57818	VBF-86	USS WASP	KYUSHU	EMPIRE		
03/18/45	82465	VBF-86	USS WASP	KYUSHU	EMPIRE	LT HAROLD R. KELLER	D
03/18/45	82673	VBF-86	USS WASP	KYUSHU	EMPIRE		
03/18/45	82305	VF-10	USS INTREPID	KYUSHU	EMPIRE	ENS LOREN S. ISLEY	M
03/18/45	82647	VF-10	USS INTREPID	KYUSHU	EMPIRE	LT WILLIAM L. LANEDRETH	M
03/18/45	82699	VF-10	USS INTREPID	KYUSHU	EMPIRE		
03/18/45	82720	VF-10	USS INTREPID	KYUSHU	EMPIRE	ENS R.W. HARRIS	M
03/18/45	57694	VF-5	USS FRANKLIN	KYUSHU	EMPIRE	ENS P.A. CASEBEE	M
03/18/45	57856	VF-5	USS FRANKLIN	KYUSHU	EMPIRE	LT R.A. NELSON	S
03/18/45	82357	VMF-112	USS BENNING-TON	KYUSHU	EMPIRE	2NDLT TIMOTHY C. CLARK	D
03/18/45	82621	VMF-221	USS BUNKER HILL	KURE	EMPIRE		
03/18/45	82334	VMF-452	USS FRANKLIN	KYUSHU	EMPIRE	2NDLT T.D. PACE	M
03/18/45	82368	VMF-452	USS FRANKLIN	KYUSHU	EMPIRE	2NDLT J.P. STODD	M
03/19/45	82727	VBF-10	USS INTREPID	HONSHU	EMPIRE		
03/19/45	82834	VBF-10	USS INTREPID	HONSHU	EMPIRE		
03/19/45	57414	VBF-83	USS ESSEX	KURE	EMPIRE		
03/19/45	57546	VBF-83	USS ESSEX	KURE	EMPIRE		
03/19/45	57601	VBF-83	USS ESSEX	KURE	EMPIRE		
03/19/45	82693	VF-10	USS INTREPID	HONSHU	EMPIRE		
03/19/45	82766	VF-10	USS INTREPID	HONSHU	EMPIRE		
03/19/45	82769	VF-10	USS INTREPID	HONSHU	EMPIRE		
03/19/45	57506	VF-5	USS FRANKLIN	HONSHU	EMPIRE	(DECK LOSS-KAMIKAZE)	
03/19/45	57721	VF-5	USS FRANKLIN	HONSHU	EMPIRE	(DECK LOSS-KAMIKAZE)	
03/19/45	57846	VF-5	USS FRANKLIN	HONSHU	EMPIRE	(DECK LOSS-KAMIKAZE)	
03/19/45	82220	VF-5	USS FRANKLIN	HONSHU	EMPIRE	(DECK LOSS-KAMIKAZE)	
03/19/45	82228	VF-5	USS FRANKLIN	HONSHU	EMPIRE	(DECK LOSS-KAMIKAZE)	
03/19/45	82369	VF-5	USS FRANKLIN	HONSHU	EMPIRE	(DECK LOSS-KAMIKAZE)	
03/19/45	82434	VF-5	USS FRANKLIN	HONSHU	EMPIRE	(DECK LOSS-KAMIKAZE)	
03/19/45	82469	VF-5	USS FRANKLIN	HONSHU	EMPIRE	(DECK LOSS-KAMIKAZE)	

DATE	BUNO	SQDRN	BASE	LOST	AREA	PILOT	FATE
03/19/45	82499	VF-5	USS FRANKLIN	HONSHU	EMPIRE	(DECK LOSS-KAMIKAZE)	
03/19/45	82503	VF-5	USS FRANKLIN	HONSHU	EMPIRE	(DECK LOSS-KAMIKAZE)	
03/19/45	82506	VF-5	USS FRANKLIN	HONSHU	EMPIRE	(DECK LOSS-KAMIKAZE)	
03/19/45	82516	VF-5	USS FRANKLIN	HONSHU	EMPIRE	(DECK LOSS-KAMIKAZE)	
03/19/45	82527	VF-5	USS FRANKLIN	HONSHU	EMPIRE	(DECK LOSS-KAMIKAZE)	
03/19/45	82529	VF-5	USS FRANKLIN	HONSHU	EMPIRE	(DECK LOSS-KAMIKAZE)	
03/19/45	82586	VF-5	USS FRANKLIN	HONSHU	EMPIRE	(DECK LOSS-KAMIKAZE)	
03/19/45	82587	VF-5	USS FRANKLIN	HONSHU	EMPIRE	(DECK LOSS-KAMIKAZE)	
03/19/45	82622	VF-5	USS FRANKLIN	HONSHU	EMPIRE	(DECK LOSS-KAMIKAZE)	
03/19/45	82672	VF-5	USS FRANKLIN	HONSHU	EMPIRE	(DECK LOSS-KAMIKAZE)	
03/19/45	82681	VF-5	USS FRANKLIN	HONSHU	EMPIRE	(DECK LOSS-KAMIKAZE)	
03/19/45	82686	VF-5	USS FRANKLIN	HONSHU	EMPIRE	(DECK LOSS-KAMIKAZE)	
03/19/45	82702	VF-5	USS FRANKLIN	HONSHU	EMPIRE	(DECK LOSS-KAMIKAZE)	
03/19/45	82719	VF-5	USS FRANKLIN	HONSHU	EMPIRE	(DECK LOSS-KAMIKAZE)	
03/19/45	57903	VMF-123	USS BENNING-TON	HONSHU	EMPIRE	MAJ T.E. MOBLEY	S
03/19/45	82339	VMF-123	USS BENNING-TON	HONSHU	EMPIRE	LT CLAUDE A. BARNHILL	S
03/19/45	82350	VMF-123	USS BENNING-TON	HONSHU	EMPIRE	CAPT WILLIAM A. CANTREL	S
03/19/45	82362	VMF-123	USS BENNING-TON	HONSHU	EMPIRE	1STLT GORDON K. WOOSTER	M
03/19/45	82473	VMF-123	USS BENNING-TON	HONSHU	EMPIRE	LT DWIGHT D. MAYO	S
03/19/45	82518	VMF-123	USS BENNING-TON	HONSHU	EMPIRE	2NDLT R.A. RUSSELL	M
03/19/45	82420	VMF-214	USS FRANKLIN	HONSHU	EMPIRE	(DECK LOSS-KAMIKAZE)	
03/19/45	82646	VMF-214	USS FRANKLIN	HONSHU	EMPIRE	(DECK LOSS-KAMIKAZE)	
03/19/45	82683	VMF-214	USS FRANKLIN	HONSHU	EMPIRE	(DECK LOSS-KAMIKAZE)	
03/19/45	82705	VMF-214	USS FRANKLIN	HONSHU	EMPIRE	(DECK LOSS-KAMIKAZE)	
03/19/45	57911	VMF-221	USS BUNKER HILL	KURE	EMPIRE		
03/19/45	57916	VMF-221	USS BUNKER HILL	KURE	EMPIRE		
03/19/45	57965	VMF-221	USS BUNKER HILL	KURE	EMPIRE	2NDLT JAMES G. TURNER	D
03/19/45	82432	VMF-452	USS FRANKLIN	HONSHU	EMPIRE	(DECK LOSS-KAMIKAZE)	
03/19/45	82403	VMF-5	USS FRANKLIN	HONSHU	EMPIRE	(DECK LOSS-KAMIKAZE)	
03/20/45	57157	VBF-83	USS ESSEX	OKINAWA	EMPIRE		
03/20/45	82658	VMF-451	USS BUNKER HILL	KURE	EMPIRE		
03/21/45	82409	COMAIR-PAC	PEARL	HAWAII	ECENPAC		
03/21/45	82718	VF-10	USS INTREPID	HONSHU	EMPIRE	LTJG RICHARD W. MASON	M

DATE	BUNO	SQDRN	BASE	LOST	AREA	PILOT	FATE
03/22/45	82826	VBF-6	USS HANCOCK	IE SHIMA	EMPIRE		
03/22/45	82536	VBF-83	USS ESSEX	HONSHU	EMPIRE		
03/22/45	82455	VF-85	USS SHANGRI-LA	PEARL	ECENPAC	ENS EDWARD F. WINTE	D
03/22/45	82551	VF-85	USS SHANGRI-LA	PEARL	ECENPAC	ENS MILTON TORMEY	S
03/22/45	57420	VMF-122		YAP	CENPAC	LT RUSSELL	S
03/23/45	57841	VBF-84	USS BUNKER HILL	OKINAWA	EMPIRE	LTJG C.S. CARTER	S
03/24/45	82665	VBF-10	USS INTREPID	OKINAWA	EMPIRE		
03/24/45	82839	VBF-6	USS HANCOCK	ENR OKINAWA	EMPIRE	LT R.B. GRAHAM	U
03/24/45	82782	VF-6	USS HANCOCK	ENR OKINAWA	EMPIRE	LTJG W.W. PARKER	S
03/24/45	57697	VMF-221	USS BUNKER HILL	OKINAWA	EMPIRE	2NDLT RICHARD WASHEY	M
03/24/45	82231	VMF-221	USS BUNKER HILL	OKINAWA	EMPIRE	1STLT JOHN E. JORGENSEN	S
03/24/45	57867	VMF-451	USS BUNKER HILL	OKINAWA	EMPIRE	MAJ EMERSON H. DEDRICK	M
03/24/45	57964	VMF-451	USS BUNKER HILL	OKINAWA	EMPIRE	CDR GEORGE M. OFFINGER	M
03/25/45	57604	VBF-83	USS ESSEX	OKINAWA	EMPIRE		
03/25/45	57651	VBF-83	USS ESSEX	OKINAWA	EMPIRE		
03/26/45	82653	VBF-10	USS INTREPID	HONSHU	EMPIRE	ENS L.R. THOMPSON	U
03/26/45	82666	VBF-10	USS INTREPID	HONSHU	EMPIRE	ENS J.C. SOUTH	U
03/26/45	82712	VBF-10	USS INTREPID	HONSHU	EMPIRE		
03/26/45	82724	VBF-6	USS HANCOCK	OKINAWA	EMPIRE	ENS R. MEYERS	S
03/26/45	82788	VF-10	USS INTREPID	HONSHU	EMPIRE	ENS ELMER S. HASSE	M
03/26/45	82797	VF-10	USS INTREPID	HONSHU	EMPIRE	ENS M.B. ALBRIGHT, JR.	U
03/27/45	82233	VBF-83	USS ESSEX	OKINAWA	EMPIRE	ENS MARCINKOSKA	S
03/27/45	82315	VF-10	USS INTREPID	OKINAWA	EMPIRE		
03/27/45	82307	VMF-112	USS BENNING-TON	OKINAWA	EMPIRE	2NDLT N.F. WHITTREDGE	M
03/28/45	57607	VBF-83	USS ESSEX	DAITO	EMPIRE		
03/28/45	57750	VBF-83	USS ESSEX	DAITO	EMPIRE		
03/28/45	57909	VBF-83	USS ESSEX	DAITO	EMPIRE		
03/28/45	82234	VBF-83	USS ESSEX	DAITO	EMPIRE		
03/28/45	82613	VMF-112	USS BENNING-TON	OKINAWA	EMPIRE	2NDLT R.W. KOONS	S
03/28/45	57496	VMF-211	ZAMBOAN-GA	MINDANAO SEA	PHIL	2NDLT MERT. GRAVERHOLTZ	D 03/28 /45
03/28/45	57952	VMF-451	USS BUNKER HILL	OKINAWA	EMPIRE	CAPT JOHN L. MORGAN, JR.	M
03/29/45	82668	VBF-10	USS INTREPID	KYUSHU	EMPIRE		
03/29/45	82236	VBF-83	USS ESSEX	SASEBO	EMPIRE	ENS J.R. KING	M
03/29/45	82847	VF-10	USS INTREPID	KYUSHU	EMPIRE	LTJG ROBERT H. HILL	S
03/29/45	57757	VMF-221	USS BUNKER HILL	OKINAWA	EMPIRE		
03/30/45	82679	VBF-10	USS INTREPID	KYUSHU	EMPIRE		

DATE	BUNO	SQDRN	BASE	LOST	AREA	PILOT	FATE
03/30/45	57656	VMF-211	ZAMBOAN-GA	ZAMBOANGA	PHIL	2NDLT DONALD H. OSTER	S
03/30/45	57901	VMF-451	USS BUNKER HILL	OKINAWA	EMPIRE		
03/30/45	82333	VMF-451	USS BUNKER HILL	OKINAWA	EMPIRE	LT M.G. HALBERT	U
03/31/45	57709	CASU(F)-51		ULITHI	WCENPAC		
03/31/45	82338	VF-84	USS BUNKER HILL	OKINAWA	EMPIRE		
04/01/45	82661	VF-10	USS INTREPID	OKINAWA	EMPIRE		
04/01/45	57900	VMF-451	USS BUNKER HILL	OKINAWA	EMPIRE	1STLT R.K. MARBLE	M
04/01/45	82217	VMF-451	USS BUNKER HILL	OKINAWA	EMPIRE	2NDLT J.K. MORGAN	M
04/02/45	82799	VBF-10	USS INTREPID	OKINAWA	EMPIRE		
04/02/45	82805	VBF-10	USS INTREPID	OKINAWA	EMPIRE		
04/02/45	57951	VF-84	USS BUNKER HILL	AMAMI	EMPIRE		
04/02/45	82349	VMF-112	USS BENNING-TON	OKINAWA	EMPIRE	2NDLT DEANE E. ERICKSON	S
04/02/45	57904	VMF-451	USS BUNKER HILL	AMAMI	EMPIRE		
04/02/45	57940	VMF-451	USS BUNKER HILL	AMAMI	EMPIRE		
04/03/45	57404	VBF-83	USS ESSEX	OKINAWA	EMPIRE		
04/03/45	82240	VBF-83	USS ESSEX	OKINAWA	EMPIRE		
04/03/45	57813	VF-84	USS BUNKER HILL	AMAMI	EMPIRE		
04/03/45	82341	VMF-112	USS BENNING-TON	IWO JIMA	EMPIRE	2NDLT H.J. STEELE, JR.	S
04/03/45	82425	VMF-112	USS BENNING-TON	IWO JIMA	EMPIRE	CAPT H.J. DEAL	D
04/03/45	82397	VMF-123	USS BENNING-TON	IWO JIMA	EMPIRE	1STLT RANDOLPH SMITH	S
04/03/45	82463	VMF-123	USS BENNING-TON	IWO JIMA	EMPIRE	CAPT W.E. ROQUES	D
04/04/45	82491	VBF-83	USS ESSEX	OKINAWA	EMPIRE		
04/04/45	57937	VF-84	USS BUNKER HILL	AMAMI	EMPIRE	LTJG JAMES A. NIST	M
04/04/45	82232	VF-84	USS BUNKER HILL	AMAMI	EMPIRE	LTJG JOHN J. SARGENT	U
04/04/45	82301	VF-84	USS BUNKER HILL	AMAMI	EMPIRE		
04/04/45	57835	VMF-451	USS BUNKER HILL	AMAMI	EMPIRE		
04/05/45	82695	VBF-10	USS INTREPID	OKINAWA	EMPIRE	ENS W.E. NORGREN	M
04/05/45	82717	VBF-10	USS INTREPID	OKINAWA	EMPIRE		
04/05/45	82767	VBF-10	USS INTREPID	OKINAWA	EMPIRE	2NDLT CARL R. MILLER	D
04/05/45	82328	VMF-112	USS BENNING-TON	NANSEI SHOTO	EMPIRE	2NDLT DEANE E. ERICKSON	D

DATE	BUNO	SQDRN	BASE	LOST	AREA	PILOT	FATE
04/05/45	82464	VMF-112	USS BENNINGTON	NANSEI SHOTO	EMPIRE	1STLT JUNIE B. LOHAN	S
04/06/45	57799	VBF-6	USS HANCOCK	OKINAWA	EMPIRE		
04/06/45	82191	VF-84	USS BUNKER HILL	OKINAWA	EMPIRE	LTJG V.P. BIDDLE	S
04/06/45	57617	VMF-123	USS BENNINGTON	OKINAWA	EMPIRE		
04/06/45	57726	VMF-221	USS BUNKER HILL	OKINAWA	EMPIRE	1STLT JARVIS H. CARPENTER	M
04/06/45	57714	VMF-451	USS BUNKER HILL	OKINAWA	EMPIRE		
04/07/45	82803	VBF-10	USS INTREPID	OKINAWA	EMPIRE		
04/07/45	57332	VBF-6	USS HANCOCK	OKINAWA	EMPIRE		
04/07/45	82657	VBF-6	USS HANCOCK	OKINAWA	EMPIRE		
04/07/45	82708	VBF-6	USS HANCOCK	OKINAWA	EMPIRE		
04/07/45	57912	VBF-83	USS ESSEX	OKINAWA	EMPIRE	2NDLT J.L. GARLOCK	M
04/07/45	82488	VBF-83	USS ESSEX	OKINAWA	EMPIRE	LT SOFFE	S
04/07/45	82525	VBF-83	USS ESSEX	OKINAWA	EMPIRE	LTJG SCHAUB	S
04/07/45	82602	VF-10	USS INTREPID	OKINAWA	EMPIRE		
04/07/45	57512	VMF-251	SAMAR	SAMAR	PHIL	CAPT FRANCIS DOUGHTY	D
04/08/45	82814	VBF-10	USS INTREPID	OKINAWA	EMPIRE		
04/08/45	57898	VBF-83	USS ESSEX	OKINAWA	EMPIRE		
04/08/45	82493	VF-84	USS BUNKER HILL	KYUSHU	EMPIRE	LTJG G.E. ROBERTS	S
04/08/45	82251	VMF-222	SAMAR	SAMAR	PHIL	LT LEASE	S
04/08/45	57518	VMF-251	SAMAR	SAMAR	PHIL	2NDLT HUGH B. IRWIN	S
04/10/45	57727	VBF-83	USS ESSEX	IWO JIMA	EMPIRE		
04/10/45	57152	VMF-224		OKINAWA	EMPIRE	2NDLT R.W. HAGER	M
04/10/45	57189	VMF-224		OKINAWA	EMPIRE	2NDLT R.M. TOUSLEY	D
04/10/45	82650	VMF-224		OKINAWA	EMPIRE	1STLT A.C. SATTLESWHITE	S
04/10/45	57379	VMF-323		OKINAWA	EMPIRE	1STLT JAMES R. BROWN	M
04/10/45	50368	VMF-441		OKINAWA	EMPIRE	LT WILLIAMS	M
04/10/45	50512	VMF-441		OKINAWA	EMPIRE	CAPT GREEN	M
04/10/45	50641	VMF-441		OKINAWA	EMPIRE	LT HARLE	M
04/10/45	50645	VMF-441		OKINAWA	EMPIRE	LT COPPEDGE	S
04/11/45	82508	VBF-10	USS INTREPID	OKINAWA	EMPIRE		
04/11/45	57922	VBF-83	USS ESSEX	TOKUNO	EMPIRE	LCDR HENRY F. GRAHAM	D
04/11/45	82193	VF-84	USS BUNKER HILL	TOKUNO	EMPIRE		
04/11/45	57828	VMF-224		OKINAWA	EMPIRE		
04/11/45	82186	VMF-311		OKINAWA	EMPIRE	2NDLT D.C. LANG	S
04/12/45	82496	VBF-10	USS INTREPID	OKINAWA	EMPIRE	LT F.M. JACKSON	S
04/12/45	57734	VBF-83	USS ESSEX	ENR OKINAWA	EMPIRE		
04/12/45	82641	VF-10	USS INTREPID	OKINAWA	EMPIRE	1STLT W.A. NICKERSON	S
04/12/45	82664	VF-10	USS INTREPID	OKINAWA	EMPIRE	ENS JOHN A. HALLE	S
04/12/45	57397	VMF-218	ZAMBOAN-GA	ZAMBOAN-GA	PHIL		
04/12/45	57299	VMF-323		OKINAWA	EMPIRE	2NDLT W.W. BOATRIGHT	S
04/13/45	57688	VF-10	USS INTREPID	OKINAWA	EMPIRE		

DATE	BUNO	SQDRN	BASE	LOST	AREA	PILOT	FATE
04/13/45	57857	VMF-112	USS BENNING-TON	IE SHIMA	EMPIRE	2NDLT VICTOR N. RUSLING	D
04/13/45	82411	VMF-112	USS BENNING-TON	IE SHIMA	EMPIRE	2NDLT E.M. DENNIS	S
04/13/45	82398	VMF-123	USS BENNING-TON	IE SHIMA	EMPIRE	CAPT GEORGE C. DEFABLE	D
04/13/45	82419	VMF-123	USS BENNING-TON	IE SHIMA	EMPIRE	1STLT FRANK KURSHINSKI	D
04/13/45	57930	VMF-221	USS BUNKER HILL	TOKUNO	EMPIRE		
04/13/45	50437	VMF-322		OKINAWA	EMPIRE		
04/13/45	50441	VMF-322		OKINAWA	EMPIRE	2NDLT RONALD T. TWITU	D
04/13/45	50536	VMF-322		OKINAWA	EMPIRE		
04/13/45	57537	VMF-323		OKINAWA	EMPIRE	2NDLT KEITH W. FOUNTAIN	S
04/14/45	82778	VF-10	USS INTREPID	OKINAWA	EMPIRE		
04/14/45	82599	VMF-112	USS BENNING-TON	OKINAWA	EMPIRE		
04/14/45	57978	VMF-311		OKINAWA	EMPIRE	2NDLT R.T. HAMNER	S
04/15/45	57869	VMF-221	USS BUNKER HILL	KYUSHU	EMPIRE		
04/15/45	57184	VMF-323		OKINAWA	EMPIRE		
04/15/45	57352	VMF-323		OKINAWA	EMPIRE		
04/15/45	82598	VMF-323		OKINAWA	EMPIRE		
04/16/45	57870	VBF-10	USS INTREPID	KOKUBO	EMPIRE		
04/16/45	82610	VBF-10	USS INTREPID	KOKUBO	EMPIRE		
04/16/45	82680	VBF-10	USS INTREPID	KOKUBO	EMPIRE		
04/16/45	82710	VBF-10	USS INTREPID	KOKUBO	EMPIRE		
04/16/45	82723	VBF-10	USS INTREPID	KOKUBO	EMPIRE		
04/16/45	82802	VBF-10	USS INTREPID	KOKUBO	EMPIRE		
04/16/45	82497	VF-10	USS INTREPID	KOKUBO	EMPIRE		
04/16/45	82715	VF-10	USS INTREPID	KOKUBO	EMPIRE		
04/16/45	82784	VF-10	USS INTREPID	KOKUBO	EMPIRE		
04/16/45	82808	VF-10	USS INTREPID	KOKUBO	EMPIRE		
04/16/45	57808	VF-84	USS BUNKER HILL	KYUSHU	EMPIRE	LT ELLIS J. LITTLEJOHN	M
04/16/45	57837	VF-84	USS BUNKER HILL	KYUSHU	EMPIRE	LT JAMES CASS DIXON	M
04/16/45	57928	VMF-221	USS BUNKER HILL	KYUSHU	EMPIRE		
04/16/45	82180	VMF-311		OKINAWA	EMPIRE	LT SEIFERT	S
04/16/45	57559	VMF-312		OKINAWA	EMPIRE		
04/16/45	57691	VMF-312		OKINAWA	EMPIRE		
04/16/45	82612	VMF-312		OKINAWA	EMPIRE		
04/16/45	50387	VMF-322		OKINAWA	EMPIRE	2NDLT J.H. PETERSON	S
04/16/45	57366	VMF-323		OKINAWA	EMPIRE	2NDLT ROBERT L. WICKSER	M
04/16/45	50421	VMF-441		OKINAWA	EMPIRE	LT C.F. BUERGER	S
04/16/45	50510	VMF-441		OKINAWA	EMPIRE	2NDLT MARION I. RYAN	S
04/16/45	50620	VMF-441		OKINAWA	EMPIRE	2NDLT RICHARD C. JOHNSON	S

DATE	BUNO	SQDRN	BASE	LOST	AREA	PILOT	FATE
04/16/45	82204	VMF-451	USS BUNKER HILL	OKINAWA	EMPIRE	MAJ H.H. LONG	S
04/17/45	57711	VF-84	USS BUNKER HILL	KYUSHU	EMPIRE	LTJG LEROY L. WALLET	S
04/17/45	57483	VMF-211	ZAMBOAN-GA	ZAMBOANGA	PHIL	2NDLT CHAPMAN	S
04/17/45	57542	VMF-211	ZAMBOAN-GA	ZAMBOANGA	PHIL	2NDLT COURNOYER	S
04/19/45	82308	VBF-83	USS ESSEX	OKINAWA	EMPIRE		
04/19/45	57456	VMF-251	SAMAR	SAMAR	PHIL	2NDLT CHARLES F. SCOTT	S
04/20/45	82627	VMF-322		OKINAWA	EMPIRE	CAPT H. CROZIER	S
04/20/45	57326	VMF-323		OKINAWA	EMPIRE		
04/21/45	57548	VMF-312		OKINAWA	EMPIRE		
04/22/45	50649	VMF-441		OKINAWA	EMPIRE	LT R.R. CORRELL	S
04/22/45	57409	VMF-441		OKINAWA	EMPIRE	2NDLT FREDERICK KOLB, JR.	S
04/23/45	57784	CASU(F)-12		GUAM	WCENPAC		
04/23/45	57897	VBF-85	USS SHANGRI-LA ENR	OKINAWA	EMPIRE	LTJG C.W.S. HULLAND	M
04/23/45	50539	VMF-322		OKINAWA	EMPIRE		
04/24/45	57770	VMF-222	SAMAR	SAMAR	PHIL	2NDLT JOHN A. RUMMEL	S
04/26/45	57946	VF-84	USS BUNKER HILL	OKINAWA	EMPIRE	1STLT R.B. WOOD	S
04/27/45	57383	VMF-251	SAMAR	SAMAR	PHIL		
04/28/45	82230	VMF-221	USS BUNKER HILL	OKINAWA	EMPIRE	1STLT E.W. LANGSTON	S
04/29/45	82414	VMF-312		OKINAWA	EMPIRE	CAPT KENNETH L. REUSSER	S
04/29/45	50545	VMF-322		OKINAWA	EMPIRE		
04/30/45	82509	CASU(F)-51		ULITHI	WCENPAC		
04/30/45	57641	POOL	PEARL	HAWAII	ECENPAC		
04/30/45	57970	VMF-311		OKINAWA	EMPIRE	1STLT WILLIAM K OUELLETTE	D
04/30/45	57551	VMF-312		OKINAWA	EMPIRE		
04/30/45	57723	VMF-312		OKINAWA	EMPIRE	CAPT JAMES E. COX	S
04/30/45	57277	VMF-423		GREEN	SOPAC		
05/01/45	82511	MAG-23		OKINAWA	EMPIRE		
05/03/45	57957	VMF-221	USS BUNKER HILL	OKINAWA	EMPIRE	1STLT E.K. NICOLALDOS	S
05/03/45	57960	VMF-221	USS BUNKER HILL	OKINAWA	EMPIRE	1STLT L.W. GOEGGEL, JR.	S
05/03/45	82745	VMF-221	USS BUNKER HILL	OKINAWA	EMPIRE	CAPT JOHN B. DELANCEY	M
05/04/45	82542	VF-85	USS SHANGRI-LA	IE SHIMA	EMPIRE	LTJG SAUL GHERNOFF	S
05/04/45	82746	VF-85	USS SHANGRI-LA	IE SHIMA	EMPIRE	LTJG F.S. SIDDALL	S
05/05/45	82824	VBF-85	USS SHANGRI-LA	IE SHIMA	EMPIRE	LTJG OWEN PAYNE	S
05/05/45	82354	VMF-323		OKINAWA	EMPIRE	MAJ ARTHUR L. TURNER	M
05/06/45	57530	VMF-312		OKINAWA	EMPIRE	2NDLT HOWARD FERGUSEN	S
05/06/45	57553	VMF-312		OKINAWA	EMPIRE	LT G.S. KARL	M
05/06/45	57839	VMF-312		OKINAWA	EMPIRE	2NDLT FRED SKREDERATER	M
05/06/45	57809	VMF-322		OKINAWA	EMPIRE		
05/06/45	82609	VMF-323		OKINAWA	EMPIRE		
05/09/45	82794	VBF-83	PEARL	HAWAII	ECENPAC	ENS GRANT A. SMITH	U
05/09/45	82479	VMF-112	USS BENNING-TON	OKINAWA	EMPIRE	2NDLT C.O. BARNHILL	U

DATE	BUNO	SQDRN	BASE	LOST	AREA	PILOT	FATE
05/09/45	82355	VMF-122		PELELIU	WCENPAC		
05/09/45	57910	VMF-224		OKINAWA	EMPIRE	2NDLT M. WALDMAN	M
05/10/45	82382	VF-85	USS SHANGRI-LA	IWO JIMA	EMPIRE	LTJG R.F. TOONGES	U
05/10/45	82387	VMF-311		OKINAWA	EMPIRE	2NDLT W.G. KNAPP	S
05/10/45	57584	VMF-312		OKINAWA	EMPIRE		
05/10/45	57611	VMF-312		OKINAWA	EMPIRE	1STLT WILLIAM R. SWENSON	M
05/10/45	82249	VMF-441		OKINAWA	EMPIRE	A.M. SMITH, JR.	S
05/10/45	82575	VMF-441		OKINAWA	EMPIRE	2NDLT D.H. EDWARDS	S
05/11/45	57823	VF-84	USS BUNKER HILL	OKINAWA	EMPIRE	(DECK LOSS-KAMIKAZE)	
05/11/45	57891	VF-84	USS BUNKER HILL	OKINAWA	EMPIRE	(DECK LOSS-KAMIKAZE)	
05/11/45	57939	VF-84	USS BUNKER HILL	OKINAWA	EMPIRE	(DECK LOSS-KAMIKAZE)	
05/11/45	57944	VF-84	USS BUNKER HILL	OKINAWA	EMPIRE	(DECK LOSS-KAMIKAZE)	
05/11/45	57945	VF-84	USS BUNKER HILL	OKINAWA	EMPIRE	(DECK LOSS-KAMIKAZE)	
05/11/45	82224	VF-84	USS BUNKER HILL	OKINAWA	EMPIRE	(DECK LOSS-KAMIKAZE)	
05/11/45	82614	VF-84	USS BUNKER HILL	OKINAWA	EMPIRE	(DECK LOSS-KAMIKAZE)	
05/11/45	82632	VF-84	USS BUNKER HILL	OKINAWA	EMPIRE	(DECK LOSS-KAMIKAZE)	
05/11/45	82838	VF-84	USS BUNKER HILL	OKINAWA	EMPIRE	(DECK LOSS-KAMIKAZE)	
05/11/45	82548	VF-85	USS SHANGRI-LA	IWO JIMA	EMPIRE		
05/11/45	57614	VMF-122		PELELIU	WCENPAC	2NDLT FRANK M. LAND	M
05/11/45	57797	VMF-122		PELELIU	WCENPAC	1STLT W.W. BURNS	S
05/11/45	57516	VMF-221	USS BUNKER HILL	OKINAWA	EMPIRE	(DECK LOSS-KAMIKAZE)	
05/11/45	57585	VMF-221	USS BUNKER HILL	OKINAWA	EMPIRE	(DECK LOSS-KAMIKAZE)	
05/11/45	57785	VMF-221	USS BUNKER HILL	OKINAWA	EMPIRE	(DECK LOSS-KAMIKAZE)	
05/11/45	57798	VMF-221	USS BUNKER HILL	OKINAWA	EMPIRE	(DECK LOSS-KAMIKAZE)	
05/11/45	57803	VMF-221	USS BUNKER HILL	OKINAWA	EMPIRE	(DECK LOSS-KAMIKAZE)	
05/11/45	57923	VMF-221	USS BUNKER HILL	OKINAWA	EMPIRE	(DECK LOSS-KAMIKAZE)	
05/11/45	57929	VMF-221	USS BUNKER HILL	OKINAWA	EMPIRE	(DECK LOSS-KAMIKAZE)	
05/11/45	57948	VMF-221	USS BUNKER HILL	OKINAWA	EMPIRE	(DECK LOSS-KAMIKAZE)	
05/11/45	82209	VMF-221	USS BUNKER HILL	OKINAWA	EMPIRE	(DECK LOSS-KAMIKAZE)	
05/11/45	82264	VMF-451	USS BUNKER HILL	OKINAWA	EMPIRE	(DECK LOSS-KAMIKAZE)	

DATE	BUNO	SQDRN	BASE	LOST	AREA	PILOT	FATE
05/11/45	82282	VMF-451	USS BUNKER HILL	OKINAWA	EMPIRE	(DECK LOSS-KAMIKAZE)	
05/11/45	82374	VMF-451	USS BUNKER HILL	OKINAWA	EMPIRE	(DECK LOSS-KAMIKAZE)	
05/11/45	82390	VMF-451	USS BUNKER HILL	OKINAWA	EMPIRE	(DECK LOSS-KAMIKAZE)	
05/11/45	82391	VMF-451	USS BUNKER HILL	OKINAWA	EMPIRE	(DECK LOSS-KAMIKAZE)	
05/11/45	82513	VMF-451	USS BUNKER HILL	OKINAWA	EMPIRE	(DECK LOSS-KAMIKAZE)	
05/11/45	82571	VMF-451	USS BUNKER HILL	OKINAWA	EMPIRE	(DECK LOSS-KAMIKAZE)	
05/11/45	82790	VMF-451	USS BUNKER HILL	OKINAWA	EMPIRE	(DECK LOSS-KAMIKAZE)	
05/11/45	82848	VMF-451	USS BUNKER HILL	OKINAWA	EMPIRE	(DECK LOSS-KAMIKAZE)	
05/12/45	82392	MAG-31		YOKOSUKA	EMPIRE		
05/12/45	57206	VMF-224		OKINAWA	EMPIRE	2NDLT L.J. MICHAELS	S
05/13/45	82594	VMF-112	USS BENNING-TON	KYUSHU	EMPIRE	2NDLT R.B. HAMILTON	D
05/13/45	57882	VMF-322		OKINAWA	EMPIRE		
05/13/45	82532	VMF-322		OKINAWA	EMPIRE	LT WARREN	S
05/13/45	82592	VMF-323		OKINAWA	EMPIRE	1STLT EDWARD F. MURRAY	M
05/14/45	57572	MAG-33	KADENA	OKINAWA	EMPIRE		
05/15/45	57565	VMF-312		OKINAWA	EMPIRE		
05/15/45	57353	VMF-323		OKINAWA	EMPIRE		
05/16/45	57555	VMF-114		PELELIU	WCENPAC		
05/16/45	57563	VMF-312		OKINAWA	EMPIRE		
05/16/45	82595	VMF-322		OKINAWA	EMPIRE		
05/16/45	57254	VMF-323		OKINAWA	EMPIRE		
05/16/45	82179	VMF-441		OKINAWA	EMPIRE	1STLT JAMES A. LILLY	S
05/17/45	57678	VMF-312		OKINAWA	EMPIRE		
05/17/45	57700	VMF-312		OKINAWA	EMPIRE	2NDLT HENRY H. KYLE	S
05/18/45	57577	VMF-312		OKINAWA	EMPIRE	1STLT BOHERD W. ALLEN	S
05/18/45	50429	VMF-322		OKINAWA	EMPIRE		
05/19/45	57658	VBF-1	KAHULUI	HAWAII	ECENPAC	LT R.B. EASON	S
05/19/45	57599	VMF-122		PELELIU	WCENPAC	2NDLT A.N. MACLEAN	S
05/19/45	50529	VMF-322		OKINAWA	EMPIRE		
05/20/45	82776	VMF-511	USS BLOCK ISLAND		EMPIRE	1STLT WALTER W. JACKSON	S
05/21/45	57570	AROU-1		MOMOTE	SW PAC		
05/21/45	82244	CASU(F)-15		SAIPAN	WCENPAC		
05/21/45	57401	VMF-113		CHIMU	EMPIRE	2NDLT LEO E. NOLAN	S
05/22/45	82395	VMF-323		OKINAWA	EMPIRE		
05/23/45	57962	VMF-115	ZAMBOAN-GA	ZAMBOAN-GA	PHIL	LT G. BRADLEY	S
05/23/45	57821	VMF-512	USS GILBERT ISLANDS	OKINAWA	EMPIRE	2NDLT EDGAR T. MILLER	D
05/23/45	57855	VMF-512	USS GILBERT ISLANDS	OKINAWA	EMPIRE	MAJ ELTON MUELLER	S
05/23/45	82842	VMF-512	USS GILBERT ISLANDS	OKINAWA	EMPIRE		
05/24/45	57270	VMF-155		KWAJALEIN	CENPAC	2NDLT WILLIAM R. LUCAS	U
05/24/45	57147	VMF-224		OKINAWA	EMPIRE		
05/24/45	57176	VMF-224		OKINAWA	EMPIRE		
05/24/45	57371	VMF-224		OKINAWA	EMPIRE		
05/24/45	82284	VMF-314		OKINAWA	EMPIRE	LT LOVIC J. MARBURY	M
05/24/45	82437	VMF-314		OKINAWA	EMPIRE	LT FURMAN H. KELLER	M
05/24/45	82441	VMF-314		OKINAWA	EMPIRE	LT CHARLES R. WHITE	M

DATE	BUNO	SQDRN	BASE	LOST	AREA	PILOT	FATE
05/25/45	82306	VBF-99	USS MAKASSAR STR.	SAIPAN	WCENPAC		
05/25/45	50408	VMF-111	ENIWETOK	ENIWETOK	CENPAC	1STLT ALOYSIUS URBANEK	D
05/25/45	57263	VMF-111	ENIWETOK	ENIWETOK	CENPAC	2NDLT HOWARD FLETCHER	S
05/26/45	82325	VMF-112	USS BENNING-TON	OKINAWA	EMPIRE	CAPT DONALD C. OWEN	D
05/26/45	82237	VMF-115	ZAMBOAN-GA	ZAMBOANGA	PHIL	MAJ RICHARD F. HARRISON	M
05/26/45	57547	VMF-211	ZAMBOAN-GA	ZAMBOANGA	PHIL		
05/27/45	82772	VBF-88	USS MAKASSAR STRAIT	SAIPAN	WCENPAC	ENS R.J. WOHLERS	S
05/27/45	82435	VMF-314		IE SHIMA	EMPIRE	1STLT JEROME K. KONZEN	D
05/27/45	50516	VMF-322		OKINAWA	EMPIRE		
05/27/45	57815	VMF-511	USS BLOCK ISLAND	IE SHIMA	EMPIRE	2NDLT ROBERT A. GOLDBERG	M
05/28/45	57384	VMF-113		OKINAWA	EMPIRE	2NDLT JOHN J. KISSEL	S
05/28/45	57925	VMF-224		OKINAWA	EMPIRE		
05/28/45	82259	VMF-312		OKINAWA	EMPIRE		
05/30/45	82768	CASU(F)-51		ULITHI	WCENPAC		
05/30/45	82759	VF-85	USS SHANGRI-LA	OKINAWA	EMPIRE	LTJG B.R. MCCRACKEN	S
05/30/45	82285	VMF-314		IE SHIMA	EMPIRE	LT VANMAESTRICHT	M
05/31/45	50501	VMF-422		IE SHIMA	EMPIRE	1STLT S.J. NICKELIE	S
05/31/45	82263	VMF-441		OKINAWA	EMPIRE	1STLT JOHN M. MENDINHALL	D
05/31/45	82561	VMF-441		OKINAWA	EMPIRE		
06/01/45	82628	VMF-112	USS BENNING-TON	OKINAWA	EMPIRE		
06/02/45	82298	VBF-85	USS SHANGRI-LA	KYUSHU	EMPIRE	LTJG R.A. FULLER	M
06/02/45	82789	VBF-85	USS SHANGRI-LA	KYUSHU	EMPIRE	LTJG CHERNOFF	M
06/02/45	82371	VF-85	USS SHANGRI-LA	KYUSHU	EMPIRE	LTJG WILLIAM HOWARD MARR	M
06/02/45	82547	VF-85	USS SHANGRI-LA	KYUSHU	EMPIRE	LT L. SOVANSKI	S
06/02/45	82751	VF-85	USS SHANGRI-LA	KYUSHU	EMPIRE	LT ATKINSON	M
06/02/45	57893	VMF-113		IE SHIMA	EMPIRE	2NDLT H.E. WENDT	S
06/03/45	57895	VBF-85	USS SHANGRI-LA	KYUSHU	EMPIRE	ENS R.J. SUNDQUIST	M
06/03/45	82636	VF-85	USS SHANGRI-LA	KYUSHU	EMPIRE	LTJG EDWARD DIXON, JR.	M
06/03/45	82753	VF-85	USS SHANGRI-LA	KYUSHU	EMPIRE	LT SIGURD LOVDAL	M
06/03/45	57508	VMF-211	ZAMBOAN-GA	ZAMBOANGA	PHIL	LT TIERNEY	S
06/04/45	82440	VF-85	USS SHANGRI-LA	KYUSHU	EMPIRE	LT R.C. WHITNEY	S
06/04/45	57175	VMF-224		OKINAWA	EMPIRE	1STLT LEO J.J. MICHAELS	D
06/04/45	57354	VMF-224		OKINAWA	EMPIRE	2NDLT J.M. FALKNER	S
06/04/45	82670	VMF-224		OKINAWA	EMPIRE	1STLT W.F. FRANKLIN	S
06/06/45	57980	VMF-311		OKINAWA	EMPIRE		
06/06/45	57388	VMF-422		IE SHIMA	EMPIRE	2NDLT L.H. CYRIL	U

DATE	BUNO	SQDRN	BASE	LOST	AREA	PILOT	FATE
06/06/45	82819	VMF-512	USS GILBERT ISLANDS	IE SHIMA	EMPIRE	2NDLT JEROME A. WINDHAM	S
06/07/45	57763	VMF-121	PELELIU	PELELIU	WCENPAC		
06/07/45	82265	VMF-311		OKINAWA	EMPIRE	2NDLT R.W. LITTLE	S
06/07/45	82549	VMF-314		IE SHIMA	EMPIRE	1STLT J.H. KLEIN, JR.	S
06/07/45	82757	VMF-441		OKINAWA	EMPIRE	1STLT JAMES F. TIGHE	S
06/08/45	82451	VF-85	USS SHANGRI-LA	KYUSHU	EMPIRE	LTJG R.L. MELTEBEKE	S
06/08/45	57163	VMF-155		KWAJALEIN	CENPAC		
06/08/45	82793	VMF-322		OKINAWA	EMPIRE	2NDLT B.D. CAMP	S
06/09/45	82596	VMF-122		PELELIU	WCENPAC	LT ROBERT L. DILKS	M
06/09/45	82460	VMF-123	USS BENNING-TON	KYUSHU	EMPIRE		
06/09/45	82500	VMF-218	ZAMBOAN-GA	ZAMBOANGA	PHIL	2NDLT JOSEPH A. EAGER	D
06/09/45	82605	VMF-323		OKINAWA	EMPIRE		
06/10/45	82290	VBF-85	USS SHANGRI-LA	ENR LEYTE GULF	EMPIRE		
06/10/45	82482	VBF-85	USS SHANGRI-LA	ENR LEYTE GULF	EMPIRE	ENS M.F. SNAVELY	S
06/11/45	82530	VMF-218	ZAMBOAN-GA	ZAMBOANGA	PHIL		
06/11/45	82286	VMF-311		OKINAWA	EMPIRE	2NDLT WILFRED W. WILHIDE	D
06/12/45	82436	VF-85	USS SHANGRI-LA	ENR LEYTE GULF	EMPIRE	LTJG L.K. MIFFLIN	S
06/12/45	50515	VMF-224		OKINAWA	EMPIRE	2NDLT S.B. VOTH	S
06/12/45	57701	VMF-312		OKINAWA	EMPIRE	2NDLT WESLIN E. O'NEAL	D
06/12/45	57526	VMF-512	USS GILBERT ISLANDS	IE SHIMA	EMPIRE		
06/13/45	50395	VMF-155		KWAJALEIN	CENPAC		
06/14/45	82427	VMF-113		IE SHIMA	EMPIRE	CAPT G.B. HERLIHY	S
06/14/45	57935	VMF-115	ZAMBOAN-GA	ZAMBOANGA	PHIL		
06/15/45	50420	CASU-11		OKINAWA	EMPIRE		
06/16/45	50504	VMF-155		KWAJALEIN	CENPAC		
06/17/45	82269	VMF-314		IE SHIMA	EMPIRE	1STLT DONALD T. MCLENNON	S
06/17/45	82442	VMF-314		IE SHIMA	EMPIRE	1STLT P.A. SCHAEFER	S
06/17/45	82562	VMF-314		IE SHIMA	EMPIRE	1STLT G.H. BERGEN	S
06/18/45	57491	VMF-211	ZAMBOAN-GA	ZAMBOANGA	PHIL		
06/19/45	57507	VMF-211	ZAMBOAN-GA	ZAMBOANGA	PHIL		
06/20/45	82372	VMF-314		IE SHIMA	EMPIRE	1STLT W.B. CALDWELL	S
06/21/45	57578	CASU-11		OKINAWA	EMPIRE		
06/22/45	82760	VMF-314		IE SHIMA	EMPIRE	1STLT J.W. LEAPER	S
06/23/45	57370	CASU-11		OKINAWA	EMPIRE		
06/23/45	82684	VBF-93	USS BOXER		CENLANT	ENS W.L. CREN	S
06/23/45	50543	VBF-99	USS MAKASSAR STR.	SAIPAN	WCENPAC		
06/23/45	82761	VMF-311		OKINAWA	EMPIRE		
06/24/45	57710	VMF-121	PELELIU	PELELIU	WCENPAC		
06/26/45	57849	VMF-322		OKINAWA	EMPIRE	2NDLT G.L. DUFFIN	S
06/26/45	57296	VMF-422		IE SHIMA	EMPIRE	2NDLT RICHARD G. TAYLOR	S
06/28/45	82276	VMF-311		OKINAWA	EMPIRE	LT EUGENE B. READE	M
06/29/45	57591	VMF-218	ZAMBOAN-GA	ZAMBOANGA	PHIL		
06/29/45	57282	VMF-422		IE SHIMA	EMPIRE	2NDLT JOHN J. LANDSBERG	D
06/29/45	82494	VMF-422		IE SHIMA	EMPIRE	2NDLT EDWARD MCCOY, JR.	D
06/29/45	82498	VMF-422		IE SHIMA	EMPIRE	2NDLT JOHN K. STEVENSON	D

DATE	BUNO	SQDRN	BASE	LOST	AREA	PILOT	FATE
06/30/45	82758	CASU(F)-12		GUAM	WCENPAC	LT L.E. SALISBURY	S
06/30/45	57781	SERVRON-22		IE SHIMA	EMPIRE		
07/01/45	82303	VMF-312		AWASE	EMPIRE	2NDLT JOHN P. FLYNN	S
07/02/45	82626	VBF-85	USS SHANGRI-LA	ENR HOKKAIDO	EMPIRE	ENS W.E. REDMON	S
07/02/45	57474	VMF-113		IE SHIMA	EMPIRE	2NDLT CHALMUS N. JONES	S
07/02/45	57783	VMF-311		IE SHIMA	EMPIRE	2NDLT JAMES FRIEL	S
07/04/45	57771	VMF-211	ZAMBOAN-GA	ZAMBOANGA	PHIL	LT BEDUNAH	S
07/08/45	82502	VMF-323		KADENA	EMPIRE	2NDLT A.F. DICHAT, JR.	S
07/09/45	82584	VMF-422		KYUSHU	EMPIRE	LT WEISS	S
07/10/45	82461	POOL	USS TRIPOLI	PEARL	ECENPAC	LTJG WARREN P. KELLEY	S
07/11/45	82378	VMF-311		OKINAWA	EMPIRE	2NDLT J.T. DOSWELL	S
07/11/45	82277	VMF-441		OKINAWA	EMPIRE	2NDLT A.J. BIBEE	S
07/11/45	82577	VMF-441		OKINAWA	EMPIRE	2NDLT J.W. FULLERTON	S
07/12/45	57422	VMF-113		IE SHIMA	EMPIRE	1STLT STANLEY L. SCHARF	S
07/13/45	82459	VMF-311		CHIMU	EMPIRE	LT EDISON	S
07/13/45	82396	VMF-441		CHIMU	EMPIRE	1STLT HOWARD K. FLETCHER	D
07/14/45	82421	VBF-1	USS BENNING-TON	HOKKAIDO	EMPIRE	ENS STEPHEN KOMAR	D
07/14/45	82512	VBF-1	USS BENNING-TON	HOKKAIDO	EMPIRE	LTJG FRANK G. KINGSTON	S
07/14/45	82633	VF-85	USS SHANGRI-LA	HOKKAIDO	EMPIRE	LTJG MCPHEE	S
07/14/45	82651	VMF-224		OKINAWA	EMPIRE	2NDLT R.F. LEE SUN	S
07/15/45	57725	CASU(F)-12		GUAM	WCENPAC		
07/15/45	82845	VBF-85	USS SHANGRI-LA	HOKKAIDO	EMPIRE	LTJG CECIL W. MOORE	S
07/15/45	82543	VF-85	USS SHANGRI-LA	HOKKAIDO	EMPIRE		
07/15/45	82384	VMF-314		IE SHIMA	EMPIRE	1STLT DONALD T. MCLENNON	S
07/16/45	57168	VMF-224		CHIMU	EMPIRE	LT R.F. SILKWORTH	S
07/16/45	57972	VMF-311		CHIMU	EMPIRE	LT O'DONNELL	S
07/18/45	82472	VBF-99	USS MAKASSAR STRAIT	SAIPAN	WCENPAC	1STLT JOHN K. SHANNON	S
07/18/45	57425	VMF-122		PELELIU	WCENPAC		
07/18/45	82475	VMF-122		PELELIU	WCENPAC	CAPT WILLIAM I. BRANAGAN	S
07/19/45	57355	VMF-113		IE SHIMA	EMPIRE	1STLT S.R. CROWELL	D
07/19/45	57429	VMF-211			PHIL	LT CORLEY	S
07/19/45	82385	VMF-314		IE SHIMA	EMPIRE	1STLT C.B. CARROL, JR.	S
07/20/45	57489	SERVRON-22		ENGEBI	WCENPAC		
07/20/45	82314	VBF-83	USS ESSEX	IE SHIMA	EMPIRE		
07/20/45	82351	VBF-99	USS MAKASSAR STRAIT	SAIPAN	WCENPAC	LTJG A.E. SALT	S
07/21/45	82418	VBF-100	HILO	HAWAII	ECENPAC	ENS IRVING B. TYSON	S
07/22/45	57696	VMF-122		PELELIU	WCENPAC	2NDLT GEO F. FARLINGTON	S
07/24/45	82468	VBF-1	USS BENNING-TON	KURE	EMPIRE	LTJG R.M. APPLEGATE	M
07/24/45	82791	VBF-83	USS ESSEX	KURE	EMPIRE		
07/25/45	82744	VF-85	USS SHANGRI-LA	KURE	EMPIRE	ENS J.H. MOORE	S
07/27/45	57461	VMF-218			PHIL	LT H.B. PERSON	S
07/28/45	57511	VMF-224		CHIMU	EMPIRE	2NDLT L.L. TRUEX	S
07/29/45	57339	VMF-155		KWAJALEIN	CENPAC	2NDLT EDWIN J. WULFF	S
07/30/45	82810	VMF-224		CHIMU	EMPIRE	2NDLT R.D. WARD	M
07/30/45	57977	VMF-441		OKINAWA	EMPIRE	2NDLT J.W. FULLERTON	D

DATE	BUNO	SQDRN	BASE	LOST	AREA	PILOT	FATE
07/31/45	57792	POOL	BARBERS POINT	HAWAII	ECENPAC		
07/31/45	82801	VBF-100		HAWAII	ECENPAC		
07/31/45	82507	VBF-85	USS SHANGRI-LA	KURE	EMPIRE		
08/04/45	82453	SERVRON-22		IE SHIMA	EMPIRE		
08/04/45	82448	VMF-314		CHIMU	EMPIRE	2NDLT JOHN J. FISHER	S
08/04/45	57973	VMF-441		CHIMU	EMPIRE	1STLT C.F. SMALLEY	S
08/05/45	57393	VMF-122		PELELIU	WCENPAC	2NDLT WILLIAM L. ARNETT	M
08/05/45	82495	VMF-422		CHIMU	EMPIRE		
08/07/45	82335	VMF-122		PELELIU	WCENPAC	LT MELIN	S
08/07/45	82807	VMF-323		AWASE	EMPIRE		
08/09/45	82567	VMF-314		CHIMU	EMPIRE	1STLT BRUCE J. THOMAS	S
08/09/45	82273	VMF-441		CHIMU	EMPIRE	2NDLT TOM J. NOLAN, JR.	S
08/10/45	50419	CASU-11		OKINAWA	EMPIRE		
08/10/45	50519	CASU-11		OKINAWA	EMPIRE		
08/10/45	57655	CASU-11		OKINAWA	EMPIRE		
08/10/45	57833	CASU-11		OKINAWA	EMPIRE		
08/10/45	57976	VMF-311		CHIMU	EMPIRE	2NDLT VINCENT J. MARSELO	S
08/10/45	82275	VMF-311		CHIMU	EMPIRE		
08/13/45	57863	CASU(F)-12		GUAM	WCENPAC		
08/13/45	82604	VMF-322		OKINAWA	EMPIRE		
08/14/45	82559	VMF-314		CHIMU	EMPIRE	2NDLT W.J. BARBANES	S
08/15/45	57761	VMF-122		PELELIU	WCENPAC		

VOUGHT F4U-4

Throughout 1943 and 1944, and into the beginning of 1945, Vought continued upgrading the F4U Corsair's "1-Series." The F4U-1, -1A, -1D and -1C, however, all shared the same core, and modifications and updates were often implemented in the field on earlier variants as they were introduced in the factory on the later models (for example, -1As still in service were retrofitted to carry the same wing-root pylons and four rocket tab positions used on the -1C). However the Corsair would soon receive a major upgrade.

While the supercharger-equipped XF4U-3 project provided unsatisfactory results, Vought would follow a different path with its contemporary and successor. At the heart of this new variant was an improved Pratt and Whitney R-2800-18(W) radial, replacing the earlier -8(W). This model of the engine would produce 2100hp on takeoff, and with the use of water-methanol injection could achieve a power rating of 2450hp. To take advantage of the increased engine power, the three-bladed paddle prop utilized since the -1A was replaced with a massive four-bladed paddle. The result was a significant increase in airspeed, rate of climb, and lateral acceleration.

The aircraft's cowling was redesigned with a distinctive chin scoop, and in addition to the exhaust stacks on the lower fuselage exhaust was vented from an additional stack on either side of the fuselage above the wings. The curved armored windscreen in most production aircraft would be replaced with a flat screen to reduce optical distortion, and the metal hood on the canopy over the pilot's head would be completely eliminated. The cockpit was completely redesigned. The "floorless" cockpit of the "1-Series" Corsairs was eliminated and replaced with a floored version. The instrument cluster was revised, as was the positioning of controls for the engine, landing gear, flaps, and other secondary systems.

Armament returned to the six Browning .50cal of the -1, -1A and 1-D, bringing to an end the experiment of all-cannon armament in the Corsair until the end of the war. Like the -1D, the aircraft was fitted with two main pylons inboard of the landing gear, and rocket tabs for four 5" HVARs on each wing, for a total of 8. The wing-mounted fuel tanks were eliminated, and even more of the fabric-covered wing surface was replaced with metal.

The new aircraft, designated the F4U-4, put up monstrous performance numbers. With a top speed exceeding 450mph at level flight at altitude she was one of the fastest propeller-driven fighters of the war. Acceleration was excellent and rate of climb was boosted to nearly 4000fpm by the uprated engine and four-bladed propeller. In combat she provided all the strengths of the previous models: excellent rate of roll, exceptional mid and high-speed maneuverability, rugged airframe and superb firepower and ordinance load. She surpassed the P-51 Mustang--widely and often considered America's finest fighter aircraft of World War II--in nearly all aspects of performance. The F4U-4 completely dominated the Japanese A6M and Ki-43; was faster than Japan's best fighter, the Ki-84, and cleanly outmatched it in vertical performance. While the "Frank" was highly maneuverable at low speeds, at mid and high speeds the F4U-4 was superior, especially with the Ki-84's tendency to suffer loss of aileron and elevator authority at higher speeds.

F4U-4s began to deploy to the Pacific during the final four months of World War II, replacing and supplementing the -1Ds and -1Cs already in the theater. However despite her gaudy performance, the F4U-4's limited action against the all but beaten Japanese Air and Naval forces meant she would make little real impact on the Pacific war. It was perhaps this late arrival that has led the "4-Hog" to be relegated by history to a place behind the P-51 Mustang as the greatest American fighter of World War II. By the time the Corsair fought her next war the age of propeller fighters was at an end, and the F4U-4 never had a real chance to truly show its capabilities as an air-to-air combatant.

F4U-4s were deployed to both Navy and Marine squadrons, and operated from carrier decks and land bases. First Corsair ace Kenneth A. Walsh finished out the war in the F4U-4, recording his final victory in the aircraft (information from Wikipedia). Aircraft lost:

DATE	BUNO	SQDRN	BASE	LOST	AREA	PILOT	FATE
00/00/00	81232	VBF-94	USS LEXINGTON				
00/00/00	81311	VBF-94	USS LEXINGTON				
03/25/45	80802	VBF-89	USS ANTIETAM		CENLANT	LT T.F. GODDING	
03/28/45	80805	VBF-89	USS ANTIETAM		CENLANT	LTJG A.S. PAULSON	
04/10/45	80799	VBF-89	USS ANTIETAM		CENLANT	ENS DAVID L. GIRARDET	S
04/15/45	80810	VBF-89	USS ANTIETAM		EMPIRE		S
05/17/45	80851	VMF-223	SAMAR	SAMAR	PHIL	2NDLT ROBERT HUXHAM	D
05/20/45	80912	VMF-212	SAMAR	SAMAR	PHIL		
05/30/45	80856	SERVRON-14		SAMAR	PHIL		
05/31/45	81553	VBF-89	USS ANTIETAM	PANAMA	CENLANT	LTJG T.F. KENDRICK	D
06/07/45	81028	VBF-94	USS LEXINGTON	PEARL	ECENPAC	ENS R.S. ISAACS	S
06/07/45	81118	VBF-94	USS LEXINGTON	PEARL	ECENPAC	LCDR L.S. WALL, JR.	S

DATE	BUNO	SQDRN	BASE	LOST	AREA	PILOT	FATE
06/09/45	81346	VBF-2	PEARL	HAWAII	ECENPAC	ENS DONALD K. HOBSON	S
06/09/45	81084	VBF-6	USS HANCOCK	PEARL	ECENPAC		
06/11/45	81000	SERVRON-14		OKINAWA	EMPIRE		
06/11/45	81173	SERVRON-14		OKINAWA	EMPIRE		
06/13/45	80892	SERVRON-14		OKINAWA	EMPIRE		
06/13/45	81493	VBF-86	USS WASP		PHIL		
06/14/45	81121	POOL	PEARL	HAWAII	ECENPAC		
06/15/45	81336	VBF-86	USS WASP		PHIL		
06/16/45	81217	VBF-94	USS LEX-INGTON	WAKE	WCENPAC	LTJG C.W. SNYDER	D
06/17/45	81116	VBF-2	HILO	HAWAII	ECENPAC	ENS LOUIS J. SMOLEY	D
06/17/45	81210	VBF-2	HILO	HAWAII	ECENPAC	LT RICHARD W. HOLLIS	D
06/18/45	81304	VBF-6	USS HANCOCK	PEARL	ECENPAC		
06/18/45	81332	VBF-86	USS WASP		PHIL		
06/20/45	81209	POOL	PEARL	HAWAII	ECENPAC		
06/20/45	81262	VBF-94	USS LEX-INGTON	WAKE	WCENPAC	LT NICHOLAS M. PAVONETTI	D
06/21/45	81066	VMF-212		OKINAWA	EMPIRE	2NDLT THOMAS H MCKAY JR.	M
06/21/45	81052	VMF-222		OKINAWA	EMPIRE	LT A.J. AUSTIN	M
06/25/45	80862	SERVRON-14		OKINAWA	EMPIRE		
06/28/45	81187	POOL	PEARL	HAWAII	ECENPAC		
06/28/45	80882	SERVRON-14		OKINAWA	EMPIRE		
06/28/45	81309	VBF-86	USS WASP	PEARL	ECENPAC		
06/29/45	80913	VMF-212		OKINAWA	EMPIRE	2NDLT JAMES B. WORTMAN	S
06/29/45	81018	VMF-212		OKINAWA	EMPIRE		
07/01/45	81061	VMF-222		AWASE	EMPIRE		
07/02/45	81303	VBF-86	USS WASP		EMPIRE		
07/02/45	81605	VBF-89		HAWAII	ECENPAC	LTJG ROBERT S.C. BAIN	S
07/02/45	81158	VBF-94	USS LEX-INGTON		EMPIRE	LTJG JOHN F. O'NEIL	D
07/04/45	81529	VBF-150	USS LAKE CHAM-PLAIN	CULEBRA IS.	CENLANT	LT J.P. HANCOCK	D
07/05/45	81760	VBF-150	USS LAKE CHAM-PLAIN	CULEBRA IS.	CENLANT	LT J.F. OLIVER	D
07/07/45	81044	VBF-6	USS HANCOCK		EMPIRE	ENS MILTON ZEHR	S
07/07/45	81012	VMF-212		AWASE	EMPIRE		
07/07/45	80817	VMF-222		AWASE	EMPIRE		
07/08/45	81671	VBF-10	USS INTREPID	HAWAII	ECENPAC		
07/08/45	81589	VBF-89		HAWAII	ECENPAC	ENS E.J. HEITINGER	S
07/09/45	81034	ACORN-30		TACLOBAN	PHIL		
07/09/45	81139	VBF-89		HAWAII	ECENPAC	ENS M.K. SPIESS	S
07/09/45	81540	VBF-89		HAWAII	ECENPAC	ENS R.L. HEARN, JR.	S
07/10/45	81180	VBF-6	USS HANCOCK		EMPIRE	LT HARVEY G. ODENBRETT	S
07/10/45	81330	VBF-94	USS LEX-INGTON		EMPIRE	LTJG EDWARD CLANCEY	D
07/11/45	81684	VBF-10	USS INTREPID	HAWAII	ECENPAC	ENS L.A. PENICK	S
07/11/45	81110	VMF-222		OKINAWA	EMPIRE	2NDLT CLARK KETCHAM	S
07/13/45	81315	VBF-2		SAIPAN	WCENPAC	ENS ROY K. SORENSEN	S
07/16/45	80875	VMF-223		AWASE	EMPIRE	CAPT DONALD L. RADWAY	S
07/16/45	80941	VMF-223		AWASE	EMPIRE	2NDLT WILLIAM V. EVERETT	M
07/17/45	81085	VBF-6	USS HANCOCK		EMPIRE	ENS N.T. EDMONDSON	D
07/17/45	80982	VMF-223		AWASE	EMPIRE		
07/18/45	80847	VBF-6	USS HANCOCK		EMPIRE		

DATE	BUNO	SQDRN	BASE	LOST	AREA	PILOT	FATE
07/18/45	80955	VBF-6	USS HANCOCK		EMPIRE		
07/18/45	81073	VBF-6	USS HANCOCK		EMPIRE		
07/18/45	81535	VBF-94	USS LEX-INGTON		EMPIRE	LTJG MILTON L. ADAMS	D
07/19/45	81298	VBF-94	USS LEX-INGTON		EMPIRE		
07/21/45	80963	VBF-6	USS HANCOCK		EMPIRE		
07/21/45	81095	VMF-212		OKINAWA	EMPIRE	2NDLT JOHN F. MCGRATH	D
07/22/45	81501	VBF-86	USS WASP		EMPIRE	LTJG ARTHUR W. ANDERSON	D
07/24/45	81253	CASU-31	HILO	HAWAII	ECENPAC		
07/24/45	81185	CVG-2		SAIPAN	WCENPAC		
07/24/45	81179	VBF-6	USS HANCOCK		EMPIRE	ENS C.L. BAUSER	D
07/24/45	81088	VBF-94	USS LEX-INGTON		EMPIRE	LTJG THOMAS BRETT	M
07/24/45	81099	VBF-94	USS LEX-INGTON		EMPIRE	LT T.A. SINCLAIR	S
07/24/45	81119	VBF-94	USS LEX-INGTON		EMPIRE	ENS H.F. DONNELLY, JR.	S
07/24/45	81319	VBF-94	USS LEX-INGTON		EMPIRE	LT RALPH E. BOGGS	M
07/24/45	81371	VMF-212		AWASE	EMPIRE		
07/24/45	80920	VMF-223		AWASE	EMPIRE		
07/24/45	80995	VMF-223		AWASE	EMPIRE		
07/24/45	81070	VMF-223		AWASE	EMPIRE		
07/25/45	80784	SERVRON-14		OKINAWA	EMPIRE		
07/25/45	81058	VBF-6	USS HANCOCK		EMPIRE	ENS E.H. DODGE	M
07/25/45	81280	VBF-86	USS WASP		EMPIRE	LTJG L.J. HOSE	U
07/25/45	80980	VBF-93	USS BOXER		CENLANT	LTJG W.L. KILLINGSWORTH	S
07/26/45	81353	CASU(F)-15		SAIPAN	WCENPAC		
07/26/45	81035	VBF-6	USS HANCOCK		EMPIRE		
07/28/45	81226	VBF-94	USS LEX-INGTON		EMPIRE	ENS HOWARD G. BELL	S
07/28/45	81396	VBF-94	USS LEX-INGTON		EMPIRE	ENS R.J. CUNNINGHAM	D
07/29/45	81214	VBF-94	USS LEX-INGTON		EMPIRE	ENS JAMES W. MINETTE	S
07/30/45	81775	CASU(F)-15		SAIPAN	WCENPAC	ENS J.E. TERHORST	D
07/30/45	80902	SERVRON-14		OKINAWA	EMPIRE		
07/30/45	80831	VBF-6	USS HANCOCK		EMPIRE		
07/30/45	80888	VBF-6	USS HANCOCK		EMPIRE		
07/30/45	81075	VBF-6	USS HANCOCK		EMPIRE		
07/30/45	81086	VBF-6	USS HANCOCK		EMPIRE		
07/30/45	81279	VBF-94	USS LEX-INGTON		EMPIRE	ENS E.W. GARRISON	D
07/30/45	81595	VBF-94	USS LEX-INGTON		EMPIRE	ENS A.L. MORRIS	M
07/31/45	80836	SERVRON-14		OKINAWA	EMPIRE		
07/31/45	80870	VBF-6	USS HANCOCK		EMPIRE		
07/31/45	80909	VBF-6	USS HANCOCK		EMPIRE		
08/01/45	81197	CASU(F)-35		ENIWETOK	CENPAC		
08/01/45	81270	CASU(F)-35		ENIWETOK	CENPAC		
08/03/45	81358	VBF-86	USS WASP	YOKOSUKA	EMPIRE		
08/03/45	81194	VBF-94	USS LEX-INGTON		EMPIRE		
08/03/45	81663	VBF-94	USS LEX-INGTON		EMPIRE		

DATE	BUNO	SQDRN	BASE	LOST	AREA	PILOT	FATE
08/04/45	81324	VBF-92		SAIPAN	WCENPAC		
08/05/45	81296	SERVRON-14		OKINAWA	EMPIRE		
08/05/45	81067	VBF-6	USS HANCOCK		EMPIRE		
08/05/45	80962	VMF-212		AWASE	EMPIRE		
08/06/45	81349	VBF-86	USS WASP	YOKOSUKA	EMPIRE	LTJG WILLIAM E. BRIDWELL	S
08/09/45	81362	VBF-6	USS HANCOCK		EMPIRE	LT MARSHALL LLOYD	S
08/09/45	80970	VF-94	USS LEX-INGTON		EMPIRE	ENS EARL W. NEFF	
08/09/45	81120	VF-94	USS LEX-INGTON		EMPIRE	LTJG GEORGE C. LANTZ	S
08/10/45	81352	VBF-6	USS HANCOCK		EMPIRE	ENS JOHN M. PETERSON	S
08/11/45	80956	SERVRON-14		OKINAWA	EMPIRE		
08/11/45	81322	SERVRON-14		OKINAWA	EMPIRE		
08/13/45	81042	SERVRON-14		OKINAWA	EMPIRE		
08/13/45	81774	VBF-86	USS WASP	YOKOSUKA	EMPIRE	LT EDWARD J. RUANE	S
08/14/45	81909	VBF-86	USS WASP	YOKOSUKA	EMPIRE		
08/14/45	81318	VF-95		HAWAII	ECENPAC	ENS DAVID C. STUCKEY	S

VOUGHT O3U-3

The Vought O2U Corsair was a 1920s biplane scout and observation aircraft. Made by Vought Corporation, the O2U was ordered by the United States Navy in 1927. Powered by a 400 hp (298 kW) Pratt & Whitney R-1340 Wasp engine, it incorporated a steel-tube fuselage structure and a wood wing structure with fabric covering. Many were seaplanes or amphibians. 76 of the O3U-3 variant were built – this variant used the 550 hp (410 kW) Pratt & Whitney R-1340-12 Wasp engine. Aircraft lost:

DATE	BUNO	SQDRN	BASE	LOST	AREA	PILOT	FATE
04/18/43	9302	VJ-3			SOPAC		
04/20/43	9303	VJ-3			WCENPAC		
04/20/43	9309	VJ-3			WCENPAC		
04/20/43	9315	VJ-3			WCENPAC		
04/27/43	9311	VJ-3			SOPAC		

VOUGHT OS2U-1

Much like the Vought OS2N-1 story written above, the Vought OS2U-1 was the initial production variant of the XOS2U-1 but powered by a 450 hp (336 kW) Pratt & Whitney R-985-48. There were 54 built. Aircraft lost:

DATE	BUNO	SQDRN	BASE	LOST	AREA	PILOT	FATE
12/08/41	1717	BB-41	USS MISSISSIP-PI	OFF ICELAND	NORLANT		
06/25/43	1699	SOSU-1	PEARL	HAWAII	ECENPAC		
05/15/44	1698	SOSU-1	PEARL	HAWAII	ECENPAC		
05/15/44	1708	SOSU-1	PEARL	HAWAII	ECENPAC		
10/31/44	1703	AWT ACTION	KODIAK	ALASKA	NORPAC		
06/08/45	1723	FAW-4	ATTU	ALASKA	NORPAC		

VOUGHT OS2U-2

Much like the Vought OS2N-1 story written above, the OS2U-2 was the production variant of the -1 with minor equipment changes and powered by a 450 hp (336 kW) Pratt & Whitney R-985-50. There were 158 built. Aircraft lost:

DATE	BUNO	SQDRN	BASE	LOST	AREA	PILOT	FATE
12/07/41	2199	PAT WING-2	KANEOHE	HAWAII	ECENPAC		
12/14/41	2208	VS-5	BERMUDA (DET 4)	BERMUDA	NORLANT	JOHN J. FITZGERALD	U
12/31/41	2207	VS-5	BERMUDA (DET 4)	BERMUDA	NORLANT	RICHARD E. BROWN	U
01/05/42	2282	FAW-10	USS CHILDS	N.E.I.	SW PAC	ENS J.O. BALDWIN	S
01/05/42	2285	FAW-10	USS CHILDS	N.E.I.	SW PAC		
01/30/42	3108	VN-7 D6	SITKA	ALASKA	NORPAC		
05/11/42	2284	VP-101		AUSTRALIA	SOPAC		
06/01/42	2192	VS-5	BERMUDA (DET 4)	BERMUDA	NORLANT	ENS JOHN J. TEDMARSH	S
06/03/42	3090	VS-5	BERMUDA (DET 4)	BERMUDA	NORLANT		
09/03/42	2194	VS-5	BERMUDA (DET 4)	BERMUDA	NORLANT	ENS LAWRENCE A. UTTER	U
11/09/42	3088		USS MACKINAC	ENR SANTA CRUZ	SOPAC		
05/17/43	3078				SW PAC		
09/12/43	2283	VS-61			SW PAC	AP1/C W.B. BECK	D
10/02/43	2281	VS-61			SOPAC		
12/31/44	2216	A.A.	PEARL	HAWAII	ECENPAC		

VOUGHT OS2U-3

Much like the Vought OS2N-1 story written above, the OS2U-3 was based on the O2SU-2 with self-sealing fuel tanks, armor protection, two .30 cal (7.62 mm) guns (dorsal and nose mounted), and able to carry 325 lbs (147 kgs) of depth charges or 100 lb (45 kg) bombs. It was powered by a 450 hp (336 kW) Pratt & Whitney R-985-AN2 engine. There were 1006 built. Aircraft lost:

DATE	BUNO	SQDRN	BASE	LOST	AREA	PILOT	FATE
12/07/41	5294	BB-36	USS NEVADA	PEARL	ECENPAC		
12/07/41	5288	BB-37	USS OKLAHOMA	PEARL	ECENPAC		
12/07/41	5289	BB-37	USS OKLAHOMA	PEARL	ECENPAC		
12/07/41	5290	BB-37	USS OKLAHOMA	PEARL	ECENPAC		
12/07/41	5305	BB-43	USS TENNES-SEE	PEARL	ECENPAC		
12/07/41	5353	BB-44	USS CALIFORN-IA	PEARL	ECENPAC		
12/07/41	5285	BB-46	USS MARYLAND	PEARL	ECENPAC		
12/07/41	5326	BB-48	USS WEST VIRGINIA)	PEARL	ECENPAC		
12/07/41	5327	BB-48	USS WEST VIRGINIA	PEARL	ECENPAC		
12/22/41	9687			PORT ARMSTRONG	NORPAC	ENS JAMES A. WAINWRIGHT	M
12/23/41	5946			BUTTON	SOPAC	ENS GEORGE H. JEWETT	S
01/26/42	5958	VS-5	RUSSELLS		SOPAC	LT PAUL S. OBNEY	S
02/03/42	5941	VS-1	(DET 14)		SOPAC		
02/03/42	5942	VS-1	(DET 14)		SOPAC		

DATE	BUNO	SQDRN	BASE	LOST	AREA	PILOT	FATE
02/13/42	5315	BB-33	USS ARKANSAS		NORLANT		
03/22/42	5329	BB-43	USS TENNES-SEE	PEARL	ECENPAC	ENS H.S. SILBERSTEIN	U
04/04/42	5777	USCG	USS NORTH CAROLINA	CARIBBEAN	CENLANT		
04/08/42		BB-40	USS NEW MEXICO	PEARL	ECENPAC	GEORGE M. COLE	U
04/25/42	5324	BB-41	USS MISSISSIP-PI	OFF SAN FRAN.	CENPAC		
05/01/42	5736	VO-3	USS IDAHO	PEARL	ECENPAC		
05/08/42	5332	BB-43	USS TENNES-SEE	PEARL	ECENPAC	ENS NORMAN MERRILL	S
05/31/42	5364	VS-1	PORT VINCENT (DET 10)		CENLANT	LT H.H. HIRSCHY	S
06/08/42	5355	VS-3	(DET 14)	HAWAII	ECENPAC		
06/09/42	5310	VO-2	USS PENNSYL-VANIA	OFF CALIFORNIA	CENPAC	ENS EDWARD P. JOYCE	S
06/11/42	5304	BB-45	USS COLORA-DO		CENPAC	(TRAINING EXERCISE)	
06/14/42	5339	VO-3	USS IDAHO	PEARL	ECENPAC		
06/23/42	5298	BB-40	USS NEW MEXICO	PEARL	ECENPAC		
06/24/42	5330	VO-4	USS MARYLAND	MIDWAY	ECENPAC		
07/01/42	5336	CL-8	USS DETROIT		ECENPAC		
07/06/42	5738		AUSTRALIA		SW PAC		
07/07/42	5818	VS-1	(DET 13)		NORPAC		
07/09/42	5748		SITKA	ALASKA	NORPAC		
07/24/42	5908	CL-6	USS CINCINNAT I	TRINIDAD	CENLANT		
08/05/42	5810	VSD-3	USS CINCIN-NATI		NORLANT	ROBERT G. LONG	D
08/06/42	5345	BB-41	USS MISSISSIP-PI	OFF SAN FRAN.	CENPAC		
08/16/42	5287	VO-4	USS MARYLAND	PEARL	ECENPAC		
08/10/42	5297	BB-40	USS NEW MEXICO	PEARL	ECENPAC		
08/20/42	5350	BB-43	USS TENNES-SEE	PEARL	ECENPAC	ENS W.J. PENDOTA	U
08/26/42	5757	VO-6	USS SOUTH DAKOTA	ENR TONGA IS.	ECENPAC		
09/02/42	5358	VO-4			ECENPAC	ENS L.A. BEARD	U
09/14/42	9634		USS ESSEX	SITKA	NORPAC		
09/21/42	5344	CL-7	USS RALEIGH		CENPAC	ENS JOHN W. GEORGE	U
09/29/42	5342	CL-5	USS MILWAU-KEE	RECIFE	BRAZIL		
10/29/42	5444	CASU(F)-12		GUAM	WCENPAC		
10/30/42	5360	VS-3	(DET 14)	HAWAII	ECENPAC		
11/15/42	5758	VO-6	USS SOUTH DAKOTA	GUADAL-CANAL	SOPAC		
11/15/42	5759	VO-6	USS SOUTH DAKOTA	GUADAL-CANAL	SOPAC		
11/18/42	5316	BB-35	USS TEXAS	PORT LYAUTEY	MOROC-CO	LT WILLIAM A. TURNER	U

DATE	BUNO	SQDRN	BASE	LOST	AREA	PILOT	FATE
11/24/42	9471	VS-2	COCO SOLO (DET 15)		CENLANT	ENS L.D. FRAME	U
12/05/42	5910		USS ERIE		CENLANT	(SHIP SANK)	
12/23/42	9688		SITKA	ALASKA	NORPAC	ENS JAMES A. WAINWRIGHT	M
01/02/43	9609	A.A.	KODIAK	ALASKA	NORPAC		
01/23/43	5963	VS-5	(DET 14)		SOPAC		
01/27/43	5349	VS-3	(DET 14)	HAWAII	ECENPAC	ENS DANIEL E. HUNT	D
02/23/43	5782	VS-4			NORLANT		
02/25/43	5343	CL-5	USS MILWAU-KEE		NORLANT	LTJG A.G. MAXWELL	U
02/28/43	9410	VS-1			NORLANT		
03/09/43	9630		DUTCH HARBOR	ALASKA	NORPAC		
03/10/43	5753	BB-33	USS ARKANSAS		NORLANT		
04/03/43	5331	VS-53	ROI		WCENPAC		
04/13/43	5321	VC-29	USS SANTEE	OFF NORFOLK	CENLANT		
05/11/43	9498	BB-35	USS TEXAS	OKINAWA	EMPIRE		
06/04/43	5450	CL-6	USS CINCIN-NATI		WCENPAC		
06/17/43	9691	VS-66			SOPAC		
06/22/43	9453	VS-40			NORLANT		
06/30/43	5317	CL-47	USS BOISE	ALGIERS	NW AFR		
06/30/43	9631	VC-70			NORPAC		
07/02/43	5496	VS-67		FIJI IS.	SOPAC	LTJG YOUNG	D
07/13/43	5641	VS-68			SOPAC		
07/16/43	5902	CL-12	USS MARBLE-HEAD	ENR MED	SOLANT		
08/05/43	5955	BB-46	USS MARYLAND		SOPAC		
08/20/43	5419	CL-4	USS OMAHA		SOLANT		
08/24/43	5732	BB-57	USS SOUTH DAKOTA	ENR EFATE IS.	SOPAC		
08/24/43	5348	CL-8	USS DETROIT	KISKA	NORPAC		
08/31/43	9476	CA-69	USS BOSTON		NORLANT		
09/14/43	5690	VS-56	KISKA	ALASKA	NORPAC		
09/23/43	9439	VS-62			NORLANT		
09/27/43	5937	VS-49			CENLANT		
09/28/43	9678	VS-56			CENLANT		
09/29/43	5611	CL-62	USS BIRMING-HAM	ENR WAKE ISLAND	WCENPAC		
10/24/43	5691	BB-58	USS INDIANA	ENR PEARL	WCENPAC		
11/01/43	5646	BB-58	USS INDIANA	PEARL	ECENPAC	ENS R.M. BATTEN	S
11/17/43	5370	VS-63	ANTIGUA		NORLANT		
11/19/43	5439	CA-27	USS CHESTER	MARSHALLS	CENPAC		
11/28/43	9664	CL-7	USS RALEIGH	ALEUTIANS	NORPAC	ENS E.D. BRACK	U
12/10/43		VCS-2	USS MARBLE-HEAD		SOLANT		
12/26/43	5711	VO-5	USS NEVADA	GREENLAND	NORLANT		
01/20/44	5697	VS-68		KOLI POINT	SOPAC	LTJG CHADWICK	S
01/31/44	5647	VCS-13	USS SANTA FE	MARSHALLS	CENPAC	ENS B.C. ZAMUCEN	S
01/31/44	9663	VO-2	USS PENNSYL-VANIA	KWAJALEIN	CENPAC		
02/01/44	9689	VCS-13	USS MOBILE	KWAJALEIN	CENPAC		

DATE	BUNO	SQDRN	BASE	LOST	AREA	PILOT	FATE
02/01/44	5750	VO-8	USS INDIANA	KWAJALEIN	CENPAC		
02/01/44	5906	VO-8	USS INDIANA	KWAJALEIN	CENPAC		
02/05/44	5693	VCS-5	USS CHESTER	MARSHALLS	CENPAC		
02/06/44	5807	VCS-5	USS CHESTER	MARSHALLS	CENPAC		
02/06/44	5954	VCS-5	USS CHESTER	MARSHALLS	CENPAC		
02/08/44	9425	SOSU-1	PEARL	HAWAII	ECENPAC	LTJG J.D. GORDON	S
02/15/44	5960	VO-4	USS COLORA-DO	KWAJALEIN	CENPAC		
02/17/44	9668	VO-2	USS PENNSYL-VANIA	ENIWETOK	CENPAC		
02/18/44	5737	VO-2	USS TENNES-SEE	ENIWETOK	CENPAC		
03/17/44	5896	VS-39		B.W.I.	CENLANT		
03/31/44	5341	CL-5	USS MILWAU-KEE	ENR MURMANSK	NORLANT		
03/31/44	5760	CL-5	USS MILWAU-KEE	ENR MURMANSK	NORLANT		
04/04/44	9680	VS-49	DUTCH HARBOR	ALASKA	NORPAC		
04/19/44	5296	VO-5	USS ARKANSAS		NORLANT		
04/26/44	9575	VCS-14	USS VIN-CENNES	CANAL ZONE	CENLANT	ENS G.A. GREENWOOD	S
04/27/44	5748	VO-3	USS NEW MEXICO	AUSTRALIA	SW PAC	LT W.C. O'MEARA	S
04/28/44	9670	VO-3	USS IDAHO	E. OF AUSTRALIA	SW PAC	H.W. WENDALL	S
04/30/44	9495	VO-6	USS NORTH CAROLINA	TRUK	CENPAC		
05/07/44	9660	VO-2	USS CALIFORN-IA	MARIANAS	CENPAC	LT R.L. LUERSON	S
05/08/44	5986	VO-4	USS MARYLAND	SAIPAN	WCENPAC	LT G.K. FRENCH	S
05/14/44	5708	HEDRON-12	BOCA CHICA		NORLANT	ENS W.R. POSTELL	S
05/22/44	5605	VS-56	ADAK	ATTU	NORPAC		
05/25/44	5430	VP-62	AMCHITKA	ALASKA	NORPAC		
05/25/44	9611	VS-48	ATTU	ALASKA	NORPAC	LTJG G.F. GOODE	S
05/28/44	5880	FAW-16		RECIFE	BRAZIL	A.I. MCDONALD	S
05/29/44	9572	VCS-14	USS HOUSTON	MARSHALLS	CENPAC		
06/10/44	9569	VCS-14	USS HOUSTON	W OF PAGAN	CENPAC	ENS H.C. MOLLECK	S
07/04/44	5363	VCS-13	USS SANTA FE	IWO JIMA	EMPIRE	LTJG N.W. HENDERSLOT	S
07/10/44	5293	BB-56	USS WASHING-TON	SAIPAN	WCENPAC	LTJG H.W. REEVES	S
07/21/44	9555	BB-64	USS WISCON-SIN	TRINIDAD	CENLANT	LT W.K. KELLER	S
07/31/44	5551	COMAIR-PAC	PEARL	HAWAII	ECENPAC		
08/21/44	5903	CL-86	USS VICKS-BURG	CARLISLE BAY	NORLANT		
08/27/44	5549	VO-7	USS NEW JERSEY	PEARL	ECENPAC	ENS ALLEN R. TRECARTIN	S
08/27/44	5935	VS-70	ATTU	ALASKA	NORPAC	LTJG R.C. BAILEY	S
09/13/44	5696	CL-81	USS HOUSTON	PELELIU	WCENPAC		
09/21/44	5309	CA-25	USS SALT LAKE CITY	ENIWETOK	CENPAC		

DATE	BUNO	SQDRN	BASE	LOST	AREA	PILOT	FATE
09/21/44	9683	CA-25	USS SALT LAKE CITY	ENIWETOK	CENPAC	ENS THOMAS W. ERICKSON	S
10/01/44	5805	CA-70	USS CANBERRA	OKINAWA	EMPIRE	LT J.D. GORDON	S
10/10/44	5547	CASU-39	ESPIRITU SANTO	NEW HEBRIDES	SOPAC	LT EDWARD J. MITCHELL	S
10/10/44	5689	CL-80	USS BILOXI	OKINAWA	EMPIRE	LTJG ROBERT L. DANA	S
10/16/44	5359	CL-81	USS HOUSTON	FORMOSA	EMPIRE		
10/17/44	9588	CL-87	USS DULUTH	TRINIDAD	CENLANT		
10/24/44	5780	CL-62	USS BIRMING-HAM	LEYTE GULF	PHIL		
10/31/44	5306	A & R	PEARL	HAWAII	ECENPAC		
11/01/44	5529	COMAIR-PAC	PEARL	HAWAII	ECENPAC		
11/01/44	5625	COMAIR-PAC	PEARL	HAWAII	ECENPAC		
11/01/44	5730	COMAIR-PAC	PEARL	HAWAII	ECENPAC		
11/08/44	5621	BB-48	USS WEST VIRGINIA	ENR MANUS	SOPAC	LT ROBERT M. ROCKASCHEL	D
11/23/44	9554	VCS-2	USS CINCIN-NATI	RECIFE	BRAZIL	LTJG JAMES R. COTTON	S
12/13/44	9507	CL-60	USS SANTA FE	ENR ULITHI	PHIL	LTJG BLASE C. ZAMUCEN	S
12/18/44	5700	CL-80	USS BILOXI	ENR LUZON	PHIL		
12/18/44	9441	CL-89	USS MIAMI	LUZON	PHIL	(DECK LOSS-TYPHOON)	
12/19/44	5377	BB-60	USS ALABAMA	LUZON	PHIL		
12/19/44	5504	BB-60	USS ALABAMA	LUZON	PHIL		
12/19/44	9686	CA-68	USS BALTI-MORE	LUZON	PHIL		
12/28/44	5745	CA-69	USS BOSTON	ENR LUZON	PHIL		
12/28/44	9581	CL-90	USS ASTORIA	LUZON	PHIL		
12/29/44	5726	CA-27	USS CHESTER	BONINS	CENPAC		
12/31/44	5286	A.A.	PEARL	HAWAII	ECENPAC		
12/31/44	5362	A.A.	PEARL	HAWAII	ECENPAC		
12/31/44	5420	A.A.	PEARL	HAWAII	ECENPAC		
12/31/44	5614	A.A.	PEARL	HAWAII	ECENPAC		
12/31/44	5905	A.A.	PEARL	HAWAII	ECENPAC		
12/31/44	5939	A.A.	PEARL	HAWAII	ECENPAC		
12/31/44	9548	A.A.	PEARL	HAWAII	ECENPAC		
12/31/44	9576	A.A.	PEARL	HAWAII	ECENPAC		
12/31/44	9669	A.A.	PEARL	HAWAII	ECENPAC		
01/05/45	5292	BB-62	USS NEW JERSEY	LUZON	PHIL		
01/18/45	5943	BB-56	USS WASHING-TON	OKINAWA	EMPIRE		
01/21/45	5533	CL-65	USS PASADENA	LUZON	PHIL	LT ROBERT W. BROWNFIELD	U
01/21/45	9553	CL-65	USS PASADENA	LUZON	PHIL	LTJG JOHN A. BOWSER	U
01/22/45	5307	CA-68	USS BALTI-MORE	OKINAWA	EMPIRE		
01/22/45	9492	CA-68	USS BALTI-MORE	OKINAWA	EMPIRE		
02/08/45	5357	A.A.	GUAM	GUAM	WCENPAC		
02/08/45	9580	A.A.	GUAM	GUAM	WCENPAC		
02/10/45	5328	A.A.	PEARL	HAWAII	ECENPAC		
02/10/45	5701	A.A.	PEARL	HAWAII	ECENPAC		
02/10/45	5728	A.A.	PEARL	HAWAII	ECENPAC		
02/10/45	9596	BB-59	USS MAKASSAR STRAIT	BONINS	CENPAC		
02/16/45	9526	BB-34	USS NEW YORK	SAIPAN	WCENPAC	ENS DONALD HARRY NITZ	S

DATE	BUNO	SQDRN	BASE	LOST	AREA	PILOT	FATE
02/17/45	5482	CA-24	USS PENSACOLA	IWO JIMA	EMPIRE		
02/18/45	9573	CL-6	USS CINCINNATI		SOLANT	LTJG SAMUEL NEWBERG	S
02/23/45	5776	BB-36	USS NEVADA	IWO JIMA	EMPIRE		
02/25/45	5936	A.A.	KODIAK	ALASKA	NORPAC		
02/28/45	5754	CL-12	USS MARBLEHEAD		CENLANT		
02/28/45	5761	CL-12	USS MARBLEHEAD		CENLANT		
03/04/45	5652	POOL	PEARL	HAWAII	ECENPAC		
03/05/45	9490	BB-56	USS WASHINGTON	IWO JIMA	EMPIRE		
03/06/45	9679	CA-25	USS SALT LAKE CITY	IWO JIMA	EMPIRE	ENS THOMAS W. ERICKSON	D
03/13/45	5944	BB-36	USS NEVADA	ENR OKINAWA	WCENPAC		
03/19/45	5543	CL-60	USS SANTA FE	KURE	EMPIRE		
03/19/45	5544	CL-60	USS SANTA FE	KURE	EMPIRE		
03/21/45	5746	COMAIRPAC	PEARL	HAWAII	ECENPAC		
03/24/45	5483	BB-59	USS MASSACHUSETTS	OKINAWA	EMPIRE		
03/24/45	9505	CL-8	USS DETROIT		WCENPAC	LT JAMES M. HOLLADAY, JR.	S
03/26/45	5651	BB-57	USS SOUTH DAKOTA	ENR PALAU	WCENPAC		
03/27/45	5441	BB-36	USS NEVADA	OKINAWA	EMPIRE		
03/27/45	5445	BB-58	USS INDIANA		WCENPAC	LTJG FRANK M. HAAS, JR.	M
03/31/45	5739	COMAIRPAC	PEARL	HAWAII	ECENPAC		
03/31/45	5740	COMAIRPAC	PEARL	HAWAII	ECENPAC		
03/31/45	5968	COMAIRPAC	PEARL	HAWAII	ECENPAC		
04/05/45	5300	BB-33	USS ARKANSAS	OKINAWA	EMPIRE		
04/14/45	5868	BB-34	USS NEW YORK	OKINAWA	EMPIRE	(DECK LOSS-KAMIKAZE)	
04/27/45	5863	VJ-16	COCO SOLO	COCO SOLO	CENLANT		
04/27/45	9610	VJ-16	COCO SOLO	COCO SOLO	CENLANT		
04/27/45	9639	VJ-16	COCO SOLO	COCO SOLO	CENLANT		
04/27/45	9463	VO-5	USS TEXAS	OKINAWA	EMPIRE	ENS JOHN R. THOMSON	S
04/30/45	9676	BB-59	USS MASSACHUSETTS	OKINAWA	EMPIRE		
05/15/45	5318	ACORN-30 PL		JINAMOC	PHIL		
05/22/45	5860	VJ-16	GUANTANAMO BAY	CUBA	CENLANT		
05/28/45	5548	BB-63	USS MISSOURI	OKINAWA	EMPIRE	LT W.K. KELLER	M
05/29/45	5347	SEAPL BASE		MANUS	SW PAC		
05/30/45	5535	CASU(F)-51		ULITHI	WCENPAC		
05/30/45	5747	CASU(F)-51		ULITHI	WCENPAC		
05/31/45	5484	BB-43	USS TENNESSEE	ULITHI	WCENPAC	(DECK LOSS-SCRAPPED)	

DATE	BUNO	SQDRN	BASE	LOST	AREA	PILOT	FATE
05/31/45	9671	BB-43	USS TENNES-SEE	ULITHI	WCENPAC	(DECK LOSS-SCRAPPED)	
05/31/45	9577	COMAIR-PAC	PEARL	HAWAII	ECENPAC		
06/01/45	5485	POOL	PEARL	HAWAII	ECENPAC		
06/02/45	5642	ACORN-30 PL		JINAMOC	PHIL		
06/02/45	5751	ACORN-30 PL		JINAMOC	PHIL		
06/02/45	9496	ACORN-30 PL		JINAMOC	PHIL		
06/02/45	9675	CL-64	USS VIN-CENNES	OKINAWA	EMPIRE	LTJG R.M. KARISCH	S
06/05/45	9658	BB-58	USS INDIANA	MARIANAS	CENPAC		
06/05/45	9604	CA-68	USS BALTI-MORE	OKINAWA	EMPIRE		
06/05/45	5486	CA-71	USS QUINCY	OKINAWA	EMPIRE		
06/06/45	9606	CASU(F)-12		GUAM	WCENPAC		
06/08/45	5311	BB-48	USS WEST VIRGINIA	OKINAWA	EMPIRE	LTJG DONALD R. WALKER	M
06/08/45	5361	CL-86	USS VICKS-BURG	KYUSHU	EMPIRE	LT CHAS. N. FEATHERSTON	S
06/09/45	5809	ACORN-30 PL		JINAMOC	PHIL		
06/09/45	9662	ACORN-30 PL		JINAMOC	PHIL		
06/11/45	5793	BB-55	USS NORTH CAROLINA	PEARL	ECENPAC	ENS WESLEY L. RENZAS	S
06/22/45	9443	ACORN-30 PL		JINAMOC	PHIL		
06/25/45	9407	FAW-16		RECIFE	BRAZIL		
06/28/45	5802	ACORN-30 PL		JINAMOC	PHIL		
06/28/45	9636	CASU(F)-12		GUAM	WCENPAC		
07/11/45	5735	ACORN-30 PL		TACLOBAN	PHIL		
07/14/45	5346	ACORN-30 PL		TACLOBAN	PHIL		
07/20/45	9652	CA-71	USS QUINCY		EMPIRE	ENS A. HUDAK	S
07/21/45	5410	POOL	PEARL	HAWAII	ECENPAC		
08/07/45	5473	BB-58	USS INDIANA	ENR PALUS	EMPIRE		
08/07/45	5870	POOL	SAN JUAN	SAN JUAN	CENLANT		
08/07/45	5871	POOL	SAN JUAN	SAN JUAN	CENLANT		
08/07/45	5875	POOL	SAN JUAN	SAN JUAN	CENLANT		
08/07/45	5876	POOL	SAN JUAN	SAN JUAN	CENLANT		
08/07/45	5882	POOL	SAN JUAN	SAN JUAN	CENLANT		
08/07/45	5883	POOL	SAN JUAN	SAN JUAN	CENLANT		
08/07/45	5886	POOL	SAN JUAN	SAN JUAN	CENLANT		
08/07/45	5887	POOL	SAN JUAN	SAN JUAN	CENLANT		
08/07/45	5888	POOL	SAN JUAN	SAN JUAN	CENLANT		
08/07/45	5971	POOL	SAN JUAN	SAN JUAN	CENLANT		
08/07/45	9474	POOL	SAN JUAN	SAN JUAN	CENLANT		
08/07/45	9620	POOL	SAN JUAN	SAN JUAN	CENLANT		
08/10/45	9593	BB-55	USS NORTH CAROLINA	EMPIRE			
08/13/45	5945	CASU(F)-12		GUAM	WCENPAC		

VOUGHT SB2U-1

The Vought SB2U Vindicator was a carrier-based dive bomber developed for the United States Navy in the 1930s, the first monoplane in this role. Obsolescent at the outbreak of World War II, Vindicators still remained in service at the time of the Battle of Midway, but by 1943, all had been withdrawn to training units. Vindicators served on four carriers, USS LEXINGTON, USS SARATOGA, USS RANGER, and USS WASP between December 1937 and September 1942. Air Group Nine, destined for USS ESSEX, trained in Vindicators aboard the auxiliary carrier USS CHARGER but transitioned to the SBD Dauntless before ESSEX joined the war. The SB2U-1 was the initial production version that was powered by an 825hp R-1535-96 engine. There were 54 built. Aircraft lost:

DATE	BUNO	SQDRN	BASE	LOST	AREA	PILOT	FATE
01/28/42	0759	VS-41	USS RANGER		CENLANT		
02/16/42	0751	VS-42	USS RANGER		CENLANT		

VOUGHT SB2U-2

The Vought SB2U-2 was basically identical to the SB2U-1 but with some minor equipment change. There were 58 built. Aircraft lost:

DATE	BUNO	SQDRN	BASE	LOST	AREA	PILOT	FATE
01/14/42	1368	VS-71	USS WASP	OFF NORFOLK	CENLANT	LT D.D. PATTERSON	M
01/27/42	1327	VS-71	USS WASP	ARGENTIA	NORLANT	ENS NORMAN KIEB	S
03/27/42	1362	VS-71	USS WASP	ENR ENGLAND	EUROPE	ENS EDWIN S. PETWAY	U
04/15/42	1364	VS-71	USS WASP	OFF GREENOCK	EUROPE	LTJG JOHN F. DUNN	U
04/23/42	1363	VS-71	USS WASP	OFF MALTA	EUROPE	ENS JACKSON	S
05/05/42	1370	VS-71	USS WASP	ENGLAND	EUROPE	JAMES F. THOMPSON	M

VOUGHT SB2U-3

The Vought SB2U-3 variant was similar to the SB2U-2 but fitted with an 825hp R-1535-102 engine, crew armor and two 0.5in guns. There were 57 built. Aircraft lost:

DATE	BUNO	SQDRN	BASE	LOST	AREA	PILOT	FATE
12/07/41	2070	VMJ-252	EWA	HAWAII	ECENPAC		
12/07/41	2047	VMSB-231	EWA	HAWAII	ECENPAC		
12/07/41	2050	VMSB-231	EWA	HAWAII	ECENPAC		
12/07/41	2051	VMSB-231	EWA	HAWAII	ECENPAC		
12/07/41	2060	VMSB-231	EWA	HAWAII	ECENPAC		
12/07/41	2063	VMSB-231	EWA	HAWAII	ECENPAC		
12/07/41	2068	VMSB-231	EWA	HAWAII	ECENPAC		
12/15/41	2069	VMSB-231	EWA	HAWAII	ECENPAC		
04/27/42	2055	VMSB-241	PEARL	HAWAII	ECENPAC	LT DELALIO	S
06/04/42		VMSB-241		MIDWAY	ECENPAC		
06/04/42	2045	VMSB-241		MIDWAY	ECENPAC	2NDLT K.O. CAMPION	S
06/04/42	2048	VMSB-241		MIDWAY	ECENPAC		
06/04/42	2066	VMSB-241		MIDWAY	ECENPAC		
06/04/42	2067	VMSB-241		MIDWAY	ECENPAC	MAJ BENJAMIN W. NORRIS	S
06/04/42	2072	VMSB-241		MIDWAY	ECENPAC	2NDLT ALLEN H. RINGBLOOM	U

VULTEE SNV-1

The Vultee BT-13 Valiant was an American World War II-era basic trainer aircraft built by Vultee Aircraft for the United States Army Air Corps (later the US Army Air Forces). A subsequent variant of the BT-13 in the US Navy was known as the SNV and was used to train naval aviators for the US Navy, US Marine Corps and US Coast Guard. The Navy adopted the Pratt & Whitney-powered aircraft as their main basic trainer. The US Navy began to show an interest in the aircraft as well and of the 6,407 BT-13A models built for the USAAF, 1,350 were transferred to the Navy and redesignated SNV-1.

Once in service, the aircraft quickly got its nickname of "Vibrator" because it had a tendency to shake quite violently as it approached its stall speed. The BT-13 served its intended purpose well. It and its successors were unforgiving aircraft to fly, but were also extremely agile. Thus the BT-13 made a good aircraft to help transition many hundreds of pilots toward their advance trainers and fighters yet to be mastered. Aircraft lost:

DATE	BUNO	SQDRN	BASE	LOST	AREA	PILOT	FATE
06/19/42	02994	VP-93			NORLANT	CHIEF MACH. HENDERSON	S

WACO YKS-6

The Waco Aircraft Company (WACO) was an aircraft manufacturer located in Troy, Ohio, USA. Between 1919 and 1947, the company produced a wide range of civilian biplanes. During World War 2, Waco produced large numbers of military gliders for the RAF and US Army Air Forces for airborne operations, especially during the Normandy Invasion and Operation Market Garden. The Waco CG-4 was the most numerous of their glider designs to be produced. At the same time Waco produced over 600 of its UPF-7 open biplanes and 21 VKS-7F cabin biplanes for the Civilian Pilot Training Program, which supplemented the output of the military training establishments. 42 privately-owned models of sixteen types were impressed into service as light transports and utility aircraft with the USAAF under the common designation C-72/UC-72.

The Waco company ceased operations in 1947, having suffered the fate of a number of general aviation companies when an anticipated boom in aviation following World War II failed to develop. There were 65 YKS-6 built with the 285 hp (213 kW) Jacobs L-5 engine. Aircraft lost:

DATE	BUNO	SQDRN	BASE	LOST	AREA	PILOT	FATE
05/04/43	09783	NAS	SITKA	SITKA	NORPAC		

WACO YKS-7

Some references state that BuNos 09783 and 09784 are both WACO YKS-7 variants. The Aircraft History Card for BuNo 09783 states it as a YKS-6 and the Aircraft History Card for BuNo 09784 states it as a YKS-7. In searching through the history of the WACO Aircraft Company I can find no reference to the YKS-7 variant, only the YKS-6. This may well be a WACO VKS-7 (21 built) but help from the readers would be appreciated.

DATE	BUNO	SQDRN	BASE	LOST	AREA	PILOT	FATE
10/31/44	09784	NAS	SITKA	ALASKA	NORPAC		

About the Author

LCDR Douglas E. Campbell, Ph.D., (USNR-R, Ret.) was born on May 9, 1954 in Portsmouth, Virginia, and grew up as a Navy Brat, traveling all over the world. He graduated from Kenitra American High School, Kenitra, Morocco, in 1972 – his 13th school. He received his Bachelor of Science degree in Journalism from the University of Kansas on May 24, 1976 and the following day was commissioned as an Ensign in the United States Navy. He joined the U.S. Naval Reserve Program as an Intelligence Officer in 1980 and was transferred to the Retired Reserves as a Lieutenant Commander on 1 June 1999. Dr. Campbell received his Master of Science degree from the University of Southern California in Computer Systems Management in 1986 and his Doctor of Philosophy degree in Security Administration from Southwest University in New Orleans, LA, in 1993. Dr. Campbell is president and CEO of Syneca Research Group, Inc., a veteran-owned small business incorporated in 1995 supporting several Government and commercial clients. He currently resides with his wife Trish in Southern Pines, NC.

Dr. Campbell is currently investigating and searching for the USS DORADO (SS-248), a World War II Gato-class submarine lost in the Caribbean in 1943. See his research at www.ussdorado.com.

OTHER BOOKS BY THE AUTHOR

Compu-terror: Computer Terrorism and Recovery from Disaster
ASIN B00071D2XO

Building a Global Information Assurance Program
(co-author Raymond J. Curts, Ph.D.)
ISBN 0-8493-1368-6

Volume I: U.S. Navy, U.S. Marine Corps and U.S. Coast Guard Aircraft Lost During World War II-Listed by Ship Attached
ISBN 978-1-257-82232-4

Volume II: U.S. Navy, U.S. Marine Corps and U.S. Coast Guard Aircraft Lost During World War II-Listed by Squadron
ISBN 978-1-257-88139-0

OTHER HISTORICAL PUBLICATIONS BY THE AUTHOR

History of Marine Corps Fighter-Attack Squadron 321 (VMFA-321)

History of Naval Air Station Anacostia (Maryland)

History of Light Photographic Squadron Two Zero Six and Three Zero Six (VFP-206 & VFP-306)

Sky Camera-History of U.S. Naval Aerial Reconnaissance

History of Shipwrecks off Pensacola, Florida

History of and Search for USS DORADO (SS-248)

TECHNICAL PUBLICATIONS ON COMMAND & CONTROL (with Dr. Curts)

"Architecture: The Road to Interoperability"

"Naval Information Assurance Center (NIAC): An Approach Based on the Naval Aviation Safety Program Model"

"Avoiding Information Overload Through the Understanding of OODA Loops, A Cognitive Hierarchy and Object-Oriented Analysis and Design"

"A Systems Engineering Approach To Information Assurance Operations"

"Analyzing C4ISR Architectures Through an Automated Data Visualization Environment"

Command & Control as an Operational Function of Information Warfare in the Context of "Information" – The Nature of Information and Information Warfare"

"Building An Ontology For Command & Control"

"Rethinking Command & Control"

"The Trouble With C2 Architectures"

"Transitioning from 'Command & Control' to 'Command & Trust'"